THE OXFORD HANDBOOK OF

THE BRITISH
MUSICAL

THE OXFORD HANDBOOK OF

THE BRITISH

MUSICAL

Edited by

ROBERT GORDON

and

OLAF JUBIN

OXFORD
UNIVERSITY PRESS

OXFORD
UNIVERSITY PRESS

Oxford University Press is a department of the University of Oxford. It furthers
the University's objective of excellence in research, scholarship, and education
by publishing worldwide. Oxford is a registered trade mark of Oxford University
Press in the UK and certain other countries.

Published in the United States of America by Oxford University Press
198 Madison Avenue, New York, NY 10016, United States of America.

Library of Congress Cataloging-in-Publication Data
Names: Gordon, Robert, 1951 November 28- editor. | Jubin, Olaf, editor.
Title: The Oxford handbook of the British musical /
edited by Robert Gordon and Olaf Jubin.
Description: New York : Oxford University Press, 2016. |
Includes bibliographical references and index.
Identifiers: LCCN 2016014652| ISBN 9780199988747 (bound book : alk. paper) |
ISBN 9780190204938 (Oxford handbooks online)
Subjects: LCSH: Musicals—Great Britain—History and criticism.
Classification: LCC ML1731 .O94 2016 | DDC 782.1/40941—dc23
LC record available at https://lccn.loc.gov/2016014652

1 3 5 7 9 8 6 4 2
Printed by Sheridan Books, Inc., United States of America

To the next generations:
Jacqui and Kathy,
Joshua and Amira

CONTENTS

PART V TRAILBLAZERS

PART VI 'THE ART OF THE POSSIBLE': ALTERNATIVE APPROACHES TO MUSICAL THEATRE AESTHETICS

ACKNOWLEDGEMENTS

THE editors wish to thank our Commissioning Editor, Norman Hirschy, for his enthusiastic support throughout the long gestation of this project; we couldn't have asked for a more helpful American counterpart in this very British endeavour. Our gratitude also goes to Lauralee Yeary, Norm's editorial assistant, for her resourcefulness in helping to secure high resolution images, musical examples, and reprint permissions as well as readying the manuscript for publication—it was a pleasure to communicate with both of them via email from London and New York, our very own version of the West End–Broadway axis.

We also wish to thank all of the contributors who brought new perspectives to topics that were either extremely well worn or virtually unresearched; special thanks must go to Ben Macpherson who stepped into the breach literally at the last minute to replace a contracted writer who was unable to deliver his essay and 'disappeared' just before the deadline. Ben delivered an excellent article on Asian and Black British musical theatre in record time.

The idea for this volume was prompted by the needs of students on the Goldsmiths MA in Musical Theatre—the first postgraduate programme ever to focus on both the writing and producing of new musicals. This book is one of a series of initiatives which include the constitution of the British Musical Theatre Research Institute (BMTRI), and are designed to address the paucity of academic research on British musical theatre by promoting academic study and publication in the field.

We are very grateful for OUP for allowing us to assemble a volume that we hope will kickstart an overdue discussion of the achievements and idiosyncracies of British musical theatre—a discussion which will be kept going by several others projects, many by contributors to this volume (and fellow members of the BMTRI), which are in various stages of preparation, writing, and publication.

We would like to thank the various photographers and photo agencies for their kind assistance in providing high resolution images and for granting reprint permission: Ellie Kurttz, Joan Marcus, Adam Sorenson as well as Mike Markiewicz and the staff at ArenaPal, Karen Fisher and Murray Melvin at the Theatre Royal Stratford East, and Saad Javed at Getty Images in London.

Our grateful acknowledgement goes to the following copyright holders for permission to use photographs. ArenaPal: Figures 1.1, 1.2, 2.2, 4.1, 5.1, 6.1, 7.1, 8.1,11.2, 12.1, 14.1, 14.2, 15.1, 15.2, 16.1, 16.2, 18.1, 18.2, 19.2, 20.2, 21.1, 21.2, 22.1, 22.2, 23.1, 24.1, 25.1, 25.2, 26.1, 26.2, 27.1, 27.2; Getty Images: Figures 2.1, 5.2, 7.2, 8.2, 9.1, 9.2, 11.1, 13.1, 13.2, 24.2; Harvard Theatre Collection, Houghton Library: Figure 3.2; Ellie Kurttz: Figure 28.2; Joan

Marcus: Figure 17.1; New York Public Library for the Performing Arts: Figure 20.1; Solo Syndication London: Figure 23.2; Adam Sorenson: Figure 17.2; Theatre Royal Stratford East Archives Collection: Figures 10.1, 19.1, 28.1.

Many of the essays in this collection were first read while the editors were guests of Dan and Michelyne Thal in Boston; they are not only the best of friends, but the most generous and accommodating of hosts—never was editorial work done in more pleasant circumstances.

Fellow musical theatre aficionados Mike and Maggie Morrow were great sounding boards; their enthusiasm, personal warmth, and sensible ideas have proved extremely useful in the development of our thinking.

Paul Sellwyn's amazing collection of cassette tapes, including even the most rare stage musicals, proved invaluable as both inspiration and primary source material.

Finally, Robert Gordon wishes to acknowledge the support of the Pinter Centre for Research in Performance and Creative Writing at Goldsmiths, University of London, which has sponsored a number of research seminars on British and German musical theatre.

Notes on Contributors

Stephen Banfield is Professor Emeritus of Music at the University of Bristol. He is the author of books on Stephen Sondheim, Jerome Kern, Gerald Finzi, and the English art song as an early twentieth-century genre. He edited the twentieth-century volume of *The Blackwell History of Music in Britain* and is currently working on two social histories of music, in the West Country of England and the British Empire.

Sarah Browne is Head of Music and Principal Lecturer at the University of Wolverhampton. She is also course leader for musical theatre. She has worked extensively as conductor, arranger, and musical director. Her research interests include the politics of race and gender in musical theatre, American musical theatre of the 1960s, and stage-to-screen transitions of musicals. Her work includes a number of papers on the musical *Hair* and the male gaze in film musicals. Sarah is currently completing a PhD at the University of Winchester, analysing the performance of rebellion in the musical *Hair*.

Dr George Burrows is Principal Lecturer in Performing Arts at the University of Portsmouth. He is co-founder of the Song, Stage and Screen international conference and founding editor of the journal *Studies in Musical Theatre* (Intellect). Although a critical musicologist by training, his research is generally interdisciplinary in approach and has a focus on musical theatre and jazz of the interwar period. His publications include the first edition of the Cello Concerto by Charles Villiers Stanford and journal articles on the likes of Duke Ellington and Cole Porter. George is completing a forthcoming monograph for Oxford University Press entitled *Andy Kirk and His Clouds of Joy*. This first complete survey of the recordings by the Kansas City-based swing band explores issues of race, gender, sexuality, and commerce that were bound up with interwar recording culture. George is also the director of the University of Portsmouth Choir, which he has conducted for more than a decade in concerts in Britain and overseas.

David Cottis is a writer, director, and lecturer. He is the Artistic Director of the award-winning Instant Classics Theatre Company, and has taught at Mountview Theatre Academy and the universities of East Anglia, Northampton, East London, and Middlesex. His adaptation of Charles Dickens's *Oliver Twist* was toured nationally by the Love and Madness Theatre Company.

David Chandler is a Professor in the English Department at Doshisha University, Kyoto. His background is in English Romanticism, but in recent years he has worked mainly on opera and musical theatre, editing books on Alfredo Catalani and Italo Montemezzi and writing pioneering articles on Roger Waters, Edward Cympson, Alan Doggett, nineteenth-century musical adaptations of Charles Dickens's stories, and other topics. He is currently working on a critical biography of Montemezzi and a history of *The Lion King*. He is a regular reviewer for *Opera, Opera Today*, and *Musicweb International*.

Ben Francis is completing a PhD on Stephen Sondheim at Goldsmiths, University of London. He has contributed essays to *the Oxford Handbook of Sondheim Studies* and has written *Christopher Hampton: Dramatic Ironist* (Amber Lane Press.) He was also a regular writer for the Radio 2 comedy show *The News Huddlines* starring Roy Hudd.

Christina Fuhrmann received her PhD in musicology from Washington University in St Louis in 2001. She is a Professor in the Department of Music at Ashland University, where she received the 2015 Taylor Excellence in Teaching Award. Her publications include articles in *Nineteenth-Century Music Review* and *Gender, Sexuality and Early Music* and a volume on Romanticism and opera. Her critical edition of Henry Bishop's adaptation of *The Marriage of Figaro* was published in 2012 by A-R Editions and her book *Foreign Opera at the London Playhouses: From Mozart to Bellini* was published in 2015 by Cambridge University Press.

Robert Gordon is Professor of Theatre and Performance and Director of the Pinter Research Centre at Goldsmiths, University of London, where he established the first MA in Musical Theatre for writers and producers in Europe. His publications include (as author) *The Purpose of Playing* (2006) and *Harold Pinter: The Theatre of Power* (2012), and (as editor) the *Oxford Handbook of Sondheim Studies* (2014). An actor, director, and playwright who has worked in South Africa, Ireland, USA, Italy, the Czech Republic, and the UK, he has recently completed the book for a children's musical and is co-author of *British Musical Theatre Since 1950* (2016).

Kathryn M. Grossman is Professor of French at Pennsylvania State University. Her research centres on nineteenth-century French literature, especially Victor Hugo's novels and other visionary prose fiction. She is the author of two books on *Les Misérables*—*'Les Misérables': Conversion, Redemption, Revolution* (Twayne Publishers-Macmillan, 1996) and *Figuring Transcendence in 'Les Misérables': Hugo's Romantic Sublime* (Southern Illinois University Press, 1994)—as well as two further studies of Hugo's early prose fiction (Droz, 1986) and his later novels (Oxford University Press, 2012). With Bradley Stephens, she has recently co-edited *'Les Misérables' and Its Afterlives: Between Page, Stage, and Screen* (Ashgate, 2015).

Dr Berta Joncus is a Senior Lecturer in Music at Goldsmiths, University of London. Her research focuses on performers, eighteenth-century music, and celebrity culture. Besides scholarly articles, her output includes an edited book on John Rich, the founder of Covent Garden, and the electronic resource *Ballad Operas Online* (Oxford Digital Library). She is senior editor of the opera *Love in a Village* (1762), a hybrid hardcopy and online music volume to be issued by Bärenreiter and the Mainz Academy of Sciences and Literature. Berta is also a music critic, principally for the BBC.

Dr Olaf Jubin is Reader in Media Studies and Musical Theatre at Regent's University London and Associate Lecturer on the MA in Musical Theatre at Goldsmiths, University of London. He gained his PhD from the Ruhr-Universität Bochum, Germany, and has written and co-edited several books on the mass media and musical theatre, including a study of the German dubbing and subtitling of Hollywood musicals and a comparative analysis of reviews of the musicals of Stephen Sondheim and Andrew Lloyd Webber. Among his forthcoming publications as author and co-author are essays on Disney's *The Hunchback of Notre Dame* and *The White Horse Inn* as well as the book *British Musical Theatre Since 1950*.

Robert Lawson-Peebles worked at the universities of Oxford, Princeton, Aberdeen, and finally Exeter. He has been, amongst others, a Fellow of the Salzburg Seminar and a Leverhulme Emeritus Fellow. He has published three books on the cultural history of the American environment, a history of earlier American literature, and articles on subjects ranging from Sir Walter Raleigh to film versions of 'classic' novels. He has a life-long interest in American music. He edited *Approaches to the American Musical* (1996), contributed to the *Oxford Handbook of Sondheim Studies* (2014), and has written essays on the cultural impact of jazz in Britain.

David Linton is a performer/theatre practitioner and Lecturer in Drama at Kingston University, London. He co-founded Prussia Lane Productions, a cooperative of performers, writers, film-makers, designers, and dancers critically engaged in the exploration of interdisciplinary approaches in the creation and realization of performance projects. His research interests include participatory arts, premodern multidisciplinary popular theatre forms and their contemporary applications, specifically mask/minstrelsy, pantomime, burlesque/neo-burlesque, cabaret, pierrot, hip-hop theatre, and revue.

Dr Miranda Lundskaer-Nielsen is a Senior Lecturer in Drama at Bath Spa University where she teaches Musical Theatre and American Drama. She has previously worked with the New York Musical Theatre Festival, Mercury Musical Developments (UK), and as a script reader for Broadway and Off-Broadway producers. Publications include *Directors and the New Musical Drama* (Palgrave Macmillan) as well as chapters in the *Oxford Handbook of Sondheim Studies* and the *Cambridge Companion to the Musical*, and articles on contemporary British musicals in *Studies in Musical Theatre*.

Ben Macpherson is Senior Lecturer and Course Leader in Musical Theatre at the University of Portsmouth. His research primarily concerns two areas: philosophies of vocal performance and the British musical, often exploring the intersection between them. As co-founder of the Centre for Interdisciplinary Voice Studies, he co-edited *Voice Studies: Critical Approaches to Process, Performance and Experience* (Routledge, 2015), and acts as co-editor for *Journal of Interdisciplinary Voice Studies* (Intellect) and the Routledge Voice Studies series. A founding member of the British Musical Theatre Research Institute, he is currently working on a monograph exploring imperialism and identity in British musical theatre, 1890–1939 (Palgrave Macmillan).

Dominic McHugh is Lecturer in Musicology and Director of Performance at the University of Sheffield. His many publications include the books *Loverly: The Life and Times of 'My Fair Lady'* (OUP, 2012) and *Alan Jay Lerner: A Lyricist's Letters* (OUP, 2014); chapters in *The Routledge Companion to Music and Visual Culture* and *The Palgrave Handbook of Musical Theatre Producers*; and articles in the *Journal of the American Musicological Society* and the *Wagner Journal*. He has appeared numerous times on BBC radio and television and has regularly acted as a consultant or guest speaker for Christie's, Lost Musicals, Encores!, and the Victoria and Albert Museum.

Stewart Nicholls is a director/choreographer, writer, and lecturer. He is also the archivist for David Heneker, Julian Slade, and George Posford, and has restored and directed/choreographed many works of British musical theatre including *Popkiss* (Electric Theatre, Guildford, 1997); *Sail Away* (Rhoda McGaw Theatre, Woking, 1998); *A Girl Called Jo, Follow That Girl, Zip Goes A Million, Vanity Fair, Grab Me A Gondola, The Amazons,* and *Ann Veronica* (all staged at the Theatre Museum, Covent Garden, London between 2000 and 2005); *Gay's The Word* (Finborough Theatre, London, 2012 and revived at Jermyn Street Theatre, London 2013); *Salad Days* and *The Biograph Girl* (both staged for the London College of Music, 2013); and *Free As Air* (Finborough Theatre, London 2014). Many of his productions have been recorded and released on CD while his restoration of Noël Coward's *Sail Away* is published by Warner/Chappell Music. Stewart also directs/choreographs new theatre works, revivals, cabarets, and pantomime: www. stewartnicholls.co.uk.

George Rodosthenous is Associate Professor in Theatre Directing at the School of Performance and Cultural Industries (University of Leeds). His research interests are the body in performance, refining improvisational techniques and compositional practices for performance, devising pieces with live musical soundscapes as interdisciplinary process, theatre directing, updating Greek tragedy and the British musical. He has edited *Theatre as Voyeurism: The Pleasures of Watching* (Palgrave Macmillan) and is currently editing *Contemporary Approaches to Greek Tragedy: Auteurship and Directorial Visions* and *The Disney Musical on Stage and Screen: Critical Approaches from 'Snow White' to 'Frozen'* (both for Bloomsbury Methuen Drama).

David Roesner is Professor for Theatre and Music Theatre at the Ludwig-Maximilian-Universität Munich. He specializes in exploring the musicality of theatre and the theatricality of music in historic and contemporary practices. Major recent publications include two co-edited books on *Theatre Noise* (Cambridge Scholars Publishing, 2011, with Lynne Kendrick) and *Composed Theatre* (Intellect, 2012, with Matthias Rebstock) and his new monograph *Musicality in Theatre* (Ashgate, 2014). David also works as a theatre-musician, sound designer, and director. Examples of his work and further publications can be seen at http://mhn.academia.edu/DavidRoesner.

Ian Sapiro is a Senior Research Fellow and Lecturer in Music at the University of Leeds, researching and teaching film music, musical theatre, orchestration, and the overlaps between them. He is author of *Ilan Eshkeri's 'Stardust': A Film Score Guide* (Scarecrow,

2013) and chapters on film-score orchestration for handbooks by Routledge and Palgrave, and is currently writing a monograph on the role of the film-score orchestrator for Routledge, as well as book chapters on screen adaptations of the musicals *Les Misérables* and *Annie*. Ian is also co-investigator on the Research Council-funded project *The Professional Career and Output of Trevor Jones*.

John Snelson is Head of Publishing and Interpretation at the Royal Opera House London. He joined the Royal Opera House as Editor in 2001 and was appointed to his current post in 2006. Snelson studied at the universities of Nottingham, Reading, and Birmingham, where he took his PhD. He was a Senior Internal Editor for the revised *New Grove Dictionary of Music and Musicians* (1994–2000) and has written widely about the lyric stage, including programme articles for many companies and for such publications as *Oxford Dictionary of National Biography, Cambridge Companion to the Musical, New Grove Dictionary of Music and Musicians*, and the *Grove Dictionary of American Music*. His books include *The Ring at Covent Garden* for Oberon/ROH and *Andrew Lloyd Webber* for Yale University Press.

Bradley Stephens is Senior Lecturer in French at the University of Bristol. His research focuses on the reception and adaptation of French Romantic literature and thought. He is the author of numerous studies and articles in this field, including his book *Victor Hugo, Jean-Paul Sartre, and the Liability of Liberty* (Legenda, 2011) and a new introduction to Hugo's *The Hunchback of Notre-Dame* (Signet Classics, 2010). He has co-edited several volumes, most recently *'Les Misérables' and Its Afterlives: Between Page, Stage, and Screen* (Ashgate, 2015) and a forthcoming entry in the MLA's 'Approaches to Teaching World Literature' series on Hugo's novel.

Dominic Symonds is Reader in Drama at the University of Lincoln. He is joint editor of *Studies in Musical Theatre* (Intellect) and founded the international conference *Song, Stage and Screen*. Publications include *We'll Have Manhattan: The Early Work of Rodgers and Hart* (OUP), *Studying Musical Theatre* (Palgrave Macmillan, co-written with Millie Taylor), *Gestures of Music Theater: The Performativity of Song and Dance* (OUP, co-edited with Millie Taylor), and *The Legacy of Opera: Reading Music Theatre as Experience and Performance* (Rodopi, co-edited with Pamela Karantonis). His monograph *Broadway Rhythm: Imaging the City in Song* (University of Michigan Press) is forthcoming.

Millie Taylor is Professor of Musical Theatre at the University of Winchester. She worked as a freelance musical director and for almost twenty years toured Britain and Europe with a variety of musicals including *West Side Story, The Rocky Horror Show, Little Shop of Horrors*, and *Sweeney Todd*. Recent publications include *British Pantomime Performance* (Intellect, 2007), *Musical Theatre, Realism and Entertainment* (Ashgate, 2012), and with Dominic Symonds, *Studying Musical Theatre* (Palgrave Macmillan, 2014), and the edited collection *Gestures of Music Theater: The Performativity of Song and Dance* (OUP, 2014). She also co-authored *British Musicals Since 1950* (Bloomsbury Methuen Drama, 2016).

Rebecca Warner is a tutor at Urdang Academy and a Visiting Lecturer at Anglia Ruskin University, and Goldsmiths, University of London. She has worked with students at both Royal Central School of Speech and Drama and Mountview Academy of Theatre Arts. She studied Music at Cambridge University and Composition for Screen at the Royal College of Music. She is a theatre composer under her maiden name of Rebecca Applin and won the Cameron Mackintosh Resident Composer Scheme in 2015 at the Mercury Theatre Colchester and the New Wolsey Theatre Ipswich.

Elizabeth A. Wells completed her doctorate in musicology at the Eastman School of Music and is now Professor and Pickard-Bell Chair of Music at Mount Allison University in Sackville, New Brunswick, Canada. She has won local and regional teaching awards and has presented over twenty papers on pedagogy. Her book on *West Side Story* was published in 2011 by Scarecrow Press and won the American Musicological Society's Music in American Culture Award. Her work on American music, and British and American musical theatre has appeared in the *Journal of the American Musicological Society* and *Studies in Musical Theatre*.

Professor Christine White started her working career as a stage manager, electrician, and lighting designer. She has worked for five UK universities and is currently Head of the School of Art and Design and Assistant Dean for the Faculty of Arts, Design & Technology at the University of Derby. She has published five books exploring theatre devices, the relationship of directors and designers and the different environments for spectating performative events, and the spaces that types of work are played out in. She is founding editor of *Scene*, an international peer-reviewed journal exploring the contexts and processes of designed environments for theatre, film, television, museums and galleries, interactive and narrative practices.

Carolyn Williams is Professor in the Department of English at Rutgers University, where she recently served as Chair. In addition to articles on Dickens, Eliot, and other Victorian authors and topics, she has published two books, *Gilbert and Sullivan: Gender, Genre, Parody* (2011) and *Transfigured World: Walter Pater's Aesthetic Historicism* (1989), and has co-edited *Walter Pater: Transparencies of Desire* (2002) with Laurel Brake and Lesley Higgins. She is currently writing on Victorian melodrama, under the working title *The Aesthetics of Melodramatic Form*.

THE OXFORD HANDBOOK OF

THE BRITISH
MUSICAL

....

INTRODUCTION

....

THIS volume endeavours to rectify the gap in scholarly and critical analysis of the British musical by providing a historical outline of its development from *The Beggar's Opera* (1728) to the present day and by promoting scholarly argument and discussion about the distinctive features of British musicals since Gilbert and Sullivan in order to better understand how these differ in their artistic intentions from American musicals, which have been extensively studied and are generally more highly regarded. Through socio-cultural analysis of a number of musicals and periods, close readings of key scores and libretti, explication of key topics, and consideration of a range of musical and theatrical styles, individual essays demonstrate the social significance and aesthetic values of British musicals. Aiming to initiate critical discussion of the specific features of British musical theatre, the volume promises a new perspective on the British musical that presents it as a cultural form complementary to the Broadway musical, rather than merely its poor relation.

If *The Beggar's Opera* is regarded as the first musical comedy, then it is patently true that from its inception the British musical has striven to represent British—usually English—social values, and to entertain audiences through both pungent and light-hearted satire of social behaviour.[1] The preferred form of British musical theatre from the eighteenth century until it was challenged in certain respects[2] by the sung-through rock operas *Tommy* (1969) and *Jesus Christ Superstar* (1970), was modelled on the structural approach of *The Beggar's Opera*. This form privileged a principle of dramaturgical organization in which songs are musically distinct and interrupt the flow of action/dialogue, rather than a more 'operatic' one that conceives all the elements of the work as a synthetic whole, musically ordered along the lines of a Wagnerian *Gesamtkunstwerk*, which has in many respects represented a paradigmatic form for the Broadway musical since *Oklahoma!* (1943).[3] It was common to hear British theatre-goers refer to musicals before the seventies generically as 'musical comedies', suggesting a lack of concern for the distinction between the 'integrated' form (musical play) and musical comedy.

The British Musical and Society: A Sociocultural Perspective

Being forms of popular culture, musicals may, at the same time as they offer social critique, advertise their function as 'only entertainment',[4] their ubiquitous utopianism either disguising or celebrating the ideology that motivates them. A critic of musical theatre is therefore obliged to be attentive towards both the hidden and overt values determining a musical's particular form. Styles of popular entertainment change as quickly as fashions and manners of social behaviour, so the topicality that made a musical popular in a particular cultural moment may render it hopelessly dated when that moment has passed. Its very ephemerality is what makes a musical such a revealing document of social and cultural history, but it also poses particular problems for the analyst. In a similar way to American scholars such as Andrea Most,[5] Raymond Knapp,[6] John Bush Jones,[7] and Stacy Wolf[8] who in the last decade have pioneered sociocultural approaches to the study of the Broadway musical that have generated new insights into its connection with American society, a number of the essays in this volume endeavour to grasp the different meanings of English musicals historically and in the present day by reading them in their relationship to British social history.

Because Britain is so much nearer to continental Europe, the British theatre—in particular, perhaps, its musical theatre—has closer ties to specific forms of European entertainment, be it opéra comique, Viennese operetta, revue, *comédie musicale*, cabaret (both in Berlin and Paris), or Brechtian theatre, than to Broadway. All of these European forms and genres were more accessible to London theatre producers and their audiences than to New York producers, and the exchange of forms between London and other European capitals was therefore more immediate, as can consistently be observed for instance in the use of song in the politically sophisticated but working-class-oriented productions of Joan Littlewood's Theatre Royal Stratford East, which evinced an aesthetic far closer to that of Brecht than to any American company or writer after the war.[9]

Of course Britain and America share the English language, which makes the two cultures teasingly similar, yet each remains perplexingly distinct from the other. The ease with which an alien cultural perspective can blind one to the aesthetic qualities of a popular form is illustrated by John Lahr's review of *Billy Elliot* in the *New Yorker*; its revealing misinterpretation of British social and cultural values might be judged as either insulting or just plain ignorant:

> Bannered across the poster for London's new hit musical *Billy Elliot* (at the Victoria Palace) [...] is an unbuttoned quotation from the usually buttoned-down British broadsheet the *Daily Telegraph*. 'The greatest British musical I have ever seen', it says. What, I wonder, are the other great British musicals? *Salad Days? The Boy Friend? Cats?* The British love musicals; they just don't do them very well. The problem, it

seems to me, is spiritual. The jazz of American optimism, which lends elation and energy to the form, is somehow alien to the ironic British spirit. At its buoyant core, the American musical is the expression of a land of plenty. England, on the other hand, is a land of scarcity—the Land of No, as a friend of mine calls it.[10]

Few other American critics have been so blindly unaware of their prejudices,[11] but Lahr's condescending views are nonetheless symptomatic of a persistent failure by theatre critics to understand and thus to acknowledge the significance of cultural differences between the USA and other English-speaking countries in analysing the peculiar features of non-American musicals, resulting in their being considered failed attempts to approximate the model established by the classic examples of the American genre.[12]

Paradoxically, the form of the Broadway musical is in many respects inherited directly from British antecedents: in the 1870s and 1880s the comic operas of Gilbert and Sullivan were, if anything, more popular in the United States than in Britain. Victorian and Edwardian musical comedy regularly succeeded on Broadway between 1892 and 1916, and provided the dramaturgical matrix from which some of the most original and distinctively *American* musical comedies were precipitated between 1915 and 1918 in the collaborative creations of two Brits (P. G. Wodehouse and Guy Bolton) and two Americans (Jerome Kern[13] and Otto Harbach) at the Princess Theatre in New York. Although the transatlantic traffic in commercial theatrical entertainments such as musicals, revues, comedies as well as in musical theatre performers continued relatively unabated after the First World War, the flow of musicals began increasingly to move eastwards from Manhattan, a consequence both of the superiority of Broadway musical comedy's jazz-inflected songs and the new importance of the USA as a world power.

After the Second World War, the London theatre continued for a number of years as it had in the 1930s. Ivor Novello and Vivian Ellis remained its most important composers, and J. B. Priestley, Noël Coward, and Terence Rattigan the major playwrights, but a clear distinction was maintained between their well-made plays[14] and the pre- and post-war operettas and musical comedies. The British musical was both lowbrow and overtly performative: musicals were so obviously influenced by farce, music hall clowning, and revue, it appeared self-evident that they would not attempt to meet the standards of verisimilitude achieved by Rattigan. In contradistinction to such middlebrow drama, operettas and musical comedies were marked by their exaggerated theatricality. For these reasons, British writers and audiences have seldom, if ever, fully embraced the Hammersteinian notion of the integrated musical play in the way that American artists did even after the triumph of *Oklahoma!* at Drury Lane in 1947.

In the 1950s a myth was perpetuated that British musicals were second-rate entertainments born of an inspired amateurism dedicated either to nostalgic recreations of pre-war grandeur or to the naive affirmation of community values, while Broadway shows were, by contrast, highly polished, well-crafted, and brilliantly staged celebrations of the American dream.[15] Yet although some of the rumbustiously energetic Broadway shows were immensely popular with London audiences, so were British musicals. Popular entertainment grows from the soil that produces it, which is why it is reductive and extremely misleading to view British musicals merely within a perspective provided by Broadway. The small-scale and nostalgic musical comedies of Sandy Wilson and Julian Slade/Dorothy Reynolds not only reflect a British tendency towards irony and under-statement in contrast with an American habit of exuberant self-expression, but also rep-resent a retreat from the confident romance of Empire that had inspired the operettas of Noël Coward and Ivor Novello and the satirical comedy of class conflict and resolution that motivated most English musical comedies between 1892 and 1939. By 1953, Britain had lost her position as a world power and was searching for a new postcolonial identity in a world increasingly controlled by American foreign policy. As John Snelson has con-vincingly argued,[16] Sandy Wilson's *The Boy Friend* (1953) and Slade and Reynolds's *Salad Days* (1954) are small-scale, archly eccentric, and nostalgic by design, reflecting not only the paucity of investment money available for theatre enterprises at the time, but also a peculiarly British approach to the musical as popular cultural form, one that invokes the special knowingness and intimacy of English pantomime, music hall, and the little revues of the forties and fifties.[17]

Camp and Queer in the British Musical of the Fifties

Under the Conservative government that came to power in 1951 the Metropolitan Police exploited the anti-Communist hysteria of the early 1950s to justify the entrapment and prosecution of individuals for homosexual soliciting. Guy Burgess had been part of a clique of Marxists and homosexuals at Cambridge in the thirties, so after the disappearance in 1951 of Burgess and his colleague Donald Maclean,[18] both of whom later turned up in Moscow, the McCarthyite assumption that homosexuals were all potential Soviet spies was fairly common in Britain, appearing to justify the victimization of homosexuals that brought misery to thousands of people and stunted the lives of countless others.[19] It is in this context that the charming, eccentric, and intimate musicals of Wilson and of Slade and Reynolds came to embody the closeted assertion of a queer space of carnival that might obliquely subvert the hegemonic insistence on conformity to bourgeois heteronormative values; *Salad Days* in fact satirized the 'hush-hush' repressiveness of Establishment culture.[20]

Sandy Wilson and Julian Slade could access a tradition of popular entertainment that stretched as far back as Gilbert and Sullivan and was archly witty, nostalgic, and self-reflexively camp,[21] although prior to the fifties its camp qualities were not neces-sarily associated with any kind of homosexual subculture.[22] The enormous West End success of *Salad Days* at the very moment that American musicals were believed to have conquered the London theatre typically illustrates the British attitude to musical thea-tre before 1970. By Broadway standards, *Salad Days* is attenuated, whimsical, silly, and singularly lacking in verisimilitude. To a West End audience the show is an amalgam of thirties musical comedy and forties revue, perfectly pitched as escapist entertainment for a society oppressed by Cold War paranoia and class privilege as it archly rejects the repressive ethos of social/sexual conformity which such circumstances were used to justify. In its context one of the show's most popular numbers, 'We Said We Wouldn't Look Back', is ironic because the musical *does* look back nostalgically to the supposedly simpler days of pre-war musical comedy typified by the shows of Vivian Ellis and Noel Gay. Opening in the West End a few weeks earlier, Sandy Wilson's *The Boy Friend* (1953) was innovative precisely *because* of its peculiar celebration of nostalgia: it was the first serious pastiche of the kind of musical comedy typified by *No, No, Nanette* (Vincent Youmans/Irving Caesar/Otto Harbach/Frank Mandel, 1925).[23]

Both *The Boy Friend* and *Salad Days* treat their audiences as privileged members of a clandestine club, gathering together in private to escape the privations of war, austerity, and bureaucratically enforced conformism. They constitute a response to the Cold War culture of the early fifties which is typically English just as *South Pacific* (1949), *The Pajama Game* (1954), or *Silk Stockings* (1955) are typically American responses to that cultural crisis. But these two idiosyncratic shows were not by any means the only British musicals to succeed in the West End after the war, and they should be considered in the context of not only the Broadway imports but also Vivian Ellis and A. P. Herbert's lavish period show *Bless the Bride* (1947, 886 performances), Novello's spectacular operetta *King's Rhapsody* (1949, 841 performances), Eric Maschwitz and George Posford's *Zip Goes a Million* (1951, 544 performances—a star vehicle for George Formby), and Hans May/Sonny Miller/Vera Caspary's *Wedding in Paris* (1954, 411 performances)—all much bigger shows in much bigger theatres.[24]

BRITISH RESPONSES TO AMERICAN MASS CULTURE

The first British musical that attempted to compete with the golden age Broadway musical comedy on its own terms was *Grab Me a Gondola* (1956). Its subject of a busty screen actress hustling to be a star at the Venice Film Festival alludes directly to British 'blonde bombshell' Diana Dors, but the reference could just as easily have been to Hollywood starlets such as Jayne Mansfield or Zsa Zsa Gabor. Julian More conceived the idea for *Grab Me a Gondola* in response to a famous publicity shot of Dors being thrown into a canal in her mink bikini at the 1956 Venice Film Festival. The show, which had a highly successful run of 687 performances, explores the mass culture phenomenon of the international film industry; its songs have a Broadway-influenced swing jazz sound with brassy orchestrations that echo American musicals rather than the quainter and more polite melodic sweetness of the English tradition. Paradoxically, the wholesale Americanization of British pop culture over the succeeding ten years provoked an upsurge of confidence in homegrown British youth culture that later led to the global dominance of the fashions and sounds of 'Swinging London'.

The phenomenon of youth culture initially became visible in Britain with the rise of the Teddy boy, whose pseudo-Edwardian dandyism was the first youth fashion to signal overt opposition to post-war conformism in the early fifties. The release of *Rock Around the Clock* in UK cinemas in 1956 signalled the full-scale introduction of American rock 'n' roll music, which was quickly imitated by British groups and soon began to rival the popularity of skiffle[25] as the new pop music. The wearing of blue jeans began to distinguish the fashion of youth from that of their parents' generation and the American word 'teenager' came into use to identify this new generation, who adopted values more akin to countercultural groups such as bohemians (or beatniks) than to those of their parents. The alternative social scene in London centred on the coffee bars and nightclubs of Soho—the area adjacent to the theatres of Shaftesbury Avenue—and soon a number of musicals were set in this milieu, including *Expresso Bongo* (1958), *Fings Ain't Wot They Use T'Be* (1959), and *The Crooked Mile* (1959).

By 1958, greater affluence allowed young people to dress completely differently from their parents, and the rise of mods and rockers as youth subcultures in the early sixties defined opposing attitudes to youthful rebellion through their extremely different styles of dress. Both popular culture and high art became more egalitarian, with large numbers of working-class artists entering the field for the first time.

HIGHBROW/LOWBROW AND POSTMODERN PASTICHE

The explosion of artistic creativity from 1956 onwards represented by the new British drama of John Osborne, Arnold Wesker, John Arden, and—later—Edward Bond at the Royal Court, Brendan Behan and Shelagh Delaney at Stratford East, and the unlikely success in the West End from 1960 of Harold Pinter and Joe Orton, was equally manifest in the striking development of new types of musical with approaches to risqué subject matter that differed substantially from that of most fifties American musicals. At Stratford East these musicals included *Fings Ain't Wot They Use T'Be*, set in an illegal gambling den in Soho; *Make Me an Offer*, a fairly dark exposé of street furniture vendors (1959); and *Oh What a Lovely War* (1963), a savage satire on the complacency that led to the slaughter of millions in the First World War. All these had successful West End transfers, joining the hard-hitting *Expresso Bongo*, a representation of the corrupt practices of the British pop industry, and *Lock Up Your Daughters* (1959), an uncensored musicalization of an eighteenth-century sex comedy, as well as *The Crooked Mile, Johnny the Priest* (1960), and *Oliver!* (1960) to constitute a corpus of shows with adult themes.

Many playwrights who aimed for recognition as 'serious' artists after the mid-fifties utilized music and song to create types of folk theatre, people's theatre, or political theatre in the manner of Bertolt Brecht, whose plays demonstrate brilliantly how songs can amplify and comment on narrative, rendering distinctions between drama and musical theatre increasingly redundant. As a result of the ubiquitous use of song in plays since 1957, British critics and audiences have tended to treat more adventurous musicals and plays with music simply as drama, which means that some innovations in musical theatre are more commonly manifest in 'legitimate drama' than within the genre of the popular musical.

John Osborne's *The Entertainer* (1957) exploits the death of the music hall as an emblem for the disintegration of the British Empire, and with it the late Victorian values that it reflected in its heyday.[26] Archie's song 'We're All Out for Good Old Number One' reveals the cynicism of the post-war generation as a betrayal of the authenticity of communitarian values that is honestly represented in the pre-war music hall style of his father, Billy. Like his camp and jaded variety performance,[27] Archie's whole life is inauthentic: 'I'm dead behind these eyes,' he admits to his daughter Jean, a confession that resonated in 1957 with the loss of faith in the whole generation of 'gentleman' politicians caused by the exposure during the Suez crisis of the patrician prime minister Sir Anthony Eden as weak, duplicitous, and ineffectual. Britain's imperial adventure in Egypt had ended in a humiliating climbdown, the final confirmation of the end of Empire.[28]

Osborne's masterful use of songs to signify the difference between authentic feeling and the lies given currency by unthinking respect for social form provides a graphic example of the dramatic possibilities of exploiting popular entertainment as a means of delineating social attitudes. Its dark and critical representation of a culture in crisis might well have inspired him to write *The World of Paul Slickey* (1959), a show that he himself categorized as a musical, and to have influenced the creation of *Expresso Bongo* (1958) and *The Lily White Boys* (1960). According to the scholar George Wellwarth, *The World of Paul Slickey* is 'pure spit and vomit thrown directly into the teeth of the audience. Commercially it has been Osborne's least successful play; artistically it is his best.'[29] The musical conducts a savage, double-edged dissection of the decadence of the aristocracy and the hypocrisy of the popular press in a style that marries a grotesque Cowardesque comedy of upper-class manners with the sleazy idiom of tabloid journalism. Offensive in its time, its satire does not seem far-fetched today.

The Lily White Boys (book by Harry Cookson, music by Tony Kinsey and Bill Le Sage) had lyrics by a major English poet, Christopher Logue. Billed as a play with music, its harshly satirical perspective on upward mobility was obviously influenced by the black humour of *Expresso Bongo* and *Paul Slickey*. Its distinguished cast included Georgia Brown, Shirley Ann Field, and Albert Finney; it was directed by Lindsay Anderson with stage designs by Sean Kenny. While never intended for a commercial production, its ambitious scope as a 'state of the nation' drama clearly reveals the seriousness of the musical as a genre within the revolutionary new tradition of British theatre. Not as bizarre as *Slickey*, its gritty milieu of a dockland council housing estate in which a bunch of unemployed boys decide to give up their criminal delinquency and pursue careers as a politician, a lawyer, and a policeman is far removed from the polite and hermetically sealed world of *Salad Days*, its gang of working-class boys ironically ending up disillusioned and unhappy with their chosen paths. Writing in *The Stage*, R. B. Marriot opined that *The Lily White Boys* was

> [t]he most interesting of the British musical shows since attempts began to be made a few years ago to fashion something authentically our own in this form of theatre [. . .] it has roots going deep enough and sufficient flavor of its own to make an impact of originality and freshness. It is angry, satirical, uncompromising and alive.[30]

The success of a large number of serious plays with music from Ewan MacColl's *Uranium 235* (1946) to *The History Boys* (2004) suggests a unique approach in British theatre, which commonly uses song and even dance within a 'highbrow' form. The great success of Osborne's *The Entertainer* (1957) ensured that this convention achieved a very high profile, as did Joan Littlewood's use of songs in her productions of Brendan Behan's *The Quare Fellow* (1954) and *The Hostage* (1958). The tradition of Brecht-influenced plays with music is represented by writers in a line initiated by the 'Royal Court revolution': many plays by John Arden (e.g. *Sergeant Musgrave's Dance*, 1957; *Armstrong's Last Goodnight*, 1965), Edward Bond (*Restoration*, 1981), and Mark Ravenhill (*Mother Clap's Molly House*, 2001) were directly inspired by Brecht's deployment of songs as a key component of dramaturgy.

In a very different vein, dramas by Peter Nicholls (*Forget-Me-Not-Lane*, 1968; *Privates on Parade*, 1977; *Poppy*, 1982) can be seen to continue the exploration of the dramaturgical possibilities of using song that bring British musical theatre and legitimate drama closer together. Peter Barnes's surreal and scabrous satire, *The Ruling Class* (1968), utilizes song and dance in startling ways which are occasionally reminiscent of *Paul Slickey*, while Alan Plater's *Close the Coalhouse Door* (1968) is a serious play about miners' lives that heralded his propensity to use song in all his work for theatre and television.[31]

Alan Bennett's hugely successful first play, *Forty Years On* (1968), originally starring John Gielgud, pioneered a new style of camp comedy, which employed songs throughout, first to evoke nostalgia and then to subvert it in order to expose the banal distortion of British history as a pageant of the past, degraded by the ritualized re-enactment of popular cultural forms that constitute a palimpsest of jingoistic clichés and half-truths. Even a relatively late play like *The History Boys* makes complex use of popular songs sung by the school boys in a series of improbable drag impersonations (e.g., Edith Piaf's 'La Vie en Rose', Gracie Fields's 'Wish Me Luck as You Wave Me Goodbye', well-worn hymns and a Pet Shop Boys hit) to excavate the process by which social history is both memorialized and transformed by the lived experience of popular culture. Victoria Wood's hilarious burlesque *Acorn Antiques* (2005), based upon a recurring sketch from her own hugely successful TV comedy series, employed camp in the English tradition of seaside 'end-of-the-pier' shows and was also filmed for the DVD market. Wood's *That Day We Sang* (2011), on the other hand, was a touching, small-scale musical that was transferred to television with a starry cast (Michael Ball and Imelda Staunton) and broadcast on Christmas Day 2014.

During the 1970s and 1980s the English propensity towards camp, pastiche, and parody continued in other more popular forms. Beginning its life in the tiny Theatre

Upstairs at the Royal Court, *The Rocky Horror Show* (1973) later transferred to an old cinema in the King's Road; it was an outrageously camp parody of the conventions of trashy horror movies that became a cult stage classic in Britain before it was made into a film which ultimately turned into a cult 'audience participation' phenomenon in the USA and elsewhere. The stage show has been touring Britain and continental Europe for decades. *Return to the Forbidden Planet* (1989) and other pastiche rock and pop actor-musician shows mixing B-movie parodies with rock 'n' roll followed in its wake, while Richard Thomas's camp and postmodern mock opera, *Jerry Springer: The Opera* (2003), had a remarkable journey from a small fringe theatre at the Battersea Arts Centre to the National Theatre, the West End, and BBC television.

In 1976, five years before *Cats* and nine years before *Les Misérables*, Trevor Nunn musicalized Shakespeare's *The Comedy of Errors* at the Royal Shakespeare Company (RSC), retaining the entire text while adding eight songs. The show, starring Judi Dench, Francesca Annis, Roger Rees, and Michael Williams, was a high point of the RSC's legendary productions in the late seventies. In an entirely different vein, Neil Bartlett wrote and staged his queer 'operas' *Sarrasine* (1990) and *A Judgement in Stone* (1992), and followed these with *Night After Night* (1993), a wonderfully camp re-viewing of fifties British musicals that 'queered' nostalgia in an extraordinary way. *Night After Night* is a pastiche of conventional fifties musicals that nudges *Shockheaded Peter* (1998), a 'junk opera' that in turn competes for attention with the Royal Opera House's production of *Anna Nicole* (2011), Mark Antony Turnage and Richard Thomas's opera based on the life of Anna Nicole Smith. So British musicals now exist in a postmodern cultural context in which Shakespeare and kitsch jostle and challenge each other to represent the current consumer society in which they are both situated.

The British Musical and Its Engagement with New Music and Subcultures

The impact of jazz, blues, and rock 'n' roll immediately transformed the idiom of British musical theatre in the late fifties, whereas the Broadway musical retained a brassy forties swing sound, remaining largely impervious to pop and rock music of the fifties and sixties until *Hair* in 1967. In Britain, the 'Swinging Sixties' expressed itself musically in the global triumph of the Beatles, the Kinks, the Rolling Stones, Genesis, the Who, Pink Floyd, and other rock and pop bands whose music knocked American rock 'n' roll and soul off the top of the charts and gave rise to the rock opera as a fashionable new form. Often debuting as concept albums, famous rock operas included Tim Rice and Andrew Lloyd Webber's *Jesus Christ Superstar* and *Evita* (1976),[32] which achieved world recognition, as well as *Tommy* by the Who, later turned into a controversial but profitable film by Ken Russell (1975). The worldwide success of Rice and Lloyd Webber's shows provided the impetus for Cameron Mackintosh's development of a system of international productions and licensing that created a new generation of globally performed musicals—*Cats* (1981), *Les Misérables* (1985), *The Phantom of the Opera* (1986), and *Miss Saigon* (1989).

As immigration began to alter the ethnic character of British cities, small-scale touring companies, community theatres, and companies appealing in the first instance to minority ethnic or diasporic communities began to create works representative of their local constituencies. Companies such as the Black British Theatre Co-op, Temba Theatre, Nitro, Tara Arts, Talawa, and Tamasha have since the late seventies used the musical languages of their diasporic communities to create diverse styles of musical theatre, while the iconic Theatre Royal Stratford East has aimed to represent the cultural diversity of the borough of Tower Hamlets, which boasts a multicultural population speaking over a hundred languages. These changes in British society and culture are reflected in works such as *Five Guys Named Moe* (1990), *Fourteen Songs, Two Weddings and a Funeral* (1998), *The Big Life* (2004), *The Harder They Come* (2005), *Into the Hoods* (2008), *Britain's Got Bhangra* (2010), *Glasgow Girls* (2012), and *The Wah Wah Girls* (2012). This progressive use of musical theatre has introduced the diversity of a multicultural society to what was in the 1950s an almost exclusively white popular theatre; many of the shows have toured extensively around Britain to audiences that include a high proportion of people from ethnic minority groups. *Bombay Dreams* (2002) helped to popularize Bollywood music and dance forms among mainstream audiences in London and the success of *Bend It Like Beckham* (2015), adapted from the screen hit, has brought the British Indian diasporic subculture to the West End.

AMERICAN PERCEPTIONS OF BRITISH STYLES AND MANNERS

The immense commercial success of *Evita, Cats, Les Misérables, The Phantom of the Opera*, and *Miss Saigon* in the late seventies and throughout the eighties provoked hostility towards British musicals from Broadway insiders. Feeling that American musicals were in danger of being commercially eclipsed by British productions on their own home territory, professionals and journalists mounted a critical counter-offensive, ridiculing the so-called British 'megamusicals' for their portentousness, their lack of traditional craftsmanship, and their alleged overuse of spectacle when compared to classic American shows.

To judge British musicals according to Broadway categories and Broadway notions of craftsmanship is misleading because British artists have never attempted to emulate those standards. Stephen Sondheim's assessment of Coward in his collection of lyrics, *Finishing the Hat*, is typically problematic in this regard. On the one hand, he reads Coward and his lyrics autobiographically, an approach that Sondheim claims is totally inappropriate when applied to himself, but more importantly he doesn't appear to understand that Coward's form of lyric writing comes from a tradition that is unrelated to the Broadway conventions taught to Sondheim by Oscar Hammerstein II.

By those standards, Coward's lyrics indeed are often lacking, but as he wasn't working with those standards in mind, why should he be judged by them? Comparing Coward to Cole Porter, Sondheim opines that 'Porter believes what he says, even at his most over-heated, and therein lies another difference; Porter is [. . .] too darn hot, but Coward, like the public persona he cultivated, is too darn chilly'.[33] This is a variation of the oft-repeated American accusation that British speech is emotionally repressed, mannered, or affected (la-di-da) but in Britain the expression of feelings is in fact codified according to the idioms of a highly stratified social discourse that is not so clearly marked in American speech. It would seem that Sondheim simply does not comprehend the way Coward articulates the nuances of class in his use of the range of English speech registers.

It is a common misconception of even some well-informed American writers and journalists that the work of British songwriters and librettists is merely a footnote in the development of the musical as it was conceived and performed on Broadway. In his coffee-table book *More Broadway Musicals*, Martin Gottfried discusses *Cats* and *The Phantom of the Opera* at length as Broadway shows based on his understanding of the art form as inherently American.[34] Would it be conceivable that *Annie Get Your Gun* or *Assassins* would ever be regarded as British musicals because they are done in London—or as German musicals for that matter, as both have been performed in Berlin?

Another classic example of the pervasive tendency to interpret British musicals within the parameters of American show business is illustrated by Gerald Mast's assertion that for '[Tim] Rice and [Andrew Lloyd] Webber, London's West End has become New Haven, where shows try out before coming to New York'.[35] It seems inconceivable for Mast that, as British citizens, Rice and Lloyd Webber have a natural desire to see their work premiered in their home country rather than thinking of a West End production merely as a stepping stone to success on Broadway.

BRITISH MUSICALS AND BRITISH AUDIENCES

As the study of popular entertainment focuses on the ways that it has connected with the audience, one indicator of its success is the number of performances a production achieved. Many shows that are dismissed or totally ignored by American scholars because they failed to repeat their success on Broadway, ran for several years in London, indicating their obvious popularity; these constitute a major manifestation of popular culture and are ripe for close readings, sociocultural or otherwise. These British hits include *Chu Chin Chow* (1916, 2,239 performances), *The Boy Friend* (1954, 2,084 performances), *Salad Days* (1954, 2,283 performances), *Oliver!* (1960, 2,680 performances),[36] *Charlie Girl* (1965, 2,202 performances), *Canterbury Tales* (1968, 2,082 performances), and *The Rocky Horror Show* (1973, 2,960 performances). Until the revival of *Chicago* in 1998, only three American musicals ever had as many as 2,000 performances—*My*

Fair Lady (London, 1958), *The Sound of Music* (London 1961), and *Fiddler on the Roof* (London, 1967). British musicals, both before and after the Second World War, have consistently been more popular with British audiences than the majority of American shows because they express explicitly *British* social and cultural values.

A rarely examined phenomenon is the way the major figures of the British musical such as writer Lionel Bart, impresario Cameron Mackintosh, and songwriting team Lloyd Webber and Rice were inspired by earlier *British* shows and composers. For example, Bart acknowledged the influence of W. S. Gilbert and Noël Coward on his lyrics; Mackintosh claims that he decided to become a producer after seeing Julian Slade's *Salad Days* when he was 8 years old, while the very first musical to be written by Lloyd Webber and Rice, *The Likes of Us*, is clearly modelled on Lionel Bart's *Oliver!*. *Billy Elliot* is indebted to the tradition of working-class political theatre that originated with Unity Theatre[37] and was then developed in less didactic ways by Joan Littlewood who had worked with Lionel Bart and later John McGrath.[38]

In the last four decades more than half of the shows constituting the corpus of musicals with which European, American, and Asian theatre-goers are most familiar, were produced in Britain.[39] There are continual revivals and tours of many British shows, while even musicals that never played on Broadway such as *We Will Rock You* (2002) are now becoming staples of the international market. Clearly British musical theatre has since the 1970s become a global phenomenon, making it increasingly important to situate it properly within a historical context, and to engage with the subject by means of aesthetic and sociocultural analysis.

The modern British musical as a field of academic study is a more or less undiscovered country. There have been only a few scholars like Andrew Lamb[40] or Kurt Gänzl[41] whose monographs pay serious attention to the British musical, mainly because the vast majority of books since the seventies restrict their attention to the Broadway musical. Other than Gänzl's encyclopaedic two-volume reference book *The British Musical Theatre* there have since the sixties been only two publications concentrating solely on the British musical: Sheridan Morley's *Spread a Little Happiness: The First Hundred Years of the British Musical* (1987) is a lavishly illustrated but superficial survey while Adrian Wright's well-informed *A Tanner's Worth of Tune* (2010), although not written as a scholarly work, points to the long lineage that culminates in the contemporary British musical.

Part I Britannia Rules: The Early British Musical and Society

The twenty-eight essays in this collection are organized in six parts and cover the subject in roughly chronological order. The first part, 'Britannia Rules: The Early British Musical and Society', focuses on the uses of song and dance in British theatre from the eighteenth century to the twentieth century between the two world wars. In Chapter 1

Berta Joncus provides an overview of ballad opera, starting with John Gay's *The Beggar's Opera* in 1728. As a genre that dominated the theatre for almost ten years (1728 to 1737, when it fell victim to the Licensing Act), even though or maybe precisely because it was full of inherent contradictions, ballad opera featured English folk song to cater to the public's 'growing appetite for celebrities, produce Britain's first star singers, [and] protest against leaders of state and industry'. Satirical ballad operas were popular not for their plots, but for witty references to public figures and political topics as well as for star performances. Women were often depicted as creatures with loose morals and lacking in rectitude. Joncus attributes to the genre's lasting legacy its insistence on 'natural' (i.e. artless) vocal delivery as more suitable to English tastes than the trained voices of Italian opera, the opportunities it offered for performers to 'step out of character and directly address audience members', as well as its combination of 'low' and 'high' music and its widespread use of pastiche.

In Chapter 2 Christina Fuhrmann charts the complicated position of music in early nineteenth-century London theatre, when it was regularly denigrated as the less valued alternative to the most widely admired form of performance, legitimate drama. The deployment of music in theatre was attacked for its persistent association with the 'frivolous, sensual and effeminate', and consequently the art form was regarded with widespread suspicion—one reason why London audiences opposed the 'lengthy intertwining of drama and song'. By comparing the uses of music across three popular genres (melodrama, British opera, and foreign opera adaptations) by one and the same composer—Sir Henry Rowley Bishop—Fuhrmann highlights their various aesthetics and what each genre contributed to the future employment of musical forms in British theatre, since these characteristics are still found in musical theatre today.

Chapter 3 provides an approach to the oeuvre of Gilbert and Sullivan—the first star songwriting team of the English stage. Carolyn Williams interrogates their much-loved comic operas for their commentaries on contemporary life as well as their representations of gender as a sociocultural category by means of sophisticated parody and burlesque of 'past literary, theatrical, and musical genres'. Through an in-depth analysis of key shows extensively related to the earlier works they spoof or ridicule, Williams reveals how the duo's unique set of character types quickly established themselves as markers of Gilbert and Sullivan's theatrical world and fosters an understanding of 'gender as culture'. Williams ends her essay with an examination of the trope of cultural encounter as it is to be found in *The Gondoliers, The Yeoman of the Guard*, and *Utopia Limited* (and at least implied in *The Mikado*), a trope that 'serves to illustrate English gender, class, and capitalism'.

In Chapter 4, Stephen Banfield examines early English musical comedy as it dominated London stages from the 'gay 1890s' to the mid-1920s by offering a close reading of *The Arcadians* (1909)—one of those shows that popular opinion regards as forgotten, 'never to be revived, its tunes no longer hummed or even remembered except in tiny pockets of cultural nostalgia'. Banfield demonstrates how *The Arcadians* offers biting social satire as well as music hall vulgarity courtesy of Edward Monckton's tunes and examines the way they are deployed in the service of the narrative. He suggests that shows from 'the West End's golden age of musical comedy' have often survived as unstable libretti and scores, whose precise forms on the London stage cannot be reconstructed with absolute certainty. Symbolizing Victorian and Edwardian confidence in Britain's worldwide colonial dominance, these musical comedies also profited from this global presence by extensively touring the Empire. Merchandising and amateur productions in Britain and elsewhere up until the 1950s testify to the shows' continuing attractiveness as commercial entertainment, even if their impact in the professional theatre began to wane with changes in public taste and attitudes after the First World War.

With the onset of that war the popularity of revue began to challenge the appeal of Edwardian musical comedy. In Chapter 5 David Linton undertakes the task of characterizing the aesthetics of the West End revue, investigating how it articulated and disseminated discourses of national identity, regeneration, and renewal. Decidedly modern in its lack of narrative, use of popular dance forms, scenic design, and jazz-inflected music, the revue tackled 'contemporary issues such as divorce, drug culture, immigration, sexual infidelity and political dissent'. Linton explains how the form established itself as a consequence of far-reaching changes in London's theatre industry and proved a perfect vehicle to combine familiar elements with experiments featuring the alternative and the new. He identifies the revue's fragmented structure as both key component and major selling point, 'marking its modernism and its difference' via 'juxtaposition and contradiction'. This structure not only allowed the genre to react promptly to changes in society, popular taste, and attitudes and to mirror the 'bewildering variety of national, racial and gender identity constructions' onstage but also offered possibilities for transgressive sketches, songs, and performance modes.

Part II British or American: Artistic Differences

The second part of the volume focuses on the years before and after the Second World War, explicating the persistent British obsession with class as well as the competitive relationship between the West End and Broadway. In Chapter 6, George Burrows considers two smash hits of the interwar years, *Mister Cinders* (1929) and *Me and My Girl* (1937) with their gender-reversed 'Cinderella-type narratives' as class-conscious examples of carnival culture as theorized by Mikhail Bakhtin. Here the carnivalistic elements on the one hand show a growing discontent with the traditional class hierarchy of British society and on the other, through their grotesque highlighting of eccentricity, embody social criticism. While the plot structure of both shows represents the need for 'increased social interaction and class mobility engendered by the impact of modernity', both *Mister Cinders* and *Me and My Girl* propose that the 'traditionally stratified structures of British society' need not be abandoned entirely as long as they are integrated within 'a refined social hierarchy built on new values'. In the final section of his essay,

Burrows also takes a look at the revivals of both shows in the 1980s, showing how the 'preoccupation with enduring class hierarchies' (which marks these shows as 'peculiarly British') was replaced by 'a reassertion of tradition' in the form of 'profound nostalgia for bygone times and clearer class-hierarchies'—as a result, abandoning what made the original productions so remarkable.

In Chapter 7, Stewart Nicholls chronicles the rise and fall of the romantic operetta from the end of the First World War to the beginning of the 1950s as epitomized by the work of Ivor Novello who had an unrivalled string of hits from *Glamorous Nights* (1935) to *Gay's the Word* (1951) as a result of his singular combination of movie star glamour and wide popular appeal as a songwriter. The overview situates his work in the context of Novello's contemporaries and competitors, such as Eric Maschwitz and George Posford, Noël Coward, Harold Purcell, and Harry Parr-Davies as well as Vivian Ellis and A. P. Herbert. Nicholls extolls the artistic virtues while occasionally exposing the shortcomings of a genre—and its most prominent composer—that has more or less completely disappeared from British stages. Typical elements of a Novello show that were often copied by other producers include 'stunning scenic effects [. . .], a grandiose ballet and [. . .] show-within-a-show sequences'. The scores and orchestrations of several of these English operettas have been lost, yet, as Nicholls convincingly argues, many of them definitely merit a proper revival.

The popular narrative concerning the conquest of the West End by the 'golden age' Broadway musical from 1947 is addressed in Chapter 8, in which Dominic Symonds interrogates its journalistic veracity to discover instead a 'far more balanced [picture] than history tells'. He also provides various explanations of how *Oklahoma!* and *Annie Get Your Gun* affected theatre-goers in a country that 'had been hit hard by the war' and consequently suffered from exhaustion, lack of spirit, and further demoralization by ongoing food rationing and a weak economy. Britain may have had an ambivalent relationship with American culture which was perceived as both 'aspirational and as a threat', but the vitality on display in the two shows, as exemplified in the energy of their performers, their unconventional portrayals of gender, as well as *Oklahoma!*'s promise of new beginnings, found a receptive audience. According to Symonds, what differentiated Broadway from West End shows was that the former were 'more vibrant, more vigorous, more up-to-date and more sexualized'. Yet if the American imports presented competition on their home turf, Symonds also demonstrates how British artists responded by taking an in-depth look at Ivor Novello's *Gay's the Word* (1951), the most obvious example of a musical that deliberately responded to the challenge of the Broadway form.

Chapter 9 focuses on those British shows which premiered between 1945 and 1955. Conceived by John Snelson as a period of 'transition and reassessment', it allowed for a broad diversity of West End shows to cater for a variety of West End audiences. Snelson identifies the politics of these musicals not merely as a response to the 'shift from Labour social inclusion to Conservative reassertion of social conformity', but also as a repeated questioning of national identity that sought to distance British culture from American social values through 'choices of subject matter, musical style, and cultural/topical reference'. The chapter illustrates how the specific talents of West End stars like Cicely Courtneidge and George Formby were showcased in star vehicles like *Gay's the Word* or *Zip Goes a Million* (both 1951) as well as considering the contributions of composers and authors such as Vivian Ellis and A. P. Herbert. These artists opted for a 'distinctly English vein of lyric theatre, especially comic opera' whose pastoral iconography in particular conjured an idealized image of the nation, its heritage and history. Those British shows that unexpectedly became smash hits (like *The Boy Friend* or *Salad Days*) often started small and that in itself already set them apart from the Broadway shows which opened at the same time. Their comforting nostalgia for a lifestyle of financial security and leisure that had never actually existed in England was 'more in tune with the decade's return to aspirational Conservative values'. Yet as Snelson reveals, *Salad Days* also allows for a reading against the grain: the show constantly challenges the status quo and is in fact subversive in its clear-eyed indictment of an increasingly repressive and rigid English society.

PART III NEW APPROACHES TO FORM AND SUBJECT MATTER

The third part of the book comprises four chapters addressing innovative musicals that appeared between the late 1950s and the early 1970s. Elizabeth A. Wells describes the changes in the genre in the wake of John Osborne's *Look Back in Anger* (1956), which ushered in a new era in British theatre. Just like the plays of the so-called 'Angry Young Men' (though there were also some women), certain London musicals reconceived their representation of working-class characters and their living circumstances at the same time as others remained content to 'merely' entertain audiences by allowing them to see their favourite stars in more traditional fare. Wells highlights how the movement to undermine the status quo was spearheaded by Joan Littlewood's Theatre Workshop and the Royal Court under the artistic direction of George Devine. Starting with the darkly satirical *Expresso Bongo* (1958), many British shows of this period—including *Fings Ain't Wot They Used T'Be* and *The Crooked Mile* (both 1959)—centred around Soho and its denizens but were less concerned with integration than the Broadway shows that reached London at the same time. With a presentational style and scores that were indebted partly to music hall and melodrama, these and other musicals of the era are testament to the desire to create an alternative to the American musicals that were believed to dominate the London stage. Soon, though, the early 1960s brought sweeping changes which 'started to make that kind of musical theatre, however challenging, seem quaint'.

To nobody's surprise the overwhelmingly positive public response to Lionel Bart's *Oliver!* (1960) led to an extended series of British period musicals that tried with varying degrees of success to emulate what had made that show unique. In Chapter 11, Ben Francis takes a closer look at seven epigones that premiered in the 1960s and early

1970s: *Half a Sixpence* (1963), *Our Man Crichton* (1964), *Jorrocks* (1966), *Ann Veronica* (1969), *Trelawny* (1972), *The Card* (1973), and *Billy* (1974). These shows have in common a return to the concentration on social class that characterized musical comedy from the Gaiety shows to *Me and My Girl*. They also share a perspective that promoted frequent revisiting of traditional music hall styles with their gentle love songs, cheeky comic numbers, and the traditional working-class social ritual of the 'knees-up'. With the hero often having to choose between working-class values and bourgeois double standards, i.e. between an authentic and a false life, the musicals allowed their protagonists upward mobility without the necessity of betraying their working-class roots, here frequently exemplified by a rebellious spirit and a naughty frankness. This liberal attitude later gave way to a less open-minded reaction to social climbing in *The Card*, reflecting the moment when conservatism regained strength in Britain after Edward Heath was elected prime minister in 1970. Nevertheless, none of these musicals wholly rejects the class system itself, presenting the middle classes with unthreatening depictions of working-class people as 'clean and hard-working' as long as they adhere honestly to the traditional values of their class. Francis's analysis also points out that the final show under discussion, the extremely successful *Billy* (904 performances), is a rare post-*Oliver!* musical to feature a leading character who is estranged from his community, a further indication of how changes in British society were reflected in the West End musical.

Chapter 12 brings to the fore three collaborations that constitute an idiosyncratic subgenre: with *Stop the World, I Want to Get Off* (1961), *The Roar of the Greasepaint, the Smell of the Crowd* (1964), and *The Good Old, Bad Old Days* (1972), Anthony Newley and Leslie Bricusse invented a kind of show that was built on minimalism, metatheatricality, and the medieval morality play. David Cottiss offers an outline of the respective careers of Newley and Bricusse, who, though close friends, came from very different backgrounds and had an artistic partnership which could best be described as 'one of checks and balances'. In many ways, *Stop the World* was not only groundbreaking but unique and therefore, as Cottiss compellingly argues, must count as 'the first British example of what has come to be known as a "concept" musical'. With integration of the musical numbers not a priority since 'Bricusse and Newley always crafted songs with one eye on the pop charts', their collaborations are difficult to revive nowadays, not least because they depended heavily on the established star persona of their original lead, Anthony Newley.

It may have taken Britain until the 1980s to re-establish a flourishing musical theatre industry after the end of the Second World War, but again in contrast to the Broadway musical after the mid-1950s it had close connections with a thriving pop-music industry. In Chapter 13, Ian Sapiro examines the significant links between pop music and the British musical as evidenced by the rise of rock opera and the increasing importance of concept albums from the late 1960s onwards. At the time, recording artists saw the potential of the long-playing vinyl record as a vehicle for a connected suite of songs that came to be known as the concept album and coincided with a movement in musical theatre away from linear narratives and towards theatrical spectacle. Sapiro explores the aesthetics of four rock operas, their concept (or subsequent) recordings and film adaptations and thus considers the Who's *Tommy* (1969), Andrew Lloyd Webber and Tim Rice's *Jesus Christ Superstar* (1970), *Jeff Wayne's Musical Version of the War of the Worlds* (1978), and Mike Batt's *The Hunting of the Snark* (1984). By analysing their respective use of rock and orchestral sounds as well as their approach to visual aesthetics, Sapiro compares the success of these shows in combining theatre and rock, explaining why the 'rock-opera-as-stage-musical [. . .] appears to have been a relatively short-lived phenomenon'.

Part IV 'The British Are Coming!'

Part IV of the book deals with key productions of the 1980s and beyond which, for whatever reason, have proved groundbreaking. In Chapter 14 Sarah Browne shows how British directors who honed their craft in subsidized theatre brought new life to classic Broadway shows through subtle and sometimes radical reinterpretation, winning widespread critical acclaim in the process and proving the advantages of working in a theatrical environment that is not predominantly geared towards profit. The National Theatre revivals of *Guys and Dolls* (directed by Richard Eyre, 1982), *Carousel* (Nicholas Hytner, 1992), and *Oklahoma!* (Trevor Nunn, 1998), as well as the Donmar Warehouse production of *Company* (Sam Mendes, 1996) re-established these musicals in the eyes of the British public not just as American musical 'standards' but also as modern classics of the American theatre, thereby winning them not only the renewed appreciation of reviewers but also new audiences. Given the opportunity 'to explore the material free from the traditions established by the original Broadway productions', these and other revivals took risks with new choreography, multiracial casting, and an exploratory approach to staging the texts that gained them huge critical and commercial success.

Regularly voted the 'most popular musical of all time', *Les Misérables* celebrated its thirtieth anniversary on the London stage in 2015. Overcoming a less-than-favourable reception upon its premiere at the Barbican in 1985, the piece has not only become the 'world's longest-running musical'[42] but was also turned into an Oscar-winning blockbuster film in 2012. In Chapter 15, scholars of Victor Hugo (Kathryn M. Grossman and Bradley Stephens) finally attempt something that neither the musical's sceptical first night reviewers nor its countless fans have done in sufficient detail: they explicitly identify the relationship between Hugo's bestseller and its musical version. Underlining that the show affectionately known (and continuously marketed) as *Les Miz* 'has perhaps done more to popularize' Hugo's epic novel than any other single adaptation, Grossman and Stephens point out the similarities and the differences in the reception of the two works. The musical's connection to its source material is 'one of correspondence rather than equivalence'; while some simplifications and omissions (such as the novel's lengthy digressions) are probably inevitable when staging a three-hour theatrical adaptation of a book that, depending on the edition, runs to more than 1,500 pages, the show nevertheless endeavours to channel 'how Hugo understood individual experience as part of a sublime collective'. For Grossman and Stephens, the musical adaptation is without doubt 'more overwhelming than it is subtle', but then it is precisely this heightening and intensifying of the original story's melodramatic elements which accounts for the show's emotional impact.

When a large number of British musicals transferred to New York in the 1980s, they were problematically named 'megamusicals' and were often criticized by American reviewers for privileging scenic style over dramaturgical content: audiences allegedly left the theatre 'humming the scenery'.[43] In Chapter 16, Christine White responds to these critics by asking whether sophisticated scenography should indeed be considered a bad thing. She outlines how the design elements of British musical theatre developed both from and in reaction to writers' theatre and agitprop and explains how practically all of the celebrated set designers since the early 1980s learned their craft not in commercial theatre, but in small-scale subsidized—and therefore often chronically underfunded—companies. Yet set designers such as John Napier, Maria Björnson, and Bob Crowley were merely reacting to two developments: on the one hand, technological advances which allowed the elaboration and movement of spectacular sets/set pieces closely aligned to the dramatic and musical climaxes of the shows, and on the other a growing sophistication on the part of the audience to interpret scenography.

In Chapter 17 Robert Gordon traces how the British musical has represented and reflected social issues in the six decades since 1954. The 'absurd disruption of social convention' in *Salad Days* can be understood not merely as whimsical fun, but also as a subversive rejection of the repression in 1950s Britain of nonconformist behaviour, such as homosexuality. With their gay/camp elements, both *Salad Days* and *The Boy Friend* are the expression of a sensibility that questions heteronormativity and is also a key ingredient of *Valmouth* (1958) and, in a postmodern context, Neil Bartlett's *Night after Night* (1993). Gordon also analyses plays that 'utilize songs in developing crucial moments of drama', referencing a history of British left-wing theatre that came to reflect working-class culture and was often based on Marxist aesthetics. These two recurrent themes of sociopolitical commentary—the queer/camp strategy and the left-wing working-class critique of hegemonic politics and culture—interact and are combined to startling effect in *Billy Elliot* (2005). With its complex portrayal of the miners' strike of 1984–5, one of the defining moments in modern British history, the show explores the effects of Margaret Thatcher's rejection of communitarian values in favour of ruthless individualism[44] while at the same time critiquing the macho, if not downright homophobic, reaction of working-class men when it comes to forms of personal and cultural expression that seem alien to their own traditions. With its 'dialectical argument around the relationship between class and gender/sexual orientation, popular and "high" art', *Billy Elliot* is a prime example of British theatre at its most socially aware.

PART V TRAILBLAZERS

The fifth part is dedicated to six artists whose work deserves special consideration because their contributions to the British musical proved to be either groundbreaking or utterly unique. The first of these 'trailblazers' is Noël Coward, multitalented star of stage and screen, who as a writer is primarily represented on English-language stages by his famous comedies—in spite of the fact that throughout his career he wrote songs and composed scores for revues, operettas, and musical comedies, which he popularized in the fifties by means of his own cabaret act. In Chapter 18 Dominic McHugh accomplishes the long overdue task of evaluating this 'elusive writer's output' in the area of musical theatre—a difficult undertaking because Coward's position within musical theatre history is contradictory and complicated. McHugh examines the influences detectable in Coward's work as well as his conception of melopoetics, before identifying the element of performativity as key to Coward's compositions. Special attention is paid to the achievements of Coward's most popular and commercially successful musical theatre work, *Bitter Sweet* (1929), and the last section of the essay reflects on the aspects of national identity and metatheatricality in the artist's revue material and final shows. McHugh arrives at the conclusion that steadfastly avoiding adherence to certain 'rules' or 'conventions' of musical theatre renders Coward's oeuvre 'sui generis'.

Diametrically opposed to Coward's aesthetics and politics is the theatre of director Joan Littlewood. Of course Littlewood is justly celebrated for her key role in British theatre from the 1950s onward, but as Ben Macpherson states at the opening of his survey of the impact of this extraordinary personality in Chapter 19, '[l]ess often is her work explored as part of British musical theatre history, with the exception of the much-feted *Oh What a Lovely War* (1963)'. He proceeds to elucidate Littlewood's achievements 'through examining [her] view of commercial success, her working processes, and the thematic and structural facets of her productions', in the context of her socialist ideal of 'a theatre for the people, by the people, with the people'. The chapter reveals how Littlewood became a major influence on the training of artists of every type in British theatre—musical or otherwise—and introduced alternative approaches to mise en scène, to plays with music, and musicals in general.

One of Littlewood's earliest success stories at the Theatre Royal Stratford East, was *Fings Ain't Wot They Used T'Be* (1959), which featured the songs of a young pop composer-lyricist named Lionel Bart who, a year later, would write *Oliver!*. Millie Taylor surveys Bart's work in Chapter 20, with specific attention to his iconic and often-revived Dickens adaptation as well as to his two other major shows, *Blitz!* (1962) and *Maggie May* (1964). Taylor explains the fact that British audiences were and continue to be far more receptive to Bart's writing than American critics and theatre-goers with reference to both his theatrical background and his particular style: his roots in East London's Jewish working class can be observed in his deployment of traditional Jewish music as well as English music hall and variety with even the ballads being composed in a 'musical range often focused around the pitch of speech rising to belted notes at the end'. Another characteristic of Bart's songs, which especially in his work for musical theatre are far more complex than he is customarily given credit for, is an often ironic juxtaposition of words and music, with lyrics depicting a harsh reality while the music takes the form of easily hummable tunes that suggest an optimism either not supported or else openly contradicted by the lyrics. Bart's best works not only reflected a British identity and idiom, but also revealed that the British musical was capable of treating more serious subjects and complex themes, while his collaboration with progressive artists like director Joan Littlewood and set designer Sean Kenny represented a bold break with traditional musical theatre.

In Chapter 21 Olaf Jubin considers the oeuvre of the man who, with the possible exception of W. S. Gilbert, may be the most successful British lyricist in the history of the musical: Tim Rice. During a career spanning nearly five decades and running the gamut from critical and commercial smash hits to flops that were appreciated by neither critics nor audiences, Rice has often been underestimated as an artist, not least because his style of lyric writing is characterized not 'by dense image clusters or startling metaphors, but rather by ingenious twists of colloquial language'. Tim Rice is shown to return time and again to certain tropes that hold a particular fascination for him and can be summed up as 'the pop star scenario': they include 'the plight of individuals who stand out from the crowd because of their talents and the way they are treated by the people that admire them—or tear them down', 'the discrepancy between public and private image [. . .], personal ambition and its cost, as well as the dissatisfaction and potential downfall after early success'. When engaged by a topic such as these, Rice's lyrics reveal him as an artist with a unique 'voice' and sensibility.

In Chapter 22, Miranda Lundskaer-Nielsen argues persuasively that perhaps the 'biggest British musical theatre star to emerge in the 1980s and 1990s' may have been the producer Cameron Mackintosh. Often praised, as well as denigrated, as the man who invented and introduced 'the so-called modern "megamusical"', Mackintosh pioneered new approaches to marketing and merchandising and opened up new global markets for the genre as a whole. In this context, Lundskaer-Nielsen chronicles the producer's success with *Cats* (1981) which was reproduced to as-yet unimagined financial gain all over the world—a producing strategy that was replicated and perfected in later Mackintosh smash hits like *Les Misérables, The Phantom of the Opera* (1986), and *Miss Saigon* (1989).

The final contribution to Part V showcases Andrew Lloyd Webber, the composer as superstar. His work combines artistry and unprecedented commercial success to such a degree that, as David Chandler puts it, no other body of music since Puccini's, or even Wagner's, has 'prompted such a combination of passionate adulation with intense, uncomprehending (and often ignorant) hostility'. Lloyd Webber's musicals are famous for their hit melodies and are ambitious in both their choice of topic and musical dramaturgy, with daring subject matter most likely to be sacrificed should the composer be forced to make a choice among the three. The all-sung musical is often regarded as the main contribution by Lloyd Webber to the compositional vocabulary of the genre as well as his 'signature style', and in Chapter 23 Chandler traces the development of this style during the composer's early years before concentrating on *The Phantom of the Opera* (1986) which is a key work in Lloyd Webber's oeuvre, not only because it may be his best-loved musical, but also because it is undoubtedly his most financially successful.

PART VI 'THE ART OF THE POSSIBLE': ALTERNATIVE APPROACHES TO MUSICAL THEATRE AESTHETICS

Part VI offers insight into a variety of more recent trends in British musical theatre. In Chapter 24, Robert Lawson-Peebles traces the ongoing influence of *The Beggar's Opera* (1728) in British drama, not just on stage but also on radio and television. The chapter reveals the varied impact the piece has made on British artists since its 1920 revival by Nigel Playfair—in the many versions of its framing device utilized by new works, in its anticipation of modern notions of musical theatre as a collaborative genre, and in its loose yet dramaturgically complex relationship between scene and song. Identifying an aesthetics of disintegration in John Gay's seminal work, the essay examines the way the radical nature of this text has repeatedly been betrayed by productions which sentimentalize and prettify its deliberately rough vernacular in speech and song. Lawson-Peebles then details the initially hostile or ambivalent British reception of the other famous work directly based on it—Bertolt Brecht and Kurt Weill's *The Threepenny Opera* (1928). After a brief discussion of Alan Ayckbourn's use of *The Beggar's Opera* in *A Chorus of Disapproval* (1984), the essay proceeds to explore the function of song in works by exponents of a socialist art form, such as Richard Hughes, Olive Shapley, Geoffrey Bridson, Joan Littlewood, and Jimmy Miller (who later called himself Ewan MacColl). The chapter ends with an analysis of the work of Alan Plater and that of Dennis Potter whose television oeuvre proved seminal in its use of popular music to frame a progressively 'darkening vision of the fate of working-class culture'.

In Chapter 25, George Rodosthenous looks at one of the least respected subgenres of contemporary musical theatre: the much maligned 'jukebox musical' might never have attained its current ubiquity if it had not been for the totally unexpected and overwhelming success of *Mamma Mia!* (1999), the first musical to prove just how much money can be earned by basing a show around the back catalogue of a famous recording artist or pop group, in this case Swedish band Abba. The show's sophisticated postmodern use of the hits exploits song placement in classic musical comedy terms to great effect. As Rodosthenous explains, British jukebox musicals come in three varieties: the semi-biographical jukebox musical, the (tribute) band jukebox musical, and the fictional jukebox musical, with *Mamma Mia!* as a prime example of the last category. The show's feminist agenda is also evident in the fact that at various points throughout its plot *Mamma Mia!* questions the importance of marriage and even rejects the obsession with biological fatherhood as an outmoded aspect of patriarchy, while still managing to remain an absolute crowd-pleaser.

Another increasingly important subgenre in today's musical theatre is the show for the whole family, and in Chapter 26 Rebecca Warner takes a closer look at what attracts 'a hybrid spectatorship' of theatre-goers from various generations. For her case studies she has chosen various shows that possess an 'archetypal British sensi-bility', although several of them have also been produced very successfully in other countries: *Just So* (1993) and *Mary Poppins* (2005) as well as two shows based on books by Roald Dahl, *Matilda* (2011) and *Charlie and the Chocolate Factory* (2013). Tony Graham, when artistic director of the Unicorn Theatre, suggested a five-step gauge for considering whether a work would appeal to children in the theatre. Warner's in-depth reading of the four musicals in question explains what forms these five elements of 'poetry, transcendence, substance, dramatic potential and a child's perspective' take in each of them.

Chapter 27 is dedicated to three productions that for different reasons each made international headlines or received international acclaim: although *Shockheaded Peter* (1998), *Jerry Springer: The Opera* (2003), and *London Road* (2011) were not classified or marketed by their creators as 'musicals', they nonetheless won prizes in the category 'best new musical'. According to David Roesner this apparent contradiction is resolved by understanding these three shows as examples that 'demonstrate the critical and even subversive potential that the musical [. . .] has'. What they also have in common is that they were nurtured originally in a subsidized theatre environment. Roesner explains that by destabilizing both the content and the form of what is commonly understood as a musical, all three productions can be seen to hark back to cultural contexts and theatri-cal traditions that are less predominantly 'British' and more generally 'European', reveal-ing that British musical theatre has been subject to influences far more wide-ranging than those of the Broadway musical and serving as a timely reminder 'that the notion of what passes as "a musical" is undergoing constant change'.

The final essay deals with the contribution of Black British and Anglo-Asian cul-ture to the musical in the UK, 'tracing attitudes and practices in both the commercial and non-mainstream sectors', which, according to Ben Macpherson, 'offer disparate versions of multicultural musical theatre'. Chapter 28 initially provides an overview of the 'long history of non-white performers on the London stage' from the early days, which evidenced a decidedly imperialistic mindset in the reception of perfor-mances by colonized subjects, before exploring the vast social changes between 1948 and 1970 that explain the subsequent impact of diasporic communities on the culture of contemporary Britain. Macpherson focuses on how the tensions that exist between 'the mainstream commercial output of London's West End, and the subsidized and fringe scene that can be seen Off-West End and regionally', are reflected in divergent representations of ethnic minorities in the UK. In this context, he discusses the cast-ing controversy triggered by *Miss Saigon* (1989) on its transfer to Broadway, *Bombay Dreams* (2002), which was marketed as a 'beacon for multicultural cosmopolitanism', as well as *The Big Life* (2004), a fictionalization of 'the history of Caribbean migrants who came to England on SS Empire Windrush' in 1948 and in certain ways attempted the first bridge between the two cultural sectors described earlier. The chapter ends with a consideration of the future of ethnic musical theatre in Britain, arguing that the recent *Bend It Like Beckham* (2015) 'suggests a major step forward' because it presents contemporary multiculturalism in the strictly commercial environment of the West End.

The different parts of this volume thus reveal alternatives to the aesthetic values of Broadway and challenge its accepted status as the epicentre of musical theatre production, foregrounding alternative cultural priorities and traditions.

Several common themes emerge from the essays in the handbook:

- the importance of the subsidized sector both as training ground and as artistic alternative;
- the pervasive influence of music hall, revue, and musical comedy;
- the innovatory nature of the sung-through musical as a type of popular opera;
- the desire to create alternative forms of musical, inspired by continental European theatre rather than by Broadway models;
- the persistent focus on the English class system and the greater interest in working-class culture and experience since the Second World War;
- the recognition of how closely popular cultural forms follow and how immediately they respond to sociopolitical events and to historical change;
- the willingness of many writers of British musicals to address failure, tragedy, and loss, e.g. *Expresso Bongo; Spend, Spend, Spend* (1998); *Billy; The Hired Man* (1984); *From Here to Eternity* (2013);
- the focus on community and communitarian values as opposed to the dream of individual success, e.g. *Me and My Girl; Salad Days; Fings Ain't Wot They Use T'Be; Maggie May; Billy Elliot; Made in Dagenham* (2014).

There is much in the field that requires the attention of scholars. A great deal of work needs to be done on identifying, editing, and preserving scores and libretti of musicals since 1892, while a number of issues and themes remain to be addressed. These include topics such as

- detailed consideration of the work of Sandy Wilson, Julian Slade and Dorothy Reynolds, Wolf Mankowitz, Monty Norman, Julian More, and Don Black;
- analysis of the work of film composers who have contributed scores for musical theatre (e. g. John Barry, David Arnold);
- consideration of the role of fringe theatres like the Finborough and the Union in keeping the history of British musical theatre alive;
- investigation of the enormous popularity of certain long-running hit shows initially disliked by the critics (e.g. *Chu Chin Chow, Charlie Girl, Starlight Express, We Will Rock You*);
- changes in the training for British musical theatre performers after the opening of *Cats* in 1981;
- star personalities such as Tommy Steele, Cliff Richard, Millicent Martin, Anthony Newley, Elaine Paige, Julia McKenzie, Michael Crawford, and Michael Ball;

- the impact of directors such as Wendy Toye, Richard Eyre, Trevor Nunn, Stephen Daldry, Mathew Warchus, and Rupert Goold on the development of new musicals;
- the contribution of new generations of writers and composers like television song-writer and comic Victoria Wood (*Acorn Antiques*, 2005; *That Day We Sang*, 2011); composer Howard Goodall (*The Hired Man*, 1984; *Love Story*, 2010; *Bend It Like Beckham*); playwrights Lee Hall (*Billy Elliot*) and Tim Firth (*Our House*, 2002; *This Is My Family*, 2013; *The Girls*, 2015); and pop stars Elton John (*Disney's Aida*, 2000; *The Lion King*, 1997; *Billy Elliot*), Damon Albarn (*Monkey: Journey to the West*, 2007; *Wonder.land*, 2015), Sting (*The Last Ship*, 2014), and Gary Barlow (*Finding Neverland*, 2015; *The Girls*).

Musicals account for the major part of the £2.7 billion spent every year by tourists on British theatre,[45] while the cultural industries generate £5.9 billion annually for the country's economy.[46] This handbook, together with other recent developments in critical writing on the British musical, aims to enhance the comprehension of what remains a vibrant form of particularly British entertainment.

NOTES

1. See Chapter 1 by Berta Joncus for a discussion of the variety of forms and aims of ballad opera.
2. *Tommy* and *Jesus Christ Superstar* originated as concept albums, so although they were sung-through, the dramaturgical structure of these shows resembles a theatricalized song cycle—closer perhaps to what soon became known on Broadway as the concept musical than to the traditional narrative musicals of Rodgers and Hammerstein.
3. See Chapter 24 by Robert Lawson-Peebles.
4. For an in-depth exploration for this term and the concept behind it, see Richard Dyer, *Only Entertainment* (London: Routledge, 2002).
5. Andrea Most, *Making Americans: Jews and the American Musical* (Cambridge, MA: Harvard University Press, 2004).
6. Raymond Knapp, *The American Musical and the Formation of National Identity* (Princeton, NJ: Princeton University Press, 2005) and Raymond Knapp, *The American Musical and the Performance of Personal Identity* (Princeton, NJ: Princeton University Press, 2009).
7. John Bush Jones, *Our Musicals Ourselves* (Waltham, MA: Brandeis University Press, 2003).
8. Stacy Wolf, *Changed for Good* (New York: Oxford University Press, 2011).
9. Indeed, in 1955 Joan Littlewood was the first actor to play Mother Courage in Britain.
10. John Lahr, 'On Your Toes', *New Yorker*, 4 July 2005, http://www.newyorker.com/critics/theatre/050704crth_theatre (subscription required) accessed 13 May 2013.
11. When *Billy Elliot* opened on Broadway in 2008, the majority of New York reviews were extremely positive.
12. Richard Kislan's *The Musical: A Look at the American Musical Theatre* (New York: Applause, 2000) and Denny Martin Flynn's, *Musical! A Grand Tour!* (Belmont, CA: Wadsworth Publishing Co., 1997) are typical of a number of publications that denigrate British musicals as failed attempts to write shows that derive from Broadway models.

13. By 1915, Kern had however worked for a number of years in London.
14. The well-made play is a genre developed by the French dramatists Eugène Scribe (1791–1861) and Victorien Sardou (1831–1908) and popularized in Britain by Arthur Wing Pinero, establishing a dramaturgical model that had by the turn of the century become ubiquitous in the West End theatre. Even playwrights as progressive as Oscar Wilde, Harley Granville-Barker, and—on occasion—George Bernhard Shaw, exploited the form of the well-made play as a vehicle for subversive ideas. The form was only directly challenged as a vehicle for serious British drama by John Osborne, Arnold Wesker, and Harold Pinter from 1956 onwards. For more on this topic, see John Russell Brown, *The Rise and Fall of the Well-Made Play* (London: Routledge, 2013).
15. '[F]or the second half of the 1950s, the most enduring image of the British musical was of something with the parochial values of the village hall in *Salad Days* or the over-refined, nostalgic atmosphere of a fictitious and glamorized 1920s in *The Boy Friend*.' John Mainwaring Snelson, ' "We Said We Wouldn't Look Back": British Musical Theatre, 1935–1960', in *Cambridge Companion to the Musical*, ed. William Everett and Paul Laird (Cambridge: Cambridge University Press, 2002), 101–119; here 116.
16. John Mainwaring Snelson, 'The West End Musical, 1947–1954: British Identity and the "American Invasion" ' (Unpublished PhD thesis, University of Birmingham, 2002).
17. The longest-running of these were *Sweet and Low* (1943), *Sweeter and Lower* (1944), *Sweetest and Lowest* (1947), at the Ambassador's Theatre, which respectively ran for 800, 670, and 791 performances.
18. Guy Burgess and Donald Maclean together with Kim Philby, Anthony Blunt, and one unidentified figure, constituted a 'Cambridge spy ring' that betrayed the Western powers to the Soviets during and after the war. Burgess made no secret of his homosexuality, and in 1955 he and Maclean were revealed as living in Moscow, while Philby defected in 1963, but it was only in the 1980s that the homosexual Anthony Blunt was publicly identified as 'the fourth man' while John Cairncross and others have been suspected of being the fifth man.
19. 'In the mid-fifties, official and public hostility to homosexuality sharply intensified [. . .]. There was an atmosphere of moral panic in which homosexuality became closely associated with national decline and political subversion [. . .]. After the defections of Burgess and Maclean [. . .] the Conservative government were keen to show their American allies that they were indeed cracking down on security risks. In this context, the bogeyman of the homosexual became a vulnerable and convenient scapegoat for broader anxieties about national security. According to the law "any act of gross indecency" between two men, whether in public or in private, was punishable by imprisonment, and it was therefore not difficult to mount a sustained drive to improve the prosecution rate, not least through the use of handsome agents provocateurs working for the Metropolitan Police in public toilets. Prosecutions for homosexual offences had already risen fourfold in the 1940s [. . .] and between 1950 and 1954 the annual prosecution rate soared from 4416 cases to 6644.' Dominic Sandbrook, *Never Had it So Good* (London: Abacus, 2006), 598–600. The two most high-profile cases of homosexuals either prosecuted or threatened with prosecution in the early 1950s were those of John Gielgud who was entrapped by an agent provocateur in a public toilet in the West End and Alan Turing. Turing was discovered to have a homosexual liaison with a man who had robbed him, and that discovery eventually led him to commit suicide.
20. The song 'Hush, Hush' in *Salad Days* is a parody of such Cold War paranoia, while the absurd appearance of the flying saucer sends up the parallel obsession of popular culture at that time with the invasion of the earth by aliens.

21. Music hall and pantomime (a form that is equally popular with middle- and working-class audiences) emphasize camp and witty by-play with the audience, crude double entendres, cross-dressing, and nostalgia for old traditions at the expense of originality and genuine modernity. With the exception of homosexual spectators who read such performance in a specially coded way, American popular culture was innocent of this type of camp until the late 1980s when gay and queer culture began to manifest itself overtly in some Broadway musicals.

22. Understandably, homosexual audiences enjoyed such camp humour in an intensely personal way, exploiting and elaborating the camp deconstruction of 'normality' in such an intense way that it exaggerated the conventional meaning of 'gay' (variously defined as 'carefree', 'jolly', 'showily dressed'); in the late sixties 'gay' became a political label to replace the then-derogatory term 'queer'.

23. In fact it deliberately references both Rodgers and Hart's *The Girl Friend* (1926) and *No, No, Nanette* (1925). Understandably, *Salad Days* did not find a home on Broadway while *The Boy Friend* succeeded in a production that turned Sandy Wilson's affectionate homage to the twenties into a vulgar burlesque. See John Snelson (Chapter 9) for a discussion of Sandy Wilson's view of the Broadway production starring Julie Andrews.

24. *The Boy Friend* (2,084 performances) and *Salad Days* (2,283 performances) far exceeded the length of run of every post-war musical until *Oliver!* but the two shows ran at the Wyndham's Theatre (759 seats) and the Vaudeville Theatre (690 seats), which are smaller West End theatres with approximately a third of the seating capacity of the Theatre Royal Drury Lane (2,196 seats) where *Oklahoma!* ran for 1,543 performances or the Coliseum (2,558 seats), home to *Annie Get Your Gun* for 1,304 performances.

25. Skiffle bands were a British phenomenon of the fifties that revived an old African American style, using banjo and acoustic guitar together with improvised instruments such as washboards, jugs, kazoos, washtub bass, the musical saw, and cigar-box fiddles to play a rough type of blues and jazz. Immensely popular between 1953 and 1958, they had a direct influence on the formation of early British rock groups such as the Beatles.

26. See Chapter 24 by Robert Lawson-Peebles for further discussion of *The Entertainer*.

27. Olivier based Archie's routines on the legendary music hall comic Max Miller.

28. Although initially successful in military terms, the opportunistic war was secretly engineered by the British and French governments who encouraged Israel to collaborate in capturing the Suez Canal in defence of British and French interests. It ultimately resulted in a humiliating climbdown; the intervention of the American government exposed the British government's post-war impotence and double standards, becoming an emblem of the dishonourable nature of the British colonial enterprise.

29. George Wellwarth, 'John Osborne: "Angry Young Man"?', in *The Theater of Protest and Paradox: Developments in the Avant-Garde Drama* (New York: New York University Press, 1964), 222–234.

30. R. B. Marriott, '*The Lily White Boys* Never Had It So Good—Or So Sad', *The Stage*, 4 February 1960, 17.

31. Lawson-Peebles's Chapter 24, 'The Beggar's Legacy', examines a tradition of using songs in stage, radio, and latterly in television plays, including analysis of the work of Alan Plater and of Alan Ayckbourn's *A Chorus of Disapproval* (1984).

32. One hardly needs to note that both *Jesus Christ Superstar* and *Evita* became enormously successful stage musicals a year or two after the concept albums were released. *Jesus Christ Superstar* was adapted into a film in 1973 and *Evita* in 1996.

33. Stephen Sondheim, *Finishing the Hat: Collected Lyrics, 1954–1981, with Attendant Comments, Principles, Heresies, Grudges, Whines and Anecdotes* (New York: Virgin Books, 2010), 230.

34. Such cultural imperialism is perpetuated in Elizabeth Wollman's *The Theatre Will Rock*, which in spite of all the evidence to the contrary, persists in regarding *Hair* as the chief progenitor of the rock and pop musical, blithely ignorant of *Expresso Bongo*'s scathing exposé of the British rock 'n' roll scene in 1958, of Jack Good's *Catch My Soul* (1967), and only vaguely acknowledging the impact of concept albums such as *Sergeant Pepper's Lonely Heart's Club Band* (1967), a piece that was toured in a concert production by Jack Good (1968) and had a direct influence on albums designated rock operas by their composers in the sixties, such as the Pretty Things' *SF Sorrow* (1968); Wollman also analyses such British rock operas or musicals as *Jesus Christ Superstar* and *Tommy* as Broadway shows.

35. Gerald Mast, *Can't Help Singin': The American Musical on Stage and Screen*, (Woodstock: The Overlook Press, 1987), 334.

36. *Oliver!* has been successfully revived three times in the West End: 1977–1980, 1994–1998, and 2008–2011. The last production toured the UK between 2011 and 2013.

37. Unity Theatre was an offshoot of the workers' theatre movement initiated in 1936 that by the 1950s had established 250 Unity Theatre clubs across Britain.

38. John McGrath was the founder and director of 7:84 company, a Marxist group named to remind audiences that 7 per cent of the population of Britain owned 84 per cent of the wealth. McGrath's aesthetic was an elaboration of Littlewood's community theatre idea, based on the popular forms of the Gaelic ceilidh in combination with entertainment in working men's clubs, touring plays that presented political protest through both working-class and folk traditions of music and theatre.

39. These are *Joseph and His Technicolor Dreamcoat, Jesus Christ Superstar, Starlight Express, The Rocky Horror Show, Evita, Cats, Les Misérables, The Phantom of the Opera, Miss Saigon, Mamma Mia!,* and, more recently, *Billy Elliot* and *Matilda*.

40. Andrew Lamb, *150 Years of Popular Musical Theatre* (New Haven: Yale University Press, 2000).

41. Kurt Gänzl, *The Musical: A Concise History* (Boston: Northeastern University Press, 1997).

42. In fact this accolade should be reserved for the Off-Broadway production of Tom Jones and Harvey Schmidt's *The Fantasticks*, which ran for a total of forty-two years, but *Les Miz* has certainly run longer than any other show in a large theatre venue.

43. This is a traditional Broadway wisecrack, often attributed to Richard Rodgers, which has repeatedly been used to denigrate British musicals of the 1980s.

44. In an interview published by *Woman's Own* in 1987, Thatcher famously asserted '[T]here's no such thing as society; there are individual men and women and there are families'. http://www.theguardian.com/politics/2013/apr/08/margaret-thatcher-quotes, accessed 25 June 2014.

45. Alistair Smith, 'Theatre Is a Greater Driver of Tourism than Sport—VisitBritain Report', *The Stage*, 4 November 2013, https://www.thestage.co.uk/news/2013/theatre-greater-driver-tourism-sport-visit-britain-report/, accessed 30 April 2015.

46. Theo Bosanquet: 'Arts Council Report Says Culture Sector Contributes £5.9 Billion to UK Economy', www.whatsonstage.com, 7 May 2013, http://www.whatsonstage.com/west-end-theatre/news/05-2013/arts-council-report-says-culture-sector-contribute_298.html, accessed 30 April 2015.

PART I

BRITANNIA RULES
The Early British Musical and Society

CHAPTER 1

....

BALLAD OPERA

Commercial Song in Enlightenment Garb

....

BERTA JONCUS

BALLAD opera transformed London theatre: through it, for the first time, English common song became crucial to the commercial success of London stage works. Ballad opera production was intense: between 1728 and 1737, authors produced some 180 works containing *c*.2,500 airs. Ballad opera's reach was long: *Flora*, created in London in 1729, became in 1735 one of the earliest documented American musical productions, in Charleston, South Carolina.[1] Ballad opera's communicative tools were sophisticated. Its melodies were in the main newly versified 'common tunes' which, being already in the public sphere, carried conventionalized associations. Ballad opera writers articulated in song the action's moral lesson by fitting new words to familiar melodies. Such songs or 'airs' could, under the pretence of moral instruction, indulge audience fancy. While the words in ballad opera seemed to address social folly, authors routinely chose titillating topics and selected music for its subversive references, focusing especially on women, politics, or members of a ruling elite.

Above all, ballad opera's airs accommodated liminal representations during which the player could step out of his or her dramatis persona and seem to represent either the playwright or the target of satire. Authoritative vocalists shaped their self-representation in the performance of ballad opera airs, while crafty authors manipulated tunes to comment on public figures. It was through its airs that ballad opera could nourish Britain's growing market in celebrities, producing the nation's first star singers, lampooning leaders of state and industry, and occasionally cashing in on scandal surrounding a person of 'Quality'. This chapter outlines the chronology of ballad opera production, probes how the practices of ballad opera shaped its development, and identifies some of the standard tropes—particularly, because of their dominance in the genre, those concerning women's 'foibles'—through which writers and theatre personnel sought to strengthen a production's appeal.

Revolution: *The Beggar's Opera*

Ballad opera burst onto the scene in 1728 with John Gay's *Beggar's Opera*, the jaw-dropping success of which other writers swiftly moved to emulate. Like other London stage productions, Gay's 'opera' and its progeny were shaped by their need for commercial success, their declared aspiration to improve spectators' morals, and their function as an outlet for political protest. The extent to which any of these elements were present in a given ballad opera suggests a typology. At London's licensed houses operating under royal patent—Lincoln's Inn Fields (Covent Garden from 1732) and Drury Lane—star vocalists were cultivated in seemingly polite works, which tended to be 'operatiz'd' versions of earlier comedies, English or French. At these houses, authors sometimes identified ballad operas as a form of native 'opera' that would rescue Town taste, putatively corrupted by Italian opera. Authors of ballad operas for non-patent theatres, or those not intended to be staged, often used them to articulate opposition politics or air court scandal; unlike patent theatre managers, they had no need to curry official favour. At fair booths, and at playhouses outside London, ballad opera's common tunes helped forge a theatre that addressed local interests and vented social criticism.

No later playwright would match the sophistication with which Gay, in *The Beggar's Opera*, mapped satire of high public officials onto a low-life story. Gay pioneered ballad opera's unique synthesis of forms literary (popular accounts of criminals, urban pastoral poetry), musical (so-called 'Old Ballads', Restoration stage song), and theatrical

FIGURE 1.1 Highwaymen or politicians? The male chorus in *The Beggar's Opera* at the Lyric Theatre, Hammersmith, London 1928.

Bertram Park and Yvonne Gregory Collection, Mander & Mitchenson, Bristol University. Courtesy of ArenaPal.

(farce, pantomimic dance, stage burlesque, sentimental comedy, Italian opera, English semi-opera, and Parisian vaudeville entertainment).[2] As in a comedy, Gay painted stereotypes from which the spectator might draw lessons for self-improvement.[3] As in a sentimental drama, the action of *The Beggar's Opera* deals with parents blocking their daughter's love marriage. Gay's protagonist Macheath was based on the celebrated thief Jack Sheppard—a cult sensation in 1724—and Macheath's father-in-law Peach'um was based on the notorious fence Jonathan Wild. Through sly allusion, Gay knitted together these underworld figures with real-life people of Quality, sometimes tantalizingly recognizable, such as the prime minister Robert Walpole.

Negatively textured stereotypes generated a compellingly subversive tale: the fence Peach'um (a stereotypical 'Father', standing also for Wild/Walpole) and his wife (a 'Bawd') keep daughter Polly ('Heroine' and 'Fine Lady'/'Italian Prima Donna') from marrying her beloved Macheath ('Lover'/'Trickster'/Sheppard/Walpole) by engineering Macheath's capture. Macheath escapes prison by charming his pregnant first 'wife' Lucy Lockit ('Jealous Rival'/'Prima Donna'), daughter of the prison warden, into unlocking his cell. Recaptured, Macheath bids his 'wives', ultimately numbering six, goodbye as he mounts the scaffold—but then receives the King's pardon, because the Beggar ('the Playwright'/Gay) who introduced the play, changes the tragic ending to a happy one at the request of the 'Player'.

In his musical selections for *The Beggar's Opera*, Gay ranged mimetic alongside seemingly didactic songs. In didactic mode, whatever lesson Gay wished audiences to draw from the stage action was communicated directly in his ballad verses. Among the social follies addressed were politicians' corruption, the justice system's double standards—rich thieves escape and use the law to quash the poor—and the hypocrisy of love vows. Stinging epigrams ('And if rich Men like us were to swing, | 'Twould thin the Land, such Numbers to string | Upon Tyburn Tree') typically brought numbers to a crisp close.[4] Such satirical lessons-in-song, packaged as a 'moral' for social improvement, were beyond the censor's remit. Audiences loved it: the success of the first season of *The Beggar's Opera* broke all theatrical records, and earned Lincoln's Inn Fields manager John Rich enough money to found Covent Garden[5]—ironically, today's dedicated home for Britain's most elite stage companies, the Royal Opera and Royal Ballet.

The popularity of 17-year-old Lavinia Fenton as Polly was perhaps the greatest sensation of all. Fenton's performances and the publicity they generated—pamphlets, poems, broadsides, mezzotint portraits—together made her London's first commercial singing star.[6] Indeed, the production of stars through common and low-style tunes proved to be one of the most enduring legacies of *The Beggar's Opera*. Fenton's success was rooted in two performance practices particular to the time: the dramatic 'point' and the manner of the street ballad singer. The 'point' is defined by Shearer West as the moment when a character's specific nature crystallizes in action that overshadows all other stage elements.[7] According to a period critic, only 'a few passages' of a stage work were worthy of 'notice', and the polite theatre-goer was expected to know 'where an actor is to exert his abilities'.[8] Gay's *Beggar's Opera* songs conveniently bracketed out for spectators the lead players' points.

While the dramatic point was a pre-existing tradition, onstage imitation of a street balladeer was new with *The Beggar's Opera*. Thanks to Gay's ballads, players could, like street singers, use 'natural'—as opposed to trained—vocal production, and step out of character to directly address the public, as a street ballad singer would. By shedding their fictional character while singing, a player could share in the playwright's diegetic authority, thanks in part to the grain of the player's 'real' voice in common song. This use of direct address and seemingly unmediated voice were noted at once. As the anonymous author of *The Touch-Stone* (1728) put it, '*The Beggar's Opera*, by robbing the Performers at Pye-corner [and] Fleet-ditch [...] of their [...] Properties, has reinstated them in Wealth and Grandeur; and what shock'd most Ears [...] at turning the Corner of a Street [...] when thrown into a regular Entertainment, charms for Hours'.[9]

Fenton used her music in *The Beggar's Opera* to great advantage. Her rendition of 'O Ponder Well', set to the ballad tune 'Chevy Case', was reported to have converted an uncertain first night audience to her cause.[10] The charms of Fenton's Polly were aided by an interpretation which undermined authorial intent: whereas on the page Polly's dialogue is increasingly cynical, Fenton's interpretation was straightforwardly sentimental.[11] Fenton's supporters celebrated the tenderness, loyalty, and sincerity that she foregrounded on stage, and her 'natural' singing, in memoirs and poems. The epigram of her mezzotint portrait assigned these qualities to her, while also implying her sexual availability.[12] She became the toast of the Town, conquering the heart of Charles Powlett, the Duke of Bolton, who by June 1728 had removed her from the stage to be his mistress.[13] Thanks to a persona born of common song and a 'natural' voice, and to large-scale print promotion, Fenton became the first popular singing star in a recognizably modern sense.

Gay copied the manner of the street ballad singer also in that he wrote new verses to common tunes that recalled their old verses. Street ballad singers used the familiarity of a melody to hook passers-by; Gay used an association between new and old verses to deepen his satire. Satirical allusion through familiar tune was not just powerful, it was also hard for censors to track. Gay and the ballad opera writers who followed him could thereby sneak naughty subtexts into songs under the cloak of melody. How did this work? Consider Air 6 of *The Beggar's Opera* (see Table 1.1). Gay reset a tune by Henry Purcell titled 'What Shall I Do to Shew [*sic*] How Much I Love Her', from John Dryden's *The Prophetess* (1690), which, as Vanessa Rogers notes, ran concurrently with *The Beggar's Opera*.[14]

In Dryden's verses, the villain sings of the purity of the heroine whom he desires. In Gay's 'Virgins Are Like the Fair Flow'r', Polly sings the same tune to lament how a woman's exchange value in the marriage market plummets once she is deflowered. Virginity in Dryden's lines transcends material forces; in Gay's, it determines the fluctuating price of a commodity. The use of Purcell's courtly minuet throws the coarseness of Gay's verses into high relief. Air 6 is just one of thirty songs about the nature of women in *The Beggar's Opera*, out of a total of sixty-nine. After Gay, ballad opera playwrights wrote hundreds more verses on the same topic.

Table 1.1 Comparison of Henry Purcell's 'What Shall I Do to Shew How Much
I Love Her' as Reset by John Gay and in Its Original Setting

John Gay, *The Beggar's Opera* (London: Printed for J. Watts, 1728), Air 6	John Dryden, *The Prophetess, or The History of Dioclesian* (1690); repr. Henry Playford, *Wit and Mirth; or Pills to Purge Melancholy*, vol. 4 (1719), v. 235
Virgins are like the fair flower in its Lustre Which in the Garden enamels the Ground: Near it the Bees in Play flutter and cluster, And gaudy Butterflies frolick around.	What shall I do to shew how much I love her How many Millions of Sighs can suffice? That which wins other Hearts, never can move her, Those common methods of Love she'll despise.
But, when once pluck'd, 'tis no longer alluring, To Covent-Garden* 'tis sent (as yet sweet,) There fades, and shrinks, and grows past all enduring, Rots, stinks, and dies, and is trod under feet.	I will love her more than Man e'er loved before me, Gaze on her all the Day, melt all the Night; Till for her own sake at last she'll implore me, To love her less to preserve our delight. Since Gods themselves could not ever be loving Men must have breathing Recruits for new Joys: I wish my Soul could be ever improving, Tho' eager Love more than Sorry destroys. In fair Aurelia's Arms leave me expiring. To be Embalm'd with the Sweets of her Breath; To the last Moment I'll still be desiring; Never had Hero so glorious a Death.

*a reference to Covent Garden's open-air markets and its brothels.

POLITE AND NATIVE ENTERTAINMENT: BALLAD OPERA AT PATENT THEATRES

Drury Lane manager Colley Cibber, who had rejected *The Beggar's Opera* when offered it, in January 1729 countered Gay's low-life tale with a polite entertainment.[15] Cibber's *Love in a Riddle* replaced Gay's gritty urban setting with a high-style Arcadia, Gay's prose with blank verse, and Gay's ruminations on corruption with pastoral sentiments. The omission of common tune titles from Cibber's wordbook meant that melodies were less likely to recall earlier settings.[16] In his prologue, Cibber created an important new ideological frame for ballad opera by arguing that 'If Songs are harmless Revels of the Heart, | Why should our Native Tongue not bear its Part? | Why after learned Warblers must we pant, | And doat on Airs, which only They can chant?'[17] Whereas Gay had exchanged Italian opera arias for common tunes flippantly, Cibber used music to aggrandize an English song tradition. In so doing, he aligned his airs with publicity praising the salutary effect of Fenton's untutored singing and her native songs.

Although a flop, *Love in a Riddle* was more indicative of the future course of productions at the patent theatres than *The Beggar's Opera* was. Explicitly in prolegomena, and implicitly in their non-satiric use of ballads, writers of patent theatre productions took up Cibber's argument that ballad opera was equal in cultural capital to its Italian counterpart. Such claims spoke to antiquarian interest in 'Old Ballads', spearheaded from 1711 by Joseph Addison in *The Spectator*, and represented in the influential *Collection of Old Ballads* published between 1723 and 1725.[18] Addison had asserted that orally transmitted ballads such as 'Chevy Chase' were like classical epics because they touched hearts universally by virtue of their directness—as Fenton's singing was later said to do.[19] Addison's convictions nourished what modern scholars have called a 'Ballad Revival'.[20] In ballad opera, however, 'Old Ballads' were little more than a deceptive branding of common tunes of diverse origin to make box-office and wordbook sales. Traditional ballads constitute only a small fraction of the music of *The Beggar's Opera* and its successors. Common tunes in ballad operas were largely sourced from London stage productions—not least Handel's Italian operas and Purcell's stage music—plus John Playford's dance collections and Thomas D'Urfey's *Pills to Purge Melancholy*.[21] London's advanced print culture fostered this mingling in ballad opera of high- and low-style melodies to create a platform for pleasingly artless vocal display, which was marketed as epitomizing British taste.

Love in a Riddle was also notable for its revelation of the talents of Catherine ('Kitty') Clive, née Raftor, who according to the prompter William Chetwood single-handedly charmed audiences enough to keep the show from being hissed off the stage.[22]

Recognizing the importance of this emerging star soprano, and capitalizing on Fenton's unexpected retirement in June 1728, Drury Lane managers subsequently cast Clive to lead practically every ballad opera they mounted.[23] Clive's portrait epigrams echoed Fenton's, broadcasting how her natural singing countered corrosive Town taste for Italian *virtuose*.[24] Unusually, the mainpiece *Love in a Riddle* was cut down to an afterpiece not by the patent theatre where it originated but by a fringe company;[25] as *Damon and Phillida*, it was the first non-patent theatre production to become a London stage staple.[26] Only when Clive forcefully exploited song's latitude for interpreting against the authorial grain, however, did Drury Lane clearly trump rival houses, patent and non-patent. In the Drury Lane summer company's *The Devil to Pay* (1731), a venal 'opera' after a Restoration farce that extolled wife-beating, Clive astonishingly managed to 'turn it & wind it & play it' to make of her submissive character Nell a sparkling, spiritedly innocent rustic.[27] Swiftly abridged to show Clive to more advantage, *The Devil to Pay* became, in its new version, the most influential ballad opera on the wider European musical stage.[28]

Clive's reward was a series of ballad opera roles which collectively came to form what critics since the seventeenth century had called a 'line' or 'walk'. The 'line' was a set of roles created for, or acquired by, a principal player, who claimed ownership of it through an inimitable stage manner. These roles coalesced into a metacharacter across works,[29] and when rivals or protégés took over parts from a principal player's line they were expected to copy each 'stroke' of the celebrity interpretation.[30] Although the 'line' was a long-standing tradition, a ballad opera line, because generated largely by English-language song, was something novel.

By 1729, playwrights, players, and managers had established the production techniques peculiar to patent theatre ballad operas. Productions were either devised as afterpieces, or cut down to an afterpiece, so as to be offered after the working day for half-price entry.[31] Plots generally revolved around a sentimental union, first thwarted, then achieved, with opportunities for reflections on the action and on women. Besides overtures and dances, ballad operas above all featured airs that articulated the action's dramatic points. Air verses typically seemed to be didactic—that is outlining a lesson that the audience should learn—and halted the action to delineate their lessons, while musical mimesis unfolded mainly during sentimental and drinking scenes. For the finale, principal players often summarized the work's moral by singing strophes in turn. In solos, the singer's voice might shift between that of the dramatis persona, the author, and indeed themselves, enabling lead players like Fenton or Clive to develop stage personalities through 'native' song. Above all, ballad operas were appreciated not as narratives, but as accretions of stock characters, situations, and melodies valued primarily for the wit of their allusions and their delivery.

After printing the *Beggar's Opera*, John Watts, London's leading theatrical bookseller, increasingly shaped ballad opera's repertory of melodies. Watts's innovation lay in merging theatrical with song publication. The copperplate engraving that he had used to print the music of *The Beggar's Opera* fell by the wayside, in favour of a woodblock cut of a melody inserted into the dialogue, without text underlay. The printed tunes were usually prepared from a series of woodcuts, each line separately cut. [32] This technique had three advantages: it lowered production costs, it let Watts reuse tunes—sometimes found also in his six-volume *Musical Miscellany* (1729–31), also from woodcuts[33]—and it linked individual players to their musical numbers. Notation is relatively rare in ballad opera wordbooks, and Watts was the only bookseller to routinely print tunes.[34] From the twenty-eight ballad operas that Watts issued with 'Musick prefix'd to each Song' emerged the tunes most frequently selected by ballad opera writers—perhaps due to their familiarity, perhaps even more to hopes that Watts would publish the ballad operas that included them, as the same woodcuts could be reused.[35] Watts's luxurious editions could also represent or enhance—sometimes misleadingly—a theatre's ownership of a production.[36]

From the first season of *The Beggar's Opera* there was stiff competition in ballad opera production between London's two licensed playhouses—those led by John Rich and Colley Cibber under royal patent—and London's non-licensed houses. Rich sought to capitalize on *The Beggar's Opera* by staging a sequel, *Polly*, which was supposed to go into rehearsal late in 1728. But the Lord Chamberlain ordered Rich not to rehearse any play not yet 'supervis'd', and following its submission to the Lord Chamberlain, *Polly* was banned, reportedly at Walpole's request.[37] Court members showed their outrage by underwriting *Polly*'s publication and, ironically, Gay earned far more from *Polly* than he had from *The Beggar's Opera*.[38] After the *Polly* debacle, Rich eschewed criminal themes to focus on sentimental ballad opera productions, typically featuring *Beggar's Opera* principals. *Polly*, titled after what had become Fenton's pseudonym, was as much a Fenton vehicle as a *Beggar's Opera* sequel; Rich also mounted Lacy Ryan's *The Cobbler's Opera*, which featured points for Fenton modelled after those of Polly in *The Beggar's Opera*,[39] though Fenton retired before this work came to the boards. John Hippisley, the original Peach'um, wrote and led Rich's only other hit ballad opera, *Flora*, adapting a vehicle by and for Thomas Dogget (*c.*1640–1721), whose comic line had depended on song.[40] Besides his own strengths, Hippisley deftly integrated into *Flora* those of John Laguerre, Rich's leading tenor.[41]

Following *Love in a Riddle*, Drury Lane forged a pastoral-inflected, polite British line of sentimental ballad operas for Clive, who was typically cast as a shepherdess, rustic, or heroine in a rustic setting. For instance, Clive led Charles Johnson's 1729 *The Village Opera* and its afterpiece version *The Chambermaid*; both omitted from their publicity any mention of the two French source comedies for Johnson's wordbook. Three Clive-led ballad operas expanded the meaning of native to include would-be Scottish and Irish representations. *Patie and Peggy* was Theophilus Cibber's adaptation of Allen Ramsay's influential pastoral comedy *The Gentle Shepherd* (1725), which in 1729 Ramsay himself had turned into a ballad opera. Cibber replaced Scots with English 'dialect', and many of Ramsay's tunes with more familiar, putatively Scots songs printed or composed in London. In his prologue, he flagged *Patie and Peggy* as a product of 'ENGLAND, the Nurse of Worth and true Desert' where tales from a 'distant SCOTLAND' could help unite 'BRITONS' in taste.[42] Joseph Mitchell's 'Scots Opera', *The Highland Fair*, led by Clive, featured the exotica of 'ancient [...] Customs, Manners and Dresses', replete with an onstage piper playing a 'March peculiar to his clan'.[43] *The Stage Coach Opera* (1730) was Irish by virtue of the source play's author, George Farquhar, whose Irish roots were touted in a 'Life' appended to the 1718 wordbook of his 1704 *The Stage Coach*.[44] With *The Stage Coach Opera*, Drury Lane competed with *Flora* at Rich's theatre by also 'operatizing' an earlier farce still in London stage repertory. Apart from William Chetwood's *The Lover's Opera* (1729), however, Drury Lane productions stumbled until Clive's stunning success in *The Devil to Pay* (1731) moved the home of ballad opera from Lincoln's Inn Fields to Drury Lane.

The phenomenal success of *Beggar's Opera* also ushered in a decade of more intense competition between these licensed theatres and their non-licensed competitors, and between the summer companies of all London's theatres. Called 'Young Companies', summer companies consisted typically of younger players who mounted productions after the Town had departed for the summer.[45] The success of *Damon and Phillida* (1729), which opened 19 August 1729 at the Little Haymarket Theatre, exemplified how a thrown-together summer company at a fringe theatre could compete with Drury Lane. Other venues for alternative ballad operas were Goodman's Fields, which had opened on 31 October 1727, as well as fair booths, and playhouses outside London.

FIGURE 1.2 A phenomenal success since 1728: Millicent Martin (Polly) and Harold Innocent (Peachum) in one of the many high-profile revivals of *The Beggar's Opera*, directed by Robin Phillips for the 1972 Chichester Festival.

Photograph by John Timbers. Courtesy of ArenaPal.

BALLAD OPERA OUTSIDE PATENT THEATRES

At fairs, Goodman's Fields, and non-London theatres, ballad opera writers tapped into local culture. Located next to the City, Goodman's Fields featured ballad operas such as *The Craftsman* (1731), *The Throwster's Opera* (1731)—a throwster was a silk-thrower—*The Sailor's Wedding* (1731), *The Mock Mason* (1733), *The Footman* (1732), *The Mad Captain* (1733), and *The Chimney Sweeper* (1736) to target tradesmen and the lower orders. At fair booths, ballad operas like *Southwark Fair* (1729), with its sheep-shearing scene and street cries, displayed community traditions. At non-London theatres like Smock Alley, local scandal sometimes drove plots, such as that of *Johnny Bow-Wow* (1732) about grave robbers. In Oxford, a 'Company of Students' used *The Oxford Act* (1733) to criticize the expense of the university's nuptial celebrations for Anne, Princess Royal and Prince William of Orange. Leading the action was a typical Oxford female 'Toast': a socially groomed, low-born woman who cruised Oxford's balls and public walks for a husband.[46]

In the text of an interview published after his death, Charles Macklin described the operation of Sadler's Wells at mid-century. Considered in tandem with *The Prisoners* [*sic*] *Opera*—possibly penned by the pugnacious Edward Ward[47]—Macklin's report shows how a ballad opera could be fitted to a fringe theatre's constraints, as well as its clientele.[48] The only ballad opera/pantomime printed with notation, *The Prisoners Opera* is sung throughout, and much of its vocal music seems to have been newly composed.[49] Uniquely among ballad operas, it opens with a chorus ('Prisoners Begging in Song, thro' a Grate'); thereafter vocal numbers are divided between protest—against debtors' incarceration, inmates' lack of food, the need to bribe to survive in prison— and cautionary tales of how the inmates came to be incarcerated. Song is interlarded with prisoners' dances, probably inspired by the *Beggar's Opera*'s 'Prisoners in Chains' dance.[50] In harlequinade episodes, Punch and Harlequin dance with the prisoners, and, unusually, sing solos. To thread together these disparate scenes, 'the Musick plays a short Lesson in the Key of the following Song':[51] a chorus of prisoners summarizes the opera's moral that debtors' prison is unjust, but that improvements to the law promise deliverance. The last scenes are multi-strophe airs by the 'Smiths', a 'drunken Miller', and 'Ragmen', plus a 'Dialogue Song' between a courtesan and a 'penurious Gentleman'.

The oddities of Sadler's Wells itself leave their mark in the density of music, the social engagement, and the episodic ending of *The Prisoners Opera*. Traditionally, Sadler's Wells was an inn and music house; this is likely why *The Prisoners Opera* has music throughout.[52] Sadler's Wells was also, in Macklin's words, a 'baiting place of thieves and highwaymen', an audience likely interested in the theme of the debtor's prison. But 'People of fashion' also visited 'occasionally', paying sixpence—double the standard price—for a place 'off to the Side' reserved for them. Entertainment was 'by daylight' with 'four or five exhibitions a day'. According to Macklin:

> The proprietor had always a fellow on the outside of the booth, to calculate how many people were collected for a second exhibition, and when he thought there were enough, he came to the back of the upper seats, and cried out, 'Is Hiram Fisteman here?' [. . .] This was the cant word agreed upon between the parties, to announce the state of the people without; upon which they concluded the entertainments with a song, dismissed that audience, and prepared for another representation.[53]

Action therefore ended early in *The Prisoners Opera*, and its series of final numbers could be cut off at any point. *The Prisoners Opera* highlights the extent to which target audience and venue could determine a ballad opera's content.

Fringe and licensed theatres alike took up this new blend of pantomime and ballad opera. Fair booths showed *The Emperor of China* (1731), *The Cheats of Scapin* (1733), and *The Fall of Phaeton* (1733), a title also used at Drury Lane for a Clive-led pantomime masque with Thomas Arne's music. One of Drury Lane's biggest hits was ballad opera/pantomime *The Harlot's Progress* (1734). This followed three fringe ballad operas—one at

Goodman's Fields, two in pamphlet form only—that dramatized Hogarth's print series *The Harlot's Progress*, from which all the productions took their titles.

Among non-licensed theatres, the Little Haymarket challenged London's two licensed playhouses most robustly.[54] As Robert Hume notes, pirate productions of *The Beggar's Opera* in 1728 at the Little Haymarket—a 'road house' for different troupes—infringed on the patent theatres' tacit claim to own successful new productions, and began the strongest third-house competition since 1642.[55] Proprietor John Potter appears to have taken little heed of what the visiting troupes performed, and by 1729 the Little Haymarket were offering the kind of provocative ballad opera, like Thomas Odell's *The Patron* of that year, that Rich seems to have avoided after *Polly*. Odell was the owner of Goodman's Fields, but mounted his ballad opera at the Little Haymarket, where he did not risk having his own theatre shut down. Dedicated to one of Walpole's bitterest opponents, Charles Spencer, third Earl of Sunderland (1675–1722), Odell's 'opera' denounced Walpole as 'the sham-Patron [. . .] corrupt, vicious and unsincere [*sic*]'.[56] Lines such as 'Cowards only can lye [*sic*], and Fools deceive: Such Talents, however fitting a Sharper or a Pimp, are very unbecoming a Gentleman, and much more a Statesman', left little to the imagination.[57] To this, Odell added the character of Peggy Lure, a prostitute who, unlike most female dramatis personae, brings about the denouement: she sexually ensnares and prevails over Sir Falcon (Walpole) to procure settlements needed by two male characters. The common tunes Odell selected let him shrewdly castigate Walpole, as in the song 'Wilely [*sic*] Politicians' set to the tune of 'Whilst the Town's Brim-full of Folly'.[58]

In 1730 the Little Haymarket hosted for the first time Henry Fielding, ballad opera's most important innovator. Fielding's wit, cynicism, and musical sophistication—he used more Handel compositions than any other ballad opera playwright[59]—caused his tune settings to weave erratically between crudity and refinement. Profligate and gifted, the young Fielding participated briskly in the vices and ambitions of London's theatrical world,[60] and his entertainments could be read as news bulletins from his own milieu. He understood that audiences relished the mockery of local and entertainment-industry figures as well as members of the establishment. Ballad opera's fluidity of voices and generic boundaries made it an ideal medium for Fielding's experiments.

With *The Author's Farce* (1730), Fielding merged ballad opera with the play-within-a-play ('an Operatical Puppet Shew, call'd the Pleasures of the Town'), styled mainly after the burlesque 'rehearsal' play pioneered by the Duke of Buckingham. That Drury Lane and Goodman's Fields were at this time both also preparing rehearsal play/ballad opera hybrids, respectively *Bays' Opera* by Gabriel Odingsells and *The Fashionable Lady* by Fielding's friend James Ralph, suggests how fierce the competition was between theatres.[61] With *The Author's Farce*, Fielding moved further than his rivals away from Gay and towards Buckingham. He included dramatis personae who comment critically on the play they are watching, and tagged by name those he was satirizing, including Drury Lane managers Colley Cibber ('Marplay') and Robert Wilks ('Sparkish'), John Rich ('Monsieur Pantomime'), and the bookseller Edmund Curll ('Curry'). [62] Fielding's ad hominem parts accommodated cast members if they wanted to 'take off' or mimic his targets, a practice we know took place in later ad hominem ballad operas.[63] To build the parody to a climax, Fielding withheld the songs until his work's concluding play-within-a-play.

The Author's Farce was London's biggest hit since *The Beggar's Opera*, establishing the 23-year-old Fielding as the town's leading comic playwright. This reputation was cemented by *The Welsh Opera* (1731) and its expanded version, *The Grub-Street Opera*, in which Fielding reinvented Gay's practices. Rather than notorious criminals, Fielding dramatized celebrity royals and their ministers. Fielding borrowed names from George Lillo's prudish ballad opera *Silvia*, recently a dismal failure at Rich's theatre.[64] By recycling Lillo's fictional characters to enact current gossip about the House of Hanover, Fielding at once mocked the court, Rich, and Lillo. The parallels were unmistakable: Lady Apshinkin (Queen Caroline) dominates Sir Owen (King George II) and rejects her rakish son Master Owen (Prince Frederick) while favouring Robin (Walpole). To *The Grub-Street Opera* Fielding added a scene about the celebrated duel between Sir William Pulteney (Will) and Sir John Hervey (John the Groom). This character defamation crystallized in common tunes, with 'Tipling John' alluding to Walpole's bibulous nature, and the 'Black Joke' referring to his sexual adventurism. The latter was especially inflammatory: the Black Joke's traditional verses praised a woman's 'coal black joke, & belly so white' which men should 'lather like soap' to make it 'draw more [. . .] rope'.[65] Fielding's smutty verses chimed with the original ones to taunt Walpole.[66] Another brilliant stroke was Fielding's selection of Purcell's 'Britons Strike Home', the pompousness of which comments archly on the duel between Pulteney and Hervey, whispered to have been pure show, engineered by Walpole.[67]

Recognizing Fielding's precocious gifts, Drury Lane management drafted him to write for Kitty Clive, and John Rich reportedly hired Edward Phillips to write ballad operas like Fielding.[68] Although never salaried at Drury Lane, Fielding wrote almost exclusively Clive vehicles for that house from 1732 until 1735.[69] Fielding's working relationship with Clive was fraught—he later defamed her—but mutually advantageous. Through his wit and command of French, he made Clive's line more sophisticated, turning comedies by Molière and Regnard into the material for her greatest successes. For her part, Clive's ability to communicate with audiences during musical numbers, of which she typically performed the most in a Fielding vehicle, gave him a new tool to work with. Fielding provided Clive with opportunities for personal engagement with her audiences both in dialogue and in song numbers.

London spectators lapped up the results: the dizzy country girl in *The Lottery* (1732), the tart-tongued wife in Molière's *Mock Doctor* (1732), and the wily chambermaid in Jean-François Regnard's *Intriguing Chambermaid* (1733) became staple ballad opera roles that Clive later passed on to her protégées. Describing Clive's acting in *The Intriguing Chambermaid*, the critic John Hill explains how she had 'three instead of two parts to play at the same time'. According to Hill, she juggled between 'pert self-sufficiency'—which he identifies as her own character—and Regnard's action for the chambermaid, while also representing an actress who shares laughs with the audience about the other dramatis personae's ignorance of plot elements of which she (the chambermaid) alone is informed. This gag, characteristic of commedia dell'arte, gave Clive the chance to insert her own persona into the action as well as the music:

> While the actress [Clive] is here construing every look and gesture of Mr Goodall into madness to Mrs Highmore [. . .] she is expressing to the audience all the while the utmost terror in the world, lest one or the other of them [Goodall or Highmore] shou'd discover her: Nay, she even adds to the necessary perplexity of her part she has to act, by blending with her very terror the pert self-sufficiency, that marks out the rest of her character [. . .] The person who understands this merit in Mrs Clive's playing this short character, will not wonder if it appear [sic] very insipid when perform'd by any body else.[70]

Another significant Clive–Fielding ballad opera was *The Old Man Taught Wisdom* (1735). Out of this work a line of Clive characters obtruded from ballad opera onto comedy. Fielding's 'Lucy' in *The Old Man Taught Wisdom* had emerged from Clive's 'Jenny' in the *Boarding House Romps* (1733); both Lucy and Jenny are silly schoolgirls, prey to suitors from lower stations. After Clive's success in *The Old Man Taught Wisdom*, several sequels starring Clive as 'Lucy' followed: by James Miller in 1739 (*Hospital of Fools*), by David Garrick in 1740 (*Lethe*, first version), and by Fielding (perhaps with others' assistance) in 1741 (*Miss Lucy in Town*).[71] All three were comedies, with occasional airs by Thomas Arne composed for Clive.[72]

Whereas the Clive–Fielding ballad operas of 1732 to 1735 were largely without allusions to current events,[73] 'pamphlet' ballad operas tended to be politically subversive, the targets of satire made clear through prefaces and standardized pseudonyms for public figures (for instance, 'Robin' for Walpole). Social and political scandal were both embraced in pamphlet ballad operas such as *Calista*, which dramatized the famous suit of Baron Abergavenny against Richard Lyddel for adultery with his wife, who may have died from shame.[74] Tattle around Prince Frederick's and John Hervey's competition for the sexual favours of one of the Queens' maids of honour, Anne Vane, nourished *The Humours of the Court* (1732) and *Vanelia, or the Amours of the Great* (1732). A versification of the tune 'A Begging We Will Go'—surely a reference to Frederick's renowned bitterness at having an allowance that was a fraction of his father's when his father had been prince—opened *The Humours of the Court*; it could escape censure because the innuendo was implied in music, rather than articulated in words.

Likewise, *The Promis'd Marriage, or The Disappointment* (1732) jeered at Anne, Princess Royal and her dwarf-like spouse, the Prince of Orange.[75] The Princess's proxy was 'Holtaria', likely pronounced 'Haught-eria' and thus-named to point up the Princess's renowned arrogance. Taken from *The Beggar's Opera*, the airs, invoking by recollection Gay's verses, flagged other satirical allusions. The tune 'If Ye'd Have a Young Virgin of Fifteen Years' spoke at once to Princess Anne being a portly, pockmarked ageing virgin, to the eagerness of her parents to see her married, and to panic about the Prince's illness, which had delayed their union.[76] Chuckling allusion to the Prince's likely future infidelity simmered beneath the tunes ''Twas When the Seas Were Roaring', 'Lass of Patie's Mill', and 'Bessy Bell', whose *Beggar's Opera* settings all thematized male perfidy. The air for 'Materna' (Queen Caroline)—'Let Ambition Fire thy Mind', likely after John Weldon's eponymous 1701 song from *The Judgement of Paris* for Juno, goddess of marriage and queen of the Roman pantheon [77]—references tattle about the Queen's dominance at court and hand in arranging the union. But *The Promis'd Marriage* was gentle compared to the gloves-off insults in *The Wedding, or The Country House-Wife*, a work Edmund Gagey discusses in detail. [78]

Small wonder that, despite the innocence of most ballad operas, officials scrutinized them for political allusions, a sometimes ludicrously off-target exercise which itself was lampooned.[79] As the 1730s progressed, however, pamphlet ballad operas undeniably grew into a medium for Opposition protest. The Excise Tax, perhaps the most toxic policy bid of Walpole's career, unleashed a spate of them. Walpole proposed the Excise Tax to offset diminished land tax income with payments from merchants trading in tobacco and wine.[80] Heated anti-Excise Tax sentiments crystallized in ballad opera pseudonyms ('Timothy Smoke', the author of *The Commodity Excis'd*) and dramatis personae ('Mr Freeman' in *The Downfal of Bribery*). Claptrap speeches and common tunes—for instance 'Here's to Thee My Boy'—celebrated English liberties.[81] Of all theatres, only the normally conservative Goodman's Fields actually mounted an anti-Excise Tax ballad opera (*A King and no King*, 1733), evidently to appeal to its City-based clientele.

In 1736 Henry Fielding largely stopped writing ballad operas, turning instead to incendiary straight comedy for his own company at the Little Haymarket.[82] In *Tumble-Down Dick*, Fielding deployed common tunes for the last time with success, in a travesty of Drury Lane's hit pantomime-masque, *The Fall of Phaeton*. While using *Tumble-Down Dick* to attack pantomime, Fielding also hit out at ballad opera. For this slight afterpiece, Fielding cross-bred two strains of theatrical writing, ballad opera versions of which predated Fielding's: the 'play about the theatre'—whose first ballad opera version had been Edward Phillips's *The Stage Mutineers* (1733)—and Ralph's *The Fashionable Lady* (1730), a rehearsal-play-cum-ballad opera lampooning ballad opera.[83] In *The Stage Mutineers*, Phillips had sharpened his ad hominem attacks by assigning richly associative common tunes to the dramatis personae, who stood for real-life players. [84] Fielding, in his airs for Clive's proxy Clymene in *Tumble-Down Dick*, did the same: air 1 referred to Henry Carey, Clive's singing teacher and songwriter, whose career had foundered;[85] air 2 was Clive's celebrated number from *The Intriguing Chambermaid*; air 3 (and perhaps 4), known as 'Our Polly Is A Sad Slut', referred to Clive as Drury Lane's Polly. Fielding set *Tumble-Down Dick*'s finale to the 'Abbot of Canterbury', ballad opera's most frequently used tune.[86] The asymmetry, obsolete modalism, lack of tonal centre, and awkward octave leap of this tune epitomized musical bad taste for the educated. Ralph had used it in the *Fashionable Lady* to represent ballad opera's musical excrescences; so, too, did Fielding in *Tumble-Down Dick*'s mock grand finale.[87]

BALLAD OPERA: PREJUDICE PEDDLED IN SONG

Fielding's attack on Clive in *Tumble-Down Dick* was hardly an isolated case of anti-female animus in ballad opera, which routinely depicted women as carriers of vices—sensuality, vanity, ambition—harmful to polite society. Titles such as *The Wanton Countess* (1733), *The Fashionable Lady* (1730), and *The Female Rake* (1736) attest to the obsessive harping in ballad opera on faults deemed innate to women. In *The Fashionable Lady*, Ralph personified ballad opera as 'Mrs Foible', and even an anti-Excise Tax ballad opera could contain a song such as 'A Woman's at Best, But a Consummate Evil'.[88] As in so many eighteenth-century fictional accounts, ballad opera's gender stereotyping betrayed deep anxieties about female empowerment. Yet playwrights also occasionally promoted female emancipation through roles such as Odell's Peggy Lure in *The Patron*, and songs like Carey's.[89]

A brief glance at the influential *Devil to Pay* (1731) shows how ballad opera playwrights could endorse brutality against women while claiming to advance manners. This was an 'operatized' version of a 1686 farce, *The Devil of a Wife*, by Thomas Jevon. In the ballad opera production of this work, the prologue's speaker Theophilus Cibber promised that *The Devil to Pay* would realize the aims of the 'ancient' muse of Comedy, 'Sworn Foe to Vice, by Virtue's Friends revered'.[90] Yet 'Virtue' is conspicuously absent in the savagery of Jevon's protagonist, the drunken cobbler Jobson: he administers five onstage beatings, boasts of whipping his wife Nell ten times a day, and threatens to run his 'Awl up to the Handle in [Nell's] Buttocks'.[91] Jevon included in his 1686 farce eight airs, three of which denigrate women, including 'The Twitcher', sung three times by Jobson. For his 1731 ballad opera adaptation, Charles Coffey left Jevon's dialogue and the Twitcher's verses intact:

> He that has the best Wife,
> She's the Burthen of his Life,
> But for her that will Scold and will Quarrel;
> Let him cut her short
> Of her Meat and her Sport,
> And ten times a Day hoop her Barrel[92]

The Twitcher melody was used for five later ballad operas airs complaining about women, denigrating them, or advocating their abuse.[93] The Twitcher's tune was mnemonic, enriching new with old verses to strengthen male complaints about women.

By playing Nell as she wanted, Clive broke through to stardom with *The Devil to Pay*. Besides becoming her signature role, Nell generated an 'abused wife' line for Clive: in Fielding's *Mock Doctor* (1732); in *The Merry Cobbler; or, The Second Part of The Devil to Pay* (1735); in *Cure for a Scold* (1735), an 'operatiz'd' version of Shakespeare's *Taming of the Shrew*, in which her abuser sings 'The Twitcher'; and in Garrick's adaption of this same play, *Catharine and Petruchio* (1754, without music), with Clive opposite Garrick. The contradiction between Clive's 'pert self-sufficiency' on stage and the abused wife she often depicted suggests that spectators tolerated the liberties she took onstage in part because she was fictionally punished.

One liberty facilitated by ballad opera was cross-dressing. Although men occasionally played bawds or old women (Mr Reynolds as Mother Pierce in *Love and Revenge*, 1729, or John Harper as Lady Termagant in *The Boarding School*, 1733), most ballad opera travesty roles were, as in other stage genres, played by women.[94] Possibly due to her vocal range—notation in wordbooks does not evidence pitch during performance—Mrs John Roberts forged herself a male line, usually playing a lover: Hunter in *Phebe or The Beggar's Wedding* (1729), Peartree in *The Country-Wedding and Skimmington* (1729), Cantato in *Bays's Opera* (1730), Moody in *The Lover's Opera* (1730), Davy in *The Highland Fair* (1731), Colin Freeman in *The Chambermaid* (1729), Patie in *Patie and Peggy* (1730), and Pert in *The Sailor's Opera* (1731). In ballad opera, the female *en travestie* joined her counterpart in spoken theatre in being a 'specular commodity' displaying her body in male dress.[95] But Roberts's persistent enactment of the male lover, strengthened by airs like 'Of All the Girls' set to the erotic 'Black Joke' (air 6 in *Phebe; or, The Beggar's Wedding*, 1729), suggests that ballad opera's suggestions of same-sex love were an anticipated draw. As Kristina Straub emphasizes, however, only the artifice of such representations made them permissible.[96]

From 1734, ballad operas enabled Charlotte Charke to enact and voice a line of male lovers that she later famously impersonated in real life.[97] A mock-tragic version of *Beggar's Opera*, led by Charke as Macheath in Roman dress, opened the 1734 summer season at the Little Haymarket. Later that season, she took the title role in Fielding's *Mock Doctor*, a part owned by her celebrity brother, Theophilus Cibber. She played Cibber ('Deputy Manager') in the ad hominem ballad opera *The Beggar's Pantomime* (1736) that dramatized the contemporary paper war between Clive and Cibber over Clive's right to play Polly.[98] As Tim the Rake in Joseph Dorman's *The Female Rake* (1736), Charke sang Macheath's tune 'Would You Have a Young Virgin' reset to bawdy verses. One imagines that this would have carried erotic overtones.[99]

While possibly tickling same-sex fancy, ballad operas viciously attacked, under the guise of 'education', Jews and Negro slaves. Hogarth's celebrated print series *The Harlot's Progress* spawned three ballad operas singling out the Jew for mockery. The eponymous Drury Lane production was fabulously popular. At its climax 'Miss Kitty'—an in propria persona role for Clive—sang a duet opening with the lines 'Farewell good Mr Jew | Now I hate your tawny Face | I'll have no more to do | With you or any of your Race.'[100] After the duet's conclusion ('Ne'er more will I come near | Such a pitiful, pimping Fool'), a scenic transformation covers the escape of 'Miss Kitty' and her lover Harlequin. Chiming with this action was Fielding's scene for the Jew 'Mr Zorobabel'—played by the celebrated Shylock Charles Macklin—and Clive in *Miss Lucy in Town*. The 'stock jobbing Pick-pocket' Jew Zorobabel fails to procure Miss Lucy's enduring attachment. As in *The Harlot's Progress*, she chooses another suitor; in Fielding's ballad opera, however, the Jew's humiliation deepens when Miss Lucy's husband kicks Zorobabel off the stage.[101]

Equally troubling is the representation of Negro slaves in Gay's *Polly*. For this *Beggar's Opera* sequel, Gay has Macheath disguise himself as Morano, a slave. As John Richardson shows, Gay stereotypes Morano/Macheath as a 'Crafty [. . .] Fraudulent' Negro, member of a race 'born and bred to be Villains'.[102] As in ballad operas featuring 'the Jew', the playwright ascribes inherently negative traits to a putatively instructive stage 'type'. So, too, did the melody selected: this was 'Mirleton', whose French provenance London audiences would have registered as suspiciously foreign.[103] In other words, Gay used music in *Polly* to represent 'Blackness' a century before the popularization of black-face musical entertainment did the same.[104] That Walpole, identified by 1729 with Macheath, likely engineered *Polly*'s stage ban may have been linked to Gay's 'blackening' of Walpole's stage proxy.

Although prejudice fuelled ballad opera's popularity, music was its chief attraction. This is rarely acknowledged, partly because most ballad opera music is lost. Of the overtures, dances, bass lines, continuo realizations, scoring, and song lead-ins and play-outs from 182 known productions, only about a dozen have dependable primary sources.[105] John Pepusch's *Beggar's Opera* overture shows how music facilitated parody through tunes even without text. In his overture, Pepusch lampooned the bombast of a French opera overture, a form Handel routinely used to open his Italian operas. Following a double-dotted homophonic first movement, French overtures traditionally feature a learned fugal second section. In his second section's fugue, Pepusch crafted the subject from Lucy's low-style air, 'I'm Like a Skiff on the Ocean Toss'd' (Air 47 in *The Beggar's Opera*). Besides the 'low' subject, Pepusch began the section by stuttering: isolated falling fifths, divided between two voices, make a false start before the subject is fully heard. Instead of composing episodic material, Pepusch took all his ideas from Lucy's tune, which he mined in curious ways. Tune fragments move alternately in parallel motion and counterpoint, rather than being spun out in a development section. The first forty bars lurch through mock-serious minor keys (submediant G minor and its subdominant, C minor) to finally cadence in a key (the dominant, F major) related to the home tonic of B flat major. Monothematic, economic, witty, and gorgeously crafted, the cleverness of the overture invites parallels with Haydn's instrumental writing.

CONCLUSION

The Licensing Act of 1737 effectively quashed ballad opera. After spiking in 1733, and dipping in 1734–5, the number of new ballad operas had begun increasing again in 1736 (see Table 1.2).

The authorities may have noted this swell, while ignoring the innocence of most works. The Licensing Act, pushed through by Walpole to clamp down on Opposition criticism, forced non-patent theatres to close, and implemented censorship of all stage productions.[106] This affected ballad opera more than any other theatrical genre, as London's non-patent theatres mounted roughly 30 per cent of all works (Table 1.3). After 1737, without competing ballad opera productions, the two patent houses ceased investing further in a form from which they had already started to move away.

Earlier ballad operas continued, however, to be performed, and ballad opera's practices informed those of later musical theatre. *The Beggar's Opera, Damon and Phillida, The Honest Yorkshireman* (1736), and Clive's vehicles—some of which grew in popularity after 1736—remained stage staples throughout the century, even as new vocalists, including Clive's protégée Jane Pope, took up her roles. The fashion, mocked by Ralph in *The Fashionable Lady* (1730), for ordering from booksellers 'all the English

Table 1.2 Ballad Operas Written 1728–1760

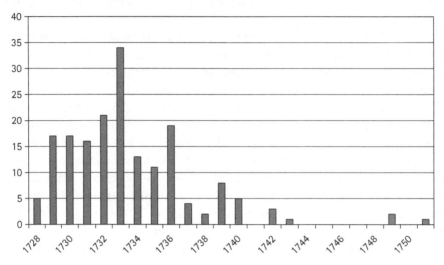

Table 1.3 Ballad Opera Productions and London Playhouses, 1728–1760

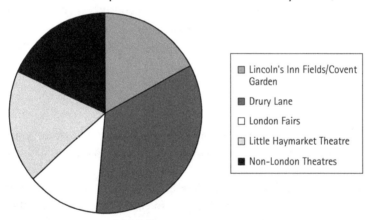

Lincoln's Inn Fields/Covent Garden

Drury Lane

London Fairs

Little Haymarket Theatre

Non-London Theatres

Operas' for an 'excellent Concert' at home, continued throughout the century.[107] Part of ballad opera's legacy was the art of pastiche, and after 1737, it remained accepted practice to draw musical numbers for a stage work from various sources. Exported to Germany, France, and the United States, ballad opera helped give rise to the Singspiel, opéra comique, and early American stage musicals. Above all, ballad opera gave vocalists like John Beard and Charlotte Brent the opportunity to cultivate vocal and dramatic techniques, thereby producing themselves as celebrities almost exclusively through music.

Ballad opera challenges modern understanding. More than the loss of its music, what blocks our grasp today of the genre is the loss of its practices. For modern audiences, tune recognition, ballad opera's chief attraction, is impossible, as is the listener's recollection of words associated with a tune. We no longer value a theatrical work or performance according to how well standard formulae—of action, versification, or stock character—are reinvented. We cannot parse ballad opera's dramatic syntax, which writers organized around musical 'points', nor can we appreciate how the characters in a principal player's 'line' related to each other, and to the player. Many preoccupations treated in ballad opera—self-improvement, normative gendering, government policy, court gossip, and the denigration of those deemed 'Other'—are either alien or repugnant to us. The desire to replace putatively corrupting Italian with morally strengthening British opera has evaporated. The use of song to stop and reflect on stage action—famously revived in Bertolt Brecht and Kurt Weill's *Die Dreigroschenoper* (*Threepenny Opera*), an adaptation of *The Beggar's Opera*—clashes with the narrative flow to which today's theatre audiences are habituated.

Yet despite its foreignness, ballad opera richly deserves study and, in some cases, revival. Practices yoked to ballad opera were integral to British musical theatre after 1737. Three in particular flourished: the production of the musical stage celebrity, the reuse of existing airs (pastiche), and the proud identification of native taste with song-and-dialogue stage works. Beard, by managing Covent Garden from 1761 and producing London's post-Clive star soprano Brent, was crucial to these practices' transmission. Playing opposite Brent, he launched her sensationally in a galant-style version of *The Beggar's Opera*. The acclaim Brent won led to a rebirth of *The Beggar's Opera* on the London stage.[108] Thereafter Beard persistently cast Brent to lead Covent Garden's musical productions, out of which her line emerged. Like Clive, Brent had a singing teacher and songwriter who composed and arranged her music in a native style: Thomas Arne, also her lover. Arne's compositions were more sophisticated than those of Henry Carey, Clive's teacher and early songwriter. This was partly because Beard had extended Covent Garden's musical theatre to encompass burletta, serious opera, dialogue opera, pastiche operas, and all-sung, newly composed afterpieces, often featuring himself in these productions.

From 1729, ballad operas had legitimated pastiche, a craft through which a playwright, by judiciously selecting existing airs, could display his own taste and that of the singers. Later writers and composers embraced pastiche, generating some of the century's most beloved productions, including the burletta *Midas* (1762), the pastiche operas *The Maid of the Mill* (1765) and *The Duenna* (1775)—the latter being Richard Sheridan's dramatization of his elopement with the celebrity soprano Elizabeth Linley—and newly composed operas with borrowed numbers, such William Shields's *Rosina* (1782) and Stephen Storace's *The Pirates* (1790). What changed after 1737 were the sources and the 'moral' of the common tune. Now selected above all from fashionable music, the common tune or 'familiar Song', once joined to 'the [poet's] moral Decree', was seen to 'Rise into its ancient Dignity and Use' and elevate the spectator's taste.[109]

Tasked with educating musically, as well as morally, post-1737 songs in operatized comedies stemmed from more diverse high-style sources, such as pleasure garden concerts, Continental Italian operas, instrumental works, and English cantatas. Ballads and ballad-style airs appeared regularly alongside these forms, and so-called 'Scotch' and 'Irish' ballads were foregrounded in works like *The Highland Reel* (1788) and *The Shamrock* (1783; revised as *The Poor Soldier*) to follow Drury Lane's model for native 'operas'. Wordbooks from patent theatres' earlier ballad operas were also reanimated with galant-style airs, some newly composed. Of these productions—*The Jovial Crew* (Covent Garden, 1760, at Drury Lane in 1770 as *The Ladies Frolick*), *Flora* (Covent Garden, 1760), *Love in a Village* (Covent Garden, 1762), *Damon and Phillida* (Drury Lane, 1768), *Achilles in Petticoats* (1773)—*Love in a Village* was most spectacularly successful, spawning a series of new rustic pastiche operas featuring Beard and Brent.

Above all, ballad opera founded the notion that spoken dialogue with song was a welcome, inherently British, art form. According to John Burgoyne, writing in 1780, a song-with-dialogue production satisfyingly 'mirrored nature' and drew its 'chief applause from reason' because music was 'restrained from having a part in [. . .] the action'.[110] In contrast to all-sung works, song-with-dialogue British stage works flourished after 1737, and followed ballad opera's model for probing, in parenthetical song numbers, topical issues such as politics, social tensions, and celebrity lives.

However distant from today's practices and concerns, ballad opera was the first modern British musical theatre—created for common spectatorship, forged from song, dance, and sentimental action, and designed around lead vocalists. Because it was founded through experiment, ballad opera held within itself the means of its own reinvention. Through ballad opera, writers and theatre personnel founded a polite and commercial British repertory which has yet to take its place in music histories. By studying ballad opera, scholars can see how a stylistically distinctive British song repertory emerged; how singing stars were produced, and produced themselves; how popular song mediated and articulated social concerns; how and why composers mixed high- with low-style music. These practices are still with us today. Henry Fielding's and Henry Carey's works merit revival, not least due to musical numbers whose source tunes these writers ingeniously reinvented.

NOTES

1. Odai Johnson and William J. Burling, *The Colonial American Stage, 1665–1774: A Documentary Calendar* (Madison, NJ: Fairleigh Dickinson University Press: London: Associated University Presses, 2002), 112–114. In Charleston, *Flora* was performed by the Holt Company in the Court Room—no dedicated theatre existing at that time—on 18 February 1735. Henry Holt was a former dancer-actor on the London stage. In London, *Flora* ran at Lincoln's Inn Fields, opening 17 April 1729. The Colonial America Stage Calendar shows that successful London ballad operas *Damon and Phillida*, *The Honest Yorkshireman*, and *The Mock Doctor* transferred to American stages about two decades after they opened in London. *The Devil to Pay* transferred more swiftly, reaching American

shores five years after opening in London. According to Johnson and Burling 'the short musical was the most popular afterpiece genre on the colonial stage [...] audiences enjoyed a selection very closely aligned with the theatres of London' (*Colonial American Stage* , 69). For details about the first London productions of ballad operas discussed in this chapter, see *Ballad Operas Online*, hosted by the Oxford Digital Library, http://www.odl.ox.ac.uk/balladoperas/.

2. The vast scholarship on Gay's *Beggar's Opera* includes some important publications such as those by Jeremy Barlow (on sources for *The Beggar's Opera* music and post-1728 productions); William Schultz (on *The Beggar's Opera* production history and original cast); John Fuller (for a critical edition of, and introduction to, Gay's wordbook); and David Nokes (on the relation of *The Beggar's Opera* to Gay's career) (see Bibliography). Dianne Dugaw elucidates how Gay drew on Restoration stage song ('critical instants'), how he deployed low-style referents to indict polite culture, and how Gay's three ballad operas—*The Beggar's Opera, Polly*, and *Achilles*—evidence the sexual and social tensions with which Gay wrestled. Her publications include, among others, '"Critical Instants": Theatre Songs in the Age of Dryden and Purcell', *Eighteenth-Century Studies* 23, no. 2 (1989): 157–181, and *Deep Play: John Gay and the Invention of Modernity* (Newark: University of Delaware Press; London: Associated University Presses, 2001). On Gay's French sources, see Vanessa Rogers, 'John Gay, Ballad Opera, and the Théâtres de la foire', *Eighteenth-Century Music* 11, no. 2 (2014): 173–213.

3. Lisa A. Freeman, *Character's Theater: Genre and Identity on the Eighteenth-Century English Stage* (Philadelphia: University of Pennsylvania Press, 2002), esp. 11–46. According to Freeman, drama, especially comedy, through its normative representations, regulated the spectator's construction of self.

4. *The Music of John Gay's 'The Beggar's Opera'*, edited and arranged from eighteenth-century sources by Jeremy Barlow (Oxford: Oxford University Press, 1990), 95 (Air 67, sung by Macheath, to the air 'Greensleeves'). Please note that quotations from this work throughout the chapter follow the original spellings.

5. Jeremy Barlow, '*The Beggar's Opera* in London's Theatres, 1728-1761,' in *The Stage's Glory: John Rich, 1692–1761*, ed. Berta Joncus and Jeremy Barlow (Lanham, MD: Rowman & Littlefield; Newark: University of Delaware Press, 2011), 169–183.

6. Berta Joncus, '"The Assemblage of Every Female Folly": Lavinia Fenton, Kitty Clive and the Genesis of Ballad Opera', in *Women, Popular Culture, and the Eighteenth Century*, ed. Tiffany Potter (Toronto: University of Toronto Press, 2012), 25–51.

7. Shearer West, *The Image of the Actor: Verbal & Visual Representation in the Age of Garrick and Kemble* (London: Pinter, 1991), 19.

8. Anon., *A Guide to the Stage: or, Select Instructions [...] towards forming a Polite Audience* (London: Printed for D. Job and R. Baldwin, 1751), 14.

9. Anon., *The Touch-Stone* (London: n.p., 1728), 16. Usually attributed to James Ralph, *The Touch-Stone* may have been by Robert Samber. See Lowell Lindgren, 'Another Critic named Samber', in *Festa Musicologica*, ed. Thomas J. Mathiesen and Benito V. Rivera (Stuyvesant: Pendragon Press, 1995), 407–434.

10. See James Boswell's entry for Tuesday, 18 April 1775, in James Boswell, *Life of Johnson*, ed. R. W. Chapman, and J. D. Fleeman (Oxford: Oxford University Press, 1980), 630. I would like to thank Jeremy Barlow for informing me of the source for this story, mentioned without citation in William E. Schultz, *Gay's Beggar's Opera: Its Content, History & Influence* (New Haven: Yale University Press, 1923), 24.

11. Joncus, 'Assemblage of Every Female Folly', 27–33.
12. Cheryl Wanko, *Roles of Authority: Thespian Biography and Celebrity in Eighteenth-Century Britain* (Lubbock: Texas Tech University Press, 2003), 51–62, 71–79.
13. Schultz, *Gay's Beggar's Opera*, 24.
14. Private communication of 24 July 2014. On the tune's source, and for its notation and verses, see *The Music of John Gay's 'The Beggar's Opera'*, ed. Barlow, 19–20, 110.
15. 'After the vast success of that new Species of Dramatick Poetry, the Beggars Opera the Year following, I was so stupid, as to attempt something of the same Kind, upon a quite different Foundation, that of recommending Virtue and Innocence.' Colley Cibber, *An Apology for the Life of Mr. Colley Cibber*, 2nd edn (London: Printed for the author by J. Watts, 1740), 199.
16. Colley Cibber, *Love in a Riddle. A Pastoral* (London: Printed for J. Watts, 1729).
17. 'Prologue. Spoken by Mr. Wilks', in Cibber, *Love in a Riddle*, not paginated.
18. Dianne Dugaw, 'The Popular Marketing of "Old Ballads": The Ballad Revival and Eighteenth-Century Antiquarianism Reconsidered', *Eighteenth-Century Studies* 21, no. 1 (1987): 71–90.
19. Steve Newman, *Ballad Collection, Lyric, and the Canon: The Call of the Popular from the Restoration to the New Criticism* (Philadelphia: University of Pennsylvania Press, 2007), 27–35. Newman notes that while Addison ascribed to 'Old Ballads' the power to express 'intrinsically English' qualities, Gay wrote ballads to let audience members see themselves 'as an individual—to "be particular" in the words of the play [*The Beggar's Opera*]' regardless of social rank. Newman, *Ballad Collection*, 17.
20. See, for instance, Albert B. Friedman, *The Ballad Revival. Studies in the Influence of Popular on Sophisticated Poetry* (Chicago: University of Chicago Press, 1961). For further literature, see Newman, *Ballad Collection*, ch. 1; Matthew Gelbart, *The Invention of 'Folk Music' and 'Art Music': Emerging Categories from Ossian to Wagner* (Cambridge: Cambridge University Press, 2007), 155–162.
21. Barlow, 'Notes on the Origins of the Songs and their Titles', in *Music of John Gay's 'The Beggar's Opera'*, ed. Barlow, 108–116.
22. 'I remember the first Night of *Love in a Riddle* [. . .] when Miss Raftor came on in the Part of Phillida, the monstrous Roar subsided'. William Chetwood, *A General History of the Stage* (London: Printed for W. Owen, 1749), 127–128.
23. Edmond Gagey, in his monograph on ballad opera wordbooks, noted, 'scarcely a ballad opera could appear at Drury Lane [. . .] without the inevitable presence of Kitty'. Edmond M. Gagey, *Ballad Opera* (New York: Benjamin Blom, 1937), 163.
24. Berta Joncus, '"A Likeness Where None Was to Be Found": Imagining Kitty Clive (1711–1785)', *Music in Art* 34, nos. 1–2 (2009): 89–106.
25. The mainpiece was the centrepiece of the evening entertainments, beginning at six o'clock; the afterpiece was a lighter, shorter work that followed. See also n. 31.
26. William J. Burling, *Summer Theatre in London, 1661–1820, and the Rise of the Haymarket Theatre* (Madison, NJ: Fairleigh Dickinson University Press; London: Associated University Presses, 2000), 94.
27. Catherine Clive, Letter of 15 December 1774; quoted in Joncus, '"Assemblage of Every Female Folly"', 40.
28. *The Devil to Pay*, once translated, inspired the Singspiel in Germany, and the opéra comique in Paris and in Vienna. See Walter H. Rubsamen, 'Mr. Seedo, Ballad Opera and the Singspiel', in *Miscelánea en Homenaje a Monseñor Higinio Anglés* (Barcelona: Consejo

Superior de Investigaciones Cientoficas, 1958–1961), 1–35; Bertil H. van Boer, 'Coffey's *The Devil to Pay*: The Comic War, and the Emergence of the German Singspiel', *Journal of Musicological Research* 8, nos. 1–2 (1988): 119–139; and Estelle Joubert, 'Songs to Shape a German Nation: Hiller's Comic Operas and the Public Sphere', *Eighteenth-Century Music* 3, no. 2 (2006): 213–230. On *The Devil to Pay* and the emergence of the opéra comique, see Bruce Alan Brown, ed., *Christoph Willibald Gluck: Le Diable à quatre, ou La Double Métamorphose*, Sämtliche Werke, Abteilung IV, Französische Komische Opern, vol. 3 (London: Bärenreiter, 1992), and Kent Smith, 'Egidio Duni and the Development of *opéra comique* from 1753 to 1770' (Unpublished PhD thesis, Cornell University, 1980).

29. Tiffany Stern, *Rehearsal from Shakespeare to Sheridan* (Oxford: Oxford University Press, 2000), chapters 5 and 6 (especially pp. 149–152 and 212–213).

30. On the tradition of players' ownership of roles, see Berta Joncus, '"In Wit Superior as in Fighting": Kitty Clive and the Conquest of a Rival Queen', *Huntington Library Quarterly* 74, no. 1 (2011): 23–42.

31. Robert D. Hume notes that 'after 1714 a one- or two-act afterpiece increasingly became the norm'. Robert D. Hume, 'John Rich as Manager and Entrepreneur', in Joncus and Barlow, *Stage's Glory*, 147. On afterpiece practices, see Leo Hughes, 'Afterpieces: Or, That's Entertainment', in *The Stage and the Page: London's 'Whole Show' in the Eighteenth-Century Theatre*, ed. George Winchester Stone (Berkeley: University of California Press, 1981), 55–70 and Kevin Pry, 'Theatrical Competition and the Rise of the Afterpiece', *Theatre Notebook* 36 (1982): 21–27.

32. Leroy J. Morrissey, 'Fielding and the Ballad Opera', *Eighteenth-Century Studies* 4 (1971): 386–402, especially 390–394. Morrissey argues against Watts being a 'major influence' on tune selection, because playwrights had 477 woodcut tunes from Watts's six-volume *Musical Miscellany* to choose from, and because Watts showed his willingness to prepare a wordbook with unfamiliar tunes by issuing George Lillo's *Silvia* (1730).

33. *The Musical Miscellany*, vols. 1–6 (London: Printed by and for John Watts, 1729–31).

34. Morrissey's assertion that 'of ninety-seven ballad operas published between 1728 and 1738, thirty-five were published with their music, but only five of the thirty-five had the music on copperplate' is incorrect. Research for *Ballad Operas Online* shows that at least 110 ballad operas were published by 31 December 1738, forty-three with music, of which ten were on copperplate.

35. Morrissey, 'Fielding and the Ballad Opera', 393.

36. Watts's editions of *The Beggar's Opera* in 1733 and 1735 with the Drury Lane cast list implied wrongly that Drury Lane's production had become London's favourite. Joncus, '"In Wit Superior"', 31. Similarly, Watts printed the Drury Lane cast for *Damon and Phillida*, although a rival company at the Little Haymarket Theatre owned this production. Joncus, '"Likeness Where None Was to Be Found"', 94–96.

37. Vincent J. Liesenfeld, *The Licensing Act of 1737* (Madison: University of Wisconsin Press, 1984), 12 and n. 14. According to Lord Hervey, Walpole objected to being depicted as a highwayman. John Fuller observes that Wapole's opponent William Pulteney may have prompted Gay to write a sequel. 'Introduction', in *Dramatic Works [of] John Gay*. Vol. 1, ed. John Fuller (Oxford: Clarendon Press, 1983), 54–55.

38. Nokes reports that by the summer of 1729 Gay's receipts had brought his personal wealth to £3,000, the interest alone from which he could live on. David Nokes, *John Gay: A Profession of Friendship* (Oxford: Oxford University Press 1995), 466.

39. Joncus, '"Assemblage of Every Female Folly"', 33.

40. 'Dogget, Thomas', in Philip H. Highfill, Kalman A. Burnim, and Edward A. Langhans, *A Biographical Dictionary of Actors*, vol. 4 (Carbondale: Southern Illinois University Press, 1975), 442–451.

41. Berta Joncus and Vanessa Rogers, 'Beyond *The Beggar's Opera*: John Rich and English Ballad Opera', in *The Stage's Glory': John Rich, 1692–1761*, ed. Berta Joncus and Jeremy Barlow (Newark: University of Delaware Press; Lanham, MD: Rowman & Littlefield, 2011), 184–204.

42. 'Prologue spoken by Mr [Theophilus] Cibber', in Theophilus Cibber, *Patie and Peggy [. . .] A Scotch Ballad Opera* (London: Printed for J. Watts, 1730). Capitals in the original.

43. Joseph Mitchell, *The Highland Fair [. . .] An Opera* (London: Printed for J. Watts, 1731), 77. The frontispiece, by William Hogarth, was titled 'A Scots Opera'.

44. *The Stage-Coach. A Comedy [. . .] By Mr. George Farquhar. To which is prefix'd, the Life and Character of Mr. George Farquhar* (London: Printed for E. Curll [. . .] and R. Francklin, 1718). Some version of this ballad opera was performed at Smock Alley, Dublin, six weeks before it opened at Drury Lane, where its adaptor, William Chetwood, included it as an afterpiece for his benefit. William J. Lawrence, 'The Mystery of *The Stage Coach*', *Modern Language Review* 27, no. 4 (1932): 392–397.

45. Burling, *Summer Theatre in London*, 24–75.

46. 'She is born [. . .] of mean estate, being the daughter of some insolent mechanic, who fancies himself a gentleman, who [. . .] resolves to keep up his family by marrying his girl to a parson or schoolmaster [. . .] to which end, he and his wife [. . .] send her to the dancing-school [. . .] this foundation laid [. . .] she frequents all the balls and public walks in Oxford [. . . to] meet with some raw coxcomb [. . .] and is at last, with some art and management, drawn in to marry her.' Nicholas Amhurst, *Terrae-Filius, or The Secret History of the University of Oxford* (London: Printed for R. Francklin, 1726); quoted in Gagey, *Ballad Opera*, 167–168. As Gagey notes, Amhurst, who later led the opposition paper *The Craftsman*, was expelled from Oxford.

47. Edward Ward (1667–1731) was a humourist of 'low extraction' condemned by Alexander Pope in *The Dunciad*. Ward's invective against the government included the *Hudibras Redivivus* (1705).

48. James Winston, *Collection of Memoranda [. . .] Relating to Drury Lane Theatre* (London, 1842), British Library, Add. MS 27,831. This bound manuscript volume was, according to its title, compiled by 'Mr Winston'—presumably the theatre historian James Winston—as 'Notes for a History of the Play Houses and the Places of Public Amusements [. . .] in November 1842'. In this volume, *The Prisoners Opera* is interleaved with Winston's transcription of the interview with Macklin that appeared in Thomas Kenrick's *The British Stage and Literary Cabinet*, cited in n. 53.

49. The music is printed as a separately-paginated appendix, and only five common tunes are identified by title: air 4 'Excuse Me', air 10 'Thomas I Cannot', air 11 'Bonny Grey-eyed Morn', air 12 'Let's Be Jovial, Fill Our Glasses', and air 13 'Dusty Miller'. Edward Ward, *The Prisoners Opera* (London: Printed at the Wells, 1730).

50. There are five dances indicated: a 'Figure or a Country-Dance' by the prisoners followed by pantomimic scene with Punch; a dance by Harlequin who mimics a Tallyman (a debt collector) 'by rattling his Bunch of Tallies [tally sticks] and his other comical Jestures [*sic*]'; a 'Marshal Dance' by 'two or more Prisoners'; a 'Scaramouche Dance'; and a 'very comical Dance performed by the Smiths'. Ward, *Prisoners Opera*, 4, 7, 9–10, and 12.

51. Ward, *Prisoners Opera*, 2, 4, and 7.

52. In his verse description of Islington's gaming, culling, and sexual advances, Ward described how he was drawn by the 'Organ' at Sadler's Wells, where 'Lady Squab [. . .] silenc'd the Noise with her Musical Note' as did a 'Fiddler in Scarlet'. Edward Ward, *A Walk to Islington: with a Description of New Tunbridge-Wells, and Sadlers Music-House* (London: no publication details, 1699), 13–15.

53. 'Sadler's Wells', in Thomas Kenrick, *The British Stage and Literary Cabinet*, vol. 1 (London: J. Chappell, 1817), 68–69.

54. Burling, *Summer Theatre in London*, 76.

55. Robert D. Hume, *Henry Fielding and the London Theatre, 1728–1737* (Oxford: Clarendon Press 1988), 37–38. On the Little Haymarket Theatre being a 'road house', see Hume, *Henry Fielding*, 52–61.

56. 'The Dedication', in Thomas Odell, *The Patron: or, The Statesman's Opera* (London: Printed by W. Pearson for J. Clarke, 1729).

57. Odell, *Patron*, 10.

58. Odell, *Patron*, 23–24.

59. Edgar V. Roberts, 'The Songs and Tunes in Henry Fielding's Ballad Operas', in *Essays on the Eighteenth-Century English Stage*, ed. Kenneth Richards and Peter Thomson, 29–49 (Manchester: Methuen & Co., 1972), and Vanessa L. Rogers, 'Writing Plays "In The Sing-Song Way": Henry Fielding's Ballad Operas and Early Musical Theater in Eighteenth-Century London' (Unpublished PhD thesis: University of Southern California, 2007), xv–xx.

60. 'Playwright and Libertine (1727–1739)', in Martin C. Battestin with Ruth R. Battestin, *Henry Fielding: A Life* (London: Routledge, 1989), 253–254.

61. Introduction to *The Author's Farce* (1730), in Henry Fielding, *Plays*, ed. Thomas Lockwood, vol. 1 (Oxford: Clarendon Press, 2004), 190–191.

62. *Author's Farce*, 242 n. 1, 262 n. 1; and 264 n. 5.

63. In the ballad opera, *The Beggar's Pantomime* (1736) 'Philo-Comicus' describes how the actor-manager William Giffard 'treated the Publick with the Resemblance, as near as he could, of another Manager [Charles Fleetwood], whom he made a spectacle of'. Joncus, ' "In Wit Superior" ', 38.

64. Introduction to *The Welsh Opera, The Grub-Street Opera* (1731), in Henry Fielding, *Plays*, ed. Lockwood, vol. 2 (2007), 12–14.

65. Paul Dennant, ' "Barbarous Old English Jig": The "Black Joke" in the Eighteenth and Nineteenth Centuries', *Folk Music Journal* 10, no. 3 (2013): 298–318.

66. Fielding used the 'Black Joke' melody for air 13 in *The Welsh Opera*, which is retained as air 15 in his second version of this work, titled *The Grub-Street Opera*. The ballad concluded, 'There's not one honest Man in Score, | Nor Woman true in Twenty four.' *The Welsh Opera*, 47. Rogers notes that audiences would surely have grasped 'the underlying smuttiness' of Fielding's setting. Rogers, 'Writing Plays "In The Sing-Song Way" ', 201.) Fielding strategically invoked or used the 'Black Joke', as a dance and a ballad, in *Don Quixote, The Lottery, The Welsh Opera, The Grub-Street Opera*, and *The Author's Farce*. See Rogers, 'Writing Plays "In The Sing-Song Way" ', 161–162, 170–176 and 199–201.

67. Curtis Price characterizes this chorus, from John Fletcher and Francis Beaumont's *Bonduca* (Act 2, Scene 2) as 'vacuous', added to a 'cheap' revival designed to incite patriotic fervour. Curtis Price, *Henry Purcell and the London Stage* (Cambridge: Cambridge University Press, 1984), 119–125. On the allusion in *The Welsh Opera* to the Pulteney duel, see Introduction to *The Welsh Opera, The Grub-Street Opera*, 1–3.

68. As Yvonne Noble shows, in the verse satire *The Dramatic Sessions*, Phillips was characterized as being supervised by Rich to write like Fielding: 'Then boldly on Theatre Ph—ll—ps appears, | With *Mock-Lawyer* in hand, and the *Stage-Mutineers*'. Yvonne Noble, 'Attributions and Misattributions to Edward Phillips, Theatre Writer of the 1730s, with Some Remarks on Thomas Phillips, Theatre Writer of the 1730s', *Restoration & Eighteenth-Century Theatre Research* 17, nos. 1–2 (2002): 73.

69. 'Table 4', in Hume, *Henry Fielding*, 257.

70. John Hill, *The Actor: A Treatise [. . .] with Theatrical Anecdotes* (London: Printed for R. Griffiths, 1750), 163. A failed actor and playwright, John Hill based this work on Pierre Rémond de Sainte-Albine's *Le Comédien* (1747). Elsewhere Hill condemned Clive for dressing herself in 'good cloathes' in her chambermaid role (p. 223) and in his 1755 revised version of this treatise, for her 'saucy and unnatural familiarity' with spectators during performance. John Hill, *The Actor [. . .] Containing Impartial Observations on the Performance, Manner, Perfections, and Defects of Mr. Garrick [. . .] &c [. . .]* (London: Printed for R. Griffiths, 1755), 222.

71. Paula O'Brien, 'The Life and Works of James Miller, 1704-1744' (Unpublished PhD thesis, University of London, 1979), 57–60; Charles Woods, 'The "Miss Lucy" Plays of Fielding and Garrick', *Philological Quarterly* 41, no. 1 (1962): 294–310; Introduction to *Miss Lucy in Town*, in Henry Fielding, *Plays*, ed. Lockwood, vol. 3 (2011), 461–465.

72. Todd Gilman, *The Theatre Career of Thomas Arne* (Newark: University of Delaware Press; Lanham, MD: Rowman & Littlefield Pub. Group, 2013), 112–113 and 185–187.

73. One exception may have been the now-lost *Deborah or A Wife for You All*, written for Clive's benefit, which may have mocked Queen Caroline. Edgar V. Roberts, 'Henry Fielding's Lost Play *Deborah, or A Wife for You All* (1733)', *Bulletin of the New York Public Library* 66 (1962): 567–588.

74. Gagey, *Ballad Opera*, 173–175; Introduction to *The Welsh Opera, The Grub-Street Opera*, 8.

75. Printed only, this was an 'interlude' in the five-act comedy *The Intriguing Courtiers* (1732) that another publisher issued (with the ballad opera interlude) the next year under its secondary title, *The Modish Gallants*. John Randall 'operatiz'd' Susanna Centlivre's *A Wife Well Manag'd*, retitling it *The Disappointment* (1732).

76. It was Lord Hervey who, as Vice-Chamberlain in the Royal Household, had to make arrangements for the marriage of the Princess Royal to William, Prince of Orange. Robert Halsband, *Lord Hervey: Eighteenth-Century Courtier* (New York: Oxford University Press 1974), 168–171.

77. Although competitively staged in four versions in 1701 by composers vying for first prize, Weldon's 'Let Ambition Fire thy Mind' was conceived, and succeeded, as a popular common air. Olive Baldwin and Thelma Wilson point out that Weldon had singers perform the air five times in his setting; unsurprisingly, it resurfaced in four ballad operas other than *The Promis'd Marriage*, and opened Thomas Arne's acclaimed pastiche *Love in a Village* (1762), based on Charles Johnson's Clive vehicle, *The Village Opera* (1729). Olive Baldwin and Thelma Wilson, 'The Singers of *The Judgement of Paris*', in *Lively Arts of the London Stage, 1675-1725*, ed. Kathryn Lowerre, 11–26 (Farnham: Ashgate Publishing Ltd, 2014).

78. Gagey, *Ballad Opera*, 186–191. The now-lost ballad opera *Barren Island, or Petticoat Government*, which ran at Bartholomew's Fair from 24 August 1734, was perhaps based on this pamphlet opera.

79. Lockwood highlights the 'mania for finding anti-ministerial designs in public entertainments' that a writer for *Fog's Weekly Journal* mocked in a 'sinister' reading of William

Chetwood's innocuous ballad opera, *The Generous Freemason*. Introduction to *The Welsh Opera, The Grub-Street Opera*, 6–7.

80. The Excise Crisis captured, according to Paul Langford, the nature of politics in Britain. Its background and impact are elucidated in Paul Langford, *The Excise Crisis: Society and Politics in the Age of Walpole* (Oxford: Clarendon Press, 1975).

81. The term 'claptrap' means pretentious, hortatory speech designed to trap audience into clapping. The air referred to was no. 9 in the *The Downfal* [*sic*] *of Bribery*, London: Printed for Sam. Pike, 1733. 'Pamphlet' ballad operas issued in 1733 include *The Honest Electors, Rome Excis'd, Lord Blunder's Confession, The Commodity Excis'd, The Downfal of Bribery* (sardonically titled '*as performed by [. . .] Players [. . .] at Taunton*'), *A King and No King*, and *The Sturdy Beggars*. Common tunes were also turned into broadsides for the cause, as in *The London Merchants Triumphant* (London: Printed for T. Reinshau, 1733), to the tune the 'Jovial Beggars'. Eustace Budgell may have written the verses.

82. 'Impresario at the Little Haymarket, 1736–1737', in Hume, *Henry Fielding*, 200–260.

83. Lockwood explains how Fielding lampooned pantomime, rather than ballad opera. Introduction to *Tumble-Down Dick*, in Henry Fielding, *Plays*, ed. Lockwood, vol. 3, 317–326.

84. Dane Farnsworth Smith, *Plays about the Theatre in England, from 'The Rehearsal' in 1671 to the Licensing Act in 1737* (London: Oxford University Press, 1936), 161–170. Although Smith dismisses the attribution of *The Stage Mutineers* to Edward Phillips, Noble shows that Phillips was indeed the author. Noble, 'Attributions and Misattributions to Edward Phillips', 71–74.

85. Norman Gillespie, 'The Life and Works of Henry Carey, 1687–1743', vol. 1 (Unpublished PhD thesis, University of London, 1982), 84–87. In debt, Carey hanged himself on 5 October 1743. The great actor Edmund Kean was his natural grandson.

86. 'Derry Down', Claude M. Simpson, *The British Broadside Ballad and Its Music* (New Brunswick: Rutgers University Press, 1966), 172–176. It was also known as 'A Cobbler There Was' and was used in twenty-seven (Simpson records the number as twenty-six) ballad operas.

87. On Ralph's parodic use of the tune, see Berta Joncus, ' "When Farce and When Musick Can Eke out a Play": Ballad Opera and Theatre's Commerce', in *The Edinburgh Companion to Literature and Music*, ed. Delia Da Sousa Correa (Edinburgh: Edinburgh University Press, forthcoming).

88. Civicus, *The Sturdy Beggars. A New Ballad Opera*, Humbly dedicated to [. . .] the Worthy Merchants and Citizens of London (London: Printed by and for J. Dormer, 1733), 45 [air 14].

89. Female emancipation was 'a recurring theme in Carey's work'. Gillespie, 'Life and Works of Henry Carey', 167–172. Carey's *Contrivances* (1729), and *Honest Yorkshireman* (1735) both evidence Carey's preoccupation.

90. 'Prologue. Spoken by Mr. Theoph. Cibber', in Charles Coffey, *The Devil to Pay* (London: Printed for J. Watts, 1731).

91. Coffey, *Devil to Pay*, 21. Jobson also 'lugs and throws down the priest' (14), beats Nell (21), straps Lady Loverule twice (37–38), and 'smacks' her (54).

92. Compare Coffey, *Devil to Pay*, 3–4 with Thomas Jevon, *The Devil of a Wife, or a Comical Transformation* (London: Printed by J. Heptinstall for J. Eaglesfield, 1686), 2.

93. Used in fifteen ballad operas from 1729 to 1743, the tune went by three titles, 'The Twitcher', 'A Damsel I'm Told', and 'He That Has the Best Wife'. Simpson traces the melody back to the Restoration ballad 'Cupid's Trepan'. Simpson, *Broadside Ballads*, 151–153. After the success

of the *Devil to Pay*, the tune, when referred to as 'The Twitcher' or 'He That Has the Best Wife', was reset to relate to Jevon's verses, as in *The Sailor's Opera* (1731), air 16 (warning men against marriage); James Worsdale's *Cure for a Scold* (1735), air 9 (wives are trouble); Matthew Gardiner's *The Sharpers* (1740), air 14 (warning men against marriage); Joseph Yarrow's *Love at First Sight* (1742), air 11 (the dramatis persona declares her intention to trade her father for a lover); and *In Court and Country; or, The Changelings* (1743), air 40 (about female promiscuity, and possibly masturbation).

94. Kristina Straub, *Sexual Suspects: Eighteenth-Century Players and Sexual Ideology* (Princeton: Princeton University Press, 1992), 127–128. In *The Rival Milliners* (1736) Mrs Talbot played the lawyer Pleadwell, and in the *Judgement of Paris*, Mrs Egleton played Juno. In *Polly* (1729) Gay included a breeches disguise intended for Fenton.

95. Straub, *Sexual Suspects*, 12.

96. Straub, *Sexual Suspects*, 130–131.

97. Scholarship on Charlotte Charke is extensive. Actress, entrepreneur, and transvestite, Charke suffered after the Licensing Act of 1737, because having alienated patent theatre managers and her father Colley Cibber she found herself without work or support. She tried a dizzying range of professions—from puppeteer to sausage maker to tavern proprietor—and was forced to go strolling. She recounted her sentimental conquests, dressed as a man, in *A Narrative of the Life of Mrs Charlotte Charke*, issued in weekly instalments. Despite the popularity of *A Narrative*, she died impoverished; according to her report, her father Colley Cibber returned unopened her letters desperately pleading for his help. See, among other items, Philip E. Baruth, *Introducing Charlotte Charke: Actress, Author, Enigma* (Urbana: University of Illinois Press, 1998), and Liberty Smith, 'Listening to the "Wives" of the "Female Husbands"', *Journal of Lesbian Studies* 6, no. 2 (2002): 105–120.

98. Joncus, '"In Wit Superior"', 23–42.

99. Joseph Dorman, *The Female Rake* (London: Printed for J. Dormer, 1736), 19 [air 5]. Dorman's verses describe how pregnancy begets prostitution: 'When a woman's been sporting as Phillis has done | When her belly grows plump and her face grows wan ...'. Mounted at the Little Haymarket Theatre on 26 April 1736, this production was for the benefit of the author Dorman. In his ballad opera, he dramatized types of 'female rakes'— women with means to indulge their concupiscence—against whom he had railed in a verse pamphlet published the previous year.

100. Theophilus Cibber, *The Harlot's Progress [. . .] the Songs made (to Old Ballad Tunes) by a Friend* (London: Printed for the benefit of Richard Cross the prompter, 1733), 10–11. As noted above, this production was a hybrid pantomime-ballad opera; the 'friend' who 'made' the song verses was likely Clive's mentor, Henry Carey.

101. *Miss Lucy in Town*, *Plays*, 489–490 and 497–499.

102. Gay contrasts the indigenous 'noble savage' (native Indians) against the black slave to highlight the latter's negative qualities; elsewhere the Negro is deployed to mirror the vices of the over-refined European man. The 'image of the African loses out both ways, since it is implicitly given all the worst characteristics of both savagery and civilization'. John Richardson, 'John Gay and Slavery', *Modern Language Review* 97, no. 1 (2002): 24.

103. Rogers, 'John Gay, Ballad Opera, and the Théâtres de la foire', 192.

104. For a provocative account of, and reflection on, this legacy, see John Strausbaugh, *Black like You: Blackface, Whiteface, Insult & Imitation in American Popular Culture* (New York: Jeremy P. Tarcher / Penguin, 2006). As Strausbaugh shows, blackface

performance is both a 'racist caricature invented by White(s)' and a manifestation of 'complex of neuroses and pathologies that mark relations between Whites and Blacks in America' which continue to inform popular culture. Strausbaugh, *Black like You*, 24.

105. Partbooks for three ballad operas are housed in the British Library and, for the *The Devil to Pay*, in the Royal College of Music. Four overtures survive in print. Roger Fiske, *English Theatre Music in the Eighteenth Century* (London: Oxford University Press, 1973), 114–116. Songsheets are highly corrupt sources, and have yet to be collated with the ballad opera wordbooks containing notation.

106. Liesenfeld, *Licensing Act of 1737*, 60–150.

107. James Ralph, *The Fashionable Lady* (London: Printed for J. Watts, 1730), 29.

108. Barlow, '*Beggar's Opera* in London's Theatres, 1728–1761', 169–183.

109. John Brown, *A Dissertation on the Rise, Union, and Power [...] of Poetry and Music* (London: Printed for L. Davis and C. Reymers, 1763), 239.

110. John Burgoyne, Preface to *Airs, Duets, Trios, &c. in the Lord of the Manor*, A Comic Opera (1780); cited in Fiske, *English Theatre Music in the Eighteenth Centry*, 263.

BIBLIOGRAPHY

Amhurst, Nicholas. *Terrae-Filius, or The Secret History of the University of Oxford*. London: Printer for R. Francklin, 1726.

Anon. *Court and Country; or, The Changelings*. London: Printed for W. Webb, 1743.

Anon. *A Guide to the Stage: or, Select Instructions [...] towards forming a Polite Audience*. London: Printed for D. Job and R. Baldwin, 1751.

Anon. *The London Merchants Triumphant*. London: Printed for T. Reinshau, 1733.

Anon. *The Musical Miscellany*. Vols. 1–6. London: Printed by and for John Watts, 1729–1731.

Anon. *The Touch-Stone*. London: n.p., 1728.

Baldwin, Olive, and Thelma Wilson. 'The Singers of *The Judgement of Paris*', 11–26. In *Lively Arts of the London Stage, 1675–1725*, edited by Kathryn Lowerre. Farnham: Ashgate Publishing Ltd, 2014.

Ballad Operas Online, http://www.odl.ox.ac.uk/balladoperas/.

Barlow, Jeremy. 'The *Beggar's Opera* in London's Theatres, 1728–1761.' In *The Stage's Glory: John Rich, 1692–1761*, edited by Berta Joncus and Jeremy Barlow, 169–183. Lanham, MD: Rowman & Littlefield; Newark: University of Delaware Press, 2011.

Barlow, Jeremy, ed. *The Music of John Gay's 'The Beggar's Opera'*. Edited and Arranged from Eighteenth-Century Sources by Jeremy Barlow. Oxford: Oxford University Press, 1990.

Baruth, Philip E. *Introducing Charlotte Charke: Actress, Author, Enigma*. Urbana: University of Illinois Press, 1998.

Battestin, Martin C., with Ruthe R. Battestin. *Henry Fielding: A Life*. London: Routledge, 1989.

Battestin, Martin C., with Ruthe R. Battestin. 'Playwright and Libertine (1727–1739).' In *Henry Fielding: A Life*, 53–254.

Boswell, James. *Life of Johnson*. Edited by R. W. Chapman and J. D. Fleeman. Oxford: Oxford University Press, 1980.

Brown, Bruce Alan, ed. *Christoph Willibald Gluck: Le Diable à quatre, ou La Double Métamorphose*. Sämtliche Werke. Abteilung IV, Französische Komische Opern. Vol. 3. London: Bärenreiter, 1992.

Burling, William J. *Summer Theatre in London, 1661–1820, and the Rise of the Haymarket Theatre*. Madison, NJ: Fairleigh Dickinson University Press; London: Associated University Presses, 2000.

Carey, Henry. *The Contrivances*. London: Printed for W. Mears, 1729.

Carey, Henry. *The Honest Yorkshireman*. London: Printed for W. Feales, 1735.

Chetwood, William. *A General History of the Stage*. London: Printed for W. Owen, 1749.

Cibber, Colley. *An Apology for the Life of Mr. Colley Cibber*. 2nd edn. London: Printed for the author by J. Watts, 1740.

Cibber, Colley. *Love in a Riddle. A Pastoral*. London: Printed for J. Watts, 1729.

Cibber, Theophilus. *The Harlot's Progress [. . .] the Songs Made (to Old Ballad Tunes) by a Friend*. London: Printed for the benefit of Richard Cross the prompter, 1733.

Cibber, Theophilus. *Patie and Peggy [. . .] A Scotch Ballad Opera*. London: Printed for J. Watts, 1730.

Civicus, *The Sturdy Beggars. A New Ballad Opera*. Humbly dedicated to [. . .] the Worthy Merchants and Citizens of London, London: Printed by and for J. Dormer, 1733.

Coffey, Charles. *The Devil to Pay*. London: Printed for J. Watts, 1731.

Dennant, Paul. '"Barbarous Old English Jig": The "Black Joke" in the Eighteenth and Nineteenth Centuries.' *Folk Music Journal* 10, no. 3 (2013): 298–318.

Dorman, Joseph. *The Female Rake*. London: Printed for J. Dormer, 1736.

Dugaw, Dianne. '"Critical Instants": Theatre Songs in the Age of Dryden and Purcell.' *Eighteenth-Century Studies* 23, no. 2 (1989): 157–181.

Dugaw, Dianne. *Deep Play: John Gay and the Invention of Modernity*. Newark: University of Delaware Press; London: Associated University Presses, 2001.

Dugaw, Dianne. 'The Popular Marketing of "Old Ballads": The Ballad Revival and Eighteenth-Century Antiquarianism Reconsidered.' *Eighteenth-Century Studies* 21, no. 1 (1987): 71–90.

Farquhar, George. *The Stage-Coach. A Comedy [. . .] By Mr. George Farquhar. To which is prefix'd, the Life and Character of Mr. George Farquhar*. London: Printed for E. Curll and R. Francklin, 1718.

Fielding, Henry. *The Author's Farce* (1730). In *Plays*, edited by Lockwood, vol. 1.

Fielding, Henry. *Plays*. Vols. 1–3. Edited by Thomas Lockwood. Oxford: Clarendon Press, 2004–2011.

Fielding, Henry. *The Welsh Opera, The Grub-Street Opera* (1731). In *Plays*, edited by Thomas Lockwood, vol. 2.

Fiske, Roger. *English Theatre Music in the Eighteenth Century*. London: Oxford University Press, 1973.

Freeman, Lisa A. *Character's Theater: Genre and Identity on the Eighteenth-Century English Stage*. Philadelphia: University of Pennsylvania Press, 2002.

Freeman, Mark. *The Downfal of Bribery; or, The Honest Men of Taunton*. London: Printed for Sam Pike, 1733.

Friedman, Albert B. *The Ballad Revival: Studies in the Influence of Popular on Sophisticated Poetry*. Chicago: University of Chicago Press, 1961.

Gagey, Edmond M. *Ballad Opera*. New York: Benjamin Blom, 1937.

Gardiner, Matthew. *The Sharpers*. Dublin: Printed for the Author by E. Jones, 1740.

Gay, John. *Dramatic Works [of] John Gay*. Vol. 1. Edited by John Fuller. Oxford: Clarendon Press, 1983.

Gelbart, Matthew. *The Invention of 'Folk Music' and 'Art Music': Emerging Categories from Ossian to Wagner*. Cambridge: Cambridge University Press, 2007.

Gillespie, Norman. 'The Life and Works of Henry Carey, 1687–1743.' Unpublished PhD thesis, University of London, 1982.

Gilman, Todd. *The Theatre Career of Thomas Arne*. Newark: University of Delaware Press; Lanham, MD: Rowman & Littlefield Pub. Group, 2013.

Halsband, Robert. *Lord Hervey: Eighteenth-Century Courtier*. New York: Oxford University Press, 1974.

Highfill, Philip H., Kalman A. Burnim, and Edward A. Langhans. *A Biographical Dictionary of Actors*. Carbondale: Southern Illinois University Press, 1975.

Hill, John. *The Actor: A Treatise [...] with Theatrical Anecdotes*. London: Printed for R. Griffiths, 1750.

Hill, John. *The Actor [...] Containing Impartial Observations on the Performance, Manner, Perfections, and Defects of Mr. Garrick [...] &c [...]*. London: Printed for R. Griffiths, 1755.

Hughes, Leo. 'Afterpieces: Or, That's Entertainment.' In *The Stage and the Page: London's 'Whole Show' in the Eighteenth-Century Theatre*, edited by George Winchester Stone, 55–70. Berkeley: University of California Press, 1981.

Hume, Robert D. *Henry Fielding and the London Theatre, 1728–1737*. Oxford: Clarendon Press, 1988.

Hume, Robert D. 'John Rich as Manager and Entrepreneur.' In *The Stage's Glory: John Rich, 1692–1761*, edited by Berta Joncus and Jeremy Barlow, 29–60.

Jevon, Thomas. *The Devil of a Wife, or a Comical Transformation*. London: Printed by J. Heptinstall for J. Eaglesfield, 1686.

Johnson, Odai, and William J. Burling. *The Colonial American Stage, 1665–1774: A Documentary Calendar*. Madison, NJ: Fairleigh Dickinson University Press; London: Associated University Presses, 2002.

Joncus, Berta. '"The Assemblage of Every Female Folly": Lavinia Fenton, Kitty Clive, and the Genesis of Ballad Opera.' In *Women, Popular Culture, and the Eighteenth Century*, edited by Tiffany Potter, 25–51. Toronto: University of Toronto Press, 2012.

Joncus, Berta. '"In Wit Superior as in Fighting": Kitty Clive and the Conquest of a Rival Queen.' *Huntington Library Quarterly* 74, no. 1 (2011): 23-42.

Joncus, Berta. '"A Likeness Where None Was to Be Found": Imagining Kitty Clive (1711–1785).' *Music in Art* 34, nos. 1–2 (2009): 89–106.

Joncus, Berta. '"When Farce and When Musick Can Eke out a Play": Ballad Opera and Theatre's Commerce.' In *The Edinburgh Companion to Literature and Music*, edited by Delia Da Sousa Correa. Edinburgh: Edinburgh University Press, forthcoming.

Joncus, Berta, and Jeremy Barlow, eds. *The Stage's Glory: John Rich, 1692–1761*. Newark: University of Delaware Press; Lanham, MD: Rowman & Littlefield, 2011.

Joncus, Berta, and Vanessa Rogers. 'Beyond *The Beggar's Opera*: John Rich and English Ballad Opera.' In *The Stage's Glory: John Rich, 1692–1761*, edited by Berta Joncus and Jeremy Barlow, 184–204.

Joubert, Estelle. 'Songs to Shape a German Nation: Hiller's Comic Operas and the Public Sphere.' *Eighteenth-Century Music* 3, no. 2 (2006): 213–230.

Kenrick, Thomas. *The British Stage and Literary Cabinet*. London: J. Chappell, 1817.

Langford, Paul. *The Excise Crisis: Society and Politics in the Age of Walpole*. Oxford: Clarendon Press, 1975.

Lawrence, William J. 'The Mystery of *The Stage Coach*.' *Modern Language Review* 27, no. 4 (1932): 392–397.

Liesenfeld, Vincent J. *The Licensing Act of 1737*. Madison: University of Wisconsin Press, 1984.

Lindgren, Lowell. 'Another Critic Named Samber.' In *Festa Musicologica*, edited by Thomas J. Mathiesen and Benito V. Rivera, 407–434. Stuyvesant: Pendragon Press, 1995.

Mitchell, Joseph. *The Highland Fair [. . .] An Opera*. London: Printed for J. Watts, 1731.

Morrissey, Leroy J. 'Fielding and the Ballad Opera.' *Eighteenth-Century Studies* 4 (1971): 386–402.

Newman, Steve. *Ballad Collection, Lyric, and the Canon: The Call of the Popular from the Restoration to the New Criticism*. Philadelphia: University of Pennsylvania Press, 2007.

Noble, Yvonne. 'Attributions and Misattributions to Edward Phillips, Theatre Writer of the 1730s, with Some Remarks on Thomas Phillips, Theatre Writer of the 1730s.' *Restoration & Eighteenth-Century Theatre Research* 17, nos. 1–2 (2002): 71–83.

Nokes, David. *John Gay: A Profession of Friendship*. Oxford: Oxford University Press, 1995.

O'Brien, Paula. 'The Life and Works of James Miller, 1704–1744.' Unpublished PhD thesis, University of London, 1979.

Odell, Thomas. *The Patron: or, The Statesman's Opera*. London: Printed by W. Pearson for J. Clarke, 1729.

Price, Curtis. *Henry Purcell and the London Stage*. Cambridge: Cambridge University Press, 1984.

Pry, Kevin. 'Theatrical Competition and the Rise of the Afterpiece Tradition 1700–1724.' *Theatre Notebook* 36 (1982): 21–27.

Ralph, James. *The Fashionable Lady*. London: Printed for J. Watts, 1730.

Richardson, John. 'John Gay and Slavery.' *Modern Language Review* 97, no. 1 (2002): 15–25.

Roberts, Edgar V. 'Henry Fielding's Lost Play *Deborah, or A Wife for You All* (1733).' *Bulletin of the New York Public Library* 66 (1962): 567–588.

Roberts, Edgar V. 'The Songs and Tunes in Henry Fielding's Ballad Operas.' In *Essays on the Eighteenth-Century English Stage*, edited by Kenneth Richards and Peter Thomson, 29–49. Manchester: Methuen & Co., 1972.

Rogers, Vanessa L. 'John Gay, Ballad Opera, and the Théâtres de la foire.' *Eighteenth-Century Music* 11, no. 2 (2014): 173–213.

Rogers, Vanessa L. 'Writing Plays "In The Sing-Song Way": Henry Fielding's Ballad Operas and Early Musical Theater in Eighteenth-Century London.' Unpublished PhD thesis, University of Southern California, 2007.

Rubsamen, Walter H. 'Mr. Seedo, Ballad Opera and the Singspiel.' In *Miscelánea en Homenaje a Monseñor Higinio Anglés*, 1–35. Barcelona: Consejo Superior de Investigaciones Cientoficas, 1958–1961.

Schultz, William E. *Gay's Beggar's Opera: Its Content, History & Influence*. New Haven: Yale University Press, 1923.

Simpson, Claude M. *The British Broadside Ballad and Its Music*. New Brunswick: Rutgers University Press, 1966.

Smith, Dane Farnsworth. *Plays about the Theatre in England, from 'The Rehearsal' in 1671 to the Licensing Act in 1737*. London: Oxford University Press, 1936.

Smith, Kent. 'Egidio Duni and the Development of Opéra Comique from 1753 to 1770.' Unpublished PhD thesis, Cornell University, 1980.

Smith, Liberty. 'Listening to the "Wives" of the "Female Husbands".' *Journal of Lesbian Studies* 6, no. 2 (October 2002): 105–120.

Stern, Tiffany. *Rehearsal from Shakespeare to Sheridan*. Oxford: Oxford University Press, 2000.

Straub, Kristina. *Sexual Suspects: Eighteenth-Century Players and Sexual Ideology*. Princeton: Princeton University Press, 1992.

Strausbaugh, John. *Black like You: Blackface, Whiteface, Insult & Imitation in American Popular Culture*. New York: Jeremy P. Tarcher / Penguin, 2006.

van Boer, Bertil H. 'Coffey's *The Devil to Pay*: The Comic War, and the Emergence of the German Singspiel.' *Journal of Musicological Research* 8, nos. 1–2 (1988): 119–139.

Wanko, Cheryl. *Roles of Authority: Thespian Biography and Celebrity in Eighteenth-Century Britain*. Lubbock: Texas Tech University Press, 2003.

Ward, Edward. *The Prisoners Opera*. London: Printed at the Wells, 1730.

Ward, Edward. *A Walk to Islington: With a Description of New Tunbridge-Wells, and Sadlers Music-House*. London: no publication details, 1699.

West, Shearer. *The Image of the Actor: Verbal & Visual Representation in the Age of Garrick and Kemble*. London: Pinter, 1991.

Winston, James. *Collection of Memoranda [. . .] Relating to Drury Lane Theatre*. London, 1842. British Library, Add. MS 27,831.

Woods, Charles. 'The "Miss Lucy" Plays of Fielding and Garrick.' *Philological Quarterly* 41, no. 1 (1962): 294–310.

Worsdale, James. *Cure for a Scold*. London: Printed for L. Gilliver, 1735.

Yarrow, Joseph. *Love at First Sight*. York: Printed for T. Gent, 1742.

CHAPTER 2

....

BETWEEN OPERA
AND MUSICAL

Theatre Music in Early Nineteenth-Century London

....

CHRISTINA FUHRMANN

MUSIC occupied an important but uneasy position in early nineteenth-century London theatre. A long tradition linked the stage with speech. The most prominent theatres in the metropolis, Covent Garden and Drury Lane, had royal patents stretching back to 1662 for 'legitimate' drama.[1] Legitimate was a vague term that essentially meant spoken drama in English and was meant to perpetuate the tradition of Shakespeare, Sheridan, and other leading British dramatists. Operating on the fringes of the territory of these two 'major' theatres were the 'minor' theatres, such as the Adelphi and Surrey. These venues, existing on yearly licences and widely regarded as catering to a lower class than the majors, were confined to 'illegitimate' drama.[2] Illegitimate was another nebulous term that encompassed dramas focused on sight, sound, and gesture as opposed to speech. The third type of theatre was the opera house, known during most of the period as the King's Theatre.[3] This house had an exclusive licence for opera in Italian, and continued to bring its largely upper-class audiences the foreign operas and singers that had first enthralled them in the early eighteenth century.[4] Such firm distinctions between repertoire became increasingly embattled and the restrictions were lifted in 1843, but they defined theatrical activity for much of the early nineteenth century. Music was an important delineator among different types of theatre and repertoire, but also fell squarely on the 'wrong' side of the most prized type of theatre: native, legitimate drama.

Music's contested position on the national stage stemmed from broader concerns about music in British culture. A persistent rhetoric styled music as frivolous, sensual, and effeminate, in contrast to more sober, masculine pursuits. James Boaden mourned that 'music triumphantly reigns over the subject reason of the country' and Henry Redhead Yorke railed against music as 'corruption, effeminacy, execrable fooleries and sing-song lullabies'.[5] Richard Leppert explains that 'the musical gentleman by his interests and actions semiotically deconstructed [. . .] the definition of gender upon which both the society and the culture ultimately depended. It is this, I believe, which justified the phenomenal attention devoted to the control of music in English society.[6] It became common to style the English language and British character as inherently inimical to music. The *Morning Chronicle* stated the prevalent idea that the English language '[did] not, without great difficulty, wind itself into the sinuosities of music.'[7] Utilizing music to define national character, Richard Mackenzie Bacon mused that '[t]he Italians depend almost wholly on the effect of the music [. . . but] we are not yet nationally speaking musical enough to melt down our other senses & faculties into the one reigning delight of combined melody & harmony.'[8] Music was thus a troublesome art, uncomfortably resonant with the feminine and the foreign.

Nevertheless, music fascinated theatre audiences. Despite repertoire laws to the contrary, it pervaded every venue and virtually every production. Given this context, British composers had plentiful but ambiguous opportunities, particularly for native opera. The London venue completely dedicated to opera, the King's Theatre, largely excluded native composers and singers in favour of foreign imports. The minor theatres were the only English-language theatres allowed to perform music, and they did employ composers heavily, but their musical resources and patrons' inclinations rarely supported full-scale opera. Unfortunately, their productions were also often so ephemeral that we can glean only a partial idea of their musical activities. Ironically, composers therefore found their most welcoming venue at the very houses that should have been most averse to music: the major theatres, who held the coveted patents for legitimate or spoken drama. While major theatre managers vigorously defended their right to legitimate drama, they found it could not solely support their ventures, particularly as they had no government subsidy. They therefore aggressively encroached on other theatres' domains, just as the minors encroached on theirs, and produced a plethora of British musical works and adapted foreign operas. Although such works were often the major theatres' most popular pieces, they still fell outside the legal repertoire of these houses, and composers had to be mindful of music's tenuous position.

The shape of native musical pieces at the major theatres, therefore—even those labelled 'opera'—diverged from Continental norms. In all productions, speech had to remain central, music ornamental. Performers tended to cultivate one sphere to the exclusion of the other. George Hogarth declared: '[I]t has been all along an impediment to the improvement of the English opera, that our singers have not been actors, nor our actors singers.'[9] Audiences rejected lengthy intertwining of drama and song. Librettist James Robinson Planché observed that 'a dramatic situation in music was "caviare to the general," and inevitably received with cries of "cut it short!" '.[10] Many British stage works therefore had little or no vocal music and relied on what was termed melodramatic music, or brief segments of instrumental music that accompanied stage gesture and action.[11] Even native operas featured spoken dialogue and often completely spoken roles. Vocal numbers were primarily light, tuneful, and accessible. Composers abjured learned ensembles, adventurous harmony, and loose forms. Foreign operas performed at the major theatres were heavily adapted to fit these parameters. In some ways, these features resonated with other vernacular operatic traditions, such as Singspiel and opéra comique. British opera was distinct even from these genres, however, with a heavier emphasis both on speech and on accessible, static music.

FIGURE 2.1 Sir Henry Rowley Bishop (1786–1865), the most prominent British theatre composer of the early nineteenth century.

Lithograph by Vigneron, Courtesy of Getty Images.

Rather than disparaging this era as unmusical and anti-operatic, as was done then
and has been done since, it is therefore more fruitful to view it in terms of a different
aesthetic, one perhaps less congruent with Continental opera than with musical theatre.
This essay explores this aesthetic through case studies of the works of the most prominent theatre composer of the time, Sir Henry Rowley Bishop (see Figure 2.1), in the three
most common musical genres at the playhouses: melodrama, British opera, and foreign
opera adaptations. These examples reveal how British composers positioned music
within a context both fascinated and repelled by it.

THE MILLER AND HIS MEN (1813) AND THE POWER OF MELODRAMATIC MUSIC

Perhaps the most prevalent and maligned genre of early nineteenth-century London
theatre was melodrama. For contemporaries, 'melodrama' indicated a theatrical genre
heavily reliant on music that first became popular in late eighteenth-century France

and quickly captivated London audiences. Its hallmark was a thrilling mixture of tragedy and comedy: tales of innocent heroines threatened by devious villains ended happily, with hero triumphant, heroine safe, and villain duly punished. A bumbling comic
or wise fool often lightened the storyline. Audiences drank in the genre's lavish scenic
effects, climactic scenes of wordless action, clear rhetoric, and obvious character types.

Music was central to melodrama. An overture and a few vocal pieces appeared in
many melodramas and all featured numerous brief passages of instrumental music.
Known as melodramatic music, these concise instrumental moments delineated characters and heightened wordless scenes of action. The use of such music stemmed from
melodrama's focus on modes of communication other than dialogue. Jacky Bratton
explains that 'the Rousseauvian appeal to the language of the heart, rejecting the potential deceptiveness of words, was effectively embodied on the melodramatic stage, where
all the resources of music, spectacle, and pantomime action could spell out the message'.[12] In this context, music, expressive yet not precisely definable, conveyed the ele-
mental message of melodrama more effectively than speech. Samuel Arnold observed
that in melodrama, 'music supplies the place of language'.[13]

While melodrama thrilled audiences, it disturbed critics. With its emphasis on sound
and sight over sense, melodrama epitomized the illegitimate drama of the minor theatres. Had melodrama appeared only at these houses, on the fringes of theatrical culture,
perhaps protests would not have arisen. Instead, the patent theatres, which were supposed to uphold the legitimate tradition of spoken drama, increasingly turned to melodrama and other illegitimate genres to support their financially precarious enterprises.
Oxberry's Dramatic Biography quipped, '[t]ragedy [. . .] has gone "clean out of fashion."
Melodrama poisoned it—operas operated on it—farce laughed at it'.[14] The prevalence
of melodrama in London theatres thus spoke to the gulf between learned and popular,
high and low, that continues to characterize discourse about popular music and theatre.

An archetypal example of melodrama is *The Miller and his Men*, by Bishop and Isaac
Pocock. Premiered in 1813 at Covent Garden, the work ran an impressive fifty-one performances in its first season, was revived every year for the next two decades, regularly
appeared at minor and provincial theatres, and was still well known enough in 1844
that Gilbert à Beckett parodied it in *Joe Miller and His Men*. The villains—a band of
robbers—appear in the novel disguise of millers. Grindoff, the robber chief, utilizes his
ill-gotten wealth to try to force the innocent Claudine into marriage and kidnaps her
when she resists. Claudine's beloved, Lothair, infiltrates the robbers' band in order to
save her and enlists the aid of another female captive, Ravina. In the climactic conclusion, Lothair battles Grindoff, carries Claudine to safety across a bridge, and instructs
Ravina to light the fuse they planted. The work ends with the spectacular explosion of
the robbers' lair (see Figure 2.2).

The music in *The Miller and his Men* is unusually well documented. Bishop's score—
piano-vocal, like all publications of British theatre music—contains not only the overture and four choral numbers, but also twenty-five pieces of instrumental melodramatic
music.[15] Publication of ephemeral melodramatic music was rare. Therefore, even though
not all music cues in the score are listed in the libretto and vice versa, and even though

FIGURE 2.2 The explosion of the robbers' lair from the final scene of *The Miller and his Men* at Covent Garden, London 1813.

Coloured print by Skelt, BAMS Collection. Courtesy of ArenaPal.

the stage directions in the two sources are not always identical, Bishop's score provides an invaluable glimpse into the possible use of music in melodrama. Broadly, Bishop's distribution of music underlines the different functions of vocal and instrumental pieces. In melodrama, instrumental music intertwined with and forwarded the action, while vocal music was primarily static. The placement of music immediately demonstrates this divide (Table 2.1). All the vocal numbers occur in Act I. In Act II, Bishop and Pocock leave these behind and offer more than twice as many cues for melodramatic music as in Act I, to help the action spiral towards the explosive climax.

While the vocal numbers were not enmeshed in the action, they served other purposes. Primarily, Bishop prepared these with an eye to the lucrative sheet-music market. Theatre composers typically received only modest payment, since managers considered that they provided 'free advertising' for composers' pieces.[16] Like most stage composers, Bishop therefore had to write numbers that both fitted the show and could easily be extracted from it. The opening chorus for the robbers disguised as millers, for example, fills two important roles onstage. First, a lengthy orchestral introduction allows audiences to appreciate the impressive stage machinery, as the millers enter on boats with a working mill in the background. Second, the number aurally lulls audiences into buying the

Table 2.1 Placement of Music in *The Miller and his Men*

Overture

Act I

Scene i: Chorus;
   Melodramatic music Nos. 1–2

Scene ii: No music

Scene iii: Sextet

Scene iv: Melodramatic music Nos. 3–4

Scene v: Drinking chorus;
   Melodramatic music Nos. 5–7;
   Chorus

Act II

Scene i: Melodramatic music Nos. 8–11

Scene ii: Melodramatic music No. 12

Scene iii: Melodramatic music Nos. 13–18

Scene iv: Melodramatic music Nos. 19–21

Scene v: Melodramatic music Nos. 22–25

millers' disguise. The pastoral key of F, the soothing 6/8 metre, the light-hearted mood, and the simple, repetitive melody, sung in a round, all signal guileless calm. This increases the shock when the millers' identity is later revealed. The number was equally at home, however, in the parlour. The published score helpfully indicates how domestic performers could shorten the lengthy introduction. The piano part offers only moderate difficulty. The vocal lines are more challenging, since they take the form of a three-part round. This was, however, a common format for the popular glee, a light choral number sold in large quantities to amateurs and various singing clubs.[17] Vocal works were thus deliberately malleable, suitable for the stage but general enough to function easily (and profitably) outside it.

In contrast, the majority of Bishop's score consists of instrumental melodramatic music created solely for specific dramatic moments onstage. Like melodrama itself, this music tended towards the obvious. Composers used clear musical gestures, since they often had only a few seconds to make their point amidst other visual and aural elements. These numbers were integral to the drama, establishing character, expressing emotion, and intertwining with the action. For example, music cues 9–11 intensify Act II, Scene i. In this scene, Grindoff and another robber, Riber, enter Claudine's house in order to abduct her and kill Count Frederick, a nobleman who has returned to the village and may recognize Grindoff as the villain Wolf. Their plan misfires and the Count's foolish servant Karl accidentally kills Riber.[18]

As Riber sneaks close to the house, tentative three-note figures, *Adagio* and *pianissimo*, gradually rise, with pauses in between. This may have coordinated with the stage action of the actor perhaps taking a few steps, pausing, then continuing cautiously. When 'the door is opened & suddenly closed', the same musical figure parallels this with an abrupt shift from *pianissimo* to *forte*. A double bar line concludes this music cue and the next is numbered separately, which suggests that the intervening dialogue was spoken with no musical accompaniment. Similarly cautious music marks cue no. 10, as tentative oscillations between two notes alternate with descending scalar figures. *Fortissimo* chords conclude the passage, presumably as Riber 'draws a poniard' to kill Count Frederick and 'Grindoff catches [his arm] and prevents the blow'. The music pauses and, in dialogue, Grindoff urges caution until he has secured Claudine and Karl talks amusingly in his sleep. After Grindoff leaves to abduct Claudine, Karl awakens, observes Riber, and surreptitiously arms himself. Music cue 11 begins as 'Riber examines his Pistol'. The same markers of caution are heard: *pianissimo*, undulating and then rising figures punctuated by rests. When Riber 'advances to the Count', the music accelerates from *Allegro moderato* to *Allegro molto*, ascending anxiously. As Karl stabs Riber, a sudden *forte* diminished triad, followed by furious descending scales, viscerally paints Riber's death. Grindoff rushes in and Frederick, awoken, 'seizes [Grindoff] by the collar, and Group stand amazed'. The scene provides a classic example of the exciting, largely wordless action of melodrama, linked with music that clearly paralleled the actors' movements and directed the audience's emotions.

The most striking scene of *The Miller and his Men* was the final catastrophe, the explosion of the robbers' den. After Lothair has carried Claudine to safety across the bridge, Ravina lights the fuse, 'the flash of which is seen to run down the side of the rock into the gully [. . .] and the explosion immediately takes place'. Claudine falls into her father's arms 'and the whole form a group as the curtain descends'.[19] Bishop wrote some of his most vivid music here. Although no stage directions are given in the score, Bishop clearly mimicked the progress of the fuse and the explosion. A quiet, murmuring line begins, a kind of primordial arpeggiation of one chord whose steadily rising range paints the progress of the fire. Cleverly, this chord turns out not to be the tonic (E), but a borrowed vi chord from the parallel minor. A surprising turn to a cadential 6/4 chord in E, after an exciting chromatic ascent, alerts listeners to the real key. Resolution is delayed by a few more measures of agitated arpeggios on the dominant, perhaps as the fuse approaches its goal. A massive outpouring of sound erupts as the tonic is finally reached, *fortissimo*, which must surely have coincided with the explosion. A long section of repeated tonic chords follows as the audience appreciates the final triumphant tableau.

For contemporary critics, pieces like *The Miller and his Men* were geared towards the lowest, most sensational common denominator. Few saw in them the glory of the British stage. The *Morning Chronicle* remarked that 'probability in a piece of this kind is of course out of the question; every thing is sacrificed to stage effect'.[20] The persistent popularity of melodrama, however, illustrates the power of effective stage music. The well-placed vocal piece in melodrama, much like the most popular numbers of opera and musical theatre alike, could charm listeners both inside and outside the theatre. As audiences heard sounds they felt capable of recreating at home, or that they perhaps had already heard excerpted in the parlour or via the organ grinder and street singers, the stage work took on an extra layer of familiarity, embedded into multiple arenas of their life outside the theatre. Meanwhile, melodramatic music, transient, brief, and perhaps not consciously noticed, established shared musical codes. Melodrama may not have used music in the same way as opera, but it popularized an effective and influential mode of musical communication.

THE SLAVE (1816) AND THE SHAPE OF BRITISH OPERA

While music appeared in most genres on the British stage, only a few pieces were designated 'operas'. These were not, however, all-sung works along the lines of the dominant Italian model. Rather, they featured the same heterogeneous mixture of speech, song, and instrumental music that characterized virtually every patent theatre production, but with a more prominent role given to song. British opera composers had to juggle the competing demands of star actors in leading spoken roles, star singers who wished to display their skills, amateur musicians eager to recreate the music at home, and critics wary of divergence from legitimate drama. Native opera was thus pulled in competing directions, with a result far from the standard image of opera.

One of the most well-known British operas of the time, *The Slave* by Bishop and Thomas Morton written for Covent Garden, exemplifies the genre. Set in Suriname during Britain's brief rule of the country, 1799–1816, *The Slave* was a sprawling piece that attempted to frame the disturbing realities of slavery within comforting dramatic conventions. Gambia, the slave of the title, is a clear example of the 'noble savage'. Although he is a slave, he helps his British masters quell a slave rebellion and sacrifices the freedom proffered to him to help his beloved Zelinda, a quadroon slave whom he altruistically cedes to her husband and father of her child, British captain Clifton. Gambia also inspires villain Lindenburg to repent through his selfless compassion. Lindenburg, who alternately acts on base desires and struggles to escape his sordid past, in the end gives up his designs on Zelinda and allows his enemy Clifton to return to Britain. A secondary love interest, between Clifton's sister Stella and Scottish naval officer Malcolm, as well as a slew of comic characters, round out the plot.

The *European Magazine* dubbed *The Slave* 'a mixture of tragedy, comedy, opera, and farce'.[21] In the smorgasbord approach typical of British theatre, *The Slave* offered something for everyone: just as in *The Miller and his Men*, there were spoken roles, sung roles, and comic roles. The difference between the scores of melodrama and opera was one of degree. As Table 2.2 demonstrates, vocal music is more prominent than instrumental music in *The Slave* and the latter is more static than melodramatic music, used primarily

Table 2.2 Placement of Music in *The Slave*

Overture

Act I

Scene i: Chorus[a];
  Solo for Malcolm

Scene ii: Solo for Zelinda

Scene iii: Instrumental music for 'Indian Procession'
  Finale for Clifton, Malcolm, Stella, Zelinda, and chorus

Act II

Scene i: Solo for Stella
  Instrumental march
  Water music
  Duet for Zelinda and Malcolm

Scene ii: Recitative and Solo for Clifton

Scene iii: No music

Scene iv: Solo for Sam[b]

Scene v: Finale for Clifton, Somerdyke, Zelinda, and chorus

Act III

Scene i: Solo for Malcolm

Scene ii: Solo for Zelinda

Scene iii: No music

Scene iv: No music

Scene v: Instrumental music 'Indian Air'
  Finale for Clifton, Fogrum, Malcolm, Sam, Stella, Zelinda, and chorus

[a] After this, the printed score contains a trio for Clifton, Malcolm, and Stella that
  is not in the printed libretto or the word book.

[b] After this, the printed score contains an additional solo for Zelinda that is not
  in the printed libretto or the word book.

for processions and dances. Vocal music also appears consistently throughout, rather than being weighted towards the beginning. Still, only some of the cast sings and there are several scenes without music. Tellingly, *The Slave* was called an 'opera' on the title page of the score, but a 'musical drama' on the title page of the libretto; both music and theatre lovers could mould it to their taste.

The 'tragic' portion of *The Slave* is entirely spoken. Both Gambia and Lindenburg, the most dramatically crucial roles in the piece, avoid all music. As Karen Ahlquist has concluded, such prominent spoken roles were common in native opera and were virtually always the most important male characters in the plot.[22] Pervasive splits between masculine speech and feminine music thus extended even to opera. Spoken roles were often designed for experienced actors of legitimate drama. Gambia, for example, was written for William Macready, a leading tragedian known for his portrayals of Hamlet, Lear, Othello, and similar roles. *The Times* felt it had been crafted 'to show off Mr. MACREADY's power of expressing the fiercer emotions'.[23] Macready could therefore easily navigate the grandiloquent rhetoric of Gambia, as he repeatedly soliloquized the central message of *The Slave*: that Britain offered a beacon of hope for any slave as obedient and self-sacrificing as Gambia. Freed by Clifton for his bravery in battle, for instance, Gambia expostulates:

> Liberty! Give me the language of the gods, to tell that I am free! the tongues of angels, to pour forth the gratitude of a heart, swelling with its dignities! [...] Generous Briton! prophetic be my tongue! when thro' thy country's zeal, the all-searching sun shall dart its rays in vain, to find a slave in Afric.[24]

The core plot of *The Slave* thus played out not only in speech, but also in the type of lofty, impassioned rhetoric that required an actor skilled in legitimate drama.

In complete contrast to such high-flown language, numerous comic characters entertained the audience. They did so primarily with spoken and physical comedy, but with a modicum of music as well. For example, comedians John Liston and John Emery played the dim-witted Fogrum and his Yorkshire mentor Sam Sharpset respectively. They provoke laughter by stupidly insulting Fogrum's wealthy aunt and being hoodwinked into trading places with another character in jail who convinces them it is a palace. Physical humour, puns, and topical jokes mark most of their comedy, but Sam also sings a comic song in a style much beloved on the British stage (Ex. 2.1). The song features a strophic form with six stanzas of text. The melody is simple, memorable, and eminently singable, both by comic actors with limited vocal abilities and by the audience, once they catch on to the repetition of 'Fol de rol'. Frequent fermatas assist the performer in making comic points and perhaps adding flourishes as the number progresses. The piano reduction firmly supports the vocal line at all times, assisting comic singer and domestic performer alike. The focus is on the lengthy comic text, which archly relates the 'seven wonders' of London, from its lawyers and belles to its tars and soldiers.

The straightforward strophic solo not only served comic purposes but also formed the bedrock of the score. *The Slave* contained solos for all of the main musical characters—Clifton, Malcolm, Sam, Stella, and Zelinda—and virtually all these follow one of the most prevalent forms in both stage and parlour: the ballad. A simple strophic song, the ballad charmed with limpid melodies, predictable harmonies, and sentimental texts general enough to transcend the stage context and sell well on the domestic market. Stella's solo exemplifies the type. It is dramaturgically peripheral and easily extractable. She and Zelinda enter and exchange a few lines commiserating with each other that their beaux are at battle. Stella then sings a ballad ruminating on the pros and cons of loving a soldier. While the song suits the plot and is a natural expression of Stella's emotions, it could be sung by virtually any woman to an actual or desired soldier. The music is similarly accessible for amateurs (Ex. 2.2).

EXAMPLE 2.1 Bishop, 'The World's Seven Wonders', *The Slave*, bars 5–18

EXAMPLE 2.2 Bishop, 'Who'd not Fall in Love with a Soldier', *The Slave*, bars 9–18

A harmonically simple accompaniment of arpeggiated quavers, punctuated by regular bass notes, highlights the vocal melody. The tune's small range, conjunct motion, and predictable periodic structure allow a focus on the text. Professional and amateur singers alike could charm with the beauty of their vocal sound rather than agile or learned passages.

Zelinda, as the primary musical character in *The Slave*, sang not only ballads but also another prominent genre on the British stage: the bravura. Zelinda, alone on stage after her beloved Clifton has agreed to marry her, hears a mocking bird and addresses it in what the score terms the 'Celebrated Mocking Bird Song'. The set-up is far-fetched, introducing a bird for no apparent dramatic reason. Once the music begins, however, the reason is revealed: a solo flute twitters with grace notes, arpeggios, and dotted rhythms, clearly representing the bird and inviting vocal mimicry (Ex. 2.3). Zelinda enters with a similarly bird-like line, frequently trilling as the flute repeats notes and then exchanging echoes with the instrument. Later, the piece moves to the typical second, fast section and the pattern of emulation continues. While this piece was not as challenging as some bravuras, it followed the expected pattern of an extended, two-tempo piece focused on vocal prowess. Listeners suspended interest in the action to focus on the fascinating powers of the performer playing Zelinda, leading soprano Catherine Stephens, as she pitted her vocal embellishments against the flute. While domestic consumers were less likely to possess the requisite skills to recreate such a piece, it could sell as a record of a memorable performance or as a challenge for the most musically accomplished amateurs.

While much of Bishop's score focuses on static miniatures, easily extractable from the plot, audiences did expect some intertwining of music and drama. This was particularly true in the finales that customarily ended each act. At the end of Act II, for example, the evil Lindenburg has Clifton, Zelinda, and their child thrown in chains, much to the scorn of Gambia and his fellow slaves. The finale begins with a flourish of repeated tonic chords. Somerdyke, who stands in musically for Lindenburg, orders the slaves to leave. The chorus of slaves responds with similar musical material, bemoaning their fate and chastising Lindenburg. A homorythmic texture prevails and each vocal line is minimally challenging, with a small range and short phrases (Ex. 2.4). A trio ensues for Zelinda, Clifton, and Somerdyke. Each sings a different text, Zelinda asking for mercy for her child, Clifton vowing vengeance, and Somerdyke continuing to order them 'thy doom obey'. The chorus joins them mid-phrase, resigned to their fate. A lengthy orchestral close solidifies the tonic and gives the audience an opportunity to enjoy the concluding tableau of virtue in distress. While the finale does not forward the plot, it extends the central conflict that concludes the act. And, while the number is not significantly challenging musically, characters' differing emotions and texts overlap in a rich texture.

Karen Ahlquist assesses *The Slave* as 'two entertainments at the same time—the plot and a concert—each having relatively little to do with the other'.[25] Most of

EXAMPLE 2.3 Bishop, 'The Celebrated Mocking Bird Song', *The Slave*, bars 22–27

EXAMPLE 2.4 Bishop, 'Strike, Strike the Oar', *The Slave*, bars 9–18

the music is easily extractable from the action, while most of the plot takes place in speech. This arrangement may appear disappointing when compared to the standards of Continental, all-sung opera, but it could also be viewed as prophetic of the shape of many musicals. In a theatrical context that places high value on both acting and music, which makes spoken dialogue the norm, which requires extractable, saleable individual numbers, and which caters to a broad audience interested in accessible entertainment, *The Slave* appears less anomalous. It is not so much a shadow of Continental opera as a distinct genre, in which music plays a circumscribed but nonetheless effective role.

EXAMPLE 2.4 Continued

Figaro: The Musical

The Slave might seem to suggest that British playhouse audiences had little interest in Continental opera, but in fact the opposite was true. Opera was an attractive commodity, able to draw London's wealthiest patrons to the King's Theatre. Major theatre managers, desirous of attracting this elite, not only cultivated native operas but also imported foreign ones, often in direct competition with the King's Theatre. For much of the early nineteenth century, however, various constraints prevented the major theatres from performing foreign operas in their original form. By law, productions had to be in English and by convention, recitative had to be replaced with spoken dialogue.[26] While the major theatres had a solid complement of orchestral and vocal musicians, they did not possess the requisite depth for foreign operas and had to cut and rework them to suit their performers.[27] Finally, the aesthetic exemplified in *The Miller and his Men* and *The Slave* did not embody the same role and style of music as Continental opera. British adaptors therefore turned foreign operas into distinctly new shapes for the playhouse stage. A representative example is Bishop's 1819 adaptation of *Le nozze di Figaro* for Covent Garden, which might perhaps best be termed *Figaro: The Musical*.[28]

For Bishop and his listeners, *Figaro* was far more malleable than today. More Londoners probably knew the Figaro tale through Thomas Holcroft's 1784 translation of the original Beaumarchais play, still playing in the 1810s, than through Mozart and Da Ponte's opera. Some patrons had been to a performance of the opera at the King's Theatre or the Pantheon, a short-lived competitor; both mounted versions of the opera in 1812 and the King's Theatre continued to revive the opera throughout the period.[29] A few complete scores were also published. The vast majority of listeners, however, experienced Mozart's *Figaro* as a series of isolated pieces, excerpted, varied, and interpolated elsewhere. Guglielmo sang 'Voi che sapete' in *Così fan tutte* at the King's Theatre in 1811, for example, while 'Non più andrai' was interpolated into *The Slave* after its premiere and became the Slow March of the Coldstream Guards.[30] *Le nozze di Figaro* was therefore already enmeshed in various adaptations, excerpts, and reworkings before Bishop brought it to Covent Garden.

Bishop amalgamated these various strands of *Figaro* into a shape congruent with his new venue's taste. Bishop relied heavily on Holcroft's translation, retaining its general outline and major changes—the original four acts are telescoped into three, the entire sub-plot for Marcellina and Bartolo disappears, and the dancing and festivities in the original Act III shrink substantially. To this story, Bishop wed approximately half of Mozart's numbers, cut all music from Count Almaviva, interpolated several of his own pieces, and included music from *Don Giovanni, Così fan tutte, Idomeneo*, and Rossini's *Tancredi* (Table 2.3). While modern readers might be struck by how little of Mozart's score Bishop kept, comparing the tables for *The Miller and his Men, The Slave*, and *Figaro* shows how much more music he included than typical playhouse productions. Bishop ambitiously included as much music as he could, explaining later: '[M]y sole object [. . .] was to improve the national taste for opera by rendering English audiences more famil-iar with truly dramatic music'.[31] His omissions and interpolations demonstrate where differences of taste and ability were too great not to require addressing.

Bishop's main task was to create the separation of music and drama that characterized native opera. This began with the cast. Count Almaviva lost his music and was portrayed by accomplished actor Richard Jones. As the *Theatrical Inquisitor* discerned, Jones thus assumed the common role in British opera, the leading spoken male who carried the dramatic or 'legitimate' portion of the production: 'Mr. JONES gave to *the Count*, all the spirit it requires, and indeed, the dramatic force of the piece principally depended on his exertions'.[32] Meanwhile, the leading female characters, the Countess and Susanna, received a disproportionate amount of the score: both sang three solos each and par-ticipated in several duets and ensembles. Comic and smaller roles, including Figaro,

Table 2.3 Placement of Music in Bishop's Adaptation of *Le nozze di Figaro*

Overture

Originally used Mozart's, but then replaced with one by Bishop, with selections from *Idomeneo*, *Così fan tutte*, and *Don Giovanni*

Act I

Scene i: Duet for Susanna and Figaro ('Cinque, dieci, venti')
   Solo for Figaro ('Se vuol ballare')
   Solo for Susanna, by Bishop

Scene ii: Duet for Barbarina and Susanna, added by Bishop[a]
   Solo for Cherubino ('Non so più, cosa son, cosa faccio')
   Chorus ('Giovani liete fiori spargete')
   Finale assembled from 'Non più andrai' and the Act I finale and 'Di scrivermi ogni giorno' from
      Così fan tutte

Act II

Scene i: Duet for Susanna and Fiorello, originally for Susanna and the Count, moved from original
      Act III ('Crudel! Perchè finora')
   Solo for Antonio, added by Bishop

Scene ii: Solo for Countess (Cherubino's 'Voi che sapete')
   Duet for Countess and Susanna ('Che soave zeffiretto')
   Solo for Susanna, added by Bishop
   Solo for Susanna ('Venite inginocchiatevi')
   Solo for Countess, added by Bishop;
   Finale ('Esci omai garzon malnato')

Act III

Scene i: Three instrumental pieces (Bolero, Pastoral March, Pas de deux), no composer listed
   Duet for Countess and Susanna, based on Italian melody 'O Pescator dell'Onde'
   Villagers' March

Scene ii: Solo for Fiorello, by Bishop

Scene iii: Solo for Countess, by Bishop

Scene iv: Trio for Antonio, Figaro, and Susanna (excerpt from 'Pian pianin le andrò più presso');
   Finale, based on 'Fra quai soavi palpiti' from Rossini, *Tancredi*[b]

---

[a] Pieces designated 'added by Bishop' are listed in the score as arranged, adapted, or partially composed by Bishop from unknown sources.

[b] This is the finale for the original happy ending, Venice, February 1813, not the new tragic ending, Ferrara, March 1813.

Antonio the gardener, Fiorello (imported from *Il barbiere di Siviglia*), and Cherubino each received one aria as well as ensembles. Much like in *The Slave*, then, Bishop congregated music around leading female roles, removed it entirely from pivotal male characters, and distributed a modest amount to other cast members.

Bishop also had to lessen the amount of drama delivered through music, especially in Mozart's lengthy ensembles. As the *Theatrical Inquisitor* noted, '[p]opular as this opera is

[. . .] we were yet inclined to doubt, whether it would be well received on the English Stage [. . .] its principal merit lies in the concerted pieces, and is obvious only to persons, who have some acquaintance with music as a science'.[33] Bishop therefore kept only six of Mozart's fourteen ensembles and altered the longest, most dramatically involved ones. The action of the Act II finale, for example, first takes place entirely in speech and then is recapped in song, using only a portion of Mozart's original. Likewise, from the long Act IV finale Bishop extracted only the trio 'Pace, Pace', with Antonio instead of the Count, and placed the bulk of the denouement in speech. To conclude the work, Bishop used Rossini's finale to *Tancredi*, which offered the same vaudeville-style format that concluded Beaumarchais's play, i.e. verses for various soloists alternating with a chorus. Playhouse audiences did expect some ensemble at the end of each act, however, and Bishop therefore augmented 'Non più andrai' with selections from *Così fan tutte* to conclude Act I with a finale.

Audiences and performers at the major theatres may have been wary of extended, dramatic ensembles, but they prized solos. Not just any solo would suffice, however, and Bishop retained only four of Mozart's fourteen arias. Some omissions simply stem from changes to the plot, but others speak to the preferred types of solos at the major theatres. In particular, Bishop worked to supply the two most popular types of solo, as seen in *The Slave*: the bravura and the ballad. The Countess, for example, sang neither of her two original arias. Bishop may have found them too formally complex and generically fluid, or perhaps the singer, Maria Dickons, wished for something more novel and suited to her abilities. Bishop wrote two entirely new pieces for her, a sentimental ballad and a new, relentlessly difficult two-tempo bravura aria. He also gave her Cherubino's 'Voi che sapete'. This was less unusual than it might seem. This particular aria had such a long history of reassignment that, in 1822, *The Times* expressed surprise when it was sung by Cherubino in a King's Theatre revival.[34] It was also not only one of the most popular excerpts from the opera but also most closely approximated the graceful, simple ballad; Bishop therefore retained it with little change. As one of the most important characters musically, the Countess thus offered listeners a variety of musical entertainment: a touching ballad, virtuosic fireworks, and one of the best-known tunes from *Figaro*.

The only British song type lacking in *Figaro* was the amusing solo for the low comic male character, as seen with Sam's solo in *The Slave*. Figaro partially fulfilled this character type, particularly in the hands of Liston, who had played Fogrum in *The Slave*, but his 'Se vuol ballare' did not quite fulfil the catchy strophic form and punning, cynical humour of this style. Rather than write a new song for Figaro, Bishop augmented the part of Antonio, the gardener. As Antonio, popular comic actor John Fawcett enjoyed an added comic scene with Barbarina that included a new solo, 'In Early Life I Took a Wife'. The number's straightforward strophic form, simple harmonic structure, catchy 6/8 rhythm, and amusing text about drunkenness typify the popular British comic song. Leigh Hunt gives us a sense of how Fawcett may have delivered such a song:

Fawcett had a harsh, brazen face, and a voice like a knife-grinder's wheel. He was all pertness, coarseness, and effrontery, but with a great deal of comic force; and whenever he came trotting on to the stage [. . .] and pouring forth his harsh, rapid words, with his nose in the air, and a facetious grind in his throat, the audience were prepared for a merry evening.[35]

One imagines Fawcett half-singing, half-speaking the number, 'whin[ing] out [the] song' in the *Theatrical Inquisitor*'s words, while the audience laughed and perhaps sang along with the refrain.[36]

Bishop crafted a new version of *Figaro* that was in many ways more congruent with early musical theatre than opera. Translation into the vernacular ensured ready comprehension. Spoken dialogue shouldered much of the dramatic responsibility. Musically, solos and small ensembles dominated, although large ensembles concluded each act. Aside from the Countess's impressive bravura, the musical style was eminently accessible and prime for extraction for the sheet music market. Bishop's *Figaro* in one sense demonstrates how vast the chasm was between Continental and native ideas of opera, and how much he had to change Mozart's work to accord with pieces like *The Miller and his Men* and *The Slave*. On the other hand, Bishop's changes should not obscure his efforts to encourage his audiences to accept more music—and often more challenging music—than in other native productions. His approach typifies the agenda of so many native composers, to expand musical taste in an often unwelcoming context.

CONCLUSION

Both contemporary and modern writers have maligned British stage music of the early nineteenth century. Richard Mackenzie Bacon argued passionately:

> [M]usic has by no means the importance in our musical drama that should appertain to it. [. . .] Nor can it be otherwise until a just perception of the intrinsic beauties of opera be generally diffused, [. . .] until indeed, a portion of that patronage which has been for a century past dedicated to the planting and maintaining a theatre for an Italian, be addressed to the establishment and support of an English opera [. . .] till this be done, our stages are not likely to exhibit any thing beyond the same anomalous jargon of dialogue and song, the same heterogeneous mixture of nonsense and show.[37]

The uneasy position of music in British theatre led to an aesthetic that frustrated those who wished for a native tradition on par with the Continent. If we look beyond such comparisons and assess these pieces on their own merits, however, important parallels to later practices emerge. The effectiveness of melodramatic music helped undermine ideas that drama could only be imparted through words and contributed to a holistic theatrical experience that encompassed sight, sound, and speech. Vocal music, meanwhile, was crafted with an eye for effectiveness both within and without the theatre.

Onstage, song balanced with speech and allowed a wide variety of cast members to entertain the audience, whether through vocal pyrotechnics, powerful acting, or comic antics. Offstage, popular numbers pervaded musical life, in the concert hall, the home, or in public via organ grinders, street singers, and pleasure gardens. Yet, native composers also strove to challenge audiences, to improve and expand their musical taste. A similar pull between song and speech, between stage context and external popularity, between accessible and challenging numbers, typifies much musical theatre. British stage music of the early nineteenth century benefits when it is removed from the shadow of Continental opera and placed somewhere between opera and musical theatre.

NOTES

1. Dewey Ganzel, 'Patent Wrongs and Patent Theatres: Drama and the Law in the Early Nineteenth Century,' *PMLA* 76 (1961): 384–396.
2. The only exception was the Haymarket Theatre, which obtained a licence for summer performances in 1776. William J. Burling, *Summer Theatre in London, 1661–1820, and the Rise of the Haymarket Theatre* (Madison, NJ: Fairleigh Dickinson University Press; London: Associated University Presses, 2000). See Jane Moody, *Illegitimate Theatre in London, 1770–1840* (Cambridge: Cambridge University Press, 2000) and Jim Davis and Victor Emeljanow, *Reflecting the Audience: London Theatregoing, 1840–1880* (Iowa City: University of Iowa Press, 2001).
3. In 1837 it was renamed Her Majesty's Theatre in honour of Queen Victoria.
4. See Jennifer Hall-Witt, *Fashionable Acts: Opera and Elite Culture in London, 1780–1880* (Durham, NH: University of New Hampshire Press; Hanover, NH: University Press of New England, 2007).
5. James Boaden, *Memoirs of the Life of John Philip Kemble, Esq. Including a History of the Stage, from the Time of Garrick to the Present Period*, 2 volumes in 1 (Philadelphia: Robert H. Small and Wilder & Campbell, 1825), 1: 81; *Political Review*, 16 September 1809, quoted in Marc Baer, *Theatre and Disorder in Late Georgian London* (Oxford: Clarendon Press, 1992), 199.
6. Richard Leppert, *Music and Image: Domesticity, Ideology, and Socio-Cultural Formation in Eighteenth-Century England* (Cambridge: Cambridge University Press, 1993), 25.
7. Anon., Review of *Fra Diavolo*, 4 November 1831. The critic may be John Payne Collier. For identifications of critics, see Theodore Fenner, *Opera in London: Views of the Press 1785–1830* (Carbondale: Southern Illinois University Press, 1994), 51–53.
8. Richard Mackenzie Bacon, '*Il Barbiere di Siviglia—MS—Rossini*', *Quarterly Musical Magazine and Review* 2 (1820), 67.
9. George Hogarth, *Memoirs of the Opera in Italy, France, Germany, and England* (1851; New York: Da Capo Press, 1972), 2: 351.
10. James Robinson Planché, *Recollections and Reflections: A Professional Autobiography*, new and revised ed. (London: S. Low, Marston & Co., 1901), 55.
11. See Michael V. Pisani, *Music for the Melodramatic Theatre in Nineteenth-Century London and New York* (Iowa City: University of Iowa Press, 2014).

12. Jacky Bratton, 'Romantic Melodrama', in *The Cambridge Companion to British Theatre, 1730–1830*, ed. Jane Moody and Daniel O'Quinn (Cambridge: Cambridge University Press, 2007), 119.
13. Quoted in Michael R. Booth, *English Melodrama* (London: H. Jenkins, 1965), 38–39.
14. [Catherine and William] Oxberry, eds., *Oxberry's Dramatic Biography* (London: George Virtue, 1825), 4: 91.
15. This score and a recording of it are on the Romantic-Era Songs website, http://www.sjsu.edu/faculty/douglass/music/album-miller.html. Musical examples referred to here can be consulted there. For discussions of Bishop's music for *The Miller and his Men*, see David Mayer, 'Nineteenth Century Theatre Music', *Theatre Notebook* 30 (1976): 115–122 and Janet Shepherd, 'Music, Text and Performance in English Popular Theatre 1790–1840' (Unpublished PhD thesis, University of London, 1991).
16. A. V. Beedell, *The Decline of the English Musician, 1788–1888: A Family of English Musicians in Ireland, England, Mauritius, and Australia* (Oxford: Clarendon Press, 1992), 60.
17. The number is not a glee in the strict definition of the term, since it is not unaccompanied, but it follows the genre in other respects and could have been performed a cappella.
18. [Isaac] Pocock, *The Miller and his Men, a Melo-drame in two acts* (London: C. Chapple, 1813), 28–29.
19. Pocock, *Miller and his Men*, 46.
20. Anon., Review of *The Miller and His Men, Morning Chronicle*, 22 October 1813. The critic may be William Hazlitt.
21. Anon., Review of *The Slave, European Magazine*, November 1816, 455.
22. Karen Ahlquist, 'Masculinity and Legitimacy on the English Musical Stage: The Mature Male, 1800–1845', *Women and Music: A Journal of Gender and Culture* 8 (2004): 1–21.
23. Anon., Review of *The Slave, The Times*, 13 November 1816. Capitals in the original. The critic may be Edward Sterling.
24. Thomas Morton, *The Slave; A Musical Drama [. . .]* (London: John Miller, 1816), 36.
25. Ahlquist, 'Masculinity and Legitimacy on the English Musical Stage', 9.
26. There were a few all-sung British operas, most notably *Artaxerxes* (1762) by Thomas Arne.
27. In 1826, Charles Dibdin indicated that the orchestra usually consisted of six to eight each of first and second violins, two violas, two cellos, three to four double basses, oboe, flageolet, two flutes, two clarinets, two horns, two bassoons, trombone, trumpet, bugle, piano, harp, bells, and kettledrums. Charles Dibdin, *History and Illustrations of the London Theatres* (London: J. Moyes, 1826), 31. Occasional playbills and libretti that list chorus members indicate that this SATB ensemble averaged seven to twelve singers per part.
28. For a modern edition of Bishop's adaptation, see Henry Rowley Bishop, *Mozart's 'The Marriage of Figaro': Adapted for Covent Garden, 1819*, ed. Christina Fuhrmann (Middleton: A-R Editions, 2012). Musical examples referred to here can be consulted there.
29. For more information on Mozart at these theatres, see Rachel Cowgill, 'Mozart Productions in the Emergence of *Werktreue* at London's Italian Opera House, 1780–1830', in *Operatic Migrations: Transforming Works and Crossing Boundaries*, ed. Roberta Montemorra Marvin and Downing A. Thomas (Aldershot: Ashgate, 2006), 145–186 and Rachel Cowgill, 'Le Nozze di Figaro Voor Het Voetlicht te Londen, 1786–1813', *Musica Antiqua* 9 (1992): 168–177.
30. See Harry R. Beard, 'Figaro in England', *Maske und Kothurn* 10 (1964): 498–513 and Tim Carter, *W. A. Mozart 'Le nozze di Figaro'* (Cambridge: Cambridge University Press, 1987), 131–132. The playbill for *The Slave* at Covent Garden on 15 May 1818 advertises that tenor John Braham will introduce 'Non più andrai'.

31. Quoted in Richard Northcott, *The Life of Sir Henry R. Bishop* (London: Press Printers Ltd, 1920), 33.
32. Anon. Review of *Le nozze di Figaro, Theatrical Inquisitor*, March 1819, 231. Capitals and italics in the original.
33. Anon., Review of *Le nozze di Figaro, Theatrical Inquisitor*, March 1819, 228–229.
34. Anon., Review of *Le nozze di Figaro, The Times*, 14 January 1822.
35. Leigh Hunt, *The Autobiography of Leigh Hunt*, ed. J. E. Morpurgo (London: Cresset Press, 1948), 130.
36. Anon., Review of *Le nozze di Figaro', Theatrical Inquisitor*, March 1819, 231.
37. Richard Mackenzie Bacon, 'Sketch of the State of Music in London', *Quarterly Musical Magazine and Review* 7 (June 1825), 204.

BIBLIOGRAPHY

Ahlquist, Karen. 'Masculinity and Legitimacy on the English Musical Stage: The Mature Male, 1800–1845.' *Women and Music: A Journal of Gender and Culture* 8 (2004): 1–21.

Anon. Review of *Le nozze di Figaro. Theatrical Inquisitor*, March 1819, 228–231.

Anon. Review of *Le nozze di Figaro. The Times*, 14 January 1822.

Anon. Review of *The Miller and His Men. Morning Chronicle*, 22 October 1813.

Anon. Review of *The Slave. European Magazine*, November 1816, 455.

Anon. Review of *The Slave. The Times*, 13 November 1816.

Bacon, Richard Mackenzie. '*Il Barbiere di Siviglia—MS—Rossini.' Quarterly Musical Magazine and Review* 2 (1820): 66–80.

Bacon, Richard Mackenzie. 'Sketch of the State of Music in London.' *Quarterly Musical Magazine and Review* 7 (June 1825): 186–211.

Baer, Marc. *Theatre and Disorder in Late Georgian London*. Oxford: Clarendon Press, 1992.

Beard, Harry R. 'Figaro in England.' *Maske und Kothurn* 10 (1964): 498–513.

Beedell, A. V. *The Decline of the English Musician, 1788–1888: A Family of English Musicians in Ireland, England, Mauritius, and Australia*. Oxford: Clarendon Press, 1992.

Biddlecombe, George. *English Opera from 1834 to 1864 with Particular Reference to the Works of Michael Balfe*. New York: Garland Publishing, 1994.

Boaden, James. *Memoirs of the Life of John Philip Kemble, Esq. Including a History of the Stage, from the Time of Garrick to the Present Period*. 2 volumes in 1. Philadelphia: Robert H. Small and Wilder & Campbell, 1825.

Booth, Michael R. *English Melodrama*. London: H. Jenkins, 1965.

Bratton, Jacky. 'Romantic Melodrama.' In *The Cambridge Companion to British Theatre, 1730–1830*, edited by Jane Moody and Daniel O'Quinn, 115–127. Cambridge: Cambridge University Press, 2007.

Burden, Michael. 'Opera in the London Theatres.' In *The Cambridge Companion to British Theatre, 1730–1830*, edited by Jane Moody and Daniel O'Quinn, 205–218. Cambridge: Cambridge University Press, 2007.

Burling, William J. *Summer Theatre in London, 1661–1820, and the Rise of the Haymarket Theatre*. Madison, NJ: Fairleigh Dickinson University Press; London: Associated University Presses, 2000.

Carter, Tim. 'Mozart in a "Land Without Music": Henry Bishop's *The Marriage of Figaro*.' In *Musikkonzepte—Konzepte der Musikwissenschaft: Bericht über den Internationalen Kongreß der Gesellschaft für Musikforschung Halle (Saale) 1998*, edited by Kathrin Eberl and Wolfgang Ruf, 1: 196–206. Kassel: Bärenreiter, 2000.

Carter, Tim. *W. A. Mozart 'Le Nozze di Figaro'*. Cambridge: Cambridge University Press, 1987.

Cowgill, Rachel. '*Le Nozze di Figaro* Voor Het Voetlicht te Londen, 1786–1813.' *Musica Antiqua* 9 (1992): 168–177.

Cowgill, Rachel. 'Mozart Productions in the Emergence of *Werktreue* at London's Italian Opera House, 1780–1830.' In *Operatic Migrations: Transforming Works and Crossing Boundaries*, edited by Roberta Montemorra Marvin and Downing A. Thomas, 145–186. Aldershot: Ashgate, 2006.

Davis, Jim, and Victor Emeljanow. *Reflecting the Audience: London Theatregoing, 1840–1880*. Iowa City: University of Iowa Press, 2001.

Davis, Tracy C. *The Economics of the British Stage, 1800–1914*. Cambridge: Cambridge University Press, 2000.

Dibdin, Charles. *History and Illustrations of the London Theatres*. London: J. Moyes, 1826.

Dideriksen, Gabriella. 'Major and Minor Theatres: Competition in London in the 1830s.' In *Le Concert et son Public: Mutations de la vie musicale en Europe de 1780 à 1914*, edited by Hans Erich Bödeker, Patrice Veit, and Michael Werner, 303–313. Paris: Éditions de la Maison des Sciences de L'Homme, 2002.

Fenner, Theodore. *Opera in London: Views of the Press 1785–1830*. Carbondale: Southern Illinois University Press, 1994.

Ganzel, Dewey. 'Patent Wrongs and Patent Theatres: Drama and the Law in the Early Nineteenth Century.' *PMLA* 76 (1961): 384–396.

Hall-Witt, Jennifer. *Fashionable Acts: Opera and Elite Culture in London, 1780–1880*. Durham, NH: University of New Hampshire Press; Hanover, NH: University Press of New England, 2007.

Hays, Michael, and Anastasia Nikolopoulou, eds. *Melodrama: The Cultural Emergence of a Genre*. New York: St Martin's Press, 1996.

Hibberd, Sarah, ed. *Melodramatic Voices: Understanding Music Drama*. Aldershot: Ashgate, 2011.

Hogarth, George. *Memoirs of the Opera in Italy, France, Germany, and England*. 2 vols. 1851. New York: Da Capo Press, 1972.

Hunt, Leigh. *The Autobiography of Leigh Hunt*, edited by J. E. Morpurgo. London: Cresset Press, 1948.

Leppert, Richard. *Music and Image: Domesticity, Ideology, and Socio-Cultural Formation in Eighteenth-Century England*. Cambridge: Cambridge University Press, 1993.

Mayer, David. 'The Music of Melodrama.' In *Performance and Politics in Popular Drama: Aspects of Popular Entertainment in Theatre, Film and Television 1800–1976*, edited by David Bradby, Louis James, and Bernard Sharratt, 49–64. Cambridge: Cambridge University Press, 1980.

Mayer, David. 'Nineteenth Century Theatre Music.' *Theatre Notebook* 30 (1976): 115–122.

Moody, Jane. *Illegitimate Theatre in London, 1770–1840*. Cambridge: Cambridge University Press, 2000.

Morton, Thomas. *The Slave; A Musical Drama [. . .]* London: John Miller, 1816.

Newey, Katherine. 'Reform on the London Stage.' In *Rethinking the Age of Reform: Britain 1780–1850*, edited by Arthur Burns and Joanna Innes, 238–253. Cambridge: Cambridge University Press, 2003.

Northcott, Richard. *The Life of Sir Henry R. Bishop*. London: Press Printers Ltd, 1920.

Oxberry, [Catherine and William], eds. *Oxberry's Dramatic Biography*. London: George Virtue, 1825.

Pisani, Michael V. *Music for the Melodramatic Theatre in London and New York*. Iowa City: University of Iowa Press, 2014.

Planché, James Robinson. *Recollections and Reflections: A Professional Autobiography*. New and revised ed. London: S. Low, Marston & Co., 1901.

Pocock, [Isaac]. *The Miller and his Men, a Melo-drame in two acts*. London: C. Chapple, 1813.

Rohr, Deborah Adams. *The Careers of British Musicians, 1750–1850: A Profession of Artisans*. Cambridge: Cambridge University Press, 2001.

Rowley Bishop, Henry. *Mozart's 'The Marriage of Figaro'; Adapted for Covent Garden*, edited by Christine Fuhrmann. Middleton: A-R Editions, 2012.

Shepherd, Jane. 'Music, Text and Performance in English Popular Theatre 1790–1840.' Unpublished PhD thesis, University of London, 1991.

CHAPTER 3

....

COMIC OPERA

English Society in Gilbert and Sullivan

....

CAROLYN WILLIAMS

To take the comic operas of Gilbert and Sullivan as seriously as they deserve, and to appreciate the complexity of their humour, we should regard them as auto-ethnographic. They provide us with an acute account of how popular conceptions of class, gender, and nation were changing in the late nineteenth century. Holding a mirror up to their national culture, these comic operas engage in satires and parodies of Victorian society. Absurd inequities of the English class system, strange constraints on gender relations, and an excess of nationalistic sentiment were not the only social ills that fell prey to their satirical dissection. In addition to these broad social problems they also focused on the process of socialization itself, a number of familiar social institutions, particular social types, and current cultural fads. Sharply pointed, their topical humour variously took aim at—or manically listed—specific details and features of social life in late Victorian England.

Parody and satire are so tightly related in the works of Gilbert and Sullivan that they are sometimes hard to separate. But a good working distinction, by way of definition, might be helpful: the chief objects of satire are the forms and foibles of social life, while the chief objects of parody are artistic or literary works, aesthetic features, or generic conventions from the past or present. The Gilbert and Sullivan operas artfully mix parody with satire—sometimes parodying social types as if they were conventional theatrical roles, and often using the parody of an individual work or a genre as a vehicle for launching trenchantly satirical social commentary. They mix real-life social types (like sailors, bureaucrats, and peers) together with fantastic figures (such as sorcerers, fairies, and 'Arcadian shepherds'), often using a realistic setting as the stage for absurd dramatic action. As spectators familiar with the operas will know, they pay close attention to the absurdities propagated by social categories such as class, gender, and nationality; in other words, they take received ideas, tacit assumptions, and abstractions regarding class, gender, and nation and subject them to critique. In the readings of their works that follow, we will see how they challenge these tacit assumptions, thereby offering criticism that both reflects and helps to cause social change.

In addition, the comic operas of Gilbert and Sullivan emphasize the theatrical nature of everyday social life. This point is not simple or one-dimensional. The trial in *Trial by Jury* (1875) is explicitly shown to be ritual theatre, while *Utopia Limited* (1893) and *The Mikado* (1885) ask their audiences to think about contemporary nineteenth-century forms of exhibition that display the culture to itself. Sociologists have emphasized the theatrical qualities of everyday life; and to some extent the discipline depends on this insight.[1] But historical changes in the eighteenth and nineteenth centuries brought this reality to the fore in a new way. The rise of social class and its correlative, social mobility, meant that social identity could be defined by means other than inherited status—for example, through wealth accumulation, manners, or education. By the late nineteenth century, certain absurdities engendered by this modern transition were familiar enough to form an object of satire. Thus Major-General Stanley in *The Pirates of Penzance* (1879) elevates himself by buying an estate, purchasing not only the property itself but also a set of ancestors buried in its chapel; he fancies himself their 'descendant by purchase'.[2] Thus at the end of *H.M.S. Pinafore* (1878), when Buttercup's baby-switching has been revealed, and Ralph Rackstraw, the common sailor, has exchanged places with his Captain, the satire turns on the process of socialization. The two have changed costume, and the Captain suddenly speaks differently, dropping his aitches and using the cockney accent of a common sailor. But a lifetime of living under specific social conditions would have been necessary to generate these speech patterns, and a slow, difficult process of education would have been necessary to change them, a premise that Shaw's *Pygmalion* (1912) will later entertain. Therefore this transformation, a satire on the absurdities of class, is also a parody of the sudden revelations that expose hidden identities at the end of Victorian melodramas.

These works have always been appreciated for poking fun at English society. The genre of English comic opera itself is founded as a national undertaking; and that process of genre formation is related to class and gender as well, for Gilbert and Sullivan set about to recapture a middle-class audience for the theatre. While their treatment of class and nation are well known, however, attention to their interest in gender as a social category has been remarkably slight.

In 1871 John Hollingshead, manager of the Gaiety Theatre, commissioned Gilbert and Sullivan to provide *Thespis*, a burlesque-style entertainment (even though their more formal collaboration did not begin until 1875, when Richard D'Oyly Carte, at the time a successful producer and talent agent, brought them together for *Trial by Jury*). By the time they began to work together, both Gilbert and Sullivan were pre-eminent in their separate fields.[3] Carte kept them together, with only brief interruptions, until 1896, claiming in retrospect that developing a school of English comic opera 'in a theatre devoted to that alone was the scheme of [his] life'.[4] In 1879, he formed a three-way partnership with them, through which they agreed to share profits equally after subtracting expenses. That financially beneficial arrangement for Gilbert and Sullivan advanced the cause of authorial rights in the theatre more generally. But it was also artistically advantageous. Because they were in full control, the partners could demand more rigorous rehearsals and invest in production values higher than the norm. Thus the Savoy operas became known for their lavish spectacle and their precision in acting, singing, and choreography, and the Savoy Theatre became known for its modern amenities.[5]

Together Gilbert, Sullivan, and Carte built their distinctive genre of English comic opera through parodies of past literary, theatrical, and musical genres—high and low, British and Continental—opera, pantomime, burlesque and extravaganza, melodrama, the minstrel show, and music hall (among others). The term 'English comic opera'—a term used at the time—captures their particularly English response to French opéra comique and opéra bouffe as well as to Italian and French 'grand opera'. All genres derive from past genres. But it is important to see that the formation of their distinctively English genre included this national twist. In the late 1870s, Gilbert and Sullivan were perhaps most interested in differentiating their works from Offenbach's opéra bouffe and from 'low' English burlesque. Their works would include no broad, coarse, or indecent humour—and no cross-dressing. Yet joking about the Victorian penchant for avoiding anything risqué allows risqué subjects to come up anyway, under the cover of light parody. Thus English comic opera can be suggestive without erring on the side of coarseness, defining itself as not-French not only because it eschews risqué themes but also because it makes fun of the English middle-class correctness that insists on being not-French.

The format of alternating passages of prose dialogue with musical numbers was familiar from opéra comique but also from native English ballad opera, best exemplified in John Gay's *The Beggar's Opera* (1728), which is also famous for its parodic deflation of Italian opera. The singing style of Savoy opera was decidedly not-Italian. Rutland Barrington later remembered that the governing idea was that 'everything connected to the venture should be English', an idea that inspired them all 'with a patriotic glow'.[6] So the 'English' part of English comic opera was a matter of genre (though of course it was a matter of content, too, as we shall see).

The 'comic' part of English comic opera is notable in two different ways. One involves the broad ethos of comedy, in which a happy ending implies the restoration of the social order, typically through marriage.[7] Even in this broad sense of the comic, we can see the parodic principle at work, however, for most of the Gilbert and Sullivan operas end with a hyperbolically multiplied array of couples, a wild and zany restoration of order that perhaps suggests a parody of the conventional comedic ending. Only *Patience* (1881) and *The Yeomen of the Guard* (1888) depart from this convention to some extent, foregrounding a lone man, left out of the wholesale marriage plot, and reminding us that the French tradition of opéra comique did not always insist on a fully 'comic' ending.

On the other hand, the Savoy operas are comic in a more colloquial sense, insofar as they are very funny. A great deal of the humour derives from the absurd premises of their plots, premises that are unfolded with extreme logical consistency, while being acted in a deadpan style that does not acknowledge the absurdity in the least. As Hamlet insists, in his advice to the players in Gilbert's parody of *Hamlet, Rosencrantz and Guildenstern* (1891):

> let there be no huge red noses, nor extravagant monstrous wigs, nor coarse men garbed as women, in this comi-tragedy; for such things are as much as to say, 'I am a comick

fellow—I pray you laugh at me, and hold what I say to be cleverly ridiculous.' Such labelling of humour is an impertinence to your audience, for it seemeth to imply that they are unable to recognize a joke unless it be pointed out to them. I pray you avoid it.[8]

This tacit acting style, never labelling the humour—which became a recognized feature of Gilbert's directorial practice—owes a debt to the English burlesque (or extravaganza) tradition, as Harley Granville-Barker pointed out.[9]

Parody always differentiates the present from the past, ostentatiously displaying a pride in its up-to-date fun-making at the expense of models that are thus made to seem old and outworn things. Thus parody is a modernizing mode, but it preserves elements of the past even while deviating from them, showing its difference from earlier models and genres even while preserving them. In this respect, parody highlights both continuity with and change from the past, and the Savoy operas are therefore deeply historical, claiming their own tradition by making fun of past traditions.[10]

THE FORMATION OF A GENRE

Their first two works were not comic operas, but they show that genre in the process of formation. *Thespis; or, The Gods Grown Old* (1871), their first collaboration, was a parody of the classical extravaganza, a genre of refined burlesque that took works of classical antiquity as a pretext, popular in England since 1831, when Madame Vestris presented James Robinson Planché's *Olympic Revels* with herself in the role of Orpheus. *Thespis* made fun of the idea that 'the gods [had] grown old', as its subtitle proclaims, with the associated implication that the genre, too, had perhaps become overly familiar and a bit threadbare. On the other hand, the work shows clearly that it intends to be seen as an English version of Offenbach, with specific reference to *Orphée aux enfers* (1858), which is itself a parody of Gluck's *Orfeo ed Euridice* (1762).

Thespis is rife with jokes about drunkenness, adultery, and even incest among the gods on Mount Olympus, practices that a band of hypercorrect English thespians— who have climbed Mount Olympus—deplore. Many of the jokes depend on a dilettantish knowledge of classical mythology, such as the reference to Lemprière's *Classical Dictionary* or the finicky debate about who is 'married' to whom among the Olympian gods. Written for the Gaiety Theatre, *Thespis* engages in many burlesque practices that Gilbert and Sullivan would soon shed. For example, the cast of *Thespis* was made up of theatrical celebrities, and the opening number (sung by a 'Chorus of Stars') plays on this fact; later, Gilbert and Sullivan would employ an ensemble specifically trained in their own aesthetic, and closely associated with the Savoy operas. Two of those stars in *Thespis*—the most famous clowns of the day—indulged in broad comic business, which would become inimical to the Savoy style. And in the role of Mercury, Nelly Farren cross-dressed, displaying her famous figure and legs in a short skirt of 'quicksilver' fabric. Gilbert and Sullivan would soon explicitly renounce theatrical cross-dressing.[11]

In 1875, Richard D'Oyly Carte commissioned Gilbert and Sullivan to provide an afterpiece—a short, humorous play that would customarily follow the theatre's main attraction—for a production of Offenbach's *La Périchole* at the Royalty Theatre, where he was manager. For that occasion, Gilbert and Sullivan supplied *Trial by Jury* (1875), a delightful one-act piece without dialogue, a revision of a short piece of comic journalism that Gilbert had previously published in *Fun* magazine.[12] The piece soon became popular, standing up very well against Offenbach. Again we see a particularly English form of outspokenness in the complex wit of *Trial by Jury*, which offers not only a satire on gender relations and on the law in general—vast social topics—but also a parody of the suit for breach of promise of marriage, and of the seduction melodramas on which those trials were often modelled.[13] The Plaintiff clearly acts the part of the 'cheated maid', who must rely on the all-male Jury to vindicate her. Throughout, justice is on the verge of miscarrying: the Jury automatically sympathizes with the Plaintiff, even before any evidence is brought; and the Learned Judge reveals (in his autobiographical song) that he has been guilty of breach of promise himself. This satire on the corruption of the law depends on the idea that people play roles in the everyday drama of gender relations. What seems merely an absurd situation is actually a trenchant critique of a system in which women become 'damaged goods' if they have been jilted. Early on, in other words, *Trial by Jury* addresses gender as a critical dimension of English society, and it shows that the performance of gender is just that: a performance.

In *Trial by Jury* we can also see that Sullivan's music participates in the parodic dynamic of the Savoy operas. The Learned Judge enters to a parody of Handel ('All hail great Judge!'). When the non-operatic voice of the comic baritone playing the Judge begs to speak, he is several times interrupted and overwhelmed by the chorus. The point is not to make fun of Handel, to be sure, but to use Handelian pomp to deflate the Judge, calling attention to the wide disparity between his importance as a representative of the law and the human reality of his small stature and petty bias. (Similarly, the near-perfect citation of Verdi's 'Anvil Chorus' in *The Pirates of Penzance* does not make fun of Verdi, but emphasizes the pirates' silly lawlessness, as they decide to 'vary piracee | With a little burglaree!' (150)).[14]

The Sorcerer (1877) was their third collaboration and their first comic opera. In it we can see a number of the features that would become hallmarks of their style and genre—such as the two-act structure that characterizes their remaining works with the one exception of *Princess Ida* (1884) which is in three acts. An ensemble of players who could act as well as sing played a set of correlated character types that soon became, as Isaac Goldberg put it, 'as stereotyped as any villain, hero or heroine in an Adelphi melodrama': the large contralto dame, the comic baritone who would usually sing the patter songs, the ingénue, and the tenor hero.[15] Most important, the chorus was fully characterized and participated in the dramatic action. Sullivan later explained the importance of this enhanced role for the chorus: 'Until Gilbert took the matter in hand choruses were dummy concerns, and were practically nothing more than a part of the stage setting.' Now, he continued, 'it seems difficult to realize that the idea of the chorus being anything more than a sort of stage audience was, at that time, a tremendous novelty'.[16]

Moreover, the Savoy chorus was often divided into male and female cohorts, making gender stand out as a structuring principle of the humour, exaggerating (and thus satirizing) the notion of the gendered 'separate spheres' and highlighting the absurdity of conceiving gender as 'opposite sexes'. It is very funny, conceptually, that a chorus of sailors is opposed to one of sisters, cousins, and aunts, a chorus of pirates to one of Wards in Chancery, a chorus of Peers to a chorus of Fairies; and these oppositions tacitly comment on Victorian gender arrangements. In addition, like the chorus of classical Greek drama, these Savoy choruses speak for society at large, but in a parodic way that emphasizes the different 'voices' and the dynamic encounters of gender. And those encounters—sometimes arguments, sometimes agreements—can be heard in the play of voice registers. This dynamic and systematic view of gender relations reaches its musical pinnacle, perhaps, in the stunning double choruses, when first one group sings, then the other, and then the two sing together, their sounds superimposed and the witty counterpoint showing how their differences interlock. One good example of this technique may be found in *H.M.S. Pinafore*, when the sailors' masculine protestations that they are 'attentive to their duty' are joined to the female chorus 'gaily tripping' as they board the ship; another good example occurs in *Patience*, when the aesthetic maidens express their rapt devotion ('Mystic poet, hear our prayer') while the Dragoon Guards express their outrage ('Now is not this ridiculous?—and is not this preposterous?').

These structural dynamics are reflected in the repetitive interactions of various individual character types—between the stout middle-aged dame and the capering comic baritone, for example, or between the high soprano ingénue and the tenor hero. Sullivan's musical characterizations add to the focus on gender, such as the feminine 'gaily tripping, lightly skipping' (the sisters, cousins, and aunts as they come aboard the *Pinafore*) and 'tripping hither, tripping thither' (the charming parody of fairy music that introduces *Iolanthe*), or the feminine 'chattering chorus' singing 'how beautifully blue the sky' to screen the lovers' duet in *Pirates* and to make it private, while '*listening eagerly all the time*' (94, 201, 130–131). Women can be warlike, too, as when Mabel enjoins the timid policemen in *Pirates* to 'go to glory and the grave!' (140). There the gender reversal is funny, as it is frequently with the dame figure. Correlatively, the male pretence to martial strength or social importance is lampooned in the music, as in the bluff military bravado of the Dragoon Guards ('When I First Put This Uniform On') or the boyish and self-involved pomposity of the Police's 'Tantara!' and the Peers' 'Tantantara! Tzing! Boom!' (167, 139–141, 208).

The Sorcerer, like *Trial by Jury*, began to unfold these strengths of the Savoy chorus. In the plot of the play, a young aristocrat idealistically hopes to break down 'the artificial barriers of rank, wealth, education, age, beauty, habits, taste, and temper' (62) and to couple everyone in the village of Ploverleigh, for love and marriage, and the union of the sexes, he believes, will be the cure of all other social divisions as well. Thus, a 'professional sorcerer' is called in to administer a love-potion sleeping-draught, which will cause each person to fall in love with the first person he or she sees upon waking. All sorts of unequal and seemingly absurd pairs result and must be set right in the end with class- and age-appropriate repairings. So much is conventional. But the notion of a 'professional sorcerer' as the linchpin of the plot is ingenious, for he is both a tradesman and a conjuror; his 'low' profession joins the everyday world to a form of magic. His self-introduction, 'My Name Is John Wellington Wells', the first of the famous patter songs, perfectly displays the mood of the assembly line, with its manic listing of pedantic specializations in multi-syllabic feminine rhymes.[17] Even though the specific parody of Donizetti's *L'elisir d'amore* (1832, which Gilbert had already parodied in *Dulcamara! or, The Little Duck and the Great Quack*, 1866) may be clearly felt, *The Sorcerer* more generally parodies the long tradition of the love potion itself—and gives it a particularly English twist, for in *The Sorcerer* the love potion is administered from a steaming teapot. This teapot philtre produces a particularly English magic, a form of measured English intoxication.

CLASS, GENDER, AND NATION
IN THE EARLY WORKS

With *H.M.S. Pinafore; or, The Lass That Loved a Sailor* (1878), Gilbert and Sullivan became an international phenomenon—first in the United States, where by early 1879 over 100 unauthorized performances were being mounted. This American craze for *Pinafore* had a reflexive effect in England and enhanced the work's popularity there. Of all the Savoy operas, *The Sorcerer* and *Pinafore* deal most pointedly with the absurdities of the class system. The plot of *Pinafore* turns on a cross-class romance between Ralph Rackstraw, a common sailor, and Josephine, his Captain's daughter, who is engaged to Sir Joseph Porter, KCB, First Lord of the Admiralty. The love triangle pits a Jolly Jack Tar, a sentimental figure who in nautical melodrama represents English duty and fidelity, a representative of the nation at its best, against a bureaucrat who rose through the ranks without merit.[18] Sir Joseph ostensibly believes in equality, but his pronouncement that 'love levels all ranks' is merely an 'official' utterance, as empty as such a thing can be (107–108, 117). The opera takes great pains to dissect his bureaucratic hypocrisy—and the fact that upward mobility can often go wrong in a bureaucracy—while considering the impossibility of real equality in a hierarchically organized navy.

The broad parody of nautical melodrama in *Pinafore* is unmistakable even today, when very few people are familiar with that genre, which flourished in the 1820s and 1830s after the Napoleonic Wars. Thus *Pinafore* stands as a good example of the way parody can keep the memory of past genres alive.[19] Throughout, Little Buttercup drops broad melodramatic hints of secrets yet to be revealed, and (as we have already seen) the plot is melodramatically resolved when her confession—that she was wet nurse to Ralph and the Captain and had 'mixed those children up'—issues in their absurd cross-class transformation and its parody of melodrama.

Even with no knowledge of the past genre, spectators still grasp the fact that Sir Joseph's insistence on the sailors' politeness is a topsy-turvy parody. Sailors swear profusely in nautical melodrama, and that's why Captain Corcoran's profession of never swearing 'a big, big D——' (and the 'What *never*? Hardly ever!' response) seemed so funny at the time (91). Later, when his politeness collapses—and he explodes with 'damme, it's too bad!'—we can see, as in *Thespis* and *Trial by Jury*, the double or triple action: getting the risqué 'Damme' into the plot, while ostensibly eschewing it and at the same time making fun of the squeamishness that would object to it in the first place (113, 46).

Melodrama depends on the convention of physiognomic legibility—the idea that spectators can identify characters' intentions by simply looking and listening. The character of Dick Deadeye in *Pinafore* lampoons this convention, for he is ugly and misshapen, and is therefore taken to be suspicious. He acknowledges: '[F]rom such a face and form as mine, the noblest sentiments sound like the black utterances of a depraved imagination' (88).[20] Yet he is the one who *should* be believed, because though he is impolite, he sees through Sir Joseph's pretensions of equality. As he succinctly puts it, 'when people have to obey other people's orders, equality's out of the question' (98). In other words, the point is satirical as well as parodic: Sir Joseph's insistence on the polite sailor shows the power structure at work ('all sailors should dance hornpipes', 97).

The most comprehensively serious point is about the theatrical nature of social life. Politeness would be merely an act on the part of the sailors, something they had learned to act out because authority had required it of them. That point is made explicit in the libretto when Sir Joseph gives the sailors a song to sing that is meant to teach them how to act the part of the British sailor.

> His foot should stamp and his throat should growl,
> His hair should twirl and his face should scowl;
> His eyes should flash and his breast protrude,
> And this should be his customary attitude—[*pose*] (99)

This wonderful glee adopts the theatrical convention of posing in 'attitudes' to show the British sailor performing his part. (We will see this self-conscious use of attitudes again in *Patience*.) Of course it is meant to be humorous. But it also makes the point that people learn the behaviours they must adopt to fit the parts they must play in social life. Authority provides one explanation for socialization; the accidental conditions of birth and upbringing provide another, and of course *H.M.S. Pinafore* takes that up, too, as we have seen.

Nautical melodrama was also famous for its nationalism and patriotism, and *Pinafore* humorously considers nationalism along with class as an aspect of socialization. To make this point, the satirical anthem 'He Is an Englishman!' adopts a naive point of view:

> For he might have been a Roosian,
> A French or Turk or Proosian,
> Or perhaps Itali-an!
>   [......]

> But in spite of all temptations
> To belong to other nations,
> He remains an Englishman! (112)

And of course 'it's greatly to his credit, | That he is an Englishman!' (112)—as if one's national origins could be chosen. But like social class, nationality is an 'accident of birth', a product of the 'force of circumstances', as the opera makes clear in its absurd ending. Thus the song provokes a critique of this sort of silly, unreflective nationalism. But because parody always depends on an imitation of its object, and it can sometimes therefore be mistaken for that object, this anthem has sometimes been taken straight. The music sounds patriotic, even though the words undercut and make fun of the automatic and unthinking nationalism (that can in fact be inspired by precisely such music).

On the other side of the nautical coin, *The Pirates of Penzance; or, The Slave of Duty* (1879) celebrates another topsy-turvy inversion of a popular type by characterizing the outlaws as sentimental orphans who can't make piracy pay because they are overwhelmed with pity when their prey claim to be orphans, too. They are 'ruthless' only in the punning sense that Frederic's nursemaid Ruth has been banished from their company. Frederic, the apprentice pirate (a figure which, like the professional sorcerer, humorously yokes two different worlds of work) is the 'slave of duty', and of course the idea of being dutiful to piracy is part of the absurd parodic inversion, but it also makes a satirical point against earnest and exaggerated Victorian middle-class dutifulness.

In general, the opera takes off on a nineteenth-century vogue for pirate melodramas and stories about pirates, brigands, corsairs, and the like. Part of the fun is the reference to the supposed sexual allure of these swashbucklers. The clever juxtaposition of Major-General Stanley's exaggeratedly innocent Wards in Chancery with the sentimental pirates on the one hand, and with the timid policemen on the other, takes part in this fun—which shows up particularly clearly in the mock-horror of the Wards at Frederic's 'effective but alarming [pirate] costume' and their complaint that the pirates want to 'marry' them: 'Against our wills, papa—against our wills!' (128, 135). In addition to this general parody, though—and like *The Sorcerer*—*Pirates* also parodies a specific work, for in 1871 Gilbert had translated the libretto to Offenbach's *Les Brigands* (1869). *The Pirates of Penzance* adopts its treatment of stealing as an occupation like any other. And like Offenbach's brigands, the Savoy pirates cannot steal effectively—though Gilbert adds the brilliant running joke about orphans. Thus *Pirates* ridicules conventions of both opéra bouffe and nautical melodrama.

Pirates offers another parody of melodramatic endings in which social identity is suddenly transformed, when it turns out that the pirates are 'all noblemen who have gone wrong', a frequent plot twist in the pirate melodramas (154). When the police charge them to 'yield, in Queen Victoria's name', they kneel, in an elaborate show of obeisance, 'because, with all our faults, we love our Queen'. They are 'the slave[s] of duty' in the end. The policemen take out their handkerchiefs and weep sentimentally at the pirates' patriotic devotion (153–154). After all, though, the hyper-logical consideration of Frederic's leap-year birthday and the question of when exactly he would be out of his indentures is another such joke on the absurdity of sudden and melodramatic transformations in identity. Sometimes it seems as if the pointed satire on the exaggerated Victorian sense of duty gets lost amid the many parodic jokes.[21]

This spoof on exaggerated patriotism undergirded by the parody of nautical melodrama returns in *Ruddigore; or, The Witch's Curse* (1887) much later in the Savoy series. The Jolly Jack Tar of that opera, Dick Dauntless, dances the obligatory hornpipe after demonstrating his naive and exaggerated patriotism in a blatantly anti-French song, 'I Shipped, D'ye See, in a Revenue Sloop'. He grossly overestimates the prowess of the British Tar, while grossly underestimating the French enemy, using a host of condescending terms for 'Froggee', who is after all 'only a darned Mounseer' (357). As in 'He Is an Englishman!' the audience should see through his unreliable narration, for he believes that the rowdy good cheer of the English sailors has 'paralysed the Parley-voo', (357), when in fact the French simply have a much bigger ship and have fired on the Revenue sloop, while the English sloop has turned about and run away. *Ruddigore* is a parodic grab-bag, ringing the changes not only on nautical melodrama and the Jolly Jack Tar figure, but also mixing them up with other forms of parody-melodrama. The governing idea of the 'witch's curse' alerts us to the element of the supernatural Gothic, which comes to fruition when the picture gallery at Ruddigore Castle comes to life—the opera's most famous scene. And when the Chorus of Bucks and Blades comes in, supposedly to marry the village maidens, we can feel the pastoral village melodrama, and a bit of seduction melodrama as well.

Thus the formation of the genre of English comic opera continues to take place through the parody of earlier genres. These early works already show an interest in gender, but in Gilbert and Sullivan's middle period, with *Patience, Iolanthe*, and *Princess Ida*, the focus on gender becomes more intense and prominent. This aspect of their wit has been much less appreciated, though it too is an important element of social life.

GENDER IN THE WORKS OF
THE MIDDLE PERIOD

Patience; or, Bunthorne's Bride (1881) is the best of many theatrical satires on aestheticism (even including F. C. Burnand's *The Colonel*, which opened a few months before *Patience*, and George DuMaurier's anti-aesthetic cartoons that ran in *Punch* from 1873 to 1882). These satirical works generally treat aestheticism as a cultural craze or fad involving certain chosen colours, fashions, hairstyles, flowers, home decor, and the collection of certain objects with an 'early English' or a Japanese provenance. Such superficial matters of fashion were portrayed as silly though innocuous for the most part, but the sharper side of some satires on aestheticism implied that aesthetes threaten the stability of the family by seducing women away from their domestic duties and husbands or husbands-to-be.[22] This conventional thread may be seen in *Patience*, when the chorus of 'aesthetic maidens' pine and sigh, following Bunthorne, the aesthetic poet, even though they are engaged to the masculine Dragoon Guards. But that thread is only one part of a complex plot structure that emphasizes gender relations in many different ways, including the humorous juxtaposition of the blindly devoted, risibly earnest aesthetic maidens against the chorus of bluff military men. Another structural feature based on gender is the love triangle around Patience, a milkmaid whose exaggerated feminine innocence amounts to ignorance; in fact, her characterization is a parody of the Victorian way of keeping maidens in ignorance of 'love' and its ways. And so, Patience in her exaggerated innocence is structurally compared to the sophisticated aesthetic maidens and their leader, Lady Jane, the most powerful and knowing woman in the plot. These characters are given as the various extremes in gender behaviour: the aesthetic maidens are ridiculous in their ardent devotion, while Patience has never loved at all; they are feminine and dependent, while Lady Jane is dominating and sensible—a great example of the powerful contralto figure, which will shortly be considered.

This structured comparison of various types of femininity is matched by a complex consideration of various masculine styles. The overarching contrast depends on the competition between the aesthetes and the conventionally masculine military men for the affections of the maidens. They are equally vain, for the Dragoons' admiration of their own costumes ('When I First Put This Uniform On') is every bit as noticeable as the aesthetes' unusual dress. Perhaps the aesthetes represent a new form of masculinity, sophisticated rather than ordinary and popular. Furthermore, the Dragoon Guards, while popular, may be seen to be a bit outmoded and old-fashioned. 'If You Want a Receipt for This Popular Mystery Known to the World as a Heavy Dragoon', the Colonel's patter song, is a wonderful name-dropping list of cultural reference points that imagines a dense form of masculinity being made from their stew: 'set them to simmer and take off the scum | And a Heavy Dragoon is the residuum!' In one famous scene, when the Dragoon Guards dress up in aesthetic garb and try to imitate the aesthetic poets, they fail miserably, implying that there is a kind of essential masculinity that absolutely cannot strike what are taken to be effeminate attitudes. Ironically, in his patter song, Bunthorne admits that he, too, is a sham; to be an aesthete is to adopt a pose, the opera seems to say.[23]

Bunthorne is paired against another poet, Grosvenor, and at his entrance, all the maidens as well as Patience flock to him. But Grosvenor is eventually persuaded to become 'an everyday young man'. The poets' duet ('When I Go out of Door'), a list-song that humorously compares the tastes of an aesthete and an everyday young man, makes that structural opposition clear, as does the contrast between their kinds of poetry: Grosvenor's simplistically moralistic poems are the very opposite of Bunthorne's aesthetic effusions. Thus Gilbert comments on a polarization in Victorian literary culture between aesthetic and idyllic poetry. When Bunthorne sets out to recite his poem, 'Oh, Hollow! Hollow! Hollow!' he calls it a 'wild, weird fleshly thing', thus making it clear that *Patience* responds to 'The Fleshly School of Poetry', a scathing attack by Robert Buchanan on the Pre-Raphaelite poets, and on D. G. Rossetti in particular. Bunthorne's poem is pretentious, billed as 'the wail of the poet's heart on discovering that everything is commonplace' (165). An illustration of the characteristics that Buchanan had despised in the Pre-Raphaelites, the sound so dominates over the sense that Bunthorne's poem is parodically dense, opaque, and hard to follow. Artful and sonorous, the surface of the poem is practically impenetrable; one can hardly tell what it means; but in fact, the poem hides a dirty joke, for the maidens in the poem might feel 'hollow' not because they are yearning or lovelorn, but because they have been 'purged' by a laxative. Thus, in addition to satirizing aestheticism in general, *Patience* offers an elaborate parody— and scatological critique—of certain kinds of Victorian poetry that might seem, to some eyes and ears, beautiful but hollow. [24]

In this contest of poetic and masculine styles, Grosvenor and the Dragoon Guards are the winners. In the end, aestheticism is literally re-dressed, as all the characters except Bunthorne change costumes and come on stage for the finale in contemporary stylish garb. Patience is paired in the end with the 'everyday young man' in a bowler hat and a suit of plaid 'dittoes', while Lady Jane—who had loyally followed Bunthorne—makes a last-minute match with the Duke. Bunthorne is left alone, and the answer to the sub-title's riddle turns out to be that 'Nobody' will be 'Bunthorne's Bride'. Many spectators have found something unsettling in the exclusion of Bunthorne from the extravaganza of multiple marriages in the end. From our point of view in historical retrospect, knowing that the Wilde trials are less than fifteen years away, it is difficult to see Bunthorne's exclusion without thinking of the punitive limelight more and more equating aestheticism with a sexuality that is in the process of being 'typed' for recognition during this period.[25] Though 'the homosexual' has not been fully typed in 1881, and though Bunthorne is represented as explicitly heterosexual in *Patience*, his character does acquire retrospective representational significance through the emergence of this social identity into explicitness, both in the theatre and out.[26]

If women seem radically unknowing in *Patience*, they are formidably in charge in *Iolanthe; or, The Peer and the Peri* (1882).[27] This opera structurally opposes its female chorus of Fairies to a male chorus of Peers and through that juxtaposition imagines that women are supernaturally powerful while men are mere sublunary, earthly, incompetent creatures. The Fairy Queen has banished her favourite, Iolanthe, from the fairy band because she broke the primary Fairy Law against marrying a mortal; Iolanthe's son, Strephon, an 'Arcadian shepherd', is the issue of that union. Responding parodically to the huge Victorian vogue for fairy painting, fairy ballet, fairy extravaganza, fairy-tale collecting, and fairy literature, the opera engages in wholesale lampooning of the House of Lords, who 'throughout the war, | Did nothing in particular' (230). The Fairy Queen's threat to throw the House of Lords open to 'Com- | Petitive Examination' (226) would overturn inherited status with a bureaucratic meritocracy. In Act 2 it turns out that all the Fairies have fallen in love with hereditary Peers, while the Fairy Queen admits her attraction to Private Willis, a sentry guard. The Lord Chancellor is revealed to be Iolanthe's mortal husband and Strephon's father. In order to resolve this difficulty—of illicit, topsy-turvy sexual attraction between the two realms—the Lord Chancellor, 'an old Equity draftsman' (244), suggests a simple change in the law. With the addition of one word, the law's meaning can be totally inverted and turned into its opposite: now

'every fairy shall die who doesn't marry a mortal' (245). Thus, arbitrarily, the law is made
to uphold cross-cultural sexual attraction rather than to oppose it.

Thus the Peers are whisked away to Fairyland, after they admit, in the person of
Lord Mountararat, that since now 'the Peers are to be recruited entirely from persons
of intelligence', they are no longer of much use 'down here' (245). (And in this respect,
Iolanthe must be seen as a parody of the fairy extravaganza, a genre that often ends with
this sort of 'transformation scene', a transfiguration and removal to a magical realm of
bliss elsewhere, often called 'Fairyland'.) In other words, the men are assimilated to the
Fairy regime, and not vice versa (as would be the case for marriages in real social life,
where the woman inevitably would take the man's class or status). Thus are the Fairies
vindicated in the end, and the plot becomes an explicit riposte to Lord Mountararat's
misogynistic claim that nothing good 'comes of women interfering in politics' (229).
And thus gender is used to make a serious political point about dysfunction and debility
in Parliament.

The figure of the Fairy Queen provides the best place for us to consider the large contralto role in Gilbert and Sullivan, represented most famously by Ruth, Lady Jane, the
Fairy Queen (see Figure 3.1), and Katisha.

FIGURE 3.1 Gender Parody: contralto Alice Barnett as the Fairy Queen in *Iolanthe*, with
Wagnerian helmet, breastplate, and spear.

Cabinet photograph by Elliott & Fry (London, 1882). Wikimedia Commons.

Our focus on parody and gender can add one important insight to the long-standing debate about whether this figure is a misogynistic representation or not. Parody always activates historical memory of its object, and in this case makes the figure more complicated than the old dame figure of pantomime and burlesque, to which she alludes. Victorian theatre was known for two forms of cross-dressing: female-to-male cross-dressing enabled women to portray princes or vulnerable waifs; they could show their figures, especially their legs, and their femininity subliminally registered as part of the character they played, etherealizing the masculine. Male-to-female cross-dressing, on the other hand, involved a low comic man playing a middle-aged female character who was overweight or fat, bossy or overbearing, plain or ugly, and always vain (see Figure 3.2).

FIGURE 3.2 An exemplary Dame figure: Frederick Robson as Medea in Robert Brough's *Medea; or, The Best of Mothers, with a Brute of a Husband* (1856).

Photograph by Herbert Watkins. Courtesy of Harvard Theatre Collection, Houghton Library.

I would argue that the large contralto figure in Gilbert and Sullivan is a parody of this dame figure. Not exactly the misogynistic cross-dressed dame of old, but a parody of that figure, she is a layered representation, a woman playing a man-playing-a-woman. Since parody must always imitate its object in order to be understood as parody, some of the misogyny of the dame figure is still detectable, and yet it is enveloped in a larger understanding that includes a critique of the misogynistic figure from the theatrical and generic past. The Savoy contralto is powerful and appealing, while at the same time humorously alluding to the dame figure's size (as in Lady Jane's opening number in *Patience*, Act 2, 'Silvered Is the Raven Hair') or even to her aggression (as in Katisha's admission that she is 'tough as a bone, | With a will of her own', 330). She is often paired, in the end, with the comic baritone, and the physical comedy of this pairing suggests both a large, bossy woman overtaking a meek, smaller man, and a sensible, forthright woman-of-a-certain-age providing a certain gravitas. In other words, as used in the Savoy operas, the figure is complex and layered—not simply the misogynistic figure of the past, but also a parody of that figure, updated with layers of present-day appreciation and critique. Thus Gilbert and Sullivan can renounce cross-dressing, but include the memory of it—under the cover of parody.[28]

A similar theatrical layering of genders occurs in *Princess Ida; or, Castle Adamant* (1884), when Prince Hilarion and his two friends dress up as women in order to penetrate the all-female precincts of Castle Adamant. That interesting case of overt cross-dressing in the Savoy operas is explicitly rationalized by the opera's plot, but the situation is complicated by the fact that the opera derives from a previous burlesque version of *The Princess*, written by Gilbert and produced in 1870. Because cross-dressing is conventional in burlesque, Prince Hilarion and his friends were played by women in that earlier version. Thus, when the men attempt admittance to Castle Adamant in *The Princess*, we have double cross-dressing: men playing women-playing-men.[29] This is especially interesting when paired with the scene of Princess Ida's three brothers taking off their armour piece by piece ('This Helmet, I Suppose'). They don't want to fight and are willing to shed their masculine, hardened outer carapace. Just like the end of *Patience*, dressing and redressing (and in this case, undressing) carries great cultural significance, as it does in Alfred Lord Tennyson's popular long poem, *The Princess: A Medley* (1847–51), of which both *The Princess* and *Princess Ida* are explicit parodies.[30]

Princess Ida, anomalous in the Savoy canon for being written in three acts and in blank verse, imagines a Princess, betrothed from birth to a neighbouring Prince, who has withdrawn, with a community of like- and strong-minded women, to Castle Adamant, where they have set up an institution of higher education for women. After the Prince and his friends invade the Castle, an actual war between the sexes ensues. The libretto makes some shocking jokes about women's lack of aptitude for higher education, which can perhaps be accounted for by the fact that the opera's libretto derives from Gilbert's earlier burlesque version of *The Princess*. (Burlesque humour conventionally employed coarse jokes and gender stereotypes.) Perhaps Gilbert intended *Princess Ida* to be a parody of his own earlier work; and since the burlesque *Princess* was already a 'respectful per-version' of Tennyson's poem, *Princess Ida* then might be seen as a parody of that earlier parody. That argument might help to justify some of the faults of *Princess Ida*, but it is a stretch.

When the Prince and his friends defeat Ida's brothers, she capitulates in *Princess Ida* (while in the Tennyson poem, the Prince is wounded and Ida nurses him back to health—a plot twist that adjusts the power imbalance). In both cases, however, the question remains: how to engineer a marriage plot within such a situation of gender separatism and antagonism? In *Princess Ida*, the rationale comes through a volley of burlesque jokes about the need to provide a future through progeny. In Tennyson's poem, the assumption is quite clear, that men will evolve toward equality with women, as humans have evolved over time. But in *Princess Ida* this understanding of history is truncated, though the Prince does ask Ida to 'try Man,' and offers her the opportunity to 'mould' his 'grosser clay' (294). However, the evolutionary logic of the Tennyson poem's view of gender shows up in a distorted way in *Princess Ida*. 'The Ape and the Lady' ('A Lady Fair, of Lineage High'), a novelty song, offers a little allegory of cross-gender, cross-class, and cross-species relations. Loving the Lady, the Ape shaves and dresses up like a human, calling himself 'Darwinian man', but his act 'would not do', for the Lady was 'a radiant Being', while Darwinian man 'at best is only a monkey shaved' (271–273). Through another little allegory about dressing and redressing, this direct critique casts doubt on the evolution of 'man'. *Princess Ida* ends, before the finale, with a quote from the Tennyson poem that echoes *Paradise Lost* in its vision of male and female walking 'yoked' through a fallen world.

LATE GILBERT AND
SULLIVAN: SOCIALIZATION AND CULTURE

The operas of the middle period, while focusing on gender, also patently analyse culture as a whole. In *Patience*, for example, an aesthetic subculture is defeated by the normative 'everyday'. In *Iolanthe* the encounter between women and men, represented by Fairies and Peers, is staged as the conflict of two cultures, each with its own set of customs and laws. This consideration of gender as culture continues in *Princess Ida*, which experiments with the idea of a separate female world. The late operas, beginning with *The Mikado; or, The Town of Titipu* (1885) often continue this meditation on culture by staging a cultural encounter. Some of what Gilbert and Sullivan want to show about English society becomes most graphically visible when juxtaposed with—and against—another culture, for in the mirror of another culture, English social conventions are defamiliarized and can be seen with a critical eye. It is in this respect as well that the overlapping concepts of 'English' and 'British' may be seen to jostle, during a time that saw not only the continued rise of empire, but also the rise of a trenchant critique of it. Thus we can see that 'Englishness' itself—and thus what Gilbert and Sullivan satirize—changes with the times.

If only *The Mikado; or the Town of Titipu* (1885)—their greatest hit—had explicitly staged an encounter between English and Japanese cultures, showing a clash and an interaction, as several of the later operas will do, then perhaps some misunderstanding could have been avoided. As it is, a traditional debate about whether *The Mikado* is making fun of Japanese or English foibles and stereotypes has often become quite heated. True, as many critics have pointed out, there are many clues in the libretto that the butt of satire is meant to be English society, but the idea that the opera trivializes Japanese customs or people periodically comes to the fore. Consequently, in the twenty-first century, staging *The Mikado* requires delicacy and care.[31]

My own reading depends upon the fact that 'the town of Titipu' is a fanciful place, *neither* English nor Japanese, but meant to suggest an encounter of the two, specifically the craze for consumption of Japanese artefacts in England and the appropriation of Japanese styles by English consumers. In this reading, *The Mikado* can be seen as a parody of Victorian *japonisme*, a fad that had begun as a high-culture phenomenon, but had moved (or was moving) into middle-class awareness.[32] As the gentlemen of Japan sing, in their opening number, they are found 'On many a vase and jar— | On many a screen and fan' (299). Indeed the opera employs stereotypes of both cultures. For example, the Mikado follows a long line of earlier burlesque characterizations of the violent 'Oriental' tyrant, while Pooh Bah clearly represents English bureaucratic departmentalization as well as English pride of ancestry. Japanese objects were popular cultural currency, in part because of the Japanese Village in Knightsbridge, a sort of proto-anthropological exhibition for metropolitan tourists, which displays another culture within the confines of the home culture, the other culture imported and made into theatre. In the programme for *The Mikado*'s original run, thanks are given for tutelage from the inhabitants of the Japanese Village, and stress is placed on the authentic nature of costumes made from real Japanese fabrics (supplied by Liberty & Co.). This realistic attention to Japanese dress may have backfired—as it may have suggested that a realistic portrait of the Japanese was intended (though no one ever thought that H.M.S. *Pinafore* was meant to be a realistic ship, no matter how accurate the setting's reproduction of H.M.S. *Victory* might have been[33]). With everyone in Japanese costume, the notion of a fruitful, conflict-inducing, or purely mercantile cultural encounter is harder to see.

One could say that the whole plot—which turns on a law stipulating that one can be put to death for flirting—makes fun of Victorian prudery (in the same way that *Pirates* makes fun of Victorian dutifulness) and that the 'three little maids from school' enact a joke about exaggerated Victorian feminine innocence. This latter idea is not far-fetched, since we have already noted that Patience is so elaborately innocent as to seem not only unworldly but ignorant. Likewise, in *Ruddigore*, Rose Maybud simplistically consults her etiquette book throughout, not knowing how to act independently of the rules; and in *Utopia Limited*, the two younger princesses are exhibited in the public square as they perform the 'correct' modest feminine behaviour during courtship. In other words, Gilbert hammers away at this point, that correctly socialized feminine innocence could reach ridiculous proportions—and above all, that femininity *is* socialized rather than natural. The three little maids are more affectionately handled than Patience or Rose

Maybud, though Yum-Yum's vanity is spotlighted when she muses about her own beauty in her 'artless Japanese way', emphasizing to the audience that in England, the 'Japanese way' was always associated with artfulness (322).

Mike Leigh's film *Topsy-Turvy* (1999) dramatizes the making of *The Mikado*, including a period of strife between Gilbert, Sullivan, and Carte leading up to it. The film may be regarded both as a biopic—much of it accurate, with notable poetic licence taken in the interpretation of the principals' private lives—and as a great work of critical reflection on what *The Mikado* is all about. Leigh emphasizes the peculiarly insular way in which the Victorians experience Japanese culture, recreating the Japanese Village in his film in order to show Gilbert and his wife observing Japanese people in little exhibition niches practising crafts of spinning and calligraphy. Gilbert watches the performance styles of the other culture, wide-eyed with wonder: two kendo fighters, a singer playing the samisen, and a kabuki drama. Then the Gilberts repair to a teahouse, where he crassly and jokingly calls the unfamiliar green tea 'spinach water'. Leigh pursues this characterization of Gilbert's attitude—his inability to understand the waitress when she asks for 'sixpence, please' and his casual superiority in nicknaming her, thereafter, 'Miss Sixpence Please'. Whether the film offers a fair characterization of Gilbert or not, Mike Leigh attempts to make him the representative of a kind of benevolent imperial paternalism, unaware of its own condescension. By relying on an apocryphal legend of Gilbert being inspired to write *The Mikado* when a Japanese sword falls from his wall, the film indulges in a historical inaccuracy that nevertheless suits Leigh's accurate historical point (that bits of Japanese culture would have come to Gilbert through his own ambient culture). When the sword falls in the film, Gilbert's eyes widen and light up with inspiration, and Leigh's point is this: Gilbert's cross-cultural wonder is both unknowing, condescending, even crude, and seriously curious and imaginative.

Topsy-Turvy reflects directly on the cross-cultural encounter, while *The Mikado* does so only obliquely. For example, the film makes the point that gender roles and norms are culturally relative. In one sequence, women from the Japanese Village come to rehearsal to show the three little maids how to walk downstage 'in the Japanese manner': the performance of Japanese femininity must be learned. Two paired scenes at the ladies' and gentlemen's costumiers emphasize the gendered ways the Savoy principals worry about their costumes. The women feel immodest because they wear no corsets under their kimonos, whereas Lely is acutely troubled by the shortness of his minstrel 'skirt', for it shows his calves.

In fact, the film makes large points about England's relation to the rest of the world (not only Japan). In one scene George Grossmith, Rutland Barrington, and Durward Lely (who played Ko-Ko, Pooh-Bah, and Nanki-Poo in the original production of *The Mikado*) are dining on oysters at a posh gentlemen's club. A caption reads: 'February 12th 1885: News reaches London of the killing of General [Charles George] Gordon by the Mahdi's troops at Khartoum.' Grossmith engages in quite blatant racism in his patriotic dismissal of the Mahdi. Lely, however, answers with a story about fifty-six families killed on the Isle of Skye by English militia, quietly making the point that barbarism exists within the nation (here understood as Britain, not England), not only outside it.

Thus Leigh juxtaposes global imperial warfare with a violent hierarchy within Great Britain herself. In other words, Leigh's film is a work of historical criticism. While many of the biographical details will always be disputed, Leigh has given us a dense weave of context within which to understand *The Mikado*, still Gilbert and Sullivan's most often-performed opera.

Other late operas, too, involve a cultural encounter or the direct consideration of another culture. In *The Gondoliers; or, The King of Barataria* (1889), Act 1 takes place in a fanciful eighteenth-century Venice, while Act 2 takes place in the mythical 'Barataria'. Through the fiction of two *gondolieri*, both of whom become one king, the opera considers the philosophical question of republicanism: how can two (or more than one) become one? In *The Grand Duke; or, The Statutory Duel* (1896), Act 1 takes place in the marketplace of Speisesaal, in the Grand Duchy of Pfennig Halbpfennig, while Act 2 takes place in the Ducal Palace. But the clash of cultures involves the invasion of an acting troupe, with the overarching argument that governing a theatrical troupe is like governing a small duchy. This last collaboration between Gilbert and Sullivan returns to the metatheatrical framework used in their first collaboration, *Thespis*, with the same mixed reference to Offenbach—this time ringing the changes on *La Grande-Duchesse de Gérolstein* (1867)— and to the classical extravaganza. Since the acting troupe is rehearsing *Troilus and Cressida*, they engage in some humorous classical pedantry. All the members of the cast are supposedly speaking German; only Julia Jellicoe, played by the beautiful Hungarian actress Ilka von Palmay, is supposed (in the plot) to be English. When she spoke with her heavy middle-European accent, the joke was about her impenetrable 'English' accent—a minor point, but another example of gazing at the English from without.

Even *The Yeomen of the Guard; or, The Merryman and His Maid* (1888; the favourite of both Gilbert and Sullivan), which is set in the sixteenth century on Tower Green, may be seen in this way. This past is both 'a foreign country' and the foundation of the present nation, whose mixed origins should not be forgotten.[34] Indeed, the Norman Conquest is celebrated, and the Tower of London stands as a symbol of this founding cultural clash and mixture, as Dame Carruthers and the Yeomen sing in 'When our gallant Norman foes | Made our merry land their own' (402). Of all the operas that deal with an English encounter with another culture, this one finds the other within the history of the nation itself, founded in a violent cross-cultural clash that, over time, has been absorbed into the very identity of the nation. The past of English theatre, too, forms a thread in this plot, which recalls the old days of strolling players and jesters.

But *Utopia, Limited; or, The Flowers of Progress* (1893) is the most explicitly developed statement of their fascination with the cultural encounter. In this opera, English society is seen from without, through the eyes of a colonized population. The premise: a South Sea Island called 'Utopia' invites a delegation of English bureaucrats—'the Flowers of Progress'—to come and teach them how to be more like England, 'the greatest, the most powerful, the wisest country in the world' (507–508). One of the Flowers of Progress is a company promoter, and he persuades the Utopians that the best way to be like England is to incorporate their island nation under the laws of limited liability. His song ('Some Seven Men Form an Association') stresses the unfair and absurd logic of limited liability.[35]

Thus this opera is trenchantly critical both of cultural colonialism and of capitalism; the latter limits the potential of Utopia, transforming it into 'Utopia, Limited'. The structure of the opera makes the opposition of Utopia to England quite graphic as the opposition of 'natural' to 'unnatural': Act 1 takes place in a 'Utopian Palm Grove,' with maidens '*thoroughly enjoying themselves in lotus-eating fashion*' (507), while Act 2 takes place in King Paramount's throne room, after the Utopians have been taught how to dress and 'act' English. Here the theatricality of everyday life and the process of socialization are again considered. The idea that someone not brought up in the ways of the culture can learn to 'act' English seems absurd—and yet it is the principle of British imperialism and the 'civilizing mission.' Indeed the Utopian King Paramount thinks it must be a practical joke: 'To a Monarch who has been accustomed to the uncontrolled use of his limbs, the costume of a British Field-Marshal is, perhaps, at first, a little cramping' (544). English costumes are so constricting, it seems unclear why anyone would voluntarily wear them.

This premise allows gender, too, to be examined as a relative and fully socialized phenomenon, especially with respect to the young princesses, whose theatrical exhibition of the correct feminine behaviour during courtship is performed in the public square. Their governess, Lady Sophy, has taught them their manners, and she guides the performance with her lecturer's wand, pointing to the finer nuances of their behaviour. To be fair, a portrait, later in the opera, depicts the 'bright and beautiful English girl', to balance this exhibition of unnatural girls who behave like 'clockwork toys' (553–554, 515). Gender doesn't have to be so artificial, this comparison seems to say, but cultural teachers like governesses pass down and enforce its scripted behaviours, which are then exhibited as illustration and education to others, who learn in their turn. The drawing room scene reinforces this idea with an elaborate display of English Society with a capital 'S', showcasing an elaborate court ritual, a presentation in the form of a procession, like a revue, of fashionable dresses and perfectly calibrated, learned behaviour. Here we may observe a complex mirroring effect involving the middle and upper classes, because most members of the Savoy Theatre audience had never been admitted to a royal drawing room, and they were as interested in this exotic dimension of their own culture as they would have been in the spectacle of another culture.

So the cultural encounter serves to illuminate and defamiliarize English gender, class, and capitalism. But the overarching lampoon of English society is nowhere better felt than in the treatment of the bureaucrats, especially when the Utopian Cabinet Council gathers in the line-up formation familiar from the Christy Minstrels to sing the minstrel number, 'Society Has Quite Forsaken All Her Wicked Courses'.[36] In this rollicking song, the Flowers of Progress claim that England could take the reformed Utopia as its model:

> It really is surprising
> What a thorough Anglicizing
> We have brought about—Utopia's quite another land;
> In her enterprising movements
> She is England—with improvements,
> Which we dutifully offer to our mother-land! (545–546)

In this burlesque of the theatrical element in political discourse, the minstrel show is important, a genre of burlesque and another genre from which the Savoy operas craft their generic mix. (In *Trial by Jury* there is another minstrel number.) But it would be difficult to ignore the American (and erstwhile colonial) derivation of the minstrel show, even if by 1896 in England it had come to seem merely a variety show like many others. Nevertheless, in the colonial context of this opera, I think racial implications are intended. And the subliminal question raised by this colonial context would be: are black subjects fully included in the purported national unity of the United States?

The opera ends with this same question: who is included and who is excluded by the borders of the nation? In 'There's a Little Group of Isles beyond the Wave', the opera zooms out to look back at England from far beyond its borders. Princess Zara and King Paramount turn their attention to the island nation that they have taken as the model for Utopia:

> Oh, may we copy all her maxims wise,
>   And imitate her virtues and her charities;
> And may we, by degrees, acclimatize
>   Her Parliamentary peculiarities!
> By doing so, we shall, in course of time,
>   Regenerate completely our entire land—
> Great Britain is that monarchy sublime,
>   To which some add (but others do not) Ireland. (560)

The admonitory refrain—'Let us hope, for her sake, | [. . .] | That she's all she professes to be!' (559–560)—comes in to interrupt and overshadow this bitter point about Ireland's uncertain status within 'Great Britain', but the acknowledgement of conflict within the nation cannot be totally disavowed. This political trenchancy of *Utopia Limited* was not popular at the time, yet its depiction of the capitalist underpinnings of global culture seems quite prescient today, hitting very close to home in the twenty-first century.

In *Utopia Limited*, then, we can see all the elements of social satire and genre parody that we have been tracing throughout this essay. Likewise, the opera focuses on gender in order to make its points about the theatrical aspects of everyday life and the process of socialization, arguing that gender behaviour need not be as unnatural as strict Victorian governesses would have it. Auto-ethnographic critique is heightened in most of the late operas, but in *Utopia Limited* it is strikingly expanded to include a canny assessment not only of British institutions (represented by the 'Flowers of Progress') but also of their larger effects in the world—since cultural colonialism and global capitalism are seen as forces that render the utopian possibilities of the island nation only 'limited.' This is the case whether 'The island nation' is taken to be Utopia or Great Britain, for within the premise of this opera, each provides a mirror for the other.

Notes

1. See, for example, Elizabeth Burns, *Theatricality: A Study of Convention in the Theatre and in Social Life* (New York: Prentice Hall, 1972) and Erving Goffman, *The Presentation of Self in Everyday Life* (New York: Anchor, 1959).

2. *The Complete Plays of Gilbert and Sullivan* (New York: W. W. Norton & Co., Inc., 1976), 139. Subsequent citations to the plays will be in parentheses and will refer to page numbers from this edition.

3. For accounts of their work before and outside their collaboration, see Michael Ainger, *Gilbert and Sullivan: A Dual Biography* (Oxford: Oxford University Press, 2002); Jane W. Stedman, *W. S. Gilbert: A Classic Victorian and His Theatre* (Oxford: Oxford University Press, 1996); Arthur Jacobs, *Arthur Sullivan: A Victorian Musician*, 2nd ed. (Oxford: Oxford University Press, 2003); and Stedman, *Gilbert Before Sullivan: Six Comic Plays by W. S. Gilbert* (Chicago: University of Chicago Press, 1967).

4. Carte to Gilbert and Sullivan, 8 April 1880, quoted in Leslie Baily, *Gilbert and Sullivan Book* (London: Spring Books, 1952), 125.

5. The works are often called 'the Savoy operas' after the Savoy Theatre was built in 1881 to house them.

6. *Rutland Barrington: A Record of Thirty-Five Years' Experience on the English Stage; By Himself*, with a Preface by William S. Gilbert (London: Grant, 1908), quoted in Isaac Goldberg, *The Story of Gilbert and Sullivan; or The 'Compleat' Savoyard* (New York: Simon and Schuster, 1928), 191.

7. In an interpretation very different from my own, Alan Fischler focuses on comedy in *Modified Rapture: Comedy in W. S. Gilbert's Savoy Operas* (Charlottesville: University Press of Virginia, 1991).

8. W. S. Gilbert, *Original Plays*, 3rd series (London: Chatto & Windus, 1923), 86.

9. On the extravaganza tradition and Gilbert's relation to it, see Harley Granville-Barker, 'Exit Planché—Enter Gilbert', in *The Eighteen-Sixties: Essays by Fellows of the Royal Society of Literature*, ed. John Drinkwater (Cambridge: Cambridge University Press, 1932), 102–148. On Gilbert's directorial style, see William Cox-Ife, *W. S. Gilbert: Stage Director* (London: Dennis Dobson, 1977).

10. For more on the dynamics of parody, see Carolyn Williams, *Gilbert and Sullivan: Gender, Genre, Parody* (New York: Columbia University Press, 2011), 6–17.

11. Ellen (Nelly) Farren was 'the *ne plus ultra* of principal boys and the idol of the Gallery', according to Terence Rees in *Thespis: A Gilbert and Sullivan Enigma* (London: Dillon's University Bookshop, 1964), 7. Unfortunately, most of the music for *Thespis* has been lost (or perhaps intentionally destroyed). The best—and nearly the only—commentary on this work is Rees's book.

12. W. S. Gilbert, 'Trial by Jury: An Operetta', which appeared in *Fun* 7 (11 April 1868), 54, is now most easily accessible in *The Bab Ballads*, ed. James Ellis (Cambridge, MA: Harvard University Press, 1980), 157–159. An intermediate version, longer than this one, preceded the libretto set by Sullivan in 1875.

13. As Susie Steinbach has shown, in 'The Melodramatic Contract: Breach of Promise and the Performance of Virtue', *Nineteenth-Century Studies* 14 (2000): 1–34. See also Susie L. Steinbach, 'Promises, Promises: Not Marrying in England, 1780–1920' (unpublished PhD thesis, Yale University, 1996).

14. Sullivan's musical parody is quite varied—sometimes, for example, spoofing operatic genres like the bel canto dilemma ensemble or Mendelssohnian fairy music, sometimes imitating national styles (Italian, Japanese, Viennese). For more on the music than space allows here, see Gervase Hughes, *The Music of Arthur Sullivan* (New York: St Martin's Press, 1960) and Williams, *Gilbert and Sullivan*, 24–29. Overall, Sullivan's brilliance in musical parody serves to emphasize his comprehensive mastery of musical idiom high and low, English and Continental, present and past. He also covers the full spectrum of parody, from fun-making critique to imitative homage (his madrigals, for example, would fall on the side of homage to a native English style).

15. Goldberg, *Story of Gilbert and Sullivan*, 197.

16. Quoted in Arthur Lawrence, *Sir Arthur Sullivan: Life Story, Letters, and Reminiscences* (Chicago: Stone, 1900), 85. For another discussion of Gilbert's use of the chorus, see Stedman, *W. S. Gilbert*, 219–220.

17. For more on the patter songs, see Williams, *Gilbert and Sullivan*, 91–94.

18. For an account of the satire on W. H. Smith, through the figure of Sir Joseph Porter, see Ian Bradley's commentary on Sir Joseph's song, 'When I was a Lad, I served a Term', in Ian Bradley, ed., *The Complete Annotated Gilbert and Sullivan* (Oxford: Oxford University Press, 1996), 134.

19. For this argument, see also Marvin Carlson, '"He Never Should Bow Down to a Domineering Frown": Class Tensions and Nautical Melodrama', in *Melodrama: The Cultural Emergence of a Genre*, ed. Michael Hays and Anastasia Nicolopolou (New York: St Martin's Press, 1996), 155.

20. Cf. Sir Despard in *Ruddigore*, which jokes on the same convention ('Why am I moody and sad?'): 'When in crime one is fully employed— | Your expression gets warped and destroyed.'

21. George Bernard Shaw argued that Gilbert did not take his own theme seriously enough, comparing *Pirates of Penzance* to Ibsen's *The Wild Duck* as a critique of the Victorian sense of duty. *Our Theatres in the Nineties*, in *Works* 24: 242, quoted in Max Keith Sutton, *W. S. Gilbert* (Boston: Twayne, 1975), 124.

22. See 'Beyond the 'Serious Family'', in Williams, *Gilbert and Sullivan*, 152–167.

23. See Ed Cohen on the importance of posing, in 'Posing the Question: Wilde, Wit, and the Ways of Man', in *Performance and Cultural Politics*, ed. Elin Diamond (London: Routledge, 1996), 35–47.

24. For more on Gilbert's elaborate parody of Victorian poetry, see Carolyn Williams, 'Parody and Poetic Tradition: Gilbert and Sullivan's *Patience*', in *Victorian Poetry* 46, no. 4 (2008): 375–403.

25. On the 'typing' of Wilde in the newspaper coverage of his trials, see Ed Cohen, 'Typing Wilde: Construing the "Desire to Appear to Be a Person Inclined to the Commission of the Gravest of All Offenses" ', in *Talk on the Wilde Side* (London: Routledge, 1992), 126–172.

26. This has given rise to much interesting critical discussion about whether or not a homosexual subtext can be read in *Patience*, even then, but certainly now. See 'Bunthorne in the History of Homosexuality', in Williams, *Gilbert and Sullivan*, 167–174.

27. It was conventional to identify fairies with women at this time, and *Iolanthe* exploits that convention.

28. For more on the dame figure, see Williams, *Gilbert and Sullivan*, 204–219.

29. With thanks to J. Donald Smith, who pointed out to me the similarity of this scene to my argument about the Fairy Queen and the tacit layering of genders found in that figure.

30. Tennyson frames his poem with an incident of cross-dressing in the Prologue, when Lilia drapes the statue of Sir Ralph with silk, creating a 'feudal warrior, lady-clad' (l. 119). At the same time, the college men recall Ralph's wife, a strong woman warrior who 'drove her foes with slaughter from her walls' (l. 123). The question of whether such women exist in the Victorian present leads Lilia to make the important feminist argument about socialization: 'There are thousands now | Such women, but convention beats them down; | It is bringing-up, no more than that' (ll. 127–129). It is within this frame that the story of Ida's separatist community unfolds, which includes the episode when the Prince and his friends dress as women in order to enter Ida's stronghold. Looking back from the poem's Conclusion, the tale's main narrator admits that the female members of the audience had wanted something less ambivalent, and 'had ever seem'd to wrestle with burlesque' (l. 116).

31. See Josephine Lee, *The Japan of Pure Invention: Gilbert and Sullivan's 'The Mikado'* (Minneapolis: University of Minnesota Press, 2010). Jonathan Miller's famous 'black and white' production for the English National Opera (1986), which placed the opera at an English seaside resort in the 1920s, avoids that particular problem—as have many other concept productions over the years, such as *The Swing Mikado* (1938), *The Hot Mikado* (1939), *The Cool Mikado* (1962), and *The Black Mikado* (1975).

32. For a discussion of 'The Town of Titipu' as neither Japanese nor English, and of *The Mikado* as a parody of Victorian *japonisme*, see Williams, *Gilbert and Sullivan*, 256–264 and 264–269 respectively.

33. On the verisimilitude of the setting for *H.M.S Pinafore*, see Bradley, *Complete Annotated Gilbert and Sullivan*, 118.

34. 'The past is a foreign country' is the first sentence of L. P. Hartley's novel *The Go-Between* (1953) and the title of an influential book on national heritage, nostalgia, and public memory by David Lowenthal (1985).

35. On the nineteenth-century history of changing laws of limited liability, see Albert I. Borowitz, 'Gilbert and Sullivan on Corporate Law', *American Bar Association Journal* 59 (1973): 1276–1281.

36. Though blackface minstrelsy began in the early 1830s, Christy's Minstrels (often called the Christy Minstrels) were launched by Edwin Christy in 1843 and set the form for the three-act minstrel show, including the minstrel 'line' that comes in Act 1. A second incarnation of the troupe (Raynor & Pierce's Christy Minstrels) opened in London at the St James's Theatre in 1857. Because of their success and celebrity, many companies claimed to be the 'original' Christy Minstrels. Starting in 1865, one such group began performing in St James's Hall (for a very long run, ending only in 1904).

BIBLIOGRAPHY

Ainger, Michael. *Gilbert and Sullivan: A Dual Biography*. Oxford: Oxford University Press, 2002.

Baily, Leslie. *Gilbert and Sullivan Book*. London: Spring Books, 1952.

Barrington, Rutland. *Rutland Barrington: A Record of Thirty-Five Years' Experience on the English Stage; By Himself*. With a Preface by William S. Gilbert. London: Grant, 1908.

Borowitz, Albert I. 'Gilbert and Sullivan on Corporate Law.' *American Bar Association Journal* 59 (1973): 1276–1281.

Bradley, Ian, ed. *The Complete Annotated Gilbert and Sullivan*. Oxford: Oxford University Press, 1996.

Burns, Elizabeth. *Theatricality: A Study of Convention in the Theatre and in Social Life.* New York: Prentice Hall, 1972.

Carlson, Marvin. ' "He Never Should Bow Down to a Domineering Frown": Class Tensions and Nautical Melodrama.' In *Melodrama: The Cultural Emergence of a Genre*, edited by Michael Hays and Anastasia Nicolopolou, 147–166. New York: St Martin's Press 1996.

Cohen, Ed. 'Posing the Question: Wilde, Wit, and the Ways of Man.' In *Performance and Cultural Politics*, edited by Elin Diamond, 35–47. London: Routlege, 1996.

Cohen, Ed. *Talk on the Wilde Side*. London: Routledge, 1992.

Cox-Ife, William. *W. S. Gilbert: Stage Director*. London: Dennis Dobson, 1977.

Fischler, Alan. *Modified Rapture: Comedy in W. S. Gilbert's Savoy Operas*. Charlottesville: University Press of Virginia, 1991.

Gilbert, W. S. *The Bab Ballads*, ed. James Ellis. Cambridge, MA: Harvard University Press, 1980.

Gilbert, W. S. *New and Original Extravaganzas*, edited by Isaac Goldberg. Boston: Luce, 1931.

Gilbert, W. S. *Original Plays*, 3rd ser. London: Chatto & Windus, 1923.

Gilbert, W. S., and Arthur Sullivan. *The Complete Plays of Gilbert and Sullivan*. New York: W. W. Norton & Co., Inc., 1976.

Goffman, Erving. *The Presentation of Self in Everyday Life*. New York: Anchor, 1959.

Goldberg, Isaac. *The Story of Gilbert and Sullivan; or The 'Compleat' Savoyard*. New York: Simon and Schuster, 1928.

Granville-Barker, Harley. 'Exit Planché—Enter Gilbert.' In *The Eighteen-Sixties: Essays by Fellows of the Royal Society of Literature*, edited by John Drinkwater, 102–148. Cambridge: Cambridge University Press, 1932.

Hughes, Gervase. *The Music of Arthur Sullivan*. New York: St Martin's Press, 1960.

Jacobs, Arthur. *Arthur Sullivan: A Victorian Musician*. 2nd ed. Oxford: Oxford University Press, 2003.

Lawrence, Arthur. *Sir Arthur Sullivan: Life Story, Letters, and Reminiscences*. Chicago: Stone, 1900.

Lee, Josephine. *The Japan of Pure Invention: Gilbert and Sullivan's 'The Mikado'.* Minneapolis: University of Minnesota Press, 2010.

Rees, Terence. *Thespis: A Gilbert and Sullivan Enigma*. London: Dillon's University Bookshop, 1964.

Stedman, Jane W. *Gilbert Before Sullivan: Six Comic Plays by W. S. Gilbert*. Chicago: University of Chicago Press, 1967.

Stedman, Jane W. *W. S. Gilbert: A Classic Victorian and His Theatre*. Oxford: Oxford University Press, 1996.

Steinbach, Susie L. 'The Melodramatic Contract: Breach of Promise and the Performance of Virtue.' *Nineteenth-Century Studies* 14 (2000): 1–34.

Steinbach, Susie L. 'Promises, Promises: Not Marrying in England, 1780–1920.' Unpublished PhD thesis, Yale University, 1996.

Sutton, Max Keith. *W. S. Gilbert*. Boston: Twayne, 1975.

Williams, Carolyn. *Gilbert and Sullivan: Gender, Genre, Parody*. New York: Columbia University Press, 2011.

Williams, Carolyn. 'Parody and Poetic Tradition: Gilbert and Sullivan's Patience.' *Victorian Poetry* 46, no. 4 (2008): 375–403.

CHAPTER 4

....

ENGLISH MUSICAL COMEDY, 1890–1924

....

STEPHEN BANFIELD

THE NARRATIVE

THE story goes something like this. Two men, Arthur Sullivan and William Schwenk Gilbert, created England's approved musical theatre, in the form of the Savoy comic operas, between the years 1875 and 1889. When they fell out, Sullivan's eye perennially on higher things, their tight cultural rein was loosened and a riot of 'gaiety' overtook the West End, as befitted the 'naughty nineties' and the frivolous, heartlessly capitalist Edwardian era that followed. This cornucopia of musical comedy, nurtured above all by the impresario George Edwardes, was served by an extraordinary welter of talent, names to conjure with that nonetheless blew away like thistledown after or in some cases before the First World War (Meyer Lutz, Edward Solomon, Sidney Jones, Alfred Cellier, Hamilton Clark, Lionel Monckton, Howard Talbot, Ivan Caryll, Paul Rubens, Leslie Stuart, Harold Fraser-Simson, Frederic Norton, Herman Finck, Arthur Wood, Ignatius de Orellana, Percy Greenbank, Owen Hall, James Tanner, Adrian Ross, Robert Courtneidge, Gertie Millar, Seymour Hicks, Ellaline Terriss, Phyllis Dare, Lily Elsie, George Grossmith Jr). The cuckoo in the nest was Broadway, first importing British musical comedies from which its creative practitioners such as Jerome Kern and the producer Charles Frohman learnt their trade, but by the 1920s exporting its own to the West End. When Kern supplied a series of scores for London's Winter Garden Theatre in 1921–3, Gershwin topping this with his *Primrose* for the same theatre in 1924, it was all over for the British. American superiority coupled with the built-in generic obsolescence of topical musical comedy (as opposed to that of the later 'integrated' musical) wiped the 'gaiety' years and its products clean from the slate, its shows never to be revived, its tunes no longer hummed or even remembered except in tiny pockets of cultural nostalgia, which means that they cannot have had the staying power—the quality?—to become standards.

Much of this story may be true, but almost every element of it, including many not mentioned above, bears cross-examination of one sort or another, with a view, first, to understanding more of the nature and dimensions of the product, including its artistic value and achievement, if any; and second, using those elements to illuminate the cultural context in new ways. This will entail delving more precisely and critically into the narrative, which has received precious little sustained research, surprising for a cultural phenomenon that has sat there like an archaeological mound for decades in full view of everybody.

THE THEATRES

First, the theatres themselves. This period of musical comedy, like every other, was a metropolitan and purely commercial phenomenon. What patrons bought into was a night in the West End or merchandise pertaining to the show that demonstrated that they had been up to town to see it or were at least aware of its currency. Investors, on their part, wanted to make money out of the show, so it needed to run as long as possible to highest capacity, which presumably also meant, then as now, that if a show was doing particularly well it might transfer to a larger theatre or to one that could charge higher ticket prices.

Table 4.1 shows which West End theatres were advertised on p. 8 of *The Times* on the day of the premiere of Gilbert and Sullivan's last comic opera (*The Gondoliers*, 7 December 1889) prior to their infamous 'carpet quarrel', and which ones were advertising exactly twenty years later. There is a lot more going on in the year of the later sample: twenty-two theatres advertise in 1889, twenty-seven in 1909, representing an overall audience capacity of about 25,000 and 32,000 respectively—an increase of 28 per cent by 1909.[1] This is more or less proportional to London's increase in population between these same years, which in itself was enormous.[2] No fewer than fourteen of the twenty-seven theatres advertising in 1909 had been built or completely rebuilt subsequent to 1889, so they will still have felt new. Yet there are actually more theatres playing what we would think of as musicals in 1889 than in 1909—six as opposed to five—and although the numerical audience capacity for these musicals has grown marginally by 1909, it represents a noticeably smaller percentage of the overall West End theatre public than in 1889: 21 per cent, as opposed to the earlier 26 per cent.

It is quite possible that the audience for musical drama has in the intervening years become smarter and more discriminating, hence limiting itself. It may also be significant that its theatres are among the newest. This was already true in 1889, when the theatres showing musicals were on average fifteen years old, as opposed to eighteen for the total of theatres advertising. In 1909 the theatres showing musicals are even newer less new than in 1889, on average fourteen years old, while the overall average is now twenty-four years old, so the difference has become more marked. Does going to

Table 4.1 West End theatres advertising in *The Times*, 7 December 1889 and 7 December 1909

Theatre	Built/ rebuilt	Capacity	Playing 7 Dec. 1889	Playing 7 Dec. 1909	Genre 1889	Genre 1909
Adelphi	1858	1,500	*London Day by Day* (George Sims)		straight play	
Alhambra	1884	2,208	*Our Army and Navy*	mixed bill	spectacular ballet (with vaudeville turns)	variety, spectacular ballet?
Apollo	1901	775		*The Follies*		revue/burlesque
Avenue	1882	679	*La Prima Donna* (H. B. Farnie and Alfred Murray)		**musical comedy**	
Comedy	1881	1,180	*Pink Dominos* (James Albery)	*Smith* (Somerset Maugham, prod. Frohman)	farce	comedy
Coronet	1898	1,143		*The Breed of the Treshams* (John Rutherford)		historical melodrama
Court	1870	465	*Aunt Jack* (Ralph Lumley, with Weedon Grossmith)		farce	
Covent Garden	1858	2,256			circus	
Criterion	1874	591	*Caste* (T. W. Robertson)	*Don* (Rudolf Besier)	comedy	sentimental comedy
Daly's	1893	1,200		*The Dollar Princess* (Leo Fall, Adrian Ross; prod. Edwardes)		**musical play**
Drury Lane	1812	2,200		*Aladdin* (Burnand) [beginning 26]		pantomime
Duke of York's	1892	650		*Arsène Lupin* (de Croisset and Leblanc; prod. Frohman, with Gerald du Maurier)		crime drama
Empire	1884	2,000		*Round the World*		spectacular ballet + variety

(continued)

Table 4.1 Continued

Theatre	Built/rebuilt	Capacity	Playing 7 Dec. 1889	Playing 7 Dec. 1909	Genre 1889	Genre 1909
Gaiety	1868 / 1903	2,000	Ruy Blas and the Blasé Roué (Meyer Lutz)	Our Miss Gibbs (Caryll and Monckton, Ross and Greenbank; prod. Edwardes)	**musical burlesque**	**musical comedy**
Garrick	1889	732	Tosca (Sardou)	Where Children Rule (Sydney Blow and Douglas Hoare; music by Edward Jones)	historical melodrama	children's play
Haymarket	1821	888	A Man's Shadow (Robert Buchanan, prod. Tree)	The Blue Bird (Maeterlinck)	melodrama	straight play
His Majesty's	1896	1,161		Beethoven (L. N. Parker, prod. Tree)		straight play, but with orch. of 50
London Pavilion*	1885	800		mixed bill		variety
Lyceum	1834 / 1904	2,100	The Dead Heart (Watts Phillips, prod. Irving)	East Lynne (Ellen Wood), then Aladdin	straight play	melodrama / pantomime
Lyric	1888	924	The Red Hussar (Stephens and Solomon)	Sir Walter Raleigh (William Devereux)	**comedy–opera**	historical romance
New Theatre	1903	872		The Woman in the Case (Clyde Fitch)		crime drama
Opera Comique	1870	862	Madcap Midge (Charles Fawcett)		comedy	
Palace	1891	1,283		mixed bill for the Cattle Show		variety
Playhouse	1907	800		Little Mrs Cummin (Richard Pryce)		comedy
Prince of Wales	1884	1,160	Paul Jones (Planquette, prod. Carl Rosa Opera Company)	Dear Little Denmark (Rubens)	**French operetta**	**musical comedy**

Theatre	Year(s)	Capacity	Production (Author)	Genre
Princess's*	1880	800	The Gold Craze (Brandon Thomas)	melodrama
Queen's	1907	990	The House Opposite (Perceval Landon)	thriller
Royalty*	1840	500	The New Corsican Brothers (Walter Slaughter)	**musical extravaganza**
Savoy	1881	1,158	The Gondoliers (Gilbert and Sullivan)	**comic opera**
Shaftesbury	1888	1,196	The Middle Man (Henry Arthur Jones)	straight play
			The Arcadians (Monckton and Talbot, prod. Courtneidge)	**musical play/ comedy**
St James's	1835	1,200	The Importance of Being Earnest (Wilde)	comedy
Strand	1882 / 1905	1,500 / 1,105	Our Flat (Mrs Musgrave)	farce
			The Merry Peasant (Leo Fall, Victor Leon)	**musical romance**
Terry's	1887	800	Sweet Lavender (Pinero)	comedy
Tivoli*	1890	1,000	mixed bill	variety
Toole's*	1882	600	The Bungalow (F. Horner)	farce
Vaudeville	1870	1,046	Joseph's Sweetheart (Robert Buchanan)	straight play
			The Brass Bottle (F. Anstey)	farce
Wyndham's	1899	750	The Little Damozel (Monckton Hoffe, with Charles Hawtrey)	comedy

Note: Musical comedies and comic operas are given in bold.

*Capacity is a guess.

Sources: See note 1.

a musical represent a particularly up-to-date experience for the audience, therefore? It probably does.

The table might tell various other stories. The range of theatrical experience on offer seems narrow. There is no Shakespeare at either date; there are no classics, old or modern (Ibsen, Chekhov, Shaw); and there is no serious opera or ballet (Covent Garden is hosting a circus). Overall, this is akin to a typical cinema bill today: a good deal of jobbing contemporaneity within standardized genres, in this case farce, domestic comedy, melodrama, crime, and extravaganza. But with hindsight, the package of musical comedy appears to have standardized itself between the earlier and the later date. In 1889, the six shows range from punning burlesque (*Ruy Blas and the Blasé Roué*), a genre soon to disappear, to *The Gondoliers*, the most sophisticated of Gilbert and Sullivan's comic operas (with the most substantial of their scores), via a French operetta produced by a visiting company and a couple of pieces whose composers' or adaptors' names now mean little.

In 1909, two shows each with music by a leading British and Austrian exponent are running: Monckton's *Our Miss Gibbs* (with Ivan Caryll) and *The Arcadians* (with Howard Talbot), and *The Merry Peasant* and *The Dollar Princess* by Leo Fall—second only to Franz Lehár in Continental eminence—and George Edwardes is producing one each of these at two of his three theatres, the Gaiety and Daly's.[3] Another big name, that of Paul Rubens, identifies the composer of the remaining show, *Dear Little Denmark*. The parallel has been drawn between this 'big name' era and the West End in the 1980s to 1990s, for as Kurt Gänzl pointed out, there was a moment in 1903 when Ivan Caryll had five shows running in the West End, just as Andrew Lloyd Webber had in 1990.[4] Caryll's shows advertised in *The Times*, 28 December 1903 were *The Earl and the Girl* at the Adelphi, *The Cherry Girl* at the Vaudeville, *The Girl from Kay's* at the Comedy, *The Orchid* at the Gaiety, and *The Duchess of Dantzic* at the Lyric. Clearly, therefore, one story that Table 4.1 does not tell of the years between 1889 and 1909 is that of peaks and troughs, for at this point in 1903 there were no fewer than nine musical comedies altogether in the West End, representing a combined audience capacity of 10,925. In addition to Caryll's five, *A Chinese Honeymoon* was running at the Strand, *My Lady Molly* at Terry's, *A Country Girl* at Daly's, and *Madame Sherry* at the Apollo, with scores respectively by Talbot (supplemented by Caryll), Sidney Jones, Lionel Monckton, and Hugo Felix. This may have been the high point of Edwardian musical comedy, as the period from 1890 to 1918 or thereabouts is by extension conveniently known.

The musical theatre industry, as we would now call it, of this period has not yet been measured, though William Archer laid the foundations for such a task as early as 1897 with his five-year analysis of currency and success in the West End. (He concluded that the preponderance of what he called 'musical farce', along with comic opera and pantomime, was 'altogether overwhelming'. But he also pointed out: 'It is impossible [. . .] without access to the books of the management, to measure with absolute precision the power of attraction exercised by any particular play.'[5]) We might start with the musicians, for whom, as Cyril Ehrlich points out, it was a major source of employment in the early twentieth century, when there were 'at least one thousand jobs' in the orchestra pits across the metropolitan area, for the largest variety theatres had bands of fifty or more (as did *Beethoven* at His Majesty's), and 'those at the Savoy, Daly's, Lyric, Gaiety, Shaftesbury, and Prince of Wales each averaged thirty'. The West End total must have been around 650–700 in 1909, while the Orchestral Association had calculated that the thirty-four pantomimes playing across London and its suburbs in February 1899 employed over 500 musicians, an average of fifteen each.[6] Unlike positions in concert and opera orchestras and their seaside counterparts during the summer, this was all-year-round employment within the metropolis, though hardly conducive to family life.

As for the composers, they were in it for the money, and the smartest of them—Monckton, Jones, Talbot—knew when to retire. At their death, these composers (Caryll, Cellier, Fraser-Simson, German, Jones, Lutz, MacCunn, Monckton, Norton, Rubens, Stuart, Sullivan, Talbot) left an average legacy of £23,855, including a staggering £79,518 on the part of Monckton and, if I have rightly understood his three probate grants to have been cumulative, £60,517 on the part of Rubens (at the age of 41). This figure includes the destitute: Hamish MacCunn, the sad case of a difficult, alienated character who left only £140, and Leslie Stuart, who squandered his fortune. Compare it with that for the British 'classical' composers of the same era (Bantock, Coleridge-Taylor, Cowen, Delius, Elgar, Goring Thomas, Holst, Mackenzie, Parry, Smyth, Somervell, Stanford, and Vaughan Williams): their average legacy was £12,075, barely half that of the musical theatre composers.[7] Elgar left £13,934, and only Vaughan Williams and Parry approached the wealth of the top four theatre composers (Monckton, Rubens, German, and Sullivan). True, longevity, lifestyle, family circumstances, and strategy all affected how people spent or saved their money and what it was worth at their death, and one would need to analyse their income patterns in order to say more. This has not yet been done except for Elgar, though something of the wherewithal for the task survives in the shape of Frederic Norton's personal account book.[8]

All but one of these composers were male, and the only women in the pit will have been the harpists, with the possible exception of a back-desk violinist. Female singing stars were another matter, with Zena Dare's legacy amounting to £63,373, Gertie Millar's £52,354, and Phyllis Dare's a more modest £8,238. The wealth at death of Florence Smithson is not known, but she was paid £30 a week for starring in *The Arcadians*, and that alone will have amounted to £3,510 over its 117-week run.[9] And chorus girls, whether 'Gaiety' or otherwise, must have numbered almost as many as the orchestral musicians, given the cheapness of labour and the tendency of the time to fill the stage with beauty (there were twenty-five girls on the stage in *Primrose*, in addition to the five female principals[10]). They opted for what was still considered a morally dubious career and could only be a short one. But they might marry into money or class, this being a leading trope of the period in both the press and the musical comedy plots themselves.[11]

THE SCORES

Composers who had undergone an expensive and painstaking musical education, including the obligatory period of study in Germany, might well begrudge the earnings of the hit songwriters, several of whom were musical amateurs born with a silver spoon in their mouth: Rubens the son of a Kensington stockbroker, Monckton of a barrister who was town clerk to the City of London; both sent to a top public school and then to Oxford to study law; both able to muster the confidence, financial support, and social networking advantages to start investing their passion for the stage until it should begin to reap dividends. The pattern is perennial, and would apply similarly on the acting front to the Monty Python team and their predecessors in the Cambridge Footlights, and to Cole Porter in particular among the 'golden age' Broadway composers, for it is not confined to England.

The divide, between aesthetic gentility and popular taste, is perceptible not just between concert and theatre composition but within the musical comedy scores. Take *The Arcadians* (1909). This show concerns a London businessman, James Smith, who crash-lands in an idyllic country forgotten by time. His mendacity immediately threatens to destabilize the Arcadians, who dip him in the Well of Truth, to emerge as Simplicitas, with whom they then travel to London in order to reform its wickedness. Simplicitas (Smith) soon cashes in on their novelty value, and when the Arcadians see through this, all parties return to their homes and ways. In *The Arcadians*, Talbot was the musical professional, having studied with Parry at the Royal College of Music, Monckton the amateur. But the divide was also the fusion; one of the great successes of Edwardian musical comedy, unrecognized though it remains in scholarship and cultural memory, was precisely this fusion of tastes which the product represented in musical terms. Let us see how it works in this particular score.

Talbot was a theatre conductor, and may even have orchestrated *The Arcadians* (it is symptomatic of the state of the subject that we do not know; another candidate would be Arthur Wood, musical director of the original production). To Talbot's musical expertise were entrusted, in addition to quite a few of the songs, most of the extended and ensemble set pieces. Of these, in Act I he wrote the music for the introduction and opening chorus, the arrival of the aeroplane, the seizure of Smith, and the finale. The shower chorus and racing finale in Act II are his, as is the extended introduction to Act III. From the outset he proves equal to the wittily gentle conceit of innocent Arcadia versus wicked London that sustains the show, unifying the two worlds musically when for the underscoring of the crucial horse race he reuses both the three-note downward scale that launches the show's opening words ('Arcadians are we') and that number's refrain motif ('In Arcady life flows along'), which has also closed the Act I finale. Moreover, when the Act I curtain rises to music audibly reminiscent of what had brought it down in that final Gilbert and Sullivan hit, 'Dance a Cachucha' from *The Gondoliers*, we are already being made aware of the fragility as well as renewal of cultural tradition. For operetta decorum will soon be under threat, though it is nicely updated too in Talbot's pastoral progressions (chords I–vi–I and parallel-triad vi–V). His masterstroke is to accompany those very first words with a diminished seventh that pulls heartbreakingly against the tonic bass (Ex. 4.1). With this, we already know that the Arcadians' world, so beautiful and delicate—and the decor must have had the audience already gasping at curtain-up eight bars earlier (see Figure 4.1)[12]—will never survive the intrusion of capitalism in the shape of Smith, his aeroplane, and his mendacity.

EXAMPLE 4.1 From *The Arcadians*, Act I, opening chorus.

FIGURE 4.1 Dan Rolyat (as James Smith) unexpectedly finds himself in Arcadia. From the original London production of *The Arcadians*, Shaftesbury Theatre 1909, showing part of the Act I setting.

BAMS Collection. Courtesy of ArenaPal.

Talbot's Act I finale is nothing short of symphonic in its emotional scope, which, were it not for the two acts to follow, would represent the moral urgency of an ecological imperative, and has all the passion of Tchaikovsky (Ex. 4.2). (At the same time it highlights Florence Smithson's soprano voice with the only top B heard in the show until

EXAMPLE 4.2 From *The Arcadians*, Act I, finale.

'Come Back to Arcady', 'My Heart Flies Homing', and 'Light Is My Heart'—most or all of these added for her at various times later in the run—showcase even higher notes in Act III.[13])

But two further acts do follow, deliciously undercutting the Arcadians' earnestness and mocking their vegetarian, free-love, communist, talk-to-the-animals pretension just as much as the Londoners' frivolity and greed. After all, at Smithson's climactic moment, which was also the climactic moment of the British Empire in terms of its extent and power, the smug Arcadians are setting out as missionaries to civilize a savage country, though Sombra finally acknowledges, in almost the final words of the show: 'He has come back to his people. Let us go to ours . . . Our mission to England has failed.'[14] This is social satire with an edge well beyond Gilbert and Sullivan.

If the edge has not been appreciated, it is because musical comedy's appeal was more demotic, more vulgar than that of the Savoy operas. Its cultural status and, more important, its cultural resilience in terms of outliving immediate fashion were correspondingly lower. The new element came from music hall, and Monckton's tunes and their dramatic function supplied it. His melodies, harmonies, and rhythms were gestural in ways more obviously aligned with star turns on the stage than with the balletic, prosy, or sentimental stances of Gilbert and Sullivan's performers. The musical theatre star had to have the audience in the palm of their hand, and would achieve this by moving around the stage and/or gesturing in irresistible ways. Millie Legarde's performance of the young Kern's hit song 'How'd You Like to Spoon with Me?' at the Palace Theatre in February 1906, as part of turn 14 in a mammoth 16-turn variety show, evoked this response from a journalist: '[She was] addressing herself to the boxes, stalls, and gallery. As I never refuse any invitation of this description I naturally left my seat after the second verse, when the question was personally addressed to me'—a moment which survives photographically, showing Legarde in a frilly dress leaning out over the cornet players in the orchestra towards four dudes in a stalls box, one of them Kern himself.[15]

Of the five or so musical encouragements or concomitants to such movement and gesturing—musicologists call them topics—that might be identified in Monckton's style as exemplified in *The Arcadians*, it is interesting that already they seem all to come from abroad, from the USA or from Lehár's Vienna. (Many of Sullivan's were indigenous or from France.) One is the military two-step, a 6/8 rhythm crying out for a stage walk-around and as a cultural topic in dance and music dating back to John Philip Sousa's 'Washington Post' march of 1889. The Act II number 'Back Your Fancy' exemplifies both the rhythm and the very idea of irresistibility, particularly in the refrain, where the off-beat 'pah's of the standard 'oompah' accompaniment have lifted themselves free of the tonic pedal drone that more sheepishly accompanied the verse section of the song in a nod back towards Sullivan, in whose comic operas such a paean to worldliness ('Come and Have a Gamble') would of course have been unthinkable (Ex. 4.3). Note, too, the snook-cocking intonation (scale degrees five to three) of the drawn-out feminine rhyme 'gamble', confirmed as burlesque when its counterpart, 'scramble', is sung to the flat sixth degree. Hubert Parry would have condemned these inflections as cockney cheek.[16] Simplicitas's Act III song 'All down Piccadilly' offers a second topic, a different kind of stage strut, this time in 2/4 metre and more of a quick march, whose almost onomato-poeic verbal element in the refrain, '-dilly, dilly, dilly, dilly', is surely meant to trigger the kind of audience handclapping that conventionally survives today in performances of the elder Strauss's 'Radetzky March'.

A third topic would be the smooth, seductive kind of melody that sits with some-what insolent freedom athwart its conventional accompaniment. Monckton writes just such a kind of melody in the refrain of 'Truth Is So Beautiful', whose words as sung by Simplicitas and his companions ring as cynically as the tune's repeated seventh and sixth

EXAMPLE 4.3 From *The Arcadians*, Act II, 'Back Your Fancy'.

degrees sound unobliged to their tonic harmony. The same thing can be heard in the 'trio' section of Monckton's Act II opening number, 'We Bow at the Altar of Fashion', whose words again reify society glitter, the tune again smoothing over any kind of harmonic difficulty its freedom might have been thought to raise. Plentiful examples of this melodic tradition can be heard in Lehár's *The Merry Widow*, which had become a huge hit in London in 1907.

The fourth topic, a matter of contrast in character and plot, is deliberately more down-market in connotation, and best labelled that of the Bowery waltz, a genre originating in the song 'The Bowery' from the American musical comedy *A Trip to Chinatown* (1891) as the self-deprecating monologue of the down-at-heel loser, trundling along seedily in 3/4 time without the dotted-note propulsions and other elements of melodic kinesis found in a good ballroom waltz. The winning—or rather losing—example of this in *The Arcadians*, 'My Motter', sung lugubriously by Peter Doody, the jockey who has never won a race, was actually composed by Talbot, but Monckton had a genius for making such tunes attractive and inventive, and 'The Girl with a Brogue', sung by Eileen in Act II, is really another Bowery waltz, its final period stopping not two bars before the end, as is standard, but one bar later, with repeated notes in between, to make it sound folky and Irish. Eileen is the down-home heroine, contrasting with the loftiness of Sombra.

One wonders whether Phyllis Dare, who played Eileen, was intended as the real star of *The Arcadians* until overtaken by Florence Smithson as Sombra, for the two numbers recorded in 1909 were hers—'The Girl with a Brogue' and 'Bring Me a Rose'—and fine recordings they are.[17] 'Bring Me a Rose' must have been dropped, for it is not in later printings of the score, but it became popular in America and its lyrics (by Monckton and Arthur Wimperis) are even quoted in John Dos Passos's huge novel *USA*.[18] A real stomper of a tune, and for Monckton relatively unusual in having a full thirty-two-bar refrain rather than a shorter one, it illustrates our fifth and final musical topic, Monckton's awareness of American syncopation, here capping the apex of the refrain's final period—just enough of it to keep the presentational dynamic up to date. Such syncopation, found also at the start of the refrain of 'Charming Weather' in Act II, is hardly noticed, but injects something, however slight, of the cakewalk's propulsion into a singer's stance.[19]

THE SCRIPTS

The scripts—book and lyrics—of these musical comedies are unstable entities, just like the scores but in certain respects more so. It is difficult to be sure whether the two lines of dialogue from *The Arcadians* quoted earlier were spoken on stage in 1909. Recourse to the Lord Chamberlain's Plays in the British Library can confirm what was drafted prior to the original production but not what was performed in the opening run. The scholar takes as his or her text whatever version of a script, if any, is available, normally an 'acting edition' published by Samuel French or Emile Littler, in which there is no way of knowing what has been updated. My copy of *The Arcadians* script is copyrighted 1945. My script of *The Country Girl* bears no date other than the original one of 1902 but must have been issued nearly fifty years later, because it advertises the libretto of *Annie Get Your Gun* on the back cover.

The scripts were generally star vehicles, as is evident from Dan Rolyat's first dialogue exchanges as Smith in *The Arcadians*, given below in the version originally presented to the Lord Chamberlain, i.e. before the first performance. But they were also wordy, as can be seen from what was later omitted or substituted (respectively crossed out and in square brackets below) to produce the current published version:

ASTROPHEL   ~~Hail, stranger!~~ Hail!
SMITH   ~~Eh, is it? I should have thought it was too warm for hail.~~ [I don't care if it snows.] But you know your own climate best. What place is this?
ASTROPHEL   This is Arcadia.
SMITH   I ~~ha'~~ve smoked your mixture, but I didn't know it was on the map. ~~Well, could~~ [Can] you recommend me to a good hotel—Mr—er—let's see, what's your name?
ASTROPHEL   Astrophel.

SMITH   [Oh! (*As if he had heard imperfectly.*)] ~~And you'll~~ Excuse me—which is Mrs ~~Astrophel~~ [Astrachan]?
ASTROPHEL   Mrs? In Arcadia we do not know what Mrs means.
SMITH   Lucky beggar![20]

Rolyat ('Taylor' backwards), who was actually married to Smithson, was an acrobatic comic. At this point he has just made his entrance in a spectacular fall from an aeroplane, and has to follow up that coup de théâtre by consolidating and intensifying his presence in whatever ways he can—a laugh in every line (including an added one in the updated version), punning ripostes that sustain the physical speed and energy (perhaps coming too fast for them all to be grasped), a maddening mutual incomprehension between the two speakers, and those vulgar asides, presumably aimed at the audience. Painful in the wrong hands, these minute textual 'events' would naturally have to be further tailored and adjusted to the contemporary techniques, including their way of speaking, of any new star recreating the role, not to mention to the changing tastes of political (in)correctness. Yet it is easy to exaggerate this theatrical instability. We still accept and enjoy the musical comedy of Astaire and Rogers, after all, whose dialogue is inexorably fixed in film, because we can still experience it with the stars for whom it was written, so it cannot simply be said that dialogue in the commercial musical theatre dies when it ceases to be contemporary popular culture.

Another consideration lies in the ongoing national traditions of humour. American humour conquered musicals, probably thanks to Mark Twain first and the global reach of sound film second, but some of the deadpan English elements of W. S. Gilbert resurfaced in Monty Python, and they are to be discovered in the interim in many an Edwardian musical comedy, as when the humourless procession of Quakers is suddenly left bawling 'our quiet meeting' (twice, in the best operatic tradition) at a gap in the texture of the opening chorus of *The Quaker Girl*. Again in Act I of *The Quaker Girl*, the silly, rapturous duet between the secondary lovers, 'Wonderful', is sung to a 9/8 tune by Monckton that is as English, redolent of country dance, as it is original. The pair have just reunited in the shires on Charteris's arrival from Paris on the 'Calais boat express', and the song is a tissue of lyrics such as these:

CHARTERIS
Like a nectar draught to me
Was the cup of Dover tea
   And the food was rapture edible—
   MATHILDE [*wondering*]
That is quite incredible!
   CHARTERIS
There was not a moment's loss
When I got to Charing Cross
   For the porters all were dutiful
   MATHILDE [*delighted*]
Oh they must be beautiful!

Jokes about railway food do not age; nor does the incongruous sound of 'Charing Cross' in a lyrical context.

The real problem with the scripts of the West End's golden age of musical comedy—let us call it that—is that we have not bothered to study them. With the notable exceptions of Len Platt and Peter Bailey,[21] few authors writing about the genre and period show evidence of opening up a script and reading it, or even of analysing the lyrics that were published profusely and attractively in the vocal scores of the shows, artefacts that can still be found second-hand at modest cost and were clearly, and deservedly, drawing-room materialities of some currency for—how long?—two generations? The individual numbers are gold mines of charm and wit in music and lyrics, and rarely can more rhymes—twelve—have been squeezed out of a vowel than Adrian Ross does in 'The Rajah of Bhong' from *A Country Girl* (1902). The cleverness here is doubled because on each occasion the syllable preceding the 'Bhong' rhyme has been prepared for by its own rhyme, so that the anticipation of how it will tie in is sustained through the whole of each triolet, as in the following:

> When I'm at home, I have bards that bring
> Poems of praise in a sort of sing-
> Song—the Rajah of Bhong.

The other eleven rhymes are '[any]thing wrong', 'sidelong', 'still strong', 'ding-dong', 'bass gong', '*vivant*', 'ping-pong', '*chantant*', 'Sou-Chong', '[gay] *Con-tin-ong*', and, capping them all, 'Hong Kong'. Have ever the earnestness of orientalism and the might of the British Empire been so delightfully punctured? But as always, one has to hear the musical rhythm to get the full comic effect. Here Monckton establishes the topic as a mock-pompous teddy-bears'-picnic march replete with long notes held up by po-faced, whole-bar suspensions on the '-ong' rhymes. More than that, one would have to be able to hear the orchestration (is that still feasible? were there gong strokes?).[22] And above all one would have had to *see* the number: the Devon villagers 'reluctantly' made to kow-tow, heads to the ground, rising every time they sing their repeated line 'The Rajah of Bhong'; the Indian Princess casting not so much 'shy and sidelong' glances at her husband-to-be but determined ones at anyone else in the 'county' milieu who may suit this iron-willed visitor better; and the Rajah himself, played by the Gilbert and Sullivan veteran Rutland Barrington (the original Pooh-Bah in *The Mikado*), seemingly in some form of blackface, its solecism neatly offloaded from the authors on to the character, for the Rajah is really the Englishman Quinton Raikes who has faked his own death mountaineering in the Himalayas in order to get away from his wife.

As for the plots, there is nothing new under the sun, and even *The Arcadians* uses many of the tropes of *Orpheus in the Underworld* (1858). *A Country Girl* works from the same premises as John Burgoyne's *The Lord of the Manor* of 120 years earlier, which was a hit at Drury Lane in 1780 with a score by William Jackson of Exeter. These two plays have the following elements in common: an Act I rural setting with the entrance to a country estate and house on one side of the stage and a farmhouse or cottage on the other; a nouveau riche tenant of the manor and his ineffectual son taking up residence; three local lasses of varying temperament who are or get entangled with the various male characters (all three suitably married off in *A Country Girl* but only one in *The Lord of the Manor*); a plot hinging on an event characteristically disruptive of rural life, military recruitment in the one case, an election in the other; a leading man returning from his enforced travels and likely to join or rejoin the service for want of being able to marry his sweetheart; a character trying to hide his true identity in a manner early made clear to the audience but only later to those around him; and a comic male servant as focus for the more farcical elements of humour. It is easy enough to imagine the slots for songs, and the types of song, as each of these characters and their histories and dilemmas are introduced, and they are not much different in 1902 from what they were in 1780. Continuity is an element of the generic story we have desperately avoided telling, yet much was interchangeable or recurrent over several centuries in the mechanics of musical comedy insofar as these boiled down to money, mistaken identity, and marriage as the dramatic stock-in-trade, deployed in terms of accommodation (or not) between classes, regions (in Edwardian musical comedy, London and the country), and lifestyles.[23] These three 'm's went together because in a capitalist society appropriate and sustaining relationships have had to be discovered in these terms, with errors demonstrated as a warning or a yardstick for true love and its ultimate purpose, propagation of the race.

The American musical, it has been said, triumphed because it could celebrate the abundance that helps solve and joyfully perpetuates this equation.[24] But belle époque England, especially London, acted out the myth of abundance too, and this certainly shows in the musical comedies. The bewildering overload of characters from the metropolis that descends on the Devon village in the course of Act I of *A Country Girl* is in itself a measure of theatrical richness, of that opulence which in the end made the Edwardian musical—indeed the Edwardian era—what it was. First enter the local harvesters, followed by the new squire and his shooting party. Already the abundance of produce, vegetable and animal, has been signalled. The squire's son has the ambition of a suffix (MP), his interlocutor the prefix 'Captain'. A rich townswoman, Mrs Quinton Raikes, enters next with her party of canvassers. Sophie her dressmaker follows, first of the local girls with metropolitan pretensions (she has put on a posh accent, succeeded in working in London, and has two assistants). Geoffrey Challoner, son of the ousted squire, then enters in naval officer's uniform with a servant, the comic lead Barry. Then comes the second local girl, the vivacious Nan, her tokens of abundance a rich Devonshire accent, praise of her county's human resources, and a fund of coquetry. Her interlocuter is titled 'Major'. Marjory, the leading woman and third local girl, is the following entrant: she has become a famous singer in London but pretends she is in service there. Finally—it has all been building up to this—the Rajah and his princess process in, having arrived, presumably at Plymouth, on the same ship as Challoner and Barry. Perhaps, then, the very point of those lengthy first acts of musicals has been freely to pile on more and more. In this case, the act contains only one set, rather than the dazzling array of new ones that would accrue with musicals borrowing from the revue mould, but new characters mean new colourful costumes, whose contrast and variety by the time most of their wearers are assembled onstage for the act finale can easily be imagined. In *A Country Girl* the second-act setting is a London ball, so that a grand suite of rooms (in the Ministry of Fine Arts), continuous music, and an even more dazzling array of costumes are implied. To the general fancy dress (*Bal à la Directoire*) are added the layers of disguise of three gate-crashers: Sophie, pretending to be a debutante, Nan (unannounced, in a crinoline), and Barry in drag, who as the star of the act sports three different costumes during the course of it.

THE CONTEXTS

The final section of this essay proposes some of the contexts within which English musical comedy of the 1890–1924 period—its moment, its history—operated. They might be grouped into three: contexts of self-celebration, self-investment, and self-destruction. Each of these can be related to a richness and variety of material trace, thus copious topics or approaches for future research easily suggest themselves (to repeat, there has not been much past research).

Self-celebration lies at the heart of the plots, the lyrics, many of the jokes in the dialogue, and the settings. The shows' 'knowingness', as Bailey analyses it, picking up on Archer, might be a dubious quality, but this was a society confident with its own role and progress, however much it might pretend to criticize its capitalism.[25] The obvious reason for the word 'girl' in so many of the titles of the shows was to demonstrate that those with youth, (female) gender, and any origin could succeed against whatever odds the plot might stack against them. The girl might be Quaker, from the country, from Yorkshire ('our Miss Gibbs'), from the Port Sunlight soap factory, or from the Gaiety chorus line; she could still expect to find a handsome, healthy, classy, and potentially prosperous man, normally in or from London. (What the lower-class man might aspire to was less clear, and in a trenchant paragraph, Bailey sums up the male characters of English musical comedy as 'in general a debilitated lot'.[26]) Metropolitan modernity was key to the enterprise,[27] and *Our Miss Gibbs* (1909) celebrates no fewer than three of London's iconic attractions. Miss Gibbs works in 'Garrod's' department store, where the first act is set (and references to Selfridge's, which opened two months after *Our Miss Gibbs*, can be found in other shows, including *The Arcadians*). Act II takes place at the White City exhibition—though setting a musical at or in relation to an international exposition was a tradition that went back at least to Offenbach's *La Vie parisienne* of 1866 and would continue long into the twentieth century. The third icon is the Crystal Palace with its national brass band contests, in one of which Mary Gibbs's cousin Timothy is competing as a euphonium player. As for self-referentiality, the final song of the West End production of *To-night's the Night* (1915, not to be confused with the 2003 Ben Elton show), 'I Could Love You If I Tried', seems to salute the entire genre in its incorporation of the names of well over a dozen musical comedy stars, along with a few from other fields of performance.

The exercise was one of consumerist mutuality, as Joel Kaplan and Sheila Stowell make clear in *Theatre and Fashion*. Couturier and department-store dress styles were depicted on stage, and the leading names supplied costumes.[28] Patrons would presumably visit the theatre wearing something comparable. There is a number called 'Hats' in the first act of *Our Miss Gibbs*, musically as well as sartorially up to date, for the parade of Parisian imports is accompanied by an uncanny foretaste of Debussy's 'La fille aux cheveux de lin'.[29] One retailer of women's clothing, Hogg & Co. of Hampstead Heath, cashed in on the consumer equation by dubbing three of its blouses the 'Sophie', the 'Marjory', and the 'Nan' (in increasing order of cost) and advertising them in the issue of *The Play Pictorial* that covered *A Country Girl* (see Figure 4.3).[30] This piece of opportunistic fatuity could be planned, because *A Country Girl* was already running when *The Play Pictorial* was founded, and the magazine did not cover the show until some months later.

Another locus for confidence, admiration, and commitment (and, as we have seen, satire) was the Empire and the armed forces needed to secure and maintain it. By the turn of the twentieth century, this was as much a matter of trade with the settler Dominions as of lordship over alien races, thus it was self-investment as well, pointed out by Archer in 1897 when he claimed that 'some five-and-twenty theatres in the West End of London are practically the only places in the British Empire where new plays of any importance are produced, [and at least since 1893] no play of any moment has been produced in the Provinces or Colonies and not seen in London'.[31] Jeffrey Richards has dealt comprehensively with this aspect of musical comedy of the period in *Imperialism and Music*, pointing out how frequently Hayden Coffin was cast as the dashing—though frankly boring—naval hero, his role in *A Country Girl*. By 1914 the character of Challoner included a patriotic song by Monckton, 'The Sailor-man', with lines such as 'He can have some fun with a twelve inch gun'.[32]

The reach and self-investment of the English musical theatre industry were impressive. Not only did Edwardes and other impresarios send out touring companies to the provinces while shows were still playing in London, but Edwardes was also able by extension to tour *A Gaiety Girl* right round the world in 1894–5; its travelling conductor, the young Granville Bantock, wrote a book about it.[33] Franchised agents such as J. C. Williamson in Australia brought the shows within their own permanent purview under licence from London.[34] For this and other reasons it would be a severe mistake to measure the cultural weight and influence of the genre of musical comedy and of individual shows within it by their West End runs alone, by their 'power of attraction' there. First, their spin-offs and merchandising were as rife then as now, which any issue of *The Play Pictorial* demonstrates: stars endorsing hand creams, dresses being copied and sold, sheet music and (already by 1902) recordings disseminating the hit numbers to living rooms and palm courts, bandstands and punts, across the country. Its October 1924 issue, covering *Primrose*, even had an article on types of car body, celebrating in passing the completion of the Great West Road, not a coincidental matter where a musical set upstream on the

609.R.   MISS GERTIE MILLAR   BEAGLES POSTCARDS
AS 'PRUDENCE' IN "THE QUAKER GIRL."

FIGURE 4.2 A new means of merchandising: picture postcard of Gertie Millar as Prudence in *The Quaker Girl*, Adelphi Theatre 1910.

Postcard provided by the editors.

Thames was concerned.[35] The picture postcard was another new merchandising outlet, which Viv Gardner has investigated in relation to Gertie Millar (see Figure 4.2).[36]

By such means, a breadth of commercial self-interest was maintained, but the second, quite different area of self-investment was a matter of length: the shows' afterlives in other countries and in amateur productions. The former were not inconsiderable, and it seems that professional productions survived longer, between the wars, abroad than in Britain. In his autobiography, Ernest Irving refers to two rival productions of *The Geisha* in Madrid in 1907, one of them by an Italian company,[37] and I possess a printed libretto of *La bella fanciulla del villaggio: Operetta inglese in tre atti*, 'Musica del Maestro L Monckton'. As for amateur productions in Britain and the English-speaking world, these

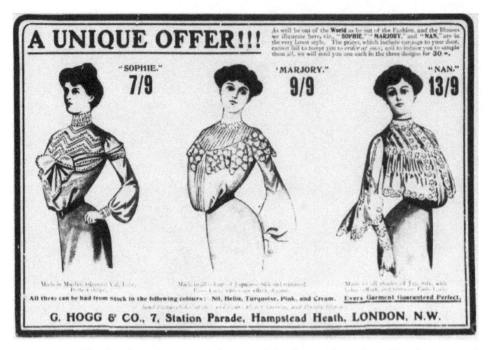

FIGURE 4.3 Merchandise relating to *A Country Girl*, advertisement from *The Play Pictorial*, November 1902.

were rarely if ever considered by scholars until John Lowerson published his *Amateur Operatics: A Social and Cultural History* in 2005, which reminded us that Baden-Powell had played the comic Chinese lead in *The Geisha* in Simla, India, within a year or so of its London premiere of 1896, and that professional directors and musical directors were much in demand around the country when amateur societies were putting on a show.[38] Thus the old musical comedies continued to generate jobs, and presumably royalties for the descendants of the original investors, for half a century or more, since productions of *A Country Girl*, to take just one example, can be found in the provinces even after the Second World War—Lichfield 1947, Dundee and Nottingham 1948, Hessle 1949, Grangetown 1950—until the earlier 1950s, when they seem rather suddenly to have stopped, though at this point so does the consolidated availability of British newspapers online, so it is difficult to be sure.[39] In Australia, where the equivalent data continues to the end of the century, an amateur production of *A Country Girl* can still be found in Brisbane in 1951, but nothing after that, although there was a studio broadcast in 1958.[40]

When values change, what has been invested in can suddenly become worthless, because nobody wants it. Self-destruction was built into the very contemporaneity of Edwardian musical comedy, whose meanings ceased to be legible with the shifts in taste that the First World War brought about. This may seem to contradict the point made earlier about the Astaire/Rogers films, and to square the two assertions would necessitate another of those research projects begging to be undertaken: the study of performance practice. Period recordings (and some later footage of one or two stars) offer ample scope for this, and the more alien or inexplicable a star's manner of speaking, singing, and projecting appears now, the further its semiotics have to be probed if anything at all is to be explained.[41] To us, a less satisfying or appropriate rendition of 'Any Old Night' than the younger George Grossmith's is scarcely to be imagined.[42] Clearly the meaning of ragtime has changed utterly, and what we might want to associate with the casual, the smug, the cool—black chic, sexual mastery—was not a performance option for him. He is simply an upper-class twit making a huge fool of himself.

The war, we are told, changed everything. Noël Coward linked it eloquently with the invasion of the new American rhythms. Praising the 'fine musical achievements' of Monckton et al. in 'scores of a quality that has never been equalled in this country since the 1914–18 war', he described how 'English composers [. . .] fell back in some disorder' at the onslaught of the 'vital Negro-Jewish rhythms from the New World'. Young English talent was otherwise occupied, and in time decimated, on the battlefields, and 'when finally the surviving boys came home, it was to an occupied country; the American victory was a fait accompli'. A moment for British talent 'to rally, to profit by defeat, to absorb and utilize the new, exciting rhythms from over the water' was lost: 'this was either beyond our capacity or we were too tired to attempt it'.[43] He was probably right, for success in the musical theatre has generally necessitated youth, and it was youth that was lacking.

Finessing this picture changes it, however. American rhythmic brashness, as we have seen, was already making inroads long before the war, and the generally demure score for *Sergeant Brue* (1904) by Liza Lehmann (the only woman among this extended team of men), contains, perhaps precisely because it was demure, an interpolated coon song by J. B. Mullen, 'Under a Panama', whose verse section is clearly ragtime. In *The Quaker Girl* (1910) the heroine actually marries 'Tony from America', and indeed the depth of his anger with her before all misunderstandings are finally sorted out seems to foreshadow that of John Kent in Kern and Harbach's *Roberta*, as do a number of other elements in the plot and setting. More important, there was surely a ripe moment not long into the war when English and American styles seemed to be fusing. The show was *To-night's the Night*, its score written by Rubens for New York, with which the Gaiety reopened in 1915 and Grossmith returned to Britain. In some respects the most sparkling of all the scores of the era, its concise first-act finale adopts Kern's later policy of building it musically around psychologically apt reprises, though Caryll was already beginning to do this in *Our Miss Gibbs*. (All such trends and precedents need further testing, preferably on the entire repertoire.) 'Boots and Shoes' and 'Pink and White' are differing 'charm' numbers of some memorability; and 'I Could Love You If I Tried' has already been mentioned. What made *To-night's the Night* stand out above all, however, was the interpolation of two songs by Kern, though by no means his first for the West End, for he had been supplying them for the best part of a decade. 'Any Old Night', which he wrote with Otto Motzan, is vintage ragtime: of the moment, but generic. The other song, 'They Didn't Believe Me', blows the stylistic world wide open. It had already appeared in New York in a British show, *The Girl from Utah*, but was new to London. David Lloyd George, soon to become prime minister, went to see *To-night's the Night*.

Backstage afterwards, he told Grossmith, who really couldn't sing it, that 'They Didn't Believe Me' was the most haunting and inspiring melody he had ever heard.[44] As the first 4/4 ballad to become the principal song in a musical, 'haunting' was a risky quality that clearly paid off, for a fulfilled love song here succeeds in evoking profound sadness through the three slow upbeats, the downward melodic seventh, the little triplet figure, the descanting thirds in the accompaniment at the mention of marriage, and above all the modulation to the mediant minor at the halfway point of Kern's long refrain (which, however, owes not a little to the even more gangly melodies of Leslie Stuart). Musical comedy had grown up.

Other questions can be raised about continuity and disruption. The extent to which the war may have destroyed the mould of musical comedy as modernity with its two big hits, Norton's *Chu Chin Chow* (1916) and Fraser-Simson's *The Maid of the Mountains* (1917), needs investigation and has probably been underestimated. The latter show was a romantic operetta about brigands set in some unspecified but presumably Mediterranean country, the former a concoction even more unrelated to anything else in this chapter—a bloodthirsty orientalist fantasy more like a pantomime than a social comedy. Was this what a new clientele wanted: escapism? Was the image smashed by an audience of privates on leave, who will have had little enough reason to wallow in social congratulation through the rituals of self-depiction? If that was the case, then the contribution of American creators after the war begins to look more like business as usual than we have thought it. Kern's *Sally*, the first of the four Winter Garden musicals (though written for Broadway), could still open with a cachucha, and its first ragtime syncopation does not arrive until p. 40 of the vocal score. His next Winter Garden show, specifically written for London the following year (1922), was called *The Cabaret Girl*, a title manifestly in the pre-war tradition. Its book and lyrics were by two Englishmen, P. G. Wodehouse and George Grossmith, and its first act was set in a London shop—a music shop, with Edward Elgar on the phone at curtain-up—followed by a second set in an English village, with two vicars complicating the finale à la Gilbert and Sullivan. Gershwin's *Primrose*, fourth and last of the Winter Garden musicals, was scarcely less in tune with British traditions, as had been a number of his earlier musical theatre numbers such as 'The Love of a Wife' from *La La Lucille* of 1919, with its echoes of 'I Do Love to Be Beside the Seaside'.

How the history of English musical comedy, 1890–1924, is told, then, will differ according to the questions being asked and the data being sought out, which should continue to unfold and develop. Many further questions already suggest themselves.[45] Where do Edward German (*Merrie England*, 1902; *Tom Jones*, 1907) and light opera fit in—or start up, in the case of the finales of the musical comedies and the types of voice singing the numbers? Should a taxonomy of genre be attempted, and if so, according to theatre (Daly's versus the Gaiety?), audience, performer, impresario, format (revue?—should *The Bing Boys Are Here* (1916) have been mentioned, as the third big wartime hit, while not a narrative musical comedy?), or some other criterion that might or might not have been culturally signalled at the time? The biggest question, of course, is whether the shows discussed in this chapter—and those for which no room was found, such as *Florodora* (1899)—have any kind of performance future. Many pundits, including Thomas Piketty, have stressed the parallels between social and economic conditions in the decades prior to the First World War and conditions now.[46] Thus some of the sharper observations in the plots, lyrics, and dialogue resonate again. One does not expect the music to do so, but one never knows.

NOTES

1. Theatre capacities and dates of erection or rebuilding are taken from a variety of Internet sources and from John Earl and Michael Sell, eds., *The Theatres Trust Guide to British Theatres 1750–1950: A Gazetteer* (London: A. and C. Black, 2000). Thomas Postlewait's article, 'George Edwardes and Musical Comedy: The Transformation of London Theatre and Society, 1878–1914', in *The Performing Century: Nineteenth-Century Theatre's History*, ed. Tracy C. Davis and Peter Holland (Basingstoke: Palgrave Macmillan, 2007), 99, refers to 100,000 people who 'poured into' the West End every evening for entertainment, but does not give precise sources; it is difficult to see how this figure relates to the 30,000-odd implied by capacity of the theatres, though music halls and early cinemas with their double showings will certainly have increased it.

2. GB Historical GIS / University of Portsmouth, London GovOf through time | Population Statistics | Total Population, *A Vision of Britain through Time*. http://www.visionofbritain. org.uk/unit/10097836/cube/TOT_POP, accessed 13 July 2016.

3. For a complete list of Edwardes's London musical shows, see Postlewait, 'George Edwardes and Musical Comedy', 84–86.

4. Kurt Gänzl, 'Caryll, Ivan (1861–1921)', in *Oxford Dictionary of National Biography*, ed. H. C. G. Matthew and Brian Harrison, vol. 10 (Oxford: Oxford University Press, 2004), 452–453. The five Lloyd Webber shows running on 14 July 1990 were *Cats, Starlight Express, The Phantom of the Opera, Aspects of Love*, and *Song and Dance*, with a concert performance of *Jesus Christ Superstar* thrown in (*The Times*, 14 July 1990, 24).

5. William Archer, 'Epilogue Statistical', in William Archer, Sydney Grundy, and Henry George Hibbert, *The Theatrical 'World' of 1897* (London: Scott, 1898), 357 and 364.

6. Cyril Ehrlich, *The Music Profession in Britain Since the Eighteenth Century* (Oxford: Clarendon, 1985), 156.

7. All 'wealth at death' figures are from the *Oxford Dictionary of National Biography*.

8. John Drysdale, *Elgar's Earnings* (Woodbridge: Boydell, 2013); Frederic Norton Archive, University of Bristol Theatre Collection, 2011/0083.

9. Rexton S. Bunnett, liner notes, *The Arcadians*, CD booklet, EMI Records, EMI 0777 7 89057 2 1, 1993, 3 and 14.

10. *Primrose*, Programme, Mander & Mitchenson Collection, University of Bristol Theatre Collection, MM/REF/TH/LO/WNT/4.

11. Wikipedia, 'Gaiety Girls', http://en.wikipedia.org/wiki/Gaiety_Girls, accessed 13 May 2014.

12. The mise-en-scène is reproduced in Wikipedia: 'The Arcadians (musical)', http://en.wikipedia.org/wiki/The_Arcadians_%28musical%29, accessed 13 May 2014.

13. Two of these numbers may be heard, complete with Smithson's trademark *pianissimi* on the high notes, on the archive recordings included in the EMI CD of *The Arcadians* (EMI 0777 7 89057 2 1, 1993).

14. Mark Ambient, Alexander M. Thompson, and Arthur Wimperis, *The Arcadians*, play-script, London, 1909, Lord Chamberlain's Plays, British Library, LCP 1909/10, Act III, p. 29 [crossed out; '103' substituted].

15. Anon. 'Players and Playthings', *Judy* 71 (10 March 1906), 116; Stephen Banfield, *Jerome Kern* (New Haven: Yale, 2006), 306; Andrew Lamb, *Jerome Kern in Edwardian London*, 2nd ed. (New York: Institute for Studies in American Music, 1985), 23 (see also 7–8).

16. C. Hubert H. Parry, *Style in Musical Art* (London: Macmillan, 1911), 114.

17. Florence Smithson, 'The Girl with a Brogue'/'Bring Me a Rose', 78 Record, His Masters Voice, HMV 03190, 1910. See Robert Seeley and Rex Bunnett, *London Musical Shows on Record 1889–1989* (Harrow: Gramophone, 1989), 9–10.

18. John Dos Passos, 'The Camera Eye 28', *1919*, Book 2 of *USA* (1932; Harmondsworth: Penguin, 1961), 350–351.

19. Caryll injects more, however, in 'My Yorkshire Lassie' from *Our Miss Gibbs*. At the beginning of the 2/4 refrain he sets the downbeat word 'Yorkshire' within a similar bar of quaver–crotchet syncopation, but real cakewalk syncopation, at double this speed, is achieved at its end, with the clincher 'You are the maid for me'.

20. Ambient et al., *The Arcadians*, Act I, p. 8 [crossed out; '22' substituted]. Stage directions omitted.

21. Len Platt, *Musical Comedy on the West End Stage, 1890–1939* (Basingstoke: Palgrave Macmillan, 2004); Peter Bailey, '"Naughty But Nice": Musical Comedy and the Rhetoric of the Girl, 1892–1914', in *The Edwardian Theatre*, ed. Michael R. Booth and Joel H. Kaplan (Cambridge: Cambridge University Press, 1996), 36–60.

22. There are indeed subtle gong strokes on the Columbia Light Opera Company's 1930 recording of a *Country Girl* selection (DX73, conducted by Charles Prentice), but on the chorus's repetitions of 'Bhong'. A later BBC broadcast had only a single, rather louder one, on the half-bar after the rhyme 'gong'.

23. Banfield, *Jerome Kern*, 71.

24. See especially John Lahr's review of *Billy Elliot*, 'On Your Toes', *New Yorker* 81 (4 July 2005), 84, characterizing England as 'a land of scarcity'.

25. Bailey, 'Naughty But Nice', 48–49.

26. Bailey, 'Naughty But Nice', 52.

27. See Platt, *Musical Comedy on the West End Stage*, 26–58, and Peter Bailey, 'Theatres of Entertainment/Spaces of Modernity: Rethinking the British Popular Stage 1890–1914', *Nineteenth Century Theatre* 26, no. 1 (Summer 1998): 5–24.

28. Joel H. Kaplan and Sheila Stowell, *Theatre and Fashion: Oscar Wilde to the Suffragettes* (Cambridge: Cambridge University Press, 1994), 131.

29. Ivan Caryll and Lionel Monckton, *Our Miss Gibbs*, vocal score (London: Chappell, 1909), 38, 44, and 110.

30. *Play Pictorial* 2, no. 8 (November 1902), 313.

31. Archer, 'Epilogue Statistical', 351.

32. Jeffrey Richards, '"Bring on the Girls": Opera, Operetta and Ballet', in *Imperialism and Music: Britain 1876–1953* (Manchester: Manchester University Press, 2001), 269.

33. Granville Bantock, *Round the World with 'A Gaiety Girl'* (London: Macqueen, 1896).

34. Warren Bebbington, ed., *The Oxford Companion to Australian Music* (Melbourne: Oxford University Press, 1997), 591.

35. Anon. ('Wheeler'), 'Players, Playgoers and the Car', *Play Pictorial* 25, no. 273 (October 1924): viii.

36. See Viv Gardner, 'Gertie Millar and the "Rules for Actresses and Vicars' Wives"', in *Extraordinary Actors: Essays on Popular Performers*, ed. Jane Milling and Martin Banham (Exeter: University of Exeter Press, 2004), 97–112.
37. Ernest Irving, *Cue for Music* (London: Dobson, 1959), 41–5.
38. John Lowerson, *Amateur Operatics: A Social and Cultural History* (Manchester: Manchester University Press, 2005), 212 and 184–92.
39. *Tamworth Herald*, 22 March 1947, 1; *Nottingham Evening Post*, 26 November 1948, 2; *Dundee Courier*, 18 March 1948, 1; *Hull Daily Mail*, 9 March 1949, 3; *Sunderland Daily Echo*, 22 November 1950, 2.
40. *Brisbane Courier-Mail*, 5 March 1951, 8; *Australian Women's Weekly*, 11 June 1958, 28.
41. See Stephen Banfield, 'Stage and Screen Entertainers in the Twentieth Century', in *The Cambridge Companion to Singing*, ed. John Potter (Cambridge: Cambridge University Press, 2000), 63–82, where a start has been made.
42. George Grossmith Jr., 'Any Old Night', 78 Record, His Master's Voice, HMV 02579, 1915.
43. Noël Coward, 'Introduction', in *The Essential Noël Coward Song Book* (1953; London: Omnibus, 1980), 9–11.
44. George Grossmith Jr., *G.G.* (London: Hutchinson, 1933), 116.
45. Postlewait ends his article 'George Edwardes and Musical Comedy' with a series of twelve research questions; they are different from mine.
46. Thomas Piketty, *Capital in the Twenty-First Century* (Cambridge, MA: Belknap, 2014).

BIBLIOGRAPHY

Ambient, Mark, Alexander M. Thompson, and Arthur Wimperis. *The Arcadians*. Playscript. London, 1909. Lord Chamberlain's Plays, British Library, LCP 1909/10.
Anon. 'Players and Playthings.' *Judy* 71 (10 March 1906): 116.
Anon. ('Wheeler'). 'Players, Playgoers and the Car.' *Play Pictorial* 25, no. 273 (October 1924): viii.
The Arcadians. Studio cast recording, 1969. CD. EMI Records, EMI 0777 7 89057 2 1, 1993.
Archer, William. 'Epilogue Statistical.' In William Archer, Sydney Grundy, and Henry George Hibbert, *The Theatrical 'World' of 1897*, 351–377. London: Scott, 1898.
Bailey, Peter. '"Naughty But Nice": Musical Comedy and the Rhetoric of the Girl, 1892–1914'. In *The Edwardian Theatre*, edited by Michael R. Booth and Joel H. Kaplan, 36–60. Cambridge: Cambridge University Press, 1996.
Bailey, Peter. 'Theatres of Entertainment/Spaces of Modernity: Rethinking the British Popular Stage 1890–1914.' *Nineteenth Century Theatre* 6, no. 1 (Summer 1998): 5–24.
Banfield, Stephen. *Jerome Kern*. New Haven: Yale, 2006.
Banfield, Stephen. 'Stage and Screen Entertainers in the Twentieth Century.' In *The Cambridge Companion to Singing*, edited by John Potter, 63–82. Cambridge: Cambridge University Press, 2000.
Bantock, Granville. *Round the World with 'A Gaiety Girl'*. London: Macqueen, 1896.
Bebbington, Warren, ed. *The Oxford Companion to Australian Music*. Melbourne: Oxford University Press, 1997.
Bunnett, Rexton S. Liner Notes. *The Arcadians*. CD Booklet. EMI Records, EMI 0777 7 89057 2 1, 1993, 1–14.
Caryll, Ivan, and Lionel Monckton. *Our Miss Gibbs*. Vocal Score. London: Chappell, 1909.

Columbia Light Opera Company. *A Country Girl.* 78 Recording. Columbia Records, DX73, 1930.

Coward, Noël. 'Introduction.' In *The Essential Noël Coward Song Book*, 9–17. 1953. London: Omnibus, 1980.

Dos Passos, John. *1919*. Book 2 of *USA*. 1932. Harmondsworth: Penguin, 1961.

Drysdale, John. *Elgar's Earnings*. Woodbridge: Boydell, 2013.

Earl, John, and Michael Sell, eds. *The Theatres Trust Guide to British Theatres 1750–1950: A Gazetteer*. London: A. and C. Black, 2000.

Ehrlich, Cyril. *The Music Profession in Britain Since the Eighteenth Century*. Oxford: Clarendon, 1985.

Gänzl, Kurt. *The British Musical Theatre*. Vols. 1–2. Basingstoke: Macmillan, 1986.

Gänzl, Kurt. 'Caryll, Ivan (1861–1921).' In *Oxford Dictionary of National Biography*, vol. 10, edited by H. C. G. Matthew and Brian Harrison, 452–453. Oxford: Oxford University Press, 2004.

Gardner, Viv. 'Gertie Millar and the "Rules for Actresses and Vicars' Wives".' In *Extraordinary Actors: Essays on Popular Performers*, edited by Jane Milling and Martin Banham, 97–112. Exeter: University of Exeter Press, 2004.

Grossmith Jr., George. 'Any Old Night.' 78 Recording. His Master's Voice, HMV 02579, 1915.

Grossmith Jr., George. *G.G.* London: Hutchinson, 1933.

Irving, Ernest. *Cue for Music*. London: Dobson, 1959.

Kaplan, Joel H., and Sheila Stowell. *Theatre and Fashion: Oscar Wilde to the Suffragettes*. Cambridge: Cambridge University Press, 1994.

Lahr, John. 'On Your Toes.' *New Yorker* 81 (4 July 2005), 84.

Lamb, Andrew. *Jerome Kern in Edwardian London*. 2nd ed. New York: Institute for Studies in American Music, 1985.

Lowerson, John. *Amateur Operatics: A Social and Cultural History*. Manchester: Manchester University Press, 2005.

Parry, C. Hubert H. *Style in Musical Art*. London: Macmillan, 1911.

Piketty, Thomas. *Capital in the Twenty-First Century*. Cambridge, MA: Belknap, 2014.

Platt, Len. *Musical Comedy on the West End Stage, 1890–1939*. Basingstoke: Palgrave Macmillan, 2004.

Postlewait, Thomas. 'George Edwardes and Musical Comedy: The Transformation of London Theatre and Society, 1878–1914.' In *The Performing Century: Nineteenth-Century Theatre's History*, edited by Tracy C. Davis and Peter Holland, 80–102. Basingstoke: Palgrave Macmillan, 2007.

Primrose. Programme. Mander & Mitchenson Collection, University of Bristol Theatre Collection, MM/REF/TH/LO/WNT/4.

Richards, Jeffrey. '"Bring on the Girls": Opera, Operetta and Ballet.' In Richards, *Imperialism and Music: Britain 1876–1953*, 248–278. Manchester: Manchester University Press, 2001.

Seeley, Robert, and Rex Bunnett. *London Musical Shows on Record 1889–1989*. Harrow: Gramophone, 1989.

Smithson, Florence. 'The Girl with a Brogue'/'Bring Me a Rose.' 78 Recording. His Masters Voice, HMV 03190, 1910.

Williams, Gordon. 'Musical Comedy and Musical Anarchy'. In *British Theatre in the Great War: A Revaluation*, 18–71. London: Continuum, 2003.

CHAPTER 5

....

ENGLISH WEST END REVUE

The First World War and After

....

DAVID LINTON

> OSBORNE This show at the Hippodrome has been running a long time.
> STANHOPE What? *Zig-Zag*?
> OSBORNE Yes. George Robey's in it.
> STANHOPE Harper saw it on leave. Says it's damn good. Robey's pricelessly funny.
> OSBORNE Wish I'd seen a show on leave.
> STANHOPE D' you mean to say you didn't go to any shows?
>
> *Journey's End* (1928) [1]

ALTHOUGH the two most successful shows of the First World War were the musical comedies *Chu Chin Chow* (1916) and *Maid of the Mountains* (1917), it was musical revue[2] that established itself at the heart of a flourishing popular entertainment zone and arguably surpassed musical comedy as the principal musical form. Why and how did this happen? What was it about revue that gave it the edge over other musical entertainment? In this chapter I will explore the emergence, popularity, and success of revue in wartime and beyond and highlight its appropriation and adaptation of different aesthetics and its engagement with specific aspects of an identity discourse of national regeneration and renewal.

As alluded to in R. C. Sherriff's seminal play about the First World War, the West End became an almost compulsory part of the soldier's itinerary whilst on leave from the front and revues were integral in creating a flourishing popular entertainment culture. However, in the late nineteenth and early twentieth century the most successful form of theatrical entertainment in London was musical comedy. A plethora of popular shows such as *The Geisha* (1896), *Floradora* (1900), *A Country Girl* (1904), *The Merry Widow* (1907), *The Arcadians* (1909), and *Our Miss Gibbs* (1910), placed musical comedy at the forefront of a vibrant and fashionable popular culture, and established the 'West End' of London as 'a modern retail and pleasure Mecca'.[3] Musical comedy emerged at the height of Britain's imperial supremacy, with the country benefiting from a combination of peace, prosperity, and wealth brought about by the Industrial Revolution and an unrivalled Empire. In this earlier period, musical comedies articulated an idealized sense of that society,[4] creating a world that was supremely confident in itself where conflicts or challenges to the status quo could be safely negotiated and assimilated, and order maintained. A key theme often elaborated within musical comedy narratives was the smooth integration between old conservative aristocratic sensibilities and the new liberal modernity of the metropolis as illustrated by George Edwardes's production of *A Gaiety Girl* (1909).

The plot of *A Gaiety Girl* concerns a group of aristocratic ladies whose ambitions of capturing the interest of military gentlemen are threatened by the entrance of a rival group of young actresses from the Gaiety Theatre. As the story progresses, these vivacious, assertive 'West End chorus girls' become emblematic of a modern world that threatens to encroach on the established order of things. However in the end, true to the narrative form of musical comedy, this modernity is made safe as the 'chorus girls' and their perceived challenge are assimilated by marriage.

During the Edwardian period London West End revue began to supplant musical comedy as the most popular theatrical entertainment. Although revue had much in common with musical comedy, it began to reconstitute a different world on its stages and at many levels rejected the world as constructed by musical comedy, poking fun at its whimsical plots. Indeed, revue's popularity in part stemmed from situating itself in direct opposition to musical comedy and its mainstream status. Where musical comedy had sought union and harmony through linear storylines, revue consciously disrupted the narrative framework and associated itself with the new popular social dances and the syncopated music that accompanied them. In contrast to musical comedy's romanticism, revue's critical, satirical commentary highlighted a world of difference and discord focusing on contemporary issues such as divorce, drug culture, immigration, sexual infidelity, and political dissent. A crucial aspect of revue's exploration of this contemporary world was the representation of national and racial identities, which provided an accessible, taxonomic shorthand for identifying characters and situations drawing on its popular theatre origins. Revue highlighted behaviours and actions that expanded traditional narratives of nation by constructing distinctive British/English and London West End identities that were to become synonymous with the form.

THE EMERGENCE OF WEST END REVUE

Allardyce Nicoll in his history of English theatre,[5] recognized revue's popularity at the beginning of the twentieth century but struggled to acknowledge its singularity, its theatrical and social frameworks, and its application as a multidisciplinary performance model. Nicoll offers a contradictory commentary that disparages revue in terms of aesthetic value but recognizes its significance as being socially reflective. At the same time he notes the difficulties in defining revue, a typical failing of conventional theatre history. Revue for Nicoll is 'an evening's entertainment made up of numerous "turns", generally short, some pointedly topical and some spectacular, presented in swift, kaleidoscopic rotation'.[6] Early British revues for Nicoll were by and large musical extravaganzas, which, 'hardly went beyond the theatrical burlesque'.[7] He observes that there was a 'certain vagueness and uncertainty concerning revue',[8] and highlights that although revue shows had been presented in the nineteenth century, the word 'revue' was not introduced until 1905 when 'J. B. Fagan's *Shakespeare v. Shaw* appeared at the Haymarket and George Grossmith Jr's show, *Rogues and Vagabonds* at the Empire music-hall the following year'.[9] Nicoll does understand that revue was intrinsically connected to changes happening across British theatre and draws attention to performance practices that had been appropriated into the form, 'the influence of the contemporary French type, the adaptation of native music-hall practice and the utilisation of the material culled from the musicals'.[10]

Nicoll sees revue's popularity with a mass audience as being as much a deciding factor in its definition and categorization as the work itself, and concludes with an astute observation of the social and cultural significance of revue:

> The revue had clearly caught the imagination and interest of the time, and there might be justification for regarding it as one of the most characteristic theatrical developments in England between its introductions in 1905 to the close of this period [1930].[11]

It is clear from Nicoll that the question of definition has proved continuously problematic for revue, as it has always incorporated many performance forms, styles, and diverse expressive elements. The word 'revue' has its origins in France, coming from the French word *revoir*—to see again—and at one time the genre was typically retrospective, established as a literal end-of-the-year 'review' of the social and cultural calendar, in the form of a theatrical production, which through a succession of scenes in dialogue and song represented incidents and individuals that had 'preoccupied the public to a greater or lesser extent during the course of the year'.[12] But in the later West End incarnations, revue's origins and influences originate from a backdrop of enormous social change, with a wide array of criss-crossing influences and huge variations.

The development of revue at the start of the twentieth century coincided with several key changes across London's theatre district. The remodelling of large areas of the district of Westminster had seen the refurbishing and sanitizing of the music halls, as the old entertainments began to decline in both reputation and economic viability.[13] The opportunity for the literal legitimization of these old entertainment centres came with the 1893 Theatre Act and the introduction of small- and medium-sized theatres. Music halls such as the Pavilion and the New Oxford became theatres and had lavish refurbishments as producers sought to reposition themselves as 'highbrow' and attract middle-class audiences into these old spaces. The 'entertainment' landscape saw various theatrical forms restructured due to social and economic pressures. An evening's entertainment now saw the rearrangement and integration of the one to three acts which had previously been split between burlesque, comedy, drama, and dancing. Some theatre managers seeking to make the change from variety entertainments to legitimate theatre exploited the revue format for their convenience and for economic reasons and simply called old variety programmes a revue. As an article in *The Stage* entitled 'Growth of Revue' observed, there grew a trend for revue 'which approximates [. . .] an ordinary variety entertainment set off with embellishments of scene and ensemble':[14]

> For the moment revue [. . .] is marked by two leading tendencies. One is to provide showy, colourful scenes especially by way of chorus workers and dancers. The other is to incorporate variety turns. By these means the transition from the music-hall programme of individual items may be in the making; and it will be well if revue can in the process give—as it is at the present doing—opportunity to a large proportion of the variety artists whom it has deprived of their regular work.[15]

Revue as a form and framework provided a vehicle for mixing the old with the new, and a space for old music hall acts, dances, comedians, and different styles to be presented in an economically efficient and diverse programme for these new West End theatres. That reality meant that some revues were a hotchpotch amalgamation and revue gained a poor reputation for being all things to all people or a catch- all term to define anything.[16] The multidisciplinary quality of revue was seriously damaged and was viewed as a sign of revue's lack of worth or aesthetic engagement. Yet those involved sought to make revue better understood, as illustrated by producer Charles Cochran (see Figure 5.1), interviewed in *The Stage*, in mapping three forms of revue:

> It occupies an intermediate place between variety art and the art of the fully organ- ised play; and in that place it has many and diverse expressions, from the revue 'intime' to the spectacular revue, with in-between, the revue that is little more than a succession of variety turns, of which the connecting link sometimes does not go beyond or even as far as the title.[17]

The main elements of revue were not imported from overseas but 'scattered among the era's stages'[18] with a 'shifting and unreliable' taxonomy. Pre-existing forms of musical theatre impacted on revue in various ways—burlesque, for example, which included the political and social topicality so important to later revue, and musical comedy, the pre- cursor of revue in terms of plotting and its obsession with fashion. James Ross-Moore refers to the significance of burletta for variety and music hall with their programmes of 'turns'. Burletta is derived from 'burla', which was a shorter form of musical farce or mockery and had become by the end of the century 'a drama in rhyme [. . .] entirely musical; a short comic piece, consisting of recitative and singing, wholly accompa- nied, more or less, by the orchestra'.[19] The concert party[20] formed a link between variety and revue by way of the bon vivant Harry Pelissier and *The Co-Optimists* (a mixture of seaside entertainment and Pierrot), while a British ballet tradition (the Alhambra's

FIGURE 5.1 Portrait of producer Charles Blake (C. B.) Cochran, a key figure in promoting the popularity of British revue, 1940s.

Mander & Mitchenson Collection, University of Bristol. Courtesy of ArenaPal.

ballet-pageants, 'owing [little] to the Russian tradition of stylised dramatic dance') was one of the elements that transformed variety bills and was also important in the development of revue by providing a link to Florenz Ziegfeld's spectacular revues 'adapted from Paris for New York in 1907 [...] which Albert de Courville brought back [to London] from Ziegfeld's Broadway five years after that'.[21] French revue and French variety also influenced West End revue, emerging from the *cafés chantants*[22] and, of course, via André Charlot—a veteran of the Folies Bergère and the Théâtre du Chatelet—who worked as a producer in London from 1912 to 1937.

Huntly Carter's *The New Spirit in the European Theatre 1914–1924* published in 1925[23] highlights critical aspects of commercial West End theatre practice and the contribution and influence of revue across genres in terms of performance. For Carter, West End revue was a conduit for burgeoning art movements often deriving from so-called 'high' art forms. Rightly he recognizes that the experimentation in fashion, design, dance, movement, non-verbal expression, and montage that was happening across continental Europe was being adapted and used in revue. Carter sees revue as multidisciplinary performance, linking it not only to the Wagnerian concept of *Gesamtkunstwerk* of 'total theatre'[24] but also directly to a British model exemplified by Sir Henry Irving and John Ruskin's 'three-fold method of play production—sound, colour and movement'.[25]

These various styles can all be seen in the revues staged in the first decades of the twentieth century. It was to be Harry Pellissier's *Follies* (1908/1911), along with George Grossmith Jr's *Hullo . . . London* (1910), *By George!* (1911), and *Kill That Fly* (1912), that initiated the expansion of and experimentation with form and narrative. These revues promoted contemporaneity and critical commentary on modern society as West End revue's defining element; however, it was Charles Cochran, Albert de Courville, and André Charlot in particular who were to brand and define a London West End revue style. Cochran and de Courville would establish revue as a popular entertainment foregrounding contemporary dance, music, sexual titillation, and spectacle. De Courville was integral to the formulation of the 'spectacular revue' style heavily influenced by Florenz Ziegfeld's New York revues, while Ziegfeld in turn had found inspiration in the Paris and Berlin spectacular revues. Ziegfeld employed hundreds of performers, stagehands, and the use of 'ultramodern technical equipment'.[26] Spectacular revue was built around singers and songs and 'opulent adornment' with lavish designs and a large chorus of dancing girls.[27] Big budget productions like *Everybody's Doing It* (1912), *Hullo Ragtime!* (1912), and *Hullo Tango* (1913) cultivated visual spectacle and titillation and began to situate revue within the consciousness of the public, firmly connected to a burgeoning dance and music culture. West End revue positioned itself at the centre of the dance crazes that swept across the country. This association in part was driven by Charles Cochran's passion for dance, which was always integral to his revues. As James Nott has argued, it is important to understand the role dancing played in people's lives and also how popular music (meaning commercial music) was connected to social dancing and entertainment.[28]

Dance was, of course, to become less central to revue's form and definition but during the early 1920s it was the dances and the dance music which helped popularize and mark revue's place as modern popular culture. *Alien Bodies*, Ramsay Burt's reconsideration of early modern dance, highlights the 'complex' interrelationships between dance as popular entertainment and dance as a serious art form, noting the 'coexistence and interdependence of many different forms of theatre dance during the interwar years, and of connections and cross-overs between them'.[29] Burt emphasizes the contribution of West End revue popular entertainment, arguing its centrality in the incubation and development of modern dance, highlighting in particular the work of Leonide Massine.

Massine started his career with Diaghilev's Ballets Russes, alongside the likes of artist Pablo Picasso and composer Eric Satie, before working with Anton Dolin (first artistic director of the English National Ballet) and Ninette de Valois (founder of the Royal Ballet) in revues such as *You'd Be Surprised* (1923), *On With the Dance* (1925), and *Whitebirds* (1927). The interwar period saw the greater commercialization of music as the emergence of 'dynamic and self-sustaining'[30] technologies enabled rapid diffusion, 'helping to bring about a mass audience'[31] for dance music. This was illustrated by Charles Cochran's *Charleston Ball and Dance Competition* at the Royal Albert Hall in December 1926, which included amongst the judges the American dancer and later

Hollywood film star Fred Astaire and Florence Mills, the star of the all-black American revue of 1926, *Blackbirds*. Ballet in particularly exercised a very strong influence on British 'stagecraftsmen [. . .] and on various forms of theatrical entertainment'. However, ballet had 'no permanent home in this country' or New York and was indeed a 'roving exhibition'.[32] Revue was pivotal in providing a space for its establishment and dissemination, employing Leonide Massine and cultivating an emerging British ballet personnel of Marie Rambert, Anton Dolin, and Ninette de Valois, all working in West End revues in the 1920s.

Revue's musical heritage enabled it to connect with extensive well-established structures of marketing and self-promotion through a range of different media, exploiting the genre's visual and aural aspects of dance, music, fashion, and design.[33]Later Charles Cochran and Albert de Courville would place revue at the forefront of the jazz dance and music era with the importation of seminal American jazz bands: Nick La Rocca's Original Dixieland Jazz Band in *Joybells* (1919), Paul Whiteman and His Orchestra in *Brighter London* (1923), and Will Vodrey and His Orchestra in *Dover Street to Dixie* (1923).

The Modern Scenographic Aesthetic of Revue: Fragmentation as Modernity

> Persons interested in the advance of stagecraft went to revue for inspiration and watched for things to flash out. The subject, the scene-painter, the costumier, the electrician, and the variety of talented artistes, some of them from the music hall, combined to produce unexpected effects, aesthetic and other, seldom to be found in the production of the drama.[34]
>
> The truth was the straight theatre had become a revue theatre.[35]

The *League of Notions* (1921) at the New Oxford Theatre opened with a theatre manager lost in the fog of London. Unable to find his way, he stumbles around until he meets a group of pantomime players, a Harlequin, a Pierrot, and a Columbine. The desperate manager begs them to show him the way and promises the trio that he will dress them in 'modern things' and put them in his show. The Pierrot retorts, 'We have very little use for any modern show'[36] and tells the manager that they still haunt the theatres where they use to hold sway. They find the modern shows 'have not advanced a bit, and we can truly say, There's nothing new.' The manager asks, 'What would you do to set the pace of modern shows?' The pantomime players take him to a tailor 'who has been sewing shows together for years'. The tailor presents a crazy patchwork quilt as an example of the necessary qualities for a modern show advocating the importance of form and content. The tailor stresses that a combination of forms and styles is what is needed and that music, song, dance, and topicality should be at its heart. 'Taking a patch from here and there [. . .] some modern tunes, some old plaintive air, a pretty face, a dance, a merry jest [. . .] they have for all mankind some interest.'[37]

Although questions of definition and taxonomy abound about revue, we do know that it sought to position and mark itself as 'modern' performance in form and content. In *League of Notions* we have revue arguing its case as the manifestation of the modern play, setting the pace of 'modern shows' through its fragmented multidisciplined form with 'a patch from here and there'. The importance of revue's fragmented structure was vital in marking its modernism and its difference, contrasting strongly with ordinary theatre's linear narratives but also reflective of life. As the programme notes for the revue *The Peep Show* (1921) explain:

> Why do we go to the Theatre? To be amused, thrilled, or roused, according to our taste; but most of us will agree that the ideal show would be one in which we experienced all these feelings—for that is life. What better entertainment could one choose than a Revue? The ordinary theatre show gives us only one side of life, but a Revue gives us comedy, and tragedy, farce—the sunshine and the shadow.[38]

The producers of *The Peep Show* promoted the revue aesthetic as something that opened up experiential possibilities on stage and pointedly associated it with a modern vitality, 'that is life'. *The Peep Show* revue itself showcased technical innovation in the form of a transforming lighting device described as having 'revolutionary possibilities in the theatre'.[39] The device enabled sets, costumes, and characters to be changed through special effects, moving from 'a snow-clad mountain gorge [. . .] into the interior of an ancient palace of India'.[40] Revue's non-linear narratives and deliberately eclectic performance style signalled something fresh and exhilarating and, as Len Platt highlights, this was a key distinctive marker between revue and musical comedy.

> Far from creating a consistent fabric, whether in terms of narrative or style, the up-and-coming form [revue] aimed for bizarre shifts and dramatic transformations at every level. Melodrama could snap into showtime glitz at any minute, film was often interpolated into performance implying not a reproduction of the modern, as in the old tradition, but a multi-media practice that emphasized difference rather than assimilation [. . .] It was not that revue was too unsophisticated to sustain traditional story, as is sometimes thought, but rather that it eschewed what it saw as the narrative simplicity and romanticism of musical comedy.[41]

Revue's ability to change and adapt gave it an advantage as it enabled it to remain current and fresh with the introduction of alternate performers, acts, and new topical scenes. *You'd Be Surprised* is a series of sketches or 'surprises' such as the 'Fearless Flipper', 'Pajama Blues', and 'Chicken Ala King', interspersed with speciality acts and the Savoy jazz band. *The Charlot Revue* (1924) was comprised of such scenes as 'Karma', a ballet by Cyril Scott, and a violent one-act drama of low-life multicultural London called 'Me Pink 'At'.

> As a form, the revue had flexibility; without being tied to a storyline or book, the producer was free to introduce performers, songs and songwriters according to his taste

or judgement and stirred a response in audiences [. . .] trad[ing] on burlesque, wit
and satire [. . . revues] were the medium par excellence of a time when a breakdown
in traditional values and established conventions prompted performers and people
to poke fun at things.[42]

In the scene 'Oh the Language' from the revue *The Whirligig* (1919), all the actors except
for a police inspector use dialect in strong opposition to the characters they play. This
scene plays with the notion of identity, where stereotypes of class, race, sex, and gender are paraded and swapped around. His lordship, 'faultlessly dressed', speaks broad
cockney ('Lord luv a duck'), the flower girl speaks in American tones ('wise guy'). The
chimney sweep uses an upper-class English accent ('Pardon me—but this sort of thing
isn't done you know. There are certain distinctions to be observed'). Mr Abrahams,
described as a 'typical Hebrew', speaks with a thick Irish brogue, while the Frenchman
speaks with a Welsh accent, and the Irish woman broken Italian. The scene is brought to
a climax by the police inspector, 'who is an everyday sort of quick-speaking Englishman',
the untainted presence and voice of reason in this multicultural gathering. Calling on
his detective to make an arrest, the detective takes off his hat to reveal a 'Chinese pigtail'
and to speak in 'pigeon English'. The final line of the scene, known as the blackout line, is
given by the 'coon waiter', speaking in a 'very high effeminate voice'.[43]

This dismantling of stage realism exemplified revue's negotiation of modernity, charting the erosion of old hierarchies of social distinction but also marking the possible new
identities that were occurring as one consequence of industrial modernization. Here is
a vision of London as a modern 'world town' as Ford Madox Ford described in *The Soul
of London* (1903):

> Mormon and Mussulman, Benedictine and Agapemonite, Jew and Malay, Russian
> and Neapolitan [. . .] [London] assimilates and slowly digests them, converting
> them, with the most potent of all juices, into the singular and inevitable product that
> is the Londoner—that is, in fact, the Modern.[44]

'Oh the Language' plays with the notion of this modern world; however, it is not necessarily a celebration of difference but rather a key into anxieties about immigration
and foreigners which had resulted in race riots in Liverpool, Cardiff, and South Shields
in the north-east of England during the summer of 1919. Fuelled by fears about rising
unemployment and lack of jobs, the disruptions resulted in the introduction of the third
Aliens Act, the earlier ones having been introduced in 1905 and 1914. This was followed
by the Aliens order in 1920 and the special restriction of 1925 severely limiting work for
black sailors.

Although presented as a unified text, West End revue's aesthetic stressed juxtaposition and contradiction, placing side by side not only the different performance styles of
popular theatre but also the contributions of numerous writers, choreographers, composers, and lyricists, each often working independently on their individual pieces and
scenes. Revue provided these separate performance styles, songs, dances, and scenes

with a syncretic, articulating frame within which they could be performed. In doing so, revue highlighted and reflected cultural crossings, montages, breaks, interruptions, and the instability and flux of the contemporary modern world. Alan O'Shea argues that the rapidity of modern living saw an 'intense time-space compression'[45] with faster transport and communication systems speeding up the experience of life. This meant that 'the process of change itself was fast, demanding rapid accommodation to new conditions'[46] as modernity bombarded people with information and sensations. This became replicated in revue as audiences were presented with a similar mixture of visual and intellectual spectacle, often out of the fear of failing to arrest the audience's attention as modern audiences seemed to suffer from durational commitment (see Figure 5.2).

FIGURE 5.2 Mirroring the faster pace of modern life: Elsa McFarlane mimicking the Silver Lady figurine of a Rolls Royce car in *The Co-Optimists*, Vaudeville Theatre 1929.

Photograph by Sasha. Courtesy of Getty Images.

As revue writer Ronald Jeans explained, 'compression became vital [. . .] It was a question not only of good art to write economically, but of dire necessity. One had to learn to unfold a situation, develop it, and come to the climax in a matter of minutes.'[47] The structure provided the opportunity for quick, direct stage performance which played with narrative storytelling, magnifying character relationships and plot lines as illustrated by the scene 'For Life'.

This scene from *The Whirligig* fuses and juxtaposes a traditional linear narrative story with theatrical experiment. A quarrelling duet is performed between a couple who tell of the breakdown of their marriage, speaking directly to the audience in rhyme, alternately and at the same time playing with timing and vocal rhythm.

HE   Just five short years ago today
    It is since we were wed—
SHE   The word wed is appropriate
    Because it rhymes with 'dead'
HE   [*looking up*] Oh! Plighted Vows.
SHE   [*hanging her head*] Oh! Blighted spouse.
BOTH   Excited rows we revelled in
    Now cupid's fled. [48]

In 'For Life' the performance structure reflects the scientific management techniques of Frederick Taylor used for rationalizing the rhythm and form of the working day of industrial workers in factories. 'Taylorism', applied here to script and character, presents a messy marriage breakdown neatly packaged in a short and concise orchestrated duologue, the emotions and actions reduced and presented staccato to the consumer/audience. In *The Whirligig* different performance styles are combined and executed with direct satirical sophisticated commentary on the 'now'. And it was this 'newness', this asociation with the themes and interests of its times, that made revue not just popular but for a time à la mode with an aspirant audience that desired and wanted to be ascribed with the fashion of the modern, as illustrated by the song 'It May Be Life' from *Riverside Nights* (1926). This tender ballad is a commentary by a maid who critiques her own existence, by comparing it to what she sees in the new media, the cinema:

I wish there weren't no washing up,
And life was like the movies are
I wish I wore a wicked hat,
I've got the face for it, I know.
I'm tired of scrubbing floors and that
It may be life but ain't it slow?
For I don't have no adventures in the street,
Men don't register e-motion when we meet.
Jack don't register love's sweet bliss,
Jack just registers an ordinary kiss and I says

'Evenin' and Jack says 'Eve-nin',
And we both stand there
At the corner of the square,
　Me like a statue and him like a bear.
　He don't make faces like the movie men,
　He just holds me tight till the clock strikes ten.
　Then I say 'Friday?' And Jack says 'Right',
　Jack says 'The same time?' And I says 'Right'
Jack just whispers and I can hardly speak.
And that's the most exciting thing that happens in the week.[49]

The piece plays on the understanding that the new mass cultural activities such as shopping in the new stores—and indeed the cinema—were, as Mica Nava argues 'main contexts in which women developed a new consciousness of the possibilities and entitlements that modern life was able to offer'.[50] We find here revue as popular culture engaging in an ambivalent social and political deliberation as the maid is provided with 'the temptations of the metropolitan world of consumption and spectacle [of the movies]—the urban phantasmagoria—which both dazzles and deceives the crowd'.[51] In an ironic observation, the 'movies' don't provide her with an 'escape' from her existence but magnify the reality of what she does not have or has never experienced. The song negotiates class, economic, and gender aspirations and highlights the development of a new consciousness. Her life does not live up to the images or stories on the big screen and this in turn connects with a sense of wanting to change the order of things. Here popular entertainment signals possible emancipation, resulting in what Walter Benjamin called the 'shattering of tradition'[52] as the monotony of the linear, the familiarity of the old order of things is exposed and challenged, inspiring a new defiant attitude to experiment and experience.

Adore us, deplore us or scatter before us
We're set upon singing our opening chorus
Our singing is not operatic
Our acting is scarcely dramatic
Our dancing as well is a bit of a sell and our memory may be erratic
So jeer us or cheer us or simply ignore us
We've set our hearts on an opening chorus.

With a lavish hand we scatter all the very oldest patter
Mouldy jokes and ancient wheezes, painted noses, comic sneezes
People falling on their faces in the most unlikely places
With fancy foible we'll struggle to please you
And show you yourselves as the other man sees you
But since you may shortly be tempted to floor us,
we'd better get on with the opening chorus.[53]

This 'Opening chorus' of the 1919 *Follies* sets out to introduce revue and in doing so situates it as a critical performance practice. Here is singing, dancing, acting, and a breadth of styles and forms, drawing on familiar traditional popular theatre techniques of direct address, self-referencing, self-parody, and burlesque.

It is a brisk and defiant opening chorus, as illustrated by the burlesquing of the coming entertainment's themes, styles, and approach. In the scene the performers challenge the audience's expectations by revealing a performance practice immersed in the routine commercial enterprise of selling entertainment. They lay bare the formulaic and repetitive nature of the entertainment that they're producing and in doing so they begin to test the notion of the passive consumer. The routine of trying to fulfil the expectations of the audience is burlesqued in an ironic display of candour and apology as they take the show apart and expose at its core an integral element of all popular theatre: the tacit understanding between the audience and performer of the reality of this unreality. Here the actuality of entertainment is laid bare as a 'struggle to please'. However, the deconstruction doesn't stop at the practice and form alone but slips in the potentially more provocative agenda of critiquing the audience and society itself. It is this central element—revue's critical commentary—that begins to distinguish it and reveals potential for being a transgressive form.

The next scene of *The Follies* takes up that theme directly. Seventeen years before *Modern Times* (1936), Charlie Chaplin's film satire on the dehumanizing effects of the labour methods in the industrial age, *The Follies* comments on the contradictions of both performance and modern life through a satire of a Russian ballet. Here the aesthetic production of a dance is shown to be just as regimented as a factory assembly line as a series of Heath Robinson contraptions sees the actors attached to a succession of complicated and exaggerated ropes and pulleys in order to perform the most mundane of tasks. The sketch provides an illustration of the often complex, subtle agential social commentaries in revue as here mass industrial labour techniques are playfully critiqued against an acknowledgement that art too is just as much a produced commodity.

Before the First World War, the association with the new dances and music allowed revue a special recognition with the public, as it marked clear generational differences and seemed to capture alternative political and social attitudes and expressions. This was to be crucial to the popularity and success of revue performances during the war as it combined patriotic entertainment with the maintenance of national morale.

WARTIME REVUE: ENTERTAINMENT AND MORALE

West End revue performance constituted a particular response to mounting social, political, and cultural insecurities over Britain's status and position at the beginning of the twentieth century. Insecurities regarding Britain's colonial rule, as exemplified in Ireland and elsewhere, were compounded by growing demands for social reform across the country: the call for women's emancipation and the growth of the labour and trade union movements all created a climate of mounting disillusion. Revue correlated the immediacy of this uncertain world with a fragmented vocabulary of performance expressed by means of a bewildering variety of national, racial, and gender identity constructions on stage. Experimenting with narrative and manifestations of speech, movement, design, and sound, revues displayed ambivalent representations that reflected social and cultural negotiations of previously essentialized identities in the modern world.

During the First World War, a renegotiation of gender roles occurred as women took up the tools of industry in war-related production. This provided opportunities for women to break free from the domestic sphere, and was pivotal in challenging patriarchal power structures and contributing to the women's suffrage movement. However, in West End revue that negotiation took on a slightly different function, for rather than revealing the breakdown of traditional gender roles and identities, as indeed could be observed in other spheres, wartime revue performance displayed a regenerative nationalism that sought a remasculinization of British culture. In often contradictory and complex representations, revues perpetuated images of British manliness and womanhood that reasserted patriarchal values and constructed a version of female virtue that sexually objectified women through the development of the chorus girl persona. This was crucial in constructing a shared rhetoric of entertainment and patriotism, as revues of this period engaged in pertinent national identity and gender formations because the political establishment called for propaganda as well as distraction and escapism.

West End wartime revue productions like *By Jingo If We Do!* (1914) and *Business as Usual* (1914) were indicative of revues in the early years of the war engaging in a celebratory discourse of national identity that championed British manhood. Both shows took their titles from prominent war catchphrases (highlighting the commercial opportunism of the revue producers), which marked their association with the ensuing national war effort. *By Jingo If We Do!* was produced by Charles Cochran and opened at the Empire Theatre in October 1914, two months after the start of the First World War. The title was drawn from the chorus of G. W. Hunt's famous 'Macdermott's War Song' (1877). *Business as Usual*, produced by Albert de Courville, derived its title from advertising manager H. E. Morgan of W. H. Smith and Son,[54] who in August 1914 'in a letter to the *Daily Chronicle* suggested that the country would do well to follow a policy of "Business as Usual".[55] It was a phrase that was taken up by the government, who believed that in order to maintain a stable functioning country, it was necessary to continue in the same manner as before the war. The implication was that any change in behaviour represented a victory for the enemy, so 'Business as Usual' became shorthand for Britain's resolve not to give in. Both productions were rousing patriotic recruitment shows that mixed jingoistic bravado with musical razzmatazz to become their own form of wartime propaganda. Revue was perfectly placed to straddle a blend of the serious and comedic because of its non-linear narratives that mixed sketches, songs, and dance, and enabled it to fulfil a crucial wartime role as an entertaining distraction which also provided a vehicle for enemy-bashing propaganda.

The employment of women in coercing men to enlist became a widespread tool in the recruitment drive at the start of the war, and revues used this to their advantage, with beauty choruses and leading ladies at the forefront of recruiting sketches. In *Business As Usual*, a scene depicting the crowded streets of Whitehall in London 'immediately after the declaration of war,' on 4 August 1914, has on stage '[b]ands of young men, hatless and otherwise [. . .] parading the streets waving flags and cheering'.[56] Here identities are performative, as the social bonds of nation are acted out. The scene portrays patriots who rush to enlist, reflecting the moment when 'many [men] joined up in groups, with their pals',[57] as we see men move from an individual to a national identity. The scene is brought to a climax with the entrance of a female recruiting sergeant (played by Violet Lorraine), who organizes the newly recruited men with the help of a group of chorus girls, who patriotically appeal for more men to sign up and fight:

> Come, take your heed of England's need of every gallant son
> That liberty and right ne'er be trampled by the Hun
> So join the colours, boys and help to lay him low at last
> Let William feel old London's heel upon him planted fast.
> Old London's hard to leave 'tis true, Old London's dear to all
> But what are London's pleasures when we hear our country's call?
> So give the games a rest until the greater fight we win
> Enlist to-day, my boys, and play your next match in Berlin.[58]

On the musical stage female representation had established a long tradition for mixing respectability and the erotic in 'very careful ways',[59] with plots that centred on female figures in shows like *A Gaiety Girl* (1893), *The Shop Girl* (1894), and *Our Miss Gibbs* (1909). Musical comedy staged femininity constructing a 'customized notion of female beauty and glamour'.[60] Wartime revue followed in that tradition, with women serving as one of the major means by which the war was imagined and represented. Women functioned in a complex mixture of roles, tacitly implicated as a sexual reward for 'serving your country', but also seen as symbols of the nation and home—the justifying factors for male action, as they needed protection. The promotion of women in West End revue mirrored Florenz Ziegfeld's New York revues, mixing patriotism and sexuality, 'increasing [the] iconicity of the female body',[61] and constructing the myth of the chorus girl. This myth perpetuated the idea of an overtly sexualized woman in the male imagination through a sanctioned display of voyeurism, reflecting 'a culture that packaged women and sold sexuality'.[62]

The pervasiveness of women on the revue stage was not universally supported by theatre critics, who voiced concern at how 'an unparalleled wave of sexuality became the predominating theatrical feature towards the end of 1916'.[63] The art critic Huntly Carter complained of a 'pornographic theatre period', in which the West End was a space 'full of erotic and aesthetic symbols capable of rousing sexual emotion'[64] through a 'vision of chorus girls'[65] and where 'gradually the individual is being quashed out, and the stage is loaded with crowds of child-aping women, called by courtesy, a beauty chorus [. . .] they dazzle the eye and blast the ear'.[66] In a letter to Huntly Carter, George Bernard Shaw was particularly disturbed by revue's growing sexualization and its effect on men:

> The dialogues and gestures are lewd and silly. The dress and decorations are sexual and suggestive. The whole thing is capable of driving men to the drinking bar at each interval, and to a brothel at the end of the play [. . .]. Someone might say, what do we expect? Ought revues to drive men to prayer?[67]

Yet doubts about the propriety of entertainment in wartime gave way to the recognition of the full possibilities of its use in the war effort, both for uplifting the nation's morale and for the dissemination of propaganda, as the West End became an 'intersection between home and front'.[68] In this respect the 'tensions between "home" and "front" and between "city" and "war" were mediated by urban entertainments with their peculiar combination of modern, nostalgic, and transgressive impulses'.[69] In one sense wartime became 'a passport to inclusion'[70] and revue stressed a social and collective national identity. Paradoxically, in another sense revue representations deepened misogyny, widened the gap between male and female equality, and regulated and sought to enforce a narrow moral economy and code of behaviour for both men and women.

Post-War Revue: 'London' Intimate Revue

The intimate aesthetics of *This Year of Grace* (1928) and *The Co-Optimists* (1926) can already be seen in earlier shows by innovative revue producers Charles Cochran and André Charlot. Stressing economy, both in production costs and performance aesthetics, these revues projected an intimacy through smaller casts, little or no set design, and by employing popular performance techniques (such as directly addressing the audience) that suggested an old music hall familiarity between the performers and audience. The chorus too, which had become a staple element of revue often consisting of twenty or more girls, was also downsized for economy ('Charlot's choruses rarely numbered more than eight'[71]) but both Cochran and Charlot emphasized that this change was also for artistic reasons. Employing performers for their skills, 'personality',[72] and versatility, rather than glamour, they developed 'revue specialists' who had 'the ability to play many characters or possibly more precisely "types" in an evening'.[73] *The Co-Optimists* consisted of just ten performers who sang, danced, and played an array of characters,[74] while Gertrude (Gertie) Lawrence, actress, singer, dancer, impressionist, and comedienne in *This Year of Grace*—along with Beatrice Lillie, Jack Buchanan, and Noël Coward—provided the 'image of revue performance that others copied for succeeding decades'.[75] Intimacy also derived from the physical space of the theatre as many of these revues were now located in smaller theatres such as the Vaudeville or Duke of York's as opposed to the spectacular revues performed at the cavernous Alhambra and

Hippodrome theatres. These elements—along with a brisk pace and a lightly comic, ironic perspective—all contributed to what producers employed to market the shows as a 'new' product for a more sophisticated and select audience. The post-war period saw André Charlot along with Charles Cochran usher in the smaller 'intimate' revue style, which promoted sophisticated satirical wordplay, with *Tabs* (1918), and *Buzz, Buzz* (1918) seeing a move away from spectacular revue with smaller sets and cast.

Revues written by Noël Coward and Ronald Jeans reflected the post-war neuroses of a decadent Mayfair society as well as the ambitions of the aspirational middle classes. Coward through his satire captured the theme 'that one now knew a little too much for happiness'[76] and started to be critical of the very dance craze and music culture that revue had spawned.[77] Charlot brought Jeans and Coward together for *London Calling* (1923) and they worked separately for both Charlot and Cochran, cementing revue's popularity with *Charlot's Revue* (1923), and Coward 's *On with the Dance* (1925), *This Year of Grace* (1928), *and Words and Music* (1932). These revues engaged in a cultural reflexivity that expressed social and cultural changes through an expansive performance vocabulary of music, movement, and verbal pyrotechnics. Both Cochran and Charlot sought to attract a 'sophisticated theatre-going public as opposed to the popular variety-music hall audience',[78] and it was through female performers such as Gertrude Lawrence, Beatrice Lillie, and Florence Mills that they were able to cultivate and situate revue at the forefront of contemporary British culture. The influence of non-European performance within revue had already been established through blackface minstrelsy and African American and Oriental music and dance. However, this was to be further emphasized by the revues featuring African American performers, *Dover Street to Dixie* and the popular series of all-black revues known as *Blackbirds*. Both revues starred the legendary performer Florence Mills, a leading figure of the Harlem Renaissance. The mixture of song, dance, drama, opera, ballet, and satire in *Riverside Nights* (1926) saw the form finding recognition as a framework by the intelligentsia. Directed by Nigel Playfair, a principal figure in the evolution of the repertory theatre movement in Britain, it was to have great influence on the Group Theatre's satirical *Dance Of Death* (1934) written by W. H. Auden and the Workers' Theatre Movement of the 1930s.

Now presented in a new intimate style, revue in this period produced complex, contradictory negotiations of class and national identities that anatomized differences and distinction. In general West End revue eschewed extremism and embraced moderation/conservatism. John Pick[79] has argued that class snobbery and the economic imperatives located at the heart of the management of West End theatres contributed to 'pervasive national snobbery' which situated itself as a monarch-loving, jingoistic, aspirational culture that sought to appeal and reflect the values, ambition, and beliefs of a middle class with similar concerns for rank and position. From this perspective, the social and political agitation of the miners, the dockers, and the railway workers was associated with revolution and portrayed as an attack on the British way of life—as Coward's lyrics for the song 'Down with the Whole Damn Lot' from the 1922 edition of the revue *The Co-Optimists* illustrate:

Down with the idle rich!
The bloated upper classes.
They drive to Lord's
In expensive Fords
With their jewelled op'ra glasses.
Down with the London P'lice!
We'll have them shot.
We'll spread destruction everywhere,
Burn things up in a fine old flare.
What about the lions in Trafalgar Square?
Down with the whole damn lot![80]

As Steve Nicholson has highlighted, West End theatre engaged in sometimes blatant and explicit propaganda at a time when the Establishment felt under threat from social-ist and communist political agitation.[81] It was in this context that, seeking to appeal to the aspirant middle class and moving away from spectacular revue to the intimate revue, Coward's shows displayed an abundance of distinctive versions of class and national identities, providing idiosyncratic depictions of class conflict and engaging and criti-quing British social life.

The 1920s saw the continued popularity of American Tin Pan Alley songs with the supremacy of the old European entertainment centres of Vienna, London, Berlin, and Paris being challenged by New York song and dance imports. However, this was never one-way traffic or a wholesale Americanization, but a complex transnational space where the dominant and the subordinate, colonizer and the colonized, old Europe and New World interacted; nowhere was this better understood and those contradictions more magnified than in revue and popular musical theatre.[82] For all the American, Viennese, Continental, orientalist, exotic, and displays of otherness in West End revue, the success and popularity of the form lay in the right mixture of the local and the global, contemporary and the old, familiar and the new, and the 'intimate' revues of the 1920s exemplify this negotiation.

It was a combination of these elements that was presented in the New York produc-tion of *Charlot's London Revue of 1924*, an amalgamation of sketches and songs pre-dominately by Ronald Jeans and Noël Coward from previous revues and past successes, which was depicted not only as a different type of revue but also as a 'London/English intimat' revue. As West End revue producer André Charlot declared:

When the American theatre-going public is given a chance to see my *London Revue*, they will understand the difference between this type of show and revue in America, which in some ways, is too subtle to put into words. Over the years we have devel-oped an intimate understanding between players and audience, such as you do not know in this country in which everyone—not just the principals—can, sing, dance [and] act, but also on lighting and scenic effects which are simple and artistic.[83]

Ironically, intrinsically implicit in this statement by a French producer, is the idea that the delineating factor for the West End intimate revue, aside from the aesthetics, was a distinct English sensibility or character in its construction. On Broadway this shift from spectacular revue to a smaller 'intimate' revue became marketed and presented as an 'English' style which became the vogue in New York and established London West End revue as the embodiment of wit, sophistication, and cool. Noël Coward's persona offstage with his quick 'clipped consonants', mirrored his caustic contemporary revue characters onstage, and combined to highlight a new 'cosmopolitan style' which became seen 'expansively as attitude, stance, posture and consciousness',[84] and seemed to connote something fresh and different. As Charlot's biographer James Ross Moore emphasizes, the impact of the show in New York was 'quick and intense', garnering praise and 'the ultimate show business compliment: imitation'.[85]

Whereas Florenz Ziegfeld's spectacular revues had provided huge sets and mass choruses, intimate revue literally sought to distinguish itself against the 'crowd' in size and content, identifying itself partly through commercial imperative, but also through a conscious aesthetic effort, as a specifically British form antithetical to American spectacular revue. The attempt to institute revue as an English national product had been crudely initiated before, by West End revue producer Albert de Courville who, seeking to explore wartime national fervour, had promoted his Hippodrome revues as 'English revue'[86] during the war. This new positioning, however, was reflective of particular contemporary and at times contradictory expressions of class, empire, and a nostalgic English identity that was key to the popularity and success of intimate revue. In part this developed as a reactionary response to national, social, and economic challenges to Britain's fading hegemony. However, revue as a form reflected the zeitgeist of the decade and West End revue was illustrative of the 'exuberance of 1920s London', 'a place plugged into global currents of energy and ideas',[87] as well as of the 'local' growing struggle between the class politics of the Left and Right.

In conclusion West End revue in the first half of the twentieth century began to enact ambiguous ideological contestation through the cultural production and construction of fictive worlds. In its (re)creation of these fragmentary, fictive worlds it played with linear bourgeois cultural frameworks challenging the idea of correspondence in performance as well as life and offering social and political critiques of the new lived experiences. However, revue's depictions of the dangers of modern living were always contradicted by the celebration and outright glorification of the West End as the centre of the entertainment district, as in 'The Curate's Song' which is part of a longer sketch:

> CURATE
> A friend of mine once took me to the theatre
> I think the piece we saw was called hot stuff
> Then we went to supper with some chorus ladies.
> Which my friend described as little bits of fluff.
> I must confess the supper was delightful
> With such a lot of fizzy stuff to drink
> But I really can't remember all we did there

> And to tell the truth
> I hardly like to think
>
> CHORUS
> But it's not the sort of thing I've been used to
> We didn't leave the place till after two
> And no doubt it may be silly but we jazzed down Piccadilly
> Well it's not what I have been accustomed to.[88]

This sketch from the revue *Splinters* (1919) exemplifies strands of revue's social and cultural registration and exploration of modernity with its focus on the individual, the city, generational difference, and theatre and entertainment. Its list of themes and issues is by no means exhaustive or exclusive. Indeed analysis of revue's exploration of modernity is problematic in that it exposes the difficulties of assembling a single narrative from the multiplicity of events, which constitute revue within British culture. However, revue's fragmented form provides a series of narratives that allow critical debate. As Mica Nava and Alan O'Shea argue, mass media narratives are

> a crucial resource in the formation of identities for the popular classes in Britain. This is not because these narratives stultify people into 'masses' but because they mull over the difficulties and contradictions of living in the modern world: they address the instabilities of modernity [. . .] and also offer utopian glimpses of transcendence over often harsh and hierarchy bureaucratic rationalism which has dominated the twentieth century.[89]

These contradictions all intersect through revue's critical exploration of modernity, which had at the centre of its world, London, a 'City in the Jazz Age [. . .] a syncopated civilisation [. . .] where no notion was too cranky to voice, no experiment too eccentric to try'. Yet it was also a city 'shot with diversity and criss-crossed with nervous energy as it stared at an uncertain future,'[90] and integral to developing that imagined community—'the West End'—as the urban metropolis. West End revue captured that dual personality and energy, eschewing the extremism of social reform (socialism) and embracing moderation (conservatism) by perpetuating a 'diffusion of acquiescent attitudes towards authority'[91] in the guise of the 'allowed disruption' as illustrated by 'The Curate's Song'. In that song we find revue dealing not only with the celebration of the city and the support of individual pleasure but also with the loss of the individual and degeneracy of the city. We find the individual, a simple country Curate, addressing 'the instabilities of modernity' as he finds himself not simply in London (the city, the urban metropolis, and a beacon of modernity) but in the very theatre and entertainment district known as the 'West End'. He catches a show, 'hot stuff', mixes with chorus girls, drinks 'fizzy stuff', before 'Jazzing down Piccadilly'. It is an assortment of encounters which displays a contradictory modern experience, as the 'West End' is constructed as a space for the allowed over-indulgence and unruly delight.

Popular theatre was one of the principal media for the communication of ideas at the start of the twentieth century. Those involved in making and producing theatre began to understand that they were engaged in the formation of particular ways of seeing the world at particular times and places and sought to explore the intricate, often coded, links between their works and the ideological worlds they inhabited. The manner of these explorations acknowledged that the agency of performance resided not only in the content but also in the process of making and creating, not only in themes, issues, and aesthetics but also through seeking new interactions with the audience. West End revue of the 1920s was a culture that was self-consciously trying to negotiate the modern world and in doing so it became symptomatic of Western modernity. Drawing on a fragmented construction of modernity, revue pursued and presented a mixture of the old, the new, the clichéd, the fresh, the progressive, and the groundbreaking. Revue started to cultivate the notion that being 'modern' involved engaging and commenting on the social and cultural action of its times and marking what was important, be that one's fashion sense, the latest dance, or striking railway workers. Its satire and social critique became a driving force of its popularity by correlating the immediacy of modern social conditions, becoming a potent symbol of the popular imagination within and outside the theatre.

As a provocative yet conservative commercial entertainment, conscious of theatre as a constructed artefact, revue expanded theatrical and social vocabularies, creating a fragmented multidisciplinary form that reflected the 'messy and uneven nature of socio-historical change'.[92]

NOTES

1. R. C. Sherriff, *Journey's End* (Oxford: Heinemann Plays, 1993), 44.
2. Among the most successful of these revues were: *Business As Usual* (1914), *Push and Go* (1915), *Flying Colours* (1916), *Zig-Zag* (1917), and *Box o' Tricks* (1918) as well as *The Red Heads* (1914), *Bric à Brac* (1915), *Vanity Fair* (1916), *Airs and Graces* (1917), *Hullo America* (1918), *Not Likely* (1914), *5064 Gerrard* (1915), and *The Bing Boys Are Here* (1916).
3. Len Platt, *Musical Comedy on the West End Stage, 1890–1939* (Basingstoke: Palgrave Macmillan, 2004), 26.
4. See David Walsh and Len Platt, *Musical Theater and American Culture* (Westport: Praeger, 2003); John Bush Jones, *Our Musicals, Ourselves: A Social History of the American Musical Theatre* (Waltham: Brandeis University Press, 2003).
5. Allardyce Nicoll, *English Drama, 1900–1930: The Beginnings of the Modern Period* (Cambridge: Cambridge University Press, 1973).
6. Nicoll, *English Drama, 1900–1930*, 169.
7. Nicoll, *English Drama, 1900–1930*, 168.
8. Nicoll, *English Drama, 1900–1930*, 169.
9. Nicoll, *English Drama, 1900–1930*, 169.
10. Nicoll, *English Drama, 1900–1930*, 170.
11. Nicoll, *English Drama, 1900–1930*, 169.

12. Raymond Mander and Joe Mitchenson, *Revue: A Story in Pictures* (London: Peter Davies, 1971), 1.
13. John Pick, *The West End: Mismanagement and Snobbery* (Eastbourne: John Offord Publications Ltd, 1983).
14. Anon., 'Growth of Revue', *The Stage*, 24, September 1925, Mander & Mitchenson Collection, University of Bristol.
15. Anon., 'Growth of Revue'.
16. Nicoll, *English Drama, 1900–1930*, 169.
17. Anon., 'Growth of Revue'.
18. James Ross Moore, 'An Intimate Understanding: The Rise of British Musical Revue 1890–1920' (unpublished PhD thesis, University of Warwick, 2000), 5.
19. Nicholson Watson, *The Struggle for a Free Stage in London* (Cambridge: Houghton, Mifflin and Company, 1906), 281.
20. The concert party was a collective name for a group of entertainers sometimes referred to as a Pierrot troupe. Popular around Britain in the late nineteenth and early twentieth century, their shows consisted of comic songs, sketches, and dancing. Simply staged with little or no props, they were usually performed alfresco as a seaside entertainment.
21. Moore, 'Intimate Understanding', 20.
22. *Cafés chantants* emerged in Paris in the eighteenth century consisting originally of small groups performing light-hearted popular songs, most famously at the Café des Aveugles (Café of the Blind).
23. Huntly Carter, *The New Spirit in the European Theatre 1914–1924* (London: Ernest Benn Ltd, 1925).
24. P. Carnegy, *Wagner and the Art of the Theatre* (New Haven: Yale University Press, 2006).
25. Carter, *New Spirit*, 10. See also Jeffrey Richards, *Sir Henry Irving: A Victorian Actor and His World* (London: Hambledon Continuum, 2006), 9.
26. Hans Ulrich Gumbrecht, *In 1926: Living at the Edge of Time* (Cambridge, MA: Harvard University Press, 1997), 191.
27. Mander and Mitchenson, *Revue: A Story in Pictures*, 26.
28. See James J. Nott, *Music for the People: Popular Music and Dance in Interwar Britain* (Oxford: Oxford University Press, 2002).
29. Ramsey Burt, *Alien Bodies: Representations of Modernity: 'Race' and Nation in Early Modern Dance* (London: Routledge, 1989), 5.
30. Nott, *Music for the People*, 3.
31. Nott, *Music for the People*, 3.
32. Carter, *New Spirit*, 130.
33. See Carter, *New Spirit*, 81.
34. Carter, *New Spirit*, 82.
35. Carter, *New Spirit*, 81.
36. *League of Notions*, Typescript, London, 1921, Lord Chamberlain's Plays, British Library, not paginated.
37. *League of Notions*.
38. Anon., *The Peep Show*, Programme, London, 1921, Mander & Mitchenson Collection, University of Bristol, not paginated.
39. Anon., *Peep Show*.
40. Anon., *Peep Show*.
41. Platt, *Musical Comedy on the West End Stage*, 134.

42. Robert Baral, *Revue: The Great Broadway Period* (New York: Fleet Press, 1962), 232.
43. *The Whirligig*, Typescript, London, 1919, Lord Chamberlain's Plays, British Library, not paginated.
44. Ford Madox Ford, *The Soul of London: A Survey of a Modern City* (London: Everyman, 1995), 12.
45. Mica Nava and Alan O'Shea, eds., *Modern Times: Reflections on a Century of English Modernity* (London: Routledge, 1996), 15.
46. Nava and O'Shea, eds., *Modern Times*, 15.
47. Ronald Jeans, *Writing for the Theatre* (London: Edward Arnold & Co., 1949), 175.
48. *Whirligig*, Typescript. This piece precedes Samuel Beckett's one-act piece *Play* (1963) which uses the same experimental format, by forty-four years. Stage directions dictate '*The lines are addressed in all cases to the audience—never to each other*'.
49. *Riverside Nights*, Typescript, London, 1926, Lord Chamberlain's Plays, British Library, not paginated.
50. Nava and O'Shea, eds., *Modern Times*, 53.
51. Nava and O'Shea, eds., *Modern Times*, 64.
52. Walter Benjamin, 'The Work of Art in the Age of Mechanical Reproduction' (1936), in *Continental Philosophy: An Anthology*, ed. William McNeil and Karen S. Feldman (Oxford: Blackwell Publishers, 1998), 245.
53. *The Follies*, Typescript, London, 1919, Lord Chamberlain's Plays, British Library, not paginated.
54. W. H. Smith and Son, is a British retailer founded in 1792 (the first chain store company in the world) which operates a chain of high street and railway shops selling amongst other things books, stationery, magazines, and newspapers.
55. Arthur Marwick, *The Deluge: British Society and the First World War* (London: Bodley Head, 1965), 39.
56. Marwick, *Deluge*, not paginated.
57. Jay Winter, 'The Practices of Metropolitan Life in Wartime', in *Capital Cities at War: Paris, London, Berlin 1914–1919*, ed. Jay Winter and Jean-Louis Robert (Cambridge: Cambridge University Press, 1999), 2.
58. *Business as Usual*, Typescript, London, 1914, Lord Chamberlain's Plays, British Library, not paginated.
59. Platt, *Musical Comedy on the West End Stage*, 105.
60. Platt, *Musical Comedy on the West End Stage*, 104.
61. Angela J. Latham, *Posing a Threat: Flappers, Chorus Girls, and Other Brazen Performers of the American 1920s* (London: Wesleyan University Press, 2000), 10.
62. Platt, *Musical Comedy on the West End Stage*, 7.
63. Carter, *New Spirit*, 33.
64. Carter, *New Spirit*, 40.
65. Carter, *New Spirit*, 41.
66. Carter, *New Spirit*, 48.
67. Quoted in Carter, *New Spirit*, 46.
68. Jan Rüger, 'Entertainments', in *Capital Cities at War*, ed. Winter and Robert, 106.
69. Rüger, 'Entertainments', 106.
70. Winter, 'Practices of Metropolitan Life in Wartime', 2.
71. Ross Moore, 'Intimate Understanding', 165.
72. See Oliver Double, *Britain Had Talent: A History of Variety Theatre* (Basingstoke: Palgrave Macmillan, 2012), 95–196.

73. Ross Moore, 'Intimate Understanding', 166.
74. This style of performance or way of making theatre is the forerunner of community theatre companies of the 1930s and, later still, companies such as Joint Stock.
75. Ross Moore, *Intimate Understanding*, 167.
76. Robert Graves and Alan Hodge, *The Long Weekend: A Social History of Great Britain 1918–1939* (London: Cardinal, 1940), 147.
77. 'Though you're only seventeen | Far too much of life you've seen | Syncopated child. | Maybe if you only knew | Where your path was leading to | You'd become less wild. | But I know it's vain | Trying to explain | While there's this insane | Music in your brain.' 'Dance Little Lady' by Noël Coward from *This Year of Grace* (1928), in Noël Coward, *The Lyrics of Noël Coward* (London: Methuen Publishing Ltd, 2002), 47.
78. Mander and Mitchenson, *Revue: A Story in Pictures*, 27.
79. Pick, *West End*, chapters 1–4.
80. Coward, *Lyrics of Noël Coward*, 93.
81. Steve Nicholson, *British Theatre and the Red Peril: The Portrayal of Communism 1917–1945* (Exeter: University of Exeter Press, 1999).
82. See Len Platt, Tobias Becker, and David Linton, *Popular Musical Theatre in London and Berlin, 1890–1939* (Cambridge: Cambridge University Press, 2014).
83. Quoted in James Ross Moore, *André Charlot: The Genius of Intimate Musical Revue* (London: McFarland & Company, 2005), 84.
84. Rebecca L. Walkowitz, *Cosmopolitan Style: Modernism Beyond Nation* (New York: Columbia University Press, 2006), 2.
85. Ross Moore, 'Intimate Understanding', 93.
86. Anon., 'A Souvenir of Push and Go: the Story of Four Revues', Theatre Programme, The Hippodrome, 1 May 1915, not paginated, Mander & Mitchenson Collection, University of Bristol.
87. Cathy Ross, *Twenties London: A City in the Jazz Age* (London: Philip Wilson, 2003), 9.
88. *Splinters*, Typescript, London, 1919, Lord Chamberlain's Plays, British Library, not paginated.
89. Nava and O'Shea, eds., *Modern Times*, 4.
90. Ross, *Twenties London*, 11.
91. Eric A. Nordlinger, *The Working Class Tories: Authority, Deference and Stable Democracy* (Berkeley: University of California Press, 1967), 210.
92. Nava and O'Shea, eds., *Modern Times*, 12.

BIBLIOGRAPHY

5064 Gerrard. Typescript. London, 1915. Lord Chamberlain's Plays, British Library.
Airs and Graces. Typescript. London, 1917. Lord Chamberlain's Plays, British Library.
Anon. 'Growth of Revue.' *The Stage*, 24 September 1925. Mander & Mitchenson Collection, University of Bristol.
Anon. *The Peep Show*. Programme. London, 1921. Mander & Mitchenson Collection, University of Bristol.
Anon. 'A Souvenir of Push and Go: the Story of Four Revues.' Theatre Programme, The Hippodrome, 1 May 1915. Mander & Mitchenson Collection, University of Bristol.
Baral, Robert. *Revue: The Great Broadway Period*. New York: Fleet Press, 1962.

Benjamin, Walter. 'The Work of Art in the Age of Mechanical Reproduction'. 1936. In *Continental Philosophy: An Anthology*, edited by William McNeil and Karen S. Feldman, 244–252. Oxford: Blackwell Publishers, 1998.

The Bing Boys Are Here. Typescript. London, 1916. Lord Chamberlain's Plays, British Library.

Box o' Tricks. Typescript. London, 1918. Lord Chamberlain's Plays, British Library.

Bric à Brac. Typescript. London, 1915. Lord Chamberlain's Plays, British Library.

Burt, Ramsey. *Alien Bodies, Representations of Modernity: 'Race' and Nation in Early Modern Dance*. London: Routledge, 1989.

Bush Jones, John. *Our Musicals, Ourselves: A Social History of the American Musical Theatre*. Waltham: Brandeis University Press, 2003.

Business as Usual. Typescript. London, 1914. Lord Chamberlain's Plays, British Library.

Carnegy, P. *Wagner and the Art of the Theatre*. New Haven: Yale University Press, 2006.

Carter, Huntly. *The New Spirit in the European Theatre 1914-1924*. London: Ernest Benn Ltd, 1925.

Coward, Noël. *The Lyrics of Noël Coward*. London: Methuen Publishing Ltd, 2002.

Double, Oliver. *Britain Had Talent: A History of Variety Theatre*. Basingstoke: Palgrave Macmillan, 2012.

Flying Colours. Typescript. London, 1916. Lord Chamberlain's Plays, British Library.

The Follies. Typescript. London, 1919. Lord Chamberlain's Plays, British Library.

Graves, Robert, and Alan Hodge. *The Long Weekend: A Social History of Great Britain 1918-1939*. London: Cardinal, 1940.

Gumbrecht, Hans Ulrich. *In 1926: Living at the Edge of Time*. Cambridge, MA: Harvard University Press, 1997.

Hullo America. Typescript. London, 1918. Lord Chamberlain's Plays, British Library.

Jeans, Ronald. *Writing for the Theatre*. London: Edward Arnold & Co., 1949.

Latham, Angela J. *Posing a Threat: Flappers, Chorus Girls, and Other Brazen Performers of the American 1920s*. London: Wesleyan University Press, 2000.

League of Notions. Typescript. London, 1921. Lord Chamberlain's Plays, British Library.

Madox Ford, Ford. *The Soul of London: A Survey of a Modern City*. London: Everyman, 1995.

Mander, Raymond, and Joe Mitchenson. *Revue: A Story in Pictures*. London: Peter Davies, 1971.

Marwick, Arthur. *The Deluge: British Society and the First World War*. London: Bodley Head, 1965.

Nava, Mica, and Alan O'Shea, eds. *Modern Times: Reflections on a Century of English Modernity*. London: Routledge, 1996.

Nicholson, Steve. *British Theatre and the Red Peril: The Portrayal of Communism 1917–1945*. Exeter: University of Exeter Press, 1999.

Nicoll, Allardyce. *English Drama, 1900-1930: The Beginnings of the Modern Period*. Cambridge: Cambridge University Press, 1973.

Nordlinger, Eric A. *The Working Class Tories: Authority, Deference and Stable Democracy*. Berkeley: University of California Press, 1967.

Not Likely. Typescript. London, 1914. Lord Chamberlain's Plays, British Library.

Nott, James J. *Music for the People: Popular Music and Dance in Interwar Britain*. Oxford: Oxford University Press, 2002.

Pick, John. *The West End: Mismanagement and Snobbery*. Eastbourne: John Offord Publications Ltd, 1983.

Platt, Len. *Musical Comedy on the West End Stage, 1890-1939*. Basingstoke: Palgrave Macmillan, 2004.

Platt, Len, Tobias Becker, and David Linton. *Popular Musical Theatre in London and Berlin, 1890–1939*. Cambridge: Cambridge University Press, 2014.

Push and Go. Typescript. London, 1915. Lord Chamberlain's Plays, British Library.

The Red Heads. Typescript. London, 1914. Lord Chamberlain's Plays, British Library.

Richards, Jeffrey. *Sir Henry Irving: A Victorian Actor and His World*. London: Hambledon Continuum, 2006.

Riverside Nights. Typescript. London, 1926. Lord Chamberlain's Plays, British Library.

Ross, Cathy. *Twenties London: A City in the Jazz Age*. London: Philip Wilson, 2003.

Ross Moore, James. *André Charlot: The Genius of Intimate Musical Revue*. London: McFarland & Company, 2005.

Ross Moore, James. 'An Intimate Understanding: The Rise of British Musical Revue 1890–1920.' Unpublished PhD thesis, University of Warwick, 2000.

Rüger, Jan. 'Entertainments.' In *Capital Cities at War: Paris, London, Berlin 1914–1919*, edited by Jay Winter and Jean-Louis Robert, 101–140. Cambridge: Cambridge University Press, 1999.

Sherriff, R. C. *Journey's End*. Oxford: Heinemann Plays, 1993.

Splinters. Typescript. London, 1919. Lord Chamberlain's Plays, British Library.

Vanity Fair. Typescript. London, 1916. Lord Chamberlain's Plays, British Library.

Walkowitz, Rebecca L. *Cosmopolitan Style: Modernism Beyond Nation*. New York: Columbia University Press, 2006.

Walsh, David, and Len Platt. *Musical Theater and American Culture*. Westport: Praeger, 2003.

Watson, Nicholson. *The Struggle for a Free Stage in London*. Cambridge: Houghton, Mifflin and Company, 1906.

The Whirligig. Typescript. London, 1919. Lord Chamberlain's Plays, British Library.

Winter, Jay. 'The Practices of Metropolitan Life.' In *Capital Cities at War: Paris, London, Berlin 1914–1919*, edited by Jay Winter and Jean-Louis Robert, 1–20. Cambridge: Cambridge University Press, 1999.

Zig-Zag. Typescript. London, 1917. Lord Chamberlain's Plays, British Library.

PART II

BRITISH OR AMERICAN

Artistic Differences

CHAPTER 6

....

MUSICAL COMEDY IN THE 1920S AND 1930S

Mister Cinders *and* Me and My Girl *as Class-Conscious Carnival*

....

GEORGE BURROWS

THE idea that the British are obsessed with class attitudes is, of course, now a well-worn cliché but like many stereotypes it has a ring of truth about it. The British poet John Betjeman wrote in 1979 that class is 'that topic all absorbing, as it was, is now and ever shall be, to us'.[1] In 1997 the Norwegian social scientist Stein Ringen wrote, 'what is peculiar to Britain is not the reality of the class system and its continued existence, but class psychology: the preoccupation with class, the belief in class, and the symbols of class in manners, dress and language'.[2]

Mister Cinders (1929) and *Me and My Girl* (1937) are particularly British musical comedies because of their preoccupation with age-old British class hierarchies in the face of the difficulty of sustaining such social strata within interwar modernity. In this context there is, as Ringen has pointed out, an enduring paradox in the fact that 'Britain is a thoroughly modern society, with thoroughly archaic institutions, conventions and beliefs'.[3] This chapter will try tease out some of that tension between the archaic and the modern and its mapping on to social class discourses in each show within its specific socio-historical context.[4]

This enterprise follows in the wake of Len Platt's seminal book on British musical comedy. Platt has argued that the apparent obsession of Edwardian shows with class discourses that revolved around the aristocracy is a sign of a particularly British struggle to come to terms with social change engendered by modernity.[5] However, Platt reads *Mister Cinders* and *Me and My Girl* merely as rare 'period-piece' successes within an era of marked decline for musical comedy.[6] For Platt, they are, in effect, outmoded anomalies requiring little critical attention because the genre was dying, if not dead.

This chapter seeks to challenge Platt's lack of detailed analysis of these interwar shows and his reading of them as anomalous by articulating a sort of Bakhtinian-British model for understanding how interwar musical comedy articulated forms of carnival that offered at least as vibrant, current and engaging discourses about contemporary class attitudes.[7] Furthermore, *Me and My Girl* arguably had an impact that far exceeded that of earlier musical comedy. This suggests the genre actually reached something of a high-point in social relevance during the interwar period.

So, this articulation of Bakhtinian carnival with musical comedy aims to highlight how such class-conscious discourse operated as a cogent form of social critique both within and beyond the musical theatre of interwar Britain, as it explores the specific forms it took in each show and also in their 1980s revivals. Ultimately, to extend Platt, the chapter aims to establish the enduring importance of British Musical comedy as a popular and powerful form of social class discourse in the period before the Second World War and also beyond it.

INTERWAR MUSICAL COMEDY
AS CLASS-CONSCIOUS CARNIVAL

The Soviet literary scholar Mikhail Bakhtin conceived of medieval carnival as a space in which the dogma of the otherwise all-powerful church was temporarily suspended in favour of enacting alternative and revitalizing social structures. This escapist or alternative medieval culture may seem a long way removed from British musical comedy of the 1920s and 1930s but Bakhtin suggests that carnival was 'transposed' into later literatures and these can include musical comedy because of similar features and functions.[8] The apparently silly and class-obsessed narratives of musical comedy, for example, invariably involve what Bakhtin calls 'carnivalistic mésalliances': unconventional combinations of 'the sacred with the profane, the lofty with the low, the great with the insignificant, the wise with the stupid.'[9] Such mésalliances mean a similarly 'free and familiar attitude spreads over everything: over all values, thoughts, phenomena and things.'[10] The subverting of social conventions means that musical comedy protagonists, like carnival's participants, tend to behave in ways that would be considered inappropriate or eccentric in contemporary society. This eccentricity, however, allows them to represent things about that society which might otherwise have been impossible.[11]

Musical comedy also shares something of the special humour of carnival, albeit in a much more genteel form. Humour is important in carnival partly because it allows for the enactment of alternative social structures without the risk of alienation or censure. Such comedy thrives on inversion, parody, and ambivalence which play on social hierarchy in such a relative way as to engender communal revitalization.[12] Carnival's bawdy language, featuring profanities and blasphemies that for Bakhtin become 'a whole system of carnivalistic debasings and bringings down to earth', is, of course, greatly refined in musical comedy.[13] However, we will see its humour similarly aims at undermining exalted attitudes by invoking contemporary modernity and the relative 'naturalism' of the working-class body in relation to social hierarchy.

At the heart of the carnivalistic rituals of musical comedy is the equivalent of the crowning and de-crowning of a carnival king, whereby an out-of-place or eccentric character becomes the focus of the narrative's mésalliances. Such a symbolic ritual is the 'primary carnival act' for Bakhtin and it is joyfully carried out in the full knowledge of its inevitable undoing (crowning always implies de-crowning). Thus carnival, like musical comedy narrative, is demarked by a symbolic birth and death (curtain up and down) that is embraced as 'the *joyful relativity* of all structure and order, of all authority and all (hierarchical) positions'.[14] In this context carnival becomes 'a pageant without footlights and without a division into performers and spectators just as audiences lose themselves in the experience of theatre'.[15] As 'its participants *live* in it', carnival blurs the divide between comedic theatre and social 'reality' to great socio-critical effect.

For Bakhtin, such relativity between the symbols of carnival and of 'real' society is crucial for the critical function of carnival humour in promoting social revitalization.[16] Thus reading a class-conscious and comedic form like British musical comedy of the interwar period as a form of carnival illuminates both its performative method of social critique and its socially revitalizing theatrics. In a period when prevailing modernity seemed increasingly at odds with the old certainties of the British social hierarchy and with musical comedy as a genre, we will see that there was much to be gained by indulging in a little carnivalistic song-and-dance about apparent class attitudes both within the theatre and beyond it.[17] Each show will thus be considered for carnivalistic resonances of hierarchical social structures and the revitalizing 'alternative' social discourses that are offered through its comical scenario.

MISTER CINDERS: SPREADING A LITTLE HIERARCHICAL HAPPINESS

Mister Cinders opened at the Adelphi Theatre in London's West End on 11 February 1929 and in time proved to be one of the most enduring shows of the late 1920s.[18] It premiered on one of the coldest nights of the year. As Vivian Ellis put it, '[t]he audience was about one degree warmer than most of the critics' and thereby ensured its success in the face of a frosty critical reception.[19] The show transferred to the Hippodrome in July 1929 to complete a run of 528 performances. It was subsequently produced in Berlin, Warsaw, Mumbai (then Bombay), and Johannesburg and was made into a film in 1934.[20]

The lyricist Clifford Grey and playwright Greatrex Newman conceived of this gender-reversed Cinderella show as early as 1927 with the West End producer Julian Wylie. Wylie had produced precious little musical comedy but was well known for his spectacular pantomimes and reviews.[21] As so many contemporary American shows had proved popular in the West End during the 1920s, Wylie thought an American score would ensure success. So Grey, who was well known in America, engaged lyricist Leo Robin and composer Richard Myers to produce songs for the show with him.[22] They collaborated on a few songs before production was halted when the British star Leslie Henson, who had been engaged to play the all-important Cinderella role, left the project to take a part in *Funny Face* starring Fred Astaire.[23]

By the time the production was back on track, the desire for a modern American score had faded in view of the urgent need to get the show on the stage. Thus a young British composer, Vivian Ellis, was employed to complete the score around the handful of extant songs. An emerging comedy performer, Bobby Howes, replaced Henson. Binnie Hale, who had enjoyed considerable success in *No, No, Nannette* (1925), was secured to play opposite him (see Figure 6.1). Ellis clearly felt it was this pairing that accounted for the success of the show. He described Hale as the epitome of a hard-working, modern woman:

> She sang, she danced, she acted, she played (piano and stock markets), she swam, she sewed, she was an efficient housewife and a wonderful mother. She talked rapidly and terrified me with her mimicry, she could kick the back of her head and

FIGURE 6.1 Appearances deceive: 'handyman' Jim (Bobby Howes) and 'maid' Jill (Binnie Hale) in *Mister Cinders*, Adelphi Theatre 1929.

Mander & Mitchenson, University of Bristol. Courtesy of ArenaPal.

touch her toes with equal facility (she still has the loveliest hands and legs I have ever seen), and oh, how she worked! She was gay but not very strong, so never wasted her energies on unnecessary parties. She would practice for hours in front of a long mirror. Everything she did was thought out, down to the smallest detail [...] she brought the full battery of her talents to her part in *Mr. Cinders* and made it live.

For Ellis, Hale was in control of all she did, whereas Bobby Howes exuded a sort of easy naturalism:

He *was* Mr. Cinders. He merely projected his own personality on to the stage. He always had an appealing singing voice, he always played the fool and had that little-boy charm. The combination was a 'natural.' Binnie Hale adored him and they were an ideal stage partnership.[24]

As we will see, just such opposing-yet-complementary characteristics spoke and, indeed, moved and sang of British class modernity in an urgent way within the carnivalistic narrative of the show. In fact, the popularity of *Mister Cinders* can be attributed to the way its carnival was attuned to contemporary British attitudes towards modernity. It appeared at the end of a decade that had ushered in a great deal of social and technological change and its carnivalistic musical comedy resonates with discourse about such change.

As carnival for Bakhtin always invokes social revitalization, the show not only reflects contemporary attitudes but also envisions an adjusted society more accepting of modernity, especially in terms of modernized hierarchical social structures. This is envisioned in the face of generally outmoded, pretentious, and oppressive figures of British aristocracy in the show. As we will see, ultimately the carnival of *Mister Cinders* suggests that if such British institutions can adjust to contemporary modernity then society will prove all the happier for it. However, while *Mister Cinders* may envision some adjustment within the British Establishment it does not suggest abandoning the traditionally stratified structures of British society but rather a strengthening of them in a refined social hierarchy built on new modern values. In this regard it reflects prevailing class politics of the mid-to-late 1920s.

In the 1924 general election, Stanley Baldwin's Conservative Party replaced Labour with a clear majority. The Conservatives had long focused on uniting individuals for the betterment of British society and by the 1920s notions of class were considered by stalwart Conservatives like Edward Wood as divisive false-concepts of collectivism resulting from 'shallow Marxist materialism'.[25] As David Cannadine has written: 'The most influential and articulate purveyor of this brand of inter-war Conservatism was Stanley Baldwin.'[26]

In essence, Baldwin rejected the division of British society into upper-, middle-, and lower-class groupings because he felt it presumed and, indeed, incited conflict between them. By contrast, he felt 'a brotherly and neighbourly feeling', such as might be found in the factory and countryside, extended 'through all classes' and thus he sought to unite the British people as 'one nation' within a more stratified social hierarchy.[27]

Baldwin was motivated by what he saw as the inflammatory class-consciousness of the years before the First World War and the enduring class politics of Bolshevism which he felt put at risk any hope of lasting peace because that required a united people. He offered instead a 'consensual, individualistic, inegalitarian, hierarchical model' for British society that involved 'the re-creation of traditional social identities in a non-traditional world'.[28]

Baldwin was aided in such hierarchical social enterprises by the Labour opposition, led by Ramsay MacDonald, which was keen to refute accusations that it was wholly class-orientated or represented only one class. However, Labour was as much influenced by the need to appeal to the growing middle-class electorate that encompassed more complex social structures engendered by the post-war economy. This cross-party consensus reflected a broader public desire for peace at the expense of more collective class identities. The effect of the tacit pact was that, as Cannadine writes, 'During the interwar years, both Baldwin and MacDonald were actively engaged in recasting and reviving hierarchical Britain'.[29]

Baldwin's government was thus quick to revamp the highly stratified and hierarchical British honours system and to reinvent the pageantry of the British monarchy (spectacular royal weddings etc.) on which the system was founded. In the face of much disconcerting modernity in the post-war period, not least the rise of fascism and communism elsewhere, reviving such institutions as central tenets of a modern Britain offered reassuring continuity, tradition, rank, and order. However, the General Strike of 1926, engendered by a depressed coal market and cross-union protests over reduced miners' pay, showed that the spectre of class groupings that Baldwin was keen to excise could not be so easily laid to rest.[30]

Although Baldwin's government ultimately triumphed over the unions in the strike, ongoing and widespread unemployment meant that by the 1929 general election class groupings were increasingly back on the agenda. That election was widely known as the 'flapper' election because it was the first in which women were given the same voting rights as men. This was a bill Baldwin had fought during 1927 in the face of stiff opposition from within his own party and on the back of several failed attempts by others. As Branson has noted, in the arguments against and for Baldwin's bill, 'nothing could have demonstrated more clearly the pre-war and post-war worlds'.[31] Among those against the bill were many 'traditional' Conservatives who struggled with the idea of the female vote and feared what it might mean for their parliamentary majority. Thus, when the 1929 election resulted in heavy losses for the Conservatives, many blamed Baldwin.[32]

As a result of a shortage of male labour, the social standing of women changed markedly during the First World War and this led towards greater equality with men during the 1920s. As the decade progressed, women gained more control over their lives (especially in terms of family planning and divorce) and broader employment possibilities. Women could mix with men more freely and this all led to a new-found confidence that was reflected in new and more daring fashions such as shorter skirts, bobbed hair, and close-fitting hats. Female fashion of the 1920s was more figure-hugging and showed more leg but the taste for short hair and flat chests meant that a very modern and boyish femininity was engendered.[33]

The carnivalistic mésalliances of *Mister Cinders* extend from the dissonant modernity of the unpretentious central characters of Jim and Jill (decidedly not James and Jillian) within the highly class-conscious pretensions of the aristocratic society that surrounds them. Jim is the nephew of the kindly but ineffective Sir George Lancaster and, as the Cinderella character of the narrative, he is oppressed by his aunt, Lady Agatha Lancaster, and her sons, Guy and Lumley.[34] Jill is an American debutante-in-waiting and the very epitome of late 1920s feminine modernity: she dresses fashionably and is on the run for dangerous driving and for evading a policeman by knocking his hat over his eyes. She shows confidence in disguising herself as Lady Lancaster's new maid to escape the police and in convincing Jim to go to the ball disguised as the Earl of Ditcham, a famous explorer of South America.

Both Jim and Jill are out of place at Merton Chase, the Lancasters' stately home, and much of the show's comedy derives from their seemingly 'eccentric' actions within its pretentiously class-conscious society. [35] Yet their carnivalistic eccentricity is precisely what enables them to speak truth to power about engrained class positions. Jill is thus always breaking things (not least the social rules) and generally subverts her assumed role as the maid to highlight Lady Lancaster's class-orientated bullying and social pretensions. Similarly, Jim, who is forced to be a handyman and to tend the grounds of Merton Chase, shows by comparison with Guy and Lumley that leisure-class affectations are never a substitute for seemingly more bodily, 'natural' and simple working-class values of hard work, directness, honesty, and integrity.[36]

While Jim, who is often depicted in bodily exertion, might be equated with an idealized 1920s image of the working classes, it soon becomes clear that he does not really belong among them and neither does Jill when she impersonates the maid. However, Jill's tomboyish modernity also means that she does not conform as a maid or a society debutante but carnivalistically 'plays' such traditional femininities to her own ends. Thus the Cinderella narrative is reconstructed through the show's carnival such that we desire the protagonists to escape their situations within the established social hierarchy and return to their rightful places among a revitalized modern-aristocratic society.

Guy and Lumley's leisure-class affectations appear highly effeminate by comparison with Jim's physical labour and down-to-earth character. They only really recover their masculinity at the end of the show when they stand up to their mother.[37] In this context the effeminate peacocking of Guy and Lumley in their costumes before the ball (amusingly rendered in the song 'Belle of the Ball') can be read as a carnivalistic representation of their emasculation in the face of Lady Lancaster's snobbish social pretensions and power.[38]

At the ball, Jim, as the Earl of Ditcham, is at his most subversively comic in 'On the Amazon', a song that he sings to a group of girls to get back at Jill, whom he thinks is humiliating herself by posing as Kemp's debutante daughter.[39] The song employs various archaic and verbose terms to describe the 'ferocious' animals that he is supposed to have encountered on his travels in Paraguay. While Jim is clearly in his element as carnival king in sending up pretentious verbosity, it is also clear that his affected status is by no means assured because the guest of honour, Donna Anna, the widow of the late president of Paraguay, is upset by his fraudulent performance. When the lights suddenly go out and Donna Anna's famous pearls are stolen, Jim is accused of stealing them and his status further diminishes.[40] Fortunately, Jim has been honest with Jill about his feelings by this point and she, as his lover-cum-fairy-godmother, also needs to escape the ball because she has been recognized as the fashionable motorist that the police are after. The couple escape on a motorcycle (a lower classed mode of transport than the expensive motor car) to the local railway station.[41]

On finding they have run out of petrol and missed the last train they head back to Merton Chase on foot to resume their identities as handyman and maid. However, they leave the real thief, Velvet Victor, who was posing as a private detective and had framed Jim for the crime, incapacitated in the sidecar with a note attached to him.[42] In the final scene a policeman unmasks the real culprit and Jim is eventually found to fit a bowler hat that was discovered with the thief in the sidecar. This utterly bourgeois replacement for the glass slipper of the fairy tale is, of course, highly symbolic of the show's class discourse. Guy suggests that Jim deserves a double reward because it was actually he who saved Kemp from drowning, but to ease the Lancasters' situation, Jill suggests Guy should still be rewarded for being such a good sport. When Kemp asks who will then reward Jim, she says 'I'll take care of that' and kisses him to effect the obligatory happy ending.

In the context of British social politics of the late 1920s the show's carnival reflects a crisis of faith in the traditional British hierarchy and thereby also the old notions of collective class structures it supported. However, the chief protagonists of *Mister Cinders* ultimately represent an adjusted, modern aristocracy based on new forms of cultural capital. Values of hard work, unpretentious honesty, self-assurance, and integrity are drawn from working-class and modern-American ethics while old-world leisure-class values are affectionately beaten back by the youthful, jazzy song-and-dance of the contemporary sensibility of the show.

This beating back is literally represented in 'Seventeenth Century Drag', an all-singing-all-dancing number, which opens Act 2 in the ballroom of the American oil tycoon's mansion. The number starts with a sedate, old-world minuet performed by the whole company. However, this rather lifeless display abruptly gives way to Ellis's version of low-down 'hot' jazz.[43] Upbeat American music thus quite literally beats back the stoical British-aristocratic culture and, as the aristocrats dance to that modern American beat, their minuet and culture is immediately updated and revitalized.

The show is thus as much a collaboration of markers of contemporary class identities, achieved through juxtaposing apparently tired British aristocratic traditions with a more vibrantly modern American culture, as it is between its various authors and performers. The aim of this collaborative enterprise is, as Ellis's most famous song in the show suggests, to 'Spread a Little Happiness' where it might otherwise be prevented by antiquated and oppressive class-stratified pretensions.[44]

To this end the song is interestingly bittersweet. As Ellis wrote:

> I wanted it to have an underlying sadness and depth [. . .] 'Spread a Little Happiness' was never an easy song, but Binnie Hale handled it beautifully. I wrote her a special counter-melody in mauscript, and very wisely she kept it. My music publishing experiences had taught me the importance of trying to suit individual artists.[45]

'Spread a Little Happiness' appears in the third scene of the show, in which the Lancaster family are all readying themselves for the ball and Jill (impersonating the maid) plots her attendance despite the seemingly impassable opposition of the all-powerful and ever-present Lady Lancaster. The lyrics of the song's AABA form refrain thus propose the importance of maintaining a sunny disposition in the face of any such depressive situation. As Jill is an American character, this sentiment would seem to represent New World optimism that contrasts with the British tradition of stiff-upper-lip acceptance.

The sunny aspect is evoked in the jaunty dotted rhythm of the opening of the refrain's melody, which ascends the first seven notes of the E flat major scale from the tonic before falling to the fifth scale degree and then bouncing back up to the tonic octave (see Example 6.1). The underlying gloom is then immediately implied via a sequence of three syncopated and falling intervals in the melody (a minor sixth, a perfect fifth, and a diminished fifth) accompanied by darker, minor-chord harmonies.[46] The last falling interval is given further pathos by flattening the fifth of the chord to produce diminished sonorities. Crucially, when the light-heartedness of the dotted rhythm is restored in the fifth bar the jaunty opening motif is reharmonized with similarly minor/diminished chords until the cadential passage is reached. Thus we are presented simultaneously with the melodic-rhythmical suggestion of Jill's upbeat carnivalistic antics and the harmonically gloomy reality of the prevailing situation that demands them.

We can hear Hale's performance of the song in a track she made with Al Starita and His Novelty Orchestra for Columbia Records in London in March 1929.[47] Her characteristically thin and fluttering voice has a vulnerable quality which is only further emphasized by the way she ornaments the melody and, in the final A section of the song, by the gaps that are introduced in the vocal line and accompaniment after 'sigh' and 'cry' that imply a highly emotive breathlessness. Her wordless counterpoint in a passage before this (sung during the dance break with Sir George in the show) also evidences a rich mix of pathos and easy-going laughter at it.[48] The effect is as much about the rhythm—long-held notes followed by quicker movement—as it is about the placement reasonably high in her almost faltering voice.

In many ways this song captures the very essence of the show's carnival atmosphere. It shows that beneath the light-hearted comedy is a profound sense of loss and nostalgia for the antiquated British class system in the face of its reinvigoration through the aegis of Anglo-American modernity. Old class pretensions seem to stand in the way of Jim and Jill's happiness and the contemporary modernity that they represent. However, by the end of the show they do not give up on aristocratic culture but take their expected places within it. Nevertheless, they bring the sunny affect of their youthful, American-British

EXAMPLE 6.1 The opening of the refrain of 'Spread a Little Happiness' (annotated).

'Spread A Little Happiness' from *Mr Cinders*.

Words by Greatrex Newman and Clifford Grey, Music by Vivian Ellis.

modern values to revive that class-conscious society. Their musical-comedy personas thus ultimately suggest a less pretentious and more integrated and highly stratified society. In the end, even the snobbish traditionalist Lady Lancaster cannot fail to feel the warm glow of the sunshine offered by the new, more Anglo-American and modern social order that Jim and Jill represent even if the old class system remains pretty much intact.

ME AND MY GIRL: REVITALIZING COCKNEY CARNIVAL

The original London production of *Me and My Girl* dates from eight years after *Mister Cinders* and sustained a far longer run of 1,646 performances.[49] It opened at the

Victoria Palace Theatre on 16 December 1937 and ran on into the war with brief inter-ruptions when it was bombed out of the theatre during the London Blitz.[50] If *Mister Cinders* ultimately preserves an adjusted aristocracy through its modern-carnival revitalization of the British social order, *Me and My Girl* puts such leisure-class gen-try and the traditional hierarchical structures supporting them much more at risk by invoking a more profound dissonance between cockney protagonists and upper-class culture.

Like *Mister Cinders, Me and My Girl* features a similar gender-inversion of the classic Cinderella narrative but it is one in which a cockney barrow boy, Bill Snibson, unex-pectedly discovers he is Lord Hareford and has inherited a large fortune. As in *Mister Cinders* there is a kindly uncle figure (Sir John) and an older-female figure of upper-class power (the Duchess). She attempts to train Bill away from his working-class upbringing and his cockney girlfriend Sally. The flirtatious Lady Jacqueline also has designs on Bill, due to his new-found wealth, and ditches her handsome upper-class twit of a fiancé, Gerald Bolingbroke, in order to make a move on Snibson.[51]

Comic situations are created by Bill's protracted attempts to escape Jacqueline's advances and to effect the transition from costermonger to aristocrat. Eventually the Duchess persuades Sally to leave Hareford Hall so as not to stand in Bill's way to becom-ing a gentleman. However, Sir John, who as a young man did not act on his own love for the Duchess, follows Sally to Lambeth and persuades her to take lessons from an elocu-tionist friend of his in order to get back with Bill. She returns to Hareford Hall having become as much a lady as Bill has a gentleman, which allows for the happy union of Bill and Sally.

Me and My Girl featured a score by Noel Gay and a libretto by L. Arthur Rose and Douglas Furber that was built around the slapstick comedy performance of actor-pro-ducer Lupino Lane who appeared in the central role of Bill Snibson (see Figure 6.2). Lane, whom Morley describes as 'the greatest cockney singer-comedian of his gener-ation', had developed the character of Snibson in 1935 in another collaboration with Rose entitled *Twenty-to-One*.[52] This started life as a comedy-play called *The Dark Horse* about betting on horse races.[53] Snibson was a peripheral character in the play until Lane started developing the role during a tour of provincial theatres.[54] Lane bought the rights to the show and by the time it opened in London it had a new musical score added by Billy Mayerl, a new title, and a new central character of Snibson. It was per-formed in London more than 400 times and, although this represents less than a quarter of the run of *Me and My Girl,* it was considered successful enough for Lane to pursue the sequel.[55]

James Dillon White's biography of Lane makes clear that the aim with *Me and My Girl* was to effect a carnivalistic scenario around Snibson that would 'shake up' the British Establishment or, at least, the enduring popular image of the leisure-class gentry.[56] As Platt has shown, by 1937 such class-orientated discourse had long been the master trope of British musical comedy and thus the show can be read as 'period-piece nostalgia'.[57] Such archaism was even noted in the review that appeared in *The Times* the day after the London opening which stated: 'As a week-end bag by some aspiring hostess this would be wonderful; as musical comedy it is just part of a 30- or it may be 50-years' tradition of kind hearts in an uphill effort against coronets.'[58]

FIGURE 6.2 Sally (Teddy St Denis) surprises Bill (Lupino Lane) in his peers' regalia just after the famous 'cape routine' in the original production of *Me and My Girl*, Palace Theatre 1937.

The archaism of the show was particularly evident for the critic in George Grave's rather old-fashioned and affected performance as Sir John, which contrasted with Lane's comparatively more 'natural' and slapstick comedy as Snibson. The reviewer remarked that once Lane overcame the seemingly tired musical comedy format he proved 'vastly superior to the piece'. The review continues:

> he takes threadbare material, turns it inside out and, though some of the seams still show, makes of it a new and fairly durable comedy. Innuendo is its strength, but it is innocent innuendo, unlike some of Graves's later gags, and his fooling is most successful when it is as irresponsible and pointless as a schoolboy's. The other prop of the evening is Mr. Graves himself, since his airs and graces of an Edwardian man about town—to-day the type has been absorbed in others—give a certain elegance to the most hackneyed wit.[59]

This suggests that the show succeeded because Lane's cockney modernity cuts across all datedness in its carnivalistic difference. Thus, while the play's genre may appear as archaic musical comedy, to describe *Me and My Girl* as merely a nostalgia piece, as Platt does, does not tell of its genre mastery and its highly modern-carnivalistic mode of performance. In fact, Lane is even described in clearly carnivalistic terms in the review for his ability to turn the tropes of the old form 'inside out' and thereby offer something of 'the reverse side of the world' of musical comedy.[60] Lane's act thus proved carnivalistically reinvigorating both within the show's narrative and with respect to the prevailing tropes of musical comedy.

The review in *The Times* points to Bill's position as the show's carnival king when it cites the most famous sequence of Lane's carnivalistic performance: '[L]eave him alone with a coronet and a mantle trimmed with miniver and he is vastly superior to the piece.'[61] The sequence that is referenced here comes in a scene when Bill is preparing to practise his maiden speech for the House of Lords and is thus dressed up in his peer's regalia. In an exchange with Sally he attempts to pass on what he has learned about the history of the Hareford family but the attempt is undermined by some funny misunderstandings. For example, when Bill mentions that one of his ancestors fought Joan of Arc, Sally replies: 'But your ancestors don't go back to the flood.'[62]

It was, however, not this 'horrible history' that made a lasting impression on audiences and critics but Lane's highly physical and comic business with his peers' regalia: he first trips on the end of his robe and then effects a series of ever more elaborate circling moves that exploit the comic potential of his billowing ermine-lined cape.[63] According to White the sequence 'was developed from an accidental movement in the try-out at Nottingham' that unexpectedly made the audience laugh and was refined 'through weeks of careful practice'.[64] In the coronation year of 1937, Lane's appearance with robes and crown immediately evoked royal pageantry and a recent constitutional crisis.

Me and My Girl appeared the year after King Edward VIII announced that he was abdicating in order to marry the American divorcee Wallis Simpson. Until the abdication, Edward was generally a popular figure: in leading a sort of playboy lifestyle as the Prince of Wales and showing concern for the unemployed he appealed as a relatively unpretentious royal to whom the public could relate.[65] However, despite some sympathy for his situation, Edward's abdication came as a shock to many British people because, until his announcement, the British media had repressed the story.[66] Thus Edward's apparently sudden decision profoundly destabilized the public's faith in the most foundational institution of the British social order.[67]

Lane's clowning, especially as it happened around potted dates in a nonsensical pseudo-royal history, thus raised topical questions about class tropes in the face of middle-class uncertainty concerning the monarchy as a defining British institution. At one point in Lane's carefully worked-out routine, Bill ends up on his back, covered in his peers' cloak and with his coronet on his stomach, as if he were lying in state.[68] When this was so easily read as a death knell for social ranking based on royal example, was it any wonder that it was met with roars of laughter and proved highly memorable even long after the show's initial run?[69]

Two contemporary critics who felt this feature was particularly telling of contemporary class attitudes were the socialist intellectuals Charles Madge (1912–96) and Tom Harrison (1911–76), the author-editors of *Britain by Mass-Observation* (1939). Madge and Harrison were in no doubt that Lane's cape routine poked 'unmistakable and uproarious fun at the coronation' in order to flag-up class politics.[70] For them this was a part of a broader methodology: 'The point of the show is essentially the contrast between the *natural* behaviour of the Lamberthians and the affectation of the upper class.'[71] They frame this view within William Empson's reading of pastoral literature, quoting it at length. The most telling part for its resonance of carnival is this:

> The simple man becomes a clumsy fool who yet has better 'sense' than his betters and can say things more fundamentally true; he is 'in contact with nature', which the complex man needs to be, [. . .] he is in contact with the mysterious forces of our own nature, so that the clown has the wit of the Unconscious; he can speak truth because he has nothing to lose.[72]

Bill, as the carnival king of *Me and My Girl*, can be seen to function in exactly this manner: his unpretentious informality is at odds with the affectations of Hareford Hall society and thus he seems eccentric (a clumsy fool). Yet it is precisely Bill's cockney eccentricity that suggests to the aristocrats that he represents a sort of 'natural' and forgotten expression of self-truthfulness. Thereby Bill leads Hareford Hall's society towards recovery of that assumedly lost 'naturalism' through a seemingly classless sensibility or, at least, one of greater class hybridity. Madge and Harrison go on to make a compelling case for the implied naturalism of the cockney characters:

> the working-class characters are 'nearer to nature' than the upper-class ones: George Graves, who takes the part of a whisky-drinking but benevolent member of the aristocracy, says to Sally the Lambeth girl: 'I like you and I like your Bill. You're two simple children of nature.' Later he says to Bill: 'Your modesty, your simplicity, proves you one of nature's gentlemen.' But Lambeth where 'the skies ain't blue and the grass ain't green,' is a far cry from 'nature' in the ordinary sense. It is the cockney character which is more 'natural' than the upper-class character.[73]

In this context of cockney naturalism, it is the body that perhaps speaks loudest, hence the importance of Lane's physical clowning. The broader concerns of Madge and Harrison's analysis are thus similarly on the embodiment of 'The Lambeth Walk', easily the most famous and enduring song from the show. At a time when dance halls were everywhere, the song sparked an unprecedented dance-craze that cut across all classes in Britain and reached continental Europe and America during 1938. For Madge and Harrison it was the song's essential 'naturalism', its simplicity and directness of self-expression, and the equally straightforward popular dance derived from Lane's original movements that accounted for its widespread consumption.[74]

Although they use other terms, it becomes clear that for Madge and Harrison it is the song's carnivalistic function in the context of the perceived social crisis engendered by King Edward's abdication that accounts for its mass appeal. In an extension of this function in the show, 'The Lambeth Walk' effectively became a 'pageant without footlights' in which dancers experienced a revitalizing shared sense of communality.[75] As Hinton explains,

> Madge and Harrison argue that the key to the Lambeth Walk's success was the fact that, reversing the usual top-down direction of cultural diffusion, it both drew on popular sources (Cockney humour, singing, and dancing) and catered to an unmet popular demand for the mix of individual self-expression and communal togetherness summed up in the words of the song.[76]

In the show the song first comes as the finale of Act 1, after Sally arrives with a gang of Bill's costermonger friends from Lambeth in a bid to show him that cockneys simply do not belong in Hareford Hall. However, it is precisely this carnivalistic mésalliance of cockneys and aristocrats that enlivens the place in song and dance because the aristocrats are ultimately drawn into the catchy cockney routine and find it rejuvenating. This affect is embodied in the otherwise peripheral character of the nonagenarian Lord Jasper Tring, who literally comes to life in the dance, unexpectedly throwing off his aged aristocratic reserve to embrace a newly remembered youthful vigour in the cockney knees-up.[77]

Cockney comedian Lane worked out the song with Cambridge-educated composer Noel Gay.[78] Their collaboration is depicted in Lane's biography:

> 'Well, I thought of it like this', Noel Gay said, and strummed a few bars on the piano. Lupino Lane grinned and shook his head. 'It's almost right', he agreed, 'but not quite. It should go *down* at the end of the first line. Something like this', and he hummed the same bars but with a different ending and a different tempo. 'Now you're turning it into a march', Noel Gay said, 'a slow march.' 'That's it. That's what I think it wants. A slow, cocky sort of march, a cockney walk!'[79]

A contrasting energetic manner ('cocky') and slow gait ('cockney walk') are thus articulated with the music's character. The famous AABA refrain of this easily singable song exemplifies how that 'cocky' energy works by rubbing up against the slow 'march' tempo in the jaunty syncopated treatment of the A section's melody (see Example 6.2). This eight-bar section is built of four two-bar motifs that in rhythmical terms have a sort of AABA structure.[80] The first two motifs open with distinctive repeated notes and an accented tied-quaver offbeat and close with descending arpeggio figures that, again, land emphatically on a tied-quaver offbeat. The third and fourth motifs really form one four-bar unit consisting of an ascending arpeggio figure in longer-breathed syncopation followed by a return to quaver–crotchet movement ahead of the cadence. The A section closes with the all-important, movement-motivating offbeat 'Oi!' which seems to invite participation. As contemporary observers noted, this is exclaimed rather than sung and that made it '[a] good dance to "break the ice", for after shouting "Oi!" to a stranger, in some ways he ceases to be one'.[81]

The melodic treatment across the whole eight bars of the refrain's A section thus evokes an enlivening and engaging feeling by going against the rhythmic grain,

EXAMPLE 6.2 The A section of the refrain of 'The Lambeth Walk'.

especially when the melody is considered against the metrical slow-two of the foxtrot/
'march' accompaniment. By contrast the 'release' of the B section of the refrain evokes
the carefree atmosphere of Lambeth: 'Ev'rything free and easy | Do as you darn well
pleasey' etc.[82] It achieves this through an ascending sequence of three two-bar motifs
featuring swung dotted-quaver–semiquaver rhythms that are contrastingly set on the
beat and in the dominant key of C major (see Example 6.3).

In something of a reawakening, the final two-bar motif of the B section builds on the
penultimate one to set the demands that we should 'Go there | Stay there' (Lambeth) in
more angular melodic intervals (a descending perfect fifth and an ascending perfect
fourth). These return us towards F major and the reprise of the jaunty A section, which
closes the refrain. The intervals are accented and operate as if to dispel any sense of indulgence or illusion: 'Don't just lose yourself in enjoying the idea of this newly-(re)discov-
ered freedom,' the music seems to say; 'get on and live in and by the Cockney carnival
of "The Lambeth Walk". Almost immediately the opportunity to do that presents itself
in a dance break, which is simply a repetition of the AABA refrain in another key (A flat

EXAMPLE 6.3 The B section of the refrain of 'The Lambeth Walk'.

'The Lambeth Walk', from *Me And My Girl*. Words by Douglas Furber and Arthur Rose, Music by Noel Gay
© Copyright 1938 Chester Music Limited trading as Cinephonic Music and Chester Music Limited trading as Richard
Armitage Music for the UK, Australia, Canada, South Africa and all so-called Reversionary Rights Territories.
Copyright renewed for the USA by Chester Music Limited trading as Richard Armitage Music. All Rights Reserved.
International Copyright Secured. Used by Permission of Chester Music Limited trading as Cinephonic Music and Chester
Music Limited trading as Richard Armitage Music.

major), in which the whole of Hareford Hall's society becomes swept up in the spirit of the song.[83]

As Madge and Harrison document, the motivation to join in with 'The Lambeth Walk' extended way beyond the confines of the show to the whole of dancing Britain and beyond. The BBC played a part in its diffusion by broadcasting an edited version of the show performed before the 'live' theatre audience that ended with a rapturous reaction to 'The Lambeth Walk' and then repeatedly played a recording of the song. However, C. L. Heimann, the manager of the Locarno chain of dance halls, achieved perhaps even greater impact when, in the spring of 1938, he commissioned Adele England to develop a simplified version of Lane's distinctive movements in 'The Lambeth Walk' for general consumption in his dance halls. She described her adaptation of Lane's 'walk' and its immediate popularity thus:

> I worked out the turns and put in the knee-slapping instead of the slight back jump and hat touching [. . .] One night we did it as a novelty dance in the Locarno here [in Streatham]. The very first night there were thousands on the floor. They kept wanting it and wanting it. . ..[84]

It seems, then, that the dance hall crowd were ready to join in with 'The Lambeth Walk' and England's simplification only made it more accessible to a broader dancing public.[85] England bemoans how the dance even escaped her adaptation as people made it their own. She stated:

> Of course people will do it their own way. In the real version you don't hold arms to start with. That's wrong until the swing-round. Whole rows of people link up together too but that's wrong. Ours was done for couples, just for couples.[86]

However, England had to admit that '[i]t's cocky. Everyone can do it, they don't have to learn it. There's never been an *English* dance success like it before.'[87]

What this shows is that people not only wanted in on 'The Lambeth Walk', they also found confidence and meaning in subscribing to the anti-hierarchical communal carnival it represented. The linking of arms thus created a sense of togetherness that was as much a safe way for non-dancers to participate, as it was appropriate to the 'cocky' character of the song's call for a 'free and easy' participation across classes. For England there was clearly something very British about this that stemmed not just from the assumed cockney origins of the 'walk' but also from its all-embracing communality.

This extends from the 'Lambeth Walk' sequence in the show that vividly demonstrates cockney song-and-dance culture enlivening upper-class stoicism to profound effect. The song comes at the midpoint of the show and it never really recovers its momentum after that until it is reprised in the finale. The last line of the show, Bill's 'Where the bloody hell have you been?', which ushers in the reprise of 'The Lambeth Walk', leaves us in no doubt that much of the cockney remains about the newly elevated Lord and his Lady. What is envisioned here then, in terms of class structures, is a much more hybrid and class-integrated British society than the one represented in *Mister Cinders* which, although envisioning a modernized aristocratic culture, ultimately retains the traditional British social hierarchy. Given that musical comedy has always been concerned with representing class issues for middle-class audiences, the mixing of upper- and lower-class identities and values in *Me and My Girl*, especially in the 'Lambeth Walk', ultimately means it is both highly topical and socially reinvigorating for everyone that experiences it, both in the theatre and beyond it.

REVIVING CARNIVALS OF CLASS HIERARCHY IN A CONSERVATIVE CONTEXT

Both *Mister Cinders* and *Me and My Girl* were revived in the mid-1980s during Margret Thatcher's eleven-year tenure as prime minister. Thatcher was elected in 1979 and soon set about privatizing state-owned industries and utilities, reforming trade unions, lowering taxes, and generally reducing social expenditure.[88] This had the effect of decreasing inflation but boosting unemployment. Such effects together with her tough line on the miners' strikes and support for individual enterprise earned her a reputation as an enemy of the working class and a champion of an ever more abundant and affluent middle class.

Thatcher's own views on class were more complex as a result of her middle-class upbringing in Grantham.[89] She, like Baldwin, was generally opposed to lumping people together in broad social classes because, as she stated, it 'sets them against one another'.[90] Like Baldwin she favoured a much more stratified and inegalitarian model of British society. Unlike Baldwin she opposed the notion of broad class groupings as a 'communist concept' that she felt ultimately engendered the sort of marked division between a ruling elite and a poor majority found within Soviet society. Nevertheless, as Cannadine puts it, 'she took a neo-liberal view, that society is a tripartite [class] construct, dominated by the laissez-faire ideology and entrepreneurial ethos of the middle classes' and 'she was a neo-populist confrontationalist, leading what was often described as "the peasants revolt" against established and entrenched élites'.[91]

Thatcher tried hard to excise all talk of class groupings during her premiership and largely succeeded but, as with Baldwin, various social crises that arose from challenging socio-economic conditions meant that the spectre of class could not be entirely exorcized in view of compelling evidence of a fundamentally divided British society.[92] In particular, the disenfranchising of the working class within Thatcher's hierarchical vision of an ever more affluent middle-class Britain meant that the class-orientated discourses of *Mister Cinders* and *Me and My Girl* were once again highly relevant. However, some adjustments to the shows were required to help them fit both contemporary expectations of musical theatre and the different sociopolitical context.

The revival of *Mister Cinders* opened at London's small King's Head theatre-pub in December 1982 and transferred to the 400-seat Fortune Theatre in April 1983 to complete a 527-performance run (one less than in 1929). The original narrative remained much the same but the score was updated, notably in utilizing synthesized instruments.[93] These represent voguish markers of 1980s popular culture but they also caricature the original score: the synthesized instruments sound particularly contrived on the 1983 revival cast recording.[94] Furthermore, the vocal style employed by the revival's performers seems something of a grotesque exaggeration of that heard in the 1920s original: a fast vibrato is particularly pronounced and is way beyond what can be heard in the recordings of Hale and Howes.

Such performative additions give the revival the character of a highly kitsch parody of the original: the characters are now all caricatures of the 1920s leisure class and thus it is hard to take any of the show, and especially any social adjustment envisioned through its classed carnival, terribly seriously. This, of course, does not mean that the revival's nostalgic-hierarchical carnival cannot still be considered fun social commentary. It is rather that its carnival is now so rooted in self-aware parody and feel-good hierarchical nostalgia that it evokes the same sort of reactions as any dessert named 'Death by Chocolate': for some, its consumption might represent a wonderfully 1980s indulgence while for others (like me) it is artificially saccharine to the point of inducing nausea.

The revival of *Me and My Girl* has also been read as 'a self-conscious play with nostalgia and a whole pastiche of "period" effects' in which 'the whole balance of the show has been tilted in favour of gentrification'.[95] It opened in the West End's Adelphi Theatre in February 1985 for what proved to be a run of 3,303 performances.[96] The revival was produced by Richard Armitage, Noel Gay's son, and featured a revised libretto by the actor and writer Stephen Fry with additions from the show's director Mike Ockrent. Fry, and no doubt Ockrent too, updated the dialogue and tightened up the structure of the play. However, in keeping with other 1980s revivals of classic shows, they added other songs from Gay's catalogue including the 1932 hit, 'The Sun Has Got his Hat On' and George Formby's 1937 hit 'Leaning on a Lamp-Post'.

The former interpolated song replaces the first reprise of 'The Lambeth Walk', which originally reopened the show after the interval with a scene in which the aristocrats show they have learned the song and dance and a mouth-organ routine from the cockneys. Alison Light and Raphael Samuel find this displaced by 'an occasion for the aristocratic house-guests to disport themselves and in some sort to match the vitality of Lambeth with their own'.[97] Similarly, 'Leaning on the Lamp-Post' is transformed from Formby's edgy class-conscious performance, evident in his famous 1937 recording, to Robert Lindsay's 1980s 'crooning': Lindsay indulges in the first 'leaning' and thereafter plays with the rhythm and phrasing to evoke a profoundly nostalgic sense emphasized by the relatively sparse musical accompaniment and his whistling refrain.[98]

Light and Samuel further argue that the revival's staging reinscribes the class-carnival of Lane's memorable cape routine in a Thatcherite social context through a 'reassertion of tradition'. They explain:

> His statesmen and warrior ancestors descend from their portraits in a pageant-like procession and the absurdity of this is forgotten in the solemnity of the music and ritualistic splendour. No doubt meant as a moving reassertion of Englishness, the anthem of *noblesse oblige* is shown to have superior claims.[99]

Given that similar civic processions featured in Margaret Thatcher's Grantham upbringing and indeed probably shaped her vision of a hierarchically structured British society centred on an ever-more gentrified middle class, it is precisely such features that speak, sing, and move of 1980s Thatcherism.[100] They do this as loudly as the original carnivals did of modernity in the 1920s and 1930s, even if it is in a rather more self-conscious way.

It was clearly as urgent for British musical theatre of the 1980s to 'Spread a Little Happiness' or to encourage 'The Lambeth Walk' among the middle classes as it was for musical comedy in 1929 or 1937. However, it would seem, then, that both revivals lack something of the carnivalistically active re-envisioning of society that is present in the originals. Instead, in the face of the social crises of the 1980s, they are both rather nostalgic for a bygone British society that their editors found represented in the original shows, one in which a more clearly demarked class hierarchy seemed to offer greater security—it seemed one knew one's place in those days and thus how to deal with the chaos of the world.

Uncertainties about class in mid-1980s Britain thus provoked period-piece revivals of *Mister Cinders* and *Me and My Girl* that are nearer Platt's vision of outmoded musical comedy than the altogether more carnivalistic and edgy originals were. This is not, of course, to suggest that the revivals were any less socially meaningful for contemporary audiences. In fact, it was precisely their outmodedness that spoke of class security in the face of much social chaos in Thatcher's Britain. In a peculiarly British way, this clinging to traditional aristocratic values of the genre shows just how flexible and adaptable British musical comedy can be relative to the social and political climate in which it is staged. Thus it is always risky to talk of the demise of British musical comedy, because that of the interwar period proves to be rather enduring in its class-conscious carnival and its adaptiveness.

Notes

1. John Betjeman, *Collected Poems*, 4th ed. (London: John Murray, 1979), 163. Also quoted in David Cannadine, *Class in Britain* (London: Penguin, 2000), ix.
2. Stein Ringen, 'The Open Society and the Closed Mind', *Times Literary Supplement*, 24 January 1997, 6. Also quoted in Cannadine, *Class in Britain*, ix.
3. Ringen, 'Open Society', 6.
4. If I fall into being overly class-conscious in this analysis it is probably because I am British and thus steeped in that culture but I hope the following analyses will prove that we British, although preoccupied with an ancient class system that might seem 'closed minded' in Stein's terms, are as able to be 'open minded' in class discourse as anyone.
5. Len Platt, *Musical Comedy on the West End Stage, 1890–1939* (Basingstoke: Palgrave Macmillan, 2004), 83–103. Platt highlights how perceived crises involving the landed gentry, engendered by economic pressures, presented a useful metaphor with which to explore the challenges of, and insecurities about, contemporary modernity in terms of social class.
6. Platt, *Musical Comedy*, 142.
7. Platt offers a comprehensive study of Edwardian musical comedy but comparatively little consideration of class discourse in the interwar period: his chapter on the trope of aristocracy, for example, concentrates on the period up to the First World War. Neither does Platt consider the material forms that this discourse took in the shows themselves beyond his highly insightful narrative readings.
8. Bakhtin writes that '[a]s a form it is very complex and varied, giving rise, on a general carnivalistic base, to diverse variants and nuances depending upon the epoch, the people, the individual festivity.' Bakhtin, *Problems of Dostoevsky's Poetics*, 122. For a consideration of *Anything Goes* in carnivalistic terms, see George Burrows, 'Anything Goes on an Ocean Liner: Musical Comedy as Carnivalistic Heterotopia', *Studies in Musical Theatre* 7, no. 2 (2013): 327–346.
9. Bakhtin, *Problems of Dostoevsky's Poetics*, 123.
10. Bakhtin, *Problems of Dostoevsky's Poetics*, 123.
11. In this vein, it is precisely the apparent frivolous and ephemeral comedy of musical comedy's carnival that makes its social discourses all the more cogent.
12. Bakhtin, *Rabelais and His World*, 20–25.

13. Bakhtin, *Problems of Dostoevsky's Poetics*, 123.

14. Bakhtin, *Problems of Dostoevsky's Poetics*, 123 (emphasis in the original).

15. Bakhtin, *Problems of Dostoevsky's Poetics*, 122.

16. Bakhtin, *Problems of Dostoevsky's Poetics*, 127.

17. The translation of Bakhtin's Soviet theory to a British interwar context is not without its problems. However, it can be argued that the hierarchical social structure of interwar Britain suggests there was as much need there for escapist ideals of the sort Bakhtin espoused with his theory of carnival. The correlation between musical comedy and carnival that this essay illuminates, suggests this to be the case.

18. Peter Hoyle, 'Mr Cinders on CD and Cassette', *The Musicals Collection* 24 (Peterborough: Orbis Publishing, 1994), 300.

19. Vivian Ellis, *I'm on a See-Saw* (London: Michael Joseph, 1953), 90.

20. Hoyle, 'Mr Cinders', 307. The show appeared just ahead of the infamous Wall Street Crash, which had effects that were felt profoundly in Britain throughout the early 1930s. This, together with a different casting, accounts for the relative failure of the 1934 film version.

21. Ellis described Wylie as 'happiest when engaged upon a production or, better still, several productions, and the more mechanical difficulties the more he liked them. If they were not in the script, he would invent them.' See Ellis, *I'm on a See Saw*, 79. Wylie's insatiable desire to represent such things as moving trains, cars, and motorcycles on the stage in an era that embraced such technologies on a mass scale for the first time, shows the apparent modernity of musical comedy. See Noreen Branson, *Britain in the Nineteen Twenties* (London: Weidenfeld and Nicolson, 1975), 220–228.

22. Ellis, *I'm on a See-Saw*, 78.

23. The first few numbers of the show were songs written by Grey, Myers, and Robin. They include the opening chorus ('Tennis'), 'True to Two', and 'I'm a One-Man Girl'.

24. Ellis, *I'm on a See-Saw*, 82–83.

25. Edward Wood, quoted in Cannadine, *Class in Britain*, 138.

26. Cannadine, *Class in Britain*, 138.

27. Baldwin, quoted in Cannadine, *Class in Britain*, 138.

28. Cannadine, *Class in Britain*, 139.

29. Cannadine, *Class in Britain*, 140.

30. Cannadine, *Class in Britain*, 132.

31. Branson, *Britain in the Nineteen Twenties*, 206.

32. Branson, *Britain in the Nineteen Twenties*, 208.

33. Branson, *Britain in the Nineteen Twenties*, 209.

34. Jim's oppression is made clear from the start of the show when he saves the American oil tycoon Henry Kemp from drowning but, at Lady Lancaster's suggestion, Guy takes the credit to gain social advantage. Lady Lancaster feels that, unlike her former husband, the late General Sir Bloodwing Beardsley (a Plantagenet), Jim and his kindly but ineffectual uncle, Sir George (her second husband), are not blue-blooded enough. This synopsis is drawn from the playscript in the Lord Chamberlain's Plays in the British Library. Clifford Grey, Greatrex Newman, Vivian Ellis, and Richard Myers, *Mister Cinders*, Playscript, London, 12 September 1928, Lord Chamberlain's Plays, British Library, LCP 1928/42, 8535.

35. The ball in Mister Cinders is very much a carnival within the carnival of life at Merton Chase.

36. This is especially clear in the highly amusing 'Belles of the Ball' ensemble number (renamed 'At the Ball' in the revival) in which each of these 'ugly sisters' bitches about what the other will wear to the ball in the face of Jim's scorn.

37. Lady Lancaster had been intent on them making a play for Jill as her father is not only moneyed but also the owner of 'The Towers', which was the former estate of Lady Lancaster's Plantagenet husband. Thus a union between one of her sons and Jill would both restore the Plantagenet connection and the ailing finances of the family. However, Guy and Lumley have their own love interests in the form of the lower-class girls Minerva and Phyllis, whom Lady Lancaster openly dismisses as socially unsuitable.

38. The Lord Chamberlain's Papers in the British Library reveal that his office demanded the removal of several references to effeminate homosexuality that stereotyped the behaviours of aristocrats mentioned in both the try-out and London productions of *Me and My Girl*. See *Me and My Girl*, Correspondence, London, 1937, Lord Chamberlain's Plays, British Library, LCP Corr 1937/57, 928.

39. Clifford Grey, Greatrex Newman, and Vivian Ellis, *On the Amazon*, Piano-vocal store (London: Chappell, 1928).

40. In the 1980s revival Donna Anna is renamed Donna Lucia and wears a diamond necklace to the ball that is subsequently stolen (in the film version Jill wears the necklace). See Vivan Ellis et al., *Mr Cinders*, Principal-chorus part, Complete vocal book (London: Boosey and Hawkes, 1982), 53–58 and 67–69, http://www.boosey.com/cr/perusals/score.asp?id=25833, accessed 29 July 2014.

41. See Branson, *Britain in the Nineteen Twenties*, 223.

42. The character of Velvet Victor was replaced by a butler named Smith in the 1982 revival. See Ellis et al., *Mr Cinders*, 67–69.

43. A fascinating video clip on YouTube, which shows silent film footage of the original production, includes the minuet section of the song but not the contrasting jazz section. Instead it cuts to the arrival of Jim as the explorer. See Anon., 'Unique Film of Stage Production of *Mr Cinders* with Binnie Hale and Bobby Howes 1929', https://www.youtube.com/watch?v=uo1iILvqglo, accessed 3 September 2014.

44. Clifford Grey and Vivian Ellis, *Spread a Little Happiness*, Piano-vocal store (London: Chappell, 1928).

45. Ellis, *I'm on a See-Saw*, 81–82.

46. In the context of otherwise minor-chord harmony the A flat major chord in bar 3 sounds to my ears rather as an accented dissonance, resolving on the F in the melody at the half-bar.

47. *Spread A Little Happiness: The Music and Songs of Vivian Ellis*, CBE, CD, Conifer Records, CDHD 257/8m 1995, track 2.

48. Such coloratura is, of course, also archaic in its evocation of old-world operetta.

49. Platt, *Musical Comedy*, 142.

50. Rex Bunnett, 'Me & My Girl' on CD and Cassette', in *The Musicals Collection 7* (Peterborough: Orbis, 1994), 79; Sheridan Morley, *Spread a Little Happiness: The First Hundred Years of the British Musical* (New York: Thames and Hudson, 1987), 87.

51. In many ways Jacqueline's character represents the supposed crisis of the contemporary aristocracy and a potential solution: to marry into money.

52. Morley, *Spread a Little Happiness*, 87.

53. James Dillon White, *Born to Star: The Lupino Lane Story* (London: Heinemann, 1957), 248.

54. White, *Born to Star*, 250.

55. Between *Twenty-to-One* and *Me and My Girl* Lane played the role of Buttons in a lavish production of the pantomime *Cinderella* at the Coliseum, the West End's largest stage. This experience undoubtedly suggested the large-scale treatment of just such a fairy-tale narrative in *Me and My Girl*. In fact, Lane proposed the idea to Rose and others in a meeting in his dressing room after one of the performances of *Cinderella*. See White, *Born to Star*, 258.

56. White, *Born to Star*, 266–267.

57. Platt, *Musical Comedy*, 148.

58. Anon., 'Victoria Palace: *Me and My Girl*', *The Times*, 17 December 1937, 14.

59. Anon., 'Victoria Palace: *Me and My Girl*'.

60. Bakhtin, *Problems of Dostoevsky's Poetics*, 122.

61. Anon., 'Victoria Palace: *Me and My Girl*'.

62. L. Arthur Rose, Douglas Furber, and Noel Gay, *Me and My Girl: A Musical Comedy* (London: Samuel French, 1954), 41.

63. Rose, Furber, and Gay, *Me and My Girl*, 42.

64. White, *Born to Star*, 278.

65. Charles Loch Mowat writes, 'he enjoyed the popularity which for years had been his as the youthful Prince Charming, the Prince of Wales'. See Charles Loch Mowat, *Britain Between the Wars: 1918–1940* (London: Methuen, 1966), 582.

66. Mowat, *Britain Between the Wars*, 582–583.

67. This much is clear from the interviews with people who remember the event that can be found on the BBC website. See 'Edward VIII: Abdication Timeline', http://news.bbc.co.uk/1/hi/uk/2701463.stm, accessed 29 July 2014.

68. Rose, Furber, and Gay, *Me and My Girl*, 42.

69. Stephen Fry quotes Noel Gay's son, Richard Armitage, as saying: 'His [Lane's] business with the cloak in *Me and My Girl* became one of the most famous sights on the London stage.' See Stephen Fry, *The Fry Chronicles* (London: Michael Joseph, 2010), 428.

70. Charles Madge and Tom Harrison, *Britain by Mass-Observation* (1939; repr. London: Hutchinson, 1986), 157.

71. Madge and Harrison, *Britain by Mass-Observation*, 157.

72. William Empson, quoted in Madge and Harrison, *Britain by Mass-Observation*, 157–158.

73. Madge and Harrison, *Britain by Mass-Observation*, 158.

74. Percy Scholes also wrote that '[t]o musicians who had listened to, and watched with dismay, the progressive deterioration of ball-room music and ball-room motion (cf. *Jazz*), the former long declined into saxophonic sentimentalities and the latter tending to a mechanical somnambulism, the freshness of the new melody and the vigour and communal spirit of the new dance came as a relief'. See Percy Scholes, 'Lambeth Walk, The', in Scholes, *The Oxford Companion to Music*, 9th ed. (Oxford: Oxford University Press, 1955), 568.

75. Bakhtin, *Problems of Dostoevsky's Poetics*, 122.

76. James Hinton, *The Mass Observers: A History, 1937–1949* (Oxford: Oxford University Press, 2013), 91.

77. According to Lane's biography the inspiration for the song was 'a sort of jaunty coster walk' that Alec Hurley used to do. See White, *Born to Star*, 269. Hurley was famously the second husband of the British star Marie Lloyd, but he had made his own career as a 'coster singer' in turn-of-the century music hall. See Anon., 'Mr Alec Hurley: Obituary', *The Times*, 8 December 1913, 13. Hurley's act even included a song called 'The Lambeth Walk' by E. W. Rogers, which, in somewhat racist-nationalistic terms, rejects the imported 'cake walk' as a 'fake walk' by comparison. See E. W. Rogers, 'The Lambeth Walk', British Library Online Gallery, http://www.bl.uk/onlinegallery/onlineex/vicpopmus/t/largeimage87770.html,

accessed 10 July 2014. So it seems the apparently authentic 'naturalism' of cockney physicality was a popular theatrical trope long before 1937.

78. If naturalism was the aim, then Noel Gay (his real name was Reginald Armitage) was clearly the right man for the job because his music was commonly praised for its seemingly unencumbered simplicity. Sheridan Morley, for example, wrote that 'Noel Gay wrote the kind of songs that people not only sang in their baths but also imagined they could write in their baths'. See Morley, *Spread a Little Happiness*, 87. Madge and Harrison reported that Gay 'did five versions of the 'Lambeth Walk', each one increasingly simple. He always aims at simplicity, 'in plugging it's absolutely necessary to stick to one or two ideas and keep on repeating them'. Madge and Harrison, *Britain by Mass-Observation*, 162.

79. White, *Born to Star*, 269.

80. A characteristic of Gay's songwriting seems to be the use of catchy short motifs, as can be seen in the title song of the show, which is also constructed from two-bar subphrases. See Noel Gay, Arthur Rose, and Douglas Furber, *Me and My Girl*, Vocal score (London: Cinephonic Music, 1937), 21–22.

81. Madge and Harrison, *Britain by Mass-Observation*, 173.

82. Gay, Rose, and Furber, *Me and My Girl*, 66.

83. Gay, Rose, and Furber, *Me and My Girl*, 67.

84. Adele England, quoted in Madge and Harrison, *Britain by Mass-Observation*, 160.

85. She knew instinctively, for example, to replace the pulling up of skirts in the show with more dignified knee slapping and, indeed, changed the dance to a point that she had to teach her version to Lupino Lane ahead of a 'big private do at Carlton House Terrace'. England, quoted in Madge and Harrison, *Britain by Mass-Observation*, 160.

86. England, quoted in Madge and Harrison, *Britain by Mass-Observation*, 161.

87. England, quoted in Madge and Harrison, *Britain by Mass-Observation*, 161 (emphasis in the original).

88. 'BBC History: Margaret Thatcher', http://www.bbc.co.uk/history/people/margaret_thatcher, accessed 28 July 2014.

89. Cannadine, *Class in Britain*, 171–175.

90. Margaret Thatcher, quoted in Cannadine, *Class in Britain*, 2.

91. Cannadine, *Class in Britain*, 175.

92. Cannadine, *Class in Britain*, 180.

93. Such instruments in a reduced scoring were, of course, also a matter of practicality, given the little space available for a band at the King's Head. However, this rationalization of the musical workforce through the aegis of technology could as much be read as a correlative of Thatcherite socio-economic politics.

94. *Mr Cinders: A Musical Comedy.* Revival London Cast Recording, 1983, CD, TER, CDTER 1069, 1993.

95. Alison Light and Raphael Samuel, 'Pantomimes of Class', *New Society* 19, no. 26 (December 1986): 17. This article was reprinted with some updating in Raphael Samuel, *Theatres of Memory*, vol. 1, *Past and Present in Contemporary Culture* (London: Verso, 1994), 390–400.

96. Bunnett, '*Me & My Girl* on CD and Cassette', 79.

97. Light and Samuel, 'Pantomimes of Class', 17.

98. Formby's recording was released on the British label Regal Zonophone on 5 September 1937. It has been rereleased numerous times including on George Formby, *George Formby: Greatest Hits*, CD, Burning Fire, 2007, track 35, and on *Me and My Girl: The Lambeth Walk Musical* (1985), Original Cast Album, 1985, CD, EMI, CDP 7 46393 2, 1992, track 14.

99. Light and Samuel, 'Pantomimes in Class', 18.
100. See Cannadine, *Class in Britain*, 171–180.

BIBLIOGRAPHY

Anon. '*Me and My Girl*: Production in Nottingham.' *The Stage*, 7 October 1937, 16.

Anon. 'Mr Alec Hurley. Obituary.' *The Times*, 8 December 1913, 13.

Anon. 'Unique Film of the Stage Production of *Mr Cinders* with Binnie Hale and Bobby Howes 1929.' https://www.youtube.com/watch?v=uo1iILvqglo, accessed 8 July 2014.

Anon. 'Victoria Palace: *Me and My Girl*.' *The Times*, 17 December 1937, 14.

Bakhtin, Mikhail. *Problems of Dostoevsky's Poetics*. Translated by Caryl Emerson. Minneapolis: University of Minnesota Press, 1984.

Bakhtin, Mikhail. *Rabelais and His World*. Translated by Hélène Iswolsky. Bloomington, IN: Indiana University Press, 1984.

BBC. 'BBC History: Margaret Thatcher.' http://www.bbc.co.uk/history/people/margaret_thatcher, accessed 28 July 2014.

BBC. 'Edward VIII: Abdication Timeline.' http://news.bbc.co.uk/1/hi/uk/2701463.stm, accessed 29 July 2014.

Betjeman, John. *Collected Poems*. 4th ed. London: John Murray, 1979.

Branson, Noreen. *Britain in the Nineteen Twenties*. London: Weidenfeld and Nicolson, 1975.

Bunnett, Rex. '*Me & My Girl* on CD and Cassette.' *The Musicals Collection* 7: 79–90. Peterborough: Orbis Publishing, 1994.

Burrows, George. 'Anything Goes on an Ocean Liner: Musical Comedy as Carnivalistic Heterotopia.' *Studies in Musical Theatre* 7, no. 2 (2013): 327–346.

Cannadine, David. *Class in Britain*. London: Penguin, 2000.

Cannadine, David. *The Decline and Fall of the British Aristocracy*. New Haven: Yale University Press, 1990.

Ellis, Vivian. *I'm on a See-Saw*. London: Michael Joseph, 1953.

Ellis, Vivien, *Spread A Little Happiness: The Music and Songs Of Vivian Ellis, CBE*. CD. Happy Days Series, A Conifer Records, CDHD 257/8, 1995.

Ellis, Vivian, Richard Myers, Clifford Grey, Greatrex Newman, Leo Robin, and Michael Reed. *Mr Cinders*. Principal-chorus part. Complete vocal book, 53–58 and 67–69. London: Boosey and Hawkes, 1982. http://www.boosey.com/cr/perusals/score.asp?id=25833, accessed 29 July 2014.

Formby, George. *George Formby: Greatest Hits*. CD. Burning Fire, 2007. Available on iTunes.

Fry, Stephen. *The Fry Chronicles*. London: Michael Joseph, 2010.

Gay, Noel, L. Arthur Rose, and Douglas Furber. *Me and My Girl*. Vocal score. London: Cinephonic Music, 1937.

Grey, Clifford, and Vivian Ellis. *Spread a Little Happiness*. Piano-vocal score. London: Chappell, 1928.

Grey, Clifford, Greatrex Newman, and Vivian Ellis. *On the Amazon*. Piano-vocal score. London: Chappell, 1928.

Grey, Clifford, Greatrex Newman, Vivian Ellis, and Richard Myers. *Mister Cinders*. Playscript. London, 12 September 1928. Lord Chamberlain's Plays, British Library, LCP 1928/42, 8535.

Hinton, James. *The Mass Observers: A History, 1937–1949*. Oxford: Oxford University Press, 2013.

Hoyle, Peter. 'Mr Cinders on CD and Cassette.' In *The Musicals Collection* 24: 299–312. Peterborough: Orbis Publishing, 1994.

Hubble, Nick. *Mass-Observation and Everyday Life*. Basingstoke: Palgrave Macmillan, 2006.

Light, Alison, and Raphael Samuel. 'Pantomimes of Class.' *New Society* 19, no. 26 (December 1986): 14–18.

Madge, Charles, and Tom Harrison. *Britain by Mass-Observation*, edited by Angus Calder. 1939. Reprint, London: Hutchinson, 1986.

Me and My Girl. Correspondence. London, 1937. Lord Chamberlain's Plays, British Library, LCP Corr. 1939/57, 928.

Me and My Girl: The Lambeth Walk Musical. Original Cast Album, 1985. CD. EMI, CDP 7 46393 2, 1992.

Mr Cinders: A Musical Comedy. Revival London Cast Recording, 1983. CD. TER, CDTER1069, 1993.

Morley, Sheridan. *Spread a Little Happiness: The First Hundred Years of the British Musical*. New York: Thames and Hudson, 1987.

Mowat, Charles Loch. *Britain Between the Wars: 1918–1940*. London: Methuen, 1966.

Platt, Len. *Musical Comedy on the West End Stage, 1890–1939*. Basingstoke: Palgrave Macmillan, 2004.

Ringen, Stein. 'The Open Society and the Closed Mind.' *Times Literary Supplement*, 24 January 1997, 6.

Rogers, E. W. 'The Lambeth Walk' (1899). British Library Online Gallery. http://www.bl.uk/onlinegallery/onlineex/vicpopmus/t/largeimage87770.html, accessed 10 July 2014.

Rose, L. Arthur, Douglas Furber, and Noel Gay. *Me and My Girl*. Playscript. London, 4 December 1937. Lord Chamberlain's Plays, British Library, LCP 1937/57, 928.

Rose, L. Arthur, Douglas Furber, and Noel Gay. *Me and My Girl: A Musical Comedy*. London: Samuel French, 1954.

Samuel, Raphael. *Past and Present in Contemporary Culture*. Vol. 1 of *Theatres of Memory*. London: Verso, 1994.

Scholes, Percy. 'Lambeth Walk, The.' In Percy Scholes, *The Oxford Companion to Music*, 9th ed., 568. Oxford: Oxford University Press, 1955.

White, James Dillon. *Born to Star: The Lupino Lane Story*. London: Heinemann, 1957.

WEST END ROYALTY

Ivor Novello and English Operetta, 1917–1951

STEWART NICHOLLS

THE great and good of the British music industry are annually presented with an 'Ivor Novello Award'. Is this prize named after Britain's most glamorous stage actor? The popular screen star of the 1920s and 1930s? The celebrated playwright, composer, writer, and star of some of the most popular of British operettas? Ivor Novello (1893–1951) was all of the above. Few people can boast such a successful and varied career in the world of entertainment; nonetheless he is practically forgotten today and almost unheard of outside of Britain. His magnetic screen persona[1] can be experienced at the occasional art house retrospective, but has only recently started to be rediscovered by the broader public thanks to new DVD releases.[2] His straight plays,[3] although generally successful in their day, are rarely, if ever, performed by amateur groups,[4] let alone professionally staged, because—unlike those of his contemporary Noël Coward[5]—they have little to offer an audience of today.[6] It is the songs from his operettas which keep his name alive, but only through concert performances, newly recorded CDs, and reissued archival recordings, not because the shows they come from are performed.

THE EARLY YEARS: NOVELLO'S STAND-ALONE SONGS, REVUES, AND MUSICAL COMEDIES

As with other theatrical composers of the same period, Novello initially found success with individually published songs, most notably his inspired 1914 war anthem 'Till The Boys Come Home', later retitled and better known as 'Keep The Home Fires Burning'. It has remained popular and established Novello as a composer. Other Novello pieces of this early period were designed for the concert platform: *The Little Damozel* (1912) in spite of its standard form features joyous soprano vocal fireworks, as does his first published piece, *Spring of the Year* (1910), clearly influenced by Edward German and Lionel Monckton—an early indication that theatre would be Novello's calling.

Revue and musical comedy allowed Novello to cut his teeth, yet with the exception of 'And Her Mother Came Too' from the 1921 revue *A to Z*, few songs from his early career have found any longevity or reveal the compositional voice for which Novello became famous. It is possible that the popularity of 'And Her Mother Came Too' is due to the witty lyric by Dion Titherage (suavely introduced by another celebrated West End male beauty, Jack Buchanan) which Novello wedded to a catchy tune. Whatever the reason, the song has stood the test of time. Johnny Mathis used it in his nightclub act and in 2001 it was sung by Jeremy Northam in Robert Altman's acclaimed film *Gosford Park*. That film also rediscovered another early Novello song: the fragile and wistful 'The Land of Might-Have-Been' (originally interpolated into the 1924 musical *Our Nell*); it received much airplay courtesy of the soundtrack recording and was republished in sheet music form, both of which promoted interest in Novello.

In the early twentieth century, it was not unusual for musical comedies and revues to be written by multiple composers and Novello often shared compositional duties with such illustrious artists as Jerome Kern and Philip Braham. It wasn't until *The Golden Moth* (1921) that he received sole credit as a composer. The piece also boasted lyrics by P. G. Wodehouse and Adrian Ross. The published vocal score reveals a set of light musical comedy songs, including 'Nuts In May' whose chirpy tune make a perfect fit for the suggestive lyric. The score also reveals glimmers of the compositional grandeur found in Novello's later works: 'If I Ever Lost You' features a soaring waltz melody over the lyric 'and found no moon'. The lines 'then you'll understand—I hope that you do' are accompanied by a signature rhythmic structure of using a long note followed by a series of short notes (in this case a dotted crotchet followed by three quavers), which gives the listener a feeling of the singer pausing on a note before falling back into the phrase.

Noël Coward and the Development of English Operetta: *Bitter Sweet*

It would be fourteen years before Novello would compose a full score for an operetta,[7] with other operetta composers of a similar vintage (George Posford, Vivian Ellis, Coward) following the same path. Coward also had individual songs published at the beginning of his career, but unlike Novello these were chirpy pieces, showing an influence of American popular song. 'The Baseball Rag' (1919, lyrics only) is a typical example, even if such words as 'tally-ho' and 'ripping' divulge his native country. Coward was soon contributing his immense wit and syncopated compositions to many successful revues, along with the occasional art song, in particular 'Parisian Pierrot' written for

London Calling! (1923). Coward persuaded theatrical producers to entrust a whole revue to him as single writer: *This Year of Grace* (1928). The subsequent success, coupled with his acclaim as author of a string of hit plays, made producers less worried about mounting an English operetta written solely by him.

By the end of the 1920s, with the exception of *Chu Chin Chow* (1916) and *The Maid of the Mountains* (1917),[8] British operetta had not produced any lasting hits by writers other than Lionel Monckton and Edward German, who ruled the West End in the first two decades of the twentieth century. There was *The Rebel Maid* (1921) which was light music[9] composer Montague Phillips's only foray into commercial theatre; it had an impressive run of 114 performances and continued to be performed by amateur companies up until the 1960s, but the score is now largely forgotten, excepting the strident Edward German-influenced baritone ballad 'The Fisherman of England'. Just as accomplished was *The Street Singer* (1924), featuring a book by Frederick Londale, lyrics by Percy Greenbank, and music by H. Fraser Simpson (almost the same writing team as *The Maid of the Mountains*), but a lack of enduring songs and recording have kept these scores out of public consciousness. Although American operetta was enormously successful throughout this period with a string of works by Sigmund Romberg, Rudolf Friml, and Jerome Kern, the costs of staging similarly huge British works made producers very wary.

Coward was regarded as the great hope. He said that the 1874 Johann Strauss work *Die Fledermaus* (*The Bat*) inspired him to write his first operetta (or 'operette' as he liked to title them); thus *Bitter Sweet* was born. Apart from a couple of comic songs—the high-class tarts belting through 'Ladies of the Town' and the effete Oscar Wildean gentlemen delicately singing about their 'Green Carnations'—the plot is pretty tragic: a girl elopes with her music teacher on the night of her wedding, he then challenges a rival to a duel, which he loses, and she returns to her jilted fiancé. The piece did not rely on great scenic designs or star casting, it was the writing that shone through. A hit both in London and on Broadway, the show survived two inferior film adaptations[10] and produced many lasting song hits including 'I'll See You Again' and 'If Love Were All'. Its commercial success paved the way for producers to present other English operettas and although none of the others achieved the international fame of *Bitter Sweet*, many found success throughout Great Britain in both professional and amateur productions, as well as lucrative sheet music and recording sales.

Novello's First Hits at Drury Lane: *Glamorous Night* and *Careless Rapture*

In the mid-1930s, the British theatre-going public were desperate for another home-grown musical theatre success. The Theatre Royal Drury Lane was desperate too: it was going through financial difficulties following a series of American musicals that failed to find an audience. Legend has it that the manager of Drury Lane lunched with Novello and described the theatre's bad fortune; Novello responded by improvising the plot of *Glamorous Night*, which was promptly commissioned.[11] It's highly likely this incident has been exaggerated over the years, but there is no doubt that a Novello operetta was welcome as the theatre needed a commercial product and Novello's name as both writer and star (bearing in mind his screen idol status) was certain to guarantee full houses. The timing was perfect for Novello: by 1934 his acting career in films had begun to falter and although he had written plays, he hadn't composed scores for the stage since the 1920s. Still, it is doubtful, whether Novello's opportunity would ever have arisen without *Bitter Sweet*.

Glamorous Night (1935) did exactly what was required of it. The theatre had a hit and Novello was once again the toast of the town and moreover was again taken seriously as a theatre composer. The score is glorious, featuring many excellent songs that are still performed today: the vocally demanding 'Fold Your Wings', the atmospheric 'When A Gipsy Played', the thrilling tenor solo 'Shine Through My Dreams', and the soaring title song for soprano. The piece introduced what would consequently become the basic set-up of almost every Novello operetta: a starring non-singing role for himself, a soprano as the female lead, a small contralto role (always played by Olive Gilbert), a comedic non-singing female, spectacular scenic effects, a plethora of soaring waltz themes, and an operetta-within-an-operetta sequence. All of these elements nestled in a romantic plot set in a mythical romantic Ruritanian country: in this case, Anthony, an English inventor of a television system, holidays in Krasnia. There, opera singer Militza who is the mistress to Krasnia's King is nearly killed during a performance by a marksman allied to the revolutionist Lydyeff. Anthony defeats the assassin, saving Militza's life. They escape on a cruise ship, which is deliberately scuttled in order to kill Militza. The two survive, reach land, fall in love, and are married in a Gipsy Wedding. They return to Krasnia where Anthony kills Lydyeff, but for the sake of her country, Militza agrees to marry the King while Anthony returns to England where he watches the royal wedding on his television invention.

Novello wrote the show rather quickly and it shows. Most likely many of the melodies in *Glamorous Night* were trunk songs[12] that allowed for the show to be put together in very short time and although he had occasionally written lyrics himself, Novello invited Christopher Hassall to pen them, thus initiating a strong collaboration that would last for years to come. Hassall's lyrics are, due to his poetical background, attractively florid, but in contrast to *Bitter Sweet*, the score shows little attempt to further the plot of the piece. In particular, 'Shanty Town' and 'The Girl I Knew', which featured the song stylings of black American singer Elisabeth Welch, with the latter number included to cover a scene change, are in a totally different musical style to the rest of the score and have no relevance to the story. The characters are two-dimensional, and in lesser hands the cracks would show, especially in Novello's dialogue. Fortunately Novello had both his looks and his natural charm to fall back on and, more importantly, he also had Mary Ellis as his leading lady. Her background in opera, her theatre experience in America, as well as her beauty and stage presence made the piece seem stronger than it is.[13]

Despite its flaws, the combination of the talented cast, spectacular stage effects (in particular the shipwreck), and soaring melodies, allowed *Glamorous Night* to become an instant hit with the public, but the run was cut short as Drury Lane had already booked its annual pantomime. Novello was furious about this; his reaction was to tour the production extensively—to enthusiastic audience response. In the following years, it continued to tour and was adapted for the screen, while its major songs were recorded countless times. The operetta itself was a popular choice with amateur operatic societies until the late 1960s.[14]

Novello's next work, *Careless Rapture* (1936), was almost not staged at all. Drury Lane initially rejected it, but had to crawl back to Novello when the piece they had chosen flopped. *Careless Rapture*, like *Glamorous Night*, is a melodramatic play with songs that barely pay any attention to the show's plot, and mostly take the form of show-within-a-show sequences. Novello employs a more lightweight approach for dialogue and story, possibly because his leading lady, Dorothy Dickson, was known for light comedy roles. The plot is simple: two feuding brothers are both in love with the same woman with the good guy getting her by the fall of the curtain. The character played by Novello, Michael, is as dashing as he is devious and even disguises himself as a Chinese prince, complete with dialogue that would now be considered both racist and sexist.[15] It must have been a thrill for Novello's admirers when the Prince revealed himself to be Michael; to keep the real identity of the Chinese prince a secret, the programme gave Novello's birth name for the 'actor' listed as playing the character: David Davies.

Various elements that were hugely popular in *Glamorous Night* could also be found in Novello's second show at Drury Lane: stunning scenic effects (here, a fairground on Hampstead Heath as well as an earthquake in Act 3), Olive Gilbert in a contralto role (which this time included some dialogue), a grandiose ballet, and two show-within-a-show sequences. This time round, though, the script was much more comedic, thanks partly to the addition of smart and sassy actress Zena Dare playing opposite Minnie Raynor (who had also portrayed a comedic role in *Glamorous Night*) in a matronly role aptly named Mrs Ripple. For himself, Novello wrote a role which once again required him to be both daring and dashing, while also allowing for wit.

Musically the piece is an interesting mix of the operatic melodies for which Novello had become known, and songs in contemporary 1930s style. There are several possible explanations for this, for instance the vocal limitations of leading lady Dorothy Dickson and the not-unfounded fear that songs by other composers might be interpolated: in 1936, the musical *Arlette*, to which Novello in 1917 had contributed seven songs, was revised and retitled *How Do, Princess* to provide product for the British touring circuit. He composed six new songs, but later discovered that his score had been beefed up with modern jazz numbers by the show's musical director. The tour was a financial disaster and *How Do, Princess* closed quickly, never to be seen again, but it is possible that following this unpleasant experience Novello felt the need to move with the times if he did not want to be pressured by his producers to include contributions by others.

Unusually for Novello, *Careless Rapture* begins with a sprightly opening number, 'Thanks to Phyllida Frame', which has its roots in Edwardian musical comedy. This is

204 BRITISH OR AMERICAN

followed by a lengthy dialogue scene featuring the two best-remembered numbers from the piece: the operatic 'Music in May' and 'Why Is There Ever Good-Bye?'.[16] Novello clearly loved his show-within-a-show sequences, and in *Careless Rapture* the first of these is titled a musical play while the second is called a musical comedy. The delightfully frivolous and catchy number in the first sequence, 'Wait For Me', sung by Dorothy Dickson and a male chorus complete with top hats and canes wouldn't have been out of place in a Fred Astaire film or a Jack Buchanan show. Hardly surprisingly, 'The Manchuko' in the second sequence is a number deliberately coined after such popular dance crazes as 'The Continental' (introduced by Ginger Rogers in the 1933 film *Flying Down to Rio*), but the composition tries too hard to be a popular melody even if it is performed by a deliberately hapless amateur operatic society.[17] The medley of three short cockney parody numbers in the Hampstead Heath scene are of interest and would not sound out of place in an East End pub—Novello is slumming a bit here, just as Coward would do in the London medley from his 1963 musical *The Girl Who Came to Supper*.

Novello normally created non-singing leading roles for himself but, perhaps because of his enormous success as the star of *Glamorous Night*, he dared to dip his toe in the water: in *Careless Rapture*, he also performs in the singing lesson scene entitled the 'Studio Duet'. It is fascinating to hear Novello on the original cast recording,[18] where he is singing in a comedic fashion. Clearly he wouldn't have been able to cope with a wider musical range which may explain why the 'Studio Duet' was shortened during the run of the show. With the exception of a short piece of simple intoning in *The Dancing Years*, he didn't sing on stage again. Novello also displayed his terpsichorean abilities in 'The Miracle of Nichaow' ballet, a dream sequence set in a Chinese Temple. Photographs attest that Novello looked very attractive in his skimpy costume and knee-high black boots, though not everyone was amused as can be gleaned from the following comment in Sandy Wilson's biography *Ivor*: 'Such—fortunately rare— errors of judgement were a source of embarrassment to most of his friends.'[19] His camp costume coupled with limited dancing skills consequently meant that Novello didn't dance on stage again either.

Drury Lane had learned their lesson and so this time did not book another Christmas pantomime; the show had a respectable run of 296 performances, followed by a national tour. The score was published, but the libretto (only available in typescript form), has all but languished on a shelf.

'A PALPABLE CHALLENGE' TO NOVELLO'S PRE-EMINENCE: *BALALAIKA*

It was inevitable that others would aim to replicate Novello's success with operettas. One such writer, Eric Maschwitz, had an expert eye for identifying the commercial elements of successful theatre productions and combining them in the creation of his own works. His composer of choice, George Posford, had a gift for melody that leaned towards the operatic but was still accessible to lovers of popular music.[20] Their collaboration began with the 1931 radio operetta *Good-Night Vienna* which Maschwitz wrote under the pseudonym Holt Marvell. The successful film version[21] a year later led to the practically unheard-of step of adapting the piece for the amateur stage before it was picked up for professional presentation in the 1940s, quickly becoming a favourite touring piece throughout the following decade.

The popularity of *Good-Night Vienna* spurred Maschwitz and Posford on to write a stage operetta, *The Gay Hussar* (1933) which was written specifically for touring. The huge Novello-sized production became economically impossible to tour and after four months the piece was abandoned, only to resurface in 1936 with considerable revisions and with a new title: *Balalaika*. Kurt Gänzl describes it as 'a palpable challenge to the Ivor Novello musicals',[22] which was evident not only in its composition, setting, and design but also because they hired Novello's director Leontine Sagan.

Maschwitz, like Novello, must have been influenced by the European operettas of Emmerich Kálmán and Franz Lehár: *Gipsy Love* (1909), *The Gipsy Princess* (1915), and *Countess Maritza* (1924). The integration of the numbers in the scripts, the importance of all characters to the story, the romantic roles for both the female and male leads, and the use of a comedic younger couple show parallels to the American operettas of the 1920s conceived by writers such as Hammerstein, Harbach, Romberg, and Friml—many of which had been long-running successes in London. The fast-paced wisecracks of the character of Nicki bear a strong resemblance to those of Benny in *The Desert Song* (1926) and the colourful Cossacks are an upmarket version of the Riffs from the same show. On the other hand, *Balalaika*'s song 'Drink to Our Friends!' was undoubtedly inspired by *The Student Prince* (1924). Maschwitz also clearly had his eye on world affairs and the recent falling of the Tsar when he referenced the influx of Russian émigrés into European countries in the show's plot.

Although he had faith is his piece, Maschwitz was nonetheless open to rewrites. Czech composer Bernard Grün was brought on board to contribute authentic-sounding music and add snatches of traditional Russian themes. Together Grün and Posford shared duties in a similar way to Edwardian composers Monckton and Talbot (or Novello and Talbot) with Posford providing the popular melodies and Grün the atmospheric musical scene setting. It is surprising that Posford's soaring love duet 'If The World Were Mine' is little known because it is glorious, but this probably is due to a lack of adequate recordings.[23] The title song (which was added to the score when the title changed) and the show itself were huge hits, outrunning many of Novello's operettas at 570 performances. *Balalaika* was next produced in Paris and Australia, published for amateurs, and later became the first British operetta to be bought and filmed by Hollywood. Unfortunately, all of the numbers were cut from the film with the exception of the title song and even then the lyrics were rewritten, perhaps to dispense with Maschwitz's weak rhyming, as in 'We were too lost in love to realise | That moonlit garden was a paradise'.[24] That this show is almost totally forgotten today is a great shame.

Maschwtiz had swiped the operetta crown from Novello, and while riding high on his success immediately started work with Posford and Grün on the Hungarian-located operetta *Paprika*. Whether it was arrogance because Maschwitz assumed that the previous

success could be duplicated or fear of repeating the disaster of touring with a large operetta, *Paprika* opened cold in London at His Majesty's Theatre in 1938 and died after eleven
performances. Refusing to be defeated, Maschwitz brought in other writers, composers,
and a new director and rewrote the piece as *Magyar Melody*. He cast the star Binnie Hale
in the leading role and took the show out of London to work on it. It came back into the
West End to the same theatre and limped along for another 105 performances. If *Balalaika*
was the first British operetta to be sold to Hollywood, *Magyar Melody* was the first British
musical to be broadcast live on television, although this was unlikely to have increased box
office takings as very few homes at that time had television sets.[25]

It is not surprising that this broad comedy with a substandard operetta score wasn't
successful. 'Mine Alone', a complex piece of music, was obviously supposed to be the
big hit of the show but the melody doesn't quite have the soaring popular qualities to be
found in Novello. The beautifully prepared detailed vocal score[26] reveals many pleasing,
if undistinguished songs, but these do not fit in easily with the dialogue, much of which
would not be out of place in a pantomime:

MIKKI   I'm a Court Photographer
JULIKA   A Court Photographer?
MIKKI   Yes, they caught me at last!
JULIKA   Oh dear, whatever happened?
MIKKI   I took a picture of a lady in her lingerie.
JULIKA   And what was the charge?
MIKKI   Over-exposure. The judge said I had too much on my plate!
JULIKA   Did the jury agree?
MIKKI   Mikki: Unanimously—they all wanted copies.[27]

Compared to Novello or Coward (or even Maschwitz in *Balalaika*), *Magyar Melody*
seems too desperate to succeed, and so Novello had no problems in regaining the operetta crown and keeping it until his death in the early 1950s.

The Late 1930s: Novello's and Coward's Failures

Novello's *Crest of the Wave* (1937) is predominantly remembered for one song—the
Elgarian anthem 'Rose of England'. One would assume this is representative of the rest
of the score, but it practically stands alone as the only operetta-style song in the piece.
The show was unpublished and assumed lost, but it turned out that Samuel French Ltd
did have the original 1937 prompt copy along with an impeccably handwritten piano/
vocal score.[28] What can now be encountered is a bright and breezy 1930s musical comedy score, nestled in a frivolous plot that features English gentry strapped for cash, mistaken identity, a villainess (who shoots Novello's character four times!), a Hollywood
movie being filmed, and the inevitable scenic spectacular—this time a train crash. It

is a lightweight comedy and Novello cast performers who had wit, pace, throwaway style, and an immense amount of charm.[29] Novello played two differing characters, the second of which—an ugly villainous film star—is jealous of Novello's first character—a penniless duke—and therefore attempts to kill him by plotting the train wreck.

Again, the musical numbers bear little relevance to the development of the plot, but they do echo the frivolity of the script. Perhaps Novello gained confidence from the more modern numbers he composed for *Careless Rapture* and tried with *Crest of the Wave* to build on this; undoubtedly he also tailored the score to Dorothy Dickson's vocal limitations. Moreover, it's likely that the all-singing, all-dancing 1930s Hollywood musicals influenced Novello and spurred him on to be up to date and to offer his take on the absurd plots and popular songs of such pieces. A ship scene features the lively song 'Nautical', the delicious duet 'Why Isn't It You?' wouldn't be out of place in an Astaire/Rogers film, while numerous numbers include exhilarating dance breaks, in particular 'The Venezuela'. Olive Gilbert's presence necessitated a contralto ballad ('Haven of My Heart') as part of the Hollywood movie sequence, which again in other hands would have sounded less operatic and may have become more popular.

The whole piece—book, music, and lyrics—is a lot of fun, but Novello did not give the audience the product they expected. Had it been written by anyone else and been produced on a more modest scale (there were seventy in the chorus!), it would most probably have run longer than 203 performances. No doubt the short run is the reason neither the score nor the libretto have ever been published, and therefore *Crest of the Wave* still awaits re-evaluation.

If there was any professional rivalry between Coward and Novello it would be in the field of operetta. It was highly unlikely that Coward would be able to top the sensational success of *Bitter Sweet*, but in 1934 he tried with *Conversation Piece*. The operette, written for French star Yvonne Printemps, lacks the heart-wrenching plot of *Bitter Sweet*. Neither story nor characters have the requisite charm while the score does not possess the musical dexterity of *Bitter Sweet*, only producing one number that has stood the test of time: the haunting waltz 'I'll Follow My Secret Heart'. One would think that at least the witty Coward patter numbers would have achieved some popularity but both 'Regency Rakes' and 'There's Always Something Fishy about the French' are perhaps not quite funny enough and are melodically uninteresting. Coward was forced to take over the male lead during rehearsals (the only case of him appearing in one of his own operettas) but when he had to leave the production, the show closed shortly afterwards at 177 performances—a considerably shorter run than the 697 performances of *Bitter Sweet*. A Broadway production was even less successful[30] and the show is now largely forgotten—not helped by the fact that the original orchestrations have been lost. This in turn means that even a concert staging could not be contemplated without commissioning new orchestrations, but since the piece is fundamentally rather dull, the question is whether that might be worth the cost.

Coward witnessed Novello's continued success and presumably thought a few years later that he should try his hand at musical theatre again. The result, *Operette* (1938), clearly follows Novello's formula: it has show-within-a-show sequences, very few songs that further the plot, and a melodramatic story. The only thing it lacks is a huge scenic spectacle, but then it wasn't presented at Drury Lane. The piece centres around a chorus girl engaged to a member of the gentry, who has the opportunity of taking over from the leading lady of her show and must thus decide whether to marry her lover and continue with her career—which for her lover means resigning his commission in the army as he would not be allowed to have an actress for a wife—or to marry him and give up the stage. Heartbroken, she breaks off the engagement and he rejoins his regiment in India. There isn't much plot, but there is a *lot* of dialogue.

The majority of songs take place in a show-within-a-show Edwardian musical comedy, 'The Model Maid', for which Coward has a lot of fun writing pastiche songs. There are so many sequences from this that the actual plot of *Operette* becomes extremely unfocused and there are very few book songs: 'Dearest Love' (which is actually a reprise of a song from 'The Model Maid' and therefore causes even more confusion), 'Where Are The Songs We Sung?', and a patter number: 'The Stately Homes of England'. The last is described by Barry Day as 'essentially an interpolated number having little or nothing to do with the plot of either play'.[31] Yet closer inspection of the two scenes on either side of the Act 2 reprise of 'The Stately Homes of England', reveals the song to be highly relevant as a comment on why the two leading characters find it difficult to contemplate marriage.[32] Apart from being confusing, *Operette* had a plot too deeply rooted in theatrical self-referentiality for the audience to fully comprehend. A run of only 133 performances (followed by an even shorter post-London run) and missing orchestrations help to explain why *Operette* is another Coward piece that is almost completely forgotten.

The Dancing Years: Novello at the Height of His Popularity

Both *Operette* and *Magyar Melody* struggled to stay open, but their closing notices soon appeared once Novello's most enduring and adored operetta, *The Dancing Years* (1939) premiered at Drury Lane. Addressing the weaker elements of his previous two shows and dispensing with any huge scenic effects, Novello this time concentrated on plot and tailored his musical composition to suit the setting of the story: Vienna in the years between 1911 and 1927. The songs are carefully integrated while the dialogue and characters are less melodramatic and more genuinely believable. Locating the story in the past necessitated composing in a period style, which forced Novello back into operetta mode and resulted in his most soaring, melodic, and unified score. All the main numbers have been recorded and performed countless times: 'Waltz of My Heart', 'The Wings of Sleep', 'My Life Belongs to You', 'I Can Give You The Starlight', 'My Dearest Dear', and 'Primrose' showcase Novello at his best—they are operatic but easily accessible. He does include the inevitable show-within-a-show, but this time the operatic sequence is integral to the plot and to Novello's character, Rudi. Opera singer Maria Ziegler discovers Rudi Kleber, a penniless composer, playing his melodies at a village inn. They are immediately attracted to each other, and soon Rudi is composing operas for Maria which are hugely successful. A misunderstanding between them sends Maria back to her previous lover, Prince Metterling, whom she marries. Years later, Maria introduces Rudi to his son, who has been bought up to believe he is heir to the Prince.

Every character in *The Dancing Years* has an interesting arc and the audience can sympathize with all of them—even Prince Metterling who could easily have become the villain of the piece. The characters have much more depth than in any other Novello operetta up to this point. His own role (much like the character in his final film *Autumn Crocus*[33]) is charming without an ounce of his usual sophistication and without reliance on lightweight comedy. Novello was also fortunate in having Mary Ellis once again appearing in one of his shows, bringing her vocal and acting talent to the role of Maria (see Figure 7.1). Minnie Raynor, who had played comedic roles in Novello's previous shows, returned in a smaller part that relied less on humorous dialogue and more on warmth and charm. One might think that Novello was simply writing parts to keep Olive Gilbert employed, but her role as Maria's singing teacher and confidante allows Novello to skilfully reveal Maria's dilemmas in duologue.

With *The Dancing Years* (1939), Novello achieved the greatest success of his career. The original run was cut short at 187 performances due to theatres being closed at the start

FIGURE 7.1 The stars of *The Dancing Years*: Ivor Novello (showcasing the famous profile) with his favourite leading lady Mary Ellis.

of the Second World War, but a morale-boosting tour, followed by a 969-performance run at London's Adelphi Theatre, secured the show's longevity. After the West End production closed, the show continuously toured for five years and was revived twice in London. The second revival in 1968, starring celebrated soprano June Bronhill, was recorded.[34] In addition, it was produced in Australia, had countless regional productions until the 1980s, and was even staged on ice at Wembley. While the 1950 film[35] is fairly faithful to the show, the 1981 television version[36] is painfully studio-bound and the dubbing of the singing voices is all too obvious. Just like Dennis Price in the film, Anthony Valentine gives a heartfelt performance as Rudi, but proves that Novello roles are notoriously hard to play due to the many elements they require: looks, charm, and star quality.

Novello conceived an important plot element for *The Dancing Years* which so far has never been analysed in detail, partly because it is not in the film and regularly has been cut from stage productions:[37] this is an epilogue set in 1938 where two officers (presumably Nazis, although that is not specified in the text) have arrested Rudi for subversive activities. Because of his actions and because of his Jewish surname, it is obvious what will happen to Rudi, but Maria, married to Prince Metterling, is able to save him. Initially, this political theme was to have been a major element of the piece, but when it premiered in 1939, the producers suppressed it due to political unrest in Europe and the likelihood that Britain would enter the Second World War. When the show later returned to London, Nazi uniforms were permitted, which gave the piece even more topicality. Novello attempted to bring a similar resonance also to his next operetta, *Arc de Triomphe* (1943).

WARTIME STORIES

Following *The Dancing Years*, anticipation was high for *Arc de Triomphe*, but ultimately the piece was a disappointment. Firstly, Novello was unable to star in it as he was still appearing in *The Dancing Years*, therefore the role was tailored to Peter Graves, who had played minor roles in all of Novello's previous operettas, but although he was charming and attractive, he was no Novello. Secondly, there was little scenic spectacle as the show was staged at the Phoenix Theatre, which was considerably smaller than Drury Lane. It was a Novello show but didn't give his audience what they came for.

What the show did have, was Mary Ellis in her final Novello role. He wrote what is possibly his most ambitious score for her, which climaxed with an opera-within-an-opera, 'Joan of Arc', featuring the purposely topical song 'Paris Will Rise Again'. For Peter Graves's lightweight baritone, Novello composed suitably debonair numbers: 'Paris Reminds Me of You' and 'You're Easy to Live With'. Elisabeth Welch, in another incidental role, introduced the atmospheric 'Dark Music' as well as the saucy 'Josephine'. The various musical styles sat uneasily next to each other and were further undermined by a rather uninspired story which seemed an amalgam of every other recent West End operetta: penniless French opera singer Marie falls for penniless cabaret singer Pierre. She leaves him to pursue her own career while he becomes a film star. When he returns to search for Marie, he finds her in a relationship with Adhémar, an opera promoter. Pierre leaves to fight in the First World War and is killed. Marie becomes an opera star, and although she is nearly thwarted at her farewell performance by Adhémar, she retires at the height of her career.

The final night of the 222-performance run was the last time *Arc de Triomphe* has ever been seen on stage. At the time only six songs were preserved in recorded or sheet music form and the score and orchestrations are lost. For someone of Novello's standing, this is incredible, but sadly not that unusual in the history of the British musical. Singer Lorna Dallas recorded 'Josephine' in 1997, having found 'a blurry work sheet of the melody in Novello's hand' in a private collection.[38] At the time of this writing, the only known copy of the music for the opera sequence and the final working script are residing in the New York Public Library to which they were bequeathed by Mary Ellis.

Preceding *Arc de Triomphe* by a few months was a show along similar lines, which has fallen into obscurity even though it was a success and was filmed, *The Lisbon Story*. Kurt Gänzl describes the show as 'a hybrid of an Ivor Novello romantic musical and a purposeful film melodrama'.[39] Its writer, Harold Purcell, had found much success in revue and musical comedy, as had composer Harry Parr-Davies.[40] Together they constructed a gripping piece that, resonating at the time of writing, would still play well today. As France is invaded by Germany, Gabrielle, an operetta star, leaves Paris for sanctuary in Lisbon. Asked to return by the German cultural department, but not wanting to collaborate with the Nazis, she refuses until realizing she can use the opportunity to get a French scientist released from a concentration camp on the pretence that he is her theatre designer and that she requires him for her operetta. On the night of the production, the scientist escapes to England, Gabrielle is found out, and as the production reaches its climax, is shot dead on stage just as Paris is liberated by the Allies.

The unsentimental, riveting, and patriotic libretto for *The Lisbon Story* is a serious affair, with a score to match: soaring, tuneful, yet not overly operatic. Purcell and Davies took two key elements from Novello but improved on them. Firstly, neither of the two leading men sang—the characters were strongly written and thus didn't require musicalization. Secondly, the operetta and ballet sequences aided the development of the plot. In addition, there are no transparent comic characters or overlong musical sequences. The only piece that potentially holds up the action is its most famous song: a lengthy set change required music to cover it, and thus 'Pedro, the Fisherman' was written which combined a self-contained story with an instantly catchy melody. The rest of the score features many glorious numbers with titles that sound as if they were from one of Novello's shows: 'Someday We Shall Meet Again', 'Never Say Goodbye', 'Music at Midnight', and a delightful rumba that opened Act 2, 'Serenade for Sale'. Unfortunately, few of the songs from *The Lisbon Story* have been recorded, and those which have are weakly delivered.[41]

Had the London Hippodrome not been closed due to bombing, it is likely that the show would have run even longer than its healthy 492 performances. National tours throughout the next few years coincided with the 1946 film adaptation.[42] Although both the libretto and the score of *The Lisbon Story* were published, not many productions of the show have been staged since the 1950s. Had there been a complete cast recording, or if the film had been more popular, the operetta may have had a life beyond its initial production. It definitely deserves rediscovery.

Purcell and Davies followed their success with a new piece in 1944, *Jenny Jones*, a Welsh whimsy. In spite of their attempt to build on the success of their previous show by incorporating the same (musical) elements, the considerable lack of plot focus in Ronald Gow's book caused the show to close early, and it has never been seen since.

Novello's next operetta, *Perchance to Dream*, tells of three generations during the Regency, the Victorian, and the then present-day periods (1945), all centred around a family home called Huntersmoon. Clearly the house is symbolic of all that is solid and strong about Britain, and as the Second World War drew to a close, the show was perfectly timed to coincide with the mood of the public. The piece is the most intimate of Novello's operettas, and although the songs and ballet sequences have little to do with furthering the plot—the latter cover scene changes and are intended to make up for the lack of scenic spectacle—they all have as an underlying theme the nature, history, and continuing strength of Britain: flag-waving framed within an operetta.

This time, there are no show-within-a-show sequences, but in Act 2 Novello played a composer, and so there was ample opportunity for various characters to perform his compositions. 'We'll Gather Lilacs' became a musical emblem for victory and is probably Novello's most famous song. It was introduced by the ever-present Olive Gilbert whose role, unlike those in all previous Novello shows, was given much more stage time, therefore allowing her less time in her dressing room—she actually had previously been running between two theatres as she had taken a small role in *Arc de Triomphe* whilst simultaneously appearing in *The Dancing Years*! Gilbert's other number, 'Highwayman Love', and the leading soprano's 'Love Is My Reason' and 'A Woman's Heart', are unmistakably Novello, yet the rest of the score sees him reverting to his earlier compositional style with set pieces that would not be out of place on a concert platform: 'A Lady Went to Market Fair', a composition for five voices, with its use of thirds and compound time perfectly sets the period, as does the duet 'The Elopement'. In his early career, Novello was occasionally credited with writing lyrics to his music,[43] and on *Perchance to Dream* he is credited as sole lyricist. Perhaps Novello after their previous collaborations by now could tap seamlessly into Hassall's style, or Hassall ghosted without credit as he was in the army.

The character of the highwayman gave Novello ample opportunity to portray a serious dashing hero, but on the whole, the piece is very funny, particularly the non-singing role of Lady Charlotte (created by Margaret Rutherford), and the suggestive lines given to Olive Gilbert as Ernestine:

ERNESTINE   I'm also to my bed. Would some gentlemen loosen my bodice for
    me? No, on second thoughts I'll do it myself—I made that mistake before.
FAILSHAM   Only once?
ERNESTINE   Well, twice.[44]

Perchance to Dream had the longest running original run of any Novello show, filling the London Hippodrome for 1,022 performances before taking the unusual step of briefly visiting South Africa. A national tour followed, as did countless amateur productions. Because it is a relatively small-scale show, it was staged by many repertory theatres up until the late 1980s before the fashion for such operettas to be presented by professional theatres dried up.

THE POST-WAR MUSICAL THEATRE SCENE

If Novello was influenced by Edwardian musical theatre, then the three post-war operettas written by Vivian Ellis and A. P. Herbert took their inspiration from Gilbert and Sullivan. Like Novello and Coward, Ellis had had considerable success composing musical comedies and for revues throughout the 1920s and 1930s including the popular shows *Mister Cinders*[45] and *Jill Darling* which brought forth the hit songs 'Spread A Little Happiness' and 'I'm on a See-Saw'. His 1938 light music composition *Coronation Scot* indicated that Ellis might have had more to offer musically, which is proven by his score for *Big Ben* (1946). Herbert on the other hand was partial to writing pieces with a political message and he may have gone too far with *Big Ben* (a shop girl becomes a Socialist Member of Parliament, eventually marrying a Conservative)—such a story was not quite what the public wanted in immediate post-war Britain which is why the show only notched up a run of 172 performances. What it did do, though, was produce some gorgeous songs, particular those for the leading soprano (especially 'I Want to See the People Happy') and consolidate Herbert and Ellis's working relationship.

It took until the mid-1950s for British writers to emulate and compete with the new slick, fast-paced, and integrated American musicals that flooded into post-war London. The year 1947 brought forth the first two of those imports, *Oklahoma!* and *Annie Get Your Gun*.[46] In this context, it would seem that Ellis and Herbert's *Bless The Bride*, a period piece with an old-fashioned title which coupled a score and a libretto that could have been written twenty or more years prior would not stand a chance against the American blockbusters, but it more than held its own. If the plot does bear similarities with *Bitter Sweet*, and if Herbert does include some laboured English versus French jokes, this time he did limit the overt politics and created a British operetta that has a great deal of heart and humour: Lucy leaves her family estate on the morning of her marriage to Thomas and flees to France with a man she has just met—a handsome French actor called Pierre. Her family follow her and bring her back to England when Pierre is drafted to fight in the Franco-Prussian War. Lucy is told by Pierre's jealous friend Suzanne that he has died in the war, but just as Thomas proposes again, Pierre reappears and Thomas gallantly steps aside allowing Lucy to marry Pierre. The piece is romantic and, at times, heartbreaking. That Pierre is believed to have died in the war must have struck a chord with many audience members at the time the show premiered. The casting of handsome Frenchman Georges Guétary opposite the new West End star Lizbeth Webb resulted in genuine chemistry and exquisite vocal performances, marrying his ringing tenor and her effortless soprano—their duets had a sound that possibly hadn't been heard in an original British operetta since *Balalaika* (see Figure 7.2).

Ellis's score comprises varying styles that nonetheless fit seamlessly together. The jubilant waltz 'I Was Never Kissed Before' perfectly evokes the feelings of first love, and 'This Is My Lovely Day' with the falling notes on the lyric 'day I'm dying' perfectly captures romantic yearning. The infectiousness of 'Ma Belle Marguerite' and the sexy rumba 'A Table for Two' with its spirited verse are wonderful expressions of Pierre's character. His march 'To France' leave no doubts that Pierre is genuine in his affection and not a gigolo. The final notes of 'Bless the Sea' expertly affirm Lucy's sexual awakening. If Herbert might have come up with a more interesting mode of escape for Lucy in the Act 1 finale,[47] at least Ellis sets the scene in an extended musical sequence that stylistically evokes Gilbert and Sullivan, as do the opening number 'Croquet', the song 'The Englishman' (with its 'fa la las'), and the occasional recitative.

Bless the Bride's healthy long run of 886 performances was cut short when its producer, C. B. Cochran closed it to open the next Ellis and Herbert 'light opera'—as

FIGURE 7.2 Romance, heartbreak, and humour: English soprano Lizbeth Webb with French singer Georges Guétary in *Bless the Bride* (1947).

Courtesy of Getty Images.

Herbert liked to call them—at the same theatre. *Tough at the Top* is the story of a boxer and a Ruritanian-esque princess falling for each other, who then have to part by the final curtain in order to return to their respective obligations; it bore more resemblance to the operettas of Novello and did not constitute a worthy successor to *Bless The Bride*. Both this score and the one of *Big Ben* are lost and therefore cannot be studied.[48] One song recorded, 'England Is a Lovely Place', showcases a ravishing melody. The show closed after 154 performances never to be seen or heard again; in contrast, *Bless the Bride* toured successfully for the next twenty years, becoming a firm favourite amongst amateur societies, and was revived at Sadler's Wells in 1987.[49]

Bless the Bride held its own against the onslaught of Broadway shows, yet Coward's 1946 Drury Lane operetta, *Pacific 1860*, closed after a minimal run of 129 performances, thus further smoothing the path for the 'American invasion'. Although *Pacific 1860* shows no change in his writing style, Coward may have sensed what was about to happen to British musical theatre, and took the precaution of casting American musical theatre star Mary Martin. But with its thin plot and undistinguished score, not even Miss Martin could save the show. Without an out-of-town try-out, the production opened cold at Drury Lane, which was still being renovated following bomb damage. Coward blamed the lack of time to get the show right before opening night for its tepid reception, but essentially, the piece is a bore. One doesn't really care about the leading characters or their story: on a fictional South Sea Island, Samolo, Kerry, the son of an expatriate family falls in love with opera singer, Elena. Not from the same social class, she concludes that she has to leave him, but during the following year she realizes that her love is so strong that she has to return. Wrongly assuming that Kerry is marrying somebody else, she takes one last glimpse at him only to discover that it is his brother who is getting married, not Kerry, and so it all ends happily.

Neither the libretto nor the score are vintage Coward. The patter numbers brighten the mood, but their impact and comic effect are dampened by the author's decision to distribute them amongst incidental characters. Coward later used two of the songs in his cabaret which secured their longevity, 'Alice Is at It Again', which was cut from the score, and 'Uncle Harry', which was also cut but then reinstated. A lesser known patter quartet, 'The Party's Going With A Swing', is very amusing, but does not compare with Coward's earlier song of a similar vein; 'I've Been To A Marvellous Party'. All in all, *Pacific 1860* has too many patter numbers, which slow up what little plot there is. The ballads are not first-rate Coward—their lengthy verses and middle sections take too long to get going—although 'This Is A Changing World' is delightful. Ronald Binge's superb orchestrations, which can be heard on the original cast recording,[50] help to elevate the score to another level, in particular the unusual 'native-style' piece 'Fumfumbolo', but unfortunately are now lost.[51]

With his final operetta, *King's Rhapsody* (1949), Novello thought he had finally found a show that could compete with the American hits, yet although it is one of his strongest pieces and had a long run at the huge Palace Theatre, it is highly unlikely that this Ruritanian tale would have stood a chance on Broadway. Nikki, prince of Murania, lives in exile with his mistress, but is obliged to take the throne and marry Princess Cristiane.

He attempts to quash the opinions of the Muranian government, but is forced out of the country and later only returns from exile to quietly observe his son's coronation. The libretto is probably Novello's strongest and the serious tone of the piece works in perfect tandem with his score. The show may have been old-fashioned, but once more Novello gave the audience what they wanted, and conceived the character of Nikki to suit his own age. The piece is less reliant on show-within-a-show sequences and on the whole, the songs help to further the plot and to develop characters. The 'Muranian Rhapsody' and 'Coronation Scene' give some idea what Novello could have achieved had he turned his hand to opera. The usual Novello ballads for soprano are back in force, including the famous 'Someday My Heart Will Awake' and 'A Violin Begins to Play', but much of the score has a touch of the art song about it: 'Fly Home Little Heart', 'The Gates of Paradise' (with its soaring vocal arrangement), and, in particular, 'Mountain Dove'. 'Take Your Girl', on the other side, which had Olive Gilbert kicking up her heels, seems a little out of place with the rest of the grandiose score, and when combined with its orchestration, feels very 1930s.

Unlike most Novello shows, *King's Rhapsody* had an out-of-town try-out, where he was able to refine the piece which undoubtedly accounts for its strength. It signalled the end of large-scale British operetta and although this is often attributed to Novello's death, both his final musical, *Gay's The Word*, and his unfinished work *Lily of the Valley* (completed by other writers and retitled *Valley of Song*[52]) show minimal operetta elements.

The other writers mentioned so far also mainly steered away from operetta in this era, falling into two camps: writing chamber works or returning back to their roots in musical comedy—although the latter in the more integrated style of contemporary American musicals. Coward wrote an underworld gangster piece, *Ace of Clubs* (1950), which was so poorly received that he momentarily fled back to operetta with *After the Ball* (1954), an adaptation of *Lady Windermere's Fan* that received a similarly tepid reception. His final piece, *The Girl Who Came to Supper* (1963), has a pastiche operetta score and quickly folded, but his penultimate show, *Sail Away* (1961), is his most successful musical comedy, as it had all the operetta excised en route to Broadway.

Vivian Ellis also left operetta behind him. His final works consisted of three chamber pieces: *And So to Bed* (1951), *Listen to the Wind* (1954), and *Half In Ernest*—the last was initially produced in America in 1957 and then in Coventry in 1958 but never reached the West End. A more elaborately conceived musical comedy, *The Water Gipsies* (1955), has amusing songs harking back to an earlier decade, but is saddled with an A. P. Herbert book full of unlikeable characters, and thus only had a short lifespan.[53]

Before Harry Parr-Davies's untimely death in 1955 he wrote two chamber pieces, both successful and yet utterly different: *Blue for a Boy* (1950), a musical romp written around character actor and comedian Fred Emney, and *Dear Miss Phoebe* (1951), an operetta version of J. M. Barrie's *Quality Street*, written with Christopher Hassall (in his only musical theatre collaboration with someone other than Novello). The latter show has a delicate score, its hit song 'I Left My Heart in an English Garden' becoming as popular as Ellis's 'This Is My Lovely Day'.

ADAPTING TO THE NEW TIMES: BRITISH
VERSIONS OF AMERICAN MUSICALS

The writer who found most success in the immediate post-war musical theatre scene was Eric Maschwitz. With composer Hans May he had a hit in 1948 with *Carissima*, although a year later he found little favour with a dated piece *Belinda Fair*, co-written with Jack Strachey. Observing where audiences were flocking, Maschwitz copied what he believed to be the winning formula and created a hit show: *Zip Goes a Million* (1951). Out went operetta and in came a British take on American musicals. The piece shows obvious awareness of all the American musicals that had flooded into the West End during that period: *Oklahoma! (1947), Annie Get Your Gun* (1947), *Kiss Me, Kate* (1951), *South Pacific* (1951)—and even an element of what was to come: *Guy and Dolls* (1953).[54] On paper it looks like Maschwitz stole many American themes, but the piece is cleverly constructed and plays incredibly well when revived.[55] George Posford's extensive melodic score is expertly arranged by Debroy Somers with exceptionally witty Maschwitz lyrics.[56] The writing, coupled with star George Formby, excelled, and the show ran at the cavernous Palace Theatre[57] for 544 performances before touring Britain for many years and finding success abroad.[58]

It is sad that the piece isn't more widely known today. Producers may be wary, assuming it was merely a vehicle for Formby, overlooking the fact that illness took him out for most of the London run and all subsequent productions. There is nothing in *Zip Goes a Million* that requires a 'Formby-type' to make it work. Had the show been written in the mid-1950s, it would have had a full cast recording, which would possibly have kept the piece alive. It deserves to be seen, unlike Maschwitz/Posford's follow-up piece *Happy Holiday* (1954), a weak adaptation of Arnold Ridley's 1925 play *The Ghost Train* that did not need musicalization. Subsequently, Posford ceased composing while Maschwitz had one last hit with *Summer Song* (1956) which, imitating the successful approach of Wright and Forrest, was an operetta conceived around the melodies of classical composer Dvořák. It was a success but, due to the provenance of the music and a script co-written with American Hy Kraft, was not strictly a British operetta.

Cicely Courtneidge, a very popular star in revue, film, and musical comedy, dominated every production in which she appeared. *Her Excellency* (1949), with a score partly by Harry Parr-Davies, struggled through a moderate run, solely on her star status. She needed a hit, and Novello provided her with one: *Gay's The Word* (1951).[59] It was to be his final show and saw him harken back to his early musical comedy days, firmly putting tongue in cheek by parodying his own style of operetta. Writing for Courtneidge and collaborating with a witty new lyricist, Alan Melville, meant that he had to adapt. The result was a revue-like piece with an outstanding list of songs wedded to a dated script that relieved heavily on Courtneidge to make it come to life. Stage star Gay Daventry's latest show flops. Penniless, she is offered money by her juvenile lead, Linda, to open a drama school at Gay's home in Folkestone. The drama school is a flop too, but Gay, thwarting two shady men who use her home as a smuggling racket, raises enough cash to put on a new show which is a hit.

The plot is thin and wouldn't be out of place in a production from the 1920s, but this was 1950. The book is officially attributed to Novello, but it is safe to assume that many sections were the work of others. Courtneidge's husband, Jack Hulbert (who directed the show), was known for reworking scripts to fit the performance style expected from his wife. Alan Melville was renowned for his excellent work in revue, and some of the revue-like sequences within the piece (such as the 'rehearsal' of the murder-mystery) are very much his mode of writing. According to cast member Elizabeth Seal, Novello was present during rehearsals and the Manchester opening, but absent throughout most the four-month pre-London tour[60] when most of the rewriting and revisions were carried out.[61] His score is top-notch and has a vibrancy and warmth that is somewhat lacking in his operettas. The opening operetta-within-a-musical sequence is very funny, particularly the opening number 'Ruritania', which offers the following comment: 'The only fellow | Is Ivor Novello | Who still believes in us'.[62] Just as witty is Courtneidge's opening number, 'Guards On Parade', which directly parodies the melodies of 'We'll Gather Lilacs' and 'Keep The Home Fires Burning' as well as referring to the 'American invasion' ('Oscar Hammerstein shows | May be mighty fine shows'[63]). It's a clever opening sequence which immediately endears the audience to the piece but also sets up and serves the plot. The same can be said of the Edwardian show-within-a-show sequence in Act 2 with the beautiful 'Sweet Thames' and the amusing 'Gaiety Glad', the latter of which furthers the plot through its onstage shenanigans.[64] The former, sung by Lizbeth Webb, is exquisite, as are her two other ballads for soprano in typical Novello style, 'On Such a Night as This' and 'Finder, Please Return'. Add to this the revue-like number, 'Teaching', the charm of 'An Englishman in Love', the infectiousness of 'A Matter of Minutes', the wistfulness of 'If Only He Looked My Way', the sauciness of 'Bees Are Buzzin'', and the showbiz pizzazz of 'Vitality', and the score stands as Novello's most varied work which is proven by recent recording of the 2012 London cast.[65] If the book had been as tight as the score and if the title were less misleading today, there is every chance that *Gay's the Word* would still be in the repertoire.

From a contemporary perspective, there are four fundamental problems with Novello's shows: the books do not stand up today, and they require a leading man of great presence, a strong operatic soprano as the female lead, as well as expensive scenic effects. There have been various attempts to revive the works, but very few have been successful. Nonetheless, some of the pieces deserve a full-scale revival, in particular *The Dancing Years*, and this would require a producer with the passion and the financial capacity to mount such an elaborate work. With this in mind, there are two British institutions which could—and perhaps should—consider a major Novello production (or any of the other fine examples of English operetta discussed in this chapter): the National Theatre and the English National Opera (ENO), the latter perhaps being the more suitable of the two due to its orchestral, vocal, and theatrical resources. One could also argue that Novello is a more appropriate choice than some of the other musical theatre works the ENO has presented in recent years.[66] Hopefully, someone will take the risk and prove to a wider and younger public that Novello is more than a composer fit only for the concert platform, small-scale fringe theatre mountings, or the occasional new recording. Unlike the presentation of an under-energized 2012 Prom,[67] the material needs good staging and singing, otherwise nobody will revise their opinion, and Novello will be undeservedly relegated to the musical theatre history books as the man who merely was once the king of British operetta.

Notes

1. A matinee idol and box-office draw, Novello can best be described as a British Rudolph Valentino.
2. Not many of his twenty-three films are commercially available on DVD. The most prominent of these few releases are *The Lodger* (1927; directed by Alfred Hitchcock), *I Lived With You* (1933; directed by Maurice Elvey and based on a play written by Novello himself), and *Autumn Crocus* (1934; Basil Dean).
3. *The Rat* (1925), *I Lived With You* (1932), *Full House* (1935), *The Truth Game* (1928), *Symphony in Two Flats* (1930), and *Fresh Fields* (1933) were his most popular works; the latter three were also produced on Broadway.
4. According to publishers Samuel French Ltd, there have only been two amateur performances of Novello plays since their computer system was introduced in 1996. Email correspondence between the author and Martin Phillips, Librarian of Samuel French Ltd London, 26 June 2014.
5. For more on Noël Coward, see Chapter 18 by Dominic McHugh.
6. Coward's comments on relationships (often the root of his plays) still have much relevance to a modern audience: the squabbling duo in 'Private Lives' and the ménage strongly hinted at in 'Design For Living' are two obvious examples. Little of comparable relevance can be found in the plots of Novello's plays.
7. Every author has their own opinion of what exactly constitutes an operetta/operette/light opera; for this essay I would like to define the term as a piece of music theatre which has dialogue as well as songs, is not sung through, and is musically in a more classical vein than a musical comedy (where the music tends to reflect the popular music of the day).
8. *Chu Chin Chow* (1916) by Oscar Asche and Fredrick Norton ran for 2,235 performances. *The Maid of the Mountains* (1917) by Frederick Lonsdale, Harry Graham, F. Clifford Harris, 'Valentine', H. Fraser-Simpson, and James Tate achieved 1,352 performances. These are phenomenal runs for West End (and Broadway) shows of this period. Both shows also were produced in New York as well as adapted to the screen.
9. The term 'light music' is generally applied to short and slightly humorous orchestral pieces written in Britain in the early twentieth century and staying popular until the late 1950s—but this is by no means a definitive categorization. Composers of note writing in this form are Eric Coates, Hayden Wood, Ronald Binge, Billy Mayerl, and Arthur Wood, to name just a few.
10. A 1933 film version was produced (for British and Dominions Imperial Studios) and directed by Herbert Wilcox; it featured Anna Neagle as the female lead. An American version by MGM was directed by W. S. Van Dyke and starred popular screen couple Jeanette MacDonald and Nelson Eddy.

11. See the Novello biography *Ivor: The Story of an Achievement* by W. Macqueen Pope (London: W. H. Allen, 1951) for a full account of this meeting.

12. A 'trunk song' is a slang term referring to an unused melody, filed by a composer in his 'trunk' for hopeful use at a later date.

13. Ellis's star quality is evident in the 1937 film adaptation (Associated British Picture Corp.) which was directed by Brian Desmond Hurst and featured Barry Mackay in the Novello role.

14. As always when new musicals are released for amateurs, those of previous eras become less attractive for those societies and consequently see less productions. In the mid-1950s many of the American musicals of the 'golden era' were made available, thus superseding amateur presentations of Novello's operettas and those of his contemporaries.

15. To give but two examples: 'The Chinese find it difficult to be flank' and 'You tly to make English ladies look beautiful? It cannot be done. I have never seen European woman who was not also a horse.' Ivor Novello and Christopher Hassall, *Careless Rapture*, unpublished typescript (London: Samuel French Ltd, 1936), 77–78.

16. Had it not been for Olive Gilbert's plummy contralto and Charles Prentice's stodgy orchestration, 'Why Is There Ever Good-Bye?' would most likely have become a very popular song in its own time.

17. There are two recordings of the song, both sung by overly operatic singers who lose the sharpness and fun of the number. While John Stoddart on the 1963 studio cast recording on World Record Club LP T214 (rereleased on CD EMI 0946 3 35968 2 1 in 2005) uses the melody from the published vocal score, with an orchestration specifically created for the recording, on the Jon Lawrenson 1968 BBC Radio recording (Columbia LP, Col TWO260) one can hear what is presumably the original orchestration, but Lawrenson sings a totally different tune. I have not been able to find any explanations as to why there are two differing melodies for a song with one and the same title.

18. 'Studio Scene (A Bit of Opera)' on HMV C2858 (1936), subsequently rereleased on numerous LPs and CDs.

19. Cyril Ritchard, quoted in Sandy Wilson, *Ivor* (London: Michael Joseph Ltd, 1975), 209.

20. Throughout his career, Posford composed many bestselling popular songs like 'Lazy Day', 'The London I Love', 'Room Five-Hundred-and-Four', as well as light music orchestral works.

21. The 1932 film was released by British and Dominions Imperial Studios and directed by Herbert Wilcox; it starred Anna Neagle and Jack Buchanan.

22. Kurt Gänzl, *British Musical Theatre*, vol. 2 (London: Macmillan, 1986), 450.

23. A very rare Australian LP of *Balalaika* on the World Record Club label (WRC ST794) recorded in the early 1960s is compromised by an anaemic orchestra and chorus, headed by very dull soloists. Only one side of the LP is given to the score of the 1936 show, the other side features *The Maid of the Mountains*.

24. The 1939 MGM film was directed by Reinhold Schunzel, starred Nelson Eddy and Ilona Massey, and featured additional music by Sigmund Romberg. Robert Wright, and George Forrest (of *Kismet* fame) reworked the lyrics.

25. It was shown on BBC TV on 27 March 1939.

26. It was published by Chappell Music in 1950, eleven years after the show closed, presumably to cater for the amateur operatic society market.

27. Eric Maschwitz, Fred Thompson, and Guy Bolton, *Magyar Melody*, Libretto (London: Samuel French Ltd, 1950), 9.

28. Samuel French Ltd also are in possession of Novello's handwritten script notes and various typed script drafts.

29. Performers included Peter Graves, Dorothy Dickson, Minnie Raynor, Olive Gilbert, and Walter Chisham. The piece would have fallen flat in lesser hands.

30. It opened in New York in October 1934 and ran for only fifty-five performances.

31. *Noël Coward: The Complete Lyrics*, ed. Barry Day (London: Methuen, 1998), 188.

32. In Refrain 4 of the song, the lyrics state: 'Our duty to the nation | It's only fair to state | Lies not in pro-creation | But what we pro-create'. *Noël Coward: The Complete Lyrics*, 188. In other words, one had to marry and procreate in the same social class.

33. Financed by Associated Talking Pictures, the 1934 film is a screen adaption of the 1931 play by Dodie Smith. The film was directed by Basil Dean and starred Novello (who had not been in the stage version) as well as Fay Compton.

34. This recording was released under RCA INTS 1049 in 1968 and also includes an interpolated song ('Rainbow in the Fountain') which was written for Novello's unfinished musical *Lily of the Valley* aka *Valley of Song*. That same year, a studio cast recording on Col TWO188 (rereleased on CD; EMI 0946 3 35985 2 2) features a song written for Olive Gilbert when the show came to the Adelphi Theatre, 'When It's Spring in Vienna'. The complete score has been recorded for the JAY label, but at present remains unreleased.

35. Released by Associated British Picture Corporation, the 1950 film was directed by Harold French and starred Dennis Price, Giselle Preville, and Olive Gilbert (reprising the role she created and proving through her charming performance that she was more than just a contralto).

36. Broadcast by ATV Television on 27 August 1981, it was directed by Richard Bramall and starred Anthony Valentine and Celia Gregory (dubbed by Marilyn Hill Smith) as well as Joyce Grant (dubbed by Ann Howard who also sings the same role on the 1968 studio cast recording).

37. There are two possible reasons for this: on the one hand, during that period, producers might have been wary of political themes within pieces that were billed as light operettas for fear of putting off potential audiences, and on the other hand, the piece is fairly long and to dispense with the epilogue offers a quick and easy way to reduce its running time.

38. Barry Kleinbort, CD Sleeve Notes, in Lorna Dallas, *The Girl I Knew ... The Music of Novello and Kern*, Harbinger Records, HCD 1501, 1998.

39. Kurt Gänzl, *The Encyclopedia of Musical Theatre*, vol. 2 (Oxford: Blackwell 1994), 867.

40. Parr-Davies also wrote two of Gracie Fields biggest song hits, 'Wish Me Luck as You Wave Me Goodbye' and 'Sing as We Go'.

41. Six songs from the score were recorded in 2005 for *Harry Parr-Davies: Songs from His Musicals, Revues and Films* (Must Close Saturday Records 3029). Three songs interpreted by Patricia Burke from the original cast are frustratingly truncated on two sides of one 78rpm record.

42. The 1946 film directed by Paul Stein and released by British National, starred Patricia Burke and Noele Gordon (both recreating their stage roles), along with David Farrar. It lacks the bite of the stage version and weakens the drama at its conclusion by opting out of the shooting of Gabrielle, preferring a happy ending. This was possibly due to censorship. At least the film offers the delight of Richard Tauber singing 'Pedro, The Fisherman'.

43. Novello and Hassall had shared lyric credit on *Arc de Triomphe*.

44. Ivor Novello, *Perchance To Dream*, Libretto (London: Samuel French Ltd, 1946), 8.

45. For a detailed discussion of *Mister Cinders*, see Chapter 6, written by George Burrows.

46. For a detailed account of the impact of those two shows, see Chapter 8, written by Dominic Symonds.
47. She disguises herself as a black male servant.
48. The Vivian Ellis archive was bequeathed to the Theatre Museum, which is now housed in the Victoria and Albert Museum, but doesn't contain scores of either piece.
49. *Bless the Bride* deserves both a complete recording and a proper revival, preferably not of the weak rewrite that was staged at the King's Head Theatre in 1999.
50. In an unusual step, Decca released the majority of the score on six 78rpm records—a huge amount for a British operetta of this period. These have been transferred to CD on CDTER 1040.
51. It is possible that Binge's orchestrations for *Pacific 1860* (along with those for other writers such as Ellis) were destroyed in the 1964 fire at Chappell Music.
52. *Valley of Song* was published by Josef Weinberger Ltd in 1963 especially for amateur operatic societies. The lyrics are by Christopher Hassall, the book is by Phil Park, and the music is adapted and arranged by Ronald Hamner, who also composed additional material.
53. Ellis found a second career in the 1960s writing amusing books such as *How to Make Your Fortune on the Stock Exchange* (1962), *How to Enjoy Your Operation* (1963), *How to Bury Yourself in the Country* (1964), *How to Be Happy in Hospital* (1964), and *How to Be a Man About Town* (1965). All of these were published by Frederick Muller Ltd.
54. The dates given here are those of the original London productions.
55. A small-scale revival directed by this author was produced at London's Theatre Museum in 2001, starring Gavin Lee; it was recorded on Bayview Recording Company, RNBW014.
56. To give but one example from the song, 'Running Away To Land': 'A wife in every port— they told me was the life | But I'd rather be back in a cocktail bar— | With a port in every wife'. (Eric Maschwitz, *Zip Goes A Million*, Script (London: The Finsbury Press Ltd, 1952), 66).
57. This theatre seats around 1,400 people.
58. There have been productions in Australia, Norway, and other countries.
59. For further discussion of *Gay's the Word*, see Chapter 8 by Dominic Symonds and Chapter 9 by John Snelson.
60. At that time, Novello was appearing in *King's Rhapsody* as well as recuperating from illness.
61. This was revealed in various conversations between the author and Elizabeth Seal during rehearsals for the *Gay's the Word* revival at the Finborough Theatre in 2012 and its later transfer to the Jermyn Street Theatre in 2013 as well as subsequent conversations during the preparation of this essay in July 2014.
62. These lyrics can be heard on the 78rpm recording of the original cast (Col DB2808) but are omitted from the published score and replaced with the following lyrics: 'We're jolly certain | The iron curtain | Will never fall on us.' Ivor Novello and Alan Melville, *Gay's the Word*, vocal score (London: Chappell and Co. Ltd. 1951), 11. As the recordings were made in the late 1950s, it is possible that these lyrics were replaced prior to the West End opening in February 1951; in any case, one wonders whether an audience today would still know what the iron curtain means in theatrical parlance.
63. Novello and Melville, *Gay's the Word*, 24.
64. Peter, a character who performs in the show-within-a-show sequence, is terrified that his father is in the audience; this farcical situation is then explored further in the following dialogue scene.

65. *Gay's the Word*, London 2012 Cast Recording, CD JAY 1425, 2013, from a production directed by this author. The recording is with solo piano, but the original orchestrations do exist and are attributed to orchestrator Harry Acres. Yet orchestrator Angela Morley told the author in a telephone conversation in 1998 that she had ghosted on the show (then known as *Wally Stott*), which makes one wonder how many of Novello's other shows were ghosted by uncredited orchestrators.
66. In particular, the critically panned production of *Kismet* (2007).
67. The songs seem to have been treated as opera rather than operetta, thus losing much of their charm.

BIBLIOGRAPHY

Coward, Noël. *Noël Coward: The Complete Lyrics.* Edited by Barry Day. London: Methuen, 1998.

Gänzl, Kurt. *British Musical Theatre.* Vol. 2. London: Macmillan, 1986.

Gänzl, Kurt. *The Encyclopedia of Musical Theatre.* Vol. 2. Oxford: Blackwell, 1994.

Kleinbort, Barry. CD Sleeve Notes. In Lorna Dallas, *The Girl I Knew . . . The Music of Novello and Kern.* Harbinger Records HCD 1501, 1998.

Macqueen Pope, Walter. *Ivor: The Story of an Achievement.* London: W. H. Allen, 1951.

Maschwitz, Eric. *Zip Goes A Million.* Script. London: The Finsbury Press Ltd, 1952.

Maschwitz, Eric, Fred Thompson, and Guy Bolton. *Magyar Melody.* Libretto. London: Samuel French Ltd, 1950.

Novello, Ivor. *Perchance To Dream.* Libretto. London: Samuel French Ltd, 1946.

Novello, Ivor, and Christopher Hassall. *Careless Rapture.* Unpublished typescript. London: Samuel French Ltd, 1936.

Novello, Ivor, and Alan Melville. *Gay's The Word.* Vocal score. London: Chappell and Co. Ltd, 1951.

Wilson, Sandy. *Ivor.* London: Michael Joseph Ltd, 1975.

CHAPTER 8

....

THE AMERICAN INVASION

The Impact of Oklahoma! *and* Annie Get Your Gun

....

DOMINIC SYMONDS

IF one characteristic stood out in West End theatre in the years immediately follow-ing the Second World War, it was that the most successful shows seemingly were all imports: the product of what was termed an 'American invasion', which in Tim Carter's words 'awakened the British theatre from its torpor of Noël Coward preciosity and Ivor Novello escapism'.[1] The first wind that came sweepin' down the plain was the long-awaited *Oklahoma!* (in 1947), already a runaway success on Broadway and eagerly anticipated in the UK; hot on its heels came *Annie Get Your Gun* (also 1947) just six weeks later, proving that anything the UK can do, the US can do better; then *Finian's Rainbow* (1947) (an American tale of the Irish), *Brigadoon* (1949) (an American tale of the Scottish), and *Carousel* (1950), bustin' out all over to kick the 1950s off with a bang. The Theatre Royal Drury Lane—intimately linked in public memory to the pre-war suc-cesses of Ivor Novello—gave itself over to the imports following Noël Coward's disas-trous *Pacific 1860* (1946), and for nine years hosted nothing but the shows of Rodgers and Hammerstein: *Oklahoma!* (1947–50), *Carousel* (1950–1), *South Pacific* (1951–3), and *The King and I* (1953–6). No wonder it seemed like an invasion; in post-war London, there really was no business like (American) showbusiness.

At least, so goes the story: as in America, *Oklahoma!* features as the groundbreaking show; Rodgers and Hammerstein reign as the exemplary creators; and British musical theatre lies dormant for thirty years before it counter-attacks with the megamusical.[2] Yet pervasive as this narrative is, in recent years it has been questioned. John Snelson's 2002 study in particular, 'The West End Musical 1947–1954: British Identity and the "American Invasion"', confronts the idea. In his view, 'too many facts sit uneasily with this accepted line of historical interpretation'.[3]

The rhetoric of an 'invasion' is key. Britain had been hit hard by the war, of course, and the prospect of invasion had been a relentless threat throughout hostilities. The changes brought about by the experience of war were very real and palpably felt. As the troops returned, it was to rebuild a country that necessarily had to readjust. Ejecting wartime leader Winston Churchill in July 1945 may have been a symbolic way of drawing a line under the past as much as it was a political gesture; but if the Britain of pre-war years was no longer tenable, the Britain the country would become was far from assured. As rationing continued and a post-war austerity descended, it would be several years before Britain would feel that it was emerging from its darkest hour.

In this climate of uncertainty, the few new British shows that appeared—Vivian Ellis's *Big Ben* (1946) and *Bless The Bride* (1947), Ivor Novello's *Perchance to Dream* (1945) and *King's Rhapsody* (1949)—may have felt like the last heroic battle-cries of an era coming to its end. *Punch* certainly thought so, calling *King's Rhapsody* 'a vast insipid musical in which Ivor Novello has pulled out most of the stops in the organ of easy sentiment'.[4] As if to confirm the impression of an old style fading away, both the producer C. B. Cochran (*Bless The Bride*) and the popular idol Novello died in 1951. With them, in Sheridan Morley's words, they took 'the last vestiges of a romantically un-American world'.[5]

The tide would turn in many ways as the 1940s turned into the 1950s. Culturally, the mood was for a more youthful expression, a more assertive aggression, and a more realistic reflection of the world. Yet despite some important cultural shifts—and despite certain attempts such as the Festival of Britain (1951) to lift British spirits following the trauma of war—the need to establish a new start for Britain was not really answered by home-grown culture or domestic exploits. As the British Empire was disintegrating, the imperial eagle of America was stretching its wings; now, the energy of American performers filled the void left by an exhausted British industry.

This chapter will explore the mythology of this 'American invasion', reflecting on why *Oklahoma!* should have been such a significant show and considering why the perception of invasion became such a deep-rooted idea. I will consider the British attitude towards America, discussing both the post-war projection of that country and the attitudes created by recent experiences of American forces being stationed in the UK. I will suggest that war-weary Britain saw America and American culture as both aspirational and threatening; and I will assess the extent to which the confident behaviour of the USA was seen to destabilize faded British notions of decency, morality, and identity, whilst redefining gender behaviours for a new post-war generation. Finally, I will consider some of the ways the West End responded to this apparent invasion as it reconceived the British musical.

'Everything's Up to Date in Kansas City'

Oklahoma! had been a resounding success when it hit Broadway in March 1943. The first collaboration of veteran writers Richard Rodgers and Oscar Hammerstein II, it was to mark the beginning not only of their immensely successful partnership, but also of a new age in musical theatre: the age of integration. This show, the histories have it, was the first to dispense with a flimsy plotline and superficial characters; instead, the musical offered believable characters in a realistic situation, and songs were woven into the dramatic fabric of the tale. This was the American musical coming of age, and in several historiographies, commentators rehearsed that metaphor until it stuck: with *Oklahoma!* American musical theatre had matured.[6] Much of that was hype, of course—the clever spin of savvy publicists, including Rodgers and Hammerstein.[7] Still, the show lived up to expectations: it 'fulfilled all the encomiums heaped on it in advance', reported the *Washington Post*;[8] and for Louis Kronenberger from *Time* it 'pretty much deserve[d] its exclamation point'.[9]

Oklahoma! is a show all about new beginnings, from its opening pastorale to the new day, 'Oh, What a Beautiful Mornin'', to its climactic paean to the new state, 'Oklahoma!'. Throughout, the infectious excitement of all things new pervades its landscape: Will Parker returns from Kansas City to celebrate the technologies and innovations of a newly emerging modernism ('Everything's Up to Date in Kansas City'); Curly and Laurey's budding relationship fizzes with the excitement of newness; and even as the show reaches its conclusion the mood is of new beginnings ('Oh, things is changin' right and left!', says Curly; 'Country achangin', got to change with it!').[10] As the community gathers to celebrate the newly forming state, themes of new beginnings merge as the new couple begin their married relationship in the new world created around them.

> AUNT ELLER   They couldn't pick a better time to start in life!
> IKE   It ain't too early and it ain't too late.
> LAUREY   Startin' as a farmer with a brand new wife—
> CURLY   Soon be livin' in a brand new state!
> ALL   Brand new state
> Gonna treat you great![11]

It's not hard to see why this idea of a new start would resonate for audiences emerging from difficult times in a nation trying to find its identity; and Raymond Knapp explores the impact *Oklahoma!* had on American audiences in that context. 'In *Oklahoma!*—with its vital images of people cheerfully "making do", overcoming conflicts and adversity, forging an enduring community, and offering homespun folk-wisdom in common direct, everyday language—America saw itself in a microcosm and acquired a vision of what it could offer the rest of the world.'[12] Against this, as a springboard from which the new could emerge, are the contrasting images of eternal verity: the farmstead, the land, the traditions, and Aunt Eller, all totemic constituents of a mythical past, reference to which, Knapp argues, is in itself significant in building identity:

> [S]ignificant remnants or 'echoes' of this lost past may be found among the folk of today's countryside [...]. From the vantage point of an imperfect present, we may look forward to a return to this alignment [...], and it is the poet/artist who articulates our position and attitude.[13]

Thus *Oklahoma!* became 'historically important for the role it played in providing America with a strongly embodied sense of a central national myth'.[14] It served to enshrine some of the most abiding beliefs sanctioned by American ideology, and in so doing it offered a powerful model for how people should live: '[T]he show was the embodiment of liberation and democracy, the creation of a new society through the voluntary coming together of different social groups for the benefit of all' (Figure 8.1).[15] Good will out, implied the narrative, and those whose psychologies are blighted by the sins of evil shall be banished from that society—the fate that befalls the social misfit Jud, and the fate that, in another theatre, the Allied forces meted out on the major protagonists of the Third Reich. In this way, *Oklahoma!* resonated not just in America but also more universally with the ideologies of the democratic West.[16]

Oklahoma! took several years to reach London, though the suggestion to transfer it to the UK had been made as early as its Broadway opening night in 1943; certain problems with immigration and tax caused the hold-up, since 'Rodgers did not want the show to be done in England unless with an American cast'.[17] When it did arrive, though, it came

FIGURE 8.1 Resonating all around the world with its story of new beginnings: the London company in 'The Farmer and the Cowman' from Rodgers and Hammerstein's *Oklahoma!*, Theatre Royal Drury Lane, 1947.

with a bang, reflecting, in Sheridan Morley's words, 'the collision of two worlds, one lost and the other so new that critics reeled back in some amazement'.[18]

> It was the vigour of the performance, its energetic gaiety, its insistence on the simple pleasures of life that lifted the hearts of its audience. Never in the history of the theatre can a show have been better timed: 'Oh What a Beautiful Morning' was just what we needed to hear just then. The sense of uplift was physical as well as spiritual.[19]

A good deal of this impact was because of the show's aesthetic innovations, qualities that have been subsumed into its identity as 'integrated', though which in fact registered with audiences simply because of their striking differences from other shows of the time. It has often been noted, for instance, that *Oklahoma!* begins not with a full opening chorus, but with a quiet pastoral scene of Aunt Eller churning butter in the yard, and a male voice singing from the wing: this was 'as simple as a folk-song', as one writer put it.[20]

> It was unusual for the curtain to rise on a simple farm scene of a woman sitting alone on the stage churning butter, with the opening song 'Oh, What a Beautiful Mornin', begun offstage by the leading baritone.[21]

Undoubtedly, this was a departure for musical theatre in general—and the fact that the female chorus doesn't even appear until halfway through the first act really was new. But this feature of the show is usually discussed in the context of integration and naturalism; few consider the simple staging of the opening as a striking element in itself. To audiences of the Theatre Royal Drury Lane, which hosted the London opening in 1947, that impact was pronounced.

Drury Lane was known for its lavish productions with large casts and extravagant set pieces. Noël Coward's *Cavalcade* (1931) had boasted a cast and crew of 400, while the series of Ivor Novello shows that occupied the theatre leading up to the war incorporated 'sensation drama',[22] living up to its reputation as a place of spectacular technical wizardry: a shipwreck in *Glamorous Night* (1935), an earthquake in *Careless Rapture* (1936), a train crash in *Crest of a Wave* (1937), and—some fifty years before a similar scene in *Miss Saigon* (1989)—a helicopter taking off from the stage in *Rise and Shine* (1936). If audiences were expecting from *Oklahoma!* a typical Drury Lane spectacular, they were in for a shock: 'No rich choirs or fiddles from the pit, no brass figures, no chords of any kind. Just golden silence and that old lady with her churn, pumping away.'[23] *Oklahoma!* was tiny: intimate, restrained, and most notably, underpopulated. 'It is remarkable [. . .] how decoratively the stage is filled with one or two figures, reinforced at exactly the right moment by a modest chorus of half a dozen,'[24] wrote *The Times*. This was 'Drury Lane's smallest production for a century', the *Daily Mail* observed; 'the company of 50 occupies only one third of the stage'.[25]

Although the spectacle was underplayed, the show was in many other ways a bold statement, not least in terms of the performances. Rodgers's restrictions on casting had been followed, and the company, led by the young Harold Keel—later to become a

Hollywood star as Howard Keel—was almost entirely American. It was to be their performances as much as any other feature that would make *Oklahoma!*'s impact (and that of subsequent shows) so impressive.

The American performance style was markedly distinct from the British style, though quite what the difference was is hard to qualify. To Snelson, it consisted of 'naturalistic acting', 'strong singing in a vernacular style', 'energetic and precise dancing', and 'a bold stage presence'.[26] Most of all, it was the American vitality that impressed the crowds: 'British performers could not match the energy of the American stars',[27] he writes. British theatre critics would emphasize this in their reviews, noting in the performances 'an absolute sureness of attack which suggests the company is a team of trained athletes. [...] Such speed and precision are rarely attained on any stage', wrote *The Times*; 'The dancing [is] exhilarating in its vigour and exactness'.[28] The *Daily Telegraph* concurred: 'For drive and vitality, I don't remember to have seen anything like it.'[29] That sense of American energy was magnified when *Annie Get Your Gun* opened within a matter of weeks (Figure 8.2); although it was cast with just two American performers in an

FIGURE 8.2 Dolores Gray, the American actress, whose warmth and vitality conquered the hearts of British audiences, as Annie Oakley in the 'I'm an Indian, Too' number from *Annie Get Your Gun*, Coliseum, 1947.

Picture Post, Hulton Archive. Courtesy of Getty Images.

otherwise British company, it still emphasized the American style—high octane energy, exuberance, and very physical dance.

In fact, the British fascination with American performance energy, and especially dance, was nothing new. Producers like C. B. Cochran visited New York regularly in the 1920s to tap into the infectious sounds of jazz and its attendant dance crazes. 'The dancing I saw for the first time in Broadway shows was quite staggering,' wrote Jack Hulbert of his experiences in New York in 1925.[30] He was captivated, and took the Tap Charleston back to London. Throughout the 1920s, all the top American writers would find their work crossing the Atlantic to bring the rhythms and energy of jazz music and dance to the UK: George and Ira Gershwin's *Lady, Be Good* (1926) introduced Fred and Adele Astaire; Rodgers and Hart's *Lido Lady* (1926)—the show they wrote for Hulbert and his wife, comedienne Cicely Courtneidge—began a near mania for the Tap Charleston. London was used to being bowled over by American energy and charisma. But following six years of war and a greatly reduced transatlantic trade, the return of this energy with the 1940s American shows threw the alternative English offerings into sharp relief.

Of course, the spirit of the British must indeed have been at a low ebb, despite the celebrated victories of 1945. The war effort had exhausted resources, and an ensuing period of retrenchment meant that families would endure food and material rationing for a number of years. The country was tired; and in its behaviour, its culture, and even its people, it reflected that weariness. Flexing its cultural and economic muscles, America would have presented a striking contrast, and it's interesting to consider in gender terms how that transatlantic cousin might have appeared in relation to Britain.

Differences between British and American masculinity in this post-war period have been explored elsewhere in terms of film; and it's fair to say that it was through quintessentially American cultural forms such as the Hollywood movie and the Broadway musical that the most striking statements about identity could be made. Mike Chopra-Gant explores this through looking at the portrayal of American men in war films and film noir, reasoning that a 'highly self-conscious performance of gender' constructed figures of bravery, heroism, and to some extent, violence.[31] Matthew Sitter draws attention to characters like Humphrey Bogart's Joe Gunn in *Sahara* (1943) and Cary Grant's Captain Cassidy in *Destination Tokyo* (1943), figures that in poster images of the time exude masculine authority, assertiveness, and aggression.[32] As Christina S. Jarvis shows, 'the US created personal and cultural narratives of military masculine embodiment that conveyed impressions of national strength and determination both at home and abroad. Images of young, white, well-muscled men circulated everywhere in the popular press.'[33] It was figures like this—not so long afterwards captured on the musical stage in the characters of Rodgers and Hammerstein's *South Pacific* (1949)— that would offer to the British public a new, sexualized masculinity, embodied by the American GI stationed on British soil. 'The soldier in the United States and elsewhere was portrayed as more physical, sculpted and aggressively masculine than in previous wars', writes Robert A. Nye,[34] and this was a masculinity that continued to assert itself in subsequent genres. Gael Sweeney considers the presentation of gender in science fiction films such as *The Day the Earth Stood Still* (1951), for example: 'American masculinity needed to set the boundaries of its difference from British masculinity in order to claim a political, physical, moral, and racial superiority to a British Empire that was now doomed and obsolete,' she writes.[35] Although an element of this involved presenting the American male within a domesticated scene, strengthening core values of the family, work, and commitment, many of the all-American heroes presented on celluloid in this period emphasized strength, size, and ability. 'America needed a new and more fitting paradigm of masculinity and power than that of their traditional model, the now discredited "English Gentleman".'[36] The English Gentleman continued to be the face of British masculinity, as British films such as *In Which We Serve* (1942) or *Brief Encounter* (1945) demonstrate. In reviewing this kind of persona, Sonya Rose refers to a kind of 'temperate masculinity' with qualities of the 'humble team-player from "ordinary" origins who enjoyed the simple pleasures of family life'.[37] Alison Light has gone even further to evoke a ' "feminised" notion of Englishness developed in inter-war years and resulting from the destruction of the heroic masculinity of the First World War'.[38] Feminized or not, the Brit was smaller and slimmer, plucky, polite and refined; the American was a product of a popular upbringing that emphasized virility and masculinity.

When American musicals appeared in London, it was such distinctions that resounded: *Oklahoma!* 'was devastating for British musical theatre, held up by comparison as a tired, outdated and retrospective form',[39] suggests Snelson; its 'aftermath turned indigenous musicals into the visible face of British theatrical failure, and by extension exposed a widespread, post-war national inadequacy'.[40]

That perception of 'British theatrical failure' may seem harsh; indeed, a number of British shows matched or even outstripped the American musicals in the late 1940s (notably *King's Rhapsody* and *Bless The Bride*). Yet as Snelson comments elsewhere, 'A crisis of confidence in the country comes through in many British shows of the period as they seek to address the long-term effects of World War II.' To him, these shows 'evok[ed] a national image that played on both the symbols of a strong and proud past and those of a tired and run-down present'.[41] Part of the perception that British theatre was outdated and inadequate was due to the way the Second World War had effectively interrupted the West End's development. Travel became dangerous and during 1940 and 1941 the heavy night-time blitzing of London by the Luftwaffe forced blackout conditions night after night. Although London's theatre scene itself was only halted briefly (between 14 and 16 September 1939), and although it sustained audience numbers throughout the war, several theatres remained closed, and the flagship venue of Drury Lane was put out of action, co-opted by ENSA (the Entertainments National Service Association) to prepare entertainment for British troops abroad. This interruption stopped in its tracks a musical theatre scene that had—in its own words—been full of glamorous nights and careless rapture, iconically reflected in the grandeur of Drury Lane productions. Lacking new material and with barely any American imports during those war years (save for a number of Cole Porter shows), producers turned to their back catalogues to dust off shows from previous generations like *The Belle of New York* (1897), *The Chocolate Soldier* (1908), and *Chu Chin Chow* (1916). In a very real sense, then, British theatre by the end of the war was 'in a time-warp of its own'.[42] When the Americans burst on to the scene with *Oklahoma!* and *Annie Get Your Gun*, it is not surprising they made a mark, presenting 'a seductive image for a demoralized Britain that began its first years of peace with bitter winters, fuel shortages, and even more harsh rationing than during the war itself'.[43] 'To us in this blessed but beleaguered island,' wrote the *Evening Standard*'s Beverley Baxter, 'there was a sub-conscious real-isation of the unbounded, unexpanded vitality of this new world-power, the United States of America. *Oklahoma!* was more than a theatrical production. It was a sym-bol',[44] one that presented 'an icon of aspiration for the British in that it was one promi-nent embodiment of an alternative and better life'.[45] Furthermore, 'the strength of the American musical as a symbol relied on there being a perceived weakness in the British musical'.[46]

In fact, that weakness was somewhat exaggerated, and the consistency of the American material likewise overstated. Yes, *Oklahoma!* made a big splash (in 1947, with 1,548 performances), and *Annie Get Your Gun* consolidated its impact (also 1947, with 1,304 performances in the enormous Coliseum). But thereafter, the imports were more modest, and several British shows stood out over and above American shows. Snelson's analysis is detailed: American imports like *Follow the Girls* (1945; 572), *Song of Norway* (1946; 526), *Brigadoon* (1949; 685), *Carousel* (1950; 566), *South Pacific* (1951; 802), *Kiss Me, Kate* (1951; 501), *Call Me Madam* (1952; 485), *The King and I* (1953; 926), *Paint Your Wagon* (1953; 478), and *Guys and Dolls* (1953; 555) certainly 'went', if length of run is the arbiter of success.[47] But *Finian's Rainbow* (1947; 55), *Romany Love* (1947; 90), and *Lute Song* (1948; 24) were simply duds. As for British shows, consider *Perchance to Dream* (1945: 1,022), *Bless The Bride* (1947; 886), *Carissima* (1948; 466), *King's Rhapsody* (1949; 881), *Blue for a Boy* (1950; 664), *Gay's the Word* (1951; 504), *Zip Goes a Million* (1951; 544), *Love from Judy* (1952; 594), and *The Boy Friend* (1953; 2,084). By this analysis, in the period 1945–53 there were twelve American hits (and three flops), compared to nine British hits. Plenty of moderately successful shows from both sides of the Atlantic also played, including *High Button Shoes* (1948, US, 291), *Wish You Were Here* (1953, US, 282) *Bob's Your Uncle* (1948, UK, 363), *Cage Me A Peacock* (1948, UK, 337), *And So To Bed* (1951, UK, 323), and *Bet Your Life* (1952, UK, 362). In summary, the picture was far more balanced than the typical historiographical narrative of British musical theatre suggests.

Yet 'there was a clear and sustained will to believe the Invasion scenario', suggests Snelson, speculating that this spin may have been 'primed by the American military presence during the war' and 'fuelled afterwards by an awareness of the American aid programme of the Marshall Plan'.[48] If the glorious British spirit had sustained the popu-lation through the struggles of conflict, it was in no small part thanks to the support of the Americans in both manpower and aid. Following the war, Britain was to be the single biggest recipient of American funding to help it rebuild itself; if this 'made tangible the dependence of Europe on America for the sustaining of its post-war reconstruction',[49] the concomitant injection of American cultural energy would serve to consolidate the impression of Britain's dependence on an emerging new power.

'OVER-PAID, OVER-FED, OVER-SEXED AND OVER HERE'

From the end of 1942, American troops had been stationed around the UK. By 1944 there were around 1.5 million US servicemen in the country (out of a total of 3 million who visited during the war), and their presence—especially during a period when many young British men were absent—inevitably had an effect on the population. In popular accounts, these GIs are remembered as 'over-paid, over-fed, over-sexed and over here':

> [T]he GIs came with saunter and swagger, with brashness and boisterousness. They came with five times the money of the British Tommy and with friendly charm which conquered the heart of many a British maiden or otherwise. [. . .] One joke heralded a new brand of knickers: 'One Yank and they're off.'[50]

Such a snapshot of the American visitors is doubtless the stuff of hyperbole; not *all* GIs were voracious sexual athletes, and not *all* British women succumbed to their charms. Nevertheless, in encountering these American servicemen—virile and masculine in contrast to the plucky Brit—the British did come to recognize Americans as different to themselves: threatening to some, though alluring to others. The combined experiences of wartime Britain, with many British men absent, many women in unfamiliar gender roles, and many American forces stationed nearby, were instrumental in a generational shift that happened throughout the 1940s. To understand this, and therefore to grasp what was at stake in what George Orwell called the American 'occupation', it is useful to get an impression of how the two countries and their representatives were perceived.

Britain's self-identity was built on already existing notions of moral virtue, Christian doctrine, family conservatism, and the British 'stiff upper lip'. According to Sonya O. Rose, 'two major themes characterized the nation during the war':

> The first was the nation as a brave and quietly (rather than bombastically) heroic people. [. . .] The second was a nation of quintessentially reasonable citizens who willingly and with good humour sacrificed their private and personal interests and desires for the collective good.[51]

It was a perception of self against which the American GIs and their attitudes stood out: Britons viewed Americans in contrast to themselves, reflecting either a dubious influence or an exciting attraction. 'For most young people in Britain,' writes David Reynolds, 'American fashions, music, even slang, were a source of fascination, epitomized above all in the movies.'[52] Americans were admired for their 'friendliness' and 'vigour', though viewed with some suspicion for their 'boastfulness' and 'materialism'.[53] Granted, these views were often superficial, born out of ignorance, and based on the depictions of Hollywood, though they came to be seen as accurate. What appealed to youngsters—the glamour, excitement, even danger of liberal America—seemed to others 'deeply subversive [. . .], a threat to English values'.[54]

Much of the influence of the American GIs, for good or ill, was played out in social and leisure contact with British women. Off-duty, servicemen would frequent the pubs, dance halls, and cinemas, bringing an alluring presence to these activities, and accelerating the spread of an already-present American culture around the UK. 'To girls brought up on the cinema,' suggests Reynolds, 'who copied the dress, hair styles and manners of Hollywood stars,' the GIs would have seemed like 'exotic creatures who stepped out of the silver screen';[55] Humphrey Bogart or Cary Grant live in the flesh, so to speak.

> [T]he sudden influx of Americans, speaking like the films, who actually lived in the magic country, and who had plenty of money, at once went to the girls' heads. The American attitude to women, their proneness to spoil a girl, to build up, exaggerate, talk big, and to act with generosity and flamboyance, helped to make them the most attractive boy friends.[56]

He continues, detailing a familiar scene from the dance halls which locates the meetings of British women and American servicemen in the social milieu, as expressions of care-free, tactile enjoyment, enacted in the physical gestures of American dance and played out to the soundtrack of American music:

> [F]or many the Yanks offered something special. There was the excitement of new dances like jitterbugging (jiving), which involved a few dance steps, performed vigorously at some distance from one's partner, punctuated by close encounters when the girl might be lifted off her feet or swung around with skirts flying. And then there was the 'big band sound'—associated with Artie Shaw, Tommy Dorsey, and above all Glenn Miller—brassy (in contrast with the frequent use of violins in British bands), sometimes ebullient, but often dreamily romantic 'smooth music'.[57]

Yet to those suspicious of American influence and wary of the dangers it posed to English morality, the activities of these dance halls were themselves threatening pursuits, and the dancing just a stylized rehearsal of the sexual act: 'The persistent advances of amorous GIs were notorious,'[58] hints Reynolds, a sentiment more pronounced in Juliet Gardiner's words: 'The Yanks were sex-mad and countless British women who had virtually no experience in this line were completely bowled off their feet,' she reports; 'almost every working girl aspired to "have a Yank".'[59]

Inevitably, there was public concern about behaviour, with some accounts expressing extreme language and hostility to both the GIs and the British women: just before GIs were stationed in Torquay in January 1944, one resident claimed, 'swarms of strange girls and smart young women *invaded* the town';[60] meanwhile, one military policeman 'never forgot the night he was approached by a "very starchy lady" [. . .] She pointed to the mail slot in her door, telling him it was for "letters of the Royal Mail variety . . . not these"', and then presented him with 'a shiny brass waste-basket at least half full of used condoms'[61] which had been forced through the letter box and into the lady's hallway.

Exaggerated though it may be in this account, the distinction between the 'starchy' older woman and the younger 'good-time girl', as they came to be called, gives an indication of the generation gap that opened up during the war years. While the pre-war generation clung to traditional values and distrusted the onslaught of modern and alien sensibilities, those growing up with the influence of American culture in their communities embraced the US: its 'friendliness' and 'vigour' were seen as charismatic; its 'boastfulness' read as charming confidence; its 'materialism' a promise of luxury that enticed young women fatigued by austerity.

More than this, though, these experiences were to reconceive traditional gender behaviours. Already, British women had been put into the situation of carrying out traditionally male jobs as they were co-opted into the workforce. With this their approach to social behaviour had also shifted. Indeed, although the encounter sketched above may satisfy our view of the dance hall as a conventional meeting place for developing romantic liaisons with the opposite sex, we should remember that we have encoded that with a contemporary sensibility towards courtship rituals. At the time, the sort of physicalized partnering that the (American) dance moves suggested was significantly more assertive for women in particular than previous codes of femininity had allowed, and the behavioural shift this invited led to a change in the way young men and women interacted. Indeed, as Reynolds's discussion of dating rituals between wartime GIs and British women reveals, this was all simply part of a changing landscape of behaviours introduced by American conduct and associated with dating as a *game*. He borrows from a contemporary report on 'dating patterns', written by the anthropologist Margaret Mead in 1943.

> Dates were 'a barometer of popularity'—the boy boosted himself by big talk, sounding as if the girl was bound to fall into his arms, whereas the girl 'proves her popularity by refusing him most or all of the favours which he asks for . . . If she kisses him back, he'll take as much as she will give and despise the girl, just as she will despise him if he doesn't ask for the kiss. A really successful date is one in which the boy asks for everything and gets nothing, except a lot of words, skilful, gay, witty words.' Mead went on to suggest that 'this game is confusing to the British.' Girls might be put off by the GI's wisecracking, speed, and assurance. Or they might confuse 'dating' with 'wooing' and kiss back 'with real warmth' or even 'think the Americans were proposing when they weren't and take them home to father.'[62]

This social foreplay—in which the rituals of traditional courtship are replaced by the charismatic tease of the dating game—could be a blueprint for the way Curly and Laurey behave in *Oklahoma!*. Thus the behaviour of romantic couples in American shows confirmed for British audiences a new, exciting type of youthful interaction, already exercised in the activities of British women with GIs in the war. In these relationships, as in wider society, traditional gender behaviours became reconceived.

'Anything You Can Do I Can Do Better'

In some ways, *Oklahoma!* is an unlikely show to have merited such an impact—so many obvious American signifiers are lacking: 'No gags, no girls, no chance,' cried the apocryphal rebuke.[63] The jazz is minimal; the brassy showbiz is muted; the show is not carried by a star; the female chorus is fully clothed; the main protagonists are morally virtuous; the romantic leads still sing in a familiar tessitura; and the girl who just cain't say no . . . well, she's just a comedy turn. Yet those deeper qualities mentioned above (friendliness, vigour, charm, confidence, and the sexual energy of the girl-meets-boy encounter) exude from the show. As American musicals continued to be imported, it was to be these traits that established themselves as endemic of the American style.

Perhaps more than anything, therefore, it is the informality of gender behaviour that contrasts in these American shows with formal Britishness. Laurey may reveal stereotypical feminine behaviour at times (in 'Many a New Day' and 'Out of My Dreams'; in her implicit 'need' to be matched with Curly), though from the start, for all that she is introduced carrying out the domestic, feminized chores (hanging out washing), she shows a confidence that startles our gender expectations.

> AUNT ELLER   Whyn't you jist grab her and kiss her when she acts thataway, Curly? She's jist achin' fer you to, I bet.
> LAUREY   Oh, I won't even speak to him, let alone 'low him to kiss me, the braggin', bowlegged, wish't he had a sweetheart bum![64]

This is a far more feisty character than was typical on the British stage. If this reconfigures the expectations of gender behaviour, it is significant. Importantly, in these narratives, the female is a character who stands up to the male.

The next show to arrive, *Annie Get Your Gun*, a musical not *by* Rodgers and Hammerstein, but *produced* by them, followed *Oklahoma!* swiftly into London, opening on 7 June 1947 at the London Coliseum. The story, set in the masculine world of sharpshooting, imagines a battle of the sexes in which 'Bad, Bad Man' Frank Butler meets his match in gun-toting Annie Oakley. 'Anything You Can Do, I Can Do Better', they argue in Irving Berlin's celebrated hit number, one of several from the show. Of course, they end up falling in love, and this therefore pitches the same sort of sparring match as *Oklahoma!*, though against the backdrop of Wild West showmanship.

Yet Annie's character is even more assertive than the (by contrast) demure Laurey. She even sings differently: no longer with the tessitura of a European soprano, but with the forceful tones of a chest belt and the syncopations of Irving Berlin's characteristic jazz. In this, the confusion of gender expectations is manifested through the stylized performance of a dating game magnified by song. When she and her sparring partner Frank trade competitive achievements in 'Anything You Can Do', this is brought into focus as the song self-consciously foregrounds singing as the performative terrain of their competition: 'Any note you can hold, I can hold longer,' challenges Frank; 'Anything you can sing, I can sing higher.' The sparring brings further tropes of masculinity to the song, though in targeting pitch, Annie wins hands down, recruiting even the biological range of her voice to showcase her assertive masculine display. As such, conventional signifiers of male and female become reconfigured, and the American musical reveals itself to be everything that the British musical is not, epitomized in the confidence it has to queer even the sound of the voice. Finally, the song concludes with 'Any note you can sing, I can sing sweeter,'[65] and the orchestration swoops into the lush stylistics of operetta, heavy on the strings and building to a European sound lost elsewhere in the score to the invasion of American song. Here, we are reminded of that other sound, and in context— in a song about masculine one-upmanship and a form stamping confident American masculinity on to the cultural landscape—that other sound really is feminized. In these cumulative gestures, can we see the American musical emasculating what went before— operetta, the European and British sounds, Coward and Novello?

I'm reminded of one striking image of Ethel Merman in the role (in the original Broadway production), used by Andrea Most as the cover image of her book, *Making Americans*. In this image, Merman sits in basque and suspenders, emphatically holding a gun aloft astride an enormous motorcycle. Annie is nothing if not an embodiment of America, but in this image she confronts, confuses, and even queers that identity. Read in the context of the American invasion, what does this suggest about American identity as a sexualizing force?

'I'm Just a Girl Who Cain't Say No'

The sexualizing of British theatre was not exactly *new* (the West End's nude revue show at the Windmill Theatre famously never closed throughout the war), but conventional British conservatism was resistant to it, and legitimate theatre was carefully policed by the censorship of the Lord Chamberlain's Office. Increasingly, that resistance became eroded, as American shows normalized a more relaxed set of sexual behaviours. Already in *Oklahoma!* the taboo of sexual intrigue is raised, in Jud's secret collection of dirty postcards and the metamorphosis of those women into embodiments of competition in Laurey's dream. Before long it was not just the antagonists who were sexualized: soon the heroes and heroines would dispense with chaperones and clothes; after all, if something had already been approved and successful on the New York stage, it was difficult for the Lord Chamberlain to veto its presentation in the West End.

Consider *South Pacific* (Drury Lane, 1951): American troops stationed abroad, local women the object of their lust, a theme of interracial relationships—this show must have seemed an ironic reminder of the GIs 'over here'. Here the exotic woman is Bloody Mary's daughter Liat, whose beauty intoxicates Lieutenant Cable. When we meet her she is already established as an example of the sexualized female object after whom the marines have been lusting. Their sentiments are couched in boisterous comedy, to be sure: 'Nothin' in the world | Has a soft and wavy frame | Like the silhouette of a dame,' they sing.[66] But when the juvenile lead encounters such a soft and wavy frame, his experience is sexualized: the music swells, the lights fade, and Cable begins to take off Liat's clothes. To Jim Lovensheimer, '[s]uch blatant eroticism was unprecedented in any musical by Rodgers and Hammerstein, and probably anyone else'.[67]

> Standing shirtless in a jungle hut after having sex with a seventeen-year-old girl, Cable represents neither marriage nor family, and his body, like the sexual act he has just experienced, suggests a transgression of post-war ideals.[68]

Even to modern sensibilities, this provocative sequence comes across as steamy; how much more transgressive would it have appeared to British post-war audiences, far more reserved about sex?

Ingrained though such reserved British attitudes may have been, the situation was changing, and generational attitudes differed both in terms of how behaviour should be policed and in terms of how morally reprehensible the new American attitudes were. And *South Pacific* was very successful, sustaining not only the Rodgers and Hammerstein occupation of Drury Lane, but also opening the doors for further even more provocative displays. Snelson details the antics of *Wish You Were Here*, a show set in an American holiday camp which opened at the Casino. This—according to his interpretation of the reviews—'was founded on the principal that young men wanted sex, and young women wanted marriage and sex, although not necessarily in that order'.[69] It involved 'long and frequent scenes with the cast wearing not much more than bathing costumes', 'many romantic liaisons presented physically as central parts of the plot or just part of the scenery', and 'a main character who boasts of his frequent sexual conquests'.[70] 'Not surprisingly,' reports Snelson, 'the sexual aspects of the show met with disapproval,'[71] and he goes on to give examples from a number of reviews describing all sorts of suggestive and/or openly sexualized acts at which the critics took offense. 'Amusing though this example of British prudery is, it highlights one of the main distinctions between the American musicals of the period and the British ones,' concludes Snelson's analysis; '[t]he Americans put sex high on the list of plot components and visual presentation; the British shows avoided it in favour of romantic but essentially chaste love.'[72]

'Gay's the Word'

The American musical had certainly made an impact, and was noticeably distinct from most British offerings: more vibrant, more vigorous, more up to date, and more sexualized. 'In terms of character motivation, humour and especially an approach to relationships,' writes Snelson, 'the American musicals were presenting a more direct and modern view of contemporary life than their British counterparts.'[73] In response to these

American shows, British writers made moves to transform their own. Astonishingly, it was Novello, the most abiding composer of the British style of old-fashioned musical theatre who would strike the biggest challenge to American musical might. As Adrian Wright comments, 'Novello regarded the American musical as "highly salutary. It defies convention, teaching us to defy convention in our own way. Americans have infused a new feeling".'[74]

The backstage *Gay's the Word* (1951), written for Cicely Courtneidge, was his swan-song—and 'one through which he made the perceived contrasts between British and American shows the substance of the show itself'.[75] It was a surprising departure for Novello to write a vehicle for Courtneidge. Although they were close friends, they were from different schools of musical theatre tradition. 'I didn't think you'd want to do my kind of music,' exclaimed Courtneidge when Novello announced he would like to write her a show;[76] but doing so was exactly the sort of riposte he envisaged to match the energy, style, and star attraction of the American shows. Courtneidge was recognized for her 'amazing'[77] 'boundless energy',[78] and in this she rivalled American performers. She wasn't the only British performer with this sort of charisma—both Arthur Askey and George Formby had successful shows written for their inimitable personalities (*Bet Your Life* and *Zip Goes a Million* respectively), though the fact that one of the songs from this new show, 'Vitality', laments the loss of the big British stars of the 1920s indicates that the sort of charisma paraded by these celebrities was seen as a quality fast dying out.

Gay's the Word was an answer to the American vitality, though: a type of show firmly British in its tone yet inspired by the American style. Morley is unequivocal: this was 'a West End answer of sorts to Broadway's *42nd Street*'.[79] The show rehearses the sort of opera versus jazz motif that had been prevalent in the Broadway musicals of the 1930s. Courtneidge plays singer Gay Daventry, who at the beginning of the show flops in an old-fashioned operetta. Desperate, she resorts to opening a drama school to restore her fortunes. By the end, she has returned to the stage, having reworked the failed show into a contemporary musical. In this storyline, Novello shrewdly recognizes the changes happening on the West End: 'Public taste is turning', goes one song,[80] its music echoing his very first hit, the patriotic First World War anthem 'Keep the Home Fires Burning' (1914).

In fact, references to his own work—and thus to the faded British style—abound. He writes the failed operetta in the style of his familiar shows, recognizing his own contribution to perpetuating that pre-war 'tosh'.[81] This may cast him as old-school, but he also deftly confirms his ability to move into the new: 'The former delights of glamorous nights | No longer constitute a raving mania,' sings the male chorus in the opening number, referring to his earlier show *Glamorous Night* (1935); 'Rhapsodical kings no longer are things | To sing about,' they continue, a nod to the then-running *King's Rhapsody* (1949), in which he was playing the King.[82]

In this unlikely volte-face, Novello acknowledges the cultural forms of West End operetta and Broadway musical—one old-fashioned, one up to date—and, as if he at least has had a wake-up call, his songs admit: 'Since *Oklahoma!* we've been in a coma |

And no-one cares for us.'[83] Moreover, he recognizes that this paradigm shift on the stage is reflective of a wider cultural need to energize post-war Britain and reboot its identity: 'To the list of faded glories must be added | Our country, which we must admit has had it,'[84] goes the opening number. Who would have thought that it would be Novello who would lead a clarion call to bring the British musical into a contemporary style? But he does—with humility, wit, and grace—and in the mock-language of war, he counters the American invasion:

> We'll gather strength in Ruritania
> When the enemy is slain
> We'll gather strength in Ruritania
> When the waltz is waltzed again.
> Oscar Hammerstein shows
> May be mighty fine shows
> But we'll gather strength in Ruritania
> With a corny old refrain
> When our song is sung again.[85]

As for the recognition of sex, *Gay's the Word* remains chaste; though taking their cue from Cole Porter, Novello and lyricist Alan Melville write a witty tour de force, 'An Englishman in Love'. 'Though passions abroad may be hot,' go the lyrics, 'In England, quite frankly, they're not.' The song whisks through a world tour of other nationalities and their sexual energies ('The Swiss never miss all the bliss of a kiss, | For romance fits a Swiss like a glove,' we are told). Although surprisingly the Americans are never mentioned (an extraordinary omission—dozens of more unlikely nationalities are), the butt of the joke remains British reserve, often given topical relevance:

> The Greeks and the Sikhs are impassioned
> And so are the Lapps and the Czechs;
> But there's nothing so heavily rationed
> As Anglo-Saxon sex.[86]

More than anything, though, it is Novello's move to embrace an American sound that affirms his adoption of the Broadway style, from the pastiche of *Annie Get Your Gun*'s 'There's No Business Like Show Business'—the far more self-effacingly British 'It's Bound to be Right on the Night'—to the hit song of the Act 1 finale, 'Vitality'. This is Novello's homage to the American invasion. As Snelson notes, it was the word 'vitality' above all that reviewers used to describe the performance style of the American shows.[87] He highlights Novello's use of 'bold and repeated syncopations' which 'create the maximum impact of energy and drive', and identifies these in particular as 'an example of the deliberate appropriation of a distinctive feature of American popular music.'[88] This song was completely unlike anything Novello had offered before, 'principally for the fact that he had never had a central character who was required to be so fundamentally defined by sheer energy.'[89] That Courtneidge gave it energy is evident from this account by the film director Herbert Wilcox, whose unnamed American companion seems bowled over:

> [A]t the first interval, [Cis] had worked—or perhaps I should say overworked—the audience into a frenzy of enthusiasm whilst she sang and danced the hit number of the show, 'Vitality.' When she came out to take a call, a chair was slipped behind the tabs for her to sit on and she sat down in a way that indicated she had given all she had to give and loved every minute of it. The producer of a new American musical turned to me and said, 'How often does she do that?' I told him eight times a week. 'They can't do that to her. They can't do it,' was all he could mutter. He was too astonished even to applaud.[90]

Sadly, Novello had no opportunity to reveal whether he could have or would have permanently transitioned from his own British style of lush romanticism to a modern American vigour: this was his last completed show.[91]

In fact, British musical theatre—and British theatre—would move in an altogether different direction. As if shaken from the torpor of the post-war years, the 1950s saw sudden awakenings: in 1951 the foundation stone for a new National Theatre was laid (though the project itself would still take years to come to fruition); in 1953, Joan Littlewood and her politically charged Theatre Workshop would take over the Theatre Royal Stratford East; in 1956 young director Peter Hall would issue an attack on the staid conventions of Britain's theatre, part of his move to inaugurate the Shakespeare Memorial Theatre (later the Royal Shakespeare Company) in Stratford which eventually formed in 1960;[92] and also in 1956 George Devine at the English Stage Company issued a call for new playscripts, which would result in *Look Back in Anger* (1956) at the Royal Court Theatre and a wave of 'Angry Young Men' playwrights offering gritty reflections of 'real' British people at their kitchen sinks. The focus was very British, and as British musicals did emerge, such as *Expresso Bongo* (1958) and *Fings Ain't What They Used T'Be* (1959), they embraced what Adrian Wright calls 'British verismo': 'the genre's attempt to offer an accurate reflection of real life.'[93] Even the wholeheartedly Broadway-inspired sound of *The Boy Friend* (1953) was such a nostalgic return to the 1920s that it didn't exactly ride the tide of the American invasion, creating instead a fond pastiche of a completely different time.

Perhaps mimicking the Broadway sound was not the way for British musical theatre to find its feet. That would be a slow process and it would be years before the West End would find another figure as dominant as Novello. Meanwhile, in any case, the influence of the theatrical score in providing the dominant sound of popular music was to wane as new voices emerged in Britain and America on radio and record.

NOTES

1. Tim Carter, *'Oklahoma!': The Making of an American Musical* (New Haven: Yale University Press, 2007), 231.

2. For more on this see the chapter entitled 'The Brits', in Mark Steyn, *Broadway Babies Say Goodnight* (London: Faber and Faber, 1997), 163–77.
3. John M. Snelson, 'The West End Musical 1947–1954: British Identity and the "American Invasion"' (unpublished PhD, University of Birmingham, 2002), 3.
4. Anon., 'At the Play', *Punch* 217, 28 September 1949, 313.
5. Sheridan Morley, *Spread a Little Happiness: The First Hundred Years of the British Musical* (London: Thames and Hudson, 1987), 116.
6. See Steyn, *Broadway Babies*, 73; Joseph P. Swain, *The Broadway Musical* (Lanham, MD: The Scarecrow Press, 2002), 81; William A. Everett and Paul R. Laird, eds., *The Cambridge Companion to the Musical* (Cambridge: Cambridge University .Press, 2002), 99.
7. See, for example, Rodgers and Hammerstein's claims to the press in Oscar Hammerstein II, 'In Re "Oklahoma!"': The Adaptor-Lyricist Describes How the Musical Hit Came into Being', *New York Times*, 23 May 1943, 11, and Richard Rodgers, 'Mr. Rodgers Insists That It Ain't Luck', *New York Times*, 1 August 1943, X1.
8. Nelson B. Bell, *Washington Post*. Quoted in Stanley Green, ed., *Rodgers and Hammerstein Fact Book: A Record of Their Works Together and with Other Collaborators* (New York: The Lynn Farnol Group, Inc., 1980), 519.
9. Louis Kronenberger, *Time*, 12 April 1943. Quoted in Green, *Rodgers and Hammerstein Fact Book*, 516.
10. Richard Rodgers and Oscar Hammerstein II, *Six Plays by Rodgers and Hammerstein* (New York: The Modern Library, n.d.), 71.
11. Rodgers and Hammerstein, *Six Plays*, 75.
12. Raymond Knapp, *The American Musical and the Formation of National Identity* (Princeton, NJ: Princeton University Press, 2005), 124.
13. Knapp, *American Musical*, 120.
14. Knapp, *American Musical*, 123.
15. Snelson, 'West End Musical', 26–27.
16. Of course, *Oklahoma!* appeared in the US before the full atrocities of the Holocaust were public knowledge, so the show can hardly be seen as a direct comment on world politics; nevertheless, Jud's unwelcome bullying of the community strikes a chord at a time when Germany is exercising its muscles over European neighbours.
17. Carter, 'Oklahoma!', 216.
18. Morley, *Spread a Little Happiness*, 112.
19. W. A. Darlington. Quoted in Morley, *Spread a Little Happiness*, 113.
20. Steyn, *Broadway Babies*, 20.
21. Stanley Green, *The World of Musical Comedy* (New York: Da Capo Press, 1980), 210.
22. Adrian Wright, *A Tanner's Worth of Tune: Rediscovering the Post-War British Musical* (Woodbridge: The Boydell Press, 2010), 25.
23. Max Wilk, *OK!: The Story of 'Oklahoma!'* (New York: Applause, 2002), 10.
24. Anon., 'Drury Lane Theatre', *The Times*, 1 May 1947, 6, http://find.galegroup.com/ttda/infomark.do?&source=gale&prodId=TTDA&userGroupName=ulh&tabID=T003&docPage=article&searchType=BasicSearchForm&docId=CS101926049&type=multipage&contentSet=LTO&version=1.0, accessed 3 May 2014.
25. Cecil Wilson, '3 Smash Hits, See Why They Run', *Daily Mail*, 30 December 1948, 2, http://find.galegroup.com/dmha/infomark.do?&source=gale&prodId=DMHA&userGroupName=ulh&tabID=T003&docPage=article&searchType=BasicSearchForm&docId=EE1864599844&type=multipage&contentSet=LTO&version=1.0 , accessed 4 May 2014.

26. Snelson, 'West End Musical', 83.

27. Snelson, 'West End Musical', 1.

28. Anon., 'Drury Lane Theatre'.

29. W. A. Darlington, *Daily Telegraph*. Quoted in Green, *Rodgers and Hammerstein Fact Book*, 527.

30. Jack Hulbert, *The Little Woman's Always Right* (London: W. H. Allen, 1975), 122.

31. Mike Chopra-Gant, *Hollywood Genres and Post-War America: Masculinity, Family and Nation in Popular Movies and Film Noir* (New York: St Martin's Press, 2006), 99.

32. Matthew Sitter, 'Violence and Masculinity in Hollywood War Films during World War II' (MA dissertation, Ontario: Lakehead University, 2012), 1. Bogart's Joe Gunn—note the name: an average Joe with a gun—is seen in a variety of action poses on the promotional material for *Sahara*; all show him commanding the field of war, in the midst of explosions and battle. Meanwhile, stills from *Destination Tokyo* show sweat glistening on Grant's open-shirted chest, an undoubted figure of determined masculinity prefiguring the sort of nonchalance epitomizing Marlon Brando or James Dean in the 1950s.

33. Cited by Robert A. Nye, 'Western Masculinities in War and Peace', *American Historical Review* 112, no. 2 (April 2007): 423.

34. Nye, 'Western Masculinities', 423.

35. Gael Sweeney, 'Impatient with Stupidity: Alien Imperialism in *The Day the Earth Stood Still*', in *Closely Watched Brains*, ed. Murray Pomerance and John Sakeris (Boston: Pearson Education, 2003), 219.

36. Sweeney, 'Impatient with Stupidity', 219.

37. Cited by Linsey Robb, *Men at Work: The Working Man in British Culture, 1939–1945* (Basingstoke: Palgrave Macmillan, 2015), 8.

38. Cited by Laura Chase, 'Public Beaches and Private Beach Huts: A Case Study of Inter-War Clacton and Frinton, Essex', in *Histories of Tourism: Representation, Identity and Conflict*, ed. John K. Walton (Clevedon: Channel View Publications, 2005), 219.

39. Snelson, 'West End Musical', 1.

40. Snelson, 'West End Musical', 2–3.

41. John Snelson, ' "We Said We Wouldn't Look Back": British Musical Theatre, 1935–1960', in Everett and Laird, *Cambridge Companion to the Musical*, 112.

42. Snelson, ' "We Said We Wouldn't Look Back" ',106.

43. Snelson, 'West End Musical', 9.

44. Quoted in Adrian Wright, *West End Broadway: The Golden Age of the American Musical in London* (Woodbridge: The Boydell Press, 2012), 43.

45. Snelson, 'West End Musical', 28.

46. Snelson, 'West End Musical', 29.

47. Length of run is certainly not the only measure of success in theatre, though it is at least one consideration. I have listed shows opening between the end of the war and 1953, when (according to the historiographies) *The Boy Friend* (1953) and *Salad Days* (1954) resuscitated the British musical. These are the subject of Chapter 9.

48. Snelson, 'West End Musical', 39.

49. Snelson, 'West End Musical', 39.

50. Quoted in David Reynolds, *Rich Relations: The American Occupation of Britain, 1942–1945* (New York: Random House, 1995), xxiii.

51. Sonya O. Rose, *Which People's War: National Identity and Citizenship in Britain, 1939–1945* (Oxford: Oxford University Press, 2003), 79.

52. Reynolds, *Rich Relations*, 38.
53. Reynolds, *Rich Relations*, 37.
54. Reynolds, *Rich Relations*, 39.
55. Reynolds, *Rich Relations*, 266–267.
56. Reynolds, *Rich Relations*, 267.
57. Reynolds, *Rich Relations*, 264.
58. Reynolds, *Rich Relations*, 201.
59. Juliet Gardiner, 'Overpaid, Oversexed, and Over Here': *The American GI in World War II Britain* (New York: Canopy Books, 1992), 108.
60. Reynolds, *Rich Relations*, 202. Italics in the original.
61. Reynolds, *Rich Relations*, 201.
62. Reynolds, *Rich Relations*, 265.
63. 'No gags, no girls, no chance' was the verdict of one commentator on seeing out-of-town try-outs of *Oklahoma!* when it first appeared as *Away We Go* in 1947. The remark is variously attributed to producer Michael Todd, newspaper columnist Walter Winchell, and Winchell's secretary Rose Bigman, though the actual circumstances are vague, and the comment may even have been 'no legs, no jokes, no chance'. Perhaps the most useful account can be found in Richard Rodgers's autobiography *Musical Stages* (New York: Da Capo Press, 2002), 225. Whatever the facts are, the show clearly proved more successful than this commentator judged.
64. Rodgers and Hammerstein, *Six Plays*, 13.
65. 'Anything You Can Do', from *Annie Get Your Gun* (1946). In *Annie Get Your Gun*, original cast recording, 1946, CD, Decca, 012 159 243-2, 2000.
66. Rodgers and Hammerstein, *Six Plays*, 289.
67. Jim Lovensheimer, *'South Pacific': Paradise Rewritten* (New York: Oxford University Press, 2010), 153.
68. Lovensheimer, *'South Pacific'*, 155.
69. Snelson, 'West End Musical', 95–96.
70. Snelson, 'West End Musical', 95.
71. Snelson, 'West End Musical', 96.
72. Snelson, 'West End Musical', 98.
73. Snelson, 'West End Musical', 99.
74. Quoted in Wright, *Tanner's Worth of Tune*, 38.
75. Snelson, 'West End Musical', 113.
76. Cicely Courtneidge, *Cicely* (London: Hutchinson and Co., 1953), 173.
77. Tony Staveacre, *The Songwriters* (London: British Broadcasting Corporation, 1980), 116.
78. Snelson, 'West End Musical', 195.
79. Morley, *Spread a Little Happiness*, 126–127.
80. 'Guards on Parade', from *Gay's the Word* (1951) by Ivor Novello and Alan Melville. *Gay's the Word*, original London cast, 2012, CD, Jay Records, CDJAY 1425, 2013.
81. Critical reviews of Novello shows were often dismissive, though the public adored them. This was *The Observer*'s reaction to *Glamorous Night* (1935): 'I lift my hat to Mr. Novello. He can wade through tosh with the straightest face.' Quoted in Staveacre, *Songwriters*, 105.
82. 'Ruritania', from *Gay's the Word*, original London cast, 2012, CD.
83. 'Vitality', from *Gay's the Word*, original London cast, 2012, CD.
84. 'Ruritania', from *Gay's the Word*, original London cast, 2012, CD.
85. 'Guards on Parade', from *Gay's the Word*, original London cast, 2012, CD.

86. 'An Englishman in Love', from *Gay's the Word*, original London cast, 2012, CD.
87. Snelson, 'West End Musical', 61.
88. Snelson, 'West End Musical', 219.
89. Snelson, 'West End Musical', 217.
90. Courtneidge, *Cicely*, 208.
91. Novello was working on a new show, *Valley of Song*, when he died. This was left incomplete and was subsequently finished by Novello's lyricist Christopher Hassall. Although not produced professionally until 2014, the show has long been available for amateur performance.
92. Peter Hall, 'Too Much Shakespeare?', *Plays and Players* 3 (1956), 5–9.
93. Wright, *Tanner's Worth of Tune*, 139.

Bibliography

Annie Get Your Gun. Original Cast Recording, 1946. CD. Decca, 012 159 243-2, 2000.

Anon. 'At the Play.' *Punch* 217, 28 September 1949, 313.

Anon. 'Drury Lane Theatre.' *The Times*, 1 May 1947, 6.

Carter, Tim. *'Oklahoma!': The Making of an American Musical*. New Haven: Yale University Press, 2007.

Chase, Laura. 'Public Beaches and Private Beach Huts: A Case Study of Inter-War Clacton and Frinton, Essex.' In *Histories of Tourism: Representation, Identity and Conflict*, edited by John K. Walton, 211–227. Clevedon: Channel View Publications, 2005.

Chopra-Gant, Mike. *Hollywood Genres and Post-War America: Masculinity, Family and Nation in Popular Movies and Film Noir*. New York: St Martin's Press, 2006.

Courtneidge, Cicely. *Cicely*. London: Hutchinson and Co., 1953.

Davis, Ronald L. *Mary Martin, Broadway Legend*. Norman: University of Oklahoma Press, 2008.

Everett, William A., and Paul R. Laird, eds. *The Cambridge Companion to the Musical*. Cambridge: Cambridge University Press, 2002.

Gardiner, Juliet. *'Overpaid, Oversexed, and Over Here': The American GI in World War II Britain*. New York: Canopy Books, 1992.

Gay's the Word. Original London Cast, 2012. CD. Jay Recordings, CDJAY 1425. Released 2013.

Green, Stanley. *The World of Musical Comedy*. New York: Da Capo Press, 1980.

Green, Stanley, ed. *Rodgers and Hammerstein Fact Book: A Record of Their Works Together and with Other Collaborators*. New York: The Lynn Farnol Group, Inc., 1980.

Hall, Peter. 'Too Much Shakespeare?' *Plays and Players* 3 (1956): 5–9.

Hammerstein II, Oscar. 'In Re *Oklahoma*!: The Adaptor-Lyricist Describes How the Musical Hit Came into Being.' *New York Times*, 23 May 1943, 11.

Hulbert, Jack. *The Little Woman's Always Right*. London: W. H. Allen, 1975.

Knapp, Raymond. *The American Musical and the Formation of National Identity*. Princeton, NJ: Princeton University Press, 2005.

Lovensheimer, Jim. *'South Pacific': Paradise Rewritten*. New York: Oxford University Press, 2010.

Milligate, Helen D. *Got Any Gum Chum? GIs in Wartime Britain 1942–1945*. Brimscombe Port: The History Press, 2009.

Morley, Sheridan. *Spread a Little Happiness: The First Hundred Years of the British Musical.* London: Thames and Hudson, 1987.

Most, Andrea. *Making Americans: Jews and the Broadway Musical.* Cambridge, MA: Harvard University Press, 2004.

Nye, Robert A. 'Western Masculinities in War and Peace.' *American Historical Review* 112, no. 2 (April 2007): 417–438.

Pomerance, Murray, and John Sakeris, eds. *Closely Watched Brains.* Boston: Pearson Education, 2003.

Reynolds, David. *Rich Relations: The American Occupation of Britain, 1942–1945.* New York: Random House, 1995.

Robb, Linsey. *Men at Work: The Working Man in British Culture, 1939–1945.* Basingstoke: Palgrave Macmillan, 2015.

Rodgers, Richard. 'Mr. Rodgers Insists That It Ain't Luck.' *New York Times*, 1 August 1943, X1.

Rodgers, Richard. *Musical Stages: An Autobiography.* New York: Da Capo Press, 2002.

Rodgers, Richard, and Oscar Hammerstein II. *Six Plays by Rodgers and Hammerstein.* New York: The Modern Library, not dated.

Rose, Sonya O. *Which People's War: National Identity and Citizenship in Britain, 1939–1945.* Oxford: Oxford University Press, 2003.

Sitter, Matthew. 'Violence and Masculinity in Hollywood War Films during World War II.' MA dissertation. Ontario: Lakehead University, 2012.

Snelson, John M. 'The West End Musical 1947–1954: British Identity and the "American Invasion".' Unpublished PhD thesis, University of Birmingham, 2002.

Staveacre, Tony. *The Songwriters.* London: British Broadcasting Corporation, 1980.

Steyn, Mark. *Broadway Babies Say Goodnight: Musicals Then and Now.* London: Faber and Faber, 2000.

Sturma, Michael. *South Sea Maidens: Western Fantasy and Sexual Politics in the South Pacific.* Westport: Greenwood, 2002.

Swain, Joseph P. *The Broadway Musical.* Lanham, MD: The Scarecrow Press, 2002.

Sweeney, Gail. 'Impatient with Stupidity: Alien Imperialism in *The Day the Earth Stood Still*.' In *Closely Watched Brains*, edited by Murray Pomerance and John Sakeris, 215–229. Boston: Pearson Education, 2003.

Walton, John K., ed. *Histories of Tourism: Representation, Identity and Conflict.* Clevedon: Channel View Publications, 2005.

Wilk, Max. *OK!: The Story of 'Oklahoma!'* New York: Applause, 2002.

Wilson, Cecil. '3 Smash Hits, See Why They Run.' *Daily Mail*, 30 December 1948, 2.

Wright, Adrian. *A Tanner's Worth of Tune: Rediscovering the Post-War British Musical.* Woodbridge: The Boydell Press, 2010.

Wright, Adrian. *West End Broadway: The Golden Age of the American Musical in London.* Woodbridge: The Boydell Press, 2012.

CHAPTER 9

....

'ORDINARY PEOPLE' AND BRITISH MUSICALS OF THE POST-WAR DECADE

....

JOHN SNELSON

BRITISH musicals in the decade after the Second World War do not readily lend themselves to clear characterization as a group. There was no single line of development or dominant creative team. The pre-war names of Ellis and Novello were in the later stages of their musical theatre work, the reputations of Sandy Wilson and Julian Slade rest essentially on one show each from the mid-1950s, while such dominant creative figures of the late 1950s–60s as Lionel Bart and David Heneker had yet to make their mark. It was a period of transition and reassessment in British musical theatre whose strands reflected national, social, and individual preoccupations, at the centre of which was a questioning of national identity.[1]

The end of the war led to a period of introspection for the country that built on attitudes engendered by the wartime experience, when the support of community was essential to survive physical and emotional damage. Community was necessary for recovery too. The 1945 general election delivered a Labour government under Clement Attlee with a majority sufficient to drive a programme of social reform that included the establishment of the collective pillars of the welfare state—mechanisms nationally administered to support the life and well-being of the individual.[2] It was a fine aim set within the major task of material, social, and psychological reconstruction of a nation, not least as some situations became worse in the five or so years following the war (food rationing, for example). But there was a reaction to the sustained post-war austerity and its associated broader national aims. In October 1951, success at the general election went to Winston Churchill and the Conservatives, and with it a trend towards pre-war and wartime values of social conformity, and defensive restriction began to be reasserted.

There was no abrupt U-turn in British attitudes in 1951. The election result demonstrated how, in the British voting system, relatively small changes in percentage support for any political party could be magnified through the number of parliamentary seats a party returned. More usefully, the election gives us a snapshot in the middle of a period of flux. British musical theatre at the time shows this flux too in the preoccupations of its creative figures, the vacillations in what appealed to audiences and hence the types of shows on which producers were prepared to risk their money. The result is a diversity of audiences that embraced a broad variety of classes and generations as well as political and moral convictions at which any work may have been aimed or to which it could have appealed.

Such overlapping strands of creation and appeal are always a factor, but the lack of a single identifiable and dominant British element in the narrative of musical theatre history at this time has led commentators repeatedly to seek one elsewhere. As a result, the British space has been filled with the conventions, preoccupations, and even repertory of American musical theatre such that the West End musical at this time is described substantially (and sometimes exclusively) in terms of the exaggerated success of Broadway imports. This distorts any sense of a British musical theatre identity while also reinforcing a set of criteria for the whole genre of the musical that by definition exclude the valuing of any Anglocentric focus. Even with today's dense and rapid exchange of news and culture, the West End is not a twin of Broadway, and Britain is not America.[3] Even less so was that the case for home-grown musicals of the mid-1940s–50s. What can be identified across British shows of this period is an active distancing from, or supplanting of, American values (not just the musical and theatrical, but the moral and political too) through choices of subject matter, musical style, and cultural/topical reference. The cultural space that British-originated musicals occupied at this time may not be entirely defined by national perspective, but is certainly incomplete without it.

THEM AND US

The most introspective musical theatre work in this period is Ivor Novello's last show, *Gay's the Word*. It opened at the Saville Theatre on 6 February 1951, a few weeks before Novello's sudden death from a heart attack, and ran until 3 May 1952. Just over half of its fifteen-month run was concurrent with a completely different sort of show also by Novello: *King's Rhapsody* had opened on 15 September 1949, at the Palace Theatre, within sight of the Saville, not closing until 6 October 1951. That *Gay's the Word* ran alongside *King's Rhapsody* chronologically and geographically made even more emphatic the differences between them. *King's Rhapsody* draws on the archetypes established within a single genre, the European locus of the Ruritanian romance of operetta, and is iconic of the distinctive style Novello had established for himself pre-war. *Gay's the Word* specifically relied upon transatlantic genre juxtapositions of British musical comedy and American musicals in the form of a backstage musical to heighten the effect of a particularly British post-war message.

The title role of Gay Daventry, a musical theatre star, was taken by Cicely Courtneidge. Her success in musical comedy (1910s), music hall (1920s), film and stage revue (1930s–40s), and musicals (1940s–50s) constitutes a monumental career across the gamut of British popular entertainment. This comment on her character from the *Sunday Express* is typical: 'For 40 years Miss Courtneidge has been the whirlwind of the theatre. She has acted, sung, danced, burlesqued in London and on tour with a unique ebullience, a warmth that is lovable and rare.'[4] She was one of the nation's favourite performers, her stage and screen persona explicitly presented as embodying patriotic British spirit.

The show's story is based on the reworking of a failing old-fashioned, operetta-style musical into a contemporary, successful musical. Although an opening scene sent up Novello's own version of the Ruritanian romance brilliantly, little of the reworking was shown, with the 'new style' presented more through the songs associated with the storyline than those of the resurrected show. Novello suggested this new style by modelling aspects of harmony, melody, or rhythm after distinctive features in Broadway successes. For example, 'If Only He'd Looked My Way' owes a debt to 'Some Enchanted Evening'; 'A Matter of Minutes' takes its lead from 'I'm in Love with a Wonderful Guy' and other Richard Rodgers waltzes; and 'Vitality', the key number of the show, is a cross between 'Another Openin', Another Show', and 'There's no Business like Show Business'. The American musical influx from 1947 on triggered a crisis of confidence as the British musical was challenged by Broadway shows. But the true cause of the problem is identified in the show and particularly in 'Vitality', in which Alan Melville's lyrics list famous performers of British theatre from Vesta Tilley, Josie Collins, George Robey, and Billy Merson right through to Gracie Fields and Courtneidge herself. The message is in effect 'we've done it before and we can do it again'. The only contemporary failing is a lack of energy and will, rather than an intrinsic national deficiency in talent. Cicely Courtneidge demonstrates just such 'Vitality' in the lengthy finale to Act 1.

The explicit use of British–American contrasts in theatrical form shown in *Gay's the Word* was extended to national traits in another British hit West End show of 1951. As with Cicely Courtneidge and her theatrical energy, the associations of the star performer in the lead role were integral to the concept. From 1937 to 1943, George Formby was the top male British screen performer. His film persona promoted the same Lancashire stereotype as his contemporary Gracie Fields: ordinary working-class folk characterized by honesty, determination, optimism, and pride, underwritten with financial prudence brought about through the necessities of deprivation.[5]

The success of Formby in romance and his eventual circumvention of the restrictions of class in the plots of his films suggested that both ordinary looks and low social status could be transcended with an honest heart and good intentions. As inadvertent heroes, Formby's characters elevated the common man. He had established himself on the stage in music hall and variety, and a venture into musical theatre in 1951 was a late development in his career, achieved with a show written for him by Eric Maschwitz with music by George Posford. *Zip Goes a Million* is one of many dramatic adaptations (stage and screen) of George Barr McCutcheon's 1902 novel *Brewster's Millions*, and even today, it is a delightful show with a fast-moving, consistently funny script, attractive musical numbers, and a strong cumulative sense of engagement with the predicament of the central character, Percy Piggott (played by Formby, the character's name changed from Montgomery Brewster to reflect Formby's regional persona).

The central premise of the farce is that the protagonist must spend an inherited fortune completely within a year in order to inherit an even larger one, but he must not reveal to anyone the conditions of the bequest. The additional dimension that this new version brought was that of cross-cultural comparison through a deceased American millionaire and a poor nephew from Lancashire, whose inheritance draws him into what is—from his perspective—the strange and foreign environment of the USA. Thus the attitudes of post-war austerity and prudence in Britain were concatenated with the Lancashire canniness with money (a stereotypical trait similar to that of the Scots), then played out against the values of American consumerism. The first act opens in

FIGURE 9.1 A symbol of shared experience: George Formby celebrating British values in *Zip Goes a Million* (1951).

Photograph by Thurston Hopkins. Courtesy of Getty Images.

Piggottsville, Texas, a town founded on the money of an oil tycoon who has left every-thing in his will to an English nephew. Percy's cautious approach to money is established in his introductory dialogue and developed in the following number 'I'm Saving Up for Sally' (independently of the show, this proved a hit song for Formby). The song's verse highlights the underlying good intentions of the character by providing the qualifica-tion that his motive to guard his cash is not avarice but the need to save up for marriage to his girlfriend.

The characters who encourage Percy to spend money (although unaware of his motive) are American; those who try to make him exercise prudence are his English friends and relatives. Throughout this show—as in so many other British ones of this period—there are small but frequent references that emphasize a mindset in which Britain viewed itself as being if not physically occupied by America then certainly pre-occupied by prevalent manifestations of its culture and ethos. It was important to keep a distance between the British and American sense of values, and *Zip Goes a Million* repeatedly does this. As one of Formby's songs in the show explained in its title, Percy Piggott was one of the 'Ordinary People', and that condition—paradoxically but per-fectly embodied by Formby, the unique performer—was also a symbol of shared expe-rience, and an invitation for those in the audience to see aspects of their own lives and British values portrayed in the drama (see Figure 9.1). Inevitably, and at the last possible moment, Percy gets the money and the girl. In 1951, any critique of British values against American ones that also sought popular affirmation (as commercially successful musi-cal theatre requires) could hardly do otherwise.

'ENGLAND IS A LOVELY PLACE'

As the 1950s began, West End–Broadway and UK–US neuroses became more promi-nent in new theatre works—especially so in musicals, where genre identity itself was subject to sustained American challenge. The comparison of American attitudes and values with British ones in these shows was principally a means to throw the national concerns into stark relief through the juxtaposition, not to present a balanced or objec-tive evaluation of the different perspectives. The timing is significant. Five years of hard post-war slog after the awful experiences of wartime itself seemed to be yielding few returns. The spirit of the nation was flagging; there needed to be something brighter on the horizon. An exhortation to that plucky British spirit (as with *Gay's the Word*) was one way. Suggesting hope in the future itself was another—1951 was the year of the Festival of Britain, created for just such a promotional purpose. Yet another was to remind people what the fight had been all about and what it was that needed to be restored, conveyed through an emotional appeal to the symbols of the nation, those special markers of a special country and especially of its countryside. This is very much the approach that Vivian Ellis and his regular librettist A. P. Herbert chose through four post-war musi-cals, beginning with *Bless the Bride* (1947). To listen to the Ellis pre-war catalogue is to encounter a succession of beautifully phrased numbers, many of which became popular with dance bands: for example, Ellis's 'She's My Lovely' (from *Hide and Seek*, 1937) was the signature tune for the British band leader Billy Ternent. Between 1927 and 1939, Ellis wrote the music to fifteen shows, twelve of them for major West End theatres, along with numerous contributions to revue and several songs for films in the 1930s. Almost all adopted a distinctly popular tone, yet Ellis's classical background—he had studied piano with Myra Hess at the Royal Academy of Music (RAM), his grandmother was the composer Julia Woolf, and his mother studied the violin with Ysaÿe—contributed to the most distinctive aspects of his popular-song writing, such as the whole-tone modality in 'The Wind in the Willows' (*Cochran's 1930 Revue*) or the almost improvisatory, art-song quality in 'Little Boat', written for the 1932 film *The Water Gipsies*. In addition, Gilbert and Sullivan was familiar territory for Ellis and Herbert, and both had written the parody 'Perseverance, or Half a Coronet' which constituted one of the sections of the revue *Streamline* (1934).

The shows *Bless the Bride, Tough at the Top* (1949), *And So To Bed* (1951), and *The Water Gipsies* (1955) draw Ellis away from his place in pre-war contemporary popular music towards a distinctly English vein of lyric theatre, especially comic opera. Herbert's librettos for the light operas *Tantiviy Towers* (1931) and *Derby Day* (1932) already provide tangible bridges to a comic opera tradition that goes back through such works as Hood and German's *Merrie England* (1902), Alfred Cellier's *Dorothy* (1886) and *Doris* (1889), and Sullivan's *Rose of Persia* (1899) and *The Emerald Isle* (1901, completed after Sullivan's death by German). Herbert's continuation of this comic opera strand in *Bless the Bride* allowed Ellis to sidestep contemporary popular music by replacing it with lyrical and harmonically rich styles that evoked aspects of British heritage.[6] If any British creative team in musical theatre could be seen as thinking in parallel to Rodgers and Hammerstein's return to the land and the past—in essence the defining of national identity as shown in *Oklahoma!* and *Carousel*—rather than portraying the urban and modern, it is Ellis and Herbert through a reinterpretation of British comic opera that reflects aspects of British social life in historical contexts. And it should be noted that the opening night of *Bless the Bride* in the West End at the Adelphi was just four days before that of *Oklahoma!* at Drury Lane. It played to packed houses alongside the American show for just over two years until its management (not its audience) decided they wanted a new show from the same successful writing partnership, and so replaced *Bless the Bride* with *Tough at the Top*.

The defining essence of Ellis is evident in the finesse of his music for *Bless the Bride*, with easy lyricism and inventive rhythmic word-setting. In the show's overarching use of pastiche, Ellis's ability to characterize each number uniquely is especially evident. But what a contrast it makes with his pre-war scores! The show provided a turning point for Ellis through subject matter that benefited from a style rooted in a specifically English past and could thus draw to significant purpose on a sense of English theatrical tradition. Elements which recall the Savoy operas, early British musical comedy, and comic opera run through the work, beginning with the characters themselves, clearly polarized as 'types' with distinctive behaviours to be mildly mocked, such as the Victorian father, bigoted grandfather, and an anti-hero (Thomas Trout), whose first number is a distinctly Gilbertian patter song of self-introduction. Moreover, the parallels in structure, music, and text suggest *Iolanthe*'s Act 1 finale as a model for *Bless the Bride*'s Act 1 *finaletto*.

Through the subsequent Ellis–Herbert shows, the dramatic settings were matched with music to create works that deliberately referenced Britain's sense of history, often with a picturesque air. *Tough at the Top* (1949) presents a contrast of Ruritanian and British class, politics, and landscape within the stylistic tradition of British comic opera. *And So To Bed* (1951) is adapted from the diaries of Samuel Pepys; its music is influenced by madrigals and employs other consciously period stylistic traits. *The Water Gypsies* (1955, adapted from Herbert's own novel of 1930), dramatizes life among the canal folk of Britain at odds with changes in the contemporary world; its musical style adopts a mixture of lyrical folksy and proto-rock 'n' roll popular idioms.

One particular form of this bolstering of national image which also runs through many other British West End musicals of the time can be seen in *Tough at the Top*: the presentation of the geographical nature of England, specifically its rural imagery and its garden metaphors. In *Tough at the Top* this gains particular expression in the Princess's song 'England Is a Lovely Place', in which the Anglophile foreign visitor extols England to her countrymen. Today it seems satiric, but was not at the time, with references in the first verse to the tropes of cricket on the village green, children on hay-wagons, ploughmen in fields, and old men at the village pub ('The George and Dragon'). Verse 2 includes daffodils, country lanes, and the scent of roses, while verse 3 adds the Oxford–Cambridge boat race and the Epsom Derby horse race. Ellis's word setting emphasizes the image of an idyllic England through a melodic and harmonic simplicity contained in an opening pentatonic phrase over a tonic pedal. The addition of an extended section of a cappella four-part chorus both in the middle and at the end, where they repeat the opening phrase (music and lyrics), confers a hymn-like quality. The use of a cappella sections is also characteristic of concerted numbers in *And So To Bed*. Four-part choral writing forms the textural basis of 'Peace and Quiet' in Ellis and Herbert's *The Water Gipsies* (1955), which also evokes the tranquillity of the countryside: the verbal imagery of church bells, larks, and flowing streams are set to a melody of hymn-like regularity with modal harmonic colouring.

All this is far from Ellis's popular-song style of the 1920s and 1930s, but also removed from the operetta style of *Bless the Bride*. Although for centuries a feature of literary descriptions, such idealized imagery—invariably of England rather than Britain—gained widespread usage during the First World War through the need for soldiers away from home to maintain some sense of identity and purpose. It continued and was strengthened over the successive decades as a means of self-definition, and the Second World War and its aftermath drew even more on such iconic symbols.[7] The shows of Ellis with Herbert responded directly to that need to bolster national self-image through potent shared iconography.

Just why such bolstering should be needed becomes even clearer when the same references are employed by Harold Purcell in his lyrics for 'Sunday Morning in England', which Cicely Courtneidge sang in *Her Excellency*, from the same year as *Tough at the Top*. While also citing the village green, pub ('The White Horse' in Purcell's version), picnics, and point-to-point racing, the last section of the lyrics referred to petrol rationing and thus introduced a tone of bitter contemporary realism that Herbert had avoided (Hugh Gaitskell was at the time minister for fuel and power in the Attlee government):

> And in a thousand little streets stand little cars with little men
> Who, having pushed them out to clean, now push them sadly back again.
> And if the tyres don't perish, p'raps August, they'll take the kids to Devon
> By saving up from nothing with the coupons dropped from Gaitskell's heaven.[8]

The final line of the song hammers the point home: 'In spite of wars and so-called peace—the English Sunday goes on still.' It was this mood of a Britain defeated in victory that prompted a need for the continuing use, even strengthening, of the idealized imagery of nation. It was in 1941 that Coward exalted a humble saxifrage as the metropolitan embodiment of national spirit in 'London Pride'. And it is no coincidence that Novello's 'We'll Gather Lilacs' (music and lyrics by him) was a major success in *Perchance to Dream* (1945): its verse establishes the scenario of a distant loved one, and hope lies in the vision of an optimistic future in which wild lilacs are gathered in the countryside and the reunited pair will 'walk together down an English country lane'. Harry Parr Davies and his lyricist Christopher Hassall included in *Dear Miss Phoebe* (1950) a duet entitled 'I Leave My Heart in an English Garden' (Act 1, Scene 1).[9] The setting adopts the same stately 4/4 pace of Novello's song and copies its structural formula of a refrain whose melody is varied by the addition of a contrapuntal second voice. Hassall's lyrics in the refrain include comforting images of the elm and oak as the 'watchmen' of the English garden and blue 'English' sky, with the verse describing 'breezes in the long grass' and 'hollyhock and bluebell scenting the air'. The floral image in the last line of the refrain is of 'the roses of England,' a potent historic and dynastic image through the Wars of the Roses that Novello had so successfully used in 'Rose of England' in *Crest of the Wave* (1937) to illustrate centuries of British historical continuity.

To reinforce the significance of the rural imagery for the recent war, 'I Leave My Heart in an English Garden' is associated in its dramatic context with the soldier abroad: it is sung by the hero, Valentine Brown, just before he goes off to fight in the Napoleonic Wars in 1806, and the scene and musical number that immediately follows is 'The March of the Redcoats'. The relationship between countryside, homeland, and war is complex, and even if by the 1940s the imagery had become the subject of cliché to many, nonetheless the connections persisted. The link of the military and the rural as seen in Valentine and his English garden is matched in *Belinda Fair* (1949, 'I Dreamed I Was at Home Again') and *The Glorious Days* (1953, 'Sing My Heart the Song of April'). One defining hit song of the wartime 'Forces' Sweetheart' Vera Lynn shares a poetic and emotional lineage with one of Vaughan William's most popular works: among symbols of British national identity it is not that far from a bluebird over a white cliff to a lark ascending.[10]

JULIAN AND SANDY

The musicals so far described were conceived and commissioned as large-scale and for the West End. They required money, which was not in generous supply in the theatre in the post-war years, and were written by composers and librettists with a pre-war record of success. Changing times and tastes determined a more risk-averse approach to theatre production: how much easier to build on the public's love of all things American (established and reinforced through the appeal of American films during the war), and import Broadway shows whose reputations could precede them to potential box-office advantage. In itself, such a process was no guarantee of commercial success. Despite the perspective often promoted even today, many imported American shows had shorter runs than their contemporary British counterparts and were embraced by neither critics nor public (such as *Finian's Rainbow* in 1947, with a run of just six weeks). But a lack of faith and an aversion to risk made the route from concept straight into the West End neither a prudent nor practical business model for a new home-grown musical.

British shows that succeeded particularly well in the West End in the 1950s and even gained some sort of afterlife demonstrate this, originating at London's Players' Theatre, the Bristol Old Vic, and—in the later part of the decade—the Theatre Royal Stratford East. Starting small (at least, considerably smaller than a major West End production) immediately imposed restrictions of scale on the cast, band, staging, and predetermined venue, as well as having the advantage of taking into account the known performing strengths and weaknesses of a familiar pool of repertory players. Such pragmatic limitations precluded emulating big Broadway-style shows and necessitated a locally focused approach that, whether intended or not, inevitably created distance from that American model. Such a response can be interpreted as a natural extension of the Novello and Ellis–Cochran post-war redefining of musical theatre through national, rather than international, elements.

The composer-lyricist of the time who best exemplifies in his approach an alternation of national and international elements is Sandy Wilson. With *The Boy Friend*, Wilson gained fame and has ever since been associated with his self-proclaimed 'valentine' to the 1920s. It began as two-thirds of a mixed evening of entertainment at a small theatre club, the Players' Theatre, performed for three weeks from 14 April to 3 May 1953. From this original form, lasting about an hour, it was expanded for a return to the Players' Theatre later the same year (13 October–22 November), and then transferred to the Embassy for a further six weeks (1 December 1953–11 January 1954). It finally reached the West End proper at Wyndham's on 14 January 1954 and ran there until 7 February 1959. Unlike the American shows that had arrived in the West End in 1953 as large-scale importations following success on Broadway, Wilson's show was not conceived for the West End or with the intention of playing a long run, but written with a specific place and an existing pool of performers in mind.

It was a deliberately nostalgic diversion ostensibly with little to relate it to the contemporary world. The Players' Theatre specialized in recreating period music-hall entertainments, the Late Joys, and Victorian pantomimes at Christmas; it was a place that took authenticity seriously. Thus, a careful recreation of a 1920s show rather than a pastiche was the intention in every part of the production. After seven years of Anglo-American competition, the British retreat comes through in the underlying sense of nostalgia: the show seemed to pretend that the previous twenty or so years had just not happened. The action is set amid the well-to-do English at a French finishing school and so does not immediately suggest any connection with other theatrical works of the 1950s or with current social themes. Instead, it presents a world that, insofar as it had ever existed, had been substantially wiped out by the war.

Such avoidance itself makes a point, for why would it be thought best to ignore the present and focus on the past, given that Wilson's reputation at that stage was for writing songs for contemporary intimate revue? The concept of *The Boy Friend* clearly fitted in well with the ethos of the Players' Theatre, which explains its creation. It does not sufficiently explain its unexpected elevation from such insular beginnings to West End hit. Part of that explanation comes from the show's elitist setting, privileged characters, and avoidance of the concerns of 1950s everyday life: it is more in tune with the decade's return to aspirational Conservative values. For example, the title of the opening number of the show is 'Perfect Young Ladies' who, as the lyrics immediately tell us, are 'preparing to take our places among the noblesse'. They discuss their dresses for the forthcoming ball, and Maisie is disingenuous about her attraction to the rich young American Bobby van Heusen who, we observe in the show, sings, dances, and swims, but never works. And even if the heroine, Polly Browne, seems to be fighting against the conventions of her class by falling in love with a delivery boy, social threat is completely neutralized when he turns out to be the Hon. Tony Brockhurst, son of Lord Brockhurst; Polly risks nothing of her upper-class lifestyle through her liaison. Through its characters, their nationality and social milieu, the show promotes the lost world of an idealized, English upper-class lifestyle of leisure and money.

By contrast, its musical locus is American, inspired by shows of the 1920s; such derivations are most apparent in the many musical references specifically to Vincent Youmans's *No, No, Nanette* (1925). The opening chorus of Wilson's show, 'Perfect Young Ladies', shares a similar melodic and rhythmic profile with the opening chorus 'How Do You Do?' in Youmans's show, even to the extent of copying its introductory orchestral phrase, and echoes specifically its lyrics in which the original 'Just flippant young flappers are we' as the closing line of the chorus becomes in Wilson's tribute 'For perfect young ladies are we', with an identical syncopated rhythm. The domestic cosiness of 'Tea for Two' was reworked by Wilson as 'A Room in Bloomsbury', while 'I Want to Be Happy' morphed into 'I Could Be Happy with You'. The chord progression of the chorus of Wilson's title song was based upon that of Rodgers's 'The Girl Friend'. Musical, structural, and thematic similarities continued in the opening to Act 2, whose number 'Sur le plage' is a reworking of *No, No, Nanette*'s similarly positioned 'The Call of the Sea'.

These were deliberate references to be recognized by the audience for whom the show was first intended, coming as such references did from a very successful show seen in London in 1925, revived at the Hippodrome for 115 performances in 1936, and a regular on the touring circuit through to the early 1950s. If Novello's constant referencing of familiar elements of British theatrical history in *Gay's the Word* was there to bolster a view that past triumphs could become the spur to potential new contemporary triumphs, *The Boy Friend* sought to place its audience back in the 1920s and return to a supposed earlier innocence. The inclusion of dance references, such as those in 'Won't You Charleston with Me?' and 'The Riviera', further placed the show in its 1926 setting. What mattered was specifically the show's 'past-ness'. While there was a transatlantic element in the originality of such shows as *No, No, Nanette* for their first West End audiences, for those in the 1950s the resonance was not especially identified as American, but as that of the now-familiar and conventional repertory of musical theatre. In this way, it furthers that strand of Ellis–Herbert's invocations that claim continuity from the past, and comfort through nostalgia. This also explains some of Wilson's extreme aversion to the changes made for the Broadway transfer of the show under the American management of Cy Feuer and Ernest Martin. (It opened in New York at the Royale on 30 September 1954 and ran until 26 February 1955; it also toured extensively in the USA.) Wilson's protests during rehearsals got him banned from the theatre as his carefully nuanced recreation of the past turned in his eyes into a vulgar, contemporary spoof.[11] London smiled with the show; New York laughed at it. Wilson's reaction reinforced an impression of his attitude as small-scale, small-minded, and dated. But the fact remains that *The Boy Friend* is the only British musical in the 1950s that ran in the West End and on Broadway at the same time; indeed, it is the only new British musical from this period to have been presented on Broadway proper at all. (A short run of *Salad Days* was given Off-Broadway in 1958 by a visiting company, the same year as a revival of *The Boy Friend* opened on Broadway that ran for more than 750 performances in comparison to the original Broadway run of 485.)

So it is unfortunate for Wilson's reputation that his show *The Buccaneer* did not make considerably more of a mark. It represents the use of British–American comparison as a means through which to examine contemporary values, seen already in *Gay's the Word* and *Zip Goes a Million*. And its first version was staged in 1953, straight after the first version of *The Boy Friend* (although substantially written before it). *The Buccaneer* opened on 8 September 1953 at the New Watergate Theatre, was subsequently revised (with the addition of six new songs) for the Lyric Hammersmith for 170 performances from 8 September 1955, and then transferred for twenty-nine performances to the Apollo from 22 February 1956, closing on 17 March.

The story concerns the battle for control of an English comic book for boys: 'Good Clean Fun' (as the opening number puts it) for the young lads of the Empire as long established by the late owner against the sensationalist, teen-gossip-and-shock preferences of an American takeover management. The impetus was a situation even debated in Parliament about the corrupting influence of American horror comics on young minds, so the story played out a current debate of British versus American values. The show's score has a wonderful popular immediacy through Wilson's unerring ear for beautifully focused literary precision animated with catchy melodic and rhythmic settings. Contemporary swing is well employed for 'It's Commercial', while 'The Good Old U.S.A.' encapsulates in miniature a pervading American-songbook quality of uplift and energy (the little 'Remember?' flick of a phrase at the line endings is a lovely touch). The elegant quasi-love duet 'Unromantic Us' exudes Rodgers and Hart at their most seductive. For Wilson, the Americans aren't coming; they're here. The home team's resistance to change is represented by the rhythmic squareness of a paean to a fantasy Empire hero 'Captain Fairbrother', and by the clipped rhythms of the boy Timothy (Kenneth Williams in the Lyric Apollo revival), especially in 'For Adults Only'. Later Wilson traits are also evident: the overt sexuality of the mature woman in 'Learn to Do One Thing Well' is a forerunner of the more outrageously diverting 'Only a Passing Phase' from *Valmouth* (1958). The 1955 revival achieved a respectable run of six months, but was inevitably in the shadow of *The Boy Friend*, which so firmly cemented audience expectations of Wilson's work that *The Buccaneer* inevitably frustrated them, as indeed did Wilson's later works. The show's contrasts of the nostalgic and the contemporary did not coalesce into something sufficient to define the show in its own right: the plot seemed local rather than symbolic, and the oppositions in the score emphasized the generational split rather than resolved it.

The West End launch of *The Boy Friend* established some of the ground that enabled *Salad Days* to follow it some months later. These two works provided their own theatrical double act of seemingly unlikely long-running successes, which made their creators appear as some sort of coherent new wave in British musical theatre. That the radio comedy sketch/parody programme *Round the Horne*, first broadcast in 1965, could name a classic pair of comedy characters Julian and Sandy after Slade and Wilson indicates how public perception elided the originators and their two most successful shows into some single identity. Julian and Sandy were a pair of out-of-work chorus boys who were constantly discovered trying different types of work. Their references were theatrical, their language full of the homosexual slang 'polari' (for example, 'Vada them bona lallies' translates as 'Look at that nice pair of legs', spoken of a man of course), their speech rhythms and intonations were overtly camp, and their dialogue was packed with gay sexual innuendo. Thus the personal qualities of the camp and self-regarding, also set within a tiny theatrical frame of reference, inevitably accreted to the reputations of Slade and Wilson. The distorted impression thus created has done neither the two composers and their works nor the British musical theatre narrative any favours.

For *Salad Days*, the originating theatre was the Bristol Old Vic, whose resident company, with Slade as musical director, had put together a light-hearted work designed around company talents. It was already a full-length work when it played at the Bristol Old Vic for three weeks in June 1954, opening soon afterwards on 5 August in London at the Vaudeville, where it remained until 27 February 1960. Its novelty lay in its importation of a small-scale work to the West End with most of the original cast and in the fact that it was part revue, part musical, written by Slade and his collaborator on book and lyrics, Dorothy Reynolds, to play to the strengths of the Bristol Old Vic performers.

The result is a mixed bag of a work whose evident popularity counters any idea that 'integration' was an essential part of a musical's identity and success in the West End at this time: it played to packed houses in London at the same time as did *West Side Story* and *My Fair Lady*. The story has Jane and Timothy between university and work looking after a magic piano that makes people dance in public spaces against their will. The Minister for Pleasure and Pastime wants the piano and its effects banned. The show is to all intents and purposes an elaborate chase for possession of the piano, and the conclusion brings everyone together under the piano's dancing spell.

Slade's role as musical director and house composer at Bristol gave him the opportunity to write to a purpose, and his compositions for a series of plays and musicals remain essentially workmanlike. His music is distanced from other shows of the time through simplified structures across all musical elements: pentatonic-based melodies in multiples of four- and eight-bar phrases, diatonic harmony with almost no chromatic colouring, standard metrical strophes, simple introductions and reprises. Any of these features alone may be commonplace in composition, but when concatenated into a single stylistic approach in such an undisguised fashion, the effect is distinguished by its unassuming directness. To strengthen this pared-down effect, musical accompaniment was provided by two pianos and percussion and not expanded for an orchestra (as also with *The Boy Friend* in London). Even the singing style was restrained, for *Salad Days* put almost all its sustained melodic charm into songs for Jane ('I Sit in the Sun' and 'The Time of My Life')—the original performer of the role, Eleanor Drew, was one of the only cast members from the Bristol Old Vic repertory company with a strong enough lyric singing voice. The cumulative effect is that of the amateur and local, putting on a show in the parish church hall with limited resources, and shared bonhomie through the self-aware result. Such an impression is evident in reviews of the show, many of which characterized the work as a type of student revue; Milton Shulman defined its social milieu by describing its humour as 'rollicking stuff for an end-of-term frolic at Harrow'.[12]

In contrast to the distilled essence of the 1920s book musical that *The Boy Friend* creates with such precision, *Salad Days* is a loose concoction whose thin story is filled out with diversionary scenes that add to the fun but not the plot. For example, the 'Beauty Parlour' scene in Act 1 is a revue sketch in which the physical and visual comedy of the process of beautification is matched by a vapid telephone conversation whose textual banality is the source of its amusement—entertainment for the moment, not narrative development. Act 2, which opens in the Cleopatra nightclub, has some minor plot advancement but is dominated first by a comic song, 'Cleopatra', for the club manager, a revue number that musically and thematically seems to echo Coward's 'Nina' from his 1945 revue *Sigh No More*; second, by a comic sequence for a many-armed oriental figure whose dance routine includes the lighting of cigarettes, sneezes, handkerchiefs, and finally excessive tickling; third, by the bluesy torch song 'Sand in my Eyes' for Asphynxia, a nightclub singer. Marking the construction of the scene as an excuse for three self-contained routines, the latter two conclude with blackouts. Equally, the introduction into the story of the alien Electrode, his flying saucer, and accompanying song which declares that 'Nobody ever saw such a saucy saucer', clearly takes its cue from pantomime, and reinforces the work's origins as a light-hearted romp—contemporary UFO sightings meet Aladdin's flying carpet.

Like *The Buccaneer*, but not *The Boy Friend*, the setting of *Salad Days* is ostensibly contemporary. However, the view it presents of the Britain of its day has a distancing element as effective as if it were the 1920s. It establishes one view of England to which many of the *Salad Days* audience aspired. A young, educated couple, Timothy and Jane, have just graduated from university. Such a focus in a musical was unusual at this time, and probably reflected the growing awareness of young adults as a distinct social group with their own developing lifestyles and expanding options for their life choices: by the end of the West End run of the show, the coffee bar and skiffle culture had become firmly established in London, while the availability of student grants for the first time allowed wider social access to, and hence an awareness of, university. That this show chose an unthreatening presentation of the potential face of the new youth is part of the work's constant displacement of social challenge beneath a surface of apparent class conformity. The dancing and singing chorus of dons who celebrate the end of term also convey the class status quo in two ways. They wear caps and gowns, those symbols of the highly educated and privileged, with heritage matched to good social status, as well as professional achievement. And although the lyrics supposedly contradict their dry and dusty image when away from students, in fact the 'mad, mad things | That are done by a don' are tame, led more by lyric rhyme than dramatic reason ('he romps and roisters | Swallowing oysters in the cloisters' or 'Turkish coffee—just for the smell of it | Cocoa parties—just for the hell of it'). Even within the supposed breaking of social conventions, there is little daring inside this academic world. Challenge will come from the outside.

Timothy has to find 'something to do'. His family is arranging a job for him through the connections provided by his educated and influential uncles: Clam in the diplomatic corps, Augustine in Parliament, General Sir Hector in the army, and Zed, a scientist. Jane is expected to get married, and her mother, Lady Raeburn, has a 'very exclusive list' of potential husbands, headed by Lord Nigel Danvers. This world is domestic and suburban: over the family breakfast table Timothy is exhorted to find his 'niche'; Lady Raeburn contemplates her daughter's marriage while at the beauty parlour; Jane visits a couture designer for a party dress; many scenes take place around a public park, peopled with a bishop, a tennis player, an artist, a butterfly catcher, and a sunbather; there is the diversion to the nightclub; and the police (PC Boot and his inspector) are involved in the plot throughout. This was the creation of an upper-class, leisured, ordered society, as recognizable in its distortion as the lower middle-class world of Coward's film *This Happy Breed* (1944) a decade beforehand. In the 1940s the fostering of a supportive spirit among and between the classes was crucial in the sustaining of morale to further the war effort, but by the mid-1950s that communal purpose had diluted in the face of individual aspirations, especially those of the ascendant suburban middle class.

Salad Days seems focused on the upper-class world to which so many of the middle class aspired: 'If there are Labour supporters in the audience [of *Me and My Girl*] with tears in their eyes at the Lambeth Walk with all its memories of the days when ordinary people (at least in make-believe) could be kings, there must be quite as many old time Tories fondly remembering *Salad Days*.'[13] It also had the advantage of caricature to give it colour, alongside the diversionary aspects of revue. But despite the impression it manages to create for some, its subtext in fact challenges the status quo at every level. Timothy prefers looking after a magic piano that makes people dance to taking up a conventional career. Far from being a welcome expression of innocent public joy and light-hearted diversion, in the plot the involuntary dancing is a seditious act of revolutionary incitement that requires police intervention and state suppression (see Figure 9.2). The involuntary aspect of the dancing the magic piano inflicts is an external corrupting force on individual characters, and thus a moral threat.

Dancing itself in popular culture has a long history of being used as a coded form of sexual engagement—for example, the waltz was at first considered immoral and suggestive in encouraging such intimate contact between partners, while the dance routines of couples in Hollywood musicals (not least those of Astaire and Rogers) are often within a dramatic setting of seduction. Additionally, the subversion of public space has resonances with sexual liaisons outdoors, heterosexual and homosexual—both were aided by wartime blackouts, and the use of parks for gay cruising was of increasing concern

FIGURE 9.2 Dancing as an act of revolutionary incitement: John Warner and Eleanor Drew in *Salad Days*, Vaudeville Theatre, 1954.

Hulton Archive. Courtesy of Getty Images.

to the authorities (with police activity to supress it) through the 1950s as a symptom of degenerating social values. Further undermining social convention, Timothy and Jane marry early in the show and in secret, not for love but convenience, and their expressions of affection to each other are perfunctory and few. The police are shown to be ineffective and increasingly camp. The various ministers of state are all suspect, emphasizing a running theme in the show that concealment of the private is an essential tool for survival in public.

These are 1950s middle-class morals and mores as through Lewis Carroll's looking glass in a period in which threats to the established order came increasingly to the fore. There was the atmosphere of Cold War paranoia with its associated spy scandals (Guy Burgess and Donald Maclean had defected to Russia in 1951, Kim Philby in 1963). There was also an increasingly visible intolerance by the law of homosexuality, and the aggressive nature of such suppression led in 1954 to the establishment of the Wolfenden Committee on Homosexual Offences and Prostitution—the juxtaposition in the title makes its own point. In theatre, censorship of plays and musicals through the Lord Chamberlain's Office became even more contentious than ever, with any threats to a conservatively dictated moral well-being expunged. The point scarcely needs to be made that theatre in particular included many who felt the impact of such constraints, and the assiduous attentions of the Lord Chamberlain's censors heightened the significance of veiled and double meanings.[14] For all its surface innocence, *Salad Days* is fundamentally subversive of the romantically dominated musical theatre of its day, and critical in its satire of an establishment that was becoming more repressive through its expectations and enforcements of conformity. The success of *Salad Days* lay not least in its ability to allow the audience's own frames of reference to dictate which reading of the drama to follow: innocent, romantic romp, or critique of contemporary oppressive right-wing values. The subtext gives dramatic bite on both levels through provoking from the outset a set of surreal juxtapositions and attitudes such as in Act 1, Scene 7 a police inspector in a ballroom clinch with his constable (Inspector: 'Getting familiar?' [PC] Boot: 'I think we're on the wrong track, Sir'), then rushing to find the magic piano not to stop it but to join in (cue the inspector holding a pair of ballet shoes).[15] As the Act 1 song 'We're Looking for a Piano' tells us, the piano in any case is 'Not just any old piano | But the one that makes you gay'.[16] And who owns the piano? It is Timothy's fifth uncle, a tramp (a long-standing symbol of social nonconformity, rather than a high-status professional as his other uncles are), the one who never married, and with the running joke whenever he is mentioned that he is 'the one we don't mention'.

What the musicals of Slade and Wilson do share is an avoidance of conventional romantic love, one of the mainstays of the musical even today, let alone in the 1950s. One only has to think of *Oklahoma!*, *Carousel*, *South Pacific*, and *The King and I* to get a sense of how they are glued together by heightened romance. That restraint evident in Slade and Wilson may have arisen from the two young gay writers' wish to avoid tackling head-on a serious love interest—it was not something they would speak about publically, so any romantic element had to be diverted or displaced. Wilson, more noticeably as he wrote both music and lyrics, adopted non-standard approaches to love relationships in his later works, and his portrayals of sexuality have been happiest at their most caricatured and unconventional: the femme fatale Madame Dubonnet first in *The Boy Friend* and then in its sequel *Divorce Me, Darling!* (1964), the aged nymphomaniac Lady Parvula de Panzoust in *Valmouth* (1958), and the self-explanatory relationship in *His Monkey Wife* (1971). These shows are not explicitly gay in their subjects or even overtly gay in the execution, but intense, heterosexual love is not a key ingredient. When this is put together with the elements of whimsy and the surreal, as well as pastiche (whether as valentine or spoof), the result heads firmly towards the concept of camp. And so Slade and Wilson became 'Julian and Sandy' as shorthand for British theatrical camp. In contrast to the continuing, priapic heterosexuality of the American contemporary canon, and the following wave of British musical theatre writers, these two figures have been repeatedly portrayed as playing to 'the keynotes of the homosexual world . . . ambivalence and ambiguity'.[17]

'ORDINARY PEOPLE'

From the examples in this chapter, it can be seen how the social and political contextualizing of the new British musicals whose premieres took place during the decade after the war is a prerequisite for gaining any sense of their significance. The internalized mindset of the post-war decade is clearly shown in the works of Ellis and Herbert, Posford and Maschwitz, Wilson, Slade and Reynolds, and indeed many others not possible to examine here. The aspects of contemporary life and attitudes these shows interpret and reflect back to the audience constitute so much of their purpose: they were written to appeal across the range of 'ordinary people' of their day. It is worth noting that the theatre audience for musicals was drawn from across all classes—literally from royalty to out-of town coach parties. In fact, the advance sales of coach-party bookings from London's surrounding counties (often arranged through local libraries as regular events) were a significant factor in any producer's deliberations on how long a show could be kept running profitably. Musical theatre had in particular retained a wide appeal, with songs from the shows providing the common currency of popular and dance band repertory. In addition, there was the huge appeal of such performers as Courtneidge and Formby, known not just for their film careers but also for lifetimes of touring nationally in theatres and music halls. (This was substantially an age before television had taken off as a broadly available form of entertainment—the televising of the Coronation in 1953 provoked such an expansion of access.) Musical hall and musical theatre had the broadest appeal of any live performance format, and popular performers of all levels toured widely, as did the shows themselves pre- and post-London. As the preoccupations and aspirations of those in the audiences changed, so did the relevance of these post-war works, and so too has the ability of later generations to read them in depth.

The shows of this time fit badly into any simple linear narrative of musical theatre for they are far from independent of their historical context, more so than now-canonical shows in many other strands of the history of the musical. The fracture of the war trans-lated into a fracture of the developmental line in British musicals. Any search for a single, dominant vision for British musical theatre by the early 1950s is frustrated by a prevailing sense of 'what are we going to do now?' Consequently, these shows are not only a vital part of the story of the British lyric stage, but also a reflection of the wider concerns of British post-war society. To revisit and reinterpret them can only add rich-ness and veracity to the narrative of a distinctly British musical theatre and similarly reveal so much more through the genre of the musical of the thoughts, desires, con-cerns, and needs of the ordinary people for whom they were intended.

NOTES

1. See John Snelson, ' "We Said We Wouldn't Look Back": British Musical Theatre, 1935–1960', in *The Cambridge Companion to the Musical*, eds. William A. Everett and Paul R. Laird (Cambridge: Cambridge University Press, 2008), 127–146 for a contextual summary complementary to this chapter. A detailed and comprehensive exploration of this period of British musical theatre and its works can be found in John Snelson, 'The West End Musical 1947–54: British Identity and the "American Invasion" ' (unpublished PhD thesis, University of Birmingham, 2003).

2. For a summary description of the welfare state in post-war Britain, see Arthur Marwick, *British Society Since 1945* (London: Penguin, 1996), 45–59. Marwick describes the essence of the idea as 'the totality of schemes and services through which the central Government together with the local authorities assumed a major responsibility for dealing with all the different types of social problems which beset individual citizens' (45). Developments in the implementation of such a purpose in Britain in the three years after the war included extensions to existing provision for social security through family allowances (support payable to mothers, regardless of class of income, for any of their children after the first), National Insurance contributions to fund old-age pensions and unemployment benefits, and a National Health Service to provide free access to a range of health needs (medical, dental, and optical). Changes to widen access to housing and education also formed part of this broadening political palette of social inclusion.

3. See John Snelson, *Andrew Lloyd Webber* (New Haven: Yale University Press, 2004), 183–200, especially 242n12, for a discussion of the lasting implications of such an approach to the establishing of a narrative of British musical theatre.

4. Anne Scott-James, 'Leading a Livelier Life: This Week – The Women!', *Sunday Express*, 28 June 1953, p. 2.

5. *Boots! Boots!* (1934) was the first of Formby's films and, as in the second film *Off the Dole* (1935), he played a character called 'John Willie', a name associated with the Lancashire regional stereotype, as promoted in songs recorded by Gracie Fields including 'John Willie's Farm' (1932), 'Mary Ellen's Hot Pot Party' (1932), and 'What Can You Buy a Nudist on His Birthday?' (1934). Formby's later films include *No Limit* and *Keep Your Seats Please* (1935), *Keep Fit* (1937), *I See Ice* and *It's in the Air* (1938), *Trouble Brewing* (1939), *Let George Do It* and *Spare a Copper* (1940), *Turned Out Nice Again* and *South American George* (1941), *Much Too Shy* (1942), *Get Cracking* (1943), *He Snoops to Conquer* (1944), *Bell Bottom George* (1943), *I Didn't Do It* (1945), and *George in Civvy Street* (1946). Invariably,

his character's forename was 'George', an assertion of the powerful Formby brand and its box-office power.

6. See Vivian Ellis, *I'm on a See-Saw* (London: Michael Joseph, 1953), 227. Ellis was also provided with inspiration through the comic opera *Carina* (1888), composed by his grandmother, whose score he 'often turned to . . . when composing *Bless the Bride*', although the clearest links between the works are more in the plot than through the music.

7. See Alun Howkins, 'The Discovery of Rural England', in *Englishness, Politics and Culture 1880–1920*, eds. Robert Colls and Philip Dodd (Beckenham: Croom Helm, 1986), 81 as well as Stephen Daniels, *Fields of Visions: Landscape, Imagery and National Identity in England and the United States* (Cambridge: Polity Press, 1993), 222–223, for the importance to national iconography in the early 1940s of Constable's paintings, including *The Hay-Wain* and especially *Willy Lot's House at Flatford*, and his use of the English sky.

8. From Harry Parr Davies, Harold Purcell, and Manning Sherwin, *Her Excellency*, unpublished playscript, 1949, Lord Chamberlain's Collection, British Library: LCP 1949/22.

9. See Harry Parr Davies and Christopher Hassall, *Dear Miss Phoebe*, vocal score (London: Sun Music Publishing Co., 1951), 26–30.

10. See Jeffrey Richards, *Films and British National Identity: From Dickens to 'Dad's Army'* (Manchester: Manchester University Press, 1997), 97–99, for the use of English rural myth in film during the Second World War as a form of morale-boosting propaganda, strengthening self-image. See also Alun Howkins, ' "Greensleeves" and the Idea of National Music', in *Patriotism: The Making and Unmaking of British National Identity*, vol. 3, *National Fictions*, ed. Raphael Samuel (London: Routledge, 1989), 89–98, for the growing significance of Vaughan Williams's *Fantasia on Greensleeves*, symbolic of this trend, such that 'by the 1950s it had assumed the role of an alternative national anthem. Only the first part was usually played, and its opening phrase, followed by the lyrical string section suggested to me, and millions of others in those wireless-dominated days, the rolling open downlands of southern England' (94). The composer's famous 'pastoral romance' for solo violin and piano or orchestra, *The Lark Ascending*, inspired by George Meredith's poem, has a similarly strong place in the repertory of nationally symbolic music even today. That such idyllic rural imagery of England should also occur in British musicals post-Second World War is consequently not surprising. Given a longer heritage that includes the paintings of Constable, the poetry of Wordsworth (especially in his elevation of the daffodil), Rupert Brooke, and A. E. Housman, the English countryside and especially its flora have long been and remain deeply embedded symbols of the idealized England. '(There'll be Bluebirds Over) The White Cliffs of Dover', the wartime anthem so identified with Vera Lynn, was in fact written in 1941 by the American songwriters Walter Kent and Nat Burton, and shares clear harmonic and melodic associations with 'Somewhere Over the Rainbow' by Harold Arlen and E. Y. Harburg. This and the fact that bluebirds (an American symbol of optimism as in Harburg's 'happy little bluebirds') are not indigenous to Britain suggests that when the need arises the vital functions of patriotic iconography can still trump ornithology and national origin!

11. See Sandy Wilson, *I Could Be Happy* (London: Michael Joseph, 1975), 173–260, for his perspective on the genesis and development of *The Boy Friend* through its various incarnations from the Players' Theatre through the West End and to Broadway. A summary of the progression is also given by Kurt Gänzl, *The British Musical Theatre*, vol. 2, *1915–1984* (London: Macmillan, 1986), 641–646. For references that illustrate how mainstream American commentators on the musical have repeatedly viewed the essence of *The Boy*

Friend, see Gerald Bordman, *American Musical Theatre: A Chronicle* (New York: Oxford University Press, 1978), 565 ('British travesty'); Stanley Green, *Broadway Musicals: Show by Show*, revised and updated by Kay Green (Milwaukee: Hal Leonard, 1994), 162 ('an affectionate send-up'); and Steven Suskin, *Show Tunes 1905–1985: The Songs, Shows and Careers of Broadway's Major Composers* (New York: Limelight, 1992), 589 ('an affectionate spoof').

12. Milton Shulman, 'Theatre Review: Mr. Slade Takes a Tip from the Vicar', *Evening Standard*, 6 August 1954, p. 6.

13. Alison Light and Raphael Samuel, 'Doing the Lambeth Walk', in *Patriotism: The Making and Unmaking of British National Identity*, vol. 3, *National Fictions*, ed. Raphael Samuel (London: Routledge, 1989), 286.

14. See Dan Rebellato, *1956 and All That: The Making of Modern British Drama* (London: Routledge, 1999), 201–205 for a broader context on homosexuality as prevalent subtext in British theatre of the 1950s.

15. Dorothy Reynolds and Julian Slade, *Salad Days*, libretto (London: Samuel French, 1961), 26–29.

16. See Alan Seinfield, *Out on Stage: Lesbian and Gay Theatre in the Twentieth Century* (New Haven: Yale University Press, 1999), 109–113 for the familiarity and duality of the use of the word 'gay' in theatre from the interwar years. Wilson describes defending *The Boy Friend* in 1954 to a journalist from accusations of it being 'queer' and 'gay' solely from its title. Wilson, *I Could Be Happy*, 238.

17. Jeffrey Weeks, 'The Idea of Sexual Minorities', in *Patriotism: The Making and Unmaking of British National Identities*, vol. 2, *Patriotism: Minorities and Outsiders*, ed. Raphael Samuel (London: Routledge, 1989), 256–269, especially 260.

Bibliography

Bordman, Gerald. *American Musical Theatre: A Chronicle*. New York: Oxford University Press, 1978.

Daniels, Stephen. *Fields of Visions: Landscape, Imagery and National Identity in England and the United States*. Cambridge: Polity Press, 1993.

Ellis, Vivian. *I'm on a See-Saw*. London: Michael Joseph, 1953.

Gänzl, Kurt. *The British Musical Theatre*. Vol. 2. *1915–1984*. London: Macmillan, 1986.

Green, Stanley. *Broadway Musicals: Show by Show*. Revised and updated by Kay Green. Milwaukee: Hal Leonard, 1994.

Howkins, Alun. '"Greensleeves" and the Idea of National Music.' In *Patriotism: The Making and Unmaking of British National Identity*, vol. 3, *National Fictions*, edited by Raphael Samuel, 89–898. London: Routledge, 1989.

Howkins, Alun. 'The Discovery of Rural England.' In *Englishness, Politics and Culture 1880–1920*, edited by Robert Colls and Philip Dodd, 62–688. Beckenham: Croom Helm, 1986.

Light, Alison, and Raphael Samuel. 'Doing the Lambeth Walk.' In *Patriotism: The Making and Unmaking of British National Identity*, vol. 3, *National Fictions*, edited by Raphael Samuel, 261–271. London: Routledge, 1989.

Marwick, Arthur. *British Society Since 1945*. London: Penguin, 1996.

Parr Davies, Harry, and Christopher Hassall. *Dear Miss Phoebe*. Vocal Score. London: Sun Music Publishing Co., 1951.

Parr Davies, Harry, Harold Purcell, and Manning Sherwin. *Her Excellency*. Unpublished play-script, 1949. Lord Chamberlain's Collection, British Library. LCP 1949/22.

Rebellato, Dan. *1956 and All That: The Making of Modern British Drama*. London: Routledge, 1999.

Reynolds, Dorothy, and Julian Slade. *Salad Days*. Libretto. London: Samuel French, 1961.

Richards, Jeffrey. *Films and British National Identity: From Dickens to 'Dad's Army'*. Manchester: Manchester University Press, 1997.

Seinfield, Alan. *Out on Stage: Lesbian and Gay Theatre in the Twentieth Century*. New Haven: Yale University Press, 1999.

Snelson, John. '"We Said We Wouldn't Look Back": British Musical Theatre, 1935–1960.' In *The Cambridge Companion to the Musical*, edited by William A. Everett and Paul R. Laird, 127–146. Cambridge: Cambridge University Press, 2008.

Snelson, John. *Andrew Lloyd Webber*. New Haven: Yale University Press, 2004.

Snelson, John. 'The West End Musical 1947–54: British Identity and the "American Invasion".' Unpublished PhD thesis, University of Birmingham, 2003.

Suskin, Steven. *Show Tunes 1905–1985: The Songs, Shows and Careers of Broadway's Major Composers*. New York: Limelight, 1992.

Weeks, Jeffrey. 'The Idea of Sexual Minorities.' In *Patriotism: The Making and Unmaking of British National Identities*, vol. 2, *Patriotism: Minorities and Outsiders*, edited by Raphael Samuel, 256–269. London: Routledge, 1989.

Wilson, Sandy. *I Could Be Happy*. London: Michael Joseph, 1975.

PART III

NEW APPROACHES TO FORM AND SUBJECT MATTER

CHAPTER 10

··

AFTER *ANGER*

The British Musical of the Late 1950s

··

ELIZABETH A. WELLS

THE year 1956 is popularly seen as a watershed in British theatre: the premiere of John Osborne's *Look Back in Anger* radically challenged British theatregoers' expectations of mainstream theatre. Although scholars have argued that there are numerous reasons why the tradition of British drama was so radically challenged at that particular juncture in its history, it cannot be denied that the tone and subject matter of British theatre was transformed by the introduction of a grittier and more confrontational style and a more inclusive and politically sophisticated representation of British society.[1] When in 1958 the West End production of *West Side Story* was offering London audiences a model of more physical, gritty musical theatre, British composers and dramatists were already assaying the same ground in shows that were meant to provoke London's theatre audience. The search for the 'great British musical' was on—one that 'could look an American one in the face and outstare it', as critic T. C. Worsley put it.[2] The first performance by Brecht's Berliner Ensemble in London in 1956 had a stunning effect on theatre creators and critics, particularly Kenneth Tynan, who was instrumental in influencing British theatrical taste, the playwright John Arden, musical theatre composer Lionel Bart, and set designer Sean Kenny (who designed a number of Bart's shows). Brecht's approach to acting style and staging would not be immediately apparent in the British musical, but the new leftist approaches of Arnold Wesker (author of the Wesker trilogy, 1956–8[3]) and John Arden, whose *Sergeant Musgrave's Dance* (1959) and other works provided Brechtian social critique, would affect a genre that prior to this time was primarily aimed at light entertainment and diversion. Like much of the new drama, new musical theatre started to focus on working-class life. The so-called 'kitchen sink drama' that took its name from Wesker's *The Kitchen* (1957) was also embraced by fledgling playwright Shelagh Delaney in her first work, *A Taste of Honey* (1958).

The New Musicals

Throughout the late 1950s and into the mid-1960s, a number of important musical theatre works challenged prevailing notions of how musicals looked and sounded, how they told their stories, and how they manipulated and extended techniques of musical theatre to reach new audiences and challenge older ones. Key to this revolution were Theatre Workshop under the leadership of Joan Littlewood and the Royal Court Theatre under George Devine. Although many of the works that premiered in this period enjoyed shorter runs or less critical acclaim than hoped for, they remain important in telling the story of Britain's musical theatre development and how it reflected changes in British culture. They also sounded the death knell for some of the more innocent and genteel musical theatre offerings that had become London's standard fare. At the same time, America continued to produce blockbusters that ran successfully in the West End and pushed the genre in new directions. British composers saw these changes as a challenge from America, and so it is telling that in many of the shows that emerged from this period, American characters feature relatively prominently. Put succinctly, one might summarize what was happening to British musical theatre during this important time—the late 1950s and early 1960s—as an indication of the desire to measure up to American standards of composition, acting, direction, and dancing while maintaining a British sensibility. Like Broadway, London developed at least two streams of musical theatre simultaneously: one including works whose function it was to simply entertain (conceived as star vehicles for box office draws) without challenging the status quo, and another including works with a more edgy, modernist approach, evidenced by more adventurous music and orchestrations, character development, subject matter, and an increase in salaciousness and stark realism. In America, charming works like *The Music Man* vied openly for kudos against the darker *West Side Story* of the same year, pitting to a certain extent a rural, idealist depiction of Americana with that of a grittier, contemporary, and racially mixed New York City.[4] In the same way, British works that harked back to an earlier time or were more innocent in their approach to subject matter (*The Boy Friend*, 1953; *Salad Days*, 1954) vied for popularity with newer works like *Johnny the Priest* (1960) or Bricusse and Newley's *Stop the World—I Want to Get Off* (1961).

To see either American or London's musical theatre culture as going through an overall revolution ignores the reality that more traditional fare continued to flourish during the same period when more modernist works were introduced to London audiences,[5] because at the same time Harry Secombe, Cicely Courtneidge, Anna Neagle, George Formby, and many others, starred in works that were written as showcases for their particular talents and personalities. For British audiences, these forms of musical theatre provided escapism with familiar faces, a sense of humour, and conventional dramatic situations.

American Harbingers

However, change was afoot and the blockbuster American shows *Oklahoma!* (West End premiere in 1947) *My Fair Lady* (1958), and *West Side Story* (1958) were among those works that left an indelible mark on the London stage and pushed creators in new directions, although the role of *Oklahoma!* as an important turning point in the British theatre has been challenged by scholars like John Snelson, who see a strong legacy emerging from British works of the same years.[6] *West Side Story's* influence on British theatre has been adequately documented elsewhere, and also points to a certain 'American Invasion' with respect to British musical theatre over the middle decades of the twentieth century.[7] What these American works offered to British producers, apart from a promise of strong box office, were better integrated ways of telling more adult stories through standard song-and-dance vehicles. With Laurie's dream in *Oklahoma!* and the second act 'Somewhere' ballet in *West Side Story*, both works incorporated serious amounts of classical or modern dance to tell parts of their stories. Each dealt with dark subject matter by featuring an onstage murder. They also both offered strong representations of what their creators thought of as quintessentially American, clearly shaped by their directors to showcase more athletic dancing and more thoroughly integrated music.

Works like *West Side Story*, which seemed to have moved audiences and creators with its radicalism on its London premiere in 1958, raised the bar for many who saw it as a new direction in musical theatre. The term 'dansical' was coined to describe its particular brand of storytelling—mainly through American-style dance.[8] Although the style of the show was quite foreign to British audiences, who had only seen such dancing on film, the cinematic quality of the work and its serious approach to serious subject matter seemed to challenge traditional British musical theatre at its very roots.

Ivor Novello's sudden death in 1951 during the run of *King's Rhapsody* (1949) was not just ironic timing: it was symbolic of how his lavish form of 'Ruritanian' operetta and the star vehicle were to fall. Novello's last produced work was a harbinger of what was to come. *Gay's the Word* of 1951, written for Cicely Courtneidge, was a behind-the-scenes musical that sent up the Ruritanian fantasy works that had become so popular. Starting the show with a number entitled 'Ruritania' and including a backstage number, 'It's Bound to Be Right on the Night', exemplifies the self-referential approach to the star vehicle by drawing attention to its inner workings. However, Novello also used more modern musical styles in the work (particularly in the overture) as a way of showing that musical theatre music was changing.[9]

THE ANGRY YOUNG MUSICAL: *EXPRESSO BONGO*

One of the first major works in a new mould and an important watershed in British musical theatre was the show *Expresso Bongo*, with a writing team consisting of Wolf Mankowitz, David Heneker, and Monty Norman. Mankowitz was a leftist artist who had been a 'scholarship boy' at Cambridge and had contributed to a number of literary genres, including the theatre. His libretto for *Expresso Bongo* was a critique of television, and of popular music, as it was emerging in Britain through stars like Tommy Steele. It was also one of the first of the 'Soho' musicals—a series of works by various artists that followed the path that the 'kitchen-sink drama' through *Look Back in Anger* and other theatre works had opened up.[10] The plot concerns the career ups and downs of a guileless young bongo player, Herbert Rudge, and his ambitious manager (the main character, played in the original production by that era's pre-eminent Shakespearean actor and later Oscar-winner Paul Scofield). Herbert is 'discovered' and signed to a record deal, but eventually is seduced and taken in other directions by a visiting rich American woman. At the end of the show, the protagonist is setting up his girlfriend, a stripper, to be the next big performer to keep the money rolling in.

Humorous in many places, and entertaining on the surface, the work is much darker, more cynical, and Brechtian in its outlook than anything mainstream British audiences or—with the exception of *West Side Story*—American audiences had been used to. The inclusion of a prominent serious actor in a work filled with so much irony and parody signalled a new direction for musical theatre, as did the inclusion of the kind of rock 'n' roll music that Herbert purveys. Songs like 'Nothing is for Nothing' did not fit in at all with the kinds of mood or tone of other musical theatre works. *Expresso Bongo*, later turned into an anodyne film featuring Cliff Richard, received enough critical and popular acclaim that it could rightly be seen as something of a turning point in what West End audiences would accept.[11] It also reflected emerging societal trends—the rise of the Soho coffee bar scene, with its excitement-seeking teenagers, ruthless talent scouts, and petty criminals—and established a new setting for musicals that better reflected the realities of London's social strata, as well as featuring Millicent Martin, the most important female British musical theatre star between 1957 and 1977, in her first starring role in a West End show.

In certain respects Noël Coward's *Ace of Clubs* (1950), although not very popular with either critics or audiences, could be seen as a precursor of this new stream of musicals, as it was set in contemporary London and included a jewel robbery along with some romance. His next show *After the Ball* (1954), based on *Lady Windermere's Fan*, was an even bigger flop, coming as it did within this new trend of more realist, contemporary theatre. The failure of Coward's post-war musicals thus left it to creators like Mankowitz, Heneker, Norman, and Bart to push the boundaries of mainstream musical theatre.

The 'Slice of Life' Musicals

Even musicals that followed standard plot developments and characterization were attempting to make themselves more contemporary. The show *Twenty Minutes South* (by Maurice Browning and Peter Greenwell) is a musical about suburban London, in which the arrival of an attractive cousin puts a conventional family through a series of challenges, although she ends up marrying the boss and everything returns to the status quo. While the setting was more contemporary (including both London and its suburbs), the plot lines and music were fairly conventional. The addition of a mambo in the dance scene is clearly a nod to Latin jazz and the incursion of social dance similar to what we see in American works. Still, the thrust of the scene—the discovery that one of the main characters came from a poor family—addresses the British preoccupation with class more directly than any Broadway musical of the period could do.

Not all contemporary works were dark and gritty: *Grab Me a Gondola* of 1956 (by James Gilbert and Julian More), which follows a reporter who seeks out a story about a starlet at the Venice Film Festival, enjoyed critical and popular success without being either very modern or edgy. Indeed, Julian More and Monty Norman, who wrote the music for *Make Me an Offer* and *Expresso Bongo*, enjoyed success as composers and lyricists and were able to write about contemporary dramatic situations without necessarily always embracing the darkness that many of those situation seemed to suggest (as in *Irma la Douce* (1956), English lyrics by Norman).

At the same time that George Devine's Royal Court Theatre was making its mark with original, modernist works, Joan Littlewood was fashioning a unique and formidable acting company at Theatre Workshop which was meant to bring working-class people to the theatre, and vice versa. Two works from these years that follow the Soho trend were *Fings Ain't Wot They Used T'Be* and *Make Me An Offer* (both 1959). The latter was from the pen of Wolf Mankowitz and his previous collaborators, and was an adaptation of his novel of the same name, which had also been filmed.[12] In it, an antiques dealer, Charlie, wrestles with the challenges of working in the Portobello Road amongst other shop owners of sometimes dubious character, life with a small family in cramped conditions, and his love of a particular Wedgwood vase (Mankowitz was an expert on Wedgwood). One of the recurring themes in the work is trying to find a place to put the pram in Charlie's small apartment. Opening the show with the song 'Damn the Pram' was seen as an obvious attempt to include more contemporary, working-class problems. *Make Me An Offer* hit a more intellectual tone than most musicals did at the time: references to Jeremy Bentham and Karl Marx might have been lost on some of the audience, and the lack of a love story (Charlie, in fact, cheats on his wife during the course of the musical) and happy ending make this a much more acerbic night of entertainment. However, it did achieve enough success to move to the West End, winning the *Evening Standard* Award for best musical of 1959. We can therefore see it not just as experimental, leftist theatre, but rather as a legitimate part of the mainstream history of London's West End.

Fings Ain't Wot They Used T'Be adheres much more closely to the kind of improvisatory, music-hall style theatre that challenged the standard West End or American fare with a new kind of energy and structure. Joan Littlewood, in her work at Theatre Royal Stratford East and with the Unity Theatre, aimed for a kind of workingmans' theatre, creating theatrical space for people who would normally not find their way into a West End theatre.[13] Her small group of dedicated actors (many of whom slept in the theatre, as they didn't make enough money to always have proper accommodation) was known to specialize in improvisation, and Joan Littlewood herself had been known to completely rewrite and rework playwright's words to suit the kind of spontaneous theatre she imagined. About Littlewood, playwright Monty Norman (who worked with her on his play *Fings Ain't Wot They Used T'Be*) states, 'Joan's mode of working and all the tensions she created were not haphazard. She left no stone unturned. She pitted actor against actor and writer against director and as the sparks flew she would stand back like some manic lightning conductor and turn the generated electricity into sparkling theatre. Very draining.'[14]

Fings was a perfect combination of this kind of improvisatory theatre with subject matter very clearly inspired by Soho, portraying morally questionable characters, and with a distinctly static plot. Instead of advancing plot and characterization following the model of American musicals, it showed a slice of life amidst Soho gamblers, prostitutes, and petty criminals that made these people seem palatable, humorous, and even somewhat heroic. The key point for the history of Soho musicals was that the style of the music and presentation was much more indebted to music hall, conventional comedy, and audience interaction than anything people previously would have accepted as mainstream musical theatre. Lionel Bart was the young composer who wrote the music (the show started as a non-musical straight play), but again, the musical numbers served the particular situations within the work, with no songs meant to become hits and no actors being set up as stars. *Fings'* move to the West End was seen as something of a sell-out for those interested in forging a new style of musical theatre, yet its success suggests that audiences were ready for something different, and something that sprang more from Britain's own music hall roots.[15] The inclusion of an openly gay character was also groundbreaking, exactly the kind of innovation that Littlewood and her crew strove for.

Although *Fings* transferred to the West End, it was not meant to be mainstream theatre. However, even within the context of standard West End fare, creators were turning to the 'slice of life' of Soho characters for both comic and dramatic effect. One of the more popular and successful works that utilizes this Soho style is *The Crooked Mile*. Written by Peter Wildblood and based on his book *West End People*, with music by Peter Greenwell, this musical came from outside London (Manchester) in 1959, but transferred to the Cambridge Theatre that same year for a modest run of a few months. In it, the creators sought to find an appropriate style and content to reflect both the characters and situations depicted in the show. The plot hinges upon an ironmonger's shop owned by Sweet Ginger. She is approached by an idealistic American who would like to buy up the entire range of properties in which the shop is located and build a giant American-style department store. In songs like 'Cousin Country' and 'Going Up' American–British political relations are particularly highlighted. Given that this work comes from a period when the 'special relationship' between Britain and America was being tested and developed,[16] the references in these songs to American expansionism, the Cold War, the nuclear threat, and the various cultural differences between the two nations are particularly topical.[17] For example, in the song 'Cousin Country', the following exchange takes place between American Mortiss and Sweet Ginger:

> MORTISS   British people think tradition
> Takes the place of ammunition
> You could have a rosy future
> But you're living in the past

SWEET GINGER   When we think of all those warheads
  Dropped on *our* heads, not on your heads
  Then we get a nasty feeling
  That each day may be our last

MORTISS   Put your trust in our discretion
  We believe in non-aggression,
  And we've got to stick together
  So we must be fair.

BOTH   Though we think you're mad as hatters,
  Only one thing really matters
  You're our cousin country
  And we're rather glad to know
  That you are there.[18]

Indeed, the inclusion of this kind of social and political commentary places this work squarely in a more intellectual milieu with perhaps a more sophisticated audience being targeted. As most musical comedies do, the show ends with some kind of positive resolution. However, listening to the opening and searching music that underlies a single voice intoning the children's song on which the title is based, gives a much darker impression of this work than that which emerges when reading the complete libretto. The inclusion of a mixed-race relationship (the primary one, between black Sweet Ginger, played by Elizabeth Welch, and white Jug Ears) and the specific reference to it in the script show a willingness to engage in contemporary race relations issues that might have been handled differently in an American musical.

JOHNNY THE PRIEST

Striking a darker tone in general is *Johnny the Priest* (1960), written by Antony Hopkins, with lyrics by Peter Powell. It was based on *The Telescope* by R. C. Sherriff, already produced as a straight play. Although it had a limited run of merely fourteen performances, this work attempted to tell a serious moral story in musical theatre terms. In it, a priest working in a tough neighbourhood tries to prevent one young juvenile delinquent (Johnny) from embarking on a criminal future. One of the key features of the work is the divide between adult and teenage worlds, as seen in *West Side Story*, and given that its opening was only two years after that show had taken the West End by storm, it is reasonable to assume that *Johnny the Priest* was a work meant to cover, in part, some of the same social and political ground. The teenagers perform 'The Burp', as both an emblem of their own identities and a way to provide more modern dance within the musical itself. This is a British version of the mambo that sets the New York gangs dancing. That it closely resembles the interactions and clashing cultures that were explored in *West Side Story* cannot be ignored. The fact that it did

so somewhat less convincingly may be the reason it had such a short run. Less preoccupied with forging a distinctive British musical theatre style and more concerned
about the subject matter (Britons were experiencing approximately the same rate of
juvenile delinquency as Americans[19]), this musical attempted to deal with a serious
social issue, but without some of the lighter moments that works like *West Side Story*
provide. Even the casting of famous Shakespearean actor Jeremy Brett as the leading man and its adventurous use of jazz were not enough to garner the work a run of
longer than two weeks.[20]

Indeed, the desire to compete with American musicals found its own catalyst
within the culture wars of the 1950s, where American styles of clothing, music,
and ultimately theatre were encroaching on a post-war audience that was not only
enamoured of these 'invasions' but also resentful of them. Exhausted from wartime
rationing and trying to build a new indigenous culture, the British were primed
for something that would allow them to make their own claim on musical theatre.
Fings went a great step towards this goal, but many other West End musicals of that
time reveal these American–British tensions more directly. *On the Level* (1966),
with music by Ron Grainer and lyrics by Ronald Miller, revolved around cheating
in university exams. The culprit, or at least the character who encourages the teens
in their illegal activity, is a coarse American. The Wedgwood dealers in *Make Me
an Offer* ultimately fleece two American buyers who have naively believed their
pitch. *Expresso Bongo*'s title character is ultimately taken away from his producer
by a rich American woman, and *The Buccaneer* (1953), by Sandy Wilson, revolves
entirely upon an American bid to take over a British boys' magazine. Such 'invasions' by American characters within a large proportion of the Soho and contemporary musicals cannot be seen as simply a casual trend or coincidence. All the
composers and creators were keenly aware of the struggle for supremacy between
American cultural interests and tastes, and the striving for a British musical style
and structure that would allow them to vie for their own place in the sun. These
struggles—as later encapsulated in general terms for instance in Richard Hoggart's
The Uses of Literacy—were played out within the plots and characters of the musicals
themselves.[21]

At the same time that these darker musicals were charting new ground, the charming musicals *The Boy Friend* and *Salad Days*, with minimal production values and not
requiring huge casts or other expensive accoutrements, were wildly successful in Britain
and (in the case of *The Boy Friend*) New York.[22] Neither of these works attempted to
stake out any kind of cultural ground; neither were obvious social statements, and certainly neither sought to advance British musical theatre. *The Boy Friend* was a pastiche
of 1920s musical comedy, ran for five years, and enjoyed over 2,000 performances.
Johnny the Priest, on the other hand, was set in modern London, and survived only a
two-week run. This discrepancy between the kind of theatre one might imagine would
attract audiences and the one that actually did raises the issue of whether there were two
distinct streams of musical theatre existing side by side while nonetheless fighting for
supremacy; the first kind, offering new incarnations of the light and entertaining fare

that British audiences had previously enjoyed and the second, more edgy variant, pursued by creators like Mankowitz and Norman.

THE ANGRY YOUNG MEN

Although British society was questioning middle-class values and patriotism after the ravages of the Second World War, it seemed that not everyone wanted to contemplate these issues within the musical theatre. They did seem ready for this contemplation, however, in the realm of literature with the new and bracing Angry Young Men movement, a poetic and literary turning away from the past that was spearheaded partly by John Osborne (much as he disliked being linked with this philosophical trend), Arnold Wesker, Harold Pinter, and a series of novelists including John Wain, Colin Wilson, and Kingsley Amis. The trend, named by commentators after the title of Osborne's iconic play, *Look Back in Anger* (1956), was famously exemplified in Amis's *Lucky Jim* (1954), a novel that had received wide critical and popular acclaim. It followed the exploits of a junior professor who sees everything around him in his university life as empty and phony. At the end of the novel he leaves his university for London with a new girlfriend and a business career ahead of him. Colin Wilson's *The Outsider*, published the same year as *Look Back in Anger*, strikes out boldly for a new political and philosophical outlook, rejecting middle-class values and tastes and calling for a new literary and cultural rebirth.

More an invention of the media than a cohesive group of artists and thinkers, the Angry Young Men can be seen not just in straight theatre, poetry, literature, and film, but also within the Soho group of musicals. Johnny, the protagonist of *Expresso Bongo*, is a perfect example of a 'Lucky Jim' type of character, cynical, unromantic, opportunistic, and shallow. Similarly, Charlie, the leading character of *Make Me An Offer*, lives in a world in which he cannot get ahead economically partly because of his love of beautiful things and unwillingness to part with them (see Figure 10.1).

He sets the tone of the musical with his first song, 'Damn the Pram' which seems to express the Weltschmerz, the generalized bitterness that the Angry Young Men seem to suffer.

> CHARLIE   The damn pram gets me every day standing on the landing
> Getting in the bloody way in the bloody way
> What are we g'n'a do about the pram
> What are we g'n'a to do about the pram
> This ornamental object hacking pieces off my skin
>
> *[puts injured ankle on table to show [Sally]*[23]

Although *Expresso Bongo* was explicitly linked to the Angry Young Men trend (it was called 'The Angry Young Musical'), vestiges of it can be seen within all the modernist

FIGURE 10.1 The Angry Young Man in musical theatre: Daniel Massey (Charlie) as a reluctant salesman in *Make Me an Offer* (1959).

Courtesy of Theatre Royal Stratford East Archives Collection.

musicals of this period, particularly *Stop the World—I Want to Get Off*.[24] In this work by Leslie Bricusse and Anthony Newley, the protagonist constantly struggles with the power of the state and capitalism to forge some kind of authentic life for himself that includes a degree of agency and authentic self-expression.[25] His social and political problems reflect the values and concerns of the Angry Young Men, but the fact that he has no real identity in the musical (even his name, Littlechap, is generic and symbolic) shows that his political struggle is more symptomatic of the time period than particular to his character.

The subculture of the 'Angry Young Men' lasted only as long as its cynical world view remained appealing, and the end of the Angry Young Musical can perhaps best be exemplified by John Osborne's *The World of Paul Slickey* (see Figure 10.2). This attempt at biting, satiric musical theatre was perhaps one of the most unusual (and certainly most short-lived) shows of the period. Although his earlier *The Entertainer* (1957) had already a lot of music in it, so much in fact that it may have prompted Osborne to write a full-scale musical, it fell to *Slickey* to constitute the only real musical in his oeuvre. The plot revolves around the dirty dealings of a newspaper reporter who writes about the goings-on of the rich and famous. Extremely negative, seeming to attack every part of society and modern media in a rather unsystematic way, Osborne went a little too

FIGURE 10.2 The sordid goings-on of the rich and famous: Dennis Lotis (Jack Oakham, alias Paul Slickey) and Maureen Quinney (Deirdre Rawley) in the provincial try-out of *The World of Paul Slickey*, Pavilion Theatre, Bournemouth, April 1959.

Photograph provided by the editors.

far and alienated audiences who might otherwise have been intrigued with his darkly humorous story.

Slickey's opening musical number, enumerates all the areas of society he is ready to embarrass and expose:

> I'm just a guy called Paul Slickey
> And the job I do is pretty tricky,
> I'm twenty-eight years old
> And practically everybody, anybody, anything
> You can think of leaves me
> Quite, completely
> Newspaper neatly
> Quite, quite cold.
> Don't think you can fool a guy like me
> The best things in life are never free!
> Guys like us who are on the inside,
> Cannot be taken for a ride.

We have professional ways and means
Of getting in behind the scenes,
To put the screw on stars in jeans.
We don't need hidden television screens.
Don't think you can fool a guy like me.
There's nothing that's not like ABC.
Guys like us who are on the spot,
Can be relied to know what's not,
Nothing's so big we can't shrink it—
We'll blot your lot and printers' ink it,
Whatever slop you want we'll see you drink it,
We can't build your boat, but we'll make damn sure you sink it![26]

The music was by a relative unknown composer (Christopher Whelen), but Osborne engaged Kenneth MacMillan, the major new ballet choreographer in Britain, to create the choreography. Despite the obvious hope that the show would hit a nerve amongst an audience sympathetic to the revolutionary new theatre, it was an utter disaster. The failure of the long, rambling, and rarely charming show was a serious turning point for Osborne, who had to live down the devastating critical and popular response (he was even chased along the Charing Cross Road by angry theatregoers).[27] Although the many targets he attacked may well have been appropriate, the show seemed to have been just a little bit too extreme to an audience that had already been exposed to too much of Osborne's bile, both on stage and in the media.

Among the many reasons why the trend of the angry musical and the Soho setting of musical theatre works might only have been short-lived was the fact that the sweeping changes of the 1960s had started to make that kind of musical theatre, however challenging, seem quaint.

THE GREAT BRITISH MUSICAL: *OLIVER!*

In 1960, *Oliver!* had finally seemingly managed to challenge the American domination of British musical theatre.[28] Although some would argue that it is stylistically derivative of American musical theatre, it seemed to signal a rebirth of musical theatre on British soil. Because the story is set amongst the poor, in a clearly British milieu, one might argue that it is the apotheosis of the working-class musical. Where it did make inroads was in the stage design and style of production, which changed and challenged the production values of other British and American shows.

Another show that ran on both continents was *Half a Sixpence* (1963), starring Tommy Steele as the protagonist in this adaptation of H. G. Wells's *Kipps*. This charming story of an ordinary man who comes into a fortune, but gives it all up for a simple life, seemed to represent British values and class consciousness and suggested that the kind of British musical that could make it both in the West End and on an international level was one that presented British people as jolly, cockney, or guilelessly delinquent with an emphasis on rousing dance scenes and a happy ending.[29]

The real turning point during this period in musical theatre was certainly the end of stage censorship in England. Although most of the musicals mentioned so far passed the Lord Chamberlain's scrutiny without too many cuts, the end of censorship at the end of the decade allowed *Hair* to open on the West End in 1968 after a few abortive attempts to produce it there. Shows like *Hair, Oh! Calcutta!* (London premiere in 1970), and *The Dirtiest Show in Town* (1971) gave audiences a very different form of entertainment than musicals set in Ruritania, star vehicles, or even dark shows like *Expresso Bongo. Hair*'s complete capsizing of standard musical theatre styles in acting, singing, and dancing changed the picture for musical theatre composers and producers.

The many musicals that followed the trend of the late 1950s seemed to return in style more to the American shows, and it would take a new generation of authors to create works that would bring to Britain the supremacy of musical theatre that came with Andrew Lloyd Webber and Tim Rice. Although the many Soho and dark musicals enjoyed less exposure than their creators might have hoped, they do constitute an important part of Britain's musical theatre history during this period, and one wonders how Joan Littlewood's temporary retirement from the theatre and the failure of *The World of Paul Slickey* have affected the development of British musical theatre during the late 1950s and early 1960s.

The search for the 'great British musical' took many creators of this period down pathways that had not been forged before in British musical theatre history. The trend of depicting Soho characters and situations was certainly pervasive and particularly British, but the appetite for these kinds of entertainments was relatively short-lived and their reception was mixed. Still, some considered *Make Me An Offer* the best musical since the war,[30] while others saw it as one in a line of groundbreaking musicals that seemed to have found their perfect subject matter. As the critic for the *Evening Standard* wrote:

> The lower down the social scale the British musical descends, the happier it seems to be. Trying to get away from the lush innocuousness of Ivor Novello and the genteel anemia of *Salad Days*, it has discovered some revitalising corpuscles in the spiv, the Cockney, the shop-girl, the racketeer and the no-good. *Expresso Bongo, The Crooked Mile*, and *Fings Ain't What They Used T'Be* revelled in the seamier aspects of London life and were clutched eagerly to the bosom of a public fed up with wholesome naivety.[31]

British composers of this period would have been delighted to see how the works of British and European musical theatre composers eclipsed American works in the 1970s and 1980s, even if the form such musicals would take may have surprised them.

Notes

1. See particularly Dan Rebellato, *1956 and All That: The Making of Modern British Drama* (New York: Routledge, 1999).
2. T. C. Worsley, 'Growing Up At Last', *New Statesman*, 3 May 1958, Harold Prince Papers, New York Public Library for the Performing Arts.
3. The trilogy consists of *Chicken Soup with Barley* (1956), *Roots* (1958), and *I'm Talking about Jerusalem* (1958).
4. The run of *West Side Story* in London was longer than the initial run on Broadway which suggests that the changes in British theatre may have paved the way for this more experimental, darker work.
5. Indeed, Cicely Courtneidge, a star of the previous decade, was still taking on star vehicles in David Heneker's *Charlie Girl* in 1965, and it was not until 1972, far into the turning point for London theatre, that Julian Slade finally retired from composition, his older style no longer so appealing to audiences.
6. John Mainwaring Snelson, 'The West End Musical, 1947–1954: British Identity and the "American Invasion"' (unpublished PhD thesis, University of Birmingham, 2002).
7. Elizabeth Wells, *West Side Story: Cultural Perspectives on an American Musical* (Lanham: Scarecrow, 2011).
8. John Thompson, 'Welcoming the Most Fantastic Opening Forty Minutes Ever to Hit the London Theatre: Enter the "Dansical" New Hit Show Era!', *Express Photo News/ Daily Express*, 13 December 1958, Harold Prince Papers, New York Public Library for the Performing Arts.
9. Snelson, 'West End Musical', 197.
10. Soho in this time period was a bohemian haven for teenagers who congregated in coffee bars, for petty criminals, prostitutes, and ne'er-do-wells, as well as for burgeoning intellectuals like Colin Wilson.
11. The film version of *Expresso Bongo* omitted most of the original music and replaced it with less acerbic and inferior songs.
12. The film was made in 1954, starring Peter Finch, Adrienne Corri, and Rosalie Crutchley. It was directed by Cyril Frankel, written by Mankowitz and W. P. Liscomb, and produced by Group 3.
13. For a detailed account of the life and work of Joan Littlewood, see Chapter 19 by Ben MacPherson.
14. Monty Norman, 'Liner Notes', *Make Me An Offer*, Original London Cast Recording 1955, CD, SEPIA 1155, 2010.
15. See Frank Norman, *Why Fings Went West* (London: Lemon Tree Press, 1975). The number of people working in British musical theatre at the time, especially in this vein, was quite small, so Norman's work and familiarity with Littlewood extended beyond this one iconoclastic model.
16. In the musical *Charlie Girl* (1965), two mothers, one American and one British, plan the marriage of their children as representing a mini 'special relationship' based on money and prestige.
17. During this time period, the testing and development of nuclear weapons was a particularly controversial topic that was reflected in musicals as well as the press. See C. J. Bartlett, *'The Special Relationship': A Political History of Anglo-American Relations Since 1945* (New York: Longman, 1992).

18. Peter Wildblood and Peter Greenwell, *The Crooked Mile*, typescript, 1959, Lord Chamberlain's Plays, British Library Manuscripts Division.
19. See Harold Conway, 'This Knocks *My Fair Lady* for Six', *London Daily Sketch*, 13 December 1958, Harold Prince Papers, New York Public Library for the Performing Arts.
20. Brett was a rising stage star, having appeared as *Hamlet*, who also worked in highly prestigious movies, such as the Hollywood epic *War and Peace* (1956; directed by King Vidor) starring Audrey Hepburn and Henry Fonda. Brett later played Freddie Eynsford-Hill in George Cukor's film of *My Fair Lady* (1964) but his most iconic role came when in 1984 he played Sherlock Holmes in a well-received British television series.
21. Richard Hoggart, *The Uses of Literacy: Aspects of Working-Class Life* (London: Chatto and Windus, 1957).
22. For a detailed analysis of these two musicals, see Chapter 9 by John Snelson.
23. Wolf Mankowitz, *Make Me An Offer* (Guilford: Biddles, 1959), 8.
24. Neil Whitcomb, 'Here is the First of the Angry Young Musicals', *Daily Mirror*, 26 March 1958, Harold Prince Papers, New York Public Library for the Performing Arts.
25. For a detailed discussion of the work of Bricusse and Newley, see Chapter 12 by David Cottis.
26. John Osborne, 'The World of Paul Slickey', in *Look Back in Anger and Other Plays* (London: Faber and Faber, 1959), 196–197.
27. For a full recounting of the disaster of this show, see John Heilpern, *John Osborne: The Many Lives of the Angry Young Man* (New York: Vintage Books, 2008), 247–252.
28. For a detailed look at the life and work of the creator of *Oliver!*, Lionel Bart, see Chapter 20 by Millie Taylor.
29. For a discussion of this musical, see Chapter 11 by Ben Francis.
30. See T. C. Worsley, 'Theatre Royal: Joan Littlewood', *Financial Times*, 20 October 1959; Angus Hall, 'The Rat Race—Set to Music', *Daily Sketch*, 20 October 1959; Bernard Levin, 'At the Theatre: Mankowitz Moves West, But His Heart Stays East', *Daily Express*, 20 October 1959. All in Harold Prince Papers, New York Public Library for the Performing Arts.
31. Milton Shulman, 'Mankowitz Comes Up with a Brash and Breezy Musical', *Evening Standard*, 20 October 1959. Harold Prince Papers, New York Public Library for the Performing Arts.

Bibliography

Allsop, Kenneth. *The Angry Decade: A Survey of the Cultural Revolt of the Nineteen-Fifties*. London: Peter Owen, 1958.

Banfield, Stephen. *Sondheim's Broadway Musicals*. Ann Arbor: University of Michigan Press, 1993.

Barker, Michael, Lionel Bart, Brendan Behan, Tom Driberg, Sean Kenny, Joan Littlewood, Ewan MacCool, Gerry Raffles, and Wole Soyinka. *Joan Littlewood and the Theatre Workshop Collection, ca. 1937–1975*. Harold Prince Papers, New York Public Library for the Performing Arts.

Bartlett, C. J. *'The Special Relationship': A Political History of Anglo-American Relations Since 1945*. New York: Longman, 1992.

Block, Geoffrey. *Enchanted Evenings: The Broadway Musical from 'Show Boat' to Sondheim*. Oxford: Oxford University Press, 1997.

Block, Geoffrey. 'The Broadway Canon from *Show Boat* to *West Side Story* and the European Operatic Ideal.' *Journal of Musicology* 11 (1993): 525–544.

Carter, Tim. *'Oklahoma!' The Making of an American Musical*. New Haven: Yale University Press, 2007.

Clum, John M. *Something for the Boys: Musical Theatre and Gay Culture*. New York: St Martin's Press, 1999.

Conway, Harold. 'This Knocks *My Fair Lady* for Six.' *London Daily Sketch*, 13 December 1958. Harold Prince Papers, New York Public Library for the Performing Arts.

Coren, Michael. *Theatre Royal: 100 Years of Stratford East*. London: Quartet, 1984.

Dornan, Reade Whiting. 'Comitted Theatre in Postwar Britain: The Approaches of Arnold Wesker and John McGrath.' Unpublished PhD thesis, Michigan State University, 1988.

Gänzl, Kurt. *The British Musical Theatre*. New York: Oxford University Press, 1986.

Gänzl, Kurt. *The Encyclopedia of the Musical Theatre*. Vols. 1–2. New York: Schirmer Books, 1994.

Goodman, Judith Lea. 'Joan Littlewood and Her Theatre Workshop.' Unpublished PhD, New York University, 1975.

Grant, Mark. *The Rise and Fall of the Broadway Musical*. Boston: Northeastern University Press, 2004.

Hall, Angus. 'The Rat Race—Set to Music.' *Daily Sketch*, 20 October 1959. Harold Prince Papers, New York Public Library for the Performing Arts.

Hischak, Thomas. *American Musical Theatre Song Encyclopedia*. Westport: Greenwood Press, 1995.

Hoggart, Richard. *The Uses of Literacy: Aspects of Working-Class Life*. London: Chatto and Windus, 1957.

Holdsworth, Nadine. *Joan Littlewood*. London: Routledge, 2006.

Johnson, John Andrew. 'Gershwin's American Folk Opera: The Genesis, Style and Reputation of *Porgy and Bess*.' Unpublished PhD thesis, Harvard University, 1996.

Kirle, Bruce. *Unfinished Showbusiness*. Carbondale: Southern Illinois University Press, 2005.

Knapp, Raymond. *The American Musical and the Formation of National Identity*. Princeton, NJ: Princeton University Press, 2005.

Lacey, Stephen. *British Realist Theatre: The New Wave in Its Context, 1956–1965*. New York: Routledge, 1995.

Lamb, Andrew. *150 Years of Popular Musical Theatre*. New Haven: Yale University Press, 2000.

Lamb, Andrew. 'From *Pinafore* to Porter: United States–United Kingdom Interactions in Musical Theater, 1879–1929.' In 'British–American Musical Interactions.' Special issue, *American Music* 4, no. 1 (Spring 1986): 34–49.

Lamb, Andrew. 'The West End Legacy and What Needs to Be Done.' The American and British Musical Conference, Bristol, 2006.

Leach, Robert. *Theatre Workshop: Joan Littlewood and the Making of Modern British Theatre*. Exeter: University of Exeter Press, 2006.

Levin, Bernard. 'At the Theatre: Mankowitz Moves West, But His Heart Stays East.' *Daily Express*, 20 October 1959. Harold Prince Papers, New York Public Library for the Performing Arts.

Littlewood, Joan. *Joan's Book: Joan Littlewood's Peculiar History as She Tells It*. London: Methuen, 1994.

Mankowitz, Wolf. *Make Me An Offer*. Guilford: Biddles, 1959.

McClung, Bruce D. 'American Dreams: Analyzing Moss Hart, Ira Gershwin and Kurt Weill's *Lady in the Dark*.' Unpublished PhD thesis, University of Rochester, 1994.

McMillin, Scott. *The Musical as Drama*. Princeton, NJ: Princeton University Press, 2006.

Meyer-Bruhl, B. 'Plays by John Arden and Peter Weiss in Their Relation to Brecht.' Unpublished PhD thesis, Oxford, 1986.

Miller, D. A. *Place for Us: Essay on the Broadway Musical*. Cambridge, MA: Harvard University Press, 1998.

Morley, Sheridan. *Spread a Little Happiness: The First Hundred Years of the British Musical Theatre*. London: Thames and Hudson, 1987.

Norman, Frank. *Why Fings Went West*. London: Lemon Tree Press, 1975.

Norman, Monty. 'Liner Notes.' *Make Me An Offer*. Original London Cast Recording, 1955. CD. SEPIA 1155, 2010.

Osborne, John. 'The World of Paul Slickey.' In *Look Back in Anger and Other Plays* (London: Faber and Faber, 1959).

Senelick, Laurence. *British Music-Hall, 1840–1923: A Bibliography and Guide to Sources, with a Supplement on European Music-Hall*. Hamden: Archon Books, 1981.

Shulman, Milton. 'Mankowitz Comes Up with a Brash and Breezy Musical.' *Evening Standard*, 20 October 1959. Harold Prince Papers, New York Public Library for the Performing Arts.

Snelson, John Mainwaring. 'The Kindness of Strangers: Using the British Sources.' The American and British Musical Conference, Bristol, 2006.

Snelson, John Mainwaring. 'The West End Musical, 1947–1954: British Identity and the "American Invasion".' Unpublished PhD thesis, University of Birmingham, 2002.

Thomas, Jennifer Renee. 'Joan Littlewood: A Director Ahead of Her Time.' Unpublished PhD thesis, University of Oregon, 2005.

Thompson, John. 'Welcoming the Most Fantastic Opening Forty Minutes Ever to Hit the London Theatre: Enter the "Dansical" New Hit Show Era!' *Express Photo News/Daily Express*, 13 December 1958. Harold Prince Papers, New York Public Library for the Performing Arts.

Walsh, David, and Len Platt. *Musical Theatre and American Culture*. Westport: Praeger, 2003.

Whitcomb, Neil. 'Here is the First of the Angry Young Musicals.' *Daily Mirror*, 26 March 1958. Harold Prince Papers, New York Public Library for the Performing Arts.

Wildblood, Peter, and Peter Greenwell, *The Crooked Mile*. Typescript, 1959. Lord Chamberlain's Plays, British Library Manuscripts Division.

Wolf, Stacy. *A Problem like Maria: Gender and Sexuality in the American Musical*. Ann Arbor: University of Michigan Press, 2002.

Worsley, T. C. 'Growing Up At Last.' *New Statesman*, 3 May 1958. Harold Prince Papers, New York Public Library for the Performing Arts.

Worsley, T. C. 'Theatre Royal: Joan Littlewood.' *Financial Times*, 20 October 1959. Harold Prince Papers, New York Public Library for the Performing Arts.

CHAPTER 11

....

'I'M COMMON AND I LIKE 'EM'

Representations of Class in the Period Musical after Oliver!

....

BEN FRANCIS

AFTER the success of *Oliver!* the West End saw a flood of shows based on famous novels and plays from the Victorian and Edwardian era. This essay will examine the representations of class in seven period musicals (including one set in 1960) that were presented in the 1960s and early 1970s: *Half a Sixpence* (1963), *Our Man Crichton* (1964), *Jorrocks* (1966), *Ann Veronica* (1969), *Trelawny* (1972), *The Card* (1973), and *Billy* (1974). Through these shows we can trace a history of how attitudes to class changed over this time.

The 1960s was an era of increased social mobility.[1] Working-class communities were being broken up, sometimes physically in slum-clearance programmes, but they were also dispersing due to the increasing affluence of much of the population.[2] Television from this era often reflected a nostalgia for the old communities, with soaps such as *Coronation Street*[3] and comedy series such as *The Likely Lads*,[4] *Till Death Us Do Part*,[5] and, with a darker tone, *Steptoe and Son*.[6] On the London stage Joan Littlewood's Theatre Workshop and the Royal Court had reacted strongly against middle-class drawing-room comedy and the West End began to tentatively reflect these changes: audiences were no longer expected to gaze in envious adoration at the sight of débutantes going to their first hunt ball. Instead, as we shall see, shows of this era portray the working class as being earthy (though not too earthy) and incapable of the sham and humbug of polite society. The shows all seem to share an underlying assumption that a working-class character could only move up the social scale at the risk of betraying his class.

Half a Sixpence (1963) with music and lyrics by David Heneker and book by Beverley Cross (679 performances) sets the tone for many of the shows to follow. Taken from H. G. Wells's 1905 novel *Kipps,* it deals with the adventures of Arthur Kipps, a draper's assistant who unexpectedly inherits £1,200 a year. At the start of the show he is in love with Ann Pornick, a parlourmaid, but, after becoming rich, he abandons her and gets engaged to Helen Walsingham, who is middle class and educated. He wants, so he thinks, to better himself.

That Kipps feels in awe of the moneyed class is expressed in the song that he sings when he dreams of Helen: 'She's Too Far above Me'. He is humble in the presence of the bourgeois woman (see Figure 11.1). Ann, however, is employed by the Walsinghams and is mistreated by them. When Kipps discovers this he breaks off his engagement to Helen and goes back to Ann. As he angrily explains to Helen: 'You people talk about her as if she was something different—as if she was a monkey in the zoo! Common Persons! Well, I'm common and I like 'em. An' I like her! I like 'er a lot! Come to think of it, I like 'er

FIGURE 11.1 The working-class man in awe of the bourgeois woman: Tommy Steele (Kipps) and Carrie Nye (Helen) in *Half a Sixpence*.

a whole lot better than what I like you . . .'[7] Kipps defiantly drops his aitches and abandons grammar to show he is abandoning the Walsingham's selfish lifestyle, a decision that the show unambiguously endorses.

THE MUSIC HALL SOUND

The notion that the working classes were full of unaffected jollity was underlined by the scores frequently using a music hall sound. The music hall was, in the Victorian and Edwardian era, a place of entertainment that was predominantly working class. If an upper-class person visited it they were assumed to be 'slumming'. The ideal of the working man propagated in the music halls was of somebody who was patriotic, loyal to the Queen, and willing to serve the Empire. Though it could be used for more subversive purposes, as we will see later, the music hall often implied that social inequality was acceptable as everyone was happy in their place and that imperialism was something to be proud of. The success of the TV series *The Good Old Days*[8] ensured that audiences of the 1960s would be familiar with music hall tropes.[9] One of the most common of these, not just in the music hall but throughout working-class culture, was the up-tempo communal number with a rousing chorus: the knees-up. The lyrics of these songs usually emphasize friendship and togetherness, often in the face of poverty: 'Consider Yourself' from *Oliver!* is a prime example. In shows and films these songs often assert identity in the face of an outside threat.[10]

Half a Sixpence has two knees-up songs: 'Flash, Bang, Wallop!' and 'The Party's on the House', and they are both sung at times when Kipps has remembered who he really is. 'Flash, Bang, Wallop!' is performed when he marries Ann, whom he should have married all along, and 'The Party's on the House' shows him getting back together with his old friends, whom he had previously abandoned. In other words, by the 1960s the knees-up songs don't just assert the main character's working-class identity to the outside world, they also remind the character himself of who he is and where he comes from—they serve to reassure him that he has not betrayed his class. With postwar Britain experiencing a prosperous economy and providing increased educational opportunities for the younger generation, there were many people in the audience who were caught between staying in their working-class environment and choosing a more affluent lifestyle.[11] Getting on in the world, with its emphasis on ambition and competitiveness, meant leaving behind a proletarian tradition and its communal values.[12] The shows discussed reflect the audience's dilemma: the main characters, like the audiences, wanted the best of both worlds, to be well-off without being la-di-da.

Take Ann Pornick's song: 'I Know What I Am' in which she rejects the genteel manners that she and Kipps had started to assume once they got married. She explains that she 'can't abide what's false and sham',[13] a sentiment which is similar to many of the famous songs from the music hall era. In songs such as 'Any Old Iron'[14] and 'Knocked 'Em in the Old Kent Road'[15] somebody from the working class puts on airs and is ridiculed by the working class themselves. 'Any Old Iron' is a chant sung by boys who are mocking the singer for wearing a gaudy watch chain, and in 'Knocked 'Em in the Old Kent Road' people make fun of the singer for driving a 'little donkey shay' that he has recently inherited. However, in Ann's song, it is notable that she does not mock herself for aping the middle classes, but rather the middle classes themselves: 'Being gents, | Don't make sense.'[16] If she doesn't want to go back to being a parlourmaid, neither is she going to live the life of frozen gentility that her mistress did.

If music hall often lent itself to perpetuating ruling-class ideology (a fact that was dramatized by *Oh What A Lovely War*[17]) it could, on the other hand, touch on subjects that were taboo at more polite entertainments, such as getting drunk ("Arf a Pint of Ale',[18] 'Don't Have Any More Mrs Moore',[19] 'I Belong to Glasgow'[20]), doing a moonlight flit ('Don't Dilly Dally on the Way'[21]), or being happy to be unemployed and put your feet up ('Wait Till the Work Comes Round'[22]). But the shows under consideration here were written not for a music hall audience, but for the West End, which wasn't used to putting on shows about characters getting drunk or skipping out of lodgings without paying the rent. The late 1950s had seen a craze for lowlife musicals such as *Expresso Bongo* (1958),[23] *Fings Ain't Wot They Used T'Be* (1959),[24] and *The Crooked Mile* (1959),[25] perhaps as a response to the phenomenon of the Teddy boy, but this had soon died down and in the 1960s there were few singing ponces, spivs or brasses on the West End stage.

The casting of Tommy Steele as Kipps is significant. Steele had started out as a rocker and imitator of Elvis Presley, but in 1957 he had topped the bill at the Royal Variety Performance at the London Palladium. Taking the lead in *Half a Sixpence* was a further step towards respectability and becoming a family entertainer. Like Kipps, Steele wanted acceptance by the middle classes without denying his origins. This pattern was later followed by Joe Brown when he appeared in Heneker's *Charlie Girl*.[26]

AUTHENTICITY VERSUS SNOBBERY

The choice was between authenticity and bourgeois double standards. This may seem unusual given that the West End audience is primarily middle class, but although England was, and remains, a class-conscious society, there has always been a stigma attached to the idea of being a snob. That the working-class lifestyle in these shows is the authentic one signifies that the working classes were shaking off the idea that they must 'know their place' and, conversely, it also signifies that the working-class culture was dying. One does not usually need to consciously commit oneself to a way of life unless that way of life is being threatened. This choice between authenticity and good breeding was often dramatized by showing the hero having to choose between two women from different classes. The hero usually realizes that the right girl is the girl from his own class (*Half a Sixpence, The Card, Our Man Crichton*). The wealthy woman represents an inauthentic lifestyle and the hero's courting of her indicates his corruption by material values. Helen Walsingham, Ruth in *The Card*, and Lady Mary in *Our Man Crichton* are all trapped in a world of repressive gentility, and Helen and Lady Mary both express regret that they are trapped and wish that they could marry the hero, precisely because he is not from their class. As Helen Walsingham says after she loses Kipps: 'I loved him just the way he was.'[27]

In *Our Man Crichton* (1964), with music by David Lee and book and lyrics by Herbert Kretzmer (208 performances), traditional class barriers are uprooted when an aristocratic family and their servants are shipwrecked on a desert island. Crichton, the family's butler, has to choose between Lady Mary, his employer's daughter, and Tweeny, the housemaid. The show (based on J. M. Barrie's 1902 play *The Admirable Crichton*) is faithful to the original play in that the butler is more snobbish than his supposedly liberal employer, Lord Loam. But whereas Barrie focused on Crichton's relationship with Lady Mary, the musical shifts the focus to Tweeny, the put-upon in-between maid.

The play had already been made into a successful film which starred Kenneth More,[28] who also played the eponymous character in *Our Man Crichton*. In the film Tweeny's role was made more important than it is in the play, but she is still relatively docile: she is shown as willing to wait for Crichton to make up his mind. In the musical version, however, we see Tweeny move from being a bullied underling in the opening song ('Tweeny!') to a liberated woman who can face the future ('My Time Will Come').

After the characters are rescued and return to England Tweeny berates Lady Mary (in a scene that is neither in the original play nor in the film) for not having the courage to marry Crichton. Instead Tweeny announces that she will marry him herself. The decision of both classes to stick to their own kind can be read as conservative (class barriers shouldn't be crossed) or egalitarian (the working classes are as good as their employers.) But, in *Our Man Crichton*, we are to be glad that Crichton will marry Tweeny, not because he should stick to his own kind, but because Tweeny is the woman with the courage to live for herself. She is a natural person, in touch with her instincts. When they are first washed ashore she prays: 'Please the Lord it may be an island as it's natural to be vulgar on!'[29] She is the character who gets a knees-up song ('London, London— My Home Town') while Lady Mary remains fraught with envy for the proletariat. In the song 'Our Kind of People' Lady Mary admits: 'Sometimes I wish I were of the common throng | Sometimes I long | To abandon all the snob set | Mingle with the mobs.'[30] Envy was now largely the preserve of the nobility. This can be read either progressively or in a more reactionary way. If the mobs are having all the fun and the nobility are jealous, then there is, perhaps, no more need for social progress, and society can stay the way it is, as the *hoi polloi* are actually the lucky ones.

David Heneker (music and lyrics) and Beverley Cross (book) followed up *Half a Sixpence* with *Jorrocks* (1966, 181 performances), based on characters created by R. S. Surtees. The show has as its main character John Jorrocks, a man whose major passion in life is fox hunting. Unusually for this era, Jorrocks and his wife are *common*: he contentedly so, while Mrs Jorrocks has pretensions to refinement. Jorrocks's plebeian joviality is contrasted with upper-class mealy-mouthed hypocrisy. He is given to saying things like 'Get your face stuffed into the trough' at elegant dinner parties.[31] His wife, however, wants to be accepted by the gentry who want her money while secretly despising her.

She is a parvenue and often uses that comic indicator of uncertain social status: the mal-apropism.[32] Jorrocks himself is wealthy—through trade: he is a tea merchant—but cares nothing for the norms of county society. He invites his huntsman, a drunken Geordie named Pigg, to sit at the dinner table of the local *grande dame*, shocking her and the other guests, who then use his egalitarian gesture as an excuse to try and have him certified as mad.

Finally Jorrocks triumphs and the aristocracy are defeated: he will not become affected like one of them, instead he will remain himself. If the common folk are now allowed to become the gentry, they don't have to behave like gentlefolk. Instead, the show claims, there is an activity where 'No-one gives a button for rank or pedigree.'[33] This activity, rather unconvincingly, turns out to be fox hunting, a bastion of aristocratic privilege that was too expensive for a working man to join. The show's unreserved endorsement of blood sports may account for its disappointing run, which is unfortunate as the show has one of Heneker's best scores.

Jorrocks has a strong and unrepentant cockney accent, which is an indicator of his unpretentious attitude. Conversely, when Kipps becomes a gentleman he tries to get Helen to correct his English. That Kipps is ashamed to drop his aitches is a sign of how he is being corrupted. In *Our Man Crichton* Tweeny tries to lose her accent in order to please Crichton, though she cannot, and it is her unaffectedness that finally wins him over. As opposed to Eliza in *My Fair Lady* (1956),[34] the characters in the later period musicals don't lose their accents. In the 1960s provincial accents were becoming acceptable for leading players: the success of film stars such as Albert Finney and Michael Caine showed that received pronunciation was no longer seen as a necessity.

ATTITUDES TO WOMEN

If men could liberate themselves from old rules then so could women. Jorrocks's niece is introduced with the song 'Belinda', a music hall-style song where her charms are praised by a chorus of working-class boys ('But Belin-Belin-Belinda beats them all').[35] She, like Ann Pornick and Tweeny, and later Ann Veronica, rejects arid forms of etiquette and good taste. Belinda sings 'I Don't Want to Behave Like a Lady' ('I don't want to sit and look pretty— | I may be pretty but I'm damned if I'll sit!')[36] while disguising herself as a man so that she can rescue Jorrocks. Gentility and old-fashioned notions of femininity are linked ideas and to rebel against one is often to rebel against the other.

Rebellion against patriarchy is taken much further by the central character of *Ann Veronica* (1969), a show with music by Cyril Ornadel, book by Frank Wells and Ronald Gow, and lyrics by David Croft, taken from the 1909 novel by H. G. Wells (forty-four performances). Ann Veronica rebels against her position and tries to live life on her own terms. In this show, in keeping with its feminist theme, it is the woman who must choose the right man. Ann Veronica has no less than four potential suitors: the good-natured

Teddy who adores her strength (reminiscent of the similarly named Freddy in *My Fair Lady*); the 'man-of-the-world' Ramage; the reverential Manning, who wants to keep Ann Veronica untouched by the world as a kind of fairy princess; and Capes, the biologist, the Wellsian man of science, who finally wins her. Her family expect her to marry the patriarchal Manning and is scandalized when she rejects his proposal. Ann Veronica makes a conscious decision to rebel against her family and background and get a job. It is a measure of the different positions of men and women that, while Kipps wants to escape work, Ann Veronica wants to get it.

The show sweetens Wells's satire on male attitudes, but does not obliterate it. In the novel Ramage loans Ann Veronica money and, as he cannot conceive of a woman taking a business loan, he thinks that she is agreeing to become his mistress. When he attempts to seduce her in a private room in a restaurant she has to fend him off. In the show, however, this is played for slapstick and Ramage comes across as a middle-aged booby.

Once again the cockney characters get a knees-up, 'Glad That You're Back', where they are welcoming and jolly: 'Pull up a chair, sit down, have some tea.'[37] The song is ironic in that the women who sing it are all in prison: they are repeat offenders and help out Ann, who has been sent to prison for suffragette activities (see Figure 11.2). The class beneath her doesn't need to worry about respectability, but Ann does and, as she has no financial means of her own, she is more trapped than she would be if she were poor. At the end she is only liberated by marriage to a man of her own class, albeit his commitment to science and social reform mean that he is not a conventional bourgeois. That she can only be liberated by a man may seem a guarded kind of radicalism but it is an accurate reflection of the lives of many women both in the Edwardian era and in the 1960s.

Trelawny (1972) with music and lyrics by Julian Slade, and a book by Aubrey Woods and George Rowell (177 performances), is a musical version of Arthur Wing Pinero's 1898 play *Trelawny of the 'Wells'*. As with *Ann Veronica* it is the woman, Rose Trelawny, who must choose between marriage and a job. Rose is an actress and, at the beginning of the show, she has chosen to retire from her profession and marry the well-to-do Arthur Gower, but when she tries to live with his family she finds the atmosphere too stultifying. The tyrannical head of the Gower household is Sir William, Arthur's grandfather, who insists on quiet and decorum. When Rose hears a barrel organ in the street playing a song from a show that she was once in she cannot resist breaking into one of her old routines.

The barrel organ is perhaps a distant relative of Minnie, the magic piano in Julian Slade's most enduring show: *Salad Days*.[38] In that show Minnie makes civil servants, policemen, and bishops dance. Repressed energies are unleashed, and the show's ad hoc story ridicules the whole notion of making characters subservient to a rigid plot, in a manner reminiscent of the way *The Goon Show*[39] tore up notions of logic to create a world of possibilities. Both *Salad Days* and *The Goon Show* reflect a post-war world where deferential attitudes to the ruling classes were starting to give way. *Salad Days* had the stuffy Minister of Pleasure and Pastime and the Goons had the cowardly and dishonest Major Bloodnok and the doddering Henry Crun who was the jealous guardian of the genteel Minnie Bannister.

FIGURE 11.2 Ann Veronica (Mary Millar, right) and her suffragette friends chaining themselves to the gates of 10 Downing Street. Cambridge Theatre, 1969.

TopPhoto. Courtesy of ArenaPal.

As it is in *Salad Days*, in *Trelawny* decorum is the enemy. Rose cannot stand living with the Gowers and returns to Sadler's Wells. When Sir William comes looking for her at her lodging house, her fellow actress Avonia Bunn berates him: 'You've brought her to beggary amongst you. You've broken her heart, and what's worse, you've made her genteel.'[40] Rose's refinement means that she can't liberate herself enough to act.

Trelawny is unusual in that it has an example of downward mobility: in order to win Rose back Arthur leaves his home and becomes an actor. Here it is the upper-class character who must change his life and conform to a new set of rules. In doing this he is doing what his grandfather had always secretly wanted to do: Sir William reveals to Rose that he used to be thrilled by seeing Edmund Kean on stage, and it is Sir William who in the end funds the play that Arthur and Rose are to star in together. As the Minister of Pleasure and Pastime is finally made to dance, so Sir William finally gets to reveal his desire to act. His repressive lifestyle has ultimately hurt only himself.

REACTION SETS IN

As the 1970s progressed, conservatism reasserted itself. In 1970 a Conservative government was elected with Edward Heath as prime minister. He repeatedly clashed with trade unions, which led to many strikes and violent confrontations. Against this background of unrest working-class solidarity became more problematic. *The Card* (1973), with music and lyrics by Tony Hatch and Jackie Trent and a book by Keith Waterhouse and Willis Hall (130 performances), is taken from a 1911 novel by Arnold Bennett. It is an unusual show in that it is about a social climber, Denry Machin, the kind of character found in novels of the era—see, for instance, Augustus Melmotte in Anthony Trollope's *The Way We Live Now* (1875) or Morris Townsend in Henry James's *Washington Square* (1880)—but generally avoided by British musicals.[41] This is not particularly surprising as social climbing is not an attractive activity for many British people as they assume that a climber will look down on the class that he came from. Although there are lots of American shows about making the big time, American shows are just as keen to prove that their heroes are not spoiled by success.[42] The creators of *The Card* try to dodge the problem by presenting the hero's selfishness and greed as charming. He works his way out of poverty, but, though he is given a couple of warnings by his dour mother, he is never made to confront the shallowness of his way of life. Arthur Kipps learns that being rich is not the solution to all his problems, whereas Denry Machin simply gets everything he wants: to be rich, to be mayor, and to be married.

Once again the hero is caught between two women: Ruth (who is made into a fortune hunter in the musical, which she is not in the novel) and Nellie, a nice (i.e. passive) girl from his own background. The show represents in fact a retrograde step (perhaps as an unconscious reaction to the growth of the women's liberation movement): Nellie waits submissively for Denry to claim her, incapable of the self-assertion of Ann Pornick or Belinda. Denry, unlike Kipps, can abandon his class with no ill effects. It is, we must assume, all right for men to be social climbers, but not for women. Social-climbing men are adventurers, women are heartless gold-diggers. And the common people are seen as grateful to Denry and acclaim him as a liberator. His egalitarian gesture is to form a thrift club (effectively a form of hire purchase) that enables poor people to shop at the local posh department store. The show never suggests that maybe the poor didn't need to shop there anyway, but then, in this musical, the lowly have no pride of their own and only exist to praise Denry.

Social climbing seems to be an impossible aspiration in the most complex show from this era: *Billy* (1974.) Taken from Keith Waterhouse's 1959 novel *Billy Liar* and the 1960 play version by Waterhouse and Willis Hall,[43] it has a score by John Barry, lyrics by Don

Black, and a book by Dick Clement and Ian La Frenais. It was one of the most successful musicals of the era, running for 904 performances. The show is set in 1960 (in the
novel the year isn't specified) and, at the beginning, Billy Fisher is trapped: his family
argue with him, his job at Shadrack and Duxbury's funeral parlour is dull, and his home
town of Stradhoughton is narrow and provincial. Billy responds by creating a fantasy
world: an imaginary land called Ambrosia, of which he is president.

In the original novel Billy is a disturbed young man whose daydreaming hardly seems
to console him anymore. The show's creators tone down the bitter comedy of the book
by making him more kid-like. He is, as he is not in the novel, nostalgic for his childhood.
In the song 'Happy to Be Themselves' he sings of

> Streamers and clowns
> And penny arcades.
> Merry-go-rounds
> And buckets and spades.[44]

The actor playing Billy in the first production of the show was Michael Crawford, at
that time a TV star in the sitcom *Some Mothers Do 'Ave 'Em*,[45] where he played Frank
Spencer, a bewildered innocent who regularly caused disaster. This casting ensured that
Billy would be seen as not really responsible for his actions, which, looked at objectively,
are pretty repulsive (he tries, for instance, to trick his fiancée Barbara into taking 'passion pills', claiming that they are energy tablets). In his 'I am' song, 'Some of Us Belong to
the Stars', we hear his gauche, unrealistic personality wittily expressed in the lyrics: 'I'll
hang my hat in ev'ry part of the atlas, | Most of the time I will be hopelessly hatless.'[46]

What is unusual in this show is that Billy does not feel part of his community: he
feels estranged from it. Usually in shows of this period only the middle class feel isolated and frustrated. But in 'Happy to Be Themselves' Billy is quite contemptuous of the
townsfolk: 'Riding in tubes | And padding their boobs.'[47] The townspeople don't hear
his complaints and sing about how contented they are. Billy also mockingly imitates the
Yorkshire accent that he hears around him, until Councillor Duxbury, his employer, tells
him to speak the way his parents have taught him to. Billy, unlike Kipps or John Jorrocks,
belongs to a generation that has lost its accent, and Billy's mockery of it may indicate a
deep-seated envy of people who can really speak that way. Duxbury is in touch with an
older past, as expressed in his song 'It Were All Green Hills', but Billy is a product of a
modern housing estate, and, unlike Kipps, Machin, or Tweeny, has no sense of belonging. He has no communal songs, except in his dreams.

That Billy feels alienated is expressed by the repeated device of having him sing
against the other characters, unheard by them. In the song 'And', his mother, father, and
grandfather all nag him while he fantasizes about killing them. When Barbara imagines
their married life together he fantasizes about killing her as well ('The Witch's Song').
This indicates his frustration, which he deals with by being a compulsive liar. He is in
fact engaged to two different women: respectable Barbara and earthy Rita (in the stage
directions she is described, without irony, as 'common'). Perhaps he is trying to sabotage

the possibility of his getting married at all and having to settle down and become like his father. Although he is caught between two women, in this show neither of them is the right girl. Instead the one who understands him is Liz, a free spirit who does what she wants. All through the show Billy claims that he is going to go to London to become a comedy scriptwriter, and it is Liz who finally offers him the chance to get on the train and come with her. Liz, we might say, is the voice of the future: she seems to foreshadow the type of the sixties woman who didn't conform to convention, while Billy is trapped in an older, more repressive world.

This may explain why he doesn't go with her, but instead deliberately misses the train and goes back home. He is a daydreamer who avoids the chance to make his dreams come true—an extraordinary ending for a musical. Is Billy's refusal to live his dream simply a negation of all that the musical as a genre stands for? Musicals can create an atmosphere of excess, joy, uplift; they often stand for the possibility of escape. One way of reading the show is that it is a period piece, and that Billy belongs to a world now gone. The year 1960 was just before the *annus mirabilis* that Larkin wrote of, when escape became a possibility for thousands of people. Perhaps by 1974 the confidence of the 1960s had evaporated. If the show had been contemporary,[48] then one might have wondered why Billy didn't escape to university. But if there were more opportunities in 1974 than in 1960, there was still the problem of belonging in a world that had nothing else to offer besides a job and a pension—disenchantment had set in.

As he walks to the station Billy sings a reprise of 'Some of Us Belong to the Stars', trying to persuade himself that he is doing the right thing, although he is abandoning his family at the time of his grandmother's death.

> If I stay here my life can only be quite good,
> But if I leave I might end up with a knighthood;
> You have to hob-nob with all those la-di-das—
> To belong to the stars.[49]

In other words Billy starts to realize that he would become a social climber. In most shows of this period 'La-di-da' is a synonym for snobbery and falsity. In *Oliver!* the Artful Dodger promises, in 'Consider Yourself', that 'Nobody tries to be lah-di-dah and uppity | There's a cup o' tea for all.'[50] In *Half a Sixpence* Ann sings disdainfully of 'Calling cards | La-Di-Dards!'[51] In *Jorrocks*, the girls jealously accuse Belinda of being "Er with 'er nose in the air, la-di-da'.[52] But only Billy faces the uncomfortable fact that in order to get on, you may have to get to know the la-di-da people, instead of sticking to your own kind.

Not that Billy is able to do this. His final song is 'I Missed the Last Rainbow', which he sings just after deciding not to escape to London.

> I missed the last rainbow,
> But what if I'm wrong?
> What if that same rainbow
> Stops further along?

> And if there's a rainbow,
> And I'm sure there's one,
> I'll get on that rainbow,
> But I'll have to run.[53]

The song seems to be trying to have it both ways: Billy is trapped now, but he might get away later on. At the station he asks (which he does not in the novel) the time of the first train to London next morning. But then he goes back home and we hear the sound of the Ambrosian National Anthem. The stage directions say:

> *As the requiem swells,* BILLY, *visibly upset, returns to his room. As the final notes sound,*
>   BILLY *addresses the audience.*
> BILLY   I'm home.
> CHORUS   . . . AND FREE.
> BILLY   *sits on his bed.*
>   *Blackout.*[54]

This scene is also not in the novel, which ends with Billy walking towards his home. What are we to make of the ideologically-charged last line 'I'm home'? What does 'home' actually mean to Billy apart from a place where he is shouted at and ignored? The ending seems to imply an acceptance of his fate: that home is best, and that it is better not to try to reach for anything, an attitude that would be unthinkable to Kipps, Machin, or Tweeny. This reading seems to be contradicted by Billy's curtain music, a reprise of 'Some of Us Belong to the Stars', which implies that he hasn't changed at all. The show seems conflicted on this point, recognizing that, although we may want him to mature, we don't want Billy to accept defeat.

If he had simply fulfilled his fantasies he would never have to confront the fact that he cannot deal with real emotions, which he begins to realize when he starts having one of his daydreams about his grandmother's death. He breaks off, shocked at himself, and asks: 'For Christ's sake, why can't I FEEL something?!'[55] His mother (and, in musicals, the mother of the protagonist is usually right) tells Billy, just before he leaves for the station, that leaving will not solve any of his problems. A more satisfactory ending might have been to have Billy being able to come home and properly communicate with his family for the first time—they could discover as a reality the community that other shows took for granted.

CONCLUSION: 'NAUGHTY AND YET QUAITE NAICE'

It is notable that, with the exceptions of *Half a Sixpence* and *Billy*, the musicals in this chapter did not achieve particularly long runs. It would be risky to speculate why any given show succeeded or failed, but, apart from *Billy*, all of these shows seem to want to have it both ways: that the working classes can get ahead without losing their class identity.[56] Not that this is an unreasonable attitude—why shouldn't the working classes get ahead if the chance is offered them? But maybe this meant that the shows became a little too polite; if they didn't accept what Alfred Doolittle would call 'middle class morality' they at least accepted middle-class standards of good taste. In *Trelawny* Avonia Bunn, the actress who always plays the maid, says that she has learned how to smile: 'To show I am "naughty" and yet "quiate naice".'[57] which, as a description, might also serve for the main characters in the period musicals of this era.

Compare *Half a Sixpence* to an earlier musical about a working man suddenly becoming rich: *Me and My Girl* (1937).[58] In this show the hero, a bookie's runner called Bill Snibson, suddenly finds that he is, in fact, Lord Hareford. Bill's low-born vitality is contrasted with glacial upper-class manners. Bill, too, has his knees-up song, 'The Lambeth Walk'. But Bill, unlike Kipps, never forgets who he is, and he sings his knees-up song to prove to the nobs that he is not ashamed of his supposedly humble origins. The toffs find Bill's uncouth energy liberating, as they discover that they enjoy doing 'The Lambeth Walk' as well. But, in the post-war shows, the blue bloods no longer join in, but instead look on enviously. Perhaps by then it was no longer necessary to make them feel included.

It might be said that *Half a Sixpence* marks an advance on the attitudes of *Me and My Girl*. In the earlier musical Bill's true love, working-class Sally, is finally accepted by the *haut monde* because she shows that she can behave 'like a lady' when required. This ending manages to please both conservatives and liberals: conservatives see that Bill and Sally present no threat to the social hierarchy, and liberals can see that class is nothing but performance.[59] But while Sally has to learn to act like a lady, Ann Pornick doesn't have to bother with all that pretence, and she can become independent without apologizing to anyone. Like Tweeny in *Our Man Crichton*, Belinda in *Jorrocks*, and the title character in *Ann Veronica*, she is, at least comparatively, a liberated woman. However, if *Half a Sixpence* displays a more egalitarian attitude than its predecessor, there is, on the other hand, something of a loss of vigour. Bill Snibson, even if he is finally willing to play the toffs' game, is far more vulgar than Kipps would ever be: Bill shoves a cream cake in the face of one of his upper-class tormentors, and he also wipes his feet on the history of the Hareford family. Kipps would never be so crass. Perhaps that smoothing away of rough edges is the price to be paid for upward mobility: the working classes weren't going to kowtow to the upper crust, but neither were they going to push a pie in their faces, as one day they might actually be working alongside them.

In this era West End theatres responded to the major social changes going on around them with caution: period shows celebrated the triumphs of characters in another era, as if to give the reassuring impression that snobbery was a thing of the past. And though the characters might mock respectability, they were never themselves disreputable. The shows no longer had cheek—the resilient, instinctively sardonic attitude that mocks all authority: the attitude that Lionel Bart captured in Nancy, Fagin, and the Artful Dodger had been discarded.[60] Perhaps audiences would still have liked to have seen common people on stage, with the licence and liberty that that implies—in capitalist society success means respectability and conformity, which explains the appeal of characters who don't care that they are on the bottom of the pile, as they are willing to be themselves. Nancy expresses this defiant attitude in her song 'It's a Fine Life'. The shows under discussion, however, seem to feature working-class characters as the middle class would like to see them: not, to be sure, doffing their caps in respect, but always clean and hardworking. If they are no longer servants, the heroes are happy to be shopkeepers (*Half a Sixpence*), fox hunters (*Jorrocks*), and mayors (*The Card.*) The middle class, after all, though they may be eager not to be thought snobbish, may also have wanted to be reassured that the new arrivals would know how to behave and wouldn't rock the boat.

After *Billy* the English period musical more or less died out in the West End: the social equality that had seemed possible in the 1960s proved elusive, and perhaps, with the increasing industrial unrest of the 1970s, many of the characters in the shows were simply too mild and optimistic to reflect the mood of the times. When by the end of the 1970s a new Conservative administration was elected under Margaret Thatcher, rampant materialism became the order of the day, the poor were to be demonized, and, within this harshly polarized society, perhaps there was no longer any room for warmhearted togetherness.

The author would like to thank Adrian Slade, and Richard Anthony Baker and Adam Borzone from the British Music Hall Society.

Notes

1. The first of these shows was put on in 1963, the year Philip Larkin in his poem *Annus Mirabilis* ironically identified as the year that life became 'A brilliant breaking of the bank, | A quite unlosable game'. Philip Larkin, *High Windows* (London: Faber and Faber, 1974), 34.
2. This process had been going on for some years: see Richard Hoggart, *The Uses of Literacy: Aspects of Working-Class Life* (London: Chatto and Windus, 1957); Michael Young and Peter Wilmott, *Family and Kinship in East London* (London: Routledge & Kegan Paul, 1957).
3. Created by Tony Warren and produced by Granada, the soap opera first aired in 1960 and is still running on ITV.
4. Created by Dick Clement and Ian La Frenais and broadcast by the BBC from 1964 to 1966. The show was about two apprentices, played by Rodney Bewes and James Bolam, with Bob Ferris (Bewes) aspiring to be middle class and Terry Collier (Bolam) being his more down-to-earth friend.
5. Created by Johnny Speight, the show could be seen on BBC from 1965 to 1975. It starred Warren Mitchell as Alf Garnett, a bigoted, reactionary London docker who regularly clashes with his more liberal-minded daughter and son-in-law (played by Una Stubbs and Tony Booth respectively).
6. This BBC show was created by Ray Galton and Alan Simpson and aired from 1962 to 1965 and then again from 1970 to 1974. It was set in a family-run scrap yard and focused on Harold Steptoe (Harry H. Corbett) who wanted to become successful and escape from his crude and bigoted father Albert (played by Wilfrid Brambell).

7. David Heneker and Beverley Cross, *Half a Sixpence*, libretto (London: Chappell Music Ltd, 1963), 56.

8. The BBC variety series that ran from 1953 to 1983 and was created by its producer Barney Colehan. Both performers and audiences wore Victorian costume.

9. George Melly in *Revolt Into Style* (London: Penguin Press, 1970), 52, wrote that 'the influence of the music-hall on British pop music has been surprisingly strong'. He cited the examples of Ray Davies from the Kinks, the Beatles, Marty Wilde, Joe Brown, and Tommy Steele himself.

10. Two examples taken from movies are the pub singalong in *Passport To Pimlico* (directed by Henry Cornelius, 1949) when the community tear up their identity cards in the face of an angry policeman and sing 'Knees Up Mother Brown', and the scene in *The Captive Heart* (directed by Basil Dearden, 1946) where a group of British POWs mock their captors by singing 'Roll Out the Barrel' to drown out the German marching song that is being played to them over the camp's loudspeakers.

11. The clash between upwardly mobile sons and fathers who belong to a working-class community was the subject of many plays of the era, such as *The Homecoming* (Harold Pinter, 1965), *Stand Up, Nigel Barton* (Dennis Potter, 1965), *In Celebration* (David Storey, 1969), and *After Haggerty* (David Mercer, 1970).

12. Dennis Potter, a miner's son who went to Oxford University on a scholarship, spoke of this tension in a 1987 television interview with Alan Yentob. 'On one level I wanted to be part of it [the working-class world of his parents], and longed for acceptance in it. On another level, I was already beginning to judge it and be the cocky scholarship boy, if you like, who's at the very moment of embracing it, compromising it.' Collected in Dennis Potter, *Seeing the Blossom: Two Interviews and a Lecture* (London: Faber and Faber, 1994), 62.

13. Heneker and Cross, *Half a Sixpence*, 68.

14. Written by Charles Collins, Fred E. Terry, and E. A .Sheppard, the song was first performed by Harry Champion in 1911.

15. Also called 'Wot Cher!', the song was written by Albert Chevalier and Charles Ingle, and first performed by Albert Chevalier in 1891.

16. Heneker and Cross, *Half a Sixpence*, 68.

17. Credited to Joan Littlewood, Charles Chilton, and the Theatre Workshop, the show was first performed at the Theatre Royal Stratford East in 1963.

18. With words and music by Charles Tempest, the song was first performed by Gus Elen in 1905.

19. Written by Harry Castling and James Walsh, the number was first performed by Lily Morris in 1926.

20. The song was written and first performed by Will Fyffe in 1920.

21. Also known as 'My Old Man (Said Follow the Van)', the song is by Fred W. Leigh and Charles Collins and was first performed by Marie Lloyd in 1919.

22. Written by Gus Elen and Charles Cornell. Elen was the first artist to perform the song, in 1906.

23. Music by David Heneker and Monty Norman, lyrics by Julian More and Monty Norman, book by Wolf Mankowitz and Julian More. It opened in 1958 and ran for 316 performances.

24. Music and lyrics by Lionel Bart, book by Frank Norman. The original 1959 production at the Theatre Royal Stratford East ran for 63 performances, while the revised version in the West End's Garrick Theatre ran for 897 performances.

25. Music by Peter Greenwell, book and lyrics by Peter Wildeblood. It opened in 1959 and ran for 164 performances.

26. Music and lyrics by David Heneker and John Taylor, book by Hugh and Margaret Williams with Ray Cooney, story conceived by Ross Taylor. It opened in 1965 and closed after 2,202 performances.

27. Cross, *Half a Sixpence*, 56.

28. *The Admirable Crichton* (1957, released in America as *Paradise Lagoon*) was directed by Lewis Gilbert, with a screenplay by Vernon Harris. Kenneth More played Crichton, the film also starred Diane Cilento as Tweeny, Cecil Parker as Lord Loam, and Sally Ann Howes as Lady Mary.

29. Herbert Kretzmer, *Our Man Crichton*, libretto (London: Hodder and Stoughton, 1965) 68. This line is also in the original play.

30. Kretzmer, *Our Man Crichton*, 39.

31. David Heneker and Beverley Cross, *Jorrocks*, libretto (London: Chappell and Co., 1966), 41.

32. She refers to one of the aristocrats as 'a man of extinction'. Heneker and Cross, *Jorrocks*, 52. This is perhaps a joke on the idea that the aristocracy will soon be extinct.

33. Heneker and Cross, *Jorrocks*, 42.

34. Music by Frederick Loewe, book and lyrics by Alan Jay Lerner.

35. Heneker and Cross, *Jorrocks*, 5.

36. Heneker and Cross, *Jorrocks*, 53.

37. Frank Wells, Ronald Gow, and David Croft. Manuscript libretto: Act 2 Scene 16, p. 20. The libretto has never been published; the manuscript consulted is the property of Ann Croft, David Croft's widow.

38. Music by Julian Slade, book and lyrics by Slade and Dorothy Reynolds. The revised version opened in the West End in 1954 and ran for 2,283 performances. For more on *Salad Days* please see Chapter 9 by John Snelson and Chapter 17 by Robert Gordon.

39. Created by Spike Milligan for BBC radio, *The Goon Show* ran from 1952 to 1960. Milligan and co-stars Harry Secombe and Peter Sellers played a variety of characters who got into wildly surreal, cartoon-like adventures.

40. Julian Slade, Aubrey Woods, and George Rowell, *Trelawny*, libretto (London: Samuel French, 1974), 55.

41. In a 1962 musical version of Thackeray's *Vanity Fair* (70 performances), with a book by Robin Miller and Alan Pryce-Jones and lyrics by Miller, Julian Slade showed an unrepentant social climber in Becky Sharpe, who points out that she is a social climber because her society has made her so. That Slade sympathizes with her is implied when he allows her a happy ending—she marries the wealthy Joseph Sedley, whereas in the novel she is reduced to selling trinkets at a fair.

42. See, for instance, Meredith Willson's *The Unsinkable Molly Brown* (1960).

43. The dramatization, directed by Lindsay Anderson, was staged with Albert Finney as Billy. There was also a film version in 1963, directed by John Schlesinger and starring Tom Courtenay and Julie Christie.

44. Don Black, Dick Clement, and Ian La Frenais, *Billy*, libretto (London: Josef Weinberger 1974; rev. 1992), 26.

45. Written by Raymond Allen, *Some Mothers Do 'Ave 'Em* ran on the BBC from 1973 to 1978.

46. Black, Clement, and La Frenais, *Billy*, 17.

47. Black, Clement, and La Frenais, *Billy*, 27.

48. There was also a contemporary version of the story on British television around that time, *Billy Liar*, which was scripted by Waterhouse and Hall and starred Jeff Rawle as Billy. It was broadcast by London Weekend Television from 1973 to 1974.

49. Black, Clement, and La Frenais, *Billy*, 79.
50. Lionel Bart, *Oliver!* (London: Oliver Promotions Ltd, 1977), 37.
51. Heneker and Cross, *Half a Sixpence*, 68.
52. Heneker and Cross, *Jorrocks*, 5.
53. Black, Clement, and La Frenais, *Billy*, 83.
54.. Black, Clement, and La Frenais, *Billy*, 84.
55. Black, Clement, and La Frenais, *Billy*, 76. Capital letters and underlining in the original.
56. In this context the American show *Darling of the Day* (1968), another musical conceived in the time frame discussed here and set in Edwardian England, reveals a telling inability to understand the English class system. The musical, with music by Jule Styne, lyrics by Yip Harburg, and a book by Nunnally Johnson, is based on Arnold Bennett's 1905 novel *Buried Alive*. The story concerns a famous artist assuming the identity of his dead manservant. In the show's finale the artist confesses his true identity, but gets the entire legal establishment to agree to a cover-up rather than admit that a servant has been buried in Westminster Abbey. (In Bennett's novel the deception is uncovered and the artist goes abroad.) The American authors see this as typical English adorable eccentricity instead of as a snobbish attitude that, by the late 1960s, people might conceivably be fed up with.
57. These lines come from the song 'Walking On'. Slade, Rowell, and Woods, *Trelawny*, 10.
58. Music and lyrics by Noel Gay, book by Douglas Furber and L. Arthur Rose. For more on *Me and My Girl* please see Chapter 6 by George Burrows.
59. A fact that was dramatized in *Oliver!* with the Artful Dodger's top hat and his insouciant first words: 'What yer starin' at? Ain't you never seen a toff?' (Bart, *Oliver!*, 36.)
60. Fagin contemplates, and finally rejects, becoming respectable in his song 'Reviewing the Situation'.

BIBLIOGRAPHY

The Admirable Crichton Directed by Lewis Gilbert, 1957. DVD. Sony Pictures, CDR11274, 2009.
Ann Veronica. Original Cast Recording, 1969. CD. Stage Door, STAGE 9042, 2015.
Barrie, J. M. *The Admirable Crichton*. London: Hodder and Stoughton, no date.
Bart, Lionel. *Oliver!* 1960. London: Oliver Productions, 1977.
Bennett, Arnold. *Buried Alive, a Tale of These Days*. London: Chapman and Hall, 1908.
Bennett, Arnold. *The Card*. London: Methuen, 1911.
Billy. Original Cast Recording, 1974. CD. CBS 472818-2, 2015.
Billy Liar. Directed by John Schlesinger, 1963. Fiftieth Anniversary Edition, DVD. Studio Canal, OPTD 2526, 2013.
Black, Don, Dick Clement, and Ian La Frenais. *Billy*. Libretto. London: Weinberger, 1974. Revised 1992.
The Captive Heart. Directed by Basil Dearden, 1946. DVD. Studio Canal Vintage Classics, OPTD 1069, 2007.
The Card. Original Cast Recording, 1973. LP. Pye Records, NSPL 18408, 1973.
The Card. London Cast Recording, 1994. CD. First Night Records, Fst CAST45, 1997.
Croft, David, Ronald Gow, and Frank Wells. *Ann Veronica*. Libretto. Unpublished manuscript, 1969.
The Crooked Mile. Original Cast Recording, 1959. CD. Reissue MCSR 3002, 2004.
Darling of the Day. Original Broadway Cast, 1968. CD. RCA Victor, 63334, 1999.

Expresso Bongo. Original Cast Recording, 1958. CD. AEI, AEI-CD-020, 2005.

Fings Ain't Wot They Used T'Be. Original Cast Recording, 1959. CD. Reissue Bayview RNBW 11, 2011.

Furber, Douglas, and L Arthur Rose. *Me and My Girl*. Libretto. London: Samuel French, 1938.

Half a Sixpence. Original Cast Recording, 1963. CD. RCA Victor, 09026-63691-2, 2000.

Heneker, David, and Beverley Cross. *Half a Sixpence*. Libretto. London: Chappell Music Ltd, 1963.

Heneker, David, and Beverley Cross. *Jorrocks*. Libretto. London: Chappell and Co., 1966.

Hoggart, Richard. *The Uses of Literacy: Aspects of Working-Class Life*. London: Chatto and Windus, 1957.

James, Henry. *Washington Square*. New York: Harper and Brothers, 1880.

Jorrocks. Original Cast Recording, 1966. LP. EMI Records, EMI CSD 3591, 1966.

Kretzmer, Herbert. *Our Man Crichton*. Libretto. London: Hodder and Stoughton, 1965.

Larkin, Philip. *High Windows*. London: Faber and Faber, 1974.

Littlewood, Joan, Theatre Workshop, Charles Chilton, and members of the original cast. *Oh What A Lovely War*. London: Methuen, 1965.

Melly, George. *Revolt into Style: The Pop Arts in Britain*. Harmondsworth: Penguin Press, 1970.

Mercer, David. *After Haggerty*. London: Methuen, 1970.

Our Man Crichton. Original Cast Recording, 1964. EMI Records, PMC 1246, 1965.

Passport to Pimlico. Directed by Herny Cornelius, 1949. DVD, Studio Canal, OPTB2446, 2006.

Pinero, Arthur Wing. *Trelawny of the 'Wells'*. London: Heinemann, 1899.

Pinter, Harold. *The Birthday Party*. London: Faber and Faber, 1965.

Potter, Dennis. *Seeing the Blossom: Two Interviews and a Lecture*. London: Faber and Faber, 1994.

Salad Days. Original Cast Recording, 1954. CD. Sepia 1061, 2005.

Stand Up, Nigel Barton. Directed by Gareth Davies, 1965. DVD. 2entertain, 2013.

Slade, Julian, George Rowell, and Aubrey Woods. *Trelawny*. Libretto. London: Samuel French, 1974.

Slade, Julian, Robin Miller, and Alan Pryce-Jones. *Vanity Fair*. Libretto. Unpublished manuscript. London, 1962.

Storey, David. *In Celebration*. London: Jonathan Cape, 1969.

Thackeray, William Makepeace. *Vanity Fair: A Novel Without a Hero*. London: Bradbury and Evans, 1848.

Trelawny. Original Cast Recording, 1972. CD. Must Close Saturday, MCSR 3007, 2003.

Trollope, Anthony. *The Way We Live Now*. London: Chapman and Hall, 1875.

Vanity Fair. Revival Recording, 2001. CD. Bayview, RNBWO13, 2001.

Waterhouse, Keith. *Billy Liar*. London: Michael Joseph, 1959.

Waterhouse, Keith, and Willis Hall. *Billy Liar: A Play in Three Acts*. London: Evans Plays, 1961.

Waterhouse, Keith, and Willis Hall. *The Card*. Libretto. London: Weinberger, 1973.

Wells, H. G. *Ann Veronica*. London: T. Fisher Unwin, 1909.

Wells, H. G. *Kipps*. London: Macmillan, 1905.

Wright, Adrian. *A Tanner's Worth of Tune*. Woodbridge: The Boydell Press, 2010.

Young, Michael, and Peter Willmott. *Family and Kinship in East London*. London: Routledge and Kegan Paul, 1957.

....

CHAPTER 12

TOWARDS A BRITISH CONCEPT MUSICAL

The Shows of Anthony Newley and Leslie Bricusse

....

DAVID COTTIS

THE three stage shows written in collaboration by Leslie Bricusse and Anthony Newley—*Stop the World—I Want to Get Off* (1961), *The Roar of the Greasepaint, the Smell of the Crowd* (1964), and *The Good Old, Bad Old Days* (1972) are unlike anything that preceded them in the British musical theatre. Minimalist, metatheatrical, and drawing on contemporary developments in literature and non-musical theatre, they were also dependent on the established persona of their co-author and star, and have proved difficult to revive without him.

ANTHONY NEWLEY: FULL-THROATEDLY THEATRICAL

Anthony Newley was already on his third (arguably, fourth) career when he began writing for the musical stage. Born in solidly working-class Hackney to a single mother in 1931, he attended the Italia Conti Stage School on a scholarship—he'd often say in later interviews that he'd financed his studies by working as the tea boy—and became a successful child actor, playing the title role in the five-part Rank serial *Dusty Bates* (1947). The next year, he appeared in David Lean's *Oliver Twist* (1948) as the Artful Dodger, a character who would remain part of his onstage persona for the rest of his life, much as Slightly in *Peter Pan* did for Noël Coward.

After a difficult period of transition, Newley re-established himself as an adult star. In 1955 he appeared in the theatrical revue *Cranks*, devised by the young South African ballet choreographer and director John Cranko, whose stripped-down aesthetic was to become a major influence on Newley's own work: 'Cranko's thing never left me. Clear the stage. Let's get back to the beginning. The only time there was any scenery, we brought it on. [. . .] He indelibly left that on me, and I worshipped him.'[1]

Newley's next career came about through his appearance in the film comedy *Idle on Parade* (1959; US title *Idol on Parade*), in which he played Jeep Jackson, a rock star called up for the last gasp of National Service. Loosely based on the military experiences of both Elvis Presley and his British imitator Terry Dene, the film included several songs mocking 1950s rock 'n' roll, one of which—'I've Waited So Long'—became a hit (no. 4, 1959), launching Newley on a chart career (like Ricky Nelson and John Leyton, he became a rock star by playing one on-screen). As Bob Stanley has pointed out, it says something about the British rock scene in the pre-Beatles era that nobody seemed bothered by the fact that the original song had been a parody.[2] (Newley himself wrote two Jerry Lee Lewis-ish numbers for the film, in collaboration with the Scottish pianist Joe Henderson.)

British rock of this period is a strange animal—half imitation of the States, half descendant of the music hall, the bastard child of Elvis Presley and Max Miller. Newley's recordings run the gamut—American covers, both rocking (Lloyd Price's 'Personality', no. 6, 1959) and teenage (Frankie Avalon's 'Why', no. 1, 1960), bel canto ('If She Should Come to You', no. 4, 1960), cockney innuendo ('Do You Mind', written by fellow East Ender Lionel Bart, no. 2, 1960), and parody folk song ('Strawberry Fair', no. 3, 1960). Newley sings in an accent that moves seamlessly between Brick Lane and mid-Atlantic, full-throatedly theatrical and often slightly camp (for a classic example of this latter quality, listen to Newley's original recording of 'Goldfinger' for which he and Bricusse wrote the lyrics[3]). It's a voice that remains influential in British pop culture—you can hear it in early David Bowie and *Parklife*-era Damon Albarn—as well as in the United States; American actors speaking and (especially) singing as Londoners, such as Johnny Depp in *Sweeney Todd* (2007), have a remarkable tendency to start sounding like Newley.

At this period, rock stardom wasn't seen as a lifetime career, and every British rocker would announce his intention of becoming 'an all-round entertainer'. Many succeeded—Cliff Richard, Tommy Steele, Jim Dale, Mark Wynter—and Newley, who was already an actor, had a head start. In 1960, he appeared in another piece that would affect his own writing, the absurdist, ahead-of-its-time television sitcom *The Strange World of Gurney Slade*. The show was written by Sid Green and Dick Hills, and directed by Newley himself, who played the title character: an over-imaginative, isolated young man in a raincoat. In the first episode, Slade literally breaks the fourth wall, as he walks off the set of a conventional situation comedy into the world outside the studio, where he muses in voice-over and converses with babies, animals, and inanimate objects. Slade is a liminal figure, who can stop the action, change the background music with a wave of his hand, and address the camera, which he often does. The second episode starts with a travelling shot across a very Beckettian wilderness, as the camera pans towards Newley; he looks at the audience and says 'Took your time getting here, didn't you?' The programme was perhaps too idiosyncratic to last more than one series (as late as 1994, it was referred to as 'one of TV's weirder offerings'[4]) but it acquired a cult following. Among those watching was a young David Bowie who said, in a 1973 *New Musical Express* interview, 'I was Anthony Newley for a year. He stopped his world and got off, which was terrible, because he was once one of the most talented men that England ever produced. Remember the *Gurney Slade* series? That was tremendous.'[5]

LESLIE BRICUSSE: CLASSICAL
AND DISCIPLINED

Although born in the same year as Newley, Leslie Bricusse was in other ways his polar opposite—suburban middle class, Cambridge-educated, and happily married. His musical tastes were formed by screenings of film versions of Broadway classics— he referred to Richard Rodgers as 'the man whose theatre music I admired above all others.'[6]

When the two men met, Bricusse had been a West End and Tin Pan Alley presence for some years, having had one of his student shows performed in the West End. *Lady At the Wheel* (Cambridge 1953; London 1958), co-written with Robin Beaumont, and with a libretto by the future novelist and screenwriter Frederick Raphael, was a Mediterranean romp in the vein of *The Boy Friend* (1953/4) or *Grab Me a Gondola* (1956), set around the Monte Carlo rally and the then-topical presence of a female British racing driver. The tone of the show is self-consciously lightweight (it includes what may well be the last ever non-ironic use of the line 'Tennis, anyone?'[7]), but the lyrics for 'We Say Oui' show a precocious fondness for globetrotting list songs and intricate rhyme-schemes:

> (Oui, oui, oui)
> We've been around
> We're widely travelled—
> We've sailed the seven seas.
> We've seen the Alps
> And we've unravelled
> The knots in the Pyrenees.
> We're hitting the heights in Europe
> Our wanderlust's hard to quench.
> The French are so warm
> We'd take them by storm—
> Except that we can't speak French.[8]

Bricusse went on to work on *Jubilee Girl* (1956) with Raphael, on *The Boy in the Corner*, an unfinished musical for Max Bygraves (for whom Bricusse had co-written the 1956 no. 18 hit 'Out of Town', winning himself an Ivor Novello Award), and as co-lyricist for the 1959 London Palladium pantomime, starring Harry Secombe as *Humpty Dumpty*. He and Newley became lifelong friends and sparring partners, beginning their collaboration with unfinished musicals based on *The Pilgrim's Progress*, the Second Coming of Christ, and—a decade before Stephen Sondheim—Ingmar Bergman's *Smiles of a Summer Night*.[9]

The pair's contrasting backgrounds and temperaments, plus the fact that each worked on both lyrics and music, make them into something of a musical theatre Lennon and McCartney. Newley was introspective, autobiographical, and sometimes melancholic (like Lennon, he grew up without a father), in contrast to the more classical, disciplined talent of Bricusse, who summed up their collaboration as one of checks and balances: 'Tony was always searching for the inner being and I did put the brakes on things sometimes when I thought they became ludicrously preachy and that we would get killed (as indeed we did more than once)'.[10] Newley said in turn that '[e]verything I know about music I owe to this man, but even he couldn't teach me how to write'.[11] It's telling that, without his collaborator, Newley's work lost this anchoring; one biographer writes of his later work that 'Newley's lyrics were, on occasion, so personal as to be utterly bewildering'.[12]

LITTLECHAP FROM BIRTH TO DEATH

In the summer of 1961, Newley was scheduled to appear in a summer season at the Brighton Hippodrome, only to be dropped when the promoter, Bernard Delfont, was offered the more saleable Max Bygraves. Newley agreed to annul his contract provided Delfont financed a new musical written by him and Bricusse, and starring himself. *Stop the World—I Want to Get Off* was written in two to four weeks,[13] and staged at the Queen's Theatre at the cost of £2,000—even then not much.

Stop the World shows the range of influences that both men (and Ian Fraser, their arranger) had been absorbing—Theatre of the Absurd, the mime of Marcel Marceau,[14] kitchen-sink films and novels, John Cranko's economical staging aesthetic, the self-referential fourth-wall breaking of *Gurney Slade*, the quest structure of the abandoned *Pilgrim's Progress*, the orchestrations of Kurt Weill and *West Side Story*. Bricusse even recycles the opening scene of *Humpty Dumpty*. As the curtain rises on Sean Kenny's circus ring set, the audience sees a gigantic egg, complete with Egg Marketing Board Lion[15]:

> *The silence is broken by an agonised female cry.*
> *The egg slowly lights from inside. It is transparent, and through it we can see the figure of* LITTLECHAP. *Slowly he flutters to life inside the egg. He gains strength and then begins to look around for a way out of the egg.*
> *The egg revolves. The back of it is open.* LITTLECHAP *toddles like a baby down the rough steps that lead from the egg. Gradually he learns to walk until he is bustling about the stage with all the exuberance of a young child.*[16]

It's clear from this non-traditional opening and symbolic use of scenery that the audience is witnessing something unusual here—the first British example of what has come to be known as a 'concept musical'. This is an easier term to use than to define, but it can broadly be described as a show where meaning is conveyed by, and cannot be separated from, the use of a specific theatrical style or convention, what Ethan Mordden calls ' a unique and thematically explanatory staging plan'.[17]

Mordden divides the birth of the concept musical into two periods. First comes the John the Baptist 1940s, when the form was invented by Rodgers and Hammerstein with the Greek-style chorus and empty stage of *Allegro* (1947), and reinforced by Kurt Weill and Alan Jay Lerner's *Love Life* (1948), with its variety interludes and never-ageing central couple. Neither of these shows was particularly successful commercially, and the form only comes into the mainstream in the 1960s, with Harold Prince's show-within-the-show framings of *Cabaret* (1966) and *Follies* (1971). *Stop the World*, the first British concept musical, is the show that bridges these two periods, with its central staging idea of the circus ring, and protagonist in unchanging white clown make-up and Marceau-style tights and braces.[18]

FIGURE 12.1 Anthony Newley in clown make-up as Littlechap, with blonde twins Jennifer (left) and Susan Baker in *Stop the World—I Want To Get Off*, July 1961.

TopPhoto. Courtesy of ArenaPal.

Stop the World, like *Allegro*, tells the story of a man's life from birth to death. Littlechap, played by Newley, is the only male character, onstage for almost the entire show, and featured in nine of its sixteen songs. There are three female characters and a chorus—the show's attitude to women can be gauged from their description as 'one blonde, one brunette, one redhead, one Slav, one Negress, one Indian and one Oriental'.[19] Staging is minimal, and interactions are presented through music: for his first job interview Littlechap 'taps timidly three times on an imaginary door, and a bad-tempered bassoon bids him enter'.[20]

Over a Shakespearean seven ages, the show takes Littlechap from office tea boy via a shotgun marriage with the boss's daughter, Evie (named after Bricusse's real-life wife, the actress Yvonne Romain), to a political career as 'Assistant Parliamentary to the Minister of Eggs and Bacon',[21] ending up as 'Lord Littlechap of Sludgepool'[22] and the winner of the 'Ignobel Prize for Outstanding Achievement in the Field of Parliamentary Doubletalk'.[23] On the way, he has affairs with Russian, German, and American women, all played by the same actress as Evie and singing a reworded version of the same song, 'Typically English'. We're told of his desire for a son: Evie only gives birth to daughters, while his one son, born to his Russian mistress Anya, dies. At the end, he realizes, Peer Gynt-style, that his true love was at home, leading to the show's biggest hit, 'What Kind Of Fool Am I?':

> What kind of clown am I?
> What do I know of life?
> Why can't I cast away
> The mask of play
> And live my life?[24]

The show originally ended with Littlechap walking off with Death as he hears the cry of his first grandson, but this was softened for the first production to faux-profundity:

> [*He draws an imaginary circle from the circus ring out into the audience.*]
>
> The wonderful thing about a circle is it's got no beginning and no end. Now, that doesn't prove anything, but it makes you think, doesn't it?
>
> [*He walks to his opening position and scratches his head as* THE CURTAIN FALLS.][25]

Stop the World remains the most successful Bricusse/Newley musical, and epitomizes both the strengths and weaknesses of their collaboration. The show combines a very 'sixties minimalism with dialogue and musical styles that draw on the music hall; the Robey-esque patter song 'Mumbo Jumbo', a teasing avoidance of swearing that suggests George Formby ('A year ago | I didn't know | Me elbow from me | —Ask just simply anyone'[26]). Littlechap is a version of Newley's established persona; Dickensian, cheeky, and Chaplinesque—Anna Quayle, who played the female lead(s) drew a parallel with one of Chaplin's forebears when she described Newley as possessing 'a Dan

Leno quality'.[27] Like Gurney Slade, he can stop the show's action, using the phrase that provides the show's title. Littlechap also incorporated features of his creator's own biography, some known to the audience, some less so—like Littlechap, Newley worked as a tea boy (or at least claimed to), was a serial philanderer, and (most remarkably) had fathered a child who died young (by his first wife, Ann Lynn). This gives certain songs an emotionalism that's rare in a male performer: 'Once In a Lifetime' and 'What Kind of a Fool Am I?' have a nakedness that's closest to that of a torch singer like Judy Garland (who recorded both the former and *The Roar of the Greasepaint*'s 'Who Can I Turn To?').

As a character, Littlechap owes something to the protagonists of the kitchen-sink novels and films of the period: like Joe Lampton in *Room at the Top* (1957, filmed 1960), he marries the boss's daughter, like Vic Brown in *A Kind of Loving* (1960), he is trapped into the marriage through an unplanned pregnancy. It also shares with many of these pieces a pre-Pill terror of female sexuality—the show depicts women as potential threats to the free-spirited male, constantly trying to entrap him through pregnancy ('Lumbered') and marriage ('Nag Nag Nag').

The innovative approach to staging and subject matter, ironically, allowed a philosophy of songwriting that was distinctly old-fashioned. Bricusse and Newley crafted songs with one eye on the pop charts, ensuring that no song was dependent on knowing its character, or dramatic context. *Stop the World* is full of take-home hits (as well as the ones already mentioned, there's the gospel-sounding 'Gonna Build a Mountain') that could attract cover versions, or be sung in cabaret. Possibly for this reason, their songs seem to stand outside the shows, in the manner that was the norm before *Oklahoma!*. All Bricusse and Newley characters, whatever their circumstances, use similar vocabulary and keep returning to the same metaphors—new days, climbing (and building) mountains, dreams and imagination, fools and clowns.

Stop the World ran fourteen months in the West End, and then decamped to Broadway, where the producer David Merrick had begun a policy of importing British hits, particularly those, like *Stop the World*, that could be staged cheaply. The show led to a US tour (with Joel Grey as Littlechap) and a film version.[28] It also established both its authors in the United States, where they both eventually settled, Bricusse as a long-time expatriate, Newley as a Las Vegas performer and one-man Rat Pack.

THE HIGH-STATUS/ LOW-STATUS DOUBLE ACT

The two reunited in 1964 for a new show which they'd been working on under the title *Mr Fat and Mr Thin*, which was described by Bricusse as 'a no man's land between a

Laurel and Hardy farce and *Waiting for Godot*.[29] The show centres round a classic high-status/low-status double act who are introduced like Beckett's Pozzo and Lucky:

> *Suddenly a bizarre sight coming over the crest of the hill sends [the chorus] scattering. The sight is of a children's boxcart being pulled by a human beast of burden. In the cart is the magnificent figure of* SIR. *The beast, almost completely enveloped by luggage of one kind or another, is* COCKY.[30]

The pair have arrived, scattering a children's chorus that included a young Elaine Paige, to play a game, the rules of which are unclear, not least because Sir can change them whenever he likes:

> For life is like cricket—we play by the rules
> And the secret, which few people know
> Which keeps men of class
> Well apart from the fools
> Is to think up the rules
> As you go.[31]

FIGURE 12.2 Anthony Newley rehearses the cast of children from *The Roar of the Greasepaint, the Smell of the Crowd*, April 1966.

Photograph provided by editors.

Cocky continues losing various forms of the game throughout the first half. In the second, there appears '*a young serious NEGRO*':

SIR   I say, haven't we met before?
NEGRO   I don't know, you all look alike to me.[32]

The Negro joins in the game and wins, leading Cocky to challenge his master:

SIR   You forget that I'm in charge of this game.
COCKY   Only because you said so![33]

Cocky plays the game and wins, leading to him declaring a new status quo: 'In future, posh upper-class players will stop pushing other poor bastard players about. Otherwise, they may find themselves playing with themselves.'[34] The show ends with an uneasy truce, as the duo exeunt the way that they came:

> *When they get to the stage right ramp, SIR wants them to turn off and go in that direction. COCKY wants to go towards stage left. They start bickering, but COCKY seems to be getting his way. The sun has by now set, the stars are out, the day is over, the last we see of SIR and COCKY is their silhouette against the setting sun, in a pose, arguing.*[35]

This synopsis doesn't really do justice to the sheer strangeness of the show, but it should make clear that this is the closest Newley and Bricusse ever came to writing about politics. Sir is a public-school patrician, quoting Latin tags (which Cocky mistranslates) and using tradition to justify his control of Cocky. One sequence suggests that religion is, indeed, the opium of the people:

> *COCKY now begins to remove his many good luck charms, religious symbols etc. one by one. Each has a string, each gets put around his neck. First a wishbone, then a four-leaf clover, a rabbit's foot, a horseshoe, an Anglican cross, an Eastern crescent, a Catholic crucifix and a star of David.*
> [. . .]

SIR   [I]t's not every man who has your faith, Cocky.
COCKY   It's not every man who needs it, sir.[36]

The game is frequently described in terms suggesting a theatrical production, hence the show's title. The musical sometimes seems like a show that's fundamentally about its own writing, and the class divide between its creators—'Cocky', after all, is an accurate description of Newley's stage persona, as well as being only one consonant away from 'cockney'. The writers even reference an earlier show about social divisions as Sir observes 'It's "Aow! Garn!" that keep her in her place. | But that's another story altogether.'[37]

Racial politics also reflect the critique of class, with Cocky's rebellion inspired by that of the Negro, played in the first production by the British/Guyanese calypso singer Cy Grant. His song of emancipation, 'Feeling Good', is the Bricusse/Newley song that has travelled furthest from its origins, becoming, like 'Ol' Man River' and 'Strange Fruit', one of the select group of black anthems written by white people. Nina Simone's 1965 cover version quickly became the standard, incidentally giving it an association with the civil rights movement.[38]

As well as 'Feeling Good', the show includes many of the pair's best-known songs, 'A Wonderful Day Like Today', 'Who Can I Turn To?' (like 'What Kind of Fool Am I?' an eleven o'clock number based round a rhetorical question), and 'The Joker', another of Newley's overwrought, possibly autobiographical ballads:

> There's always a funny man
> In the game
> But he's only funny by mistake
> But everyone laughs at him
> Just the same
> They don't see his painted heart break.[39]

The Roar of the Greasepaint sums up the paradox of Bricusse/Newley—a deathless score stuck within a book that manages to be simultaneously pretentious and twee. The original British production, with Willoughby Goddard as Sir and Norman Wisdom as Cocky, closed before coming to London; on Broadway, with Newley bowing to the inevitable and taking the latter part himself, it fared a little better. The show wasn't seen in London until a 2011 production at the intimate Finborough Theatre, when Lyn Gardner in *The Guardian* described it as 'hover[ing] uneasily between the facetious and the winsome'.[40]

THE DEVIL MEETS GOD

The two men didn't collaborate for another seven years. Bricusse wrote for several troubled screen musicals—*Goodbye, Mr. Chips* (1969), *Scrooge* (1970), and *Doctor Dolittle* (1967), which includes, in 'Talk to the Animals', the only really successful character song either man ever wrote.[41] Newley co-wrote (with Herbert Kretzmer), directed, and starred in *Can Hieronymous Merkin Forget Mercy Humppe and Find True Happiness* (1969), a film about the making of a film which is either Fellini-esque or grotesquely self-indulgent, depending on the critic's degree of tolerance. Newley here takes his autobiographical tendencies to new extremes, casting his own daughters and then-wife Joan Collins—the latter as Merkin's second wife, Polyester Poontang—and even including a witty self-criticism: 'Oh, I dunno. I've always liked the chap's work. A lot of it is scatological and loosely put together. But it's fun and the *music* is nice.'[42]

The two men re-established their collaboration on-screen, writing the songs for *Willy Wonka and the Chocolate Factory* (1971); by this time they lived so far apart that they communicated by letter and telephone, never actually meeting face-to-face. The score isn't one of their best—Henry Blinder wrote that '[w]hen [the songs] come on, children in the audience inevitably take the opportunity to run up and down the aisles',[43] though it does include two take-home hits in 'Pure Imagination' which was judged so integral to the story that it was inserted into the 2013 stage adaptation by Marc Shaiman and Scott Wittman, and 'The Candy Man', which became a US Number 1 for Newley's friend Sammy Davis, Jr.[44]

The pair's final stage collaboration, *The Good Old Bad Old Days* (1972), originally entitled *It's a Funny Old World That We Live In—But the World's Not Entirely to Blame*, was described by Bricusse as 'a modest little saga about Man, Life, Death, God and the Devil, with the history of the world thrown in (nothing pretentious!)'.[45] Newley, speaking before the show opened, was a little more forthcoming:

> This is not a religious musical. The story is of a meeting between the Devil (Bubba) and God (Gramps) at which God says he is fed up with Man. The Devil turns advocate for Man and says that humanity is more the victim than the criminal. There are a lot of heavy questions raised during the piece in a very Light Comedy way, which we wouldn't even pretend to know the answers to [. . .] It's a pantomime, really, for grown-ups.[46]

If *Stop the World* drew on *Peer Gynt* and *The Roar of the Greasepaint* on *Waiting for Godot*, the model for the new show seemed to be either Shaw's *Back to Methuselah* or, closer to home, Irwin Allen's film *The Story of Mankind* (1957), in which a loose series of historical vignettes are linked by a debate between God and the Devil (played by Ronald Colman and Vincent Price) over the continued existence of mankind. *The Good Old Bad Old Days* borrows this structure, with the significant difference that, in this case, it's the Devil (or Bubba), played by Newley, who is humanity's advocate.

Again, the tone is set by the opening moments—Bubba surveys a collage of newspaper headlines showing 'murder, rape, violence, war, bloodshed, hijackings, genocide, earthquakes, droughts, famines, sexual aberations [sic]' and remarks: 'Isn't it wonderful to see people enjoying themselves?'[47]

The suggestion that sexual aberrations (however you spell them) are morally equivalent to war and genocide gives some indication of how out of touch the writers were with the zeitgeist. That they were also out of touch with their own skill is suggested by the show's only big hit, the title song:

> Seems to me
> You're either out or you're in!
> You lose or you win!
> In these sad old glad old days!
> You're poor or you're rich

> Who knows which is which
> Anyways?
> We're living on time
> We're having to borrow!
> No one knows if we will live
> To see tomorrow!
> Nevertheless
> I guess we have to confess
> These are the good old bad old days![48]

It's difficult to imagine a younger version of either writer (especially the fastidious Bricusse, who complained when a censor made him change the lyrics in 'What Kind of Fool Am I?' from 'Till I don't give a damn' to 'Like any other man', because it created a false rhyme with 'am'[49]) being satisfied with the awkward inversion of 'living on time | We're having to borrow', or the sheer desperation of 'Who knows which is which | Anyways?'—surely the answer is 'Almost everybody'?

The structure allows scenes set in ancient Rome, the Dark Ages, Shakespearean England,[50] the courts of Louis XIV and Napoleon, the American Civil War, with an ironic minstrel-show celebration of 'nigger-lynching',[51] and Bubba's star witness, the twentieth century, including the Wright brothers[52] and—in a moment that owes a lot to *Oh What a Lovely War*—the Battle of the Somme.[53]

On the way, we get a few glimpses of Newley/Bricusse philosophy, as when Bubba paraphrases Feste:

GRAMPS   Tell, me Jester, why are men fools?
BUBBA   Oh, that's easy, sir. Because they believe themselves to be wise.
GRAMPS   Are no men wise?
BUBBA   Oh yes, sir. But only them as plays the fool.[54]

There's even a touch of Gnostic theology, as Bubba reveals himself to be Gramps's son, incubated by Eve, and then questions his own existence:

So one night, while she was sleeping, I slithered into Eve's sweet womb, and clung there like a leech until she gave me life! I was Eve's first-born, not Cain! And that's why there's a little bit of the Devil in all of you! [. . .]

[*To* GRAMPS]

You know as well as I do that *Man* created *you*! And me! We only exist in his Imagination! He only created you because he was scared, and he created me because he wanted to have a good time! You don't think that's funny?[55]

Like Cocky and Sir, Bubba and Gramps finally decide to leave the matter unsettled, going off for a holiday together.

As before, the show is tailored heavily towards its star/co-writer—Bubba is in ten of the sixteen songs—and this show suffers from it. Newley's singing voice was showing the strain of cabaret performance and an overindulgent lifestyle, and his stage persona was beginning to take on the quality of self-parody; Ian Fraser said that 'if Anthony Newley entered an Anthony Newley impersonation contest, he would come in third'.[56]

This awkward, unfocused show would probably have failed at any time. In a West End that had recently seen the opening of *Jesus Christ Superstar* (1972), it was a dinosaur. Critics were especially harsh on its attempted profundity, the reviewer from *The Times* speaking for many:

> To fortunate clowns like Charlie Chaplin it only occurs late in life that they have a message for the world. Anthony Newley contracted this delusion at an early age on *Stop the World—I Want to Get Off* and in the ten years since his last appearance on the London stage this malady has spread to the terminal state visible in this unspeakable musical.[57]

Newley vowed that it would be 'no more books for Bricusse and Newley. From now on, it's just the scores'.[58] The two men worked on a dull television version of *Peter Pan* (1976), their last completed collaboration, and an unstaged musical about Jack the Ripper. Newley co-wrote (with television scriptwriter Stanley Ralph Ross) and starred in *Chaplin* (1982), a notorious flop that closed before its planned Broadway opening. He also worked at various times on musicals based on the story of Napoleon and Josephine (intended as a vehicle for himself and Shirley Bassey, and later Barbra Streisand, with whom he was having an affair[59]), *Around the World in Eighty Days* (collaborating again with Herbert Kretzmer), and *Richard III*, a show that he and his collaborator Mike McKenzie referred to as *Hump!*.[60] His last years, before his death in 1999, were characterized by a number of false starts and misguided acting roles, and a return to the musical stage as a performer, including a 1989 revival of *Stop the World* which led even Ian Fraser, the show's original orchestrator, to acknowledge that it was now 'a period piece'.[61] Fittingly, one of his last stage appearances was in the title role of Bricusse's show *Scrooge* in 1996.

BRICUSSE WITHOUT NEWLEY: *PICKWICK* AND AFTER

Throughout all of their work neither man ever showed an aptitude for (or even much interest in) creating characters through music—Newley always wrote for a version of himself, while Bricusse preferred to hitch a lift on characters who were already iconic.[62] Bricusse's most successful show in this vein was *Pickwick* (1963), part of the Dickensian feeding frenzy that followed the success of *Oliver!* (1960), even using that show's director and designer, Peter Coe and Sean Kenny. The idea for *Pickwick* originated with its star, Harry Secombe. The actor/singer suggested it to its adaptor, Wolf Mankowitz, and producer, Bernard Delfont, who reunited the *Humpty Dumpty* team of Bricusse and Cyril Ornadel.

All adaptors of *The Pickwick Papers* need to find a way through the episodic narrative of the original book (it's misleading to call it a novel). Noel Langley's 1952 film finds a through-line in Pickwick's battles with the Machiavellian Jingle. Mankowitz, more charitably, locates it in friendship rather than rivalry, structuring his show round the title character's double-act with his valet/coachman, Sam Weller, who announces the show's debt to *Oliver!* with his Artful Dodger-ish 'I am' song, 'Talk'. Bricusse and Ornadel base one song on street cries, à la 'Who Will Buy?' and borrow the atmosphere of *A Christmas Carol* by setting Pickwick and Sam's first meeting at Christmas. Pickwick even quotes that novella's street urchin, referring to 'Turkeys bigger than I am'.[63]

Compared to *Oliver!*, this is a much lighter, less troubled story, albeit one that's told in flashback from a debtor's prison, where Pickwick has been incarcerated after losing a trial for breach of promise. The paper-thin plot is an excuse for theatrical effects—Pickwick skating and falling through the ice (the first act curtain)—and comic turns, like Peter Bull's second act appearance as the prosecutor Sergeant Buzfuz, whose role is limited to a single scene for a two-page speech. Again, the take-home hit was one that could be detached from its context—'If I Ruled the World' (perhaps the most un-Dickensian sentiment that could be imagined[64]) is associated more with its star Harry Secombe than its character.

Pickwick ran for eighteen months in the West End before going to Broadway, where it failed to imitate the success of either *Oliver!* or *Stop the World*, closing after fifty-six performances. It still made a small profit, thanks to a long pre-New York tour—it was rumoured that David Merrick used this show as a bargaining chip for theatres seeking preferential bookings for his blockbuster of the same time, *Hello, Dolly!*.[65]

Sean Kenny's adaptable set was described by his director as resembling 'children's blocks that fit together in various ways',[66] and that's the key—this is a world of childhood, where characters are defined by their gangs, and nothing is to be taken too seriously. It's also very much a male world, in which female entrapment is something to be avoided, and the important relationships are between men—*Pickwick* must be the only musical (apart from drag shows) in which every single song is written for a male lead vocal.

Bricusse's fixation with commitment-phobic men[67] reached some kind of climax in *Kings and Clowns* (1978), a project that had first been mooted in 1971, under the title *Great Harry!*,[68] and which made it to the stage with Frank Finlay miscast as Henry VIII. The show is narrated by another of Bricusse's wise fools, in this case Will Somers, the King's real-life jester, who sets the show's tone (and level of invention) with his opening song:

> Kings and Clowns—Kings and Clowns
> The magic world of Kings and Clowns.
> Like yours, it's full of ups and downs,
> Fate and smiles and frowns, Of Kings and Clowns[69]

At times the uxoricidal monarch sounds rather like Littlechap ('I wanted a son. A man is entitled, surely, to his one small piece of immortality'[70]) and at other times like a saloon-bar bore ('Before I went into the marriage business, my life was filled to overflowing with wonderful, loyal, devoted, true friends—men'[71]). The vein of misogyny that had been present in Bricusse's work since *Stop the World*'s 'Nag, Nag, Nag', is back, to an almost unbelievable extent—at one point Anne Boleyn says 'EVERY woman is a bitch. Some of them just never get a chance to prove it, that's all'[72]—and is accompanied by some of his more lackadaisical lyrics:

> There was a young Henry named Tudor
> When he saw a woman he wooed her
> [.......]
> He prayed for a son to succeed him
> And that was the passion that keyed him.[73]

The show's closing, after a month, was followed soon after by that of *The Travelling Music Show* (1978), a Newley/Bricusse songbook show starring Bruce Forsyth and Derek Griffiths.

Bricusse's most commercially successful show has never been seen in the West End, where it might feel a little like coals to Newcastle. *Jekyll and Hyde* (1997), with music by Frank Wildhorn, is a Broadway version of a Lloyd Webber-ish megamusical. Its take-home hit 'This is the Moment' (a sentiment that long-time Bricusse fans would recognize from *Stop the World*'s 'Once in a Lifetime') was frequently played at what Jessica Sternfeld refers to as 'such anthem-friendly contexts as the Miss America pageant, the Olympics and the 1996 Democratic National Convention'.[74] As Sternfeld waspishly comments, the very non-specificity of the lyric was what made it so ubiquitous; unlike 'Memory' (too literary) or 'Don't Cry For Me, Argentina' (too locked into its dramatic source), 'This is the Moment' boasted rather general inspirational lyrics and no bitter-ness and irony, and so was a ready-made hit'.[75] The show ran for 1,543 performances on Broadway, where it attracted its own group of cult followers, called 'Jekkies'.

Much of Bricusse's recent work has focused on properties that would seem to have lit-tle to gain from musicalization, such as *Kennedy* (2013, first seen as *One Shining Moment*, 1983, co-written with Allan Jay Friedman) and *Cyrano de Bergerac* (an ongoing col-laboration with Wildhorn, first staged in Tokyo, 2009). *The Revenge of Sherlock Holmes* (1988) may seem, at first glance, to be part of this tendency, but is actually a spoof—it shares its central premise (the villain turns out to be Moriarty's daughter) with Charles Marowitz's 1987 Broadway hit *Sherlock's Last Case*. Characteristically, Bricusse included a song, 'London is London', that was recycled from the film *Goodbye, Mr. Chips*.

Bricusse also wrote a number of stage versions of his less successful films. *Goodbye, Mr. Chips*, staged in 1982 at Chichester Theatre, proved irredeemable, while *Doctor Dolittle* (1998) enjoyed a long run at the too-large Hammersmith Apollo, largely on the strength of its star (Phillip Schofield) and over a hundred animatronic animals provided by the Jim Henson creature shop. *Scrooge* (1992) actually improved on the film version, with Bricusse adding new songs for each revision, and doubling Isabel, Scrooge's lost love, with Helen, his nephew's wife, adding a wistful quality to Scrooge's backstory.

The legacy of Bricusse and Newley is not easy to assess. *Stop the World—I Want to Get Off*, though probably unstageable now (if only for its sexual politics), is an important show historically, as the first commercially successful concept musical. Its staging techniques anticipate those of *Cabaret* and *Company* (1970)—another show about a commitment-phobic male—and its rough-and-ready aesthetic was to prove influential on early rock musicals like *Hair* (1967/8) and *Godspell* (1971), which even used the clown make-up. The Bricusse/Newley back catalogue still inspires cover versions, and the lyrics turn up in odd places—the line 'What kind of fool am I?' was used by Neil Bartlett in his 1990 National Theatre translation of *Bérénice* by the seventeenth-century French playwright Jean Racine,[76] while the near-quote 'stop the world and let me off' appears in the play-within-the-play in Anna Washburn's *Mr Burns*.[77] Newley remains alive in pop culture—as I write this, British cabaret star Lenny Beige is touring a one-man show about him. Bricusse, a more controlled and conventional talent, is a difficult writer to like—there's a quality of calculation to even his best work, with its focus on pre-sold properties and deliberately non-specific lyrics, though its commercial success is undeniable. As with many British writers of musicals, Newley and Bricusse in the end are more interesting for their potential than what they actually achieved.

Notes

1. Quoted in Garth Bardsley, *Stop the World … The Biography of Anthony Newley* (London: Oberon Books, 2003), 32.
2. Bob Stanley, *Yeah Yeah Yeah: The Story of Modern Pop* (London: Faber and Faber, 2013), 75.
3. This track can be found on the album *The Best of Bond*, 30th Anniversary Limited Edition, EMI Records USA, 0777 7 98413 25, 1992 or on YouTube. According to Dylan Jones, who describes it as 'supremely arch', this version 'was considered too camp for inclusion in the movie, so the producers opted for the more strident Shirley Bassey'. Dylan Jones, *Easy! The Lexicon of Lounge* (London: Pavilion Books Ltd, 1997), 99.
4. Tise Vahimagi (ed.), *British Television: An Illustrated Guide* (Oxford: Oxford University Press, 1994), 96.
5. Charles Shaar Murray, 'Interview', *New Musical Express*, 24 February 1973, quoted in Dick Fiddy, DVD Notes, *The Strange World of Gurney Slade*, DVD, Network, No. 7953388, 2011, 3.
6. Leslie Bricusse, *The Music Man: The Life and Good Times of a Songwriter* (London: Metro Publishing, 2006), 177.
7. Leslie Bricusse and Robin Beaumont. *Lady at the Wheel*, Act 1, Scene 3, Typescript 1958, Lord Chamberlain's Plays, British Library, p. 3.
8. Bricusse and Beaumont, *Lady at the Wheel*, no page number. Bricusse reused the opening line of the chorus in 'Never Seen Anything like It' from *Dr Dolittle*.
9. The two men referenced the director in their nicknames for each other, Newberg and Brickman.
10. Quoted in Bardsley, *Stop the World*, 82.

11. Quoted in Bardsley, *Stop the World*, 204.

12. Bardsley, *Stop the World*, 173.

13. Most accounts, including Bardsley, say two weeks, but Newley himself, when he appeared on *This Is Your Life*, said that it was four. The original typescript, among the Lord Chamberlain's Plays in the British Library, also shows that the two men carried on revising it for another two months. It also gives the title as *Stop the World, I* Wanna *Get Off*.

14. Kenneth Tynan, in a generally damning review, was especially harsh on the Marceau-inspired opening: 'When he spoke, one was startled; it was like being present at a miracle cure.' Kenneth Tynan, *Tynan Right and Left* (London: Longmans, Green and Co., 1967), 80.

15. Between 1956 and 1971, all eggs produced in Britain were sold through a governmental organization called the Egg Marketing Board, which stamped them with a small lion logo as a guarantee of quality. The board was responsible for the famous slogan 'Go to work on an egg.'

16. Anthony Newley and Leslie Bricusse, *Stop the World, I Wanna Get Off*, Act 1, p. 1, Typescript 1961, Lord Chamberlain's Plays, British Library.

17. Ethan Mordden, *Rodgers and Hammerstein* (New York: Harry N. Abrams Inc., 1992), 96.

18. Newley was initially resistant; 'Sean, you're not going to put me in whiteface. Man as a clown is the oldest, dullest gag in show business.' Quoted in Bardsley, *Stop the World*, 86. His attitude seems a little churlish here, given that Kenny was presumably inspired by the line 'What kind of clown am I?'

19. Newley and Bricusse, *Stop the World*, Act 1, p. 1.

20. Newley and Bricusse, *Stop the World*, Act 1, p. 1.

21. Newley and Bricusse, *Stop the World*, Act 2, Scene 1, p. 8.

22. Newley and Bricusse, *Stop the World*, Act 2, Scene 2, p. 13.

23. Newley and Bricusse, *Stop the World*, Act 2, Scene 2, p. 14.

24. Newley and Bricusse, *Stop the World*, Act 2, Scene 3, p. 20.

25. Newley and Bricusse, *Stop the World*, no page number.

26. Newley and Bricusse, *Stop the World*, Act 1, p. 3. Bricusse and Newley repeated this joke in the song 'Where Would You Be Without Me?', in Anthony Newley and Leslie Bricusse, *The Roar of the Greasepaint, the Smell of the Crowd*, Act 1, p. 35, Typescript 2001, Finborough Theatre Archive.

27. Quoted in Bardsley, *Stop the World*, 88.

28. The film version, directed by television director Philip Saville, was released in 1966, and featured Tony Tanner, in his one major film role, imitating Newley's vocal mannerisms as Littlechap. The film is a strangely subdued affair; filmed onstage at the Lyric Theatre, Hammersmith, with hardly any concession to the medium, it's mainly of interest as a record of the original staging.

29. Bricusse, *Music Man*, 125.

30. Newley and Bricusse, *Roar of the Greasepaint*, Act 1, p. 1.

31. Newley and Bricusse, *Roar of the Greasepaint*, Act 1, p. 20.

32. Newley and Bricusse, *Roar of the Greasepaint*, Act 2, p. 13.

33. Newley and Bricusse, *Roar of the Greasepaint*, Act 2, p. 28.

34. Newley and Bricusse, *Roar of the Greasepaint*, Act 2, p. 22.

35. Newley and Bricusse, *Roar of the Greasepaint*, Act 2, p. 37.

36. Newley and Bricusse, *Roar of the Greasepaint*, Act 1, p. 15.

37. Newley and Bricusse, *Roar of the Greasepaint*, Act 1, p. 19.

38. When George Michael covered the song on his 2014 live album *Symphonica*, it was as a soul classic rather than a show tune written by two white Englishmen, one an East Ender, one a Cambridge graduate—he even said onstage: 'It's too much to expect a white man to do it like Nina.' Quoted in Caroline Sullivan, Review of *Symphonica, The Guardian*, 14 March 2014, G2/23.

39. Newley and Bricusse, *Roar of the Greasepaint*, Act 1, p. 47.

40. Lyn Gardner, Review of *The Road of the Greasepaint, the Smell of the Crowd, The Guardian*, 14 June 2011. http://www.theguardian.com/stage/2011/jun/14/the-roar-of-the-greasepaint-review, accessed 20 May 2014.

41. Bricusse wrote this song as his audition for the film's star, Rex Harrison, and drew on the persona that the actor (and Alan Jay Lerner) had created for *My Fair Lady*. Bricusse writes in his autobiography that 'To this day, I am not sure whether I wrote that song for Doctor Dolittle or for Henry Higgins, but, since they were both Rex Harrison, it didn't much matter'. Bricusse, *Music Man*, 163. This remark perhaps says rather more than Bricusse intended about his attitude to character.

42. Quoted in Bardsley, *Stop the World*, 139.

43. Henry Blinder, 'Willy Wonka and the Chocolate Factory', in Danny Peary, *Cult Movies 2* (London; Vermilion, 1984), 169.

44. Newley reportedly disliked Aubrey Woods's performance of this song in the film so much that he offered to play the part himself without a fee. See Fred Bronson, *The Billboard Book of USA Number One Hits* (New York; Billboard Publications, Inc., 1988), 313.

45. Quoted in Bardsley, *Stop the World*, 159.

46. Quoted in Bardsley, *Stop the World*, 165.

47. Anthony Newley and Leslie Bricusse, *The Good Old, Bad Old Days*, Act 1, p. 1, Typescript 1972, British Library Manuscripts Collection.

48. Newley and Bricusse, *Good Old, Bad Old Days*, Act 1, p. 2.

49. Bardsley, *Stop the World*, 87.

50. One character, witnessing an offstage performance of *Twelfth Night*, says 'Twelfth Night? He'll be lucky if he has a *second* night!'

51. The satirical television show *That Was the Week That Was* had done this better a decade earlier, in a number written by Newley collaborator Herbert Kretzmer. See Humphrey Carpenter, *That Was Satire That Was: The Satire Boom of the 1960s* (London: Victor Gollancz, 2000), 255.

52. Another very typical joke: 'Let's hope two Wrights don't make a wrong!' Newley and Bricusse, *Good Old, Bad Old Days*, Act 2, p. 20.

53. '[S]ixty thousand men a day sacrificed to the great God of War! And they say show business is dead! They certainly don't write them like *that* any more!' Newley and Bricusse, *Good Old, Bad Old Days*, Act 2, p. 28. The same figure is quoted in *Oh What a Lovely War*, although this may just indicate that the two sets of writers used the same sources. See Theatre Workshop, Charles Chilton, and Members of the original cast, *Oh What a Lovely War* (London; Methuen and Co. Ltd, 1965).

54. Newley and Bricusse, *Good Old, Bad Old Days*, Act 1, p. 22.

55. Newley and Bricusse, *Good Old, Bad Old Days*, Act 2, pp. 23–25.

56. Quoted in Bardsley, *Stop the World*, 178.

57. Quoted in Kurt Gänzl, *The British Musical Theatre* (London: Macmillan, 1986), 2: 950.

58. Quoted in Bardsley, *Stop the World*, 163.

59. Newley seems to have felt an especial fascination with the character of Napoleon; as well as featuring in *The Good Old, Bad Old Days*, he is mentioned in the dialogue of *The Roar of the Greasepaint, the Smell of the Crowd* (Act 1, p. 44).

60. This, together with the Jack the Ripper musical, means that, in later life, Newley worked on the same ideas for musicals as both sets of comic characters in the films *This Is Spinal Tap* (1984) ('Saucy Jack') and *The Tall Guy* (1989) ('Got a Hunch That I'm Gonna Be King').

61. Quoted in Bardsley, *Stop the World*, 204.

62. I don't mean simply that he preferred to adapt existing works, more that he didn't add anything to them. Whereas Bart's Fagin and Bond/Wheeler/Sondheim's Sweeney Todd are new variations on an existing character, Bricusse leaves Pickwick, Cyrano de Bergerac, and Sherlock Holmes exactly as he found them.

63. Wolf Mankowitz, Leslie Bricusse, and Cyril Ornadel, *Pickwick* (London: Samuel French Ltd, 1991), 9.

64. 'His [Dickens's] radicalism is of the shallowest kind and yet one always knows that it is there. That is the difference between being a moralist and a politician. He has no constructive suggestions, nor even a clear grasp of the nature of the society he is attacking, only an emotional perception that something is wrong [. . .]. What he is against is not this or that institution, but as Chesterton put it "an expression on the human face".' George Orwell, 'Charles Dickens', in *The Penguin Essays of George Orwell* (Harmondsworth: Penguin, 1984), 81.

65. Steven Suskin, *Second Act Trouble: Behind the Scenes at Broadway's Big Musical Bombs* (New York: Applause, 2006), 287.

66. Introduction to Mankowitz, Bricusse, and Ornadel, *Pickwick*, no page number.

67. Bricusse shares this fixation with Alan Jay Lerner, though, unlike Lerner's, his doesn't seem to be reflected in his own life—where Lerner had eight wives, Bricusse has been married to the same woman since 1958.

68. Bricusse had actually discussed a Henry VIII musical years earlier, as a possible collaboration with Richard Rodgers, but their idea foundered on Bricusse's commitments to *Doctor Dolittle*. Rodgers later wrote his own unsuccessful show on the subject, *Rex* (1979), in collaboration with Sheldon Harnick, and with an equally inappropriate star in Nicol Williamson.

69. Leslie Bricusse, *Kings and Clowns*, Act 1, Typescript 1978, British Library Manuscripts Collection, p. 1.

70. Bricusse, *Kings and Clowns*, Act 1, p. 8.

71. Bricusse, *Kings and Clowns*, Act 1, p. 3.

72. Bricusse, *Kings and Clowns*, Act 2, p. 6. Capital letters in the original.

73. Bricusse, *Kings and Clowns*, Act 1, p. 2.

74. Jessica Sternfeld, *The Megamusical* (Bloomington, IN: Indiana University Press, 2006), 313.

75. Sternfeld, *Megamusical*, 313.

76. Neil Bartlett, *Bérénice, Le Misanthrope, The School for Wives* (Bath: Absolute Classics, 1990), 41.

77. Anna Washburn, *Mr. Burns* (London: Oberon Books, 2014), 47.

BIBLIOGRAPHY

Bardsley, Garth. Stop the World ... The Biography of Anthony Newley. London: Oberon Books, 2003.

Bartlett, Neil. Bérénice, Le Misanthrope, The School for Wives. Bath: Absolute Classics, 1990.

Blinder, Henry. 'Willy Wonka and the Chocolate Factory.' In Danny Peary, Cult Movies 2, 167–169. London: Vermilion, 1984.

Bricusse, Leslie. Kings and Clowns. Typescript, 1978. British Library Manuscripts Collection.

Bricusse, Leslie. The Music Man: The Life and Good Times of a Songwriter. London: Metro Publishing, 2006.

Bricusse, Leslie. The Revenge of Sherlock Holmes. London: Samuel French, 1994.

Bricusse, Leslie. Scrooge: The Musical. London: Samuel French, 2008.

Bricusse, Leslie, et al. Humpty Dumpty. Typescript, 1959. Lord Chamberlain's Plays, British Library. LCP 1959/58.

Bricusse, Leslie, Robin Beaumont, and Frederick Raphael. Lady at the Wheel. Typescript, 1958. Lord Chamberlain's Plays, British Library. LCP 1953/60.

Bronson, Fred. The Billboard Book of USA Number One Hits. New York: Billboard Publications, Inc., 1988.

Carpenter, Humphrey. That Was Satire That Was: The Satire Boom of the 1960s. London: Victor Gollancz, 2000.

Fiddy, Dick. DVD Notes. The Strange World of Gurney Slade. DVD. Network, No. 7953388, 2011.

Gänzl, Kurt. The British Musical Theatre, 2 vols. London: Macmillan, 1986.

Gardner, Lyn. Review of The Roar of the Greasepaint, the Smell of the Crowd. The Guardian, 14 June 2011. http://www.theguardian.com/stage/2011/jun/14/the-roar-of-the-greasepaint-review, accessed 20 May 2014.

Jones, Dylan. Easy! The Lexicon of Lounge. London: Pavilion Books Ltd, 1997.

Mandelbaum, Ken. Not Since Carrie: Forty Years of Broadway Musical Flops. New York: St Martin's Press, 1991.

Mankowitz, Wolf, Leslie Bricusse, and Cyril Ornadel. Pickwick. London: Samuel French Ltd, 1991.

Marowitz, Charles. Potboilers: Three Black Comedies. New York: Marion Boyars, 1986.

Mordden, Ethan. Open a New Window: The Broadway Musical in the Sixties. New York: Palgrave, 2001.

Mordden, Ethan. Rodgers and Hammerstein. New York: Harry N. Abrams Inc., 1992.

Morley, Sheridan. Spread a Little Happiness: The First Hundred Years of the British Musical. New York: Thames and Hudson, 1987.

Newley, Anthony, and Leslie Bricusse. The Good Old Bad Old Days. Typescript, 1972. British Library Manuscripts Collection.

Newley, Anthony, and Leslie Bricusse. The Roar of the Greasepaint, the Smell of the Crowd. Typescript, 2011. Finborough Theatre Archive.

Newley, Anthony, and Leslie Bricusse. Stop the World, I Wanna Get Off. Typescript, 1961. Lord Chamberlain's Plays, British Library. LCP 1961/31.

Orwell, George. 'Charles Dickens.' In The Penguin Essays of George Orwell, 35–77. Harmondsworth: Penguin, 1984.

Stanley, Bob. Yeah Yeah Yeah: The Story of Modern Pop. London: Faber and Faber, 2013.

Sternfeld, Jessica. The Megamusical. Bloomington, IN: Indiana University Press, 2006.

Sullivan, Caroline Review of Symphonica. The Guardian, 14 March 2014, G2 and G23.

Suskin, Steven. *Second Act Trouble: Behind the Scenes at Broadway's Big Musical Bombs.* New York: Applause, 2006.

Theatre Workshop, Charles Chilton, and Members of the Original Cast. *Oh What a Lovely War.* London: Methuen and Co. Ltd, 1965.

Tynan, Kenneth. *Tynan Right and Left.* London: Longmans, Green and Co., 1967.

Vahimagi, Tise, ed., *British Television: An Illustrated Guide.* Oxford: Oxford University Press, 1994.

Washburn, Anna. *Mr. Burns.* London: Oberon Books, 2014.

Wright, Adrian. *A Tanner's Worth of Tune: Rediscovering the Post-War British Musical.* Woodbridge: The Boydell Press, 2010.

CHAPTER 13

....

THE POP-MUSIC INDUSTRY AND THE BRITISH MUSICAL

....

IAN SAPIRO

DISCUSSIONS of the relationship between musical theatre and the pop-music industry tend to focus on pop- and rock-influenced stage works, particularly *Hair* (1967) and the 'rock musicals' that followed it through the 1970s. Andrew Lloyd Webber and Tim Rice's *Jesus Christ Superstar* (1970) is usually included, often as the sole British contribution, and is almost always singled out as deriving from a 'concept album'.[1] While there is little doubt that *Superstar* is the best-known work to fall into both of these categories, it is by no means the only British rock opera produced in the years following *Hair*; nor can *Hair* necessarily take sole credit for the formulation of the rock opera genre. Close links between theatre (and film) and the British pop-music industry reach back into the 1950s when performers like Tommy Steele and composers such as Lionel Bart and John Barry first started in the music industry, and the Beatles' album *Sgt Pepper's Lonely Hearts Club Band*—which, like *Hair*, dates from 1967—was a natural development of the band's musical films from the mid-1960s. The album was produced at a time when British artists were starting to see the potential of the LP to realize longer and more interconnected songs and projects, and such experiments in pop music ran parallel with attempts in theatre to move away from a reliance on narrative linearity and make increased use of technology to generate spectacle.[2] Taken together, these developments led to the formulation of what became known as the concept album, with those containing narratives (no matter how weak) termed 'rock operas'.

This chapter considers a sample of works from across the genre to explore this aspect of the relationship between the pop-music industry and the British musical. The chapter begins with a detailed investigation of the rock operas *Tommy* (1969) and *Jesus Christ Superstar*, followed by consideration of the stage and screen adaptations of these works in the years following their releases. Finally, the discussion focuses on *Jeff Wayne's Musical Version of the War of the Worlds* (1978) and Mike Batt's *The Hunting of the Snark* (1984), works that have received little scholarly attention, examining the musico-narrative structures and processes evident in each and, briefly, their reception and legacies.

Rock Messiahs: *Tommy* and *Jesus Christ Superstar*

Conceived by Pete Townshend in 1968 and produced the following year, *Tommy* was the Who's first full-length concept album. It has a narrative premise and a synopsis was published following the album's release, but the lack of any spoken dialogue between or during the musical numbers and the decision to have all the characters voiced by Townshend, Roger Daltrey, and John Entwistle creates an ambiguity about precisely how and why the story proceeds as it does. The creation of the album is perhaps at least partially responsible for this effect, since Townshend wrote several of the songs before the concept itself came into being, and, as Richard Barnes explains in his sleeve notes for the CD reissue of the album, 'songs were written, changed, dropped and old ones slotted in' as the project took shape.[3] By contrast, Lloyd Webber and Rice turned to the concept album for *Jesus Christ Superstar* having failed to secure financial backing for a stage production.[4] However, despite the change of medium the concept remained the starting point for the creators, and while Lloyd Webber may have turned to his back catalogue for some parts of the project, most of the material in *Superstar* was written explicitly for the album. Accordingly, there is a much clearer narrative structure behind the work, though this is also helped by the use of an existing story (albeit with significant dramatic licence being taken in places). Additionally, since there was never any intention that *Superstar* would be performed by its creators, the album features a much wider range of voices, with each character played by a different singer and no principal singer taking on more than one role.

Since *Tommy* and *Superstar* are both narrative works, the description 'rock opera' is not entirely inappropriate, but one clearly leans more towards rock and the other towards opera. Townshend views *Tommy* as 'the prime example of Rock and Roll throwing off its three-chord musical structure, discarding its attachment to the three-minute single [. . .] and yet hanging grimly on to the old ways at the same time', though quite how successfully innovation and ancestry are balanced is debatable.[5] Individual song lengths range from twelve seconds ('Miracle Cure') to the ten-minute 'Underture' but average at around three minutes, and it is notable that the most successful stand-alone hits from the album are 'Pinball Wizard' (3′02″), 'I'm Free' (2′40″), and 'See Me, Feel Me' (actually the last 3′30″ of the finale, 'We're Not Going to Take It'). The shedding of rock 'n' roll's typical three-chord musical structure is more apparent, with the album permeated by unusual and unexpected modulations and harmonic progressions, though there remains a lack of musical development across or within tracks. There is still a reliance on the 'old way' in 'Captain Walker', 'Sparks', 'Go to the Mirror', 'Sally Simpson', the verses of

'Christmas', and the famous 'Pinball Wizard' riff, but these contrast markedly with the chromaticism and harmonic invention found in '1921', 'Cousin Kevin', 'Do You Think It's Alright?', and 'Fiddle About'. It is not only through harmonic development that *Tommy* pushes the musical boundaries of rock 'n' roll; just as the Beatles did in 'Lucy in the Sky with Diamonds', time signatures of 4/4 and 3/4 are juxtaposed in *Tommy*'s 'Fiddle About', but rather than existing in two different tempi the crotchet beat is consistent throughout the number, resulting in a lopsided rhythmic pulse that increases the discomfort of the song for the listener. The same is also true when considering the occasional 5/4 bars in '1921', when Tommy's parents persuade the 4-year-old boy that he did not see or hear and will never speak about the murder he has just witnessed, unwittingly initiating his deaf, dumb, and blind state.

   Such musical invention pales in the light of Lloyd Webber's handling of material in *Superstar*, however, which demonstrates a more operatic approach. The repetition of material and the relating of different parts of the work through the music enables Lloyd Webber to connect similar scenes and points of emotion, even if he falls short of establishing particular leitmotifs, and perhaps embodies the difference in musical education between himself and Townshend. Lloyd Webber draws heavily on his classical background and training to seamlessly integrate the rock band and the symphony orchestra, and the use of irregular and changing time signatures is more developed in *Superstar* with significant musical phrases in 5/4 and 7/8. The album is also far less one-paced than *Tommy*, incorporating ballads as points of musical and narrative relief within the overarching and otherwise fairly persistent rock style. Indeed, while both shows leave gaps in the narrative owing to the omission of dialogue and recitative, *Superstar*'s greater musical cohesion results in a stronger sense of direction through the work.[6]

Adapting the Album: Sound, Screen, and Stage

Such was *Tommy*'s popularity that the Who would often play most or all of it at gigs in the years following its release. Advantageously for the band, and in contrast to the Beatles' specific use of studio effects on *Sgt Pepper* such as the multilayered orchestral crescendi and extended fade-out in 'A Day in the Life' which meant they could not have performed it live (even if they had still been touring), *Tommy* was restricted to the performing abilities of the Who members, with John Entwistle's occasional French horn the only departure from a typical rock 'n' roll sound. *Tommy* was first adapted for performance by Les Grands Ballets Canadiens in 1971 but, although this introduced a new interpretative aspect to the narrative, the music itself was not performed live. Of greater significance is a second album released the following year, featuring the rock opera performed by the London Symphony Orchestra (LSO) with the various characters played by a raft of rock 'n' roll stars including Rod Stewart and Ringo Starr. While alterations

FIGURE 13.1 The star-studded concert presentation of rock opera *Tommy* at The Rainbow Theatre, London, 9 December 1972. Left to right: Rod Stewart, Merry Clayton, Peter Sellers, Sandy Denny, Graham Bell, Steve Winwood, Roger Daltrey, Pete Townshend, John Entwistle, and Keith Moon.

Photography by Gijsbert Hanekroot/Redferns. Courtesy of Getty Images.

might have been expected during Will Malone and James Sullivan's process of arranging the tracks for a symphony orchestra, some parts of the album are subject to greater changes than are necessary, indicating that some songs were merely arranged but others were changed to a larger degree, i.e. adapted.

The 'Underture' that marks the end of the first half of the rock opera is reduced to less than half the length, largely through the omission of repetitions from within the original track, and although the timbral and textural variety of the orchestra (which far exceeds that available to the rock band) means that such a reduction was not necessary to sustain musical interest, it impacts positively on the pacing of the album. Conversely, the translation of strummed guitar chords to repeated string notes in 'Pinball Wizard' results in the song having a significantly slower tempo than the original, adversely affecting its drive and impetus. The orchestral track is around forty-five seconds longer than the rock band version (equating to an additional 25 per-cent running time), and Rod Stewart's vocals often push ahead of the beat in the verses, almost pleading with the conductor for a little more pace. Further to this, the chorus, performed by the English Chamber Choir, dispenses with the close harmonies of the original in favour of a more 'classical' four-part arrangement that almost completely nullifies the song's rock 'n' roll power and presence. The creative decisions taken during this particular adaptation perhaps demonstrate a corporate shortage of orchestral knowledge among those responsible, since neither of the arrangers held any significant credits for orchestration or arranging prior to the album and the Who had not written any material for orchestra. 'Pinball Wizard' inadvertently draws attention to the lack of the electric guitar on the album, and typifies the different sound of the two *Tommy* recordings: one is rock and the other is an orchestral adaptation of rock music, but apart from the drum kit it is devoid of the instrumental timbres that are such a key component of the style. Such a discrepancy demonstrates the difficulty of adapting rock music for a non-rock ensemble, though *Tommy* is the only album for which this situation occurred, with all the other works discussed in this chapter that feature the orchestra being originally conceived for hybrid musical forces.

A brief consideration of similar matters in *Superstar* shows how Lloyd Webber's greater command of orchestral and choral language (through both composition and orchestration) is used to benefit rather than hamper the final result. The rock band is at the heart of the *Superstar* sound, with the orchestra used largely to enhance and develop the timbral palette and increase the scale of some of the material. For example, the driving 7/8 rhythm at the start of 'The Temple' is initially propelled by guitars and drums but, as the emotional intensity of the song builds, Lloyd Webber adds held strings to thicken the texture and as a contrast to the otherwise rapid movement. Shortly after this, brass is introduced doubling the vocal harmonies, lending the music a new sense of grandeur and importance but without detracting from what is fundamentally a rock-based track (albeit one not in a typical rock time signature). Similarly, in 'This Jesus Must Die', the rock-styled musings of the priests are interrupted by brief snippets of chorus demanding 'Jesus Chris, Superstar, | Tell us that you're who they say you are'.[7] Just as in the orchestral adaptation of 'Pinball Wizard' the chorus are heard in four-part harmony, but Lloyd Webber's careful crafting of the material and the vocal arrangement ensures that the interjections intrude on the characters' thoughts but not on the audience's listening experience.

Despite the early adaptations and the band's performances of the complete album, Townshend and the Who never conceived of *Tommy* as anything more than a recording.[8] As has already been noted, *Superstar*, by contrast, was initially intended as a stage project and, following the release of the album, Australian impresario Robert Stigwood (who had previously turned down the advances of the writers) purchased the performing rights. As a result, Lloyd Webber and Rice's concept album was adapted three times in as many years following its release, with the first official stage production opening on Broadway in 1971, a London stage show in 1972, and a film musical produced in 1973, though all three demonstrate the difficulty of converting musico-narrative works from the purely audio domain into the audio-visual. Directors faced significant challenges developing and maintaining visual aesthetics that were convincing on stage or screen without completely destroying the imagined settings conjured by fans through repeated listening to the albums. They were also often hamstrung by the structure of the source works, which did not always lend themselves easily to theatrical translation. Stigwood approached Frank Corsaro to direct *Superstar* on Broadway, but was reputedly concerned that Corsaro's vision for the work—minimally staged, using monitors and projectors for set, and with the music and lyrics presenting most of the story as they had done on the album itself—would not achieve the impact he sought for the stage musical. Corsaro worked on the production without a contract and when he was injured in a vehicle accident Stigwood took the opportunity to replace him with Tom O'Horgan.[9] O'Horgan was a Drama Desk Award winner for Outstanding Direction (for *Futz* in 1969), and had been nominated for a Tony Award in 1969 for his direction of *Hair*, the show and production widely acclaimed as the one that first brought 'rock' to the Broadway stage. Indeed although MCA-Decca took on *Jesus Christ Superstar* in the hope it would be the next *Tommy*, Lloyd Webber and Rice always maintained that their biggest influence when writing the album was O'Horgan's production of *Hair*,[10] seemingly making him a natural choice to direct a stage adaptation of their rock opera.

Initial discussions between the composer and director determined that more material was needed for the stage show than had been necessary for the album, which had no dialogue linking the narrative's musical episodes. However, aside from 'Could We Start Again, Please?', Lloyd Webber and Rice did not provide anything new for O'Horgan to work with and he rapidly lost interest in their views, instead creating a stage show that presented his interpretation of their take on the story. In stark contrast to Corsaro's approach, O'Horgan's solution to the problem of converting the album for the stage was to employ large amounts of visual spectacle, light shows, special effects, and elaborate stage tricks and costuming, seemingly to compensate for the fact that none of these things were possible on the original album. In this respect, O'Horgan's *Superstar* can be seen as the climactic moment in the intersection between the British musical and the pop-music industry,[11] the ultimate combination of an expanded rock-styled musical narrative and excessive theatricality, drawing on large amounts of spectacle and technology.[12] However, the combination missed its mark significantly and, instead of promoting an ideal marriage of theatre and rock, offered twice the opportunity for criticism. His attempts to give *Superstar* narrative direction and impetus were not met positively by critics or audiences, and in addition to the overblown visual effects that dwarfed the characters the production was unable to match the sound of the album. Influential *New York Times* critic Clive Barnes noted in his opening-night review that the sound was 'rather blurred'. Indeed, though he praised some of O'Horgan's work, Barnes was also critical of the production's visual excesses, concluding that the stage musical paled in comparison to the album from which it was derived.[13] Observations of this nature are common in reviews of theatrical adaptations of rock operas, and the idea of a stage show or film being seen (and heard) as inferior to the album is a constant and consistent theme across the genre. The reviews for *Superstar* certainly contributed to the musical's relatively poor run on Broadway—it closed within two years, having offered large numbers of discounted tickets for much of the run—but advance sales of over US$1 million had already ensured that the show would be financially successful, and even before the Broadway opening Stigwood had contracted Norman Jewison to direct a film version of the musical.

The West End staging of the show was sandwiched between the Broadway and Hollywood adaptations, and having despised O'Horgan's over-flamboyant production, Lloyd Webber and Rice selected the director for London themselves.[14] They chose Jim

Sharman, who had brought both *Hair* and *Superstar* to the Australian stage to great critical acclaim (the latter in May 1972, three months before the scheduled West End opening), and the resulting production refocused the story on the characters' thoughts and feelings as Lloyd Webber and Rice had attempted to do with the album itself. Shorn of the overwhelming spectacle of the Broadway show, the London production allowed the motivations of the various protagonists to push the action forward, and the breaks in the narrative caused by the concept album format were largely smoothed away by the fact that most audience members already knew the story. Indeed in his opening night review, *The Times* critic Irving Wardle commends Lloyd Webber and Rice for having 'entirely dispensed with a book—notoriously the weakest element in modern musicals', also noting that the biblical story is overlaid with 'the image of a declining star, first idolized and then torn apart by the fickle ravers'.[15] By placing the emphasis on the characters rather than the staging, Sharman's London production of *Superstar* effectively became a new adaptation of the concept album rather than merely a transatlantic translation of the Broadway show. Visual effects and the use of multimedia technologies proclaimed the contemporary theatrical aesthetic of O'Horgan's rock 'n' roll production, but Sharman's musical unified rock and theatre more successfully by presenting the story through the metaphor of the fading pop star, superimposing contemporary pop and biblical narrative.

The success of the London production matched the hype that had surrounded the Broadway opening, with the show covering its costs within six months and running for eight years. While the differences in directorial perspective are clearly fundamental to understanding the vastly different responses to *Superstar* on Broadway and in London, it must also be noted that the concept album itself was far less successful in the UK than it had been in the US. Whereas American reviewers had found the show inferior to the album, Wardle raises some concerns about the ability of the London cast to maintain their vocal performances but does not draw any comparisons with the album in terms of sound quality or vocal style, indicating the altered hierarchy of the various versions of the show in the UK.

As has already been noted, Norman Jewison was approached to direct the film of *Superstar* before the musical opened on Broadway, and production was started before work began on the London stage version. Jewison had experience of screen adaptations of stage works having previously directed the film of *Fiddler on the Roof*, and recalls that, although Lloyd Webber and Rice originally intended the film to be 'pure *King of Kings*, with all the trappings; a cast of thousands',[16] he defined his own vision of the concept album, just as O'Horgan had done on Broadway.[17] The resulting picture contains a curious mix of elements drawn from the worlds of biblical epic and contemporary drama, a quasi-show-within-a-show that suffuses ancient and modern in what Ellis Nassour and Richard Broderick describe as 'vignettes of the passion play as seen through the eyes of the troupe'.[18] These scenes are bookended by shots of the cast (the aforementioned 'troupe') arriving in a bus at the start of the film and departing the scene in the same vehicle at its conclusion, though Ted Neeley, who plays Jesus, is conspicuous by his absence in the closing sequence, implying some sort of metaphorical blurring of the two

FIGURE 13.2 Paul Nicholas as the crucified Messiah in the spare and character-driven London production of *Jesus Christ Superstar*, Palace Theatre, 1972.

Photograph by Leonard Burt/Central Press. Courtesy of Getty Images.

stories. The film opened six weeks after the Broadway show had closed, and such close proximity must have damaged its impact. Stigwood's initial intention had clearly been to release the picture while the stage show was still running so that each would promote the other, but the failure of the theatrical production instead tarnished the film before it was even on general release. As with O'Horgan's Broadway staging, many reviewers disliked Jewison's visualization of the story, and some critics also attacked Neeley's performance. Writing in the *New York Times*, Howard Thompson declared 'it doesn't work, even with a perspiring cast clambering around crags and caves, grimacing soulfully and singing their heads off'. *The Guardian*'s Michael McNay was even less impressed, bemoaning Jewison's crucifixion scene as a 'souped-up Sunday-school picture-postcard vision, sun throwing a nimbus around Christ's head and all' and describing Neeley's Jesus as 'incidental': 'When everything is effect, nothing is effective.'[19] While the film was the last of these three adaptations to be released, it was the London stage show which was the last to go into production and therefore had the greatest opportunity to reflect upon the strengths and weaknesses of the Broadway musical. O'Horgan and Jewison were both chosen by Stigwood and their productions favour visual overstimulation as compensation for any gaps in the narrative or inadequacies in the vocal performances.[20]

By contrast, Sharman—Lloyd Webber and Rice's pick to direct the London production—created more of an adaptation than a full reimagining of the work, leading to greater critical and financial success.

ROCK FLOPERAS

Over the next five years a mix of new and adapted theatrical rock works, some British and others derived from British music, were created for the London and New York stages and for the screen, though not all were successful. Jim Sharman directed *The Rocky Horror Show* in London in 1973 and, although it was not derived from a concept album, his experience on *Superstar* made him well placed to interpret another rock-styled stage work. The show was an instant success and transferred to Los Angeles in 1974 where it again played well, though the run was ended to enable the filming of *The Rocky Horror Picture Show* featuring the same cast. Just as Stigwood had intended with *Superstar*, American producer Lou Adler set the film's release date to fall during a planned Broadway run of the musical, but in a curious case of symmetry the New York production of *Rocky Horror* closed before the film opened, and neither did as well as had been hoped.[21]

Sandwiched between the London and New York openings of *Rocky Horror* was *Sgt Pepper's Lonely Hearts Club Band on the Road*, an Off-Broadway musical that constructed a loose narrative around songs from the Beatles' *Sgt Pepper* and *Abbey Road* albums. The show was produced by Robert Stigwood and directed by Tom O'Horgan, and the title character was played by Ted Neeley. All three men had emerged rather battered and bruised from their *Superstar* experiences and were hoping that this British pop-music-based show would yield a more successful outcome.[22] However, despite the optimism of the production team and the support of the Beatles, *Sgt Pepper's Lonely Hearts Club Band on the Road* was, perhaps unsurprisingly, plagued with many of the same difficulties as *Superstar*. O'Horgan had simply failed to learn the lessons of *Superstar* in terms of staging a concept album, and if anything *Sgt Pepper* offered even greater visual excess than its predecessor. Mel Gussow's *New York Times* review concluded that the Beatles' songs were 'submerged', and also bemoaned the use of numerous giant puppets, projections, lighting effects, smoke, and other technological paraphernalia.[23]

Given the failures of *Sgt Pepper* and *Rocky Horror* (in America, at least), mounting a rock-themed adaptation was perhaps not the most prudent of strategies in early 1975, but even as the Beatles were being drowned Off-Broadway, Pete Townshend and the Who were shooting the film of *Tommy*, directed by Ken Russell. As with the symphonic *Tommy*, the film has an all-star cast, with Roger Daltrey in the title role. The rest of the company comprises film-musical icon Ann-Margret (Nora Walker); screen actors Oliver Reed (Frank Hobbs), Jack Nicholson (the Specialist), and Robert Powell (Captain Walker); stars from the pop-music industry, including Elton John (the pinball wizard), Tina Turner (the Acid Queen), and Eric Clapton (the Preacher); and musical theatre performer Paul Nicholas (Cousin Kevin), who had originated the roles of Claude and Jesus in the London productions of *Hair* and *Superstar*.

The film features three new songs, two further songs based on other tracks from the album, and several changes to the sequence of musical numbers.[24] All three new numbers, 'Champagne', 'Mother and Son' (the opening of which is actually based on 'Tommy Can You Hear Me' followed by a snippet based on 'Tommy's Holiday Camp'), and 'T.V. Studio' appear in the latter half of the film. The first celebrates Tommy's unknowing rise to fame and stardom; the second heralds the return of Tommy's sight, hearing, and speech and his mother providing a brief explanation of his life to date; and the last features his parents' dreams of Tommy's worldwide fame and recognition as a spiritual leader and redeemer. 'Bernie's Holiday Camp' is based on 'Tommy's Holiday Camp' and 'Extra, Extra, Extra' uses the music of 'Miracle Cure'; as the following discussion demonstrates, in both cases there are clear narrative reasons for the reuse of musical material for these additional tracks. The film is effectively bookended by Bernie's and Tommy's camps and both are turning points in the story, marking the end of a happy time in Tommy's life and the start of a descent into mental trauma and isolation. It is at Bernie's that his mother, Nora, meets and begins the relationship with Frank that will lead to the murder of Tommy's father and the boy's subsequent catatonic state, and the guests at Tommy's camp rebel against his pinball doctrine, murder Nora and Frank, and cause Tommy to regress again to being deaf, blind, and dumb. 'Extra, Extra, Extra' and 'Miracle Cure' both herald some aspect of Tommy's unusual and incredible success: the former announces his rise to pinball prominence ahead of his competition with the 'Pinball Wizard', while the latter raises him further, from man to messiah, with the release from his mental prison.

The symphonic arrangement of *Tommy* had added some clarity to the story, thanks to the different characters being performed by different people, and it might be expected that adapting the album on film would decrease the ambiguity and vagaries of the narrative further. However, Russell's approach to the picture, which has no dialogue, does relatively little to clarify matters. While some questions are answered—Captain Walker is shown to be Tommy's guide on his 'Amazing Journey', for instance—the passing of time is occasionally hard to gauge, and the action moves from scene to scene with little by means of explanation. Furthermore, in many respects, the film follows the O'Horgan school of thought regarding the visualization of rock opera—Russell's use of cinematography and editing often favour visual effects and computer-generated graphics over narrative content, resulting in a barrage of audio-visual material[25]—and it is notable that the picture was produced by the Robert Stigwood Organization. As a fixed medium, the film was able to overcome the issues of sound quality that hampered the Broadway production of *Superstar*, with a new quintaphonic sound system used for recording the songs. Stigwood oversaw the installation of quintaphonic reproduction systems in several major cinemas ahead of the film's release so that the full effect could be realized by the audience, meaning that the film of *Tommy* was perhaps the first adaptation of a rock opera to boast better sound than the album on which it was based—at least in those cinemas equipped to deliver it. However, as with the other Stigwood-produced adaptations of the 1970s, *Tommy* did not receive particularly positive reviews,[26] and while the soundtrack sold well, reaching no. 2 in the Billboard 200 (the original album had peaked at no. 4 in 1970), the project again raised questions about the suitability of rock operas for theatrical and cinematic presentation.

In the years following *Tommy*, Stigwood produced the successful rock-musical films *Saturday Night Fever* (1977) and *Grease* (1978), but on his return to rock opera in 1978 with *Sgt Pepper's Lonely Hearts Club Band* he suffered a similar fate. While *Superstar* and *Tommy* were based on extremely successful albums, *Sgt Pepper's* film origins were more closely linked to the failed Off-Broadway show *Sgt Pepper's Lonely Hearts Club Band on the Road* than to the original Beatles hits, and once again the production was undermined by a weak book. Plans to release the soundtrack album ahead of the film's launch were hampered by Universal's desire for the picture to open in the summer rather than at Christmas, giving the album limited time for radio broadcast before the premiere. In the event the plan backfired completely, with the picture's disastrous reviews quickly curtailing airplay of the album.[27] Even a cast that featured rock stars Peter Frampton, the Bee Gees, Aerosmith, Alice Cooper, and Earth, Wind & Fire alongside stage performers Paul Nicholas and Frankie Howerd was not enough to prevent the film from receiving savage criticism. Reviewers disliked just about every aspect of the production, with the reputations of some performers—notably Frampton and the Bee Gees—tarnished significantly by their involvement in the project.[28]

In contrast to the difficulties encountered by rock-influenced theatre, theatrical rock enjoyed significant success in the early to mid-1970s. Live performances of concept albums were an important part of this scene, with David Bowie (*The Rise and Fall of Ziggy Stardust and the Spiders from Mars*), Pink Floyd (*Dark Side of the Moon*), and Genesis (*The Lamb Lies Down on Broadway*) among Britain's leading artists in this regard. Kevin Holm-Hudson identifies two approaches to theatrical spectacle in rock concerts of the time, which he terms *totalist* and *particularist*: 'totalist theatrics direct one's attention to the total performance space by providing a "larger-than-life" theatrical spectacle [. . .] which invariably serves to distract one's attention from the performers themselves', whereas 'particularist theatrics [. . .] focus one's attention on a particular person on stage'.[29] He associates Bowie and Peter Gabriel with the particularist approach (acknowledging that while this applies to Gabriel, it is not true of the rest of Genesis), and equates the totalist designation with bands such as Pink Floyd, whom Kimi Kärki notes 'inaugurated a new era in the unification of music, theatrical elements, and the latest audiovisual technology' on their *Dark Side of the Moon* tour in 1973.[30] Indeed, while Bowie and Gabriel adopted stage personas using masks, costumes, and physicality to draw the audience's attention, Pink Floyd's concerts featured large-scale lighting and visual effects (such as a flying pig and an aeroplane crash) and advanced use of a quadrophonic sound system, with technology employed to generate and maintain the significant spectacle required for the large venues in which they tended to perform. It is notable that Pink Floyd achieved success in America much sooner than Bowie or Genesis,[31] possibly indicating greater public interest in the multisensory totalist style of spectacle than the more nuanced, personal, particularist approach. This being the case, it perhaps gives some justification for Tom O'Horgan's persistence with prominent audio-visual technologies and effects in his stage productions throughout the mid-1970s despite negative criticism from reviewers, though Holm-Hudson warns that 'the danger of totalist theatre is that it runs the risk of being arbitrary, having little to do with the music that is ostensibly the focus of the performance'.[32] His observation relates to theatrical rock but applies equally to rock theatre, though given the narrative and musical issues underpinning most of O'Horgan's productions, it is possible that such distraction may have been his intention.

Indeed, the only truly financially and critically successful rock-opera adaptation of the early 1970s was Sharman's London production of *Superstar*, and Lloyd Webber and Rice repeated their success with their next (and last major) collaboration, *Evita*, which was released as an album in 1976, reaching the London stage in 1978 and Broadway the following year. However, *Evita* is a slightly misleading inclusion in this set of works since the creators always envisaged it as a sung-through stage work and released it as an album first because that strategy worked so effectively with *Superstar*. While the public's first engagement with *Evita* was as a concept album, the creative process involved in devising and writing the show meant that in many respects this functioned more like an original cast album than an entity in its own right, though not all of the performers on the album reprised their roles on stage. Accordingly, apart from noting its creation and success, and the fact that despite the commercial failure of *Tommy* Ken Russell was lined up to direct a film version in the late 1970s, nothing more will be said about *Evita* here. Instead, the closing section of this chapter focuses on two late rock operas that present themselves quite differently to those already discussed.

THE CONCEPT ALBUM AS ROCK NON-OPERA

Jeff Wayne's Musical Version of the War of the Worlds and *The Hunting of the Snark* have followed very different paths but share a remarkable number of characteristics. Initially conceived by Wayne in 1975, *War of the Worlds* took three years to come to fruition and was released in 1978, within the roughly ten years following the release of the Beatles' *Sgt Pepper* during which concept albums were relatively common in the pop-music industry and rock operas were being adapted for stage and screen. *Snark* also had a reasonable gestation period, with Mike Batt discovering Lewis Carroll's poem in 1982 and bringing it to the stage in 1984 in a concert with the LSO before recording the album later that year. Accordingly, *Snark* falls well outside the principal period when rock operas were in vogue and, although the concept albums of *Chess* and *Time* also date from the 1980s, can be seen as somewhat behind its time in this respect.[33] Nonetheless, the similarities that can be observed between *War of the Worlds* and *Snark* are quite surprising.

Although Lloyd Webber and Rice could claim that *Superstar* was based—perhaps loosely—on the Gospels, a common feature of the concept albums considered thus far is the lack of a pre-existing literary text that underpins the narrative. *War of the Worlds* and

Snark buck this trend, drawing on the work of well-known and respected writers H. G. Wells and Lewis Carroll respectively, and in doing so they establish two presentation strategies absent from previous rock operas: spoken word and the narrator. Critically both albums feature passages of dialogue, usually—though not exclusively—delivered by a narrator, giving greater flow and continuity to the storylines and addressing one of the key criticisms levelled at some of the older concept albums: vagaries in and fragmentation of the story. The *War of the Worlds* narrator is the journalist of Wells's story, though in contrast to the original source the entire story is told from the journalist's perspective in the manner of a recollection of the events. The narration is a paraphrase of Wells's novel, pared down to the bare bones in order to compress the plot into a manageable length, and the opening of the album is, unusually, devoted to the unaccompanied spoken voice of Richard Burton as he establishes the historical and social context for the story. This introduction is followed by the now iconic *War of the Worlds* motif played by string orchestra that is allowed to fade before being repeated first by rock and electronic instruments and then by the combined ensemble. The first two minutes of the album thus not only establish the sound-world (rock band with electronics and strings) but also, by opening with an unaccompanied narration, assert the primacy of speech over music, emphasizing the difference between this album and those that preceded it.

Throughout the album the narration is set against songs with original lyrics that comment on characters and points of action but do not always progress or develop the plot. While music is relegated to the background as underscoring during narrated passages, the voice of the narrator is modified by music during songs. The spoken narration is delivered by Burton, but the recognizable tone and timbre of his voice is replaced by that of Moody Blues singer and guitarist Justin Hayward when the journalist is called upon to sing. With this brief substitution in the opening number, 'The Eve of War', the general casting strategy for the album becomes apparent: dialogue is delivered by actors and songs are performed by performing pop artists. In addition to Hayward, the latter include singer and lead guitarist from Manfred Mann's Earth Band, Chris Thompson ('Thunder Child'), and Thin Lizzy singer and bass player Phil Lynott (the Parson), emphasizing the rock credentials of the album and its sound. The other sung parts are performed by Julie Covington (Beth) and David Essex (the Artilleryman), who brought to the album's sound some experience of musical theatre, notably through other rock musicals. Both had appeared in the original London production of *Godspell* (Essex in the lead role as Jesus), Covington originated the role of Janet in *The Rocky Horror Show*, and both were involved with *Evita* (Covington sang Eva on the concept album, and Essex originated the role of Che on the London stage shortly before recording *War of the Worlds* with Wayne). The Artilleryman straddles the speech–song divide significantly, Essex's dual identity as an actor and pop musician making him eminently suitable for the role without excessively damaging the album's casting convention, though since both Beth and the Parson have spoken dialogue during their duet 'The Spirit of Man', there are clearly some flaws in the overarching strategy.

A similar premise is evident in *Snark*. Batt extracted parts of Carroll's poem for spoken delivery by a narrator, and interspersed songs with original lyrics that expand on the characters' thoughts and feelings. The cast for the concert performance of *Snark* also combined an established actor as the narrator with performing pop artists as the characters on the expedition, and Batt drew on his significant experience in the British pop-music industry to gather his performers, having written and produced hits for a number of different artists over the course of his career.[34] The concert featured Christopher Cazenove as the narrator and former Manfred Mann vocalist Paul Jones played the Baker, arguably the lead character in the piece; for the album Batt augmented the roster considerably. The role of the narrator was split between Sir John Gielgud and John Hurt, both established stage and screen actors with recognizable voices, with the narration expanded to include all the dialogue spoken by the various characters. The hunting party consisted of Cliff Richard (Bellman), Art Garfunkel (Butcher), Roger Daltrey (Barrister), US artist Deniece Williams (Beaver), Julian Lennon (Baker), and Captain Sensible (Billiard-Marker), with instrumental solos performed by former Beatle George Harrison and virtuoso violinist Stephane Grappelli. Batt reverted to a single narrator for a filmed concert at the Royal Albert Hall in 1987, retaining the services of Hurt in this role, with Lennon, Garfunkel, Daltrey, Williams, and Captain Sensible also reprising their album roles in this costumed, semi-staged production. Billy Connolly replaced Cliff Richard as the Bellman, his comic delivery and acting compensating somewhat for an unsurprisingly inferior singing voice (the highest notes in particular are amusing to watch on the film), and former Thin Lizzy and Ultravox guitarist Midge Ure performed Harrison's solo in 'Children of the Sky'.

Despite the involvement of prominent musical theatre performers, *War of the Worlds* is arguably the least theatrical work of all those considered here. It is therefore perhaps surprising to find that it presents the most theatrical score in terms of the way in which Wayne uses the musical material to maintain the narrative and guide the listener through the story. There is significant use of leitmotif (or at least a simplified form of thematic linkage): in addition to the *War of the Worlds* motif there are themes for the invasion, the Martians, the dreaded heat ray (for which the slightly overdriven guitar timbre is a second narrative marker), the narrator's relationship with his 'beloved' Carrie ('Forever Autumn'), the warship Thunderchild, the Parson and his wife Beth, and the Artilleryman's 'Brave New World'. There are also two themes each for the Martians' fighting machines and the red weed, and a motif of descending octaves that can be heard as representing radio communications. While some melodies feature only in individual numbers (such as the material for the Parson and Beth in 'The Spirit of Man'), others permeate the album, supporting the story and guiding the listener in conjunction with the spoken narration. There are often long passages with no dialogue or lyrics in which the music is the sole storytelling element, and the placement and interaction of Wayne's various themes enable the listener to create the story in their own imagination based on the thematic content of the album tracks. For example, in 'Thunderchild' a battle is played out in the music through the use of the two fighting machine themes being interspersed with the sung material of the Thunderchild melody, with the *War of the Worlds* motif used to underscore some parts of the narrative, to link the themes together (so that they flow musically), and to lead from the Martian victory to the radio signal motif that closes the track. Likewise, 'Dead London' begins with a variation of the second fighting machine melody as the narrator decides to give himself up to the invaders, though the slower pace of the theme indicates that all is not well with the Martians. After it transpires that the Martians are all dead (killed by bacteria), the rest of the number is constructed from sections of the opening 'Eve of War', with one short passage taken from 'The Artilleryman and the Fighting Machine', the recapitulation of the music marking a return to the position of human dominance on Earth, as was the case at the beginning of the story. This triumph is emphasized in 'Epilogue Part 1' through frequent use of a motif first heard in the Artilleryman's deluded dream of a utopian 'Brave New World' underground and away from the Martian conquerors, but here it represents an actual rather than fictional way forward for the human race.

Batt's musical storytelling is generally more simplistic, though he still provides some aural signposts on the quest for the snark. The instrumental 'Introduction' establishes four motifs and two main themes, and elements from this small set of musical ideas are sprinkled liberally across the album to create a vague macrostructure for the work. In addition to exposing this musical material, the 'Introduction' also features two prominent aspects of the musical strategy that permeates the album: instrumentation and harmony. The track and album open with pounding bass notes on string and electric basses, piano and percussion followed by a short snare-drum burst and a one-bar phrase of orchestral scoring, showcasing all the ensemble's constituent parts within the first two bars of music. The interactions between the orchestra and the rock band are varied: at times the two seem to exist as separate entities with whole passages or sections of numbers scored for just one or the other, and yet in other places their integration is what gives the music its particular character and originality. Indeed, the film of the Albert Hall concert shows the rock band placed near the heart of the LSO (who played in both concerts and on the album), positioned behind the woodwind, on a level with the orchestral brass. Batt often uses the orchestra to echo the band and vice versa, and the album has a similar advantage to *Superstar* in that it was originally conceived for this combination of instrumental forces. The 'Introduction' also highlights the unusual harmonic language of the album, which frequently juxtaposes widely contrasting tonal areas and makes extensive use of movement between chords a third apart, but also draws on closed eight-bar (and sometimes six-bar) chord progressions in the manner of a pop song. The result is a restless quality to the music, which seems constantly to be searching for a point of resolution but often does not even reach such a conclusion at the end of a song, in a way mirroring the characters' ongoing and somewhat surreal quest for the snark.

The influence of pop music is evident in the thematic structures of almost all of the main songs in *Snark*. The first vocal number on the album, 'Children of the Sky' (sung by Batt himself as the invented character of the Bandmaster, in keeping with the B-titled roles of Carroll's poem), presents a verse and chorus that are repeated after a short bridge, a guitar solo based around the harmonic progression of the chorus, a modulation up one semitone for a full orchestral chorus, with the voices returning for a final chorus after another semitone step up. The song displays a number of pop-influenced characteristics in its structure, though Batt's propensity for unusual phrase lengths—the verse is twenty bars and the chorus just fourteen—and occasional half-length bars prevent it from sounding particularly formulaic. 'The Bellman's Speech', 'Midnight Smoke', 'The Snooker Song', and 'Dancing Towards Disaster' are all based around alternating verses and choruses, with 'The Pig Must Die' and 'As Long as the Moon Can Shine' both utilizing variations on this structure, but with the exception of 'Dancing Towards Disaster', none of them feature the sort of predictable phrase lengths that might be anticipated in pop music.

Whereas most of Wayne's songs are characterized by recurring melodies, in general it is only in *Snark*'s longer tracks that Batt's musical signposting appears, with 'The Escapade' and 'The Vanishing' exposing and drawing on a number of themes and motifs to help progress the narrative. 'The Escapade' follows directly from 'The Bellman's Speech' and introduces three new melodies, two of which reappear later in the album. The escapade theme is sung by the Beaver (to whom we have not yet been introduced), who muses on the futility of the trip and the low likelihood of success, though these negative thoughts are swiftly repelled, firstly by an instrumental burst of the chorus from the rousing 'Children of the Sky', and then more explicitly by the Bellman who rallies his crew in a short passage of music that seems to channel Gilbert and Sullivan through progressive rock.

The result of this optimism is the full-blooded hunting theme which sets the driving guitar, bass, and drums of the rock band alongside a fanfare melody that opens on horns and adds trumpets and low brass before a repeat of the theme introduces a sweeping countermelody on violins, high woodwind, and piano. The hunting theme surrounds the character theme used to introduce the Baker, Butcher, and Beaver, and while such sharing of material could indicate a relationship or similarity between the characters, in this case it appears to be more a question of musical economy than strict narrative connectivity. The hunting theme is used similarly to highlight the character of the Barrister in his only solo appearance, 'The Pig Must Die', with the song opening and closing with an orchestration of the theme for strings with solo oboe and muted trumpet. Despite the fact that the Barrister's song contains some of the most overtly progressive rock moments of the whole score, by surrounding it with a light version of the hunting theme Batt almost separates it from the rest of the album, a hermetically sealed number that brandishes its rock credentials (particularly since it was performed in both concerts and on the album by Roger Daltrey), but makes no meaningful contribution to the ongoing story. The final occurrence of the hunting theme is in the closing number, 'The Vanishing', which brings together several of the album's key themes for the narrative and musical climax of the piece. It opens with the Bellman's chorus melody and several musical motifs and themes from the 'Introduction' before the escapade theme returns, this time sung by the Baker whose thoughts reflect those originally voiced by the Beaver, but with greater certainty that the snark will soon be found. The return of the hunting theme confirms these feelings but, as the Baker nears his end at the hands of the snark, the theme turns from its normal path and descends into a sustained underscore for the narration of his fatal encounter. The song, album, and quest finish with a return to 'Children of the Sky' in multiple iterations ending with a final chorus for tutti orchestra celebrating the tragic failure of the hunt—and, with hindsight, of Batt's *Snark* project.

Both *War of the Worlds* and *Snark* are inextricably linked to the CBS record label, though in very different ways. When Wayne created *War of the Worlds* he did so with no certainty that CBS would release the work, and ultimately CBS UK bought out the 50 per-cent share held by Columbia in order to secure the album's launch. *War of the Worlds* entered the UK album chart at no. 24 and although it peaked at no. 5 it has spent 313 weeks in the Official UK Album Chart since its release, most recently that ending 6 December 2014, some thirty-six years after it first went on sale.[35]

Batt recorded *Snark* in the months following the LSO concert in 1984, but withdrew from a contract with CBS owing to artistic disagreements over the album's content. He moved the project to a smaller label on the promise of a mass advertising campaign, but the company went into liquidation and it took Batt some time to recover the album from the liquidators. By this time he had already organized the filmed Albert Hall concert, which he has quipped was 'one hell of an expensive evening to promote a record that was not even on release'.[36] Indeed, apart from a short time in 1986 when First Night records produced a limited run, the 2010 Dramatico CD was the first proper album release of *Snark*, at least in the UK.

CONCLUSION

Some bands continued to experiment with concept albums into the 1980s, notably Pink Floyd and Peter Gabriel, but the idea had all but disappeared from pop music by 1990. The rock-opera-as-stage-musical also appears to have been a relatively short-lived phenomenon, and even (or perhaps because) within this canon successful theatrical adaptations are few and far between. Batt put a greatly expanded *Snark* on the London stage in October 1991, the culmination of nearly a decade of work turning the surreal poem into a sophisticated concept musical. He successfully advertised for financial backing of £1.6 million,[37] with investors including Cameron Mackintosh and Andrew Lloyd Webber,[38] but like so many of its predecessors *Snark* closed after a short run, having been criticized by reviewers who objected to the show's incessant and insistent audio-visual effects, the high volume level of the music, and the resulting unintelligibility of most of the lyrics.[39] Indeed *Snark*'s enduring legacy is probably 'The Snooker Song', used as the theme for all fourteen series of the BBC television show *Big Break* between 1991 and 2002. *The Who's Tommy*, a 1993 stage adaptation of the album, ran for two years on Broadway with a shorter run in the West End but was plagued by similar issues, notably being viewed as inferior to the album in terms of musical performance.[40]

Notwithstanding *Evita* for reasons given earlier, with the exception of *Jesus Christ Superstar* stage and screen interpretations of rock operas have failed to reach the heights of the original albums, and even in that case both the Broadway and Hollywood versions were criticized for visual and vocal shortcomings. In 2010 the American band Green Day put their rock opera *American Idiot* on to the Broadway stage, but like so many before it the show lasted just a year. The musical did tour in the UK, playing eight one-week runs in October–December 2012, but there was no West End transfer and a mooted film version scheduled for 2013 has not yet materialized.[41] Perhaps the model to follow is that employed initially by Wayne, creator of the most successful of these albums. The thirtieth anniversary of *The War of the Worlds* saw the launch of an immensely successful live tour with life-size fighting machines, projections, and pyrotechnics—ironically precisely the sort of visual effects for which O'Horgan's Broadway adaptations were castigated—and Wayne retained this format over an eight-and-a-half year period before finally developing the work into a stage musical. The show ran from February to April 2016 at London's Dominion Theatre, but the visual elements that had been so effective on the tour were not well received by critics who felt that the production, like its forebears, was ill-conceived and suffered poorly by comparison to the album.[42] Indeed, the event (and perhaps the whole genre) is most succinctly summarized by the title of the unattributed review in *The Telegraph*: 'How do you stage *Jeff Wayne's War of the Worlds*? You don't.'[43] And yet despite all of the difficulties and disappointments that stalked rock opera, its legacy is still felt keenly within the world of British (and wider) musical theatre. 'Jukebox musicals'—stage shows created around a band's or artist's existing songs—are perhaps the most readily recognizable development of the idea of rock opera. Indeed, the strength of the connection between these forms of theatre can be seen in the criticisms received by many jukebox musicals for their weak narratives and, to a lesser extent, the presentation and reinterpretation of established songs.[44] Although there have been a number of high-profile flops, notable successes in both the West End and on Broadway include *Mamma Mia!* and *Jersey Boys*, while *Buddy—the Buddy Holly Story* and *We Will Rock You* both played well in London.[45] A wider impact of rock opera can be seen in the increased use of narrative song and a corresponding reduction in dialogue in many contemporary rock musicals, with shows such as *Rent, Bare: A Pop Opera, Jerry Springer: The Opera, Repo: The Genetic Opera*, and *Next to Normal* containing little or no dialogue between or within musical numbers (the operatic claims in the subtitles of three of these musicals also bearing testament to their heritage). Lloyd Webber continued to use song as the principal narrative device in his musicals through the 1980s in *Starlight Express, Aspects of Love*, and *The Phantom of the Opera*, each of which features a rock-influenced score (if sometimes only in part) with a largely sung-through narrative, and the idea of continuous song can also be found in the musicals of Alain Boublil and Claude-Michel Schönberg, notably *Les Misérables* and *Miss Saigon*.

Nearly fifty years after the creation of the concept album, the pop-music industry continues to impact on the British musical, with a number of prominent artists becoming creators of musical theatre works. Having worked with Tim Rice on songs for Disney's *The Lion King* and *Aida*, Elton John wrote the score for *Billy Elliot: The Musical*, which opened in the West End in 2005 and also ran for three years on Broadway, and Jeff Lynne, founder member of the Electric Light Orchestra, co-wrote music and lyrics for the Broadway adaptation of *Xanadu* in 2007. Sting began working on a semi-autobiographical musical, *The Last Ship*, in 2011 with *Next to Normal* lyricist Brian Yorkey.[46] The show arrived on Broadway in late 2014 but closed after only a short run,[47] a circumstance Gary Barlow is hoping will be avoided by his co-composed stage adaptation of *Finding Neverland*, which opened on Broadway on 15 April 2015. The idea of engaging leading pop musicians to create songs for the stage extends beyond Britain and the British industry, with recent examples including *Spider-Man: Turn Off the Dark* with songs by Bono and The Edge of Irish pop band U2, and Cyndi Lauper's music for *Kinky Boots*, which serves as further affirmation of rock opera's ongoing legacy, the relationship between the pop-music industry and musical theatre, and the impact of the British musical on the genre more widely.

NOTES

1. In his chapter in *The Cambridge Companion to the Musical*, for example, Scott Warfield singles out *Superstar* as an exemplar of 'works that began as concept albums'. See Scott Warfield, 'From *Hair* to *Rent*: Is "Rock" a Four-letter Word on Broadway?', in *The Cambridge Companion to the Musical*, 2nd ed, ed. William A. Everett and Paul R. Laird (Cambridge: Cambridge University Press, 2008), 236.
2. Sternfeld and Wollman discuss developments in aural spectacle, noting the introduction of microphones and amplification as well as suggesting that 'visual spectacle took a turn toward the mechanical and electronic' in the early 1970s. See Jessica Sternfeld and Elizabeth L. Wollman, 'After the "Golden Age"', in *The Oxford Handbook of the American Musical*, ed. Raymond Knapp, Mitchell Morris, and Stacy Wolf (New York: Oxford University Press, 2011), 115. See also Elizabeth L. Wollman, *The Theater Will Rock: A History of the Rock Musical, from* Hair *to* Hedwig (Ann Arbor: University of Michigan Press, 2006), 75–78; Virginia Anderson, 'Sets, Costumes, Lights and Spectacle', in *Oxford Handbook of the American Musical*, ed. Knapp, Morris, and Wolf, 294–308.
3. Richard Barnes, 'Deaf, Dumb and Blind Boy', Liner Notes to The Who, *Tommy* (1969), CD, Polydor 5310432, 1996.
4. Wollman, *Theater Will Rock*, 91.
5. Richard Barnes and Pete Townshend, *The Story of 'Tommy'* (Twickenham: Eel Pie Publishing, 1977), 129.
6. There is insufficient space to consider it in detail here, but an argument might be made that *Tommy* is more revolutionary in terms of dramaturgical conception, and this could also affect its musical coherence relative to *Superstar*. My thanks to Robert Gordon for drawing my attention to this aspect of the two works.
7. This can be heard at 0'55"–1'09" on track 5 of the original concept album: *Jesus Christ Superstar* (1970), Decca, 5339271, 2012.
8. Denisoff and Romanowski note that 'The Who were reluctant to see their "masterpiece" turned into a film'. See R. Serge Denisoff and William D. Romanowski, *Risky Business: Rock in Film* (New Brunswick, NJ: Transaction Publishers, 1991), 214–15.s
9. Denisoff and Romanowski claim that Corsaro 'worked extensively on the production' prior to his accident, though Wollman states that he suffered his injuries 'shortly after casting had begun'. Regardless of which account is more accurate, it is clear that nothing of Corsaro's conception was retained in the Broadway production. See Denisoff and Romanowski, *Risky Business*, 209; Wollman, *Theater Will Rock*, 94.
10. Keith Richmond quotes Rice as saying 'our real influence wasn't *Tommy*, it was *Hair*', and Barbara Lee Horn notes that Lloyd Webber and Rice 'freely admit their decision to

write a rock show came immediately after they attended a performance of *Hair*'. See Keith Richmond, *The Musicals of Andrew Lloyd Webber* (London: Virgin Publishing Limited, 1995), 27; Barbara Lee Horn, *The Age of Hair: Evolution and Impact of Broadway's First Rock Musical* (Westport: Greenwood Press, 1991), 130.

11. Notwithstanding that O'Horgan's directorial career was centred entirely on and off Broadway, and that he likely had little if any idea of trends in British theatrical productions, *Superstar* remains a British musical.

12. British and American artists such as Screamin' Jay Hawkins, Screaming Lord Sutch, Arthur Brown, Alice Cooper, and other proponents of 'shock rock' often included elements of theatricality in their live gigs in the late 1960s and early 1970s, an approach further developed through the 1970s by 'prog rock' bands including Pink Floyd and Genesis. See, for example, Meg Fisher, 'Hawkins, Screamin' Jay', in *Encyclopedia of the Blues*, vol. 1, ed. Edward M. Komara (New York: Routledge, 2006), 415; Deena Weinstein, 'Alice Cooper', *Grove Music Online. Oxford Music Online* 2013, http://www.oxfordmusiconline. com/subscriber/article/grove/music/A2240019, accessed 26 August 2015.

13. Clive Barnes, 'Theater: Christ's Passion Transported to the Stage in Guise of Serious Pop: *Jesus Christ Superstar* Billed as Rock Opera Music's Vitality Asset to O'Horgan Work', *New York Times*, 13 October 1971, 40.

14. Denisoff and Romanowski suggest Lloyd Webber and Rice 'had been far from satisfied with O'Horgan's stage presentation', while Nassour and Broderick quote Lloyd Webber as saying 'I don't agree with what O'Horgan has done. Tom's production is not the definitive version by any means'. See Denisoff and Romanowski, *Risky Business*, 211; Ellis Nassour and Richard Broderick, *Rock Opera: The Creation of 'Jesus Christ Superstar' from Record Album to Broadway Show and Motion Picture* (New York: Hawthorn Books Inc., 1973), 177.

15. Irving Wardle, 'Little Here for Card-carrying Christians', *The Times*, 10 August 1972, 11.

16. *King of Kings* is the title of two biblical epics, a silent Cecil B. DeMille picture from 1927, and a 1961 MGM film. It seems most likely that the reference here is to the latter, though doubtless both featured large casts. See Nassour and Broderick, *Rock Opera*, 228.

17. This is despite Jewison originally claiming that, in contrast to the Broadway production, 'author Tim Rice and composer Andrew [Lloyd] Webber will personally supervise every frame of the film'. See Nassour and Broderick, *Rock Opera*, 216.

18. Nassour and Broderick, *Rock Opera*, 232.

19. Howard Thompson, 'Mod-Pop *Superstar* Comes to Screen', *New York Times*, 9 August 1973, 28; Michael McNay, 'US Calvary', *The Guardian*, 23 August 1973, 10. Denisoff and Romanowski cite a *Rolling Stone* review in which Neeley's Jesus is similarly considered to be a 'gaping hole in the centre of [the] movie'. See Denisoff and Romanowski, *Risky Business*, 213.

20. Such criticisms were not levelled at all members of the cast, with *The Times* reviewer David Robinson asserting that Judas is 'dazzlingly played by Carl Anderson', and *Variety* calling Anderson 'outstanding as Judas in the film's best performance'. Indeed, a comparison of the various soundtrack releases reveals that Anderson's voice can be considered warmer and richer than either Murray Head or Ben Vereen (the respective Judases on the original album and on Broadway), with better tone throughout his whole vocal range. However, it is equally conceivable that the relative lack of roughness in his singing might be a cause for criticism for some listeners familiar with the original concept album. See David Robinson, 'Crucified Again', *The Times*, 24 August 1973, 7; Variety Staff, 'Review: *Jesus Christ Superstar*', *Variety*, 31 December 1972, http://variety.com/1972/film/

reviews/jesus-christ-superstar-4-1200423014/, accessed 26 August 2015. Details of record-ings are given in the Discography of this chapter.

21. Clive Barnes criticized the Broadway production for being too 'flashy, expensive and overstaged', going on to ask 'why did not someone understand [. . .] that the entire point of *The Rocky Horror Show* in London was that it was tacky? Tacky, tacky, tacky!', which perhaps explains why it failed to attract similar audiences in New York. See Clive Barnes, 'Stage: A Flashy *Rocky Horror Show*', *New York Times*, 11 March 1975, 26.

22. A rather 'rose-tinted' recollection of the *Sgt Pepper* experience is given by one of the origi-nal cast members, B. G. Gibson, in the Autumn 1994 issue of the Beatles fanzine *Good Day Sunshine*. The text of the account is available online at Sara Schmidt, 'Sgt Pepper's Lonely Hearts Club Band on the Road', *Meet the Beatles for Real*, 21 February 2014, http://www.meetthebeatlesforreal.com/2014/02/before-there-was-beatles-love-in-las.html, accessed 26 August 2015.

23. Mel Gussow, 'Stage: *Sgt Pepper* Goes on the Road', *New York Times*, 18 November 1974, 74.

24. Russell is credited as the screenwriter, but Denisoff and Romanowski suggest that 'Russell and Townshend spent a year working together on the script', also quoting from a *Rolling Stone* article from April 1975 in which Townshend states 'everything Ken Russell has done with the story and music has my full blessing'. See Denisoff and Romanowski, *Risky Business*, 215.

25. Cinematography on *Tommy* was done by Dick Bush and Ronnie Taylor, with Robin Lehman credited with work on 'special material'. The film editor was Stuart Baird. See '*Tommy* (1975): Full Cast and Crew', *Internet Movie Database* 2014, http://www.imdb.com/title/tt0073812/fullcredits?ref_=tt_ov_st_sm, accessed 26 August 2015.

26. Critic Vincent Canby concluded his review stating '*Tommy* is not the sort of movie you may ever want to see again, but it's an unforgettable souvenir of a time in our history when the only adequate dose was an overdose', and Charles Michener described it as 'the loud-est, most assaultive movie musical ever made [. . . a] phantasmagorical nightmare'. See Vincent Canby, 'When Too Much is Just About Right', *New York Times*, 30 March 1975, 91; Charles Michener, 'The New Movie Musicals', *Newsweek*, 24 March 1975, 54.

27. Indicative reviews include Janet Maslin, 'Screen: Son of *Sgt. Pepper*: Many Forms Involved', *New York Times*, 21 July 1978, C16; Tom Zito, '*Sgt. Pepper*: Homogenized Memories', *Washington Post*, 21 July 1978, C4; David Ansen, 'Stigwood's Home Movie', *Newsweek*, 31 July 1978, 42. For discussion of the marketing plan linking the album and movie see Susan Peterson, 'Key Label Executives Analyse Their Approach to the Marketing of Movie Music', *Billboard*, 6 October 1979, ST2.

28. Denisoff and Romanowski quote Paul Nelson's *Rolling Stone* review in which he states that the film 'managed to trash whatever rock and roll reputations such Seventies artists as Peter Frampton and the Bee Gees had', and they also comment that 'The *Sgt. Pepper* deba-cle seemed to mark the end of the Bee Gees' eminence'. See Denisoff and Romanowski, *Risky Business*, 248.

29. Kevin Holm-Hudson, *Genesis and 'The Lamb Lies Down on Broadway'* (Aldershot: Ashgate, 2008), 32.

30. Kimi Kärki, ' "Matter of Fact It's All Dark": Audiovisual Stadium Rock Aesthetics in Pink Floyd's *Dark Side of the Moon* Tour, 1973', in *'Speak to Me': The Legacy of Pink Floyd's 'The Dark Side of the Moon'*, ed. Russell Reising (Aldershot: Ashgate, 2005), 27.

31. *Dark Side of the Moon* reached no. 1 on its release in March 1973, and Pink Floyd enjoyed a hugely successful tour down the US East Coast that summer. See Mark Blake, *Pigs Might*

Fly: The Inside Story of Pink Floyd (London: Aurum Press Limited, 2007), 207, 209. By contrast, *Ziggy Stardust* had only reached no. 75 a year earlier, and *The Lamb* peaked at no. 41 the following year.

32. Holm-Hudson, *Genesis and 'The Lamb Lies Down on Broadway'*, 33.

33. Mike Batt comments that Tim Rice, Benny Andersson, and Björn Ulvaeus attended the concert premiere of *Snark* in 1984, having just completed the album of *Chess*, but none of these 1980s rock operas reached the benchmarks set by *Superstar* and *Evita*. *Time*, written by pop musician Dave Clark, opened in April 1986 and ran for two years at the Dominion theatre, and *Chess* opened a month later at the Prince Edward and ran for three years but closed after just two months on Broadway in 1988, losing over $6.5 million. See Mike Batt, Liner Notes for *The Hunting of the Snark*, Dramatico: DRAMCD0030, 2010 [CD/DVD]; 'History of the Theatre: The Rock and Roll Years', *Dominion Theatre*, not dated, http://www.dominiontheatre.com/theatre/about-the theatre/history-of-the-theatre/the-rock-and-roll-years/, accessed 26 August 2015; Warfield, 'From *Hair* to *Rent*', 244.

34. Batt wrote the music and lyrics for Art Garfunkel's 'Bright Eyes' and 'Please Don't Fall in Love' for Cliff Richard, created arrangements for and produced Justin Hayward's album *Classic Blue*, and produced the music for the ITV series *The Dreamstone*, the performers on which included Billy Connolly. He also had an existing relationship with the LSO, having recorded two albums with them in the late 1970s.

35. 'Jeff Wayne', *The Official UK Charts Company*, 2016, http://www.officialcharts.com/artist/28762/jeff-wayne/, accessed 26 July 2015.

36. Batt, Liner Notes for *The Hunting of the Snark*.

37. See Vivien Goldsmith, 'The *Hunting of the Snark* Angels: A Stage Version of Lewis Carroll's Nonsense Epic Is Not for Nervous Investors', *The Independent*, 3 March 1991, 20.

38. Ian Katz, 'Raiders of the Lost *Snark*', *The Guardian*, 16 December 1991, 21.

39. Benedict Nightingale, reviewing for *The Times*, notes that 'the audience's eyes and ears get no rest. Flats and gauzes never stop dropping from the flies, to show [. . .] visual trickiness galore', going on to comment that the music 'is almost always too loud, and accompanied by lyrics which, when audible, do nothing for the narrative'. *The Observer*'s Michael Coveney similarly considered the show to have 'lyrics, music and staging of unmitigated direness'. See Benedict Nightingale, 'Rhyme but Little Reason', *The Times*, 26 October 1991, 5; Michael Coveney, 'Utterly, Totally Batt's', *The Observer*, 27 October 1991, 58.

40. John Pareles expresses his disappointment that 'Broadway's *Tommy* subdues most of the music, trading Roger Daltrey's rock belting for conventional Broadway emoting and taming the Who's glorious power chords with unnecessary keyboard doodling', and Michael Kuchwara concludes his Associated Press review by suggesting that '*Tommy* is an assault of sound, light and color. Don't go expecting anything more, and you'll have a reasonable, if uninvolving, time. Then go home, put on the old Who album—assuming you still have something as antiquated as a turntable—and listen to the real stuff'. See John Pareles, 'Damping 60's Fire of *Tommy* for 90's Broadway', *New York Times*, 27 April 1993, C13; Michael Kuchwara, 'The Who's *Tommy* Arrives—Loudly—on Broadway', *Associated Press*, 22 April 1993, http://www.nexis.com, accessed 26 August 2015.

41. Details of the tour can be found at 'Green Day Musical *American Idiot* to Tour the UK', *Daily Telegraph*, 1 December 2011, http://www.telegraph.co.uk/culture/theatre/theatre-news/8928221/Green-Day-musical-American-Idiot-to-tour-the-UK.html, accessed 26 August 2015. The proposed film is listed on the Internet Movie Database as 'in development'.

See 'American Idiot', *Internet Movie Database* 2014, http://www.imdb.com/title/tt1623740/
?ref_=nv_sr_1, accessed 26 August 2015.

42. See, for example, Tim Auld, 'Waging War on our Ears', *Daily Telegraph*, 18 February 2016,
25; Henry Hitchings, 'You Can't Help but Root for the Martians in this Overblown Display
of Prog Rock Pomp', *The Evening Standard*, 18 February 2016, 33; Ann Treneman, 'It's a
World of Pain: the Martians Should Sue', *The Times*, 18 February 2016, 19, http://www.
nexis.com, accessed 26 July 2016.

43. 'How Do You Stage *Jeff Wayne's War of the Worlds*? You Don't', *The Telegraph*, 18 February
2016, http://www.nexis.com, accessed 26 July 2016.

44. Examples include *Good Vibrations*' 'blockheaded comic strip of a book' (Ben Brantley,
New York Times) and 'sketchy, almost non-existent plot' (Michael Kuchwara, *Associated
Press*), *All Shook Up*'s 'story that causes all the trouble' (Clive Barnes, *New York Post*), and
vocal performances that 'range from painfully self-conscious to outright clueless', leading
to a 'false, sterile feel' in several songs (Elysa Gardner, *USA Today*), *Never Forget*'s 'book
[that] feels as if it is being stretched to shoehorn in the next ballad' and for which 'it is
clear that nobody got round to writing the second half' (Lyn Gardner, *The Guardian*), and
Viva Forever! in which 'what really scuppers the show—and it is nearly always the case
with dud musicals—is the book [which] is almost insultingly banal' (Charles Spencer,
Daily Telegraph). None of these shows, which featured the music of the Beach Boys,
Elvis Presley, Take That, and the Spice Girls respectively, achieved 250 performances. See
'IBDB Reviews: *Good Vibrations*', *Internet Theatre Database*, 2005, http://www.ibdb.com/
reviews.php?id=388139, accessed 26 August 2015; 'IBDB Reviews: *All Shook Up*', *Internet
Theatre Database* 2005, http://www.ibdb.com/reviews.php?id=383114, accessed 26 August
2015; Lyn Gardner, 'Review: Theatre: *Never Forget*', *The Guardian*, 23 May 2008, Review,
p. 44; Charles Spencer, 'Spice Girls Come to Grief in This Fatuous and Tawdry Musical',
Daily Telegraph, 12 December 2012, 27.

45. See Robert Viagas, 'Long Runs on Broadway', *Playbill*, 3 August 2015, http://www.playbill.
com/celebritybuzz/article/long-runs-on-broadway-109864, accessed 26 August 2015; The
Society of London Theatre, 'The Top 20 Longest-Running Musicals in West End History',
The Society of London Theatre, 24 September 2014, http://solt.co.uk/top-20-longest-
running-musicals, accessed 26 August 2015.

46. See Dave Itzkoff, 'Sting and Brian Yorkey Embark on a New Musical, *The Last Ship*', *New
York Times*, 1 September 2011, http://artsbeat.blogs.nytimes.com/2011/09/01/sting-and-
brian-yorkey-embark-on-a-new-musical-the-last-ship/, accessed 26 August 2015.

47. See 'Sting's Broadway Musical to Close, as Theatres Report Blockbuster Year', *BBC*, 6
January 2015, http://www.bbc.co.uk/news/entertainment-arts-30698228, accessed 26
August 2015.

Bibliography

'American Idiot.' *Internet Movie Database* 2014. http://www.imdb.com/title/tt1623740/?ref_
=nv_sr_1, accessed 26 August 2015.
Anderson, Virginia. 'Sets, Costumes, Lights and Spectacle.' In *The Oxford Handbook of the
American Musical*, edited by Raymond Knapp, Mitchell Morris, and Stacy Wolf, 294–308.
New York: Oxford University Press, 2011.

Anon. 'Green Day Musical *American Idiot* to Tour the UK.' *Daily Telegraph*, 1 December 2011. http://www.telegraph.co.uk/culture/theatre/theatre-news/8928221/Green-Day-musical-American-Idiot-to-tour-the-UK.html, accessed 26 August 2015.

Ansen, David. 'Stigwood's Home Movie.' *Newsweek*, 31 July 1978, 42.

Barnes, Clive. 'Stage: A Flashy *Rocky Horror Show*.' *New York Times*, 11 March 1975, 26.

Barnes, Clive. 'Theater: Christ's Passion Transported to the Stage in Guise of Serious Pop: *Jesus Christ Superstar* Billed as Rock Opera Music's Vitality Asset to O'Horgan Work.' *New York Times*, 13 October 1971, 40.

Barnes, Richard, and Pete Townshend. *The Story of 'Tommy'*. Twickenham: Eel Pie Publishing, 1977.

Batt, Mike. Liner Notes to *The Hunting of the Snark*. CD. Dramatico Records, DRAMCD0030, 2010.

Blake, Mark. *Pigs Might Fly: The Inside Story of Pink Floyd*. London: Aurum Press Limited, 2007.

Canby, Vincent. 'When Too Much Is Just About Right.' *New York Times*, 30 March 1975, 91.

Coveney, Michael. 'Utterly, Totally Batt's.' *The Observer*, 27 October 1991, 58.

Denisoff, R. Serge, and William D. Romanowski. *Risky Business: Rock in Film*. New Brunswick, NJ: Transaction Publishers, 1991.

Fisher, Meg. 'Hawkins, Screamin' Jay.' In *Encyclopedia of the Blues*, vol. 1, edited by Edward M. Komara, 415. New York: Routledge, 2006.

Gardner, Lyn. Review of *Never Forget. The Guardian*, 23 May 2008, Review, p. 44.

Goldsmith, Vivien. 'The *Hunting of the Snark* Angels: A Stage Version of Lewis Carroll's Nonsense Epic Is Not for Nervous Investors.' *The Independent*, 3 March 1991, 20.

Gussow, Mel. 'Stage: *Sgt Pepper* Goes on the Road.' *New York Times*, 18 November 1974, 74.

'History of the Theatre: The Rock and Roll Years.' *Dominion Theatre*, not dated. http://www.dominiontheatre.com/theatre/about-the-theatre/history-of-the-theatre/the-rock-and-roll-years/, accessed 26 August 2015.

Holm-Hudson, Kevin. *Genesis and 'The Lamb Lies Down on Broadway'*. Aldershot: Ashgate, 2008, 32.

Horn, Barbara Lee. *The Age of 'Hair': Evolution and Impact of Broadway's First Rock Musical*. Westport: Greenwood Press, 1991.

The Hunting of the Snark (Concert). Dramatico: DRAMCD0030, 2010.

IBDB Reviews: *All Shook Up. Internet Theatre Database* 2005. http://www.ibdb.com/reviews.php?id=383114, accessed 26 August 2015.

IBDB Reviews: *Good Vibrations. Internet Theatre Database* 2005. http://www.ibdb.com/reviews.php?id=388139, accessed 26 August 2015.

Itzkoff, Dave. 'Sting and Brian Yorkey Embark on a New Musical, *The Last Ship*.' *New York Times*, 1 September 2011. http://artsbeat.blogs.nytimes.com/2011/09/01/sting-and-brian-yorkey-embark-on-a-new-musical-the-last-ship/, accessed 26 August 2015.

Jesus Christ Superstar. Directed by Norman Jewison, 1973. Starring Ted Neeley, Carl Anderson, and Yvonne Elliman. Universal Pictures UK, 2005.

Kärki, Kimi. ' "Matter of Fact It's All Dark": Audiovisual Stadium Rock Aesthetics in Pink Floyd's *Dark Side of the Moon* Tour, 1973.' In *'Speak to Me': The Legacy of Pink Floyd's 'The Dark Side of the Moon'*, edited by Russell Reising, 27–42. Aldershot: Ashgate, 2005.

Katz, Ian. 'Raiders of the Lost *Snark*.' *The Guardian*, 16 December 1991, 21.

Kuchwara, Michael. 'The Who's *Tommy* Arrives—Loudly—on Broadway' *Associated Press*, 22 April 1993. http://www.nexis.com, accessed 26 August 2015.

Maslin, Janet. 'Screen: Son of *Sgt. Pepper*: Many Forms Involved.' *New York Times*, 21 July 1978, C16.

McNay, Michael. 'US Calvary'. *The Guardian*, 23 August 1973, 10.

Michener, Charles. 'The New Movie Musicals.' *Newsweek*, 24 March 1975, 54.

Nassour, Ellis, and Richard Broderick. *Rock Opera: The Creation of 'Jesus Christ Superstar' from Record Album to Broadway Show and Motion Picture*. New York: Hawthorn Books Inc., 1973.

Nightingale, Benedict. 'Rhyme But Little Reason.' *The Times*, 26 October 1991, 5.

Pareles, John. 'Damping 60's Fire of *Tommy* for 90's Broadway.' *New York Times*, 27 April 1993, C13.

Peterson, Susan. 'Key Label Executives Analyse Their Approach to the Marketing of Movie Music.' *Billboard*, 6 October 1979, ST2.

Richmond, Keith. *The Musicals of Andrew Lloyd Webber*. London: Virgin Publishing Limited, 1995, 27.

Robinson, David. 'Crucified Again.' *The Times*, 24 August 1973, 7.

The Rocky Horror Picture Show. Directed by Jim Sharman, 1975. Starring Tim Curry, Susan Sarandon, and Barry Bostwick. 20th Century Fox Home Entertainment, 2006.

Schmidt, Sara. 'Sgt Pepper's Lonely Hearts Club Band on the Road.' *Meet the Beatles for Real*, 21 February 2014. http://www.meetthebeatlesforreal.com/2014/02/before-there-was-beatles-love-in-las.html, accessed 26 August 2015.

Sgt Pepper's Lonely Hearts Club Band. Directed by Michael Shultz, 1978. Starring Peter Frampton and the Bee Gees. Universal Studios Home Entertainment, 2003.

The Society of London Theatre. 'The Top 20 Longest-Running Musicals in West End History.' *The Society of London Theatre*, 24 September 2014. http://solt.co.uk/top-20-longest-running-musicals, accessed 26 August 2015.

Spencer, Charles. 'Spice Girls Come to Grief in This Fatuous and Tawdry Musical.' *Daily Telegraph*, 12 December 2012, 27.

Sternfeld, Jessica, and Elizabeth L. Wollman. 'After the "Golden Age".' In *The Oxford Handbook of the American Musical*, edited by Raymond Knapp, Mitchell Morris, and Stacy Wolf, 111–126. New York: Oxford University Press, 2011.

'Sting's Broadway Musical to Close, as Theatres Report Blockbuster Year.' *BBC*, 6 January 2015. http://www.bbc.co.uk/news/entertainment-arts-30698228, accessed 26 August 2015.

Swain, Joseph P., *The Broadway Musical: A Critical and Musical Survey*. 2nd ed. Lanham, MD: Scarecrow Press, 2002.

Thompson, Howard. 'Mod-Pop *Superstar* Comes to Screen.' *New York Times*, 9 August 1973, 28.

Tommy. Directed by Ken Russell, 1975. Starring Roger Daltrey, Ann-Margret, and Oliver Reed. Odeon Entertainment Limited, 2012.

'*Tommy* (1975): Full Cast and Crew.' *Internet Movie Database* 2014. http://www.imdb.com/title/tt0073812/fullcredits?ref_=tt_ov_st_sm, accessed 26 August 2015.

Variety Staff. Review of *Jesus Christ Superstar*. *Variety*, 31 December 1972. http://variety.com/1972/film/reviews/jesus-christ-superstar-4-1200423014/, accessed 26 August 2015.

Viagas, Robert. 'Long Runs on Broadway.' *Playbill*, 3 August 2015. http://www.playbill.com/celebritybuzz/article/long-runs-on-broadway-109864, accessed 26 August 2015.

Wardle, Irving. 'Little Here for Card-Carrying Christians.' *The Times*, 10 August 1972, 11.

Warfield, Scott. 'From *Hair* to *Rent*: Is "Rock" a Four-Letter Word on Broadway?' In *The Cambridge Companion to the Musical*, 2nd ed., edited by William A. Everett and Paul R. Laird, 235–249. Cambridge: Cambridge University Press, 2008.

Weinstein, Deena. 'Alice Cooper', *Grove Music Online. Oxford Music Online* 2013. http://www. oxfordmusiconline.com/subscriber/article/grove/music/A2240019, accessed 26 August 2015.

Wollman, Elizabeth L. *The Theater Will Rock: A History of the Rock Musical, from 'Hair' to 'Hedwig'.* Ann Arbor: University of Michigan Press, 2006.

Zito, Tom. 'Sgt. Pepper: Homogenized Memories.' *Washington Post*, 21 July 1978, C4.

Discography

The discography includes important British (and some American) rock operas/concept albums first released in the period 1960–90 (those marked with * are featured in this chapter), as well as original cast recordings and film soundtracks for the stage and screen musicals considered. Albums are ordered by composer/band name followed by year of original release (shown in parenthesis where this differs from the listed recording).

The Alan Parsons Project. *Eye in the Sky* (1982). 25th Anniversary Edition. Arista/Arista Legacy/RCA/Sony Music Distribution, 82876815272, 2007.

The Alan Parsons Project. *I Robot* (1977). 30th Anniversary Edition. Arista/Arista Legacy/Sony Music Distribution, 82876815242, 2007.

Batt, Mike. *The Hunting of the Snark* (1984). Dramatico Records, DRAMCD0030, 2010 [concept album].*

The Beatles. *Sgt Pepper's Lonely Hearts Club Band* (1967). EMI Records, 863793, 2009 [concept album].*

The Beatles. *Sgt Pepper's Lonely Hearts Club Band* (1978). Original Motion Picture Soundtrack. Polydor Records, 5570762, 1998 [film soundtrack; no cast recording was ever made of the 1974 Off-Broadway musical *Sgt Pepper's Lonely Hearts Club Band on the Road*].*

The Bee Gees. *Odessa* (1969). Polydor Records, #E8254512, 1987.

Bowie, David. *The Rise and Fall of Ziggy Stardust and the Spiders from Mars* (1972). EMI Music Distribution, 3577, 1990.

Brooks, Joe. *Metropolis.* Original Cast Recording (1989). Jay Records, 1248, 1997 [musical].

Clark, Dave. *Time* (1986). Dave Clark Productions via iTunes. https://itun.es/i6Bh7nw (Act 1), https://itun.es/i6BY2cL (Act 2), 2012.

Frank Zappa. *Joe's Garage: Acts I, II and III* (1979). Rykodisc, RCD 10530/31, 1995.

Genesis. *The Lamb Lies Down on Broadway* (1974). Atlantic/Rhino Records, 516782, 2014.

Green Day. *American Idiot* (2004). Reprise Records, 9362487772 [concept album].

Green Day. *American Idiot* (2010). Original Broadway Cast Recording. Maverick/Reprise/ Warner Bros., 23724, [musical].

Iron Maiden. *Seventh Son of a Seventh Son* (1988). EMI Music Distribution, 7902582.

Jethro Tull. *Thick as a Brick* (1972). 40th Anniversary. Chrysalis Records, 04619, 2012.

The Kinks. *Arthur (Or the Decline and Fall of the British Empire)* (1969). Essential Records, ESMCD511, 1998.

Lloyd Webber, Andrew, and Tim Rice. *Evita* (1976). MCA Records, 11541, 1996.

Lloyd Webber, Andrew, and Tim Rice. *Jesus Christ Superstar* (1970). Decca, 5339271, 2012 [concept album].*

Lloyd Webber, Andrew, and Tim Rice. *Jesus Christ Superstar.* Decca Broadway Original Cast Album (1971). Decca, 067734, 2003 [musical—Broadway].*

Lloyd Webber, Andrew, and Tim Rice. *Jesus Christ Superstar* (1972). 20th Anniversary London Cast Recording. RCA Victor/RCA, 61434, 1992 [musical—London].*

Lloyd Webber, Andrew, and Tim Rice. *Jesus Christ Superstar.* Original Motion Picture Soundtrack (1973). 25th Anniversary Reissue. Geffen/MCA Records, 11757, 1998 [film soundtrack].*

Marillion. *Misplaced Childhood* (1985). EMI Music Distribution, 7461602.

The Moody Blues. *Days of Future Passed* (1967). Polydor Records, 8200062, 1986.

Nirvana. *The Story of Simon Simopath* (1967). Edsel, EDCD465, 1996 [Nirvana was a British psychedelic rock band active principally in the 1960s and 1970s, and should not be confused with the Seattle-based grunge band of the late 1980s and early 1990s fronted by Kurt Cobain].

O'Brien, Richard. *The Rocky Horror Show.* Original London Cast (1973). Snapper/Original Masters, 15606, 2002 [musical].*

O'Brien, Richard. *The Rocky Horror Picture Show* (1975). Ode Records 1, 2013 [film soundtrack].*

Pink Floyd. *Dark Side of the Moon* (1973), EMI, 679180.

Pink Floyd. *Wish You Were Here* (1975). EMI Music Distribution, 5099952243325, 2012.

Pink Floyd. *The Wall* (1979). EMI Music Distribution, 028944, 2011.

Pink Floyd. *The Final Cut* (1982). Columbia, CK-38243.

The Pretty Things. *S.F. Sorrow* (1968). JVC Compact Discs, 64266, 2008.

Rice, Tim, Benny Andersson, and Björn Ulvaeus. *Chess* (1984). Polydor/Decca, 847445, 1996.

Styx. *Kilroy Was Here* (1983). A&M, AA7502137342, 1990.

Wakeman, Rick. *Journey to the Centre of the Earth* (1974). A&M: AA7502131562, 1988.

Wayne, Jeff. *Jeff Wayne's Musical Version of the War of the Worlds* (1981). Columbia/Sony Music Distribution, 35290, 1986.*

The Who. *Quadrophenia* (1973). MCA Records, 11463, 1996.

The Who. *Tommy* (1969). Polydor Records, 5310432, 1996 [concept album].*

The Who. *Tommy—As Performed by the London Symphony Orchestra & Chamber Choir* (1972). Ode Records/Rhino, R2-71113, 1989 [concept album arranged for orchestra].*

The Who. *Tommy.* Original Soundtrack (1975). Polydor Records, 8411212, 2001 [film soundtrack].*

The Who. *The Who's Tommy.* Original Cast Recording (1993). RCA Victor, 61874 [Broadway cast recording].*

PART IV

'THE BRITISH ARE COMING!'

CHAPTER 14

'EVERYBODY'S FREE TO FAIL'

Subsidized British Revivals of the American Canon

SARAH BROWNE

In June 1945, the British government established a permanent body recognized by royal charter as the Arts Council. Previously known as the Committee for Encouragement of Music and the Arts (CEMA), the enterprise had been initiated with financial assistance from the private sector. Britain's post-war government acknowledged that reliance on such funding of the arts would be inadequate in continuing to provide the invaluable recreational and cultural activities that had become a mainstay of community life during the war. Through the achievements of CEMA and similar bodies, the arts began to be seen as a vital part of the war effort[1] and their work was varied and wide-ranging. In an attempt to develop new audiences, CEMA ensured that national orchestras and ballet companies toured the country and established non-profit repertory theatre companies whose productions frequently played to capacity audiences. With ten regional offices, and headquarters based in London, CEMA provided the administrative framework for the Arts Council of Great Britain.

The aims and objectives of the Arts Council since its inception have broadly related to fostering excellence in the arts and ensuring access for all. Indeed, their most recent strategic framework document, released in 2010, seems to echo this same philosophy in its title, *Great Art and Culture for Everyone*, proposing to achieve this by investing in 'artists and organisations that practice ambitious programming, encouraging audiences and users to expand their horizons and explore new ideas'.[2] Such a declaration suggests that subsidy offers artists, directors, and theatrical enterprises the freedom to explore and to be daring in their choice of material and the ways in which they approach it. Similar luxuries are rarely, if ever, afforded to the commercial sector, which relies solely on funds from private investors. The risk undertaken by these investors is significant: unlike the producers of subsidized ventures, they often have little control of the creative elements of the production and any return on their investment is dependent on the ever-changing tastes of the audience. Once the production has recouped, the producer is then required to return the unit value purchased by each investor. The producer/investor division of profits is often subject to negotiation in the United Kingdom as opposed to a more common 50/50 split in the United States. The economic imperative is such that reviving a much-loved musical classic is often considered a safer financial bet than mounting a new work. Revivals of musicals, therefore, are often little more than imitations of their premier productions, replicating elements of the initial incarnation in an attempt to recreate its original success: the 1980 touring and West End revival of *Oklahoma!*, for example, adapted the original De Mille choreography. The same approach was taken for the 1957 and 1965 New York productions of *Carousel*.

During the 1980s and 1990s, the subsidized sector in Britain turned its attention to reviving the work of Broadway composers and playwrights. From a financial perspective, this form of programming may not be considered particularly ambitious, but for one of the institutions examined in this chapter, it was certainly a divergence from their established programming model. In his chapter in the *Oxford Handbook of Sondheim Studies*, surveying Stephen Sondheim and the subsidized sector, Keith Warner argues that Arts Council funding allows companies to tackle the most 'esoteric and controversial' musicals from the composer's catalogue, asserting that the luxury of public funding allows producers and directors to explore the material in a different fashion to that of the commercial sector. The safety net provided by such funding allows companies to spend a greater amount of time exploring the material in rehearsal and, as Warner suggests, the production team can 'spread its wings'.[3] This, as some critics propose, has allowed directors to dispense with the more bromidic elements of these American classic musicals, revisiting the material in new and dynamic ways, which results in a production that bears little or no resemblance to its original stage version or its incarnation on screen. The investigation of examples of such revivals, the director's approach to the material, and the subsequent audience response offers an insight as to how British subsidized venues established a standard for treating certain musicals as classics of the American theatre.

'MANY A NEW DAY'

Spurred on by the support for and the success of CEMA's cultural enterprises throughout the 1940s, the London County Council urged the government to establish a national theatre. Wartime efforts had stimulated pride in British culture and it was perhaps this increased sense of national identity that contributed to the ease with which the National Theatre Bill was introduced in November 1948 and passed in the subsequent year (although it should be noted that the first proposal for such a theatre was made in 1848). The Bill authorized a Treasury contribution of £1 million to aid in building a theatre on the South Bank of the River Thames, which would set a standard for the production of drama worthy of the British tradition.

The proposed building would not in fact be completed until 1976, by which time the National Theatre had already established a regular programme of international classics and serious new plays while housed at the Old Vic Theatre. Following a phased move into each of the three theatres housed on the South Bank site, the National continued to produce a steady diet of the work of British playwrights (such as Ben Jonson, Tom Stoppard, and Peter Shaffer) interspersed with occasional productions from continental European playwrights (Brecht, Tolstoy, Chekhov, and Ibsen). So it seems unsurprising that in 1982, when the National's new artistic director, Richard Eyre, was asked to direct a 'major popular classic', the response to his suggestion of *Guys and Dolls* (a musical that Laurence Olivier had originally planned to produce and star in as Nathan Detroit at the National in 1970) was cautious at best. Eyre recalls the criticism levelled at the National as a result of his choice to stage an American musical theatre classic; 'the National Theatre was dropping its standards; it was going commercial; the piece wasn't good enough to earn its place in the NT's repertoire; it would be treated patronisingly'.[4]

A fan of American culture but initially not of musicals, Eyre was aware of the risk that lay ahead. He recognized that the National's first musical 'had to be true to its genre but [...] true to whatever the values were embodied within the National Theatre'. It was a risk that could have only been taken as a result of the safety net provided by arts subsidy. The aim of the production was to 'end the apartheid between practitioners of musicals and those of plays by marrying the two within a subsidised context devoted to the truthful examination of the text'.[5]

Eyre's *Guys and Dolls* delivered a Manhattan steeped in American mythology. By night, John Gunter's neon set design illuminated the monotone seediness of the city; the illuminated signs, proclaiming the merits of Wrigley's chewing gum and 'Maxwell House' coffee provided 'a comforting overlap of economies [and] cultures'.[6] Gunter's neon world could have created a Times Square that alienated a British audience but the familiar brands brought the audience closer to an understanding that, although this was a fairy-tale setting of New York, it was not one that was steeped in the artificiality that has often typified musicals. Eyre assembled a cast of British actors, some of whom had little experience of performing in musicals; all had to learn a tap routine for the finale. The majority of the cast (with the exception of Julia McKenzie and Julie Covington), not necessarily skilled in singing and dancing, were encouraged to approach their characters through the text. A dialect coach was employed to ensure that accents were authentic, while a professional croupier was also on hand to teach the cast to shoot craps. Eyre recalls that he wanted actors to 'play truthfully' and, as a result, all of the performers immersed themselves in the stories of Damon Runyon.

The original West End production of *Guys and Dolls* had opened in 1953. With a hiatus of nearly thirty years between the original production and Eyre's revival, British audiences had probably only been exposed to the film version of the musical (released in 1955, starring Marlon Brando as Sky Masterson, the British actress Jean Simmons as Sarah Brown, and Frank Sinatra as Nathan Detroit). In casting Bob Hoskins as Nathan Detroit (see Figure 14.1), Eyre had chosen an actor who was not only far removed from Sinatra's portrayal but who could also bring humanity to the role. Reminiscent of Sam Levene (Nathan Detroit in the original Broadway production), Hoskins's raucous, growling portrayal of 'Sue Me' gave the audience a Nathan that reserved the crooning

FIGURE 14.1 The late Bob Hoskins as a decidedly human Nathan Detroit and Julia McKenzie as his long-suffering fiancée Adelaide in Richard Eyre's famous 1982 production of *Guys and Dolls* at the National Theatre, Olivier.

Photograph by Laurence Burns. Courtesy of ArenaPal.

for moments when he needed to be his most charming; he implores Adelaide to 'call a policeman [. . .] I love you' in his dulcet tones, but barks the final 'shoot bullets through me, I love you',[7] with an added accelerando, reminding us that, much to Adelaide's disbelief, he still has to hastily depart for a prayer meeting.

Guys and Dolls was received with uncharacteristic elation from British theatregoers, evident in 'Sit Down, You're Rocking the Boat', which was reprised seven times to appease the audience. Set designer John Gunter felt that the musical had been staged at just the right time, adding that as Britain was embroiled in the Falklands conflict and in the later stages of a recession, 'it's extremely hard to think at all positively [. . .] the public needs it'.[8] The success of this production was such that it ran again two years later at the National and, following a UK tour, transferred to the West End. Although many of the production values remained the same, an entirely new cast was assembled; McKenzie's understudy, Imelda Staunton, now headlined as Adelaide (her performance received critical acclaim and established her as a star performer), Clarke Peters stepped into the role of Sky Masterson, and in the show's final reprise at the National in 1996 Clive Rowe gave an Olivier Award-winning portrayal of Nicely-Nicely Johnson. Both actors were black and reviews seized on the multiracial casting element of the 1996 production, proclaiming 'Sky turns black'. In response to the critics, Clarke Peters exclaimed;

> I know people get upset when they see a black man kissing a white woman on stage but that is their problem. This show is not about black and white; it's not a racial issue. It's about men's hearts—their relationship with women—and that's the bottom line.[9]

Eyre's production seemed to have provided the blueprint for tackling classics of the American musical theatre at the National and Nicholas Hytner, appointed as Eyre's associate director in 1990, confirmed this to be the case with his 1992 production of Rodgers and Hammerstein's classic, *Carousel*. In an innovative move, mirroring the appointment of Agnes de Mille in the 1940s, Cameron Mackintosh suggested Sir Kenneth MacMillan as choreographer. A leading choreographer of his generation, MacMillan believed that ballet should reflect the 'complicated truths of people's lives', with many of his heroes and heroines portrayed as outsiders.[10] From the opening bars of 'The Carousel Waltz' it was clear that this production would present a re-envisaging of this classic of the American stage.

Rodgers's waltz, which serves as the overture, is significantly slower in tempo than in previous productions and cast recordings. Centre stage is a huge clock face, designed by Bob Crowley (working on his first musical), which towers over several female workers operating machinery. The dull monotony of their daily work is reflected in the tempo of the waltz and it is clear why the central heroine, Julie Jordan, is given to 'gaze absentminded[ly] at the roof'.[11] As the bell sounds, signalling the end of the workday, the female mill-workers erupt joyously through the gates, and the fairground (and eventually, the carousel) are erected in full view of the audience (see Figure 14.2). Hytner's opening scene refuses to present the audience with a pristine carousel of painted horses, instead showing us numerous grizzly sideshows and the very bowels of the machinery as the canopy slowly descends.

This sets the stage for Hytner's significant reimagining of *Carousel*'s two central characters. No longer presented as two young lovers who flirtatiously dance around each other, Julie and Billy are 'aged by drudgery and snubbed by respectable society [. . .] old and achingly lonely before their time'.[12] Michael Hayden's Billy Bigelow is a somewhat angry young man, self-centred and volatile. His behaviour and demeanour towards Julie in the bench scene forewarns of the troubled and violent relationship they will briefly share. His portrayal serves as a stark contrast to the renowned performances of John Raitt and Gordon MacRae; in Hayden, Billy is closer to Molnar's *Liliom*. The original script of *Liliom* leaves much of the central character's thoughts unspoken, whereas Rodgers and Hammerstein chose to express these same thoughts in song. In doing so, as Scott McMillin proposes, they illustrate Billy's complicit role in the community. As much as Billy wishes to remain an outsider, his musical material and the implication of his sung moments indicate his attachment to those around him.[13] Consequently, much of the original Molnar character is often lost during Billy's musical numbers, but in 'Soliloquy', Hayden's portrayal was one that combined both characters to full effect. Billy's humanity is apparent, particularly in the final section when aggression,

FIGURE 14.2 The fairground as designed by Bob Crowley in Nicholas Hynter's 1992 revival of *Carousel* at the National Theatre, Lyttleton.

Photograph by Clive Barda. Courtesy of ArenaPal.

desperation, and confusion are combined to shape his concluding thoughts; he is unsure how he will provide for his child but he recognizes he is prepared to die trying. In response to this darker portrayal, we also understand that Julie, as portrayed by Joanna Riding, is much more worldly-wise concerning men like Billy. The tempo of the song 'What's the Use of Wonderin'' is significantly slower than in previous recordings and productions. Julie's weariness is evident in the way the phrases are drawn out; the dotted rhythms no longer propel the emotion forward, instead delaying the inevitable ending of each cadence point, signalling her resignation and offering a musical acknowledgement that her relationship with Bigelow is doomed. The privation experienced by both central characters and the simplicity of the New England community that form the ensemble is reflected in Bob Crowley's set designs. Reminiscent of the paintings of Edward Hopper, his backdrops reflect the folk-like modesty of the community, whilst also seeming to communicate the isolation and solitude of Billy.

CASTING *CAROUSEL*

As with its predecessor *Guys and Dolls*, Hytner's production of *Carousel* grabbed headlines for its interracial casting. Clive Rowe as Enoch Snow brought humour and exuberance to the part, counting out muffins as he explained his plans for a large family. Critics were divided in their response to the casting of Rowe; although many remarked on his outstanding performance, a number labelled the choice of actor as 'misplaced liberalism of subsidised theatre', historically inaccurate, and an 'insult to Rodgers and Hammerstein'.[14] The racial transformation of this character may have been a shock to the audience at the time (the added double joke of assigning a black actor to the role of Mister Snow did not go unnoticed), but to Hytner, who had been determined to assemble a cast of actor-singers, it was merely a case of choosing the right actor for each role.[15]

Carousel proved to be another success for the National Theatre. A donation from the Mackintosh Foundation (established in 1988 by Cameron Mackintosh) encouraged the National to stage classic musicals with a view to transferring them to the commercial sector. This was indeed the case with the Rodgers and Hammerstein classic: reopening at the Shaftesbury Theatre in 1993, the production then moved to Broadway the following year. Following a move by the Actors' Equity Association which prevented a transfer of the British cast, a completely new cast was assembled (with the exception of the American Hayden, a graduate of Juilliard, who retained the role of Billy) and New York critics and audiences responded enthusiastically to Hytner's reimagining of this musical play. The key to his success was an approach which echoed that of Eyre's: choosing actors to take on challenging roles and allowing them to analyse the part in the same manner in which they would approach the text of a play.

Five years later, the new artistic director of the National, Trevor Nunn, chose another Rodgers and Hammerstein classic as his first musical on the South Bank: Oklahoma!. No stranger to musicals, having previously directed Cats, Starlight Express, Les Misérables, Chess, and Sunset Boulevard, Nunn believed that an 'artificial barrier' had been established between musical theatre and plays. Commenting that he felt there should not be any such division, Nunn proposed that 'a national theatre is very well served by doing the whole spectrum'.[16] He approached the Rodgers and Hammerstein Organization with a view to replacing Agnes de Mille's original choreography as both he and Susan Stroman (the choreographer) wanted the principals to also dance the dream ballet at the end of Act 1. It is highly likely that the success of MacMillan's choreography for Carousel aided in the organization granting this request; in addition, as the production was to be staged in London, the reputation of Oklahoma! on Broadway could remain intact should Nunn's experiment fail. Removing the dream counterparts of the three lead roles (Curly, Laurey, and Jud) allowed for a greater exploration of character, whilst, as with the original production, it also progressed the narrative. Nunn wanted to create a production of Oklahoma! that focused on community—one that explored a fledgling country, its origins, conflicts, and priorities—and to flesh out the elements of the story that he felt had been neglected by the 1955 film.[17] Directed by Fred Zinnemann, the feature film was the first to be shot using the Todd-AO 70 mm widescreen technique and was, the trailer declared, 'big and colourful as all outdoors'.[18] Anthony Ward's set design managed to evoke the same Technicolor vistas, using the revolve of the National to full effect. But that is where the similarities ended.

CASTING OKLAHOMA!

Casting a then unknown Hugh Jackman in the lead role, the creative team felt they had found a Curly with strength and vulnerability; Stroman remarks that *Oklahoma!* had been 'shaped through the eyes of Curly, and audiences saw it through his eyes'.[19] Jackman's portrayal of Curly is indeed vulnerable, aided primarily by Josefina Gabrielle's feisty portrayal of Laurey. In the opening scene, as with the original production, the audience hears Laurey's strains of 'Oh, What a Beautiful Mornin'' before the character appears on stage. Her reprise of Curly's musical material at this point aurally connects the two lead roles and prepares the audience for what will eventually be their joyful union. Visually, however, this is a Laurey who will be hard to win. No longer the pristine young maiden, dressed immaculately in ribbons and bows, Laurey appears, wearing worn, drab dungarees and work boots. This is a young woman who works the land, her future foreshadowed by her aunt who sits centre stage churning butter in her weathered and dirty apron. In previous incarnations, in addition to numerous amateur productions, Laurey had been presented as a ladylike figure of femininity: virtuous, pure, and free from the banal tedium of everyday life. In Nunn's version, Laurey is presented as a woman who understands the humdrum and difficult nature of a life in the territory. Her costume suggests she works the land and places her outside the feminine order established by the female chorus. This is exemplified in Stroman's choreography for 'Many a New Day', significantly different from de Mille's. As the scene opens, Laurey is set apart from the rest of the female community, signified by the use of costume, and is an observer of their dialogue. The song is performed in response to this dialogue and Laurey's exasperation is clear. The female chorus are no longer her confidantes but her tutees and the first verse is delivered as an admonishment to the woman who 'blubbers like a baby' at the thought of her man leaving her. What follows presents an interesting dichotomy in terms of gender performance. Members of the female chorus act as Laurey's male suitors (represented by the hat that is passed from one to the other). As they dance their respective duets, Laurey brushes off each suitor with increasing boldness, at one point completely subduing her partner by winning an arm wrestling match. Laurey's costume provides an added signifier of her performance of masculinity. Although she is the female counterpart of each couple, her actions suggest she is adopting the dominant (read: masculine) position. Her role as tutor to the female chorus is further emphasized in the final verse, where she uses a horse whip as a teacher's cane. She maintains this position throughout the vocal number; her final solo refrain shows she is even more resolute than at the opening of the scene. In previous versions, and in the well-known 1955 film version, Laurey's final refrain is marked by indecision and uncertainty. She has to repeat the final few bars of material in order to convince herself that she must remain firm and resolute in her assertions. There is no such indecision in the revival; instead, Laurey offers the final few bars as a warning, reiterating her feminist rallying cry that has so clearly been communicated throughout the scene.

The 'Dream Ballet' also serves to develop the lead characters and presents a more complex portrayal of the relationship between Laurey and Jud. Stroman and Nunn's decision not to use dance counterparts subsequently allowed for a deeper exploration of the three lead characters and their motives. Stroman's choreography dispenses with the symbolic motifs of De Mille's work; gone are the staircases leading to nowhere and the fluttering, pulsating flat palms representing Laurey's beating heart. In Stroman's ballet, Laurey runs through a cornfield, unlocking her unconscious and allowing her fears to haunt her dreams. The score for the ballet (newly arranged by David Krane and orchestrated by William David Brohn) uses fewer motifs than the original. The developing love story between Laurey and Curly is portrayed through the use of Curly's musical material, but culminates in the use of 'People Will Say We're in Love', written in waltz time. This section, vaguely reminiscent of the meeting scene in 'Dance at the Gym' from *West Side Story*, is hesitant and tender and allows both the audience (and the lead characters) to explore this possible union. Furthermore, this provides a starker contrast when Jud enters to disrupt the marriage.

Nunn and Stroman's use of the community throughout the ballet adds a further element to the narrative. Ado Annie and Will Parker are present during the wedding procession, revealing the community's assent to the union between Laurey and Curly. Each member of the female chorus is assigned a male counterpart and it is clear that this is the foundation upon which the new state should be built. However, when Jud enters, the community still continue to play a crucial role in the scene. Jud's entrance is heralded by strains of 'Oh, What a Beautiful Mornin'', juxtaposed with fragments from 'Lonely Room'. The music summarizes Laurey's dilemma perfectly. The two themes are never quite resolved, both striving to reach a perfect cadence. Jud is accompanied by burlesque dancers, seated on chairs which are dragged onto the stage by the male ensemble. Accompanied by a honky-tonk piano, the burlesque girls perform their lascivious dance and the entire ensemble appears complicit in Jud's world of debauchery, corralling Laurey back into their circle of iniquity. She is dragged around on stage and manipulated like a doll into dancing in the burlesque kick-line. It is at this point that Laurey's fascination with Jud is communicated clearly. The beaming grin which spreads across her face shows she likes dancing in this fashion and exploring elements of her sexuality which are not yet fully known to her. In this world, she is the outsider—an interesting contrast to Jud's role outside the real-world community. Jud is no longer the Other; rather than assimilate himself, he has created a world in which others must assimilate or face the consequences administered by his hand. The male ensemble reiterate this; having previously revealed their sexual promiscuity, their choreographed movements now urge the fight between Jud and Curly to continue and they block the ensemble from reaching the ensuing action. Curly's dead body is then placed on the same chairs used by the burlesque dancers and slowly dragged away by the male ensemble who now represent a funeral cortège. Thus, when Laurey awakes, her tacit approval in allowing Jud to accompany her to the box social now has a double meaning: she can believe that she is saving not only Curly but also the community.

The opening of Act 2 ('The Farmer and the Cowman') is now also more poignant. The territory of Oklahoma, on the brink of becoming a state, has to decide its future: to become domesticated and settled (shown through Laurey's relationship with Curly) or to entertain the possibility of being ruled by the untamed ego, characterized by hedonism and personified in the character of Jud. The dream ballet has reinforced Nunn's exploration of this young community and, in doing so, has introduced the idea that it is the threat posed by Jud's world (albeit one imagined in Laurey's dream) that allows the citizens of *Oklahoma!* to cast aside their differences in order to form the foundations for their new state.

Like Eyre and Hytner before him, Nunn approached *Oklahoma!* in the same way as he would a straight play, encouraging his cast to do the same. With no singing allowed in early rehearsals, all lyrics were delivered as dialogue, resulting in the cast examining the text in the same level of detail as the *Guys and Dolls* cast did sixteen years earlier. The production received generally positive critical reviews, with one exception that caused Nunn to pen a letter in response to the criticisms levelled at his decision to stage a Rodgers and Hammerstein classic. Writing in *The Guardian* newspaper, Michael Billington accused the National of lowering expectations and being 'driven by cautious pragmatism', proposing that the theatre would have been better served by ending the year with a £2 million deficit in order to prove that the current level of public funding was unsustainable. Nunn branded the critic's suggestion as 'pompous and idiotic', declaring that *Oklahoma!* was an important work in the last hundred years of theatre and the National must cater to all tastes.[20]

Oklahoma!'s sell-out run had averted financial disaster, allowing the theatre to operate on a surplus. The following year, *Oklahoma!* transferred to the West End with a Broadway production scheduled for the autumn, but Nunn's plans for the latter production were impeded when Actors' Equity refused to allow him to import his National Theatre cast.[21] Nunn's schedule did not allow time to rehearse with a new American cast, and although he proposed that the original cast would be replaced four months into the run, Actors' Equity could not 'allow English actors to be cast in a Broadway production of the quintessential American musical'.[22] Although the National's production of *Carousel* had received critical acclaim when it reached Broadway, the reviews for *Oklahoma!* were decidedly lukewarm, disappointing both critics and fans who perhaps felt that this was one Broadway classic that did not require a British reimagining. Writing in the *New York Observer*, John Heilpern asserts that Nunn's production 'takes itself all too solemnly, earnestly over-mining the subtext and presumed erotic undercurrent [. . .] and stops short of igniting the joyful spirit of a new American dawn'.[23]

The response of Actors' Equity is perhaps key to understanding the approach adopted by Nunn and his predecessors. All three directors were able to explore the material, free from the traditions established by the original Broadway productions. Audience responses to the premieres of *Oklahoma!* and *Carousel* in 1943 and 1945 respectively, had largely been influenced by the context in which the pieces were presented: Rodgers and Hammerstein's works had served as reminders of national pride in a country emerging from the Depression and the effects of the Second World War. Subsequent Broadway productions (*Oklahoma!* was revived in 1951, 1953, and 1979: *Carousel* in 1949, 1954, and 1957) appeared to pay homage to this, preserving de Mille's choreography, with directorial credit frequently taken by the original director, Rouben Mamoulian. Although it seemed that Eyre's *Guys and Dolls* was a precarious choice for the National, licensing restrictions meant his successors often had much more at stake when choosing to stage iconic musicals that had become the mainstay of the American musical theatre. In addition, the National had only staged two musicals in the decade between *Guys and Dolls* and *Carousel*: *Jean Seberg* (1983) and *Sunday in the Park with George* (1990), directed by Steven Pimlott. *Jean Seberg* was a disaster and *Sunday in the Park with George* had not managed to replicate the success of Eyre's production. Yet the freedom provided by working in a subsidized environment meant that these directors, supported by an in-house production team, could spend more time exploring the material and often did so through detailed analysis of the text.

For the National Theatre, musicals brought financial security, often in the form of lucrative West End transfers. *My Fair Lady* (2001) and *Anything Goes* (2002), both directed by Nunn, enjoyed successful transfers to the Theatre Royal Drury Lane with the former subsequently going on tour throughout the UK. Other Broadway productions in the National's repertoire were premieres (*Sunday in the Park with George*, 1990) or revised versions; both *Candide* (1999) and *South Pacific* (2001) were subject to revisions—the former rewritten and directed by John Caird, the latter by Trevor Nunn. Although this has meant the choice of repertoire has, at times, been subjected to critical disdain, it indicates that the programming at the theatre is reflective of the tastes of middle-class British audiences and also fulfils the National's remit to present a diverse array of world theatre.

'ONLY MAYBE SLIGHTLY REARRANGED'

> My association with the Donmar Warehouse has been a joy from its inception in 1992 with *Assassins* through its productions of *Company, Merrily We Roll Along, Into the Woods* and *Pacific Overtures*. Our collaborations over the years have been professionally fulfilling and personally gratifying.
>
> Stephen Sondheim[24]

When the Donmar Warehouse opened its doors in October 1992, it did so without funding from the Arts Council. The newly renovated space in Covent Garden came rent-free for the first five years and all productions in the first three years had been underwritten by investment from the property owners. The freedom afforded by such financial support allowed artistic director Sam Mendes and his creative team to choose a programme, for at least the first few years, which capitalized on the artistic possibilities of the intimate space.[25]

The theatre's first production, *Assassins*, had been suggested to Mendes by Richard Eyre. The Sondheim musical was new to British audiences and this production allowed the composer and book writer, John Weidman, the opportunity to revisit their work after receiving a less-than-favourable reception of its Off-Broadway premiere in 1991, resulting in the insertion of a new eleven o'clock number, 'Something Just Broke'. Mendes was convinced that such a rewrite would enable British audiences to understand the kind of America that *Assassins* portrayed, whilst also communicating the sense of grief that had united Americans following the assassination of Kennedy and other US presidents.

The British premiere of *Assassins* opened at the Donmar in October 1992 and reviews indicated that the venue was perfectly suited to material of this nature. Mendes had assembled a cast of musical theatre veterans (Louise Gold) alongside actors with extensive experience of the classical repertoire (Ciaran Hinds) and actors who were at home in both genres (Henry Goodman). The intimate nature of the venue supported the requirements of a chamber musical, but also added an extra dimension that could not have been achieved in larger West End theatres. Goodman's passage to the gallows as Charles Guiteau brought uncomfortable laughter from the audience; the close proximity to the action afforded an eerie insight into the assassin's final moments. The only production in the season to turn a profit[26] Mendes's *Assassins* established the reputation of the Donmar and forged a collaboration with a composer whose work had found a comfortable home in the venue.

In 1995, the Donmar opened its fourth season with another Sondheim chamber production, *Company*. The production could have been the Donmar's last had an emergency payment from the Arts Council not been granted the following year; the capacity of the venue meant that very few productions had been able to transfer easily to the West End and the financial support that had been provided by private investors could not continue forever. Repeating a similar casting pattern to *Assassins*, Mendes assembled Shakespearean actors (Adrian Lester as Bobby and Sophie Thompson as Amy) alongside those with experience of musical theatre (Clive Rowe as Harry and Teddy Kempner as David). In a similar vein to the National's production of *Carousel*, Mendes cast black actors in the roles of both Harry (Rowe) and Bobby (Lester), the latter being the first black male actor to take a lead role in a Sondheim production. Both the casting of Lester and the timeless, non-specific geographical nature of the setting removed what Mendes refers to as 'the white middle-class chic New York curse, which is the thing that above all dates *Company* the most'.[27] The action takes place in Bobby's loft (designed by Mark Thompson) whereas Boris Aronson's Tony award-winning set for the original production suggested the frantic quality of life in Manhattan, whilst also managing to incorporate the respective apartments of each couple. Stacy Wolf's excellent feminist reading of the original production argues that this raises questions about 'the meaning of home and domesticity [. . .] when women's liberation was becoming part of mainstream society'.[28] In Mendes's version, the choice to stage *Company* in Bobby's loft liberates the musical from the decade of the 1970s and all the resulting implications, in addition to informing the audience that Bobby is central to the action.

In the opening scene, the married couples appear to function as a Greek chorus, commenting on Bobby's birthday celebrations, whilst he watches, unacknowledged from a chair placed centre stage. Upon initial scrutiny, this opening scene may reinforce the notion that Bobby is the outsider, separate from the action and never anything more than on the sidelines. The chorus voices remain disembodied until Bobby invites them in and it becomes clear in the following scene that the action takes place in Bobby's imagination; he is listening to the messages his married friends have left on his answering machine. This device is further reinforced throughout, particularly in 'Poor Baby', when Bobby is in bed with April, but somewhat egotistically imagines how his other female friends are spending their time in bed—thinking about him.

In this production of *Company*, although Bobby is often seemingly depicted as the outsider because of his marital status, there is a clear sense that he is the controlling force in the narrative. Mendes places him central to each scene and Bobby enters the action at his own bidding, transitioning seamlessly from the chair placed downstage centre, into the lives of the married couples. The techniques employed by Mendes ensure that Bobby is never quite the outsider. In Act 1, the scene featuring Bobby, Harry, and Sarah uses the intimate setting of the Donmar to full effect. The camaraderie established between Harry and Bobby is unmistakable and so when Harry and Sarah begin their energetic karate-chopping display in their metaphoric battle for supremacy, the audience are experiencing the discomfort that Bobby must also feel by intruding into the lives of his married friends. This is further reinforced when the scene is underscored by the song 'The Little Things You Do Together'. In her comprehensive journal article, Natalie Draper recognizes that Bobby steps outside the scene to observe Joanne's scathing commentary on marriage, as expressed in this song. In doing so, Draper asserts that 'the audience is allowed to enter Bobby's stream of consciousness and empathize with his ambivalence about relationships'.[29] However, this was established much earlier in the scene. As Bobby witnesses the dialogue between Sarah and Harry that culminates in their physical display, there is a clear sense that he is already an observer. The dialogue excludes Bobby; as Wolf indicates, the married couple's conversational repartee focuses on their respective addictions and Mendes's staging of this scene places Bobby in the central position, over whose head Harry and Sarah lob their volleying shots. Bobby is both central and apart. Whilst cueing much of the action by his own thoughts, he is also capable of performing the role of critical observer, coaxing the audience into both sharing and examining the moment.

Placing Bobby central to the story and action could have proved problematic when tackling the staging of 'Side by Side/What Would We Do Without You'. In this production, the song is conjured from Bobby's cocaine-fuelled thoughts, singing the lyrics 'parallel lines who meet'[30] as he prepares the drug with his credit card. He remains central to the whole scene; when the momentum of the song wanes, Bobby snorts another line and the chorus are once again driven into a frenetic song and dance routine. Bobby attempts to replicate the dance routines executed by his married friends but finds he has no partner to respond to his solo dance. Upon initial examination it would appear that the song reinforces his loneliness and isolation, but it should not be forgotten that the whole scene was conjured at his bidding and at numerous points throughout the sequence, Bobby has refused to assimilate himself into the choreographic world created by his friends. The song ends with Bobby surrounded by his friends—after all 'one's impossible, two is dreary'— and so he chooses to end his 'trip' with option number three: 'company, safe and cheery'.[31] This would suggest that he is yet to reach his epiphany, reserved instead for the final scene.

Sheila Gish's performance of 'The Ladies Who Lunch' is delivered directly to the audience who, at close quarters, have no choice but to witness her emotional breakdown in fine detail. When she screams, 'Watch! Did you just hear yourself? Watch . . . WATCH!' the audience understands that they have been voyeurs: they have witnessed both Joanne's breakdown and Bobby's pain and distress up close and personal—a privilege afforded by the production's venue. As with *Assassins* and his 1993 revival of *Cabaret*, Mendes revises the eleven o'clock number. Gone is the anthemic life-affirming portrayal of 'Being Alive', replaced instead with 'a hymn to desperation and need'.[32] Lester's interpretation of the text, particularly when the lyrics switch to the more personal plea ('Somebody hold *me* too close'), presents a broken man who takes little joy in acknowledging his loneliness. At this point the audience witness a man who is desperate; they share in his pain and anguish but also recognize that they too have ended their journey and can now dissolve their partnership with Bobby as he has with both bachelorhood and his married friends.

As with other revivals of American musical classics at the National, the production made a West End transfer to the Albery Theatre in March 1996 (where the seating capacity was more than three times the size of the Donmar), but was unable to repeat the success of its original sold-out run, where the intimate setting in which the production had first been presented brought the audience closer to Bobby, thus fostering a deeper understanding of the character and his motivations. Since its production of *Company*, the Donmar Warehouse has staged some thirteen musicals, four of which were Sondheim revivals: *Into the Woods* (1998, director: John Crowley), *Merrily We Roll Along* (2000, director: Michael Grandage), *Pacific Overtures* (2003, director: Gary Griffin), and *Passion* (2010, director: Jamie Lloyd). In 1997, two new musicals premiered at the Donmar (*The Fix*, directed by Sam Mendes, and *Enter the Guardsman*, directed by Jeremy Sams) but neither did particularly well at the box office. Mendes asserts that rediscovery appears to be the Donmar's forte, and that Sondheim's musicals in particular are apt for this type of treatment. The subsidy received by the Donmar has provided the freedom to programme ambitiously, to rediscover and reimagine some of the least commercial works in the American canon. Speaking of his collaboration with the theatre, Sondheim himself admits that this form of financial independence at the Donmar has been invaluable: 'I never felt I would sink them or that anything depended on it, except doing the production well.'[33]

'You've Been Given the Freedom . . . to Work Your Way'

Frank Rich opens his review of the National Theatre's production of *Carousel* with the declaration that 'even in the age of Andrew Lloyd Webber, the British remain in awe of the Broadway musical'.[34] Removing the adverb 'even' may offer some insight as to why these, and many other, British revivals of Broadway classics were so warmly received by British audiences. During the late 1980s and early 1990s, the West End hosted an array of Lloyd Webber shows, that later were labelled—and denigrated as—'megamusicals' (*Cats, Starlight Express, The Phantom of the Opera, Sunset Boulevard*). Whilst these musicals did contribute a great deal to the financial success of the West End, drawing millions of tourists to the theatre every year, the subsidized sector needed to offer an alternative to the commercial sector. Eyre's choice to revive *Guys and Dolls* in 1982 was daring and ambitious; the reputation of the National was at stake as critics felt that this hallowed institution should not mimic the commercial sector and that, under the auspices of public funding, the theatre had both the freedom to fail and the task to innovate. Merely reviving a much-loved Broadway classic was not considered innovation enough. Innovation, however, came in the form of how directors chose to approach the material.

By stripping the musicals back to the text, all four directors discussed in this chapter were able to approach these works in the same way they would a play by Arthur Miller or Edward Albee. They encouraged their casts to do the same, often casting actors who had not trained in musical theatre but had established a career in repertory and Shakespeare and had voices good enough to cope with the demands of the musical score. Lyrics became monologues and choreography was released from the fetters of original Broadway productions and the numerous US revivals that prescribed duplication. In adopting this approach, director and actor were able to realize afresh the intention of each piece and consider how the musical material functioned to serve the plot. For Nunn, this meant that *Oklahoma!* became a piece about a community and its priorities, shifting the focus from the (simplistic) question of who the lead female character would take to a social gathering. Similarly, for Mendes at the Donmar, *Assassins* allowed British audiences to understand the failure of American neo-liberalism, whilst *Company* managed to convey loneliness and isolation in the most intimate of spaces.

It is also interesting to note that whilst these musicals may have been revived on Broadway several times since their inaugural production, this was not the case in the West End. The Donmar's *Assassins* was a British premiere and *Company* had not been seen on the professional London stage for twenty-three years. The National Theatre productions tell a similar story: *Guys and Dolls* had been absent from the British stage for nearly thirty years, while *Carousel*'s last professional production in the West End had been mounted forty-two years earlier. (*Oklahoma!* toured in 1980 and settled in the West End the following year, some thirty-three years after the London premiere.) The musicals staged at the National had also been released in film adaptations during the 1950s and it is probably this medium that had subsequently attracted an audience in the UK. The undoubtedly limited exposure of British audiences to this material on the professional stage was probably a key factor in the success of these productions. So refreshingly different from the film versions (notwithstanding the obvious differences between live performance and cinema), these British revivals appealed to new audiences, perhaps introducing some of them to Rodgers and Hammerstein, Loesser and Sondheim for the very first time, and attracting these new audiences to subsidized venues.

The appetite for Broadway musicals amongst British audiences is also reflected in the success of such productions in other subsidized venues. During Hytner's stretch as artistic director at the National, there was only one major production of a Broadway musical (*A Funny Thing Happened on the Way to the Forum* in 2004), allowing other venues to take on the task of reviving classic American musicals. The Menier Chocolate Factory, opened in 2004, has offered a repertoire which intersperses London premieres of musicals (*Tick, Tick . . . Boom!*, *The Last Five Years*, *Take Flight*, and *Road Show*) with revivals of Broadway classics. Of the latter, many have transferred to the West End including three Sondheim musicals: *Sunday in the Park with George*, *A Little Night Music*, and *Merrily We Roll Along*. Another subsidized venue enjoying similar success is Chichester Festival Theatre, which since its opening in 1962 under the auspices of artistic director Sir Laurence Olivier, had produced a steady diet of plays, adding the occasional Broadway musical revival to its repertoire by the mid-1980s. In recent years, its musical revivals have received critical acclaim and often transferred to the West End. In the last four years alone, under the artistic directorship of Jonathan Church, four productions have either moved to the West End or have toured (*Singin' in the Rain*, *Sweeney Todd*, *The Pajama Game*, and *Barnum*) and the 2014 revival of *Gypsy* transferred to the Savoy Theatre in March 2015. Under the artistic directorship of Rufus Norris, the National Theatre appears set to return to the tradition of reconceiving Broadway musicals. His style is diverse and inclusive and his direction of *Cabaret* and the 2011 verbatim musical *London Road*, seem to hint that he is willing to consider both new and revised existing material for the National's repertoire.

British theatre now appears to be entering an era in which cross-fertilization between the subsidized and commercial sectors is relatively commonplace. The three National Theatre productions explored in this chapter all transferred to the West End or Broadway and it is worth noting that a similar relationship between the subsidized and commercial sector brought *Les Misérables* to the West End stage nearly thirty years ago. Cameron Mackintosh identified Trevor Nunn as the ideal director for such a piece and in turn, Nunn agreed, insisting that he should work with the Royal Shakespeare Company and co-direct with John Caird, further explored in the chapters by Kathryn M. Grossmann, Bradley Stephens, and Miranda Lundskaer-Nielsen.[35] This relationship between the sectors appears to be one that will be further developed by Mackintosh who plans to turn the Ambassadors Theatre into a receiving house for subsidized productions, renovating the space to emulate the non-proscenium layout favoured by many of the subsidized companies. Such plans are not without their risks; subsidized houses may feel tempted to produce a final product that is more akin to the demands of the commercial sector in order to secure a successful transfer and this, in turn, may mean that fewer artistic risks are taken.

Reviving a musical is an onerous task; often, the restrictions placed upon directors and producers by the estates of the writers and composers have too great an influence for the creative team to fully liberate the material (although it should be noted that the geographical advantage of reviving in London, as opposed to Broadway, meant that some licence holders were perhaps more lenient in their demands). If the composer or playwright is still alive, then revivals can often appear as rewrites. Public taste will have significantly changed since the original production was first staged and whilst the change in context may allow for a greater exploration of some of the more complex issues of certain plots, there is no guarantee that the reception will be favourable. It may be that audiences on either side of the Atlantic possess a different understanding of what constitutes a reimagining of old material, exemplified in the response of British critics to the transfer of the Lincoln Center's production of *South Pacific,* directed by Bartlett Sher. Whilst it was received with huge acclaim in the US, reviews in the UK claimed that this 'faintly bland and traditional treatment' suggested that 'New York has little to teach us about resurrecting the Broadway past'.[36]

The success of the productions examined in this chapter lies in the approach that the directors adopted towards the material. British directors had interrogated the Broadway musical in the same way they would a Shakespearean or Chekhov classic. Such classics are open to reinterpretation and innovation. By trusting in the dramatic narrative to tell the story, using design and music to reinforce the same rhythmic language, the bold, imaginative approaches adopted by British directors have proved the classic status of the American musical.

NOTES

1. Janet Minihan, *The Nationalization of Culture* (London: Hamish Hamilton, 1977) cites the BBC and ENSA (Entertainments National Service Association) as two of the main publicly funded bodies that helped stimulate public interest in live theatre and music during the 1940s. ENSA, financed by Treasury funds administered through the Army, Royal Air Force, and Royal Navy, was established to provide light entertainment to the armed forces and factory workers during the Second World War.

2. Arts Council England, *Great Art and Culture for Everyone: 10 Year Strategic Framework* (London: Arts Council England, 2013), 44.

3. Keith Warner, 'And One for Mahler: An Opera Director's Reflections on Sondheim in the Subsidized Theater', in *The Oxford Handbook of Sondheim Studies,* ed. Robert Gordon (New York: Oxford University Press, 2014), 230–232.

4. Richard Eyre, 'Love Letter to Broadway', *The Guardian,* 14 May 2005, http://www.theguardian.com/stage/2005/may/14/theatre.broadway, accessed 28 July 2014.

5. Eyre's recollections of the production are drawn from Matt Wolf, *The 'Guys and Dolls' Book* (London: Nick Hern, 1997), 34–38.

6. An earlier publication of the similarly titled *'Guys and Dolls' Book* (London: Methuen, 1983) by Frank Loesser et al. features a review from Russell Davies (quoted here), interviews with Eyre, and photographs of the National Theatre production. The full libretto is also included.

7. Frank Loesser, *Guys and Dolls* (London: MPL Communications Ltd, 1950), 103–104.

8. Quoted in Daniel Rosenthal, *The National Theatre Story* (London: Oberon, 2013), in the chapter 'Deputies and Dolls'.

9. Quoted in Matt Wolf, *'Guys and Dolls' Book,* 100.

10. The MacMillan Estate, 'Kenneth MacMillan Biography', http://www.kennethmacmillan.com/kenneth-macmillan/biography.html, accessed 8 December 2014.

11. Oscar HammersteinII, *Carousel* (New York: Williamson Music, 1945), 38.

12. Frank Rich, 'London Makes a Revelation of *Carousel*', *New York Times*, 17 December 1992, http://www.nytimes.com/1992/12/17/theater/review-theater-london-makes-a-revelation-of-carousel.html, accessed 27 August 2014.

13. Scott McMillin, *The Musical as Drama* (Princeton, NJ: Princeton University Press, 2006), 85–86. The discussion here focuses on community as a theme emerging from the drama itself. McMillin's observations relate to a number of Rodgers and Hammerstein musicals, although he notes that *Carousel* is unusual in that it opens on a large scale as opposed to the more intimate openings of *Oklahoma!*, *The King and I*, and *South Pacific*.

14. Otis Baxter, 'All the World's a Stage' (*Weekly Journal*, 25 February 1993, 8) offers a summary of many of the reviews. Similar views were also shared by Richard Ingrams, Review of *Guys and Dolls*, *The Observer*, 24 January 1993, 20 and Lynn Barber, Review of *Guys and Dolls, Independent on Sunday*, 24 January 1993, 23. With thanks to Daniel Williams for his assistance in summarizing many of these reviews.

15. During his appearance on *Desert Island Discs* (broadcast 11 July 1993), Hytner compared Rowe to Stubby Kaye, calling him 'the perfect musical performer'.

16. Broadcast on 2 November 2013, *Live from the National Theatre: 50 Years on Stage* featured an interview with Nunn.

17. Rosenthal, *National Theatre Story*. See the chapter entitled 'From Prison to the Prairies' for a detailed description of Nunn's vision for *Oklahoma!*

18. *Oklahoma!*, movie trailer (online video) https://www.youtube.com/watch?v=V6uD9-aLCps, accessed 8 December 2014.

19. Quoted in John Crook, 'Jackman Is Better than OK in *Oklahoma!*', *Los Angeles Times*, 16 November 2003, http://articles.latimes.com/2003/nov/16/news/tv-coverstory16, accessed 15 December 2014.

20. Michael Billington, 'Oh No: Not *Oklahoma!*', *The Guardian*, 12 August 1998, 16. Nunn's letter of response was printed five days later: '*Oklahoma!* Is the Price to Keep National from Nobs and Snobs', *The Guardian*, 17 August 1998, 17.

21. In 1999, Equity rules governing the transfer of British and American actors to opposite sides of the Atlantic stated that permission must be sought from both Equity organizations and that the exchange of actors should be balanced. Highlighting that costs of production in the UK are generally lower because of government subsidy, the American union, Actors' Equity, believe that bringing British actors into Broadway transfers of revivals reduces job opportunities for American actors. Felicia R. Lee, 'British Group Urges Freer Exchange of Actors with U.S.', *New York Times*, 3 February 1999, http://www.nytimes.com/1999/02/03/theater/british-group-urges-freer-exchange-of-actors-with-us.html, accessed 20 August 2015.

22. Michael Riedel, 'No OK for Brit Revival', *New York Post*, 22 January 1999, http://nypost.com/1999/01/22/no-ok-for-brit-revival/, accessed 15 December 2014. The Broadway transfer of *Oklahoma!* opened at the George Gershwin Theatre in 2002 and ran for 388 performances. It featured only two members of the original cast: Josefina Gabrielle as Laurey and Shuler Hensley as Jud.

23. John Heilpern, 'There's a Dark, Rainy Cloud on the Meadow', *New York Observer*, 4 January 2002, http://observer.com/2002/04/theres-a-dark-rainy-cloud-on-the-meadow/, accessed 20 August 2015. Steven Suskin in his *Broadway Yearbook 2001–2002: A Relevant and Irreverent Record* (New York: Oxford University Press, 2002) also highlights Ben Brantley's reviews of both the original London production and the Broadway transfer,

declaring that 'audiences who didn't see the London version may wonder what the fuss was about'.

24. Quoted in Alistair Smith, 'Adrian Lester and Daniel Evans Join Donmar's Sondheim Celebration', *The Stage*, 10 July 2010, http://www.thestage.co.uk/news/2010/07/adrian-lester-and-daniel-evans-join-donmars-sondheim-celebration/, accessed 30 July 2014.

25. The Donmar Warehouse has a seating capacity of 251.

26. Matt Wolf, *Sam Mendes at the Donmar: Stepping Into Freedom* (London: Nick Hern, 2002), 26.

27. Matt Wolf, *Sam Mendes*, 29.

28. Stacy Wolf, 'Keeping Company with Sondheim's Women', in *The Oxford Handbook of Sondheim Studies*, ed. Robert Gordon (New York: Oxford University Press, 2014), 368.

29. Natalie Draper, 'Concept Meets Narrative in Sondheim's *Company*: Metadrama as a Method of Analysis', *Studies in Musical Theatre* 4, no. 2 (2010), 176.

30. Stephen Sondheim, *Company: A Musical Comedy* (Winona: Hal Leonard Publishing, 1970), 108.

31. Sondheim, *Company*, 114.

32. Matt Wolf, *Sam Mendes*, 29.

33. Quoted in Matt Wolf, *Sam Mendes*, 25. Wolf devotes a chapter of his book to the relationship between the Donmar and Sondheim in which he cites Mendes as proposing that the box office failures of new musicals fell prey to the 'Why isn't it Sondheim?' mentality.

34. Rich, 'London Makes a Revelation of *Carousel*'.

35. For more information on *Les Misérables* and Cameron Mackintosh, please consult the essays by Kathryn M. Grossmann and Bradley Stephens as well as by Miranda Lundskaer-Nielsen, in this volume.

36. Paul Taylor, '*South Pacific*'s Magic Is Swept Away on Trip Across Atlantic', *The Independent*, 24 August 2011, http://www.independent.co.uk/arts-entertainment/theatre-dance/reviews/first-night-south-pacific-barbican-london-2342755.html and Michael Billington, Review of *South Pacific*, *The Guardian*, 23 August 2011, http://www.theguardian.com/stage/2011/aug/23/south-pacific-review, both accessed 23 December 2014.

BIBLIOGRAPHY

Arts Council England. *Great Art and Culture for Everyone: 10 Year Strategic Framework*. London: Arts Council England, 2013.

Barber, Lynn. Review of *Guys and Dolls*. *Independent on Sunday*, 24 January 1993, 24.

Baxter, Otis. 'All the World's a Stage.' *Weekly Journal*, 25 February 1993, 8.

Billington, Michael. 'Oh No: Not *Oklahoma!*' *The Guardian*, 12 August 1998, 8.

Billington, Michael. Review of *South Pacific*, *The Guardian*, 23 August 2011. http://www.the-guardian.com/stage/2011/aug/23/south-pacific-review, accessed 23 December 2014.

Crook, John, 'Jackman Is Better than OK in *Oklahoma!*' *Los Angeles Times*, 16 November 2003. http://articles.latimes.com/2003/nov/16/news/tv-coverstory16, accessed 15 December 2014.

Draper, Natalie. 'Concept Meets Narrative in Sondheim's *Company*: Metadrama as a Method of Analysis.' *Studies in Musical Theatre* 4, no. 2 (2010): 171–183.

Eyre, Richard. 'Love Letter to Broadway.' *The Guardian*, 14 May 2005. http://www.theguardian.com/stage/2005/may/14/theatre.broadway, accessed 28 July 2014.

Hammerstein II, Oscar. *Carousel*. New York: Williamson Music, 1945.

Heilpern, John. 'There's a Dark, Rainy Cloud on the Meadow.' *New York Observer*, 4 January 2002. http://observer.com/2002/04/theres-a-dark-rainy-cloud-on-the-meadow/, accessed 20 August 2015.

Ingrams, Richard. Review of *Guys and Dolls*. *The Observer*, 24 January 1993, 20.

Lee, Felicia R. 'British Group Urges Freer Exchange of Actors with U.S.' *New York Times*, 3 February 1999. http://www.nytimes.com/1999/02/03/theater/british-group-urges-freer-exchange-of-actors-with-us.html, accessed 20 August 2015.

Loesser, Frank. *Guys and Dolls*. London: MPL Communications Ltd, 1950.

Loesser, Frank, et al. *The 'Guys and Dolls' Book*. London: Methuen, 1983.

The MacMillan Estate. 'Kenneth MacMillan Biography.' http://www.kennethmacmillan.com/kenneth-macmillan/biography.html, accessed 08/12/2014.

McMillin, Scott. *The Musical as Drama*. Princeton, NJ: Princeton University Press, 2006.

Minihan, Janet. *The Nationalization of Culture*. London: Hamish Hamilton, 1977.

Nunn, Trevor. '*Oklahoma!* Is the Price to Keep National from Nobs and Snobs.' *The Guardian*, 17 August 1998, 17.

Rich, Frank. 'London Makes a Revelation of *Carousel*.' *New York Times*, 17 December 1992. http://www.nytimes.com/1992/12/17/theater/review-theater-london-makes-a-revelation-of-carousel.html, accessed 27 August 2014.

Riedel, Michael. 'No OK for Brit Revival.' *New York Post*, 22 January 1999. http://nypost.com/1999/01/22/no-ok-for-brit-revival/, accessed 15 December 2014.

Rosenthal, Daniel. *The National Theatre Story*. London: Oberon, 2013.

Smith, Alistair. 'Adrian Lester and Daniel Evans Join Donmar's Sondheim Celebration.' *The Stage*, 10 July 2010. http://www.thestage.co.uk/news/2010/07/adrian-lester-and-daniel-evans-join-donmars-sondheim-celebration/, accessed 30 July 2014.

Sondheim, Stephen. *Company: A Musical Comedy*. Winona: Hal Leonard Publishing, 1970.

Suskin, Steven. *Broadway Yearbook 2001-2002: A Relevant and Irreverent Record*. New York: Oxford University Press, 2002.

Taylor, Paul, '*South Pacific*'s Magic Is Swept Away on Trip Across Atlantic.' *The Independent*, 24 August 2011. http://www.independent.co.uk/arts-entertainment/theatre-dance/reviews/first-night-south-pacific-barbican-london-2342755.html, accessed 23 December 2014.

Warner, Keith. 'And One for Mahler: An Opera Director's Reflections on Sondheim in the Subsidized Theater.' In *The Oxford Handbook of Sondheim Studies*, edited by Robert Gordon, 227–238. New York: Oxford University Press, 2014.

Wolf, Matt. *The 'Guys and Dolls' Book*. London: Nick Hern, 1997.

Wolf, Matt. *Sam Mendes at the Donmar: Stepping into Freedom*. London: Nick Hern, 2002.

Wolf, Stacy Ellen. 'Keeping Company with Sondheim's Women.' In *The Oxford Handbook of Sondheim Studies*, edited by Robert Gordon, 365–383. New York: Oxford University Press, 2014.

....

CHAPTER 15

LES MISÉRABLES

From Epic Novel to Epic Musical

....

KATHRYN M. GROSSMAN AND BRADLEY STEPHENS

By 1978, when Alain Boublil and Claude-Michel Schönberg began reworking Victor Hugo's epic novel *Les Misérables* for musical theatre, the story of the convict Jean Valjean and his journey towards redemption in post-Revolutionary France was already one of Western literature's most adapted works. After the immense success of its international publication in 1862, the renown of *Les Misérables* had been enhanced thanks to a wide range of adaptations in print, on stage, across the airwaves, and on screen, extending from the Americas to the Far East.[1] Although Schönberg himself has noted that Puccini abandoned his own operatic treatment of *Les Misérables* because Hugo's novel was too vast,[2] he and Boublil were certainly not the first to set the text to music, with versions having appeared in the United States and Italy before either artist was even born.[3] Yet no single adaptation has perhaps done more to popularize Hugo's bestseller than the work that is today universally known as *Les Miz*. The London production that opened on 8 October 1985 has become the epicentre of an international phenomenon as the world's longest-running musical.[4] Garnering over 140 major theatre awards and playing across nearly 350 cities in forty-four countries, the show has been seen in person by more than seventy million people.[5] Those oft-cited figures potentially do not account for the yet broader audiences that have experienced *Les Misérables*: various album recordings and filmed concerts have sold by the millions, while the 2002 School Edition and the 2012 Hollywood film version have both extended the musical's reach into popular culture. For Boublil and Schönberg, this success maintains Hugo's legacy: '[O]ur musical of *Les Misérables* is now following in the footsteps of Victor Hugo's novel; embraced by different nations in different languages all over the world.'[6]

One inheritance they might have preferred to do without was the hostile critical response that Hugo's epic initially received. When France's Goncourt brothers proclaimed that 'a man of genius had written a novel intended for the *cabinets de lecture* (i.e., the uneducated people who visited the reading rooms)'[7] their observation had been meant as a criticism rather than a prediction of the novel's mass popularity. Like many

French critics, they saw *Les Misérables* as a return to outdated Romantic tastes. Idealism and contrived characterization threatened to devalue the contemporary investment in realist poise and literary craftsmanship.[8] Such objections made little difference: the global market was instantly swept up in the very same sentimentalism that had irked so many commentators. Over 120 years later, the musical's London debut uncannily soured the same cultural tastes that privilege supposed artistic integrity over popular sentiment. In London *The Times* derided the show's 'push-button emotionalism' and *The Guardian* labelled it 'middlebrow entertainment rather than great art'. Ironically, however, Hugo's novel had by now accumulated greater artistic credit thanks to its enduring status, leading several critics to declare that the show trivialized its source and 'emasculated Hugo's Olympian perspective', as *The Observer* claimed.[9] Benedict Nightingale for the *New York Times* numbered among the few who could anticipate the fervour of the paying audiences, as if aware of the lessons that history offers through such changes of fortune. He articulates the public experience when remembering that first night: 'I was transported as I've seldom been in a career in which I reckon I've reviewed some 12,000 shows: transported into a world of beggary and heroism, evil and self-sacrifice.'[10] A mass marketing machine—not dissimilar from the one launched by Hugo and his publisher—would capitalize on such sensations. For all of the musical's achievements, the ability to unsettle critics but to bring audiences together makes it recognizably Hugolian in character.

This telling line of continuity between page and stage rests upon a shared aesthetic character and universal appeal. In this chapter, we trace that line through an analysis of the novel's transfer to the stage so as to explore its relationship with Hugo's text as one of correspondence rather than equivalence. To borrow Linda Hutcheon's influential theory of how adaptations work, we see Boublil and Schönberg's musical not as 'a copy in any mode of reproduction, mechanical or otherwise', but as 'repetition without replication, bringing together the comfort of ritual and recognition with the delight of surprise and novelty'.[11] Scholarly attention to the relationship between the musical and its literary source has been limited, arguably owing to two unhelpful if persistent critical discourses: the qualitative distinction between high and popular culture on the one hand, and the tendency to consider adaptations as secondary products to their sources on the other.[12]

Thankfully, some insightful investigations have been carried out, in spite of the general suspicion. In *The Megamusical* (2006), Jessica Sternfeld included a chapter on *Les Misérables* that richly detailed its production history and carefully analysed the score. Elsewhere, in a chapter from his co-authored study *Adapting Nineteenth-Century France* (2013), Andrew Watts returned Hugo to the discussion by exploring how the novel and its musical adaptation each borrow from different theatrical sources for melodramatic effect. Notwithstanding these respective lenses on the commercial musical and literary adaptation, our essay sharpens the focus that both approaches afford. We further scrutinize the English libretto's collaborative development in order to create a clearer aesthetic and cultural portrait of what has become one of Britain's most beloved musical exports. Such scrutiny will be strengthened by recapping two contexts that tend to be underplayed but that have important roles: first and foremost, the epic character of Hugo's novel, which reflects both the author's Romantic world view and his literary diversity, and which for that reason cannot be conceptualized solely through models of adaptation or simply labelled with vague clichés of 'greatness'; and second, the French version of *Les Misérables* that Boublil and Schönberg recorded as a concept album and staged in Paris some five years before the English musical, itself constituting a significant prototype for their worldwide hit.

Our intention is to tease out the similarities and differences between the novel and the musical in order to clarify the ways in which the latter at once mirrors the former while projecting its own individual identity. Given that the show's length equals the time it takes most people to read less than 5 per cent of Hugo's text, this is hardly surprising, but such extensive abbreviation need not be understood in strictly reductive terms. The comparatively short runs of the many stage plays based on the book, beginning with that of Hugo's son Charles in 1863, indeed suggest that the musical form draws far greater verve from the novel than any strictly theatrical production has done. The novel's spiritual and sentimental tones necessarily become simpler and more forceful in a sung-through musical that is played out on a theatrical stage. The musical echoes Hugo but understands that his narrative range and depth could not merely be recited if it were to succeed as a modern opera.

HUGO AND HIS ADAPTORS

Both the literary form and narrative content of *Les Misérables* have travelled across different generations, cultures, and media by fascinating audiences and adaptors alike. Hugo's sensory descriptions generate an obvious interest for the visual and performing arts. In famous scenes such as Jean Valjean's flight through the sewers, Hugo displays an imagination that is 'both impressionistic and cinematic' in its attention to light and shifting viewpoints.[13] At the same time, he relies on what has been called his 'highly developed auditory sensitivity':[14] music is everywhere in the novel, from Fantine's maternal lullaby to Gavroche's rebellious songs, while the narrative frequently calls upon sound, noticeable for example when Inspector Javert traverses eerily silent streets to happen upon the invisible but audibly mighty swell of the Seine beneath him.[15] This narrative style is made to serve a story that is both sweeping in its scope as a work of historical fiction and universal in its nature as an allegory of human suffering. The co-dependency between good and evil and the reality of social injustice are broad themes with general relevance, just as the novel's primal emotions such as love and despair can be universally experienced. Hugo saw the fates of all living things—irrespective of their grandeur or depravity—as entwined individual threads, knotting together into a twisting whole that at once tightens and unravels. Such a viewpoint is articulated in the novel's opening part through Bishop Myriel: he contemplates a universe in which everything is connected by a mysterious divine power that is infinite in its reach and transcendent in its effects (I.i.14).[16] Hugo's brief prologue—a single unfolding sentence that concisely illustrates his ever-expanding but always connected thought processes—talks not of the future of France but of every living soul.[17] The plight of the *misérables* is that of the world entire, in which an individual descent into wretchedness can still find deliverance through altruism and humanity. Invoking such a belief, Hugo foresees that his novel will be constrained neither by national nor temporal borders in its universal and timeless appeal.

In short, he had fashioned *Les Misérables* to be a classic in the vein of such greats as Homer, Milton, and Dante, whose works themselves reverberate through his writing.[18] He offers a poetic vision of modernity rather than an academic musing on it, knowing that basic principles rather than political intricacies would capture a global popular imagination. The 1832 Paris insurrection is therefore positioned as the direct result of poverty rather than specifically within the complicated ideological debates of the July Monarchy.[19] Furthermore, Hugo drew on the contemporary styles of historical and urban novels from writers such as Sir Walter Scott and his friend Honoré de Balzac, lending his work a modern attitude that would engage and entertain readers in an age when they were becoming increasingly accustomed to the thrills of narrative fiction. His own literary credentials allowed his imagination to thrive when writing the novel.[20] As both a highly successful playwright and the most celebrated French poet of the century, Hugo was fully qualified to excite and entice his readers with his combination of melodramatic plotting and epic dimensions—already seen three decades earlier in his hugely popular novel *Notre-Dame de Paris* (1831). Crucial to this emotional and literary scale were the characters themselves, who quickly entered into the public consciousness. 'By making them the means—and not the ends—for the transmission of a larger message,' as Isabel Roche has observed,[21] and with Hugo's encouragement of illustrators such as Gustave Brion for popular editions, figures like Valjean and Cosette struck an instant connection as emblems of Hugo's argument in favour of compassion and spirit over self-interest and desolation.

These various characteristics all facilitated *Les Misérables'* rebirth as a lyrical drama in the hands of Boublil and Schönberg. The challenge of translating Hugo's sprawling 1,500-page novel into a stage musical was considerable—all the more so when we consider that Charles Dickens's *Oliver Twist*, the musical of which (Lionel Bart's *Oliver!*) inspired Boublil during its 1978 London revival by reminding him of Hugo's characters, is only one-third as long. But musical theatre, as much as Hugo's writing, motivated the two Frenchmen. As a librettist, Boublil had been attracted to the medium's potential since he had seen *West Side Story* in 1959 in Paris. The New York premiere of *Jesus Christ Superstar* twelve years later convinced him that 'an all-sung musical with an historical theme, mixing the tradition of Italian opera with contemporary musical and literary styles', had enormous artistic potential.[22] Convincing the composer Schönberg of this interest, he produced *La Révolution française* in Paris in 1973: a rock opera whose subject created a precedent for their next collaboration. Importantly, the three musicals that had so enthused Boublil were themselves adaptations of monumental works—Dickens's social fiction, Shakespeare's *Romeo and Juliet*, and the Bible itself. They each demonstrated that well-known tales could find new life within the musical genre, and each conveyed themes found in *Les Misérables*, including social unrest, star-crossed lovers, and salvation. One other show may also have had its part to play, even if it has yet to figure in the orthodox narrative of the musical's creation. Intriguingly, in the autumn of the same year that Boublil and Schönberg began their project, a big-budget spectacle of Hugo's *Notre-Dame de Paris* was being staged (with orchestral music) at the same Parisian venue—and under the guidance of the same director, Robert Hossein—where the coursing four-note arpeggios that recur throughout *Les Misérables* would be played live for the first time. In hindsight, adapting *Les Misérables* seems an almost predetermined choice.

Where Hugo had taken the best part of two decades to write his novel, Boublil and Schönberg would need only two years to create their musical. The poet Jean-Marc Natel helped Boublil with the libretto, while the English composer John Cameron recorded the original concept album in London in early 1980.[23] However, the result was not the show with which the vast majority of audiences are familiar today, but the original French iteration that premiered at the 4,500-seat Palais des Sports on 17 September 1980. The album had sold over a quarter of a million copies and helped to finance a sell-out run of over 100 performances, which were seen by nearly half a million people before the engagement came to an end.[24] Though Hossein's heavily stylized production has yet to be given even partial consideration in the history of *Les Misérables*, it will not be our concern here. It seems that none of the British collaborators who would eventually bring the musical to London had seen Hossein's staging, since their contact with the material was through the 1980 album alone.

That album contains all the underpinnings of what would become *Les Miz*, marking a major development in the musical's backstory. Rereading Hugo, Boublil and Schönberg closely detailed the main character interactions and emotional responses. Much as the novel's title would eventually be compressed into the musical's colloquial nickname, they dismissed the numerous detours within Hugo's text, straightening out its twists and turns for the sake of brevity and focus. Large swathes of the narrative were jettisoned while the essential features of its plot, characters, themes, and imagery were retained. The novel's lengthy digressions, which constitute well over a quarter of the book— on subjects ranging from the Battle of Waterloo to Restoration salons to King Louis-Philippe, French slang, convent life, and the history of the Paris sewer system—had to go. Likewise, for a story in which the technique of narrative coincidence was exaggerated rather than concealed so as to highlight the connectivity in which Hugo believed, less credible details of the plot needed to be skipped, such as Thénardier's improbable ties to Marius through his father on the battlefield of Waterloo.

Having distilled the text, the duo began drafting the necessary lyrics and musical signatures to find a counterpart for Hugo's voice. Just as Hugo had merged classic styles with contemporary modes, Boublil and Schönberg mixed the soaring stringed overtures and intimate poignancy of traditional opera with the modern pulse of popular music, including rock and even echoes of disco. In keeping with an operatic style, there was no dialogue and all songs were held together by recitative and orchestral bridges, showcasing the mindsets of individual characters and at key dramatic moments drawing them together into ensemble pieces. The score recalled Beethoven's choral writing and Verdi's dramatic intensity, as well as elements of the stage musicals that had inspired the French pair. Most conspicuously, the ensemble 'Demain' ('Tomorrow'), which would be retitled 'One Day More' in English and become a signature anthem, echoed the 'Tonight' quintet from *West Side Story* (itself a play on the quartet 'Bella figlia dell'amore' from Verdi's *Rigoletto*—which was based on Hugo's 1832 play, *Le Roi s'amuse*). Each of the main characters, except for the deceased Fantine, contemplates the future in individual solos that reuse motifs from previous songs but that are sung in counterpoint, ranging back and forth from A major to C major, and building towards a rousing chorus. Located at the heart of the show, the unification and interaction of the different melodies perfectly exhibit Boublil and Schönberg's dedication to channelling how Hugo understood individual experience as part of a sublime collective.

This famous track's arpeggios were the first sounds that Cameron Mackintosh heard when he listened in November 1982 to the album, which started with the song 'La Journée est finie' ('At the End of the Day'). Instantly enamoured, the British producer put together a collaborative team that became integral to how Boublil and Schönberg's musical morphed from a French concept album into a worldwide phenomenon. From the start, all three were actively involved in shaping a fresh musical adaptation: much as Hugo's original manuscript for his novel would considerably change between 1848 and 1861, so too did the musical undergo noticeable alteration. Mackintosh looked to the Royal Shakespeare Company for the experience and ingenuity necessary for a major adaptation of this kind, hiring Trevor Nunn and then John Caird as co-directors, and John Napier as set designer. In 1979, this team had been responsible for a successful theatrical adaptation of Dickens's *The Life and Adventures of Nicholas Nickelby*, while Nunn had also directed the popular musical *Cats* (1981).

Following Boublil and Schönberg's example, Nunn and Caird began by reading Hugo's novel and drafting their own list of vital elements in order to identify what could be added to—and cut from—the French prototype. The contraction of narrative that had led to Boublil and Schönberg's album was now being countered by a strategy of dilation. With the co-directors' revised plotting in place, half of the original French version was reworked and 50 per cent more material was added over the next couple of years. Over three hours long, the result embraced a more thematically audacious interpretation that still displayed what Caird called a 'heightened form of concentration' in its abridgement and simplification of Hugo's storyline.[25] Acutely aware that a British audience would not be as familiar with the novel as the French, Nunn and Caird wanted more context for the musical's story and its central characters, especially Valjean and Javert. Furthermore, they became convinced that the musical's stirring potential to move an audience could be maximized only by stressing the theme of spirituality. They had initially veered towards a radical political tone, no doubt in tune with the political unrest in Britain since 1975 that resulted in the Thatcher government coming to power in 1979 and culminated in the Miners' Strike of 1984. But they eventually decided that a notion of God was more important to the work's meaning, believing that '*Les Misérables* is ultimately a piece about sacrifice'.[26] Additions included new solos for the characters of Valjean and Javert—the prayer-like 'Bring Him Home' and the regal 'Stars'—to communicate their respective beliefs in a forgiving and an avenging God, with Thénardier also receiving another solo in the form of 'Dog Eats Dog' to convey his depraved rejection of any religious morality. At the same time, 'L'Air de la misère' ('The Look of Misery'), one of Fantine's early songs that decried social inequality, was reframed into Eponine's 'On My Own', shifting the focus on to unrequited love to give the character's selflessness more substance. A new solo, 'Empty Chairs at Empty Tables', was likewise developed for Marius to lend more insight into the grief of sacrifice, while the rock touches were softened to give the score a more timeless quality.

Fresh episodes were also inserted as revealing bookends to the musical's narrative: a prologue to depict Valjean's release from prison and his life-changing encounter with Myriel, condensing the novel's opening sections and stressing the difference between Old and New Testament values; and the return of the fallen characters to accompany Valjean to 'the Garden of the Lord' in the climax, creatively building upon the novel's intuition that the bishop's spirit was with Valjean on his deathbed. Crucial to the emotional impact of these changes were Herbert Kretzmer's lyrics. The poet James Fenton first worked on the libretto, but his lyrics proved too exacting, and he was replaced by Kretzmer, who employed idiomatic English to prioritize the audience's immediate understanding over any poetic sophistication. 'Any lyric that is self-regarding, by definition, is going to distract attention away from the narrative,' he argued,[27] leading to clear wording that aimed to compress Hugo's world view into easily digestible ideas. Most relevant in light of the emphasis on religion would be the famous line 'To love another person is to see the face of God'. In comparing the English libretto to Hugo's novel, we thus see both imitation and innovation. *Les Misérables* is transformed into an epic stage spectacle, aided in no small part by Napier's shifting sets and the famous hydraulic barricade.

A DUET BETWEEN BOOK AND LIBRETTO

Hugo's narrative voice may at first appear absent, but his commentaries on the Parisian gamin and the construction of the 1848 June insurrection barricades undergird the portrayal of Gavroche's character and of the students' 1832 barricade. Hence, Gavroche's cocky claim, '[I]t's me who runs this town! | And my theatre never closes | And the curtain's never down'[28] captures the irrepressible spirit of 'Paris Atomized' (III.i). The higgledy-piggledy fortification fabricated on stage to protect the young revolutionaries taps into Hugo's depiction of the 1848 Saint-Antoine barricade as having 'something of the cloaca in this redoubt, and something of Olympus in this jumble. [. . .] It was a garbage heap, and it was Sinai' (pp. 1172–3).

Commemorating the moment as significant for the drama itself, Enjolras sings:

> Here upon these stones
> We will build our barricade,
> In the heart of the city
> We claim as our own. (libretto, 182)

FIGURE 15.1 The young revolutionaries raising the red flag over their street barricade in *Les Misérables*, Palace Theatre, 1985.

Photograph by Chris Davies. Courtesy of ArenaPal.

In these ways, the show allows glimpses of some digressions to be seen even when direct reference has been stripped away.

Whereas the novel enjoys an expansive rhythm, with long descriptive periods alternating with (sometimes equally long) periods of action and high drama, the musical moves quickly from one major episode to another. Pauses for reflection are key, as with Gavroche's death, but these do not linger, as Sternfeld summarizes: 'With constant underscoring during set changes, passages of time, and other transitions, the story moves perpetually. The revolving stage rolls new sets on and off and carries people with it. Things swing in and out of view; days and years fly by.'[29] Different groups—the prisoners at Toulon, the poor in Montreuil-sur-Mer, M. Madeleine's factory workers, the 'whores' in town, the drinkers at Thénardier's inn, the Parisian beggars, the revolutionaries, the women of Paris after the battle—play the role of the chorus in counterpoint to solos, duets, trios, and so forth in order to create visual and auditory variety. Hugo's work itself can be seen as operatic, because of his tendency to stage scenes with distinct voices that offset each other, but the musical greatly magnifies this tendency. The support for all of these occasions to feature and combine a range of voices in songs such as 'Do You Hear the People Sing?' and 'A Heart Full of Love' is, of course, the narrative thread that holds everything together.

Given such a pace and the need for tight exposition across a seventeen-year storyline, many characters from the novel disappear, and with them the backstories for several of those who remain. The opening book in part I ('An Upright Man') ostensibly devoted to Bishop Myriel, but also presenting some of the main themes of the text, completely vanishes, along with Fantine's happier days in Paris ('In the Year 1817'; I.iii). Her feckless lover, the ageing law student Tholomyès, is anonymously romanticized in 'I Dreamed a Dream':

> He slept a summer by my side.
> He filled my days
> With endless wonder.
> He took my childhood in his stride,
> But he was gone when autumn came. (libretto, 168)

That he fits the profile of other verbose, materialistic, and self-centred bourgeois characters, who likewise disappear in the musical, cannot be deduced from the lyrics. The musical's sights thereby shift from the whole class of antagonists represented (and defended) by Javert to the Inspector himself. Marius, for his part, arrives on the scene a ready-made rabble-rouser: his sad childhood; the tragic fate of his father, Colonel Pontmercy; the comic portrait of his well-meaning but ultraconservative grandfather, M. Gillenormand; his own struggles with poverty (III.ii–v)—all give way to an instantly heroic figure. And of Thénardier's five children, only one, Eponine, is so identified here; Gavroche loses that marker and all the episodes linked to it in the text (as when he rescues his father from atop a prison wall in IV.vi.3); and their sister Azelma and two nameless younger brothers are not even mentioned. As a result, Thénardier's despicable behaviour as a father not just to Cosette but also to his own children lies fully on the shoulders of Eponine. When Gavroche first introduces her—'That's Eponine, she knows her way about' (libretto, 175)—we are hard-pressed to guess that the line might echo textual allusions to her father offering her services to people he attempts to bilk. What results from both reducing the cast of characters and narrowing the behavioural range of those featured is the removal of some of the novel's darker notes, found in its subplots and background scenes.

Of the five parts of *Les Misérables*, four bear the names of key protagonists: 'Fantine' (I), 'Cosette' (II), 'Marius' (III), and 'Jean Valjean' (V). There is no part dubbed 'Javert' or 'Thénardier'—two characters whose presence looms large throughout the musical—but Javert has two books, 'Javert' (I.vi), which highlights his moral integrity and heroism, and 'Javert Off the Track' (V.iv), which is devoted to his demise; another book, 'The Noxious Poor,' (III.viii) depicts Thénardier at his most vicious. Despite the latter's menace to Eponine, 'You wait my girl, you'll rue this night | I'll make you scream. You'll scream alright!' (libretto, 181), when she prevents him and his bandits from attacking Valjean and Cosette's house on the Rue Plumet, Thénardier is largely depicted as a comic figure on stage. This depiction arguably bears Boublil and Schönberg's fingerprints in particular, given their familiarity with the comic actor Bourvil's performance as Thénardier in Jean-Paul Le Chanois's well-known 1958 French film. From his outlandish appearance, to Mme Thénardier's satirical take on his song, 'Master of the House', to his

ineptitude in ambushing Valjean and in blackmailing Marius, to his self-absorbed 'triumph' at the wedding party, Thénardier provides the production's primary comic relief
as a nemesis to Valjean far less threatening than Javert. This characterization, though
exaggerated, accurately conveys the villain's role in the novel as the quintessentially
comic 'duper duped.' When the innkeeper is outfoxed by the 'awful pauper' (libretto,
401) who produces not just abundant banknotes but also a signed letter from Fantine
entrusting Cosette to the bearer (a detail silently staged in the musical), it is but the prel-
ude to a series of encounters—notably in the Gorbeau ambush (III.viii.20) and the Paris
sewers (V.ii.8)—where Valjean gets the better of Thénardier. Even the climactic scene,
when Thénardier tries to prove to Marius that his father-in-law is a robber and an assassin, only to reveal him as 'a hero, . . . a saint' (p. 1447), 'the convict . . . transfigured into
Christ' (p. 1452), feeds into this portrayal of a clueless malefactor. Yet Thénardier's textual
afterlife as a 'slave trader' (p. 1451) reintroduces his malignant side, whereas the musical
shows him as a comic foil right to the end.[30] His deeper political significance as a shadow
figure in the book for Hugo's arch-enemy, Louis-Napoléon Bonaparte (Napoleon III), is
predictably elided for a twentieth-century audience.

Javert merits more complex treatment in the musical than Thénardier, in part influenced by Mackintosh's memories of Charles Laughton's famous performance as the
Inspector in Richard Boleslawski's 1935 Hollywood film.[31] The Valjean/Javert rivalry is
vocally implied in their respective tenor and baritone ranges, and the careful attention
given to Javert reflects his role in the novel. Hugo makes it clear from the outset that the
rigidly law-abiding Inspector, the offspring of a 'fortune teller whose husband was in
the galleys', carries the germ of conflict within: '[H]e felt that he had a powerful foundation of rectitude, order, and honesty based on an irrepressible hatred for that gypsy race
to which he belonged' (p. 170). Javert's origins had been so thoroughly repressed that he
was fated to suffer a crisis of identity. The libretto has Javert disclosing this information
directly to Valjean as they confront each other at Fantine's deathbed: 'I was born inside
a gaol | I was born with scum like you, | I am from the gutter too' (libretto, 172). The
revelation enriches both Javert's declaration just beforehand that 'Every man is born in
sin | Every man must choose his way' (libretto, 172). Anyone condemned by the law, to
his way of thinking, has chosen to do wrong, and for this reason, as he sings in his key
solo, 'Stars':

> Those who falter
> And those who fall
> Must pay
> The price. (libretto, 177)

Hugo's character applies this logic to himself early on, when he attempts to resign for
having falsely denounced the town's mayor, M. Madeleine, as Jean Valjean: 'I have
caught myself doing wrong. [. . .] I must be sent away, broken, dismissed—that is just'
(p. 211). Though the scene is cut from the musical, Javert's absolute identification with
the forces of good in 'Stars' adumbrates his final 'Soliloquy', after the ex-convict saves

his life on the barricades, by showing that his black-and-white world cannot tolerate any ambiguity.

To the policeman's mind, being spared by '[t]his desperate man that I have hunted' (libretto, 188) suggests a superior form of justice that eludes his understanding:

> Shall [Valjean's] sins be forgiven?
> Shall his crimes be reprieved?
> And must I now begin to doubt,
> Who never doubted all those years? (libretto, 188)

Condensing Hugo's twelve-page chapter on Javert's suicide into just forty-two lines, the lyrics lose the sweeping movement of his identity crisis, whereby he is forced to see Valjean 'exalted' and himself 'degraded' (p. 1323), unable to determine the right course of action. His protracted dilemma is only alluded to in the lines, 'And my thoughts fly apart, | [. . .] | As I stare into the void | Of a world that cannot hold' (libretto, 188). At the same time, these destructive centrifugal forces vividly figure, in just a few words, the ruined sense of self so thoroughly examined in the text[32]—and whose collapsing reality is further evoked by the twisting violin chords and the irregular tempo. This collapse is also expressed visually through the dramatic lighting effects on stage as he jumps from the bridge.

FIGURE 15.2 His sense of self ruined, Javert (played by Roger Allam) commits suicide, Palace Theatre, 1985.

Photograph by Michael Le Poer Trench. Courtesy of ArenaPal.

Though Jean Valjean's identity is vastly more complicated than Javert's, he succeeds where the other fails in reconciling all his potentially conflicting selves. His string of name changes in the novel—from 24601 to M. Madeleine, then Ultime Fauchelevant, and finally Urbain Fabre—are simplified on stage to just Madeleine, doubtless to avoid confusing the audience. Since the curtain rises on his release from the Toulon galleys by Javert, rather than on Bishop Myriel's journey of faith and awakening political consciousness, we are immediately launched into the protagonist's dark world. His bitterness—

> Never forget the years, the waste.
> Nor forgive them.
> For what they've done.
> They are the guilty—everyone. (libretto, 165)

—turns to astonishment when Myriel saves him from returning to prison, gives him the silver candlesticks he had stolen, and claims, 'I have bought your soul for God!' (libretto, 166). This challenge to Valjean's vengeful mindset leads, in the musical, to his first soliloquy, 'What Have I Done?'—reflections that do not appear explicitly in the book itself. Setting up the counterpoint to Javert's later crisis through similar lyrics and melody, Valjean discovers in being forgiven and redeemed that 'there's another way to go. | [. . .] | And I stare into the void— | To the whirlpool of my sin' (libretto, 167). But while both characters vow to 'escape now from the world[,] | From the world of Jean Valjean' (libretto, 167 and 188), Javert maintains, 'There is nowhere I can go. | There is no way to go on . . .' (libretto, 188), before plunging into the abyss of the Seine. Valjean, however, declares, 'Another story must begin' (libretto, 167). One man's despair is musically confirmed as another's hope.

Valjean's transformation into the saintly Madeleine in turn allows a new narrative; Javert's perceived dead end illustrates his lack of similarly (re)inventive imagination, a point that Hugo makes as well. In one of the novel's most famous chapters, 'A Tempest Within a Brain' (I.vii.3), the ex-convict mayor undergoes an excruciating moral dilemma between two equally fraught actions: to denounce himself as Jean Valjean to save the innocent Champmathieu arrested in his place (but then to reduce his workers and the town to ruin) or to embrace his identity as M. Madeleine (but then to lose his soul). His rousing solo, 'Who Am I?' concisely captures his quandary: 'If I speak, I am condemned. | If I stay silent, I am damned!' (libretto, 171). When he answers his own question in both the book and the musical by informing the court in Arras, 'I am Jean Valjean', he demonstrates that the good Madeleine has become part of a richer, more totalizing identity. Subsequent dilemmas in the text—whereby Valjean must decide whether to stay hidden with Cosette in the Petit-Picpus convent or to allow her to experience the world outside; then later, whether to let Marius die on the barricades or to go to his rescue; and finally, whether to reveal his true identity to Marius at the expense of seeing Cosette—are bypassed on stage as heroic action replaces inner struggles. Valjean's existential crisis is therefore resolved once and for all in Montreuil-sur-Mer, whereas his journey to sainthood in the novel follows a more recursive (and reflective) path, with much deeper evidence of martyrdom than the show itself conveys. When he prays 'Bring Him Home' on the barricade, enjoining God to spare Marius's life, we see a kinder, gentler Valjean than the one that Hugo paints looking soon thereafter 'with inexpressible hatred' (p. 1291) at the unconscious young man in the sewer below. The labyrinthine trial of the sewer, like that of his night-time escape with Cosette through the city streets and, earlier yet, of unravelling his tortuous thoughts in the Champmathieu affair, figures the triumph of conscience in the novel. Conversely, in the musical it caps Valjean's status as an action hero.

As with the older generation, the younger characters—Fantine, Marius, Eponine, Enjolras, Cosette, and Gavroche—are drawn in large strokes that capture essential aspects of Hugo's work while avoiding many of its subtleties. Fantine's degradation is far more graphic under Hugo's pen: her sacrifices and inexhaustible dedication serve as examples to Valjean, who in the novel succeeds her not just as Cosette's father but also as her mother. Yet the grotesque scene where Fantine begins to sell her few possessions and then her body parts on a rigged market reflects Hugo's satire in this and other episodes of the exploitation of the have-nots by the haves. And when she laments regarding her customers, 'Don't they know | They're making love to one already dead?' (libretto, 169), she echoes his dystopian image of *les misérables* as the living dead.[33] Her presence in the end at Valjean's deathbed—replacing that of Myriel—both lends visual symmetry to the musical, given that Valjean was earlier at her side before she died, and signals her own salvation.

The plight of little Cosette at the Thénardiers' inn, doomed to a form of slavery like her mother, is compressed on stage to references to domestic chores and enduring Mme Thénardier's verbal and emotional abuse. Her ugliness, 'anguish' (p. 399), and potential fate in the book as either 'an idiot or a demon' (p. 400) give way to the simple pathos of a child dreaming of a better life, as had her mother, in 'Castle on a Cloud'. We have only the slightest hint of Hugo's lyrical passage describing her terror in the 'sinister darkness' (p. 389) of the woods at night when Valjean shows up with her at the inn remarking, 'I found her wandering in the wood | This little child, I found her trembling in the shadows' (libretto, 174). But we miss the miraculous overtones of their encounter, just as she is praying 'Oh God!' (p. 390), that marks her sense of the divine entering her life. Emerging fully formed as a lovely young woman in the next scene ten years later, Cosette reveals nothing of her education by Valjean in Paris, or of her flight from Javert with him to the convent, where her schooling continues, or of their long afternoons in the Luxembourg Gardens after they leave. Rather, her life appears to begin, as does Marius's, the day their paths first cross. Her yearning for 'a world that I long to see' (libretto, 179) sets up the generational conflict with Valjean more fully discussed in the book as the process of a seventeen-year-old's psychological self-discovery. Where she connects deeply with Marius through the prose poems he leaves on her garden bench before they hold their first conversation, the medium in the musical is not textual but human: Eponine brings them together at Cosette's garden. After their duet, then trio with Eponine, followed by their joining the other main characters for 'One Day More' at the end of Act 1, Cosette disappears for most of the rest of the show, making room for the action-filled scenes on the barricade and in the sewers.

Cosette's wait in the wings allows the production to focus more closely on Eponine, whose fall in life has accompanied the other's rise. Spoiled by her mother in Montfermeil, she is now a street urchin in Paris who recoils when her memory is jogged during the ambush: 'Cosette! How can it be[?] | We were children together | Look what's become of me . . .' (libretto, 177). The contrast in their fortunes is reinforced by Eponine's less feminine persona and courageous deeds for love of Marius, much as in the novel. Her big solo, 'On My Own', expresses feelings not fully articulated in the text but easily guessed by Hugo's reader—the dream of a love that can never be. Although Eponine dies in the book before Gavroche summons Valjean to the barricade, having her instead deliver Marius's letter to Cosette's father enhances her active, selfless character. But this sacrifice is not followed by the key scene in the novel when she takes a bullet meant for Marius. Rather, she is shot as she approaches the barricade on her way back from the Rue Plumet, dying in Marius's arms, as she does in the novel, but without the same order of heroism. Spared the need to explain this new sacrifice, she can simply enjoy her first and last embrace from him, punctuated by a touching duet and Marius's fraternal 'Hush-a-bye' (recalling Fantine's maternal 'Come to Me'). As the 'first to fall' she rallies the revolutionaries to 'fight here in her name' (libretto, 184), although the honour belongs to the destitute old bibliophile Mabeuf in the novel.

In many ways, then, the musical belongs to the young. It shifts Hugo's intergenerational emphasis that runs from toddlers to the very old to a mere one-generation gap. Aside from the function of Jean Valjean's gripping story in focusing and organizing the musical's narrative, much of the appeal of the show adheres to the younger action figures: Eponine, Marius, Gavroche, Enjolras, and the other insurgents. Marius, for example, is not Hugo's half-starved, daydreaming student but a firebrand co-equal with Enjolras, the group's leader in Hugo's text. Though he waxes poetic in 'Red and Black' about the 'breathless delight' (libretto, 178) of encountering Cosette, he is soon won over to his friends' revolutionary frame of mind, joining in the stirring chorus. In the novel, he embraces their cause as a kind of suicide when he finds the house on the Rue Plumet closed and Cosette vanished—'He wanted to die, the opportunity presented itself' (p. 1118)—yet he enters the barricade with guns blazing, killing two Municipal Guards to defend his friends. This is the Marius largely presented on stage, a worthy successor in Cosette's life to Jean Valjean, who like him shoots to kill on the barricade (whereas in the novel Valjean preserves as many lives as possible). By later agreeing that his father-in-law-to-be 'must be gone' (libretto, 189) in order to protect Cosette, he sets up the comic presence of both Thénardiers at their wedding, along with the revelation that it was Valjean who had saved Marius's life on the barricades by carrying him through the sewers. Hugo's own tragicomic ending to the novel, spread out over five or six months, is thus compressed into a single day during which the young couple is married and the forlorn Valjean dies after they rush to his side to offer (and receive) forgiveness.

The vigorous characters of Enjolras and the other 'Friends of the ABC'—Grantaire, Combeferre, Courfeyrac, Joly, Feuilly, Prouvaire—likewise offset the tension between

Valjean, Javert, and Thénardier, opening the scope of the musical to include, beyond Marius and Cosette's love story, the political dimension so prominently displayed in the novel. In the absence of leaders willing to address the 'hunger in the land' (libretto, 167) lamented by the poor in Montreuil-sur-Mer and echoed ten years later by Parisians begging for 'a crust of bread', Enjolras wonders, 'How long before the judgement day? | Before we cut the fat ones down to size?'[34] Condensing the novel's many images of starvation and of its corollary, the overstuffed bourgeois complacent in their comfort and indifferent to the suffering of others, the libretto cuts to the heart of Hugo's argument against social inequality. As in the novel, the young men are determined to challenge the powers that be, leading immediately from the emphatic chorus of 'Red and Black'—

> Red—the blood of angry men!
> Black—the dark of ages past!
> Red—a world about to dawn!
> Black—the night that ends at last! (libretto, 178)

—to the even more electrifying 'Do You Hear the People Sing?' where the citizens of Paris take up the anthem. This 'music of a people | Who will not be slaves again' (libretto, 178) is the song of Jean Valjean, of Fantine, of little Cosette, of Eponine and Gavroche, all of whom have supplied concrete examples of the students' more abstract sociopolitical principles. Their dream of 'a new world to be won' (libretto, 181)—of 'a life about to start | When tomorrow comes' (libretto, 178)—constitutes a reply to the dreams shared elsewhere by the individual characters within a wider context. In light of the exiled Hugo's hidden call to action in *Les Misérables* against Napoleon III's Second Empire,[35] it is fitting that Enjolras's utopian vision of a happier future in 'What Horizon is Visible from the Top of the Barricade' (V.i.5) provides key imagery for both the Act 1 finale, 'One Day More', and the two versions of 'Do You Hear the People Sing?', the second of which closes Act 2. If the novel ends with Jean Valjean's death, the intimations of resurrection that accompany his passing recall Enjolras's message: 'Brothers, whoever dies here dies in the radiance of the future, and we are entering a grave illuminated by the dawn' (p. 1191). That Valjean is joined by the spirits of the fallen revolutionaries in the final chorus demonstrates that the librettists fully understood the connection between these two narrative strands.

CONCLUSION

There is no doubt that Boublil and Schönberg's musical is more overwhelming than it is subtle. The closing technique of brightening white light descending from the rafters on to the souls of the fallen is in use from the start: each time a character dies, the body is immersed in a blinding beam to signify a door opening into the beyond.

The mysterious presence felt by Myriel in his garden—and that watches from the shadows as Valjean frets over revealing the truth to Marius (V.vi.4)—is made much more tangible on stage; the 'radiance' that Enjolras beholds on the future's horizon is taken to an extreme. While Hugo ends his novel with the image of Valjean's headstone to signify both closure and the continuing march of time, the musical reunites the downtrodden in a defiant display of unity for a sentimentalized finish. Such is the nature of the chosen medium, which shapes the adaptation as much as the adaptors themselves: '[M]usical theatre welcomes big emotions but not always complicated or ambivalent ones.'[36] The depth of Hugo's grand visions can only be alluded to at best, but their emotional scale adapts into a thoroughly exuberant form that is less superficial than it is rhapsodic.

Whether personal taste accommodates the megamusical genre or not, the fact remains that Les Misérables has become the foremost example of this musical form by successfully intensifying the original novel's melodrama. Mackintosh has frequently cited the instantaneous connection that the musical makes with audiences and the 'often under-appreciated perception of the public': '[They] see in Les Misérables what many a professional scribe could not.'[37] At the same time, and implicitly countering the accusation that the musical trivializes its own social themes in favour of bathos: 'No other play, in the history of theatre, has generated such social concern, or raised so much money for charity.'[38] The musical's emotional impact strengthens its bond with Hugo's novel, which prompted even the French Emperor to bring philanthropy back into fashion, and which championed what would become much of the agenda for social welfare in France's Third Republic. As the show evolves—running times cut back under three hours, updated staging, streamlined orchestration, and ever-changing star casts—much of its vitality continues to share the DNA of Hugo's literary behemoth.

Notes

1. See Kathryn M. Grossman and Bradley Stephens, eds., 'Les Misérables' and Its Afterlives: Between Page, Stage, and Screen (London: Routledge, 2016); for the musical's importance to this legacy, see Stephens's chapter 'Les Misérables in the Twenty-First Century', 191–204.
2. Claude-Michel Schönberg, quoted in Matthew Westwood, 'Les Misérables Goes Beyond the Barricade', The Australian, 28 June 2014, http://www.theaustralian.com.au/arts/review/les-miserables-goes-beyond-the-barricade/story-fn9n8gph-1226967684193?nk=0d789e2854c57c126d3c52460dedd5ba, accessed 4 July 2014.
3. These versions are noted by Andrew Watts in 'Les Misérables, Theatre, and the Anxiety of Excess', in Adapting Nineteenth-Century France: Literature in Film, Theatre, Television, Radio, and Print, ed. Kate Griffiths and Andrew Watts (Cardiff: University of Wales Press, 2013), 117–118.
4. Andrew Lloyd Webber's The Phantom of the Opera holds the record as Broadway's longest-running musical and enjoys the highest worldwide gross receipts in history, but its London debut came a year after Les Miz.

5. Statistics are being continually updated at the musical's official webpage: http://www. lesmis.com.

6. Boublil and Schönberg, 'Beyond Our Dreams', in 'Les Misérables': The Musical Phenomenon, Souvenir Programme (London: Dewynters, 2013), 2–3.

7. Julie Rose, 'Victor Hugo', in Les Misérables, trans. Julie Rose (London: Vintage, 2008), xiii.

8. Kathryn M. Grossman, 'Les Misérables': Conversion, Revolution, Redemption (New York: Twayne, 1994), 16. For the novel's critical reception, see 14–22.

9. Such reviews are comprehensively covered by Jessica Sternfeld in The Megamusical (Bloomington: Indiana University Press, 2006), 185–188.

10. Benedict Nightingale, 'A Supremely Improbable Winner', in Les Misérables, Souvenir Programme (2013), 16–17.

11. Linda Hutcheon, A Theory of Adaptation, 2nd ed. (London: Routledge, 2012), 173.

12. Literary adaptations are especially prone to these criticisms, through which recycled texts (not least on screen) become 'impure'; see Deborah Cartmell and Imelda Whelehan, 'Introduction', in Carmell and Whelehan, eds., Screen Adaptation: Impure Cinema (Basingstoke: Palgrave, 2010), 1–9. For more on how these discourses have been challenged, see Hutcheon, Theory of Adaptation, especially chapter 1 (1–32).

13. Laurence M. Porter, Victor Hugo (New York: Twayne, 1999), 29–30.

14. Arnaud Laster, Pleins feux sur Victor Hugo (Paris: Comédie-Française, 1981), 360. For a perceptive illustration of this 'auditory sensitivity', see Watts, 'Les Misérables', 126–127.

15. Victor Hugo, Les Misérables, trans. Lee Fahnstock and Norman MacAfee (New York: Signet Classics, 1987), 1319–1320. Pages for citations from the novel will hereafter appear in the text, prefaced by pp. References to Hugo's subdivisions of the novel into part, book, and chapter will appear in the text and notes in the form, e.g. I.i.1.

16. Late at night, Myriel sometimes walks in his garden alone to appreciate 'creation's universal radiance': 'moved in the darkness by the visible splendors of the constellations and the invisible splendor of God [. . .] he felt something floating away from him, and something descending upon him; mysterious exchanges of the soul with the universe' (I.i.13, pp. 54–55).

17. 'So long as there shall exist, by reason of law and custom, a social condemnation which, in the midst of civilization, artificially creates a hell on earth, and complicates with human fatality a destiny that is divine; so long as the three problems of the century—the degradation of man by the exploitation of his labor, the ruin of woman by starvation, and the atrophy of childhood by physical and spiritual night—are not solved; so long as, in certain regions, social asphyxia shall be possible; in other words, and from a still broader point of view, so long as ignorance and misery remain on earth, there should be a need for books such as this' (Hugo, Les Misérables, p. xvii).

18. See Victor Brombert, Victor Hugo and the Visionary Novel (Cambridge, MA: Harvard University Press, 1984), chapter 4 (86–139).

19. See Michael Sibalis, 'Who Were Les Misérables?', Fiction and Film for French Historians, 3, no. 4 (2013), http://h-france.net/fffh/the-buzz/who-were-les-miserables/, accessed 21 May 2016.

20. For more on Hugo's suitability for fiction, see Bradley Stephens, Victor Hugo, Jean-Paul Sartre, and the Liability of Liberty (Oxford: Legenda, 2011), 85–105.

21. Character and Meaning in the Novels of Victor Hugo (West Lafayette, IN: Purdue University Press, 2007), 11.

22. Edward Behr, The Complete Book of 'Les Misérables' (New York: Arcade, 1989), 47.

23. Behr, *Complete Book*, 51.
24. See Benedict Nightingale and Martyn Palmer, *'Les Misérables': From Stage to Screen* (London: Carlton, 2013), 6–11.
25. Quoted in Margaret Vermette, *The Wonderful World of Boublil and Schönberg* (London: Applause, 2006), 133.
26. Caird, quoted in Vermette, *Boublil and Schönberg*, 134.
27. Quoted in Vermette, *Boublil and Schönberg*, 69.
28. Behr, *Complete Book*, 177. Page references from the libretto will hereafter appear in the text, prefaced by 'libretto'.
29. Sternfeld, *Megamusical*, 190.
30. The Thénardiers indeed reveal one of the most striking changes between the novel and the musical, especially since in Hugo's text Madame Thénardier dies in prison. The musical's reconfiguring of the Thénardiers makes narrative sense, however: their presence at the wedding banquet necessarily lifts the mood and provides some respite before the death-bed reconciliation between Valjean, Cosette, and Marius, in addition to serving as the catalyst for that denouement. Given the predominantly British character of the creative team, this reconfiguration may well also reflect a reaction to Thatcher's contested 1987 idea that 'there is no such thing as society': the Conservative government's insistence on individual responsibility and disregard for the underclass is unsettled by the persistence of the Thénardiers as an exploitative force.
31. Nightingale and Palmer, *'Les Misérables': From Stage to Screen*, 16.
32. See Kathryn M. Grossman, *Figuring Transcendence in 'Les Misérables': Hugo's Romantic Sublime* (Carbondale: Southern Illinois University Press, 1994), 88–95.
33. See Grossman, *Figuring Transcendence*, 35, 38, and 59–60.
34. These lines are missing from the libretto available in Behr's volume. They are included in the inlay booklet for the original London cast recording (Kretzmer, not paginated), although they are attributed to Feuilly rather than Enjolras, reflecting ongoing changes in the production. See Herbert Kretzmer, Libretto, *Les Misérables*, original London cast, 1985, CD, First Night Records, Encore CD1, 1986.
35. See Grossman, *Figuring Transcendence*, 224–225 and 252–253.
36. Adam Gopnik, 'The Persistent Greatness of *Les Misérables*', *New Yorker*, 28 December 2012, http://www.newyorker.com/online/blogs/books/2012/12/the-persistent-greatness-of-victor-hugos-les-miserables.html, accessed 9 May 2016.
37. Cameron Mackintosh, 'Storming the Barricade', in *Les Misérables*, Souvenir Programme (2013), 24.
38. Behr, *Complete Book*, 157.

BIBLIOGRAPHY

Behr, Edward. *The Complete Book of 'Les Misérables'*. New York: Arcade, 1989.
Boublil, Alain, and Claude-Michel Schönberg. 'Beyond Our Dreams.' In *'Les Misérables': The Musical Phenomenon*. Souvenir Programme, 2–3. London: Dewynters, 2013.
Brombert, Victor, *Victor Hugo and the Visionary Novel* (Cambridge, MA: Harvard University Press, 1984).
Cartmell, Deborah, and Imelda Whelehan, eds. *Screen Adaptation: Impure Cinema*. Basingstoke: Palgrave, 2010.

Gopnik, Adam. 'The Persistent Greatness of *Les Misérables*.' *New Yorker*, 28 December 2012. http://www.newyorker.com/online/blogs/books/2012/12/the-persistent-greatness-of-victor-hugos-les-miserables.html, accessed 9 May 2016.

Grossman, Kathryn M. *Figuring Transcendence in 'Les Misérables': Hugo's Romantic Sublime*. Carbondale: Southern Illinois University Press, 1994.

Grossman, Kathryn M. *'Les Misérables': Conversion, Revolution, Redemption*. New York: Twayne, 1996.

Grossman, Kathryn M., and Bradley Stephens, eds. *'Les Misérables' and Its Afterlives: Between Page, Stage, and Screen*. London: Routledge, 2016.

Hugo, Victor. *Les Misérables*. Translated by Lee Fahnstock and Norman MacAfee. New York: Signet Classics, 1987.

Hutcheon, Linda. *A Theory of Adaptation*, 2nd ed. London: Routledge, 2012.

Kretzmer, Herbert. Libretto. *Les Misérables*. Original Cast Recording, 1985. Music by Alain Boublil and Claude-Michel Schönberg. CD. First Nights Records, Encore CD1, 1986.

Laster, Arnaud. *Pleins feux sur Victor Hugo*. Paris: Comédie-Française, 1981.

Mackintosh, Cameron. 'Storming the Barricade.' In *'Les Misérables': The Musical Phenomenon*. Souvenir Programme, 24–25. London: Dewynters, 2013.

Nightingale, Benedict. 'A Supremely Improbable Winner.' In *'Les Misérables': The Musical Phenomenon*. Souvenir Programme, 16–17. London: Dewynters, 2013.

Nightingale, Benedict, and Martyn Palmer. *'Les Misérables': From Stage to Screen*. London: Carlton, 2013.

Porter, Laurence M. *Victor Hugo*. New York: Twayne, 1999.

Roche, Isabel. *Character and Meaning in the Novels of Victor Hugo*. West Lafayette, IN: Purdue University Press, 2007.

Rose, Julie. 'Victor Hugo.' In *Les Misérables*. Translated by Julie Rose, xi–xiii. London: Vintage, 2008.

Sibalis, Michael. 'Who Were *Les Misérables*?' *Fiction and Film for French Historians* 3, no. 4 (2013). http://h-france.net/fffh/the-buzz/who-were-les-miserables/, accessed 21 May 2016.

Stephens, Bradley. *Victor Hugo, Jean-Paul Sartre, and the Liability of Liberty*. Oxford: Legenda, 2011.

Sternfeld, Jessica. *The Megamusical*. Bloomington: Indiana University Press, 2006.

Vermette, Margaret. *The Wonderful World of Boublil and Schönberg*. London: Applause, 2006.

Watts, Andrew. '*Les Misérables*, Theatre, and the Anxiety of Excess.' In *Adapting Nineteenth-Century France: Literature in Film, Theatre, Television, Radio, and Print*, by Kate Griffiths and Andrew Watts, 114–142. Cardiff: University of Wales Press, 2013.

CHAPTER 16

....

'HUMMING THE SETS'

Scenography and the Spectacular Musical from Cats *to* The Lord of the Rings

....

CHRISTINE WHITE

THE Broadway musical *The Producers* (2001) was adapted from the Mel Brooks film of the same name (1967), which revolves around two producers overselling interests in a Broadway flop as their 'get rich quick' plan. What they don't count on is the show's overwhelming success. This would seem unlikely at the outset as they have discovered what they perceive to be the worst play ever written: its subject matter is outrageous and the show includes offensive stereotypes of people of various nationalities, religions, and sexual orientations as well as an unforgettable love letter to Adolf Hitler in the song 'Springtime for Hitler'. As a spoof of musical theatre, however, *The Producers*—both in its film and stage incarnations—touches some interesting chords: sometimes, the most unlikely production turns into a success, while brilliant scenography lends itself as often to box office hits as to catastrophic failures. In *The Producers*, Brooks jokingly explores the economics of musical theatre where profit and loss sometimes depend on mere circumstance rather than the artistic qualities that distinguish a 'good' from a 'bad' musical.

Throughout the 1980s the dominance in Britain of what had become known and widely accepted in the previous decades as 'writers' theatre' was challenged by the rise of 'spectacle theatre', a term referring to theatre which is primarily visual and whose producers, while possibly still aiming to enable good writing, have as their main concern the sales of their show as an event. The profit motive and concomitant commercialization of the theatre as a leisure industry has been at the centre of stage production since the nineteenth century; however, the business aspect became ever more critical in the late twentieth century because large-scale musicals require extensive amounts of funding (implying a large number of investors) in order to guarantee an exciting experience for an audience demanding value for money. Yet, since audiences as long ago as the eighteenth century enjoyed all manner of special effects created by instantaneous changes of elaborate scenery, sometimes in full view of the audience, it has been recognized that '[o]ne cannot argue that the emphasis on scenes and machines came solely as a response to commercial drive. Rather the impulse was, at least in the beginning, theatrical.'[1]

THE INFLUENCE OF 'WRITERS' THEATRE' AND AGITPROP

Most often associated with the Royal Court Theatre, 'writer's theatre' employed minimalist staging, initially exemplified by the designs of Jocelyn Herbert in the late 1950s, that by the 1970s was recognizable as politically oriented theatre which could come from the back of a van.[2] It was a theatre exploiting a visual aesthetic that was symbolic yet realist, influenced by Bertolt Brecht's house designer at the Berliner Ensemble, Casper Neher, whose work made a great impact on theatre professionals when first seen in London in 1956. Instead of providing spectacle and visual stimulation, the staging was usually minimal: scenes were indicated by means of a single piece of cloth, a bit of flooring, and some lights. In fact, expressive lighting design was a significant part of the visual palette; productions were quite dark as they utilized only a few lights to evoke time and place.

The heyday of agitprop stretched from the late 1960s to the late 1970s, its sole purpose being to communicate a political message effectively by means of a 'pared down' aesthetic. Political playwright David Edgar lamented the rise during the 1980s of sets he perceived to be 'distracting', believing that they were the result of a paucity of good writing. Edgar complained that a theatre without new plays is a theatre of sensation and spectacle: a theatre merely celebrating performance skill, with no higher aspirations than to be a circus. Edgar's idea of new work with a political imperative did not encompass the musical. Nevertheless the British musical has not only increased in popularity, but has also been informative, educational, provocative, and in some cases downright political with regard to its subjects and reflections on society. During its rise in the 1980s, however, British musical theatre was seen by some theatre reviewers to represent the triumph of shallow, escapist entertainment for the masses, in line with the political landscape, which had been radically transformed by the advent of Thatcherism in the UK and Reaganism in the USA.[3] West End producers began to see scenographic virtuosity as a valid box office lure,[4] while some subsidized theatres developed musical theatre in collaboration with commercial producers for the purpose of building up reserves of funds by which to support other work.[5]

The 'doing something with nothing aesthetic' might have had an economic imperative in agitprop and touring theatre in the UK, but the 'pared down' aesthetic, striving to be both emblematic and metaphorical, also brought about the a new trend of disjointed and abstract features of a set sometimes referred to in design circles as 'the wobbly set'. This type of scenery traded on expressionist ideas: angular, sloping, utilizing machines of operation, thereby reflecting a sense of the diminished human, as it had done in 1920s and 1930s Europe. The change of artistic director at the Royal Court from Max Stafford-Clark (1979–93) to Stephen Daldry (1992–8) signalled a movement away from minimalism in the subsidized theatre of the 1990s towards an exploration of a full range of scenographic means. There was also a new emphasis on music, recognizing its unique power and resulting in the underscored play as exemplified by Stephen Daldry's stagings of J. B. Priestley's *An Inspector Calls* and Sophie Treadwell's *Machinal* at the National Theatre in 1992 and 1994 respectively, and in the work of touring companies such as Cheek by Jowl and Shared Experience. Plays were presented with operatic scores that underscored and accompanied physical movement as well as enhancing and punctuating the drama; these productions were also unapologetic examples of theatricality.

This changing aesthetic was confronted by certain theatre critics who often wrote of the tussle between word and image on stage.[6] Many of these reviewers came from the same Oxbridge stable as the directors (e.g. Michael Billington and Irving Wardle) and conceived of theatre criticism as a sister discipline to literary criticism. These critics struggled with a visual iconography that they had no training to interpret, often referring to sets as distractions. The development of screens in cinema, television, and computing has meant that since the start of the twenty-first century the entertainment industry has become dominated by the visual emphasis of the media. As a consequence the scenography of stage environments is interpreted by the viewer with as much sophistication as the written text. The audience now expects a complex visual experience from any production, and technology has played its part in creating an appetite for elaborate visual staging. This process had started much earlier: the 'white heat of technology' advocated by Prime Minister Harold Wilson in the 1960s had by the 1980s enabled scenographers to astound audiences with spectacle that drew delighted gasps of 'How did they do that?'

Style as Commodity

If we look back at the 1980s, we can observe how the commodification of style for musicals became significant. The training ground for the theatre practitioners responsible for these shows was the stable of major subsidized companies, such as the National Theatre and the Royal Shakespeare Company (RSC). The design style of the RSC's *Nicholas Nickleby* (1980) was conceived by Trevor Nunn and John Caird (co-directing), John Napier (set and costume design), and David Hersey (lighting design) working as a team. The style of *Les Misérables* (1985) followed a similar pattern, with an abstract and minimalist aesthetic that employed emblematic features to imply a whole image, relying on audience imagination rather than full-scale representation of place. The basic team remained the same, but was joined by Andreane Neofitou (costume designer) and Dermot Hayes (co-designer). *Cats* was produced in 1981 with the same core team but with the accompanying publicity for Napier's radical alteration of any theatre that this work was shown in, such as the surprise revolve and flying trapeze which caught the imagination of both critics and the audience.

Cats and *Les Misérables* are still being performed today, having transferred to Broadway and around the world. What they also have in common is a specific style of branding in the form of scenography and marketing, which has become recognizable as that of 'megamusicals',[7] globally successful without using vast amounts of technology—at least none that is obvious to the theatre spectator. In contrast to this, other British musicals of that era such as *Time* (1986), *Chess* (1986), *Metropolis* (1989), and *The Hunting of the Snark* (1991) tried to 'wow' their audience with the externals of design, which involved complex scenographic mechanisms, but failed to capture the interest of audiences sufficiently to ensure long runs. John Napier was interviewed about the marriage of approaches which he developed in both the subsidized and the commercial sector:

> For Napier, designing the show was a process of cross-breeding the flat-out glitz of his commercial work with his lower-key RSC style. In the West End, where design can virtually be an end in itself, Napier is known for the flash and the clever; that final twist as a show comes brilliantly together, as in the ascent of Cat Grizabella on her junkyard tire to paradise. In both genres, his hallmark is massive, self-transforming sets: His design for *Henry VI*, which opened the Barbican in 1982, focused on four 25' high siege towers converging to form an elaborate inner court and village. But there is a qualitative difference in the way Napier works in the two situations. In classical repertory, the design supports and intentionally recedes behind text and performance. It is also a context in which ensemble acting is of paramount importance, and Napier, Nunn, and Caird take advantage of it at the RSC by having the ensemble appear to build their environments in view of the audience. *Les Misérables* successfully marries the two approaches: creating enough visual excitement to make it a West End sellout, while sticking to the RSC's low-hype, high-fidelity treatment of the text.[8]

The production teams for the early megamusicals created work that exploited stylized realism, which John Bury had first utilized with Joan Littlewood's Theatre Workshop at Stratford East in the 1950s; it is no coincidence that Bury was head of design at the RSC from 1963 and later when Nunn and Napier worked there. We begin to see an approach which has emerged as the established 'house style' for musical theatre and has its roots, ironically, in a radical 'poor' theatre. The inception of this style can be traced to Sean Kenny's constructivist sets for his work with Joan Littlewood between 1957 and 1960 and then in the musicals he designed, using a frame which, depending on budget, would become more mechanized and animated the larger the funds. The frame was therefore a scaffold or skeleton set which would be used to provide a sense of entrances and exits through its structural openings. As Kenny trained in architecture with Frank Lloyd Wright it is no surprise that he not only designed sets but also engineered them and understood the use of cantilever, balance, and line. In the 1980s the alternative/fringe theatre was copying this style of design and using it in the flexible ways Kenny had envisaged with the manipulation of sets and movement of pieces being undertaken by actors and stage managers as part of the performance when expensive engineering wasn't affordable.

The need for design to create a realistic ambience or world is often regarded as the main job of the designer, unless s/he is working in a more traditional form, for example, in a three-set opera. These kinds of sets need to be both innovative and spectacular. The technology can be seen in the articulated set, which is dynamic and able to move, perhaps including a double revolve, moving in both vertical and horizontal planes, with the artistic purpose of these technologies at the centre of each show's performance dynamic. The revolve changes the space and time of the narrative as well as the 'play' of movement on the stage; its changing of the dimension of time adds a surreal quality to a performance, which in reviews has been called 'filmic'.

In *Les Misérables* the technology which enabled the movement of the scenery was highly sophisticated with remote bolts locking the revolve in position before the 1-ton trucks moved on to it; the hydraulic trucks were driven by a driver, the trucks switched over from motors to battery power to then become the barricades which was amazing to see as it looked like they were moving on their own. From the very beginning *Les Miz* (as it was affectionately known), was designed to transfer to other venues in Britain and around the world. The fluid scene changing was recognized as part of a product that could be sold, even though the production team might not have predicted the terrible reviews it received initially.

This 'Disneyfication' of theatre involves the use of design as a component part of the production's marketability: just as Disney produced not only animated films but also a host of other commodities that were sold alongside it, scenography itself became commodified in the 1980s as yet another aspect of the marketing for the show. It became customary to produce high-tech sets, which acted as branding for the production. In *Sunset Boulevard* (1993) the detail of the stage set was displayed for audience scrutiny in the theatre programme, as this couldn't be seen from the stalls. There is little abstraction or use of symbol; any representation of the real aims at environmental verisimilitude. Most of the sets looked like film sets, with a nod to both stylization and the hyperreal. The level of detail was beautiful but audiences did not have to interpret its meaning; it became visually unstimulating because it was too finished. In these contexts some musicals have become theme-park experiences, with *Starlight Express* (1984) being pre-eminent: designed by John Napier, the show had an all-encompassing roller-skate track wrapped around the curves of the auditorium at the Apollo Victoria Theatre London, where a 6-ton bridge tilted and moved to provide extra dramatic tension for the races.

The musical *Time* is another illustration of the musical as theme park attraction; here, the Dominion Theatre was gutted and rebuilt to accommodate the massive steel set and hydraulic lift demanded by Napier's design. The music came from Dave Clark's concept album which in turn derived from the 1970s musical *The Time Lord* by David Soames and Jeff Daniels. As a sci-fi multimedia rock musical it relied heavily on special effects, light show, and lasers as well as a fake hologram of Sir Laurence Olivier. John Gill complained in *Time Out*: 'The effects are stunning; however, even these are thanks to the twin cities of Sensurround and Stroboscope [. . .] If you can afford a second mortgage, go for the effects. Otherwise, make way for the coach parties and Motörhead fans.'[9] The London critics were pretty much in agreement about how to evaluate what was going on at the Dominion in 1986, with some describing the show as demonstrating the victory of technology over art—and that clearly was blamed on the set design (see Figure 16.1).

Michael Billington wrote in *The Guardian*: 'It rather saddens me to see the theatre following Hollywood movies in using ever vaster resources to say less and less. This is design taking over the theatre and becoming a substitute for hard thought. Maria Björnson did this no less effectively in *Donnerstag aus Licht* at Covent Garden.'[10] The opera by Karlheinz Stockhausen was produced in 1985 and also divided the critics as some felt that its theatrical conception worked against the music, which proves that the accusation of providing 'mere spectacle' in Britain at least was not aimed solely at musicals.

However, there is a different interpretation of what occurred which is that, as design in the theatre has developed, the audience has become much more accepting of the designer's art and consequently theatregoers' visual literacy nowadays is much more attuned to the synergies of musical score and scenic movement. This is in contradiction to some critics' views of the damage design was doing to the theatre during the late twentieth

FIGURE 16.1 The victory of technology over art? John Napier's spectacular set design for *Time*, featuring Jeff Shankley (as Lord Melchisedic, The Time Lord), Clinton Derricks-Carroll (as Captain Ebony), and David Cassidy (as The Rock Star, Chris Wilder) at the Dominion Theatre, 1986.

Photograph by Nobby Clark. Courtesy of ArenaPal.

century, when many reviewers complained of being subjected to aesthetic overkill and to scenic bombardment. Admittedly there were some disasters along the way:

> By the time of *Time*, opinion was starting to turn: for many, state-of-the-art computerised technology and lasers did not a musical make, and Napier seemed to have been hoisted on the very petard of an aesthetic which he helped beget. His [. . .] West End show, the John Caird/Stephen Schwartz *Children of Eden*, expired early in 1991: self-important visuals were no longer enough without a quality experience to enfold them.[11]

Time is often used as the prime example of the gratuitous use of spectacle but should also be seen in context: the design and use of technology onstage—in particular hydraulics, lasers, and new lighting instruments—were all typical of this period and were part of a designer's palette. *Time* was simply a useful vehicle for using these technologies, which were appropriate for its sci-fi aesthetic.

Scenography as Part of the Total Theatre Experience

In 'The 1991 Prague Quadrennial', Arnold Aronson highlights the problem of what happens when the techniques of theatre scenography and design are deconstructed:

> The case of the written text is, of course, well known: the words become the property of literary analysts and the inquiry shifts to questions of language, meaning, and structure divorced from the realities of performance. More recently, however, the elements of design have become a focus of collections and exhibitions as well as a subject for analysis. This is a good thing insofar as it heightens spectator awareness of the contributions of design and the inseparability of the performance (i.e. actors and language) from the physical space. But it also elevates the processual icons— the models, renderings, plans, and sketches—to the level of art objects. The moment this is done, the object ceases to be viewed and evaluated as a tool for achieving a production—as part of a process—and is instead appreciated for aesthetic principles similar to those applied to painting and sculpture; it becomes an end in itself [. . .]. The result of this emphasis upon the object or some extra-theatrical scale of aesthetic principles contributes to the valorisation of painters in the theatre—Pablo Picasso and David Hockney are prime examples—when in fact they are not always particularly good, let alone innovative, theatrical designers.[12]

What Aronson points out here is a problem for anyone discussing design for the stage outside the combined sense of the environment and the live performance. Reflection on only the part of the staging that can be shown separately from the performer always gives us a limited sense of the event itself.

Most musicals maintain the viewing perspective of the proscenium arch for what they present. However, the nature of theatre venues has been explored by practitioners to include non-traditional spaces and to embrace the notion of total theatre, which some twenty-first-century musical theatre staging explores. That notion partly goes back to Norman Bel Geddes (1893–1958), the American designer-director, who was able to reveal his expertise in the total organization of action, sound, light, and space. He discovered that it was possible for light to abstract the significant areas of human action and to imbue each with emotive colour. He found that the action itself is shaped by the spatial design into meaningful wholes, so that what is done and what is seen both reinforce the symbolic significance of speech and sound in a script.[13]

Bel Geddes's output in design for industry (aerodynamics and industrial design), architecture, film, and theatre was prodigious, but it must be remembered that his career coincided with a time of mass production and technological advances. He promoted the transition from ornate and tawdry decor to streamlined functionalism. Bel Geddes's approaches to the designing of stage space and to the multiplicity of scene changes has its heritage in the kind of staging which has been embraced in the genre of musical theatre, where the machines of the stage have been used to great effect to enhance the stage transformations of space and time. Bel Geddes designed over 100 Broadway productions and his influence cannot be underestimated.[14] In the form of his work for the Metropolitan Opera his design style also migrated to Britain. My research suggests that rather than a generically British style of design for musical theatre, there is an osmotic relationship between Broadway and the West End: *Cats*, for instance signalled the rebirth of musical theatre in London during the 1980s, yet it had a simplicity of staging that harked back to Bel Geddes's streamlined concepts of design.

The use of music and moving mechanisms as well as of light and shade to exploit the drama, or—to put it another way—the tonal echoing of music in the staging of a show in order to produce the kind of spectacle that may lead to commercial success, is widely recognized and employed in a choreographed fashion throughout musical theatre. Some typical features became iconic moments of scenic and musical synergy such as, 'You must see the helicopter/the barricades/the underground lake/the way the world opened up and revolved' (*Miss Saigon*, *Les Misérables*, *The Phantom of the Opera*, and *Cats* respectively) These were actually exploited as part of each show's marketing strategy.

STYLE OVER SUBSTANCE? RESPONSES OF BRITISH REVIEWERS TO SPECTACULAR SCENIC DESIGN

The notion of 'humming the scenery'[15] suggests that scenic design is the most memorable aspect of the experience of seeing a musical, and can be taken to imply that the show's set caught the eye of the critic to a disproportionate degree, thereby distracting from a more profound meaning. But it can also mean that the set caught the eye of the regular theatregoers and helped to enhance their experience.

In contrast to the poor reviews for *Les Miz*, reviews for the original production of *Cats*, which opened at the New London Theatre on 11 May 1981 and marked a new departure as the whole cast used radio microphones, were fairly generous, including favourable comments on the design. In fact, the critics specifically extolled the virtues of the show's staging. In the *Daily Telegraph* John Barber wrote:

> *Cats* is the concatenation of multi-media theatrical talent [...]. Trevor Nunn has lav- ished a fortune on dazzling effects, using enough shadows and fairy lights, masks, giant fans, smoke-hidden lifts, roving spotlights and conjuring tricks to turn the round stage into a three-ring circus [...]. If I have a criticism it is that the voices seem to come from loud-speakers instead of throats.[16]

The Guardian's Michael Billington felt it was '[a]n exhilarating piece of total theatre [...]. John Napier has designed a wonderful environmental rubbish-dump set'.[17] What is interesting about these reviews is the response of the critics to the way the staging changed the space and created the appropriate atmosphere for the story being told. In the *Financial Times* Michael Coveney raved: 'We find an auditorium that is like a dream conjunction of the Olivier and the Round House [...]. [Elaine] Paige [as Grizabella] is transfigured by David Hersey's coloured lighting'.[18] What became evident, and was noted at the time by designers and technicians working in London's West End, was that the critics were writing about the design elements of productions in their reviews. This was new. Witness Francis King's detailed report in the *Sunday Telegraph*:

> When the houselights dim, the 60-foot circle revolve begins to carry with it a whole section of the stalls, and eyes of innumerable cats glitter out of the surrounding dark- ness [...]. I'm not sure where Trevor Nunn's responsibility as director branches off Miss Lynne's; but it seems reasonable to credit him with the show's technical excel- lence (David Hersey's lighting, Abe Jacob's sound, both superb) [...] the giant tyre on which [Grizabella's] ascent [to the Heaviside Layer] is accomplished and the huge ramp lowered from the sky to meet it, are reasons in themselves for seeing the show.[19]

Finally, there was Jack Tinker's unadulterated praise in the *Daily Mail*: 'the entire New London Theatre has been brilliantly converted into one huge refuse dump. Surely no auditorium can ever have been more effectively or dramatically used'.[20]

In considering the impact of changing aesthetics of presentation, of more immersive stage environments, and also of new technologies on theatre productions, especially on musicals, critics have referred to the development of an aesthetic that they frequently denigrate as visual style over dramaturgical substance. However, in this context we should also consider that certain sophisticated musicals straddle the genres of musical theatre and opera—an art form where visual style has always been paramount, espe- cially in Europe. The two examples selected here for discussion are two British produc- tions of musicals by Stephen Sondheim who once memorably stated that if one of his shows plays in an opera house, then it is an opera and if it plays in a regular theatre, it is a musical. To some extent his definition seems as appropriate as any other.

The year 1990 saw the London premieres of two of Sondheim's musicals: *Sunday in the Park with George* (National Theatre, set designed by Tom Cairns) and *Into the Woods* (Phoenix Theatre, set designed by Richard Hudson and costumes by Sue Blane); both received mixed responses to their metaphorical visual stagings. The production of *Sunday in the Park with George* imaginatively referenced some of Georges Seurat's paintings, culminating in the characters recreating one of Seurat's best-known pointillist paintings, *A Sunday Afternoon on the Island of La Grande Jatte*, on stage. This was extremely impressive in terms of the design as the shades of the costumes and the set managed to convey the post-impressionistic atmosphere of the art work, a concept which clearly steered both the costume design and the staging of the production.

For Sondheim there are two types of musical theatre,

> revivals and the same kind of musicals over and over again, all spectacles [...] You get your tickets for *The Lion King* a year in advance, and essentially a family comes as if to a picnic, and they pass on to their children the idea that that's what the theater is—a spectacular musical you see once a year, a stage version of a movie. It has nothing to do with theater at all. It has to do with seeing what is familiar. We live in a recycled culture.[21]

Sondheim's commentary is relevant here in that it highlights a change of perceptions that is also related to British musical theatre as an art form, to its popularity, and to the production policies of many regional theatres in Britain, which are predicated on only producing musicals once a year—usually a pantomime, i.e. already familiar material, which then pays for the theatre's other productions during the rest of the season. The need to create a display of visual spectacle when putting on a musical has become an important feature of staging a commercially successful production not just in London's West End, but all around the country.

The understanding that his musicals can be staged in many fascinating ways is an important part of Sondheim's thinking when writing his shows, and some of his favourite theatre companies are amongst the more avant-garde, such as Théâtre de Complicité and Cheek by Jowl.[22] Both use the stage in innovative and radical ways, combining perceived simplicity of staging with density of signification. For *Into the Woods*, designer Richard Hudson created a flat view of the interior of the fairy-tale characters' houses for Act 1, which then morphed into the frightening and dark woods of Act 2, using the proscenium arch as a frame to great effect. The staging was sophisticated and its references to certain artists and aesthetics did not go unnoticed by critics. In *The Guardian* Michael Billington informed his readers:

> the evening's triumph belongs also to director Richard Jones, set designer Richard Hudson and costume designer Sue Blane who evoke exactly the right mood of haunted theatricality. Old-fashioned footlights give the faces a sinister glow. The

woods themselves are a semi-circular, black-and-silver screen punctuated with nine doors and a crazy clock: they achieve exactly the 'agreeable terror' of Gustave Doré's children's illustrations. And the effects are terrific: doors open to reveal the rotating magnified eyeball or the admonitory finger of the predatory giant.[23]

RECLAIMING THE VISUAL

Twenty-first-century technology offers many new ways of powering and operating changes in stage spaces, be it illumination, film projection screens, stage platforms, lifts, and scene changes. This variety is also reflective of the sophisticated staging that is possible in musicals, site-specific staging or immersive venues, all of which are part of the stage designer's armoury, even if most commercial musicals are still presented in and remain determined by the proscenium arch stage. To use the stage to maximum effect has of course been a major incentive for spectacle and was already demanded more than nine decades ago by Fernand Léger (1881–1955), a painter, sculptor, and film-maker who believed that 'there must be a maximum of stage effects'.[24] For Léger, whose theory was influenced by an inveterate fondness for the circus, actors had always been a barrier to complete scenic homogeneity, their 'authoritative personalities' standing out too much. In his eyes the theatre of spectacle was first and foremost a startling display of colour, lights, icons, and moving objects with the actor's value no greater than that of any other object seen on stage.

Léger's essay, *The Spectacle: Light, Color, Moving Image, Object-Spectacle*, written in 1924, describes a hypothetical ideal performance: what was called for, according to the artist, was a shallow stage with most movement and action taking place on a vertical plane. The background consisted of object-scenery, which was movable and participated in the stage action. Overhead, films were to be projected on the tops of the scenery and these filmic presentations would contribute to the animated stage, since they showed luminous, metallic objects shifting and pulsating in the air. The performers were to be used in groups, moving in parallel or contrasting rhythms, on condition that the general effect was in no way sacrificed. What he was describing has the potential to reclaim spectacle as a means to enchant and mesmerize rather than something that could pejoratively be described as mere decoration.

So we arrive at *Lord of the Rings: The Musical* (*LotRM*), a more recent spectacular musical, which at first glance might appear as a prime example of a show that has its audience 'humming the sets'. The show was based on Tolkien's epic novel, which in the early 2000s had been turned into three commercially successful, Oscar-winning movies. The musical version was first performed in Canada, representing the transatlantic exchange of musical theatre between North America and Britain. As comparisons with the multiple Oscar-winning film versions were inevitable, the musical opted for extravagant staging.

LotRM seems to have created a huge stir amongst critics and audience alike, if for different reasons: this time even websites referred pejoratively to 'chewing the scenery', echoing Groucho Marx's critique of television as chewing gum for the eyes, i.e. as a passive occupation where the eyes but not the mind are engaged. The musical was first staged with the support of the Canada Council for the Arts, opening in Toronto in February 2006. It was widely praised for its visual spectacle but it was also ridiculed as 'bored of the rings'[25] by a number of critics who used the spoof title to denigrate the length of the production. It was felt by some that the hype surrounding the sixty-five performers, the record-breaking cost of production, and the excess of commercialization ruined it as a show. The music was composed by A.R. Rahman, the Indian composer best known in the West for the music for the musical *Bombay Dreams* and his Oscar-winning soundtrack to the film *Slumdog Millionaire*, and Värttinä, a Finnish folk music band; the lyrics were penned by Matthew Warchus, its British director and dramatist, and Shaun McKenna, another British writer and dramatist. Set and costume designer Rob Howell and Warchus had both previously worked at the RSC and then went on to collaborate on many West End and Broadway productions.[26]

Warchus's intention was to overcome the constraints of existing conventions:

> We have not attempted to pull the novel towards the standard conventions of musical theatre, but rather to expand those conventions so that they will accommodate Tolkien's material. As a result, we will be presenting a hybrid of text, physical theatre, music and spectacle never previously seen on this scale. To read the novel is to experience the events of Middle-earth in the mind's eye; only in the theatre are we actually plunged into the events as they happen. The environment surrounds us. We participate. We are in Middle-earth.[27]

The set was noted for being both wonderful and expensive, the latter mainly because the producers had released information about the budget as part of their publicity campaign in the hope that extravagance might add to the attraction. However, even though the production claimed to offer an immersive experience within the auditorium, the Canadian press was not impressed, with *Toronto Star*'s Richard Ouzounian one among many to condemn the show as lacking excitement.[28] The subsequent West End transfer of the £19 million show opened at the Theatre Royal Drury Lane where the auditorium was designed so that the whole theatre became part of the spectacle: the auditorium and the proscenium stage were merged, so that it was no longer possible to recognize where one ended and the other began. This all-encompassing design created the sense of entering Middle-earth, the feeling that Warchus had originally aimed for. In this production we see both the need for the proscenium arch and its disruption via the use of staging techniques deriving from the environmental staging contexts of earlier decades, with the various elements used to make this an immersive experience: 'Halflings frolic in the stalls—actually on the seats—and downstage in front of the curtain; catching dragonflies in a net, having a bit of a dance—you know, Hobbity things.'[29]

The intention of director Matthew Warchus was to present a production that could best be described as Shakespeare-meets-Cirque du Soleil and the audience response suggests that he and his creative team succeeded:

> [Let's praise] the sheer beauty of the production; the scenes flow together seamlessly, the staging [is] in many ways a wonder of modern theatre. The use of every single theatrical trick, magic, participation, puppetry, projections, aerial work—the list goes on—ensured that whilst the plot may feel slow or stale, there is always plenty to look at, especially in the big 'production scenes'. In the third act interval, for which the audience stayed seated, Orcs prowl through the stalls and dress circle, scaring audience members half to death—including me when one jumped out of nowhere, behind my seat![30]

With three revolves, sixteen hydraulic lifts, and continually changing stage lighting the musical was a challenge for the lighting designer Paul Pyant. His design complemented Howell's multilayered scenographic elements perfectly, with an extensive use of textures and projected patterns throughout to create a lifelike environment, accentuating the changing seasons, the passing of time, and varying moods (see Figure 16.2).

FIGURE 16.2 'Wonderful and expensive': the design of *The Lord of the Rings*—sets and costumes by Rob Howell, lighting by Paul Pyant, featuring Michael Hobbs on stilts as Treebeard at the Theatre Royal Drury Lane, 2007.

On the Internet, members of the public expressed their delight:

> I was unsure that *Lord of the Rings the Musical* could be produced as a 'short' musical but was blown away by the performance, the visuals and the music. I thoroughly enjoyed it and would love to be able to see it again. I am sad that it is considered a 'flop' because it was worth every penny of the ticket price.[31]

It is interesting that the negative comments of the London theatre critics focused on the book, the acting, the length of the show, and the money spent, not the staging or the music. Indeed, reviewers and audience wanted more music and for the show to 'come out' as a proper musical rather than having much of the action underscored as in a traditional movie. In this case, both professional critics and regular theatregoers had no problem at all with the spectacle as that element of the show was widely praised: they actually wanted a full-blown spectacular musical.

So here the scenery did not make the musical but it did make the experience memorable and contributed greatly to the appeal of the musical. *LoRM* was a feat of both the imagination and the technology used to create its own visual poetry. It was announced in 2013 that it would relaunch as an epic new production and embark on a world tour in 2015, but this has not yet come to pass.[32]

What Makes Scenic Design Memorable?

And so, as the popular cultural form of the musical and the production teams who create them travel between countries, what results is a cross-fertilization of practices and aesthetics which are often showcased in large international touring productions that support and sustain commercial musical theatre as a genre and an art form. Nonetheless it is worth remembering that the world's longest-running musical is *The Fantasticks* which premiered at the Sullivan Street Playhouse in New York 1960 and was put together on a very low budget: the producers spent $900 on the set and $541 on costumes, at a time when major Broadway shows would cost $250,000.[33] The original set designer, costumer, prop master, and lighting designer was Ed Wittstein, who performed all four jobs for a total of only $480 plus $24.48 a week. The set was sparse on a semicircular stage, which created an intimate performance space, consisting of a raised stationary platform anchored by six poles. It was a highly stylized production and combined old-fashioned showmanship, classic musical theatre, and some techniques from commedia dell'arte and Noh theatre.[34] The stage resembled an English medieval pageant wagon, with different false curtains drawn across the platform at different times during the performance. There was a sun/moon made out of cardboard with one side painted bright yellow (the sun) and the other black with a crescent of white (the moon). That sun/moon was hung from a nail in one of the poles. The production closed in 2002, after 17,162 performances, a musical theatre record that is still unbroken.

One of the most memorable songs from the show is 'Try to Remember'. What *do* you remember when you see a show? Do you come out humming the sets? And what's so bad if you do?

NOTES

1. Shirley Strum Kenny, ed., *British Theatre and Other Arts 1660–1800* (Washington, DC: Associated University Presses Inc., 1984), 18.
2. Catherine Itzin, *Stages in the Revolution* (London: Methuen 1980).
3. Vera Gottlieb, 'Thatcher's Theatre—or, After *Equus*', *New Theatre Quarterly* 4, no. 14 (May 1988): 99–104; Jonathan Burston, 'The Megamusical: New Forms and Relations in Global Cultural Production' (Unpublished PhD thesis, Goldsmiths, University of London, 1998); and NTQ Symposium, 'Theatre in Thatcher's Britain: Organizing the Opposition', *New Theatre Quarterly* 5, no. 18 (May 1989), 113–123.
4. This also coincided with a need for the subsidized theatre to find a way of developing commercial income as budgets shifted from public subsidy towards a mixed economy of funding, due to funding cuts.
5. Richard Eyre and Trevor Nunn at the Royal Shakespeare Company and the National Theatre, London used this as their business model during their tenures. For more information on these and other musical theatre productions which started at subsidized theatres, please see Chapter 14 by Sarah Browne.
6. Clive Hirschhorn opined: 'In a victory of technology over art, Napier's eye-full of a space age set with its twinkling galaxies, dazzling light show, dancing lasers and a flying saucer that can do almost anything required of it, is the eighth wonder of the world. What it cannot do is save the book, the music and the lyrics from boggling banality.' Clive Hirschhorn, Review of *Time*, *Sunday Express*, 13 April 1986, Cuttings file, V&A Museum.
7. Jessica Sternfeld, *The Megamusical* (Bloomington, IN: Indiana University Press 2007).
8. Bethany Haye, 'Les Misérables', *Theatre Crafts* 20, no. 9 (November 1986): 33–34.
9. John Gill, Review of *Time*, *Time Out*, 16 April 1986, Cuttings file, V&A Museum.
10. Michael Billington, Review of *Time*, *The Guardian*, 10 April 1986, Cuttings file, V&A Museum.
11. Matt Wolf, 'Recent Tendencies in Design', in Strum Kenny, *British Theatre and Other Arts 1660–1800*, 224.
12. Arnold Aronson, 'The 1991 Prague Quadrennial', *Drama Review* 1 (Spring 1993): 61.
13. His conception of the artistic integration of theatrical means was realized even more completely when he worked with Max Reinhardt on *The Eternal Road* by Franz Werfel in 1937. The play required thirty-five distinct scene changes including a recurring synagogue. It took two years to produce and had 245 actors and singers and nearly 1,800 costumes. The New York Manhattan Opera House had to be gutted and rebuilt to accommodate the simultaneous sets of the synagogue interior, which was designed into the orchestra pit, alongside the biblical scenes to be performed on the rest of the stage (which was structured into five tiers). Gilbert Gabriel reviewed the Bel Geddes and Reinhardt production in the *New York American*: 'The Eternal Road is a spectacle of such grandeur and beauty as we have never seen before [...]. Norman Bel Geddes' scheme for its swift, but stately succession of scenes is an amazing one [...]. His burly genius has a playground of sufficiently vast size here. And what he works

with, the theatre's simple materials of carpentry, canvas, paint, people and streaming lights which burrow down towards the subway and upward towards the clouds, must be hailed as the garnerings of genius.' Gilbert Gabriel, 'Review of *The Eternal Road*', *New York American*, 24 January 1937, 3, http://norman.hrc.utexas.edu/nbgpublic/, accessed 20 February 2015.

14. Among his many celebrated designs are those for *Lady Be Good* (1924), *Ziegfeld Follies of 1925* (1925), *The Five O'Clock Girl* (1927), *Fifty Million Frenchmen* (1929), *Lysistrata* (1930), *Hamlet* (1931), and *Dead End* (1935).

15. This saying is often attributed to Richard Rodgers, although its actual origin is impossible to source.

16. John Barber, Review of *Cats*, *Daily Telegraph*, 12 May 1981, Cuttings file, V&A Museum.

17. Michael Billington, Review of *Cats*, *The Guardian*, 12 May 1981, Cuttings file, V&A Museum.

18. Michael Coveney, Review of *Cats*, *Financial Times*, 12 May 1981, Cuttings file, V&A Museum.

19. Francis King, Review of *Cats*, *Sunday Telegraph*, 12 May 1981, Cuttings file, V&A Museum.

20. Jack Tinker, Review of *Cats*, *Daily Mail*, 12 May 1981, Cuttings file, V&A Museum.

21. Frank Rich, 'Conversations with Sondheim', *New York Times Magazine*, 12 March 2000, http://www.nytimes.com/library/magazine/home/20000312mag-sondheim.html, accessed 10 October 2014.

22. Rich, 'Conversations with Sondheim'.

23. Michael Billington, 'In the Thickets of Thought—Michael Billington Sings the Praises of Sondheim and Lapine's Fairy Tale Attempt to Push the Musical into New and Daring Direction', *The Guardian*, 27 September 1990, Cuttings file, V&A Museum.

24. Henning Rischbieter, 'Fernand Léger and the Theatre of Spectacle', in *Art and the Stage in the 20th Century*, ed. Henning Rischbieter (Boston: New York Graphic Society, 1968), 97.

25. See Harry Zing, 'What Went Wrong? #1 *The Lord of the Rings*. Musical Retrospective 30/07/2012', https://chewingthescenerydotcom.wordpress.com/tag/chewing-the-scenery/, accessed 10 October 2014.

26. At the RSC, Rob Howell designed *The Shakespeare Review, The Painter of Dishonour, Little Eyolf, Richard III*, and *The Family Reunion*, while Matthew Warchus directed *The Unexpected Man, Hamlet, Henry V, The Devil Is an Ass*, and *The Winter's Tale*. They later worked together on *Buried Child* (2004), *Boeing-Boeing* (2008), *The Norman Conquests* (2008), *Ghost: The Musical* (2011), and *Matilda* (2010); the last four productions all moved from the West End to Broadway, where—with the exception of *Ghost*—they were very successful, winning several Tony Awards.

27. Anon. '*The Lord of the Rings* Cast Announced', https://www.londontheatredirect.com/news/113/The-Lord-Of-The-Rings-cast-announced.aspx, accessed 19 December 2014.

28. Quoted in Zing, 'What Went Wrong?'

29. Zing, 'What Went Wrong?'

30. Zing, 'What Went Wrong?'

31. Zing, 'What Went Wrong?'

32. As of December 2015, the official website, www.lotr.com, is still under construction.

33. Donald C. Farber and Robert Viagas, *The Amazing Story of 'The Fantasticks': America's Longest-Running Play* (Pompton Plains, NJ: Limelight Editions, 2005),158.

34. Farber and Viagas, *The Amazing Story of 'The Fantasticks'*, 157.

BIBLIOGRAPHY

Anon. 'The Lord of the Rings Cast Announced.' https://www.londontheatredirect.com/news/113/The-Lord-Of-The-Rings-cast-announced.aspx, accessed 19 December 2014.

Archer, William. 'The Dying Drama.' New Review 9 (1888): 382–389.

Aronson, Arnold. American Set Design. London: Theatre Communications Group, 1985.

Aronson, Arnold. 'The 1991 Prague Quadrennial.' Drama Review 1 (Spring 1993): 61–73.

Barber, John. Review of Cats. Daily Telegraph, 12 May 1981. Cuttings file, Victoria and Albert (V&A) Museum.

Billington, Michael. 'In the Thickets of Thought—Michael Billington Sings the Praises of Sondheim and Lapine's Fairy Tale Attempt to Push the Musical into New and Daring Direction.' The Guardian, 27 September 1990. Cuttings file, V&A Museum.

Billington, Michael. Review of Cats. The Guardian, 12 May 1981. Cuttings file, V&A Museum.

Billington, Michael. Review of Time. The Guardian, 10 April 1986. Cuttings file, V&A Museum.

Booth, Michael R. Prefaces to English Nineteenth-Century Theatre. Manchester: Manchester University Press, 1980.

Burston, Jonathan. 'The Megamusical: New Forms and Relations in Global Cultural Production.' Unpublished PhD thesis. Goldsmiths, University of London, 1998.

Coveney, Michael. Review of Cats. Financial Times, 12 May 1981. Cuttings file, V&A Museum.

Dyal, Donald H. Norman Bel Geddes: Designer of the Future. Monticello: Vance Bibliographies, 1983.

Farber, Donald C., and Robert Viagas. The Amazing Story of 'The Fantasticks': America's Longest-Running Play. Pompton Plains, NJ: Limelight Editions, 2005.

Fergusson, Francis. The Idea of a Theater: A Study of Ten Plays; The Art of Drama in a Changing Perspective. 1948. Reprint, Princeton, NJ: Princeton University Press, 1968. Page references are to the 1968 edition.

Gabriel, Gilbert. Review of The Eternal Road. New York American, 24 January 1937, 3. http://norman.hrc.utexas.edu/nbgpublic/, accessed 20 February 2015.

Gill, John. Review of Time. Time Out, 16 April 1986. Cuttings file, V&A Museum.

Goodwin, John, ed. British Theatre Design: The Modern Age. London: Weidenfeld & Nicolson, 1998.

Gottlieb, Veral. 'Thatcher's Theatre—or, After Equus.' New Theatre Quarterly 4, no. 14 (May 1988): 99–104.

Haye, Bethany. 'Les Misérables.' Theatre Crafts 20, no. 9 (November 1986): 33–34.

Hirschhorn, Clive. Review of Time. Sunday Express, 13 April 1986. Cuttings file, V&A Museum.

Itzin, Catherine. Stages in the Revolution. London: Methuen 1980.

King, Francis. Review of Cats. Sunday Telegraph, 12 May 1981. Cuttings file, V&A Museum.

Léger, Fernand. The Spectacle: Light, Color, Moving Image, Object-Spectacle. 1924. Translated by Alexandra Anderson in Functions of Painting, edited by Edward F. Fry, 35–47. London: Thames and Hudson, 1973.

NTQ Symposium. 'Theatre in Thatcher's Britain: Organizing the Opposition.' New Theatre Quarterly 5, no. 18 (May 1989): 113–123.

Rich, Frank. 'Conversations with Sondheim.' New York Times Magazine, 12 March 2000. http://www.nytimes.com/library/magazine/home/20000312mag-sondheim.html, accessed 10 October 2014.

Rischbieter, Henning. 'Fernand Léger and the Theatre of Spectacle.' In Art and the Stage in the 20th Century, edited by Henning Rischbieter, 92–7. Boston: New York Graphic Society, 1968.

Scott, Clement. 'A Few Words for the Unseen.' *The Theatre* 13 (January–June 1889). http://archive.org/stream/s4theatre13londuoft/s4theatre13londuoft_djvu.txt, accessed 20 February 2015.

Stokes, John. Resistible Theatres: *Enterprise and Experiment in the Late Nineteenth Century* London: ELEK, 1972.

Sternfeld, Jessica. *The Megamusical.* Bloomington, IN: Indiana University Press 2007.

Strum Kenny, Shirley, ed. *British Theatre and Other Arts 1660–1800.* Washington, DC: Associated University Presses Inc., 1984.

Tinker, Jack. Review of *Cats. Daily Mail*, 12 May 1981. Cuttings file, V&A Museum.

Wilde, Oscar. 'As You Like It at Coombe House.' *Dramatic Review*, 6 June 1885, 296–297.

Wolf, Matt. 'Recent Tendencies in Design'. In Strum Kenny, *British Theatre and Other Arts 1660–1800*, 223–231.

Zing, Harry. 'What Went Wrong? #1 *The Lord of the Rings*. Musical Retrospective 30/07/2012.' https://chewingthescenerydotcom.wordpress.com/tag/chewing-the-scenery/, accessed 10 October 2014.

CHAPTER 17

BILLY ELLIOT AND ITS LINEAGE

The Politics of Class and Sexual Identity in British Musicals since 1953

ROBERT GORDON

BILLY ELLIOT: THE MUSICAL IN ITS SOCIAL AND ARTISTIC CONTEXTS

AFTER the experiments in new musico-dramaturgical forms in British musicals from the 1970s to the 1990s,[1] *Billy Elliot: The Musical* (2005) returns to older forms of popular entertainment in order to evoke a disappearing world of northern working-class culture. Remarkably, the musical sets the tacky showbiz glitz and camp comedy of stage and television variety shows[2] in dialectical opposition to the rude vitality and political directness that typified the 'rough' aesthetic of British socialist theatre between the 1950s and the early 1980s to create a synthesis that comprises a new kind of folk aesthetic. Critiquing the rigidly sexist and homophobic paternalism of working-class culture while at the same time lamenting the destruction of the communitarian values that sustained it, the show's dramaturgical strategies owe as much to the utopian ethos of fifties musical comedies such as *The Boy Friend* (1953) and *Salad Days* (1954) as to the revolutionary politics of working-class drama from the seventies.

Without some understanding of its political context, *Billy Elliot* makes sense only as a version of the well-worn story in which a poor but talented youngster battles to realize his/her dreams of success. Yet this is precisely the way in which the musical has been interpreted by the New York critic John Lahr. Amidst a chorus of approval for the show by London critics after its premiere—and by Broadway reviewers three years later—Lahr's review of the West End production of *Billy Elliot* in the *New Yorker* (July 2005) stands out for its ethnocentric blindness to the distinctively British context that informs the musical:

> The British love musicals; they just don't do them very well. [...] The jazz of American optimism, which lends elation and energy to the form, is somehow alien to the ironic British spirit. At its buoyant core, the American musical is the expression of a land of plenty. England, on the other hand, is a land of scarcity—the Land of No, as a friend of mine calls it.[3]

Lahr's refusal to comprehend the specific forms of British entertainment as expressive of a wholly other cultural identity betrays a reflex of American imperialism that neatly inverts the historical posture of British colonial superiority. Nowhere in Lahr's review is there an acknowledgement that the miners' eventual capitulation in 1985 was a defining historical moment, symbolizing the Thatcher government's victory over trade union power and the triumph of monetarist policy. A British audience will, however, be profoundly aware of how the consequent destruction of Britain's industrial base created an opposition between the devastated mining and manufacturing regions of Wales and the north, and the wealthy south of England, leaving a legacy of class hatred that festered for decades. Paradoxically, Lahr's condescending critique of *Billy Elliot* serves merely to underline the deeper cultural differences between British and American musicals too often ignored in their frequent transatlantic crossings:

> By nature, the musical genre deals with fantasy, not fact; it is at its most political when it delivers pleasure, not dogmatic persiflage. [Lee] Hall doesn't seem to understand this, and his prolix, repetitive book quickly loses its way. When the miners are the issue—and their story eats up a fair portion of the saga—the musical stalls; the proletariat here really *are* lumpen. When Billy dances, however, everything comes alive.

Lahr appears to presume that, as entertainment, the skilful representation of exceptional individuals by gifted performers creates stage magic, whereas the convincing enactment of the mundane lives of workers is simply boring. Articulating the deeply rooted credo of American liberalism, Lahr implies that, rather than unfolding coherent and believable narratives, musicals should provide opportunities for virtuoso performers to demonstrate their special talent: 'When Billy is doing his twists and twirls, his youthful entrechats and jetés, the immanence of the extraordinary is credible. When he tap-dances, it isn't; Savion Glover he ain't.'[4] Inherent in Lahr's judgement is the assumption that it is the chief function of the musical to valorize the star system. While it is true that the majority of Broadway musicals celebrate the success of the extraordinary individual both in fact and in fiction, British musicals are usually motivated by more communitarian aims. In sociocultural terms, *Billy Elliot* is interesting precisely because its dramaturgical structure opposes the capitalist ideology of acquisitive individualism against the collectivist values of social welfare.

THE CAMP SENSIBILITY IN POPULAR
BRITISH ENTERTAINMENT

It is notable that *Billy Elliot* exploits conventions of drag and camp performance from music hall, pantomime, and end-of-the-pier shows to destabilize patriarchal notions of the biological determination of gender and sexual identity. It is the first British musical to explore the connection between homophobic anxiety and the cultural implications of homosexual orientation within a society that prizes masculine strength as a heroic virtue. By distinguishing between homosexuality and effeminacy and undermining the incorrect assumption that ballet is a profession for women and gay men, the musical has achieved historical significance in being the first mainstream British entertainment to directly interrogate homophobic prejudice as a function of patriarchal society.[5] In doing so *Billy Elliot* employs a long tradition of camp in British popular culture as a strategy for undermining patriarchal assumptions of gender and sexuality.

A number of British entertainment forms that originated in the nineteenth century exhibited a sensibility that might today be labelled 'camp': pantomime, burlesque, farce, music hall (later variety) performance, and end-of-the-pier concerts were character- ized by eccentric stage personalities, cross-dressing, parody, and comic drollery that was both deadpan and facetious. Such types of entertainment persisted until the advent of broadcast television transformed many popular kinds of stage entertainment into TV comedy and variety shows[6] in the late fifties. As had been the case with Edwardian music hall stars like Marie Lloyd and George Robey, the biggest stage stars between the 1920s and 1950s, such as Gracie Fields and George Formby, achieved popularity with working- and middle-class audiences alike, perhaps through the success of their films.[7] On the other hand, musical comedy appealed predominantly, if not wholly, to middle- and upper-class audiences, tending to employ singers, dancers, and comic actors trained as theatre performers rather than music hall artistes.[8]

The camp sensibility that formed an important component of predominantly working-class types of entertainment was arch and facetious, ridiculing clichés and fet- ishizing outmoded forms by means of both nostalgia and parody, but during the 1890s the attitude was adopted and elaborated by a queer subculture. Camp's knowing empha- sis on sexual innuendo may well have lent itself to the subversive satire of a queer milieu in which the fixity of gender positions was undermined by unrestricted sexual role-play. The interwar period witnessed the gradual development of a hidden gay subculture in British cities; this was even more pronounced during the war years but repressive policing after 1951 ensured that this bohemian subculture, shared perhaps by artists and theatre people, remained more or less invisible to the bourgeois majority. There was an invented language called Polari by which one insider could recognize another, allowing apparently innocent behaviour to be interpreted in a coded way.

In the mainstream forms of variety, pantomime, revue, cinema, and 'light enter- tainment' programmes on radio and television, the queer potential of camp became progressively more emphatic between the 1950s and the 1980s. A line of queer performers became household names, including Frankie Howerd, Kenneth Williams, Charles Hawtrey, Larry Grayson, and Julian Clary, while a few much-loved drag performers such as Danny La Rue and Paul O'Grady, aka Lily Savage, were complemented by overtly 'straight' male performers who were famous for their varied uses of transvestite performance (e.g. Barry Humphries, aka Dame Edna Everage, Stanley Baxter, and Les Dawson).

MUSICAL COMEDY AND CAMP SINCE 1953

Although deriving from the more 'respectable' middle-class theatre tradition, Sandy Wilson's *The Boy Friend* has a tongue-in-cheek quality that is inherently camp, its charming and nostalgic pastiche of twenties musical comedy making it the first entirely retro musical comedy.[9] Its lack of any genuinely sexual romance heightens the camp effect in which the accurate pastiche of twenties musical comedy empties the original form of any emotional content—perhaps a sign of Sandy Wilson's queer sensibility. The fact that its love songs deliberately echo popular antecedents renders them *de trop*: 'A Room in Bloomsbury' reproduces the style of Coward's definitive 'A Room with A View'[10] without any of its romantic yearning. The title song lends itself so easily to camp parody:

> We've got to have,
> We plot to have;
> For it's so dreary not to have,
> That certain thing called the boy friend.
>
> We're blue without,
> Can't do without,
> Our dreams just won't come true without,
> That certain thing called the boy friend.

Here the female chorus sing of the 'boy friend' as of any attractive man, a generalized image of a male as sex object, which reverses the usual order of musical comedy courtship in which men pine after women. The potential boy friends somewhat narcissistically collude in the process of being admired:

> Life without us
> Is quite impossible
> And devoid of all charms,
> No amount of idle gossip'll
> Keep them out of our arms.

In an era when musicals were resolutely hetero-normative, when boy met girl and usually got her after negotiating a number of obstacles, Sandy Wilson's camp disruption of generic expectations invites a degree of playfulness that might encourage a homosexual man to place himself in the girls' position of desiring a generic 'boy friend'. Such a coded reading might have been even more obviously implied in 1953 when most of the West End chorus boys would have been gay and many effeminate, though no doubt the doubleness of the signification, which allowed both 'straight' and 'camp' readings would have been maintained.[11]

In an equally playful though even more absurd vein, the plot of *Salad Days* (1954) exploits the episodic structure of an intimate revue,[12] thinly disguised as a coming-of-age narrative in which Jane and Timothy, having newly graduated with BA degrees, attempt to find something to do with their lives ('We Said We Wouldn't Look Back'). At face value, the wild eccentricity of *Salad Days* might simply appear charming to most British audiences but its questioning of authority is particularly resonant for those who may have had occasion to fear it. As in revues and pantomimes of the period, the camp innuendo of *Salad Days* appealed especially to a bohemian class of theatre professionals and closeted homosexuals in the form of 'in-jokes'.

In *Salad Days*, Jane's parents are pressuring her to find a suitable husband and Timothy's are harassing him to find a proper job ('Find Yourself Something to Do') so the two decide to get married without any suggestion of passionate attachment on either side and without any idea how they will earn a living.[13] A series of adventures is initiated through their chance encounter with a tramp in a London park; he asks the couple if they will look after his old portable piano for £7 a week: it is a magic piano that makes anyone who hears it dance ('Oh Look at Me'). The outbreaks of dancing that interrupt the dialogue a number of times offer an experience of utopian pleasure, joyously shared by the audience.

On the surface a fantastical folk tale, *Salad Days* metaphorically represents the malaise of young middle-class people in Britain nine years after the war. Expected to follow conservatively in the footsteps of their parents, and lacking any distinct identity as young people, university graduates were trapped in a repressive and puritanical environment that demanded dull but comfortable conformity. The post-war dispensation denied young people the pleasure that in different ways characterized the romantic escapism of personal relationships during the war and the more subversive hedonism of the rock 'n' roll culture of Teddy boys and teenagers soon to come.

The startling transformation by the magic piano of a most unlikely assortment of individuals into dancers prompts a carnivalesque disruption of social convention that promotes gaiety in the old-fashioned sense of the word, but also gestures towards the more modern meaning of 'being gay'. A scene set in Gusset Creations, the fashionable dress shop frequented by Jane's mother, features the only obviously homosexual character in *Salad Days*. While contributing little if anything to the elaboration of the plot, Act 2, Scene 5 presents a dress parade organized by the flamboyantly effeminate fashion designer, Ambrose, that goes horribly wrong, eventually being interrupted by the news that the piano has been lost again. Ambrose's pretentious attitudes and histrionically

exaggerated closing line, 'I'm drained of all emotions. I'm a husk. Leave me' (53) reinforces a camp stereotype of the hysterical homosexual. When read 'against the grain,'[14]
this revue-like scene's tangential connection with the central narrative discloses the
absence in the text of any realistic representation of homosexuality—a result of the
regime of censorship and police repression being satirized in the show.

It does not require a great leap of the imagination to view the ironically titled Minister
of Pleasure and Pastime as a satire on the hypocritical and censorious regime of the
Conservative government: while puritanically attempting to put a stop to the subversive gaiety of the magic piano he spends his evenings at the club 'Cleopatra'. Also very
apt as a satirical target is the police officer whose secret passion for all forms of dance
expresses itself in an extremely camp and funny scene where he demonstrates his hidden terpsichorean skills by partnering his constable. The chief joke in *Salad Days* is the
repeated revelation that the Dionysian enemy lies *within* the Establishment. In their different ways, both *The Boy Friend* and *Salad Days* respond to the change from a post-war
Labour to a Conservative government in 1951, which confronted artists with the contradiction between the social consensus upholding the liberal values of a welfare state and
the increasingly oppressive political climate of Cold War paranoia.

Although the strain of camp irreverence and humour extends into the work of Slade/
Reynolds and, even more obviously, that of Wilson in the late 1950s and the 1960s,[15]
overt references to homosexuality were forbidden by stage censorship and, with the odd
exception,[16] gay or queer culture was an underground phenomenon while camp was
largely confined to radio and television comedy, films,[17] and entertainment on the club
circuit. The demi-monde of Soho and the East End does infiltrate the musical after 1956
by way of shows such as *Expresso Bongo* (1958), *The Crooked Mile* (1959), and *Fings Ain't
Wot They Used T'Be* (1959), whose intermingling of gamblers, policemen, gangsters,
prostitutes, and effeminate interior decorators, while more inclusive in representing a
bohemian environment, nevertheless marginalizes homosexual characters as comic
stereotypes. By the early 1960s serious young playwrights such as Shelagh Delaney, Joe
Orton, and Harold Pinter were offering subtle challenges to censorship by their more
honest and adult portrayal of gay characters. It was only in 1966, however, that John
Osborne's *A Patriot for Me*, a historical drama about the homosexual Colonel Redl, was
so explicit that, together with other plays at the Royal Court, it provoked calls for the
outright abolition of theatre censorship, which occurred in 1968.[18]

Mainstream British musicals have until the beginning of the millennium generally
avoided representing overtly homosexual characters. Sandy Wilson's *Valmouth* (1958)
and Richard O'Brien's *Rocky Horror Show* (1973) might appear as exceptions, but each
was conceived as a 'fringe' show addressing a minority audience, and the latter only
really became a mainstream entertainment once the screen version had established
itself as a cult classic. *Valmouth* is a musical adaptation of Ronald Firbank's outrageously
camp novel. It is not difficult to interpret the decadent town of Valmouth—which is
eventually destroyed by an erupting volcano—as an emblem of the bohemian demi-
monde, a self-contained milieu with its own bizarre norms of behaviour. *The Rocky
Horror Show* deliberately addressed a younger, more progressive audience, paying

homage to the much-vaunted androgynity of seventies 'glamrock' icons such as David Bowie and Marc Bolan through the transvestite and bisexual machismo of Tim Curry's Frank'n'furter and subverting bourgeois expectations by exposing Brad and Janet, the generic 'straight' couple from fifties B-movies, as sexually repressed neophytes desperately in need of the liberation achieved during the succeeding carnival of homo- and heterosexual seductions.

Aiming to appeal to an older and mainstream audience demographic, Lee Hall and Elton John's *Billy Elliot: The Musical* is far subtler than *The Rocky Horror Show* in its treatment of sexual difference. The stage show transforms the tightly focused depiction of a Geordie[19] mining community on strike in Stephen Daldry's film (2000) by making extensive use of ballet and several other types of dance in order both to enhance the show's entertainment value as a musical and to place greater emphasis on the trope of gender and sexuality. The musical's more complex interrogation of sexism and homophobia reflects the concerns of an epoch during which Western countries have made progress in gender and sexual politics by recognizing discrimination against women and LGBT individuals and legislating to remove it. The central focus of the film on the politics of class is dialectically counterpoised in the musical with a critique of working-class masculine identity. The opposition between the 'rough' (implicitly masculine) aesthetic of politically engaged leftist theatre and the refined (supposedly feminine) but politically uncommitted 'high art' form of ballet is resolved in the popular form of variety. The pleasure of such variety entertainment is generated by an exploitation of the inherent subversiveness of camp, which has since the 1970s made audiences complicit in the acceptance of alternative sexualities—a quintessentially British way of affirming the equality of all individuals within a community.

MARXIAN AESTHETICS AND WORKING-CLASS CULTURE: 'A GOOD NIGHT OUT'

The rough theatre aesthetic inscribed in both the subject matter and form of *Billy Elliot* invokes the socialist theatre movement which made a significant impact on musical theatre of the late 1950s. Emblematic of this approach is the work of Joan Littlewood who must be reckoned one of the two most important directors in the British theatre since 1945.[20] From her days with Unity Theatre in the thirties, she and her partner, the folk singer Jimmy Miller (who later called himself Ewan McColl), pioneered the development of Marxian aesthetics in British theatre and radio through the use of popular and folk songs within plays (the best-known was Brendan Behan's *The Hostage*, 1958) to create a unique type of community drama that faithfully depicted the harsh realities of working-class life.[21] Revealing the influence of Brecht well before his approach to theatre became fashionable in Britain during the late 1950s, Littlewood's vision of working-class culture represented a direct attack on what was from her perspective a decadent society sanctioned by a corrupt authority; today one might recognize the cultural marginalization of the working class in the fifties as parallel to the suppression of homosexuality by both the police and the institution of censorship.

Littlewood's revelatory framing of *Oh What a Lovely War* as an end-of-the-pier Pierrot show motivated the ironic deployment of popular songs from the First World War to satirize the blindly sentimental way in which the horrific slaughter of men had been memorialized. Her concept of popular theatre foreshadowed the folk aesthetic ('a good night out') of John McGrath's company, 7:84 Scotland (there was also a 7:84 England).[22] These two groups presented musicals or plays with songs in community centres, village halls, and pubs, during the 1970s and early 1980s with the aim of exposing the inequalities of British society from a Marxist perspective.[23] Most successful was the groundbreaking and influential *The Cheviot, the Stag and the Black Black Oil* (1973), which dramatized the ruthless exploitation of the Highlands by capitalists between 1746 and 1973, while also telling stories of local resistance. McGrath drew on an eclectic mix of entertainment traditions, including music hall, pantomime, farce, the ceilidh,[24] and folk song as well as a range of theatrical techniques—documentary, verbatim, and revue—to construct radically left-wing shows that engaged audiences both through direct political argument and by appealing to the visceral pleasure of traditional folk entertainments.

A BRECHTIAN FABLE: *BLOOD BROTHERS*

Not as radical as the work of 7:84 but very much in the tradition of a 'good night out', Willy Russell's *Blood Brothers* (1983)[25] premiered at the Liverpool Playhouse and then transferred to the Lyric Theatre in London where it had a short engagement in 1983. However, Bill Kenwright's touring production was extremely successful around the country and when it played again in London in 1988 it was a huge hit, running until 2011. As a playwright who loved pop music, Russell's Liverpool background helped him tap into a rich vein of music and stories and he alternated between writing plays and musicals with apparent ease. Written near the end of Margaret Thatcher's first term of office as prime minister, *Blood Brothers* expresses some of the anger and impotence felt by working-class people in the north of England, who saw their traditional industries being abandoned, leaving towns and villages derelict in the wake of the new monetarist policies of the Conservative government. The piece illustrates the harsh realities of northern working-class existence just before the events represented in *Billy Elliot* actually took place.

The story of *Blood Brothers* is told by a narrator as an urban folk tale, the score consisting of emotive pop ballads and rhythmically driving satirical rock songs: it contrasts the lives of twin brothers, one of whom has been given over for adoption by the cleaner Mrs Johnstone, to her wealthy and childless employer, Mrs Lyons ('My Child'). Mrs Johnstone's story reveals the archetypal destiny of a single working-class mother. An

FIGURE 17.1 A working-class mother in 1980s Liverpool: Petula Clark as Mrs Johnstone with David Cassidy as her son Mickey in the Broadway production (1993) of Willy Russell's *Blood Brothers*.

Photograph by Joan Marcus. Courtesy of Joan Marcus.

uneducated woman with seven children, her husband had left her while she was pregnant with the twins:

> Then, of course, I found
> That I was six weeks overdue
> We got married at the registry
> An' then we had a do
> [......]
> They said the bride was lovelier than Marilyn Monroe
> And we went dancing
> Yes, we went dancing
> [......]
> My husband, he walked out on me
> A month or two ago
> For a girl they say who looks a bit like Marilyn Monroe
> And they go dancing
> They go dancing. (81–82)

As in *Salad Days* and *Billy Elliot*, dancing provides an image of utopian pleasure, signifying the joy of escape or liberation from a harsh or repressive environment, the difference being that the aforementioned musicals display dance on stage at every opportunity, whereas virtually no dancing is actually presented in *Blood Brothers*, because much of the story is told in song rather than enacted on stage.

The narrative structure of the musical conforms precisely to Brecht's notion that in epic theatre the story (*fabel*) should be constructed in the complicated shape of a narrative rather than directly embodied in dramatic action. Not only does a narrator figure appear throughout the course of *Blood Brothers*, but many of the characters also narrate their own histories in song. This is designed to promote critical reflection and, ultimately, judgement by the spectator, rather than simple and immediate identification with the central characters.

While Mickey, the charming but aimless son, remains stuck in an impoverished environment that offers no opportunities, his brother Eddie is brought up as a conventional scion of the upper middle class and eventually attends university. Despite Mrs Lyons's determination to keep the boys apart, they meet, become friends, and—not knowing their true relation—declare themselves 'blood brothers' ('My Friend'). In order to put an end to the friendship Mrs Lyons moves away from the area, but, by chance, the council rehouses the Johnstone family in the same suburb, so the boys meet again ('That Guy'), both falling in love with the same girl, Linda, who marries Mickey when Eddie goes away to university. Mickey eventually becomes a thief and is caught and sent to prison ('Madman'), during which time Eddie becomes first Linda's comforter and then her lover. When Mickey is released he jealously confronts Eddie but when his mother informs him in a bid to stop him from shooting Eddie that they are twin brothers, he screams, 'You! Why didn't you give me away? (. . . *almost uncontrollable with rage.*) . . . I could've been him!' (158). Mickey accidentally kills Eddie, while the police shoot Mickey to prevent him from doing any harm to Mrs Johnstone or Linda ('Tell Me It's Not True').

The musical is a simple but powerful examination of the effects of class in British society, its representation of the interaction between genetics and social environment revealing an almost Sophoclean notion of destiny. Clearly *Blood Brothers* struck a chord with the kind of British audiences who might have found Sondheim's musicals alien in terms of both subject matter and musical style. Russell's ability to evoke the idiom and manners of a 'Scouse'[26] environment is remarkable, as is his talent for writing songs redolent of the era and milieu, while the melodramatic plot structure, although somewhat contrived, has proved very attractive to a broad audience. Significantly, the exclusive focus on class politics in *Blood Brothers* precludes any use of the camp strategies of variety: correspondingly, neither sexual orientation nor gender is problematized in any way.

EARLY RESPONSES TO THE POLITICAL LEGACY OF THATCHERISM

Our Day Out, originally a television play (1977) but rewritten as a musical for the Liverpool Everyman (1983) with music by Bob Eaton, Chris Mellor, and Russell himself, continued the exploration of working-class subjects in a demotic idiom.[27] Willy Russell followed the majority of leftist male writers of his generation in concentrating exclusively on the politics of class rather than gender, race, or sexual identity. Howard Goodall and Melvyn Bragg's *The Hired Man* (1984), a musical based on Bragg's historical novel, also focuses exclusively on the representation of the exploitation of working-class men by capitalist farm owners and businessmen. In the early 1970s newly established feminist[28] and gay theatre groups began to create performances with the aim of demonstrating that 'the personal is political'; these companies, however, had limited impact on mainstream theatre, remaining largely ghettoized until the 1990s.

The examination of the relationship between characters and their local communities in several films, plays, and musicals since the mid-1980s represented opposition to the radical social transformation engendered by the manifold failure of Conservative policies to maintain social harmony. Two works by Jim Cartright directly exposed the devastation of northern communities caused by the Thatcher government's policy of closing mines and privatizing national industries. These were plays with songs rather than full-blown musicals, but their use of popular songs was extremely evocative. *Road* (1986) deployed an eclectic range of popular songs to invoke emotionally charged 'folk' memories at key dramatic moments. *The Rise and Fall of Little Voice* (1992) included even more songs in its representation of a painfully shy young woman's ('Little Voice') transformation into a surprisingly confident performer when channelling a range of iconic fifties and sixties singers that her late father had loved. Set in a cheaply over-decorated house and a tawdry northern working-class club, the show anatomized a dying world whose characters inhabit their fantasies of the past or future as an escape from the ugly reality of the present. Both shows achieved great commercial success in theatres around the country and were later filmed.

BILLY ELLIOT AS BRITISH HISTORY PLAY

With its location in a mining village in County Durham between 1984 and 1985, *Billy Elliot* cleverly refunctions the strategies of socialist theatre of that epoch in conjunction with the variety entertainment of the time, thereby initiating a complex play of intertextuality. Brechtian effects frame the openings of both Act 1 and Act 2: the action begins with the entrance through the auditorium of a very small boy who then sits at the front of the stage to watch newsreel footage proclaiming the nationalization of the mining industry by the newly elected Labour Party soon after the Second World War. The second act opens with a performance by members of the Easington community reminiscent of the kind of political agitprop produced by John McGrath's 7:84 company before the Thatcher government removed its funding in the mid-1980s.

Thatcher's ruthless determination to establish an unregulated free-market economy without any state intervention, revealed a total lack of concern for the well-being of working-class towns and villages[29] and the resulting political unrest was regarded as justification for the increased deployment of the police force as a nationally coordinated arm of government authority.[30] In *Billy Elliot*, images of social division and economic disintegration are presented through a mixture of Brechtian 'epic' and dialectical techniques as the show exploits popular British forms of entertainment in order to construct an unusually coherent musical revealing the profound irony that Billy's success coincides with the community's failure to prevent the destruction of its way of life.

Political history becomes a frame for the narrative from the first moment of the performance, the anthem-like 'The Stars Look Down' clearly expressing the political solidarity of the village in opposition to the government's decision to close unprofitable coal mines. The tradition of such pit communities is enacted in the singing of this anthem; implicit in that tradition is the assumption that boys such as Billy are destined to be miners, like Billy's brother Tony, his father Jackie, and his father's father before him. A scene in which strikers leave the Elliot house to man the picket line, is followed by one in the community hall, in which the masculine culture of the miners is ironically indicated by the comedy of a few small boys, including Billy and his friend Michael, lamely going through the motions of a boxing lesson.

MASCULINE VERSUS FEMININE CULTURES

Having failed to register any enthusiasm for the typically masculine sport of boxing, Billy stays to give the keys of the hall to the ballet teacher and gets caught up in the conventionally feminine activity of learning ballet. As performed by Mrs Wilkinson and her class, 'Shine' depicts the clumsy attempts of a gaggle of naughty and untalented girls to learn a dance routine. Its humour stems from the teacher's sarcastic commentary on the hopeless nature of her task as, cigarette in mouth, she exhorts her pupils to 'smile', the lyrics at times becoming a rueful 'voice-over' of her observations of the class:

> Doesn't matter if you're short or squat,
> Cerebrally challenged, completely shot;
> You might have it or might not,
> All you really have to do is,
> All you really have to do is shine.
> Give 'em that old razzle dazzle and shine.[31]

With the aid of a hand-held smoke machine the dance sequence metamorphoses into a rather ramshackle dress rehearsal for which the girls have donned pink ballet tutus in an attempt at showbiz sparkle.[32]

The action is progressed and the character of the sardonic, world-weary Mrs Wilkinson is developed in the song, whose music and lyrics evoke the stale clichés of endlessly recycled showbiz numbers that by the 1980s were ubiquitous in working-class pubs and budget holiday resorts and which became the staple of television variety and game shows of the period. The number perfectly exemplifies the amateur entertainment of small communities without immediate access to professional theatre. Such second-hand and second-rate

FIGURE 17.2 Showbiz razzle dazzle in a northern community centre: Mrs Wilkinson (Ruthie Henshall) and her ballet class, including a baffled Billy (Elliot Hanna) in 'Shine' from *Billy Elliot* at the Victoria Palace Theatre, 2014.

Photograph by Adam Sorenson. Courtesy of Adam Sorenson.

commercial entertainment provides a kitsch soundtrack to the humdrum lives of once-proud miners, the sounds of whose true culture have earlier been voiced in the familiar choral convention of the opening song, redolent of an authentic folk tradition of community singing that predates the mass-produced 'hits' of the popular music industry.

Traditional working-class values are illustrated in a rather different way in the haunting flashback to the dance halls of the forties and fifties that accompanies Billy's grandmother's song of reminiscence ('Grandma's Song') in which the strong-willed old woman who says she can remember the General Strike of 1926, concludes that 'if I had my time again, / Oh I'd do it without the help of men'. Here the superb musical staging by Peter Darling creates the ghost-like atmosphere of courting rituals in vanished dance halls of thirty-five years previously when 'women were women and men they were men' in order for the grandmother to share her memories of an abusive relationship while offering a darkly comic critique of the life allotted to her within a rigidly patriarchal society.

> But we'd go dancing, he was me own Brando
> [......]
> But we were free for an hour or three,
> From the people we had to be,
> But in the morning, we were sober.

The delightful and complex performance of Ann Emery[33] provided the audience with an extraordinarily vivid portrayal of the resilience of working-class women of an earlier era, whose potential talent and intelligence went unnoticed and therefore remained unfulfilled.

SONG-AND-DANCE AS POLITICAL METAPHOR

If 'Grandma's Song' exhibits the sophistication of the staging as an element of *Billy Elliot's* musical dramaturgy, 'Solidarity' represents a model of how musical theatre writing can be integrated with choreography to express the complex meaning of historical narrative.[34] Conflating the ballet class with a stylized representation of the battle between the striking miners and the police, the music, lyrics, and choreographic patterns suggest the multiple meanings of 'solidarity': for the miners, it means keeping faith with their trade union and its opposition to an oppressive regime of government-backed bosses; for the police it signifies a legitimate defence of social order as a bulwark against rioters; for the girls it simply means keeping in step together in their dance routine. In the most general sense, the repetition of 'solidarity' in the song ironically implies the traditional working-class solidarity that should unite both miners and police against exploitation by capitalist employers, but which has been deliberately broken by the Conservative government's unfounded promise of a new classless form of meritocracy.

> POLICE   Keep it up till Christmas lads,
>   It means a lot to us
>   We send our kids to private school
>   On a private bus
>
>   We've got a lot to thank you for
>   Geordie you're a corker:
>   A nice extension on the house and a fortnight in Majorca.
>   Solidarity, solidarity
>   Solidarity forever

In a virtuoso deployment of stage props, including chairs, policeman's helmets and clubs, rolled-up newspapers and miner's helmets, Peter Darling creates a dialectically complex piece of staging that indicates the effect of the large police presence on the life of the striking village. The face-off between straight lines of police and pitmen singing at each other enacts the way police and miners (traditionally linked as working-class comrades) have been set against each other:

> MINERS   Don't worry lads, we're on your side;
>   Solidarity forever.
>   Solidarity, solidarity
>   Solidarity forever
>   We're proud to be working class,
>   Solidarity forever.

The extraordinarily witty and detailed musical staging in which pitmen and policeman alternately wear their own and their opposed counterpart's helmets exposes the inter-changeability of warring policemen and miners beneath their uniforms. The irony that both groups of men are unknowingly partnering the girls in their dance while actually going about the business of the strike is a clever way of depicting the way the life of the community continues in spite of the disruptive events of the strike:

GIRLS   We're proud to be working class,
   Solidarity forever.

POLICE   You fucking worms
   You fucking moles
   You fucking Geordie shits
   We're here to kick your Geordie arse
   You little Geordie gits.

MINERS   We're terrified,
   We're petrified,
   Those words are so obscene.
   We'll boot your fuckin' cockney skulls,
   Right back to Bethnal Green

WILKINSON   Shine, just shine
   All you have to do is shine
   [.....]

GIRLS   12345678

The dainty steps that both burly miners and aggressive policemen unwittingly perform as part of the girls' rehearsal mockingly highlight the hyper-masculinity of their working-class culture as mere role play: their unexamined homophobia is thereby implicitly exposed as a macho fear of femininity, which manifests itself in their prejudice against ballet as an elitist art form for middle-class women and effete men. During the number Billy progressively exhibits his growing skills as a dancer until at its culmination he takes centre stage in an exciting display of his talent. Ironically, the complexity of the song-and-dance sequence is a refutation of Margaret Thatcher's infamous assertion in 1987 that 'there is no such thing as society. There are individual men and women and there are families.'[35]

WORKING-CLASS MASCULINITY AND INDIVIDUAL SELF-EXPRESSION

The patriarchal construction of masculinity is more overtly challenged by the irresist-ibly camp paean to individuality, 'Expressing Yourself'. Initially afraid of the stigma of effeminacy, Billy reveals to his eccentric young friend Michael that he has been attending ballet classes; Michael in turn persuades Billy to join him in dressing up in his sister's clothes. Completely shameless in his love of drag ('Me Dad does it all the time') Michael draws Billy into the song-and-dance duet, which climaxes with the neophyte tap dancers being accompanied by a group of giant women's 'dresses' who tap along with them in carnivalesque defiance of gender conformity:

> What the hell is wrong with expressing yourself?
> For trying to be free.
>
> If you wanna be a dancer, dance,
> If you wanna be a miner, mine . . .

The number succinctly contrasts the unique personality of each boy. Although Michael may be gay he thinks ballet is 'weird'; Billy's instinctive attraction to dance certainly does not make him gay, yet each boy has a strong need to assert his own identity in the face of a restrictive society that by policing traditional norms of masculinity offers no creative outlet for men.

When Billy's father finds out he is missing boxing sessions in order to attend ballet classes, he bans him outright from attending but Billy accepts Mrs Wilkinson's offer to tutor him secretly in preparation for an audition for the Royal Ballet School. When she devises a new dance for Billy, the thickset accompanist Mr Braithwaite progressively strips off his outer garments during the exhilarating song-and-dance number 'Born to Boogie' to reveal himself as a rather nimble dancer in tracksuit trousers and a skintight T-shirt. The routine is an expression of the pure joy of dance to a song that sounds like a typical Elton John rock 'n' roll hit from the early eighties—exactly the kind of music that was ubiquitous on radio and television in 1984:

> From the day of creation
> We were the dance sensation.
> Come on and shake yer bootie,
> Cos we were born to boogie.

Billy's father and brother, Tony, prevent him from sneaking off to Newcastle for the audition as the battle between police and striking miners intensifies. On entering the house to enquire after Billy, Mrs Wilkinson is trapped into a confrontation with these two angry men who are incensed that she has ignored Jackie Elliot's wishes.

During the ensuing argument Tony calls her 'a middle class cow', while Mrs Wilkinson bluntly criticizes the men's pig-headed and antediluvian working-class pride. After she leaves, the men go out to join the pickets while Billy storms upstairs, flinging himself on his bed in black despair and resentment, his kicking and shouting segueing into the 'Angry Dance'. Brilliantly swathed in flashes of red light on a set whose individual sections move upwards and downwards, revealing Billy stamping down the stairs from his bedroom and jumping down a manhole into the sewers while he rages helplessly both against the war of police and pitmen around and above him and against the miners' prejudices, the combined forces of which have conspired to prevent him from doing what he loves most deeply. The violence on the street that actually occurred in towns like Easington is graphically depicted when the policemen form a line of fibreglass riot shields to halt protesting strikers, against which Billy repeatedly throws himself as part of his furious clog dance. Eventually exhausted by his futile efforts, Billy collapses downstage centre; his angry protest dance has failed to stop the advance of the riot police. As the audience begins to applaud the boy playing the role, he gets up and it is the actor, not Billy, who gives a challenging look at the audience as he simply walks offstage—a Brechtian 'distancing' device to effect a separation between actor and character.[36]

MUSICAL THEATRE AND POLITICAL PROTEST

The opening of the second act brings two miners—the boxing teacher and Billy's brother Tony—in front of the stage curtain. Incongruously dressed as Santa Claus and his elf they address the theatre audience as if they are working-class spectators at a camp Christmas pantomime. This instantly places the spectators in the position of members of the mining community. The makeshift show-within-a-show ('Merry Christmas Maggie Thatcher') comes as a complete surprise, illustrating the life of a community united in its hatred of the prime minister, caricatured as a demonic marionette bestriding an entire stage filled with miniature glove puppets of Conservative politicians such as Michael Heseltine, trade union leaders including Arthur Scargill,[37] and even a cow representing the free milk that Mrs Thatcher has now 'stolen' from schoolchildren:[38]

> They've come to raid your stockings
> And to steal your Christmas pud
> But don't be too downhearted
> Cos it's all for your own good.
> The economic infrastructure
> Must be swept away
> To make way for business parks
> And lower rates of pay

The sadness beneath the surface of the jollification is revealed when Jackie Elliot is asked to sing; instead of obliging with the requested 'Big Spender' or another such cabaret-style pop song, he somewhat drunkenly performs a rendition of 'Deep into the Ground', a moving folk lamentation for his deceased wife, in the chorus of which he is later joined by the other revellers.

> Oh once I loved a woman,
> She meant all the world to me.
> Saw ourselves a future
> As far as I could see
> But she was only thirty-seven
> When they took her down from me,
> And buried her deep in the ground.
>
> Oh the winter wind can blow me colder
> Oh the summer's heat can parch me dry
> But I'll love these dark, dark hills forever,
> And I won't leave them until I die.

After the others have straggled off home, Billy completes the song for his sobbing, inebriated father as they stand in the deserted and cold community hall. Jackie leaves his son alone with Michael who makes a touching if somewhat clumsy romantic advance. Although Billy declares he is 'not a poof,' his response is sensitive because he doesn't shy away from physical contact; he even makes Michael a gift of a ballet tutu.

'He Could Be a Star': Individual Success at the Expense of Solidarity

Left alone, Billy plays a tape of *Swan Lake*, during which a vision of his future self as a professional dancer appears to perform a fantasy ballet, in which the young and the adult Billy together offer a glimpse of the aesthetic accomplishment towards which Billy aspires. This extraordinary piece of drama has in this particular moment the strangely magical effect of a transformation scene in a pantomime: on the verge of seeming kitsch, Tchaikovsky's overfamiliar music nevertheless evokes all the idealized and heroic beauty of ballet as Billy 'flies' with the aid of theatre technology. The sequence never fails to elicit ecstatic cheers and applause from the audience as Billy ends it standing in front of his perplexed father who has re-entered to take him home. Having directly witnessed Billy's talent, Jackie decides to visit Mrs Wilkinson as he now wishes to help Billy get to London for a Royal Ballet School audition.

Jackie's determination to earn money to pay for his son's trip to London himself rather than accept Mrs Wilkinson's financial aid—a typical example of the crippling effects of the masculine working-class pride she has accused him of earlier—obliges him to cross the picket line so he can return to work, thereby causing a direct confrontation with Billy's brother Tony in the song 'He Could Be a Star'. Anthem-like verses sung alternately by Jackie and Tony concisely express the opposed ideologies of socialism (the communitarian values of social welfare) and capitalism (success as a reward for the exceptional individual) that have motivated the entire plot:

TONY   This isn't about us Dad
    It's not about the kid
    It's all of us, it's everybody's chance
    It's everybody's future
    It's everybody's past
    It's not about a bairn who wants to dance.
[....]
DAD   He could be a star for all we know
    We don't know how far he can go,
    And no one else can give what I can give

The miners' agreement to donate money to help Billy signifies the traditional solidarity of comrades in their struggle against the ruling class:

> We're all in this together Jack
> There is another way
> All for one
> And one for all

Contrasting with Billy's desire to 'shine' as a ballet star is the miners' pride in the altruism and courage that helps them to shine in fighting for justice:

> We will go and we will shine
> We will go and seize the time
> We will all have pride in how we live.

A 'scab' (strike-breaker) generously offers Billy money to cover all his expenses but Tony and the miners are reluctant to let him take it, even though the amount they themselves are able to muster is not nearly sufficient. The incident is poignant because the fact that Billy finally takes the cash suggests that the miners' strike is about to fail, indicating the crumbling of the workers' solidarity in their struggle against the selfish individualism of the capitalist system.

When Billy and his father arrive at the Royal Ballet in Covent Garden, they feel out of place in the posh surroundings and somewhat intimidated by the rarefied and seemingly elitist atmosphere, but when they leave, the female chair of the audition panel wishes them good luck with the strike, nicely revealing the solidarity of the metropolitan arts world with the socialist battle for justice being fought in the industrial north.[39] In answer to her question of what Billy feels when he is dancing, he sings 'Electricity', a celebration of the feelings of power and freedom generated by dance as a form of artistic expression, a number that then segues into an exhilarating physical demonstration of the significance of the lyrics. Tellingly, in the following scene the happy news of Billy's acceptance by the Royal Ballet School is immediately undermined by the announcement that the strike has collapsed; by contrast, a Broadway musical would, typically, delay the news of Billy's success until *after* the sad realization of the miners' failure in order to provide the conventional showbiz uplift.

As Billy prepares for his departure to London, the miners accompany his leave-taking by singing the deeply nostalgic 'Once Were Kings'—a lament for the loss of their liveli-hood and way of life due to the imminent closure of the pits. The men's reticence makes the scene profoundly moving for what is left unsaid and the final image of the pitmen, with their helmet lamps shining into the auditorium from the darkness as they descend underground, is a devastating symbol of their heroism in defeat. The play ends with Billy bound for London, walking off the stage into the auditorium on his own but leaving his gay friend Michael alone on his bike[40] in the dystopian wasteland of a doomed mining community. As the curtain slowly descends, this final image of abandonment symbol-izes the tragic destruction of a traditional way of life. There is no celebration of indi-vidual triumph, only a harsh realization that the miners and the isolated young gay man share the fate of being on the wrong side of history.

Billy Elliot is a great work of popular art, not only because its success story of a boy who wants to become a ballet dancer is told in a thoroughly heartfelt and entertaining way, but also because the sociocultural dimensions of a turning point in British political history are so authentically conveyed in action, speech, song and dance. As a perfor-mance text it is sophisticated and densely wrought: the scenography always contributes to the significance of the action. The rather ramshackle appearance of what is actually a superbly designed set[41]—which characters give the illusion of pushing and pulling into place by hand—evokes the milieu of a poor but respectable household with its make-do-and-mend decoration and dated electrical appliances, as well as utilitarian public halls in Victorian buildings that have been successively adapted for multiple purposes in an eclectic concatenation of styles. In the picket line scene the authentic Conservative party poster against the rear wall of the stage with its cunningly manipulative head-line *LABOUR ISN'T WORKING*, precisely pinpoints the historical moment with the uncanny percipience of hindsight.

In *Billy Elliot* the traditionally macho aspects of left-wing working-class popular culture are subverted by a long-standing British habit of camp innuendo to undo the repression of femininity that is commonly manifest in British culture as reflex homo-phobia. The stage musical brings to the surface of attention what is merely a subtext of the film—a complex focus on masculinity that introduces the perspective of the twenty-first century to recognize that the political includes the personal. While the politics of social reform and revolution are the film's overt subject, in the musical version the psy-chology motivating the routine sexism and homophobic anxieties of the miners consti-tutes an important aspect of Billy's conflict in his gradual realization that he wants to be a ballet dancer; the staging/choreography 'queers' the hyper-masculinity of the miners, relativizing what this particular society regards as universal, thereby initiating a dialecti-cal argument around the relationship between class, gender, sexual orientation, popular and 'high' art. These themes are comically reprised in the finale—not a part of the action but a theatrical coda to the final narrative moment which presents a Dionysian celebra-tion of the unrepressed, in which dancing miners in white tutus worn over orange boiler suits join the whole cast in a joyous and extended curtain call.

As a musical adaptation it seizes the opportunity to let dance do the work of evoking an aspirant dancer's passion for the art, representing the thrill of dancing by creating dance that itself thrills us. If, as Richard Dyer has claimed, musicals generate pleasure in the momentary contemplation of utopia, *Billy Elliot*'s deeply political use of an array of entertainment forms to critique the inhumanity of unregulated capitalism in the 1980s while engaging its audiences in celebrating the possibilities for personal freedom in the future, knowingly exemplifies the idea that the genre is always more than 'only entertainment'.[42]

Notes

1. These included rock operas like *Jesus Christ Superstar* (1970), sung-through epics such as *Evita* (1976) and *Les Misérables* (1985), musical melodramas such as *The Phantom of the Opera* (1986), and jukebox shows like *Buddy—the Buddy Holly Story* (1989) and *Mamma Mia!* (1999).
2. British variety is a form of concert entertainment derived from music hall in the late nineteenth century that survived until the early 1960s but was largely replaced as a form of popular entertainment by television; the annual Royal Variety Performance on television is the last remaining trace of the form.
3. John Lahr, 'On Your Toes', *New Yorker*, 4 July 2005, http://www.newyorker.com/critics/theatre/articles/050704crth_theatre, accessed 10 July 2015.
4. Young performers who have recently played Billy have been superb tap dancers; the choreography is in fact adapted to suit the special talents of each individual boy.
5. Peter Nicholls's *Privates on Parade* (1977) had focused on an army entertainment corps led by a sergeant who was a drag queen, but that was a play with music which was premiered by the Royal Shakespeare Company and not a commercial musical.
6. The most famous television variety show of the early 1960s was *Sunday Night at the London Palladium*, while many TV comics who had started in pubs, working men's clubs, and variety became household names on TV comedy and variety shows.
7. These stars achieved international fame in English-speaking countries outside the United States on radio, film, and later TV shows.
8. Such stars as Cicely Courtneidge, Jack Hulbert, Noel Coward, Gertrude Lawrence, Jack Buchanan, Jessie Matthews, Peggy Wood, Hermione Gingold, Hermione Baddeley, Evelyn Laye, Dorothy Dickson, Olive Gilbert, Bobby Howes, and Lupino Lane were trained theatre performers who made their names in revue and musical comedy.
9. Coward and Novello had for years been writing 'retro' operettas.
10. The song was first performed in the 1928 revue *This Year of Grace*.
11. Wilson's trenchant criticism of the crudely camp production that the show received on Broadway where it starred Julie Andrews is evidence that he wished the show to maintain a surface innocence.
12. Intimate revue was the most ubiquitous form of musical theatre during and immediately after the Second World War.
13. The asexual nature of the relationship is in marked contrast to the overtly heterosexual attraction of the central characters in contemporary American musicals, and gives credence to the notion of a gay subtext in *Salad Days*.

14. This is one of the chief strategies of literary deconstruction.
15. See, in particular, Wilson's *Valmouth* (1958) and *His Monkey Wife* (1971).
16. Sung by a very effeminate interior decorator, Lionel Bart's song 'Contemp'ry' in *Fings Ain't Wot They Use T'Be* is a rare example.
17. The series of *Carry On* films, running from 1958 until 1978, is one of the most famous examples of the camp comic tradition that has persistently represented sex according to the conventions of seaside postcards as 'naughty' and ridiculous.
18. Shelagh Delaney's *A Taste of Honey* (1958), Joe Orton's *The Ruffian on the Stair* (1963), and Harold Pinter's *The Collection* (1964) were among the earliest plays to represent homosexual characters and relationships as aspects of ordinary life.
19. Person from the Newcastle area.
20. Her only rival is Peter Brook.
21. See Ben Macpherson on Joan Littlewood, Chapter 19, and Robert Lawson-Peebles, Chapter 24, on the use of song in socialist drama.
22. The company was named after the fact that 7 per cent of the population owned 84 per cent of its wealth.
23. These plays include *Trees in the Wind* (1971), *The Fish in the Sea* (1972), *The Cheviot, the Stag and the Black Black Oil* (1973), and *Blood Red Roses* (1980).
24. The ceilidh is a traditional Gaelic entertainment.
25. All quotations from *Blood Brothers* are taken from Willy Russell, *Educating Rita, Stags and Hens, and Blood Brothers: Two Plays and a Musical* (London: Methuen Modern Plays, 1986). Further page references will be given within the text.
26. A 'Scouser' is a working-class person from Liverpool.
27. The narrative of deprived schoolchildren being taken by their teachers on an outing depicts a day of anarchic fun in a café, a zoo, Conway Castle, and the beach; it provides a realistic insight into the joy and pain of growing up. Underlying the humour, a darker theme emerges—the realization that this day of escape from their depressing existence is likely to be the happiest these children will ever experience: 'Why can't it always be this way / Why can't it last for more than just a day / The sun in the sky and the seagulls flying by / I think I'd like to stay / Then it could always be this way.' Willy Russell, *Our Day Out: The Musical* (London: Methuen, 2011), 62.
28. The pre-eminent feminist theatre companies established in the 1970s included Red Rag, Cunning Stunts, Mouth and Trousers; Gay Sweatshop was the first and for some years the only gay theatre group in Britain.
29. 'Mrs Thatcher and her ministers made it conclusively clear that they felt no responsibility for the promotion of social harmony and that, in the pursuit of longer-term aims, they found confrontation and violence entirely acceptable.' Arthur Marwick, *British Society Since 1945* (Harmondsworth: Penguin, 2003), 289.
30. Although railwaymen and other industrial unions did not universally support the coal miners, there was widespread sympathy for the hardships suffered by miners and their families throughout the country, which even extended to the managers of some of the mines. See Marwick, *British Society Since 1945*, 288–289.
31. Quotations of lyrics from *Billy Elliot: The Musical* are taken from www.themusicallyrics.com/b/177-billy-elliot.html, accessed 22 October 2013.
32. John Lahr's comment on 'Shine' revealingly illustrates his blindness to the cultural context. Although his dismissal of the song as 'a third-generation Xerox of *Chicago's* "Razzle Dazzle"' (Lahr, 'On Your Toes') is in some respects apt, it misses the point of Elton John's

clever pastiche of seventies and eighties pop-style versions of Broadway show music, the kind of music that Elton John himself was writing during that era.

33. Astonishingly, Ann Emery has played this role for ten years in London with only a few months' break to perform in *Betty Blue Eyes* (2011).

34. Without didacticism, the number alludes to the complex conflicts of interest motivating the events of the coal miners' strike: this was the first time in British history the police had been deployed against strikers in riot gear and using riot shields and, while there was violence on both sides, these events acquired powerful symbolic value in demonstrating the successful strategy of the Thatcher government in breaking the traditional solidarity of workers to create divisions within and between trades unions by setting one section of workers against others through a manipulation of the occasionally conflicting financial interests of each, as 'Solidarity' and other songs in *Billy Elliot* indicate.

35. Anon., 'Margaret Thatcher in Quotes: Key Comments from Britain's First Female Prime Minister', *The Guardian*, 8 April 2013, http://www.theguardian.com/politics/2013/apr/08/margaret-thatcher-quotes, accessed 13 August 2015.

36. Lahr's failure to understand the Brechtian techniques exploited throughout the show can be seen in his lame criticism of the end of Act 1: '[A]fter Billy's sensational explosion at the police, Daldry can't properly clinch the moment. Billy lies back on the ground, then simply gets up and walks offstage: end of Act I. Fatigue seems to have blinkered Daldry's critical ability.' Lahr, 'On Your Toes'.

37. Arthur Scargill was president of the National Union of Miners (NUM) from 1982 to 2002 and therefore an iconic figure in the opposition to the Thatcher government.

38. Apart from failing to identify the tradition of working-class Christmas entertainment cleverly exploited in the scene, Lahr's criticism of its puppets—hardly avant-garde!—reveals a total ignorance of its political significance, 'But, out of a kind of narrative desperation, Daldry is forced to borrow from the tattered grab bag of avant-garde tricks: behemoth puppets, masks on the backs of heads—any surprise to cover up the lacklustre book and music.' Lahr, 'On Your Toes'.

39. The metropolitan arts world was as directly opposed to the Thatcher government's policies as was the NUM, as it threatened savage cuts to government subsidy for the arts.

40. The term 'on yer bike' became a catchphrase in the 1980s, indicating the need for unemployed youngsters to stop loitering and move on, but with the implication that they should get on their bicycles to seek gainful employment in another town or village—a reflection of the devastation of the economy that by the end of the 1980s had left entire towns and villages derelict.

41. The set was designed by Ian McNeil.

42. See Richard Dyer, *Only Entertainment* (London: Routledge, 1992).

BIBLIOGRAPHY

Anon. 'Margaret Thatcher in Quotes: Key Comments from Britain's First Female Prime Minister.' *The Guardian*, 8 April 2013. http://www.theguardian.com/politics/2013/apr/08/margaret-thatcher-quotes, accessed 13 August 2015.

Dyer, Richard. *Only Entertainment*. London: Routledge, 1992.

Lahr, John. 'On Your Toes.' *New Yorker*, 4 July 2005. http://www.newyorker.com/critics/theatre/articles/050704crth_theatre, accessed 10 July 2015.

Marwick, Arthur. *British Society Since 1945*. Harmondsworth: Penguin, 2003.

Russell, Willy. *Educating Rita, Stags and Hens, and Blood Brothers: Two Plays and a Musical*. London: Methuen Modern Plays, 1986.

Russell, Willy. *Our Day Out: The Musical*. London: Methuen, 2011.

www.themusicallyrics.com/b/177-billy-elliot.html, accessed 22 October 2013.

PART V

TRAILBLAZERS

CHAPTER 18

....

NOËL COWARD

Sui Generis

....

DOMINIC MCHUGH

ALTHOUGH dubbed 'The Master' by many of his admirers, Noël Coward's detractors were quick to retort that he was, on the contrary, a 'jack of all trades, master of none'.[1] The polarity of these labels perhaps helps to explain his unusual position in twentieth-century culture: a number of his plays (such as *Blithe Spirit* (1941) and *Private Lives* (1930)) have never left the repertoire, yet the perception by his detractors of his lack of 'mastery' arguably denies his entry into the musical theatre canon. Coward's theatre so often gravitates to its delicate surface—humour through the selection, timbre, and order of the language; pace and flow; melody; comic situations—that questions of form and substance clouded the reception of his work in his own time and beyond.[2] The 'jack of all trades' quality of his career also gives rise to a hermeneutic problem in categorizing the character and meaning of his output. As an actor, singer, composer, lyricist, director, cabaret performer, playwright, screenwriter, and diarist, his artistry finds coherence more within itself than in relation to exterior values (see Figure 18.1).

On the one hand, Coward's identity was and is clearly formed through reference to his personality, class, nationality, and sexuality; on the other, the multifaceted nature of his activities defies convention. When dealing with his contribution to the development of the musical, this is especially problematic: the success of the 1929 *Bitter Sweet* (in particular) and the endurance of numerous of his songs demands attention, yet the absence of an overarching 'plan' and the inconsistency of his engagement with the musical stage calls into question his historical position.

Genre especially becomes a fallible tool in the exegesis of Coward's musicals. He flitted deftly from revue to operetta, from original comedy to adaptation, from British to American models—an impressive feat that should not be underestimated. Yet just as genre is often retrospectively extrapolated from key works to provide a framework for the scholar rather than a tangible taxonomy from the point of view of the artist, for Coward it might be argued that genre was a loose mode of reference rather than the essence of his musicals. In this chapter, I outline his stated influences and his approach to songwriting

FIGURE 18.1 'The Master': Noël Coward directing a rehearsal of *Sail Away* at the Savoy Theatre, London 1962.

Photograph by John Timbers. Courtesy of ArenaPal.

before exploring key issues in the generation and reception of his musical theatre output. Through this discussion, it emerges that Coward's musicals shaped his identity as much as his identity shaped his musicals—biography acts as an agent of creation and interpretation equal to genre and generic markers—and though success on the musical stage eluded him in the latter part of his career, an enquiry into his total body of work in this field helps better to situate this paradoxically present but elusive writer's output.

INFLUENCES: EDWARDIAN OPERETTA, OSCAR HAMMERSTEIN II, AND INTEGRATION

Growing up in the early decades of the twentieth century, Coward's early exposure to music on the stage mainly consisted of Edwardian operetta and musical comedy. Coward himself was open about his tastes and influences, referring in particular to the scores of Lionel Monckton, Paul Rubens, Ivan Caryll, and Leslie Stuart as being 'of a quality that has never been equalled in this country since the 1914–18 war'.[3] Written in 1953, this reactionary statement helps to explain why Coward's relationship to the musical stage became problematic as the decades wore on: he was resistant to the various aesthetic shifts in popular music and theatre that occurred as British musicals explored other influences. Nevertheless, his admiration for these early works was sincere, and not without good foundation. His point of view was that of a composer: with *Our Miss Gibbs* (1909), *Miss Hook of Holland* (1907), and *The Arcadians* (1909), he said, 'over and above the artists who performed them, the librettists who wrote them, and the impresarios who parented them, their music was the basis of their success'.[4] He could also say on a technical level why these pieces were of substance: 'It was in the completeness of their scores that their real strength lay: opening choruses, finales, trios, quartettes and concerted numbers—all musicianly, all well balanced and all beautifully constructed'.[5]

By privileging complexity, Coward showed a flagrant preference for the elements of these works that derived from or most resembled art music. This is a vital insight into a different point of view about musicals: whereas discussions of the Broadway musical tend to promote the idea that musicals took on 'work identities' during the 1940s and 1950s,[6] demonstrated particularly by the proliferation of revivals in this period, Coward reveals that this model already existed in Edwardian comedy. That several of his musicals were published in complete piano-vocal scores—including *This Year of Grace* (1928), *Bitter Sweet, Words and Music* (1932), *Operette* (1937), and *Pacific 1860* (1946)[7]—rather than just in individual song sheets or vocal selections provides another link back to the operettas of the previous generation, many of which were similarly published complete; it also suggests he was happy to see his texts disseminated in permanent form, confounding the idea that he regarded his music as merely 'light' or even 'cheap'—Amanda's line from *Private Lives* about the 'potency of cheap music' has often been misleadingly invoked as self-commentary—even though these labels have been applied to his musical oeuvres in blanket fashion.

In part, Coward's taste could also be said to be motivated by his vigorous nationalistic perspective: he contrasted the quality and integrity of these operettas with an American musical he had seen 'in which the hit number was reprised no less than five times during the performance by different members of the cast', a pattern he described as 'assaulting of the ear by monstrous repetition'.[8] Elsewhere, he refers to 'the American invasion' (by which he denotes pre-First World War songwriters such as Irving Berlin rather than the post-*Oklahoma!* period) and outlines how 'conservative musical opinion was shocked and horrified by such alien noises', going on to berate British musical theatre for failing to 'absorb and utilize the new, exciting rhythms from over the water and to modify and adapt them to its own service'. Though he was eager to commend the talents of Ivor Novello ('rich in melody and technically expert . . . For years he upheld, almost alone, our old traditions of musical Musical Comedy') and Vivian Ellis (who 'proved over the years that he can handle a complete score with grace and finesse'),[9] clearly Coward felt frustrated by what he perceived as the lack of continuity in the development of the British musical during his career. That Coward was so ambivalent about his forebears and contemporaries—problematizing or distancing himself from many of the models associated with other writers—again suggests that genre may not always provide the most satisfactory framework for the discussion of his achievements in this area.

Nonetheless, Coward *was* interested in and influenced by some of the other writers of his own time. He even attempted a collaboration with Jerome Kern in 1923–4 on a show called *Tamaran*, which would have been his first book musical;[10] though it was abandoned, Coward frequently wrote of his admiration for Kern (he was 'cheer-fully enchanted' by *Sally* (1920), for instance), and was 'deeply touched' when the composer dedicated 'The Last Time I Saw Paris' to him (he went on to record it himself).[11] Furthermore, it is striking that he employed the rhetoric of the 'integrated musical' when evaluating his own output in the preface to the published edition of his complete lyrics in 1967, thereby (perhaps unexpectedly) aligning himself with Rodgers and Hammerstein (the latter arguably Kern's most important lyricist-librettist, of course):

> The late Oscar Hammerstein wrote wisely and accurately in the preface to his own published book of selected lyrics, that the perfect lyric for a musical should be inspired directly by the story and the characters contained in it. In fact, ideally, a song in a musical should carry on whenever the dialogue leaves off. Apart from one or two rare exceptions I concur with him entirely. Revue writing is of course different because there is no definite story line on which to hang the numbers. But any young potential lyric writer should learn early that if he wishes to write a successful 'book show' he must eschew irrelevance and stick to the script.[12]

Coward's association with Rodgers and Hammerstein led to their approaching him to direct and appear in their forthcoming show *The King and I* (1951) opposite Gertrude Lawrence (he and Lawrence were already, of course, close friends and celebrated collaborators), though he turned them down; he did eventually appear in Rodgers's television musical *Androcles and the Lion* (1967). His diaries also reveal that even when he felt critical of some aspects of their work, he considered Rodgers and Hammerstein to be the best:

> I went to *The Sound of Music* with Ginette [Spanier] [. . .] There were too many nuns careering about and crossing themselves and singing jaunty little songs, and there *was*, I must admit, a heavy pall of Jewish-Catholic schmaltz enveloping the whole thing, but it was far more professional, melodic and entertaining than any of the other musicals I've seen.[13]

Importantly, the degree to which Coward's work was 'integrated' became the key criterion for his own reflection on it. He said he had written 'three integrated scores of which I am genuinely proud. These are *Bitter Sweet, Conversation Piece*, and *Pacific 1860*.'[14] By contrast, he considered *Operette* (1938) to be 'sadly meagre' with the exception of three numbers ('Dearest Love', 'Where Are the Songs We Sung?', and 'The Stately Homes of England'); he said that although *Ace of Clubs* (1950) 'contained several good songs', it could 'not fairly be described as a musical score'; and admitted that *Conversation Piece* (1934) was 'less full and varied'. From the point of view of composition, he also regarded the revue as a lower genre that defied integration, even though he was prolific within it: he was especially dismissive of *London Calling* (1923), *On With the Dance* (1925), and *Sigh No More* (1945) because they contained contributions from other composers, thereby undermining the opportunity of an integrated whole flowing organically from a single creative source (his preference for writing book, music, and lyrics is obvious from the pieces he chose to promote in his late-career reflections). That Coward himself was a little dismissive of his work in revue can only have fuelled the prevailing marginalization (and attendant alienation) of the genre in the literature on musicals; consequently, this aspect of his musical theatre work is rarely valued, let alone revived. Nevertheless, 'although [they were] revues'[15] he confessed he was happy with his work on *This Year of Grace* (1928) and *Words and Music* (1932), both of which he wrote in their entirety. It is hardly surprising, either, that when assessing his final musical *The Girl Who Came to Supper* (1963), which was written for Broadway rather than London, he said that 'Most of the lyrics in this were inspired, as they should be, by the book'.[16]

COWARD'S CONCEPTION OF MELOPOETICS

Integration, of course, has implications for the composer and lyricist when it becomes a specified priority. Stephen Banfield has written compellingly about the importance of approaching songwriting (or 'melopoetics') in a way that considers the 'interplay between verbal and musical factors giving rise to a unitary perception dependent upon them both'.[17] In the case of Coward, the same person served as both composer and lyricist, and often librettist too, and this would seem on the surface to make the potential tensions between words and music evaporate in the search for integration. Yet the purpose of the musical number is almost always to deliver the pleasure of contrast on some level; it provides a welcome juxtaposition to the other parts of the experience, something Coward does not clearly acknowledge.

A further problem emerges when we start to look more closely at the reality of the creative process of Coward's scores, namely his resistance to becoming musically educated (and therefore musically literate). He was completely open about his reliance on an amanuensis, acknowledging in his songbook that with complex works such as *Bitter Sweet* and *Conversation Piece*, 'Miss Elsie April, to whom I dictated them, was a tremendous help to me both in transcribing and in sound musical advice'.[18] Indeed, he plugged the idea that his lack of technical knowledge was helpful because it allowed his 'natural talent' to flourish. 'To be born with a natural ear for music is a great and glorious gift,' he said. 'It is either there or it isn't.'[19] With lyric writing too, he commented that 'I can only assume the compulsion to make rhymes was born in me'.[20] In the latter cases, he suggests that his genius was best nurtured by being undistracted by external models (i.e. the technical development that education would have provided). But most interesting of all, perhaps, was his feeling that his greatest scores were the product of developing music and lyric in tandem:

> If you happen to be born with a built-in sense of rhythm, any verse you write is apt to fall into a set pattern and remain within its set pattern until it is completed. This is perfectly satisfactory from the point of view of reading or reciting, but when you attempt to set your pattern to a tune, either the tune gives in and allows itself to be inhibited by the rigidity of your original scansion or it rebels, refuses to be dominated

and displays some ideas of its own, usually in the form of unequal lines and unexpected accents. This is why I very seldom write a lyric first and set it to music later.
I think that the best lyrics I have written are those which have developed more or less
at the same time as the music.[21]

Along similar lines, he describes how he wrote the patter song 'Mad Dogs and
Englishmen' 'when I was driving, in February 1930, from Hanoi in Tonkin to Saigon [. . .]
I wrestled in my mind with the complicated rhythms and rhymes of the song until finally
it was complete, without even the aid of pencil or paper.'[22] The song's ingenious rhymes
include 'But Englishmen detest a siesta' and 'The toughest Burmese bandit | Can never
understand it.'[23] 'Nina', 'Uncle Harry', and 'I Wonder What Happened to Him', meanwhile,
were products of needing material at short notice with which to entertain the troops during the Second World War (i.e. for a specific function),[24] while the music of 'I'll Follow
My Secret Heart' came to him abruptly one night when he was turning off the lamp on
his piano, having decided to go to bed: 'I walked automatically to turn it off, sat down and
played [the song] straight through in G flat, a key I had never played in before.'[25]

To the musicologist, the latter story is reminiscent of one of Stravinsky's famous
accounts of the genesis of *The Rite of Spring*: 'I am the vessel through which *Le Sacre*
passed', he once suggested, as if he had played a passive role in its creation, rather than
crafting it with full consciousness.[26] Coward's story is particularly ironic given the carefully layered setting of the words: for example, the chilling rising diminished seventh
on 'fol-low' gives way to a falling line on 'secret heart', underlining the picture of frustrated passion in the lyric. Yet the significant aspect of Coward's commentaries on this
subject is the way in which they help his songs become personal and autobiographical.
In contrast to his ambition to make his musicals integrated, he suggests the songs often
derive from his own experiences and imagination rather than being constructed from
their dramatic context. Their reception became even more intertwined with biography
when—to his 'own and every one else's astonishment'—he became a major cabaret performer in the 1950s. Appearing at the Café de Paris in London and at the Desert Inn in
Las Vegas, he renewed his career by presenting his songs to the public in person (just
as he had done by appearing in several non-musical plays). Thus by writing the words
and music, explaining how the songs had been conceived, and then performing them,
Coward had found a moment where his musical work could become performative: part
of the essence of his life and then of his identity.

The Performativity of Song
in Coward's Musicals

In a coruscating critique of Coward's career as a playwright, John Lahr suggested he
was '[a] man who spent a lifetime merchandising his de-luxe persona . . . [I]n his songs,
plays and public performances, Coward lived up to the responsibility of making a proper

spectacle of himself.'[27] Lahr rightly points to Coward's image as an artistic phenomenon, his particular flavour, the piquancy of a career that ranged from writing a ballet to starring in Hollywood movies; yet his most important observation is that Coward's plays and songs were 'primarily vehicles to launch his elegant persona on the world'.[28] Artifice is a major theme throughout his writing, as Frances Gray observes in a fascinating essay on Coward and movement: '[I]t has long been acknowledged that Coward is at his most assured and most poignant when showing the relationship between the performed self and the performer.'[29] His songs were public conduits for his interior experiences, though in some instances this resulted in ironies and contradictions: his association with the aristocracy and the upper classes (typified, needless to say, in songs such as 'The Stately Homes of England' and 'Mad Dogs and Englishmen') belied the financial insecurity and lower middle-class ambience of his family background, while his 'high camp' style (again Lahr's assessment)[30] contrasted with nervous breakdowns and various periods of depression and melancholy.[31]

Coward's construction of self is reflected in various reported accounts of his wariness about revealing his sexuality too obviously in his own performances of his work. Alan Sinfield discusses how although, to many, 'Coward, [Cecil] Beaton, [Marlene] Dietrich and the entire set have always seemed as camp as Christmas', Coward himself moderated what he revealed to the public. He even advised Beaton that the latter's sleeves were 'too tight', his voice 'too high and too precise', and asked Dietrich to inform him 'if you see me being at all "queer"'.[32] He was well aware of the way in which he presented himself: 'The indeterminacy over effeminacy and sexuality was both the anxiety and the opportunity for Coward,' Sinfield goes on to explicate. 'He tried to maintain a distance between himself and manifest queerness. Nonetheless, a strategic cultivation of effeminacy enabled him first to stake out an oppositional stance, then to invoke and partly to constitute an emergent gay sub-culture.'[33] Thus whenever characters play 'roles' in his musicals—whether in metatheatrical contexts, as husbands and wives, or as footmen and maids—some part of the theatrical effect feeds into the frequent sense that everything in Coward's theatre is intended to be read as constructed, or in inverted commas, reflecting his moderated public persona. One of the most obvious examples of this is the song 'I'll Follow My Secret Heart' (mentioned above), a number about impossible desires that could be read as a homosexual's expression of hidden passion (the 'secret heart'), displaced for theatrical purposes onto a female character. The verse is especially indicative, with sentiments such as '[T]here is nowhere we could go, | Where we could hide from what we know | Is true'.[34]

In Coward's revues this idea of 'playing roles' is especially intense because the non-linear, non-narrative, anti-integration element of the genre draws attention to the fact that each performer appears in several disconnected sketches and numbers that are unified only through the performer's body. In *Set to Music*, for instance, Beatrice Lillie appeared as a Valkyrie in 'A Fragonard Impression', the Schoolgirl in 'Mad About the Boy', a jaded socialite in 'Weary of it All', and the Party Girl in 'I Went to a Marvellous Party'.[35] In the New York version of *This Year of Grace* (1928) Coward himself performed 'Dance, Little Lady', 'A Room With a View', 'Lilac Time', and 'Love, Life and

Laughter', each completely different in scenario and tone, thereby explicitly revealing his ability to adopt different identities within the same body. Accordingly, though he was inclined to discuss revue as a lower form of music theatre because of its resistance to dramatic integration, he clearly revelled in the opportunity to exploit this aspect of the genre—that the disconnect of the sequence of scenes is integrated through the presence of the performers—to lend coherence to the multifaceted construction of his personal identity.

BITTER SWEET: TIME, MEMORY, NOSTALGIA

Yet not every aspect of Coward's theatre was entirely driven by his performative strategy. In *Bitter Sweet* particularly, his musico-dramatic achievement was considerable, incorporating clever employment of diegetic musical numbers, a sophisticated narrative structure, and contrasts of both musical and lyric diction to convey the potency of the plot's social commentary. As noted earlier, Coward treasured the operetta genre above all else, and the three-act structure here played to his strengths. He directed the piece himself, no doubt relishing the opportunity to manage the complexity of the material in its first production. It is set in both the nineteenth and twentieth centuries: the first act opens in 1929 (the present day for the original audience), revealing a dance at the Marchioness of Shayne's house in Grosvenor Square, where the engaged couple Dolly Chamberlain and Henry Jekyll are heard debating their relationship. But when Henry storms off, it emerges that Dolly is in love with Vincent Howard, the pianist in the band at the dance. Lady Shayne disturbs them in the midst of a warm embrace, but she regards the scene with partial amusement, observing, 'I laugh at almost everything now—it's only when one is very old indeed that one can see the joke all the way round [. . .] Life and death and happiness and despair and love.'[36]

This comment serves as something of a keynote for the operetta as a whole: Lady Shayne has seen all of this before, when as a young girl—then known as Sarah Millick—she eloped with Carl Linden, her singing teacher (Act 1, Scenes 2 and 3 are set in 1875 and depict this sequence of events). In Act 2, the tragic consequences of Sarah's consummation of her passion for Carl are enacted when the now-married couple is shown struggling financially in a seedy café in Vienna, in 1880. Carl is conductor of the orchestra, and is seen quarrelling with a former lover, Manon, a singer at the café; in the second scene, Sarah (now called Sari, and also employed as a singer) is forced to dance with an army captain who forces himself on her. Carl is outraged when he sees the man kiss his wife, but in an ensuing duel the musician is inevitably slain by the military man. The final act shifts in year and place again, this time to London in 1895. At a reception at Lord Shayne's house, it emerges that he has proposed marriage to Sari in various cities all over Europe, where she has become famous for singing Carl Linden's songs. He now proposes again, observing that although she may not love him, he could perhaps make her a little happier; she promises to think about it, and then proceeds to perform two

FIGURE 18.2 Time, memory, and nostalgia: Peggy Wood in *Bitter Sweet*, His Majesty's Theatre, 1929.

Photograph by Mander & Mitchenson, University of Bristol. Courtesy of ArenaPal.

songs for the company. At the end of the second, a blackout takes the audience back to the scenario of the first scene of the operetta, where Sari is now Lady Shayne; the curtain falls as she performs a final refrain of 'I'll See You Again'.

Time is a leitmotif of Coward's lyrics for the piece. Both the hit songs from the score focus heavily on this theme: in 'I'll See You Again', Carl and Sarah sing of 'remembering knowing you' and 'memories that must fade',[37] while in 'If Love Were All' Manon admits that 'Nobody here can say | To what, indeed, | The years are leading'.[38] Memory and reminiscence also crop up in 'That Wonderful Melody' ('play me | A romantic memory'),[39] 'The Call of Life' ('glamour fades away'),[40] 'Tell Me, What is Love?' ('Live your life, for time is fleeting'),[41] 'Ladies of the Town' ('before it's too late'),[42] 'Alas, the Time is Past' ('We sometimes look aghast | Adown the lanes of memory'),[43] and 'Evermore and a Day' ('Time's on the wing, my love, and time is fleet'),[44] to name just six of the many instances. This semantic project maps on to the scenic structure of the work as a whole, of course, where the outer tableaux signify the elderly Sari remembering moments from her varied past: the operetta is telescoped through her memory. Particularly effective is the re-enactment of her youth through the lens of Dolly's romance with Vincent, a ritual of the new generation inheriting the impulses of the old that calls to mind a similar idea in the Magnolia–Kim relationship in *Show Boat* (a work with which Coward must have been familiar, though there is no reason to think this is a conscious allusion). Again, Lahr's analysis is insightful:

> He puts the old and new tempos at loggerheads in *Bitter Sweet* (1929) when old world comments on new, operetta on jazz. At a London society dance in 1929, where 'a swift dance tune' plays and young couples 'jig about', Lady Shayne puts a stop to the new sound and the new dances [. . .] In her final reprise of 'I'll See You Again', the word 'goodbye' is a farewell not only to her memory of romance but to an age.[45]

Indeed, the work is full of endings and beginnings. Act 3 is especially poignant: when Madame Sari Linden is being anticipated as the special guest of Lord Shayne's party, his friends are unaware that she is the former Sarah Millick, whom they had heard to be dead. Yet when she arrives and they recognize her, Sari herself admits that in one sense she 'did die. Fifteen years ago to be exact. Things happened and I couldn't come back. I didn't want to come back, so I thought I'd better die, vaguely and obscurely.'[46] In other words, Sari/Sarah/Lady Shayne—three different identities within one body—represents the character in *Bitter Sweet* who 'plays with the audience' (to adopt Jean Chothia's astute observation about a common pattern in Coward's theatre works),[47] both inside and outside the plot. In this speech, Coward communicates the character's ability to shift her identity in terms of name, rank, and occupation, factors that are amplified by the fact that Sari is a singer and performer (she has diegetic numbers to sing in two of the three acts). As such, she emblematizes Coward's own life and career, in which, as Chothia observes, he 'necessarily wore a mask.'[48] Meanwhile, in the unambiguously camp sensibility of 'We All Wore a Green Carnation', with its lines such as 'Haughty boys, naughty boys, every pore | Bursting with self-inflation',[49] he found yet another space for the projection of his own identity.

Bitter Sweet was a major breakthrough for Coward, proving he had the flair and technical control to build a complex musical theatre work (three acts, six scenes) with an episodic structure and several concerted numbers. Its romantic escapism was perhaps risky at a time when the American musical stage could now encompass the comparative realism of *Show Boat* and the jazz elements of *Funny Face*, both seen in London the year before *Bitter Sweet* opened. Yet the large budget of £20,000 helped to provide a production of high quality, as well as an excellent cast that included Peggy Wood (see Figure 18.2). The reviews were slightly mixed: the *Sunday Times* said Coward had done 'a thundering job,' but *The Times* called the score 'naïve'[50] and Coward himself complained that the press notices were 'remarkable for their tone of rather grudging patronage.'[51] Two movie versions of the piece were heavily altered and do not do it justice, much to Coward's chagrin.[52] His own view of the overall quality of his work on *Bitter Sweet* once again indicated a prioritization of integration: it was 'a musical that gave me more complete satisfaction than anything else I had yet written', he commented. 'Not especially on account of its dialogue, or its lyrics, or its music, or its production, but as a whole [. . .] [It] achieved and sustained the mood of its original conception more satisfactorily than a great deal of my other work.'[53]

National Identity and Metatheatre
in the Revues and Later Musicals

While *Bitter Sweet* focuses on performance as a device for character development, the theatre itself is an imposing presence in several of Coward's other works. His earliest important revue, *London Calling!* (1923), for which he wrote about half the material in the score, opened with a paean to the Duke of York's Theatre ('We must treat it respectfully'), where the revue was housed. It also contained an amusing burlesque number, 'There's Life in the Old Girl Yet', and the most important song in the show, 'Parisian Pierrot', invoked yet another theatrical tradition, the commedia dell'arte. A further revue, *Words and Music* (London, 1932; revised for Broadway as *Set to Music*, 1939), which was produced by Charles B. Cochran, opened wittily with an uptempo choral number in which Cochran's chorus girls complain about the way he (like his American counterpart, Florenz Ziegfeld) sends them on to distract the audience whenever the show gets boring: 'For every scene he cuts out | He says, "Just send the Sluts out".'[54] This critique of Cochran's objectification of women is turned around later in the piece in 'Mad About the Boy', when a Society Woman, a Schoolgirl, a Cockney, and a Tart are seen queuing outside a cinema to see the latest movie of their favourite heartthrob. Coward's setting is especially haunting, with its neurotic melodic line and resistance to harmonic resolution. The lyric offers a sense of the theatrical: four women of different ages and backgrounds are paying to pursue a source of desire they know to be nothing but an illusion, yet they feel compelled to do it anyway. Coward's play on the artifice of class divisions is particularly striking: the Society Woman is 'ashamed' of how her impossible desire causes her to have 'sleepless nights' ('On the Silver Screen | He melts my foolish heart in ev'ry single scene'); the Schoolgirl thinks her infatuation is 'scrumptious' ('I know that quite sincerely | Housman really | Wrote *The Shropshire lad* about the boy'); the Cockney sees the boy's face 'in all the brushes and brooms' as she goes about her daily chores ('Last week I strained me back | And got the sack, | And 'ad a row with Dad about the boy'); and the Tart feels 'enchained' by the image of his eyes as she walks the streets ('Walking down the street, | His eyes look out at me from people that I meet').[55] The play *Cavalcade* (1931) also contains metatheatrical elements (the characters go to watch an operetta called *Mirabelle*), and Coward would also explore the show-within-a-show idea in *Ace of Clubs* and *The Girl Who Came to Supper*.

But it was with *Operette* (1938) that he would delve into this area most extensively. Opening at Her Majesty's Theatre, London, on 16 March 1938, the musical would run only 132 performances—a disappointment in comparison to the 697 performances achieved by *Bitter Sweet*, which it was partly trying to emulate. Once again, Peggy Wood would star, but the metatheatrical element overwhelmed the drama on this occasion: rather than framing the notion of performed identity, it simply rendered large swathes of the plot rather vacuous, in comparison to the elegiac *tinta* of *Bitter Sweet*. Coward regarded it as 'the least successful musical play I have ever done', damning it as 'over-written and under-composed', and in particular dismissing the music as 'mea-gre'. He admitted that 'the plot which should have been the background, became the foreground', suggesting that the interior entertainment he placed at the operetta's heart lacked substance, overwhelming the framing device.[56] Despite Coward's negative assessment, though, there are signs of ambition and imagination in the score and struc-ture. For example, there is both an outer opening number, 'Prologue', which acts as a kind of Greek chorus, and an 'Opening Chorus', which represents the beginning of *The Model Maid* (the show-within-a-show). Act 2 also starts with a self-reflexive 'Prologue', in which the chorus admit 'That though you get a little wit through us | It's hard to have to sit through us | Once more'.[57]

Adrian Wright comments negatively on the piece—'*Operette* carried the show-within-a-show format to excess [. . .] Reading the script today, one has the impression that its author spent too much time in theatres'[58]—yet the sense that Coward's experi-ences shaped the content of the musical is perhaps the best way to understand it, regard-less of its flaws. *Operette* also contains 'The Stately Homes of England', in which a quartet of lords bemoan the fate of the aristocracy; the number had little bearing on either of the musical's plots, but its jaunty march setting helped it quickly to became one of Coward's most popular songs.

Throughout his career in musicals, Coward foregrounded national identity, whether in the gender satire of 'Britannia Rules the Waves' from *This Year of Grace* ('We'll put a frill on the Union Jack'), 'Regency Rakes' from *Conversation Piece* (1934), or the unin-tentionally controversial 'Don't Let's Be Beastly to the Germans' (1943).[59] Class struc-tures come to the fore in both *After the Ball* (a disappointing adaptation of Wilde's *Lady Windermere's Fan* (1954)) and *The Girl Who Came to Supper* (another disappointment, this time based on Rattigan's *The Sleeping Prince* (1953); unusually, Coward did not write the book), especially pungent in the latter's dichotomy between Tessie O'Shea's cockney sequence and the scenes depicting royalty.[60]

A different kind of ambition can be seen in the lengths to which he went in creat-ing *Pacific 1860* (1946), a 'musical romance' that starred a sadly miscast Mary Martin as a fading opera singer.[61] British imperialism is invoked in the mythical setting of the South Sea island of Samolo, which Coward invented and became obsessed with to such an extent that he devised both a history and a language for it (he set *We Were Dancing* from *Tonight at 8.30* (1935) and his novel *Pomp and Circumstance* there too). Coward's partner Graham Payn, who appeared in the musical, observed that 'Noël used the island as a forum for his humour about spent colonialism, which he mingled with a touch of nostalgia for happier days'.[62] As with *Bitter Sweet*, the past intermingles with the pre-sent, while the setting of the fictional island—representing both the national (a specific colonial British reference) and the personal (it was a figment of his imagination)—again provides a connection with Coward's use of musical theatre to project his personal and public identities. At the other end of the spectrum from the fantastical *Pacific 1860* was *Ace of Clubs* (1950): the Soho nightclub setting was part of his strategy to write in 'an idiom entirely different from [his] other musical plays'.[63] This attempt to inhabit a more contemporary style was certainly bold: for instance, the sexually provocative song

'Chase Me, Charlie' ('Love in the moonlight can be sublime') was censored by the BBC,[64] and Coward had to rewrite the show several times before its seedy world became acceptable to a producer.[65] However, neither audiences nor critics warmed to the piece, which closed after a few months, much to Coward's bitterness.[66]

Changing direction later in his career, Coward wrote *Sail Away* (1961) for Broadway, viewing the American model through a British lens. His persona was unmistakable behind sardonic lyrics such as 'The Customer's Always Right' and 'Why Do the Wrong People *Travel*?', their wit providing an irresistible connection to the social commentary of the British musical comedy (in the latter song, he writes: 'What compulsion compels them and who the hell tells them | To drag their bags to Zanzibar instead of staying quietly in Omaha?');[67] but in 'Come to Me' and 'Go Slow, Johnny', he also proved that he could devise buoyant rhythm numbers that would have seemed at home in several American shows of the time. Coward strove hard to make the musical work: an early version called *Later Than Spring* was replaced with a new concept, initially written with Kay Thompson in mind and then heavily revised for Elaine Stritch.[68] The Broadway run lasted a rather modest 167 performances, but a London transfer the following year did somewhat better with 252 performances. Naturally, Coward was disappointed that it was not more of a hit: in both New York and Broadway in this period, American shows such as *My Fair Lady* and *The Sound of Music* each ran for several years, and *Sail Away* made a modest impression by comparison. Ironically, Coward felt on reflection that his attempt to create something commercial (for once) was a problem—he admitted he was 'wrong' in having 'deliberately kept the 'book' down to the minimum, in the belief that the public would be relieved at not having to sit 'through acres of dialogue between numbers'— though he also conceded that 'the lyrics are just a bit too clever'.[69]

Conclusion: Situating Coward's Musicals

A dismissive comment in Gervase Hughes's book on operetta, though written more than fifty years ago, unwittingly provides a key to the problem of situating Coward's musicals: he refers to them as 'a handful of operettas or what-you-will'.[70] Because the cause and effect of his work on the British musical repertoire in general is complex, a satisfactory generic term for it proves elusive; 'what-you-will' *almost* does very nicely as a term for his musicals, seemingly evoking a similar taxonomical issue with the 'problem' plays of Shakespeare (*What You Will* is the subtitle of *Twelfth Night*, of course). Coward's contribution to musical theatre spanned roughly two generations, during which time he witnessed two waves of American influences on the British stage (the jazz musical of the 1920s and the Rodgers and Hammerstein musical of the 1940s). Amongst British writers, he watched the rise of Novello, was impressed by the work of Vivian Ellis, saw the nostalgic comedies of Wilson and Slade, and continued working during the grittier work of Lionel Bart. Yet it is only in the broadest terms that Coward's musicals reveal the impact of his British contemporaries in the field, or indeed that he had a significant impact on them. Adrian Wright's somewhat damning chapter on Coward's musicals in his book *A Tanner's Worth of Tune* is headed 'Mastering Operetta'—a misleading label for a writer who demonstrably took his work in directions other than simply a single genre (operetta). Wright also comments that 'he did not easily learn lessons, at least when it came to musical theatre',[71] but again, if we view his musicals as part of his self-constructed career (and by extension, his persona), perhaps he simply did not believe that his own style had to adhere to others' rules or lessons.

Stephen Citron has attempted to identify an analogue for Coward's output in his American contemporary Cole Porter, branding them 'The Sophisticates'. Yet in trying to connect their childhood circumstances as a reason for discussing their careers in tandem, Citron accidentally draws attention to a major difference between the pair. He explains that '[b]oth had ineffectual fathers and strong, determined and ambitious mothers', and concludes that '[c]oming from such a classically twisted psychological situation, it is not surprising that both Noël and Cole were homosexual'.[72] But just as this 'explanation' of their sexuality is awkward, so too must it be recognized that the ways in which the two figures presented their sexuality were completely different: Porter married a woman and constructed a heterosexual biography for himself, whereas Coward undertook no such charade.[73] Thus some of the apparent connections between Coward and Porter's lives and work are superficial or misleading. Notwithstanding his self-consciousness about being too effeminate in public, Coward's sexuality (unspoken rather than actively concealed) formed part of his broader project of presenting aspects of his life through his work. The vibrant colours of his individualized palette, though without name, comprise his 'talent to amuse'.[74] As such, his musicals are not anachronistic but sui generis: the transience of identity experienced by the principal characters in key works such as *Bitter Sweet*, combined with leitmotifs such as nationalism and class, provided his personalized generic framework.

NOTES

1. In his autobiography, Coward describes 'suffering a good deal' from the latter tag even around his late teens. See Noël Coward, *Autobiography* (London: Methuen, 1986), 69.
2. Summing up how celebrity overwhelmed substance in Coward's career, John Lahr concludes: 'Coward, who was as old as the century, personified all its deliriums. His obsession with output, industry, fame, momentum, enchantment were those of modern life that his stage success made glorious.' Lahr, *Coward: The Playwright* (New York: Avon Books, 1983), 161.
3. Noël Coward, 'Introduction', in *The Noël Coward Songbook* (London: Michael Joseph Ltd, 1953), 9.
4. Coward, 'Introduction', 9.
5. Coward, 'Introduction', 9.

6. See, for instance, Jim Lovensheimer, 'Texts and Authors', in *The Oxford Handbook of the American Musical*, eds. Raymond Knapp, Mitchell Morris, and Stacy Wolf (New York: Oxford University Press, 2011), 20, and Kim Kowalke, Review-Article, *Journal of the American Musicological Society* 60, no. 3 (Fall 2007), 691. In general, it is suggested that musicals developed the status of permanent 'works' as opposed to ephemeral 'events' during this period, indicated by the increasing status of the writer, the increase in revivals, and the publication of more scripts and vocal scores of musical, the latter two concepts suggesting permanence.

7. Years of publication: *This Year of Grace*, 1928; *Bitter Sweet*, 1929; *Words and Music*, 1932; *Operette*, 1938; *Pacific 1860*, 1947.

8. Coward, 'Introduction', 9.

9. Coward, 'Introduction', 9.

10. See Graham Payn (with Barry Day), *My Life With Noël Coward* (New York: Applause Books, 1994), 103–105, for details of the collaboration; and *Noël Coward: The Complete Lyrics*, ed. Barry Day (Woodstock: The Overlook Press, 1998), 60–65, for the surviving lyrics from the aborted project.

11. Graham Payn reveals the importance of this gesture; see Payn, *My Life With Noël Coward*, 187.

12. Noël Coward, *The Lyrics of Noël Coward* (Garden City, NY: Doubleday, 1967).

13. *The Noël Coward Diaries*, ed. Graham Payn and Sheridan Morley (London: Macmillan, 1983), 455.

14. Coward, 'Introduction', 11.

15. Coward, *Lyrics of Noël Coward*, 3.

16. Coward, *Lyrics of Noël Coward*, 361.

17. Stephen Banfield, 'Stephen Sondheim and the Art That Has No Name', in *Approaches to the American Musical*, ed. Robert Lawson-Peebles (Devon: University of Exeter Press, 1996), 138.

18. Coward, *Noël Coward Songbook*, 12. The published vocal score of *Bitter Sweet* is dedicated to April 'in gratitude for all the unfailing help and encouragement you have given me in music'. *Bitter Sweet*, vocal score (London: Chappell, 1929), not paginated.

19. Coward, 'Introduction', 13.

20. Coward, 'Introduction', vii.

21. Coward, 'Introduction', vii.

22. Coward, 'Introduction', 103.

23. Coward, 'Introduction', 58.

24. Coward, 'Introduction', 205.

25. Coward, 'Introduction', 15.

26. See Igor Stravinsky and Robert Craft, *Expositions and Developments* (Berkeley: University of California Press, 1981), 148.

27. Lahr, *Coward: The Playwright*, 1.

28. Lahr, *Coward: The Playwright*, 1.

29. Frances Gray, 'Moving with Coward', in *Look Back in Pleasure: Noël Coward Reconsidered*, eds. Joel Kaplan and Sheila Stowell (London: Methuen, 2000), 96.

30. Lahr, *Coward: The Playwright*, 1.

31. See Philip Hoare, *Noël Coward: A Biography* (London: Sinclair-Stevenson, 1995), esp. 63–64 (on his nervous breakdown), 168–169 (on depression), and 274 (a further breakdown).

32. Alan Sinfield, 'Noël Coward and Effeminacy', in Kaplan and Sheila Stowell, *Look Back in Pleasure*, 33–34.

33. Sinfield, 'Noël Coward and Effeminacy', 42.

34. Coward, 'Introduction', 66.

35. The lyrics are reproduced in *Noël Coward: The Complete Lyrics*, 193–197.

36. Noël Coward, *Collected Plays: Two* (London: Methuen, 1979), 98.

37. Coward, 'Introduction', 36–37.

38. Coward, 'Introduction', 29.

39. *Noël Coward: The Complete Lyrics*, 105.

40. *Noël Coward: The Complete Lyrics*, 106.

41. *Noël Coward: The Complete Lyrics*, 106.

42. *Noël Coward: The Complete Lyrics*, 107.

43. *Noël Coward: The Complete Lyrics*, 114.

44. *Noël Coward: The Complete Lyrics*, 114.

45. Lahr, *Coward: The Playwright*, 58–59.

46. Coward, *Collected Plays Two*, 168.

47. See Jean Chothia, 'Playing with the Audience', in Kaplan and Sheila Stowell, *Look Back in Pleasure*, 103–113.

48. Chothia, 'Playing with the Audience', 103.

49. *Noël Coward: The Complete Lyrics*, 114.

50. Sheridan Morley, 'Introduction', in Coward, *Collected Plays Two*, not paginated.

51. Quoted in *Noël Coward: The Complete Lyrics*, 115.

52. See Morley, 'Introduction'. The first version starred Anna Neagle, Fernand Gravey, and Ivy St Helier, and was released by United Artists in 1933 (director: Herbert Wilcox). The second version was reconceived as a vehicle for the popular duo of Nelson Eddy and Jeanette MacDonald, and was released in 1940 by MGM (director: W. S. Van Dyke).

53. Quoted in Morley, 'Introduction'.

54. *Noël Coward: The Complete Lyrics*, 148.

55. *Noël Coward: The Complete Lyrics*, 158–160.

56. Coward, 'Introduction', 12.

57. *Noël Coward: The Complete Lyrics*, 191.

58. Adrian Wright, *A Tanner's Worth of Tune: Rediscovering the Post-War British Musical* (Woodbridge: The Boydell Press, 2010), 51.

59. See Day in *Noël Coward: The Complete Lyrics*, 205–208 for a useful discussion of the varied reception of the song during the war.

60. For more information on these shows, see Stephen Citron, *Noël and Cole: The Sophisticates* (London: Sinclair-Stephenson, 1992), 226–228 (on *After the Ball*), and 255–257 (on *The Girl Who Came to Supper*).

61. The casting was inappropriate since she was near the beginning of her career as a star and never had the vocal prowess for opera.

62. Payn, *My Life with Noël Coward*, 38. The section on 37–45 of Payn's book gives a useful insight into the degree to which Samolo was personal to Coward, as well as the troubled genesis and reception of the show.

63. Coward, 'Introduction', 267.

64. *Noël Coward: The Complete Lyrics*, 267.

65. *The Letters of Noël Coward*, ed. Barry Day (London: Methuen, 2007), 549.

66. As Barry Day notes, it cannot have escaped Coward's notice that Frank Loesser's contemporaneous *Guys and Dolls* managed to achieve commercial success with its corresponding depiction of lowlifes. (*Letters of Noël Coward*, 565.)
67. Coward, 'Introduction', 157.
68. See Coward, 'Introduction', 157, for more information.
69. Both quotations are reproduced from *Noël Coward: The Complete Lyrics*, 333.
70. Gervase Hughes, *Composers of Operetta* (Westport: Greenwood Press, 1962), 234.
71. Wright, *Tanner's Worth of Tune*, 59. Here, Wright refers to Coward's swift descent from overconfidence during the writing of the musical to his apparent indifference to its fate after it had proved a critical disappointment.
72. Citron, *Noël and Cole*, 2.
73. My thanks to Hannah Robbins for pointing out this crucial difference, which is also a problem in the dual analysis of Joseph Morella and George Mazzei, *Genius and Lust: The Creative and Sexual Lives of Cole Porter and Noël Coward* (New York: Robson Books, 1996).
74. A well-known quotation from 'If Love Were All' (from *Bitter Sweet*). *Noël Coward: The Complete Lyrics*, 110.

Bibliography

Banfield, Stephen. 'Stephen Sondheim and the Art That Has No Name.' In *Approaches to the American Musical*, edited by Robert Lawson-Peebles, 137–160. Devon: University of Exeter Press, 1996.

Chothia, Jean. 'Playing with the Audience.' In Kaplan and Stowell, *Look Back in Pleasure*, 103–114.

Citron, Stephen. *Noël and Cole: The Sophisticates*. London: Sinclair-Stephenson, 1992.

Coward, Noël. *Autobiography*. London: Methuen, 1986.

Coward, Noël. *Bitter Sweet*. Vocal Score. London: Chappell, 1929.

Coward, Noël. *Collected Plays: Two*. London: Methuen, 1979.

Coward, Noël. 'Introduction.' In *The Noël Coward Songbook*. London: Michael Joseph Ltd, 1953.

Coward, Noël. *The Letters of Noël Coward*. Edited by Barry Day. London: Methuen, 2007.

Coward, Noël. *The Lyrics of Noël Coward*. Garden City, NY: Doubleday, 1967.

Coward, Noël. *The Noël Coward Diaries*. Edited by Graham Payn and Sheridan Morley. London: Macmillan, 1983.

Coward, Noël. *The Noël Coward Songbook*. London: Michael Joseph Ltd, 1953.

Coward, Noël. *Noël Coward: The Complete Lyrics*. Edited and annotated by Barry Day. Woodstock: The Overlook Press, 1998.

Gray, Frances. 'Moving With Coward.' In Kaplan and Stowell, *Look Back in Pleasure*, 91–102.

Hoare, Philip. *Noël Coward: A Biography*. London: Sinclair-Stevenson, 1995.

Hughes, Gervase. *Composers of Operetta*. Westport: Greenwood Press, 1962.

Kaplan, Joel, and Sheila Stowell, eds. *Look Back in Pleasure: Noël Coward Reconsidered*. London: Methuen, 2000.

Kowalke, Kim. Review-Article. *Journal of the American Musicological Society* 60, no. 3 (Fall 2007): 688–714.

Lahr, John. *Coward: The Playwright*. New York: Avon Books. 1983.

Lovensheimer, Jim. 'Texts and Authors.' In *The Oxford Handbook of the American Musical*, edited by Raymond Knapp, Mitchell Morris, and Stacy Wolf, 20–32. New York: Oxford University Press, 2011.

Morella, Joseph, and George Mazzei. *Genius and Lust: The Creative and Sexual Lives of Cole Porter and Noël Coward*. New York: Robson Books, 1996.

Morley, Sheridan. 'Introduction.' In Coward, *Collected Plays*.

Payn, Graham (with Barry Day). *My Life with Noël Coward*. New York: Applause Books, 1994.

Sinfield, Alan. 'Noël Coward and Effeminacy.' In Kaplan and Stowell, *Look Back in Pleasure*, 33–43.

Stravinsky, Igor, and Robert Craft. *Expositions and Developments*. Berkeley: University of California Press, 1981.

Wright, Adrian. *A Tanner's Worth of Tune: Rediscovering the Post-War British Musical*. Woodbridge: The Boydell Press, 2010.

CHAPTER 19

JOAN LITTLEWOOD

Collaboration and Vision

BEN MACPHERSON

IN 1969, John Russell Taylor declared in *Anger and After: A Guide to the New British Drama*: 'Of all the producers and directors intimately connected with the staging of the new dramatists, Joan Littlewood has had the most far-reaching effect on the actual texts we know on the stage.'[1] This is a common narrative regarding the influence of director Joan Littlewood, and one echoed by many scholars, historians of British theatre, journalists, and theatre critics.[2] Problematically, although perhaps unsurprisingly, Littlewood, and her work with Theatre Workshop at the Theatre Royal Stratford East (see Figure 19.1), is often discussed with reference to her working practices, which share many commonalities—as well as many differences—with avant-garde European theatre, such as that produced by Bertolt Brecht, Vsevolod Meyerhold, and Erwin Piscator. Her 'theatre of the [political] left' is commonly situated as part of a dramatic turn in twentieth-century British theatre that includes John Osborne, John Arden, and Arnold Wesker.[3] Less often is her work explored as part of British musical theatre history, with the exception of the much-feted *Oh What A Lovely War* (1963), and her directing and producing of several of Lionel Bart's works, discussed in Chapter 20 of this volume. In fact, in Adrian Wright's *A Tanner's Worth of Tune: Rediscovering The Post-War British Musical* (2010) Theatre Workshop isn't even indexed, and the enduring legacy of *Oh What A Lovely War* is only mentioned in passing.[4] Yet, whilst a lot of Littlewood's practice may be seen as marking a particular point in British theatrical history as a whole, a closer consideration may also suggest much that has directly and indirectly influenced musical theatre in Britain and elsewhere. Using *Oh What A Lovely War* as an exemplar of all her ideals and practice, together with references to other key works throughout her career, this chapter interrogates her contribution to British musical theatre through examining her view of commercial success, her working processes, and the thematic and structural facets of her productions.

FIGURE 19.1 Joan Littlewood in the rubble in front of the Theatre Royal Stratford East.
Courtesy of Theatre Royal Stratford East Archives Collection.

LIFE AND CAREER: A PRECOCIOUS PARADOX

Maudie Joan Littlewood was born out of wedlock in Stockwell, south London on 6 October 1914. She was raised by her grandmother, a larger-than-life storyteller who actively encouraged Littlewood's literary instincts. In fact, Littlewood blamed only getting one vote at a talent show in Ramsgate during a family holiday on her choice of song: 'My Mother's Arms'. She concluded it was a mistake because 'I would have hated to be in my mother's arms'.[5] Her most influential period of schooling was a scholarship to a convent school, an experience she described as 'a bit of a bore' despite her intellect and her success at inadvertently inducing the Mother Superior to faint during her dynamic production of *Macbeth*.[6] After her expulsion from the school, she was awarded a second scholarship to study at the Royal College of Art. Instead, she briefly attended the Royal Academy of Dramatic Art (RADA) after secretly writing them a letter and applying for a scholarship. Nevertheless, following a pattern established when she moved to the convent school from a council-run school in Stockwell, she did not complete her studies at RADA, leaving early because she judged the Academy 'a waste of time'.[7] Years later, stories would be told by former actors of Theatre Workshop about Littlewood's contrary nature: how she could not abide the formalities and 'representationalism' of drama training common in Britain at the time, but how her regime for training was more tortuous than that of drama school; how she would deliberately and forcibly reduce an actor's stage time throughout the rehearsal process to teach them humility and give them the momen-tum needed when, on the first night, she handed back all the roles to them for the first performance.[8] After a trek to Manchester in 1934, she met singer Jimmie Miller—later to become Ewan MacColl and Littlewood's husband of sixteen years—and joined his socialist Theatre of Action group, part of the Workers' Theatre movement in the UK. Two years later, they would establish the Theatre Union and, after the Second World War in 1945, founded Theatre Workshop. Eight years of nomadic touring ensued, and in 1953 the Theatre Workshop became the resident company at the Theatre Royal Stratford East.

A somewhat charming picture of Littlewood is often painted; a small woman in a woollen cap, with a cigarette permanently stuck between her front teeth, who swore profusely, would scream for more coffee as she sat in the front row of the dress circle 'bellowing instructions through a megaphone in terms that would shame a Fascist traf-fic cop',[9] and who was vehemently opposed to the commercial transfers of her major successes, all of which might be called 'music theatre' through their inclusion and use of song and dance.[10] Yet, while avowedly socialist, she became a close companion to Baron Philippe de Rothschild in her later life, often spent time relaxing aboard a yacht owned by Theatre Workshop business manager Gerry Raffles, and regarded herself as an authority on caviar.[11] In her memoirs, she humorously recalled that despite being under-whelmed by RADA and its ideals of naturalistic drawing-room theatre, when called upon by American producer Carol Sax in Manchester she immediately gave him the full rendition of Lady Macbeth's monologue. Inevitable resonances might be identified here with her convent school production of Shakespeare's play and her classical train-ing, which it appears she never fully relinquished.[12] Such contradictions and paradoxes in Littlewood's nature, I will argue, embody a particular and peculiar part of the British psyche, relating to a simultaneously latent sense of discomfort and pride in the nation's imperial heritage—a paradoxical perspective that might be seen as a defining charac-teristic of 'Britishness'.[13] These facets of Littlewood's personality can be seen in her con-tribution to the history of British musical theatre, and to begin exploring this in more detail, her complicated relationship to commerce will situate her theatrical practice and socialist agenda in a broader economic and cultural context.

COMMUNITY, COMMERCE, AND CONTRADICTION

The driving force throughout Littlewood's career was the ideal of a theatre for the peo-ple, by the people, with the people: 'People ask why I came into theatre. I didn't come into it. We're all part of it, because theatre is the soul of the people', she said.[14] In 2002, the BBC's online obituary of Littlewood emphasized her mantra that 'Theatre should be free, like air or water or love', [15] not commercially or economically driven—a credo seen in her unfulfilled plans with Cedric Price for a Fun Palace, a mobile undercover arcade where 'nothing is obligatory, anything goes'.[16] Littlewood's rationale for this was to encourage a socialist utopia freed from the servitude of the factories and the state, in which art would be seen as part of free expression.[17] This sense of community and socialism was evident in the way she included the local community at the Theatre Royal Stratford East throughout Theatre Workshop's tenure. For example, the public dress rehearsal of *Oh What A Lovely War* prompted friends and neighbours to 'come on stage bringing memories and mementoes, even lines of dialogue which sometimes turned up in the show'.[18] Such a sense of community, and the desire she had for working-class audiences in the E15 postcode to feel kinship with the characters that represented them in her work, bears distinct echoes of Brecht's desire for his epic theatre to inspire the proletariat. Yet, just as Brecht's audiences were very often those he sought to criticize, the Theatre Royal Stratford East quickly became a reputable producing house, with a white middle-class audience demographic.

Between the years 1959 and 1961, this contradiction grew increasingly complicated, as a combination of audience demand, critical reputation, and the need for financial sustainability led to five of Theatre Workshop's musical productions transferring to West End playhouses. 'Success was going to kill us', bemoaned Littlewood, as her company became bifurcated between the Theatre Royal Stratford East and the West End.[19] Yet, whilst traditional narratives might echo the *Daily Telegraph*'s claim that Littlewood despised such transfers, the extent to which this is true is open to debate.[20] If Littlewood's personality was a peculiar mixture of socialist ideals with an enjoyment of economic success, then it was surely reflected in her difficult relationship with commerce. Whilst it is true that she left Theatre Workshop in 1961 to work abroad in children's theatre, seemingly unable to reconcile the need for commercial profit to fund her unsubsidized organization, it is also true that the Wolf Mankowitz/Monty Norman musical *Make Me An Offer* (1959) was produced explicitly with a transfer in mind. The same dichotomy could be seen in her involvement with the Robin Hood-inspired musical farce *Twang!!* (1965) (the two exclamation marks are obligatory). Originally conceived by composer Lionel Bart and writer Harvey Orkin as 'a rollicking romp through Sherwood, combining the bawdy laughs of a *Carry On* film with the attitude of spontaneity of [Bart's earlier Littlewood-directed success] *Fings*',[21] the musical famously ran for only forty-three performances with an estimated loss of nearly $40,000.[22] Orkin—an American comedy writer who had dabbled in the British television industry—was attached to the project as the result of a card game at which Bart suggested to Littlewood that he would 'cut Orkin in' in order to pay his debts.[23] In one biography of Bart, the resultant script is described as having 'no proper storyline, coherent style, characterisation, structure, through-line or reason to exist'[24]—a scenario which prompted Littlewood to rewrite Orkin's work entirely.[25] The rewritten version had a disastrous try-out in Manchester, and Littlewood resigned from the project before it transferred to London—again rewritten—with Burt Shevelove at the helm. The negotiation of commerce, profit, and art was evidently not easily reconcilable in Littlewood's case.[26]

As Robert Leach has noted, in transferring *Oh What A Lovely War* to the West End, 'the original ending—a bitter comment about the ongoingness of war'—was

changed to a 'safer' version for commercial consumption as part of the British culture industry.[27] The extent to which Littlewood consented to this change perhaps
demonstrates the paradox that defined her character and career. The alteration
of the final episode of *Oh What A Lovely War* suggests something about the attitude towards satirical socialist commentary of the British Establishment. While
the musical was still avowedly an anti-war piece, its political message was amelio-
rated by its own success. In her book on British pantomime, Millie Taylor draws on
Mikhail Bakhtin's theoretical construction of 'carnivalesque', a lens through which
burlesque, parody, and satire may be seen to subvert and transform authority.[28]
Importantly here, Taylor's discussion implicitly acknowledges these subversions
as being 'socially contained' within the culture industry and its associated political discourse.[29] The consequence of this is that satire—such as *Oh What A Lovely
War*—is only political in that it is sanctioned or allowed by the Establishment. Such
a precarious and paradoxical situation is perhaps not only embodied by Littlewood's
relationship with socialism and success, but also tellingly demonstrated in an anec-
dote recounted by Victor Spinetti, one of the original actors in *Oh What A Lovely
War* at the Theatre Royal Stratford East:

> One evening Princess Margaret came with [the] Lord Chamberlain [who had
> authority at that time to censor material in all performances]. Afterwards Princess
> Margaret came backstage and said 'Well Miss Littlewood those things should have
> been said many years ago—don't you agree, Lord Cobbold?' [the Lord Chamberlain].
> He gave a thin smile and said 'Oh yes ma'am'. And Joan knew that was our permission
> to go into the West End.[30]

Interestingly, the context for both the stage show and the movie in Britain included a
reappraisal of the popularity of the First World War poets. Vincent Dowd highlights a
move away from a focus on the doubts and darkness of Wilfred Owen, and on to the
more patriotic national identity seen in the poems of Rupert Brooke.[31] Whatever the case
for this, *Oh What A Lovely War* can be found parochial, doggedly nostalgic, and even
though the entire raison d'être of the project was to critique and challenge the national
British mythology of the hapless Tommy fighting the enemy with a spring in his step
and a sense of cosy camaraderie, Littlewood's greatest musical success only attempted to
debunk this myth within the firmly held constraints of the British cultural landscape. To
this end, her ideals are complex and paradoxical when considering the commercial success of her output, a success that, later, Ewan MacColl would suggest rendered the effect
of the material a failure: 'Theatre, when it is dealing with social issues, should hurt'[32]—
something that didn't happen at the end of *Oh What A Lovely War* when it played at
the Wyndham's Theatre after transferring. However, complicated her relationship with
commerce may have been, her focus on community and her ideology were very much
apparent in her working practices and in the dramatic concerns of the productions for
which she is best known. The elements may not have a direct parallel with today's musical theatre, but they are vital in situating how the musical in Britain reflected a change in

practice and form, representing similar changes taking place in the broader landscape of British theatre at the time.

PROCESSES, APPROACHES, PRACTICES

All aspects of Littlewood's working practices during rehearsal and production demonstrated her belief that theatre should be a collaborative process, not a hierarchy. Indeed, the notion of ensemble extended from the training regime and warm-up exercises, through approaches to rehearsal, to the final performance; as a result, Theatre Workshop's reputation and standard of performance largely remained uniform throughout its lifetime.[33] Rosalie Williams, who joined the then-named Theatre Union in 1938, recalls that actors underwent a 'quite extraordinary' training programme, which only grew in intensity when Theatre Union reformed as Theatre Workshop after the war: 'We started each evening with relaxation exercises [. . .] Then voice production, Stanislavsky, ballet, movement, and mime.'[34] The rigour of the training undertaken by Theatre Workshop was notable in itself, as Littlewood, MacColl, and their movement expert Jean Newlove dispelled the perception that once an actor graduated from drama school there was no more training required. More groundbreaking, however, was the type of training used.

The training programme that Littlewood and MacColl developed derived its heritage, not in classical acting techniques used during Littlewood's time at RADA, but rather from Europe, and particularly from Russia.[35] Whilst in Manchester as Theatre Union, Littlewood and MacColl read Léon Moussinac's *The New Movement in the Theatre* (1931) and later Littlewood would discover Mordecai Gorelik's *New Theatres for Old* (1947). In fact, there are specific annotations in Littlewood's copy of Gorelik's text that demonstrate the development of her working practices, with evident influences from Sergei Eisenstein (the use of episodic montage seen in *Oh What A Lovely War*) and Rudolf von Laban (the dance-like physicality of *John Bullion* (1940)), along with the epic theatre of Brecht (the use of song as political commentary in much of Theatre Workshop's output) and Piscator (the integrity of lighting and set design to the themes of *Uranium 235* (1946) or *The Other Animals* (1948)). Likewise, the use of Stanislavskian techniques was unusual, as Robert Leach notes that at this point in British theatre practice, 'no other theatre [. . .] was even interested' in practices from the Continent, despite the fact that in 1937 Elizabeth Hapgood Reynolds translated Stanislavksy's *An Actor Prepares* into English, which may perhaps suggest more of an interest than Leach intimates.[36] What is certain is that the focus on creating an ethos of ensemble improvisation using movement, mime, and acting—techniques that, according to Howard Goorney, 'would often merge into genuine rehearsal, improvisation providing the bridge'—became a hallmark of Littlewood's approach to creating musical plays.[37]

Littlewood's training and rehearsal processes are already well documented and in many ways are not explicitly related to a discussion of her contribution to musical theatre, aside from acknowledging the use of such practices in heightening the physicality of performance—a discourse that often focuses on the American musical theatre innovations of Agnes de Mille, Bob Fosse, Jerome Robbins, and Michael Bennett. What is of interest here is the observation from Howard Goorney quoted above regarding the lack of delineation between training exercises, improvisation, and rehearsal. As Leach has elsewhere noted, Littlewood appropriated Stanislavksy's round-the-table method of textual analysis, informed by thorough research in the tradition of Meyerhold, discussions which would often be physicalized using Laban's effort actions, returning to Meyerhold's approaches of improvisation.[38] All discussions, research, and development were carried out by the company—and not solely by Littlewood as an auteur. She certainly enabled and facilitated the collaborations and ultimately drove the company with her vision; it was in the end, however, very much about the collegial sharing of expertise, talent, and ideas.

This means of working extended beyond the physical staging and development of work; it was a core methodology in the way texts were approached in-process, and consequently had particular ramifications for the way song and dance were developed in rehearsal. In short, Littlewood rejected ideas of the definitive urtext in rehearsal. As warm-ups led to improvisation, and round-table discussions led to rehearsals, the written play-text was often altered in response to the creative process Littlewood facilitated. Frank Norman's original text for the play *Fings Ain't What They Used T'Be* (1959) was initially fifteen pages long. In Littlewood's workshops it was extended, improvised around, and musicalized, in an intensive process with composer Lionel Bart, who was integral to the devising process even at this early stage: 'I had to report in every morning with at least two new songs which had developed out of their improvisations [. . .] They were all clowns.'[39] Later, Frank Norman would refer to *Fings Ain't Wot They Used T'Be* as 'A play Joan Littlewood put on based on a line I wrote'.[40]

This sense of improvisatory development explicitly included alternative and antithetical approaches to dramaturgy, established in Littlewood's production of Brendan Behan's *The Hostage* just a year prior to *Fings*. Set in a Dublin brothel in the late 1950s, *The Hostage* satirized the IRA's sense of nationalism as they plan for the execution of the titular protagonist, Leslie, a young British man, in retaliation for the imprisonment of IRA members being held in a Belfast prison. The fact that the play is set in a brothel perhaps demonstrates the satirical mode within which Littlewood was working at this time. Constantly shifting between comedy, direct address, and political commentary, in a manner reminiscent of Brechtian techniques, it was also in this production that Littlewood's use of music hall techniques and repertoire to punctuate the narrative was first seen—pre-empting the political use of such a low cultural idiom in *Oh What A Lovely War* (1963).

In the final scene, police raid the brothel after news of a hanging in Belfast. Leslie is killed in the gunfight, but then immediately comes to life singing the popular wartime song 'The Bells of Hell Go Ting-a-ling-a-ling' (used once more by Littlewood in *Oh What A Lovely War*). As noted in the article 'Laughing Boy, Serious Girl: *The Hostage* Reconsidered', *The Hostage* has 'less a structure than a framework around which action is improvised [with] interruption of its action by songs'[41] and thus, even though the sudden reversal of Leslie's death at the end may have seemed farcical, it serves as a demonstration of Littlewood in action, switching effortlessly between the harsh reality of Irish politics and a call for resolution:

> This it does through Leslie's coming to life and being joined in song by all the other characters. The fact that Leslie is dead one moment and alive the next is the culmination of the play's intermingling of the tragic and the comic, is itself affectionate mockery of conventional dramatic form, of conventional dramatic seriousness. Life and the comic spirit of exuberance and reconciliation are *made* to prevail in the end.[42]

Reportedly, Behan was perfectly willing to work with this approach—then almost unique in British theatre—along with Shelagh Delaney, author of the kitchen-sink drama *A Taste of Honey* (1958), which was extended by Littlewood, and given the addition of a jazz trio to underscore a story of sexual promiscuity and challenges to class, gender, and race, once again demonstrating a subversive use of music akin to Brecht's idea that music should have a 'gestic' quality in its relation to the theme of the drama.[43] In this context, the use of a jazz trio may have even been seen as a form of the 'cheap' music that Brecht claimed epic theatre required.[44] Yet, whilst the interpolation of music or song into the often-episodic nature of Littlewood's plays has Brechtian overtones, it should be noted that in his epic theatre, Brecht championed the 'strict separation' of music from all other elements.[45] Such stringent delineation does not feature so explicitly in Littlewood's approach. A closer consideration of the published playscripts for productions which might be thought of as plays-with-songs (including *Johnny Noble* (1945), *The Other Animals* (1949), *The Hostage* (1958), or indeed *Oh What A Lovely War*) generally demonstrates a more intimate thematic and narrative connection between the choice of song and the scenario than Brecht strove for. Perhaps in this sense it was less the content that Littlewood intended to be Brechtian, and more the approach to dramaturgical structures and the significance of stylistic choices.[46] There may be no greater example of this than Theatre Workshop's most enduring success: *Oh What A Lovely War*. The following section will consider how this work exemplified all Littlewood's concerns, approaches, innovations, and techniques, exploring its structure, thematic content, and the politics inherent in its presentation.

THEMES, TROPES, AND ATTITUDES TOWARDS 'THE TEXT'

Presented in the epic style of Brecht or Piscator, *Oh What A Lovely War* is a montage of (loosely chronological) events from the First World War, the episodes linked by using well-known British war songs, and focusing on the young men conscripted through propaganda to fight for their country—many of whom would never return. The initial conception of this work came from a radio play by Charles Chilton and was developed by Littlewood and all members of the Theatre Workshop. What makes *Oh What A Lovely War* an exemplar of Littlewood's overall contribution to the British theatrical landscape, and particularly that of musical theatre, is the use of irony and juxtaposition in its narrative construction, and the use of music hall conventions, all framed as a very British end-of-pier seaside Pierrot show. The representation of the British military as a seaside variety attraction already hints at the antithetical strategies that Littlewood used to such great effect. Yet this stylistic decision has broader implications for our understanding of the piece dramaturgically.

One day, on holiday in Ramsgate, the young Littlewood was bored with sitting on the beach. Going off to explore, she came upon a troupe of Pierrots who were singing and dancing as a traditional end-of-the-pier seaside entertainment. Professional troupes were a draw at the seaside, and the clowning often celebrated inept happenings, in a similar manner to circus acts or music hall comedians. Enchanted, Littlewood returned every day to watch them perform, particularly enraptured by the Carnival Night that took place on the last night of her holiday: 'I went early to watch them putting up coloured lights round their stand. The place was transformed. So were we.'[47]

Littlewood's use of Pierrots in *Oh What A Lovely War* (see Figure 19.2) perhaps suggests something deeply personal, which—in thrall to the songs, dances, and coloured lights—evidently had a profound effect on Littlewood's love for what Russell Taylor called the 'magnified realism' seen in the majority of her works.[48] As with all of Littlewood's decisions, it was undoubtedly also motivated by a desire to get inside the piece they were trying to create, and in this particular case it engaged with a sociopolitical narrative peculiar to Britain and its involvement in the two world wars: a narrative that itself epitomizes the sense of Britishness that Littlewood championed and embodied.

In his chapter '"Who Dies If England Live?": Masculinity, the Problematics of "Englishness" and the Image of the Ordinary Soldier in British War Art 1915–1928', J. A. Black discusses this narrative as being one which represented 'First World War soldiers as passive victims mutely suffering affliction', exploring the readily accepted view of the British Tommy as an easy-going, polite, and somewhat ineffectual buffoon who 'did not hate the enemy enough'.[49] Likewise, in later radio and television broadcasts in Britain, such as the successful BBC television comedy *Dad's Army*, Stuart Ward has noted that the 'British military were portrayed as nincompoops'.[50] In this sense, on the one hand, Littlewood's choice to dress the soldiers as seaside clowns embodied a peculiarly British ideology of the lovable but amateurish Tommy in a manner that drew on her established onstage celebration of the lower classes. On the other hand, John Bury's set design included a ticker-tape newsreel which antithetically provided the audience with the cold, shocking facts, figures, and images of the First World War; how many soldiers were killed in each major offensive, or how much ground was lost. In an approach that has obvious links with Piscator and early Brecht, this use of multimedia served as a counterpoint to the characters it set in relief, exposing the officers and political leaders as clowns, and reinforcing the reality of the ordinary soldiers as often naive victims. Simultaneously and ironically, the

FIGURE 19.2 End-of-the-pier entertainment: the Pierrots in *Oh What a Lovely War*, played by Murray Melvin, Fanny Carby, Avis Bunnage, and Victor Spinetti, Theatre Royal Stratford East, 1963.

Photography by Mander & Mitchenson, University of Bristol. Courtesy of ArenaPal.

costuming and use of war songs also allowed a sense of mockery of the generals who sent men to their deaths.

In this respect, one scene of note is the song-and-dance routine for 'Are We Downhearted?'.[51] This patriotic celebration of camaraderie is undermined when the new army recruits complain to the bullish and abusive Drill Sergeant (also in Pierrot costume) that 'We've no rifles'.[52] The soldiers are subsequently told they have to use anything they can find; some use the umbrellas they have been dancing with. Following this exchange, one soldier gets so frustrated during the drill (a drill the Sergeant describes as 'Tragic'), that he chases one of the dancing girls into the audience 'as she screams for help'.[53] This sense of ineptitude was given particular comedic value through the improvising and devising process. As Littlewood recalls, the fact that the Drill Sergeant was directed to speak 'gibberish' served to mock the aggression which often accompanies that rank, and demonstrated irreverence towards the hierarchy of the British army as a whole.[54] What must this depiction have suggested within the jingoistic narrative of British military superiority?

Similarly, the first scene of Act 2 in the original play-script depicts countries represented by actors on a grouse-shooting picnic. Dressed all in Pierrot costumes, they are distinguished from each other only by their headgear. Scotland, France, Germany, England, America, and Switzerland are all present. America—evidently making money from arms deals—is portrayed as disabled at this point (and only later joins the war effort), and Switzerland is represented by a banker. When asked whether Britain would like to buy improved poison gas and new weapons, the British Pierrot politely replies: 'If it's all the same to you, old boy, we'll stick to the dear old Enfield Rifles, cheap and easy to make', suggesting too that rather than employ new gas initiatives, '[t]he old chlorine's pretty good'.[55] This nostalgic determination to carry on with relatively outmoded means of warfare seems inherently British here, and as Andrew Spicer has observed, British military satires portraying life during the world wars often indicate 'a deep seam of irreverence towards militarism and [...] enjoyment of unofficial, alternative images [...] that were suppressed by official discourse'.[56] Such irreverence is perhaps most clearly seen in a further technique used by Littlewood in the devising process.

During their round-the-table discussions, extensive research was collated about the role of Field Marshal Sir Douglas Haig. As a result, his character was developed through verbatim techniques, a device that moves Littlewood's musical play ever more into the realm of serious social commentary and suggests even stronger links to European practice.[57] Thus, the satirical bite of this work is seen most clearly when his declaration that the wounded are 'very cheery' is contrasted with the men digging a mass grave, singing 'The Bells of Hell'.[58] *Oh What A Lovely War*, portrayed as that most nostalgic and parochial of seaside entertainments, subverts the status quo—the British national narrative of its army as 'well-meaning but rather hapless'—by exposing the horrors of reality.[59] It displays irreverence toward the myth that is still perpetuated today: the cosy, warm, British community spirit, evidenced by stoic citizens who sat in their bomb shelters singing songs, went to church on Sunday, and who made do and mended. A key part of this comes from the use of period songs interpolated into the episodes. In his discussion of music hall conventions, Colin Chambers suggests that music hall was in fact the earliest form of 'alternative theatre', with its spiritual home in the East End, arguing that it is 'to some degree always political in the broadest sense, because of the relationship to its audiences through representation of how they relate to their own lives'.[60] Placing alternative theatre and the roots of the music hall in this location as far back as the reign of King Charles II, Chambers continues to suggest that: 'A sense of the outsider/alternative was therefore inscribed in the theatres of the East End and their permitted repertoires'.[61] The use of music hall songs—each political or satirical in its own right—further enhanced Theatre Workshop's position as a creator of 'alternative theatre'. *This* was Littlewood's ideology embodied through song, dance, costume, and the antithetical dramaturgies she borrowed from Europe.

Yet, despite the evident ideological position Littlewood's practices demonstrate, and the content of her work suggests, questions remain regarding the consistency of this position, when considering the contradictions in her own personality. Voicing his cautious reservations about the theatrical practices of Brecht, Adorno once suggested that the theatricalization of reality negates the very goal of presenting its 'true hideousness'.[62] The fact that Russell Taylor has already identified a 'magnified realism' in Littlewood's work, and that it was the stylized juxtapositions of physicality, improvisation, and song that became her trademarks, suggests an inherent theatricalization of the themes and social issues she sought to address.[63] This is not to suggest that Chambers's earlier assertion of East End theatre having a political or 'alternative' agenda is incorrect. Yet, in drawing attention to working-class characters and political issues through theatre, Littlewood creates a magnified theatricalization of the British national narratives she was attempting to subvert. The anti-war message of *Oh What A Lovely War* is readily acknowledged, and its influence is clearly seen through its enduring presence in drama studies education syllabuses in the UK today. However, presented through parochial and irreverent nostalgic content, did this production inadvertently serve to reinforce the narrative of nostalgia and buffoonery, so deeply embedded that any subversion of it may ultimately be seen as a story the nation did not want to hear? Theatre Workshop expert Robert Leach has suggested that the dramas of Ewan MacColl (and to an extent Theatre Workshop at large) were a 'fight against the "culture industry"',[64] yet in the case of *Oh What A Lovely War* this fight actually become more of a sanction, as demonstrated by the visit of Princess Margaret discussed earlier. To this end, whilst Littlewood always wanted to fight the system through her use of European theatre techniques, costuming, and song and dance, her ability to do this seemed always tempered by her awareness of the need for success to achieve her objective. The woman who loved caviar, sailed on yachts, set up a fund with Gerry Raffles to ensure all profits from *Oh What A Lovely War* fed back to Theatre Workshop, and who conceded to commercialism for profit in producing *Make Me An Offer*, was also the woman who left the company in frustration at the need for a transfer model to ensure financial viability, who dreamed of a Fun Palace where art and culture would mean free expression for the masses, and whose love of working-class values were always in evidence, and thus was indeed a very British paradox: 'a ragamuffin, a nuisance, and a wonder', as Philip Hedley so lovingly recalls.[65]

Having considered her paradoxical approach to life, and some key aspects of her theatrical practices and methodologies, we must consider what impact this woman has had on British musical theatre at large.

LITTLEWOOD'S LEGACY

It should not be overlooked that in the history of theatre directors, there are precious few women who have received acclaim for their visionary approach or landmark successes. In this respect, Joan Littlewood occupies a space all of her own. Additionally, her legacy at the Theatre Royal Stratford East has been actively kept alive by her successors. Philip Hedley, who served as Littlewood's assistant director for two and a half years, worked as artistic director for the theatre between 1979 and 2004. His time with Littlewood inspired him to continue promoting works that were socially conscious, regionally specific, and politically motivated. In 2005 he was an associate producer on *The Big Life*—the first black British musical to play in the West End—and was responsible for the Theatre Royal Stratford East staging more black and Asian works than any other theatre in Britain during his tenure. In 1990 he was honoured with a Prudential Award for Drama for his work with audiences 'mixed in age and race and class', and again in 2004 the Theatre Management Association Arts Council Eclipse Award was given to him for his services to combating institutional racism in theatre.[66] Retaining Littlewood's commitment to new work, the Theatre Royal Stratford East produced many new works by writers including Tunde Ikoli, Barrie Keeffe, and Tom Kempinski, and in 1999 this included the introduction of the Theatre Royal Stratford East Musical Theatre Initiative, which has since spawned musical theatre successes such as *The Big Life* (2005), *Wah! Wah! Girls* (2012), and *Glasgow Girls* (2013). In this sense, new British musical theatre writing which deals with community and social concerns is still alive and well at Littlewood's spiritual home.

Although space has not permitted a full coverage of it here, many of the accounts of Littlewood's career mention the constant wrangling she had with Arts Council Grant provisions and other sources of subsidy for her independent and experimental theatre. Today, organizations now exist to support new work, and new music(al) theatre writing in the UK, and whilst it may not be tangible or explicit, the influence of Littlewood's love of community-based regional initiatives, and her careful (if at times problematic) relationship with commerce, can perhaps be understood in light of current working models of contemporary regional producing houses such as the West Yorkshire Playhouse, which produced a revised version of Boublil and Schönberg's *Martin Guerre* in 1999; the Watermill Theatre in Berkshire, whose productions have included reimaginings of classic musical theatre works using the actor-musician aesthetic; Liverpool's Everyman Theatre, which premiered a hip-hop musical, *Melody Loses Her Mojo*, in September 2013; or the Menier Chocolate Factory—an Off-West End venue that produces works exclusively for a specific audience demographic, or concentrates on smaller-scale reimaginings of 'classic' works which then transfer into larger commercial houses in the West End. Elsewhere, Margaret Walker (first wife of Theatre Workshop set designer John Bury) established the influential East 15 theatre school in 1961, with Jean Newlove. Currently offering courses under the auspices of the University of Essex, East 15 still delivers a syllabus that was originally based upon an integrated approach of Stanislavskian character work and Laban movement-training. The result of this is that many of today's actors, directors, writers, and producers—working in all areas of performing arts—have trained in a manner that grew directly from Littlewood's methods.

Methods of actor training, and approaches to mise en scène, have been attributed to Littlewood as their pioneer—including the open stage, and the use of montage and episodes. Many musical theatre works might be considered as following in this tradition, including Stephen Sondheim and John Weidman's *Assassins* (1991) which is set at a fairground and framed with a balladeer in the same vein as the Master of Ceremonies from *Oh What A Lovely War*, or even Kander and Ebb's *Cabaret* (1966) and *Chicago* (1975). *Cabaret* was directed by Hal Prince, who was consciously influenced by the same Russian theatre practitioners that also influenced Littlewood and MacColl in the early days of Theatre Union. *Oh What A Lovely War* played on Broadway in 1965, only a year before *Cabaret*, and may have influenced the way in which the 'concept' musical developed. Certainly, Littlewood was instrumental in bringing the epic theatre of Bertolt Brecht to Britain, when in 1955 she originated the role of Mother Courage in *Mother Courage and Her Children*, a work of European theatre that—as with the majority of Theatre Workshop's output—could be seen as a musical play.

Some further, more subtle instances of influence might be inferred as well. The metatheatrical and carnivalesque construction of the 2001 Off-Broadway production *Urinetown* can be seen as bearing similarities to Littlewood's work, and likewise during the improvisatory development of many of the works she was involved in, the documentary approach involved drawing on interviews or the use of verbatim quotations in developing representations of real-life personalities such as Haig in *Oh What A Lovely War*. In 1975, a decade after *Oh What A Lovely War* appeared on Broadway, Michael Bennett used verbatim techniques in writing his episodic dance musical *A Chorus Line*, and as recently as 2011, the National Theatre on the South Bank developed *London Road*—a verbatim musical by Alex Cork and Alecky Blythe, which dealt with the reaction of a parochial community in Ipswich to the murders of five prostitutes on the London Road. In these instances, there may not be an explicit connection, but the influence of Littlewood in alternative approaches to musical plays is certainly undeniable.

A chapter of this length can only explore a few specific aspects of Littlewood's work, approach, and influence. She was a sprawling, chaotic impresario, who was simultaneously singular in vision, methodical and rigorous in approach, with a clear sense of integrated training, theatrical ethos, and love of music hall traditions. While it may be too much to suggest an explicit and direct legacy in the development of the British musical, her influence is far-ranging. One thing is certain: Littlewood's work influenced British theatre in all areas, and while I have used it to exemplify her legacy in this instance, her approaches to the development of the musical play deserve attention, recognition, and consideration, far beyond the pages of this book.

NOTES

1. John Russell Taylor, *Anger and After: A Guide to the New British Drama* (London: Methuen, 1969), 120.
2. Prior to Russell Taylor's study, Kenneth Tynan lauded Littlewood, claiming that 'when the annals of the British theatre in the middle years of the century come to be written [her] name will lead all the rest'. Kenneth Tynan, *Profiles*, ed. Kathleen Tynan and Ernie Eban (London: Nick Hern Books, 2007), 179.
3. Raphael Samuel, Ewan MacColl, and Stuart Cosgrove, *Theatres of the Left, 1880–1935: Workers' Theatre Movements in Britain and America* (London: Routledge and Kegan Paul, 1985).
4. Adrian Wright, *A Tanner's Worth of Tune: Rediscovering the Post-War British Musical* (Suffolk: Boydell and Brewer, 2010), 16.
5. See Joan Littlewood, *Joan's Book: The Autobiography of Joan Littlewood* (London: Methuen, 2003), 56.
6. Littlewood, *Joan's Book*, 58.
7. In her own words, Littlewood was scornful of Sir John Gielgud's performances during her time at RADA. Although he was hailed as the doyen of acting, Littlewood thought his approach 'too decorative', leaving her bemused as to why an author of George Bernard Shaw's calibre—who bequeathed a third of all his royalties to RADA upon his death—would 'waste his time on such a place'. See Littlewood, *Joan's Book*, 69.
8. This happened to Larry Dann during an American tour of *Oh What A Lovely War*. He recalls: 'I floated through that show'. Georgina Brown, 'Sightings of the Invisible Woman', *The Independent*, 12 May 1993, 12.
9. Tynan, *Profiles*, 179.
10. Robert Leach, *Theatre Workshop: Joan Littlewood and the Making of Modern British Theatre* (Exeter: University of Exeter Press, 2006), 143. In fact, between 1959 and 1961, five of her musical plays—*A Taste of Honey, The Hostage, Fings Ain't Wot They Used T'Be, Make Me an Offer*, and *Sparrers Can't Sing*—transferred from Stratford East to London's West End playhouses, and even to Broadway or on to film.
11. Tynan, *Profiles*, 179.
12. Littlewood, *Joan's Book*, 85.
13. Richard Osborne, *Up The British* (London: Zidane Press, 2009), 71.
14. Quoted in Tynan, *Profiles*, 178.
15. Anon., 'Theatre's Defiant Genius', BBC News online, http://news.bbc.co.uk/1/hi/uk/1628351.stm, accessed 21 July 2013.
16. Cedric Price and Joan Littlewood, 'The Fun Palace', *TDR: The Drama Review* 12, no. 3 (Spring 1968): 127–134.
17. Price and Littlewood, 'The Fun Palace', 129.
18. Littlewood, *Joan's Book*, 693.
19. Littlewood, *Joan's Book*, 547. The difficulty of finance is illustrated by the fact Littlewood reports that in an eleven-year period between 1944 and 1955, Arts Council England

only provided Theatre Workshop with the sum total of £4,150 worth of funding. Yet, she records, at the same time in Frankfurt am Main, West Germany, there existed an annual fund of £8,500,000 for theatre. See *Joan's Book*, 551.

20. Anon., 'Joan Littlewood Obituary', *Daily Telegraph*, http://www.telegraph.co.uk/news/obituaries/1408012/Joan-Littlewood.html, accessed 15 August 2013.

21. Caroline Stafford and David Stafford, *Fings Ain't Wot They Used T'Be: The Lionel Bart Story* (London: Omnibus Press, 2011), 173.

22. Michael Fiener, 'Bart's *Twang!!*—Most Expensive Flop in London', *Montreal Gazette*, 2 April 1966, 20.

23. Stafford and Stafford, *Fings Ain't Wot They Used T'Be*, 173.

24. Stafford and Stafford, *Fings Ain't Wot They Used T'Be*, 178.

25. Fiener, 'Bart's *Twang!!*', 20.

26. It should be noted that the infighting during the development of *Twang!!* also meant that Littlewood's usual practices of facilitating ensemble-led exploration of the material were somewhat compromised—another possible reason for its failure. Fiener in his newspaper article recorded that '[Paddy] Stone rehearsed his dancers in another room, [Oliver] Messell in yet another corner worked on his designs, and Bart sent instructions to everyone'. Fiener, 'Bart's *Twang!!*', 20.

27. Leach, *Theatre Workshop*, 162.

28. Millie Taylor, *British Pantomime Performance* (Bristol: Intellect, 2008), 17.

29. Taylor, *Pantomime*, 17.

30. Vincent Dowd, 'The Birth of *Oh! What A Lovely War*', http://www.bbc.co.uk/news/magazine-15691707, accessed 3 May 2011.

31. Dowd, 'Birth of *Oh! What A Lovely War*'.

32. Quoted in Howard Goorney, *The Theatre Workshop Story* (London: Eyre Methuen, 1981), 128.

33. It was the lack of regulation in the Workshop being spread too thinly between Stratford and the West End that was part of Littlewood's problem with commercial transfers.

34. Quoted in Leach, *Theatre Workshop*, 78.

35. It should be acknowledged here that Littlewood's only positive experience at RADA involved a Laban dance class, which she spoke very favourably about.

36. Leach, *Theatre Workshop*, 79.

37. Howard Goorney, 'Littlewood in Rehearsal', *Tulane Drama Review* 11, no. 2 (Winter 1966): 102–103.

38. Robert Leach, quoted in Jonathan Pitches, ed., *Russians in Britain: British Theatre and the Russian Tradition of Actor Training* (Oxford: Routledge, 2012), 131–136.

39. Quoted in Stafford and Stafford, *Fings Ain't Wot They Used T'Be*, 64.

40. Quoted in Stafford and Stafford, *Fings Ain't Wot They Used T'Be*, 63.

41. Bert Cardullo, 'Laughing Boy, Serious Girl: *The Hostage* Reconsidered', in *Dramatic Considerations: Essays in Criticism, 1977–1987*, American University Studies, vol. 26, no. 11 (New York: Peter Lang, 1992), 97–104.

42. Cardullo, 'Laughing Boy, Serious Girl', 102.

43. Delaney and Behan's willingness to work in this collaborative fashion was not shared, however, by writing team Wolf Mankowitz and Monty Norman, widely noted as disliking Littlewood's improvisatory and—as they saw it—irreverent techniques in producing (and revising) *Make Me an Offer* (1959), Theatre Workshop's only production deliberately intended to transfer from Stratford to the West End to earn money.

44. Bertholt Brecht, *Brecht on Theatre: The Development of an Aesthetic*, trans. John Willett (London: Methuen, 1974), 87.

45. *Brecht on Theatre*, 85.

46. There are, perhaps, strong similarities in this between Littlewood's approach and that of Stephen Sondheim and George Furth in *Company* (1970). Sondheim has been explicit in his dislike of Brecht's political didacticism, and yet readily acknowledges the Brechtian approach to song in his own episodic musical.

47. Littlewood, *Joan's Book*, 56.

48. Quoted in Nadine Holdsworth, *Joan Littlewood* (Oxford: Routledge, 2006), 81.

49. J. A. Black, '"Who Dies If England Live?": Masculinity, the Problematics of "Englishness" and the Image of the Ordinary Soldier in British War Art, 1915–1928', in *Relocating Britishness*, eds. Steven Caunce et al. (Manchester: Manchester University Press, 2004), 163, 150.

50. Stuart Ward, 'No Nation Could Be Broker: The Satire Boom and the Demise of Britain's World Role', in *British Culture and the End of Empire*, ed. Stuart Ward (Manchester: Manchester University Press, 2001), 95.

51. Joan Littlewood, *Oh What A Lovely War* (London: Methuen Drama, 2000), 17.

52. Littlewood, *Lovely War*, 18.

53. Littlewood, *Lovely War*, 18.

54. Littlewood, *Joan's Book*, 682.

55. Littlewood, *Lovely War*, 47.

56. Andrew Spicer, 'The "Other War": Subversive Images of the Second World War in Service Comedies', in *Relocating Britishness*, eds. Steven Caunce et al. (Manchester: Manchester University Press, 2004), 168.

57. As noted at the end of this chapter, the use of verbatim in musical theatre is not unique in this context. Another recent British musical, *London Road* (2011), along with the 1975 American musical *A Chorus Line*, used this technique to achieve a particular poignancy of magnified realism in a similar manner to Littlewood's use here, as mentioned by Russell Taylor in Holdsworth, *Joan Littlewood*, 81.

58. Littlewood, *Lovely War*, 79.

59. Black, '"Who Dies If England Live?"', 149.

60. Colin Chambers, 'More than Music Hall, or How the Alternative Is Not So New', keynote paper presented at the East Through Performance conference, Victoria and Albert Museum, 29 January 2009.

61. Chambers, 'More than Music Hall'.

62. Theodor Adorno, 'Commitment', in *Marxist Literary Theory: A Reader*, eds. Terry Eagleton and Drew Milne (Oxford: Blackwells, 1996), 192.

63. Russell Taylor, quoted in Holdsworth, *Littlewood*, 81.

64. Leach, *Theatre Workshop*, 64.

65. Anon., 'Theatre's Defiant Genius'.

66. Philip Hedley, 'Biography', http://philiphedley.com/, accessed 1 September 2013.

Bibliography

Adorno, Theodor. 'Commitment.' In *Marxist Literary Theory: A Reader*, edited by Terry Eagleton and Drew Milne, 187–203. Oxford: Blackwells, 1996.

Anon. 'Joan Littlewood Obituary.' *Daily Telegraph*, 23 September 2002. http://www.telegraph. co.uk/news/obituaries/1408012/Joan-Littlewood.html, accessed 15 August 2013.

Anon. 'Theatre's Defiant Genius.' http://news.bbc.co.uk/1/hi/uk/1628351.stm, accessed 21 July 2013.

Black, J. A. '"Who Dies If England Live?": Masculinity, the Problematics of "Englishness" and the Image of the Ordinary Soldier in British War Art, 1915–1928.' In *Relocating Britishness*, edited by Steven Caunce, Ewa Mazierska, Susan Sydney-Smith, and John K. Walton, 148–167. Manchester: Manchester University Press, 2004.

Brecht, Bertholt. *Brecht on Theatre: The Development of an Aesthetic.* Translated by John Willett. London: Methuen, 1974.

Brown, Georgina, 'Sightings of the Invisible Woman.' *Independent*, 12 May 1993, 12.

Cardullo, Bert. 'Laughing Boy, Serious Girl: *The Hostage* Reconsidered.' In *Dramatic Considerations: Essays in Criticism, 1977–1987*, 97–104. American University Studies, vol. 26, no. 11. New York: Peter Lang, 1992.

Chambers, Colin. 'More than Music Hall, or How the Alternative is Not So New.' Keynote paper presented at the 'East through Performance Conference'. Victoria and Albert Museum, London, 29 January 2009.

Dowd, Vincent. 'The Birth of *Oh! What A Lovely War.*' http://www.bbc.co.uk/news/magazine-15691707, accessed 3 May 2011.

Fiener, Michael. 'Bart's *Twang!!*—Most Expensive Flop in London.' *Montreal Gazette*, 2 April 1966, 20.

Goorney, Howard. 'Littlewood in Rehearsal.' *Tulane Drama Review* 11, no. 2 (Winter 1966): 102–103.

Goorney, Howard. *The Theatre Workshop Story.* London: Eyre Methuen, 1981.

Hedley, Philip. 'Biography.' http://philiphedley.com/, accessed 1 September 2013.

Holdsworth, Nadine. *Joan Littlewood.* Oxford: Routledge, 2006.

Leach, Robert. *Theatre Workshop: Joan Littlewood and the Making of Modern British Theatre.* Exeter: University of Exeter Press, 2006.

Littlewood, Joan. *Joan's Book: The Autobiography of Joan Littlewood.* London: Methuen, 2003.

Littlewood, Joan. *Oh What A Lovely War.* London: Methuen Drama, 2000.

Osborne, Richard. *Up The British.* London: Zidane Press, 2009.

Pitches, Jonathan, ed. *Russians in Britain: British Theatre and the Russian Tradition of Actor Training.* Oxford: Routledge, 2012.

Price, Cedric, and Joan Littlewood. 'The Fun Palace.' *TDR: The Drama Review* 12, no. 3 (Spring 1968): 127–134.

Russell Taylor, John. *Anger and After: A Guide to the New British Drama.* London: Methuen, 1969.

Samuel, Raphael, Ewan MacColl, and Stuart Cosgrove. *Theatres of the Left, 1880–1935: Workers' Theatre Movements in Britain and America.* London: Routledge and Kegan Paul, 1985.

Spicer, Andrew. '"The 'Other War": Subversive Images of the Second World War in Service Comedies.' In *Relocating Britishness*, edited by Steven Caunce, Ewa Mazierska, Susan Sydney-Smith, and John K. Walton, 167–182, Manchester: Manchester University Press, 2004.

Stafford, Caroline, and David Stafford. *Fings Ain't Wot They Used T'Be: The Lionel Bart Story.* London: Omnibus Press, 2011.

Taylor, Millie. *British Pantomime Performance.* Bristol: Intellect, 2008.

Tynan, Kenneth. *Profiles.* Edited by Kathleen Tynan and Ernie Eban. London: Nick Hern Books, 2007.

Ward, Stuart, 'No Nation Could Be Broker: The Satire Boom and the Demise of Britain's World Role.' In *British Culture and the End of Empire*, edited by Stuart Ward, 91–110. Manchester: Manchester University Press, 2001.

Wright, Adrian. *A Tanner's Worth of Tune: Rediscovering the Post-War British Musical.* Suffolk: Boydell and Brewer, 2010.

CHAPTER 20

LIONEL BART

British Vernacular Musical Theatre

MILLIE TAYLOR

TODAY Lionel Bart (1930–99) is best remembered for *Oliver!* (West End 1960, Broadway 1963, film 1968). He himself adapted the book from the novel *Oliver Twist* by Charles Dickens and wrote the music and lyrics. In this he was one of the few artists who successfully conceived of a whole show alone—a huge and improbable achievement for someone relatively new to musical theatre. For this work he was awarded an Ivor Novello award (now called Ivors) for Outstanding Contribution to the Score of a Stage Play, Film, TV or Radio Programme in 1960 and a Tony in 1963. Nancy's ballad from *Oliver!* 'As Long As He Needs Me' also won an Ivor for The Best Selling and Most Performed Song of 1960. Bart had previously won an award for the score of *Lock Up Your Daughters* and in 1985 he was lauded with the Jimmy Kennedy Award at the Novello Award Ceremony for his lifetime contribution to the British music industry.[1] Bart also wrote a number of other musicals and many hit songs; 'A Handful of Songs' for Tommy Steele won an Ivor as early as 1957, while his final award was for the Abbey Endings TV/Radio Commercial campaign in 1989. Outside a musical theatre show, and internationally, his most widely known song is without doubt 'From Russia with Love', the theme song for the 1963 James Bond film of that name.[2]

Through his songs, such as 'Living Doll', but more specifically through his shows, Bart's musical and lyrical language altered the way British musical theatre spoke to a local audience. His works, perhaps because of his lack of musical training, were contemporary, gritty, working class, more musically and lyrically direct, and his musicals were more in tune with the political theatre being developed at the Theatre Workshop than the West End musicals of Ivor Novello, Julian Slade, Sandy Wilson, and (arguably) David Henneker. His songs and shows speak in a vernacular language and accent about locally specific working-class subjects, and use pastiche and nationally identifiable musical references. Bart's musicals were quite different from the musicals arriving from the USA, and didn't always translate well to Broadway: his use of musical genres and lyrical complexity was often subtly and specifically British, as were the locales within which the narratives were placed and the issues with which they dealt.

Because of his lack of formal musical education Bart wrote lyrics with sol-fa notation identifying the notes of the scale to which each syllable should be attached and then, working with musical directors, arrangers, and orchestrators, he was very specific about what the sound of a melody and the accompanying harmony should be. However, the exact contribution of some of those musical directors, orchestrators, and arrangers is hard to quantify. It could easily be argued that the melody, harmony, and structure of each song was clear in Bart's mind, though others assisted not only in writing down his musical ideas and clarifying the orchestral arrangements, but also perhaps in developing the larger scale formal structures of the works. What can certainly be said is that his musical expression, honed through his cultural background in London's East End, and later at Theatre Workshop, produced a body of work with certain identifiable characteristics that has subsequently had a marked influence on British musical theatre.

'What Makes a Star': Bart's Beginnings

The roots of Bart's work lie in the Jewish working-class traditions of his home life. He was the youngest of eleven children of Jewish immigrants to London's East End 'rag trade' (his father and all his surviving siblings were tailors). Bart (whose real surname was Begleiter) is likely to have been aware of the music hall and variety songs of his youth, the Jewish harmonies and melodic ornamentation of his family's cultural background, the musical theatre and jazz influences abounding in London from the late 1950s onwards, but his first successes as a songwriter were in the newly imported genre of rock 'n' roll as he teamed up with Tommy Steele and others in writing a series of hit songs.[3] However, it was the diversity of musical styles that he employed to represent character, using vernacular musical and verbal languages and dialects, that became a feature of his subsequent work in musical theatre.

At the same time that he was beginning to achieve success as a pop song writer, Bart began contributing songs to shows by the amateur working-class theatre company Unity Theatre, including for *Cinderella* in 1953. He went on to write the musical *Wally Pone* (based on Ben Jonson's *Volpone*) for Unity Theatre in 1958.[4] He was spotted at Unity Theatre in 1953 by Joan Littlewood, who recruited him into her Theatre Workshop that had arrived at the Theatre Royal Stratford East the same year. At Stratford he became part of the regular company and established relationships with collaborators and performers with whom he would work on many of his future shows. There he wrote the music and lyrics for Frank Norman's play *Fings Ain't Wot They Used T'Be* (1959), followed by lyrics for *Lock Up Your Daughters* (1959) by Bernard Miles and Laurie Johnson at the Mermaid Theatre. Then began the most successful period of his career with *Oliver!* (1960), *Blitz!* (1962) (with Joan Maitland collaborating on the book), and *Maggie May* (1964) (book by Alun Owen).

The show that led to his financial collapse was *Twang!!* (book by Harvey Orkin) which followed in 1965, and into which he poured his own money despite a disastrous production process and universally bad reviews. He even sold the rights to *Oliver!* to finance this ill-fated show. This was followed in 1969 by a musical version of the Fellini film *La Strada* where all that remained of his contribution was two songs when it played for just one night on Broadway. In 1972 he declared himself bankrupt but contributed songs to two further musicals at Stratford East, *The Londoners* and *Costa Packet*, in the same year, before falling victim to the drink, drugs, and ill health that plagued the rest of his life, though he continued to work on several shows and advertising campaigns. At his death in 1999 there remained an unfinished version of *The Hunchback of Notre-Dame* called *Quasimodo* that was completed and performed in 2013 at the fringe venue The King's Head in Islington, north London, as well as materials for *Gulliver's Travels* and *Golde*.[5]

'BE WHAT YOU WANNA BE': NEGOTIATING THE THEATRICAL CONTEXT

In the immediate post-war years the West End became home to an influx of new and exciting musical theatre productions from the United States. In the 1950s these imports included *Carousel, Kiss Me, Kate, South Pacific, Guys and Dolls, The King and I, Pal Joey, Wonderful Town*, and in 1958 *West Side Story*. John Snelson argues that British writers (Novello, Coward, Slade, Wilson, Henneker, Cyril Ornadel) tended to maintain continuity with the pre-war and wartime years in their light-hearted musical comedies, while the Americans were embracing change in their musical language and the content of their musicals.[6]

However, alongside a new type of realism in theatre that is canonically focused around the production of John Osborne's iconic *Look Back in Anger* at the Royal Court in 1956, two musicals moved in a new direction. The first, *Expresso Bongo* (David Henneker and Monty Norman, 1958), brought amplified guitar-based pop music and a more cynical narrative to the theatre. It told the story of a predatory agent in the pop industry and an older actress keen to revive her career by association with a rising young star, both of whom preyed on the rather limited talents of the singer, Bongo Herbert. In its cynicism it was reminiscent of *Pal Joey* and its pop music reflected contemporary tastes, but the censorship of the stage play by the Lord Chamberlain's Office and the adaptation into a vapid film version retaining few of the punchier numbers has led to it being overlooked in musical theatre history, despite it being voted Best British Musical of the Year in a *Variety* annual survey of shows on the London stage. As Snelson remarks, 'A London view of the musical in 1958 reverses the usual historical assumption in that the new American success was a costume and period work [*My Fair Lady*] whereas the new British success was utterly contemporary in its characters, setting, plot, language and music.'[7]

The second of the two musicals that articulated a change in musical theatre followed in 1959: *Fings Ain't Wot They Used T'Be*. The use of regional accents and dialect in works set in local and regional communities was a new development in mainstream British theatre from the mid-1950s and arose from a grittier realism in the representation of locally specific narratives—the so-called kitchen-sink drama.[8] This is one of the practices Bart developed as a result of expressing his own East End background, and later his detailed research into other dialects and regional music.

Aiming to produce a genuine working-class theatre, Joan Littlewood often used writers and actors from the local area, which, at this time, was east London. In situation and accent audiences could see themselves represented in the somewhat stereotypical characters portrayed onstage. Littlewood reports that Frank Norman and Lionel Bart were at the rehearsals of *Fings* each day where they could ad-lib new lines or songs in the vernacular as the rehearsals progressed. *Fings* packed the Theatre Royal at Stratford with audiences who 'enjoyed identifying themselves with these ponces, lags and layabouts. Frank's language, learned on the streets, in the nick or in Soho spielers, was a change from the drama school cockney, suitable for faithful batmen and moronic maids.'[9] The work created a sense of community among the performers and with the audience at Stratford whose language and environment were presented onstage.[10] Although there was a certain naivety about the stereotypical characterizations, a very limited dramaturgy, and rather too much predictability in the music-hall style songs, *Fings* did two things: it developed the reputation of its composer/lyricist, Lionel Bart, and it took a musical about East End working-class life, developed through the Theatre Workshop company process, into the West End. The show moved from Stratford East to the Garrick Theatre in London's West End where it ran for 886 performances and won the *Evening Standard* award for Best Musical. Milton Shulman described it in the same newspaper as 'a brawling, bawling, bawdy, sentimental and chaotic affair as far removed from *Salad Days* as a police raid is from a fit of the vapours. It is the first British musical actually proud of its sweat glands.'[11]

Almost simultaneously with *Fings* Bart was writing the lyrics for *Lock Up Your Daughters* (1959). The songs contain many examples of Bart's witty run-on and internal rhymes, such as in 'There's a Plot Afoot' (Act 2, No. 12) which contains the lines 'which involves a little lady | and a shady | local inn.'[12] In the same song Bart artfully rhymes 'swill on' with 'villain,'[13] while in 'It Must Be True' the line 'If they tell as fact' is rhymed with 'How a Pterodact | yl's about to hatch.'[14] In 'When Does the Ravishing Begin', 'Tho' her smile is coy and winsome' continues 'it's fixing in a grin'[15] to articulate a change of mood in very few words while demonstrating significant lyrical acuity. Noël Coward is later reported to have given Bart a rhyming dictionary on which he wrote, 'Do not let this aid to rhyming | Bitch your talent or your timing.'[16] Clearly, right from the beginning of his career, Bart's lyrics were inspiring comment.

The vocal aesthetic of the choral singing in this and Bart's subsequent shows might be regarded as democratic. Song delivery used the raucous vocal character of popular variety and music hall, and even in ballads the musical range often focused around the pitch of speech, rising to belted notes at the end. Certainly the classical-sounding soprano range for heroines and tenor range for heroes was ignored. Company songs had a somewhat 'shouty' quality and company singing tended to be predominantly in unison. These are all features that arose from the democratic, socialist agenda, and the use of untrained performers. Both of these resulted from the inclusive, local, company ethos at the Theatre Workshop and Unity, and these were some of the formative influences Bart took forward in his subsequent work for the musical stage.

'It's a Fine Life': Success with *Oliver!*

After twelve rejections by London managements, *Oliver!* was produced by Donald Albery at the New Theatre, directed by Peter Coe and designed by Sean Kenny (two collaborators from *Lock Up Your Daughters* at the Mermaid Theatre). It cost just £14,000.[17] The show ran for six years or 2,618 performances in London and 774 on Broadway, holding the long-run record for a musical in London until overtaken by *Jesus Christ Superstar* and the record for the longest running import to Broadway until overtaken by *Evita*.[18] Sean Kenny's set, consisting of multilevel scaffolding built on a revolve with two rotating side pieces, was hugely important because it gave the production a fluidity that allowed scenes to 'tumble onwards'[19] as characters could move from one scene to the next turning up in different places—Fagin's hideout, the funeral parlour, the misty streets of London's East End, or the bedroom at Mr Brownlow's.

However, the sets alone don't make a show, and for *Oliver!* Bart wrote music that reflected characters and as he put it, 'people's walks'.[20] The *Oliver!* theme was a reflection of the Beadle's walk, while Fagin's music was described by Bart as 'like a Jewish mother-hen clucking away'.[21] This feature of the musical, which creates a sympathetic star of the show in the anti-hero Fagin, alongside the cherubic Oliver, the mischievous Dodger, and the gang of appealing ruffian children, gives audiences plenty of characters with whom to empathize and plenty of tuneful songs to remember as they leave the theatre.

However, the music and lyrics are not just simple tunes to hum on the way home. Nancy is introduced by the rather ironic song 'It's a Fine Life', whose sentiments are epitomized by the opening words of the chorus: 'If you don't mind having to go without things, | It's a fine life!'[22] The music is an upbeat music-hall song that the boys join in, singing 'It's a fine life!' in a rousing repetition, but the reality of Nancy's life is revealed as she sings of the upper-class ladies who with their 'Fine airs and fine graces don't have to sin to eat'.[23] Already one can perceive the paradoxical layering of a conservative morality and the bleak reality in the words with a superficially upbeat and singable tune whose musical 'hook' and atmosphere belies the content of the song. This became one of the features of Bart's writing style.

The same paradox is evident in the waltzing singalong in a music hall style that is 'Oom-Pah-Pah' (pictured in Figure 20.1). Each verse tells a story of drunkenness, debauchery, or prostitution, concluding with the tale of 'Pretty little Sally' who allowed men to 'see her garters, | but not for free and gratis'.[24] Naively she 'let a feller feed 'er,

FIGURE 20.1 Georgia Brown and company on the famous Sean Kenny set for the original London production of *Oliver!*.

Photograph by Eileen Darby Images Inc., Astor, Lenox and Tilden Foundation, Billy Rose Theatre Division. Courtesy of The New York Public Library for the Performing Arts.

| then lead 'er along'. Nancy concludes her tale of Sally, singing 'She is no longer the same blushing rose. | Ever since Oom-pah-pah!'.[25] Nancy might equally have been referring to herself, demonstrating character not only in lyrics but also through the raucous delivery of this song.

'I'd Do Anything' is very different as it sends up the politeness of the gentry in a gavotte—a musical form and performance designed to pastiche the archaic manners the boys and Nancy see being demonstrated by the upper classes. As the song progresses, however, it also demonstrates the much closer relationship between Fagin, Nancy, and the boys, and the quieter, gentler melody allows the audience to empathize with this community that sings and play-acts together.

Fagin's songs, too, offer surprising insights; they offer opportunities for empathy with a character that in Dickens is much more villainous.[26] Bart was from a Jewish background, but not a practising Jew. Perhaps because the Jewishness was in his cultural background rather than being a religious practice, Fagin's Jewishness appears in melodic phrases and rhythms, but isn't articulated as the anti-Semitism of which Dickens was accused (though some productions have focused on this aspect of the character). Fagin isn't a good character, but his situation is presented in a more nuanced and complex way in the musical through the three songs he sings (two with the boys). In the first, 'Pick a Pocket or Two', Fagin and the boys teach Oliver in a comic song the tools of a trade by which he can be a member of the gang and have food and shelter. Although the trade is illegal it reveals the workings of a capitalist economy and the opportunities available to the dispossessed within it (in a similar style to the narratives of John Gay's *The Beggar's Opera* and Bertolt Brecht and Kurt Weill's *The Threepenny Opera*). The minor key (F minor), the strong emphasis on the opening beat of the bar (e.g., 'In this life'—which could be compared with 'If I were a rich man' from *Fiddler on the Roof* (Bock and Harnick, 1964)), the chromaticism of the title phrase ('you've got to pick a pocket or two') are all reminiscent of Jewish traditional music, as is the opportunity for a little cadenza by Fagin on the word 'boys', just before the final line of the song. Not only are there Jewish motifs in the melody and harmony, but the song is also cheerful and upbeat, depicting a happy family atmosphere among the gang that might be somewhat misplaced. Fagin's second song, also with the boys, is 'Be Back Soon'. This is an even more cheery song with open diatonic harmonies and a marching-pipe-band sound as the boys leave for work, almost turning Fagin into a pied piper or community band leader.

Fagin's final song (his soliloquy) is the most overtly Jewish in style. It is in F minor again, but more importantly it goes 'from free tempo to a slow *boom-chick* that accelerates in typical Klezmer fashion'.[27] Klezmer is an eastern European style of dance music that is partly improvised and may derive from the Ashkenazi Jews. It is used at weddings throughout the diasporic community and is the clearest signifier of Fagin's racial background in the show. This is particularly interesting as the pace changes are used here to represent Fagin's indecision rather than as dance moves. Each acceleration occurs as he gets carried away with a fantasy building to a climax that he suddenly realizes is impossible for him, and he backtracks in the descending phrase 'I think I'd better think it out again'.[28] In a sense this extends Bart's own observation that he created music based on the way people walk to how people think—this scene of indecision sees Fagin thinking slowly, developing an idea, and then getting carried away. In parallel the music speeds up before the pause and descent/decline of the final phrase. One form of music Bart knew that contained those changes of pace was the Klezmer, articulating both Bart's and Fagin's cultural context in the mental changes of pace in the monologue. In all these examples the musical form is used in ways that serve and complement the dramatic moment, demonstrating Bart's sophisticated incorporation of his own diverse musical contexts into character and action.

The dramaturgy of the work as a whole was quite original in musical theatre at the time, building on the 'poor theatre' aesthetic that was already being practised at the Theatre Workshop. Locales shifted frequently and fluidly through the use of the revolving stage and Kenny's innovative set design, making it possible for a long novel to be reduced to less than three hours of stage time. Characters were suggested in action, dialogue, and music, reducing the need for novelistic description. Scene changes were integrated into the action, allowing greater continuity and momentum to build. Although many details in the novel were cut, and a particular focus established, the musical version managed to contain the main elements of the plot, including drama and comedy and a 'flavour of London and of the period'[29] through clear musical and lyrical articulation of character and a strong sense of the social inequities that drove Dickens's politics and later inspired Bart in his adaptation of this work.

The majority of the reviews were positive. Milton Shulman in the *Evening Standard* suggests that *Oliver!* could 'stimulate an avalanche of Dickens musicals' since 'the flamboyant theatricality of Dickens fits in admirably with the florid and melodramatic techniques of the musical'. His argument is that Dickens can't lose credibility by having music added—it's already incredible enough. He goes on to describe Lionel Bart's music as 'a zestful, unabashed blending of Tin Pan Alley, Yiddish folk melodies and the rhythms of the Old Kent Road. They not only button hole you; they practically slug you.'[30]

By this time the West End of London had been overwhelmed by the rhythmic complexity, choreographic brilliance, and tragic story of *West Side Story*. What was exciting about *Oliver!* was that it didn't attempt to follow that route or compete with what American musicals were doing, but used a different British historical and political context and a British/European devising and design concept to represent the Dickensian story. Rather than the rock 'n' roll or jazz-inflected harmonies of Bart's popular songs, this work used a musical language that represented the Dickensian characters for a 1960s audience. In fact, in place of the fascination with American culture that could be seen in Bart's popular songs, through Littlewood's influence Bertolt Brecht, Kurt Weill, and Caspar Neher featured among the show's performative and dramaturgical inspirations. Its politics encompassed a socialist critique of a capitalist world derived from John Gay, Dickens, and Brecht that spoke to a somewhat straitened post-war British context.

Very quickly the stage show, and more importantly the film, became a British folk classic and to some extent replaced the novel in the popular imagination. In fact it had such impact that Sharon Aronofsky Weltman argues that not only the costuming and camera angles for the cartoon, but even the title of the Disney-animated *Oliver & Company* (1988), is a homage to the designation in the score that certain songs are to be sung by 'Oliver and Company'.[31] Weltman also notes the influence of *Oliver!* on both the 1979 production of Sondheim and Hugh Wheeler's *Sweeney Todd* and Tim Burton's 2007 film adaptation in scenic design, characterization, and even casting. She identifies a number of other popular cultural references before concluding that 'particularly for a twentieth- or twenty-first-century American audience—Victorian simply means Dickensian, and Dickensian means *Oliver!*'.[32]

The show was a remarkable achievement and a monumental popular and commercial success that changed the perception and direction of British musical theatre. On seeing a revival of *Oliver!* in London, the French lyricist of *Les Misérables*, Alain Boublil, remarked that 'As soon as the Artful Dodger came onstage, Gavroche came to mind. It was like a blow to the solar plexus. I started seeing all the characters of Victor Hugo's Les Misérables—Valjean, Javert, Gavroche, Cosette, Marius, and Éponine—in my mind's eye, laughing, crying, and singing onstage.'[33] In an even stronger statement, Andrew Lloyd Webber identified 'Lionel [Bart as] the father of the modern British musical'.[34]

'As Long as This Is
England': Remembering *Blitz!*

Bart's next show was *Blitz!*, a show set amid the bombing of London during the Second World War, which opened at the Regal Edmonton on 12 April 1962 and transferred to the Adelphi Theatre on 9 May 1962 after two charity previews, and following Hugh Hastings's wartime play *Seagulls over Sorrento*. The show was directed by Bart with Eleanor Fazan as co-director and Joan Maitland, Bart's former secretary, helping him with the book. The score was transcribed and arranged by Bob Sharples, who orchestrated the majority of the score, though other orchestrators were involved, including Ray Jones who worked on the jazz numbers.[35] Explaining the writing process for *Blitz!*, Bart described how he made a tape of the score singing some of it with other singers and piano, bass, and strings. Afterwards he explained how rhythm and pointing were to be added, then harmony, then texture, all in collaboration with the orchestrator.[36]

In contrast with the £15,000 or so spent on *Oliver!* the *Daily Mail* records that *Blitz!* cost £100,000 to mount,[37] while a later reviewer for the same paper remarked that 'some say it has cost £200,000, and certainly it can hardly have cost less than £100,000. A cast of 60, dozens of dances, 27 songs, sets by Sean Kenny . . . even Noël Coward's *Cavalcade* was not so lavish as this.'[38]

Blitz! tells the story of two East End families during the London Blitz. One is the immigrant Jewish family of Mrs Blitzstein who runs a pickled herring stall, the other is the family of the adjoining white cockney market trader Alfred (Alf) Locke, who runs the fruit stall. The matriarch of the Blitzsteins and the patriarch of the Lockes don't even speak directly to each other, as demonstrated in the song 'Tell Him—Tell Her'. Their two children, Carol and Georgie fall in love, despite opposition from their racially, politically, and personally divided parents, but Carol is blinded in an air raid and Georgie returns from war embittered. Carol's mother realizes that Georgie's love for Carol will help them both to settle down and, despite her animosity towards Alf, pushes them back together. The wedding party ends with a bomb shattering the café and Alf rescuing Mrs Blitzstein, but there is no real reconciliation of opposites among the parents even as the children are happily settled.

For *Blitz!* Sean Kenny's set consisted of four multilevel scaffolds on rolling wagons and two towers that rolled upstage and downstage connected by a bridge that raised and lowered. These pieces moved into ever new formations representing the East End streets with pubs, a view of Petticoat Lane, an underground station with trains, or fires around St Paul's Cathedral, which were created using back projections and a tiny cardboard cut-out of the cathedral that was enlarged many times.[39] An elaborate mechanism meant that there were realistic explosions to create a lifelike replica of the London bombing. The height of the set also gave actors and audiences the sensation of East End tenements as huge blocks of flats were propelled around the stage. In fact Gänzl's assessment of *Blitz!* is that the story was built around the 'pictorial concept of the piece'[40] creating 'a magnificent piece of stagecraft'[41] that according to the acerbic Noël Coward was 'twice as loud and twice as long as the real thing'.[42]

Contemporary interviews suggest that Bart aimed to move beyond developments in the American musical, which, he said, 'with the exception of *West Side Story*—became stereotyped in *Oklahoma!*'.[43] Bart used period pastiche to create the atmosphere of the 1940s and saw 'nothing incongruous in surrounding it with music and dramatic statement which belongs to the '60s'.[44] In fact, he deliberately used two different types of music: period pastiche which created the atmosphere and context for the work, and dramatic statements which he regarded as 'his own, and timeless'. For the period material and atmosphere he researched English folk groups, street cries, and nursery rhymes which he incorporated with his own East End Jewish background and jazz. As he said

> Jazz is unavoidable; it means today, 1962; it means civilization or decadence, whichever is the right word. I'm not a musical scholar but I have a good ear and I've gone into musical origins. Jazz, real African jazz, isn't far from Jewish music, which is closer to Gregorian, and leads on to Celtic music and then to English folk songs and Cockney street chants.[45]

Since jazz, for Bart, was the current music of 1962, he used it to represent the young people in this score, saving cockney, Jewish, and musical theatre influences for the older characters, thus not only differentiating the generations but also articulating the connection between Carol and Georgie in music.

Bart's ability to recreate moods and atmospheres by pastiching musical styles features throughout this musical. Music hall community singing is remembered in 'Who's this Geezer Hitler?' while Vera Lynn's sentimental wartime ballads are recreated in 'The Day After Tomorrow' which was sung by Vera Lynn herself and orchestrated by her own orchestrator. Andrew Jarrett described each character as having a unique musical sound that reflected their age, just as characters' walks were imagined and signified in *Oliver!*. Mrs Bernstein's characterization draws on the sounds of Jewish culture in 'Be What You Wanna Be' and 'Bake a Cake' with melodic and harmonic patterns reminiscent of 'Reviewing the Situation'—the latter even has a little cadenza at the end. Alfred has quasi-patriotic tunes with lyrics such as 'As Long As This Is England'. The lovers, Carol and Georgie, share 'Opposites', and 'Magic Doorway' (which doesn't appear on the cast recording) uses syncopated rhythms and jazz/blues-inflected harmonies. By contrast the other young women, who can be seen led by Toni Palmer in Figure 20.2, are rather raucous but contemporary in 'Leave It to the Ladies', which has a walking bass, syncopation, and big band interjections. Carol also sings the beautiful Act 2 ballad 'Far Away' (later recorded by Shirley Bassey), while Georgie becomes more of a 'jack the lad' character in the popular, jazz-inflected music of 'I Want to Whisper Something' and 'Who Wants to Settle Down'.

Market cries create a nostalgic atmosphere in this score as they did in *Oliver!*. In this case 'Petticoat Lane' suggests an idealized community market just as 'Who Will Buy' did in *Oliver!*. Also similar to *Oliver!* is the use of paradoxically cheerful music disrupted by

FIGURE 20.2 Recreating the mood and atmosphere of wartime London: Toni Palmer leading the company of *Blitz!* in the number 'Down the Lane' (1962).

Photograph by TopPhoto. Courtesy of ArenaPal.

unexpected harmony and lyrical or melodic invention to add complexity. 'We're Going to the Country' is a good example; it is a marching song for the children being evacuated whose cheery bright melody contains some foreshortened intervals and dissonant harmonies that suggest the complex emotions and circumstances that require the evacuation, and the rather uncertain futures the children will face in the country. The music the parents sing at the end is even more dissonant in what appears to be an uptempo cheery 6/8 song. Equally disturbing is the children singing 'Mums and Dads' to a music box tune, as they embody their parents' arguments and drunkenness, thus representing the children's dysfunctional family lives. At the same time as each musical number is distinctive, the score as a whole is imbued with the discordant air-raid sirens that then feature in the dissonance and rising phrases of songs such as 'We're Going to the Country'. 'Magic Doorway' and 'Bake a Cake' begin with the same augmented-fourth interval in the melody—Bart's homage to *West Side Story* and a feature that provides a thematic centre for the score as a whole.

The show, like *Oliver!*, was very successful with audiences, running for 568 performances, but despite negotiations, it didn't transfer to Broadway. This may be due to the fact that Americans couldn't relate to the experience of the Blitz in the way British people, and especially Londoners, did. More importantly, even though the music in this score incorporated jazz, it was within a score derived from British cultural influences, and in the service of a rather thin story using stereotypical characters and melodramatic events. While the (British) reviewer for *Punch* called it a 'warm and sentimental account of what life was like in the East End of London during the six months beginning September 1940' with 'spirited harmony and music',[46] the (American) reviewer Norman Nadel reported in the *New York World Telegram and Sun* that it had 'jingle jangle music, much of it [sounding] like a mediocre American musical of thirty years ago'.[47] However, although he found it 'sentimental and common' he remarked that 'time and again *Blitz!* gets through to you—and the sum of those times makes Bart's musical entertainment something to see when you're in London'.[48] This show demonstrates Bart's skill at depicting time, place, emotion, and character in music and lyrics, but reveals that his skill as director and dramatist were rather more limited.

Pat Wallace of *The Tatler* praised it as '[o]ne of ours [. . .] a full blooded entertainment of which liveliness and unashamed sentiment are the keynotes'.[49] The reviewer for *Queen* didn't like the sentimentality, calling it a 'mammoth, sentimental bellows-machine of a musical'.[50] Vincent Mulchrone wasn't overly optimistic about its likely success based only on word from the previews: 'Previews suggest it will be a failure. It is slow, they say. And diffuse. And mawkish. And tuneless'.[51] The run of 568 performances can hardly be considered a failure, and the show was subsequently performed in Australia (1985), revived in the UK by the National Youth Music Theatre (1990) and on tour (by the Northern Stage Company). Listening to the CD now allows one to reflect that, although it is certainly somewhat sentimental, some of the songs might have an enduring appeal.

'THE WORLD'S A LOVELY PLACE': CRITICAL SUCCESS WITH *MAGGIE MAY*

The final successful musical in the series was *Maggie May*. With a book by Alun Owen, and directed by Ted Kotcheff, it opened at the Opera House, Manchester on 19 August 1964 and transferred to the Adelphi Theatre in London on 22 September. It ran for 501 performances and is regarded as Bart's best work, perhaps partly because of the politics of Alun Owen's book that gave Bart strong material and complex characters to depict. The story is set in Liverpool, a setting that required Bart to study the dialects that appear comically in the tongue-twisting jazz waltz 'Dey Don't Do Dat T'day'. He also incorporated sounds of the city, like the street cries of his previous musicals, in 'Shine You Swine', but the show's social comment mostly arises from Alun Owen's book. The story concerns Patrick Casey, son of a famous union leader, and his love for the local prostitute Maggie May. Casey doesn't want to follow in his father's footsteps, so runs away to sea, leaving Maggie to follow the oldest profession. When he returns decades later he gets involved in wild cat strikes and wants to destroy a cargo of guns destined for South Africa, but Casey is killed in a confrontation leaving Maggie with no hope for the future.

Once again the music was made up of an eclectic mix of styles, a mix that Rexton Bunnett praises as 'interestingly diverse and lyrically the most mature' of Bart's works.[52]

Some songs were in a folk idiom, such as 'The Ballad of the Liver Bird' sung by the balladeer who opened and ended the show,[53] and the working song 'Right of Way'. The storytelling song 'Stroll On' was also performed by the male chorus and drew on folk traditions. Other songs had a stronger rhythmic drive, such as 'We Don't All Wear the Same Size Boots' (music hall singalong style), 'Dey Don't Do Dat T'day' (jazz waltz), and 'There's Only One Union' (cha cha cha) but *The Times* critic remarked that the most memorable songs were those derivative of the folk tradition. The review was positive about the 'vigorous orchestrations', concluding that 'there is a good deal to be rapturous about'.[54] The reviewer for *The Stage* concurred, beginning his piece with the statement '*Maggie May* is brassy, vigorous and tuneful!'[55] Certainly the score stands up well to contemporary listening, reflecting, once again, Bart's uncanny ability to write in many genres, to speak in many voices, and especially to represent complex characters through paradoxical juxtapositions of music and lyrics.

The ballad 'The Land of Promises'[56] is one of the songs that opens with a dissonance between melody and harmony, in the augmented fourth (a melodic B natural over the chord of F7) that also featured in *Blitz!*. This beautiful song begins with a wide-ranging melodic phrase that is followed by an augmentation of its range at the repetition. The middle section contains a series of sequences extending the range upwards again, before the line 'open to ridicule' falls down on an unrelated chord. The song then modulates before a sequence of falling phrases returns to the tonic though deferring resolution until the last moment. This is sophisticated songwriting that contains some quite simple elements of word painting, but also demonstrates Bart's understanding of melody and harmony in the creation of song structure.

In a completely different mood the pastiche cha cha 'There's Only One Union' is much more focused on lyrics as it conveys the sexual innuendo depicted in the verbal double entendres: 'There's only one Union I approve of | Which entre-nous only two can create'[57] and later 'it doesn't need a show of hands | When both agreed the motion stands', concluding with 'Who needs a chair to declare we've begun | No minutes read but the bed's over there man!'[58] Nonetheless there are some unexpected intervals that make the melody interesting to listen to and tricky to sing, as in the falling phrases of 'two can create' and 'likely candidate' or the unexpected harmony also at 'Who'll be the likely candidate'.

The augmented fourth between melody and chord appears again in the uptempo community song 'We Don't All Wear the Same Size Boots' where the melodic D natural appears over the chord of A flat. This is a passing dissonance that colours the word 'don't' but it has, by now, apparently become a feature of Bart's writing, and it appears again in 'The World's a Lovely Place'. The unexpected semitone movements, and especially the chromatic rising phrases at 'The stars are free' and 'with all this free it's hard to see how love can be so dear',[59] make the beautiful melody very difficult to sing absolutely in tune, but these details turn a simple waltz into something much more complex. Overall this score incorporates a wide range of musical genres handled deftly to represent character, atmosphere, and situation.

On 27 August *The Stage*'s reviewer commented that the work was 'stark, vivid, and saltily down-to-earth',[60] though noting that 'it is the book which gives the show a great deal of its bite' because of the Liverpool dockland milieu which made it distinctive—this was the era of the Beatles and everything from Liverpool had a certain currency. Bart only 'nearly matches this in his shanty or blues-like songs' for example when the dockers sing 'Right Of Way' while shifting cargo, or when Casey sings 'Stroll On' with a shanty chorus. The sentimental numbers were poorly received—here described as 'mawkish'. This was not aided by the fact that neither of the two leading performers (Rachel Roberts and Kenneth Haigh) were strong singers.[61] Their voices on the cast recording appear to be adequate, but Roberts's performance was apparently somewhat unpredictable[62] and she left the show early to be replaced by Georgia Brown who was more kindly received. Despite the somewhat mixed reviews the show had a more than respectable run.

Milton Shulman in the *Evening Standard* was rather unkind about the show. He worried that the descent of the British musical from the 'Ruritanian palaces of Ivor Novello to the kafes [*sic*] of *Fings Ain't Wot They Used T'Be* has been rather sharpish'. This was not a move of which he approved, though, in a rather supercilious comment, he felt sure that *Maggie May* would be popular with 'charabanc audiences', while those 'looking for something really adventurous or novel in a British musical will be disappointed'.[63] Perhaps, more than anything, this demonstrates the conservative views of critics when comparing home-grown offerings with American imports, even though Sean Kenny's sets that represented streets, warehouses, docks, a ferryboat, and the New Brighton Fairground were once again praised as 'a show in themselves'.[64] But reviews such as these did affect the historical perception of the innovation contained in this musical. What the reviewers perhaps didn't appreciate on first hearing was the development of Bart's style: his use of an eclectic mix of genres to represent character, mood, and atmosphere; and his use of dissonance, word painting, lyrical complexity, pastiche, and playfulness. These are the features that, with hindsight, can be perceived to be distinctive elements of Bart's style, but the musical language was, by then, going out of fashion.

'Unseen Hands': Who's in Charge of *Twang!!*

For *Twang!!*, a Robin Hood story that seems to have been closer to British pantomime or the British series of *Carry On* films than musical theatre,[65] Bart envisaged 'a spectacular extravaganza that combined Theatre Workshop techniques with all the trappings of commercial theatre'.[66] Script and score changed daily during rehearsals and the result was a disaster of epic proportions at its previews in Manchester with Littlewood resigning as director on opening night. Burt Shevelove was brought in as show doctor, but the show closed after just forty-three performances in the West End. Since Bart had ignored his friend Noël Coward's advice and invested his own money in keeping the show running for those forty-three performances, his fortune was damaged to the extent that he had to declare himself bankrupt in the early 1970s.

According to Nadine Holdsworth, 'many held Littlewood responsible for the failures of *Twang!!*'.[67] As director she attempted to use the techniques of the Theatre Workshop in a commercial working environment, employing many of her regular actors but in a different type of production. The content and order of scenes and songs were constantly altered in a devising process that was unsuited to a situation in which orchestral parts needed to be written, dancers needed to learn routines, and singers, songs. The result was chaotic in the extreme with performers unsure of the order of scenes and songs, or even which scenes and songs would be performed on any given occasion.[68] However, the book and music must hold some of the blame, too. The score contains a number of catchy tunes, but since the book has no political or social relevance, the lyrics and music don't create the ironic juxtapositions apparent in Bart's previous works and tend towards the obvious. In fact, Gänzl comments that 'simplicity turned into childishness and banality, humour into pure silliness and the composer of *Oliver!* and *Maggie May* came up with a score which sounded like a mixture of nursery rhymes and bad television themes'.[69]

For example, in the song 'Make An Honest Woman Of Me' Barbara Windsor as Delphina sings that she would 'give up all previous delights, delectable, to spend my mornings, afternoons and nights, respectable'.[70] She requests a chastity belt so that someone can 'make an honest woman' of her. The music has a jazzy big-band feel that slows to the tempo and style of *The Stripper* as the women portray themselves as sexually desiring and desirable, but passive in the pursuit of personal happiness. This chimes with the stereotypical and patriarchal representations of female sexuality that had been imposed on/adopted by Barbara Windsor in the *Carry On* films in which she became famous, and may have been replicated in this role as a result. However, the male characters are equally simplistically presented with repeated references to size in the songs of the Merry Men. Such simplistic representations in no way compare with the complexities of characters such as Maggie May or Nancy. Altogether the show appears to have more in common with saucy postcards than the sophistication of Bart's previous lyrics. However, the music is tuneful and sometimes jazzy, in the style of imported American popular music so that the music and lyrics appear to have entirely different levels of sophistication—a dissonance that, on this occasion, entirely fails to convince.

La Strada, developed from the 1954 Federico Fellini film, was an even bigger disaster, though at least it didn't have Bart's money in it. The music for the original demo is available on CD with lush orchestration and a large group of singers.[71] It is clear that these songs are to some extent a return to form for Bart, containing dissonance and unsettling lyrics in pastiches of circus and other music to reflect the dark story. Children are present again, singing 'The Seashell Song' with Gelsomina. This is a much more straightforward melody and harmony than Bart had given children to sing in previous musicals, though perhaps the simplicity of the melody is designed to represent Gelsomina's simplicity. On the other hand, the presence of increasingly complex genres demonstrates Bart's sophistication, as, for example, in the tango 'The Pick of the Bunch'.[72] The soliloquy Zampano sings when considering leaving Gelsomina by the roadside 'Tan-tan-ta-ra! Farewell!' demonstrates an increase in complexity from the song which might be considered its antecedent, Fagin's 'Reviewing the Situation'. In Zampano's number there are numerous changes of mood articulated through changes of genre, tempo, time signature, and style as Zampano decides how to proceed. There is enormous rhythmic complexity, too, as Zampano reflects on his own mortality—and Gelsomina's—to fast, upbeat music. This is followed by a slower passage in which he affectionately remembers his life with her; the section 'Sometimes' is a useful example of the dreamlike quality of the score as a whole. Bart's use of dissonance in melody and orchestration continues in this score: using the seventh or augmented fourth on the downbeat occurs, for example, in 'To Be a Performer', which also exemplifies the use of extended melodic sequences.

Bart's lyrical acuity was also undiminished as can be seen in the song 'My Turn To Fall' in which Marita sings of her love for Mario in a lyric with internal rhymes, sequences, run-on phrases, alliteration, and circus metaphors: 'He walks that slender tight rope high overhead | And on the slender slight hope | That he might have meant all he said | I cry, yes I love you, silently in my soul.'[73] In this song Bart's lyrics might appear to be out of step with the relatively unsophisticated character. This juxtaposition, which we've seen in the writing for Nancy and Maggie May, may be one of the reasons why Bart isn't regarded as a great writer of musical theatre. But, of course, such a charge makes the assumption that the Broadway understanding of writing 'in character' for an 'integrated' musical is the only way forward, and as Kander and Ebb and Sondheim were proving on Broadway simultaneously, musical theatre can be written in many different ways. On the other hand, a workshop production/rehearsed reading of La Strada directed by Fiona Laird in about 2002 was not well received by the major West End directors and producers who attended. The performers seem to have found the dialogue a bit comical in its naivety and the music rather pedestrian for a road movie set in Italy—but of course this is a twenty-first-century commentary on a 1960s musical that clearly had not stood the test of time. What Bart appears to have brought to the British musical in the 1960s was a different aesthetic quality derived from his own history and context that didn't always sit well with the increasing desire for musical and formal innovation in musical theatre.

Bart's illness and addiction prevented him from travelling to Detroit and all but two of his songs were removed by the time the show arrived on Broadway at the Lunt-Fontanne Theatre on 14 December 1969. It closed the same night.

Bart continued writing throughout the rest of his life, with songs for two further shows performed at the Theatre Royal Stratford East in 1972, as he returned to his roots. The first was a stage version of the film Sparrers Can't Sing,[74] for which Bart had written the original theme song. The show was called The Londoners and depicted 'the inhabitants of a condemned slum terrace and their rumbustious community spirit, [which] spoke volumes in the context of the loss of two thousand such homes in the immediate vicinity of the Theatre Royal.'[75] It was unexceptional and completed its anticipated season of sixty-three performances at Stratford East. Costa Packet[76] saw Bart working with Frank Norman (book) and Joan Littlewood (director)[77] once more; the team with whom he had written Fings in 1959 was reunited. The show ran for two months (sixty-five performances) at the Theatre Royal Stratford East.[78] Bart's working life had come full circle. However, his songs for these two shows did not receive the critical acclaim or achieve the financial rewards of his earlier work since by now they were perceived to be unexceptional; British musical theatre had moved on with the opening of *Jesus Christ Superstar* in 1972 following the 1970 UK opening of the American *Hair*.

Beyond this there were revivals of *Oliver!* especially from 1994 onwards, produced by Cameron Mackintosh who used the opportunity to provide financial support to Bart by returning a royalty to him. Finally there was a posthumous completion of *Quasimodo* in 2013, which contained some beautiful music but offered a predictable and rather dull version of the story. The musical was begun in 1963[79] after the success of *Oliver!*. My own assessment of this adaptation corresponds with that of Paul Taylor in *The Independent*:

> The narrative element is a little cheesy [...] but the score, with an excellent reduced orchestration for piano, accordion, and an oily Klezmer-tinged clarinet, has an uplifting directness, characteristically swinging on an axis between the Jewish cantor tradition and the kind of Catholic hymn that sounds like a pub sing-a-long. The lyrics are, at points, mildly ludicrously top-heavy; by and large, though, the songs each have a strongly distinctive personality—from the madly catchy 'Abracadabra' through the belting ballad 'So Let It Be' [...], to 'Introducing You' in which Quasimodo introduces his bells as if they were individuals.[80]

Jane Shilling remarked that 'the musical numbers are tremendous, with the catchy lyrics and haunting melodies of a composer utterly at ease with his ability to write a hit'[81] while Edward Seckerson, who regards Bart as 'the quirkiest, the most extraordinary, and potentially greatest musical theatre talent that this country has ever produced', noted the distinctive character of each song as well as their profusion.[82]

'SOMETHING SPECIAL': IDENTIFYING BART'S INFLUENCE

Lionel Bart's musicals, especially *Oliver!* because of its widespread fame, rerouted the British musical theatre away from lightweight fantasies to something more contemporary, more gritty, more musically direct, and more in tune with the political theatre being developed at the Theatre Workshop and elsewhere. I'm not sure I would go as far as Edward Seckerson (quoted in the previous paragraph) in praising Bart's talents, but his influence has certainly been substantial. His collaborations with designer Sean Kenny resulted in a shift in musical theatre spectacle from the use of 'realistic' perspective behind the proscenium arch to something much bolder, more stylized, and more fluid. The backgrounds of the creative teams meant that these settings were urban, often focusing on political subjects through the presentation of dysfunctional or complex situations and relationships. This type of approach, and the political relevance of the work it spawned, could easily be argued to have influenced later epics such as *Les Misérables* and *The Hired Man* (1984).

The incorporation of gritty dissonance, and Bart's articulation of a British identity through a stylized pastiche of folk, music hall, East End Jewish, and contemporary idioms alongside downbeat, sometimes overly sentimental, but always specifically British situations and nostalgia locates his work in its time and place. The vocal presentation of song was often not aesthetically pleasing and incorporated idioms, dialects, and accents of the British regions; the 'shouty' quality found on the cast recordings is a move away from trained voices and is designed to represent the voices of the urban working classes. Bart's works are very specifically British representations using techniques he acquired aurally and beyond the confines of American musical theatre stereotypes, which may account for the limited interest in these works (apart from *Oliver!*) in the United States.

Bart's work is not like that of his American peers. We might notice, for example, that Annie's song 'Tomorrow' (from the US musical *Annie* (Charles Strouse, Martin Charnin, and Thomas Meehan, 1977)) and Oliver's song 'Where is Love?' (from the UK musical *Oliver!*) demonstrate something about the difference in our two countries in those decades: American optimism that assumes things will improve ('The Sun'll Come Out') contrasts with British pessimism ('Where is Love?'), which perhaps reflects a society resigned to the difficulties, absences and losses that were endured in the post-war years. Alternatively we might remark on how melodramatic stories, epic novels, the 1960s obsession with the Victorian/Edwardian English novel and play have subsequently infiltrated British works such as *Pickwick* (1963), *The Matchgirls* (1966), *Half A Sixpence* (1963), *Trelawney* (1972), *The Card* (1973, updated 1994),[83] *The Good Companions* (1974), *Les Misérables* (London 1985), *The Phantom of the Opera* (1986), and *Scrooge* (1992). Equally, we might comment on the reference to the politics of inequality and unionization of the working classes in *The Hired Man* and *Billy Elliot* (stage, 2005). The sophisticated use of pastiches of musical idioms to articulate paradoxical or complex situations or simply as shorthand to signify character stereotypes can be discovered in a number of works including *Joseph and the Amazing Technicolor Dreamcoat* (cantata 1968, London 1973), *Jesus Christ Superstar* (concept album 1970), *Honk!* (Newbury 1993, West End 1999), *Betty Blue Eyes* (2011), and *Soho Cinders* (showcase 2008, Soho Theatre 2012) (the last three by Stiles and Drewe). Bart's epic approach to the representation of history using popular theatre forms was to feature later in *Privates on Parade* (1977) and *Poppy* (RSC 1982, West End, 1983).

Lionel Bart's work (other than *Oliver!*) has since been somewhat overlooked in theatre history,[84] but it may be that this is the result of the specificity of his subjects, music, references, and its audiences. This is particularly true of *Blitz!*, reminding audiences of a very specific experience of the war; *Maggie May* that was in no way glamorous as it negotiated images of the north-west of England, working-class unionization and prostitution; and *Twang!!* which directly referenced the slapstick and innuendo of a 1960s British comedy film franchise. Much of his work seems to have appealed specifically to a British audience with none of the glamour of contemporary American imports. However, it did appeal to that audience: it seems that his instincts, honed in the London clubs, the pop music industry, the East End Jewish community, and the politics of left-wing-devised theatre practices rather than through an academic training allowed Bart to communicate with a contemporary British audience. His lack of formal musical education, rather than hindering his development, allowed him to incorporate all these experiences and to popularize a new type of politically conscious musical idiom that had a profound influence on the subsequent development of a British vernacular in musical theatre.

NOTES

1. The Jimmy Kennedy awards were given out during the 1980s and 1990s.
2. With thanks to Brenda Evans for her invaluable help in finding source materials at the Lionel Bart Archive. Also thanks to Fran Matthews at the British Academy of Songwriters, Composers and Authors (BASCA) for information about the Ivor Novello Awards, and to Alexander Carter who worked as my research assistant in the early stages of this research.
3. Songs include 'Rock with the Caveman' (UK No. 13, 1956), 'Butterfingers' (UK No. 7, 1957), 'Water Water' (UK No. 5, 1957), 'Hey You' (UK No. 28, 1957), 'Little White Bull' (UK No. 6, 1959) and 'Happy Guitar' (UK No. 20, 1958; sung by Tommy Steele), 'Living Doll' (UK No. 1, 1959; sung by Cliff Richard and The Shadows), 'Walkin' Tall' (UK No. 28, 1959; sung by Frankie Vaughan), 'Do You Mind?' (UK No. 1, 1959; sung by Anthony Newley), 'Hide and Seek' (UK No. 47, 1961; sung by Marty Wilde), 'Easy Going Me' (UK No. 12, 1961; sung by Adam Faith), and 'Choose' (US No. 112, 1964; sung by Sammy Davis Jr).
4. Unity Theatre was an association of working-class theatre groups in major cities that developed in the 1930s. The plays they performed had a left-wing political agenda and were designed to appeal to working-class audiences.
5. Some songs from these musicals are available on the third of a three-CD box set *The Genius of Lionel Bart* (Sepia 1201, 2012) on which tracks 8–11 and 23 are from *Quasimodo*, 12–17 are from *Gulliver's Travels*, and 18 is from *Golde*.
6. John Snelson, '"We Said We Wouldn't Look Back": British Musical Theatre, 1935–1960', in *The Cambridge Companion to the Musical*, 2nd ed., ed. William A. Everett and Paul R. Laird (Cambridge: Cambridge University Press, 2008), 145.
7. Snelson, '"We Said We Wouldn't Look Back"', 144.
8. Scott Miller makes the claim that *Fings* was the first time real cockney was spoken on stage (Scott Miller, *Strike Up the Band: A New History of Musical Theatre*, (Portsmouth, NH: Heinemann, 2007), 80)—a rather unlikely claim given that Theatre Workshop had been using local actors for some years already, speaking with their own regional accents, and Unity Theatre had been using amateur performers. It is possible, though unlikely, that it might lay claim to the first genuine cockney accent on the West End stage since *A Taste of Honey* that preceded it in transferring from Theatre Workshop to the West End as that was set in Salford, Manchester.
9. A spieler was a seedy Soho gambling den and brothel. The term derives from the German *spielen*, meaning 'to play'. Joan Littlewood, *Joan's Book: Joan Littlewood's Peculiar History as She Tells It* (London: Methuen, 1994) 545.
10. The show was revived at the Theatre Royal Stratford East in 2014 using a similar aesthetic to similar effect.
11. Milton Shulman, 'Not One for the Matinee Set . . .', *Evening Standard*, 12 February 1960, Cuttings file, V&A Museum.

12. Bernard Miles, Lionel Bart, and Laurie Johnson, *Lock Up Your Daughters* (London: Samuel French, 1967), 40.

13. Miles, Bart, and Johnson, *Lock Up Your Daughters*, 42.

14. Miles, Bart, and Johnson, *Lock Up Your Daughters*, 9.

15. Miles, Bart, and Johnson, *Lock Up Your Daughters*, 28.

16. Quoted in Mark Steyn, *Broadway Babies Say Goodnight: Musicals Then and Now* (London: Faber and Faber, 1997), 174.

17. Samantha Ellis claims that it cost £15,000. Samatha Ellis, 'Lionel Bart's *Oliver!* June 1960', *The Guardian*, 18 June 2003, http://www.guardian.co.uk/stage/2003/jun/18/theatre.samanthaellis/print, accessed 12 June 2013. Kurt Gänzl reports that Donald Albery raised £14,000 to capitalize the venture including £3,000 of his own money. For more about the development of the first and subsequent productions see Kurt Gänzl, *The British Musical Theatre*, volume 2, *1915–1984* (London: Macmillan, 1986) 770–774 and 777–779.

18. Stanley Green, *Broadway Musicals: Show by Show* (Milwaukee: Applause Books, 2008), 201.

19. Gänzl, *British Musical Theatre*, 771.

20. Quoted in Steyn, *Broadway Babies*, 173.

21. Steyn, *Broadway Babies*, 173.

22. Lionel Bart, *Oliver!*, vocal score (by John Evans) (London: Lakecview Music Publishing Co., n.d.), 59.

23. Bart, *Oliver!*, vocal score, 60.

24. Bart, *Oliver!*, vocal score, 85.

25. Bart, *Oliver!*, vocal score, 87.

26. For an in-depth discussion of the changes the character of Fagin underwent in the musical adaptation see Sharon Aronofsky Weltman, '"Can a Fellow be a Villain All His Life?": *Oliver!*, Fagin, and Performing Jewishness.' *Nineteenth-Century Contexts* 33, no. 4 (September 2011): 375.

27. Weltman, '"Can a Fellow"', 377.

28. Bart, *Oliver!*, vocal score, 114, 116, 117, 119.

29. Gänzl, *British Musical Theatre*, 770.

30. Shulman, 'First Night—*Oliver!*'

31. Weltman, '"Can a Fellow"', 371 and 383 n. 1.

32. Weltman, '"Can a Fellow"', 373.

33. Boublil, quoted in Edward Behr, *The Complete Book of 'Les Misérables'* (New York: Acrcade, 1989), 50.

34. Lloyd Webber quoted in Miller, *Strike Up the Band*, 81.

35. Thanks for this and other information about the musical scores goes to Andrew Jarrett. Jarrett transcribed the score of *Blitz!* from the cast album for a production in Australia in 1984 when the score had been lost. Bart went to see the production and invited the young Jarrett back to the UK to work on National Youth Music Theatre productions of *Blitz!* and *Maggie May*. He worked with Bart on other productions until Bart's death, and is still involved with reviving material from the archive.

36. Anon., '*Blitz!*', *The Times*, 8 May 1962, Cuttings file, V&A Museum. Of course, the fact that Bart saw it that way doesn't mean that others didn't feel differently. Another story is told anecdotally that his collaborators—especially directors, musical directors, and arrangers—contributed enormously to the success of both *Oliver!* and *Blitz!* by structuring and adapting the bare materials (personal communications with the MD of the *Oliver!*

revival, Tony Britten, 10 July 2013). However, Andrew Jarrett also attests to Bart's ability to be very specific about what he wanted to hear, and his ability to work in great detail with orchestrators and arrangers.

37. Cecil Wilson, 'Blitz!', Daily Mail, 6 March 1962, Cuttings file, V&A Museum.
38. Anon., 'Blitz!', Daily Mail, 13 April 1962, Cuttings file, V&A Museum.
39. Jolyon Wimhurst, 'Blitz!', The Sphere, 19 May 1962, Cuttings file, V&A Museum.
40. Gänzl, British Musical Theatre, 797.
41. Gänzl, British Musical Theatre, 798.
42. Quoted in Gänzl, British Musical Theatre, 798.
43. Lionel Bart, 'Lionel Bart on an "Epic" Musical', Interview: From Our Special Correspondent, The Times, 22 March 1962, not paginated.
44. Bart, 'Lionel Bart on an "Epic" Musical'.
45. Bart, 'Lionel Bart on an "Epic" Musical'.
46. Anon., 'Blitz!', Punch, 16 May 1962, not paginated, Cuttings file, V&A Museum.
47. Norman Nadel, 'Blitz!', New York World Telegram and Sun, 27 May 1963, not paginated, Cuttings file, V&A Museum.
48. Nadel, 'Blitz!'.
49. Pat Wallace, 'Blitz!', Tatler, 23 May 1962, Cuttings file, V&A Museum.
50. Anon., 'Blitz!', Queen, 8 May 1962, Cuttings file, V&A Museum.
51. Vincent Mulchrone, 'Will Bart's Blitz! Go Off with a Bang?', Daily Mail, 3 May 1962, Cuttings file, V&A Museum.
52. Rexton S. Bunnett, 'Sleevenotes', Maggie May, original cast recording, Bayview Recording Company, RNBW020, 2002.
53. This was an early appearance by Barry Humphries who later created the character Dame Edna Everage. Even earlier Humphries had also appeared as the undertaker Mr Sowerbury in the original cast of Oliver!.
54. Anon., 'Maggie May', The Times, 23 September 1964, Cuttings file, V&A Museum.
55. Anon., 'Maggie May', The Stage, 27 August 1964, 4, Cuttings file, V&A Museum.
56. Lionel Bart, Maggie May Song Book (London: Apollo Music, 1964), 11–13.
57. Bart, Maggie May Song Book, 22.
58. Bart, Maggie May Song Book, 22–23.
59. Bart, Maggie May Song Book, 19.
60. Anon., 'Maggie May', The Stage, 27 August 1964.
61. Anon., 'Maggie May', The Stage, 27 August 1964.
62. See Gänzl, British Musical Theatre, 834.
63. Milton Shulman, 'First Night—Maggie May', Evening Standard, 23 September 1964, Cuttings file, V&A Museum.
64. Anon., 'Maggie May', The Times, 23 September 1964. A reported £178,500 advance on the film and Broadway rights of the musical had been received from United Arts and the Peter Sellers–John Bryan organization Brookfield Productions, but the Broadway transfer and the film never transpired. Anon., 'Maggie May', Daily Mail, 22 September 1964, Cuttings file, V&A Museum.
65. The Carry On films consisted of thirty-one low-budget comic films all made at Pinewood Studies that specialized in seaside postcard humour and sexual innuendo. The films featured a consistent group of actors including Barbara Windsor who starred in Fings and was also booked to star in Twang!!
66. Nadine Holdsworth, Joan Littlewood (London: Routledge, 2006), 39.

67. Holdsworth, *Joan Littlewood*, 39.
68. For more on the disastrous production see Gänzl, *British Musical Theatre*, 854–855.
69. Gänzl, *British Musical Theatre*, 855.
70. Transcribed from *Twang!!*, original London cast 1955, CD, Jay Productions Ltd, DDJAY7004, 2011.
71. The CD was originally recorded as a Studio Demo of the songs in 1967 but never released. In 2004 the demo was remastered and released.
72. Not on the demo CD, but available as a score in the archive.
73. Transcribed from *Twang!!*, original London cast 1955, CD.
74. This was a 1962 British film based on a play by Stephen Lewis, which had been directed at Stratford East by Joan Littlewood. The film, also directed by Littlewood, starred James Booth, Barbara Windsor, and Roy Kinnear. It was produced by Don Taylor.
75. Holdsworth, *Joan Littlewood*, 41.
76. The show dealt with the package tourism industry that was burgeoning at the time. A review of Bart's life in *The Independent* on the occasion of a new show about his life (*It's A Fine Life*), considers the songs 'unmemorable' and the show 'predictable'. Anon., 'Lionel Bart: Appetite for Destruction', *The Independent*, 31 August 2006, http://www.independent.co.uk/arts-entertainment//theatre-dance/features/lionel-bart-appetite-for-destruction-414120.html, accessed 6 July 2014.
77. It is interesting that they were working together again despite the disputes and recriminations over *Twang!!*. This may say something about Bart's need to work, or about Littlewood's regret for the position in which she had left him.
78. Gänzl, *British Musical Theatre*, 951.
79. Jane Shilling in *The Telegraph* records its inauguration as 1963 (Jane Shilling, 'Quasimodo, The King's Head, London: Review', *Daily Telegraph*, 27 March 2013, Cuttings file, V&A Museum), whereas Paul Taylor in *The Independent* suggests it was begun in 1965 (Paul Taylor, 'Quasimodo, King's Head, London', *The Independent*, 25 March 2013, http://www.independent.co.uk/arts-entertainment/theatre-dance/reviews/quasimodo-kings-head-london-8547799.html#, accessed 27 March 2013).
80. Taylor, 'Quasimodo'.
81. Shilling, 'Quasimodo'.
82. Edward Seckerson, 'Lionel Bart's Quasimodo, King's Head Theatre (Review), 27 March 2013, http://www.edwardseckerson.biz/reviews/lionel-barts-quasimodo-kings-head-theatre-review/, accessed 27 March 2013.
83. For a detailed discussion of these five shows, see Chapter 11 by Ben Francis.
84. At the time of writing Bart's estate was attempting to revive some of his lesser known works. Revivals had appeared of *Fings Ain't Wot They Used T'Be* (2014) and *Quasimodo* (2013) and an adaptation of *Twang!!* was written by Julian Woolford and Richard John and performed at the GSA (Guildford School of Acting) in 2013.

BIBLIOGRAPHY

Anon. 'Blitz!' *Daily Mail*, 13 April 1962. Cuttings file, Victoria and Albert (V&A) Museum.
Anon. 'Blitz!' *Punch*, 16 May 1962. Cuttings file, V&A Museum.
Anon. 'Blitz!' *Queen*, 8 May 1962. Cuttings file, V&A Museum.
Anon. 'Blitz!' *The Times*, 8 May 1962. Cuttings file, V&A Museum.

Anon. '*Maggie May.*' *Daily Mail*, 22 September 1964. Cuttings file, V&A Museum.

Anon. '*Maggie May* is Brassy, Vigorous and Tuneful!' *The Stage*, 24 September 1964, 14. Cuttings file, V&A Museum.

Anon '*Maggie May.*' *The Stage*, 27 August 1964. Cuttings file, V&A Museum.

Anon '*Maggie May.*' *The Times*, 23 September 1964. Cuttings file, V&A Museum.

Anon '*Oliver!*' *Independent London News*, 16 July 1960. Cuttings file, V&A Museum.

Anon. Review of *Oliver! The Tatler*, 27 July 1960. Cuttings file, V&A Museum.

Anon. 'Lionel Bart: Appetite for Destruction.' *The Independent*, 31 August 2006. http://www.independent.co.uk/arts-entertainment/theatre-dance/features/lionel-bart-appetite-for-destruction-414120.html, accessed 6 July 2014.

Bart, Lionel. 'Lionel Bart on an "Epic" Musical.' Interview: From Our Special Correspondent.' *The Times*, 22 March 1962, not paginated.

Bart, Lionel. *Maggie May Song Book*. London: Apollo Music, 1964.

Bart, Lionel. *Oliver!* Vocal Score (by John Evans). London: Lakeview Music Publishing Co., n.d.

Behr, Edward. *The Complete Book of 'Les Misérables'*. New York: Arcade, 1989.

Blitz! Original London Cast Album, 1962. CD. EMI Records Limited, 00946 311282 2 6, 2005.

Britten, Tony. Personal communication with the author. 10 July 2013.

Bunnett, Rexton S. 'Sleevenotes.' *Maggie May*. Original Cast Recording. Bayview Recording Company: RNBW020, 2002.

Ellis, Samantha. 'Lionel Bart's *Oliver!* June 1960.' *The Guardian*, 18 June 2003. http://www.guardian.co.uk/stage/2003/jun/18/theatre.samanthaellis/print, accessed 12 June 2013.

Fings Ain't Wot They Used T'Be. Original London Cast Recording, 1959. CD. Pickwick Group Limited, Hallmark 710032, 2011.

Gänzl, Kurt. *The British Musical Theatre*. Volume 2, *1915–1984*. London: Macmillan, 1986.

The Genius of Lionel Bart. CD. Sepia Records, SEPIA 1201, 2012.

Green, Stanley. *Broadway Musicals: Show by Show*. Milwaukee: Applause Books, 2008.

Holdsworth, Nadine. *Joan Littlewood*. London: Routledge, 2006.

La Strada. A Selection of Songs from the Musical. Bayview Recording Company, RNBW028, 2004.

Littlewood, Joan. *Joan's Book: Joan Littlewood's Peculiar History as She Tells It*. London: Methuen, 1994.

Lock Up Your Daughters. Original Cast Recording, 1959. CD. Pickwick Group Limited, Hallmark 710532, 2011.

Maggie May. Original Cast Recording, 1964. Bayview Recording Company, RNBW020, 2002.

Miles, Bernard, Lionel Bart, and Laurie Johnson. *Lock Up Your Daughters: A Musical Play*. London: Samuel French, 1967.

Miller, Scott. *Strike Up the Band: A New History of Musical Theatre*. Portsmouth, NH: Heinemann, 2007.

Mulchrone, Vincent. 'Will Bart's *Blitz!* Go Off with a Bang?' *Daily Mail*, 3 May 1962. Cuttings file, V&A Museum.

Nadel, Norman. '*Blitz!*' *New York World Telegram and Sun*, 27 May 1963. Cuttings file, V&A Museum.

Oliver! An Original Cast Recording, 1960. CD. Decca Recording Company Limited, DERAM 820590-2, 1989.

Seckerson, Edward. 'Lionel Bart's *Quasimodo*, Kings Head Theatre (Review).' http://www.edwardseckerson.biz/reviews/lionel-barts-quasimodo-kings-head-theatre-review/, accessed 27 March 2013.

Shilling, Jane. '*Quasimodo*, The King's Head, London: Review.' *Daily Telegraph*, 27 March 2013. Cuttings file, V&A Museum.

Shulman, Milton. 'First Night—*Maggie May*.' *Evening Standard*, 23 September 1964. Cuttings file, V&A Museum.

Shulman, Milton. 'Not One for the Matinee Set . . .' *Evening Standard*, 12 February 1960. Cuttings file, V&A Museum.

Snelson, John. ' "We Said We Wouldn't Look Back": British Musical Theatre, 1935–1960.' In *The Cambridge Companion to the Musical*. 2nd ed., edited by William A. Everett and Paul R. Laird, 127–146. Cambridge: Cambridge University Press, 2008.

Steyn, Mark. *Broadway Babies Say Goodnight: Musicals Then and Now*. London: Faber and Faber, 1997.

Taylor, Paul. '*Quasimodo*, King's Head, London.' *The Independent*, 25 March 2013. http://www.independent.co.uk/arts-entertainment/theatre-dance/reviews/quasimodo-kings-head-london-8547799.html#, accessed 27 March 2013.

Twang!! Original London Cast, 1965. Jay Productions Ltd, DDJAY7004, 2011.

Wallace, Pat. '*Blitz!*' *Tatler*, 23 May 1962. Cuttings file, V&A Museum.

Weltman, Sharon Aronofsky. ' "Can a Fellow Be a Villain All His Life?": *Oliver!*, Fagin, and Performing Jewishness.' *Nineteenth-Century Contexts* 33, no. 4 (September 2011): 371–388.

Wilson, Cecil '*Blitz!*' *Daily Mail*, 6 March 1962. Cuttings file, V&A Museum.

Wimhurst, Jolyon. '*Blitz!*' *The Sphere*, 19 May 1962. Cuttings file, V&A Museum.

CHAPTER 21

TIM RICE

The Pop Star Scenario

OLAF JUBIN

RIGHTLY or wrongly, the general public usually associates works of music theatre with their composer: it is Giuseppe Verdi's *Otello* (1887), Frank Lehár's *The Merry Widow* (1905), and Benjamin Britten's *Peter Grimes* (1945). In spite of the general consensus that musicals are among the most collaborative of art forms,[1] this tendency is almost as pronounced when it comes to Broadway or West End shows, and so *West Side Story* (1957) is mainly attributed to Leonard Bernstein just as *The Phantom of the Opera* (1986) is commonly identified as a piece by Andrew Lloyd Webber.[2] This in turn has consequences not just for the reputation of whoever provides the words to the songs of a production, but also for the show's marketing. As David Benedict put it pithily in his review of *From Here to Eternity* (2013), a musical that was advertised as the latest work by Tim Rice, the man who wrote the lyrics: 'When was the last time anyone booked a ticket on the basis of a lyricist?'[3]

This implies that, at least in the opinion of the audience, the composer of a show shapes it to a larger degree than its lyricist, whose authorial voice and/or trademarks may be more difficult to detect. Is it then possible to describe what makes a musical 'typical' of a particular wordsmith? This question is especially intriguing with regard to the chequered career of the English writer Tim Rice, in certain respects the most successful British lyricist in the history of musical theatre: he has won thirteen Ivor Novello Awards, four Tony Awards, three Academy Awards. and one Grammy Award.[4] In 1999 he was inducted into the Songwriters Hall of Fame and in the following year, Rice had four shows running simultaneously on Broadway,[5] something that no other lyricist has ever achieved.

Tim Rice has been in the public eye for more than four decades and throughout his career has experienced the full range of critical and audience responses, achieving early acclaim and affluence, then suffering middle-aged disappointments and staging spectacular comebacks; his oeuvre includes classics of musical theatre (*Jesus Christ Superstar*, 1970;[6] *Evita*, 1976), cult shows (*Chess*, 1984), financial flops (*Blondel*, 1983;

From Here to Eternity, 2013), musicals that were never fully staged (*Tycoon*, 1992; *King David*, 1997), musicals that were professionally produced all over the world, but not once in his home country (*Aida*, 1999), and commercial hits that were widely panned by the critics (*Heathcliff*, 1997). One of his shows (*The Lion King*, 1997) is now the highest-grossing stage entertainment of all time with worldwide revenue of more than $6.2 billion/£4,03 billion.[7]

The Broadway musical *The Lion King* is of course the theatrical version of the Disney animated cartoon musical of the same name. Released in 1994, it remains one of the most lucrative family movies ever made, with global box-office receipts of $987.5 million.[8] Other forays of the lyricist into the same film genre, like *The Nutcracker in 3D* (2010) or *Jock* (2011),[9] however, proved far less effective, with the former earning a meagre $195,459 in North America on a budget of $90 million,[10] and the latter not even being released in cinemas in most countries (including the US, UK, and the rest of Western Europe, where the film is only available on DVD).[11]

What exactly is a 'Tim Rice musical', and does it include more than just a recognizable 'turn of phrase'? The wide range of his successes and failures and the extreme eclecticism of source material that Rice has used—the Bible, biographies, French musicals, classic novels, operas, original stories—as well as the numerous forms of presentation through which he has chosen to acquaint the public with his work—concept recordings, concert stagings, animated cartoon musicals, stage musicals—make it difficult to discern styles, themes, and topics that are unmistakably his own.

It is customary to distinguish between the Richard Rodgers of Rodgers and Hart and the Richard Rodgers of Rodgers and Hammerstein, as well as between the Kurt Weill of the Weimar Republic (and frequent collaborator of Bertolt Brecht) and the American Kurt Weill, the man who single-handedly tried to change the direction in which the Broadway musical was heading. These distinctions reflect the fact that certain artists adapt their style of writing to their collaborators. As a rule of thumb, though, this already seems questionable when it comes to certain *composers* of musical theatre— Jerome Kern is always recognizable by his strong musical signature, and it is never difficult to identify a song as having been written by Alan Menken. Such distinctions seem especially problematic when it comes to lyricists: is there really that much difference between Oscar Hammerstein II's lyrics for *Show Boat* (1927) and those for *South Pacific* (1949)? Aren't Comden and Green always recognizably Comden and Green, regardless of whether the melodies they set to words are by Leonard Bernstein, Jule Styne, or Cy Coleman?[12]

Let us assume for a moment that Tim Rice's oeuvre can best be subdivided according to his collaborators, which as an organizing principle suggests that his style of lyric writing changes depending on whether he works with Andrew Lloyd Webber, Elton John, Alan Menken, Stephen Oliver, Benny Andersson and Björn Ulvaeus, Michel Berger, John Farrar, or Stuart Brayson. But even a cursory analysis of Tim Rice's work proves that a categorization based on his composers is too limiting when trying to distil the style of the English lyricist, as there clearly are themes that recur throughout Rice's career, regardless of who he is working with.

Table 21.1 The Works of Tim Rice

Year	Work	First Presentation	Composer	Source Material
1965	*The Likes of Us*	concert staging	Andrew Lloyd Webber	original story
1968	*Joseph and the Amazing Technicolor Dreamcoat*	school cantata	Andrew Lloyd Webber	the Bible (Book of Genesis)
1970	*Jesus Christ Superstar*	concept recording	Andrew Lloyd Webber	the Bible (the Four Gospels); Fulton J. Sheen's *The Life of Christ* (1958)
1973	*Jacob's Journey*	one-act stage musical	Andrew Lloyd Webber	the Bible (Book of Genesis)
1976	*Evita*	concept recording	Andrew Lloyd Webber	the life of Eva Perón (1919–52); Frank Owen's *Perón: His Rise and Fall* (1957); and Richard Bourne's *Political Leaders of Latin America* (1969)
1981	*1984*	concept recording	Rick Wakeman	George Orwell's *Nineteen Eighty-Four* (1949)
1983	*Blondel*	stage musical	Stephen Oliver	original story
1984	*Chess*	concept recording	Benny Andersson and Björn Ulvaeus	original story
1986	*Cricket*	one-act stage musical	Andrew Lloyd Webber	original story
1992	*Tycoon*	concept recording	Michel Berger	original story; English translation of the French musical *Starmania* (1978; French lyrics by Luc Plamondon)
1992	*Aladdin* (additional lyrics by Howard Ashman)	animated cartoon musical	Alan Menken	freely adapted classic fairy tale
1994	*Beauty and the Beast* (additional lyrics by Howard Ashman)	stage musical	Alan Menken	freely adapted classic fairy tale; stage version of the 1991 film
1994	*The Lion King*	animated cartoon musical	Elton John	original story very loosely based on Shakespeare's *Hamlet* (c.1601)
1995	*Heathcliff*	concept recording	John Farrar	Emily Brontë's *Wuthering Heights* (1847)
1997	*King David*	concert staging	Alan Menken	the Bible (Book of Samuel)

(*continued*)

Table 21.1 Continued

Year	Work	First Presentation	Composer	Source Material
1998	*Aida*	concept recording	Elton John	Giuseppe Verdi's opera (1871)
2000	*The Road to El Dorado*	animated cartoon musical	Elton John	original story
2010	*The Nutcracker in 3-D*	live action film musical in 3D	Pyotr Tchaikovsky	Pyotr Tchaikovsky's ballet (1892)
2010	*The Wizard of Oz* (additional songs)	stage musical	Andrew Lloyd Webber	stage version of the 1939 film
2011	*Jock—the Hero Dog*	animated cartoon musical in 3D	Johnny Clegg, Craig Hinds, Alan Menken, and others	Percy Fitzpatrick's *Jock of the Bushveld* (1907)
2013	*From Here to Eternity*	stage musical	Stuart Brayson	James Jones's 1951 novel in its uncensored, restored version of 2011.

FINDING HIS OWN STYLE

Maybe one can get a clearer sense of the 'Rice mode of expression' by exploring how his craft developed throughout his formative years. His very first finished score for *The Likes of Us* (1965) shows a Tim Rice (and Andrew Lloyd Webber) trying very hard to follow in the footsteps of Lionel Bart's *Oliver!*, with a story about philanthropist Dr Thomas Barnardo, the nineteenth-century founder of homes for destitute children, a more comfortable fit for the composer than the lyricist. As Rice himself concurs: 'The music was definitely more sophisticated than the words, although in some of the humorous numbers I held my own.'[13]

The lyricist does indeed do nicely with some of the comic songs like 'Lion-Hearted Land' and especially 'Going, Going, Gone'—the first number Rice and Lloyd Webber ever wrote together—which opens with the line 'Here I have a lovely parrot, sound in wind and limb' and later praises the parrot as 'a healthy bird with plumage fine and rare | Fluent in five languages and never known to swear.'[14]

But the more earnest songs are often marred by anachronistic colloquialisms ('If you stagnate in semi-slumber | You will never make your mark | No slacker has ever succeeded | Since the days of Noah's Ark';[15] 'I'll fall in love a hundred times | I shall refuse to believe in the blues today'[16]) that seem at odds with the sentimental approach to the subject matter as evidenced by the title song, which is performed by a chorus of homeless 'rooftop children'.[17] The love songs never move beyond non-specific clichés such as 'Though I feel today | Love is here to stay | Is this just a dream in my mind?'.[18]

TIM RICE: THE POP STAR SCENARIO   511

Rice seems more at home with the all-for-fun *Joseph and the Amazing Technicolor Dreamcoat* (1968); writing for schoolchildren already excited by the prospect of the end of term, Rice found a natural outlet for his droll irreverence. Whether he is expressing the early envy of the title character's brothers ('Being told we're also-rans | Doesn't make us Joseph fans'[19]) or their later struggle for survival ('No one comes to dinner now | We'd only eat them anyhow'[20]), his use of words is pitched perfectly at the target audience—these witticisms seem to have been thought out by a very clever youngster with a love for words which may explain why it is one of the most popular of all musicals among children between the ages of 8 and 12 who can easily relate to the language in the piece, not least because of the deliberately anachronistic relationship between the lyrics and subject matter.

Kurt Gänzl is wrong in claiming that Rice was the first lyricist to use sarcasm and colloquial phrases in musical theatre,[21] but Rice *was* the first to use these stylistic tools in musicals based on the Bible. Since then, his cheeky and effervescent, sometimes flippant turn of phrase has become something of a trademark—not for nothing does Rice claim the most widely recognized couplet he ever wrote is 'Prove to me that you're no fool | Walk across my swimming pool'[22] from 'The King Herod's Song' in *Jesus Christ Superstar*.[23] This deliberately ahistorical, anachronistic, and disrespectful treatment of subject matter and character is especially prominent in the youthful *Joseph* and no doubt was one of the reasons why the Disney company in the early 1990s decided to ask Rice to work on their animated cartoon musicals *Aladdin* and *The Lion King*, as they have a similar postmodern, knowing, and hip sensibility.

This humorous approach is probably at its best in *Blondel* (1983), where the title character, a medieval minstrel, asserts that he nearly had a hit with 'Send in the Jesters'.[24] Yet a similar attitude is mainly or completely absent from *Evita, Chess, Tycoon*, or *Heathcliff*, only to resurface in spurts in *Aida*, where an orderly is advised: 'Put 5,000 slaves on stand-by.'[25] In the first two of these shows it is replaced with a razor-sharp satirical indictment of political manoeuvres that will only bring bitterness and resentment.

That his lyrics in general are characterized less by dense image clusters or startling metaphors and more by ingenious twists of colloquial speech, is probably one of the reasons why Rice is often underestimated as an artist, leaving listeners with the mistaken impression that anybody could have come up with these lines. US reviewers and authors in particular are frequently acerbic in their evaluation of his work: *Variety*'s reviewer of the New York production of *Chess* called Rice's lyrics 'flat, unadorned by imagery, pedestrian,'[26] while Denny Martin Flinn denigrates his 'vapid pop lyrics' for *Evita* as 'virtually illiterate'.[27]

Another danger of using vernacular expressions is that they may not just be *of* the moment, but also merely *for* that particular moment, i.e. that they do not age well. Tim Rice has escaped this problem throughout most of his career, although there is the odd exception such as '"What's the Buzz", a phrase I don't think I invented, but if I did I wish I hadn't. While I maintain that most of the words in *Superstar* have not dated a great deal, it's hard to deny that "What's the Buzz" is hardly common linguistic currency these days, it if ever was.'[28]

In addition, comments like 'I have never been accused of allowing my work to dominate my life'[29] seem to hint at a fairly casual or even lackadaisical approach to the task of lyric writing[30] and tend to obfuscate the hard work and ingenuity observable in Rice's best songs. As media commentators pointed out repeatedly,[31] there were thirteen years between the Broadway premiere of *Aida* (2000) and the West End production of the next new Tim Rice musical *From Here to Eternity* (2013). While this does not suggest an artist driven by the desire to work incessantly, the long time-lapse between (theatre) projects[32] is also the result of the fear that any new collaboration, especially when it results in a financial flop (as was the case with *From Here to Eternity*), may have a negative impact on whatever standing one has earned in the theatrical community and the public eye, or, in Rice's own words, 'As you go on you get a bit worried about reputation.'[33]

It may have taken several years before Rice found a style of lyric writing that would suit him, but once he had, he soon started raising his own stakes with *Jesus Christ Superstar* and *Evita*. One can feel the fun Rice had writing *Blondel*, and the hard work he put into *Chess*—which contains many of his best lyrics such as 'Where I Want to Be', 'Nobody's Side', 'Pity the Child', and 'Someone Else's Story'—is obvious, while *From Here to Eternity*, based on James Jones's bestselling novel, includes some of the most ingenious examples of Rice writing in character.

Rendering Character in Song

Jones's wartime epic, first published in 1951 and restored to its uncensored original form in 2011, representing in vivid detail army life in the months leading up to the attack on Pearl Harbor on 7 December 1941, may at first sight have seemed a rather unusual choice of source material for the lyricist. Yet its sharply delineated characters and clear-eyed view of the frustrating day-to-day lives of soldiers who have enlisted for all sorts of reasons—patriotism not being among them—offered Rice and his collaborators, Bill Oakes (libretto) and Stuart Brayson (music), the chance to create something increasingly rare in this day and age: a musical for adults.

Tackling subjects like the abuse of power, adultery, prostitution, homosexuality, murder, and death, the show, which opened in the West End on 23 October 2013, seasons its more dramatic moments with scenes and songs suffused with black humour—a more fitting modification of Rice's usual jokiness—exposing the fallibility of both individuals and institutions. In 'I Love the Army', Private Angelo Maggio, incarcerated for insubordination and then bullied and beaten up by the prison warden, takes to task the three value systems that are supposed to sustain him—the army, his country, and religion—only to arrive at the sobering realization that they have all failed him. The other soldiers, each and every one of whom signed up to the army for life, let us know that contrary to their unrealistic expectations they have 'screwed more boilerplates than hookers'.[34] With a soldier's life therefore definitely not as exciting as they assumed it would be and no way out because 'it's getting far too dark to find the door', the privates can only resort to sarcasm about their profession: 'if this is all they muster | They can give it back to Custer'.[35]

Rice's favourite number in the score is 'Ain't Where I Wanna Be Blues' which was written in less than an hour[36] and features the two male protagonists, both totally drunk yet cognizant that they are wailing in self-pity, complaining to each other about their rotten lives. The title is reminiscent of the 'God-Why-Don't-You-Love-Me Blues' from Stephen Sondheim's 1971 musical *Follies*, and a comparison between the two songs shows a telling difference in the way that Sondheim and Rice typically portray their characters: whereas the energetic vaudeville shtick of the *Follies* number barely manages to mask the pain beneath the hyperactive surface, the duet between Warden and Prewitt shows the men reacting to their predicament more with incredulity and fatalism (i.e. with cynicism) than with blank despair.

A Passion for Pop and Rock

What rankles with many observers in the field of musical theatre is that the English lyricist wilfully ignores several of the conventions so carefully adhered to by Broadway, for which there is a simple explanation: Tim Rice's major passion has always been pop music,[37] not the stage or film musical.[38] Tellingly, his creative influences are not necessarily found among the giants of American (or British) musical theatre—he revealed in a 2003 interview that in spite of his adoration for certain artists who have written for the stage like Alan Jay Lerner[39] and revue performer Michael Flanders,[40] his favourite songsmiths are Jerry Leiber, Bob Dylan, and Paul Simon, stating: 'In the last 40 years the lyricists I admired were in the record field/rock field.'[41]

This ardour for anything relating to pop music and the charts not only led Rice to co-edit the immensely successful *Guinness Book of British Hit Singles*—an idea that resulted in thirty bestselling publications[42]—but may also account for his lack of interest in seeing musicals on stage when he was growing up—although he loved *listening* to cast recordings and soundtracks.[43] Moreover, it explains his marked preference for concept recordings—seven of his works were first introduced to the public via albums or CDs—and although the very idea of a concept recording may seem utterly anachronistic in the era of iTunes and YouTube, he still obviously prefers the more easily controllable environment of a recording studio to the imponderables of the musical theatre stage, conceding that he would love to cut a studio album of *From Here to Eternity* (which is only available as a live recording).[44]

Then there is the fact that most of his major collaborators, such as Elton John, Rick Wakeman, Benny Andersson and Björn Ulvaeus, John Farrar, Michel Berger, and Stuart Brayson, came to prominence (and continue to work) in the area of international rock and pop.[45] This in turn is closely connected to his insistence that rock music has a place on the Broadway (and West End) stage, partly because rock has become increasingly theatrical,[46] wryly advising those who complain about the level of amplification shows with this kind of music often utilize: 'If it's too loud, you're too old.'[47]

But with the stance that, for him, there is no difference between show tunes and regular pop music,[48] and even with the score for his latest musical *From Here to Eternity* striving for a 'rock sort of feel'[49] albeit set in 1941, he places himself between two stools. For lovers of traditional musicals (including many an older theatre reviewer) who prefer what has become known as 'show music', he imports a sound-scape that they consider unsuitable for proper storytelling whereas for rock fans, musicals aiming for commercial reasons at a predominantly white and middle-class audience, lack the authenticity and raw power and thus the rebelliousness of true rock 'n' roll. As a consequence, he isn't taken seriously by members of either constituency, although his acceptance by the former camp seems to increase as time goes on as theatre-goers nowadays consist more and more of people who grew up with rock and pop.

RICE'S ATTITUDE TO BROADWAY CONVENTIONS OF LYRIC WRITING

As a result, Rice has often been criticized, sometimes unjustly, for not adhering to what are generally regarded as the basic rules of lyric writing: witness the many examples of unclean rhymes—such as 'beginning/dimming',[50] 'enough/stuffed' and 'magazines/been',[51] 'store/ensure',[52] 'pretending/endings',[53] or 'Horus/for us'[54]— throughout his career, although the lyricist nowadays professes to being a 'purist' about rhyming who 'shudder[s]' at some of the word choices in his early songs.[55] Other conventions that Rice does not always follow are writing in character and in period, or providing lyrics that are perfectly geared towards the target audience and are in essence simple.

It seems safe to assume that at the beginning of his career Tim Rice was simply oblivious to the principles of lyric writing that, for instance, Stephen Sondheim so carefully adheres to[56]—and it also seems logical to conclude that he is not thoroughly invested in some of the Broadway 'rules' for songwriting in musical theatre, partly because his collaborators may not always have (had) the same concerns. Stuart Brayson, the composer of *From Here to Eternity*, whose background is in rock 'n' roll, questioned Rice's endeavours at providing rhymes at certain moments, citing many famous rock stars (like David Bowie) who found both critical acclaim and financial success without that kind of stylistic device.[57] Furthermore the lyricist's observation that 'pure rhymes and rock are almost mutually exclusive',[58] throws a telling light on those instances of Rice's work that do feature unclean rhymes.

One can definitely find examples where Rice's choice of words might be considered inappropriate for the character singing: would a 16-year-old, even one wise beyond her years, really use the phrase 'that I'm immune to gloom'[59] as Juan Perón's unnamed mistress does in 'Another Suitcase in Another Hall'?[60] The Nubian princess Aida on the other hand concurs in 'Elaborate Lives': 'Too many choices tear us apart',[61] which is rather puzzling considering that she is a slave in captivity.

Still, the mistake of writing out of character can happen to the best of lyric writers, such as Sondheim—witness Swedish maid Petra in *A Little Night Music* dreaming of marrying the Prince of Wales in her solo 'The Miller's Son'. It should also be pointed out that Tim Rice is English and thus comes out of a completely different tradition of songwriting. This likewise might help to explain why his definition of craft doesn't necessarily conform to the Broadway style of lyric writing as defined by Lehman Engel who initiated (and for many years ran) the BMI workshop.

That Tim Rice has a different understanding of how lyrics should be crafted also becomes obvious when comparing his work for Disney and Alan Menken with the lyrics of Howard Ashman, whom he was called in to replace. Ashman had the unique talent of writing childlike lyrics without alienating adults; his phrases are witty and appropriate without resorting to words that children might not understand—like the best of Broadway lyricists, he never wrote above the heads of his target audience. Not so Tim Rice: 'One Jump Ahead' (from *Aladdin*, 1992), for instance, contains the line 'Next time, gonna use a Nom de Plume'.[62] Rice explains his reasoning as follows:

> When I included words and phrases such as 'quid pro quo' [*The Lion King*] and 'fratricide' [*Joseph*] in those of my own efforts that were written primarily for young children,[63] I never worried about whether or not they would understand every syllable at the time. As long as they enjoyed the whole, the extra fun of enjoying some of the details could easily be postponed for a while.[64]

Rice bowed out of writing the lyrics for the P. G. Wodehouse adaptation *Jeeves* (1975)—later to be called *By Jeeves* (1997)—because he felt he would not be able to do justice to the source material.[65] Thus it is surprising that he agreed to work on *Heathcliff*, a project initiated by its painfully miscast star, Cliff Richard. The lyricist always was a rather peculiar choice to transform Emily Brontë's nineteenth-century Romantic classic *Wuthering Heights* into lyrics—the novel's vibrant, passionate characters and the brooding, Gothic atmosphere seem miles away from Rice's defiantly ironic, self-aware, quick-witted sensibility. Nothing in his work prior to *Heathcliff* suggested that he would find a way of creating an idiom that could vividly and convincingly render the Yorkshire moors and their inhabitants, and he didn't. *Heathcliff* is a good example of the variable quality of Rice's output[66] containing his least interesting lyrics, which often—as in 'Mrs Edgar Linton'—are inappropriate for both the characters and the period.[67]

This failure to stay true to the source material and to faithfully transpose the language of the original into the lyrics of an adaptation—a task so brilliantly achieved by Alan

Jay Lerner in *My Fair Lady*, who mimicked George Bernard Shaw to a degree that it is sometimes hard to tell who came up with what—might be considered a severe short-coming with respect to one of the major talents expected of a lyric writer. It must none-theless be recognized that Rice would later turn out to be more than equal to the task of rendering perfectly in song the milieu and characters of James Jones's *From Here to Eternity*.

Occasionally, Rice also has disregarded Stephen Sondheim's dictum that lyrics should be 'underwritten',[68] at times at his own peril. Realizing that 'The Lady's Got Potential' may be overly ambitious in its attempt to cover multiple topics at once—the state of Argentinian politics and Juan Perón's position within them, Che's scheme to become rich by inventing an insecticide, and Eva Duarte's advances towards her future husband—Rice contends that '[m]uch of these messages would pass a listener by in one hearing, but if followed with the lyric sheet, they are not too incomprehensible'.[69] While this may work for a concept recording as buyers can be assumed to listen to the songs while at the same time perusing the lyrics booklet, it potentially poses a grave prob-lem for any stage presentation, which may explain why director Harold Prince cut 'The Lady's Got Potential' when he adapted *Evita* for the theatre.

Rice's confidence that audiences will also read what they hear reduces one of the most original conceits in *Blondel* where at one point during 'Ministry of Feudal Affairs' the first letters of each line form the name Margaret Thatcher[70] to an in-joke, doomed to go unnoticed by anyone not familiar with the printed libretto. Although any show can sur-vive if theatre-goers fail to grasp one particular witticism, no musical will leave an audi-ence satisfied when they cannot understand what is going on, which is the case with one of the last numbers in *Chess*: the lyrics of 'Endgame' are so convoluted that even prior knowledge of the words does not prevent confusion as to what exactly is happening in this very complicated scene.[71]

Rice has admitted that he had hoped to improve certain lyrics in *Jesus Christ Superstar* and *Evita* which displeased him and which were written under enormous time pressure while preparing the original concept recording in time for a stage production. The most famous example of these last-minute glitches is probably the non sequitur in 'Don't Cry for Me, Argentina', where the song title is followed by the line 'The truth is I never left you'.[72] But this and other songs that contained problematic lyrics had already become so popular when the musicals were finally staged that fans didn't want him to change the lines he considered problematic,[73] and so in the case of *Evita*'s most famous song he never did. When in 1996 Rice actually did adjust certain expressions and rhymes for Gale Edwards' London revival of *Jesus Christ Superstar*, he was criticized by several enthusiasts for rendering flavourless what had been unique.[74]

Putting audience pleasure above artistic considerations is certainly not unknown in musical theatre, yet Rice, although acutely aware of them,[75] seems to be far less bothered by these lapses of craftsmanship than for instance Stephen Sondheim, who throughout his career has chastised himself publicly for some of his lyrics in *West Side Story*, specifi-cally 'I Feel Pretty', which he considers substandard as they misrepresent the character, thereby violating his highly developed sense of professional standards.[76]

RICE'S THEMES

The response of the general public to outstanding talent

When contemplating the whole corpus of Rice's work several themes emerge; these run through more or less all of the shows he initiated or conceived, and sometimes find their way into the films and stage musicals he was commissioned to write. First and foremost among them is the plight of individuals who stand out from the crowd because of their talent and their treatment at the hands of the people who admire them—or tear them down. I wish to call this the 'pop star scenario', even though Rice's exploration of the topic is rarely limited to the field of music, with the exception of *Blondel*, in which the title character and his trio of back-up singers 'are revealed as rock stars'[77] in the last scene.

It is helpful in this regard to remember that Rice himself tried to make it in the music business as a *performer* before settling for a career as lyricist. On 8 July 2014, the writer was celebrated with a gala concert 'Tim Rice: A Life in Song' at London's Royal Festival Hall, where in conversation with Michael Grade he once again admitted that his original

FIGURE 21.1 A medieval rock star and his backing group: Paul Nicholas as the title character in *Blondel* (1983) with Christine Cartwright, Jan Lloyd, and Rachel Izen (the Blondettes) at the Old Vic Theatre, 1983.

Photograph by Conrad Blakemore. Courtesy of ArenaPal.

ambition was to become a teenage pop idol. This confession also can be found at the beginning of his 1999 autobiography:

> I wanted to be a pop star, for all the healthy reasons—women, money and fame. It seemed to me that plenty of other blokes around my age (twenty) and not overburdened with talent were making it and I wished to be one of their number.[78]

This ambition, not entirely abandoned even much later in his life,[79] may never have been achieved, but Rice acknowledges that he nonetheless experienced certain aspects of a rock star's life if on a less exalted scale, from the opportunities for casual sex[80] and the preferential treatment as a celebrity[81] to the inconstancy of the public's acclaim and the self-doubt of those who have become successful very quickly.

The pop star scenario invariably includes such aspects as the unpredictable behaviour of crowds, the discrepancy between public image and private self and the danger that the latter will be consumed by the former, the cost of personal ambition, as well as the dissatisfaction and potential downfall that often follow early success. These elements play an important role in all of the shows that Rice initiated and/or co-conceived, such as *Joseph*, *Jesus Christ Superstar*, *Evita*, *Blondel*, *Chess*—and, to a lesser degree, *King David* and *Aida*.

Rice's lifelong preoccupation with the rock star phenomenon, his 'irresistible fascination with pop stars',[82] becomes evident as early as *Joseph*, where the ability to decipher dreams leads not just out of prison but to great personal wealth and influence. As the Narrator points out, '[a] man who can interpret | Could go far—could become a star | Could be famous | Could be a big success'.[83] When moving from the boy wonder of the Old Testament to the main character of the New Testament, and borrowing freely from Andy Warhol and his entourage, Tim Rice came up with a catchy term that signalled the approach he would take when telling the story of the last seven days of the Son of God. *Jesus Christ Superstar* already referred in its very title to the pop star scenario, and throughout the musical, Jesus is variously described as 'cool', 'top of the poll', as a person whose 'glamour increases' and who has given rise to 'Jesusmania'.[84] Accordingly, King Herod treats Jesus like the latest C-list celebrity who tries to impinge on his own genuine royal status.

The 15-year-old Eva, so keen to provide 'a little touch of star quality', comes to Buenos Aires to seek fame, fortune, and political influence, equating Argentina's pulsating capital with the centre of Western show business, New York: 'I wanna be a part of B.A. | Buenos Aires—Big Apple'.[85] Blondel, the 'talented troubadour'[86] with his own back-up group, searching for his true king, Richard, all over Europe is pursued by an assassin who has been hired to kill the monarch before he has a chance to return to England, an assignment that the murderer describes as 'the gig to make me a star'.[87] Even chess champion Freddie Trumper displays 'typical' rock star behaviour, throwing tantrums, making unreasonable demands and sulking when he does not get his way.

Talent may be the prerequisite to fame, but it is not enough. One cannot be a 'spiritual leader' on one's own: it takes someone (often creative) to lead the way and someone to follow, which is why a rock star is nothing without his/her audience. The phenomenon of people adoring someone they don't know personally is especially bizarre from an outsider's perspective. Rice had the opportunity to observe the perplexing behaviour of fanatical admirers on several occasions: 'One of the strangest feelings I know is to be in the presence of someone famous, but not to you. The reaction of fans to the celebrity whom you don't know from Adam seems beyond all comprehension and logic.'[88]

But the masses are unreliable and adoration easily can turn to apathy, disdain, or violent rejection: the same people who cheer Jesus when he arrives in Jerusalem are the ones who later demand his crucifixion. It is Juan Perón, military man turned dictator who points out to his wife Eva: 'The people belong to no one | They are fickle, can be manipulated | Controllable, changeable . . .'[89] In 'Westminster Abbey' from *Blondel*, the crowds who earlier celebrated Prince John with shouts of 'You're a star! That's what you are', shortly afterwards try to convince Richard the Lionheart: 'No, no you do us wrong | We were with you all along.' Richard, however, isn't fooled, sarcastically addressing his subjects as 'my fickle friends'.[90] As *Jesus Christ Superstar* exposes, there is also often an element of calculation in the people's adoration, the hope of receiving a reward: 'Christ you know I love you | Did you see I waved? | I believe in you and God | So tell me that I'm saved.'[91]

In the 1980s Rice would understand an additional consequence of having several hit songs and hit musicals with respect to the behaviour of regular fans, which is that many people, often self-designated 'experts', wish to get involved in your projects, undoubtedly hoping to participate in 'the next big thing', but ultimately subverting and thereby sabotaging the initial impulses and original ideas.[92] The reporters in *Chess* are accused of basking in the 'reflected glory'[93] of world champion Freddie Trumper, and his rival for the title, Anatoly Sergievsky, is warned to beware of the crowds of chess fans and fanatics: 'Your deeds inflame them | Drive them wild, but then | Who wants to tame them? | If they want a part of you | Who'd really blame them?'[94] Finally, in 'The Caravan Moves On' from *King David*, we learn that '[e]ven the best slip from favour'.[95] Rice himself realized early on in his career how quickly media praise can turn to public vilification, especially when one's work brings one both prominence and prosperity: as soon as the double album of *Jesus Christ Superstar* topped the Billboard charts in the United States, reviews of and reports on the recording and its creators changed from magnanimous and appreciative to harshly pejorative.[96] The same happened once *Evita* started to climb up the British charts in 1976.[97]

In a Tim Rice musical, the masses always rapaciously move in on the star because they hope for glory and admiration through association, a notion that is brusquely rejected by the Russian in *Chess*. When his second Molokov reminds him that 'winning or losing reflects on us all', Anatoly states clearly: '*I* win—no one else does | And *I* take the rap if I lose . . .'[98] But the adoring fans should be careful for what they wish for: Evita's invitation 'So share my glory | So share my coffin . . .'[99] points to the fact that even second-hand renown comes at a price as fame and (spiritual?) death are closely linked or—at least in this case—are one and the same.

The dangers of having a public persona

One unavoidable result of being in the spotlight is the creation of a public image or persona that can easily endanger or replace any sense of private self—a process that Rice is concerned about as early as *Jesus Christ Superstar*. When Judas confronts the man he once admired unconditionally because '[y]ou've begun to matter more than the things you say',[100] he accuses Jesus of having fallen for his own myth—like many a pop star—and of having replaced the religious and political message with a messianic cult.

When by chance Florence and Anatoly in *Chess* find themselves alone with each other in 'Mountain Duet' they come to realize to their utter amazement that their media-fuelled and ideologically led preconceptions about each other are completely wrong: 'You—you are so strange—why can't you be | What you ought to be? | You should be scheming, intriguing, | Too clever by half . . .'[101]

Eva Duarte approaches Juan Perón because she assumes he can deliver what she craves for, an assumption that is entirely based on his public image: 'I've heard so much about you' refers to both the public image any celebrity exploits and the trap s/he is caught in. At the end of the musical it becomes clear that Evita is consumed by the public persona she herself so carefully created. Her ambitions thwarted by both her political opponents and her own body, all that finally remains is a frozen simulacrum for everyone to gaze at: 'Still life displayed forever . . .'[102]

What is it that makes all these different characters seek the spotlight in spite of the many potential risks this entails? Several people have pointed out the similarities between the eponymous characters of *Jesus Christ Superstar* and *Evita*, such as the fact that both Jesus and Eva Perón died at the age of 33 and that both were admired and criticized by their contemporaries.[103] Yet that is where the similarities end. Jesus' religious belief and sense of a God-given mission are replaced by a turn to the secular with Evita's breathless requests: 'All I want is a whole lot of excess' and 'a lifetime of success'.[104] The wife of Argentina's president and self-styled 'spiritual leader of the nation', combines in her person show business, religion (or rather personality cult), and politics to an even larger degree than Jesus, as is made clear right from the beginning in the opening number, 'Requiem for Eva/Oh What a Circus', which is described in the liner notes as 'majestic, a combination of the magnificent excesses of Hollywood and the Vatican',[105] thereby introducing early on the unique combination of glamour factory and pious iconography, of the star and the saint, that won Eva Perón so many admirers.

This melange of potentially destructive forces also threatens to overwhelm and/or destroy the main characters in two other musicals with lyrics by Tim Rice, *Chess* and *Tycoon*, the English version of a French musical with the more-than-fitting original title *Starmania*. Both again show that with success comes power and opportunities. Neither of these bring out the best in people—not everyone is able to resist 'sirens of fame and possessions'.[106] Blondel may describe himself and his fellow artists without a hint of irony as 'tragic and sensitive souls',[107] but his girlfriend Fiona begs to differ as is shown in the following exchange:

BLONDEL   I'm just a minstrel—
[. . .]
FIONA   You're a self-centered, arrogant—
BLONDEL   Star.[108]

The disadvantages of early success

The tendency to keep 'looking out for number one'[109] may be directly related to the puzzling question of what is left to do, where to go once one has reached the top—yet another consequence of achieving eminence in your chosen field. For many artists 'overnight success', no matter how long it actually takes to arrive, causes doubts to set in, and Tim Rice was no exception, pondering even several decades after his breakthrough with *Jesus Christ Superstar*, why he (and Lloyd Webber) were fortuitous where others failed to gain recognition: 'I often wonder where we went right. Obviously, Andrew had a great gift for melody and I had a feel for a turn of phrase that occasionally amused or intrigued, but so did many others.'[110]

In Rice's case the apprehension and doubt that arose with fame and fortune not only triggered hypochondria,[111] but were also exacerbated by his first-hand observation that financial rewards in the entertainment industry are anything but fair. An unpublished essay (written in September 1971 and titled 'A Year of Superstar') sees Rice reflecting on his own meteoric rise in just a couple of months as a result of what was quickly turning into the biggest-selling British album in history.[112] He underlined that '[i]n the glittering world of show business you are either ridiculously underpaid or ludicrously overpaid for your talents—neither is a satisfactory position to be in'.[113]

The lyricist's ambivalence about his new position and concerning his future found expression in the number 'High Flying, Adored', 'one of the few songs in *Evita* [written] from a personal perspective',[114] not least because Eva Perón, the new First Lady of Argentina, was exactly the same age as the lyricist when he hit it big. On the one hand, early success is bound to bring lifelong disappointment at what comes next. As Che warns Eva in 'High Flying, Adored': 'A shame you did it all at 26 | Nothing can thrill you | No one fulfil you',[115] sentiments mirrored in *King David*'s 'You Have It All': 'It's very hard when things come easy | You start to fear a bitter end | [. . .] | This is our golden age | We will recall | [. . .] | In safer times than these that we once had it all.'[116]

On the other hand, when you can't climb any higher, all you can do is hang on to the crest, and never gaze back at your humble beginnings: 'Don't look down | It's a long, long way to fall . . .',[117] because the only other alternatives are retreating or being pushed aside—which in this case means being pushed off the summit. In 1971, Rice saw only one solution to this quandary and that was not to stop working: 'When you work for something for a long time and achieve your goal it will all mean nothing at all if you don't find a new target fairly quickly.'[118]

Yet even keeping oneself occupied is no safeguard against existential doubts, for after roughly ten years when everything he touched turned to gold, Rice personally experienced the vagaries of fortune with two shows to which he once again not only contributed the lyrics, but for which he also conceived the problematic storylines—neither show in its London production credited a librettist. Fatally misjudging the prevalent general mood of the early 1980s and accordingly failing to recognize that musical theatre audiences had begun to embrace darker subjects, the lyricist had his 'first important stage flop'[119] courtesy of the witty and irreverent, if dramaturgically highly uneven, *Blondel*. With its playfulness and self-reflexivity the show anticipates by nearly twenty years the wave of self-referential shows that flooded Broadway in the early 2000s, such as *The Producers* (2001), *Urinetown* (2001), *Spamalot* (2005), and *The Drowsy Chaperone* (2006), and thus could be argued to have been ahead of its time. Examples of Rice's exuberant facetiousness abound throughout the show: there are references to *Salad Days*[120] (the song 'Saladin Days'), *Evita*,[121] *Grease* ('Peace is the Word'), as well as metatheatrical comments such as 'Who says this piece wasn't educational?' or 'This is only a two-act play'.[122]

Chess in turn ran for 1,109 performances in London, but barely made its money back,[123] and then flopped spectacularly in New York, where it closed after a mere sixty-eight performances, which must have been especially heartbreaking for its lyricist because he approached the project full of enthusiasm, and afterwards conceded that '[t]here is a lot of me in *Chess*'.[124] With *Blondel* and *Chess*, the lyricist thus had two major flops in a row; ironically, this reversal of fortune occurred at a time when his former writing partner Lloyd Webber, with whom he had split up as he later sarcastically explained, because they were 'certain that they could never top'[125] their earlier successes, seemingly could do no wrong by composing one smash hit after another with *Cats* (1981), *Starlight Express* (1984), and *The Phantom of the Opera* (1986). Feeling 'a bit depressed' and wondering whether he 'blew it',[126] Rice was 'saved' a few years later by the Disney Studios;[127] his work for their animated cartoon musicals *Aladdin* (1992) and *The Lion King* (1994) as well as for the stage productions of *Beauty and the Beast* (1994), *The Lion King*, and *Aida* led to 'another immensely high-profile decade'.[128]

The inevitability of disappointment

In its original incarnation, *Chess*, probably the most bitter musical of the 1980s, takes one step further the theme of life leading inevitably to dissatisfaction, with protagonists who have achieved most of what they ever dreamed of, only to realize that success doesn't bring contentment. 'Where I Want to Be' may be a place that is both unreachable and undesirable, partly because it is lonely at the top, and partly because success is always threatened by people just waiting for a mistake, a chance to usurp one's position: 'Running for my life and never looking back in | Case there's someone right behind to | Shoot me down and say he always knew I'd fall.'[129] Thus there is no one you can trust, which is why female protagonist Florence advises herself bluntly: 'Never lose your heart, use your head | [. . .] | Never be the first to believe | Never be the last to deceive | Nobody's on nobody's side'[130] because, as expressed more than a decade later in *Aida*: 'We don't know whose words are true . . .'[131]

In *Chess*, all the protagonists wind up in situations where they 'could be choosing | No choices whatsoever',[132] and even the attempt to objectify the dilemma by reflecting on oneself in the third person fails,[133] because nothing can prevent the ultimate acknowledgement of being trapped; as Florence realizes in 'Someone Else's Story': 'Trouble is, the girl is me.'[134] In the world of high-stakes board games and high-stakes politics, ultimately everything is for sale,[135] as the number 'The Merchandisers' Song' reminds us, and nothing is sacred, least of all human beings and their feelings, because self-preservation rules both countries and individuals. Consequently, it is not surprising when people refrain from baring their souls because emotional honesty may only lead to exploitation. As Florence asks herself: 'What if he saw my whole existence | Turning around a word, a smile, a touch?'[136] It is also not surprising that the score for *Chess* is permeated by sarcasm, both right on target ('Merano', 'The Merchandisers Song', and 'Embassy Lament') and woefully off the mark (the drinking song 'Der Kleine Franz', performed in German, a supposedly funny collection of German and Austrian clichés,[137] contains so many grammatical errors as to be virtually incomprehensible).

King David, the last of three full-length Tim Rice musicals based on stories from the Bible, retells the story of the man who defeated Goliath as another cautionary tale of thwarted ambition, accompanied by the grim realization that, despite affirmation to the contrary, fame, power, and love are fleeting, as the deceived party has to learn the hard way: 'Words count for nothing | Only for show . . .'[138] In Tim Rice's books, this is another side effect of success: relationships do not last; betrayal, often brought about by the boredom bred by the familiarity and the everyday, is unavoidable because the intimacy engendered by both long-term relationships and the daily grind are detrimental to sustaining passion[139] and in the end weaken commitment: 'Heaven help my heart | The day that I find | Suddenly I've run out of secrets | Suddenly I'm not always on his mind.'[140]

Only the ruthless young starlet Eva Duarte on her way to the top can discard her former lovers with cynical words such as: 'Oh, but it's sad when a love affair dies | The decline into silence and doubt. | Our passion was just too intense to survive . . .'[141] Older and wiser Tim Rice characters are less likely to be this cruel, having experienced heartbreak and disillusion themselves. The resignation of Fiona, the female protagonist of *Blondel*, unable to leave a man she knows to be egocentric and flawed, in the Act 1 finale 'Running Back for More' speaks volumes: 'Half the world says leave him be | Makes it sound so very easy | They don't know the half of me | How I've tried a thousand times | How my love defeats me | How my love defeats me.'[142]

The lovers in *Chess*, not able to shield their love from political intrigues, confess to each other, 'I'd give the world for that moment with you | When we've thought we knew | That our love would last | But the moment passed | With no warning far too fast.'[143] *Aida* opens with the statement that 'Every story is a love story', only to proceed to the conclusion that 'Every story | [. . .] | [is a] tale[s] of human failing.'[144] The Nubian heroine tries to reconcile herself to the prospect of never being with the man she loves by reminding herself that 'Love's an ever-changing situation | Passion would have cooled | And all the magic would have died' and that it is 'better the contempt of the familiar cannot start.'[145]

In Tim Rice's musicals, it's usually the women who realize that 'Nothing is so good it lasts eternally | Perfect situations must go wrong' and that 'No-one in your life is with you constantly | No-one is completely on your side,'[146] although Heathcliff expresses similar sentiments in 'Each to His Own', when he sings: 'Nothing can be permanent | Nothing's set in stone. | Never try to fool yourself | That you are not alone.'[147] It is the

'Enemy Within', as a song in *King David* terms it, which invariably leads to 'the lover's first deception'.[148] Up until *Chess* this might be seen as a fault of personality or a character defect, but later, in the world view evinced in Tim Rice's musicals from the 1990s onwards, it appears more benignly as simply human nature: 'We make our promises of love without a thought | That infidelity will ever touch our lives | And then the everyday procession | Ensures no certainty survives . . .'[149]

In *Tycoon* Rice returns to this theme in the song 'Nobody Chooses': 'He lies, she lies, and really try to care | Make love, fake love | And no-one's getting very far | Nobody chooses what they are.'[150] No wonder that the last number of the score leaves the audience with the message: 'You Have to Learn to Live Alone.' In 'My Heart Dances', a number written for but not used in the animated movie *The Road to El Dorado* (2000), the singer confesses: 'I long to love you better, but I swear I don't know how' and then comes to the sorrowful conclusion: 'The things we love completely we are fated to destroy.'[151]

The two love affairs in *From Here to Eternity* between Sergeant Warden and Karen Holmes, the wife of his superior officer, and between Private Prewitt and the prostitute Lorene, are prime examples of the unlucky relationships in a Tim Rice musical, as both are doomed, if for different reasons. Karen, unable to bear children after her husband infected her with syphilis, is desperately looking for 'a reason to exist before I die' in various extramarital flings, even though she doesn't fully believe that lasting happiness is possible: 'We do our best to screw things up, because we can.'[152] At the end, in spite of strong

FIGURE 21.2 A prime example of the doomed relationships in the musicals of Tim Rice: Rebecca Thornhill (Karen) and Darius Campbell (Sergeant Warden) in *From Here to Eternity* at the Shaftesbury Theatre, 2013.

Photograph by Johan Persson. Courtesy of ArenaPal.

feelings for him she splits from Warden, reflecting: 'Maybe, I played him and the situation badly | Too restless, too impatient, too demanding | Too much in love to let him be.'[153]

The mutual attraction between Lorene and Prewitt is neatly summed up with 'wrong place, wrong girl, wrong guy':[154] she is a prostitute with a game plan and he a destitute soldier without any chance for a career in the military because he cannot suffer injustice and refuses to be forced into the boxing ring. Suspecting that their liaison has no future with war on the horizon ('we long for love, but life gets in the way'[155]), they decide to live only in the here and now: 'There ain't no time on our side | [. . .] | Just how long can we last? | A year [. . .] maybe two, | Who can say? | So love me forever today.'[156]

All of the above led Michael Walsh to conclude that '[i]n Tim's universe, lovers used each other, no one could be trusted, and in the end they all came to grief'.[157] When confronted with Walsh's statement, Rice admitted that he was indeed 'a bit cynical about that dreaded word relationships', but then relativized his comment by insisting this should not be mistaken for his 'philosophy'.[158] He takes a correspondingly ambivalent position regarding the 'somewhat misanthropic chorus'[159] of 'Goodnight and Thank You' in *Evita*, where Eva Duarte and her rejected lovers announce to the audience:

> There is no one, no one at all
> Never has been and never will be a lover
> Male or Female
> Who hasn't an eye on
> Tricks they can try on their partner
> They're hoping their lover will help them or keep them
> Support them, promote them
> Don't blame them
> You're the same.[160]

Rice claims to have 'some (not total, and not always) sympathy'[161] for the negative view of human nature expressed here, and this intermittent cynicism surfaces at times in the most unexpected of places: the lyricist has called attention to the fact that even the opening number of the family musical *The Lion King* has 'a dark side to it [and] a few pessimistic moments'.[162]

RECURRING PHRASES
AND SUBJECTS REVISITED

Tim Rice has emphasized rather grudgingly that composers have the advantage of being able to reuse the melody of a discarded song whereas their lyricists are stuck with a number that is usually too specific to fit into another context and thus into another show.[163] While it is undoubtedly rather difficult to find later use for a finished set of lyrics, it should be pointed out that Rice at least has found further use for certain striking formulations and images in other songs which on a less elevated level also contributes to a certain consistency in his output.

For instance, the line 'I just can't wait to be king',[164] which Rice would later choose as the title for one of the most popular numbers in *The Lion King*, can first be heard in *Blondel*. The entrance song of Amneris, the Pharaoh's daughter, in *Aida* is 'My Strongest Suit' which is an expression that already turned up in the song 'Hearts, Not Diamonds'[165] (written for the 1981 film *The Fan*, with music by Marvin Hamlisch). The song 'Julia' on the concept album *1984*, which was released in 1981, features two images that would recur in the musical *Chess* three years later: the title of the no. 1 hit 'I Know Him So Well' is prefigured in the line 'Barely a trace of the place where I knew him well',[166] while 'I had it all in one grand afternoon'[167] is reconceived as the angry advice 'Never waste a hot afternoon'[168] in 'Nobody's Side'.

Furthermore, what also seems typical of Tim Rice is that with all the shows that had rewrites, either extensive ones such as *Chess* or minor ones such as *Evita*, the lyricist has a tendency to go back to his first vision in the end. Just as the 1996 movie version of the latter reinstated several of the original lyrics that were discarded or replaced for the 1978 Harold Prince stage production, the latest incarnation of *Chess* approved by Rice, the 2009 Royal Albert Hall concert, reverted to the 1984 concept recording, although in this case the lyricist of 'May I return to the beginning . . .'[169] did nothing to solve the various problems of the book and its inconsistent characterizations.

In a comparable way, Rice does not like to let go of specific subjects that he is intrigued by; this tenacity has had both positive and negative consequences. On the one hand it helped him to eventually persuade Lloyd Webber to follow his instinct that the life of Eva Perón would make a great topic for a musical, 'that by far the best way to capture the melodramatic, almost unbelievable, glamorous and ruthlessly populist characteristics of Eva Peron [sic] was through the melodramatic, almost unbelievable, glamorous and ruthlessly populist characteristics of a musical'.[170] On the other hand, his 'daft obsession'[171]—as he ruefully describes it—with the medieval tale of Richard the Lionheart, king of England from 1189 to 1199, induced him first to start work on a musical with Lloyd Webber in 1969, *Come Back Richard Your Country Needs You*, which they then abandoned, before it resurfaced fourteen years later with *Blondel*. Another subject that Rice contemplated as early as the late 1960s and then revisited twenty-five years later with composer Alan Menken, is the biblical story of King David.[172]

CONCLUSION: THE 'REAL TIM RICE'

There can be no question that there are subjects, motifs, and attitudes that unequivocally characterize the work of an artist who may be, apart from W. S. Gilbert, the most famous English lyricist ever. The 'real Tim Rice' or at least the lyricist with an easily discernible and highly sophisticated voice, though, is most prominently at work in those musicals that he initiated himself rather than joined subsequently as a 'hired hand'. Considering how generic some of Rice's lyrics are in certain of his less well-known songs, he obviously needs to be fired up by a topic to rise above mere competence and come up with lyrics that are startlingly original. In this respect, *From Here to Eternity* is proof that the lyricist has recently found a way of channelling his preoccupations and favourite themes, when the material inspires him, into writing that is brilliantly in character. The lyricist may have expressed this most aptly himself in *Blondel*: 'I can't change at someone's whim—my soul is not for hire | I have to write about and for a subject I admire.'[173]

NOTES

1. Stephen Sondheim insists that 'The musical, more than any other kind of theatrical piece, is a collaborative effort'. Stephen Sondheim, 'The Musical Theatre', in *Broadway Song and Story: Playwrights, Lyricists, Composers Discuss Their Hits*, ed. Otis Guernsey Jr. and Terrence McNally (New York: Dodd Mead, 1985), 232. This sentiment is echoed by his fellow composer Jule Styne: 'The most important thing is: if you're not a collaborator, you'd better never write a show'. Quoted in Al Kasha and Joel Hirschhorn, *Notes on Broadway: Conversations with the Great Songwriters* (Chicago: Contemporary Books, 1985), 294.

2. See Olaf Jubin, *Entertainment in der Kritik, Eine komparative Analyse von amerikanischen, britischen und deutschsprachigen Rezensionen zu den Musicals von Stephen Sondheim und Andrew Lloyd Webber* (Herbolzheim: Centaurus Verlag, 2005), 1035–1045.

3. David Benedict, 'West End Review: *From Here to Eternity*', *Variety*, 23 October 2013, http://variety.com/2013/legit/reviews/west-end-review-from-here-to-eternity-1200755273/, accessed 24 October 2013.

4. David Benedict, 'Auds Still Hungry for Rice. Profile in Excellence: Sir Tim Rice', http://variety.com/2012/legit/news/auds-still-hungry-for-rice-1118052243/, accessed 16 April 2012.

5. http://www.timrice.co.uk/bio.html, accessed 6 November 2014.

6. Here and throughout I will refer to those Tim Rice shows which were first released as a concept album by the year in which that recording was released.

7. Jeremy Gerard: 'Hakuna Matata, Baby: Disney Claims Record $6.2 Billion Gross for *Lion King*', 22 September 2014, http://deadline.com/2014/09/disney-lion-king-highest-grossing-show-at-6-2-billion-838482/, accessed 6 November 2014.

8. http://www.boxofficemojo.com/movies/?id=lionking.htm, accessed 6 November 2014.

9. The film is alternatively known as *Jock of the Bushveld* (title of the cinema release in South Africa) and *Jock—the Hero Dog* (title of the US DVD release), http://www.imdb.com/title/tt1822239/releaseinfo?ref_=tt_ql_9, accessed 6 November 2014.

10. http://www.boxofficemojo.com/movies/?id=nutcracker3d.htm, accessed 6 November 2014.

11. The film was only released theatrically in South Africa (the country in which it was made), the Ukraine, Georgia, Estonia, and Israel, (http://www.imdb.com/title/tt1822239/releaseinfo?ref_=tt_ql_9, accessed 6 November 2014.

12. It could be argued that Comden and Green were at their least effective when they consciously tried to write outside their comfort zone as with the misbegotten sequel to Henrik Ibsen's *A Doll's House*, the 1982 musical *A Doll's Life* (with music by Larry Grossman).

13. Tim Rice, *Oh, What a Circus: The Autobiography* (London: Hodder & Stoughton, 1999), 107.

14. *The Likes of Us*, Live From the Sydmonton Festival, CD Booklet, Really Useful Recordings 987 4834, 2005.

15. From 'I'm a Very Busy Man', *Likes of Us*, CD Booklet.

16. From 'This Is My Time', *Likes of Us*, CD Booklet

17. 'We don't mind the things we got | And we ain't gonna fuss | This is what we know is proper | For the likes of us.' *Likes of Us*, CD Booklet.

18. From 'Will This Last Forever?', *Likes of Us*, CD Booklet.

19. From 'Jacob and Sons/Joseph's Coat', *Joseph and the Amazing Technicolor Dreamcoat*, CD Booklet, Really Useful Recording 511 130-2, 1991.

20. From 'Those Canaan Days', *Joseph*, CD Booklet.

21. 'Rice's words were not quite like anything else that had existed up till now in the musical theater. They were thoroughly colloquial.' Kurt Gänzl, *The Musical: A Concise History* (Boston: Northeastern University Press, 1997), 341.

22. *Jesus Christ Superstar*, double disc set, CD Booklet, MCA Records MCD 00501-1, 1970.

23. Rice, *Oh, What a Circus*, 167, 210.

24. From 'Artists Are Tragic and Sensitive Souls', *Blondel*, original cast album, Lyrics Booklet, MCA Records, MAPS 11504, 1983.

25. *Aida*'s 'My Strongest Suit' already *contains* the element of camp that usually is only *brought to* 'King Herod's Song' by the performer, if he chooses to apply it.

26. Anon. ['Humm'], 'Broadway Review: *Chess*', *Variety*, 4 May 1988, 552 + 556.

27. Denny Martin Flinn, *Musical! A Grand Tour* (New York: Schirmer Books, 1997), 399. The lyricist disavowed Flinn's charges in a statement, which is both eloquent and witty, in the comment section of Internet company Amazon. Tim Rice, 'Extremely Miffed That I Got Slagged Off', http://www.amazon.com/Musical-Grand-Denny-Martin-Flinn/dp/002864610X/ref=pd_cp_b_0, accessed 7 November 2014.

28. Rice, *Oh, What a Circus*, 200.

29. Quoted in Benedict, 'Auds Still Hungry for Rice'.

30. In his autobiography Rice defends himself vigorously against accusations of laziness and explains how his hesitancy to appear unequivocally invested in their projects, which he attributes to being 'too English and too middle class', might have been misconstrued as indifference by his then writing partner Lloyd Webber. Rice, *Oh, What a Circus*, 290, 369.

31. See, for instance, the reviews of *From Here to Eternity* by Dominic Cavendish (*Daily Telegraph*, 24 October 2013), Henry Hitchings (*Evening Standard*, 24 October 2013), Alexander Gilmore (*Financial Times*, 26 October 2014), Susanna Clapp (*The Observer*, 27 October 2014), and Andrzej Lukowski (*Time Out London*, 29 October 2013), collected in *London Theatre Record*, 22 October–4 November 2013, 992–996. In the same time period his former writing partner Andrew Lloyd Webber composed no less than four completely new shows: *The Beautiful Game* (2000), *The Woman in White* (2004), *Love Never Dies* (2010), and *Stephen Ward* (2013).

32. Between 2000 and 2013, Rice also wrote the lyrics for two film musicals, *The Nutcracker in 3D* and *Jock*, and several individual songs, such as 'Wake up Call' (2000; music: Andrew Farris), 'Whatever Happened to Peggy Sue' (2002; Bobby McVee), 'A Touch of Love' (2004; Andrew Lloyd Webber), 'Dance the Dance' (2005; Andrew Lloyd Webber), 'Running for You' (2005; composer unknown); 'Who'll Speak for Love' (2007; Burt Bacharach), and 'Peterloo' (2009; Malcolm Arnold), http://www.timrice.co.uk/songs.html, accessed 3 November 2014.

33. 'Theatre Talk: Tim Rice', video, New York Public Library for the Performing Arts, NCOX2406, 2008. With this concern Rice is not alone amongst musical theatre writers of a certain age as Stephen Sondheim, fourteen years his senior, has expressed similar

trepidation to begin a new project late in his career: 'One of the problems is that I get more frightened each time I write because people are expecting so much. That slows me down.' Quoted in Frank Rich, 'Conversations with Sondheim', *New York Times Magazine*, 12 March 2000, http://partners.nytimes.com/library/magazine/home/20000312mag-sondheim.html, accessed 7 November 2014.

34. From 'Thirty Year Man (Reprise)', *From Here to Eternity: The Musical*, live cast recording 2013, CD Booklet, Absolute Records OVCD11, 2014.

35. From 'Thirty Year Man (Reprise)'.

36. Pat Cerasaro, 'InDepth Interview: Sir Tim Rice on *From Here to Eternity* Story to Stage to Screen Plus *Chess, Aladdin* & More', http://www.broadwayworld.com/article/InDepth-InterView-Sir-Tim-Rice-On-FROM-HERE-TO-ETERNITY-Story-To-Stage-To-Screen-Plus-CHESS-ALADDIN-More-20140925, accessed 2 October 2014.

37. Rice, *Oh, What a Circus*, 71.

38. 'I don't consider myself particularly a theatre person. I mean, I enjoy writing for it very much. But I don't think I ever said, "I must go into theatre".' Tim Rice, quoted in Kasha and Hirschhorn, *Notes on Broadway*, 231.

39. The Alan Jay Lerner and Frederick Loewe songs for *My Fair Lady* (1956) form Rice's favourite musical theatre score. Rice, *Oh, What a Circus*, 51.

40. Rice, *Oh, What a Circus*, 3. For more information on the life and career of Michael Flanders (1922–75), see http://en.wikipedia.org/wiki/Michael_Flanders.

41. 'Interview with Tim Rice', video, New York Library for the Performing Arts, NCOX 2175, 2003. When asked which lyricists working for musical theatre he holds in high esteem, Rice also mentioned Cole Porter and Ira Gershwin.

42. Rice, *Oh, What a Circus*, 303–304. The other three editors were Paul Gambaccini, Joel Whitburn, and Mike Read.

43. Rice, *Oh, What a Circus*, 52.

44. Cerasaro, 'InDepth Interview'.

45. Rice has also written the lyrics to songs by Freddie Mercury, Paul McCartney, Mike Batt, and Burt Bacharach, among others.

46. 'Interview with Tim Rice'.

47. 'Theatre Talk: Tim Rice'.

48. 'I've never thought of anything I've written [. . .] as Broadway or not-Broadway or rock. It's just stuff I like.' 'Interview with Tim Rice'.

49. Cerasaro, 'InDepth Interview'.

50. From 'Any Dream Will Do', *Joseph*, CD Booklet.

51. Both examples from 'Goodnight and Thank You', *Evita: An Opera Based on the Life Story of Eva Peron* [sic] *1919–1952*, 20th Anniversary Edition, CD Booklet, MCA Records DMCX 503, 1996. The first example was subsequently replaced while the latter was changed to a clean rhyme: see 'Goodnight and Thank You', *Evita*, libretto, London cast recording, Really Useful Recordings 9855975, 2006.

52. From 'Economic Acrostic', *Blondel*, Lyrics Booklet.

53. From 'You and I', *Chess*, concept recording, CD Booklet, Polydor Records, 847 445-2, 1984.

54. From 'Another Pyramid', Elton John's and Tim Rice's *Aida*, original Broadway cast recording, CD Booklet, Buena Vista Records 60671-1, 2000.

55. Rice, *Oh, What a Circus*, 138.

56. As Rice freely acknowledges in his autobiography, regarding the time when *Jesus Christ Superstar* conquered the USA in 1970, the very year in which Stephen Sondheim and

Harold Prince ushered in the era of the concept musical with their ground-breaking Company: 'I was lamentably ignorant about both these giants of the musical [at that time].' Rice, *Oh, What a Circus*, 217.

57. Carrie Dunn, 'BWW Interviews: Composer Stuart Brayson on *From Here to Eternity and More!*', http://www.broadwayworld.com/westend/article/BWW-Interviews-Composer-Stuart-Brayson-On-FROM-HERE-TO-ETERNITY-And-More-20140508, accessed 19 May 2914.

58. Rice, *Oh, What a Circus*, 138.

59. *Evita*, CD Booklet.

60. Michael Walsh voices similar concerns in his discussion of the song: 'The world-weary lyric is far too sophisticated for a 15-year-old schoolgirl.' Michael Walsh, *Andrew Lloyd Webber: His Life and Works* (London: Abrams, 1989), 102. Even Rice himself has conceded that the lyrics are 'probably too sophisticated for the character'. Rice, *Oh, What a Circus*, 360.

61. Elton John's and Tim Rice's *Aida*, CD Booklet.

62. *Aladdin*, original motion picture soundtrack, CD Booklet, Walt Disney Records 60846-2, 1992.

63. Other examples can be found in the score to the animated cartoon *The Road to El Dorado* (released in the year 2000), where the songs '16th Century Man' (not used in the finished film) and 'It's Tough to Be a God' employ words such as 'anti-diluvian' and 'noveau riche' respectively. Elton John's *The Road to El Dorado*, CD Booklet, DreamWorks Recording 250 219-2, 2000.

64. Rice, *Oh, What a Circus*, 51.

65. Gerald McKnight, *Andrew Lloyd Webber* (New York: Granada Publishing, 1984), 153.

66. Another instance is 'The Morning Report', a comic number that fails to generate any laughs, from *The Lion King* and also has the dubious distinction of having been voted the 'worst animated cartoon song of all time' by *Empire* magazine. Andrew Osmond, 'The Top 10 Cartoon Songs', *Empire* 239 (May 2009): 152–153.

67. 'Mrs Edgar Linton' features rhymes such as 'viable/undeniable/pliable', 'suitable/inscrutable/mootable' as well as lines such as 'Think of him in bed! Touching you in bed' which are both too sophisticated and too modern for the young Yorkshire girls singing the song. *Heathcliff Live (The Show)*, CD Booklet, EMI Records 7243 8 54766 2 2, 1996.

68. Stephen Sondheim, 'Theater Lyrics', in *Playwrights, Lyricists, Composers on Theatre: The Inside Story of a Decade of Theater in Articles and Comments by Its Authors, Selected from Their Own Publication, the 'Dramatists Guild Quarterly'*, ed. Otis GuersneyJr. (New York: Dodd, Mead, 1974), 64.

69. Rice, *Oh, What a Circus*, 358.

70. *Blondel*, Lyrics Booklet.

71. This is based on personal observations: in March 2013 I took twenty-five students to see a production of *Chess* at the Union Theatre, a London fringe venue. In spite of sitting very close to the actors, afterwards not one of my students was able to describe what was going on during 'Endgame'. Consequently they had grave difficulties in understanding how the show ended.

72. *Evita*, CD Booklet. Rice explains in detail how and why the lyrics were changed during the recording session in his autobiography: Rice, *Oh, What a Circus*, 365–366.

73. Rice, *Oh, What a Circus*, 366.

74. Rice, *Oh, What a Circus*, 193.

75. Rice refers to the subject of changing less-than-perfect lyrics of widely known and beloved songs three times in his autobiography. Rice, *Oh, What a Circus*, 138, 193, 366.

76. See, for instance, Craig Zadan, *Sondheim & Co.* 2nd, updated ed. (New York: Nick Hern Books, 1989), 22 and Stephen Sondheim, *Finishing the Hat: Collected Lyrics (1954–1981), with Attendant Comments, Principles, Heresies, Grudges, Whines, and Anecdotes* (London: Virgin Books, 2010), 48. Sondheim was especially irked that he wasn't allowed to change the lyrics in question, because his collaborators preferred the original ones.

77. From 'I'm Monarchist (Reprise)', *Blondel*, Lyrics Booklet.

78. Rice, *Oh, What a Circus*, 2.

79. 'I wanted to be a pop star (still do)'. Rice, *Oh, What a Circus*, 257; see also 52, 'I still await my chart début as a vocalist'.

80. 'Since my first brush with celebrity, my love life had been fairly hectic, if not in the Division One rock star league, time-consuming and erratic'. Rice, *Oh, What a Circus*, 315.

81. 'I was not actually a proper star, but this was a minor detail as we lapped up the glamorous treatment [while promoting *Jesus Christ Superstar* in the USA in 1971]'. Rice, *Oh, What a Circus*, 228.

82. Rice, *Oh, What a Circus*, 298.

83. From 'Pharaoh Story', *Joseph*, CD Booklet.

84. In her 1996 London revival of the show which later moved to Essen/Germany and New York, Australian director Gale Edwards found a striking stage picture to reinforce the way in which the imagery in *Jesus Christ Superstar* links the nearly religious adoration that certain rock stars inspire to the New Testament: the cross onstage was made up of spotlights.

85. From 'Buenos Aires', *Evita*, CD Booklet.

86. From 'Monks' Introduction', *Blondel*, Lyrics Booklet.

87. From 'Assassin's Song', *Blondel*, Lyrics Booklet.

88. Rice, *Oh, What a Circus*, 282n.

89. From 'Dice Are Rolling', *Evita*, CD Booklet.

90. From 'Richard's Return', *Blondel*, Lyrics Booklet.

91. From 'Hosanna', *Jesus Christ Superstar*, CD Booklet.

92. Rice, *Oh, What a Circus*, 251.

93. Benny Andersson, Björn Ulvaeus, Tim Rice, Richard Nelson, *Chess*, Libretto, Broadway Version (New York: Samuel French, Inc., 1991), 14.

94. From 'Endgame', *Chess*, Concept Recording, CD Booklet.

95. Alan Menken and Tim Rice's *King David*, a world premiere concert event, highlights from the live performance, CD Booklet, Buena Vista Records 60944-7, 1997.

96. Rice, *Oh, What a Circus*, 240.

97. Rice, *Oh, What a Circus*, 382.

98. From 'The Russian and Molokov', *Chess*, concept recording, CD Booklet; emphasis suggested by the music and the performance by Tommy Körberg.

99. From 'Requiem/Oh, What a Circus', *Evita*, CD Booklet.

100. From 'Heaven on Their Minds', *Jesus Christ Superstar*, CD Booklet.

101. From 'Mountain Duet', *Chess*, concept recording, CD Booklet. The song 'Farewell to a Sex Symbol' from *Tycoon* deals with exactly the same topic, the split between public and private image.

102. From 'Lament', *Evita*, CD Booklet.

103. See, for instance, Michael Skasa, 'Schauspieler im politischen Gewerbe—Politik als Show', *Theater heute* 3 (1981): 5.

104. From 'Buenos Aires'.

105. From 'Buenos Aires'.

106. From 'Endgame', *Chess*, concept recording, CD Booklet.

107. From 'Artists Are Tragic and Sensitive Souls'.

108. From "Trio" (*Blondel*, Lyrics Booklet).

109. From 'Argument', *Chess*, concept recording, CD Booklet.

110. Rice, *Oh, What a Circus*, 421.

111. Rice, *Oh, What a Circus*, 248.

112. Rice, *Oh, What a Circus*, 240.

113. Tim Rice, 'A Year of Superstar', unpublished manuscript, Tim Rice Clippings, New York Public Library of the Performing Arts.

114. Rice, *Oh, What a Circus*, 368.

115. *Evita*, CD Booklet.

116. From 'You Have It All', in Alan Menken and Tim Rice's *King David*, CD Booklet.

117. From 'High Flying, Adored', *Evita*, CD Booklet.

118. Rice, 'A Year of Superstar'.

119. Rice, *Oh, What a Circus*, 68.

120. Rice 'loved' the Julian Slade/Dorothy Reynolds musical when he saw it in 1954. Rice, *Oh, What a Circus*, 32.

121. Just like Eva Perón, Blondel embarks on a disastrous tour through the European countries Spain, Italy, and France.

122. *Blondel*, Lyrics Booklet.

123. 'Theater Talk # 212: Tim Rice on *King David*'. Video, New York Public Library for the Performing Arts, NCOX 1405, 1997.

124. 'Theater Talk # 212'.

125. 'Tim Rice: Lyricist', in *Evita*, London revival 2006, Programme May–June 2006 (London: Adelphi Theatre Company Ltd, 2006), not paginated.

126. 'Theater Talk # 212'.

127. That Rice lived through more than a decade when his best work (or at least his best received work) seemed to be behind him, may explain why he once stated: 'Most people do their best work when they're young.' 'Theater Talk # 212'.

128. Benedict, 'Auds Still Hungry for Rice'.

129. From 'Where I Want to Be', *Chess*, concept recording, CD Booklet.

130. From 'Nobody's Side', *Chess*, concept recording, CD Booklet.

131. From 'Elaborate Lives', Elton John's and Tim Rice's *Aida*, CD Booklet.

132. From 'Someone Else's Story', *Chess*, Original Broadway Cast Recording, CD Booklet, BMG Records BD87700, 1988.

133. The same approach is taken by Marie-Jeanne in the song 'Working Girl' in *Tycoon*.

134. From 'Someone Else's Story'.

135. In this context, it seems significant that two other Tim Rice musicals, *Joseph* and *Aida*, deal with the ultimate form of using humans for profit: slavery.

136. From 'Heaven Help My Heart', *Chess*, concept recording, CD Booklet.

137. Among those stereotypical terms and symbols mentioned are 'Prosit', 'Hofbräuhaus', 'Gemütlichkeit', 'Tannenbaum', 'Lorelei', 'Bratwurst', 'Sauerkraut', und 'Heidelberg'. To add insult to injury, the first three items are misspelled in the Samuel French edition.

Benny Andersson, Björn Ulvaeus, and Tim Rice, *Chess: The Musical*, London stage version (London: Samuel French Ltd, 1994).

138. From 'Never Again', Alan Menken and Tim Rice's *King David*, CD Booklet.

139. Tim Rice experienced this when he was in his early twenties with his then girlfriend, Juliet Simpkins: '[A]fter two years [...] the point of all the passion, if not the passion itself, almost imperceptibly cooled.' Rice, *Oh, What a Circus*, 105.

140. From 'Heaven Help My Heart', *Chess*, concept recording, CD Booklet.

141. From 'Goodnight and Thank You', *Evita*, CD Booklet.

142. *Blondel*, Lyrics Booklet.

143. From 'You and I'.

144. Elton John's and Tim Rice's *Aida*, CD Booklet.

145. From 'Easy As Life', *Aida*, CD Booklet.

146. From 'I Know Him So Well', *Chess*, concept recording, CD Booklet.

147. *Heathcliff Live*, CD Booklet.

148. Alan Menken and Tim Rice's *King David*, CD Booklet.

149. From 'When in Love', *Aida*, CD Booklet.

150. *Tycoon*, CD Booklet, Epic Records 471923 2, 1992.

151. Elton John's *The Road to El Dorado*, CD Booklet.

152. From 'Another Language', *From Here to Eternity: The Musical*, live cast recording, 2013, CD Booklet, Absolute Records OVCD11, 2014.

153. From 'Maybe', *From Here to Eternity*, CD Booklet.

154. From 'Run Along, Joe', *From Here to Eternity*, CD Booklet.

155. From 'Love Me Forever Today', *From Here to Eternity*, CD Booklet.

156. From 'Love Me Forever Today'.

157. Walsh, *Andrew Lloyd Webber*, 99.

158. 'Theater Talk # 212'.

159. Rice, *Oh, What a Circus*, 357.

160. *Evita*, Libretto.

161. Rice, *Oh, What a Circus*, 357.

162. 'Interview with Tim Rice'. Perhaps Rice refers to the lines 'There is more to be seen that can ever be seen | More to do than can ever be done' which imply that in the end all (human) endeavour may prove insufficient and is therefore doomed from the start. *The Lion King*, CD Booklet.

163. This topic is broached not once but twice in his 1999 autobiography. Rice, *Oh, What a Circus*, 290, 402.

164. From 'Saladin Days/I Can't Wait to Be King', *Blondel*, Lyrics Booklet.

165. The exact use of the phrase is 'Hearts were not my strongest suit'. 'Hearts, Not Diamonds: Lyrics'. *The Fan*, Paramount Home Video 01469, 1981.

166. http://lyrics.wikia.com/Rick_Wakeman:Julia, accessed 28 July 2014.

167. http://lyrics.wikia.com/Rick_Wakeman:Julia, accessed 28 July 2014.

168. *Chess*, original concept recording, CD Booklet.

169. From 'Any Dream Will Do'.

170. Rice, *Oh, What a Circus*, 415.

171. Rice, *Oh, What a Circus*, 168.

172. Rice, *Oh, What a Circus*, 168.

173. From 'Trio', *Blondel*, Lyrics Booklet.

Bibliography

Aladdin. Original Motion Picture Soundtrack. CD Booklet. Walt Disney Records 60846-2, 1992.

Alan Menken and Tim Rice's *King David*. A World Premiere Concert Event. Highlights from the Live Performance. CD Booklet. Buena Vista Records 60944-7, 1997.

'All Things Considered: Lyrics.' http://www.vangelislyrics.com/vangelis-lyrics-collaborations/ elaine-paige-love-hurts-lyrics.htm, accessed 26 October 2014.

Anderson, John Anderson. 'The Nutcracker in 3D. Review.' http://www.variety.com/review/ VE117944081, accessed 23 November 2010.

Andersson, Benny, Björn Ulvaeus, and Tim Rice. *Chess: The Musical*. London Stage Version. London: Samuel French Ltd, 1994.

Andersson, Benny, Björn Ulvaeus, Tim Rice, and Richard Nelson. *Chess*. Libretto. Broadway Version. New York: Samuel French, Inc., 1991.

Anon. ['Humm']. 'Broadway Review: *Chess.*' *Variety*, 4 May 1988, 552 + 556.

Beauty and the Beast: A New Musical. Original Broadway Cast Recording, 1994. CD Booklet. Walt Disney Records 60861-7, 1994.

Benedict, David. 'Auds Still Hungry for Rice. Profile in Excellence: Sir Tim Rice.' http://variety. com/2012/legit/news/auds-still-hungry-for-rice-1118052243/, accessed 16 April 2012.

Benedict, David. 'West End Review: *From Here to Eternity.*' http://variety.com/2013/legit/ reviews/west-end-review-from-here-to-eternity-1200755273/, accessed 24 October 2013.

Blondel. Original Cast Album, 1983. Lyrics Booklet. MCA Records. MAPS 11504, 1983.

Cerasaro, Pat. 'InDepth Interview: Sir Tim Rice on *From Here to Eternity* Story to Stage to Screen Plus *Chess, Aladdin* & More.' http://www.broadwayworld.com/article/InDepth-InterView-Sir-Tim-Rice-On-FROM-HERE-TO-ETERNITY-Story-To-Stage-To-Screen-Plus-CHESS-ALADDIN-More-20140925, accessed 2 October 2014.

Chess. Concept Recording. CD Booklet. Polydor Records 847 445-2, 1984.

Chess. Original Broadway Cast Recording. CD Booklet. BMG Records BD87700, 1988.

'Christmas Dream: Lyrics.' http://www.metrolyrics.com/christmas-dream-lyrics-perry-como. html, accessed 26 October 2014.

Dunn, Carrie. 'BWW Interviews: Composer Stuart Brayson on *From Here to Eternity and More!*' http://www.broadwayworld.com/westend/article/BWW-Interviews-Composer-Stuart-Brayson-On-FROM-HERE-TO-ETERNITY-And-More-20140508, accessed 19 May 2914.

Elton John's and Tim Rice's *Aida*. Original Broadway Cast Recording, 2000. CD Booklet. Buena Vista Records 60671-7, 2000.

Elton John's *The Road to El Dorado*. CD Booklet. DreamWorks Recording 250 219-2, 2000.

Evita: An Opera Based on the Life Story of Eva Peron [sic] 1919–1952. 20th Anniversary Edition. CD Booklet. MCA Records DMCX 503, 1996.

Evita. Libretto. London Cast Recording, 2006. Really Useful Recordings 9855975, 2006.

'The Fallen Priest: Lyrics.' http://www.metrolyrics.com/the-fallen-priest-lyrics-freddie-mercury.html, accessed 26 October 2014.

Flinn, Denny Martin. *Musical! A Grand Tour*. New York: Schirmer Books, 1997.

From Here to Eternity. Reviews. *London Theatre Record*, 22 October–4 November 2013, 992–996.

From Here to Eternity: The Musical. Live Cast Recording, 2013. CD Booklet. Absolute Records OVCD11, 2014.

Gänzl, Kurt. *The Musical: A Concise History*. Boston: Northeastern University Press, 1997.

Gerard, Jeremy. 'Hakuna Mataka, Baby: Disney Claims Record 6.2 Billion Gross for *Lion King*', 22 September 2014. http://deadline.com/2014/09/disney-lion-king-highest-grossing-show-at-6-2-billion-838482/, accessed 6 November 2014.

'The Golden Boy. Lyrics.' http://www.azlyrics.com/lyrics/freddiemercury/thegoldenboy.html, accessed 26 October 2014.

Heathcliff Live (The Show). CD Booklet. EMI Records 7243 8 54766 2 2, 1996.

'Hearts, Not Diamonds: Lyrics.' *The Fan*. Directed by Edward Bianchi; starring Lauren Bacall, James Garner, and Michael Biehn. Paramount Home Video 01469, 1981.

'Hot As Sun: Lyrics.' http://www.metrolyrics.com/christmas-dream-lyrics-perry-como.html, accessed 26 October 2014.

'Interview with Tim Rice.' Video. New York Public Library for the Performing Arts, NCOX 2175, 2003.

'It's Easy for You: Lyrics.' http://www.metrolyrics.com/its-easy-for-you-lyrics-elvis-presley.html, accessed 26 October 2014.

Jesus Christ Superstar. Double Disc Set. CD Booklet. MCA Records MCD 00501-1, 1970.

Joseph and the Amazing Technicolor Dreamcoat. CD Booklet. Really Useful Recordings 511 130-2, 1991.

Jubin, Olaf. *Entertainment in der Kritik, Eine komparative Analyse von amerikanischen, britischen und deutschsprachigen Rezensionen zu den Musicals von Stephen Sondheim und Andrew Lloyd Webber*. Herbolzheim: Centaurus Verlag, 2005.

Kasha, Al, and Joel Hirschhorn. *Notes on Broadway: Conversations with the Great Songwriters*. Chicago: Contemporary Books, 1985.

'Legal Boys: Lyrics.' http://www.metrolyrics.com/legal-boys-lyrics-elton-john.thml, accessed 26 October 2014.

The Likes of Us. Live from the Sydmonton Festival, 2005. CD Booklet. Really Useful Recordings 987 4834, 2005.

The Lion King. Original Broadway Cast Recording, 1997. CD Booklet. Walt Disney Records WD 608022, 1997.

McKnight, Gerald. *Andrew Lloyd Webber*. New York: Granada Publishing, 1984.

'Missing: Lyrics.' http://www.vangelislyrics.com/vangelis-lyrics-cover-versions/elaine-paige-cinema-lyrics.htm, accessed 26 October 2014.

Nikkhah, Roya. 'Clash of Musical Titans over Lloyd Webber's Plans for Television Search for "Jesus".' *Daily Telegraph*, 22 January 2012, http://www.telegraph.co.uk/culture/theatre/theatre-news/9029789/Clash-of-musical-titans-over-Lloyd-Webbers-plans-for-television-search-for-Jesus.html, accessed 22 January 2012.

'One of My Best Friends: Lyrics.' http://www.metrolyrics.com/one-of-my-best-friends-lyrics-michael-crawford.html, accessed 26 October 2014.

Rice, Tim. 'A Year of Superstar.' Unpublished manuscript, September 1971. Tim Rice Clippings, New York Public Library of the Performing Arts.

Rice, Tim. 'Extremely Miffed That I Got Slagged Off.' http://www.amazon.com/Musical-Grand-Denny-Martin-Flinn/dp/002864610X/ref=pd_cp_b_0, accessed 7 November 2014.

Rice, Tim. *Oh, What a Circus: The Autobiography 1944–1978*. London: Hodder & Stoughton, 1999.

Rich, Frank, 'Conversations with Sondheim.' *New York Times Magazine*, 12 March 2000. http://partners.nytimes.com/library/magazine/home/20000312mag-sondheim.html, accessed 7 November 2014.

Skasa, Michael. 'Schauspieler im politischen Gewerbe—Politik als Show.' *Theatre heute* 3 (1981): 4–7 + 10.

Sondheim, Stephen. *Finishing the Hat: Collected Lyrics (1954–1981), with Attendant Comments, Principles, Heresies, Grudges, Whines, and Anecdotes.* London: Virgin Books, 2010.

Sondheim, Stephen. 'The Musical Theatre.' In *Broadway Song and Story: Playwrights, Lyricists, Composers Discuss Their Hits,* edited by Otis GuernseyJr. and Terrence McNally, 228–250. New York: Dodd Mead, 1985.

Sondheim, Stephen. 'Theater Lyrics.' In *Playwrights, Lyricists, Composers on Theatre: The Inside Story of a Decade of Theater in Articles and Comments by Its Authors, Selected from Their Own Publication, the 'Dramatists Guild Quarterly',* edited by Otis GuersneyJr., 61–97. New York: Dodd, Mead, 1974.

'Theater Talk: Tim Rice.' Video. New York Public Library for the Performing Arts, NCOX 2406, 2008.

'Theatre Talk # 212: Tim Rice on *King David.*' Video. New York Public Library for the Performing Arts, NCOX 1405, 1997.

'Tim Rice: Lyricist.' In *Evita.* London Revival 2006. Programme May–June 2006, not paginated. London: Adelphi Theatre Company Ltd, 2006.

Tycoon. CD Booklet. Epic Records 471923 2, 1992.

Walker, Tim. 'Sir Tim Rice's Musical Puts Gay into the Fray in *From Here to Eternity.*' *Daily Telegraph,* 28 January 2012. http://www.telegraph.co.uk/active/8887178/Sir-Tim-Rices-musical-puts-gay-into-the-fray-in-From-Here-to-Eternity.html, accessed 28 January 2012.

Walsh, Michael. *Andrew Lloyd Webber: His Life and Works.* London: Abrams, 1989.

'Who'll Speak for Love: Lyrics.' http://www.justsomelyrics.com/1875515/trijntje-oosterhuis-who'll-speak-for-love-lyrics.html, accessed 26 October 2014.

'A Winter's Tale: Lyrics.' http://lyricsplayground.com/alpha/songs/xmas/awinterstale.shtml, accessed 4 November 2014.

The Wizard of Oz. London Palladium Recording, 2011. CD Booklet. Really Useful Recordings 2770131, 2011.

Zadan, Craig. *Sondheim & Co.* 2nd, updated edn. New York: Nick Hern Books, 1989.

....

CAMERON MACKINTOSH

Control, Collaboration, and the Creative Producer

....

MIRANDA LUNDSKAER-NIELSEN

> I never intended to be innovative, or to put on great productions in coun-
> tries that have never seen a West End or Broadway show. It just happened
> because I wanted my shows to be as good as possible, not because I had
> a dream.
>
> Cameron Mackintosh, 2011[1]

THE biggest British musical theatre star to emerge in the 1980s and 1990s was arguably not a performer, director, or writer but a producer. The extraordinary global success of Cameron Mackintosh's shows—particularly *Cats* (1981), *Les Misérables* (1985),
The Phantom of the Opera (1986), and *Miss Saigon* (1989)—made him an internationally
recognized brand name and revolutionized the perception of British musicals abroad,
replacing the image of quirky, nostalgic, one-off hits like *Me and My Girl* (1937), *The Boy
Friend* (1953), and *Oliver!* (1960) with a string of confident, polished new musicals with
bold storylines, a contemporary sound, and dramatic designs that were marketed with
flair and ingenuity.[2]

By the mid-1990s Mackintosh was one of the most recognizable names in British theatre: as well as heading *The Stage*'s annual list of most powerful individuals in the theatre
industry, he was listed in the *Evening Standard*'s 1992 list 'The 25 People Who Really
Run London'[3] and in 1994 his shows formed the theme of the annual Regent Street
Christmas lights. The cultural and economic impact of his success has been officially
acknowledged in honours that include a 1996 knighthood, the 2005 Queen's Award for
Export Achievement, and the 2006 National Enjoy England Award for Outstanding
Contribution to Tourism. Mackintosh himself has exuberantly celebrated the scale of
his success, admitting cheerfully that 'I don't think I was ever humble. [. . .] Even as a
stage manager I made a nuisance of myself and insisted on having my name on the play
bill.'[4] This propensity for self-promotion was evident in the boasts of long-running success on show posters ('*Cats* –Now and Forever'); in the extravagant gala performances

to mark milestone anniversaries; and in the huge billboard erected in New York's Times Square proclaiming *Les Misérables* as the world's most popular musical with a changing digital display showing attendance figures worldwide.

This flair for flamboyant marketing and the international impact of his shows might explain the common depiction of Mackintosh as the pioneer of the so-called modern 'megamusical'—a label that is explored in some detail in Jessica Sternfeld's book *The Megamusical*[5] but is more commonly used as a dismissive shorthand for shows that prioritize style over substance. This depiction of his shows also underpins the notion of his shows as 'McTheatre'—a term used by, among others, scholars Jonathan Burston[6] and Dan Rebellato,[7] to draw a parallel between the McDonald's franchise model and Mackintosh's meticulous replication of productions around the globe. Specifically, Rebellato compares a McDonald's spokesman talking about the volume of burger sales with a book that cites the numbers of headache pills, posters, radio mics, etc. used by *Cats* and *Miss Saigon*, leading to his assertion that these musicals are 'commodities and the attitudes behind them are nakedly about capital accumulation [. . .]. Any pretence at cultural value or artistic worth is crowded out by sheer reverence at the statistical scale involved.'[8]

However, while there is no doubt that Mackintosh takes great pride in his commercial success, his relationship to producing is far more personal than a simple moneymaking enterprise. In 2000 he commented about the subsidiary rights to his shows: 'I could probably sell [them]for an enormous amount of money but I have no interest in doing so: a) I don't need the money, and b), what is the point, having fought my entire life to be independent?'[9] In fact, throughout his career Mackintosh has revealed himself to be both a romantic and pragmatist, arguing that 'you have to get the art right first but you always have to do that within practical limits. A show has to have a strong emotional thread to sustain two and a half hours in the theatre and a rattling good story. My basic philosophy is that if I fall in love with something I will do it, but within bounds.'[10]

THE EARLY YEARS

Mackintosh's fascination with theatre started early and, importantly, included both British and American influences. He has often cited an early trip to the light, nostalgic British musical *Salad Days* (1954) as a formative moment and a fondness for *Oliver!* (1960) that has resulted in several productions of Bart's musical. He also developed an early interest in the Broadway canon thanks to a great-uncle in New York who sent him cast albums of Broadway shows like *The Sound of Music* (1959) before they were generally available in the UK.[11]

After attending Prior Park—a private school in Bath—where he was deeply involved in the drama productions, Mackintosh started the stage management course at Central School of Speech and Drama but was impatient with the academic course content and dropped out to start working his way up within the theatre business, initially as a stagehand and cleaner at Drury Lane theatre. In 1965 he got his break as an acting assistant stage manager in a tour of *Oliver!* which taught him both the magic of live performance and also his own limitations as a performer:

> My Pie Boy, in fact, became something of a showstopper. Eventually I had to be slapped down because, while all eyes were meant to be on Oliver during the big chase at the end of act one, I was getting a lot of attention at the side hurling boys and pies in the air. The real truth is that I loved performing but I was no good at it. But being part of a big show and belting out a song in a house going bananas was something I've never forgotten.[12]

This exuberant, almost childlike enthusiasm for his chosen career is a recurring theme among his colleagues, with Stephen Sondheim calling him 'an over-excited, boundlessly and unabashedly enthusiastic child in the playground of musical theatre'[13] and British theatre critic Michael Billington characterizing him as 'a bouncy, boyish enthusiast' with 'a totally uncynical love of theatre', going on to describe Mackintosh's venture into West End theatre ownership as 'a Peter Pan who has managed to create a Never-Never Land to his own exacting specifications'.[14] It is hard to imagine any other contemporary producer throwing themselves into some of the flamboyant and tongue-in-cheek stunts that Mackintosh has engaged in, such as the anniversary performance of *Cats* where Mackintosh the millionaire came onstage sweeping with a broom in a coy, humorous reference to his early job as a theatre cleaner; or the tenth anniversary performance of *Miss Saigon* where, after the curtain call, Mackintosh drove onstage in a car with the director and writers serenaded by Jonathan Pryce singing 'The American Dream';[15] or his impromptu decision, during a holiday cruise to Antarctica, to stage and choreograph 'One Singular Sensation' from *A Chorus Line* with forty crew members dressed as penguins.[16]

Mackintosh quickly worked his way up from his early jobs to co-producing and marketing, learning his craft in the hands-on, unglamorous world of the British touring scene. As the advertising manager for a national tour of *Hair*, he came up with 'Hair Rail', a combined rail and theatre ticket, and under the mentorship of the actor-manager Patrick Desmond he learned the art of thrifty producing: when their tour of Agatha Christie's *Murder at the Vicarage* (using borrowed scenery from the Nuffield Theatre) started flagging, they worked out that another Christie piece, *Black Coffee*, had the same number of characters and toured the two plays as a 'Festival of Christie' with the same cast and set, 'though we did move the French windows from stage left to stage right and put a new cover on the sofa to give the public a taste of novelty'.[17]

From the mid-1960s until 1980—at a time when 'it was still possible to put on a touring play with a basinful of chutzpah and 200 quid'[18]—Mackintosh went on to produce a string of shows with varying levels of success, learning through mistakes as well as achievements. Mackintosh later claimed to treasure the pithy feedback from director Malcolm Farquhar on his 1967 production of *Little Women* ('The only advice I can give is that the next one shouldn't be quite as bad'[19]) and humorously recalled the feminist revue *After Shave* that ran for all of two weeks the same year: 'It was by some university friends of the girl I was going out with. Like a female revue. I tried it out in Leicester. Then we put it on at the Apollo. The moment we got the set on to the stage I realised it was a disaster.'[20] In 1969, his first West End musical *Anything Goes* ended up £40,000 in debt[21] followed by *At Home with the Dales*: based on the radio show *Mrs Dale's Diary*, he had booked it into the 2,000-seater Winter Gardens in Blackpool for two weeks but ticket sales were so poor that his bank manager gave him £500 to pay the actors 'because he said if I didn't, Equity would bar me and I'd never work in the theatre again.'[22]

While his initial work was with a wide range of theatre, Mackintosh soon realized that his main passion lay in musical theatre and his early work also included *The Card* (1973), his first new musical from scratch, and *Side by Side by Sondheim* (1976), a revue based around the work of composer and lyricist Stephen Sondheim that provided him with his first real hit, although the initial financing had required some pragmatic lateral thinking: '[A]ctors don't turn up for rehearsals before 2pm. I had to be in the dole queue before 10am. So I would stand in line for the dole early in the morning, then get back to the theatre and pay the cast.'[23] And in 1979 his production of *My Fair Lady* was an early trailblazer for collaboration between the commercial and subsidized sectors when the Arts Council approached him to help fill a series of large regional houses they had just acquired—a collaboration that was all the more remarkable given that it was another thirty years before the Arts Council finally recognized musical theatre as an art form deserving of public funding.[24]

Towards the end of this period, in the late 1970s, Mackintosh was also looking to New York for inspiration. Nick Allott, his long-term managing director, recalls that 'Cameron was at that time a completely unknown producer [. . .] finding his feet and creating his business. He would scrape together his pennies to fly to New York to see the shows and bang on people's doors and was sort of adopted by Bernie Jacobs who was one of the great legendary Shuberts.'[25] Indicatively, Allott notes that a major inspiration was the legendarily idiosyncratic and flamboyant Broadway producer David Merrick: 'Merrick was very much Cameron's role model—in fact Merrick was incredibly kind to Cameron round about the time of *42nd Street* just before *Cats* in the late 1970s/early 1980s. Merrick insisted on seeing him and gave him an afternoon of time, a masterclass in generations of experience.'[26]

While many discussions of Mackintosh centre around his later successes on the world stage, these first fifteen years as a jobbing producer provide a valuable insight into his often unconventional approach to developing, marketing, and licensing his musicals. His formative years within the British touring circuit, together with his detailed understanding of both the West End and Broadway, have led to marketing strategies, collaborative partnerships, and approaches to the audience experience that diverge from the established traditions of both the West End and Broadway. One example of this was his 1990 transfer of *Five Guys Named Mo* from the more informal ambience of the Theatre Royal Stratford East in London's East End to the West End. Philip Hedley, then the artistic director of the Theatre Royal Stratford East, recalls the way in which Mackintosh responded pragmatically and efficiently to his concerns around the transfer between very different theatre environments:

> He said what do we need to do to make it work as well as it did in your theatre? I said well, we have younger and jollier ushers than in the West End. He said he'd change that. He didn't sack the ones he had; he moved them to another theatre, and we got younger staff in. Then he said—what else? I said our seats are obviously cheaper, but you can't do anything about that, can you? He asked how much are your cheapest tickets—£3?—he'd charge that for the gallery: what else? I said well, the audience is more polite in the West End than our audiences. He said he'd hire a meeter and greeter.[27]

The show ran for four years in the West End and opened on Broadway in 1992, where Mackintosh again created a less formal ambience by knocking through the back wall of the theatre to the bar next door, renaming it 'Moe's Bar', and serving drinks throughout the performance.

Another lasting legacy of these early pragmatic years was to reinforce Mackintosh's innate sense of fiscal hawkishness. His brother Nicky has traced this back to their mother: 'She was born in Malta and her experiences gave her the ability to make everything go a long way. A chicken that was supposed to be for two she made last for six.'[28] This early frugal influence is reflected in Mackintosh's 1992 comments that, despite now being a millionaire, 'I lead as normal a life as I can. I think something rubs off on you if you never have to queue. I go shopping and it is one of my great joys going to [British supermarket chain] Tesco's and being beady about prices. That's what everyone has to do to find £28 to buy a ticket to a show.'[29] While he has clearly enjoyed his wealth in both his professional and personal lives—mounting large-scale productions, throwing lavish parties, buying and renovating theatres, owning multiple homes—his business approach remains fiscally conservative. In 1990, as Broadway producers increasingly spoke about the difficulties of producing and recouping costs on Broadway, Mackintosh's response was: 'You just have to know what you are doing. I'm a pro and whatever else people may say, after all those years of operating on shoestring budgets, I am not profligate with money.'[30] This outlook can also be seen in his statements in 2010 about government arts policy and the arts bureaucracy, arguing that 'there must be a more straightforward way of running things. I'm running a worldwide enterprise with 45 people working for me, including the accountant.'[31]

CATS AND INTERNATIONAL SUCCESS

By the end of the 1970s Mackintosh was building a reasonable reputation as a touring producer in the UK. Then in 1980 a lunch meeting with composer Andrew Lloyd

Webber led to the two teaming up as producer and composer of an unconventional new musical (see Figure 22.1), and when *Cats* opened the following year it provided Mackintosh with a springboard on to the international stage. The scale of the show's success, and that of *Les Misérables* afterwards, came as a surprise to everybody. Mackintosh later recalled that '[w]e didn't even know what we had there. It was just settings of T. S. Eliot poems. In fact, everybody thought it was Andrew Lloyd Webber's one bad idea. Only later did we realise that its theme was universal: the tribe with an outsider.'[32]

The scale of this success can be attributed to a number of factors. One was that musical theatre itself was at a crossroads. Mackintosh recognizes that 'Andrew [Lloyd Webber] and I were brought up on the end of the heyday of the American musical. We were stage struck about it. But we came to our fruition when there was a hunger for seeing new things, in the same way as Spielberg and Lucas were in the cinema. It isn't that we discovered a secret mine: it's just that people were ready for change.'[33] On a practical level, Mackintosh's major shows came at a time when air travel was becoming more accessible to the general public and so broadening the audience base to include international visitors. Culturally, Nick Allott notes that Mackintosh's breakthrough coincided with a decade of conspicuous consumption when musical theatre became part of the cultural zeitgeist.

FIGURE 22.1 A surprise hit: celebrating at the first night party of *Cats* on 23 April 1981. From left to right: Cameron Mackintosh, Elaine Paige, Brian Blessed, Andrew Lloyd Webber, and Wayne Sleep.

Photograph by PA/TopPhoto. Courtesy of ArenaPal.

Another explanation for the broad appeal of Mackintosh's shows is that his own tastes are unapologetically populist. He has cited his adherence to the advice of British producer Charles Cochran to 'never try and put a show on for the public: always put it on for yourself and then perhaps the public will like it'.[34] Given this approach, it has clearly helped that his personal tastes are, in his own words, 'stylishly common'[35] and 'pretty general public' with a fondness for spy novels, popular fiction, and the classics.[36] While there are strong stylistic and thematic differences between the shows he has produced, he is clearly more interested in big stories, arguing that 'George Bernard Shaw's *Pygmalion* was responsible for *My Fair Lady*; Victor Hugo for *Les Misérables*. Take a massive story and you have the right start. *Oliver!* we owe to Dickens'[37] Mackintosh's interest seems to lie in creating a viscerally and emotionally exciting night at the theatre rather than exploring complex and/or political ideas. While some of the shows that he has been involved in developing and producing have been based on quite highbrow sources (T. S. Eliot's *Old Possum's Book of Practical Cats*, Victor Hugo's *Les Misérables*, Puccini's *Madama Butterfly*), the style of the storytelling in the musical adaptations has been very accessible, and he has argued openly that

> [m]usicals are not the best place to make political points. *South Pacific* was very adventurous, and indeed won the Pulitzer Prize, but I don't think it was particularly illuminating on the subject of the Second World War, although it used that specific historical setting, as does *Miss Saigon* in [sic] Vietnam, as a background. But it was a great musical.[38]

This stance makes his long-standing association with Stephen Sondheim an interesting one. Mackintosh clearly has a deep respect for the composer, helping to establish Sondheim in Britain with *Side by Side by Sondheim* (1976) and the UK premiere of *Follies* (1987), featuring a Sondheim section in *Hey, Mr Producer!* (itself named from a Sondheim lyric in *Follies*) and even naming one of his West End theatres after him in 2014. Nevertheless, he remains ambivalent about the widely admired complexities of his shows that have served as role models for many of the next generation of writers: 'People often ask why I don't do more Sondheim but, actually, even though I admire a huge amount of virtually everything he has written, he writes about people who are just not me. You know that song at the end of *Into The Woods*, "No One Is Alone"? I am not that introspective. I don't have to find myself. I don't need analysis.'[39] Elsewhere he clarifies: 'It's not the music, nor the libretto, nor the story that I don't like. It's those characters! I couldn't stand being in the same room with those Sondheim characters for more than five minutes. They're vile. They're malcontents.'[40]

However, while Mackintosh is unapologetic about his populist tastes, he has strongly refuted accusations that his shows are all about technology and big sets, arguing that 'all we are doing is employing modern technology to replace manpower [...]. We're not doing anything that the Victorians and other people haven't done before. It's like saying you shouldn't watch a modern television. We use the best technology to make it work. That's different from technology taking over.'[41] In a nod to the holistic theory of the Wagnerian *Gesamtkunstwerk*, he emphasizes that 'what I know better than anyone is that a great set doesn't make a good show. I also know that in order to sound good it's got to look good.'[42]

Control and Collaboration

Whatever the contributing factors, the success of *Cats*, followed closely by *Les Misérables* and *The Phantom of the Opera*, had a profound effect on Mackintosh's career trajectory, giving him financial and therefore artistic freedom. He chose to exercise this freedom by adopting a very personal approach to producing. Mackintosh's head office is an elegant pair of town houses in a tranquil, leafy square in Bloomsbury. His company is commonly portrayed as a family-like environment, albeit clearly a patriarchy, that combines high expectations and exacting standards with a sense of loyalty and fun. His first secretary Sue Higginson later recalled that '[h]e wants his own way, but he created this family thing at work. He was a fantastically good employer'[43] while his former managing director Martin McCallum notes: 'His style is to interpose. That's what keeps the company's vitality. Everyone is very clear about what they want to achieve; it's a mixture of fun and hard work.'[44] It is certainly noticeable that many of Mackintosh's core staff have remained with the company for years, in some cases decades, and that current and former employees largely speak of him with respect and affection, openly and humorously referring to him as 'matron'. There is also a sense of familial loyalty in Mackintosh going back to his early investors even when he didn't need outside backing[45] and in his decision to voluntarily give Lionel Bart a percentage of the profits on his West End production of *Oliver!* (see Figure 22.2)[46] Writing team George Stiles and Anthony Drewe publicly acknowledged in 1999 that he 'never drops you, there's always something going on in the background';[47] in 2013, Drewe still described the relationship as an 'ongoing mentorship'.[48]

Mackintosh's status as sole producer on most of his shows has secured him an unusual level of financial control. This has in turn given him great flexibility to respond to the specific needs of each production. Creating pressure on ticket availability has been a key to his marketing strategy—in 1999 he reflected that '[i]f *Cats* had been in a 2,000-seat theatre, it would have come off years ago.'[49] Thus for the Broadway productions of *Les Misérables* and *Miss Saigon* (which played in much bigger theatres) he adopted the strategy of buying unsold seats and giving them to charity to make it appear a sell-out and so boost its appeal. Usually, this is only done to keep the show above the stop clause (the weekly gross required by the theatre landlord to allow the show to continue) with unsold seats otherwise being sold half-price from the TKTS ticket booth. This tactic has drawn disapproval from other producers, including Andrew Lloyd Webber, on the grounds that it distorts official audience figures, but Mackintosh simply calls it 'a marketing strategy for a megamusical in its first year', pointing out the crucial factor that 'as

FIGURE 22.2 Cameron Mackintosh and Lionel Bart at a rehearsal for the 1994 London revival of *Oliver!*.

Photograph by Colin Willoughby. Courtesy of ArenaPal.

I am the sole producer and both a major investor and royalty participant, the real cost to me is very low for the control it gives me.'[50]

The extent of Mackintosh's creative control within the development process has also set him apart in an industry that increasingly consists of producing teams. On Broadway today, large commercial musicals are almost always produced collaboratively by multiple investor-producers, while in the subsidized sector the journey of a show from inception to production often entails a series of readings and workshops, each of which is followed by detailed feedback from directors, theatre producers, and dramaturges. By contrast, Allott notes, Mackintosh collaborates through choice rather than necessity: '[W]e work with other people on a fairly regular basis but there always needs to be a creative reason for doing so. It's not a financial reason—which is why most Broadway producers co-produce.'[51] Although Mackintosh has chosen to engage in producing partnerships with major organizations like the Royal Shakespeare Company (RSC), the National Theatre, and Disney[52] as well as British regional theatres like Chichester and the West Yorkshire Playhouse, he retains a high level of involvement, with colleagues citing his 'extraordinary'[53] and even 'forensic'[54] attention to detail and West End producer Nica Burns characterizing him as 'enthusiastic, committed and totally ruthless about getting what he wants.'[55] Mackintosh himself is very open, indeed cheerful, about describing his producing style as 'interfering'[56] and acknowledging that 'I am a meddler.

I meddle in every phase of the musical. I help rewrite, I help direct, I approve of the lighting. I am what they call an active producer.'[57] While acknowledging that he is not the easiest person to work with, Mackintosh is unapologetic, arguing that '[a]lthough theatre is utterly collaborative, it is impossible when the producers are a group of people. You've got no one definite batting for the production team to go against [. . .]. Not many great shows come out of having a sewing circle.'[58]

Inevitably, this approach takes its toll on his artistic collaborators. A 2013 documentary captured Mackintosh in rehearsals for *Barnum*, a co-production with the Chichester Festival Theatre. It shows Mackintosh as an intensely focused and often impatient presence, getting involved in every aspect of the show from the delivery of individual lyric lines and musical phrases to the staging of key numbers. The latter ranges from small details ('I love what you've got. They just need to do one more thing— flying like that', gesturing with arms) to invoking rules of musical staging ('we can't take the cast off in the middle of a number and leave just two people on it. It just isn't the way to do a production number') and dramaturgical notes ('I think the opening is wrong. I feel incredibly strongly [. . .] you just have to be so careful in those first five minutes of a show of how you give the audience a language. And simplicity is always better. There's just too many things coming in too fast. You know what they mean in the show but an audience doesn't').[59] The director Tim Sheader is repeatedly seen looking subdued and taken aback as Mackintosh demands changes on the grounds that 'this looks shambolic' and the proposed costumes are 'no good'.[60] He reflects to the camera: 'I can't lie—it's quite difficult. If you're a director in a subsidized sector if it's a matter of taste the director wins. In the commercial world the producer is the boss [. . .]. I love getting notes but you want to be able to put it together a bit before you get too many notes. It's only different because it's Cameron—it's a different pressure and a different level of management.'[61]

Even Mackintosh's long-time collaborators often combine respect and affection with exasperation. This relationship is humorously captured by Stephen Sondheim and Andrew Lloyd Webber in their musical tribute to Mackintosh in *Hey, Mr Producer!* with new lyrics set to the tune of 'The Music of the Night': 'Night time falling | Cameron keeps calling | Posing questions | Questions with suggestions | Suddenly appearing | Forever interfering . . .'.[62] Julia McKenzie, director and co-creator of *Putting it Together* (1976), later recalled his participation as 'monstrous. He wants to do everything. When we were putting this show together he wouldn't stay away',[63] while Sondheim has noted that Mackintosh 'loves to interfere—it drives me crazy—in every individual department' before going on to acknowledge that 'it is his major contribution. You feel that there is a captain of the ship—there's a boss who is looking out for everybody's interests.'[64] Similarly, director Eric Schaeffer reflected that sometimes 'you've just got to beat him off with a stick' before conceding: 'Actually he's terrific. He's unusual for a producer in his enthusiasm.'[65] Richard Eyre describes him as a 'genial bully' but notes that there's a dialectic between Mackintosh and the rest of the creative team: 'However autocratic his instincts may be, in the end he does collaborate. Much as he would like to be the writer/ composer/director/designer—and sometimes thinks that he is—in the end he recognizes the way that things are put together.'[66]

In 2013, after working with Mackintosh on several shows alongside writing partner George Stiles, Anthony Drewe reflected that 'Cameron's involvement with everything we've done has made us better writers,'[67] because of the way in which he challenges them creatively:

> He's always been very good at pointing a finger at an area of the show that's not working or which can be improved—which isn't funny enough or isn't snappy enough, or is too ponderous at that point in the act [. . .]. What he's not so great at—and I think he admits himself—is coming up with the solution. He will come up with *a* solution, but that doesn't necessarily mean that you have to adhere to [it] . . . I remember once saying to him when he came up with a solution: 'Cameron, I totally disagree', and he said 'Oh good dear—now tell me why.' What he's trying to do is to prod you out of your slumber into challenging him and coming back with something better.[68]

This insistence on robust creative dialogue also extends to the rest of the creative team and Chris Grady argues that Mackintosh enjoys being challenged and is open to being persuaded.[69] It is characteristic that rather than hiring musical theatre veterans his directorial choices have often been major figures from the British subsidized sector like Trevor Nunn, John Caird, Nicholas Hytner, and Richard Eyre who are highly experienced and articulate practitioners used to working in a variety of theatrical genres (classical theatre, contemporary drama, opera, musicals) and to working dramaturgically with new writing. As Mackintosh noted in 1994, 'nearly every person I have ever worked with successfully in the musical theatre has had one thing in common with me: we learned our trade through, or because of, the subsidised theatre'.[70]

The development process for *Mary Poppins* (2005) provides an interesting insight into Mackintosh's proactive involvement. [71] The show was co-produced with Disney, but the extent of Mackintosh's involvement was reflected in his credit not just as producer but also as a co-creator. The show's director Richard Eyre confirms that Mackintosh was very much a partner in the development of the show, along with the writers, choreographer, and himself.[72] Lyricist Anthony Drewe recalls that Mackintosh and Disney's Tom Schumacher spent a weekend creating a sixty-four-page synopsis with extracts from the books, the screenplay, and the songs from the film which gave the writers 'a wonderful seedbed in which to plant our own thoughts'.[73] In the ensuing writing period Schumacher would check in on the show's progress from time to time while Mackintosh had the writers come and see him every week with their work-in-progress. Drewe notes that this process came as a bit of a shock to Fellowes who, fresh from winning an Oscar for the screenplay of *Gosford Park* (2002), was 'not used to having a producer telling him how to make a scene funny'.[74] Throughout the development period there was an ongoing dialectic between the writers and producer, with Mackintosh giving notes on songs as they were written and serving as an editor: at one point Stiles and Drewe played three possible songs for a certain moment in the show—Mackintosh rejected one as 'too wordy' and then invited them to choose one of the remaining two which became 'Anything Can Happen'. He also insisted on being part of the presentation of songs to Eyre and later to the co-producers: Drewe fondly recalls a presentation of three *Mary Poppins* songs to their Disney co-producers in which Mackintosh played the role of Michael Banks.[75] At the end of the development process, Mackintosh built in extended time at the Bristol Hippodrome before the London opening in a throwback to the days of the out-of-town try-outs that have largely been abandoned on Broadway—a decision that Eyre claims was 'absolutely vital' as it allowed the time to rework the show in front of live audiences.[76]

Inevitably, there are sometimes less favourable repercussions to having the producer—who is ultimately responsible for the commercial success of a show—taking such a central role in the creative process. There are times when Mackintosh's personal taste for theatrical excitement and big stories, coupled with his ultimate control of the project, have blurred or derailed the writers' original intentions in a way that retrospectively may have been unhelpful to the show. Two examples of this are *Just So* and *Betty Blue Eyes*—both with music and lyrics by Stiles and Drewe and, interestingly, both much more modest shows than the epic stories that have made Mackintosh a household name.

On *Just So*, their first full collaboration with the producer, Drewe recalls a lack of authorial control in the developmental process where he didn't always agree on the script changes made by Mackintosh and director Julia McKenzie. In particular, he cites how McKenzie and Mackintosh's idea of introducing an environmental angle started 'to make the show into something different from what we intended it to be [. . .] suddenly it became this thing about green issues and suddenly it became a show of two halves rather than a whole'.[77] While there was a process of 'barter' he recalls that 'it's hard to jump on board a train that you're not driving yourself'. Ultimately Drewe agreed with reviews that said Act 2 was a bit of a mess; he also felt that the show was overproduced for the small Tricycle Theatre—with too much smoke, light, and sound that made it 'claustrophobic'.[78] He and Stiles subsequently did a rewrite of the show which Drewe calls 'our version'.

Betty Blue Eyes (2011) is an adaptation of Alan Bennett's screenplay *A Private Function* (1984)—also the original title of the musical. When Mackintosh asked to hear it there was already a plan to do it in a workshop at the West Yorkshire Playhouse, although the theatre was looking for an enhancement deal.[79] Anthony Drewe recalls that he was 'reticent' to let Mackintosh hear it as he was happy with the show and didn't want Mackintosh to 'unpick it'.[80] In the event, Mackintosh stepped in and offered to help with the workshop but on condition that no other producers were to attend. Afterwards, he agreed to produce the show but decided that it was to open in the West End rather than at the West Yorkshire Playhouse. Drewe notes that while this made financial sense, it also denied them the out-of-town try-out that had proved so helpful on *Mary Poppins* and the chance to build an audience. Most contentiously, Mackintosh took the unilateral decision to change the title to *Betty Blue Eyes*: the writers first learned about this at the poster presentation. Both Drewe and director Richard Eyre maintain that the title change was a mistake, alienating the Bennett fans and selling the show on the animatronic pig when it is fundamentally quite an intimate show about a marriage.[81] In the event, the show got strong reviews but didn't find an audience and had to close early. Subsequently, the writers reworked the show for a 2014 co-production between four regional theatres: Mercury Theatre Colchester, Liverpool Everyman and Playhouse, Salisbury Playhouse, and West Yorkshire Playhouse.

But while hindsight may have proved Mackintosh guilty of some misjudgements, few would question his genuine dedication to creating the best possible work. Indeed, Mackintosh's fierce protectiveness of his shows has led to some dramatic battles such as his legendary (and ultimately successful) battle with American Equity over bringing Jonathan Pryce to Broadway in *Miss Saigon*—a stand-off that saw him publicly announce the cancellation of the Broadway production and promise to refund all advance tickets before the union backed down.[82] And while Mackintosh's career has encompassed great successes as well as commercial flops, it is indicative that he often seems as passionate about the ones that didn't meet with great critical or box office success as those that did. After *Martin Guerre* opened to mixed reviews in 1996, the creative team reworked the show and Mackintosh closed it down for a few days (at considerable expense) before reopening in a substantially revised version that went on to win the 1997 Olivier Award for Best Musical. Subsequently the show was reworked again at the West Yorkshire Playhouse in 1998 before touring the UK and US. In summer 2014, Mackintosh confirmed that the show was being comprehensively rewritten again for a new production.[83]

LICENSING

The sense of personal attachment to his shows is undoubtedly also a key reason for Mackintosh's unconventional approach to licensing them internationally once they are up and running. Nick Allott points out that a British producer before Mackintosh typically had only limited control over the afterlife of their shows:

> If he had no clout at all he would just have had the rights for the UK and then the author's agents would have taken it back and licensed it all over the world. If he had a little bit of clout he may have had some sort of participation in the first couple of productions. Or if he'd had considerable clout he would have been sort of involved in the New York production and maybe sort of involved in Australia but after that again it would be down to the agents to actually license it. What Cameron did was to persuade third party licensees like Theater an der Wien in Vienna that they should be taking a reproduction of the London production. Because traditionally people would do their own.[84]

In practice, licensing Mackintosh's shows can take two forms. Smaller 'local' productions have to be different from the West End original for copyright reasons although Mackintosh has approval of everything from set and poster designs to casting. However, for major productions, the licensee is required to replicate the original production exactly, with permission required for any changes. The production team credentials and theatres are rigorously examined and a Mackintosh team is sent out to work with the local producers throughout the casting and rehearsal process. With overseas productions, Mackintosh will himself attend the final stages of rehearsals or an early preview, make some changes, and then return to see the show again.[85] Chris Grady notes that as head of licensing he had twenty minutes with Mackintosh every two weeks in which to go over designs and plans for the various productions of his shows: his job was to make sure that Mackintosh was never surprised when he dropped in on rehearsals unexpectedly.[86]

It is partly this level of creative control and the franchise business model that have led to labelling the shows 'McTheatre', with the implicit criticisms that it stifles artistic freedom for the new production team and subjects audiences to something that is a carbon copy rather than an original and authentic piece of theatre. In response to these criticisms, Mackintosh's colleagues and staff highlight the issue of audience expectations, with Nick Allott arguing that when there is a hit show in one country, audiences elsewhere want the original—a claim that is confirmed by producer Mariko Kojima of TOHO in Tokyo.[87] Allott further points out that the physical staging (which the advent of YouTube has made more visible) is a part of this and the only way to ensure that audiences experience the original production is to exercise tight artistic control. As an example, he cites an early Polish production where the local producer was given freedom to reconceive the staging but simply ended up doing a cheap imitation of the original.[88] Similarly, Kojima points out that TOHO also licenses shows from Vereinigte Bühnen Wien with whom they have an open brief to restage the shows: the result is that the Austrian shows are done more cheaply and therefore more often in Japan than the Mackintosh shows, but at the loss to Japanese audiences of the original production values.[89]

In practice, it seems that the extent of dialogue and negotiation can vary from one production to another. This can partly be explained by who is supervising the show: Kojima notes that at TOHO they can work more organically when the original director is in charge. When it's an assistant director who has learned the show they may explain to the actors why they are doing a particular move, and the performers may try to build characters around that, but ultimately they have to fit in with the existing staging.[90] Kojima cites the end of *Miss Saigon* where Ellen in the original production simply stood still onstage: they found that the TOHO audiences had no sympathy for her but in order to make the change they had to write a letter to Mackintosh asking whether she could extend her hand.[91] Perhaps inevitably, translation is also an issue that can create complications with the franchise model due to cultural and linguistic differences: in Japanese they can only fit 30–50 per cent of the original words into the same musical phrases and this sometimes creates issues with staging and choreography as that is based on the English words. Thus Kojima notes that while sometimes they can fit the translation to the staging, there are other times when the two simply don't match.[92]

While the level of control exercised by Mackintosh can undoubtedly be challenging, it is not completely inflexible. Chris Grady emphasizes that Mackintosh looks for local teams to inspire him and even surprise him with their ideas, and that sometimes he does approve changes[93]. Willem Metz, Executive Producer at Stage Entertainment in Holland, concurs that although Mackintosh is very strict, he wants his overseas collaborators to be hands-on theatre producers and if they are doing everything they can, he is very respectful if they need help.[94] He cites the 2010 Dutch production of *Mary Poppins* at the Circus Theater in Scheveningen in which they negotiated a number of changes to suit their venue which was very different to the Victorian West End theatres, such as making some of the numbers bigger and inventing new ways of coming into the audience that made good use of the specific shape of the theatre. And while the translation was generally very faithful, the word 'supercalifragilisticexpiallydocious' had to be changed because 'docious' only has five rhymes in Dutch, while the new ending '-dasties' rhymes with useful words like 'fantastisch'. This also meant changing the choreography because the dancers were spelling out the word with their bodies. He notes that while Mackintosh wanted an explanation of why they were changing a fantasy word, he listened to the rationale.

One important by-product of Mackintosh's revolutionary approach to licensing has been to develop new markets for musical theatre, and while this was never Mackintosh's primary goal he has stated that '[w]hat I am most proud of having done is to have raised the standard of the musical by putting on shows to a Broadway and London standard in parts of the world which have never seen that'.[95] This includes opening up a new market in the East (which Allott now sees as the future) with Japan being a particularly strong market through their relationship with Shiki (*Cats* and *The Phantom of the Opera*) and TOHO (*Les Misérables* and *Miss Saigon*). In Europe, the Mackintosh shows also broke new ground in many countries, bringing West End quality musical productions to audiences who couldn't travel to London and presenting them in the local language. Founded in 1998 by producer Joop van den Ende, Stage Entertainment is today one of the biggest producing organizations in Europe. Metz (a former Mackintosh employee) openly acknowledges Mackintosh's influence in both their development of new shows and their approach to international licensing. At the writing stage this can be seen in the producers' 'detail-oriented' involvement in the development process as well as in the common use of the Mackintosh shows as shared reference points among the writers. He also recognizes Mackintosh's influence in Stage Entertainment's engagement with new international markets and in its adoption of the franchise model of licensing: starting in one place and then rolling out productions from there in the confident belief that the same show can work in different markets and cultures.[96]

MANAGING LONG RUNS

Another by-product of Mackintosh's popular success has been unusually long—in some cases record-breaking—runs, with the accompanying challenges of adapting an ongoing production to changing economic climates, new technologies, and the dangers of artistic stagnation. On several occasions he has made it clear that while he has a sense of being part of a theatre community his first allegiance is to keeping his shows fresh and financially viable.

Interestingly, while both industry members and the press are quick to complain about the long-running musicals dominating West End and Broadway theatres at the expense of new material, his attempts to keep them fresh have sometimes met with resistance. This includes the decision to undertake a major recasting of *Les Misérables* on Broadway in the run-up to the tenth anniversary celebrations in October 1996. In support of Mackintosh, co-director John Caird argued publicly that 'the production just feels a little stuck, a little bit stale. Some people have been in it for a very, very long time, and nobody can keep things fresh forever. Long-run-itis is a disease that can really kill a show'.[97] However, the decision played out in the press under emotional headlines like 'Bloodbath on *Broadway* as Mackintosh Sacks *Les Mis* [sic] cast'[98] and 'Les Mis [sic] Purge Causes Fury on Broadway'[99] which reported that 'Mr. Caird told the cast of 37 they looked like "Madame Tussaud's waxworks" and were too old to play students'. Interestingly, *The Independent*'s David Lister chose to frame Mackintosh's attention to ongoing quality control in negative terms, arguing that '[p]art of the problem is Sir Cameron's perfectionism—he likes to see his blockbuster shows kept fresh with regular cast renewals even when they are displaying house-full notices'.[100] In the event, some cast members were fired, some were asked to reaudition, and some were invited to stay with the show.[101] But the fact that a cast change in a long-running show met with such an astonished and indignant response is indicative of the extent to which Mackintosh's shows had come to be perceived as steady employment in a traditionally volatile profession.

THE MACKINTOSH LEGACY

Cameron Mackintosh has unquestionably made an enormous impact on the development of musical theatre through his revolutionary approach to licensing, his synthesis of commercial musicals with the traditions of British subsidized theatre, and his development of new audiences and new global markets for contemporary musicals. The combination of producing, licensing existing productions, and ownership of multiple theatre buildings resulted in a very powerful theatrical organization. In recognition of the size of his operation, and the responsibility that comes with it, Mackintosh appointed Alan Finch as co-managing director with Nick Allott in April 2015, noting both the need for another person to shoulder the growing workload and a pragmatic approach to succession planning: 'I am coming up to my 70th birthday. Nick is younger than me but not that much, and it's a vast amount of work. [. . .] If anything, God forbid, happened to either me or Nick, we need a massively strong structure to take on this responsibility'.[102]

Perhaps inevitably, Mackintosh's close personal involvement with looking after existing shows has limited his time and energy for new productions. It is tempting to speculate how he might have further advanced the cause of new musical development in the

UK if *Cats* and *Les Misérables* had simply been modest successes, leaving him free to develop new projects. A 1982 interview with Mackintosh and Andrew Lloyd Webber offers a glimpse of a different kind of impact that he might have had through their plans for a theatre school with theatre attached in which to try out new and existing musicals in a reasonably risk-free environment—an idea born from their experiences on *Cats* which took nine months to cast due to a lack of singer-dancers. Mackintosh described their vision for 'the sort of place [where] it doesn't really matter if a show hits or misses but you can have an interesting experiment. Too big an auditorium is a noose round your own neck. We want to set up somewhere like Joan Littlewood's place at Stratford East, absolutely bursting with life. If a show was any good, it could transfer out.'[103] In an ironic reversal of the critical reactions to his own shows as spectacle, Lloyd Webber argued: 'I think that now is the time to do it, when our big rivals—the Broadway producers—are not finding material that is phenomenally exciting. Their shows depend to an enormous extent on production values.'[104] In the event, this venture never materialized and it was the American non-profit theatres that developed the kind of low-risk development opportunities in the 1980s and 1990s that fulfilled this role.[105]

Nonetheless, Mackintosh has made a significant contribution to developing new talent and new work. The number of hit productions that he produced in the West End and around the world provided the impetus for a proliferation of serious musical theatre training programmes outside the US. In addition, the Cameron Mackintosh Foundation—as well as giving millions to charities working with causes like AIDS, children, and the homeless—has provided substantial sums to support new musical theatre development. In the US, he set up a $1.5 million endowment with the *New York Times* in 1991 to fund musical theatre development at three New York theatres. In the UK, he has supported opportunities within existing organizations, such as establishing the Cameron Mackintosh Chair of Contemporary Theatre at St Catherine's College, Oxford (a one-year appointment first held by Stephen Sondheim); funding a young director traineeship at Greenwich Theatre under the Regional Theatre Young Director Scheme (with the proviso that the theatre put on a musical in that year); and supporting the Cameron Mackintosh Resident Composer Scheme in collaboration with Mercury Musical Developments which funds placements in midsized British producing theatres for emerging musical theatre writers. In 2015, Mackintosh provided financial backing and became a shareholder in director Jonathan Church's new production company on his departure from Chichester Festival Theatre.[106]

While critics will no doubt continue to debate Mackintosh's legacy in terms of both achievements and lost opportunities, he himself has long professed himself at peace with his life and career, stating in 2015 that 'I never expected to be producing shows in my sixties'.[107] Certainly Mackintosh has always made a point of nurturing his interest outside the high-octane, volatile world of musical theatre producing—including spending time at his houses in France, Scotland, and Somerset—which has allowed him to retain a sense of perspective. In public, at least, he has philosophically accepted the inevitability of being replaced as the pre-eminent musical theatre producer, noting that 'I know enough about the history of the theatre to know it goes in cycles. There is a period in which you learn your craft. You meet people with a similar interest and for fifteen to twenty years you are firing on all cylinders and then there is a new audience for something else.'[108] He cites a touching moment watching *Godspell* with the legendary producer Hugh 'Binkie' Beaumont sitting behind him: 'At the end, we all went wild. Binkie, in his seventies by then, just sat there, looking rather sad. I could see that he smelt a hit but I could also see he couldn't understand why. And I've always remembered that for myself.'[109]

However, there is little indication that Mackintosh is planning to leave the musical theatre arena anytime soon. His successful first foray into film musicals with *Les Misérables* (2012) represented a new creative direction, and as the majority shareholder of Music Theatre International (the largest owner of secondary rights to musicals) he continues to play a key role in the business of international licensing. In addition, his move into owning and renovating theatres (in which, inevitably, he takes a close personal interest) has ensured that he will remain a physical presence within the West End for as long as he wants. As he pointed out in 1992: 'I know at some point no one will like my shows—not even my mother. But I'll still want to work in theatre. Supervising a building is a safety net to keep me in the play-pen.'[110]

NOTES

1. David Thomas, 'I Always Think I'm Tigger', *Sunday Telegraph*, 8 July 2011, 5.
2. This is, of course, an overseas perspective—in fact, London had been a thriving centre of musical theatre for decades, with long-running hits by writers such as Ivor Novello, Julian Slade, and many more. For an overview, please see John Snelson, ' "We Said We Wouldn't Look Back": British Musical Theatre 1935–1960', in *The Cambridge Companion to the Musical*, eds. William A. Everett and Paul R. Laird (Cambridge: Cambridge University Press 2002), 101–119.
3. Valentine Low, 'The 25 People Who Really Run London', *Evening Standard*, 1 September 1992, London Life section, 21–22.
4. Valerie Grove, 'The Valerie Grove Interview', *The Times*, 16 December 1994, 14.
5. Jessica Sternfeld, *The Megamusical* (Bloomington: Indiana University Press, 2006), 1–4.
6. J. I. Burston, *The Megamusical: New Forms and Relations in Global Cultural Production* (Goldsmiths, University of London, UMI Dissertations Publishing 1998).
7. Dan Rebellato, 'Playwriting and Globalization: Towards a Site-Unspecific Theatre', *Contemporary Theatre Review* 16, no. 1 (2006): 97–113.
8. Rebellato, 'Playwriting', 101.
9. Helena de Bertodano, 'Can't Dance, Can't Sing, Can Do', *Sunday Telegraph*, 16 July 2000, 3.
10. Heather Farmbrough, 'The Virtues in Showing Off', *Voyager Magazine*, July/August 1994, 14.
11. David Lister, 'Bard of the West End', *The Independent*, 21 July 2001, V&A Theatre & Performance collections.
12. Michael Billington, 'Total Theatre Nut', *The Guardian*, 9 December 1992, A4.
13. Simon Fanshawe, 'Mister Musical', *The Guardian*, 23 October 1999, 6.
14. Billington, 'Total Theatre Nut'.

15. Lister, 'Bard of the West End'.
16. Charles Spencer, 'Cameron's Musical Laboratory', *Daily Telegraph*, 12 February 1992, V&A Theatre & Performance collections.
17. Billington, 'Total Theatre Nut'.
18. Billington, 'Total Theatre Nut'.
19. Billington, 'Total Theatre Nut'.
20. www.alanfranks.com/Sir_Cameron_Mackintosh.html, accessed 2 September 2014.
21. Fanshawe, 'Mister Musical'.
22. Fanshawe, 'Mister Musical'.
23. Harry Rolnick, 'Magician of the Musical', *Regent Magazine*, 1996, 36.
24. I have discussed the cultural debates leading up to this shift in more detail in Miranda Lundskaer-Nielsen, 'The Long Road to Recognition: New Musical Theatre Development in Britain', *Studies in Musical Theatre* 7, no. 2 (2013), 157–173.
25. Nick Allott, Personal interview with the author, 11 June 2013.
26. Allott, Personal interview.
27. John Cunningham, 'Production Numbers', *The Guardian*, 17 June 1996, 7.
28. Fanshawe, 'Mister Musical'.
29. Geordie Greig, 'Has the Curtain Come Down on Cameron?', *Evening Standard*, 2 November 1992, V&A Theatre & Performance collections.
30. Michael Coveney, 'A Lot of Money Gives a Chap Something to Croon About', *The Observer*, 8 July 1990, V&A Theatre & Performance collections.
31. Arifa Akbar, 'Cuts Needn't Be Bad for Creativity', *The Independent*, 20 September 2010, 19.
32. Andrew Billen, 'The Billen Interview: Cameron Mackintosh Talks *Cats*, Dogs and Morality', *The Observer*, 11 December 1994, 6.
33. Billington, 'Total Theatre Nut'.
34. Quoted in Farmbrough, 'The Virtues in Showing Off'.
35. Emily Bearn, 'The Showman Must Go On', *Sunday Telegraph*, 25 January 2004, 3.
36. Billington, 'Total Theatre Nut'.
37. Edwards, 'Putting the ! into *Oliver!*'.
38. Coveney, 'A Lot of Money'.
39. Billen, 'The Billen Interview'.
40. Rolnick, 'Magician of the Musical'.
41. Neil Norman, 'The Wise Owl behind *Follies*', *Evening Standard*, 23 July 1987, 29.
42. Edwards, 'Putting the ! into *Oliver!*'.
43. Fanshawe, 'Mister Musical'.
44. Farmbrough, 'The Virtues in Showing Off'.
45. Rolnick, 'Magician of the Musical'.
46. Bart had sold his rights some years earlier in a period of personal financial crisis.
47. Fanshawe, 'Mister Musical'.
48. Anthony Drewe, Personal interview with the author, 25 July 2013.
49. Michael Wright, 'And for His Next Trick . . .', *The Times*, 3 October 1999, 17.
50. Andrew Alderson, 'Mackintosh Buys Seats to Ensure Broadway Hit', *Sunday Times*, 29 March 1992, V&A Theatre & Performance collections.
51. Allott, Personal interview.
52. The partnership with Disney, while ultimately a creative one, was also one of practical necessity since they held the rights to the *Mary Poppins* film, including all the songs, while Mackintosh held the rights to the books.

53. Chris Grady, Personal interview with the author, 27 March 2013.
54. Allott, Personal interview.
55. *The Sound of Musicals*, Episode 2, Channel 4, first broadcast 19 November 2013.
56. Rolnick, 'Magician of the Musical'.
57. Rolnick, 'Magician of the Musical'.
58. Bertodano, 'Can't Dance, Can't Sing, Can Do'.
59. *The Sound of Musicals*, Episode 2.
60. *The Sound of Musicals*, Episode 2.
61. *The Sound of Musicals*, Episode 2.
62. http://www.theatermania.com/new-york-city-theater/news/03-2013/happy-birthday-to-the-dueling-divos-of-broadway_64671.html, accessed 10 September 2014.
63. Fanshawe, 'Mister Musical'.
64. Fanshawe, 'Mister Musical'.
65. Bertodano, 'Can't Dance, Can't Sing, Can Do'.
66. Richard Eyre, Personal interview with the author, 12 August 2013.
67. Drewe, Personal interview.
68. Drewe, Personal interview.
69. Grady, Personal interview.
70. Cameron Mackintosh, 'Letter to the Treasury', *Evening Standard*, 20 October 1994, V&A Theatre & Performance collections.
71. Drewe, Personal interview.
72. Eyre, Personal interview.
73. Drewe, Personal interview.
74. Drewe, Personal Interview.
75. Drewe, Personal Interview.
76. Eyre, Personal interview.
77. Drewe, Personal interview.
78. Drewe, Personal interview.
79. A deal in which a commercial producer pays some of the development and initial production costs for a new show at a producing theatre in exchange for a share of the commercial rights to the show. This enables theatres to undertake more expensive work and cuts the commercial producer's development costs and thus the financial risk.
80. Drewe, Personal interview.
81. Drewe, Personal interview, and Eyre, Personal interview.
82. For further details on this and the subsequent battle over Lea Salonga, see http://articles.philly.com/1991-01-08/news/25818496_1_lea-salonga-miss-saigon-englishman-jonathan-pryce, accessed 12 September 2014.
83. http://www.broadwayworld.com/article/Cameron-Mackintosh-Confirms-MARTIN-GUERRE-Being-Revised-for-West-End-Run-20140505, accessed 10 September 2014.
84. Allott, Personal interview.
85. Allott, Personal interview.
86. Grady, Personal interview.
87. Mariko Kojima, Personal interview with the author, 13 August 2013.
88. Allott, Personal interview.
89. Kojima, Personal interview.
90. Kojima, Personal interview.
91. Kojima, Personal interview.

92. Kojima, Personal interview.
93. Grady, Personal interview.
94. Willem Metz, Personal interview with the author, 15 August, 2013.
95. Geordie Greig, 'On the Crest of a Wave', *Sunday Times*, 1 December 1994, 3.
96. Metz, Personal interview.
97. Laurette Ziemer, '*Les Mis* [*sic*] Purge Causes Fury on Broadway', *Evening Standard*, 30 October 1996, V&A Theatre & Performance collections.
98. Quentin Letts, 'Bloodbath on Broadway as Mackintosh Sacks *Les Mis* [*sic*] Cast', *The Times*, 30 October 1996, V&A Theatre and Performance Collection.
99. Ziemer, '*Les Mis* [*sic*] Purge'.
100. David Lister, 'Maestro with Midas Touch Faces Toughest Challenge Yet', *The Independent*, 12 November 1996. http://www.independent.co.uk/news/maestro-with-midas-touch-faces-toughest-challenge-yet-1351922.html, accessed 5 September 2014.
101. Ziemer, '*Les Mis* [*sic*] Purge'.
102. Matthew Hemley, 'Cameron Mackintosh Appoints Alan Finch in Bid for Global Expansion', *The Stage*, 15 April 2015. https://www.thestage.co.uk/news/2015/cameron-mackintosh-appoints-alan-finch-bid-global-expansion/, accessed 7 September 2015.
103. John Barber, 'Making a Song and Dance', *Daily Telegraph*, 26 April 1982, V&A Theatre & Performance collections.
104. Barber, 'Making a Song and Dance'.
105. I have written about this more extensively in Miranda Lundskaer-Nielsen, *Directors and the New Musical Drama* (New York: Palgrave Macmillan, 2008), 73–87.
106. Matthew Hemley, 'Jonathan Church Productions to Form with Delfont Mackintosh Backing', *The Stage*, 3 June 2015, https://www.thestage.co.uk/news/2015/jonathan-church-productions-form-delfont-mackintosh-backing, accessed 10 September 2015.
107. 'The Sound of Musicals'.
108. Andrew Billen, 'The Billen Interview: "I've been Living on Borrowed Time for Years"', *Evening Standard*, 4 April 2001, 29–30.
109. Billen, 'Billen Interview', 30.
110. Quoted in Billington, 'Total Theatre Nut'.

BIBLIOGRAPHY

Akbar, Arifa. 'Cuts Needn't Be Bad for Creativity.' *The Independent*, 20 September 2010, 19.
Alderson, Andrew. 'Mackintosh Buys Seats to Ensure Broadway Hit.' *Sunday Times*, 29 March 1992. V&A (Victoria and Albert Museum) Theatre & Performance collections.
Allott, Nick. Personal interview with the author, 11 June 2013.
Barber, John. 'Making a Song and Dance.' *Daily Telegraph*, 26 April 1982. V&A Theatre & Performance collections.
Bearn, Emily. 'The Showman Must Go On.' *Sunday Telegraph*, 25 January 2004, 3.
Bertodano, Helena de. 'Can't Dance, Can't Sing, Can Do.' *Sunday Telegraph*, 16 July 2000, 3.
Billen, Andrew. 'The Billen Interview: Cameron Mackintosh Talks *Cats*, Dogs and Morality.' *The Observer*, 11 December 1994, 6.
Billen, Andrew. 'The Billen Interview: "I've Been Living on Borrowed Time for Years".' *Evening Standard*, 4 April 2001, 29–30.
Billington, Michael. 'Total Theatre Nut.' *The Guardian*, 9 December 1992, A4.

Burston, Jonathan. *The Megamusical: New Forms and Relations in Global Cultural Production.* Goldsmiths, University of London, UMI Dissertations Publishing, 1998.

Coveney, Michael. 'A Lot of Money Gives a Chap Something to Croon About.' *The Observer*, 8 July 1990. V&A Theatre & Performance collections.

Cunningham, John. 'Production Numbers.' *The Guardian*, 17 June 1996, 7.

Drewe, Anthony. Personal interview with the author, 25 July 2013.

Edwards, John. 'Putting the ! into *Oliver!*.' *Daily Mail*, 18 October 1994. V&A Theatre & Performance collections.

Eyre, Richard. Personal interview with the author, 12 August 2013.

Fanshawe, Simon. 'Mister Musical.' *The Guardian*, 23 October 1999, 6.

Farmbrough, Heather. 'The Virtues in Showing Off.' *Voyager Magazine*, July/August 1994, 14.

Grady, Chris. Personal interview with the author, 27 March 2013.

Greig, Geordie. 'Has the Curtain Come Down on Cameron?' *Evening Standard*, 2 November 1992. V&A Theatre & Performance collections.

Greig, Geordie. 'On the Crest of a Wave.' *Sunday Times*, 1 December 1994, 3.

Grove, Valerie. 'The Valerie Grove Interview.' *The Times*, 16 December 1994, 14.

Hemley, Matthew. 'Cameron Mackintosh Appoints Alan Finch in Bid for Global Expansion.' *The Stage*, 15 April 2015. https://www.thestage.co.uk/news/2015/cameron-mackintosh-appoints-alan-finch-bid-global-expansion/, accessed 7 September 2015.

Hemley, Matthew. 'Jonathan Church Productions to form with Delfont Mackintosh backing.' *The Stage*, 3 June 2015. https://www.thestage.co.uk/news/2015/jonathan-church-productions-form-delfont-mackintosh-backing, accessed 10 September 2015.

Kojima, Mariko. Personal interview with the author, 13 August 2013.

Letts, Quentin. 'Bloodbath on Broadway as Mackintosh Sacks *Les Mis* [sic] Cast.' *The Times*, 30 October 1996. V&A Theatre & Performance collections.

Lister, David. 'Bard of the West End.' *The Independent*, 21 July 2001. V&A Theatre & Performance collections.

Lister, David. 'Maestro with Midas Touch Faces Toughest Challenge yet.' *The Independent*, 12 November 1996. http://www.independent.co.uk/news/maestro-with-midas-touch-faces-toughest-challenge-yet-1351922.html, accessed 5 September 2014.

Low, Valentine. 'The 25 People Who Really Run London.' *Evening Standard*, 1 September 1992, London Life section, 21–22.

Lundskaer-Nielsen, Miranda. *Directors and the New Musical Drama.* New York: Palgrave Macmillan, 2008.

Lundskaer-Nielsen, Miranda. 'The Long Road to Recognition: New Musical Theatre Development in Britain.' *Studies in Musical Theatre* 7, no. 2 (2013): 157–173.

Mackintosh, Cameron. 'Letter to the Treasury.' *Evening Standard*, 20 October 1994. V&A Theatre & Performance collections.

Metz, William. Personal interview with the author, 15 August 2013.

Norman, Neil. 'The Wise Owl behind *Follies*.' *Evening Standard*, 23 July 1987, 29.

Rebellato, Dan. 'Playwriting and Globalization: Towards a Site-Unspecific Theatre.' *Contemporary Theatre Review* 16, no. 1 (2006): 97–113.

Rolnick, Harry. 'Magician of the Musical.' *Regent Magazine* (1996), 36. V&A Theatre & Performance collections.

The Sound of Musicals, Episode 2. Channel 4. First broadcast 19 November 2013.

Spencer, Charles. 'Cameron's Musical Laboratory.' *Daily Telegraph*, 12 February 1992. V&A Theatre and Performance collections.

Sternfeld, Jessica. *The Megamusical*. Bloomington: Indiana University Press, 2006.

Thomas, David. 'I Always Think I'm Tigger.' *Sunday Telegraph*, 8 July 2011, 5.

Wright, Michael. 'And for His Next Trick . . .' *The Times*, 3 October 1999, 17.

Ziemer, Laurette. '*Les Mis* [*sic*] Purge Causes Fury on Broadway.' *Evening Standard*, 30 October 1996. V&A Theatre & Performance collections.

CHAPTER 23

ANDREW LLOYD WEBBER

Haunted by the Phantom

DAVID CHANDLER

WHEN Tim Rice first met Andrew Lloyd Webber (b. 1948) in 1965 he found him 'the acme of paradox':

> He oozed contradiction. Aspects of this were instantly apparent; he seemed at once awkward and confident; sophisticated and naïve; mature and childlike. Later I discovered that he was also humorous and portentous; innovative and derivative; loyal and cavalier; generous and self-centred; all these characteristics to the extreme.[1]

Lloyd Webber's career similarly abounds in contradictions. He has composed a body of work at once groundbreaking and safely commercial; he has shown a Puccini-like ability to be both profoundly moving as well as thoroughly banal—sometimes, remarkably, at the same time; his musicals are the product of a distinctively British sensibility, yet they have had unprecedented international appeal; and though widely recognized as pioneering the rock-style musical, he has also been, perhaps more importantly, a conduit for classical and operatic influences. To this list we might add the fact that no other body of musical theatre work since Puccini's, or even Wagner's, has prompted such a combination of passionate adulation with intense, uncomprehending (and often ignorant) hostility. And further, while Lloyd Webber has often been described as immersed in the world of music—'I think about music all the time' he stated in 1988[2]—his critics have often suggested, not without reason, that he is more businessman than artist. The acme of paradox? It would certainly seem so.

Two things are very clear though: Lloyd Webber—who became Lord Lloyd-Webber in 1997, the hyphen added according to House of Lords convention—has had more success in the field of musical theatre than anyone before him; and no other composer or writer has had more influence on the modern, globalized culture of big-budget musicals designed for long runs.

To Glance Behind

In discussing Lloyd Webber we are talking about someone who is not only an artist but also a commercial phenomenon, and the complex relationship between the two. My starting point is 'The Music of Evita [sic]', an essay Lloyd Webber wrote in 1978 when he already had three extremely successful musicals behind him—*Jesus Christ Superstar, Joseph and the Amazing Technicolor Dreamcoat*, and *Evita* itself—and when he was, in the judgement of several of his most astute critics (including Tim Rice), at the height of his powers. The essay amounts to a statement of how Lloyd Webber, at that time, understood himself in history. His attraction to the form of the musical, he explains, rested particularly on the way 'music can cut corners and say something quite quickly that it would take far longer to say in words'. He then proceeds to offer a little historical sketch of the practical working-out of the idea:

> Although many opera composers, particularly the romantic ones, were brilliant at cutting corners, lately it has been in the post-war American musical that the technique of really using music as more than the source of a 'hit tune' has blossomed. For me it was Rodgers and Hammerstein who started this ball rolling. There had been attempts before the Second World War to move the musical out of the world of chorus girls or of revue, notably Rodgers and Hart's *Pal Joey* and of course Gershwin who in his opera *Porgy and Bess* anticipated much that I would like to see from contemporary opera by about forty years. But it was *Oklahoma* [sic] which first introduced a down-to-earth subject to the musical.
>
> Following *Oklahoma*, the Americans produced a whole string of musicals which continually have pushed the frontiers further forward. *Guys and Dolls, West Side Story*, and more recently *Cabaret* and *Company* are serious subjects handled in such a way as to suggest that it is in the popular musical theatre that much of the best contemporary theatre music has been composed, and where, significantly, words have equal importance to the music.[3]

The argument is confused, but revealing. The expressive power of music to 'cut corners' and the need for music and text to somehow meet as equals have been much debated since the emergence of opera around 1600. In that history, it is music which has often claimed the upper hand, and there have been repeated calls for it to be 'disciplined' by greater adherence to the text. Lloyd Webber is unspecific regarding the 'romantic' opera composers he was thinking of, but in my understanding he uses 'romantic' to signify deliberately emotive and (accordingly, in his view) pre-modernist. He and his father have both expressed a particular enthusiasm for Puccini, the composer who, in a certain simplified reading of musical history, can be taken as the culmination of this particular 'romantic' tradition. But here artistic and commercial issues get confused. The young Lloyd Webber knew enough of classical music to know that opera composers did not stop 'cutting corners' after Puccini's death; Benjamin Britten was as adept at it as anyone.

What opera composers lost, or forsook, was not this form of musical shorthand but the ability to market themselves to a large audience through the use of popular melodies and their commercial reproduction. Hence the movement, in Lloyd Webber's historical sketch, from 'romantic' opera (perhaps ending with *Turandot*, 1926) to the emergence of the 'serious' musical in the middle decades of the twentieth century. Rodgers and Hammerstein are the heirs of Puccini, for in a sort of historical twist they elevated popular musical theatre to the realm of serious art, whereas Puccini had managed to arrest the slide of opera away from popular culture. Lloyd Webber has consistently named Rodgers his greatest inspiration, though he has also stated categorically that '[t]he all-time greatest musical is *West Side Story*'.[4] The fact that *West Side Story* was composed by a 'classical' composer who also wrote opera carries considerable resonance in the tradition being staked out here.

A good deal becomes clear about Lloyd Webber's musicals if we imagine him coming to think of Richard Rodgers as his artistic father, Puccini as his artistic grandfather, and Leonard Bernstein as an older cousin. 'Hit tunes' combined with 'serious subjects' (though hardly 'down-to-earth' ones) and some of the artistic ambition of opera have generated much of his best work. Of these three elements, he has been most willing to sacrifice the 'serious subject', and had he written his essay after *Cats* (1981)—for all its T. S. Eliot pedigree—and *Starlight Express* (1984) he might have expressed himself differently. By the 1980s, in the eyes of his detractors, 'seriousness' had become a matter of style and publicity rather than content. There is some truth in this, but it was probably inevitable that Lloyd Webber would experience a conflict between the Rodgers and Hammerstein impulse to raise his art and the Puccini and Bernstein impulse to democratize it; in any case, it is debatable whether a musical like *Cats* suffers from a lack of seriousness or an excess of it. In the matter of 'hit tunes' and artistic ambition Lloyd Webber has consistently delivered and surprised. In these areas he need not fear comparisons with Puccini or Rodgers.

Lloyd Webber's 1978 essay proposes that musical theatre is an evolving art form and holds out the possibility that opera and the musical may be meaningfully combined (or recombined), as in the exemplary case of Gershwin's *Porgy and Bess*. Moreover, it suggests that Lloyd Webber's own works represent a new evolutionary stage, and read in combination with *Evita* itself, suggests exactly this kind of synthesis. *Evita* had been promoted as 'An Opera', and was making a bid to reinstall opera in popular culture. Its claim to be an opera rested largely on the fact that it was all sung, and the 1978 essay reveals that Lloyd Webber considered the elimination of spoken dialogue to be his major departure from, and refinement of, the American musical:

> I find a snag with the musical. Even in the very finest shows I find worrying that awkward moment when you see the conductor raising his baton and the orchestra lurching into life during the dialogue which indicates the impending approach of music. [...] I like to write something where the music and words can get uninterrupted attention without jolts from one style to another.[5]

This 'snag' had only recently revealed itself to Lloyd Webber, though, and was perhaps associated in his mind with the complete failure of his more traditional musical with dialogue, *Jeeves* (1975). Nevertheless, the all-sung style subsequently became central to claims for the innovatory, indeed revolutionary, style of Lloyd Webber's musicals, and its development is worth exploring at some length.

RETURNING TO THE BEGINNING

The 1978 essay is remarkable for making no mention of any earlier British work. This may have been partly a sop to the large American audience who had avidly embraced *Jesus Christ Superstar*, but in general Lloyd Webber seems to have been unwilling or unable to see any connection between his musicals and the British tradition which preceded him. The confident young heir to popular Italian opera and the serious American musical had a far from straightforward apprenticeship, however; the position he staked out at the age of 30 had probably not been even imagined a decade earlier.

Lloyd Webber has been, by all accounts, passionate about making musicals all his life, and even as a boy he wrote several for a toy theatre, certain tunes for which were reused in his mature work. In 1965 he composed *The Likes of Us*, the earliest of his musicals which can be critically assessed today: it had lyrics by Tim Rice, and a book—there was no thought yet of an all-sung musical—by Leslie Thomas. The story was very loosely based on the life of the young Thomas Barnardo (1845–1905), the Victorian philanthropist, and set in the 1860s. In 1978 Rice described it, succinctly and accurately, as 'a bit of an *Oliver* [*sic*] rip-off, with a rotten plot'.[6] The influence of Lionel Bart's *Oliver!*, well into its record-breaking run at the New Theatre, is felt all over *The Likes of Us*, and clearly inspired the choice of subject: Victorian London with its dens of vice and choruses of street urchins. Lloyd Webber's melodies, ably supported by Rice's lyrics, are strong and memorable, yet the sense of deep familiarity with lower-class culture that Bart so successfully infused into all his musicals is absent, and the moral earnestness emanating from Barnardo sits unsatisfactorily beside the rowdy scenes of imaginary cockneydom. *The Likes of Us* is interesting now chiefly for what it reveals of the young Lloyd Webber. He was concerned with success rather than innovation, focused on the home market, and more than willing to copy the most successful British musical of the decade. Attempts to interest theatres in *The Likes of Us* proved unsuccessful, though, and on the whole this early failure appears to have been propitious. Indirectly, it led Lloyd Webber to try something new.

In 1967 Alan Doggett, the music teacher at Colet Court School who had participated in a demo recording of *The Likes of Us*, suggested that Lloyd Webber and Rice write a 'pop cantata' in the style of Herbert Chappell's very popular *The Daniel Jazz* (1963). Doggett had conducted a performance of Chappell's work for BBC television in 1966 and recorded the work for HMV later in the year, so the rewards were potentially considerable, but the first step was simply to have something ready for his school choir to perform in the following Easter term. *The Daniel Jazz* is a ten-minute choral piece telling the Old Testament story of Daniel in the lions' den in a mixture of pop, jazz, and traditional Sunday school-style choruses. Though mostly narrated, an extended solo part takes the form of 'a schmaltzy waltz-song'.[7] Chappell's fluid shifting between different musical styles and combination of narration with dramatic parts arguably influenced Lloyd Webber more than almost any other single piece of music. He and Rice produced a comparable work on another Old Testament story: the first, fifteen-minute version of *Joseph and the Amazing Technicolor Dreamcoat*. The extended solo part now became the 'Pharaoh's Song', a wonderful Elvis Presley parody, and stood out rather more strongly. This first *Joseph* was premiered at Colet Court on 1 March 1968. The modest nature of the occasion, with an audience of bemused parents, has been made much of in subsequent publicity, but the important thing is that Doggett had invited a representative from Novello & Co. Ltd, the publisher of *The Daniel Jazz*. He liked what he saw and Novello bought the rights to *Joseph*. A second performance, at Westminster Central Hall on 12 May, produced equally good results: Decca decided to commission a recording, for which Lloyd Webber and Rice prepared a longer, thirty-minute version of the piece, with more inset songs and a prominent role for an (adult) narrator. This was released in early 1969.

The 1968–9 *Joseph* has long been recognized as the foundation of Lloyd Webber's subsequent career in musical theatre, but it cannot be emphasized too strongly that it was not a musical, nor, bearing in mind his subsequent construction of a tradition for himself, does it seem to have anything to do with Rodgers and Hammerstein, let alone Puccini. The shorter version is strongly indebted to Chappell and is clearly a 'pop cantata'; the LP version defies easy categorization, and Derek Jewell's sleeve notes call it 'in effect, a pop oratorio, probably the first of its kind'.[8] Rice and Lloyd Webber were breaking new ground here, effectively crossing the pop cantata with the concept album, though this seems to have had less to do with conscious innovation than the commercial imperative to somehow stretch their little work to LP length (*The Daniel Jazz* had been squeezed on to a forty-five record). The final result was a complete departure from *The Likes of Us*: whereas that work had attempted to carry its audience into an imaginary past with its spoken dialogue and Bart-style songs, the all-sung *Joseph* simply reimagined the Bible story in terms of modern pop, modern attitudes, and its creators' own 'dreams' of success. There was no mention of God, and only the most superficial treatment of the psychological depths of the story. But, though consciously 'light' and unserious, this early *Joseph* conveys an exuberant sense of fun and showcases Lloyd Webber's extraordinary melodic gifts and ability to synthesize diverse styles of music into a convincing, seamless whole.

The LP version of *Joseph* was the major inspiration for Lloyd Webber's next important work with Rice, and the one that established them as leaders in their field: *Jesus Christ Superstar*. This was begun in late 1969, written quite quickly, recorded as a double LP in spring and summer 1970, and released in September. It was promoted as a 'rock opera'— a term nicely highlighting the overall synthesis taking place in Lloyd Webber's music, as well as defining the new work's movement beyond the 'pop cantata', or 'pop oratorio', of *Joseph*. The term 'rock opera' had been variously used in popular music circles since 1966, in fact, but Lloyd Webber appears to have been the first composer of such a work actually to have known much about opera, and the first to produce something more or less suitable for staging. *Jesus Christ Superstar* developed the all-sung style of *Joseph* in a theatrical context and thus represents the point in Lloyd Webber's career at which, in his own interpretation of his achievement, he made the decisive artistic break away from musicals with spoken dialogue. In a very important passage in his autobiography, however, Rice confesses that this came about by accident:

> Although we knew we were writing something for a record album, we still felt that our ultimate aim was the theatre. Consequently we originally entertained the idea that the show would have a considerable amount of spoken dialogue between each number. This however would be absolute death on a record, unlistenable to after one hearing [. . .]. We decided that for the album only, we would write the piece in operatic form, i.e. tell the entire story through song and music, and even after we had completed the recording, still thought it possible that we would have to alter large chunks of it in order to accommodate spoken scenes for a stage version. Ditching the book turned out to be a masterstroke (just as issuing the score on record before the show proved to be), though impelled upon us by circumstances and never a conscious artistic decision.[9]

It was thus the unauthorized productions of *Jesus Christ Superstar* that began to be staged in the United States in summer 1971 which demonstrated that spoken dialogue was in fact unnecessary—in large part, because the basic story was already so well known. Not until the latter half of 1971 can Lloyd Webber have grasped that he had, unwittingly, affected a revolution in the form of the popular musical, and it would be several more years before he accepted that this was to be his signature style.

Even without the innovation of what Rice calls 'operatic form', *Jesus Christ Superstar* was a landmark work. The choice of subject was brave and inevitably controversial (though the controversy turned out to be good publicity). Rice's lyrics are intelligent and thought-provoking—even the one obviously comic number, 'King Herod's Song', neatly expresses, and seemingly ridicules, a conventional attitude to the miraculous. Lloyd Webber's searingly powerful score captures the glory, the anguish, and the doubts experienced by Christ and his followers in music on the one hand bristling with the possibilities of the emerging rock style of the early 1970s and on the other supported by an expansive, classical sense of melody. No other Lloyd Webber score sounds so entirely of its moment, or, arguably, responded so acutely to the spiritual needs of a particular moment. And because that moment (poised between the Beatles on one hand and Led Zeppelin on the other) has a seminal status in our collective sense of how the sounds and themes of modern popular music developed, *Jesus Christ Superstar* still impresses as fresh and exciting. Like the best pop art, it is iconoclastic, leading its audience into new places and new relationships with the familiar rather than satisfying an existing market. As a piece of storytelling, *Jesus Christ Superstar* has a certain cubist, fragmented quality—there is no single, controlling perspective—that reflects its origins as a sort of concept album, but even this, though born of inexperience, arguably works, keeping the audience intellectually engaged. Altogether, *Jesus Christ Superstar* deserved its huge international success, and in my judgement it stands with *The Phantom of the Opera* at the summit of Lloyd Webber's achievement.

AND THE MONEY KEPT ROLLING IN

Jesus Christ Superstar made Lloyd Webber a rich man, allowing him to adopt the sort of affluent, landed lifestyle he had always desired. Artistically, it proved a difficult work from which to move on. Lloyd Webber was not ready to accept the artistic consequences of what his 'rock opera' had achieved, and his next two musicals, both unsuccessful, employed spoken dialogue and a much less contemporary style. *Jacob's Journey* (1973) was written as a 'prequel' to *Joseph*, with dialogue supplied by the experienced comic writers Ray Galton and Alan Simpson. It played for several months (alongside *Joseph*), but Lloyd Webber and Rice withdrew it, apparently deciding against the 'low' humour Galton and Simpson had brought to this intriguing collaboration; it was neither published nor recorded. The aforementioned *Jeeves* (1975), a much more ambitious work with book and lyrics by Alan Ayckbourn, simply flopped. The programme included the striking claim that '[t]he musical *Jeeves* fulfils Andrew Lloyd Webber's long standing ambition to write a musical specifically for the theatre',[10] but the critics were near unanimous in condemning it as, above all, untheatrical. The answer to this career slump was clearly to return to the successful model of *Jesus Christ Superstar*, and this is what Lloyd Webber and Rice did in *Evita*, released as a recording in 1976 and first staged in 1978.

Evita tells the story of Eva Perón (1919–52), the controversial former first lady of Argentina. It was Rice's choice of subject, and a brave and unusual one; Lloyd Webber took some time to accept that it was suitable material for a musical. Unlike the case of *Jesus Christ Superstar*, the story was little known and the collaborators knew they were writing an all-sung work suitable for staging: therefore much more care had to be taken to construct a credible, coherent narrative, and this in turn led to a more thoughtfully through-composed score. *Evita* impresses as the more sophisticated of the two musicals at every level, and the loss of exuberant youthful brashness is compensated with more dramatic and musical subtlety. If the subject of *Jesus Christ Superstar* made people want to see the musical, in this case it was the musical which made people interested in the subject (as Rice points out, many books on Eva Perón followed in the musical's wake[11]).

In his 1978 essay 'The Music of Evita', Lloyd Webber states: 'In my view Rodgers and Hammerstein never really topped *Oklahoma* [*sic*] artistically and started to become sentimental.'[12] This is an arresting judgement given that much the same could be said of his own work after *Jesus Christ Superstar*. The rise of sentiment is an audible fact in *Evita*, and the attentive listener can detect the sort of tension between words and music often found in the works of Gilbert and Sullivan. Ironically, this seems to have emerged from a principle of overcompensation on Lloyd Webber's part. He had no attraction to the historical Eva Perón, unlike Rice, who is reported to have encouraged the doubtful composer with the words: 'I know you think she's a bitch, but make her wonderful.'[13]

Lloyd Webber followed this advice by imagining Eva as a sort of tragic Puccinian heroine (he subsequently claimed, dubiously, 'that Puccini would have adored her'[14]). He composed the most radiantly beautiful music he had yet written for her, and at times this breaks away from the much more sardonic undertow in Rice's words to create sentimental moments that complicate, without spoiling, the overall drama. This is most notable in Eva's great 'Don't Cry For Me Argentina', where the lyrics are, as Rice says, deliberately 'a string of meaningless platitudes,'[15] and yet Lloyd Webber's melody, composed before the lyrics were written, transmits an air of rapt, timeless, almost mystical profundity to the song that for a brief interlude at least transports all but the most cynical listeners, placing them, against their better judgement, on Eva's side (see Figure 23.1). This sort of sentiment, deriving from the pursuit of the moving 'hit tune' that Lloyd Webber has been perennially fascinated by, and has regularly composed with scant regard to specific dramatic function (hence the movement of many melodies from one musical to another), would become central to his later work.

Meanwhile, the 1969 *Joseph* had been considerably expanded. In 1972, Doggett, the original commissioner, had suggested that it could be easily adapted for the theatre by changing some of the third-person narration into first-person dramatized song. Lloyd Webber and Rice accepted this, and enlarged the overall work again, now taking it to just

FIGURE 23.1 A heroine Puccini would have adored? Elaine Paige as Eva Perón in *Evita*, Prince Edward Theatre, 1978.

Photograph by Chris Davies. Courtesy of ArenaPal.

under an hour. This played alongside *Jacob's Journey*, but when the latter work was abandoned they made an attempt to stretch *Joseph* much further so that it could (loosely) 'fill' an evening. Three new songs were added, and, in Rice's words, they 'elongated several of the other songs to their absolute limit with new verses, instrumental passages or blatant repetition of existing lines. [. . .] Finally we encored about a third of the show at the end [. . .] a desperate attempt to fill time.'[16] As this description suggests, there was no attempt to deepen or strengthen the story, which was still as flimsy and upbeat as it had been in its 1960s incarnation. This did not prevent the new *Joseph* from proving very popular, and the lesson Lloyd Webber seems to have taken away is that, at the box office level, his public did not necessarily want 'serious subjects' but would be happy with something tuneful, diverting, and well presented. It is with the expanded *Joseph* that the conflict between Lloyd Webber the artist and Lloyd Webber the businessman becomes significant. In the early 1980s he told his first biographer that '[*Joseph's*] level really is that of a show that is close to children, and I don't therefore believe its home is a West End theatre at peak times.'[17] Despite such belated scruples, Lloyd Webber soon comfortably adjusted to the position that if audiences were happy to pay for big theatre productions of *Joseph* then such productions should be encouraged.

The extended *Joseph*, in a medley of musical styles, with one song plumbing greater emotional depths than the rest ('Close Every Door to Me'), provided a general model for *Cats* (1981), Lloyd Webber's next major musical (between *Evita* and *Cats* had come the delightful dramatized song cycle, *Tell Me on a Sunday* (1979)). *Cats* began life as a song cycle, a setting of poems from T. S. Eliot's *Old Possum's Book of Practical Cats* (1939), and represented a new challenge for Lloyd Webber, who had in the past preferred to have his lyricists fit words to tunes he had already written. It was one he met with great aplomb, matching Eliot's lively rhythms and rhymes with appropriate ear-catching music. The song cycle was privately performed in summer 1980, and plans for a stage musical then evolved with astonishing rapidity. Cameron Mackintosh was asked to produce the show, and by 25 September he was telling the press that *Cats* (the title had already been chosen) would be the 'first English dance-musical'.[18] Trevor Nunn was chosen to direct, and when he was shown some unpublished fragments of poems connected with *Old Possum* that Valerie Eliot, T. S. Eliot's widow, had made available to Lloyd Webber, he sensed the possibility of an overarching narrative. One fragment concerned the faded 'Glamour Cat' Grizabella, and another referred to a mysterious 'Heaviside Layer'. What, Nunn reasoned, if one cat each year was selected to ascend to the 'Heaviside Layer' and in this particular year that cat was Grizabella? What if she were 'the emotional climax of the show'?[19] The 'dance-musical' thus became a story of redemption.

Cats opened in London on 11 May 1981. No British musical had ever been offered to the public with less of a plot; this, and the fact that the performers were to be dressed in cat costumes, meant that few people initially believed in its commercial viability, and shares were sold in the show to raise the £500,000 needed to produce it. Yet *Cats* soon became an extraordinary commercial phenomenon; by February 1989, according to Michael Walsh's calculations, it had become 'the most profitable theatrical venture in history' (not factoring in inflation),[20] and it went on to become easily the longest-running musical ever in both the West End and on Broadway. Whereas the London productions of *Jesus Christ Superstar* and *Evita* had run for 3,357 and 3,176 performances respectively—both comfortably ahead of the 2,618 managed by *Oliver!*—the London *Cats* managed an utterly unprecedented 8,949 performances, closing only in 2002, and redefined the idea of what a 'long run' could mean. The fact that the story comprised only a little of the whole, and that Grizabella's suffering and redemption sat rather oddly alongside the basically happy, festival atmosphere, did not deter audiences: they loved the novelty and fun of it all and embraced, or at least accepted, the kitsch sentiment. In fact, in an unlikely way, *Cats* made a strength out of weakness, for if there was little story there had to be a great show, and Nunn's innovative production, with John Napier's remarkably effective set and costumes and Gillian Lynne's brilliantly inventive choreography, offered a new kind of theatrical experience, one that almost anyone could enjoy. It is noteworthy, for example, that the veteran opera critic Stan Meares judged *Cats* the 'outstanding' one among Lloyd Webber's 'many shows'.[21]

Starlight Express (1984), the musical which followed *Cats*, was quickly dubbed 'Cats on Tracks', and was the closest Lloyd Webber ever came to repeating himself. He had in fact planned a musical about trains, based on Wilbert Awdry's *Railway Series* stories, long before there was any thought of *Cats*, and as originally conceived it was to have been the more modestly-scaled work. In the hands of Trevor Nunn, to whom the production was again entrusted, *Starlight Express* finally became something quite different, a 'spectacular total theatre' experience (Nunn's description[22]) in which singers on roller skates pretending to be engines and carriages race around the audience: a sort of cross between a musical and a theme park ride. Although in some ways a natural extension of the *Cats* model, *Starlight Express*, with lyrics by the popular poet Richard Stilgoe, lacked a good deal of the charm of the earlier musical, and paid heavily for it on Broadway, where it ran for a disappointing 761 performances. In London, however, *Starlight Express* proved very durable, settling in behind *Cats* as the West End's second longest-running musical, and not closing until 2002.

Cats and *Starlight Express* did not demand a great deal of Lloyd Webber beyond a string of catchy songs (some of them subsequently rewritten and updated). The job of working those songs into something like a coherent piece of theatrical storytelling was largely entrusted to Nunn and his design team. In the terms of Lloyd Webber's 1978 essay, this was really a regression to pre-Rodgers and Hammerstein standards, and he knew that, ultimately, he did not want to be judged by those. His next musical, *The Phantom of the Opera* (1986), was accordingly an ambitious attempt to return to, and surpass, the 'operatic', musico-dramatic aspirations of *Evita*. 'I knew I wanted to write a big romantic score,' he later explained, 'something in the direction of Rodgers and Hammerstein, and *Phantom* had the potential to be a great operatic love story'.[23] The setting of the story, an opera house, naturally encouraged an operatic treatment, and the period, the late 1800s, was a time when 'romantic' opera still reigned supreme and Puccini's genius was gradually revealing itself. The soaring melodies are consistently among Lloyd Webber's finest, and in no other of his musicals is his sense of himself as an artist in history so clearly revealed: the score, while including some contemporary rock elements, also looks back through Rodgers to Puccini and contains clever parodies of earlier operatic styles as remote as that of Mozart's period. The overall impression is certainly 'operatic', in a more traditional sense than *Evita*, and *The Phantom*'s appeal to its huge audience has rested a good deal on its ability to exude a sense of privileged access to 'high' art in the most sumptuous European tradition. Much of that audience has enjoyed thinking of *The Phantom* as 'an opera' with none of the negative connotations often associated with the older art form in popular culture.

Lloyd Webber's source for his new musical was Gaston Leroux's novel, *Le Fantôme de l'Opéra* (1910), first published in English in 1911, and he was influenced by Ken Hill's theatrical version, which had included clever adaptations of real nineteenth-century operatic music. Leroux's famous novel tells the story of how Erik, 'the Phantom', a brilliant but disfigured man with an angelic voice, has constructed a fortress for himself in the lowest basement of the Paris Opera House. He becomes besotted with a young chorus girl, Christine Daaé, whom he teaches to sing, without however revealing himself; she believes him to be the 'Angel of Music' her deceased father had told stories about. When Christine falls in love with Raoul de Chagny, a young aristocrat, Erik resorts to a series of increasingly violent plots to force her to be his. Eventually, when she shows sympathy for his torments, Erik relents and lets her go. Lloyd Webber became fascinated with the story, but also very critical of the way Leroux had told it. As Frederick Forsyth, who discussed the matter at great length with the composer, subsequently reported:

> [Lloyd Webber] saw that it was not basically a horror story at all, nor one based on hatred and cruelty, but a truly tragic tale of obsessive but unrequited love between a desperately disfigured self-exile from the human race and a beautiful young opera singer who eventually prefers to give her love to a handsome aristocratic suitor. [. . .] he] extracted the true essence of the tragedy.[24]

Whatever one thinks of the suggestion that Lloyd Webber somehow understood the story better than the man who wrote it, there can be little doubt that *The Phantom of the Opera* is his defining musical, not just in the sense that it is easily his most commercially successful work—it is still running in the West End and on Broadway at the time of writing—but because, of all his successful musicals, it is the one in which he invested most of himself, and took most creative control over (see Figure 23.2). His new writing partner, the young Charles Hart (b. 1961), was given the task of essentially translating the composer's thoughts into words—poetic, romantic words with none of the subversive playfulness of Rice's style. Although *The Phantom of the Opera* is still rich in spectacle like its predecessors—the falling chandelier is particularly famous—the spectacle is no longer an end in itself, but an attempt to intensify the emotional drama of the story, as reimagined by Lloyd Webber. Here, more than in the previous musicals, the story *as* music, and therefore the composer, is the centre of everything.

Yet the most remarkable thing about *The Phantom of the Opera*, given its astonishing success, is how perilously it navigates a dramatic tightrope to which Lloyd Webber appears to have been blind. In the novel it is obvious that Erik, elderly, physically

FIGURE 23.2 The composer linked with his most famous creation: Andrew Lloyd Webber posing with the Phantom's mask on the cover of the *Daily Mail Weekend* magazine, 24 September 2011.

Photograph by Charlie Gray. Reprint courtesy of Charlie Gray and Solo Syndication London.

repellent, and shabby (and presumably not very hygienic), cannot be an object of romantic or sexual attraction to Christine: it is simply his voice she loves. In the musical, by contrast, the Phantom, who is never referred to as Erik, is much younger and presented immaculately dressed and groomed, with only part of his face disfigured (and, famously, masked): the general tendency of the retelling is to push the story towards an intense love triangle in which Christine is attracted to both Raoul and the Phantom. This structure allows Christine, and through her, the audience, a dark, 'Gothic' fantasy of violation, of succumbing to the obsessive, reckless love of the sexualized Phantom lurking in the darkness, but this fantasy is crucially enacted within, and to an extent enabled by, the safe framework of her fairly conventional Cinderella-like romance with the rich, titled, handsome—though perhaps not very exciting—Raoul. The balance between fantasy and reality is very effective, partly because it tends to disguise the fact that the 'reality' on offer here—Raoul's love and all the social advantages it brings—is itself a fantasy. But the balance is also very delicate: if Raoul is too obviously the superior option we lose sympathy for the Phantom, who then appears primarily as a dark *threat* to Christine's happy destiny; on the other hand, if we are led to believe that Christine really would be happier with the Phantom, her eventual, conventional choice disappoints. Puccini would have quickly recognized how important this balance is for dramatic effect; Lloyd Webber, by contrast, appears to have reached it somewhat fortuitously by identifying with the Phantom and not feeling much interest in Raoul. He clearly believed that Christine might, or even *should*, choose the Phantom—and hence, eventually, his badly judged sequel, *Love Never Dies*, discussed later. But in *The Phantom of the Opera* itself the imaginative constraints imposed by Leroux's basic storyline checked the composer's potentially self-destructive desire to transform the Phantom into the romantic hero of the story.

The underlying superficiality of Lloyd Webber's response to Leroux's novel was highlighted when, after years of discussion, the composer's Really Useful Group finally produced a big-budget movie version of the musical in 2004. Gerard Butler, known for his strikingly handsome looks and muscular physique (at the time of his audition in 2003 he was most associated with the role of Attila the Hun in the American TV miniseries *Attila* (2001)) was cast as the Phantom, despite having virtually no singing experience and no means of persuading any but the most deluded that he was the 'Angel of Music'. Butler himself has left an account of the rather surreal moment when he auditioned in Lloyd Webber's drawing room:

> I treated this whole thing as an interesting idea because it was kind of unusual that they came to me in the first place. [. . .] Andrew was sitting in the back with his arm clapped over his face. I suddenly thought, 'what the hell am I doing here?' I had never had a singing lesson in my life and it was all new to me.[25]

The 'arm clapped over his face' may suggest that the artist in Lloyd Webber was struggling with the businessman, attempting not to be swayed by Butler's looks, but if that was the case the businessman emerged triumphant and an outstandingly cynical decision was made that a handsome Phantom (displayed advantageously with a smaller mask) would be a bigger box office draw than the presence of a great singer in the role. This decision, and the ensuing direction (by Joel Schumacher) designed to establish Butler as an object of *visual* desire, imperilled the precarious balance of the story and represented a significant step towards its inversion in *Love Never Dies*. Much of the popular reaction to the movie predictably consisted of female enthusiasts extolling Butler's attractiveness (clearly preferring him to Patrick Wilson's conventional pretty-boy Raoul), but many existing fans of the musical took exception to Schumacher's glossy superficiality, his constant emphasis on spectacle over substance. Although it made substantial profits, the movie was not nearly so successful as an expensive screen version of the world's then most popular musical could, and should, have been, and the reason is clear: many people had invested more deeply in Leroux's story, as reinterpreted in the musical, than the film allowed. The businessman in Lloyd Webber had underestimated his public. Ironically, but revealingly, the film most pleased those least likely to be content with the existing storyline: those who felt that Christine should have chosen the Phantom, or at least succumbed to some ravishing. *Love Never Dies* would give expression to that feeling.[26]

THE PHANTOM NEVER DIES

By the 1990s Lloyd Webber had become, in a virtually unprecedented way, his own worst enemy. With *Cats, Starlight Express*, and *Phantom* apparently more or less permanently encamped in the West End, and *Cats* and *Phantom* equally well established on Broadway, any new Lloyd Webber musical faced formidable competition from his older ones.

The first, and perhaps greatest, casualty of this situation was *Aspects of Love* (1989), based on David Garnett's novel of the same name (1955). This ran for 1,325 performances in the West End: a good run by pre-*Cats* standards, but by 1992, when it closed, regarded as something of a failure. On Broadway it fared much worse, managing a mere 377 performances and losing over US$8 million. The diagnosis of this failure offered in Lloyd Webber's 2001 *Now & Forever* career retrospective is very interesting, for James Inverne's obsequious booklet notes are innocent of anything approaching an independent critical standpoint and can be read, in effect, as an officially sanctioned account of the composer's own thoughts on his works and their reception. *Aspects of Love*, the booklet says, was 'an intimate tale [. . .] the characters were too subtle to capture the public imagination'. It was, further, a 'chamber work', not really suited to big theatres (an echo of Lloyd Webber's earlier doubts about *Joseph*).[27] Subsequent smaller-scale revivals have shown, in fact, that the 'too subtle' nature of the work rather than its comparative size was the main reason *Aspects* failed to capture the very large audience of the earlier musicals. It certainly has a claim to be Lloyd Webber's most sophisticated and emotionally complex theatre work, yet had it immediately followed *Evita* it would probably have been accepted as part of a natural artistic progression. It was the earlier 1980s musicals that had taught audiences to expect, and prefer, unsubtle, undemanding, spectacular entertainment. As the *Now & Forever* booklet puts it, with complicated irony, *Aspects of Love* contains 'no crashing chandeliers'. For some, this was a welcome change, and Kurt Gänzl, a notable champion, records that it 'became a particular favorite with those looking for relief from the current fashion for heavily spectacular or glitzy musical shows'.[28] Relief then, as much as anything, from Lloyd Webber.

Aspects of Love was the only post-*Phantom* Lloyd Webber musical not shaped in some way by the overwhelming cultural presence of the 1986 work. Planned and partly composed before *Phantom*, it was completed well in advance of any conclusive demonstration that the latter musical would be critically and popularly accepted as Lloyd Webber's defining achievement. The other post-*Phantom* musicals, by contrast, all seem to be either clearly related to *Phantom* (*Sunset Boulevard*, *The Woman in White*, *Love Never Dies*) or rather desperate attempts at something completely different (*Whistle Down the Wind*, *The Beautiful Game*, *Stephen Ward*, *School of Rock*). The first of these, *Sunset Boulevard* (1993), based on the cult film of the same name (1950), offered unmistakable plot similarities with *The Phantom of the Opera* but it ultimately told a far more cynical story without anything equivalent to the wholesome love of Raoul and Christine and their happy ending. Moreover, while the Phantom's antics and the Paris Opera House had offered many integral opportunities for spectacle in the earlier musical, in *Sunset Boulevard* the large quota of spectacle seemed there to please the audience rather than serve the story. These were substantial disadvantages, and though *Sunset Boulevard* was slightly more successful than *Aspects of Love*, its high cost meant it lost a great deal of money in America.[29] For all this, there is no doubt that the level of musical inspiration is very high: *Sunset Boulevard* stands, with *Aspects of Love*, as one of the most underrated Lloyd Webber musicals.

Sunset Boulevard, mainly, it would seem, in deference to the film on which it was based, began reintroducing spoken dialogue into the Lloyd Webber musical. This was taken much further in his next two efforts, *Whistle Down the Wind* (1996) and *The Beautiful Game* (2000), which also marked an unexpected return to social realism and 'down-to-earth subject[s]'. The main problem, as with the early *The Likes of Us*, was that neither Lloyd Webber nor his rather unlikely lyricists—Jim Steinman for *Whistle* and Ben Elton for *The Beautiful Game*—had much natural feeling for, or understanding of, the particular historical contexts that shape these stories: God-fearing Louisiana in the 1950s and Belfast with its sectarian violence in the 1960s. *Whistle*, despite spawning a huge hit single in 'No Matter What', was markedly less successful than *Aspects* and *Sunset*, and did not open on Broadway at all. A much simpler production, it did not actually lose money; nevertheless, it is a remarkable comment on Lloyd Webber's post-*Phantom* decade that the *Now & Forever* booklet emphasizes this point, as though 'stay[ing] in the black' was now a sort of triumph for the composer who had enjoyed overwhelming commercial success in the 1970s and 1980s.[30] *The Beautiful Game* fared even worse, again failing to make it to Broadway and running for less than a year in London. This latter musical, based on an original story by Ben Elton, saw Lloyd Webber attempting to remap his relationship to Rodgers and Hammerstein and by extension the entire preceding tradition of musical theatre. He felt that '[i]t was the kind of story that Rodgers & Hammerstein in their early days would have seriously thought about setting'—i.e. in their best, unsentimental period according to Lloyd Webber's reading of their career.[31] The fact that Lloyd Webber regards two such very different musicals as *The Phantom of the Opera* and *The Beautiful Game* as extending the Rodgers and Hammerstein legacy says much about the way he has consistently been inspired by, and judged himself against, the works of the American partnership, and in the latter musical he was presumably trying to connect with the realistic, homespun quality of *Oklahoma!*, even though the more obvious influence is his beloved *West Side Story*. Yet the realism of *The Beautiful Game* consists primarily of a rather moralizing demonstration of the way positive human values and ordinary human lives are corrupted by sectarian violence: a heavily politicized plot of a kind Rodgers and Hammerstein never attempted, nor showed any aptitude for (witness the treatment of National Socialism in *The Sound of Music*). This was not natural Lloyd Webber territory either; after being confronted with the dismal box office returns, he decided not to pursue the new vein further.

The next musical, *The Woman in White* (2004), was a clear swerve back towards *Phantom* territory, and might have succeeded better had it immediately followed the 1986 work. Based on Wilkie Collins's classic novel of the same name, it was a return to nineteenth-century imaginative material of a kind clearly more congenial to the composer than the subjects of his three previous musicals. (Lloyd Webber, it is worth noting, has amassed one of the world's finest collections of Victorian art and is a recognized authority on the subject.) But the much greater complexity of the plot, and the fact that it was not a naturally musical story, made for less satisfying theatre than *Phantom*; Trevor Nunn's staging, with the use of projections, also proved unpopular. *The Woman in White* managed just 500 performances in London and a mere 109 in New York. The much-hyped *Love Never Dies* (2010) (discussed at the end of this chapter), the sequel to *Phantom*, again failed to reverse the general downward trajectory of Lloyd Webber's career, and *Stephen Ward* (2013) was a complete flop, running for just four months.

This extraordinary run of comparative failures presents interpretative problems, especially as, throughout his post-*Phantom* period, Lloyd Webber has been consistently able to depend on extensive publicity and to draw on the talents of leading writers, producers, and performers (whether he has chosen them wisely is obviously another matter). Apart from *Aspects of Love*, and parts of *Sunset Boulevard* and *Love Never Dies*, these later musicals do not represent the composer at his best, perhaps, but they are not obviously inferior work either, and one is forced to the conclusion that their reception has been shaped by both extrinsic and intrinsic factors. The fresh young talent of the 1970s had, by the mid-1980s, become the Establishment, and there was an inevitable reaction. *Spitting Image*, a highly successful satirical puppet show first aired by ITV in 1984, took aim at him from the beginning. One early sketch showed him composing his music on a cash register and categorized him, in contradistinction to 'composers who fart a lot', as 'a fart who composes a lot'.[32] The 1989 film, *The Tall Guy*, written by Richard Curtis and featuring several of Britain's leading comic actors, included a ferocious parody of the Lloyd Webber style, and especially of *Phantom*, in the form of a spoof musical called *Elephant* (based on the life of Joseph Carey Merrick, the so-called 'Elephant Man'). Roger Waters's 1992 song, 'It's a Miracle' (on his *Amused to Death* album), included the line 'Lloyd Webber's awful stuff runs for years and years and years'.[33] Long runs were increasingly taken as evidence that Lloyd Webber had pandered to the lowest popular taste, producing the theatrical equivalent of the high-salt, high-fat junk food which, in various standard, branded forms, spread rapidly across much of the developed world in the 1980s: a 1995 BBC Two documentary specifically compared Lloyd Webber's business practice to that of the burger chain McDonald's.[34] Thus the later musicals did not obtain an unprejudiced hearing, being rejected on one hand by those who had already written Lloyd Webber off as an out-and-out populist, and on the other by those who had fallen in love with *Cats* and *Phantom* and wanted more of the same. This of course is unfair, though any such argument tends to invite the reasonable riposte that, overall, Lloyd Webber has been rewarded according to, and perhaps much beyond, his deserts.

There is also the complex question of the role of the Really Useful Group in Lloyd Webber's career. This was a company he created in 1977 to manage and license productions of his musicals (and, subsequently, a few other works). It was floated on the stock exchange in 1986, but Lloyd Webber soon decided that he hated the way this 'lessened his authority and exposed him to the vagaries of the marketplace'[35] and from 1990 he embarked on a series of manoeuvres to reacquire complete financial control. The Really Useful Group has guaranteed him productions of all his musicals subsequent to *Evita* on his own terms and effectively meant that everyone connected with those productions is his employee. This enabled the situation Michael Walsh evokes in a succinct and prescient sketch of Lloyd Webber's decline written as early as 1997: 'The theater may be a cooperative enterprise, but Lloyd Webber had worked all his life to make it a one-man show, and over the years he had become increasingly indifferent to anyone's opinion but his own.'[36] It is noteworthy that of Lloyd Webber's six musicals which have enjoyed spectacular success at the box office, three were produced in equal partnership with Tim Rice, two in more or less equal partnership with Trevor Nunn, and the last, *Phantom*, was produced by Cameron Mackintosh and directed by Hal Prince: powerful men capable of standing up to the composer. Of these major collaborators, only Trevor Nunn has been significantly involved in Lloyd Webber's post-*Phantom* career, directing *Aspects of Love*, *Sunset Boulevard*, and *The Woman in White*, but, as Vagelis Siropoulos has well said, 'his role was significantly reduced, resembling now more that of a handsomely paid stage manager, handling the busy stage traffic and blocking out the scenes, rather than conceptualizing the performance.'[37] In general, since *Phantom* more and more aspects of each musical, from the storyline to the casting and advertising, have come under Lloyd Webber's personal control. A positive interpretation of this, of course, is that he now gets to write the musicals he wants to write without having to worry too much about their commercial viability as his earlier musicals remain immensely lucrative. Nevertheless, it is surely significant that many of the newer musicals which have moved in to address the market he once dominated have been much more collaborative affairs: *The Lion King* (1997), *Mamma Mia!* (1999), and *Wicked* (2003) are obvious examples.

Whether Lloyd Webber will compose any more massive hits on the scale of those he produced in the 1970s and 1980s must remain an open question. At the time of writing it appears that his future reputation as a composer for the theatre will continue to rest primarily on *Joseph and the Amazing Technicolor Dreamcoat*, *Jesus Christ Superstar*, *Evita*, *Cats*, *Starlight Express*, and *The Phantom of the Opera*. Rodgers and Hammerstein also produced six major hits, as did Puccini.

It is worth concluding with a more extended look at *Love Never Dies*, the sequel to *The Phantom of the Opera*. Of all his musicals, this is the one in which Lloyd Webber made the largest imaginative and emotional investment: '*Love Never Dies* is, I am unashamed to say, the most personal of all my stage works to date', he stated in 2011.[38] It is filled with passionate, fiery music that shows his melodic talents quite undimmed. Unfortunately, the very idea of a sequel to *The Phantom*, especially one that reunites all the major characters, tends to strike most people as preposterous—a bit like there being a sequel to *Oliver!*. Nevertheless, Lloyd Webber conceived of such a sequel to his greatest hit as early as 1990, perhaps partly because of the sort of Hollywood culture that always sees lucrative possibilities in sequels, but mainly, it would appear, because of his compulsive desire to make the Phantom the true love of Christine's life. He imagined the Phantom, who dies in Leroux's novel but simply disappears at the end of the musical, making his way to New York, there to be subsequently joined by Christine and, weirdly, *their son*. This plot sketch was perhaps influenced by the fact that Broadway had become Lloyd Webber's second home; here, too, was a chance to join up the European opera-operetta tradition with the American musical. The composer discussed his idea with the novelist Frederick Forsyth, who did his best with it and published *The Phantom of Manhattan* in 1999, crediting the germ of the novel to Lloyd Webber. The latter found Forsyth's version unsuitable for musical development, however, and the project was put on hold for several years. In 2006, Ben Elton, who had written *The Beautiful Game* (and been widely criticized for it), was asked to help reshape the story, and did so to Lloyd Webber's satisfaction. The eventual book was credited to 'Andrew Lloyd Webber & Ben Elton / With Glenn Slater [the lyricist] & Frederick Forsyth'.

Lloyd Webber's 'most personal' work turns on a stunning, and to many a disillusioning, absurdity: that the Phantom impregnated Christine before she married Raoul. In *The Phantom of Manhattan* the fact that Christine and the Phantom (Erik) have a son drives the plot, but Forsyth says as little as possible about how this came to be, merely suggesting that Christine was raped after Erik abducted her from the theatre. At the very end of the novel she tells him: 'I was so afraid I thought I would die of fear. I was half swooning when what happened . . . happened'.[39] This was an intelligent storyteller's solution to the yawning plot hole in Lloyd Webber's scenario. It did not satisfy the composer at all, however, as it directly contradicted the central idea motivating a sequel. In the musical, Lloyd Webber got what he longed for: here we are invited to believe that, on the eve of her wedding to Raoul, Christine stole away to see the Phantom, somehow knowing where he was hiding, and that they enjoyed passionate, consensual, outdoor sex. Christine awoke in the morning ready to swear eternal love to the Phantom, but found him gone—and so married Raoul in a fit of pique. In *The Phantom of Manhattan* Raoul is still the kind, noble man found in *The Phantom of the Opera*; in *Love Never Dies* he is a gambler, an alcoholic, and a thoroughly unpleasant individual. To solve the weighty problems of Christine being married, and domestic bliss between her and the Phantom being (to most people) strictly incredible, she is accidentally shot dead at the end of the sequel by Meg Giry, her friend from Paris days: an extraordinarily contrived demonstration of the fact that fantasy can only be fantasy.

That Lloyd Webber kept faith for so many years with the absurd notion that the Phantom is Christine's true love, and was willing to sacrifice Raoul's character, a good part of Christine's character, and even her life on that altar, is less a comment on his artistic judgement in general—which has frequently been very shrewd—than on his particular obsession with reinterpreting *The Phantom of the Opera* story. The point of *Love Never Dies* may be that Christine could never get the Phantom out of her head and her life; the significance of the work is that Lloyd Webber had not been able to get the Phantom out of his. Yet *Love Never Dies*, strong as it is musically, must be one of the oddest sequels in theatrical history, shaped by a peculiar love–hate relationship to its original. On one hand it shores up the position *The Phantom of the Opera* occupies as Lloyd Webber's central, defining musical; on the other it seems intent, in a rather Freudian way, on displacement, on destroying the authority of the earlier work (which is scrupulously respected in Forsyth's novel), and as such perhaps dramatizes the older composer's frustration at having to keep competing (unsuccessfully) with his younger self. Lloyd Webber has indeed prophesied that he will be eventually remembered as the composer of *Love Never Dies*, not *Phantom*: 'I think, in the end, if I was a betting man—which I'm not—the musical that I'd say will be remembered in 100 years' time is Love Never Dies [*sic*].'[40] As sequel and original are erected on such different imaginative premises that they cannot both be true (as though a sequel to *Oliver!* were to show Oliver choosing, after all, a life of crime with Fagin, in defiance of Charles Dickens), this implies audiences gradually rejecting Leroux's residual authority over the characters he created and corresponding acceptance of the fact that they are now completely Lloyd Webber's. So far, however, all the evidence suggests that the vast majority of the composer's many fans will remain loyal to the earlier musical and that 'in 100 years' time' he is likely to be remembered above all for *The Phantom of the Opera*.

Whether Lloyd Webber will ever emerge from the shadow of *The Phantom* is unclear, but perhaps with *Love Never Dies* now completed to his satisfaction he will find himself able to move on decisively and rediscover the freshness, unpredictability, and art of leading and directing popular taste that allowed him to stamp his personality so compellingly on the modern musical in the 1970s and 1980s. At the time of writing, in late 2015, Lloyd Webber's newest musical, *School of Rock*—following the current fashion for musicals based on recent films—is due to premiere on Broadway. This is his most commercial choice of subject since *Phantom*, and if the balance between diegetic and non-diegetic music is satisfactorily worked out, it is likely to prove his most successful musical of the new century. But whatever it adds to his existing achievement, the past five decades remain Lloyd Webber's era, and in Britain, especially, there is no obvious inheritor of his mantle as a creator and enabler of musical theatre with global appeal and a global reach.

Notes

1. Tim Rice, *Oh, What a Circus: The Autobiography 1944–1978* (London: Hodder and Stoughton, 1999), 1.
2. Quoted in Michael Walsh, 'Magician of The Musical', *Time* (US ed.), 18 January 1988, 61.
3. Andrew Lloyd Webber, 'The Music of Evita', in Andrew Lloyd Webber and Tim Rice, *Evita: The Legend of Eva Peron 1919–1952* (London: Elm Tree Books, 1978), not paginated.
4. Quoted in Andrew Lamb, 'What's the Greatest Musical Ever Written?', *Theatregoer*, September 2003, 23.

5. Lloyd Webber, 'Music of Evita'.

6. Quoted in John Coldstream, 'High Flying', *Evita*, programme (London: Prince Edward Theatre, 1978), not paginated.

7. Basil Ramsey, Sleeve Notes, *The Southend Boys' Choir: Three Pop Cantatas*, LP, Vista VPS 1009, 1974.

8. *Joseph and the Amazing Technicolor Dreamcoat*, LP, Decca SKL 4973, 1968.

9. Rice, *Oh, What a Circus*, 191.

10. Andrew Lloyd Webber, 'Andrew Lloyd Webber', *Jeeves*, programme (London: Her Majesty's Theatre, 1975), not paginated.

11. Rice, *Oh, What a Circus*, 319.

12. Lloyd Webber, 'Music of Evita'.

13. Quoted in Michael Walsh, *Andrew Lloyd Webber: His Life and Works*, extended ed. (New York: Harry N. Abrams, 1997), 97.

14. Lloyd Webber, 'Music of Evita'.

15. Rice, *Oh, What a Circus*, 366.

16. Rice, *Oh, What a Circus*, 289.

17. Quoted in Gerald McKnight, *Andrew Lloyd Webber* (London: Granada, 1984), 87.

18. Quoted in Anon., 'T. S. Eliot Musical: Nunn Joins Forces with Andrew Lloyd-Webber [*sic*]', *Stage and Television Today*, 25 September 1980, 2.

19. Quoted in McKnight, *Andrew Lloyd Webber*, 209.

20. Walsh, *Andrew Lloyd Webber*, 115.

21. Stan Meares, '"From Disaster to Triumph": A Selection of British Operas Composed During the Reign of HM Queen Elizabeth II', *British Music* 34 (2012): 100.

22. Quoted in Keith Richmond, *The Musicals of Andrew Lloyd Webber* (London: Virgin, 1995), 88.

23. Quoted in Richmond, *Musicals of Andrew Lloyd Webber*, 103.

24. Frederick Forsyth, *The Phantom of Manhattan* (New York: St Martin's Press, 1999), xii.

25. Wilson Morales, 'Andrew Lloyd Webber's *The Phantom of The Opera*: An Interview with Gerard Butler', blackfilm.com features, December 2004, http://www.blackfilm.com/20041217/features/gerardbutler.shtml, accessed 19 June 2014.

26. This point is well illustrated by some videos on YouTube that take footage from *The Phantom of the Opera* film and combine it with Christine and the Phantom's account of their lovemaking in *Love Never Dies* ('Beneath a Moonless Sky'). The combination suggests, of course, that Butler's Phantom *was* sexually irresistible to Christine.

27. James Inverne, Booklet Notes, *Andrew Lloyd Webber, Now & Forever*, not paginated, CD, The Really Useful Group, 314 589 393-2, 2001.

28. Kurt Gänzl, *The Encyclopedia of Musical Theatre*, 2nd ed., 3 vols. (New York: Schirmer Books, 2004), 1:76.

29. The financial losses *Sunset Boulevard* suffered in America had much to do with Lloyd Webber's personal casting decisions and the expensive legal suits and bad publicity they prompted. See Walsh, *Andrew Lloyd Webber*, 262–263.

30. Inverne, Booklet Notes.

31. Andrew Lloyd Webber, untitled essay, *The Beautiful Game*, programme (London: Cambridge Theatre, 2000), not paginated.

32. *Spitting Image*, directed by Bob Cousins, Peter Harris, and Andy de Emmony, broadcast on ITV on 10 March 1985.

33. Roger Waters, *Amused to Death*, arranged for voice, piano, and guitar (Esher: Pink Floyd Music Publishers Ltd, 1992), 71.
34. *The Business*, directed by Helen Richards, broadcast on BBC Two on 20 July 1995.
35. Walsh, *Andrew Lloyd Webber*, 232.
36. Walsh, *Andrew Lloyd Webber*, 233–234.
37. Vagelis Siropoulos, 'The Ideology and Aesthetics of Andrew Lloyd Webber's Musicals: from the Broadway Musical to the British Megamusical' (unpublished PhD thesis, Aristotle University of Thessaloniki, 2008), 279–280.
38. Andrew Lloyd Webber, 'A Note from the Composer', *Love Never Dies*, programme (Melbourne: Regent Theatre, 2011), not paginated.
39. Forsyth, *Phantom*, 250.
40. Quoted in Rebecca Hardy, '*Love Never Dies* . . . (Ask My Ex-wives!)', *Daily Mail Weekend*, 24 September 2011, 9.

Bibliography

Anon. 'T. S. Eliot Musical: Nunn Joins Forces with Andrew Lloyd-Webber [*sic*].' *Stage and Television Today*, 25 September 1980, 2.

The Business. Directed by Helen Richards. Broadcast 20 July 1995 on BBC Two.

Coldstream, John. 'High Flying'. *Evita*, Programme, not paginated. London: Prince Edward Theatre, 1978.

Forsyth, Frederick. *The Phantom of Manhattan*. New York: St Martin's Press, 1999.

Gänzl, Kurt. *The Encyclopedia of Musical Theatre*, 2nd ed. 3 vols. New York: Schirmer Books, 2004.

Hardy, Rebecca. '*Love Never Dies* . . . (Ask My Ex-wives!).' *Daily Mail Weekend*, 24 September 2011, 8–9.

Inverne, James. 'Booklet Notes.' *Andrew Lloyd Webber, Now & Forever*, not paginated. CD. The Really Useful Group, 314 589 393-2, 2001.

Jewell, Derek. Sleeve Notes. In *Joseph and the Amazing Technicolor Dreamcoat*. LP. Decca SKL 4973, 1968.

Lamb, Andrew. 'What's the Greatest Musical Ever Written?' *Theatregoer*, September 2003, 20–24.

Lloyd Webber, Andrew. 'Andrew Lloyd Webber.' *Jeeves*, not paginated. Programme. London: Her Majesty's Theatre, 1975.

Lloyd Webber, Andrew. 'The Music of Evita.' In Andrew Lloyd Webber and Tim Rice, *Evita: The Legend of Eva Peron 1919–1952*, not paginated. London: Elm Tree Books, 1978.

Lloyd Webber, Andrew. Untitled essay. In *The Beautiful Game*, not paginated. Programme. London: Cambridge Theatre, 2000.

Lloyd Webber, Andrew. 'A Note from The Composer.' In *Love Never Dies*, not paginated. Programme. Melbourne: Regent Theatre, 2011.

McKnight, Gerald. *Andrew Lloyd Webber*. London: Granada, 1984.

Meares, Stan. ' "From Disaster to Triumph": A Selection of British Operas Composed During the Reign of HM Queen Elizabeth II.' *British Music* 34 (2012): 85–109.

Morales, Wilson. 'Andrew Lloyd Webber's *The Phantom of the Opera*: An Interview with Gerard Butler.' blackfilm.com features, December 2004. http://www.blackfilm.com/20041217/features/gerardbutler.shtml, accessed 19 June 2014.

Ramsey, Basil. Sleeve Notes. In *The Southend Boys' Choir: Three Pop Cantatas*. LP. Vista VPS 1009, 1974.

Rice, Tim. *Oh, What a Circus: The Autobiography 1944–1978*. London: Hodder and Stoughton, 1999.

Richmond, Keith. *The Musicals of Andrew Lloyd Webber*. London: Virgin, 1995.

Siropoulos, Vagelis. 'The Ideology and Aesthetics of Andrew Lloyd Webber's Musicals: from the Broadway Musical to the British Megamusical.' Unpublished PhD, Aristotle University of Thessaloniki, 2008.

Spitting Image. Directed by Bob Cousins, Peter Harris, and Andy de Emmony, broadcast 10 March 1985 on ITV.

Walsh, Michael. 'Magician of the Musical.' *Time* (US ed.), 18 January 1988, 54–61.

Walsh, Michael. *Andrew Lloyd Webber: His Life and Works*. Extended ed. New York: Harry N. Abrams, 1997.

Waters, Roger. *Amused To Death*, Arranged for Voice, Piano, and Guitar. Esher: Pink Floyd Music Publishers Ltd, 1992.

PART VI

··

'THE ART OF THE POSSIBLE'

Alternative Approaches to Musical Theatre Aesthetics

··

CHAPTER 24

THE BEGGAR'S LEGACY

Playing with Music and Drama, 1920–2003

ROBERT LAWSON-PEEBLES

INTRODUCTION: DISINTEGRATING
THE MUSICAL

THE *Beggar's Opera* is a rough work about tough lives. In the original 1728 production John Gay's satire revealed the intimate relation between the underworld and the upper crust. The inhabitants of his criminal subculture put the quietus to the fashion for Italian opera by singing well-known British songs, turning the ballad opera into a popular if controversial form and Gay into 'the Orpheus of highwaymen'.[1] By 1886 *The Beggar's Opera* had ceased to captivate. The play had been superseded by the licensed tomfoolery of the Savoy operas and their proletarian relations, the music halls. Yet, as I will argue, thirty-four years later, *The Beggar's Opera* provided both a subject adaptable to modern cultural politics and a related organizing principle allowing for the flexible interaction of music and text.

There are three reasons why *The Beggar's Opera* has proved so influential. Firstly, it is surrounded by a framing device. The Beggar and the Player underline the play's parodic structure. The Beggar's desire for 'a most excellent moral' for the opera is squashed by the Player's demand that it complies 'with the taste of the town'.[2] They then double as dei ex machina, saving Macheath from his fate. Secondly, Gay recruited many (unwitting) contributors, who provided the sixty-nine 'Airs'. *The Beggar's Opera* thereby anticipates the collaborative ethos, not only of theatre, but also of film and television. Thirdly, *The Beggar's Opera* initiated a loosely articulated dramaturgy, enabling many adaptations and recreations.[3]

This chapter is organized into two main parts, each beginning with the work of the actor-manager Nigel Playfair (1874–1934). I will discuss the influence of *The Beggar's Opera* on a group of authors who work against the generic grain of the musical. They are against enchantment. They treat the musical as omnivectoral, protean, transitory, subject to multiple interventions, conceived in hybridity and condemned to instability. They undermine any kind of homogeneity, whether it be the dramatic unities; or Eugène Scribe's well-made play; or the organic tours de force of Wagner's music dramas; or the integration of song, character, and plot that informs the 'Broadway canon' from *Show Boat* to *West Side Story*.[4] They disintegrate the mainstream musical to expand the range and potential of the form.

PART ONE: PLAYFAIR SETS A PRECEDENT

My argument begins with the 1920 revival of *The Beggar's Opera*. When it opened at the Lyric Theatre on 5 June, the Nigel Playfair–Frederic Austin production completed the transformation of Gay's criminal, bitingly satirical subculture into jolly robber gentility, an urban update to the Robin Hood method of wealth redistribution. The novelist Arnold Bennett toned down Gay's language (words like 'whore' being too coarse for fastidious ears). Two articles in *The Times* prepared the audience for its opening night. *The Beggar's Opera* is 'a fierce kind of comedy, but a comedy all the same'. It is 'the 18th century equivalent to a *revue*', poking fun at 'lordly' institutions. Since its first production, 'this forerunner of the music-halls' has acted as an honest, indigenous remedy to the superficial fashion for foreign opera. Moreover, *The Beggar's Opera* is a morality tale, for its 'Gilbertian' heroine Polly, 'the one decent person in a sea of infamy', insists that Macheath marry her. *The Times* concluded that this revival should appeal to 'the plain Englishman'.[5] It did. The production ran for three-and-a-half years. It ensured the continuance of the Lyric Theatre. When *The Beggar's Opera* closed on 17 December 1923, an editorial in *The Times* triumphantly proclaimed that 'the nation has regained a classic'.[6] And that is how it was treated. The production was revived for a broadcast from the studio of 2LO (the London station of the BBC) on the fifth anniversary of its opening; and it was revived again at the Lyric as a bicentennial obeisance to Gay in 1928, the year in which Playfair was knighted.

The articles in *The Times* suggest that *The Beggar's Opera* has a role in the English Musical Renaissance. This renaissance has largely been seen as pastoral in style, abiding by the rustic socialism of William Morris and folk-song collector Cecil Sharp.[7] Yet the composer most associated with the pastoral, Ralph Vaughan Williams, suggested that urban music had its place. He identified *The Beggar's Opera* as a landmark in English music, to be included as a source of national art with music hall songs, Welsh hymns, Salvation Army bands, 'children dancing to a barrel organ [. . .] the cries of street pedlars, the factory girls singing their sentimental songs'.[8] In *Some Versions of Pastoral* (1935), the literary critic William Empson included *The Beggar's Opera* in an argument expanding the definition of pastoral to include all 'low' people, urban and rural. He wrote that 'it is a fine thing that the play is still popular', for it made 'the classes feel part of a larger unity'.[9] Yet there was dissent on musicological and ideological grounds. H. C. Colles, chief music critic of *The Times*, thought that the music of *The Beggar's Opera* was inadequate for the role it had been given. 'A distinctive musical style' could only be created by 'the union of language and music' in song. He praised Schubert's gift of transforming everyday sounds—such as 'the whirr of Gretchen's spinning wheel [. . .] the wheezy grind of the hurdy-gurdy'—into art song.[10] Unlike Schubert, words and music in *The Beggar's Opera* did not 'share responsibilities for the drama'. Ultimately, its music was 'really only decorative'.[11] Later, Wilfrid Mellers suggested that Gay's work had become 'a typical manifestation of middle-class culture', prompting the audience to jeer at the rich and sneer at the poor.[12] The cultural critic Raymond Williams added that both Sharp and Empson indulged in 'a dream of England', based on 'a deep desire for stability, served to cover and to evade the actual and bitter contradictions of the time'.[13]

Some Versions of Urban Pastoral

The fissile connection between music and drama meant that each new production of *The Beggar's Opera* involved complex negotiations between the differing demands of high style and low life; or of venue—opera house and theatre, cinema and television. Playfair used opera singers, while Austin (who played Peachum) added an 'authentic' touch with an eight-piece ensemble, including a harpsichord, viola d'amore, and viola da gamba.[14] Thus, according to *The Times*, 'the airs have been reset with dainty accompaniments which appeal at once to the modern ear, though the 18th century feeling is preserved'.[15] The 1940 Glyndebourne production updated the action to the nineteenth century, omitted the harpsichord (to the dismay of Frank Howes, music critic of *The Times*), and had the actor Michael Redgrave sing the part of Macheath.[16] Benjamin Britten's 1948 production continued his flirtation with folk song and low life that began with *Plymouth Town* (1931). He recomposed *The Beggar's Opera* as an intimate if sometimes acid chamber opera. Tyrone Guthrie, its first producer, complained that Peter Pears played Macheath as if the highwayman had strayed into 'Stainer's *Crucifixion* on skates at Scunthorpe'.[17] In 1952, Peter Brook for his first film wanted 'a rough energetic film in black and white, with a coarse and virile highwayman in the lead'. He hoped to get Richard Burton. He got Laurence Olivier, a Technicolor project for the Coronation Year, and 'a deep conflict' that turned his movie production 'into an ugly battlefield'. The film barely survives the split between 'the urbane and stylish jeu d'esprit' wished for by Olivier and his co-producer, Herbert Wilcox (best known today for *Spring in Park Lane*, starring Wilcox's wife Anna Neagle), and Brook's desire for a 'violent and harsh work' that 'breathed the stinking air' of Hogarth's cartoons.[18] The chubby Macheath of Hogarth's famous painting of the opera is transformed by Olivier's handsome star status. Yet Brook's wish for greater realism can still be seen in the mob sequences, in Filch as an evil dwarf, and in the Beggar and the Player combined into Hugh Griffith's jailbird author, who reprieves his hero by inciting a prison riot. At least the filmic device of lip-synching averted a vocal anomaly. Only Olivier and Stanley Holloway (Lockit) both sang and spoke their roles.[19]

A mismatch between spoken and sung voices affected Sir Malcolm Sargent's 1955 recording. A cast of distinguished opera singers graced Bennett's bowdlerized lyrics with bel canto, jarring against the demotic dialogue spoken by actors lionized as 'Members of the Old Vic Company'.[20] The score was rearranged for a symphony orchestra. Sargent gave the modest Austin edition the treatment normally reserved for his monster *Messiahs*. Like Richard Eyre's 1982 National Theatre production, Jonathan Miller's 1983 BBC production replaced such proprieties with fidelity to Hogarth's spirited, swarming London. Miller's close-up camera shots reveal a filthy and claustrophobic environment, cluttered with bodies and loot. Jeremy Barlow's arrangement for Miller conveys eighteenth-century style.[21] Roger Daltrey, lead singer of The Who, puts his cocky voice to good use, and emphasizes Macheath's sexual potency by groping his doxies. Patricia Routledge's Mrs Peachum sports with Filch.[22] Bob Hoskins's importunate Beggar adds a brief Prologue insisting that the work's 'most excellent moral' remain as he 'at first intended'.[23] The Hangman misunderstands the signal of Graham Crowden's foppish Player and Macheath sings his final 'Air' from another place, suitably equipped with an echo chamber.[24]

A 1981 recording, based on a Sydney Opera production that had, controversially, been set in a 1930s film studio, employs the divas Joan Sutherland (Lucy Lockit) and Kiri Te Kanawa (Polly Peachum), with Angela Lansbury (Mrs Peachum) fresh from her triumph as Nellie Lovett in Sondheim's *Sweeney Todd*, and Alfred Marks (Peachum) and Warren Mitchell (the Beggar), camping up their cockney credentials. Douglas Gamley's arrangement for full-size modern orchestra celebrates the opera's vital, disjunct nature in a wide range of allusions from Stravinskian neoclassicism to a palais de danse saxophone. Richard Bonynge makes the music bounce with vigour. The Gamley–Bonynge notes on the recording highlight the connections between eighteenth-century ballad opera and twentieth-century musical comedy, and mock authenticity by treating everything as pastiche. The result is aurally an appealing version of the opera, but with nothing of the darkness that Peter Brook had wished to portray.[25]

Die Dreigroschenoper

Two recreations of *The Beggar's Opera* move the work firmly away from its status as a comic opera. The better-known is *Die Dreigroschenoper*. Its first 1928 production was advertised as an update of *The Beggar's Opera*. Caspar Neher's poster displays both titles, in front of a Chaplinesque figure with a cane and unfortunate teeth, while the playbill announces that it is 'after the English of John Gay'.[26] It is, rather, an imaginative transformation of the Playfair–Austin production in terms of Bertolt Brecht's epic theatre and Kurt Weill's dislike of the Wagnerian *Gesamtkunstwerk* (unified, total work of art).[27] Their differing interests were united by the socio-economic realities of 1920s Berlin. Macheath is no longer 'a gentleman of the road', but a businessman who knows that founding a bank is more profitable than robbing one. He is a career murderer and, as 'Die Moritat von Mackie Messer' ('The Ballad of Mack the Knife') makes clear, a pimp for paedophiles. One of his first acts is to have the legs sawn off a stolen harpsichord in order to create a bench.[28] A little woodwork thus reduces Frederic Austin's attempt at eighteenth-century authenticity into a site for *Bänkelsang* (literally bench-song, or street singing), a more lurid aspect of the German ballad tradition.[29] In 1956, Lotte Lenya recalled that Brecht had quickly written the verses for 'Die Moritat'. They were

> modelled after the *Moritaten* ('Mord' meaning murder, 'tat' meaning deed) sung by singers at street fairs, detailing the hideous crimes of notorious arch-fiends. Kurt not only produced the tune overnight, he knew the name of the hand-organ manufacturer [. . .] who could supply the organ on which to grind out the tune for the prologue.[30]

It is fitting that in the 1929 recording of the 'Mack the Knife', a barrel organ should introduce the melody before accompanying Brecht's raw voice as he sings the first two verses.[31] It is as if Schubert's hurdy-gurdy man has been resurrected after a century in the chill of winter. On the centenary of Schubert's death, Weill wrote that Schubert had achieved 'the fusion of genuine popularity with the highest artistic perfection' because his songs 'arise from folk-like experience'.[32] In addition to *Die Winterreise*, Weill drew on Ernst Křenek's 'jazz opera' *Jonny spielt auf* (*Johnny Strikes Up*, 1927). At a critical moment Křenek's black protagonist, Jonny, steals an Amati violin, leaving a banjo instead. So Weill replaced Austin's sweet viola d'amore with a strident banjo.

The description of the production at the Theater am Schiffbauerdamm by Norman Ebbutt, the Berlin correspondent of *The Times*, shows how far Brecht and Kurt Weill had deviated from the Playfair–Austin production. Primitive scenery and ultra-modern lighting and projection techniques had turned *The Beggar's Opera* into expressionist theatre. Weill's music was played by an onstage band, including saxophones and the 'more startling of present-day dance music instruments'. Ebbutt was so nonplussed that he failed to notice that Weill had retained Gay's first 'Air' as 'Peachum's Morning Hymn' (No. 3). Yet he approved this update of Gay's burlesque: everything in *Die Dreigroschenoper* was 'a movement towards freeing music, acting and the cinematograph from the ruts of Italian opera, Wagnerian music-drama, drawing-room comedy, and Hollywood, and creating something new with them'.[33] *Die Dreigroschenoper* was a phenomenal success in Europe and Scandinavia. Thanks to the Playfair–Austin production, only Britain remained immune. In 1929 an Englishwoman wrote from Vienna complaining that *Die Dreigroschenoper* 'has no single thing to recommend it—neither text, costumes, nor one of the charming airs which are so essential a characteristic of *The Beggar's Opera*'. 'This work', she continued, 'would disgust and revolt any English man or woman who had the pleasure of knowing the original.'[34] *Die Dreigroschenoper* first appeared in English translation in a BBC broadcast on 8 February 1935. Critics dismissed the broadcast in terms similar to those of six years before.[35]

There was one exception: Alfred Einstein. When he introduced the 1935 BBC broadcast, the music critic praised 'the hurdy-gurdy tune [as] one of Weill's most brilliant inventions'. While Gay had used popular song as 'mitigation' of his criticism of society,

Brecht and Weill had produced a work 'more biting, more bitter, more unconcealed, less considerate of social misunderstandings'. Einstein hoped that *Die Dreigroschenoper* was 'the beginning of a new type of opera as yet unknown in England, which might have led to a resuscitation of the traditional and obsolete form'. *The Tuppeny-Ha'penny Opera*, as he called it, had a simple form 'based on the "Lied"' which 'would appeal to the masses'. Not surprisingly, the work had been suppressed in Germany. Like Weill, Einstein had left Berlin because of Nazism, and believed that Britain was 'probably the only country where it can at any rate still be broadcast'. He concluded by expressing hope that Weill would one day be able to continue his experiment.[36] Yet *The Threepenny Opera* did not appear on the British stage until 1956, six years after Weill died.[37]

A Chorus of Disapproval

In comparison with *The Threepenny Opera, A Chorus of Disapproval* (1984) appears tame, at first sight depicting parochial peccadillos. Yet it too uses the articulated structure of *The Beggar's Opera* to experiment with the resources of theatre. Alan Ayckbourn's play functions as a complex backstage musical which ends where it begins; as a provincial comedy of errors, undercut by Chekhovian longing; and as a mousetrap wherein, ironically, no consciences are caught. It concerns the attempt by the Pendon Amateur Light Operatic Society to perform the *The Beggar's Opera*. The framing device, the final 'Air' with Macheath and his doxies (69), sets the ironic tone. The action in the *Opera* is mirrored in the play, and eleven of the original sixty-nine 'Airs' provide a commentary. Therefore, Crispin Usher, the initial Macheath, sings 'How happy could I be with either, | Were t'other dear charmer away' (Air 35) while his two girlfriends roll around the floor in a vicious fight. When Usher quits, it seems as if the production will collapse. As the Director, Dafydd ap Llewellyn, remarks, 'trying to do *The Beggar's Opera* without a Macheath is a bit of a non-starter even for Peter Brook'.[38] (See Figure 24.1.)

So the new arrival, Guy Jones, becomes Macheath. Ayckbourn creates further ironies from the performance history of *The Beggar's Opera*, for Guy has none of the star status of Olivier. Instead, he is prepared for his part through affairs with Fay Hubbard, the local swinger, and Hannah, Dafydd's neglected wife. Guy's audition song, 'All Through the Night'/'Ar Hyd y Nos' (*not* one of the original sixty-nine 'Airs', but instead from a 1784 collection of Welsh music[39]) introduces no 'pure and holy feeling' into the assembly, but is rather a vehicle for Dafydd to strut his Welsh identity. Ayckbourn remarked in a newspaper interview before the first London run of the play (at the Olivier in the National Theatre) that 'Guy is [. . .] a vacuum, a giant slate that everyone scribbles on'.[40] They scribble with relish, projecting on to him their lust and greed, propelling him up the criminal and acting hierarchy, and in the process commenting on contemporary politics.

A Chorus of Disapproval confirms Michael Billington's insight that 'Ayckbourn was the first dramatist to pin down an essential contradiction of Thatcherism: its worship of family values and its sanctification of individual greed'.[41] Dafydd asserts that *The Beggar's Opera* is 'as relevant as it was' in 1728. Indeed, its vitality reflects badly on the present. As Dafydd adds: 'Can you imagine Captain Macheath purchasing marital aids [. . .]?' The antipode of Macheath is Councillor Jarvis Huntley-Pike. As his wife remarks, 'six years

FIGURE 24.1 John Gay's *The Beggar's Opera* recreated as a provincial comedy of errors: Rob Brydon (centre; as Dafydd ap Llwewellyn) and company in the West End revival of *A Chorus of Disapproval*, Harold Pinter Theatre, 2012.

Photograph by Marilyn Kingwill. Courtesy of ArenaPal.

sharing a mattress with Jarvis' has cured her of sex. Jarvis follows in his forebears' footsteps as a monster of market economics. He cuts himself off from the others by listening to recordings of steam engines and, in the most chilling words in the play, has 'paid off' everyone, even his family. Guy, too, has been 'paid off', in two senses of that phrase: he has been rewarded by Jarvis for a corrupt land deal and sacked by the multinational firm which employed him. There is therefore a hollow ring to the second, more positive, conclusion to the play-within-a-play. Guy, the rejected 'Wretch of To-day' in the opening scene, suffering a chorus of hypocritical disapproval, will not be 'happy To-morrow'.[42]

In this and a number of other respects Michael Winner's film version of *A Chorus of Disapproval* presents a different view. Slapstick replaces irony. The framing device is changed to fit with a linear, realist narrative. The film begins as Guy arrives at Scarborough railway station. It ends at the station with Guy, relocated rather than sacked, waltzing with a trolley in gamesome anticipation of a part in *The Merry Widow* at Blackpool. Ayckbourn co-wrote the screenplay, but became unhappy with the film— although well acted and directed, it has none of the acid tone, political bite, or complexity of the stage original.[43]

Part Two: Playfair Embarks on an Experiment

On 14 December 1923, three days before the Playfair–Austin production of *The Beggar's Opera* completed its triumphant first run at the Lyric Theatre, Nigel Playfair wrote in the fledgling *Radio Times* that radio offered 'a wonderful opportunity for playwrights and others who will direct their abilities to the production of material specially suitable for broadcasting'.[44] On 15 January 1924 2LO broadcast Playfair's production of Richard Hughes's *Danger*, the first play written specifically for broadcasting. Hughes would shortly 'ghost' Playfair's first volume of memoirs, *The Story of the Lyric Theatre, Hammersmith* (1925). Today he is best remembered for *A High Wind in Jamaica* (1929). *Danger* concerned three visitors to a Welsh coal mine who become trapped when a generator fails. The announcer recommended that listeners switch off the lights in order to sympathize with their predicament. A photograph in *The Times* showed Playfair, in evening dress, 'directing the production of incidental "effects" '. These included primitive sound-effect devices, including a suspended bucket, into which the actors spoke to create the echo of a cavern.[45] A Welsh male voice choir sang from behind a soundproof door, which was occasionally opened to admit the strains of 'Aberystwyth' or 'Ar Hyd y Nos' ('All Through the Night', used in *A Chorus of Disapproval*).[46]

BBC Manchester

It took time to build upon this modest if imaginative experiment. From 1923 the BBC had run landlines from Covent Garden (for opera) or the Savoy Hotel (for dance music) to their London studio, but it was only in 1935 that BBC Manchester began to use what John Grierson, the pioneer of film documentary, called the 'art of microphone sound' to capture 'actuality', the drama of ordinary life, in combination with text and music.[47] In 1932 Archie Harding (1903–53), a producer, had been banished from London to Manchester because one of his programmes had caused a diplomatic incident. In the course of four years in Manchester, Harding revolutionized broadcasting by giving voice to ordinary people.[48] Among the actors he recruited were Joan Littlewood[49] and Jimmie Miller, a radical autodidact who was spotted busking folk songs outside a Manchester cinema. Harding's writers and producers included Giles Playfair (son of Sir Nigel), Olive Shapley (an Oxford Marxist like Harding), and Geoffrey Bridson. In May 1935, Bridson (1910–80) began a series of programmes mixing his verse with ballads sung by a local choir and the voices of ordinary people. These led to more adventurous programming, including one broadcast on May Day 1936. It was, Bridson wrote, 'a pleasantly varied mosaic' to answer the 'maypole tradition', where 'Tennyson, in the role of an increasingly hysterical Queen of the May, found himself cross-cut against a rising tide of industrial militancy'. Sounds of machine guns in Berlin and loudhailers in Red Square gave way to Bridson's poem on the 3 million unemployed in Britain, 'snarled out in seething anger by a vigorously proletarian voice'.[50] It was Jimmie Miller's. Bridson would go on, now with Manchester's new Mobile Recording Unit, to write *Steel*, with music for choir and symphony orchestra, broadcast in 1937, and—with the assistance of Joan Littlewood— *Johnny Miner: An Opera for Coal* (1947), using Tyneside Colliery songs.

Shapley (1910–99) started with *Children's Hour*, and moved to documentary programming with Littlewood and Miller. Two programmes made in 1939 illustrate Shapley's method. *They Speak for Themselves* mixed studio commentary with recorded actuality, dramatized reconstructions, and linking music. This was followed by *The Classic*

Soil, produced with Littlewood, its title taken from Friedrich Engels's description of Manchester in 1844, and suggesting how little the city had changed in the succeeding ninety-five years. Between them, Bridson and Shapley developed methods of regional programme-making that wrenched, as she later put it, 'John Reith's BBC from the grip of the stuffed shirts by taking the microphone out of the studio and into the country at large'.[51]

Theatre Workshop

Littlewood and Miller (who changed his name to Ewan MacColl) followed Shapley's precept by bringing theatre to an audience with little or no experience of the stage. The manifesto of Theatre Workshop, inspired by the landslide Labour victory in the general election, announced a popular yet experimental theatre 'which reflected the dreams and struggles of the people'.[52] Its first production, a ballad opera entitled *Johnny Noble*, opened at a girls' school in Cumbria in August 1945.[53] The plot concerned the love affair between a young woman and the eponymous hero from the 1930s up to 1945. The treatment was, however, far from conventional. The curtains open on a completely dark stage. Two narrators are illuminated by spotlights:

> 1ST NARRATOR   *[Singing]* Here is a stage—
> 2ND NARRATOR   *[Speaking]* A platform twenty-five feet by fifteen.
> 1ST NARRATOR   *[Singing]* A microcosm of the world.
> 2ND NARRATOR   *[Speaking]* Here the sun is an amber flood and the moon a
>   thousand-watt spot.
> 1ST NARRATOR   *[Singing]* Here shall be space,
>   Here we shall act time.
> 2ND NARRATOR   *[Speaking]* From nothing everything will come. . . ..
>   *Up boogie-woogie music. A woman enters, dances across the stage and off. Fade out*
>   *music.*[54]

This is a striking instance of the simplicity that Peter Brook would call 'an act of theatre', but it is part of a complex dramaturgy.[55] MacColl later explained that their 'technical resources' included two state-of-the-art consoles, one to control lighting and the other (with six turntables) to play 'factory noises, ships' engines, aeroplanes, artillery and bombs' as well as instrumental music. 'The contrast between this and the *a capella* singing of the narrators', he continued, 'was a sure way of altering the perspective of a scene.' Their ensemble work drew upon past productions that 'had been refined and stripped [. . .] in much the same way that the text of a traditional ballad is stripped down by passing through the mouths of generations of singers'.[56]

The ballad genre was important for two reasons. Firstly, it provided a model of transmissive practice, with the plot of *Johnny Noble* recycling MacColl's earlier work on theatrical documentaries and the work about women in wartime that Shapley and Littlewood had prepared for the BBC. The device of two narrators comes from *The Beggar's Opera*.

The portable lighting and audio systems were the latest evolution of work begun with Playfair's rudimentary 1924 2LO broadcast and developed by BBC Manchester. In addition, the imaginative dramaturgy of *Johnny Noble* is indebted to Sergei Eisenstein's theory of montage, Rudolf von Laban's choreography, Adolphe Appia's stage lighting; to productions like Erwin Piscator's *The Good Soldier Schwejk*, Brecht's *The Rise and Fall of the City of Mahagonny*, which MacColl had seen depicted in Léon Moussinac's well-illustrated tome, and Stravinsky's *The Soldier's Tale*, which had its British premiere in Newcastle upon Tyne in 1926. *Johnny Noble* ends with a confrontation between two commedia dell'arte capitalists, '*grotesque figures wearing black tights and bowler hats*' who demand a return to business as usual, and an actor, planted in the audience, who reasserts the socialist idealism of the Labour landslide (62–66).[57]

This indicates the second—political—reason for the importance of ballads. Singing had always been an important part of socialist pedagogy. MacColl used his self-taught and wide-ranging musical knowledge as a concise mode of exposition. Some songs were written for the production; some adapted from earlier sources. Music cues 12 and 22 (pages 49, 62, 68 of the text) adapt 'On Top of Old Smoky', a well-known ballad of lost love, probably from the Appalachians, which now celebrates the fidelity of lovers separated in wartime. MacColl himself wrote music cue 23 (pages 62–63, 71), announcing Johnny's return from the war. It is a variation of 'The Manchester Rambler', written in 1932 after a campaign for access to the countryside, its melody in turn adapted from the Minuet from Haydn's Symphony No. 94 in G major.[58] In sum, *Johnny Noble* exemplified 'a flexible theatre-art' that was well adapted to touring conditions that were often difficult. It remained in the repertoire of Theatre Workshop for five years, and the company performed it throughout Britain, Norway, Sweden, West Germany, and Czechoslovakia.[59] In 1982 John McGrath restaged it with his 7:84 Company. More widely, it pioneered a radical method of blending words and sounds to be developed in the Radio Ballads and, later, in the work of Alan Plater and Dennis Potter.

The Radio Ballads

Committed to the pedagogy inherent in a touring company, MacColl quit Theatre Workshop after it settled at the Theatre Royal Stratford East. He returned to his old trade, writing and performing folk songs. His work was transformed by the arrival of Alan Lomax, who had a commission to record folk music in the Old World. Lomax had recorded oral histories of folk music and jazz for the Library of Congress and, at the suggestion of Geoffrey Bridson, had compiled three American ballad operas for the BBC. Together, MacColl and Lomax contributed significantly to the second renaissance in folk music, which was notably different from the first. To overstate the case: if the patron saint of the first renaissance was William Morris and its nuncio Vaughan Williams, the patron saint of the second was Karl Marx and its nuncio Lonnie Donegan. The folk song movement was transformed from rural and nationalist to vernacular and cosmopolitan.[60] It led to a period of popularity, to increased airtime on the BBC, and to the Radio Ballads.

Charles Parker (1919–80), a BBC producer in Birmingham, commissioned MacColl for 'a dramatic ballad treatment'[61] about John Axon, the driver of a runaway goods train who, in the words of the citation for his posthumous George Cross, 'remained at his post and [. . .] gave his life in an attempt to prevent a collision'.[62] This story of 'an ordinary Englishman of our own times', Parker wrote when introducing the programme, was 'something to sing about'. *The Ballad of John Axon* exploited the Anglo-American folk-song tradition, multi-source 'actuality', and an ensemble style. In place of actors and 'formal narrative', Parker and MacColl used 'real people [. . .] to tell their story simply and directly'.[63] It was a complex and time-consuming process, involving the collection and editing of many hours of voices and sound effects. MacColl then wrote songs and plain-chant, and the production was completed in the studio by musicians and audio technicians under the direction of the American folk-singer Peggy Seeger.[64]

Between 1958 and 1964, a total of eight Radio Ballads sang about the experience of ordinary people. The historian Eric Hobsbawm, writing under his jazz nom de plume of Francis Newton, praised them as 'the most valuable products of the folk-music movement', providing 'cultural populism' as yet unadulterated by commercialism.[65] The ballads were carefully constructed. *The Ballad of John Axon* presents a working-class hero within a tragic framework, composed of the title ballad, plainchant, the 'official' voice of a radio announcer, and the sound effects of a train crash. The railway career is narrated by the voices of Axon's workmates, and by another thematic ballad, 'The Iron Road Is a Hard Road'. MacColl adapts the call-and-response pattern of African American worksong to create a duet between the chorus and the rasp of a fireman's shovel. The *Ballad* mixes such imagery with factuality to evoke the frowst of a community at work. Yet leisure is part of an integral whole. One driver says that 'railways go through the back of your spine like Blackpool goes through rock'.[66] Axon goes dancing and rambling, the latter allowing MacColl to recycle 'The Manchester Rambler'. In real life, Axon liked watching television and was a fan of the crooner Ronnie Hilton; but MacColl suppresses any evidence of Axon's attachment to modern transatlantic mass culture.[67] The final composition was received with acclaim by the press. The *Manchester Guardian* wrote that the programme was 'a powerfully effective way of telling the story' of 'a hero of the people and the tradition of service out of which his heroism grew, and to do this in something like the idiom of the people'.[68] That was exactly how I felt when, as a teenager, I heard the first broadcast in 1958.

In 1972 Parker gave MacColl credit for the 'overall conception' of the Radio Ballads, due to his work for BBC Manchester and Theatre Workshop.[69] MacColl also used his wide reading to understand the relation of archetypal forms and the vernacular. For instance, reading William Empson could have prompted him to include a driver's memory of a nocturnal footplate journey, related as a pastoral soliloquy. In the next Radio Ballad, *Song of a Road* (1959), about the construction of the M1 motorway, MacColl understood that the varied dialects of the labourers contained common rhythms and dramatic imagery missing from the articulate yet circumscribed speech of the white-collar staff. Tragedy had been the appropriate form for *The Ballad of John Axon*. In the next four ballads, Epic valorized the struggles of ordinary people in shifting earth (*Song of a Road*), or with the sea (*Singing the Fishing*, 1960), or in mining (*The Big Hewer*, 1961), or with disability (*The Body Blow*, 1962). Paradigms were changed for the last three ballads: the quest format conveyed the experiences of teenagers (*On the Edge*, 1963), while allegory was used to ironize the world of professional boxing (*The Fight Game*, 1963). MacColl thought that the last ballad, *The Travelling People* (1964), had a perfect subject in the Travellers, whom he regarded as 'the chief carriers of the English and Scots folksong traditions'.[70] But this was a bitter final solution. Its climactic song, 'The Winds of Change', is an angry gloss upon Macmillan's apparently liberal 1960 South African speech. Holocaust imagery informs *The Travelling People*, with a Birmingham councillor suggesting their extermination. At that precise moment, Parker makes his sole intervention in eight ballads: 'You can't really mean that?' The ballad ends with the councillor's response, 'Why not?'[71] Parker was radicalized by his work on the ballads. Eventually, he was fired by the BBC in 1972, and in his remaining years devoted his energies to teaching and to radical theatre.

The Threepenny Opera, 1956

MacColl's most significant theatrical appearance, appropriately, was as the Street Singer in the British premiere of *The Threepenny Opera*. The lyrics which MacColl sang the first night at the Royal Court Theatre, 9 February 1956, were written by Marc Blitzstein, and are so widely performed that they have a life independent of the *Opera*:

> Oh the shark has pretty teeth, dear
> And he shows them pearly white,
> Just a jackknife has Macheath, dear
> And he keeps it out of sight.[72]

Blitzstein had been listening to Brecht's recording, for in the 1954 Off-Broadway recording that first stanza was also accompanied by a barrel organ.[73] The lyrics confirm Aaron Copland's opinion that Blitzstein was the first American composer to create a convincing vernacular musical idiom, and only a few changes were needed to convert to English vernacular.[74] Sam Wanamaker, the director of the English production, adopted Blitzstein instead of the Desmond Vesey–Eric Bentley translation, which was more accurate but, according to Lotte Lenya, 'unsingable'.[75] Blitzstein—perhaps with Brecht's vocal in mind—advised Wanamaker to find an English equivalent for Louis Armstrong's 'fabulous' recent version; it epitomized 'the world of the work'.[76] So Wanamaker hired MacColl who, as Littlewood put it, 'had abandoned his own good baritone for the cracked voice of some old farm labourer'.[77]

   After six weeks at the Royal Court, *The Threepenny Opera* transferred to the West End, where it continued for another three months. Reviews were divided. Frank Howes thought that *The Beggar's Opera* was still the benchmark; Weill's 'offensive' music only served to exaggerate 'the sordid text'.[78] Hans Keller responded that Weill's music was 'a demonstrable masterpiece' which, by creating 'new forms out of eclectic material', united the prestigious with the popular. Its success, in the West End as well as on recordings such as Louis Armstrong's, was a sign of 'a torrential revival that has swept right across our musical world'. The failure of critics like Howes to appreciate the event showed that they were becoming 'psychotic'—'isolated' from society.[79] Keller's language emphasized his familiarity with psychoanalysis and sociology, and his belief that theatre music was undergoing a sea change, part of a general cultural change characterized, as he suggests, by division and anger. Richard Hoggart's *The Uses of Literacy* (1957) and Raymond Williams's *Culture and Society* (1958) extended the definition of culture to include groups previously disqualified. The monopoly of the BBC was upset by the arrival of the more demotic independent television, ITV. The 'old leisured classes' (Williams's caricature[80]) were dismayed by dissident youth and their portrayal in such films as *Momma Don't Allow* and *The Blackboard Jungle* (both 1955), featuring respectively trad jazz and its future nemesis rock 'n' roll. The theatrical 'old guard' (Billington's phrase[81]) were disturbed by the Brechtian dramaturgy of the visiting Berliner Ensemble and productions at the Royal Court, by *The Threepenny Opera*, and by two John Osborne plays, *Look Back in Anger* and *The Entertainer*.[82]

The Entertainer

Osborne claimed that Brecht had no influence on *The Entertainer*. Instead, he said that the theme had been suggested by some music-hall mummery while waiting for his hero, Max Miller, to come on. He added that a Bunk Johnson record of a Scott Joplin rag provided the title.[83] This sounds right, for Johnson, too, was something of the mummer. With new teeth, a fallible trumpet technique, and a dubious claim to have played alongside the first jazzman (Buddy Bolden), Johnson became the figurehead of revivalism. Both Bunk Johnson and Archie Rice 'have a go' at recreating a dying form. *The Entertainer* deals more or less exclusively in the second hand. Laurence Olivier, just five years after the roistering Macheath, memorably played Archie as morally and financially bankrupt in both the stage premiere and the film (see Figure 24.2).[84]

Archie vividly remembers a real spiritual rendered by an elderly African American, but at the play's emotional climax he can only croak a poor imitation (70–71, 73). The play focuses on Archie's immediate family, but its disembowelling is nothing like *Long Day's Journey into Night* (published in Britain in 1956 but not staged until two years later); and poor drunken Phoebe (Archie's wife) is hardly the addict in the attic. The real world is elsewhere, whether it is the Suez Canal or the protest of Archie's daughter Jean in Trafalgar Square on 4 November 1956. The play is precise in its moral location. Aneurin Bevan's Trafalgar Square speech accused the government of 'a policy of bankruptcy and despair'.[85] *The Entertainer* demonstrates the impact of that policy on a divided family. For, as Michael Billington pointed out, there was 'a symbiotic link' between the Empire and the music halls

FIGURE 24.2 Music hall as metaphor: Laurence Olivier as sleazy and disillusioned seaside entertainer Archie Rice in *The Entertainer* (1957).

Photograph by Express Newspapers. Courtesy of Getty Images.

so often named for it.[86] Osborne's 'Note' prefacing the play laments the decline of the 'folk art' of the music hall, yet adopts its techniques ([7]). It is here that *The Threepenny Opera* provided a relevant model, for *The Entertainer* is both a political commentary and (unlike *Look Back in Anger*) a decisive break with naturalist drama. Its songs fall into two kinds. Archie's 'turn numbers' were written by Osborne and John Addison, and are performed at the edge of the proscenium. With titles like 'Why Should I Care' (24–25) and 'We're All Out for Good Old Number One' (32–33), they provide an ironic counterpoint to the songs sung by other members of the family. Phoebe sings 'The Boy I Love Is Up in the Gallery' (66), written by George Ware in 1885 and made famous by Marie Lloyd. Frank sings 'The Absent-Minded Beggar' (64–65), written by Rudyard Kipling and Arthur Sullivan in 1899 to raise money for soldiers in the Boer War. Both Brecht and Osborne appreciated Kipling for his use of music hall idiom: vitality and direct contact with an audience.

Plater's Provinces

In *The Last Days of the Empire* (2003), Alan Plater (1935–2010) paid homage to *The Entertainer*. His play is set in 1957, and concerns the misfortunes of Pedro Gonzales and his Caribbean Rhythm. Like many 'exotic' music-hall turns, the band is a complete fake, fronted by Mike and Peggy Gorman, from Solihull. Then a last-minute stand-in appears. He has just arrived, part of the Windrush generation, from Jamaica. This feint towards authenticity is doomed, for the next day the Empire will be turned into a bingo hall, and this will be their last appearance. Plater's theme is, again, the last days of imperialism and of the music halls. Yet this isn't simply a rehash of *The Entertainer*. In his autobiography Plater suggested there was 'genuine nobility in people like the Gormans, who carried on fighting to the end'. Their act may be threadbare, but they are not morally bankrupt, and this is reflected in the music. Plater wrote the lyrics of a calypso, the Gormans' one-time hit celebrating the 1953 Coronation, to music by John Dankworth. It ends: 'And oh what a happy day | God save the Queen and hip hip hooray.' Equivocally trite lyrics are used as a subtle entry to a complex debate on questions of nationalism and multiculturalism.[87]

Plater was fond of quoting his first 'rave notice', about his 1962 television play, *A Smashing Day*: 'It had the voice of *Coronation Street* but the spirit of Chekhov.'[88] This is also a good description of much of his subsequent work, with a northern locale and emphasis on character rather than plot. The television play, *Land of Green Ginger* (1973), is set in Hull. The plot is simple: a young woman, working in London, returns home and decides not to marry her boyfriend because his work on a trawler involves too much absence and danger. The emotional cruces are carried by songs and shanties, including the traditional air 'A North Country Maid', sung by a local folk-singing family, the Watersons.[89] Many of Plater's plays are set in other, sometimes fictional, northern areas that might be called Platerland. Its inhabitants are defiantly provincial, with a quirky underdogged humour occasionally rising to anger. In 1968 Plater wrote *Close the Coalhouse Door*. The play uses techniques derived from Theatre Workshop, but replaces idealism with intimacy. This was achieved by a set that placed a front room alongside a looming pithead; by an insistence on Geordie dialect; and by interweaving a history of mining with a golden wedding anniversary, with songs and music-hall cross-talk. There are no archetypal heroic miners, as in the Radio Ballad *The Big Hewer*, but instead a tribute to the virtue of a dissident humour in the face of vicious exploitation and industrial decline. When the play was restaged in 1994 it had become an elegy for the years of strikes and closures. Plater's original dedication, 'To the Pitmen of Tyne and Wear', had disappeared.[90] The testimonial to their courage and resilience, though, remains in the playscript, and in the voice of Alex Glasgow, the son of a miner, who wrote the songs for the play. The songs may still be heard.[91]

Plater's Jazz

Plater said he had developed 'an instinctive approach' which was 'akin to that of a jazz musician, improvising'.[92] It made him sensitive to a writer like Anthony Trollope, despite their many differences. It also meant that, if there was no chemistry, the result was leaden-footed. This happened, surprisingly, with Plater's adaptation of J. B. Priestley's *The Good Companions* (1980). Although both were northerners, Priestley's well-known irascibility and dislike of jazz caused tensions, seen most clearly in the documentary about the musical.[93] In his autobiography, Plater describes the jazz view of the world as 'suspicion of authority, a taste for bleak jokes, respect for eccentricity [and] a reluctance to wear a tie'.[94] Priestley wore a tie. Whether or not that was sufficient to destroy the relationship between Plater and Priestley, *The Good Companions* is not a triumph. Its happiest moment, celebrating the joy of release from dreary circumstances, is the song 'We Are On Our Way', to a tramping march written by David Fanshawe.[95]

The adaptation of Priestley was followed by Plater's first work with a jazz view of the world. *Get Lost!* inverts the plot of Priestley's *The Good Companions*. It concerns a reluctant search for a husband who has disappeared from a dreary environment, somewhere near Leeds. The amateur detectives on his trail are his wife, a politically active English teacher, and her colleague, a jazz-loving woodwork teacher. A pastiche of a Duke Ellington small group provides the musical accompaniment. The success of *Get Lost!* prompted a further play with the same characters (although different actors), *The Beiderbecke Affair*. In turn this success prompted two sequels. Jazz played a greater role in what has become known as *The Beiderbecke Trilogy*. Leon Bismarck Beiderbecke (1903–31) is one of a handful of jazz musicians known, thankfully, by his nickname. Bix was a legend, partly because his cornet style became the first clear alternative to Louis Armstrong's, and partly because he drank himself to death. The search for Bix recordings provides the spur of the plot, while Bix's exotic legend and a recreation of his cool, elegant music counterpoints the events in what Plater called 'a parallel universe, set in the moonstruck outer limits of Leeds, where only the bizarre was commonplace'.[96]

Four other works gave jazz an even greater role. In *Prez: The Opera* (1985), Plater worked with bass player Bernie Cash to tell the story of Lester Young, another jazz antihero known by his nickname. Plater's libretto deployed a testing technique known as vocalese, setting lyrics to Prez's recorded tenor saxophone solos. The opera focused on three key episodes in the life of Prez, and was performed by four voices and an onstage sextet. *Misterioso* (novel 1987, BBC TV play 1991) tells of a woman's search for her jazz musician father. The key to her identity is in the title blues, by Thelonious Monk. *Rent Party* (1989), staged at the Theatre Royal Stratford East, deals with time-warp travel from 1989 Guildford to 1940s Harlem. Finally, *The Last of the Blonde Bombshells* (BBC TV 2000) is a retrospect to the proto-feminist time when all-girl swing bands became heroic symbols of the People's War. (The first group to play in Berlin after its capture was Ivy Benson and Her All Girls Band.) Plater turns the plot into a riposte against ageism: a widow takes up her saxophone and overcomes the obstacles of convention by recreating the band she had played in almost forty years earlier.[97] Plater once more uses his enthusiasm for jazz as a commentary on a contemporary political issue.

Potter's Pop Songs

First musical memories sometimes shape whole careers. Alan Plater's was 'Mood Indigo', by Duke Ellington.[98] Dennis Potter's was a popular sentimental ballad of the Great War, 'Roses of Picardy', sung by his mother when he was a child, and performed at his memorial service.[99] In his incandescent first publication, *The Glittering Coffin*, Potter echoed the fears of Richard Hoggart and J. B. Priestley that working-class culture was being suffocated by American consumerism. Yet he quoted an article by his future collaborator Kenith Trodd in the Oxford undergraduate magazine *Isis* that pop songs capture 'the "atmosphere" of their mood and period to a degree which seems to contradict the shoddiness of their raw materials'. Potter added:

> a great deal of that which is true and valuable in traditional working-class culture is *still* reflected in the slicker, cheapened 'pop' culture, however obliquely, however much like a ray of light sliding through a filthy window.

Potter valued the records of Al Bowlly, the South African crooner killed in the Blitz, as 'genuine artefacts of the past'. [100] Bowlly often sang with Lew Stone, the bandleader admired by Trodd who, rather than writing a biography, compiled 'a bundle of material' about the bandleader's career. Potter, who tended to give his works song titles, used a 1938 Bowlly-Stone recording for the title of his 1969 TV drama, *Moonlight on the Highway*.[101] It was the first to be produced by Trodd, and concerns a disturbed man so mesmerized by Bowlly that at one point he lip-synchs the crooner's song.[102]

Potter's Lip-Synch Trilogy

Amanda, the female protagonist of Noël Coward's *Private Lives* (1930), thought it was 'extraordinary how potent cheap music is'.[103] Potter, who otherwise despised Coward, used that potency by means of lip-synching in his TV serial *Pennies from Heaven* (1978). In the era of the Hollywood studio musicals, it was normal practice for a trained singer to 'ghost-sing' the vocal part of an established, if musically incompetent, star. Potter reverses the convention. Actors mime recordings made some thirty years earlier, sustained by a stagy mise en scène that comments on their song. Lip-synching had a twofold result. The actor's performance is a simulation with no pretence to authenticity; while the impact, as Trodd put it, 'was to dislocate us firmly from the entrenched naturalism of television drama'.[104] Brecht, you could say, pranced arm in arm with Jean Baudrillard, particularly in the courtroom scene, where the lyrics of 'Whistling in the Dark' are used to convict an innocent man; and in the final scene, where the convict obtains a posthumous reprieve on Hammersmith Bridge.

Arthur Parker, the ill-fated sheet-music salesman in *Pennies from Heaven*, believes that songs 'tell the truth'. It is the brand mark of his deadly self-deception. Yet a residual honesty remains in the sheer force of Arthur's belief, like that 'ray of light sliding through a filthy window'. There is a particularly close relationship between Arthur and the Accordion Man (called the Hiker in the published screenplay). The Accordion Man is surrounded by Christian images, and plays hymns to unheeding passers-by. He mimes the title recording, by one of the few American singers on the soundtrack, Arthur Tracy, who used the pseudonym of the Street Singer. The Accordion Man is a spectral figure, stigmatized by a speech defect, an outsider who acts as Arthur's alter ego.[105] He owes his origin to the Street Singer who performs Mack the Knife, and before him the hurdy-gurdy man in *Winterreise*, the despised musician who cranks his organ to Schubert's final song.

Potter's project continued with *The Singing Detective* (1986) and *Lipstick on Your Collar* (1993). They record a darkening vision of the fate of working-class culture. *The Singing Detective* contains four interweaving narrative strands that reflect on 1945. Potter said that the songs helped Marlow, the leading character in *The Singing Detective*, make sense of his life.[106] There is little to celebrate: the Accordion Man is replaced by 'a pathetic old busker playing an achingly melancholy "Peg o' My Heart" on a mouth-organ' in a street that is now empty.[107] The children at a crumbling village school sing 'It's a Lovely Day Tomorrow', a popular Vera Lynn wartime song (92). The disfigured Marlow instead recalls another popular song of the war, 'Lili Marlene', sung by Lale Andersen in the 1945 bilingual version (118–120). The famous military love song is mimed by Marlow's mother, and it leads into old George's recollection of the occupation of Hamburg in 1945, where the going rate was a 'couple of fags . . . for a shag' (108). George had earlier mimed Dick Haymes's song of young love, 'It Might As Well Be Spring' (70), but the memory of spring in Hamburg prompted a fatal heart attack. The Ink Spots' 'Do I Worry?' creates in Marlow's mind a humiliating image of his father miming the song as part of a trio with his wife and her lover (118). The songs in *The Singing Detective* reflect the painful life of Marlow.

The title sequence of *Lipstick on Your Collar* 'ends on a big, glitzy juke-box, drawing all eyes into its shining depths', then segues into a newsreel of H-bomb precautions in New York.[108] Potter reconfigures Richard Hoggart's 'aesthetic breakdown', caused by

American commercialism, into a straightforward narrative of youthful frustration.[109] Potter suggested that the music of the play was 'dangerous'.[110] In *The Beggar's Opera* and *The Threepenny Opera* the songs were used to attack an external adversary. Now the conflict is fought out within the play. The generations are divided by music. The youngsters indulge their fantasies to doo-wop groups like the Platters ('Only You') and the Crew-Cuts ('Earth Angel'), while the older generation is still beguiled by the faded orientalism of 'By a Sleepy Lagoon' and 'In a Persian Market', peddled by dirty old organist Harold Atterbow. The division is terminal for British imperial aspirations, for this is 1956 and the generation gap is widest between the frustrated National Service language clerks (once including Potter) and the deluded career officers. Private Hopper begins to mime Elvis Presley's 'Heartbreak Hotel' as he walks the corridors of the War Office (175). A general drones on about the projected invasion of Suez, while the squaddies dream about Diana Dors (156). Hopper brings squaddies and officers together for some community singing to 'I See the Moon' by the Stargazers, once the comic staple of the BBC forces request show, *Two-Way Family Favourites* (124). The choreography barely controls a manic cast of soldiers, belly dancers, Arab brigands, and a stage camel. On instruction, the camel covers the camera (and hence the viewer) with projectile diarrhoea, but still deposits enough faeces for the squaddies to pelt the officers. Emotionally, if not chronologically, this was the beggar's last legacy, both to British politics and to the mainstream musical.

NOTES

1. John Courtenay, quoted in James Boswell, *Life of Johnson*, ed. George Birkbeck Hill, revised and enlarged by L. F. Powell, 6 vols. (Oxford: Clarendon Press, 1934–50), 2: 367n.

2. Gay, *The Beggar's Opera*, III. xvi–xvii, ed. Edgar V. Roberts and Edward Smith (1968; London: Edward Arnold, 1969), 82–83.

3. See Uwe Böker, Ines Detmers, and Anna-Christina Giovanopoulos, eds., *John Gay's 'The Beggar's Opera' 1728–2004: Adaptations and Re-Writings* (Amsterdam: Rodopi, 2006); and Dianne Dugaw, *'Deep Play': John Gay and the Invention of Modernity* (Newark: University of Delaware Press, 2001).

4. Geoffrey Block, 'The Broadway Canon from *Show Boat* to *West Side Story* and the European Operatic Ideal', *Journal of Musicology* 11, no. 4 (1993): 525–544.

5. Anon., 'The Beggar's Opera', *The Times*, 4 June 1920, 18; and Anon., 'Operatic Politics', *The Times*, 5 June 1920, 12.

6. Anon., 'Exit the Beggar', *The Times*, 17 December 1923, 13. Original cast recordings are on 'The Beggar's Opera' and 'Polly', CD, Symposium 1307, 2002.

7. See Georgina Boyes, *The Imagined Village: Culture, Ideology and the English Folk Revival* (Manchester: Manchester University Press, 1993), particularly 44–57; Paul Harrington, 'Holst and Vaughan Williams: Radical Pastoral', in *Music and the Politics of Culture*, ed. Christopher Norris (London: Lawrence & Wishart, 1989), 112–115.

8. Ralph Vaughan Williams, 'Who Wants the English Composer?' (1912), reprinted in *Vaughan Williams on Music*, ed. David Manning (Oxford: Oxford University Press, 2008), 41–42.

9. William Empson, *Some Versions of Pastoral* (1935; London: The Hogarth Press, 1986), 65–67, 195, 199, 250.
10. H. C. Colles, *Voice and Verse: A Study in English Song* (London: Oxford University Press, 1928), 140, 144–148, 154–167.
11. H. C. Colles, 'The Beggar's Opera', *The Times*, 28 January 1928, 10.
12. Wilfrid Mellers, *Music and Society: England and the European Tradition*, 2nd ed. (London: Dobson, 1950), 139–140.
13. Raymond Williams, *The Country and the City* (1973; London: The Hogarth Press, 1985), 258, 45.
14. John Gay, *The Beggar's Opera, as It Is Performed at the Lyric Theatre, Hammersmith, with New Settings of the Airs & Additional Music by F. Austin* (London: Boosey, 1926). This and the next paragraph were suggested by three talks by the composer and conductor Guy Woolfenden, 'John Gay's The Beggar's Opera in Performance', BBC Radio 3, 29 November, 6 and 13 December 1993. See also Jeremy Barlow, 'Published Arrangements of The Beggar's Opera, 1729–1990', *Musical Times* 131 (1990): 533–538.
15. Anon. 'The Beggar's Opera', *The Times*, 7 June 1920, 10.
16. Frank Howes, *The English Musical Renaissance* (London: Secker and Warburg, 1966), 110.
17. Humphrey Carpenter, *Benjamin Britten* (London: Faber & Faber, 1992), 266–267.
18. Peter Brook, *Threads of Time* (London: Methuen, 1999), 99–102.
19. *The Beggar's Opera*, directed by Peter Brook, music arranged by Sir Arthur Bliss, Warner Bros., 1953; DVD Studio Canal, OPTD 1191, 2004.
20. *The Beggar's Opera*, 2CD, Classics for Pleasure 575 9722, 1997.
21. Jeremy Barlow subsequently produced a scholarly edition: *The Music of John Gay's 'The Beggar's Opera'* (Oxford: Oxford University Press, 1990). He recorded it with the Broadside Band in 1991 on 2CD Hyperion CDA 66591/2.
22. Routledge would later exchange metropolitan slap and tickle for suburban propriety when she played Hyacinth Bucket in *Keeping Up Appearances*, BBC, 1990–1995).
23. Gay, *The Beggar's Opera*, ed. Roberts and Smith, III. xvi. 20–24, p. 82.
24. *The Beggar's Opera*, directed by Jonathan Miller, BBC, 1983; DVD Metrodome, MTD5192, 2005.
25. Richard Bonynge and Douglas Gamley, 'A Note on the Present Version', CD Booklet, *The Beggar's Opera*, 2CD, Decca Eloquence 442 8629, 2013.
26. *Kurt Weill: The Threepenny Opera*, ed. Stephen Hinton (Cambridge: Cambridge University Press, 1990), front cover + 10.
27. See Kim H. Kowalke, *Kurt Weill in Europe* (Ann Arbor: UMI Research Press, 1979), 144–157.
28. Bertolt Brecht, *The Threepenny Opera*, trans. Ralph Manheim and John Willett (London: Eyre Methuen, 1979), 4, 14, 76–77.
29. See Tom Cheesman, *The Shocking Ballad Picture Show* (Oxford: Berg, 1994), 1–3, 25–33.
30. Lotte Lenya, 'August 28, 1928', in Bertolt Brecht, *The Threepenny Opera*, English book by Desmond Vesey, English lyrics by Eric Bentley (New York: Grove Press, 1960), xii.
31. Brecht, accompanied by Theo Mackeben and his Orchestra, 'Die Moritat von Mackie-Messer.' May 1929; reissued on CD, *Die Dreigroschenoper*, Berlin 1930, Telefunken Legacy 0927 42663-2, 1991.
32. Weill, 'Schubert-Feiern' (1928), translated in Kowalke, *Kurt Weill in Europe*, 154. *Der Leierkasten* is German both for the hurdy-gurdy and the barrel organ, although they are different instruments.

33. Norman Ebbutt, 'The Threepenny Opera: A Berlin Burlesque', The Times, 25 September 1928, 12, reprinted in Kurt Weill: The Threepenny Opera, 126–128.

34. Muriel Lynch, 'The Beggar's Opera', The Times, 20 May 1929, 16.

35. Stephen Hinton, 'The Première and After', in Kurt Weill: The Threepenny Opera, ed. Hinton, 50–73.

36. Alfred Einstein, 'A German Version of The Beggar's Opera', Radio Times 46, no. 592 (1 February 1935), 13.

37. It will be discussed later in the subsection 'The Threepenny Opera, 1956'.

38. Alan Ayckbourn, A Chorus of Disapproval (London: Faber & Faber, 1986), 71–76.

39. Edward Jones, Musical and Poetical Relicks of the Welsh Bards [. . .] Never before Published (London: Printed for the author, 1784), 56–57.

40. Anon., 'Craft Chronicler of Middle Mind', The Times, 27 July 1985, 18.

41. Michael Billington, State of the Nation: British Theatre Since 1945 (London: Faber & Faber, 2007), 316.

42. Ayckbourn, Chorus of Disapproval, 33–34, 80, 75, 9–11, 90.

43. A Chorus of Disapproval, directed by Michael Winner, Curzon Films, 1988; DVD, Slam Dunk Media SDMD2079, 2007.

44. Nigel Playfair, 'How Plays Will be Broadcast', Radio Times 1, no. 12 (14 December 1923), 429.

45. The Times, 11 January 1924, 13.

46. Richard Hughes, Danger, in A Rabbit and a Leg: Collected Plays (New York: Alfred A. Knopf, 1924), 150. Richard Perceval Graves, Richard Hughes: A Biography (London: André Deutsch, 1994), 100–103, 111, 122, 124.

47. John Grierson, 'Preface', in Paul Rotha, Documentary Film (London: Faber & Faber, 1936), 8–9.

48. Paddy Scannell and David Cardiff, A Social History of British Broadcasting, vol. 1. 1922–1939: Serving the Nation (Oxford: Basil Blackwell, 1991), 138–140, 333–355.

49. For more information about the later work of Joan Littlewood at the Theatre Royal Stratford East, see Chapter 19 by Ben Macpherson.

50. D. G. Bridson, Prospero and Ariel: The Rise and Fall of Radio (London: Victor Gollancz, 1971), 22, 32–39.

51. Olive Shapley with Christina Hart, Broadcasting a Life (London: Scarlet, 1996), 48–54, 186.

52. Howard Goorney, The Theatre Workshop Story (London: Eyre Methuen, 1981), 41–42.

53. Ben Harker, Class Act: The Cultural and Political Life of Ewan MacColl (London: Pluto Press, 2007), 37–69.

54. MacColl, Johnny Noble, in Agit-Prop to Theatre Workshop, ed. Howard Goorney and Ewan MacColl (Manchester: Manchester University Press, 1986), 36. Further page references are given in parentheses in the text.

55. Peter Brook, The Empty Space (1968; Harmondsworth: Pelican Books, 1972), 11; Billington, State of the Nation, 23–25.

56. MacColl, 'Introduction', in Agit-Prop to Theatre Workshop, ed. Goorney and MacColl, lii.

57. Goorney, Theatre Workshop Story, 158–161; Raphael Samuel, 'Theatre and Socialism in Britain (1880–1935)', and MacColl, 'Theatre of Action, Manchester', in Theatres of the Left 1880–1935, ed. Raphael Samuel, Ewan MacColl, and Stuart Cosgrove (London: Routledge & Kegan Paul, 1985), 11–12, 42–44, 242–249; Léon Moussinac, The New Movement in the Theatre: A Survey of Recent Developments (1932; New York: Blom, 1967), plates 41, 59–60. See also Robert Leach, Theatre Workshop: Joan Littlewood and the Making of Modern British Theatre (Exeter: Exeter University Press, 2006).

58. Harker, *Class Act*, 35.

59. Goorney, *Theatre Workshop Story*, 18–48.

60. Ewan MacColl, *Journeyman: An Autobiography* (London: Sidgwick and Jackson, 1990), 268–274; Bridson, *Prospero and Ariel*, 101–115; John Szwed, *The Man Who Recorded the World: A Biography of Alan Lomax* (London: William Heinemann, 2010), 206–208, 254, 290–292; Boyes, *Imagined Village*, 198ff.

61. Parker, letter 12 July 1957 to MacColl, quoted in Peter Cox, *Set into Song: Ewan MacColl, Charles Parker, Peggy Seeger and the Radio Ballads* ([London]: Labatie, 2008), 1.

62. Supplement to the *London Gazette*, 3 May 1957, 1.

63. Parker, 'The Ballad of John Axon', *Radio Times* 139, no. 1807 (27 June 1958), 33.

64. MacColl, *Journeyman*, 311–335.

65. Francis Newton, 'Two Cheers for Folk-Song', *New Statesman* 66, no. 1689 (26 July 1963), 119.

66. *The Ballad of John Axon*, CD, Topic TSCD 801, 1999.

67. Ben Harker, 'Class Composition: *The Ballad of John Axon*, Cultural Debate and the Late 1950s British Left', *Science & Society* 73, no. 3 (2009): 344–348.

68. 'WLW', *Manchester Guardian*, quoted in Cox, *Set into Song*, 58–59.

69. Charles Parker, 'Radio Ballads', *The Times*, 20 November 1972, 17.

70. Ewan MacColl, quoted in Cox, *Set into Song*, 155. Travellers is a collective noun for English Gypsies, Scottish tinkers, indeed anyone who embraces the alternative, nomadic mode of life.

71. *The Travelling People*, CD, Topic, TSCD 808, 1999.

72. Howard Pollack, *Marc Blitzstein: His Life, His Work, His World* (New York: Oxford University Press, 2012), 354.

73. The original cast recording, 1954, is available on CD, Decca 012 159 463-2, 2009.

74. For instance, 'kick-up-the-arse' replaces 'kick-in-the pants'. See Pollack, *Marc Blitzstein*, 363.

75. Pollack, *Marc Blitzstein*, 352.

76. Pollack, *Marc Blitzstein*, 365.

77. Joan Littlewood, *Joan's Book* (1994; London: Methuen, 2003), 434–435.

78. Frank Howes, 'Royal Court Theatre', *The Times*, 10 February 1956, 4.

79. Hans Keller, 'The Threepenny Opera' (1956), reprinted in *Kurt Weill: The Threepenny Opera*, ed. Hinton, 146–148.

80. Raymond Williams, *Culture and Society 1780–1950* (1958; Harmondsworth: Penguin, 1963), 307.

81. Billington, *State of the Nation*, 92.

82. A relevant analysis of the period is in John Caughie, *Television Drama: Realism, Modernism, and British Culture* (Oxford: Oxford University Press, 2000), 57–71.

83. John Osborne, *Almost a Gentleman: An Autobiography*, vol. 2, *1955–1966* (London: Faber & Faber, 1991), 35–42.

84. John Osborne, *The Entertainer* (1957; London: Faber & Faber, 1961). Further page references are given in parentheses in the text. *The Entertainer*, dir. Tony Richardson, Woodfall Film Productions, 1960; released on DVD by MGM, 10001026, 2004. See also Robert Gordon, '*The Entertainer* as a Text for Performance', in *John Osborne: A Casebook*, ed. Patricia D. Denison (New York: Garland Publishing, 1997), 91–114.

85. Bevan, speech 4 November 1956, quoted in Nicklaus Thomas-Symonds, *Nye: The Political Life of Aneurin Bevan* (London: I. B. Tauris, 2015), 2.

86. Billington, *State of the Nation*, 103–109.
87. Alan Plater, *Doggin' Around* (London: Northway Publications, 2006), 187–191. Plater's calypso lightly carries a heavier freight, let's say, than the 'Victory Calypso' ('Cricket, lovely cricket'), written for the West Indies' defeat of England in 1950 by the Trinidadian Aldwyn Roberts, better known under his imperial stage name of Lord Kitchener.
88. Plater, *Doggin' Around*, 59.
89. Plater, *Doggin' Around*, 81–83.
90. Alan Plater, *Close the Coalhouse Door* (London: Methuen, 1968), not paginated; Plater, *Close the Coalhouse Door* (Newcastle-upon-Tyne: Bloodaxe, 2000).
91. *The Songs of Alex Glasgow*, CD, MWM Records, MWMCDSP14, 1997.
92. Alan Plater, *Hearing the Music*, Time Shift, BBC Bristol, 2004.
93. 'On the Road: The Making of *The Good Companions*', special feature in *The Good Companions*, DVD Network 7953583, 2011.
94. Plater, *Doggin' Around*, 103.
95. *The Good Companions*, Yorkshire TV, 1980; DVD Network 7953583, 2011.
96. *Get Lost!*, Yorkshire TV, 1981; *The Beiderbecke Trilogy*, Yorkshire TV, 1985–1988, DVD Network 7952536, 2008; Plater, *Doggin' Around*, 107. See also William Gallagher, *The Beiderbecke Affair* (London: Palgrave Macmillan, 2012).
97. *Prez: The Opera*, in *The South Bank Show*, Season 8, Episode 24, London Weekend Television, 2 June 1985; Plater, *Misterioso* (London: Methuen, 1987); Plater, *Doggin' Around*, 126–127, 144–150; *The Last of the Blonde Bombshells*, directed by Gilles MacKinnon, Universal Studios 2000; DVD Boulevard Entertainment, BVAR0617, 2011).
98. Plater, *Doggin' Around*, 2.
99. Humphrey Carpenter, *Dennis Potter: A Biography* (London: Faber & Faber, 1998), 13, 582.
100. Dennis Potter, *The Glittering Coffin* (London: Victor Gollancz, 1960), 121; Kenith Trodd, 'Introduction', in Dennis Potter, *Pennies from Heaven* (London: Faber & Faber, 1996), ix.
101. Kenith Trodd, *Lew Stone—a Career in Music* (London: Joyce Stone, 1971), 4, 69.
102. Carpenter, *Dennis Potter*, 13, 582, 226–235. See also Vernon W. Gras and John R. Cook, eds., *The Passion of Dennis Potter: International Collected Essays* (New York: St Martin's Press, 2000).
103. Noël Coward, *Private Lives* (1930; London: William Heinemann, 1932), 30.
104. Trodd, 'Introduction', in Potter, *Pennies from Heaven*, xi.
105. Potter, *Pennies from Heaven*, 24, 60, 238–239, 247. See also John Baxendale and Chris Pawling, *Narrating the Thirties* (Basingstoke: Palgrave Macmillan, 1995), 171–187; and Glen Creeber, *Dennis Potter between Two Worlds: A Critical Reassessment* (Basingstoke: Macmillan, 1998), 111–148.
106. Graham Fuller, ed., *Potter on Potter* (London: Faber & Faber, 1993), 87.
107. Potter, *The Singing Detective* (London: Faber & Faber, 1986), 1. Further page references are given in parentheses in the text. '*The Singing Detective*': Music from the BBC TV Serial, LP, BBC Records, BBC REN 608. See also Glen Creeber, *The Singing Detective* (London: British Film Institute, 2007).
108. Potter, *Lipstick on Your Collar* (London: Faber & Faber, 1993), 1. Further page references are given in parentheses in the text. *Lipstick on Your Collar*, directed by Renny Rye, Channel 4, 1993; Acorn Media DVD AV9798, 2010.
109. Richard Hoggart, *The Uses of Literacy* (1957; Harmondsworth: Pelican, 1958), 247.
110. Fuller, *Potter on Potter*, 98.

BIBLIOGRAPHY

Anon. 'The Beggar's Opera.' The Times, 4 June 1920, 4.

Anon. 'The Beggar's Opera.' The Times, 7 June 1920, 10.

Anon. 'Craft Chronicler of Middle Mind.' The Times, 27 July 1985, 18.

Anon. 'Exit the Beggar.' The Times, 17 December 1923, 13.

Anon. 'Operatic Procedures.' The Times, 5 June 1920, 12.

Ayckbourn, Alan. A Chorus of Disapproval. London: Faber & Faber, 1986.

The Ballad of John Axon. CD, Topic TSCD 801, 1999.

Barlow, Jeremy. 'Published Arrangements of The Beggar's Opera, 1729–1990.' Musical Times 131 (1990): 533–538.

Barlow, Jeremy, ed. The Music of John Gay's 'The Beggar's Opera'. Oxford: Oxford University Press, 1990.

Baxendale, John, and Chris Pawling, Narrating the Thirties. Basingstoke: Palgrave Macmillan, 1995.

The Beggar's Opera. Directed by Peter Brook, music arranged by Sir Arthur Bliss, Warner Bros., 1953. DVD. Studio Canal, OPTD 1191, 2004.

The Beggar's Opera. Directed by Jonathan Miller, BBC 1983. DVD. Metrodome, MTD5192, 2005.

The Beggar's Opera. Recorded 1955. 2 CD. Classics for Pleasure, 575 9722, 1997.

'The Beggar's Opera' and 'Polly'. Original Cast Recordings, 1920 and 1923. CD. Symposium 1307, 2002.

The Beiderbecke Trilogy. Yorkshire TV, 1985–1988. DVD. Network, 7952536, 2008.

Billington, Michael. State of the Nation: British Theatre Since 1945. London: Faber & Faber, 2007.

Block, Geoffrey. 'The Broadway Canon from Show Boat to West Side Story and the European Operatic Ideal.' Journal of Musicology 11, no. 4 (1993): 525–544.

Böker, Uwe, Ines Detmers, and Anna-Christina Giovanopoulos, eds. John Gay's 'The Beggar's Opera' 1728–2004: Adaptations and Re-Writings. Amsterdam: Rodopi, 2006.

Bonynge, Richard, and Douglas Gamley. 'A Note on the Present Version.' CD Booklet. The Beggar's Opera, 2CD, Decca Eloquence, 442 8629, 2013.

Boswell, James. Life of Johnson. Edited by George Birkbeck Hill, revised and enlarged by L. F. Powell. 6 vols. Oxford: Clarendon Press, 1934–50.

Boyes, Georgina. The Imagined Village: Culture, Ideology and the English Folk Revival. Manchester: Manchester University Press, 1993.

Brecht, Bertolt. The Threepenny Opera. English book by Desmond Vesey. English lyrics by Eric Bentley. New York: Grove Press, 1960.

Brecht, Bertolt. The Threepenny Opera. Translated by Ralph Manheim and John Willett. London: Eyre Methuen, 1979.

Bridson, D. G. Prospero and Ariel: The Rise and Fall of Radio. London: Victor Gollancz, 1971.

Brook, Peter. The Empty Space. 1968. Harmondsworth: Pelican Books, 1972.

Brook, Peter. Threads of Time. London: Methuen, 1999.

Carpenter, Humphrey. Benjamin Britten. London: Faber & Faber, 1992.

Carpenter, Humphrey. Dennis Potter: A Biography. London: Faber & Faber, 1998.

Caughie, John. Television Drama: Realism, Modernism, and British Culture. Oxford: Oxford University Press, 2000.

Cheesman, Tom. The Shocking Ballad Picture Show. Oxford: Berg, 1994.

A Chorus of Disapproval. Directed by Michael Winner, Curzon Films, 1988. DVD. Slam Dunk Media, SDMD2079, 2007.

Colles, H. C. 'The Beggar's Opera.' The Times, 28 January 1928, 10.

Colles, H. C. Voice and Verse: A Study in English Song. London: Oxford University Press, 1928.

Coward, Noël. Private Lives. 1930. London: William Heinemann, 1932.

Cox, Peter. Set into Song: Ewan MacColl, Charles Parker, Peggy Seeger and the Radio Ballads. London: Labatie, 2008.

Creeber, Glen. Dennis Potter between Two Worlds: A Critical Reassessment. Basingstoke: Macmillan, 1998.

Creeber, Glen. The Singing Detective. London: British Film Institute, 2007.

Die Dreigroschenoper. Berlin 1930. CD. Telefunken Legacy, 0927 42663-2, 1991.

Dugaw, Dianne. 'Deep Play': John Gay and the Invention of Modernity. Newark: University of Delaware Press, 2001.

Ebbutt, Norman. 'The Threepenny Opera: A Berlin Burlesque.' The Times, 25 September 1928, 12.

Einstein, Alfred. 'A German Version of The Beggar's Opera.' Radio Times 46, no. 592 (1 February 1935), 13.

Empson, William. Some Versions of Pastoral. London: The Hogarth Press, 1986.

The Entertainer. Directed by Tony Richardson, Woodfall Film Productions, 1960. DVD. MGM, 10001026, 2004.

Fuller, Graham, ed. Potter on Potter. London: Faber & Faber, 1993.

Gallagher, William. The Beiderbecke Affair. London: Palgrave Macmillan, 2012.

Gay, John. The Beggar's Opera. Edited by Edgar V. Roberts and Edward Smith. 1968. London: Edward Arnold, 1969.

Gay, John. The Beggar's Opera, as It Is Performed at the Lyric Theatre, Hammersmith, with New Settings of the Airs & Additional Music by F. Austin. London: Boosey, 1926.

The Good Companions. Directed by Bill Hays and Leonard Lewis, 1980. DVD. Network, 7953583, 2011.

Goorney, Howard. The Theatre Workshop Story. London: Eyre Methuen, 1981.

Goorney, Howard, and Ewan MacColl, eds. Agit-Prop to Theatre Workshop. Manchester: Manchester University Press, 1986.

Gordon, Robert. 'The Entertainer as a Text for Performance.' In John Osborne: A Casebook, edited by Patricia D. Denison, 91–114. New York: Garland Publishing, 1997.

Gras, Vernon W., and John R. Cook, eds. The Passion of Dennis Potter: International Collected Essays. New York: St Martin's Press, 2000.

Graves, Richard Perceval. Richard Hughes: A Biography. London: André Deutsch, 1994.

Grierson, John. 'Preface.' In Paul Rotha, Documentary Film, 8–9. London: Faber & Faber, 1936.

Harker, Ben. Class Act: The Cultural and Political Life of Ewan MacColl. London: Pluto Press, 2007.

Harker, Ben. 'Class Composition: The Ballad of John Axon, Cultural Debate and the Late 1950s British Left.' Science & Society 73, no. 3 (2009): 340–355.

Harrington, Paul. 'Holst and Vaughan Williams: Radical Pastoral.' In Music and the Politics of Culture, edited by Christopher Norris, 112–115. London: Lawrence & Wishart, 1989.

Hinton, Stephen, ed. Kurt Weill: The Threepenny Opera. Cambridge: Cambridge University Press, 1990.

Hoggart, Richard. The Uses of Literacy. 1957. Harmondsworth: Pelican 1958.

Howes, Frank. The English Musical Renaissance. London: Secker and Warburg, 1966.

Howes, Frank. 'Royal Court Theatre.' The Times, 10 February 1956, 4.

Hughes, Richard. A Rabbit and a Leg: Collected Plays. New York: Alfred A. Knopf, 1924.

John Gay's 'The Beggar's Opera'. 2 CD. Hyperion Records, CDA 66591/2, 1991.

John Gay's 'The Beggar's Opera' in Performance. BBC Radio 3. Broadcast 3 November, 29 November, 6 December, and 13 December 1993.

Jones, Edward. *Musical and Poetical Relicks of the Welsh Bards [. . .] Never before Published*. London: Printed for the author, 1784.

Kowalke, Kim H. *Kurt Weill in Europe*. Ann Arbor: UMI Research Press, 1979.

The Last of the Blonde Bombshells. Directed by Gilles MacKinnon, Universal Studios 2000. DVD. Boulevard Entertainment, BVAR0617, 2011.

Leach, Robert. *Theatre Workshop: Joan Littlewood and the Making of Modern Theatre*. Exeter: Exeter University Press, 2006.

Lenya, Lotte. 'August 28, 1928.' In Bertolt Brecht. *The Threepenny Opera*. English Book by Desmond Vesey. English Lyrics by Eric Bentley, xii. New York: Grove Press, 1960.

Lipstick on Your Collar. Directed by Renny Rye, Channel 4, 1993. DVD. Acorn Media, AV9798, 2010.

Littlewood, Joan. *Joan's Book*. 1994. London: Methuen, 2003.

Lynch, Muriel. 'The Beggar's Opera.' *The Times*, 20 May 1929, 16.

MacColl, Ewan. *Journeyman: An Autobiography*. London: Sidgwick and Jackson, 1990.

McMillin, Scott. *The Musical as Drama: A Study of the Principles and Conventions Behind Musical Shows from Kern to Sondheim*. Princeton, NJ: Princeton University Press, 2006.

Mellers, Wilfrid. *Music and Society: England and the European Tradition*. 2nd ed. London: Dobson, 1950.

Moussinac, Léon. *The New Movement in the Theatre: A Survey of Recent Developments*. 1932. New York: Blom, 1967.

Osborne, John. *Almost a Gentleman. An Autobiography*. Vol. 2, *1955–1966*. London: Faber & Faber, 1991.

Osborne, John. *The Entertainer*. 1957. London: Faber & Faber, 1961.

Parker, Charles. 'The Ballad of John Axon.' *Radio Times* 139, no. 1807 (27 June 1958), 33.

Parker, Charles. 'Radio Ballads.' *The Times*, 20 November 1972, 17.

Plater, Alan. *Close the Coalhouse Door*. Newcastle upon Tyne: Bloodaxe, 2000. First published 1968 by Methuen.

Plater, Alan. *Doggin' Around*. London: Northway Publications, 2006.

Plater, Alan. *Hearing the Music*. Time Shift. BBC Bristol, 2004.

Plater, Alan. *Misterioso*. London: Methuen, 1987.

Playfair, Nigel. 'How Plays Will Be Broadcast.' *Radio Times* 1, no. 12 (14 December 1923), 429.

Pollack, Howard. *Marc Blitzstein: His Life, His Work, His World*. New York: Oxford University Press, 2012.

Potter, Dennis. *The Glittering Coffin*. London: Victor Gollancz, 1960.

Potter, Dennis. *Lipstick on Your Collar*. London: Faber & Faber, 1993.

Potter, Dennis. *Pennies from Heaven*. London: Faber & Faber, 1996.

Potter, Dennis. *The Singing Detective*. London: Faber & Faber, 1986.

Prez: The Opera. In *The South Bank Show*. Season 8, Episode 24. Broadcast 2 June 1985.

Samuel, Raphael, Ewan MacColl, and Stuart Cosgrove, eds. *Theatres of the Left 1880–1935*. London: Routledge & Kegan Paul, 1985.

Scannell, Paddy, and David Cardiff. *A Social History of British Broadcasting*. Vol. 1, *1922–1939: Serving the Nation*. Oxford: Basis Blackwell, 1991.

Shapley, Olive (with Christina Hart). *Broadcasting a Life*. London: Scarlet, 1996.

'The Singing Detective': Music from the BBC-TV Serial. LP. BBC Records, BBC REN 608, 1986.

The Songs of Alex Glasgow. CD, MWM Records, MWMCDSP14, 1997.

Szwed, John. *The Man Who Recorded the World: A Biography of Alan Lomax.* London: William Heinemann, 2010.

Thomas-Symonds, Nicholas. *Nye: The Political Life of Aneurin Bevan.* London: I. B. Tauris, 2015.

The Threepenny Opera. Original Cast Album, 1954. CD. Decca, 012 159 463-2, 2009.

The Travelling People. CD. Topic, TSCD 808, 1999.

Trodd, Kenith. *Lew Stone—A Career in Music.* London: Joyce Stone, 1971.

Vaughan Williams, Ralph. 'Who Wants the English Composer?' In *Vaughan Williams on Music*, edited by David Manning, 41–42. Oxford: Oxford University Press, 2008.

Williams, Raymond. *The Country and the City.* 1973. London: The Hogarth Press, 1985.

Williams, Raymond. *Culture and Society, 1780–1950.* 1958. Harmondsworth: Penguinn, 1963.

CHAPTER 25

....

MAMMA MIA! AND THE AESTHETICS OF THE TWENTY-FIRST-CENTURY JUKEBOX MUSICAL

....

GEORGE RODOSTHENOUS

INTRODUCTION

....

IN April 1970, ABBA's career began on a small Mediterranean island when the two couples who were to form the band were visiting the island of Cyprus on holiday. 'What started as singing for fun on the beach ended up as an improvised live performance in front of the United Nations soldiers stationed on the island.'[1] Twenty-nine years later, on 6 April 1999, *Mamma Mia!*, a jukebox musical set on a Greek island and built around the many hits of the Swedish pop group, conceived by producer Judy Craymer and her all-female team (director Phyllida Lloyd and writer Catherine Johnson), opened in the West End.

Mamma Mia! has since become a global phenomenon with more than thirty-two productions all over the world and has seduced more than 54 million audience members to date.[2] David Savran discusses the politics of pleasure in musical theatre and its power to seduce the audience:

> No theatre form is as single-mindedly devoted to producing pleasure, inspiring spectators to tap their feet, sing along, or otherwise be carried away. This utopian—and mimetic—dimension of the musical (linked to its relentless reflexivity) makes it into a kind of hothouse for the manufacture of theatrical seduction and the ideological positions to which mass audiences can be seduced.[3]

The musical resembles British TV holiday/wedding abroad Reality TV programmes and creates a space for the ABBA songs to be included: the karaoke competition, the hen night, and the stag do. Within this setting, the musical reinforces a metatheatrical use of the ABBA songs and allows the audience to relate it to their own experiences of when they sang and danced to the pop tunes in their own lives.

The musical's narrative might, at first, seem to be about a quest for Sophie's identity but is really about female empowerment and liberation. *Mamma Mia!* is full of symmetries: three former members of the Dynamos, three female friends (including Sophie), three male friends (including Sky), and three possible fathers. It is an attempt to break away from the imposed dualities of most musical theatre and offers a progressive narrative trope of relationships by focusing on multiple sub-narratives. Thus, it achieves a more contemporary dramaturgical treatment of the traditional boy-meets-girl model.[4]

The jukebox musical is a subgenre of the musical genre and, as Millie Taylor asserts, 'the songs function differently in a jukebox musical than in an "integrated" musical, in that rather than simply amplifying and expanding on their context, they leap from it and make connections with other parts of the audience's lived experience.'[5] This chapter will explore the aesthetics of the jukebox musical subgenre, and by taking *Mamma Mia!* as a key example will explore the dramaturgy of the piece to show how its narrative and musical structure reflects the interlocking themes of the break-up of the nuclear family, mother–daughter relationships, and the problems of single mothers. By examining how *Mamma Mia!* evokes on stage the sunny atmosphere of a beach holiday on a Greek island, the article demonstrates the way in which the show exploits the jukebox format to express the utopianism of musical comedy through the pleasure derived from its artful deployment of ABBA's greatest hits.[6] The essay will consider the jukebox structure of *Mamma Mia!* and compare it with other British examples of the subgenre, namely the jukebox musicals *Our House* (2002), *Taboo* (2002), *Never Forget* (2007), and *Viva Forever!* (2012).

The Provenance of the Jukebox Musical

One could trace the jukebox musical's history from *The Beggar's Opera* (1728) to two of MGM's greatest successes—*An American in Paris* (1951) and *Singin' in the Rain* (1952)—as in all these famous works pre-existing songs were used to counterpoint a new narrative.[7] 'Since the 1920s familiar songs have been reintroduced into other narratives to express love, anger, frustration, desire, and so on through the sung words.'[8] *Mamma Mia!* is one of the successful attempts to create a narrative around an existing back catalogue of songs. Other notable jukebox musicals predating *Mamma Mia!* are the crowd-pleasing *Five Guys Named Moe* (1990), *Buddy—The Buddy Holly Story* (1989), *Smokey Joe's Cafe* (1995), *Boogie Nights* (1997), *Saturday Night Fever* (1998), and *Disco Inferno* (1999), while after 2000, there have been *We Will Rock You* (2002), *Our House* (2002), *Taboo* (2002), *The Boy from Oz* (2003), *Tonight's the Night* (2003), *Thriller Live* (2006),

Desperately Seeking Susan (2007), and *Never Forget* (2007). This trend also included a series of works that were later adapted into film musicals such as *Jersey Boys* (2005/2014) and *Rock of Ages* (2006/2012).[9]

Bud Coleman associates the jukebox musical with the musical revue[10] and describes it as

> an assemblage of pre-existing songs where the emphasis is clearly on the songs, not on plot and/or character. Unlike earlier elaborate revues put on by the likes of Ziegfeld and George White, late twentieth century revues tend to focus on the music of one composer and generally do not showcase stars.[11]

Not all jukebox musicals are as successful as *Mamma Mia!* and together with composer-lyricist Michael John LaChiusa one could lament that the jukebox musical as a form of popular entertainment has replaced the creation of new musicals on Broadway and in the West End:

> The familiar songs from the repertoires of famous pop and rock stars never seem to rise organically from the story at hand, and the music does little to advance action, much less explore character. But audiences and some critics apparently enjoy these concerts masquerading as musicals. They can go into the theater humming the tunes. What drama there is seems to come from the moment when the audience recognizes a familiar song.[12]

And indeed, the weaker ones become a mere puzzle of simplistic, interlocking narratives in order for the songs to be presented within a contrived dramaturgical framework. Jukebox musicals very often use pop songs and in doing so, they deny the audience songs which can in a subtle way portray character and communicate their thoughts. On some occasions, the amalgamation of narrative and existing music does not go beyond the cliched plot of the development of a band/tribute band and this does not allow for exciting new storylines or dramaturgical complexity. Due to the nature of the songs, easy narratological devices such as karaoke and concerts lead to predictable metatheatrical narratives.[13] These introduce the form to music fans who would not otherwise attend the theatre. The experience is compromised by the use of music that is often encountered in, and more suited to, the concert arena rather than the theatre and promotes a non-organic narrative development. In the jukebox musical some crucial dramaturgical concerns remain for musical theatre purists like songwriter Michael John LaChuisa: why do these characters actually sing? Who do they sing to? And why do they use existing songs?

LaChiusa continues his attack on jukebox musicals by calling them 'faux musicals' and insisting that '[a]ll sense of invention and craft is abandoned in favor of delivering what the audience thinks a musical should deliver.'[14] He opines that

> the idea of 'using' or 'placing' pre-existing songs into a story-line isn't a new device; it's certainly an easier one than allowing a song to spring indigenously [*sic*] from the

drama. *Mamma Mia!* inserts its catalogue of ABBA hits into the thinnest of librettos, but it does so with a modicum of sly wit. Those who wish to imitate its success had better think long and hard about it, or the result can be disastrous.[15]

Jukebox musicals focus on the theatrical composition which in this context refers to the power of the mise en scène, instead of on the composition of new musical material, and in this respect, they threaten the development of new musical theatre composers. Barbara Ellen calls them 'hybrids of pop nostalgia and theatrical sawdust'.[16] Three British examples from the early twenty-first century reflect three distinct approaches to the subgenre: the fictional jukebox musical (*Our House*), the semi-biographical jukebox musical (*Taboo*), and the (tribute) band jukebox musical (*Never Forget*).

Our House (2002) is a fictional jukebox musical using the music of the band Madness with a book by Tim Firth which takes the concept of the film *Sliding Doors* (1998; directed by Peter Howitt):[17] it presents a narrative which explores the consequences of two different choices. The two paths are fully fleshed out in sequence and are introduced by a narrator figure—a device also used in *Blood Brothers* (1983). Its tongue-in-cheek metatheatrical language is typical of the genre's self-reflexivity; in-jokes too are used to wink at the musical theatre audience's knowledge of existing hits: for example, the use of the gondola in the second half is a homage to *The Phantom of the Opera* (1986). *Our House*, with its rather predictable book, relied too much perhaps on the youthful exuberance of its (unknown) cast rather than the eccentric music of Madness, which has an eclectic audience anyway and thus did not have the appeal of, for instance, *We Will Rock You* (2002) with its songs by Queen.

Taboo (2002) is a semi-biographical musical based around the life of the composer/performer Boy George. It combines existing chart hits such as 'Do You Really Want to Hurt Me' and 'Karma Chameleon' with songs written specifically for the show and creates a semi-autobiographical fantasy which revolves around the London club life of the 1980s. The musical explores the protagonist's sexuality and places the song 'Stranger in This World' at the centre of its narrative. The show was reworked in 2013 for a new production in a Brixton nightclub and enjoyed a successful, if limited, run with two casts. *Taboo* is unique because it combines new and well-known songs with autobiographical elements to sketch an important part of the British pop milieu.

Never Forget (2007), on the other hand, presents a fictional story about the trials and tribulations of a Take That tribute band. It uses a range of narrative motifs in order to incorporate the songs, such as auditions, rehearsals, walks in the rain, and fully performed concerts and, like many other musicals of its kind, tries to recreate the feeling of watching a band which has broken up. *Never Forget* offers the audience a 'copy' of the successful boy band Take That performing live and allows them to dig deep into their memory to recreate their initial excitement at watching that band.[18] The difficulty with this kind of tribute band narrative is that they are rather predictable (especially if they follow the lives of real bands and the inevitable progress to their break-up).

In viewing these musicals, the audience 'seems curiously situated between the presence of the now (watching the current musical) and the absence of something that previously existed [...] This works as a palimpsest in which there are reverberations between what we hear and our "historical" involvement with the original song"[19] and, as a phenomenon specific to jukebox musicals, will be further explored in the *Mamma Mia!* case study. [20]

Mamma Mia! in Academic Discourse

The musical *Mamma Mia!* has received a lot of academic interest. Since the release of the film, there has been substantial academic discourse on *Mamma Mia!*. Louise FitzGerald and Melanie Williams in their edited volume on *Exploring a Cultural Phenomenon: 'Mamma Mia! The Movie'* conclude that *Mamma Mia!* is 'doing something quite revolutionary, in that it is actively reforming and reconstructing popular memory, and making us see the recent past in a fresh and positive light'.[21] In 'Work, Family, Romance and the Utopian Sensibilities of the Chick Megamusical *Mamma Mia!*', Elaine Aston provides a feminist reading of the work. She analyses how shows aimed predominantly at women (therefore 'chick' megamusicals) create a strong audience reaction and believes that 'the emotionality and affectivity of the musical is produced chiefly through its women-centred choreographies (aural, physical, and dramatic)'.[22] She closes her article by reminding us that *Mamma Mia!*

> effects its own kind of feminist intervention into the entertainment industry, and the affectivity of the chick megamusical is paramount in enabling 'so many different types of women' to come together [... in] a celebratory sense of being transported into a world that imagines more inclusive, heterogeneous modalities of 'belonging' than those encountered elsewhere, socially and culturally. Such sensibilities comfort and discomfort, fulfil and yet are unfulfilled, are made present in the temporal, temporary moment of the performance and are *still yet absent*.[23]

Jill Dolan states that *Mamma Mia!* presents us with 'a string of ABBA songs never meant for the theatre that are stuck along a plot no more than a millimeter thick'.[24] But, in a way, what the show does is to bridge the gap between concert lovers, musical theatre lovers, and haters of musicals and seduce them into the world of theatre. Millie Taylor comments on the often abrupt and unprepared-for renditions of ABBA songs and states that 'these devices are comic, create distance from identification with the story, and create a new camp context for the songs'.[25]

Malcolm Womack analyses *Mamma Mia!* from a feminist angle and suggests that part of its success is the work's 'reflection of generalized nostalgia for the 1970s'.[26] He continues by describing the ABBA songs as a 'ventriloquial act where the female singers used first person lyrics to describe themselves in ways that were patriarchal, condescending, and in some cases just short of insulting'.[27] He demonstrates how Catherine Johnson reworks these songs, giving them a new meaning, and how the new performativity of the words empower the female singers to celebrate their individuality and freedom from cultural norms.[28]

Stacy Wolf writes that 'when the songs are heard outside the musical itself, they are always ghosted by the original voice'.[29] This creates an interesting dynamic and provides a surprise for the audience who enjoy the recontextualization of the songs,[30] which is how the musical manages to import the songs into a new fictional world where they are used with humour, comic timing, and an element of surprise.[31] The reinterpretation of the songs plays with audience expectations and preconceptions. The songs set up a specific expectation and then subvert it.[32] Dolan writes that 'musicals' complicity in gender arrangements is insidious, but it's also very easy to turn familiar songs against their own meanings through parodic juxtaposition'.[33]

For Kelly Kessler the genre's integration of pop songs provides a 'reflexivity' and 'a similar sense of nostalgic reminiscence and intertextuality while embracing a stronger sense of gratification and irony'.[34] The transitions into song in *Mamma Mia!* can indeed be described as ironic and surprising.[35] Although recontextualizing a hit is a well-tested basic strategy for using existing songs in jukebox musicals, here a moment of surprise precedes each number, as if cueing the audience teasingly to guess which song will be used next. This playful approach has its rewards as it allows the audience to be titillated through this suggestive interaction, which is enhanced by the fact that the show's programme lists the musical numbers alphabetically, not chronologically. On the other hand, the show has been criticized by Ceri Hovland for having 'characters burst into song with little provocation; in song-mode they express their emotions with unrealistic transparency and fluency; they can stand side by side without hearing each other sing'.[36]

THE MOTHER–DAUGHTER RELATIONSHIP

In order to understand the dramaturgical workings of *Mamma Mia!*, it might be useful to apply Richard Dyer's notion of utopia and build on Aston's and Dolan's writings. Donna (Sophie's mother) has very clearly rejected her lifestyle in England and has created a new world for her daughter and herself in Greece: 'I am free, I am single and it's great!'[37] She is the manager of a taverna and organizes everything. This 'escape'—both literal and metaphorical—is now her reality and she feels that this is a better way of living for her and by extension her daughter Sophie.

Dyer proposes three reasons why audiences seek entertainment in theatre and elsewhere: social tension, inadequacy, and absence. Donna abandons the British lifestyle in order to carry out her 'revolution' on a Greek island and starts afresh by becoming an entrepreneur with a local business. The show offers a reflection on the tourist industry and the situation of the British expat abroad and how this 'new life' is integrated within the new environment. This jukebox show can be seen as a representation of utopia and fulfils Dyer's definition because 'energy, abundance, intensity, transparency and community'[38] are crucial elements of the musical. What is more, Dolan highlights that the three female leads (Donna and the Dynamos) have merely 'tenuous connections to conventionality [. . .] Their spirit of anti-establishment female hell-raising becomes infectious.'[39] This is one of the major selling points of the show: in spite of what the poster of *Mamma Mia!* promises, this is not a musical about a young girl finding happiness, but a show about older women having fun and being the main centre of the attention in the narrative.

Donna claims 'I need a holiday', even though she is on a dream island designed for taking vacations. The unrealistic presentation of a local woman idly knitting, while the British one is active earning her living is rather jarring, but is used to strengthen the representation of Donna as a hard-working 'monster' that the men are afraid of.[40] Her hysterical welcoming of her two old friends and former members of the Dynamos on the island adds a more human touch to her character and offers the perfect excuse for reminiscing about their days as a band. In this context, Donna makes a strong claim for independence: 'Marriage is an institution for people who belong in an institution' which is then juxtaposed with females-behaving-badly 'fun' and a comic treatment of the song 'Chiquitita'. Donna hates the suggestion that she is like her own mother because she aims to be a modern mother who raises her daughter Sophie without adhering to patriarchal principles. Visually, there is also a fleeting comment on the re-enactment of a lesbian wedding when Rosie and Tanya hold hands as if to be married. A serious moment is given comic spin with a feminist agenda. Through the music, the ex-Dynamos members are transported back in time to their youth and are allowed (together with the audience) to be their younger selves. It may feel like silly holiday fun, but the creative team's message remains ultimately political: the modern woman does not need a man—and this message is imparted just before a wedding day.

In spite of *Mamma Mia!*'s many comic moments and funny situations, the mother and daughter relationship is the main focus.[41] Millie Taylor, when writing about Stephen Sondheim's *Sweeney Todd* (1979), explains that we often empathize to a larger degree with people who sing the more lyrical songs in a musical. 'The combination of beautiful music, slow, lyrical singing, and the understanding generated through the lyrics gives audiences the opportunity to empathize with [the protagonist] and so the complexity of his character begins to be revealed.'[42] In the case of Donna and Sophie, the ballad 'Slipping Through My Fingers' leads to one of the many duets of the second act—the most powerful in the whole narrative (see Figure 25.1).

The mother–daughter relationship is laid bare and it is one that many female theatre-goers can relate to. In many countries, but especially in Greece, this moment is a precious one: 'giving the daughter away' often involves many tears and in this case it works on a deep emotional level. With the lyrical 'Slipping Through My Fingers', this situation now acquires a new global context: it is the feeling of a mother 'losing' a daughter and becomes a genuinely moving moment in the show:

> Slipping through my fingers all the time
> Do I really see what's in her mind?
> Each time I think I'm close to knowing
> She keeps on growing
> Slipping through my fingers all the time[43]

FIGURE 25.1 Siobhan McCarthy (Donna) and Lisa Stokke (Sophie) in the number 'Slipping Through My Fingers' from *Mamma Mia!*, Prince Edward Theatre, 1999.

Photography by Richard Mildenhall. Courtesy of ArenaPal.

The magical moment of putting on the wedding dress is not sugary, as in most musicals featuring a wedding, but has a more sombre, humane simplicity and dryness—it brings the mother and daughter back to reality, and then when Sophie utters the words 'Mum, I am proud of you', the audience's empathy is triggered by their own personal associations.

ON MARRIAGE, NUCLEAR FAMILY, AND THE PATERNITY ISSUE AS DRAMATURGICAL DEVICE

Mamma Mia! destablizes the convention found in many musicals that the boy marries the girl at the end of the show. The message is contrary to that of most traditional musicals:[44] marriage should not only be an option for young people.[45] Even though this could be described as just as clichéd and formulaic in its approach, it is nonetheless still extremely successful. Womack claims that Sophie, the daughter, 'journeys from post-feminist to feminist, cheerfully rejects both husband and father, eschews marriage and dismisses the importance of patriarchy'.[46]

The fact that the characters are behaving as if they were on holiday is explicitly linked to the music of ABBA[47] and provides many of the musical's highlights. *Mamma Mia!* almost completely fails to acknowledge any presence of the 'local' population (with the exception of an old *yiayia*[48] knitting on the side and some local young men playing backgammon) and does not explore the fact that this single mother would not have been accepted easily by the close-knit Greek village community. Constant questions would have been asked about the identity of the father and why he is absent, and the woman's assumption of stereotypical male roles such as the running of a coffee shop (a classic masculine occupation) or indeed a taverna. Some of the humour of Brits abroad is encapsulated in the comic moments of the show,[49] but, basically, the local Greek community is summarily represented by the new British taverna owner Donna.[50]

The permanent absence of the father figure is something that is not often discussed between the mother and daughter, but it is an underlying source of hidden tension between them. Just before the interval, we get a karaoke rendition of the Dynamos' return gig (see Figure 25.2). Karaoke is an indispensable activity in holiday resorts and here functions to enhance the flow of the narrative. The audience feels very much part of this karaoke concert, which extends beyond the proscenium arch.

FIGURE 25.2 Karaoke as narrative means: Kim Ismay, Vivien Parry, and Lara Mulcahy as 'Donna and the Dynamoes' in *Mamma Mia!*, Prince of Wales Theatre, 2004.

Photograph by Pete Jones. Courtesy of ArenaPal.

The camp costumes and the music make the audience believe that they are partici-
pating in the all-female hen party by feeling the vibrations of the music through the
thumping bass lines and the disco lights. But when the men join in, we witness a huge
celebration as the song 'Gimme! Gimme! Gimme! (A Man after Midnight)' becomes a
hymn to women having fun, during which Sophie announces to each one of the possible
fathers her concerns about fatherhood. With the help of crafty dramaturgical manipulation, the family drama is interspersed with and unfolded within the pandemonium of
dancing. 'I don't know who my dad is,' says Sophie in the most climactic moment before
the interval; 'I have to know I'm a curious child.'[51] Still, because of the final number featuring the male cast topless with their ankle-length swimsuits, revealing soaking-wet
inches of bare flesh, thrusting pelvic movements,[52] floor lighting patterns flashing wildly
and clumsy attempts at Greek dancing with both clockwise and anticlockwise circular
patterns, the audience is left elated to go and buy their interval drinks having just joined
in the celebrations on the island.

According to Womack the men are 'pleasant but passive in the face of female assertion,'[53] and indeed it is the women in *Mamma Mia!* who carry the narrative forward;
the men are mere stereotypes. The male chorus is there to provide the bachelor party
antics and deliver some of the erotic titillation via the obligatory (semi-)nudity of TV
holiday programmes, holiday videos, and photographs. This provides visual pleasure
to the straight women and gay men.[54] The men are decorative and also contribute to the
show's comedy; by making them wear flippers, the director allows the choreography to
incorporate elements of slapstick. With the exception of Pepper who acts as the local
kamaki,[55] the production ridicules the whole ritual of flirting with over-elaborate adjec-
tives of admiration for the female sex. But *Mamma Mia!* is really about women behaving
badly and so the men are used as ciphers, as decorative bodies who are prevented from
exhibiting their customary alpha-male machismo. They are not the chief focus of the
evening; they are not why women flock to this show: the largely female spectators go to
experience sisterhood and female empowerment.

The dream sequence at the beginning of the second half uses the song 'Under Attack'
similar to the dream sequence in *Oklahoma!* (1943) by borrowing some of its nightmarish qualities. Taking place on a bed, the number addresses the question of paternity, with
Sophie imagining her mother in a foursome with the three possible suitors who could
be her father. Sophie also sees herself, in an out-of-body experience, as the bride being
given away by the three fathers, only that the young bride is actually Sky in a bridal dress,
thus reversing the audience's expectations. The wedding is treated to a parodic reversal in which Sophie's future husband is the one wearing a wedding dress, which gives a
nightmarish quality to the dream sequence and further destabilizes traditional gender
representations.

The rest of the second half includes a formulaic series of duets between the following characters: Pepper, the young stallion, and Tanya;[56] Donna and Harry; Donna and
Sophie; and Rosie and Bill. In the church, there is a moment of musical chairs, where
the older characters are allowed to behave in a childish manner. Their flirting adds
another element of unorthodoxy to the narrative. British audiences, like most, love a

good wedding. So, the mise en scène provides everything from hats to gowns in the final scene, but the wedding does not go as expected. One wedding is cancelled, while another takes place leading to the taking of the 'essential' wedding picture. The young couple rejects the values associated with a wedding and walk away into the sunset,[57] while the older couple finally gets their well-deserved chance at happiness. The show achieves full symmetry with Donna remaining on the island.[58] However, Donna now has a husband and Sophie decides to leave the island. Sophie never finds her real dad, but departs and goes on an adult journey with the man of 'her' life.[59] *Mamma Mia!* breaks away from centuries of narratives which all revolve about finding out who the true father is by suggesting that, actually, biological paternity is unimportant.

The creators of a good jukebox musical know how to select a strong song, to make it appropriate for the narrative by referencing the source, but then to transcend that source. The original context of ABBA's music is crucial for our discussion because the music itself has an inherent theatricality. Their music has been often used in cabaret acts, discotheques in the 1980s, and nostalgia nights by a young contemporary generation (who approaches this music with a sense of historical distance).[60]

Although the piece has a very clear feminist agenda and creates a female (writing) space, it can be enjoyed by everybody because of the music's ability to seduce the viewer and stimulate the senses to involve the whole body. It is no secret that at the end of each show the entire audience is on its feet dancing and giving a standing ovation to the cast of *Mamma Mia!*.[61] It is not the ending of the narrative, but the additional final concert (with its rendition of three bonus tracks 'Mamma Mia', 'Dancing Queen', and 'Waterloo') that elevates the spirits and triggers the standing ovation. This after-show concert is still framed within the narrative as a 'Dynamos' concert and closes the musical with an upbeat coda, yet as a show-within-a-show it also fulfils the audience's wish to see a recreation of ABBA's songs without any pretence of additional narrative.

Conclusions: Musical Theatre as Seduction

Even though the jukebox musical[62] has reintroduced the musical to a wider audience, it is also partly responsible for the stagnation of musical theatre as an art form. LaChiusa bemoans the fact that '[w]ith big box-office from shows such as *Contact* and *Mamma Mia!* there was bound to be the inevitable imitation of product: musicals that use songs, rather than invent them'[63] and that imitation limits the space of exposure[64] for new musical theatre songs.[65] One can only hope that audiences sometime will again demand new original musicals with which they can associate—with original scores and narratives which are not adapted from well-known films, novels, or children's books—and which are reflecting contemporary issues, trends, and realities.[66]

David Savran celebrates the responses of contemporary audiences and postulates that '[t]he laboring bodies onstage produce not a thing to be ingested but an experience as elusive and polyvalent as it is ephemeral . . . [the] ticket for a musical . . . will buy them "goose bumps", dazzle, unpredictability, and at least the signs and sweat of liveness, transcendence and authenticity'.[67] The ever-growing audiences of *Mamma Mia!* have proved that they respond positively to the challenge of live entertainment with repeat visits to the same show.

Mamma Mia! is so successful because it reflects a modern feminist sensibility that is far more relevant to women today than the old-fashioned portrayals of gender that feature in most other musicals (jukebox or original). Unfortunately, for the producer of *Mamma Mia!*, one success did not guarantee the next one. So, when Judy Craymer decided to produce the opportunistic *Viva Forever!* in 2012, a musical based on the music of the Spice Girls, it was a critical and financial disaster. Tim Walker from the *Daily Telegraph* deplored the fact that it was

> [t]hrown together without any great thought, and [that it was] ugly in every respect, the show . . . [being] a fitting symbol of the me-me-me generation, whose members take the Spice Girls as their role models because they demonstrate that fame and fortune can these days be quickly, easily and pointlessly obtained by just about anybody.[68]

He also claimed that he would happily award it 'a minus-star rating. This show is not just bad, it is definitively, monumentally and historically bad'.[69] The *New York Times* was not any more welcoming and made a specific reference to *Mamma Mia!* and that show's central dynamic: '[O]nce again is a single mother locked in tetchy if eventually loving combat with her daughter, both of whom will impart easily digested life lessons on the way to the preordained megamix finale'.[70]

The film of *Mamma Mia!* has received extensive criticism about its commercialized casting. Although the stage version of *Mamma Mia!* is an exhilarating, sun-drenched comedy full of infectious energy, its film adaptation made some unfortunate casting decisions by placing enormous emphasis on the marketability of the cast and zero emphasis on whether they can actually sing.[71] Still, it is the music of ABBA, with its diachronic, refreshing, and celebratory qualities, that is mainly responsible for *Mamma Mia!*'s success, both the stage musical and its film adaptation: people have been listening and dancing to this music for the past forty years. To translate that from a visceral, private experience to the stage environment and appropriate it to the musical theatre genre was always a big challenge. But the show's all-female team of producer, writer, and director managed to find a market for their product; it has a strong dramaturgical structure, even if it is underuses the ensemble[72] and resorts to objectifying men as peripheral entities[73] to a quartet of women seeking to live their lives in an unorthodox way. *Mamma Mia!* allows the women in the audience to dream and to hope like contemporary Shirley Valentines for a more vibrant, sunny lifestyle, away from the 'the tyranny of (traditional) wedlock'.

For Aston, *Mamma Mia!* breaks 'the glass ceiling of the male-dominated musical industry as an all-women's team [and], in turn counters the utopian impulse of a mainstream postfeminist culture that sees gender power relations as already having made a difference'.[74] *Mamma Mia!* has the gifts of witty dialogue, slick stage direction, and a plausible if slightly exaggerated narrative conceit. It banks on the popularity of its songs and because of its family-friendly appeal attracts an audience from a wide range of demographics[75] which is there to have a good time and experience the musical as a form of escapism.[76] And, it is the best next thing to a holiday on a Greek island they could get!

At the end of the day, as Dolan believes, 'theatre can move us toward understanding the possibility of something better, can train our imaginations, inspire our dreams and fuel our desires in ways that might lead to incremental cultural change'.[77] *Mamma Mia!* does what other jukebox musicals (and there is an abundance of them) do not. It provides a space for the audience to associate with the utopian fantasy of escaping from the daily routine and troubles of a constricted urban existence and redefines 'living the dream'[78] as being on a Greek island[79] full of warmth, sun, and romantic opportunities.[80]

Notes

1. www.abba.bewithmusic.com, accessed 31 July 2014.
2. The audiences are mostly women (as is the case for other female-focused musicals such as *Wicked, Legally Blonde*, or *Dirty Dancing*).
3. David Savran, 'Toward a Historiography of the Popular', *Theatre Survey* 45, no. 2 (2004): 215.
4. Ben Brantley has pointed out, as did other early reviewers, that parts of the narrative are very similar to the film *Buona Sera, Mrs Campbell* (1968) in 'Mom Had a Trio (and a Band, Too)', *New York Times*, 19 October 2001, http://www.nytimes.com/2001/10/19/movies/theater-review-mom-had-a-trio-and-a-band-too.html, accessed 15 August 2014. *Buona Sera, Mrs Campbell* was directed by Melvin Frank and featured Gina Lollobrigida, Shelley Winters, Phil Silvers, Peter Lawford, and Telly Savalas.
5. Millie Taylor, *Musical Theatre, Realism and Entertainment* (Surrey: Ashgate Publishing Ltd, 2012), 162.
6. The Greek island has associations with Shakespeare's *The Comedy of Errors*, and its reversals of fortune and mistaken identities. However, it would be safe to assume that Catherine Johnson chose the location partly because Greece is one of the main tourist destinations for Brits.
7. The two film musicals *Moulin Rouge!* (2001) and *Across the Universe* (2007) have also encouraged audience expectations that film and stage musical theatre may use pre-existing music as their score and create a narrative around those well-known songs.
8. George Rodosthenous, 'Re-locating the Song: Julie Taymor's *Across the Universe*', in *Gestures of Music Theatre: The Performativity of Song and Dance*, ed. Dominic Symonds and Millie Taylor (New York: Oxford University Press, 2014), 43.
9. *Hunky Dory* (2011) and *Sunshine on Leith* (2013) are examples of British film musicals that employ the jukebox format.

10. It should be pointed out, though, that most twentieth-century revues had songs specially written for them.

11. Bud Coleman 'New Horizons: The Musical at the Dawn of the Twenty-first Century', in *The Cambridge Companion to the Musical*, ed. William A. Everett and Paul R. Laird (New York: Cambridge University Press, 2011), 287. Coleman refers to the jukebox musical as a 'disguised pop/rock concert' and divides the genre into semi-biographical ones, 'story album musicals' or 'anthology with a story' musicals, and musicals with non-biographical plots (Coleman, 'New Horizons', 287–289).

12. 'Open Season', *Opera News* 1 (August 2014), http://www.operanews.com/Opera_News_ Magazine/2014/8/Features/Open_Season.html, accessed 1 November 2014.

13. At the time of writing, there are three musicals in the West End, which could be defined as tribute band musicals: *The Jersey Boys*, *The Commitments*, and *Sunny Afternoon*.

14. Michael John LaChiusa, 'The Great Gray Way: Is It Prognosis Negative for the Broadway Musical?', *Opera News* 1 (August 2005): 32.

15. LaChuisa 'Great Gray Way', 33.

16. Barbara Ellen, 'I Want to Break Free . . . Now', *The Observer*, 16 April 2006, http://www. theguardian.com/stage/2006/apr/16/theatre.musicals, accessed 1 November 2014.

17. The 2014 Broadway musical *If/Then* also uses this concept.

18. One of the problems of shows like *Never Forget* is that in the end the audience has to realize that watching a tribute band perform the material does not come anywhere near the excitement they felt watching the original band.

19. For a more detailed discussion of gender relocations, see Rodosthenous, 'Re-locating the Song', 42–43.

20. The 2013 London cast featured Leon Cooke who used to be Billy in *Billy Elliot*. It was fascinating to rewatch *Mamma Mia!* with that extra level of (emotional) memory as part of the viewing experience. It created extra layers of meaning (and associations) about the performer's career, which I could not disassociate from my viewing experience, thus adding another level of nostalgia.

21. Louise FitzGerald and Melanie Williams, eds., *Exploring a Cultural Phenomenon: 'Mamma Mia! The Movie'* (London: I. B. Tauris, 2013). Although this chapter focuses solely on the stage version, it will still reference some of the writings on the film.

22. Elaine Aston, 'Work, Family, Romance and the Utopian Sensibilities of the Chick Megamusical *Mamma Mia!*', in *A Good Night Out for the Girls*, ed. Elaine Aston and Geraldine Harris (Basingstoke: Palgrave Macmillan, 2013), 114–133.

23. Aston 'Work, Family, Romance', 131–132. Emphasis in the original.

24. Jill Dolan, '*Mamma Mia!* on Screen', *Feminist Spectator*, 24 July 2008, http://feministspec- tator.blogspot.co.uk/2008/07/mamma-mia-on-screen.html, accessed 30 July 2014.

25. Taylor, *Musical Theatre*, 161.

26. Malcolm Womack, ' "Thank You for the Music": Catherine Johnson's Feminist Revoicings in *Mamma Mia!*', *Studies in Musical Theatre* 3, no. 2 (2009): 201.

27. Womack, ' "Thank You for the Music" ', 203.

28. Richard Dyer's full discussion of utopia is also fascinating; see Dyer, *Only Entertainment* (London: Routledge, 2002).

29. Stacy Wolf, *A Problem Like Maria: Gender and Sexuality in the American Musical* (Ann Arbor: University of Michigan Press, 2002), 42.

30. For an analysis of the recontextualization of songs in the jukebox musical (specifically in *Across the Universe*), see Rodosthenous, 'Re-locating the Song'.

31. An example would be the treatment of the song 'Does Your Mother Know' by Tanya and Pepper which will later be discussed in detail.

32. The film version of *Mamma Mia!*, in a way, negates this effect because it allows for repeated viewing, which means the subversion/surprise becomes expected, especially in cases where regular repeated viewing becomes the norm (as with the 1975 cult movie *The Rocky Horror Picture Show*).

33. Jill Dolan, *Presence and Desire: Essays on Gender, Sexuality, Performance* (Ann Arbor: University of Michigan Press, 1993), 118.

34. Kelly Kessler, *Destabilizing the Hollywood Musical: Music, Masculinity and Mayhem* (Basingstoke: Palgrave Macmillan, 2010), 198. See also Naomi Graber, 'Memories That Remain: *Mamma Mia!* and the Disruptive Potential of Nostalgia', *Studies in Musical Theatre* 9, no. 2 (2015): 187–198.

35. Only one of the songs in the show, 'Does Your Mother Know', was originally performed by a male singer, composer-lyricist Björn Ulvaeus.

36. Ceri Hovland, 'Embracing the Embarrassment: *Mamma Mia!* and the Pleasures of Socially Unrestrained Performance', in Fitzgerald and Williams, *Exploring a Cultural Phenomenon: 'Mamma Mia!' The Movie*, 110.

37. http://www.scribd.com/doc/140818692/Mamma-Mia-the-Musical-Script#scribd, accessed 14 July 2014.

38. Dyer, *Only Entertainment*, 20–21.

39. Dolan, '*Mamma Mia!* on Screen'.

40. This has clear associations with the feisty Katharina in *The Taming of the Shrew* and *Kiss Me Kate* respectively, as well as feminist Emilia in *Othello*: 'Let husbands know | Their wives have sense like them. They see, and smell, | And have their palates both for sweet and sour, | As husbands have. What is it that they do | When they change us for others? Is it sport? | I think it is. And doth affection breed it? | I think it doth. Is't frailty that thus errs? | It is so, too. And have not we affections, | Desires for sport, and frailty, as men have? | Then let them use us well, else let them know | The ills we do, their ills instruct us so.' Act 4, Scene 3, lines 92–100.

41. It explores the presence of mothers and the absence of fathers (and thus constitutes a reversal of the plot of *Billy Elliot*).

42. Millie Taylor, '*Sweeney Todd*: From Melodrama to Musical Tragedy', in *The Oxford Handbook of Sondheim Studies*, ed. Robert Gordon (New York: Oxford University Press, 2014), 340.

43. Benny Andersson and Björn Ulvaeus, 'Slipping Through My Fingers' (1981), http://www.metrolyrics.com/slipping-through-my-fingers-lyrics-abba.html, accessed 15 November 2014.

44. *Mamma Mia!* can be linked to Sondheim's *Company* and its controversial/unorthodox views on marriage since that show 'explores themes relating to marriage and social isolation in a modern, urban environment'. Natalie Draper, 'Concept Meets Narrative in Sondheim's *Company*: Metadrama as a Method of Analysis', *Studies in Musical Theatre* 4, no. 2 (2010): 172.

45. As it is Donna who marries in the end, the message here is that 'you are never too old to marry and find happiness' which must be quite a comfort for many women in the audience.

46. Womack, ' "Thank You for the Music" ', 202.

47. It is interesting to note again here that ABBA started their career when on holiday in Cyprus.

48. Greek for Grandmother.
49. The banter of the hen night party, the unavoidable karaoke session, and the compulsory attempts to dance the local syrtaki dance are all part of this holiday-abroad culture.
50. This raises issues about what Deleuze refers to as 'territorialisation' and can open up a postcolonialist analysis, which does not explicitly concern this author here.
51. http://www.scribd.com/doc/140818692/Mamma-Mia-the-Musical-Script#scribd, accessed 15 November 2014.
52. It is interesting to note that all the couples featured here are boy-girl, going against the feminist political messages and agenda of the show. It could open up another discussion about how this links with the strong gay following of the musical and seemingly creates a paradox about musical content and audience empathy.
53. Womack, '"Thank You for the Music"', 210.
54. *Mamma Mia!* is a show that is remarkably unconcerned with visually pleasing straight men.
55. *Kamaki* 'is the special name of the Greek men who spend time in tourist-heavy places courting women. Kamaki are less active today than a decade ago, but the fact is there are still men who are looking to have sex with as many foreign women as possible', http://www.greeceindex.com/various/greek-kamaki.htm, accessed 15 November 2014.
56. Tanya, the older woman, represents a comic Jocasta-like figure. 'I am old enough to be your mother' is one of many jokes referring to Oedipus.
57. On all three viewings of the stage musical, I found this ending rather unsatisfactory as it does not bring a sense of real closure to the narrative, but instead resorts to a 'neutral', unexciting, unresolved conclusion. That is perhaps why the uplifting quality of the final coda with the three added bonus tracks seems even more satisfying.
58. The musical accompaniment here sounds like *Zorba the Greek* to remind us of the locality.
59. For a comparison of Sophie's journey with Baby's journey in *Dirty Dancing*, see George Rodosthenous, 'Dirty Dancing and Its Jukebox Stage Dancical Adaptation: The Dancing Male in a Teenage Female Fantasy of Desire and Sensuality', in *The Time of Our Lives: Dirty Dancing and Popular Culture*, ed. Y. Tzioumakis and S. Lincoln (Detroit: Wayne State University Press, 2013), 297–314.
60. Some of the songs have a water (liquid)/summer holiday quality to them that transports us to a sea, thus letting the utopian fantasy dominate the imagination; on the other hand Björn Ulvaeus has also often pointed out that what makes their songs to poignant is the undercurrent of melancholy which he attributes to his and Benny Andersson's Scandinavian sensibility.
61. This is perhaps also triggered by the fact that the audience is already on its feet dancing during the three bonus songs of the finale.
62. In the case of *Mamma Mia!*, its filmic rendition as well.
63. LaChiusa, 'Great Gray Way', 34.
64. Jukebox musicals have been commercially successful since the 1970s, e.g. *Ain't Misbehavin'* (1978), *Buddy—The Buddy Holly Story* (1989), *Five Guys Named Moe* (1990), as well as the stage versions of *Jelly's Last Jam* (1991), *Smokey Joe's Café* (1995), and *Saturday Night Fever* (1998).
65. There has been a disproportionate number of jukebox musicals that have proliferated in the last two decades compared to shows with an original score: http://www.newyorker.com/culture/cultural-comment/lets-rock-defense-jukebox-musicals, accessed 15 February 2015.
66. And consequently producers invest in such works.

67. David Savran, 'Trafficking in Transnational Brands: The New "Broadway-Style" Musical', *Theatre Survey* 55, no. 3 (2014): 334–335.

68. Tim Walker, '*Viva Forever!*', *Daily Telegraph*, 19 December 2012, http://www.telegraph.co.uk/culture/theatre/theatre-reviews/9756534/Viva-Forever-Piccadilly-Theatre-review.html, accessed 15 November 2014.

69. Walker, '*Viva Forever!*'.

70. http://www.nytimes.com/2013/01/09/arts/09iht-lon09.html?_r=0, accessed 1 November 2014.

71. The casting of non-singers as part of a marketing strategy in major film musical adaptations such as *Mamma Mia!* and *Les Misérables* (2012) raises a host of ethical questions which fall outside the scope of this study.

72. In both the film and the stage version, the use of the chorus in *Mamma Mia!* is intentionally underwhelming and not explored to its full potential.

73. Some audience members might find it refreshing that it is the men who are objectified here by strong females. Women are allowed and encouraged to look at handsome, semi-naked athletic men. This gratuitous 'exhibitionism' was too rare an offer within (jukebox) musicals in 1999. And because it is done with a wink, it is not really felt to be objectionable by most of the audience.

74. Aston, 'Work, Family', 120.

75. *Mamma Mia!* cleverly attracts various segments of the public: ABBA fans from the 1970s–80s, mothers and daughters, middle-aged women and their friends, as well as gay men.

76. This is, of course, one of the main features of most successful musicals.

77. Jill Dolan, 'Performance, Utopia, and the "Utopian Performative"', *Theatre Journal* 53 (2001), 460.

78. An important aspect of *Mamma Mia!* is the very redefinition of that dream itself—it is no longer the traditional boy-marries-girl scenario, but a life that allows women to be strong, independent, good mothers (even if they are single parents), and to have close female friends. It promotes the idea that none of this must necessarily prevent anybody from achieving emotional and sexual fulfilment (whether you are married or not).

79. Its recent advertising campaign promises this 'Escape to a Greek island', which is rather ironic, if we consider Greece's current financial climate.

80. With many thanks to the editors Robert Gordon and Olaf Jubin, and my colleagues on the IFTR Music Theatre Working group that I co-convene, for their comments and feedback on this chapter, as well as to Matthew Lockitt, Millie Taylor, Jordan Taylor, Alex Hammond, Ricky Waite, and Demetris Zavros.

BIBLIOGRAPHY

Aston, Elaine. 'Work, Family, Romance and the Utopian Sensibilities of the Chick Megamusical *Mamma Mia!*' In *A Good Night Out for the Girls*, edited by Elaine Aston and Geraldine Harris, 114–133. Basingstoke: Palgrave Macmillan, 2013.

Brantley, Ben. 'Mom Had a Trio (and a Band, Too)'. *New York Times*, 19 October 2001. http://www.nytimes.com/2001/10/19/movies/theater-review-mom-had-a-trio-and-a-band-too.html, accessed 15 August 2014.

Coleman, Bud. 'New Horizons: The Musical at the Dawn of the Twenty-First Century'. In *The Cambridge Companion to the Musical*, edited by William A. Everett and Paul R. Laird, 284–302. New York: Cambridge University Press, 2011.

Dolan, Jill. 'Mamma Mia! on Screen.' Feminist Spectator, 24 July 2008. http://feministspectator. blogspot.co.uk/2008/07/mamma-mia-on-screen.html, accessed 30 July 2014.

Dolan, Jill. 'Performance, Utopia, and the "Utopian Performative".' Theatre Journal 53 (2001): 455–479.

Dolan, Jill. Presence and Desire: Essays on Gender, Sexuality, Performance. Ann Arbor: University of Michigan Press, 1993.

Draper, Natalie. 'Concept Meets Narrative in Sondheim's Company: Metadrama as a Method of Analysis.' Studies in Musical Theatre 4, no. 2 (2010): 171–183.

Dyer, Richard. Only Entertainment. London: Routledge, 2002.

Ellen, Barbara. 'I Want to Break Free . . . Now.' The Observer, 16 April 2006. http://www.the-guardian.com/stage/2006/apr/16/theatre.musicals, accessed 1 November 2014.

FitzGerald, Louise, and Melanie Williams, eds. Exploring a Cultural Phenomenon: 'Mamma Mia! The Movie'. London: I. B. Tauris, 2013.

Graber, Naomi. 'Memories That Remain: Mamma Mia! and the Disruptive Potential of Nostalgia.' Studies in Musical Theatre 9, no. 2 (2015): 187–198.

Hovland, Ceri. 'Embracing the Embarrassment: Mamma Mia! and the Pleasures of Socially Unrestrained Performance.' In FitzGerald and Williams, Exploring a Cultural Phenomenon: 'Mamma Mia! The Movie', 109–126.

Kessler, Kelly. Destabilizing the Hollywood Musical: Music, Masculinity and Mayhem. Basingstoke: Palgrave Macmillan, 2010.

LaChiusa, Michael John. 'The Great Gray Way: Is It Prognosis Negative for the Broadway Musical?' Opera News 1 (August 2005): 30–35.

LaChiusa, Michael John. 'Open Season.' Opera News 1 (August 2014). http://www.oper-anews.com/Opera_News_Magazine/2014/8/Features/Open_Season.html, accessed 1 November 2014.

Larson, Sarah. 'Let's Rock: In Defense of Musicals.' New Yorker, 22 July 2014. http://www.new-yorker.com/culture/cultural-comment/lets-rock-defense-jukebox-musicals, accessed 15 February 2015.

Rodosthenous, George. 'Dirty Dancing and Its Jukebox Stage Dansical Adaptation: The Dancing Male in a Teenage Female Fantasy of Desire and Sensuality.' In The Time of Our Lives: Dirty Dancing and Popular Culture, edited by Y. Tzioumakis and S. Lincoln, 297–314. Detroit: Wayne State University Press, 2013.

Rodosthenous, George. 'Re-locating the Song: Julie Taymor's Across the Universe.' In Gestures of Music Theatre: The Performativity of Song and Dance, edited by Dominic Symonds and Millie Taylor, 41–53. New York: Oxford University Press, 2014.

Savran, David. 'Toward a Historiography of the Popular.' Theatre Survey 45, no. 2 (2004): 211–217.

Savran, David. 'Trafficking in Transnational Brands: The New "Broadway-Style" Musical.' Theatre Survey 55, no. 3 (2014): 334–335.

Taylor, Millie. Musical Theatre, Realism and Entertainment. Surrey: Ashgate Publishing Ltd, 2012.

Taylor, Millie. 'Sweeney Todd: From Melodrama to Musical Tragedy.' In The Oxford Handbook of Sondheim Studies, edited by Robert Gordon, 335–349. New York: Oxford University Press, 2014.

Walker, Tim. 'Viva Forever!' Daily Telegraph, 19 December 2012. http://www.telegraph.co.uk/culture/theatre/theatre-reviews/9756534/Viva-Forever-Piccadilly-Theatre-review.html, accessed 15 November 2014.

Wolf, Matt. '"Viva!" but Maybe Not Forever.' *New York Times*, 8 January 2013. http://www. nytimes.com/2013/01/09/arts/09iht-lon09.html?_r=0, accessed 1 November 2014.

Wolf, Stacy. *A Problem Like Maria: Gender and Sexuality in the American Musical.* Ann Arbor: University of Michigan Press, 2002.

Womack, Malcolm. '"Thank You For The Music": Catherine Johnson's Feminist Revoicings in *Mamma Mia!' Studies in Musical Theatre* 3, no. 2 (2009): 201–211.

CHAPTER 26

···

ATTRACTING THE FAMILY MARKET

Shows with Cross-Generational Appeal

···

REBECCA WARNER

INTRODUCTION

···

IN recent decades the family musical has become of increasing importance in Britain; the success of shows such as *Matilda the Musical* (2011) and *Charlie and the Chocolate Factory* (2013) in the West End indicates that it is a form which continues to be highly successful in Britain, within an industry culture which would seem to perceive the family show as a serious art form. The political, financial, and creative factors which have potentially given rise to the 'family epic' have been discussed by Garry Lyons in his article 'The Generation Game' (2013). While Lyons acknowledges that some mainstream musical theatre is encompassed within his definition of the term 'family epic' (*Matilda the Musical* being one such example) his 'focus is on theatre that aims to be culturally enriching rather than entertainingly populist' and he therefore states that he is 'differentiating the family epic from the commercial musical'.[1] However, some of the ideas found in Lyons's paper relating to the crossover audience, and the importance of cross-generational shared experience, are of direct interest to a study of the family musical. This essay seeks to explore how the family musical may provide a strong appeal to all generations, by examining some of the creative factors that are often found in the genre. It will be considered how the genre of musical theatre itself offers a peculiarly appropriate vehicle for cross-generation audiences, thus making the family audience a particularly important market.

THE FAMILY MUSICAL IN THE WEST END

The importance of family musicals in Britain is not a new development; historically a variety of British theatre makers have created musicals which appeal to a family audience or which involve child protagonists. Some notable examples of family musicals that have originated in London include Lionel Bart's *Oliver!* which premiered in the West End in 1960 and has seen a number of London revivals, including the most recent at Drury Lane in 2009 followed by a UK tour in 2011. Two of Andrew Lloyd Webber's long-running musicals might be seen as particularly suitable for a family audience: *Cats* which premiered in the West End in 1981 and *Starlight Express* which played from 1984 onwards, finally closing in 2002. Two stage adaptations of family musical films have also been of particular note in the West End: *Chitty Chitty Bang Bang*, based on the 1968 film and opening at the London Palladium in 2002, and *Mary Poppins*, which was based on the 1964 film and premiered at the Prince Edward Theatre in 2004. These latter two musicals have seen a collaboration between American and British creative forces: both films engaged the American songwriting team of the Sherman Brothers, with British writing team George Stiles and Anthony Drewe reimagining and augmenting the score for the stage version of *Mary Poppins*. *Chitty Chitty Bang Bang* was produced as a British film, while the film of *Mary Poppins* was produced by Disney in America, but both stage adaptations originated in the West End. The foundation of Disney Theatrical Productions has meant that since 1997, when *Beauty and the Beast* opened in the West End, there has also been a significant presence in London of family shows which originated on Broadway, perhaps most significantly *The Lion King* which has been playing at the Lyceum since 1999. However, as particularly demonstrated by *Matilda*, the success of the Disney blockbusters does not seem to have dampened the burgeoning success of family musicals of British origin.

ROALD DAHL AND THE FAMILY MUSICAL

At the time of writing, two musicals based on Roald Dahl's work have a high profile in the West End: *Matilda* and *Charlie and the Chocolate Factory* playing at the Cambridge Theatre and Theatre Royal Drury Lane respectively. Dahl's importance in the current world of the family musical is perhaps no surprise given that his stories appeal to children and adults alike; Jeremy Treglown identifies that '[o]ne of his features as a writer is the lack of a clear boundary-line between his work for adults and for children'.[2] The box-office success of Tim Burton's film version of *Charlie and the Chocolate Factory* starring Johnny Depp (2005) will also have had a marked impact on the popularity and resurgence of Dahl's work as source material. Dahl's *Matilda* similarly enjoyed a highly successful American film adaptation in 1996. The typically British characteristics of Dahl's writing provides ideal source material for the home-grown family musical with a style that feels representative of an idealized sense of British eccentricity. This can be seen in *Charlie and the Chocolate Factory* in the inventions of Mr Bucket, and in Willy Wonka's play on words and ability to turn the world on its head. The incorporation of eccentric invention is also seen in *Chitty Chitty Bang Bang* through the creations of Caractacus Potts and it is perhaps noteworthy that Dahl wrote the original screenplay to the 1968 film, capturing similar themes of the family unit and austerity alongside the quirky aesthetic found in his stories. The 'make do and mend' attitude of the Buckets, and the rise of the underdog—seen in both *Charlie and the Chocolate Factory* and in *Matilda*—can also be seen as representative of an archetypal British sensibility.

STILES AND DREWE AND THE FAMILY MUSICAL

The fact that British writers and producers of musical theatre have fully embraced the family show, is particularly evident in the work of George Stiles and Anthony Drewe: the musicals *Honk!* (1999) and *Just So* (1989) appeal to all ages, as does their reworking of the family classic *Mary Poppins* for the musical stage. All three of these musicals have origins in children's literature: *Mary Poppins* is based on both the Disney film and the original P. L. Travers stories, while *Honk!* is an adaptation of Hans Christian Andersen's 'The Ugly Duckling'. *Just So* is adapted from Rudyard Kipling's *Just So Stories* in which the Elephant's Child and the Kolokolo Bird travel to find the rebellious Pau Amma crab and challenge him to stop flooding the lands which is causing havoc for the other animals. The 'family audience' to which these shows might appeal most, is a hybrid spectatorship and this chapter seeks to draw out key aspects of family musicals which enable them to appeal on multiple levels to a crossover audience of children and adults alike. Particular attention will be given to four stage musicals which have originated in Britain: *Honk!* (Anthony Drewe and George Stiles, 1993), *Mary Poppins* (Sherman Brothers, Julian Fellowes, Anthony Drewe, and George Stiles, 2004), *Matilda* (Dennis Kelly and Tim Minchin, 2011), and *Charlie and the Chocolate Factory* (David Grieg, Marc Shaiman, and Scott Wittman, 2013).

THE FAMILY AUDIENCE

In *Theatre for Young Audiences,* James Reynolds discusses non-musical theatre that has grown from crossover literature, and particularly the National Theatre's role in this development, quoting Susannah Clapp's (2004) view of an 'approach to a serious-minded young audience'.[3] Productions such as *His Dark Materials* (2003) and *War Horse*

(2007), both based on crossover literature, have enjoyed the success of appealing on a variety of levels across generations. In the family musicals being considered here, a slightly different process comes into play, which is creating a crossover show adapted from a piece of literature more specifically aimed at children. The ideal audience for the family musical would seem to be identified by book writer and lyricist Anthony Drewe: 'My favourite audience with *Honk!* is when you get three generations; you get grandparents, parents and kids all getting something different out of it.'[4] There is both an artistic and commercial satisfaction in theatre which has such a wide potential audience. As Lyons states with regard to the 'family epic': 'In an era when theatre professionals are constantly being told they are serving a contracting audience that is fragmenting into niche groups, there is an excitement about a form that brings those groups together as one.'[5]

In *The Young Audience*, Matthew Reason includes a piece by Tony Graham, written when he was artistic director of Unicorn Theatre, a theatre specifically dedicated to work for children. Graham discusses the means by which the Unicorn assessed potential pieces of children's theatre during his time as artistic director and suggests a particularly useful five-step gauge for considering whether a work will appeal to children in the theatre: '[W]e have devised a five-pronged chart for writers and makers which helps us to gauge scripts. The five prongs (think of a star as they are all connected) are: poetry, substance, transcendence, dramatic potential and a child's perspective.'[6] These five prongs will form the basis of the discussion of the family musical here. Although Graham's focus is on theatre for *children*, and our concern is the crossover *family* musical, these five points are still of relevance. Graham makes the point that 'theatre for young audiences, if it's to be any good, must by definition be theatre for all of us. We live in the same world as children. It's no less complex and baffling for children than it is for the rest of us.'[7] The five points will be considered alongside the idea of a 'universal theme' as a potential primary factor to the wide appeal necessary for the family musical.

POETRY

The first of Graham's criteria for children's theatre is 'poetry'. The musical is an inherently poetic genre in that no matter what the subject matter of a show, there must be a number of opportunities to sing. Song can be seen as an elevated performance mode in which word becomes more formalized, regularized, and expressive in lyric while the voice achieves a heightened form of expression, all of which can be said to constitute 'poetry' of a kind. In *Writing a Musical* Richard Andrews considers the significant differences between poetry and lyrics: 'Poetry is meant to be read; lyrics are meant to be heard with music, and they are incomplete without it . . . Poetry should reveal greater depths the more it is studied, but lyrics that require study inevitably fail.'[8] However, as Andrews explains, there are key similarities between the two forms, two particular similarities being the use of imagistic expression and the use of metaphors and similes. Such poetic techniques abound in the musical lyric, as can be seen in the lyrics of Anthony Drewe, for example in his use of imagery in 'Now I've Seen You' from *Honk!*: 'I've seen waterfalls cascading, sparkling in the light. | Damsel flies that dance their dance from morning til night',[9] and his use of simile in 'Practically Perfect' from *Mary Poppins*: 'I'm practically perfect, not slightly soiled | Running like an engine that's just been freshly oiled'.[10] In an interview for the podcast *Musical Talk*, Drewe talks about the adult wit found in *Honk!* and also in Stiles and Drewe's style in general. He considers that the writers' generation appreciates this form of wit, and therefore thought their children would also respond to it. Drewe comments: 'It strikes me that the children respond to the punning nature of the lyrics.'[11] Such punning wordplay can be found readily in *Honk!*, for example: 'He is gawky in whatever he does, Oh! | He really is an ugly oiseau' from 'Look at Him',[12] 'You can chivvy your chow before you chew' from 'Play With Your Food',[13] and 'Though I'm tyrannosaurus rexy | Some will find me sexy in my way' from 'Warts and All'.[14]

In addition to the techniques which poetry and lyric may share, the multidisciplinary nature of the genre of musical theatre gives rise to what Stephen Banfield has called 'melopoesis'—the reciprocal play between music and words.[15] In *The Musical Theatre Writer's Survival Guide*, David Spencer describes this as the 'poetic connection',

> The more you study musical theatre scores of all kinds, the more you'll find that with the best ones, the ones that stay in the literature and become classic, there is almost always a poetic connection between the music and the lyric and/or the drama of the lyric . . . The poetic connection is the reason that music is aesthetically wedded to its context; and it's often the difference between a perfectly nice score and a score that resonates.[16]

'Poetry' can be seen as what is created in the symbiotic relationship between words and music and vice versa. As Aaron Frankel suggests: 'The words must rise out of the plot into crystal shapes. They must make music every time; the lyricist must be a musician by instinct, if not by training. Then, above all, in union with the music, the words must create a thing done, drama.'[17]

Taking the term 'poetry' on a less literal level than the construction of poetic lines, or of the poetic union of integrated elements, the idea of poetic substance as an *essence* can be seen as fundamental to the musical genre. In *How Musicals Work* Julian Woolford provides a helpful framework in which the creation of musical theatre can be viewed. Drawing on Aristotle, Lehman Engel, and his own considerations of 'produce-ability', he proposes eighteen elements of the musical as a guide to engaging with an audience (intended in the first instance for shows addressed to adults).[18] In this conceptualization of the word, the term 'poetry' can be seen to be related to Engel's discussion of the importance of 'feeling' in the musical, which Woolford subsequently incorporates into his proposed eighteen elements of the musical. As regards feeling and subject matter, Engel points to the fact that the musical must have something to break into song and dance for, a factor which Howard Kissel's commentary highlights as 'what may be the single most important question about a musical: what is there to sing about?'[19] Song gives rise to poetry not only in terms of poetic techniques but also in terms of achieving a kind of 'poetic state' in which song becomes an appropriate, and needed, mode of expression. Engel himself highlights that 'feeling' cannot necessarily be easily identified,[20] and each individual spectator will respond to such emotional stimuli in his/her own way. This is even more pertinent to the family audience where different generations of spectators will find the evocation of feeling in different places. The degree of empathy and emotional investment, however, would seem to be a key factor to experience the poetic essence of a show: 'To feel is to experience and in order to experience any kind of emotion from a play or musical one has to care about the characters and the situations.'[21] This provides a link to Graham's categories of 'poetry' and of 'substance'.

Substance

The question of what subject matter may appeal to children in the theatre is addressed in detail by David Wood in *Theatre for Children*. He suggests that there are particular 'themes, ideas and stories' which children particularly respond to, some of which include 'fantasy within reality', 'myths and legends', what Wood calls 'old wine in new bottles', 'tales of the anthropomorphic', 'the quest', 'toys and inanimate objects', and 'fairy tales'.[22] The shows in question can be seen to bear close relation to several of these topics. *Honk!* for example is based on the 'fairy tale' of 'The Ugly Duckling', and in its reworking can be considered 'old wine in new bottles'. Its quest structure is revealed in the search of Ugly's mother, Ida, for her son, and in its simultaneous expression of humans as animals it is a tale of the anthropomorphic. As Drewe states, however, it is 'as much about people as it is about ducks . . . the main message that we wanted the audience to go away with is that being different is OK, it is something to be welcomed, embraced and celebrated rather than feared, misunderstood or persecuted'.[23]

This last statement raises the question of the prevalence of an 'issue' or intended 'message' in the family musical. While this would seem to be an important factor of the family musical, in order to truly reach a cross-generational audience, the key would seem to be that there are multiple layers of meaning. At the same time as the adults may find themselves appreciating levels of meaning which the child discovers, they themselves may see other interpretations relevant to themselves. Lyn Gardner's comment on another of Stiles and Drewe's family musicals, *Just So*, that 'like all good family shows it's multi-layered and open to many meanings',[24] is indicative of the importance of this particular level of substance in the family musical. *Mary Poppins* holds an appeal for the adult who remembers seeing the musical film as a child from the perspective of its being about Jane and Michael Banks and the re-establishing of their relationship with their parents, and then may be surprised by their adult selves focusing on the particular dilemmas of Mr Banks and his wife as they may have even more to learn than the children. The addition of the song 'Being Mrs Banks' in the stage version of *Mary Poppins*, reprised later as

Mrs Banks's understanding of her husband grows, highlights the adult predicament, and elevates this to the same level of seriousness as that of the children's situation.

A similar pattern can be found in *Matilda* in its exploration of complex issues related to both the child and adult protagonists: the attempted repressing of Matilda's intellect and creativity by her family, and the past and continued terrorization of Miss Honey by her aunt Miss Trunchbull, are both situations which explore ideas of oppression, neglect, and intimidation. Two songs which can be seen as the characters' respective 'I am' songs reflect their position but are telling in terms of their character's response to the oppression. Matilda reveals herself to be the braver of the two in 'Naughty': 'If you sit around and let them get on top, you might as well be saying you think that it's okay | and that's not right',[25] whereas Miss Honey categorizes herself as 'Pathetic': 'Look at you hesitating, hands shaking. | You should be embarrassed. | You're not a little girl. | It's just pathetic'.[26] As far as bravery goes, it is for the child to teach the adult in this case—something which may provide inspiration or empowerment to the children in the audience.

DRAMATIC POTENTIAL

Graham lists 'dramatic potential' as another of the important factors in a piece of children's theatre. One such source for 'dramatic potential' might be found in the exploration of complex issues. Shifra Schonmann explicates in *Theatre as a Medium for Children and Young People* the idea that 'theatre—the only art whose precondition is that human beings confront one another—can uniquely stand for life and thus is inexhaustible'.[27] In both *Mary Poppins* and *Matilda* there is an underlying theme that is larger than the specific issues being faced by both child and adult characters, and it is this fundamental theme that then has cross-generational and indeed universal appeal. In *Mary Poppins*, the final glorious number 'Anything Can Happen' has the potential to inspire all generations: '[I]f you reach for the stars | All you get is in the stars, | But we've got a whole new spin | If you reach for the heavens, | You get the stars thrown in.'[28] What unites both Matilda and Miss Honey on the other hand is the profound realization 'that you can control your own story, and rebellion and protest can defeat the bullies'.[29]

The life-affirming experience of the family musical would seem to be vital to its appeal—it is in such sweeping numbers as 'Anything Can Happen' that some of the 'rush that comes from truly great musical theatre'[30] can be found. However, also of importance is that any implication of didacticism might be almost approached 'sideways', seeing as any labouring of a 'take home' meaning would seem to be counterproductive in that it takes the audience out of the theatrical moment. Dennis Kelly, the bookwriter of *Matilda*, states that it is important for the audience to be able to explore the theme for themselves: 'I'm not trying to teach anyone lessons. I just pose questions I don't know the answers to, and then use plays to explore them.'[31] A related factor which may help to explore such life-affirming sweeping themes without being didactic, is stimulating the imagination. Jonathan Levy states how important a theatre-maker's nurturing of the

imagination is for the child as 'we hold their imaginations in trust'.[32] The adult characters in the shows in question also nurture this imagination: Mary Poppins through visiting new worlds, Mrs Phelps by encouraging Matilda's storytelling, Willy Wonka with his
Imagining Room. The imagination not only plays a key role in the characters' journeys,
but also evokes the audience's imagination as regards the universal theme. This in turn
is closely linked to the idea of transcendence, an idea which is developed further below.

The way in which a child or adult is encouraged to explore substantial themes in the
shows in question is of course closely bound up with characterization. Engel argues that
it is primarily empathy for the character's predicament that draws in the audience and
therefore sustains their engagement in the show:

> Doesn't one factor emerge? The character (or plural) is caught up in a conflict and we
> care because he is unable to escape. (We abhor the sight of a wounded bird. We care.)
> In comedies it is also the conflict which imprisons the characters. We would like to
> free them. In every case it is the situation in which the characters find themselves that
> elicit our empathy.[33]

In the case of 'Naughty' already discussed, Matilda draws on the audience's empathy
because she has to live with her abhorrent parents, but 'Naughty' secures the audience's engagement even further through her approaching the situation with a childlike
sense of fun and rebellion, coupled with a mature sense of argument and a spirit that
refuses to be dampened. In this one number alone she elicits sympathy for her situation,
empathy through the use of a child's language such as 'sometimes you have to be a little
bit naughty',[34] and admiration for her determination to make the best of her life, also
brought about by the joyful dotted lilt to the song.

The choice of characters themselves in the musicals in question is of course closely
related to the suitability of a particular theme for engaging children. Certain recurring tropes are established by means of characterization: the animal or non-human
protagonist is one such trope, and ties in closely with Wood's suggestions of the suitability of anthropormorphic tales, toys, and inanimate objects. *Honk!* is of the anthropomorphic variety, as is Stiles and Drewe's *Just So*, whereas other family musicals such
as *Starlight Express* feature the toy/inanimate object as protagonist. The idea of engaging
with toys coming to life can also be found in *Mary Poppins* in the nursery courtroom
sequence deploring the children's 'Temper Temper'. The child protagonist would seem
to be key to allowing a child to empathize with the character, and even in the anthropomorphic examples above, the protagonist is still a child of the species. Matilda, Charlie
Bucket, and Jane and Michael Banks all provide this crucial element of identification
for the young audience. In addition to the child protagonist, there is a strong trope of
the predicament of the 'outsider', which can also engage an audience's empathy. Ugly
is very strongly an outsider to his companions, and Matilda is an outsider within her
own family who consider her intelligence, enquiring mind, and lack of interest in television unacceptable. While we only see Charlie within his loving family environment,
there is an implication that the whole Bucket family is on the outside of society due to

their financial hardship. This is an element which is strong in the source material for *Charlie and the Chocolate Factory* and *Matilda* as discussed by John Grigsby: 'In his best stories Dahl presents skillfully composed plots that convey powerful insights into the frequently negative depths of the human psyche. His stories often satirize the conventional norms, institutions, and hierarchies of society from the point of view of [. . .] "an outsider".[35]

Similarly fundamental to the family show is the child protagonist's relationship with a parental or adult figure. The dual-protagonist situation combining an adult character and a child character furthers a shared spectatorship experience between adult and child, reflecting the joining of forces of the child and adult characters onstage. Crucially, the onstage relationship is often two-way in terms of the idea of the action being a psychological journey and personal development: Miss Honey supports Matilda and Matilda helps her to be courageous (see Figure 26.1), Grandpa Joe supports Charlie's imagination and inventing, and Charlie gives him the will to get out of bed and continue to live. Again, the nurturing of imagination seems to be an important source for the power and drive of each character.

FIGURE 26.1 Adult and child joining forces: Adrianna Bertola (Matilda) and Lauren Ward (Miss Honey) in *Matilda—the Musical*, Courtyard Theatre, Stratford-upon-Avon, 2010.

Photograph by Nigel Norrington. Courtesy of ArenaPal.

TRANSCENDENCE

We have seen that the imagination is perhaps a primary ingredient of the family musi-cal. David Wood suggests that magic is also important: 'Achieving the impossible by magic is intrinsically theatrical. It follows that a story with magic as part of the plot can make good children's theatre.'[36] It is a well-established trope in fairy tale and children's literature that the use of imagination may enable protagonists to unlock ability, power, self-belief, courage, and limitless possibilities of life-affirming action. These are all often substantiated in 'magic'. Both imagination and magic can perhaps be seen as symbolic of various kinds of 'transcendence'. *Charlie and the Chocolate Factory*'s 'Pure Imagination' encapsulates in its lyrics three potential levels between imagining and transcend-ence: first the imagination is ignited ('Come with me | And you'll be | In a world of pure imagination'); secondly, this can lead to the power of doing good or improving life and the world ('Want to change the world? There's nothing to it'); and thirdly, by living in this way you can transcend earthly ways ('Living there you'll be free | If you truly wish to be').[37] The manifestation of what is seemingly fantasy and magic in the factory is finally revealed as having a nucleus in the Imagining Room, a completely empty room which allows the mind's imagination to be the source of everything. It is therefore this room that is the source of all possibility for Charlie which leads to the epiphany of the glass elevator breaking free from its casing and soaring into the sky. *Matilda* makes significant use of the child's gift for storytelling and seems to elevate its importance above that of her magical abilities. This is perhaps indicative of the fact that Matilda's magical power comes from her anger and frustration, whereas the power unleashed by her storytelling which enables her and Miss Honey to find the confidence to take charge of their own destiny, comes more strongly from the imagination.

Another trope of transcendence is the idea of a fantastical location, or of journeying to 'other' places, perhaps metaphorically of being lifted up by such journeys. The outings of Mary Poppins, which become fantastical adventures, can be seen as such transpor-tation. The idea of transcendence on a smaller-scale, everyday level is shown through the adventure in the park in the 'Jolly Holiday' sequence. While in P. L. Travers's book and also in Disney's musical film version, this adventure involves a transportation via chalk paintings into another world, a similar effect of transportation and elevation of the spirits is brought about in the stage version. The change from dull monochrome tones to glorious colour and the bringing to life of the statues in the theatre adaptation both achieve such an elevation and prove that this can be found in the most ordinary of locations, such as the park. In this way *Mary Poppins* conveys the optimistic idea that transcendence can occur in ordinary life, again through the power of imagination (see Figure 26.2).

These everyday occurrences become more and more frequent in the stage musical as the show progresses, with the 'Step in Time' sequence being of particular importance for the theme of transcendence. According to Stiles and Drewe there is a recurring motif

FIGURE 26.2 The family reunited by the transcendent force of imagination: (clockwise from top left) David Haig (George Banks), Linzi Hately (Winifred Banks), Charlotte Spencer (Jane Banks) and Harry Stott (Michael Banks) in *Mary Poppins* at the Prince Edward Theatre, 2004.

Photograph by Marilyn Kingwill. Courtesy of ArenaPal.

in *Mary Poppins* of being up in the air: 'P. L. Travers had a huge belief in there being a higher level as she referred to it.'[38] The metaphor of being up on the roof already includes the notion of an elevated position. The stage version of 'Step in Time' involves a seemingly gravity-defying moment of Bert climbing and dancing along the proscenium arch, and hanging upside down from its apex. As George Stiles explains, in *Mary Poppins* there is a suggestion that 'chimney sweeps are like guardian angels looking over children wherever there's a chimney pot'.[39] By this point in the show, Mary's ability to enable others to transcend has literally reached the sky. By the end of the musical this level of elevation has truly attained a cosmic significance through the celestial visual imagery and lyrics in 'Anything Can Happen'. Mary's work is done, having led the Banks family and the audience to a comprehension of celestial transcendence by way of an experience of transcendence in the everyday.

For Charlie Bucket, the chocolate factory represents an 'other' world, somewhere magical, because although it is a working factory, nobody ever goes in or out. It is a place where inventions can become reality and fantasy can become actuality. For the Charlie of Act 1, the factory represents the ability to transcend his family's impoverished existence and to discover the place where his imaginings can become truth. Crucially, for

Charlie, his ability to transcend the everyday is already established in the opening number 'Almost Nearly Perfect' highlighted by such lyrics as 'Your trash is my treasure'[40] which show his ability to find good in, and a use for, other people's rubbish; the outwardly useless is given worth and substance in Charlie's mind. The point when Charlie loses his ability to imagine and stops drawing and inventing, when—in other words—he stops believing in the ability to transcend, is a nadir for the whole family in Act 1. This manifests itself in 'If Your Mother/Father Were Here' in which Charlie's parents' lack of time together and their despair at not knowing what to do for their son is highlighted. Physical elevation in *Charlie and the Chocolate Factory* is brought about by the symbolic escaping of the glass elevator. However, similarly to *Mary Poppins*, the true transcendence is achieved by the fusion of everyday life with Charlie's family at the end of the musical living permanently in the location which symbolized transcendence for Charlie. The factory holds this symbolism because it gives him the ability to make his imaginings reality. Graham suggests that transcendence is one of the key factors for children's theatre, and the examples analysed above suggest the same is true for the family market. It is often in the moments of numinous experience in these musicals that the underlying theme is fully explored, therefore turning such sublime events into key moments in the show.

PERSPECTIVE

Tony Graham's fifth and final criteria for children's theatre is that of the child's perspective. It has already been discussed that the youth of the particular protagonists of the shows in question enables a child to readily engage with their stories purely from the perspective of identification through age. It has also been pointed out that the dual-protagonist relationships of a child and their counterpart adult protagonist widens this perspective for the family market as opposed to the children's market. Moreover it has been shown that the themes of the shows are often explored from multiple perspectives so that they can be interpreted differently by different generations in the audience. However, there is a further major consideration here and that can be found in the implications of the word 'perspective', i.e. in the consideration of whose perspective the events of the story are ultimately told *through*. It would seem, again, that the important factor here for family theatre as opposed to that aimed solely at engaging children, is that it offers more than one perspective. As may be expected, much of the unfolding of the story is seen from a child's perspective: it is Charlie who we follow from searching through the rubbish heap, encountering the 'old man', running home, watching the TV broadcasts of the golden tickets, through to entering the factory. For much of *Mary Poppins* we encounter the daily life of Jane and Michael, and after Mary Poppins's arrival there are some incidents such as the aforementioned nursery sequence with the toys where Mary is not present and we are aware of seeing events unfold from the children's perspective. In *Matilda*, there is a great emphasis on the children's point of view, of course seeing events through Matilda's eyes, but also through those of the other children as manifested in some of the production numbers such as 'Miracle', 'School Song', and 'When I Grow Up'. The last of these, particularly given its place in the show and its status as one of the anthemic, almost lyrical numbers in the musical, firmly roots the show as a consideration of the world through a child's eyes—wondering about the future and all it could be when grown up. For adults, 'When I Grow Up' also creates nostalgia, as it reminds you of your own dreams of what being a grown-up would be like when you were a child.

There are many instances in all of the shows being considered when the perspective of the adult characters is given as much room as the child's. The aforementioned 'Being Mrs. Banks' from *Mary Poppins*, and 'If Your Mother/Father Were Here' from *Charlie and the Chocolate Factory* are examples of this, as is 'Every Tear A Mother Cries' from *Honk!* in which Ida's grief as a mother is every bit as three-dimensional as Ugly's pain at being 'Different'. One further aspect to the idea of the family musical employing multiple perspectives, only one of which being the child's, lies in the importance of whose 'world vision' it is which ultimately wins out. Again, this comes back to the concept of the underlying universal theme with cross-generational appeal being perhaps the strongest key to the family musical's attractiveness. In *Honk!*, the championing of being different is a stance of both Ugly and his mother. In *Matilda*, it is the eponymous heroine's fight for freedom which wins out, with Matilda encouraging Miss Honey to share her vision. From the start, Charlie shares Willy Wonka's belief in the world-changing power of imagination and when they finally meet, the child and his adult counterpart at last find their kindred spirit. In *Mary Poppins* it is Mary's world view which is prevalent and one which she gradually manages to impart to both generations of the Banks family. In all of these shows, the prevalent world vision is one that is *shared* cross-generationally. There are differences in terms of the direction in which the influence travels—in *Matilda* it is largely from child to adult, while in *Mary Poppins* it is from adult to child, and also from adult to adult. In *Charlie* the world vision is equally shared between child and adult but Wonka and Charlie only gradually come to realize this. Despite these differences in the direction of influence, the resulting effect is of multiple generations being able to share a positive world view—an experience which may easily be shared by the several generations which make up a family audience.

In *Theatre for Young Audiences*, Nellie McCaslin discusses the shared experience between generations in theatre-going and proposes that in being with a child who is experiencing something for the first time, the older generation also experiences it as if for the first time: 'One of the most wonderful things you can do for your own child is to invite him to discover with you every new thing [...], every significant life experience.'[41] She goes on to point out that 'the opportunities for such a communion among the human family are far more rare today than they used to be ... I believe that one means of restoring this broken community exists—potentially at least—in theatre.'[42] Although McCaslin was writing more than thirty-five years ago, her evaluation seems to be just as relevant to the present day. There are two important thoughts here: one is the idea of communion between adult and child in the experience of theatre-going and in the shared experience of the event together; the second is that for the adult the experience is also enhanced by drawing on embedded sensations of discovery from their own childhood:

> What is mutually appealing to this heterogenous gathering? I believe that the things of childhood stay with us. Somehow it seems to me that if we think children's theatre is a good thing for our children—and indeed for us—it's because we think it will have something to do with those sensations and perceptions and feelings and involvements of our collective childhoods.[43]

The idea of collective experience is pertinent here; the source material for each of the musicals in questions is widely familiar to adults and children and thus constitutes a common experience across the generations. The stories of 'The Ugly Duckling', *Charlie and the Chocolate Factory*, *Matilda*, and *Mary Poppins* are known to the majority of the adult audience from their own childhoods and in various retellings, from the original stories to classic films. Indeed in the case of *Mary Poppins* and *Charlie and the Chocolate Factory* some of the songs themselves are part of this shared experience and collective memory ('Pure Imagination' in *Charlie and the Chocolate Factory* being from the 1971 Gene Wilder film version *Willie Wonka and the Chocolate Factory*, and approximately half of the *Mary Poppins* stage score being reworked from the 1964 Disney film). The adult is able to rediscover their own associations from childhood in addition to exploring the stage version alongside their own children or grandchildren. All of the family musicals that have been discussed here involve the element of a juvenile character discovering the world for the first time alongside an adult character discovering it anew with them: Matilda alongside Miss Honey, Michael and Jane alongside Mary Poppins and Bert, Charlie alongside Grandpa Joe, Ugly alongside his mother. In each case the child discovers something afresh which then also teaches the adult; it is not just a simple case of the juvenile character learning what the adult already knows. The mixed audience of a child who is experiencing the elements of theatre and the story of the show for the first time, alongside their adult companion brings about a sense of communion through shared discovery, which is also reflected in the show itself. To return to McCaslin's thoughts,

> I would like to think of [theatre] as a place in the community where all these profound and mysterious things that children know are affirmed and rejoiced over instead of denied or made to seem of little worth. And I would like to think of it as that place in the community where, for older people, these sensations, remembrances, vague associations, and deeply felt emotions—which have never died—can be returned to. Referred to. Shared. In a communion which brings children and adults together and makes them one.[44]

There is an implication here that the fundamental appeal in the family musical for the adult is one of nostalgia for childhood and that it caters to the 'inner child' in the adult.

This is reflected in the questioning lyrics of *Just So*: '[T]he child inside won't have to take another knock or a fall | Makes me wonder if anyone ever really grows up at all.'[45] Or as *Time Out* commented in October 2012 with reference to *Matilda*: 'For kids, yes, but also for the children that we all remain at heart.'[46] However, there would seem to be something even more fundamental to the appeal of the family musical across generations, and that is in the shared experience of a profoundly universal theme. As discussed earlier, while there is a plane on which themes are explored in each of the shows from a child's perspective and concurrently from the adult's perspective, what binds them together is usually a theme that strikes right at the heart of the human condition. At such a level, age ceases to be important, and the theme is appreciated from whatever perspective each individual person has. As Anthony Drewe remarks, 'People say "who's it for" and I say "it's for anyone who likes going to the theatre".'[47] In addition, the family musical is often profoundly uplifting and its fundamental elements of song and dance only enhance this. Far from being frivolous, songs such as 'Let's Go Fly A Kite', 'Anything Can Happen', 'Pure Imagination', and 'Warts and All', are life-affirming celebrations of fundamental themes of love, acceptance, and transcendence which are endemic to the human experience irrespective of age.

Notes

1. Garry Lyons, 'The Generation Game: The Rise of the Large-Scale Family "Epic" and Its Role within Publicly Funded Theatre in Britain', *Studies in Theatre & Performance* 33, no. 3 (2013): 349.
2. Jeremy Treglown, 'Introduction', in Roald Dahl, *Collected Stories* (New York: Knopf, 2006), xvi.
3. Quoted in James Reynolds, 'Theatre for Young Audiences at London's National Theatre', in *Theatre for Young Audiences: A Critical Handbook*, ed. Tom Maguire and Karian Schuitema (London: Institute of Education Press, 2012), 40.
4. '*Honk!* to *Mary Poppins*: Stiles and Drewe Interview', *Musical Talk*, online podcast, no. 0033, 2007, http://podbay.fm/show/190005618/e/1180555320, accessed 24 August 2014.
5. Lyons, 'Generation Game', 357.
6. Quoted in Matthew Reason, *The Young Audience: Exploring and Enhancing Children's Experiences of Theatre* (London: Institute of Education Press, 2010), 31.
7. Quoted in Reason, *Young Audience*, 32.
8. Richard Andrews, *Writing a Musical* (London: Robert Hale Ltd, 1997), 92.
9. Anthony Drewe and George Stiles, *Vocal Selections from 'Honk!'* (London: The Music Trunk Publishing Co. Ltd, 1997), 100.
10. Anthony Drewe et al., *Mary Poppins*, vocal selections (Burbank, CA: Wonderland Music Company Inc., 2005), 25.
11. '*Honk!* to *Mary Poppins*.'
12. Drewe and Stiles, *Vocal Selections from 'Honk!'*, 51.
13. Drewe and Stiles, *Vocal Selections from 'Honk!'*, 63.
14. Drewe and Stiles, *Vocal Selections from 'Honk!'*, 115.

15. See Stephen Banfield, *Sondheim's Broadway Musicals* (Ann Arbor: University of Michigan Press, 1995).

16. David Spencer, *The Musical Theatre Writer's Survival Guide* (Portsmouth: Heinemann, 2005), 68.

17. Aaron Frankel, *Writing the Broadway Musical* (Boston: Da Capo Press, 2000), 118.

18. Julian Woolford, *How Musicals Work* (London: Nick Hern Books, 2012).

19. Quoted in Lehman Engel, *Words with Music: Creating the Broadway Musical Libretto*, updated and revised by Howard Kissel (New York: Applause Theatre & Cinema Books, 2006), 37.

20. Engel states: 'The evocation of feeling seems to be a many-sided thing.' Engel, *Words with Music*, 78.

21. Engel, *Words with Music*, 78.

22. David Wood, *Theatre for Children* (London: Faber and Faber, 1997), 30–37.

23. 'Honk! to Mary Poppins.'

24. Lyn Gardner, 'Honk! The Ugly Duckling Musical', *The Guardian*, online, 2009, http://www.theguardian.com/stage/2009/dec/13/honk-review, accessed 30 August 2014. Gardner suggests that some of the meanings which might be taken from the musical include a 'straightforward farmyard fairytale, a gay coming-out story or a tale of fierce mother love and sibling rivalry'.

25. Tim Minchin, *Matilda the Musical*, vocal selections (London: Wise Publications, 2012), 35.

26. Minchin, *Matilda the Musical*, 53.

27. Shifra Schonmann, *Theatre as a Medium for Children and Young People* (New York: Springer, 2006), 19.

28. Drewe et al., *Mary Poppins*.

29. Lyn Gardner, 'Matilda Review', *The Guardian*, online, 2011, http://www.theguardian.com/stage/2011/nov/25/matilda-review, accessed 30 August 2014.

30. Woolford, *How Musicals Work*, 74.

31. Quoted in Eleanor Turney, 'Dennis Kelly: Writing *Matilda*', online, 2012, www.ideastap.com/ideasmag/the-knowledge/dennis-kelly-interview, accessed 30 August 2014.

32. Quoted in Schonmann, *Theatre as a Medium for Children and Young People*, 61.

33. Engel, *Words with Music*, 79.

34. Minchin, *Matilda the Musical*, 34.

35. John L. Grigsby, 'Roald Dahl', in *British Short-Fiction Writers, 1945–1980*, ed. Dean Baldwin, Dictionary of Literary Biography 139 (Detroit: Gale, 1994), 43.

36. David Wood, *Theatre for Children* (London: Faber and Faber, 1997), 51.

37. Anthony Newley and Leslie Bricusse, 'Pure Imagination', in *Charlie and the Chocolate Factory*, Theatre Royal Drury Lane, April 2014.

38. 'Honk! to Mary Poppins.'

39. 'Honk! to Mary Poppins.'

40. Marc Shaiman, Scott Wittman, and David Greig, *Charlie and the Chocolate Factory*, Theatre Royal Drury Lane, April 2014.

41. Nellie McCaslin, *Theatre for Young Audiences* (New York: Longman Inc., 1978), 80.

42. McCaslin, *Theatre for Young Audiences*, 80.

43. McCaslin, *Theatre for Young Audiences*, 81.

44. McCaslin, *Theatre for Young Audiences*, 81.

45. Drewe and Stiles, *Vocal Selections from 'Honk!'*.

46. *Time Out*, online, 2012, http://www.timeout.com/london/theatre/matilda-the-musical, accessed 30 August 2014.
47. '*Honk!* to *Mary Poppins*.'

BIBLIOGRAPHY

Andrews, Richard. *Writing a Musical*. London: Robert Hale Ltd, 1997.

Drewe, Anthony, and George Stiles. *Vocal Selections from 'Honk!'*. London: The Music Trunk Publishing Co. Ltd, 1997.

Drewe, Anthony, Richard Sherman, Robert Sherman, and George Stiles. *Mary Poppins*. Vocal Selections. Burbank, CA: Wonderland Music Company Inc, 2005.

Engel, Lehman. *Words with Music: Creating the Broadway Musical Libretto*. Updated and revised by Howard Kissel. New York: Applause Theatre & Cinema Books, 2006.

Frankel, Aaron. *Writing the Broadway Musical*. Boston: Da Capo Press, 2000.

Grigsby, John L. 'Roald Dahl.' In *British Short-Fiction Writers, 1945–1980*, edited by Dean Baldwin, 40–8. Dictionary of Literary Biography 139. Detroit: Gale, 1994.

'*Honk!* to *Mary Poppins*: Stiles and Drewe Interview.' *Musical Talk*. Online podcast, no. 0033, 2007. http://podbay.fm/show/190005618/e/1180555320.

Lyons, Garry. 'The Generation Game: The Rise of the Large-Scale Family "Epic" and Its Role within Publicly Funded Theatre in Britain.' *Studies in Theatre & Performance* 33, no. 3 (2013): 347–363.

McCaslin, Nellie. *Theatre for Young Audiences*. New York: Longman Inc., 1978.

Minchin, Tim. *Matilda the Musical*. Vocal selections. London: Wise Publications, 2012.

Reason, Matthew. *The Young Audience: Exploring and Enhancing Children's Experiences of Theatre*. London: Institute of Education Press, 2010.

Reynolds, James. 'Theatre for Young Audiences at London's National Theatre.' In *Theatre for Young Audiences: A Critical Handbook*, edited by Tom Maguire and Karian Schuitema, 35–46. London: Institute of Education Press, 2012.

Schonmann, Shifra. *Theatre as a Medium for Children and Young People*. New York: Springer, 2006.

Spencer, David. *The Musical Theatre Writer's Survival Guide*. Portsmouth: Heinemann, 2005.

Treglown, Jeremy. 'Introduction.' In Roald Dahl, *Collected Stories*, ix–xxi. New York: Knopf, 2006.

Turney, Eleanor. 'Dennis Kelly: Writing *Matilda*.' www.ideastap.com/ideasmag/the-knowledge/dennis-kelly-interview, accessed 30 August 2014.

Wood, David. *Theatre for Children*. London: Faber and Faber, 1997.

Woolford, Julian. *How Musicals Work*. London: Nick Hern Books, 2012.

....

CHAPTER 27

GENRE COUNTERPOINTS

Challenges to the Mainstream Musical

....

DAVID ROESNER

INTRODUCTION

....

SEEN from a distance (which is still the chosen or preferred perspective of most scholars in musicology, theatre or performance studies, or cultural studies), the mainstream musical[1] is often regarded as a particularly coherent and consistent group of works and performances. This is certainly partly a consequence of the aesthetic and promotional strategies of its producing industry, which place consistency of experience, recognizability of its brands, stars, and aesthetics at the centre of what it promises. Nonetheless, the mainstream musical as an art form is always on the lookout for new material (more often adaptations than original stories, though), new vehicles for stars, new spectacle, but it is not necessarily known for pushing its boundaries with respect to its genres—some exceptions excluded. Whilst the discourse in the main academic disciplines which *should* be interested in the musical (musicology, music theatre studies, and theatre studies) has recently been dominated by investigations into their respective core subjects, questioning the ontologies of theatre and music and their accepted boundaries, the discourse on musicals has—at least in my view—been much less concerned with these questions.

One plausible reason for this might be found by looking at the respective artistic landscapes, which in the case of, for example, contemporary European theatre or art music show high degrees of blurred boundaries, self-referential theatricality, bridges and fusions between art and life, and other interart tendencies,[2] all of which have challenged the epistemological and methodological paradigms of their disciplines, in contrast to the presumed absence of these tendencies in 'the musical' here and across the pond.

In this chapter I aim to question this assumption by analysing three striking examples of the British musical. Although all of them were successful in terms of both critical acclaim and audience attendance within their original subsidized theatre context, each individually rubs against and challenges some of the core traditional expectations we associate with 'the musical' and does so in different ways and to different effect. I will explore the aesthetic, performative, and dramaturgical strategies with which these musicals as performances exploit precisely the boundaries and genre conventions as sites of creating friction, meaning, and also pleasure—thus adding to the more established modes of conveying narrative sense and emotional coherence, which still act as hallmark qualities for the repertoire of successful musicals.

My case studies form exceptions to the rulebooks of 'How to write/stage/perform a musical' in that they are instances where 'the musical' interrogates, parodies, and subverts its own status. I will explore them with particular reference to 'genre'—which as a theoretical framework allows me to take into account both 'qualities of artworks and qualities of experiences,'[3] or in other words characteristics of the works and their performances *in relation to* a horizon of expectation on the part of the audience, 'sanctioned by convention,' as Jim Samson puts it:[4]

> A genre title is integral to an artwork and partly conditions our response to its stylistic and formal content, but it does not create a genre nor will a taxonomy of shared characteristics of itself define a genre. It is the interaction of title and content that creates generic meaning. Clearly, within this interaction, the content may subvert the expectations created by the title, but can do so only where a sufficient correspondence of title and content has been established in the first place.[5]

I will argue that some current British musicals use this 'interaction of title and content', this interplay between genre expectations and actual mise en scène to innovate, disrupt, and entertain.[6]

Genre as a Framework

While genre has declined as an epistemological tool to help make, describe, analyse, or sell Western 'classical' music or contemporary theatre in the twentieth century,[7] it is, I would argue, still an important factor and useful analytical instrument when looking at popular forms such as the musical. Genre has always been strongly underpinned by economic interests (of both producers and consumers) and the British musical is no different to its relatives in North America or continental Europe when it comes to placing commercial considerations centre stage.

With regard to film, where genre theory has been adumbrated with particular coherence, Rick Altman notes that by 'assaying and imitating the money-making qualities of their most lucrative films, studios seek to initiate film cycles that will provide successful, easily exploitable models'.[8] He emphasizes (as do many other authors[9]) the cyclical and constantly evolving nature of the process by which consensus over the identity of a genre emerges: this is 'a never-ceasing process, closely tied to the capitalist need for product differentiation'.[10]

Genre is thus characterized as an ever-changing *process* rather than an agreed set of criteria. The eminent scholar of film genre Stephen Neale argues that 'the repertoire of generic conventions available at any one point in time is always *in* play rather than simply being *re*-played'.[11] *In* play are thus 'instances of repetition and difference',[12] which have 'firstly to be understood in their relationship to desire, pleasure and *jouissance*, i.e. as modalities of the process of the subject'.[13] It is also important to note that difference and repetition, however, do not form a dichotomy, but instead 'function as a relation [...]. There is hence not repetition *and* difference, but repetition *in* difference.'[14] This relation strongly guides an audience's expectations, which refers not only to the film (or in our case: the musical) itself, but also to its paratexts, metadiscourses, and 'packaging': from the paper quality of the ticket stub to the cast list, from the available refreshments in the foyer to the design of the musical's logo, there are endless conscious and unconscious triggers and expectations all of which have in common that they form a 'double layer', as Neale calls it: 'As far as genre is concerned, expectations exist both to be satisfied, and also, to be redefined.'[15]

I should be clear about how I position the challenges to the genre, how I gauge their experimental and innovative impact; it is after all quite a relative judgement—today's experiment may well be tomorrow's mainstream. I was reminded of this when reading Bud Coleman's 2008 account of 'new horizons' for the musical[16] and the list of musicals and subgenres he suggests were breaking the mould:

> With the New York premieres of Stephen Sondheim's *Company* (1970), Andrew Lloyd Webber's *Jesus Christ Superstar* (1971), Michael Bennett's *A Chorus Line* (1975), and John Kander, Fred Ebb and Bob Fosse's *Chicago* (1975), several new artists found audiences for their disparate visions of what a musical could be, sing and/or dance about. Experimentation continued as the concept musical, the jukebox musical, the revisal, the dansical and the megamusical came to be.[17]

The differentiation I would make here is that while all these examples and forms certainly introduced innovation to the genre, none of them fundamentally questioned its genre affiliation; the framework of the musical remains intact and they actually all quite happily (sometimes even calculatingly) initiated other cycles of 'regular novelties', as Peter Stanfield calls them.[18]

In contrast to and against this theoretical backdrop, I will now investigate three particularly noteworthy examples of British musicals, which do twist and bend the frame provided by their generic (self-)attribution substantially. I will do so chronologically, but without suggesting a linear development from one to the other. The productions in question are *Shockheaded Peter*, by Phelim McDermott and Julian Crouch, first seen at the West Yorkshire Playhouse in Leeds in 1998; *Jerry Springer: The Opera* by Richard Thomas and Stewart Lee[19], which premiered at the National Theatre, London in 2003; and *London Road* by Alecky Blythe and Adam Cork, also first produced at the National Theatre, London in 2011. It should be said from the outset that none of these three was branded as a 'musical': *Shockheaded Peter* was subtitled 'a junk opera', *Jerry Springer:*

The Opera supposedly carries its categorization in its title, while *London Road* refrained from indicating any generic affiliation altogether. However, Wikipedia, for example, seems to have had no reservations about labelling all three as 'musicals'.[20]

SHOCKHEADED PETER

Shockheaded Peter[21] is playfully subverting 'genre' in a number of ways. This starts already at the level of its conception: while being the brainchild of a single individual, the producer Michael Morris—who thought it might be interesting to combine a controversial children's book, Heinrich Hoffmann's *Struwwelpeter* from 1845, with its dark, even sadistic moral tales with the English cult band The Tiger Lillies—it became an unusually multi-authored affair. The original production credits *all* the actors and musicians as co-authors, twelve altogether including the two directors McDermott and Crouch. McDermott mentions this as one of the show's 'greatest achievement[s]': '[I]t's in the West End, and yet you can't really say who wrote it'.[22] Most musicals are of course multi-authored, but the extent to which this production challenges the conventional divisions of labour remains noteworthy.

This is reflected in its dramaturgy and form: the show lacks an overarching narrative, but instead offers episodic vignettes all of which—even more radically than the book—end with the death of the misbehaving child in question. While not all musicals have happy endings, this proliferation of narrative misery is certainly unique: 'There is no resolution. This is not a play for children but a play to prick the conscience of adults'.[23]

Furthermore, *Shockheaded Peter* makes some unusual choices in terms of its dramatic delivery: it offers multiple literal and metaphorical 'framing' devices. Visually this is delivered through the 'frame of the Victorian toy theatre',[24] a stage upon the stage, which offers multiple windows, portholes, hatches, and doors, some even embedded in or above the secondary proscenium arch, through which characters and musicians appear, perform, and disappear. The theatre, it seems, is a porous affair with performance 'leaking' out of it, rather than being contained and presented by it.

The music, which I will discuss in more detail later, is *dramaturgically* unconventional in that it is both diegetic and non-diegetic at the same time: the lead (and only) singer, Martyn Jacques and the Master of Ceremonies, Julian Bleach (see Figure 27.1) as the *two* narrators of the show consciously use, produce, and refer to the music as part of the theatrical action, while the characters and puppets depicted in the dramatic scenes are not aware of it. The age-old question of how to justify why characters *sing* in musicals is solved here very directly: the characters simply don't sing with the exception of a singing narrator who feeds off well-established traditions of this kind of delivery, such as the troubadour, the ballad-monger, the vaudeville performer, the minstrel, or the *Moritatensänger* (itinerant balladeer). The *Moritatensänger* used to deliver a *cantastoria* (Italian) or *Moritat* (German) 'where a performer tells or sings a story while gesturing

FIGURE 27.1 Gothic and grotesque: Julian Bleach in *Shockheaded Peter*, Albery Theatre, 2002.

Photograph by Pete Jones. Courtesy of ArenaPal.

to a series of images'[25]—often depicting a tragic or gruesome event. But neither the seamless interweaving of singing and acting, music and images that the framework of the musical leads us to expect nor their clear separation that the *Moritat* tradition suggests are upheld. The three-piece band is very mobile and far from restricted to an orchestra pit or the side of the stage. They are very much part of the play that frames the play within, walking in and out of scenes and interfering quite directly in the performance.[26] Music, narration, characterization, and visualization don't remain distinct, as they would in a *Moritat* or murder ballad.[27] They witness, narrate, underscore, and comment, and are at the same time an integral part of the metafictional device of the bumbling actor and inept master of ceremonies who pulls the strings.

This leads us to the performative style, which is characterized, I would argue, by an unusual degree of ambiguity paired with an exceptionally overt theatricality, both somewhat at odds with the generic frame.

At the centre of the show (and at the heart of its creation process) is the band The Tiger Lillies, who bring not only their already unusual musical idiom to the show, but also their well-established 'musical personae',[28] which combine British eccentricity with grotesque, clownesque, and Gothic elements of make-up; costume elements that seem to be a hotchpotch of the colonial Victorian Empire with an air of the uncanny.

All of this leaves a strong mark on the overall aesthetics of the show significantly and blurs the lines between their roles as accompanying musicians, semi-fictional characters, and star personae. What adds significantly to the uncanny ambiguity is singer Martyn Jacques's use of his falsetto voice. In stark contrast to conventional musical theatre singing, which seeks to combine beauty of tone, agility, virtuosity, and characterization but is in most cases contained within the realms of professional and popular style of delivery, Jacques's voice is excessive, disturbing, at times piercingly uncomfortable while at others eerily sweet. It is shriekingly cruel, both uncanny and funny:

> Appalling as Martyn's lyrics can be, the tender simplicity of the melodies and his disembodied falsetto singing give the songs a haunted longing quality. Listeners are kept off kilter—they don't know whether to laugh or cry.[29]

At times this ambiguity in tone and delivery tips over into transgressiveness (which is also a strong feature of *Jerry Springer: The Opera* as we will see): *Shockheaded Peter* takes the dark moral tales of Hoffmann with their 'poisonous pedagogy'[30] into the realm of horror and sadism and does not offer closure or absolution to the viewer. This makes for a 'perverse delight'[31] as Jack Zipes calls it. The musical is not ordinarily a place for the kind of confrontation that *Shockheaded Peter* provides and which pushes the boundaries not just with regard to subject matter, but also with regard to the equivocal stance of its treatment.

Musically, there is further stylistic ambiguity due to the high levels of intertextuality (or better: intermusicality) and pastiche. In a genre, which normally fetishizes the singular star composer (from Richard Rodgers to Stephen Schwartz, from Andrew Lloyd Webber to Stephen Sondheim), the music by The Tiger Lillies is deliberately and self-consciously eclectic: harmonies, melodies, orchestration, and delivery make strong references to Weimar cabaret, English music hall, freak show and circus, Gypsy music, French chanson, and a good dollop of Bertolt Brecht and Kurt Weill.[32]

The Tiger Lillies' bass player Adrian Stout describes the effect as follows:

> Martyn's music . . . uh . . . It's nice, simple, very simple, but it can do a lot of things. It can be emotional and then very crass, and it can be very profane and then very sacred. You know, it can be things at the same time, it can be very sort of moving and very funny, but it is usually 'very something'. Hopefully it is never very comfortable and hopefully it's not just pedestrian, hopefully it is something different and unlike anything people have heard.[33]

It is part of the phenomenon of The Tiger Lillies and this theatrical production that it is on the one hand utterly unique and unlike anything one will have heard or seen and on the other hand completely familiar as it evokes such a range of popular styles and idioms.

There is a final major departure from genre expectations, particularly with respect to those musicals which are characterized by an escapist tendency of creating self-contained, fantastical worlds: *Shockheaded Peter* instead is characterized by a sustained self-referential use of mise en abîme. It constantly plays with and exposes various frames as proscenium arches and theatrical conventions: It treats theatrical devices such as stage design or puppetry in a deliberately artless and tongue-in-cheek fashion making no attempts to try to disguise their mechanics and manufacturedness. In the 'Silly Little Bully Boys' scene, for example, there are marionettes which at some point visibly have their strings cut to signify their death in the storyline. The show continuously exposes itself as 'just theatre':

> The macabre impact of these tales is consistently sabotaged by the manner of their telling. The evening's M.C. [...], while looking like a Victorian variation on the Nosferatu, is a bumbler—a self-important ham actor plagued by clumsy timing and reduced to railing at an audience that refuses to take him seriously.[34]

Given that in the mainstream discourse about the musical (in audience forums and fan sites, for example) tropes of 'believability',[35] 'immersion', and being 'overwhelmed' still feature strongly, this 'junk opera' is deliberately anti-illusionist, anti-immersive, anti-escapist, and anti-virtuosic.

Almost none of this can be said about my next example, *Jerry Springer: The Opera*, which is slick, polished, virtuoso, and in some ways utterly escapist (following in the footsteps of its daytime TV source material).

Jerry Springer: The Opera

Jerry Springer[36] defies genre conventions in a number of ways that are not incidental but central for its success and significance as a piece pushing at the boundaries of what we might consider the contemporary British musical.

In contrast to other musicals, it didn't even set out to be one, initially: the show developed out of an interest by its composer Richard Thomas in absurd short operatic sketches which attracted comedian Stewart Lee to join him in the idea to write an opera based on the (in)famous *Jerry Springer Show*—an American TV show which has run with great success since 1991. The first results of their collaboration were presented in a short work-in-progress performance at the Battersea Arts Centre in 2001. It was thus initially contextualized firmly as an experimental fringe phenomenon, confirmed through a stint at the Edinburgh Fringe Festival in 2002, only then to be received into the ranks of high art through being adopted and developed by the National Theatre, London in 2003. Finally, it was transferred into the heart of Europe's commercial musical theatre scene, the West End, in the same year and saw two concert performances at Carnegie Hall, New York in 2008. The filmed version, which is commercially available,[37] is based on the West End version of the show which I will refer to when discussing the show's challenges to the musical genre.

The genre-defying uniqueness of *Jerry Springer: The Opera* is captured already in its title. On the one hand it enters new thematic territory by adapting a daytime trash television format.[38] In the way it does this it also undermines the tacit pact with the audience that a musical should have an entertaining feel-good factor or at least a cathartic quality: *Jerry Springer: The Opera*—while described unanimously as entertaining and evidently successful both with reviewers and at the box office—offers neither in a pure sense. The feelings of enjoyment and/or catharsis are somewhat tainted by the awareness of one's voyeuristic position and the middle-class guilt one may well experience—neither are at play when watching, say, *The Lion King. Jerry Springer: The Opera*, however, 'challenges us to confront our own complicity as spectators of ritualised humiliation.'[39]

On the other hand it works with sustained and highly transparent incongruities and juxtapositions like 'The Jerry Springer Show' (with its associations of low culture, cheap production values, mass popularity, etc.) and 'The Opera' (high culture, virtuoso performances, artistic elitism, etc.). It combines musical sophistication and lyrical intertextuality[40] with an unprecedented amount of 'bad' language and profanities and was famously accused of blasphemy causing demonstrations and threats by Christian fundamentalists.[41] It fuses a highly voyeuristic show on dysfunctional lower class relationships with biblical stories and the fight between heaven and hell.[42] It contrasts taboos with show business culminating in routines like that of the step-dancing Ku Klux Klan.

Furthermore it creates a continuous incongruity between our generic expectations and the music-dramatic form(s) it chooses and uses. Putting 'opera' in its title is of course a red herring, but much more than a quick joke.[43] I have already cited Samson's observation that genre titles are integral to artworks and shape our expectations and responses.[44] Unsurprisingly, then, the generic title in the case of *Jerry Springer: The Opera* has created some debate: Mark Swed insists that it is 'hardly an opera, but neither is it a musical. It is something new. It is a religious operetta posing as anti-opera, silly words and music working hand in hand in pseudo-sacrilege.'[45] Kevin Gustafson calls it 'a frothy mix of disparate dramatic and musical forms'[46] and offers a critical view on its generic status:

> It is in one sense appropriate to call *Jerry Springer: The Opera* an opera, a form that has long been used to indulge in spectacles of moral and emotional excess. But *Jerry Springer: The Opera* is actually more indebted to musical comedy, even pastiche, in that it derives humour as well as emotional distance from the improbable juxtaposition of serious forms (requiem, mass, oratorio) and prestige styles (baroque, classical) with exuberant vulgarity of language. *Jerry Springer The Opera* has such a wide range of influences—from Handel and Mozart to Busby Berkeley, Mel Brooks, and Andrew Lloyd Weber [sic]; from *bel canto* to Gospel and Jazz—that it is best to think of the show as opera in the etymological rather than a generic sense: a collection of diverse musical works that tells a story.[47]

While *Shockheaded Peter* amalgamated old musical and theatrical forms and idioms into a new and exceptional style, *Jerry Springer: The Opera* in contrast constantly plays with and reminds us of its hybridity,[48] two core aspects of which have been described by Jay David Bolter as 'multiplicity and fragmentation'.[49] If we focus on the use of voice, for example, it is striking how in *Shockheaded Peter* its many influences and traces seem to become united in the unique voice of Martyn Jacques, which, while multifaceted and variable, is instantly recognizable, but amounts to a provocation to our genre expectations with its genderless quality and its broken and imperfect beauty. *Jerry Springer: The Opera*, however, juxtaposes a multiplicity of voices in rapid and fragmented succession, from operatic bel canto and coloraturas (as in 'Fuck You Talk'[50]) to musical theatre *belt* (e.g. 'Talk to the Hand'[51]) to the way that actors sing in a post-Brecht/Weill fashion (part of warm-up man David Bedella's delivery of 'Ladies and Gentlemen Have Yourselves a Good Time' is in that vein, for example): favouring dramatic expression over pitch-perfect intonation or timing.

But the show also requires its performers to embrace hybridity *within* their own voices. Notably the onstage choir (the 'audience' of the depicted *Jerry Springer Show* episode), switches quickly between quite different vocal idioms, from baroque and classical tones to funky riffs and shouts. Millie Taylor suggests that

> the hybrid voice arises [. . .] in the relationships between performer and work, and as a result of the interactions of vocal technique, genre and musical language, and as such is the product of cultural knowledge alongside collaborative process.[52]

The composer and librettist make a point about continuously changing register in their writing and simultaneously cite and undermine genre classifications, thus offering a genre hybrid and a highly intertextual deconstruction by overloading it with genre signifiers, both musically and thematically/narratively. Samson plausibly points out the potential effects of this 'mixing or blending of genres', which may well

> confuse the classifier, but [. . .] greatly strengthens the commutative and programmatic potential of genre. Since genres possess certain recognisable identifying traits (genre markers), they can be counterpointed within an artwork to generate a 'play' of meanings which may, in some later style systems, extend into irony or parody[53]

There is no doubt that *Jerry Springer: The Opera* makes ample use of such humorous strategies, but it doesn't limit itself to them: at the heart of the show is after all the attempt to look at the 'otherness' of its characters, at the desires, hopes, rejections, and hurt of those who are seemingly caricatured rather than portrayed through the prism of 'opera' in order to 'create a form capable of expressing profound revelations of the human condition'.[54] By elevating the seemingly absurd and abject constellations and fetishes of a certain class of people—who are being watched by a more privileged audience as a 'guilty pleasure'—to the level of the 'operatic', by creating grandeur of emotions and complexity of the musical treatment, and by suggesting a biblical universality of its themes and conflicts, the show provokes us to think twice about pigeonholing and labelling too quickly. So amongst other things, *Jerry Springer: The Opera* uses genre to interrogate our very need for genre and the kind of unreliable certainty it provides.

LONDON ROAD

London Road[55] offers an interesting third example, as it contrasts substantially with both previous case studies in terms of its creation process, its musical and textual style, and its performance.

The project developed from an unlikely encounter between writer Alecky Blythe and composer Adam Cork during an exploratory workshop organized by the National Theatre, London aiming to bring together writer and composers 'to see whether any interesting discoveries were made by the end of it'.[56] Blythe comes from a background of verbatim theatre, which in her case means a method of conducting, recording, and editing interviews with people and then directing actors to speak these lines following the cadence, speech patterns, and their idiosyncrasies as closely as possible, often aided by having the recordings played into the actors' earpieces even during the final performances. Words like social responsibility, verisimilitude, faithfulness, community, and documentary are strongly associated with this method—all of which sit uncomfortably with most of what the musical theatre genre stands for. The choice to use the recorded interviews in order to create a musical style, which tries to 'represent the music of the speech rhythms with [. . .] forensic zeal'[57] are on the other hand a challenge to the more purist principals of verbatim theatre. Two genres with their respective 'rules', expectations, and methods of creation meet here and create a 'third stream'[58] which challenges and enriches both.

I want to analyse in more detail now how this unusual piece materializes on the stage and how employing certain performative strategies further adds to its appeal as a work that defies categorization.

In contrast to the previous two examples, *London Road* avoids any generic classification and has only been called or labelled a musical by others (for example, by winning the Critic's Circle's Award for Best Musical), but not by the makers themselves—it is also much less obviously indebted to existing genres or firm theatrical traditions but instead merely uses certain elements in pursuit of a new and original form.

The narrative premise and perspective are unusual and interesting to begin with. *London Road* captures the impact that the presence of a serial killer in Ipswich in Suffolk had on the neighbourhood he lived in. What could have been a whodunnit with a good measure of sex and gore thrown in (all victims were prostitutes and were found naked and strangled), becomes instead a kaleidoscopic view of the bystanding community: the musical shows neither the victims nor the perpetrator, but different strata of the community affected in different ways: neighbours of the killer, teenagers, other prostitutes, police officers, reporters. It focuses on the fear, the speculation, the reputation of a town, the damaging air of suspicion, etc. and avoids a clear distinction between 'goodies and baddies'; it confronts us with the moral ambiguities of the case without resolving them. Do the murdered girls deserve sympathy ('They certainly weren't [. . .] angels'[59])? Are the people of Ipswich the victims ('The biggest problem, was—is getting ye car here'[60])? While the musical genre normally relies heavily on the clear juxtaposition of antagonists and the telling of a moral tale of sorts,[61] here the moral message remains open, not least because all involved parties are problematic and flawed protagonists: they deserve our sympathies, but not necessarily our approval since they are at times annoying, ordinary, prejudiced, racist, and selfish—in other words: human.

Theatrically, we are both drawn in and kept at arm's length in Rufus Norris's original staging—the former is achieved by a striking, almost continuous use of direct address, which is motivated from the beginning by the framing device of a community hall meeting, to which we, the audience, sitting in a horseshoe formation in the relatively intimate Cottesloe (now Dorfman) stage at the National Theatre,[62] feel invited to and part of. The small musical ensemble (percussion, guitar, keyboard, and three woodwinds) is visible on a small platform at the back of the stage and thus established as a diegetic musical accompaniment. The latter manifests an almost 'epic' approach to the theatrical action (despite occasional moments of theatre magic—moments of great intensity and audiovisual imagination such as the appearance of a sky full of flower pots, shown in Figure 27.2): everything is transparently set up, transitions between the simple, often stylized settings are undertaken by the actors, no illusions or stage effects aim to dazzle the audience.

For the song/scene 'That's When It All Kicked Off',[63] for example, actors quickly create a web of police 'crime scene—do not cross' tape, which they then have to step over and under, symbolizing the intrusion and complication of navigating the blocked roads, interrogations, and press attention for the community.

The performance style is unlike the psychological naturalism of many musicals but also distinct from the abstract formalism of a Robert Wilson piece, for example. In insisting on the strictly 'verbatim' use of text—with all its grammatical flaws, half-finished sentences, and fillers—it already paradoxically creates a further element of defamiliarization: conventionally, we are used to dramatic language being more artificially 'correct' and eloquent. By setting much of the half-spoken, half-sung dialogue to music, the verbatim language is then heightened and estranged, and while the composition follows and amplifies the musicality of the individual and local idiomatic colour of the interviewees, it also occasionally violates the principles of linguistic importance or coherence by rhythmically stressing fill words or subordinate clauses ('That's When It All Kicked Off' ends with 'But uhm—'), or by repeating individual textual and musical phrases extensively (as in the same scene, in which the phrase 'And that's when it all started' is repeated and varied six times).

And finally, it challenges our genre expectations yet again, by denying us most familiar musical structures and forms and thus the element of recognizability and orientation: while a substantial part of the book is set to music, the 'numbers'—identified as 'songs' with titles in the libretto—are hardly songlike in their structure: instead of offering hummable tunes, hook-lines, refrains, verses, or bridges, the music meanders with

FIGURE 27.2 A sky full of flower pots: the inhabitants of London Road try to rebuild their community. Duncan Wisbey (Gordon) and Claire Moore (Ward Councillor Carol) in *London Road*, at the National Theatre, Cottesloe, 2011.

Photograph by Marilyn Kingwill. Courtesy of ArenaPal.

only a minimum of memorable motifs or phrases, which are repeated and offer some structural coherence.

What the piece features instead is an extensive use of layering and juxtaposition—dramaturgically, musically, and vocally. There is, for example, a continuous interweaving of the banal and the tragic: the 'London in Bloom' competition award ceremony at the community centre is intercut with memories of the terrible event that shook up the neighbourhood (Act 1, Section 1), a monologue by Mark in the section 'Shaving Scratch'[64] on the serial killer's profile is overlaid with a choral singers' rendition of 'Silent Night', and the musical setting for the reporting of the verdict is polyphonic to the point of rendering the details of the verdict almost unintelligible; instead it captures the sensationalist tone of the press, adding to the anxiety and the adrenaline of the moment in stark musical and thematic contrast, for example, to the church hall meeting of the community.

Vocally, this piece of 'choric theatre',[65] as Cork calls it, is characterized by a hybrid use of voice, which also denies us an easy pigeonholing of its genre or idiom. In contrast to *Jerry Springer: The Opera*, however, *London Road* is not a mixture and citational web of recognizable vocal styles, but an in-between that emerges from the encounter of a local dialect with a musical language that borrows from European Sprechgesang traditions (from Arnold Schönberg and Alban Berg to Kurt Weill), without adopting their often considerable degrees of artificiality, delivered by an ensemble of singing actors rather than vocal virtuosos. 'The end result', says Millie Taylor, 'is different from the musical writing in either musical theatre or contemporary opera, and the vocal delivery is equally unique.'[66]

Where *Shockheaded Peter* and *Jerry Springer: The Opera* found originality in how they nostalgically revisited traditional forms of music-theatrical performance in the former case or, in the latter, cited, sampled, and mashed up idioms and aesthetic surfaces of mainstream musical genres to create effects of contrast, surprise, and irony, *London Road* establishes a truly new quality of music-theatrical tone, structure, and delivery. Cork himself refers to it as 'an inspiring new approach to songwriting' before correcting himself modestly to calling it 'an exciting development of an existing way of composing songs.'[67] Despite the influences mentioned earlier, the musical language is very specific to the original context of the story. It is this specificity, I would argue, which makes it so remarkable, when (commercial) musical theatre is conventionally so preoccupied with finding stories and musical styles that are universally relatable and where time and location may offer colour and flavour, but are either interchangeable or have become tropes with a worldwide currency (such as 'a French revolution' in *Les Misérables* (1985), 'the Shtetl' in *Fiddler on the Roof* (1964), 'the 1950s/1960s in America' in *Grease* (1971) or *Hairspray* (2002)).

It is a musical without protagonists as such, without a tidy narrative, without a love story, and with an absence at the centre: the serial killer everyone is looking for and who lives amongst the residents of London Road. Fittingly (and also unusually), there are no individual curtain calls and bows—the choric ensemble received the (enthusiastic) applause as an ensemble of equals, which is perhaps also noteworthy in a genre and an industry that rather fetishizes the individual star.

CONCLUSION

Mainstream musicals tend to be affirmations of cultural hegemonies, to use Antonio Gramsci's term, subscribing to the core values of the dominant class and its ideologies. Even when they discuss (potentially) controversial topics (homosexuality in *Bare* (2000), state torture in *Kiss of the Spider Woman* (1992), bipolar disorder in *Next to Normal* (2008)) they tend to embed them within familiar dramaturgies, musical idioms, and performance aesthetics. In the productions discussed in this chapter, however, there is a more profound destabilization of content *and* form, as I have sought to demonstrate, which ultimately highlights the innovative and critical potential that the musical has and which, due to commercial constraints and genre conventions, remains too often unexplored. Hegemonies of an old-fashioned sense of punitive parenting and education (which at the time of writing seem to experience an eerie renaissance in British cultural policy), of the quasi-religious mass entertainment of a class-exploitative

TV programme, or of the chasm between twenty-four-hour news sensationalism and a local community striving for normality are all being interrogated by the shows analysed in this chapter—not just because they choose unlikely subject matter for British musicals, but also in the way each production plays with citations and innovations of music-theatrical form and performance.

The cultural context from within which this happens is perhaps less a uniquely *British* one, but evidently informed by a strong *European* tradition of theatre,[68] cabaret and music theatre: forms of circus, Sprechgesang, opera, music hall, epic theatre, murder ballads, and ballad operas provide readily available viewpoints from which the conventions of 'the musical' are dissected and the genre is read against its grain. In the case of *London Road* this led to a profoundly new way of exploring the relationship between theatre and music, in *Shockheaded Peter* to a particularly self-reflexive play with theatricality and modes of musical and vocal delivery, whereas for *Jerry Springer: The Opera* the fast-paced intermusical jump-cuts between well-established music-theatrical idioms and the sheer incongruity between subject, language, and music-dramatic treatment undermined any sense of affirmation.

I do not, however, suggest that these examples have a lasting destabilizing or undermining effect on our notion of 'the musical'. Instead, they function as the kind of indispensable deviations that ultimately provide a reinvigorating consolidation of the genre, as Theodor Adorno already described in his *Aesthetic Theory* (even though certainly not thinking of the musical in particular!): 'Universals such as genres [. . .] are true to the extent that they are subject to a countervailing dynamic.'[69]

The greater context, in which this needs to be seen perhaps, is one in which most forms of music-theatrical performance experience some tearing and tugging at their seams: in contemporary theatre, the form, function, and phenomenology of incidental music has changed significantly in a number of ways: we have seen what Petra Maria Meyer has coined an 'acoustic turn', i.e. an increased interest in and awareness of theatre as a sonic event;[70] we can observe a tendency towards 'liveness' of incidental music by using live musicians and/or playback technologies, which react in real time and are determined by live parameters; and we can witness increasing dissolutions between actors and musicians, theatre and concert, or theatre and radio play. In Britain alone all this is exemplified by companies such as Propeller, Sound and Fury, Shunt, Fine Chisel, and Filter.

In opera, the sacrosanct nature of the score is beginning to give way to more experimental approaches to operatic staging, including experiments with the physicality and (inter)mediality of operatic performance, all of which 'challenge the hierarchical metaphysis of music theatre', as Nicholas Till has put it.[71]

In dance and dance theatre the strict separation between the acoustic stage of the music and the visual stage of the choreography is dissolving in many performances as choreographers like Akram Khan or Sidi Larbi Cherkaoui explore new forms in their works, as is true for many choreographers and companies on the Continent (for example, Sasha Waltz, Alain Platel, and Anne Terese de Keermaekers).

And even in forms of popular entertainment that are beginning to be analysed as music-theatrical events,[72] such as music-based video games, we can observe that the complex and layered interplay between musical and performative aspects is at the heart of challenges to the genre and the medium, rendering games like *RockSmith* or *Sound Shapes* liminal phenomena between gaming, performing, and music-making.

In essence, then, what I have tried to demonstrate and argue in this chapter towards the end of a thick volume on the 'British Musical', is that the notion of what passes as 'a musical' is undergoing constant change and that while the musical as an art form retains a quite consistent core of works, conventions, and genre expectations, there are also forces at work to continuously test and challenge our habits of making and watching musicals, which in my view is highly 'Willkommen, Bienvenue, Welcome'.[73]

NOTES

1. When I speak of the mainstream musical, I do not refer to a specific, canonical group of works or artists and do not suggest such an essential definition exists, but refer to a widespread shared understanding of what 'a musical' is in common terms, even if this understanding will vary from person to person and context to context. This understanding is corroborated by a plethora of books, giving instructions and providing formulas on how to write/stage/perform in a musical (examples appear at the end of this note). In reality, the musical as an art form has proved to be rather open and inclusive and now consists of many genres (like the book musical, mega musical, meta musical, jukebox musical), which differ quite significantly from each other. It isn't quite comparable to the wealth of genres and forms that film, for example, has proliferated, but is certainly wider than the general discourse on musicals would suggest. See, for example, Aaron Frankel, *Writing the Broadway Musical* (1977; Cambridge: Da Capo Press, 2000); Ruthie Henshall and Daniel Bowling, *So You Want to Be in Musicals?* (London: Nick Hern Books, 2012); Julian Woolford, *How Musicals Work and How to Write Your Own* (London: Nick Hern Books, 2012).

2. See, for example, Christa Brüstle, *Konzert-Szenen: Bewegung, Performance, Medien; Musik zwischen performativer Expansion und medialer Integration 1950–2000* (Stuttgart: Franz Steiner Verlag, 2013); David Cecchetto et al., eds., *Collision: Interarts Practice and Research* (Newcastle upon Tyne: Cambridge Scholars Publishing, 2008); Erika Fischer-Lichte, Kristiane Hasselmann, and Markus Rautzenberg (eds.), *Ausweitung der Kunstzone: Interart Studies; Neue Perspektiven der Kunstwissenschaften* (Bielefeld: transcript, 2010); Troy Thomas, 'Interart Analogy: Practice and Theory in Comparing the Arts', *Journal of Aesthetic Education* 25, no. 2 (Summer 1991): 17–36.

3. Jim Samson, 'Genre' in *New Grove Dictionary of Music and Musicians*, 2nd ed., vol. 9, ed. Stanley Sadie (London: Macmillan, 2001), 657.

4. Samson, 'Genre', 657.

5. Samson, 'Genre', 658.

6. Please see my comments on how genre titles were avoided or subverted in the three case studies, which, I argue, did not diminish the presence of a strong sense of 'genre'.

7. Samson, 'Genre', 659.

8. Rick Altman, *Film/Genre* (London: British Film Institute, 1999), 60.

9. See, for example, Amy J. Devitt, 'Generalizing about Genre: New Conceptions of an Old Concept', *College Composition and Communication* 44, no. 4 (1993): 573–586; Stephen Neale, *Genre* (London: British Film Institute, 1980); Peter Stanfield, 'Regular Novelties: Lawrence Alloway's Film Criticism', *Tate Papers* 16 (Autumn 2011), http://www.tate.org.uk/research/publications/tate-papers/regular-novelties-lawrence-alloways-film-criticism, accessed 02 May 2014.

10. Altman, *Film/Genre*, 64.

11. Stephen Neale, *Genre and Hollywood* (London: Routledge, 2000), 219 (original emphasis).

12. Neale, *Genre*, 48.

13. Neale, *Genre*, 48.

14. Neale, *Genre*, 50.

15. Neale, *Genre*, 54.

16. Bud Coleman, 'New Horizons: The Musical at the Dawn of the Twenty-First Century', in William A. Everett and Paul R. Laird, eds., *The Cambridge Companion to the Musical* (Cambridge: Cambridge University Press, 2008), 284–302.

17. Coleman, 'New Horizons', 284.

18. Stanfield, 'Regular Novelties'.

19. While I don't suspect that the makers of *Jerry Springer: The Opera* planned for starting a trend or even new a subgenre, it should be noted that a series of musicals have since emerged which share the strong satirical vein of *Jerry Springer* such as *Spamalot* (2005), *Book of Mormon* (2011), and *I Can't Sing! The X Factor Musical* (2014).

20. See https://en.wikipedia.org/wiki/Shockheaded_Peter_(musical); https://en.wikipedia.org/wiki/Jerry_Springer%3A_The_Opera; https://en.wikipedia.org/wiki/London_Road_(musical), all accessed 21 March 2014.

21. '*Shockheaded Peter* is a 1998 musical using the popular German children's book *Der Struwwelpeter* (1845) by Heinrich Hoffmann as its basis. Created by Julian Bleach, Anthony Cairns, Julian Crouch, Graeme Gilmour, Tamzin Griffin, Jo Pocock, Phelim McDermott, Michael Morris and The Tiger Lillies (Martyn Jacques, Adrian Huge, and Adrian Stout). For further information on such topics as production history and awards see https://en.wikipedia.org/wiki/Shockheaded_Peter_(musical), I should note that *Shockheaded Peter* has since been restaged a number of times internationally by different companies (and bands)—it was very popular in Germany, for example—and that many of the specific characteristics I mention here are thus only valid for the original production.

22. Quoted in Duška Radosavljević, *The Contemporary Ensemble: Interviews with Theatre-Makers* (London: Routledge, 2013), 199. The show transferred to the West End after two successful runs at the subsidized Lyric Hammersmith.

23. Jack David Zipes, 'The Perverse Delight of *Shockheaded Peter*', *Theater* 30 no. 2 (2000): 142.

24. Zipes, 'Perverse Delight', 142.

25. https://en.wikipedia.org/wiki/Moritat#Picture_stories_in_Europe_and_the_Middle_East, accessed 25 March 2014.

26. Blurring the role descriptions between actor and musician has, it should be noted, increasingly become a stylistic device, often known as 'actor/muso': the cast then largely accompanies itself by playing a variety of instruments. This has been used to particular acclaim by Scottish director John Doyle both on Broadway (starting with Sondheim's *Sweeney Todd* (2005) and followed by *Company* (2006)) and in the West End (Stewart and Herman's *Mack and Mabel* (2006)). There is now even an 'Actor Musicianship' degree programme at Rose Bruford College, London.

27. The Tiger Lillies' latest theatre work, based on *Lulu* (West Yorkshire Playhouse, February 2014) is subtitled 'a murder ballad', clearly a format they are invested in.

28. I follow Philip Auslander's distinction here between 'the real person (the performer as human being), the performance persona (the performer's self-presentation), and the character (a figure portrayed in a song text)'. Philip Auslander, *Performing Glam Rock: Gender and Theatricality in Popular Music* (Ann Arbor: University of Michigan Press, 2006), 4.

29. Documentary feature from the DVD *Shockheaded Peter and Other Songs from The Tiger Lillies*, https://www.youtube.com/watch?v=XYS7-P2Vg1Q, 2005 at 14'40", accessed 27 March 2014.

30. Stemming from the German notion of *Schwarze Pädagogik*, as first outlined by Katharina Rutschky in her eponymous book from 1977 (reprint Munich: Ullstein, 2001), this notion describing a punitive, manipulative, and repressive method of parenthood was further analysed and developed by Alice Miller in her book *For Your Own Good* (New York: Farrar Straus Giroux, 1983) as 'poisonous pedagogy'.

31. Zipes, 'Perverse Delight'. See his article for a more in-depth discussion of the history of pedagogic values behind the book and their treatment in the musical.

32. Jacques quotes specifically the *Dreigroschenoper* and German cabaret as strong influences, https://www.youtube.com/watch?v=mA7yio5BfK8. See also the documentary feature from the DVD *Shockheaded Peter*.

33. Documentary feature from the DVD *Shockheaded Peter* at 43'08".

34. Ben Brantley, 'The Kiddie Show Goes Dark', *New York Times*, 1 May 2005, http://www.nytimes.com/2005/05/01/theater/newsandfeatures/the-kiddie-show-goes-dark.html?_r=0, accessed 27 March 2014.

35. Here are a few quotations to support this assertion, but similar results can be found for the other terms cited. From a newspaper interview: 'Not all musicals contain dance numbers, but for those that do, greatness depends on the believability of characters breaking into song and dance [...]' (http://www.nytimes.com/2001/04/15/magazine/15FIVEFROM.html, accessed 22 April 2014); from a website for teaching musicals: 'This principle also creates a presence onstage and within the actor that helps in the creation and believability of a scene/number' (http://www.theatreteachers.com/lesson-plans/performance-principles-musical-theatre, accessed 22 April 2014); from a High School Musical page: 'Acting Auditions are judged on the following criteria: [...] Does the actor effectively engage the audience through their passion, believability and willingness to take creative risks?' (http://millsmusic.org/Mills_Music/Musical.html, accessed 22 April 2014); from a fan-site: 'The characters lost any shred of believability in the transition from play to musical.' (http://everythingmusicals.com/everything_i_know_i_learn/2009/12/the-worst-musicals-of-the-2000s.html, accessed 22 April 2014).

36. See https://en.wikipedia.org/wiki/Jerry_Springer%3A_The_Opera, for a synopsis, cast list, and comprehensive production history.

37. *Jerry Springer: The Opera* (directed by Peter Orton), BBC 2005, ASIN: B000B3MIWO.

38. For an overview of some of the discourses around these see Andrew Tolson, ed., *Television Talk Shows: Discourse, Performance, Spectacle* (London: Routledge, 2001).

39. Kevin Gustafson, Review of Jerry *Springer: The Opera* by Richard Thomas and Stewart Lee, *Theatre Journal* 55, no. 4 (2003): 726–728.

40. These are outlined by Marshall Sella in the *New York Times*: 'The work contains traces of many of Thomas's formative influences: Bach, Miles Davis, Harrison Birtwhistle [*sic*], Arvo Part, Burt Bacharach, the Sex Pistols, Mozart and even the French composer Olivier

Messiaen's blend of religious harmonics and bird song. Stewart Lee's contribution, besides a shared comic sensibility with Thomas, is a surprising dose of John Milton, William Blake and Samuel Beckett.' Quoted in Donna Soto-Morettini, ' "The Clowns of God": *Jerry Springer: The Opera*', in 'Adventures in Music Theatre', special issue, *Contemporary Theatre Review* 14, no. 1 (2004): 76.

41. In London, organizations like Christian Voice attacked the show and more specifically it being broadcast by calling for e-mail complaints and by trying to bring criminal action against the BBC. According to IMBD, 'the BBC received over 50,000 complaints about the screening of this show (most of them before it aired), making it the most complained about TV broadcast in British television history'. (http://www.imdb.com/title/tt0441324/ trivia?ref_=tt_trv_trv, accessed 13 June 2014). See also the dedicated section 'Protests and controversy' on the Wikipedia site, https://en.wikipedia.org/wiki/Jerry_Springer:_ The_Opera#Protests_and_controversy, accessed 13 June 2014. In the US, the 'American Society for the Defense of Tradition, Family and Property' called for a public rally in pro- test against 'insults to the Faith' (http://www.tfp.org/current-campaigns/anti-blasphemy/ when-opera-is-offensive-protesting-a-jerry-springer-production.html, accessed 13 June 2014). It was also condemned by the Catholic League.

42. Gustafson elaborates: 'Here, as tabloid television meets mediaeval mystery play, *Jerry Springer: The Opera* becomes highly original.' Gustafson, Review of *Jerry Springer: The Opera*, 727.

43. It also didn't prevent *Jerry Springer: The Opera* to win several awards as Best *Musical*, such as the Evening Standard Award 2003, Critic's Circle Theatre Award 2004, and the Laurence Olivier Award 2004.

44. Samson, 'Genre', 658.

45. Mark Swed, 'Anti-Opera Review: *Jerry Springer: The Opera*' *Los Angeles Times Online*, 10 July 2011, http://latimesblogs.latimes.com/culturemonster/2011/07/anti-opera-review- jerry-springer-the-opera-.html, accessed 4 April 2014.

46. Gustafson, Review of *Jerry Springer: The Opera*, 727.

47. Gustafson, Review of *Jerry Springer: The Opera*, 728.

48. While there is something of a tradition of 'operatic musicals' in the history of the American musical—from Gershwin's *Porgy and Bess* (1935), via Bernstein's *Candide* (1956), to Sondheim's *Sweeney Todd* (1979)—I would argue that none of them wear their hybridity quite as prominently on its sleeves.

49. Jay David Bolter, 'The Desire for Transparency in an Era of Hybridity', *Leonardo* 39, no. 2 (2006): 109.

50. Richard Thomas and Stewart Lee, *Jerry Springer: The Opera*, songbook (London: Wise Publications, 2003), 67–73.

51. Thomas and Lee, *Jerry Springer*, 16–23.

52. Unpublished manuscript of a research talk entitled 'Hybrid Voices of Music Theatre: *Deep Blue, Bombay Dreams* and *London Road*' given by Millie Taylor at Performance Culture Industry PSI Annual Conference Leeds, 27 June–1 July 2012.

53. Samson, 'Genre', 658.

54. Soto-Morettini, 'Clowns of God', 78.

55. See https://en.wikipedia.org/wiki/London_Road_(musical) for detailed information about the show.

56. Alecky Blythe, quoted in Alecky Blythe and Adam Cork, *London Road* (London: Nick Hern Books, 2011), v.

57. Adam Cork, quoted in Blythe and Cork, *London Road*, ix.
58. This is a term employed by Gunther Schuller which he coined in a lecture at Brandeis University in 1953 to refer to the way in which he and other composers fuse elements of classical concert music and jazz. See Gunther Schuller, *Musings: The Musical Worlds of Gunther Schuller; A Collection of Writings* (New York: Oxford University Press, 1986), 114.
59. Blythe and Cork, *London Road*, 64.
60. Blythe and Cork, *London Road*, 29.
61. *West Side Story* (1957), for example, tells the story of the rivalry of two street gangs and two star-crossed lovers, whose love and sacrifice ultimately transcends the feud. *Les Misérables* (1985) is dominated by the lifelong conflict between Valjean and Javert and is a tale of idealism in the face of an oppressing social order. *Wicked* (2003) shows an outsider's struggle for friendship, acceptance, and loyalty, celebrating the transformative effect people can have on each other when they overcome their prejudices.
62. The musical was later revived in the larger Olivier Theatre, following its critical and box office success.
63. Blythe and Cork, *London Road*, 26–28.
64. Blythe and Cork, *London Road*, 23.
65. Cork, quoted in Blythe and Cork, *London Road*, x.
66. Taylor, 'Hybrid Voices'.
67. Cork, quoted in Blythe and Cork, *London Road*, viii.
68. It should be added that part and parcel of this tradition is not just the aesthetic palette these shows draw upon, but also the economic reality of generous public subsidy for theatres, which allows for these experiments to be honed at venues which are largely non-commercial.
69. Theodor W. Adorno, *Aesthetic Theory* (London: Routledge, 1984), 242.
70. See Petra Maria Meyer, ed., *Acoustic Turn* (Tübingen: Fink, 2008); Ross Brown, *Sound: A Reader in Theatre Practice* (Basingtoke: Palgrave, 2010); Lynne Kendrick and David Roesner, eds., *Theatre Noise: The Sound of Performance* (Newcastle upon Tyne: Cambridge Scholars Publishing, 2011); and Mladen Ovadija, *Dramaturgy of Sound in the Avant-Garde and Postdramatic Theatre* (Montreal: McGill-Queen's University Press, 2013).
71. In his presentation at the AHRC network meeting on Composed Theatre in Hildesheim 15 May 2009, documented for Exeter Digital Archives (http://spa.exeter.ac.uk/drama/research/exeterdigitalarchives/media_searchresults.php?search=Nicholas+Till&Submit=Search, accessed 2 May 2014. See also his chapter in *Composed Theatre: Aesthetics, Practices, Processes*, ed. Matthias Rebstock and David Roesner (Bristol: Intellect, 2012).
72. Melanie Fritsch's PhD project at the University of Bayreuth, for example, takes a decidedly music-theatrical approach to game music. See Melanie Fritsch, 'Live Performance Games? Musikalische Bewegung Sehen, Hören Und Spielen', in *Bewegungen zwischen Hören und Sehen: Denkbewegungen Über Bewegungskünste*, ed. Stephanie Schroedter (Würzburg: Königshausen & Neumann, 2012) as well as Kiri Miller, *Playing Along: Digital Games, YouTube, and Virtual Performance* (Oxford: Oxford University Press, 2012) and Karen Collins, *Playing with Sound: A Theory of Interacting with Sound and Music in Video Games* (Cambridge, MA: MIT Press, 2013).
73. I would like to thank Patrick Reu for his generous and insightful comments on an early draft of this chapter.

BIBLIOGRAPHY

Adorno, Theodor W. *Aesthetic Theory*. London: Routledge, 1984.

Altman, Rick. *Film/Genre*. London: British Film Institute, 1999.

Auslander, Philip. *Performing Glam Rock: Gender and Theatricality in Popular Music*. Ann Arbor: University of Michigan Press, 2006.

Blythe, Alecky, and Adam Cork. *London Road*. London: Nick Hern Books, 2011.

Bolter, Jay David. 'The Desire for Transparency in an Era of Hybridity.' *Leonardo* 39, no. 2 (2006): 109–111.

Brantley, Ben. 'The Kiddie Show Goes Dark.' *New York Times*, 1 May 2005. http://www.nytimes.com/2005/05/01/theater/newsandfeatures/the-kiddie-show-goes-dark.html?_r=0, accessed 27 March 2014.

Brown, Ross. *Sound: A Reader in Theatre Practice*. Basingtoke: Palgrave, 2010.

Brüstle, Christa. *Konzert-Szenen: Bewegung, Performance, Medien; Musik zwischen performativer Expansion und medialer Integration 1950–2000*. Stuttgart: Franz Steiner Verlag, 2013.

Cecchetto, David, Julie Lassonde, Dylan Robinson, and Nancy Cuthbert, eds. *Collision: Interarts Practice and Research*. Newcastle upon Tyne: Cambridge Scholars Publishing, 2008.

Coleman, Bud. 'New Horizons: The Musical at the Dawn of the Twenty-First Century.' In *The Cambridge Companion to the Musical*, edited by William A. Everett and Paul R. Laird, 284–302. Cambridge: Cambridge University Press, 2008.

Collins, Karen. *Playing with Sound: A Theory of Interacting with Sound and Music in Video Games*. Cambridge, MA: MIT Press, 2013.

Devitt, Amy J. 'Generalizing About Genre: New Conceptions of an Old Concept.' *College Composition and Communication* 44, no. 4 (December 1993): 573–586.

Fischer-Lichte, Erika, Kristiane Hasselmann, and Markus Rautzenberg, eds. *Ausweitung der Kunstzone: Interart Studies—Neue Perspektiven der Kunstwissenschaften*. Bielefeld: transcript, 2010.

Frankel, Aaron. *Writing the Broadway Musical*. 1977. Cambridge: Da Capo Press, 2000.

Fritsch, Melanie. 'Live Performance Games? Musikalische Bewegung, Sehen, Hören und Spielen.' In *Bewegungen zwischen Hören und Sehen: Denkbewegungen über Bewegungskünste*, edited by Stephanie Schroedter, 609–624. Würzburg: Königshausen & Neumann, 2012.

Gustafson, Kevin. Review of *Jerry Springer: The Opera* by Richard Thomas and Stewart Lee. *Theatre Journal* 55, no. 4 (2003): 726–728.

Henshall, Ruthie, and Daniel Bowling. *So You Want to Be in Musicals?* London: Nick Hern Books, 2012.

Kendrick, Lynne, and David Roesner, eds. *Theatre Noise: The Sound of Performance*. Newcastle upon Tyne: Cambridge Scholars Publishing, 2011.

Meyer, Petra Maria, ed. *Acoustic Turn*. Tübingen: Fink, 2008.

Miller, Kiri. *Playing Along: Digital Games, YouTube, and Virtual Performance*. Oxford: Oxford University Press, 2012.

Neale, Stephen. *Genre*. London: British Film Institute, 1980.

Neale, Stephen. *Genre and Hollywood*. London Routledge, 2000.

Ovadija, Mladen. *Dramaturgy of Sound in the Avant-Garde and Postdramatic Theatre*. Montreal: McGill-Queen's University Press, 2013.

Passow, Wilfried. 'Whom Do They Love?' In *Performance Theory*, edited by Henri Schoenmakers, 85–92. Amsterdam, 1992.

Radosavljević, Duška. *The Contemporary Ensemble: Interviews with Theatre-Makers*. London & New York: Routledge, 2013.

Rebstock, Matthias, and David Roesner, eds. *Composed Theatre: Aesthetics, Practices, Processes*. Bristol: Intellect, 2012.

Samson, Jim. 'Genre.' In *New Grove Dictionary of Music and Musicians*, 2nd ed, vol. 9, edited by Stanley Sadie, 657–659. London: Macmillan, 2001.

Schuller, Gunther. *Musings: The Musical Worlds of Gunther Schuller; A Collection of Writings*. New York: Oxford University Press, 1986.

Soto-Morettini, Donna. '"The Clowns of God": *Jerry Springer: The Opera*.' 'Adventures in Music Theatre', special issue, *Contemporary Theatre Review* 14, no. 1 (2004): 75–88.

Stanfield, Peter. 'Regular Novelties: Lawrence Alloway's Film Criticism.' *Tate Papers* 16 (Autumn 2011). http://www.tate.org.uk/research/publications/tate-papers/regular-novelties-lawrence-alloways-film-criticism, accessed 27 March 2014.

Swed, Mark. 'Anti-Opera Review: *Jerry Springer: The Opera*.' *Los Angeles Times*, http://latimes-blogs.latimes.com/culturemonster/2011/07/anti-opera-review-jerry-springer-the-opera-.html, accessed 10 July 2011.

Thomas, Richard, and Stewart Lee. *Jerry Springer: The Opera*. Songbook. London: Wise Publications, 2003.

Thomas, Troy. 'Interart Analogy: Practice and Theory in Comparing the Arts.' *Journal of Aesthetic Education* 25, no. 2 (Summer 1991): 17–36.

Tiger Lillies, The, *Shockheaded Peter and Other Songs from the The Tiger Lillies*. DVD 2005. https://http://www.youtube.com/watch?v=XYS7-P2Vg1Q, accessed 27 March 2014.

Tolson, Andrew, ed. *Television Talk Shows: Discourse, Performance, Spectacle*. London: Routledge, 2001.

Woolford, Julian. *How Musicals Work and How to Write Your Own*. London: Nick Hern Books, 2012.

Zipes, Jack David. 'The Perverse Delight of *Shockheaded Peter*.' *Theater* 30, no. 2 (Summer 2000): 129–143.

CHAPTER 28

SOME YESTERDAYS ALWAYS REMAIN

Black British and Anglo-Asian Musical Theatre

BEN MACPHERSON

INTRODUCTION

WHEN the new film-to-stage musical adaptation of Gurinder Chadha's movie *Bend It Like Beckham* (2002) opened at the Phoenix Theatre in London on 24 June 2015, the Web magazine Whatsonstage.com described the Anglo-Asian girl-power football show as 'a joyous new British musical about where we are now. [. . . W]ith a Punjabi kick, it brings a unique cultural fusion of musical theatre to the stage for the first time'.[1] In addition, Holly Williams of *The Independent* drew attention to the Anglo-Asian texture of the work: 'While [Howard] Goodall's music should provide plenty of sweeping showtunes, it also naturally reflects the British–Asian context. The original score is seriously spiced up, Goodall using Punjabi tabla rhythms in his music to bring an Indian inflection. Bhangra pioneer Kuljit Bhamra was also brought on board to help it go with a bang.'[2]

The visibility of Asian and other cultures on the London stage is not, as Whatstonstage. com suggests, 'unique'. In fact, it is not even something unusual in the context of the British musical.[3] This chapter examines the development of Anglo-Asian and black British musical theatre in the UK, tracing attitudes and practices in both the commercial and non-mainstream sectors, which I argue offer disparate versions of multicultural musical theatre. After a brief historical context, the chapter will primarily consider the growth in diasporic black British and South Asian performances in the second half of the twentieth century, arriving back on the football pitch of *Bend It Like Beckham* in conclusion, tracing the shifts in British cultural discourses from the initial rejection of colonial practices to the celebration of multiculturalism and diasporic communities as part of contemporary British cultural life.

A Historical Context of Performing 'the Other' in British Musical Theatre

Because of its global reach and geographic, cultural, and economic power, Britain has a long history of non-white performers on the London stage. In the eighteenth century, for example, the artist Hogarth included black actresses in his engravings of London life, such as *Strolling Actresses Dressing in a Barn* (1738) which pictured black actresses preparing for a production in South London.[4] In the early nineteenth century, African American performers such as Ira Aldridge (1807–67) and Samuel Morgan Smith (1832–82) were well known, with Aldridge even assuming British citizenship. Yet, such performers and performances were often popular *because* of their perceived exoticism or Otherness—an imperial celebration of that construction of Britain's self-representation in popular culture as an inclusive and global nation that at the same time reinforced an underlying sense of white English ideological supremacy.

This simultaneity can be observed in historical attitudes towards African American, Afro-Caribbean and South Asian performances in London, revealing a complex landscape of colonial, imperial, and postcolonial attitudes. David Linton and Len Platt have noted that there is 'a long history of African-American acts and performers in the West End'.[5] Such a description already hints at the distinction between British acts and those from elsewhere on the English stage, the cultural signifier 'African American' explicitly rendering such acts culturally and racially separate. Cultural delineation is not merely semantic. This separation was evidently practised in performance; in 1928, the home-grown English musical comedy *Virginia* was performed at the Palace Theatre on Shaftesbury Avenue and included a second act set in American's Deep South performed entirely by black actors. Such dramaturgical conventions were 'deeply imbricated in the politics of race and Otherness', as Linton and Platt suggest.[6] While C.B. Cochran's biographer James Harding described attitudes towards black performers in *From Dover Street to Dixie* as 'ambiguous',[7] an article in the March 1988 issue of British jazz journal *Storyville* presented evidence of a much less ambivalent stance during the 1920s. The article cited a correspondence from the Actors' Association to the Home Office in December 1922, protesting against the growing number of 'Plantation Revues' in London and expounding the alleged after-effects of the African American revue *In Dahomey* (1903):

> Unfortunately, [when *In Dahomey* closed] a large number of the Negroes did not leave the country, but settled down, chiefly in London, [and] it is a well-known scandal in theatrical circles that most of these people who stayed behind have lived on white women and are responsible for a great number of evils of this kind.[8]

Further criticism and suspicion was seen in an exposé written by theatre critic Hannen Swaffer, bemoaning the amount of white British artistes who remained unemployed while 'Sir Alfred Butt and C. B. Cochran are quarrelling apparently about which niggers they have got'.[9] This vitriol emanated from a growing insecurity about Britain's place in the world after the First World War, as its colonial reach in India, China, Africa, and the Caribbean began to evidence an instability that would take a further two decades to fracture, concomitant with America's ascension to global prominence and its own appropriation of white racial superiority from the 'old and exhausted island' of Britain.[10]

Of course, it was not just African American acts and performances that were seen on the London stage at this time. Reviews of Niranjan Pal's South Asian play with music, *The Goddess* (1922, Ambassador's Theatre) was received with mixed reactions. The lavish Indian costumes were praised, but Pal was criticized for his 'imperfect command' of English by *The Spectator*,[11] and the music in the work was viewed as 'characteristically plaintive' in *The Stage,* invoking words like 'dirge' in its further analysis of the work.[12] Likewise, Stanley Rice, a critic for *Asiatic Review*—an English magazine of the East India Association that sought to document and analyse South East Asia's relationship with Britain—considered the performances of Pandit Shyam Shankar at the Court Theatre, London in January 1922.[13] Whilst Rice's tone is generally positive, suggesting that English audiences have yet to grasp the 'excellence' of Indian music in performance, he asserts that this results in an audience who must remain 'rather interested than enthusiastic', echoing *The Spectator*'s review of *The Goddess* by confirming that 'no Indian production can fail to please the eye'. However, for an audience 'accustomed to the finished production of the English stage, there was somewhat of an amateur flavour in the performance', and Rice continues to suggest—rather presumptuously—that for Shankar, 'a more careful study of technique will lead to improved productions in the future'.[14] The critic does not display the vitriolic aggression towards South Asian performance seen in the Actors' Association's letter, or Swaffer's exposé noted above. Yet, along with the admitted sense of exoticism and appreciation for performance from a colony in the far-flung reaches of the Empire, the assertion of amateurishness and recommendation for Shankar to learn professionalism from the English evidences British imperialism towards colonized South Asia of the time.

While a sense of colonial paternalism can be identified towards South Asian performers, and opinion remained divided on black performers from America, John Cowley notes that 'documentary material on the activities of black Caribbean musicians in London is scanty throughout the 1920s'.[15] Indeed, while documents show that active West Indian and African musicians in Britain included pianist George Ruthland Clapham, and reed-player Sidney Bechet (who was deported in 1922) and that Guyana-born Rudolph Dunbar and Ken 'Snakehips' Johnson were prominent figures in British West Indian music in the 1930s, Adrian Wright notes that—even with the opening of *Calypso* at the Playhouse Theatre a month before SS *Empire Windrush* docked at Tilbury in 1948—it was difficult for Jamaican immigrants in Britain to find work on stage. Wright suggests: 'It was as if an unofficial apartheid ruled in British musicals'.[16] Nevertheless, the ideology of white British supremacy was soon to become challenged, diminished through a series of social shifts in Britain's world role and cultural landscape that would facilitate greater multiculturalism in British musical theatre.

SOCIAL CHANGE: 1950–1970

Following Egypt's independence from the Empire in 1922 and the Balfour Declaration of 1926 that constituted the genesis of the Commonwealth, the concept of British colonial subjects and British-born ethnic minorities became a political conundrum that would take years to negotiate and define. In 1947, India also gained independence from the British, tangibly signalling the decline of British colonial and imperial dominance on the world stage following the atrocities of the Second World War. In that same year, London hosted the Commonwealth Conference, where the change from 'British subject' to member-state citizenship, distinct but concomitant with 'Commonwealth citizen', was agreed. Importantly, as Lawrence J. Butler suggests, this change sought to achieve greater mobility and preferential treatment for Commonwealth citizens over 'foreigners', in social and economic migration and mobility from Britain to the colonies, and—importantly—from Commonwealth and colony *to* Britain, an island with a severely depleted workforce following the conflicts of 1939–45.[17] The growth in immigration *to* Britain in the decades following the 1948 British Nationality Act that affected these changes of citizenship can in many ways be seen as the beginnings of what might be called an 'indigenous' black British and Anglo-Asian cultural presence.

Since 1951, the changing social and cultural demography of Britain, particularly England and Wales, reveals a huge shift towards multicultural indigeneity, with second- and third-generation UK-born communities growing and spreading as a result of immigration. According to the Office of National Statistics, two years after the British Nationality Act came into effect, the UK population totalled around 50 million, yet only 4.3 per cent of residents (1.9 million) in England and Wales were recorded as 'foreign born', with the vast majority of these being white European or Irish emigrants.[18] However, between 1951 and 2011, the total population of England and Wales increased by 28 per cent, within which the non-UK born population almost quadrupled. As the Office of National Statistics notes, migration has therefore contributed to 45 per cent of population increase and diversification; the theatrical and artistic landscape would inevitably change as a result of such cultural pluralism.[19] In fact, as the box shows, information from the census paints a complex picture of cultural diversification in the UK with regard to growing black British and Anglo-Asian populations.[20]

The Office of National Statistics and Multicultural Britain, 1951–2011

African migration

- The Kenyan-born population of England and Wales increased from 6,000 in 1961 to 58,000 in 1971. Many of these were East African Asians who were escaping discrimination in Kenya.

- Between 1971 and 1981, there was a notable increase in other African-born immigrants: Ugandan-born residents of the UK increased by 270 per cent during this decade, whilst 10,850 Tanzanian-born immigrants arrived in the UK between 1971 and 1980.

(continued)

- Zimbabwean-born residents increased by over 100 per cent during the 1970s.

Asian migration

- In 1951, India was the third highest non-UK country of birth. Between 1961 and 1971, the Indian-born population of England and Wales almost doubled, and in 2011, the Indian-born demographic became the largest foreign-born population.
- The Bangladeshi-born population more than doubled between 1981 and 1991.
- Between 1961 and 1971, the Pakistani-born population more than quadrupled and has been ranked third largest foreign-born population in censuses since 1981.
- Over half (55 per cent) of Vietnamese-born residents in 2011 (29,000) arrived during the 1970s and 1980s, following the end of the Vietnam War in 1975. Subsequent arrivals were a result of the Vietnam–China war of 1979–80.
- Around 47% of those listed as having Bangladeshi ethnicity arrived between 1981 and 2000, largely as a result of the Bangladeshi war of independence (1971) and other military unrest.
- In the census year of 2011, 6.6% of the British population was comprised of a non-UK born Pakistani diaspora.

Caribbean migration

- Between 1951 and 1971, the Jamaican-born population saw a sixteen-fold increase, from 6,000 to 100,000.

The reasons for migration to the UK are many and varied but, as the report notes, include 'push' factors such as civil conflict, political instability, and poverty, and 'pull' factors such as employment and education opportunities, along with familial and cultural links. Unsurprisingly, the groundswell of immigration from the 1950s onwards brought a new set of reference points within British culture: immigrant writers and, crucially, new audiences.

In tandem with this groundswell, government policy sought to encourage integration and multicultural relationships through a series of Race Relations Acts in 1965, 1968, 1976, 2000 (Amendment), and the Equality Act of 2000. As a result—and not-withstanding the simultaneous institutional mechanisms that obstructed the freedom of black British and Asian performers in Britain[21]—here was a gradual growth in black British and Asian performers of first-, second-, and even third-generation immigrant communities. For example, the 1970s saw the growth of black British theatre companies such as Black Theatre Co-operative (now Nitro), Carib Theatre, Strange Fruit, and Talawa, followed in the 1990s by the Tamasha Theatre Company, and regional initiatives focused particularly in England, such as New Writing venues including The Drum (Birmingham), The Oval House (London), and the Nia Centre (Manchester).

Why, then, did Whatsonstage.com suggest that *Bend It Like Beckham*'s musical soundscape and representation of a Southall Anglo-Asian community was 'unique'? It would appear that the answer to this question can be best understood by examining the separate cultural spheres of British musical theatre: the mainstream commercial output of London's West End, and the subsidized and fringe scene that can be seen Off-West End and regionally. The final sections of this chapter, therefore, examine the paradoxes of representation and tensions that exist between these two areas.

COMMERCIAL CONSTRUCTIONS OF COLONIAL CARICATURES

As a 'commodity-led industry', an artefact which at one extreme end of the market is global and catering for millions',[22] commercial musical theatre in the UK often privileges broad appeal and stereotypical constructions of society above nuanced or complex representations of the cultural and political zeitgeist. Concomitant with the criticism of the production-line ethos often seen in the West End,[23] the commercial representations of contemporary multiculturalism are accordingly broad, and often essentialized in ways that are perceived by the white middle-class demographic of producers and directors to be most commercially viable.

For example, when Alain Boublil and Claude-Michel Schönberg's retelling of *Madama Butterfly* opened at the Theatre Royal Drury Lane as *Miss Saigon* (1989), the lead role of Kim—a virgin Vietnamese bargirl run by a pimp known as The Engineer—was played by Filipina actress Lea Salonga. In her article 'The Transnational Vision of *Miss Saigon*: Performing the Orient in a Globalized World', Tzu-I Chung noted that while the producers went to Manila in search of an actress to play Kim, and were reportedly 'close to tears' when they found 'the one' for what Chung calls 'their performance of this heteropatriarchal fantasy of the Oriental woman', the search for an Asian actor to play her pimp was far less extensive.[24] The Engineer, described publicly as 'Eurasian', was played by English actor Jonathan Pryce. Considering potential performers for the role, director Nicholas Hytner suggested Pryce and, as the actor recalls: 'They offered me the job then and there.'[25]

In a reflection of the market forces and capitalist star-system that dominated the West End during the 1980s, Chung continued to note that 'the announcement of [Pryce's] casting in *Miss Saigon* drew much press attention in Britain, some on the front page [...] Pryce's star status and fame thereby attracted the initial publicity that no Asian or Asian American performer would have been able to achieve in the late 1980s due to the long history of role segregation and role stratification in the Western entertainment industry'.[26]

While Cameron Mackintosh did hire eight Filipino men to augment the chorus and provide a sense of 'authenticity', the overriding sense of white British hegemony caused a media furore when *Miss Saigon* transferred to Broadway—with its original cast, including Pryce in 'yellow-face'. Chung's analysis suggests that it was finally market forces that determined Mackintosh's need to benefit from the Philippines' labour market:

> In dire need of a large number of 'authentic' Asian looking females to play Kim and other bar girls, the Mackintosh company institutionalized the market to regulate the source of labor. In a way that can be theorized by extending [Lucy] Burns's idea of 'corporeal colonization' to that of corporeal neocolonization, the company established The Miss Saigon School in Manila, which gives students a free six-month crash course in singing, dancing, and acting. Many of these students then join one of the international tours.[27]

This sense of neocolonization is endemic of an essentialism that prevails backstage, and not simply in the performance of Otherness onstage each night. The cultural awkwardness that existed in this entire production in London is perhaps also seen in Hytner's reflection of the rehearsal process:

> Lea Salonga [...] had no real theatre experience. She'd been a child star in the Philippines but now she was literally in a foreign country, so it was all very different [...] All of the Filipino cast were very anxious do well. They couldn't have worked harder to adjust themselves to a new culture [...] and a new way of working.[28]

While there seems to be an evident and implicit respect in Hytner's words here, cultural differences are respected seemingly because they are reinforced, rather than embraced or renegotiated. Of course, Miss Saigon was written by two Frenchman, directed by an English Jew, and produced by a Scottish-Maltese impresario. Set during the US–Vietnam conflict of the 1950s–70s, it was not, and did not claim to be, a British musical about British–Asian experiences. Yet, the problems and attitudes that underpinned the casting and production processes of this show give evidence of a latent imperialism in the West End as the twentieth century headed into its final decade. In some ways, the role stratification that Chung identifies above was played out in the original British production of this show. It is also telling that following the Broadway production of Miss Saigon in 1991, all subsequent performers to embody The Engineer have been of Asian ethnicity. In the record-breaking 2014 London revival, Filipino actor Jon Jon Briones assumed the role to great critical acclaim. Reflecting on the original 'yellow face' controversy, Briones suggests that 'back then, I'm not sure there was enough trust in Asian actors that they could be given a lead role, so a lot of the Engineers that followed Jonathan began as covers and after a while it was, like, "Yeah, OK, we can give the role to them." Suddenly there was a demand for Asian performers that there hadn't been before, and it took everything that happened to help get it to this point.'[29] Quite where this 'point' is, however, is a matter of some debate: Briones is not new to Miss Saigon, having been chosen especially for the role—he was one of the original eight Filipino male ensemble members brought to London in 1989 to add 'authenticity' to the original production, and has subsequently played the role in other revivals of the work.

Notwithstanding the somewhat problematic production history of *Miss Saigon*, a more explicit collaboration between British and Asian creatives seemingly heralded a twenty-first-century fusion of East and West on the London stage in 2002. Premiering at the Apollo Victoria on 19 June 2002, *Bombay Dreams* was created by an Anglo-Asian team of Indian composer A. R. Rahman, British lyricist Don Black, and British-Asian writer Meera Syal, with choreography by British choreographer Anthony Van Laast and Indian Farah Khan. Directed by Stephen Pimlott, the production grew from a concept by Indian film director Shekhar Kapur, and was produced by Andrew Lloyd Webber. A Bollywood-inspired spectacular, it utilized that genre's cinematic tropes to tell the story of slum-dweller Akaash and his rise to fame in the Hindi film industry. Caught up in his celebrity and his love for the daughter of a movie mogul, Akaash is in danger of forgetting where he came from. The slums are slated for demolition, and the story thus unfolds, seeing Akaash stuck between fulfilling his dreams and betraying his roots.

Rather than evidence role stratification or 'corporeal neocolonization', *Bombay Dreams* was sold by its marketing and creative team as a beacon for multicultural cosmopolitanism.[30] In her paper 'Hybrid Voices of Music Theatre: *Deep Blue, Bombay Dreams* and *London Road*', Millie Taylor has subsequently explored the construction of cosmopolitanism in the vocal performance of *Bombay Dreams*. Yet, Taylor notes that while *Bombay Dreams* may have been ideologically intercultural, its primary audience was the diasporic community that shared the sense of Anglo-Asian identity embodied in the performers, and members of the creative team.[31] In this sense, the hybridity seen in *Bombay Dreams* seemingly appealed to a specific community, and did not extend overtly across a broader cultural demographic, despite its initial visibility and the attendant political discourses of multiculturalism proffered at the time by the centre-left ideology of Tony Blair's New Labour administration.

When considered in the light of Homi Bhabha's concept of hybridity in postcolonial theory, *Bombay Dreams* seems to occupy a peculiar place in the pantheon of Anglo-Asian musical theatre.[32] While most press reviews at the time lauded it as a 'joyous tribute to Bollywood movies', 'ingenious, inventive and radical [and] a musical step in the right direction', with a score that 'couldn't be more authentic [. . .] a glorious crossover',[33] the dynamics that contributed to its development evidence both *hybridity* and what Jerri Daboo has termed 'the hegemony of the imperialism of globalization'.[34] The points at which global hegemonic factors concomitant with the populist consumerism of the West End collide with hybridity in this work provide a fascinating picture of the commercial representations of Anglo-Asian British musical theatre at the turn of the twenty-first century.

In many ways, Taylor's assertion of hybridity is correct, and along with the vocal textures and timbres of the performance, *Bombay Dreams* offered two further representations of hybridity. First, the dramaturgy and design values drew heavily on aesthetics and tropes of the Hindi film industry. According to film scholars M. Koti Gokulsing and

Wimal Dissanayake, Bollywood films can be broadly defined by a set of tropes and conventions, including

- an insistence on spectacle, song, and dance;
- a blend of realism and fantasy;
- a sense of melodrama in tone and structure;
- unrealistically instantaneous changes of location or costume mid-production number;
- songs which comment on the action, externalize character's thoughts or emotion, progress the plot, or presage events.[35]

Tellingly, these conventions share structural, cultural, or aesthetic similarities with Western musical theatre. In particular, such conventions in *Bombay Dreams*—with its huge sets, gaudy costume, and overt attempt at spectacle—are reminiscent of a particular genre of Western musical theatre that has evidently influenced Bollywood through transnational borrowings. Paul Prece and William Everett have observed that megamusicals 'merge aspects of human suffering and redemption with matters of social consciousness', two key tenets of *Bombay Dreams*'s narrative.[36] Jessica Sternfeld has further identified megamusicals as being big: a big plot, big music, big sets, big marketing. Once again, *Bombay Dreams* fits comfortably into that definition.[37] It was, after all, produced and financed by Lloyd Webber, regularly seen as the doyen of the megamusical production values. The fact that the musical was financed by a member of the British Establishment, and developed with his oversight, might suggest a claim of ownership by the hegemonic white middle class, redolent of the neocolonialism seen when casting Jonathan Pryce in *Miss Saigon*. Yet, the production values—and process—of *Bombay Dreams* must be read in the context of a history of cultural borrowings between Bollywood and Western entertainment forms. While it might be true that Bollywood has succumbed to Westernization in recent decades, Rekha Sharma and Carol A. Savery draw on Antonio Gramsci's cultural theory to suggest that such borrowings should not be seen as 'evidence of cultural imperialism, but as indicative of the complex interaction of global and local forces'.[38] The interpretative and abstract settings, redolent of the fantasy world Bollywood creates; the structural nods to Bollywood staples, such as the 'wet sari' number, and the constant costume changes; the pre-recorded, mimed, soundtrack on three occasions in the London production; and the pantomimic archetype villains—albeit 'homogenized' within Andrew Lloyd Webber's marketing machine—did go some way towards creating a 'hybrid' of East and West in the production of the show, where Bollywood opulence met megamusical spectacle. Further examples of such hybridity are also evident in Rahman's musical score, in its compositional process, and in the musical features it employs.

The working practices of Rahman—who has a degree in Music from Oxford University—often involved praying for inspiration, lighting candles, and showing respect for the sanctity of the creative space by removing shoes and meditating, working from ideas rather than fully formed lyrics or structures, free improvisation, and long hours with regular breaks. Veteran lyricist Don Black reflects that 'it was a long, laborious job to get actual shapes of songs that could be right [. . .] Rahman is very unorthodox'.[39] Presumably, Black's use of 'unorthodox' here is used in reference to his own unfamiliarity with Rahman's sacred approach to composition. Nevertheless, the lyricist formed a close friendship with the composer, flying to New York to attend Rahman's sold-out one-off appearance in the city in 2001. For his part, Rahman described working with Black—who constantly guided him to shape, hone, and focus his music into musical theatre forms—as 'a privilege'.[40] In this respect, then, there appeared to be a genuine and mutual interchange of experiences, approaches, and aesthetics between Bollywood and Broadway traditions during the creative process.

The musical score that resulted included the adaptation of pre-existing music by Rahman—for the songs 'Love's Never Easy', 'How Many Stars', 'Chaiyya Chaiyya', 'Closer Than Ever', and 'Wedding Gawwali'—a hallmark of the Bollywood tradition of transposition, once again evidencing a sense of hybridity in cultural practice. It was a score that drew on Indian traditions in its harmonic constructions, rhythm, and as highlighted by Taylor, voice—at certain points. In each case, a sense of hybridity can be identified between Eastern musical practices and Western conventions in further examples of transcultural borrowing and fusion. Rahman's use of the tonic drone as a harmonic marker in 'Love's Never Easy',[41] or the nasal vocality heard throughout the piece in brief moments such as the beginning of 'Like An Eagle' or the 'Wedding Gawwali' (utilizing the high-chest register of ragas and ghazal) are contrasted with the circle of fifths that harmonically form the bedrock for 'The Journey Home' and the use of the tonic/ submediant tonality of 'Closer Than Ever', often employed in standard Western ternary song forms. In this case, Rahman borrowed Western styles of music, and then repackaged them back to a Western audience in a contemporary Bollywood aesthetic. If this is the case, and an Indian composer with a Western classical music background repackages Western borrowings under the guise of fusion, then it would seem the 'hybridity' in Bombay Dreams offered a Westernized mediation of Indian influences, rather than a negotiation or bridge between them, so the show is dominated by a heavily Western aesthetic.

Jerri Daboo has argued that the Asian identity staged in Bombay Dreams was 'homogenized', 'stereotypical', 'conforming [sic] to an imperialist definition of identity'.[42] In a similar vein, when the review of the Bombay Dreams cast recording appeared on the BBC website, reviewer Chris Jones concluded his analysis by suggesting that 'Rahman seemed unable to break free of his producer's spell [. . .] talent seems to have been wasted in giving us just another one for the tourists'.[43] In his review of the opening night performance, Michael Billington seemed to confirm this assertion, observing that while Bombay Dreams sets out to critique ambition and the plastic smiles of Bollywood films, it does so through replicating them without a shred of irony.[44] Such criticisms of commercial populism essentializing the hybrid potential of this work seemed to be aimed at Lloyd Webber as the primary hegemonic force in the process, and once again echo the power structures and production teams that cast a white Welsh actor as an Asian pimp. Of course, by the early twenty-first century, Lloyd Webber was also an easy target for derision and criticism in the popular press, leading to a somewhat inevitable mixture of journalistic praise and blame. In addition, the Hindi film industry itself has been increasingly controlled by hegemonic forces of (inter)national capital, enabling a sense of comparison in this sense with the hegemonic theatre system in London.

Perhaps, then, the reading of *Bombay Dreams* as an Anglo-Asian hybrid musical is more ideological rather than factual. While Lloyd Webber had a genuine interest in the 'melodic genius' of A. R. Rahman,[45] and developed the concept in conversation with Kapur, certain aspects of the process—and the reflections on the process by the team—hint at latent neocolonialist attitudes. In the biography of Don Black, writer John Inverne recalls a performance at which Chris Nightingale—musical director for *Bombay Dreams,* who in practice had significantly more input in shaping the piece than might traditionally be the case as musical director—summarized the Asian community as a 'noble yet chaotic race'.[46] Further, having rehearsed with Asian co-choreographer Farah Khan, Anthony Van Laast freely expressed his surprise that dancers in Mumbai 'did not know' how to warm up, do exercises, and have 'no technique [...], none', while associate choreographer Nicola Treherne bemoaned the fact that Khan's dance troupe did not know anything about techniques of the body, implying that Khan will benefit from a 'nice break' by getting to rehearse in London on sprung floors, rather than concrete.[47] To borrow from Rustom Bharucha, 'I do not believe that there is an overriding [...] pervasive "orientalism"' here. This is not to suggest that Black, Nightingale, Treherne, Lloyd Webber, or Van Laast were racist, or even that this production sought to Anglicize an Eastern popular form.[48] Yet, in both written documentation of the process and in the documentary film *Salaam Bombay Dreams*, one gets an evident sense that true hybridity was a difficult task for a work that would always be mediated through the culturally hegemonic forces of the West End.

Indeed, one might go so far as to say that the very title of the show—*Bombay Dreams*—refers explicitly to the British colonial name of the city, derived from seventeenth-century occupation, rather than the official Marathi name, Mumbai, reassigned to the city in November 1995. As Daboo has observed, if this musical represented India, it was surely a homogenized, *British version* of India—determined and developed with input from Asian practitioners, but presented within a narrative of latent imperialist attitudes, wherein the psychological decolonization of post-imperial British culture might be identified; the British appropriation of the cultural milieu of *Bollywood*, itself a moniker created by the West to 'commercialize' culture of the East (after Said). This is not to suggest that *Bombay Dreams* did not have benefits for the diaspora in the UK. In fact, anecdotally, the creative team at the time reflected on the positives: Asian actors who auditioned were at times ashamed to tell their parents where they were going for fear of recrimination, but became increasingly vocal and proud of their association with the show. Additionally, as Daboo cautiously acknowledges: 'The encouragement of Asian audiences into West End theatres could be seen as a significant achievement.'[49] From this perspective, *Bombay Dreams* represented a huge leap forward in the cultural diversity of a West End audience—something still relatively unusual in commercial venues.

Cynically, Dahoo continues to warn that such encouragement 'can also lead to a "new audience" itself becoming a commodity for the purposes of marketing and commercialism' within a dominant ideology that idealizes the positive effects of mass globalized cultural hegemony.[50] Yet, notwithstanding the inevitable conclusion that such a situation would serve to reinforce white middle-class hegemony, the fact remains that without *Bombay Dreams*, perhaps a new West London musical celebrating girl power and football would never have seemed possible.

Progressive Constructions of Postcolonial Pluralism

Outside the neocolonial capitalism of the West End, a much more vivid representation of Anglo-Asian and black British identity can be seen in regional and Off-West End producing houses. Original music(al) theatre that explores diasporic and multicultural community experience in Britain has developed over the past forty years at venues such as the Theatre Royal Stratford East. Encouragingly, three years after a 1976 Arts Council report that condemned theatre for its lack of support for theatre from British ethnic minorities,[51] theatre companies such as Nitro (established in 1979 under its original name, the Black Theatre Co-operative) began to build a reputation for celebrating and engaging with minority ethnicities and the pluralism of British creative culture.

As described on their website, Nitro 'creates dynamic music theatre events that explore the contemporary black British experience [. . .] From musicals to oratorios, from dance shows to opera, Nitro's productions celebrate black music, inspired and driven by a wealth of styles from reggae, calypso, salsa, soul, jazz and hip-hop to contemporary opera.'[52] Crucially, it is in this mix of styles and approaches that innovative biographical music theatre is seen.

Since their inception, Nitro's work has focused on constructing an ethnography of the black British experience. Recent projects include *The God Racket* (2013), which saw the company collaborate with community theatre project Cardboard Citizens, to develop a musical loosely based on the biblical account of the suffering of Job, set in London in the 1960s. The choice of narrative themes (suffering without knowing why, loss, determination, redemption, belonging, and identity) were both universally familiar and thematically pertinent to the communities involved in the development of the work.[53] The fact that a full showcase was presented, not in London, but at Birmingham's Rep Theatre, demonstrates the demographic and community reach of Nitro's work. Community engagement is core to Nitro's activity, further seen in 2013 when the *Afropolitan* project—supported in collaboration with Theatre Royal Stratford East and the National Theatre—brought together writer Oladipo Agboluaje, director Mpumelelo Paul Grootboom, and composer and artistic director of Nitro, Felix Cross. Drawing on their own cultural influences from the Caribbean, Nigeria, Somalia, South Africa, and

Britain, they created *Tides*, a music theatre work that told a love story set in a fishing village in Somalia. While the narrative was set elsewhere, the creative team are all from ethnic minorities in the UK. In fact, in this instance, it is not the work itself that proves interesting but the process of minority ethnic practices freed from the commercial considerations and constraints of the West End. After the initial presentation of *Tides,* the creative team were invited to further develop the work a year later, culminating in a showcase event on 18 October 2014.

This event was not a performance, but a forum in which the creators were able to reflect on the ways a sense of plurality in their cultural identities could come together in storytelling. Using folk oration, poetry, and contemporary music, along with video and performance, the work politicized the creation of performance, reflecting on the varied diasporic experiences that contributed to it. Indeed, such a critical engagement with creative process, alongside the diasporic narratives represented on stage, could be further seen in a public discussion at the Theatre Royal Stratford East, less than a month earlier, on Monday 22 September 2014. This forum sought to reflect on the 'discussions, lessons and legacy' of *Exhibit B*, an art installation by South African artist Brett Bailey that was forcibly closed at the Barbican after being accused of racism.[54] This sense of community engagement and sociopolitical discourse is becoming part of Nitro's ethos, as they seek to 'redefine black musical theatre'.[55]

While Nitro's community engagement is prolific, and other companies such as Talawa and Tamasha Theatre produce work that curates increasingly multicultural experiences, these companies still exist in large measure outside the mainstream. In fact, the overt community ethos appears to echo Farrukh Dhondy's observation from the 1980s: minority ethnic theatre was 'an off-shoot of the political phenomenon of immigrant settlement'.[56] In part, this perhaps suggests that the neocolonial hegemony of the West End still reduces multicultural musical theatre to the margins, as applied theatre for various diasporas, denying—rather than embracing—the heterogeneous experience of contemporary Britain. Yet, the encouragement to engage with a progressive music(al) theatre culture that reflects the postcolonial experience of pluralism in the UK has not always quietly occupied these margins. In particular, Nitro's regular collaboration with the National Theatre through the development of their work in collaboration with other Arts Council-funded initiatives says much about the growing visibility and importance of black British theatre in the twenty-first century. Of course, there is still some way to go in this respect. Crucially, in the examples outlined above, Nitro also partnered with the Theatre Royal Stratford East, a theatre with a long history of social engagement and projects that seek to represent diasporic and local communities.

For example, in April 2004, the Theatre Royal Stratford East premiered *The Big Life*.[57] With a book and lyrics by Paul Sirett and music by Paul Joseph, the production sought to fictionalize the history of Caribbean migrants who came to England on SS *Empire Windrush* (see Figure 28.1). The men concerned make a pact not to become involved with women for the first three years in England but, of course, things do not work out quite as planned. Its success at Stratford East saw it revived in February 2005. The social situation which led to the development of *The Big Life*, along with its theatrical and

FIGURE 28.1 A fictionalized account of the first Caribbean migrants to Britain: the company of *The Big Life* recreating the 1948 arrival of the SS *Empire Windrush*, Theatre Royal Stratford East, 2004.

Courtesy of Theatre Royal Stratford East Archives Collection.

musical strategies, evidenced what might be seen as a midpoint between the neocolonialism of the West End and the indigenous experience of black Britain. In this sense, *The Big Life* is an appropriate show to act as a bridging point between the two cultural spheres in the British musical.

First, the cultural composition of the neighbourhood within which the Theatre Royal is located has an important bearing on the many 'Urban' initiatives the theatre has pursued in the last two decades, under the guidance of Philip Hedley. At the time of its production, 61 per cent of Newham (the location of the Theatre Royal) were from ethnic minorities, with a high percentage of these being younger people.[58] The need arose to embrace ethnic diversity and a broad range of ages, and subsequently, the Urban Musical Initiative was started at the Theatre Royal, which facilitated the development of *The Big Life*.[59]

The content of the musical utilized specific cultural signifiers that would appeal to a diverse urban population of all ages, and to a white English demographic beyond the geographical boundaries of E15. Subtitled 'The Ska musical', *The Big Life* drew on reggae and ska music in a deliberate endeavour to engage with, and to some extent represent, the community served by the venue. As Barbara Korte and Eva Ulrike Pirker have observed, the musical strategically utilized 'retro music that is black in origin but also already appealed to whites in the 1950s and 60s—and still does to older as well as younger audiences, being both culture-specific and also universal'.[60] In addition, the narrative drew on Shakespeare's *Love's Labour's Lost* and framed it within the context of the Caribbean immigrant experience. Both narrative and music therefore had dual-appeal and allowed the show to perform the post-immigrant trope of lost hope and disenchantment in a narrative that ameliorates the reality through the conventions of an upbeat musical language and a traditional love story. Yet, unlike the universal ambitions of *Bombay Dreams* or *Miss Saigon, The Big Life* offered a less rose-tinted, if at times incredibly funny, vision of its subject, presenting a black history in Britain for both white British and diasporic audiences.

Although written by a white British male, the use of pidgin and dialectical inflections in the book and lyrics (the first song features the refrain 'Inglan Big time We comin' Inglan' as a choral gospel number) operates differently to other theatricalized representations of dialect.[61] Without a pretence to 'authenticity', the linguistic inflections of this show become ironic, performed by actors who have direct familial connections to the very boat they are seen arriving on at the top of Act 1—a pertinent comment about the reception such immigrants received when they arrived at Tilbury.

While the script may have been penned by a white Briton, the sense of the diaspora performing its own experience was perhaps nowhere more poignant than in the casting and the character of Mrs Aphrodite, who acts as a Greek chorus providing commentary on the progress of the men. Yet, it was not this theatrical device that was most significant; it was the placement of Aphrodite-as-audience-member. The commentary that she provides—criticizing the folly of abstinence but praising the men's desire to work hard and succeed—constructs a performance of spectatorial collusion in reclaiming the Afro-Caribbean immigrant experience for that community. The actress that originated the role of Mrs Aphrodite (Jamaican Tameka Empson) was of the Windrush generation, and the sense of the present retelling being deconstructed through the eyes of those that were there created a powerful sense of theatricality and biography to this production.

In fact, it is the biographical nature of this musical that separates it from *Bombay Dreams* or *Miss Saigon*. In performing the black experience, director Clint Dyer expressly wanted

> a way of paying homage to my parents' generation without the usual serious, po-faced attitude. By doing this in such a comic, exuberant and loving way, we've really got to the essence of black people as opposed to the external things that affect us. [...] The irony here is that we make it funny because normally we're never allowed to laugh at ourselves. I also think white people will learn about themselves in a non-threatening way.[62]

This revisioning of postcolonialism through music, song, dance, comedy, and a sense of knowingness on the part of the performers and their diasporic audiences proved such a success that the musical transferred to the West End, playing at the Apollo Theatre from 23 May to 1 October 2005.

Continuing their practice of staging postcolonial pluralities, a decade after *Bombay Dreams*, the Theatre Royal Stratford East collaborated with Kneehigh Theatre to present a new Anglo-Asian musical, *Wah! Wah! Girls*. Directed by Emma Rice, and written by Tanika Gupta with music by Niraj Chag, it opened at the Peacock Theatre on 24 May 2012. Set in the East End, the musical concerned a clash of cultures: Soraya, an Indian-born immigrant who is familiar with the culture of Mujra and Kathak dancing clashes with the British Asian Sita, who arrives at Soraya's club with her Westernized Bollywood dance style. The use of dance idioms to represent the clash and negotiation of cultures was an effective theatrical device redolent of the ska music employed in *The Big Life*. Yet the critical reception was mixed. Laura Thompson of the *Daily Telegraph* suggested the show brought the multicultural vibrancy of the East End to life with 'droll economy' in a manner that 'has conjured an entertainment to make the ghost of Joan Littlewood applaud'[63] while *The Guardian*'s Lyn Gardner bemoaned the fact that 'in its search for contemporary references to multicultural London [it] makes some excruciating Polish detours', in reference to the immigrant handyman character.[64] Finally, Thompson concluded that *Wah! Wah! Girls* was, 'in essence, a remarkably traditional musical', notwithstanding that it offered a contemporary representation of the East End.[65] While Thompson indicates the use of conservative theatrical forms here, a contemporary representation of multiculturalism in the UK was not staged in *Miss Saigon*, or *Bombay Dreams*, or even in *The Big Life*. Indeed, it is the ability of the work to perform *contemporary* multiculturalism in a commercial venue that perhaps suggests a major step forward—a sense of progress seen once again in 2015, when the sounds of Southall were set to music in *Bend it Like Beckham*.

Breaking Borders: The Future of Multicultural Musical Theatre

In the end, *Bend It Like Beckham* is an inherently populist musical, adapted from a surprise cinematic success, which offers broad-brushstroke characters and comedic stereotypes. Nevertheless, the readiness of the press to praise this new 'British' musical may indicate a changing commercial landscape, increasingly tolerant and comfortable with contemporary representations of multicultural pluralities on the popular musical stage.[66] What the musical successfully achieves—in a similar manner to *Wah! Wah! Girls*—is the theatrical representation of Southall, an area known for its cultural pluralism; it is a musical that constructs Otherness *at home*, and not in Bollywood, or the Caribbean, or Vietnam.

In a torch song sung by the hero of *Bombay Dreams*, Akaash reflects on the fact that such journeys home will, for a time at least, carry with them a remnant of the struggles of 'yesterday'.[67] In this case, while regional companies like Nitro and others are still tangential to mainstream popular culture, they *are* thriving, using community engagement, social issues, and a breadth of cultural practices not seen in British commercial theatres to negotiate, construct, and perform contemporary minority ethnic experience in

FIGURE 28.2 Celebrating multicultural life in London: the company of *Bend It Like Beckham* in the number 'UB2', Phoenix Theatre, 2015.

Photograph by Ellie Kurttz. Courtesy of Ellie Kurttz.

the UK. Scholar Simon Shepherd poignantly observes that such practices, which surely include Nitro's use of African folklore and oral storytelling traditions in *Tides*, 'are definingly associated with black arts practice and, hence, *not available to white theatre*. In its staging of them, therefore, black theatre may be said to have developed forms that extend the language and practice of all theatre'.[68]

This is a provocative statement, and indicates the potential cross-fertilization of artistic practices in British theatre as a whole in the twenty-first century. As the cast of *Bend It Like Beckham* suggests in the lyrics to the opening song 'UB2' (see Figure 28.2), Britain now hosts splashes of saffron on a grey backdrop,[69] and while the institutional and neocolonial mechanisms of history still impact attitudes and practices in many areas of the commercial musical, the pluralities of postcolonial British popular culture are increasing, and the vital signs are looking more robust than at any time in the nation's past.

NOTES

1. Anon., '*Bend It Like Beckham*', Whatsonstage.com, http://www.whatsonstage.com/west-end-theatre/shows/bend-it-like-beckham_50121, accessed 1 July 2015.
2. Holly Williams, 'Can *Bend It Like Beckham* Succeed in the West End?', *The Independent*, 19 May 2015, http://www.independent.co.uk/arts-entertainment/theatre-dance/features/can-bend-it-like-beckham-succeed-in-the-west-end-10261680.html, accessed 1 July 2015.
3. As this chapter is primarily concerned with diasporic communities and their indigenous theatrical practices as part of the growing multiculturalism of the British musical stage,

the discussion does not include the representational strategies or colonial appropriations most often seen in late nineteenth-century musical comedy. The imperial politics of race during the fin de siècle, which saw English playwrights and composers creating characters such as geishas, Japanese emperors, and Indian princes to be performed by English actors, has been considered elsewhere in this volume, and in other publications: see Brian Singleton, *Oscar Asche, Orientalism and British Musical Comedy* (Westport: Praeger, 2004); Martin Clayton and Bennett Zon, eds., *Music and Orientalism in the British Empire 1780s–1940s: Portrayal of the East* (Farnham: Ashgate, 2007). Rather, the relationship between British diasporic communities and musical theatre offers a separate—albeit related—history of British attitudes towards race and Otherness.

4. William Hogarth, *Strolling Actresses Dressing in a Barn*, engraving, 1738, British Museum no. S.232-2009.

5. David Linton and Len Platt, 'Dover Street to Dixie and the Politics of Cultural Transfer and Exchange', in *Popular Musical Theatre in London and Berlin 1890 to 1939*, ed. Len Platt, Tobias Becker, and David Linton (Cambridge: Cambridge University Press, 2014), 175.

6. Linton and Platt, 'Dover Street to Dixie', 173.

7. James Harding, *Cochran: A Biography* (London: Methuen, 1988), 100.

8. Howard Wry, 'The Plantation Revues', *Storyville* 133 (1 March 1988), 5.

9. Hannen Swaffer, 'The Scandal of Negro Revues', *Daily Graphic*, 5 March 1923, 7.

10. Ralph Waldo Emerson. Quoted in Kariann Akemi Yokota, *Unbecoming British: How Revolutionary America Became a Postcolonial Nation* (New York: Oxford University Press, 2011), 242.

11. Stanley Rice, *The Spectator*, 22 July 1922. Quoted in Sumita Mukherjee, 'The Representation and Display of South Asians in Britain, 1870–1950', in Ruvani Ranasinha et al., eds., *South Asians and the Shaping of Britain, 1870–1950: A Sourcebook* (Manchester: Manchester University Press, 2012), 221.

12. *The Stage*, 22 June 1922. Quoted in Mukherjee, 'South Asians in Britain, 1870–1950', 221.

13. The *Asiatic Quarterly Review* was founded by Sir Lepel Griffin in 1885, and ceased publication in 1952. The journal included articles on matters relating to Asia, along with book reviews and comments on international affairs. It was politically engaged and a valuable resource in encouraging multicultural interrelationships.

14. Stanley Rice, 'Indian Plays in London', *Asiatic Review* 18, no. 53 (1922), 129.

15. See John Cowley, 'London Is the Place: Caribbean Music in the Context of Empire 1900–1960', in Paul Oliver, ed., *Black Music in Britain: Essays on the Afro Asian Contribution to Popular Music* (Milton Keynes: Open University Press, 1990), 58. Troublingly, in contrast with European and Asian populations, an accurate picture of the Caribbean population in the UK is also difficult to obtain through official records.

16. Adrian Wright, *A Tanners Worth of Tune: Re-discovering the Post-war British Musical* (Suffolk: Boydell and Brewer, 2010), 144.

17. Lawrence J. Butler, *Britain and Empire: Adjusting to a Post-Colonial World* (London: I. B. Tauris, 2002), 68.

18. Anon., 'Immigration Patterns of Non-UK Born Populations in England and Wales in 2011', Office of National Statistics, 17 December 2013, http://www.ons.gov.uk/ons/rel/census/2011-census-analysis/immigration-patterns-and-characteristics-of-non-uk-born-population-groups-in-england-and-wales/story-on-immigration-patterns-of-non-uk-born-populations-in-england-and-wales-in-2011.html?format=print, accessed 15 July 2015.

19. Anon., 'Immigration Patterns', 2013.

20. Anon., 'Immigration Patterns', 2013.

21. These obstructions and the subsequent difficulties they created are outlined in 'Progressive Constructions of Postcolonial Pluralism', later in this chapter.

22. Paul Barker, '"Putting It Together": Teaching Musical Theatre in UK Higher Education', March 2006, https://www.academia.edu/169228/_Putting_It_Together_Teaching_Musical_Theatre_in_UK_Higher_Education, accessed 25 July 2015.

23. For a discussion of this, see Dan Rebellato's consideration of 'McTheatre' in *Theatre and Globalization* (Basingstoke: Palgrave Macmillan, 2009), 39–49.

24. Tzu-I Chung, 'The Transnational Vision of *Miss Saigon*: Performing the Orient in a Globalized World', *MELUS: Multi-Ethnic Literature of the U.S.*, 36, no. 4 (2011), 67.

25. Angela Pao, 'The Eyes of the Storm: Gender, Genre and Cross-Casting in *Miss Saigon*', *Text and Performance Quarterly* 12, no. 1 (1992), 26.

26. Chung, 'Transnational Vision', 67–68.

27. Chung, 'Transnational Vision', 68.

28. Quoted in Margaret Vermette, *The Musical World of Boublil and Schönberg* (New York: Applause, 2006), 145.

29. Quoted in Matt Wolf, 'West End Star Jon Jon Briones on His 25-Year Journey in *Miss Saigon*, From Ensemble Member to Engineer', 7 May 2014, http://www.broadway.com/buzz/175829/west-end-star-jon-jon-briones-on-his-25-year-journey-in-miss-saigon-from-ensemble-member-to-engineer/, accessed 4 July 2015.

30. Chung, 'Transnational Vision', 68.

31. Millie Taylor, 'Hybrid Voices of Music Theatre: *Deep Blue, Bombay Dream* and *London Road*', Performance Culture Industry PSI Annual Conference Leeds, 27 June–1 July 2012.

32. Homi Bhabha, *The Location of Culture* (Oxford: Routledge, 1994), 5.

33. See Anon., Reviews of *Bombay Dreams*, http://www.reallyuseful.com/shows/bombay-dreams/reviews/, accessed 1 August 2015; Nicholas de Jongh, '*Bombay*'s Epic Night of Dreams', *Evening Standard*, 20 June 2002, http://www.standard.co.uk/goingout/theatre/bombays-epic-night-of-dreams-7434254.html, accessed 1 August 2015.

34. Jerri Daboo, 'One Under the Sun: Globalization, Culture and Utopia in *Bombay Dreams*', *Contemporary Theatre Review* 15, no. 3 (2005): 331.

35. See Tejaswini Ganti, *Bollywood* (New York: Routledge, 2004); K. M. Gokulsing and W. Dissanayake, *Indian Popular Cinema: A Narrative of Culture Change* (London: Trentham Books, 2004), 98–99.

36. Paul Prece and William Everett, 'The Megamusical: The Creation, Internationalisation and Impact of a Genre', in *The Cambridge Companion to the American Musical* 2nd ed., ed. William A. Everett and Paul Laird (New York: Cambridge University Press, 2008), 250.

37. See Jessica Sternfeld, *The Megamusical* (Bloomington, IN: Indiana University Press, 2006), 2–3.

38. Rekha Sharma and Carol A. Savery, 'Bollywood Marriages: Portrayals of Matrimony in Hindi Popular Cinema', in *Heroines of Film and Television: Portrayals in Popular Culture*, ed. Norma Jones, Maja Bajac-Carter, and Bob Batchelor (Lanham: Rownam and Littlefield, 2014), 154.

39. James Inverne, *Wrestling with Elephants: The Authorised Biography of Don Black* (London: Sanctuary, 2003), 191.

40. Inverne, *Wrestling with Elephants*, 193.

41. It is worth noting the Western association with drones to evoke a sense of the archaic and the rural. One might think of Beethoven's 'Pastoral' Symphony No. 6 or Mahler's Symphony No. 1, both of which use a drone to evoke the idea of nature. The drone—in the Western classical tradition—might therefore be associated with a sense of indigenous authenticity, appropriate here in both the exotic overtones and the borrowing from Western constructions.

42. Daboo, 'One Under the Sun', 331.

43. Chris Jones, Review of A. R. Rahman, *Bombay Dreams*, BBC music online, http://www.bbc.co.uk/music/reviews/wvhj, accessed 10 September 2014.

44. Michael Billington, '*Bombay Dreams*.' *The Guardian*, 20 June 2002, http://www.theguardian.com/stage/2002/jun/20/theatre.artsfeatures, accessed 12 September 2014.

45. BBC News online, 'Madras Maestro Backing Brum', 10 April 2003, http://news.bbc.co.uk/1/hi/england/west_midlands/2937655.stm, accessed 1 August 2015.

46. Inverne, *Wrestling with Elephants*, 193.

47. Really Useful Group, 'The Making of *Bombay Dreams*', (particularly 0'00"–0'38"), https://www.youtube.com/watch?v=vxziGozMuvM, accessed 10 September 2014.

48. Rustom Bharucha, *Theatre and the World: Performance and the Politics of Culture* (New York: Routledge, 1990), 13.

49. Daboo, 'One Under the Sun', 334.

50. Daboo, 'One Under the Sun', 334.

51. In 1976, Naseem Kham published the Arts Council report on minority ethnic arts. It was poignantly entitled *The Art That Britain Ignores*, and has since been praised as the document that 'revolutionised the Arts Council [. . .] and financially engaged with the work of artists from ethnic minorities', in Dominic Hingorani, *British Asian Theatre: Dramaturgy, Process and Performance* (Basingstoke: Palgrave Macmillan, 2010), 188.

52. Nitro, 'About Nitro', http://www.nitro.co.uk/about/, accessed 28 July 2015.

53. A YouTube clip from rehearsals offers some pertinent personal experiences from the cast, as they reflect on the disparate religious and social backgrounds that effect the performance: Nitro, 'The GOD RACKET: Stand Up Bites! Episode 2.' https://www.youtube.com/watch?t=108&v=CHv5L3nNOHQ, accessed 30 July 2015.

54. Stella Odunlami and Kehinde Andrews, 'Is Art Installation Exhibit B Racist?', *The Guardian*, 27 September 2014, http://www.theguardian.com/commentisfree/2014/sep/27/is-art-installation-exhibit-b-racist, accessed 28 July 2015.

55. Nitro, 'Projects: *Tides*', http://www.nitro.co.uk/projects/now/tides/, accessed 28 July 2015.

56. Quoted in Alda Terracciano, 'Mainstreaming African, Asian and Caribbean Theatre: The Experiments of the Black Theatre Forum', in *Alternatives within the Mainstream: British Black and Asian Theatre*, ed. Dimple Godiwala (Newcastle: Cambridge Scholars, 2006), 31.

57. The title is taken from the landmark immigrant author Sam Selvon's novel *The Lonely Londoners*: 'One day the ship dock in London and he went to Piccadilly Circus and watch the big life.' (1956; London: Penguin, 2006), 84.

58. Akin Ojumu, 'Reach for the Ska', *The Guardian*, 18 April 2004, http://www.theguardian.com/stage/2004/apr/18/theatre1, accessed 20 July 2015.

59. A year prior to *The Big Life*, artistic director Philip Hedley presented *Da Boyz* (2003)—a hip-hop version of the Rodgers and Hart musical *The Boys from Syracuse*.

60. Barbara Korte and Eva Ulrike Pirker, *Black History—White History: Britain's Historical Programme between Windrush and Wilberforce* (New York: Columbia University Press, 2011), 239.

61. For example, one might consider the language of the stevedores in *Show Boat* (1927).
62. Quoted in Ojumu, 'Reach for the Ska', 18 April 2004.
63. Laura Thompson, Review of *Wah! Wah! Girls*, Peacock Theatre, 1 June 2012, *Daily Telegraph* online, http://www.telegraph.co.uk/culture/theatre/theatre-reviews/9306061/ Wah-Wah-Girls-Peacock-Theatre-review.html, accessed 19 July 2015.
64. Lyn Gardner, Review of *Wah! Wah! Girls*, 1 June 2012, *The Guardian* online, http://www. theguardian.com/stage/2012/jun/01/wah-wah-girls-review, accessed 19 July 2015.
65. Thompson, Review of *Wah! Wah! Girls*.
66. For example: Dominic Cavendish, '*Bend It Like Beckham*, Phoenix Theatre Review, "Irresistible"', 24 June 2015, http://www.telegraph.co.uk/culture/theatre/theatre-reviews/ 11693987/Bend-It-Like-Beckham-Phoenix-Theatre-review-irresistible.html;   Michael Arditti, 'Theatre Reviews: *Bend It Like Beckham* and *Luna Gale*', *Daily Express*, 28 June 2015,   http://www.express.co.uk/entertainment/theatre/587301/Bend-it-like-Beckham-Luna-Gale-theatre-review; Quentin Letts, 'An End-to-End Joy Packed with Melodrama . . . The Girl Done Great! Quentin Letts Reviews *Bend It Like Beckham, The Musical*', *Daily Mail*, 25 June 2015, http://www.dailymail.co.uk/tvshowbiz/article-3138381/An-end-end-joy-packed-melodrama-girl-great-QUENTIN-LETTS-reviews-Bent-Like-Beckham-Musical.html, all accessed 1 August 2015.
67. Quoted in Really Useful Group, 'The Journey Home'. See https://www.youtube.com/ watch?v=6TgSwFmTseQ, accessed 11 September 2014.
68. Simon Shepherd, *The Cambridge Introduction to Modern British Theatre* (Cambridge: Cambridge University Press, 2009), 210, my emphasis.
69. Taken from a lyric in the opening song, 'UB2'. See https://www.youtube.com/ watch?v=K4Dk9ml8_FQ, accessed 30 July 2015.

BIBLIOGRAPHY

Anon. 'Bend it Like Beckham.' http://www.whatsonstage.com/west-end-theatre/shows/bend-it-like-beckham_50121, accessed 1 July 2015.
Anon. 'Immigration Patterns of Non-UK Born Populations in England and Wales in 2011.' Office of National Statistics, 17 December 2013. http://www.ons.gov.uk/ons/rel/ census/2011-census-analysis/immigration-patterns-and-characteristics-of-non-uk-born-population-groups-in-england-and-wales/story-on-immigration-patterns-of-non-uk-born-populations-in-england-and-wales-in-2011.html?format=print, accessed 15 July 2015.
Anon. Reviews of *Bombay Dreams*. http://www.reallyuseful.com/shows/bombay-dreams/ reviews/, accessed 1 August 2015.
Anon. 'UB2.' https://www.youtube.com/watch?v=K4Dk9ml8_FQ, accessed 30 July 2015.
Arditti, Michael. Reviews of *Bend It Like Beckham* and *Luna Gale*. *Daily Express*, 28 June 2015. http://www.express.co.uk/entertainment/theatre/587301/Bend-it-like-Beckham-Luna-Gale-theatre-review, accessed 1 August 2015.
Barker, Paul. ' "Putting It Together": Teaching Musical Theatre in UK Higher Education.' March 2006.   https://www.academia.edu/169228/_Putting_It_Together_Teaching_Musical_ Theatre_in_UK_Higher_Education, accessed 25 July 2015.
BBC News online. 'Madras Maestro Backing Brum.' 10 April 2003. http://news.bbc.co.uk/1/hi/ england/west_midlands/2937655.stm, accessed 1 August 2015.
Bhabha, Homi. *The Location of Culture*. Oxford: Routledge, 1994.

Bharucha, Rustom. *Theatre and the World: Performance and the Politics of Culture*. New York: Routledge, 1990.

Billington, Michael. '*Bombay Dreams*.' *The Guardian*, 20 June 2002. http://www.theguardian.com/stage/2002/jun/20/theatre.artsfeatures, accessed 12 September 2014.

Butler, Lawrence J. *Britain and Empire: Adjusting to a Post-Colonial World*. London: I. B. Tauris, 2002.

Cavendish, Dominic. '*Bend It Like Beckham*, Phoenix Theatre Review, "Irresistible".' *Daily Telegraph*, 24 June 2015. http://www.telegraph.co.uk/culture/theatre/theatre-reviews/11693987/Bend-It-Like-Beckham-Phoenix-Theatre-review-irresistible.html, accessed 1 August 2015.

Chung, Tzu-I. 'The Transnational Vision of *Miss Saigon*: Performing the Orient in a Globalized World.' *MELUS: Multi-Ethnic Literature of the U.S.*, 36, no. 4 (2011): 61–86.

Clayton, Martin, and Bennett Zon, eds. *Music and Orientalism in the British Empire 1780s–1940s: Portrayal of the East*. Farnham: Ashgate, 2007.

Cowley, John. 'London Is the Place: Caribbean Music in the Context of Empire 1900–1960.' In *Black Music in Britain: Essays on the Afro Asian Contribution to Popular Music*, edited by Paul Oliver, 57–76. Milton Keynes: Open University Press, 1990.

Daboo, Jerri. 'One Under the Sun: Globalization, Culture and Utopia in *Bombay Dreams*.' *Contemporary Theatre Review* 15, no. 3 (2005): 330–337.

De Jongh, Nicholas. '*Bombay*'s Epic Night of Dreams.' *Evening Standard*, 20 June 2002. http://www.standard.co.uk/goingout/theatre/bombays-epic-night-of-dreams-7434254.html, accessed 1 August 2015.

Ganti, Tejaswini. *Bollywood*. New York: Routledge, 2004.

Gardner, Lyn. Review of *Wah! Wah! Girls*. *The Guardian*, 1 June 2012. http://www.theguardian.com/stage/2012/jun/01/wah-wah-girls-review, accessed 19 July 2015.

Gokulsing, K. M., and Dissanayake, W. *Indian Popular Cinema: A Narrative of Culture Change*. London: Trentham Books, 2004.

Harding, James. *Cochran: A Biography*. London: Methuen, 1988.

Hingorani, Dominic. *British Asian Theatre: Dramaturgy, Process and Performance*. Basingstoke: Palgrave Macmillan, 2010.

Hogarth, William. *Strolling Actresses Dressing in a Barn*. Engraving, 1738. British Museum no. S.232-2009.

Inverne, James. *Wrestling with Elephants: The Authorised Biography of Don Black*. London: Sanctuary, 2003.

Jones, Chris. Review of A. R. Rahman, *Bombay Dreams*. http://www.bbc.co.uk/music/reviews/wvhj, accessed 10 September 2014.

Korte, Barbara, and Eva Ulrike Pirker. *Black History—White History: Britain's Historical Programme between Windrush and Wilberforce*. New York: Columbia University Press, 2011.

Letts, Quentin. 'An End-to-end Joy Packed with Melodrama . . . The Girl Done Great! Quentin Letts Reviews *Bend It Like Beckham, The Musical*.' *Daily Mail*, 25 June 2015, http://www.dailymail.co.uk/tvshowbiz/article-3138381/An-end-end-joy-packed-melodrama-girl-great-QUENTIN-LETTS-reviews-Bent-Like-Beckham-Musical.html, accessed 1 August 2015.

Linton, David, and Platt, Len. '*Dover Street to Dixie* and the Politics of Cultural Transfer and Exchange.' In *Popular Musical Theatre in London and Berlin 1890 to 1939*, edited by Len Platt, Tobias Becker, and David Linton, 170–185. Cambridge: Cambridge University Press, 2014.

Mukherjee, Sumita. 'The Representation and Display of South Asians in Britain, 1870–1950.' In *South Asians and the Shaping of Britain, 1870–1950: A Sourcebook*, edited by

Ruvani Ranasinha, Rehana Ahmed, Sumita Mukerherjee, and Florian Stadtler, 205–225. Manchester: Manchester University Press, 2012.

Nitro. 'About Nitro.' http://www.nitro.co.uk/about/, accessed 28 July 2015.

Nitro. 'Projects: Tides.' http://www.nitro.co.uk/projects/now/tides/, accessed 28 July 2015.

Nitro. 'The GOD RACKET: Stand Up Bites! Episode 2.' https://www.youtube.com/watch?t=108&v=CHv5L3nNOHQ, accessed 30 July 2015.

Odunlami, Stella, and Andrews, Kehinde. 'Is Art Installation Exhibit B Racist?' *The Guardian*, 27 September 2014, http://www.theguardian.com/commentisfree/2014/sep/27/is-art-installation-exhibit-b-racist, accessed 28 July 2015.

Ojumu, Akin. 'Reach for the Ska.' *The Guardian*. 18 April 2004. http://www.theguardian.com/stage/2004/apr/18/theatre1, accessed 20 July 2015.

Pao, Angela, 'The Eyes of the Storm: Gender, Genre and Cross-Casting in *Miss Saigon*.' *Text and Performance Quarterly* 12, no. 1 (1992): 21–39.

Prece, Paul, and Everett, William A. 'The Megamusical: The Creation, Internationalisation and Impact of a Genre.' In *The Cambridge Companion to the American Musical*. 2nd ed., edited by William A. Everett and Paul Laird, 250–269. New York: Cambridge University Press, 2008.

Really Useful Group. 'The Journey Home.' https://www.youtube.com/watch?v=6TgSwFmTseQ, accessed 11 September 2014.

Really Useful Group. 'The Making of *Bombay Dreams*.' https://www.youtube.com/watch?v=vxziGozMuvM, accessed 10 September 2014.

Rebellato, Dan. *Theatre and Globalization*. Basingstoke: Palgrave Macmillan, 2009.

Rice, Stanley. 'Indian Plays in London.' *Asiatic Review* 18, no. 53 (1922): 129.

Selvon, Sam. *The Lonely Londoners*. 1956. London: Penguin, 2006.

Sharma, Rekha, and Savery, Carol A. 'Bollywood Marriages: Portrayals of Matrimony in Hindi Popular Cinema.' In *Heroines of Film and Television: Portrayals in Popular Culture*, edited by Norma Jones, Maja Bajac-Carter, and Bob Batchelor, 147–162. Lanham: Rownam and Littlefield, 2014.

Shepherd, Simon. *The Cambridge Introduction to Modern British Theatre*. Cambridge: Cambridge University Press, 2009.

Singleton, Brian. *Oscar Asche, Orientalism and British Musical Comedy*. Westport: Praeger, 2004.

Sternfeld, Jessica. *The Megamusical*. Bloomington, IN: Indiana University Press, 2006.

Taylor, Millie. 'Hybrid Voices of Music Theatre: *Deep Blue, Bombay Dream* and *London Road*.' Performance Culture Industry PSI Annual Conference Leeds, 27 June–1 July 2012.

Terracciano, Alda. 'Mainstreaming African, Asian and Caribbean Theatre: The Experiments of the Black Theatre Forum.' In *Alternatives within the Mainstream: British Black and Asian Theatre*, edited by Dimple Godiwala, 22–60. Newcastle: Cambridge Scholars, 2006.

Thompson, Laura. Review of *Wah! Wah! Girls*, Peacock Theatre. *Daily Telegraph*, 1 June 2012. http://www.telegraph.co.uk/culture/theatre/theatre-reviews/9306061/Wah-Wah-Girls-Peacock-Theatre-review.html, accessed 19 July 2015.

Vermette, Margaret. *The Musical World of Boublil and Schönberg*. New York: Applause, 2006.

Williams, Holly. 'Can *Bend It Like Beckham* Succeed in the West End?' *The Independent*, 19 May 2015. http://www.independent.co.uk/arts-entertainment/theatre-dance/features/can-bend-it-like-beckham-succeed-in-the-west-end-10261680.html, accessed 1 July 2015.

Wolf, Matt. 'West End Star Jon Jon Briones on His 25-Year Journey in *Miss Saigon*, From Ensemble Member to Engineer.' 7 May 2014. http://www.broadway.com/buzz/175829/

west-end-star-jon-jon-briones-on-his-25-year-journey-in-miss-saigon-from-ensemble-member-to-engineer/, accessed 4 July 2015.

Wright, Adrian. *A Tanners Worth of Tune: Re-discovering the Post-war British Musical.* Suffolk: Boydell and Brewer, 2010.

Wry, Howard. 'The Plantation Revues.' *Storyville* 133 (1 March 1988).

Yokota, Kariann Akemi. *Unbecoming British: How Revolutionary America Became a Postcolonial Nation.* New York: Oxford University Press, 2011.

BIBLIOGRAPHY

Adiseshiah, Siân. '"We Said We Wouldn't Look Back": Utopia and the Backward Glance in Dorothy Reynolds and Julian Slade's *Salad Days*.' *Studies in Musical Theatre* 5, no. 2 (2011): 149–161.

Agate, James. *Immoment Toys: A Survey of Light Entertainment on the London Stage, 1920–1943*. London: Jonathan Cape, 1945.

Ahlquist, Karen. 'Masculinity and Legitimacy on the English Musical Stage: The Mature Male, 1800–1845.' *Women and Music: A Journal of Gender and Culture* 8 (2004): 1–21.

Ainger, Michael. *Gilbert and Sullivan: A Dual Biography*. New York: Oxford University Press, 2009.

Anderson, Virginia. 'Sets, Costumes, Lights and Spectacle.' In *The Oxford Handbook of the American Musical*, edited by Raymond Knapp, Mitchell Morris, and Stacy Wolf, 294–308. New York: Oxford University Press, 2011.

Aston, Elaine. 'Work, Family, Romance and the Utopian Sensibilities of the Chick Megamusical *Mamma Mia!*' In *A Good Night Out for the Girls*, edited by Elaine Aston and Geraldine Harris, 114–133. Basingstoke: Palgrave Macmillan, 2013.

Auslander, Philip. *Performing Glam Rock: Gender and Theatricality in Popular Music*. Ann Arbor: University of Michigan Press, 2006.

Bacon, Richard Mackenzie. 'Sketch of the State of Music in London.' *Quarterly Musical Magazine and Review* 7 (June 1825): 186–211.

Baer, Marc. *Theatre and Disorder in Late Georgian London*. Oxford: Clarendon Press, 1992.

Bailey, Peter. '"Naughty But Nice": Musical Comedy and the Rhetoric of the Girl, 1892–1914.' In *The Edwardian Theatre*, edited by Michael R. Booth and Joel H. Kaplan, 36–60. Cambridge: Cambridge University Press, 1996.

Bailey, Peter. 'Theatres of Entertainment / Spaces of Modernity: Rethinking the British Popular Stage 1890–1914.' *Nineteenth Century Theatre* 26, no. 1 (Summer 1998): 5–24.

Baily, Leslie. *The Gilbert and Sullivan Book*. London: Spring Books 1966.

Bardsley, Garth. *Stop the World . . . The Biography of Anthony Newley*. London: Oberon Books, 2003.

Barlow, Jeremy. '*The Beggar's Opera* in London's Theatres, 1728–1761.' In *The Stage's Glory: John Rich, 1692–1761*, edited by Berta Joncus and Jeremy Barlow, 169–183. Newark: University of Delaware Press; Lanham, MD: Rowman & Littlefield, 2011.

Barnes, Richard, and Pete Townshend. *The Story of 'Tommy'*. Twickenham: Eel Pie Publishing, 1977.

Barrington, Rutland. *A Record of Thirty-Five Years' Experience on the English Stage; By Himself*. London: Grant, 1908.

Behr, Edward. *'Les Misérables': History in the Making*. Updated ed. New York: Arcade 1996.

Behr, Edward, and Mark Steyn. *The Story of 'Miss Saigon'*. New York: Arcade, 1991.

Boaden, James. *Memoirs of the Life of John Philip Kemble, Esq. Including a History of the Stage, from the Time of Garrick to the Present Period.* 2 volumes in 1. Philadelphia: Robert H. Small; New York: Wilder & Campbell, 1825.

Böker, Uwe, Ines Detmers, and Anna Giovanopoulos, eds. *John Gay's 'The Beggar's Opera' 1728–2004: Adaptations and Re-writings.* Amsterdam: Rodopi, 2006.

Bowers, Julie. *Stan Laurel and Other Stars of the Panopticon: The Story of the Britannia Musical Hall.* Edinburgh: Birlinn Ltd, 2007.

Bradley, Ian, ed. *The Complete Annotated Gilbert and Sullivan.* New ed. New York: Oxford University Press, 2001.

Bradley, Ian. *Oh Joy! Oh Rapture! The Enduring Phenomenon of Gilbert and Sullivan.* New York: Oxford University Press, 2007.

Bradshaw, Jon. 'The Truth about *Twang!!' Plays and Players* 14, no. 4 (April 1966): 51–52; no. 5 (May 1966): 51–54 and 72–73.

Brahms, Cary, and Ned Sherrin. *Song by Song: The Lives and Work of Fourteen Great Lyric Writers.* Bolton: Ross Anderson, 1984.

Bratton, J. S., ed. *Music Hall: Performance and Style.* Milton Keynes: Open University Press, 1986.

Bratton, J. S., Richard Allen Cave, Brendan Gregory, Heide J. Holder, and Michael Pickering. *Acts of Supremacy: The British Empire and the Stage, 1790–1930.* Manchester: Manchester University Press, 1991.

Bricusse, Leslie. *The Music Man: The Life and Good Times of a Songwriter.* London: Metro Publishing, 2006.

Burling, William J. *Summer Theatre in London, 1661–1820, and the Rise of the Haymarket Theatre.* Madison: Fairleigh Dickinson University Press; London: Associated University Presses, 2000.

Burston, Jonathan. *The Megamusical: New Forms and Relations in Global Cultural Production.* PhD thesis, UMI Dissertations Publishing, 1998.

Carlson, Marvin. ' "He Never Should Bow Down to a Domineering Frown": Class Tensions and Nautical Melodrama.' In *Melodrama: The Cultural Emergence of a Genre,* edited by Michael Hays and Anastasia Nicolopolou, 147–166. New York: St Martin's Press 1996.

Carter, Huntly. *The New Spirit in the European Theatre 1914–1924.* London: Ernest Benn Ltd, 1925.

Castle, Charles. *Noël.* London: Abacus, 1974.

Chandler, David. ' "Everyone Should Have the Opportunity": Alan Doggett and the Modern British Musical.' *Studies in Musical Theatre* 6, no. 3 (2012): 275–289.

Cheshire, D. F. *Music Hall in Britain.* Devon: David & Charles, 1974.

Chung, Tzu-I. 'The Transnational Vision of *Miss Saigon:* Performing the Orient in a Globalized World.' *MELUS: Multi-Ethnic Literature of the US* 36, no. 4 (2011): 61–86.

Citron, Stephen. *Noël and Cole: The Sophisticates.* London: Sinclair-Stevenson, 1992.

Citron, Stephen. *Sondheim and Lloyd-Webber: The New Musical.* Oxford: Oxford University Press, 2001.

Clayton, Martin, and Bennett Zon, eds. *Music and Orientalism in the British Empire 1780s–1940s: Portrayal of the East.* Farnham: Ashgate, 2007.

Coren, Michael. *Theatre Royal: 100 Years of Stratford East.* London: Quartet, 1984.

Courtneidge, Cicely. *Cicely.* London: Hutchinson and Co., 1953.

Coveney, Michael. *Cats on a Chandelier: The Andrew Lloyd Webber Story.* London: Hutchinson, 1999.

Coward, Noël. *Autobiography*. London: Methuen, 1986.

Coward, Noël. *The Lyrics of Noël Coward*. London: Methuen Publishing Ltd, 2002.

Coward, Noël. *The Noël Coward Diaries*. Edited by Graham Payn and Sheridan Morley. London: Macmillan. 1983.

Cowley, John. 'London is the Place: Caribbean Music in the Context of Empire 1900–1960.' In *Black Music in Britain: Essays on the Afro Asian Contribution to Popular Music*, edited by Paul Oliver, 57–76. Milton Keynes: Open University Press, 1990.

Cox, Peter. *Set into Song: Ewan MacColl, Charles Parker, Peggy Seeger and the Radio Ballads*. London: Labatie, 2008.

Cox-Ife, William. *W. S. Gilbert: Stage Director*. London: Dennis Dobson, 1977.

Creeber, Glen. *Dennis Potter Between Two Worlds: A Critical Reassessment*. Basingstoke: Macmillan, 1998.

Daboo, Jerri. 'One Under the Sun: Globalization, Culture and Utopia in *Bombay Dreams*.' *Contemporary Theatre Review* 15, no. 3 (2005): 330–337.

Davis, Jim, and Victor Emeljanow. *Reflecting the Audience: London Theatregoing, 1840–1880*. Iowa City: University of Iowa Press, 2001.

Davis, Lee. *Bolton and Wodehouse and Kern: The Men Who Made Musical Comedy*. New York: James H. Heineman Inc., 1993.

Davis, Tracy C. *The Economics of the British Stage, 1800–1914*. Cambridge: Cambridge University Press, 2000.

Dideriksen, Gabriella. 'Major and Minor Theatres: Competition in London in the 1830s.' In *Le Concert et son public: Mutations de la vie musicale en Europe de 1780 à 1914*, edited by Hans Erich Bödeker, Patrice Veit, and Michael Werner, 303–313. Paris: Éditions de la Maison des sciences de l'homme, 2002.

Donaldson, Frances. *P. G. Wodehouse*. New York: Alfred A. Knopf, 1982.

Double, Oliver. *Britain Had Talent: A History of Variety Theatre*. Basingstoke: Palgrave Macmillan, 2012.

Dugaw, Dianne. ' "Critical Instants": Theatre Songs in the Age of Dryden and Purcell.' *Eighteenth-Century Studies* 23, no. 2 (1989): 157–181.

Dugaw, Dianne. *Deep Play: John Gay and the Invention of Modernity*. Newark: University of Delaware Press; London: Associated University Presses, 2001.

Dugaw, Dianne. 'The Popular Marketing of "Old Ballads": The Ballad Revival and Eighteenth-Century Antiquarianism Reconsidered.' *Eighteenth-Century Studies* 21, no. 1 (1987): 71–90.

Eden, David, and Meinhard Saremba, eds. *The Cambridge Companion to Gilbert and Sullivan*. Cambridge: Cambridge University Press, 2009.

Ellis, Vivian. *I'm on a See-Saw*. London: Michael Joseph, 1953.

Elsom, John. *Post-War British Theatre Criticism*. London: Law Book Company of Australasia, 1981.

Fischler, Alan. *Modified Rapture: Comedy in W. S. Gilbert's Savoy Operas*. Charlottesville: University Press of Virginia, 1991.

Fiske, Roger. *English Theatre Music in the Eighteenth Century*. London: Oxford University Press, 1973.

FitzGerald, Louise, and Melanie Williams, eds. *Exploring a Cultural Phenomenon: 'Mamma Mia! The Movie'*. London: I. B. Tauris, 2013.

Gagey, Edmond M. *Ballad Opera*. New York: Benjamin Blom, 1937.

Gammond, Peter. *A Guide to Popular Music*. London: Phoenix House, 1960.

Gänzl, Kurt. *The British Musical Theatre*. 2 vols. London: MacMillan, 1986.

Gänzl, Kurt. *The Complete 'Aspects of Love'*. New York: Viking Studio Books, 1990.

Gänzl, Kurt. *The Encyclopedia of Musical Theatre*. 3 vols. 2nd ed. New York: Schirmer Books, 2004.

Gänzl, Kurt. *Song & Dance: The Complete Story of Stage Musicals*. London: Carlton Books Ltd, 1995.

Goldberg, Isaac. *The Story of Gilbert and Sullivan; or The 'Compleat' Savoyard*. New York: Simon and Schuster, 1928.

Goodman, Judith Lea. 'Joan Littlewood and Her Theatre Workshop.' Unpublished PhD, New York University, 1975.

Goodwin, John, ed. *British Theatre Design: The Modern Age*. London: Weidenfeld & Nicolson, 1998.

Goorney, Howard. *The Theatre Workshop Story*. London: Eyre Methuen, 1981.

Gordon, Robert, Olaf Jubin, and Millie Taylor. *The British Musical Since 1950*. London: Bloomsbury Methuen Drama, 2016.

Graber, Naomi. 'Memories That Remain: *Mamma Mia!* and the Disruptive Potential of Nostalgia.' *Studies in Musical Theatre* 9, no. 2 (2015): 187–198.

Grandage, Michael. *A Decade at the Donmar, 2002–2012*. London: Constable, 2012.

Granville-Barker, Harley. 'Exit Planché—Enter Gilbert.' In *The Eighteen-Sixties: Essays by Fellows of the Royal Society of Literature*, edited by John Drinkwater, 102–148. Cambridge: Cambridge University Press, 1932.

Graves, George. *Gaieties and Gravities*. London: Hutchinson, 1931.

Grossman, Kathryn M., and Bradley Stephens, eds. *'Les Misérables' and Its Afterlives: Between Page, Stage, and Screen*. Farnham: Ashgate, 2015.

Harding, James. *Cochran: A Biography*. London: Methuen, 1988.

Harding, James. *Ivor Novello*. London: W. H. Allen, 1987.

Hoare, Philip. *Noël Coward: A Biography*. London: Sinclair-Stevenson, 1995.

Holden, Stephen. 'Lloyd Webber: Hits But No Hit Songs.' *New York Times*, 3 July 1983, H15–H16.

Holdsworth, Nadine. *Joan Littlewood*. London: Routledge, 2006.

Hollingshead, John. *Gaiety Chronicle*. London: Constable, 1898.

Hollingshead, John. *Good Old Gaiety*. London: The Gaiety Theatre Co. Ltd, 1903.

Huffman, James R. '*Jesus Christ Superstar*: Popular Art and Unpopular Criticism.' *Journal of Popular Culture* 6, no. 2 (1972): 259–269.

Hughes, Gervase. *The Music of Arthur Sullivan*. New York: St Martin's Press, 1960.

Hulbert, Jack. *The Little Woman's Always Right*. London: W. H. Allen, 1975.

Hunt, Leigh. *The Autobiography of Leigh Hunt*, edited by J. E. Morpurgo. London: Cresset Press, 1948.

Hyman, Alan. *The Gaiety Years*. London: Cassell, 1975.

Inverne, James. *Wrestling with Elephants: The Authorised Biography of Don Black*. London: Sanctuary, 2003.

Jacobs, Arthur. *Arthur Sullivan: A Victorian Musician*. 2nd ed. Oxford: Oxford University Press, 2003.

Jeans, Ronald. *Writing for the Theatre*. London: Edward Arnold & Co., 1949.

Joncus, Berta. ' "When Farce and When Musick Can Eke out a Play": Ballad Opera and Theatre's Commerce.' In *The Edinburgh Companion to Literature and Music*, edited by Correa Delia Da Sousa. Edinburgh: Edinburgh University Press, forthcoming.

Joncus, Berta, and Vanessa Rogers. 'Beyond *The Beggar's Opera*: John Rich and English Ballad Opera.' In *The Stage's Glory: John Rich, 1692–1761*, edited by Berta Joncus and Jeremy Barlow, 184–204. Newark: University of Delaware Press; Lanham, MD: Rowman & Littlefield, 2011.

Jubin, Olaf. 'Experts Without Expertise? Findings of a Comparative Study of American, British, and German-Language Reviews of Musicals by Stephen Sondheim and Andrew Lloyd Webber.' *Studies in Musical Theatre* 4, no. 2 (2010): 185–197.

Kaplan, Joel, and Sheila Stowell. *Look Back in Pleasure: Noël Coward Reconsidered.* London: Methuen, 2000.

Lamb, Andrew. *150 Years of Popular Musical Theatre.* New Haven: Yale University Press, 2000.

Lamb, Andrew. 'From *Pinafore* to Porter: United States–United Kingdom Interactions in Musical Theater, 1879–1929.' *American Music* 4, no. 1 (1986): 34–49.

Lawrence, Arthur. *Sir Arthur Sullivan: Life Story, Letters, and Reminiscences.* Chicago: Stone, 1900.

Leach, Robert. *Theatre Workshop: Joan Littlewood and the Making of Modern British Theatre.* Exeter: University of Exeter Press, 2006.

Lee, Edward. *Folksong & Music Hall.* London: Routledge & Kegan Paul Ltd, 1982.

Lee, Josephine. *The Japan of Pure Invention: Gilbert and Sullivan's 'The Mikado'.* Minneapolis: University of Minnesota Press, 2010.

Lesley, Cole. *Remembered Laughter: The Life of Noël Coward.* New York: Alfred A. Knopf, 1976.

Lesley, Cole, Graham Payn, and Sheridan Morley. *Noël Coward and His Friends.* London: Weidenfeld & Nicolson, 1979.

Light, Alison, and Raphael Samuel. 'Doing the Lambeth Walk.' In *Patriotism: The Making and Unmaking of British National Identity*, vol. 3, *National Fictions*, edited by Raphael Samuel, 261–271. London: Routledge, 1989.

Light, Alison, and Raphael Samuel. 'Pantomimes of Class.' *New Society* 19, no. 26 (December 1986): 14–18.

Linton, David. 'New Insecurities, New Form, New Identity: National Identity and Raciologies in *Eightpence a Mile* (1913).' *Studies in Musical Theatre* 7, no. 1 (2013): 9–22.

Lippert, Richard. *Music and Image: Domesticity, Ideology, and Socio-Cultural Formation in Eighteenth-Century England.* Cambridge: Cambridge University Press, 1993.

Littlewood, Joan. *Joan's Book: Joan Littlewood's Peculiar History as She Tells It.* London: Methuen, 1994.

Lloyd Webber, Andrew, and Tim Rice. *Evita. The Legend of Eva Perón.* New York: Drama Book Specialists, 1978.

Lundskaer-Nielsen, Miranda. *Directors and the New Musical Drama: British and American Musical Theatre in the 1980s and 1990s.* Basingstoke: Palgrave Macmillan, 2008.

Lundskaer-Nielsen, Miranda. 'The Long Road to Recognition: New Musical Theatre Development in Britain.' *Studies in Musical Theatre* 7, no. 2 (2013): 157–173.

MacDonald, Laura: '"Sometimes You Have to Make a Little Bit of Mischief": Matthew Warchus' Hybrid Approach to Musical Theatre Directing.' *Studies in Musical Theatre* 6, no. 3 (2012): 355–362.

Macqueen Pope, Walter. *Gaiety: Theatre of Enchantment.* London: W. H. Allen, 1949.

Macqueen Pope, Walter. *Ivor. The Story of an Achievement: A Biography of Ivor Novello.* London: W. H. Allen, 1951.

Mander, Raymond, and Joe Michenson. *Musical Comedy: A Story in Pictures.* London: Taplinger Publishing Company, 1969.

Mander, Raymond, and Joe Mitchenson. *Revue: A Story in Pictures.* London: Peter Davies 1971.

Mantle, Jonathan. *Fanfare: The Unauthorized Biography of Andrew Lloyd Webber.* London: Michael Joseph Ltd, 1989.

Matthews, Jessie. *Over My Shoulder.* London: W. H. Allen, 1974.

Mayer, David. 'Nineteenth Century Theatre Music.' *Theatre Notebook* 30 (1976): 115–123.

McKee, Alison L. ' "Think of Me Fondly": Voice, Body, Affect and Performance in Prince/Lloyd Webber's *The Phantom of the Opera.' Studies in Musical Theatre* 7, no. 3 (2013): 309–325.

McKnight, Gerald. *Andrew Lloyd Webber*. New York: St Martin's Press, 1984.

Moody, Jane. *Illegitimate Theatre in London, 1170–1840*. Cambridge: Cambridge University Press, 2000.

Moore, James Ross. 'Girl Crazy: Musicals and Revue Between the Wars.' In *British Theatre Between the Wars 1918-1939*, edited by Clive Barker and Maggie B. Gale, 88–112. Cambridge: Cambridge University Press, 2000.

Morley, Sheridan. *Our Theatres in the Eighties*. London: W & N, 1990.

Morley, Sheridan. *Spread a Little Happiness: The First Hundred Years of the British Musicals*. London: Thames and Hudson, 1987.

Morley, Sheridan. *A Talent to Amuse*. London: Pavillon Books, 1985.

Morley, Sheridan, and Ruth Leon. *Hey, Mr Producer! The Musical World of Cameron Mackintosh*. New York: Art Books International, 1998.

Morrissey, Leroy J. 'Fielding and the Ballad Opera.' *Eighteenth-Century Studies* 4 (1971): 386–402.

Nassour, Ellis, and Richard Broderick. *Rock Opera: The Creation of 'Jesus Christ Superstar' from Record Album to Broadway Show and Motion Picture*. New York: Hawthorn Books Inc., 1973.

Naylor, Stanley. *Gaiety and George Grossmith: Random Reflections on the Serious Business of Enjoyment*. 1913. London: Kessinger Publishing, 2007.

Newey, Katherine. 'Reform on the London Stage'. In *Rethinking the Age of Reform: Britain 1780–1850*, edited by Arthur Burns and Joanna Innes, 238–253. Cambridge: Cambridge University Press, 2003.

Nicholson, Steve. British *Theatre and the Red Peril: The Portrayal of Communism 1917–1945*. Exeter: University of Exeter Press, 1999.

Nicoll, Allardyce. *English Drama, 1900–1930: The Beginnings of the Modern Period*. Cambridge: Cambridge University Press, 1973.

Noble, Peter. *Ivor Novello: Man of the Theatre*. London: The Falcon Press, 1951.

Norman, Frank. *Why Fings Went West*. London: Lemon Tree Press, 1975.

Northcott, Richard. *The Life of Sir Henry R. Bishop*. London: Press Printers Ltd, 1921.

Nott, James J. *Music for the People: Popular Music and Dance in Interwar Britain*. Oxford: Oxford University Press, 2002.

Pao, Angela. 'The Eyes of the Storm: Gender, Genre and Cross-Casting in *Miss Saigon.' Text and Performance Quarterly* 12, no. 1 (1992): 21–39

Parker, Alan. *The Making of 'Evita'*. New York: Collins, 1996.

Parker, Derek, and Julia Parker. *The Story and the Song: A Survey of English Musical Plays, 1916–1978*. London: Arts Books International, 1979.

Payn, Graham, and Barry Day. *My Life with Noël Coward*. New York: Applause Books, 1994.

Pearson, Hesketh. *Gilbert: His Life and Strife*. London: Hamish Hamilton, 1957.

Pearson, Hesketh. *Gilbert and Sullivan*. London: Hamish Hamilton, 1935.

Peck, Ellen Marie. 'Artistic Freedom through Subsidy: The British Model of Reviving American Musicals.' *Studies in Musical Theatre* 5, no. 1 (2011): 85–97.

Perry, George C. *The Complete 'Phantom of the Opera'*. New York: Henry Holt, 1988.

Perry, George C. *'Sunset Boulevard': From Movie to Musical*. New York: Henry Holt, 1993.

Pick, John. *The West End: Mismanagement and Snobbery*. Eastbourne: John Offord Publications Ltd, 1983.

Planché, James Robinson. *Recollections and Reflections: A Professional Autobiography*. New and rev. ed. London: S. Low, Marston & Co., 1901.

Platt, Len. *Musical Comedy on the West End Stage, 1890–1939*. Basingstoke: Palgrave Macmillan, 2004.

Platt, Len, Tobias Becker, and David Linton. *Popular Musical Theatre in London and Berlin, 1890–1939*. Cambridge: Cambridge University Press, 2014.

Postlewait, Thomas. 'George Edwardes and Musical Comedy: The Transformation of London Theatre and Society, 1878–1914.' In *The Performing Century: Nineteenth-Century Theatre's History*, edited by Tracy C. Davis and Peter Holland, 80–102. Basingstoke: Palgrave Macmillan, 2007.

Prece, Paul, and William A. Everett. 'The Megamusical: The Creation, Internationalisation and Impact of a Genre.' In *The Cambridge Companion to the American Musical*, 2nd ed., edited by William A. Everett and Paul R. Laird, 250–269. New York: Cambridge University Press, 2008.

Price, Cedric and Joan Littlewood. 'The Fun Palace.' *Drama Review* 12, no. 3 (Spring 1968): 127–134.

Ramsey, Burt. *Alien Bodies, Representations of Modernity: 'Race' and Nation in Early Modern Dance*. London: Routledge, 1989.

Rebellato, Dan. *1956 and All That: The Making of Modern British Drama*. London: Routledge, 1999.

Rees, Terence. *Thespis: A Gilbert and Sullivan Enigma*. London: Dillon's University Bookshop, 1964.

Rice, Tim. *Oh, What A Circus: The Autobiography 1944–1978*. London: Hodder and Stoughton, 1999.

Richards, Jeffrey. *Imperialism and Music: Britain 1876–1953*. Manchester: Manchester University Press, 2001.

Richmond, Keith. *The Musicals of Andrew Lloyd Webber*. London: Virgin Publishing Ltd, 1995.

Robb, Linsey. *Men at Work: The Working Man in British Culture, 1939–1945*. Basingstoke: Palgrave Macmillan, 2015.

Rodosthenous, George. '*Billy Elliot: The Musical*: Visual Representation of Working-Class Masculinity and the All-Singing, All-Dancing Bo[d]y.' *Studies in Musical Theatre* 1, no. 3 (2007): 275–292.

Rogers, Vanessa L. 'John Gay, Ballad Opera, and the Théâtres de la foire.' *Eighteenth-Century Music* 11, no. 2 (2014): 173–213.

Rohr, Deborah Adams. *The Careers of British Musicians, 1750–1850: A Profession of Artisans*. Cambridge: Cambridge University Press, 2001

Rohr, Deborah Adams. 'Writing Plays "In the Sing-Song Way": Henry Fielding's Ballad Operas and Early Musical Theater in Eighteenth-Century London.' Unpublished PhD, University of Southern California, 2007.

Roper, David. *Bart! The Unauthorized Life and Times, Ins and Outs, Ups and Downs of Lionel Bart*. London: Pavillion Books Ltd, 1994.

Rose, Richard. *Perchance to Dream: The World of Ivor Novello*. London: Leslie Frewin, 1974.

Ross, Cathy. *Twenties London: A City in the Jazz Age*. London: Philip Wilson, 2003.

Ross Moore, James. *André Charlot: The Genius of Intimate Musical Revue*. London: McFarland & Company, 2005.

Ross Moore, James. 'An Intimate Understanding: The Rise of British Musical Revue 1890–1920.' Unpublished PhD thesis, University of Warwick, 2000.

Rubsamen, Walter H. 'Mr. Seedo, Ballad Opera and the Singspiel.' In *Miscelánea En Homenaje a Monseñor Higinio Anglés*, 1–35. Barcelona: Consejo Superior de Investigaciones Cientoficas, 1958–1961.

Rüger, Jan. 'Entertainments.' In *Capital Cities at War: Paris, London, Berlin 1914–1919*, edited by Jay Winter and Jean-Louis Robert, 101–140. Cambridge: Cambridge University Press, 1999.

Schultz, William E. *Gay's 'Beggar's Opera': Its Content, History & Influence*. New Haven: Yale University Press, 1923.

Seeley, Robert, and Rex Bunnett. *London Musical Shows on Record 1889–1989*. Harrow: Gramophone, 1989.

Seinfield, Alan. *Out on Stage: Lesbian and Gay Theatre in the Twentieth Century*. New Haven: Yale University Press, 1999.

Senelick, Laurence. *British Music-Hall, 1840–1923: A Bibliography and Guide to Sources, with a Supplement on European Music-Hall*. Hamden: Archon Books, 1981.

Shepherd, Jane. 'Music, Text and Performance in English Popular Theatre 1790–1840.' Unpublished PhD thesis, University of London, 1991.

Short, Ernest. *Fifty Years of Vaudeville*. London: Eyre & Spottiswoode, 1946.

Simpson, Claude M. *The British Broadside Ballad and Its Music*. New Brunswick: Rutgers University Press, 1966.

Siropoulos, Vagelis. 'Andrew Lloyd Webber and the Culture of Narcissism.' *Studies in Musical Theatre* 4, no. 3 (2010): 273–291.

Siropoulos, Vagelis. 'Megamusicals, Spectacle and the Postdramatic Aesthetics of Late Capitalism.' *Studies in Musical Theatre* 5, no. 1 (2011): 13–34.

Slattery-Christy, David. *In Search of Ruritania: The Life and Times of Ivor Novello*. Milton Keynes: Author House, 2008.

Snelson, John. ' "We Said We Wouldn't Look Back": British Musical Theatre, 1935–1960.' In *The Cambridge Companion to the Musical*, 2nd ed., edited by William A. Everett and Paul R. Laird, 127–146. Cambridge: Cambridge University Press, 2008.

Snelson, John. 'The West End Musical 1947–1954: British Identity and the "American Invasion".' Unpublished PhD thesis, University of Manchester, 2003.

Stafford, Caroline, and David Stafford. *Fings Ain't Wot They Used T'Be: The Lionel Bart Story*, London: Omnibus Press, 2011.

Staveacre, Tony. *The Songwriters*. London: British Broadcasting Corporation, 1980.

Stedman, Jane W. *W. S. Gilbert: A Classic Victorian and His Theatre*. Oxford: Oxford University Press, 1996.

Sternfeld, Jessica. *The Megamusical*. Bloomington: Indiana University Press, 2006.

Steyn, Mark. *Broadway Babies Say Goodnight: Musicals Then and Now*. London: Faber and Faber, 1997.

Stone, Harry. *The Century of Musical Comedy and Revue*. Milton Keynes: AuthorHouse, 2009.

Sutton, Max Keith. *W. S. Gilbert*. Boston: Twayne, 1975.

Taylor, Millie. *British Pantomime Performance*. Bristol: Intellect, 2008.

Taylor, Millie. ' "Don't Dream It, Be It!": Exploring Signification, Empathy and Mimesis in Relation to *The Rocky Horror Show.' Studies in Musical Theatre* 1, no. 1 (2007): 57–71.

Thomas, Jennifer Renee. 'Joan Littlewood: A Director Ahead of Her Time.' Unpublished PhD thesis, University of Oregon, 2005.

Vermette, Margaret. *The Musical World of Boublil and Schönberg*. New York: Applause, 2006.

Walsh, David, and Len Platt. *Musical Theater and American Culture*. Westport: Praeger, 2003.

Walsh, Michael. *Andrew Lloyd Webber. His Life and Works*. Updated and enlarged ed. New York: Harry N. Abrams, 1997.

Walsh, Michael. 'Lloyd Webber: Now, But Forever?' *New York Times*, 9 April 2000, section 2, 1 and 9.

Warfield, Scott. 'From *Hair* to *Rent*: Is "Rock" a Four-letter Word on Broadway?' In *The Cambridge Companion to the Musical*, 2nd ed, edited by William A. Everett and Paul R. Laird, 235–249. Cambridge: Cambridge University Press, 2008.

Watson, Nicholson. *The Struggle for a Free Stage in London*. Cambridge: Houghton, Mifflin and Company, 1906.

Watts, Andrew. '*Les Misérables*, Theatre, and the Anxiety of Excess.' In *Adapting Nineteenth-Century France: Literature in Film, Theatre, Television, Radio, and Print*, edited by Kate Griffiths and Andrew Watts, 114–142. Cardiff: University of Wales Press, 2013.

Webb, Paul. *Ivor Novello: Portrait of a Star*. Rev. ed. London: Haus Publishing Ltd, 2005.

Weltman, Sharon Aronofsky. '"Can a Fellow Be a Villain All His Life?": *Oliver!*, Fagin, and Performing Jewishness.' *Nineteenth-Century Contexts* 33, no. 4 (September 2011): 371–388.

White, James Dillon. *Born to Star: The Lupino Lane Story*. London: Heinemann, 1957.

Williams, Carolyn. *Gilbert and Sullivan: Gender, Genre, Parody*. New York: Columbia University Press, 2011.

Williams, Carolyn. 'Parody and Poetic Tradition: Gilbert and Sullivan's *Patience*.' *Victorian Poetry* 46, no. 4 (2008): 375–403.

Williams, Gordon. *British Theatre in the Great War: A Revaluation*. London: Continuum, 2003.

Williams, Michael. *Ivor Novello: Screen Idol*. London: BFI Publishing, 2003.

Wilmeth, Don B. *American and English Popular Entertainment: A Guide to Information Sources*. Detroit: Gale Group, 1980.

Wilson, Robin, and Frederic Lloyd. *Gilbert and Sullivan: The D'Oyly Carte Years*. London: Weidenfeld & Nicolson, 1984.

Wilson, Sandy. *I Could Be Happy: An Autobiography*. London: Michael Joseph, 1975.

Wilson, Sandy. *Ivor*. London: Michael Joseph, 1975.

Windsor, Barbara. *All of Me*. London: Headline, 2000.

Wodehouse, P. G. *Author! Author!* New York: Simon and Schuster, 1954.

Wodehouse, P. G., and Guy Bolton. *Bring on the Girls!* New York: Simon and Schuster, 1953.

Wolf, Matt. *Stepping into Freedom: Sam Mendes at the Donmar*. London: Nick Hern, 2002.

Wollman, Elizabeth L. *The Theater Will Rock: A History of the Rock Musical, from 'Hair' to 'Hedwig'*. Ann Arbor: University of Michigan Press, 2006.

Womack, Malcom. '"Thank You for the Music": Catherine Johnson's Feminist Revoicings in *Mamma Mia!*' *Studies in Musical Theatre* 3, no. 2 (2009): 201–211.

Wren, Gayden. *A Most Ingenious Paradox: The Art of Gilbert and Sullivan*. New York: Oxford University Press, 2006.

Wright, Adrian. *A Tanner's Worth of Tune: Rediscovering the Post-War British Musical*. Woodbridge: The Boydell Press, 2010.

Wright, Adrian. *West End Broadway: The Golden Age of the American Musical in London*. Woodbridge: The Boydell Press, 2012.

Zipes, Jack David. 'The Perverse Delight of *Shockheaded Peter*.' *Theater* 30, no. 2 (Summer 2000): 129–143.

Index